F

N(

The
NATURE
AND PROCESS
OF LAW

The
NATURE
AND PROCESS
OF LAW

An Introduction to Legal Philosophy

EDITED BY

Patricia Smith

New York   Oxford
OXFORD UNIVERSITY PRESS
1993

Oxford University Press

Oxford   New York   Toronto
Delhi   Bombay   Calcutta   Madras   Karachi
Kuala Lumpur   Singapore   Hong Kong   Tokyo
Nairobi   Dar es Salaam   Cape Town
Melbourne   Auckland   Madrid

and associated companies in
Berlin   Ibadan

Published by Oxford University Press, Inc.
200 Madison Avenue, New York, New York 10016

Oxford is a registered trademark of Oxford University Press

Library of Congress Cataloging–in–Publication Data
The nature and process of law : an introduction to legal philosophy
edited by Patricia Smith
p.   cm.
ISBN   0–19–507697–4
1. Law — Philosophy. 2. Law — United States.   I. Smith, Patricia, 1956–
K231.N37   1993
340'.1 — dc20   92–15723

9 8 7 6 5 4 3 2 1

Printed in the United States of America
on acid-free paper

Preface

After teaching legal philosophy for quite a few years I became dissatisfied with the textbooks available for my subject. Although there are a few very good ones, there are not many to choose from, and none of them does certain things that I wanted to be able to do. First, I wanted materials basic enough for an introductory course that requires no background in philosophy or law. Second, I wanted to focus on the nature of law as a decision-making process and as a social institution. Third, I wanted to provide a well-balanced coverage of civil law as well as criminal law, or private law as well as public law. And fourth, I wanted materials that are genuinely different from anything on the market. I wanted a change, a real alternative.

Philosophy texts tend to approach law in terms of discrete, abstract concepts. This is not illegitimate. In fact, it is useful for certain purposes, especially, for example, to challenge advanced students who already have a good grasp of how legal concepts function within legal systems. Unfortunately, my experience is that many students have no such understanding and that this has two important consequences. First, students often have trouble appreciating the distinctively legal features of many issues raised in the abstract (for example, they often think of discrimination or paternalism in moral rather than legal terms). Second, some important issues are difficult to raise at all; they do not come up naturally, without focusing on the formal or systemic aspect of law (for example, problems of judicial review, constitutional rights, and the distribution of power or jurisdiction).

Given these problems, I undertook to assemble teaching materials that would aim at the special objectives I wanted to achieve—namely, to provide a philosophical approach to the idea of a legal system and to analyze legal concepts within that framework. Once these objectives are adopted certain other ideas follow. A legal system has two important dimensions, which I will call "formal" and "environmental," for reasons that should become apparent. Both require examination in a legal philosophy course.

Any legal system has a formal structure or constitution. It is put together in some particular way, and the way it is put together matters—it has implications and consequences. Furthermore, this constitution or structure includes a formal process—a way of functioning—which also matters. A helpful way to think of this formal dimension is to imagine an evolving conceptual framework. One legal scholar described it nicely as a moving classification system. This is an oversimplification, of course, but it conveys the general idea. These formal elements (the structure and process) of law are important, basic, and not easily conveyed unless the materials are set up to do so. This is not the sort of thing an instructor can effectively raise as an aside. Once the formal dimension is effectively raised, however, basic questions naturally come up that do not otherwise surface. How, if at all, does form affect content in law? How does the process of law affect its substance? These are basic philosophical questions. They are widely recognized as having central importance in law schools. Yet they are rarely addressed in philosophy courses. I think that they should be.

The environmental dimension of law refers to the fact that a legal system is a social institution. Just as legal concepts do not function in a vacuum, legal systems do not function in a vacuum. They reflect the needs, values, commitments, and assumptions of society. They are not value neutral. Every legal system is connected to and affected by a complex social environment—the general belief system of a society—which includes political, economic, moral, and cultural assumptions, among other things. Unlike process issues, most issues of environment can easily be raised by the instructor without special materials. The problem is that the environmental connections overwhelm the legal issues in the minds of many students. Too often students lapse into discussing legal issues simply as moral or economic issues: They lose sight of (or never see) the distinctively legal dimension of these problems. Such a response indicates (among other things) that students need a better understanding of law as a functioning system, and that they need a powerful counterbalance to the issues of social environment. I try to meet both these needs by using our own legal system as a model. This approach has the advantage of providing a rather rich, extensive, and fairly concrete context within which all issues get raised and organized. It also provides a vehicle for demonstrating certain elusive features of law, such as its complex, interwoven, historical, evolutionary character.

The format of the book has been carefully worked out to facilitate the objectives set out earlier. The book opens with a general introduction, highlighted by Oliver Wendell Holmes, Jr.'s rather inspiring lecture on the study of law as requiring a study of history, philosophy, and function or purpose. In these materials I undertake to meet Holmes's challenge, using American law as a model. The idea is to examine the form and nature, the presuppositions and implications of this model with a view to better understanding law as a functioning conceptual system and as an evolving social process or institution.

The materials are divided into three units reflecting major distinctions in law. The first division reflects the distinction between form and content or process and substance. Unit I focuses on the formal aspect of law by confronting issues of structure (or constitution) and process directly in terms of a model or example. We examine first the fundamental form or composition of government—how is the political process constituted in this model, and why? What is presupposed by constituting government in a particular way? What follows? From general considerations of the nature of law and political structure we move to an examination of legal process as such. What is the nature of a judicial process or a legislative process in our example? How does it function? What is it for? How does it fit into the general structure? What are its limits? Why have it this way rather than some other way? This first unit is intended to provide the student with a good beginning sense of law as process. That beginning sense is then bolstered by demonstrating the effects of process throughout Units II and III. This is done by organizing the materials to do it and then simply asking incidental questions in the introductory materials throughout the book.

Units II and III deal with substantive issues and reflect a second major distinction—that between private law and public law. The distinction between private law and public law is a natural way to raise issues of the social environment within a clearly legal context. Perhaps the most fundamental of these issues is the tension between the individual and the social nature of human beings. This tension is manifested in a fundamental question of political philosophy: how to reconcile individual rights with social welfare. Legal systems, of course, are shot through with specific instances of this general problem. Thus, it is easy and natural to raise such issues within the specific context of problems of a legal system. The introduction to each unit sets out the overall concern of the unit—as well as the overarching themes of the book. What is the nature of law? How does its form or process affect its substance or content? What makes something a private (that is, individual) matter or a public (community) concern?

Each unit is divided into two or three chapters that represent important areas of law relevant to the overall concern of the unit as well as topics of independent interest. The selection of materials is designed to give the student a good overview of the area and the problems associated with it. The introduction to each chapter raises general issues, provides background, fills in gaps, and explains the organization and selection of material.

Each chapter is divided into three or four sections that raise rather specific issues by using (largely) short reading selections drawn from history, law, and philosophy and complemented by political documents and/or court cases. The introduction to each section briefly places and explains the readings and provides critical commentary. Each article is preceded by "Notes and Questions," a set of study questions for the student to consider while reading the selections.

I use "Notes and Questions" to illustrate the interwoven, systematic nature of law. For example, court decisions in one time period and area of law often affect decisions in another time and area, so throughout the book I refer the student to other sections of the book that refer to different times and areas affected by interwoven lines of decisions. An example might be, what could the right to contract in 1937 (as discussed in Unit II, Chapter Three) have to do with the right to privacy in 1965 (as discussed in Unit III, Chapter Seven)? The answer is, quite a lot if you are talking about American law decided by courts (as discussed in Unit I, Chapter Two). In another system one has nothing to do with the other. But in any legal system the formal process and cultural environment affect the content of law. I also use "Notes and Questions" to point out comparisons. What is the difference between a tort (Unit II, Chapter Five) and a crime (Unit III, Chapter Six)? Or what is the difference between a contract right, a property right, a free speech right, and a civil right to Social Security benefits? The idea is to make the organization of material mirror major distinctions and the systematic nature of a legal system, and to use the materials very specifically to focus the issues clearly in the minds of students by giving them lots of examples. It is a simple idea, really, but it works. My own students have been extremely enthusiastic about this approach, and I believe it has facilitated a better learning situation for them and produced a higher level of discussion in my classes.

Since the book is organized around several themes, on several different levels, it can be used in a number of ways. I have used the materials differently every time I have used them. For example, one year I tried them out on advanced students, using Units II and III on the distinction between public law and private law and focusing on models of adjudication. Another year I organized the course around the nature of rights, emphasizing different parts of the same materials. My intended audience is not primarily graduate students. Nevertheless, it is interesting to test for versatility. So far my advanced students (graduate philosophy and third-year law students) seem happily challenged by these materials. My advanced course is cross listed with the law school and is taken by law students, graduate students, and undergraduate seniors. So it presently appears to me that the book can be suitable for advanced philosophy courses or for jurisprudence and possibly legal process courses as well as undergraduate courses. The materials are flexible. The level of difficulty depends on the interests and approach of the instructor and on student ability.

The aim of the book, however, is introductory. Its intended audience is the student with no particular background in philosophy or law. The way I like to use the materials for that purpose is to use Unit I (on the formal structure and process of law) plus selections from Units II and III, depending on the length of the course. One good format, for example, is to use Unit I plus tort law (from Unit II, private law) and criminal law (from Unit III, Public Law). Many combinations are possible. The book could be used for a year-long (for example, two semesters or three quarters) course by covering the whole thing, front to back. It could be used for special topics courses by selecting various chapters in various combinations. Every chapter can be used alone. Each makes sense by itself and is of independent interest. My arrangement of the materials overall enables a teacher to do more than examine discrete issues in isolation from one another by asking how the subject matter of the chapters in this book relate to one another as a system. If that is not the interest, then it need not be done. One might do other things instead. Most teachers are pretty individualistic about their courses and will quickly devise their own uses. In any case, it seems to me that the book could be used for a course of any length (a quarter, a semester, or a year), at any level of difficulty, and for a number of different purposes. The reason that this is possible is that although many of the readings and topics are challenging, I provide basic explanations and study questions to guide the beginning student through every assignment. Because of this approach my materials are more basic than anything else on the market. My introductory course is aimed at undergraduates with no background from sophomore through senior level.

The book is flexible because it is aimed at accommodating a wide range of students. When I started teaching legal philosophy twelve years ago I had only one course (a typical situation in many universities), which had to cover all students from beginning sophomores through third-year law students. This is a frustrating teaching situation, since the beginners are lost or the advanced students are bored, or both. This book is my effort to handle this problem.

The book requires no special expertise to use. Although I include legal materials in it, they are basic and carefully explained. No legal training is required of the instructor. I assume that most legal philosophers are familiar with legal materials, but I also realize that a nonspecialist might teach a legal philosophy course. If so, the materials should be perfectly accessible. I try to make the materials relatively self-contained. The focus of the book and the questions asked are always philosophical, but the readings are not. Students do not understand issues of legal philosophy well unless they have a minimal understanding of legal doctrine and legal history. Instead of assuming that they have it, I supply it. I include legal and historical as well as philosophical materials. I find that philosophical issues can be raised in the classroom just as easily using legal and historical materials as by using readings designed to be philosophical. This mix has been effective and popular with the students.

I use numerous other learning aids as well. Included are legal documents, cases, and lines of cases for illustration and for ease of research (if the relevant document is in the book the students will read it; if they have to go to the library they will skip it). Specific cases and documents can also be effective in class discussion. Lines of cases may be used to illustrate reasoning and the development of concepts about them. This is particularly important in legal philosophy. Although many books include cases (that is currently a popular feature), they are used individually, in much the way hypothetical cases are used in philosophy. However, I use lines of cases or sets of cases to illustrate the development of ideas or to set out conflicting interests or contradictions. This is something like the law school approach to cases. In any event, the eclectic use of materials, the inclusion of study questions, and the interactive use of public documents and lines of court cases is an unusual set of features that students seem to find exciting.

The most unusual feature of this book is its basic rationale, which is that legal process is fundamental to the nature of law. The presumption is that you do not understand law if you do not understand it as a system. Making this idea clear to students turned out to be a complicated and time-consuming project overall. So I want to express my appreciation for the unwavering support of my colleagues at Kentucky even as this book took many years to complete. I want to thank the Oxford team, who not only made the book possible but actual: Cynthia Read for believing in the potential of the concept before anyone else did; Peter Ohlin for patient encouragement and careful attention to so many important details; an anonymous reviewer who wrote enormously helpful comments; and Fran Bartlett for amazing editorial acumen and outstanding diplomatic skill. Because of their efforts it is a much better book. And finally, I want to thank my students for their enthusiastic participation and feedback toward the completion of this project over the years. This book is really theirs.

Lexington, Kentucky   P. S.
December 1992

Acknowledgments

Oliver Wendell Holmes. "The Path of the Law," 10 *Harvard Law Review* 457. Copyright © 1897. Reprinted by permission of the publisher.

George Dargo. "Law, the Revolution, and the Constitutional Movement." From *Law in the New Republic* by George Dargo. Copyright © 1983. Reprinted by permission of McGraw-Hill Publishers.

Edward S. Corwin. From "The 'Higher Law' Background of American Constitutional Law," *Harvard Law Review* XLIII (1928–29). Copyright © 1928. Reprinted by permission of the Harvard Law Review.

Laurence Tribe. From *American Constitutional Law* by Laurence Tribe, Chapter 1. Copyright © 1988 by Laurence Tribe. Reprinted by permission of the author.

Lawrence C. Becker. From "Individual Rights." From *And Justice for All*, edited by T. Regan and D. Van de Veer. Copyright © 1982. Reprinted by permission of Rowman and Littlefield Publishing Company.

Wesley Newcomb Hohfeld. From *Fundamental Legal Conceptions* by Wesley Newcomb Hohfeld. Copyright © 1919. Reprinted by permission of Yale University Press.

Joel Feinberg. From *Social Philosophy*. Copyright © 1973 by Prentice-Hall. Reprinted by permission of the publisher.

Robert Paul Wolff. "The Solution of Classical Democracy." From *In Defense of Anarchism* by Robert Paul Wolff. Copyright © 1970 by Robert Paul Wolff. Reprinted by permission of Harper-Collins Publishers.

Benjamin Cardozo. From *Paradoxes of Legal Science* by Benjamin Cardozo. Copyright © 1928, Columbia University Press, New York. Used by permission.

Edward Levi. From *An Introduction to Legal Reasoning* by Edward Levi. Copyright © 1948 by the University of Chicago Press. Used by permission.

Julius Stone. From *Legal System and Lawyers' Reasonings* by Julius Stone. Copyright © 1964 by Julius Stone. Reprinted by permission of the publisher, Stanford University Press.

David Kairys. "Legal Reasoning." From *The Politics of Law* by David Kairys. Copyright © 1982 by David Kairys. Reprinted by permission of Pantheon Books, a division of Random House, Inc.

Robert Bork. "The Original Understanding." From *The Tempting of America: The Political Seduction of the Law* by Robert H. Bork. Copyright © 1990 by Robert H. Bork. Reprinted with the permission of The Free Press, a Division of Macmillan, Inc.

Frederick Schauer. "An Essay on Constitutional Language," 29 *UCLA Law Review* 797. Copyright © 1982 by The Regents of the University of California. All rights reserved. Reprinted by permission of the author and the publisher.

John Hart Ely. "Policing the Process of Representation: The Court as Referee." From *Democracy and Distrust* by John Hart Ely. Reprinted by permission of the publishers (Cambridge, Mass.: Harvard University Press). Copyright © 1980 by the President and Fellows of Harvard College.

Martha Minow. From "Justice Engendered," 101 *Harvard Law Review* 10. Copyright ©1987 by Martha Minow. Reprinted by permission of the publisher and the author.

H. L. A. Hart. From *The Concept of Law* by H. L. A. Hart. Copyright © 1961 by Clarendon Press, Oxford. Reprinted by permission of Oxford University Press.

Ronald A. Dworkin. From "'Natural' Law Revisited," *University of Florida Law Review* 34 (1982):165–88. Reprinted by permission of the University of Florida Law Review.

John Chipman Gray. From *The Nature and Sources*

of Law. Copyright © 1921 by Roland Gray (New York: Macmillan Company, 1921), pp. 84–103. Reprinted with permission.

Janet Rifkin. "Toward a Theory of Law and Patriarchy," 3 *Harvard Women's Law Journal* 83. Copyright © 1980 by the President and Fellows of Harvard College. Reprinted by permission of the publisher.

Lon L. Fuller. From *The Morality of Law* by Lon L. Fuller. Copyright © 1969 by Yale University Press. Reprinted by permission of the publisher.

Jerome Frank. From *Law and the Modern Mind.* Copyright 1930, 1933, 1949 by Coward McCann, Inc. Copyright © 1930 by Brentano's Inc., used by Anchor Books edition (Landover Hills, MD: Anchor, 1963). Copyright renewed 1958 by Florence K. Frank. Reprinted 1977 by Dickenson Publishing Company, by permission of the estate of Barbara Frank Kristein.

Table 1, page 291. From "Premarital Pregnancy in America, 1640–1971: An Overview and Interpretation," *Journal of Interdisciplinary History,* 5 (1975), 561. Reprinted with the permission of the editors of the *Journal of Interdisciplinary History* and the M.I.T. Press, Cambridge, Massachusetts. Copyright © 1975 by the Massachusetts Institute of Technology and the editors of the *Journal of Interdisciplinary History.*

Charles Fried. From *Contract as Promise* by Charles Fried. Reprinted by permission of the publishers (Cambridge, Mass.: Harvard University Press). Copyright © 1981 by the President and Fellows of Harvard College.

Patrick S. Atiyah. From *Promises, Morals and Laws* by Patrick S. Atiyah. Copyright © 1981 by Oxford University Press. Reprinted by permission of Oxford University Press.

M. E. Tigar and M. R. Levy. "Contract: A Study of Law and Social Reality." From *Law and the Rise of Capitalism* by M. E. Tigar and M. R. Levy. Copyright © 1977 by Michael E. Tigar. Reprinted by permission of Monthly Review Foundation.

Max Radin. "Contract Obligation and the Human Will," 43 *Columbia Law Review* 575 (1943). Copyright © 1943 by the Directors of the Columbia Law Review Association, Inc. All rights reserved. Reprinted by permission.

"A Legal, Moral, Social Nightmare" and "A Surrogate's Story" reprinted from TIME Magazine, September 10, 1984. Copyright © 1984 Time Inc. Reprinted by permission.

"'Baby M' Contract Illegal, Court in New Jersey Rules" reprinted by permission of the Associated Press. Copyright © 1988 by the Associated Press, all rights reserved.

A. M. Honoré, "Ownership." From *Oxford Essays in Jurisprudence.* Copyright © 1977 by Oxford University Press. Reprinted by permission of Oxford University Press.

Henry George. From *Progress and Poverty* by Henry George. Copyright © 1955. Reprinted by permission of the Robert Schalkenbach Foundation.

Robert Nozick. From *Anarchy, State and Utopia* by Robert Nozick. Copyright © 1974 by Basic Books, Inc. Reprinted by permission of Basic Books, a division of HarperCollins Publishers, Inc.

A. M. Honoré. "Property, Title and Redistribution." From *Equality and Freedom: Past, Present and Future,* edited by Carl Wellman, published by Archiv für Rechts- und Sozial-philosophie. Copyright © 1977. Reprinted by permission of the publisher.

Dan B. Dobbs. From *Torts and Compensation* by Dan B. Dobbs. Copyright © 1985; reprinted by permission of the West Publishing Company.

William Prosser. "Negligence." From *The Law of Torts.* Copyright © 1956 by Little, Brown and Company. Reprinted by permission of the publisher.

Fowler Harper and Fleming James. From *The Law of Torts,* Vol 2, by Fowler Harper and Fleming James. Copyright © 1956. Reprinted by permission of the publisher, Little, Brown and Company.

H. L. A. Hart and A. M. Honoré. From *Causation in the Law,* second ed., 1985. Reprinted by permission of Oxford University Press.

Douglas N Husak. From "Omissions, Causation and Liability," *Philosophical Quaterly* 30 (1980):318–26. Published by Basil Blackwell Inc. Reprinted by permission of the publisher.

Susan J. Hoffman. From *Statutes Establishing a Duty to Report Crimes or Render Assistance to*

Strangers by Susan J. Hoffmann. Copyright © 1984 by the University of Kentucky Law Journal. Reprinted by permission of the publisher.

Abram Chayes. "The Role of the Judge in Public Law Litigation," 89 *Harvard Law Review*. Copyright © 1976. Reprinted by permission of the author.

John Kleinig. "Crime and the Concept of Harm," *American Philosophical Quarterly*. Copyright © 1987. Reprinted by permission of the publisher.

Lawrence Friedman. From *A History of American Law* by Lawrence Friedman. Copyright © 1973 by Lawrence Friedman. Reprinted by permission of the author and the publisher, Simon & Schuster.

Louis B. Schwartz. From "Moral Offense and the Model Penal Code," 63 *Columbia Law Review* 669 (1963). Copyright © 1963 by the Directors of the Columbia Law Review Association, Inc. All rights reserved. Reprinted by permission.

Richard B. Brandt. "The Principles of Criminal Law." From *Ethical Theory* by Richard B. Brandt. Copyright © 1959. Reprinted by permission of the author.

From the Model Penal Code. Copyright © 1956 by The American Law Institute. Reprinted by permission.

Jerome Hall. From *General Principles of the Criminal Law,* second edition. Copyright © 1960. Reprinted by permission of the Michie Company. All rights reserved.

Herbert Packer. "Culpability and Excuses." From *The Limits of the Criminal Sanction* by Herbert Packer. Copyright © 1968 by Herbert Packer. Reprinted by permission of the publisher, Stanford University Press.

Edmund L. Pincoffs. From *The Rationale of Legal Punishment* by Edmund L. Pincoffs. Copyright © 1966 by Edmund L. Pincoffs. Reprinted by permission of the Estate of Edmund L. Pincoffs.

Jeffrie G. Murphy. "Marxism and Retribution," *Philosophy and Public Affairs,* 2(3). Copyright © 1973 by Princeton University Press. Reprinted by permission of Princeton University Press.

Karl Menninger. From *The Crime of Punishment* by Karl Menninger. Copyright © 1966, 1968 by Karl Menninger. Used by permission of Viking Penguin, a division of Penguin Books USA Inc.

Randy E. Barnett. "Restitution," *Ethics* 87(4). Copyright © 1977. Reprinted by permission of the publisher, The University of Chicago Press, and the author.

Fred R. Berger. "Symbolic Conduct and Freedom of Speech." From *Freedom of Expression* by Fred R. Berger. Copyright © 1980 by the author. Reprinted by permission of the publisher, Wadsworth Publishing Company.

Nat Hentoff. "The Enemy Within," *The Village Voice,* August 8, 1977. Copyright © 1978. Reprinted by permission of the author and The Village Voice.

Judith Wagner DeCew. "The Scope of Privacy in Law and Ethics," *Law and Philosophy* 5 (1986), pp. 145–73. Copyright © 1986 by Kluwer Academic Publishers. Reprinted by permission of Kluwer Academic Publishers.

John Rawls. "Justice as Fairness," *Philosophical Review,* Vol. 67. Copyright © 1958 by John Rawls. Reprinted by permission of the publisher and the author.

Kimberlé Williams Crenshaw. From "Race, Reform and Retrenchment," 101 *Harvard Law Review* 1331. Copyright © 1988 by Kimberlé Williams Crenshaw. Reprinted by permission of the Harvard Law Review.

Frank I. Michelman. From "On Protecting the Poor," 83 *Harvard Law Review* 7. Copyright © 1969 by Frank Michelman. Reprinted by permission of the Harvard Law Review.

L. J. Barker and T. W. Barker, Jr. From *Civil Liberties and the Constitution,* third edition. Copyright © 1978. Reprinted by permission of Prentice Hall, Englewood Cliffs, New Jersey.

Contents

CHAPTER TWO   The Nature of the Judicial Process and the Concept of Law,   137

SECTION 1   Judicial Review and the Common Law,   140

SECTION 2   The Concept of Law,   218

CHAPTER SEVEN   The Nature of Civil Rights,   658

SECTION 1   Civil Rights and the Value of Freedom,   660

APPENDIX

The
NATURE
AND PROCESS
OF LAW

The Path of the Law

OLIVER WENDELL HOLMES, JR.

When we study law we are not studying a mystery but a well-known profession. We are studying what we shall want in order to appear before judges, or to advise people in such a way as to keep them out of court.

* * *

I wish, if I can, to lay down some first principles for the study of this body of dogma or systematized prediction which we will call the law, for men who want to use it as the instrument of their business to enable them to prophesy in their turn, and, as bearing upon the study, I wish to point out an ideal which as yet our law has not attained.

The first thing for a business-like understanding of the matter is to understand its limits, and therefore I think it desirable at once to point out and dispel a confusion between morality and law, which sometimes rises to the height of conscious theory. . . .

* * *

You can see very plainly that a bad man has as much reason as a good one for wishing to avoid an encounter with the public force, and therefore you can see the practical importance of the distinction between morality and law. A man who cares nothing for an ethical rule which is believed and practised by his neighbors is likely nevertheless to care a good deal to avoid being made to pay money, and will want to keep out of jail if he can.

I take it for granted that no hearer of mine will misinterpret what I have to say as the language of cynicism. The law is the witness and external deposit of our moral life. Its history is the history of the moral development of the race. The practice of it, in spite of popular jests, tends to make good citizens and good men. When I emphasize the difference between law and morals I do so with reference to a single end, that of learning and understanding the law. For that purpose you must definitely master its specific marks, and it is for that I ask you for the moment to imagine yourselves indifferent to other and greater things.

I do not say that there is not a wider point of view from which the distinction between law and morals becomes of secondary or no importance, as all mathematical distinctions vanish in presence of the infinite. But I do say that distinction is of the first importance for the object which we are here to consider — a right study and mastery of the law as a business with well understood limits, a body of dogma enclosed within definite lines. I have just shown the practical reason for saying so. If you want to know the law and nothing else, you must look at it as a bad man, who cares only for the material consequences which such knowledge enables him to predict, not as a good one, who finds his reasons for conduct, whether inside the law or outside of it, in the vaguer sanctions of conscience. The theoretical importance of the distinction is no less, if you would reason on your subject aright. The law is full of phraseology drawn from morals, and by the mere force of language continually invites us to pass from one domain to the other without perceiving it, as we are sure to do unless we have the boundary constantly before our minds. The law talks about rights, and duties, and malice, and intent, and negligence, and so forth, and nothing is easier, or, I may say, more common in legal reasoning, than to take these words in their moral sense, at some stage of the argument, and so to drop into fallacy.

* * *

So much for the limits of the law. The next thing which I wish to consider is what are the forces which determine its content and its growth. You may assume, with Hobbes and Bentham and Austin, that all law emanates from the sovereign, even when the first human beings to enunciate it are the judges, or you may think that law is the voice of the Zeitgeist, or what you like. It is all one to my present purpose. Even if every decision required the sanction of an emperor with despotic power and a whimsical turn of mind, we should be interested none the less, still with a view to prediction, in discovering some order, some rational explanation, and some principle of growth for the rules which he laid down. In every system there are such explanations and principles to be found. It is with regard to them that a second fallacy comes in, which I think it important to expose.

The fallacy to which I refer is the notion that

the only force at work in the development of the law is logic. In the broadest sense, indeed, that notion would be true. The postulate on which we think about the universe is that there is a fixed quantitative relation between every phenomenon and its antecedents and consequents. If there is such a thing as a phenomenon without these fixed quantitative relations, it is a miracle. It is outside the law of cause and effect, and as such transcends our power of thought, or at least is something to or from which we cannot reason. The condition of our thinking about the universe is that it is capable of being thought about rationally, or, in other words, that every part of it is effect and cause in the same sense in which those parts are with which we are most familiar. So in the broadest sense it is true that the law is a logical development, like everything else. The danger of which I speak is not the admission that the principles governing other phenomena also govern the law, but the notion that a given system, ours, for instance, can be worked out like mathematics from some general axioms of conduct. This is the natural error of the schools, but it is not confined to them. I once heard a very eminent judge say that he never let a decision go until he was absolutely sure that it was right. So judicial dissent often is blamed, as if it meant simply that one side or the other were not doing their sums right, and, if they would take more trouble, agreement inevitably would come.

This mode of thinking is entirely natural. The training of lawyers is a training in logic. The processes of analogy, discrimination, and deduction are those in which they are most at home. The language of judicial decision is mainly the language of logic. And the logical method and form flatter that longing for certainty and for repose which is in every human mind. But certainty generally is illusion, and repose is not the destiny of man. Behind the logical form lies a judgment as to the relative worth and importance of competing legislative grounds, often an inarticulate and unconscious judgment, it is true, and yet the very root and nerve of the whole proceeding. You can give any conclusion a logical form. You always can imply a condition in a contract. But why do you imply it? It is because of some belief as to the practice of the community or of a class, or because of some opinion as to policy,

or, in short, because of some attitude of yours upon a matter not capable of exact quantitative measurement, and therefore not capable of founding exact logical conclusions. Such matters really are battle grounds where the means do not exist for determinations that shall be good for all time, and where the decision can do no more than embody the preference of a given body in a given time and place. We do not realize how large a part of our law is open to reconsideration upon a slight change in the habit of the public mind. No concrete proposition is self evident, no matter how ready we may be to accept it. . . .

* * *

So much for the fallacy of logical form. Now let us consider the present condition of the law as a subject for study, and the ideal toward which it tends. We still are far from the point of view which I desire to see reached. No one has reached it or can reach it as yet. We are only at the beginning of a philosophical reaction, and of a reconsideration of the worth of doctrines which for the most part still are taken for granted without any deliberate, conscious, and systematic questioning of their grounds. The development of our law has gone on for nearly a thousand years, like the development of a plant, each generation taking the inevitable next step, mind, like matter, simply obeying a law of spontaneous growth. It is perfectly natural and right that it should have been so. Imitation is a necessity of human nature, as has been illustrated by a remarkable French writer, M. Tarde, in an admiral book, *Les Lois de l'Imitation*. Most of the things we do, we do for no better reason than that our fathers have done them or that our neighbors do them, and the same is true of a larger part than we suspect of what we think. The reason is a good one, because our short life gives us no time for a better, but it is not the best. It does not follow, because we all are compelled to take on faith at second hand most of the rules on which we base our action and our thought, that each of us may not try to set some corner of his world in the order of reason, or that all of us collectively should not aspire to carry reason as far as it will go throughout the whole domain. In regard to the law, it is true, no doubt, that an evolutionist will hesitate to affirm universal validity for his social ideals, or for the principles which he thinks should be embodied in legislation. He is content if he can prove them best for here and now. He may be ready to admit that he knows nothing about an absolute best in the cosmos, and even that he knows next to nothing about a permanent best for men. Still it is true that a body of law is more rational and more civilized when every rule it contains is referred articulately and definitely to an end which it subserves, and when the grounds for desiring that end are stated or are ready to be stated in words.

At present, in very many cases, if we want to know why a rule of law has taken its particular shape, and more or less if we want to know why it exists at all, we go to tradition. We follow it into the Year Books, and perhaps beyond them to the customs of the Salian Franks, and somewhere in the past, in the German forests, in the needs of Norman kings, in the assumptions of a dominant class, in the absence of generalized ideas, we find out the practical motive for what now best is justified by the mere fact of its acceptance and that men are accustomed to it. The rational study of law is still to a large extent the study of history. History must be a part of the study, because without it we cannot know the precise scope of rules which it is our business to know. It is a part of the rational study, because it is the first step toward an enlightened scepticism, that is, towards a deliberate reconsideration of the worth of those rules. When you get the dragon out of his cave on to the plain and in the daylight, you can count his teeth and claws, and see just what is his strength. But to get him out is only the first step. The next is either to kill him, or to tame him and make him a useful animal. For the rational study of the law the black-letter man may be the man of the present, but the man of the future is the man of statistics and the master of economics. It is revolting to have no better reason for a rule of law than that so it was laid down in the time of Henry IV. It is still more revolting if the grounds upon which it was laid down have vanished long since, and the rule simply persists from blind imitation of the past.

* * *

We must beware of the pitfall of antiquarianism, and must remember that for our purposes our only interest in the past is for the light it throws upon the present. I look forward to a time when the part played by history in the explanation of

dogma shall be very small, and instead of ingenious research we shall spend our energy on a study of the ends sought to be attained and the reasons for desiring them. As a step toward that ideal it seems to me that every lawyer ought to seek an understanding of economics. The present divorce between the schools of political economy and law seems to me an evidence of how much progress in philosophical study still remains to be made. In the present state of political economy, indeed, we come again upon history on a larger scale, but there we are called on to consider and weigh the ends of legislation, the means of attaining them, and the cost. We learn that for everything we have we give up something else, and we are taught to set the advantage we gain against the other advantage we lose, and to know what we are doing when we elect.

There is another study which sometimes is undervalued by the practical minded, for which I wish to say a good word, although I think a good deal of pretty poor stuff goes under that name. I mean the study of what is called jurisprudence. Jurisprudence, as I look at it, is simply law in its most generalized part. Every effort to reduce a case to a rule is an effort of jurisprudence, although the name as used in English is confined to the broadest rules and most fundamental conceptions. One mark of a great lawyer is that he sees the application of the broadest rules. There is a story of a Vermont justice of the peace before whom a suit was brought by one farmer against another for breaking a churn. The justice took time to consider, and then said that he had looked through the statutes and could find nothing about churns, and gave judgment for the defendant. The same state of mind is shown in all our common digests and text-books. Applications of rudimentary rules of contract or tort are tucked away under the head of Railroads or Telegraphs or go to swell treatises on historical subdivisions, such as Shipping or Equity, or are gathered under an arbitrary title which is thought likely to appeal to the practical mind, such as Mercantile Law. If a man goes into law it pays to be a master of it, and to be a master of it means to look straight through all the dramatic incidents and to discern the true basis for prophecy. Therefore, it is well to have an accurate notion of what you mean by law, by a right, by a duty, by malice, intent, and negligence, by ownership, by possession, and so forth. I have in my mind cases in which the highest courts seem to me to have floundered because they had no clear ideas on some of these themes. I have illustrated their importance already.

* * *

The advice of the elders to young men is very apt to be as unreal as a list of the hundred best books. At least in my day I had my share of such counsels, and high among the unrealities I place the recommendation to study the Roman Law.

* * *

No. The way to gain a liberal view of your subject is not to read something else, but to get to the bottom of the subject itself. The means of doing that are, in the first place, to follow the existing body of dogma into its highest generalizations by the help of jurisprudence; next, to discover from history how it has come to be what it is; and, finally, so far as you can, to consider the ends which the several rules seek to accomplish, the reasons why those ends are desired, what is given up to gain them, and whether they are worth the price.

We have too little theory in the law rather than too much, especially on this final branch of study.

* * *

I have been speaking about the study of the law, and I have said next to nothing of what commonly is talked about in that connection — textbooks and the case system, and all the machinery with which a student comes most immediately in contact. Nor shall I say anything about them. Theory is my subject, not practical details. The modes of teaching have been improved since my time, no doubt, but ability and industry will master the raw material with any mode. Theory is the most important part of the dogma of the law, as the architect is the most important man who takes part in the building of a house. The most important improvements of the last twenty-five years are improvements in theory. It is not to be feared as unpractical, for, to the competent, it simply means going to the bottom of the subject. For the incompetent, it sometimes is true, as has been said, that an interest in general ideas means an absence of particular knowledge. I remember in army days reading of a youth who, being examined for the lowest grade and being asked a question about squadron drill, answered that he never had considered the evolutions of less than ten thousand men. But the weak and foolish must be left to their folly. The danger is that the able and practical minded should look with indifference or distrust upon ideas the connection of which with their business is remote. I heard a story, the other day, of a man who had a valet to whom he paid high wages, subject to deduction for faults. One of his deductions was, "For lack of imagination, five dollars." The lack is not confined to valets. The object of ambition, power, generally presents itself nowadays in the form of money alone. Money is the most immediate form, and is a proper object of desire. "The fortune," said Rachel, "is the measure of the intelligence." That is a good text to waken people out of a fool's paradise. But, as Hegel says, "It is in the end not the appetite, but the opinion, which has to be satisfied." To an imagination of any scope the most far-reaching form of power is not money, it is the command of ideas. If you want great examples, read Mr. Leslie Stephen's *History of English Thought in the Eighteenth Century*, and see how a hundred years after his death the abstract speculations of Descartes had become a practical force controlling the conduct of men. Read the works of the great German jurists, and see how much more the world is governed to-day by Kant than by Bonaparte. We cannot all be Descartes or Kant, but we all want happiness. And happiness, I am sure from having known many successful men, cannot be won simply by being counsel for great corporations and having an income of fifty thousand dollars. An intellect great enough to win the prize needs other food besides success. The remoter and more general aspects of the law are those which give it universal interest. It is through them that you not only become a great master in your calling, but connect your subject with the universe and catch an echo of the infinite, a glimpse of its unfathomable process, a hint of the universal law.

Introduction

On January 8, 1897 Oliver Wendell Holmes, Jr., then justice of the Supreme Court of Massachusetts, addressed the students and faculty of Boston University Law School regarding the study of law. The preceding selection is an excerpt from that lecture. Much of what Holmes had to say that day is of lasting value for students in a broader range of subjects than the one he addressed, but it is especially apt for the student of law. It is also an extremely insightful statement on educational method. Holmes astutely directs the student to approach the law as a bad man. Why? The approach serves several purposes.

First, it sets out the beginnings of a particular philosophical theory of law that focuses on the decisions of courts as central to the nature of law. That purpose should be bracketed for the time being. We will deal with it later; it is simply one theory among several about the nature of law, which is no reason at all to use Holmes's lecture as the general preface to a whole set of materials about the nature and process of law. Ignore it for now.

Second, and more important for our purposes, Holmes's approach is a focusing device. It is a technique that reminds anyone who uses it to do two things: (1) Be specific, and (2) be pragmatic. These may seem like surprising suggestions for a philosophy course, and they are not intended as a statement of everything you will need to do, but there are good reasons for keeping them in mind. Many of the ideas and issues in this course are very abstract, so it is a good counterfoil to try to put the abstract ideas and issues in a specific context. One way to do this is Holmes's way. The point is to ask yourself exactly what you need to know and why you need to know it. Who are you, anyway? Are you a bad man — a criminal? What do you need to know to keep yourself out of trouble? Are you a lawyer? What do you need to know to protect your client? From your perspective the law is whatever the courts will say about your case. The law is whatever the courts say it is, and that is what you will want to predict. But perhaps you are not a lawyer. Are you a legislator, a member of a city council or a representative in Congress? What do you need to know about law? Not the same thing a lawyer or a bad man needs to keep in mind. Among other things, you will want to consider what will be good for all the people you represent. What will promote the general welfare as well as protect the rights and interests of individuals? In other words, you will have to consider not only what law is but what it ought to be. That is quite a different perspective. It raises different issues. Suppose you are a judge. Are you more like a lawyer or a legislator? What should inform your decision? Perhaps you are in business. Maybe you are a property owner or a tenant, a manufacturer or a consumer, a man or a woman, a member of a minority group or the "silent majority." Whatever position you assume, it will focus your inquiry and make some issues clear and others less clear. Law touches vast areas of life and produces innumerable concrete effects. On the one hand, at its most abstract level, law is an idea — a very complex idea. On the other hand, law is a concrete, social institution that serves highly specific, particular, practical purposes. To understand law well, you must understand both sides.

Holmes expresses the point very well when he notes that an understanding of theory is crucial for the practical lawyer, even though abstraction can be a pitfall that masks incompetence. Law has both a practical and a theoretical side. Understanding of both is needed. Either without the other is crippling. So restricting yourself to only one aspect of law is like restricting yourself to the use of only one leg. You may in fact learn to hop outstandingly well. But you cannot be as swift or as steady as a runner. If you were in a law course (which this is not) you should remember theory in the face of much practical detail. In a philosophy course you should remember the particularity of law in the face of much abstract theory. Holmes is urging his students to do both—which, of course, is best of all.

A third purpose of Holmes's approach corresponds to an ancient ideal of philosophical method, advocated by thinkers as early as Socrates and Plato. If you would like to understand what something is, a good first step is to eliminate everything that it is not. This is what Holmes has in mind when he sets down as a first principle of the study of law the understanding of its limits. As Holmes would put it, law is not morality or logic. Nor is it custom or power. Even if it involves all these things (and just how much and in what way it involves them is a matter of great controversy) it should not be identified or conflated with them. Understanding the limits of a concept or an institution will not explain everything, but it goes a long way toward clarifying our thinking about it. So adopting thought devices that clarify limits is a useful study technique.

A fourth purpose of Holmes's approach, and the explicit objective of the lecture, is to set out what Holmes takes to be certain first principles for the study of law. The first of these, understanding the limits of law, has just been mentioned. Holmes's second basic principle is to study law as it is—to "consider the present condition of law and the ideal toward which it tends." That means we need to understand the grounds, the foundations, the reasons and justifications for having certain legal institutions and not others. It also means we need to understand the implications and presuppositions of legal institutions; that is, what follows from and what is assumed by having certain legal institutions rather than others. Why is all this important? Holmes thinks it is important because he believes it will make law (that is, any legal system) better if those who primarily work with law try to make it rational and articulate. Why is it important for the student of philosophy? The philosophical perspective seeks to understand not a particular legal system but the nature of law itself. Now, how do you suppose we should go about studying Law itself? Well, we could start by eliminating what we do not want to study. We do not want to study scientific law— the laws of physics. That is not our subject matter. Nor is mathmatical law—the laws of logic. Nor is moral law or divine law, assuming there are such things. The law that is our subject matter is sometimes called human law or positive law. What is that? It is the law human beings devise in order to govern themselves or one another. The only way that kind of law manifests itself is in terms of particular legal systems. That is the only way it exists. Furthermore, it is the only way the concept makes sense. Positive law presumes human society. Positive law is a human institution. Since we cannot study all existing (or historical) examples, we will study one.

The idea behind these materials is to study legal concepts in light of a concrete example: the legal system of the United States. To approach the subject this way is to concentrate on understanding one particular instance of a general idea, recognizing that it is just that, one instance among many. This approach uses the legal system of the United States as a model. To view law (or Law, if one likes to think big) on the model proposed here is to think of it as a working system or an evolving process for accomplishing certain ends. Holmes approaches law this way in his lecture, and we will take some of his suggestions quite seriously. We will, for example, study some history to see how we came to have our present institutions and processes. We will study jurisprudence—that is, philosophy, to inquire into the meaning of legal concepts, as well as the implications and justifications of legal institutions and processes. In any case, we will not consider concepts in a vacuum but as part of a complex conceptual structure with a history, a purpose (or many purposes), and a connection to social and political life. We will also follow Holmes's suggestion to consider what aims are sought and at what cost.

Our model presumes that law is not an isolated concept, nor even an isolated system. There are many connections to be identified. And that is just about all we will manage to do here: identify them. These materials are introductory only. We cannot make our study in depth, nor can we make it as comprehensive as ideally it should be. So keep in mind that the model is incomplete. This is just a sketch of a real legal system. The readings are necessarily selective and in some cases highly edited. But they are intended to be representative of a real legal system and thus representative of the problems faced by a legal system. The general idea is to provide the student with enough background, breadth, and skill to be able to pursue the topics as long as the interest is there to be pursued.

One important aim is to provide a picture of law as a complex, interwoven, dynamic system. Present features evolved from past ones. Decisions in one area of law often produce surprising effects in other areas. It is a sensitive system affected by politics, economics, individuals, particular circumstances, general trends, arguments, attitudes, ideas, events, fads — certainly intellectual fads and possibly many other fads as well — stock market fluctuations, books, theories, shortages, surpluses, wars, and natural disasters. The system of law is also affected, structured, and limited by its basic composition or constitution. It matters how a government is put together. Is it a constitutional democracy or a totalitarian monarchy? What are the procedures and roles? How are powers and duties distributed? The way a government is constituted carries with it implications about the society it structures and reflects. A particular form of government implies a commitment to certain values and a rejection of others. Such implications in turn provide justification for and limitation of the decision making of officials and the conduct of citizens. Thus it is very important to recognize the many interconnections and to understand their implications. At the same time most constitutional features of government are compatible with an enormous range of decisions, acts, and policies regarding particular issues, problems, or cases. Hence the impact of the random factors mentioned earlier.

This holistic view of law is often missed by students, especially when they are presented with concepts, issues, or cases abstracted from the system as a whole and considered in isolation from it. These materials are arranged to try to avoid that problem. Furthermore, I encourage students to consider these remarks an invitation to join in the effort. Keep in mind the breadth and interconnectedness of the system of ideas you will be studying. We cannot, of course, cover a legal system comprehensively, but we can at least represent its scope and composition.

The general organization of a legal system is represented here by the arrangement of the materials in three parts, reflecting three major functions or divisions of any full-blown legal system. There are certain purposes that any legal system must accomplish and, indeed, for which purpose the legal system exists. One is to set out rules of organization and function. Law associated with this purpose is often called *procedure* or *process* and is distinguished from the substance or content of law. We will have much more to say about this distinction as we go along. Unit I is concerned with issues of form, structure, and process.

A second function of law is to facilitate interpersonal transactions. These are laws that enable private parties to do things with each other that they want to be able to do — such as transact business, form corporations, own or sell property, or make contractual agreements regarding an enormous range of objectives, including, for example, professional services, employment conditions, and marriage. Unit II is concerned with this area of law, often called *private law*, as manifested in the law of the United States. Remember that U.S. law is only an example. We could have chosen a different example. The basic question to keep in mind is what sorts of objectives ought to be considered matters of private transaction, and why? The answer may depend on the example, or it may transcend any particular system.

A third function of law is to protect the public interest, or the general welfare, by prohibiting certain acts or protecting certain others as a matter of public policy. Public law presupposes (correctly or incorrectly) a common value or commitment to or against whatever it requires or prohibits. A crime, for example, is by definition a "public harm." Unit III is concerned with public law. As with private law the basic question is what sorts of objectives ought to be included in this category, and why? What makes a harm a public harm or an interest a public interest?

Finally, we will represent the specificity of law. We will utilize specific cases, problems, and documents to focus and test ideas, arguments, and theories. A broad overview is necessary but not sufficient for a good understanding of philosophical issues in law. Implications emerge when arguments are considered carefully and in detail. Many diverse issues are examined in these materials, but certain general questions run through them as well. One is a question that many people regard as the fundamental issue of political philosophy. How can individual rights be reconciled with public welfare? This is a fundamental problem for law and legal philosophy, and investigating it is a general theme of this book. However, a second and related question distinguishes legal from political philosophy. It is the problem of achieving particular justice with general rules. Given that laws, or legal rules, must be general, how can they be made to accommodate all diverse, particular, individual cases? Investigating this question requires us to understand law as a system. There is a third question that is the most fundamental and the most abstract. What is the nature of law? We will approach this question by aiming primarily at the other two, but asking, as we wind our way through the maze of problems produced by the question of rights and the question of rules, Is this problem particular to a given legal system or would some form of it occur sooner or later in any legal system? Considering these three questions overall is the motivating force behind these materials.

UNIT I

Formal Foundations of Law

To understand the nature of law we must first understand the distinction between form and content, or as it is frequently described, the distinction between the process of law and its substance. Beginning students often overlook this crucial distinction or fail to realize its importance. If we overlook it or ignore it we will fundamentally distort the nature of the legal issues we consider.

What exactly does this distinction amount to? Works of art embody the same distinction and may provide us with a useful illustration. Poetry, paintings, plays, and novels, for example, all involve both form and content. Consider poetry. The form of a poem is the way it is put together, the patterns of rhythm, meter, rhyme, and so on. It is the structure or arrangement of words and lines on a page. We can symbolize and diagram these patterns to demonstrate the formal properties of the poem without any reference to the particular words or at least to the meanings of the words used. So any poem can be viewed as a set of formal properties structured in a certain way.

A poem can also be viewed as a particular artistic process. That is, this formal structure can also be described as a set of artistic (or communicative) devices (rhythm, meter, rhyme, alliteration) that perform certain functions, to accomplish certain objectives, such as quickening or slowing a tempo, creating a lively mood or a reflective one, evoking a sense of patriotism or a feeling of dread, and so on. The point is that the structure of a poem makes a difference in the way the poem works or functions.

The formal properties of a poem, then, are the way it is put together and the way it functions. By contrast, the content (or substance) of a poem is its subject matter, what it is about—war, love, autumn, time. The form of a poem, such as Shakespeare's "Passionate Pilgrim," is that of a sonnet, and its content or subject matter is love. Many sonnets are about love. That form seems to be especially suitable for the subject of love. This is not to say that form determines content (or vice versa) but that in art form and content definitely interact, and certain poetic forms are more appropriate to expressing certain perspectives than others and therefore more conducive to accomplishing certain artistic goals and purposes than others. In other words, form matters.

Similarly, law has both form and content (usually called *process* and *substance*). The extent to which each affects the other is a matter of dispute. It has been argued that these connections are tenuous. But even so, it appears that certain forms of government are particularly amenable to promoting certain ends and/or retarding others. For example, it is commonly thought that democratic forms of government express and promote freedom and possibly equality better than other forms of government (such as monarchy or oligarchy). On the other hand, democracy is probably not an efficient form.

In any case, every government has a basic structure that is not a necessary feature of law itself but a political foundation. The political structure of the United States is that of a constitutional democracy, limited by a Bill of Rights and a doctrine of separated powers. These are all formal devices that are fundamental structural features of that particular legal system. These structural devices can also be viewed as part of a political (or legal) process. To say that a legal system is democratic is to say something important about the way the system functions. Structure and

11

process are thus two ways of looking at formal features of a legal system. They actually refer to the same thing, namely, the form of the law or legal system.

By contrast, the substantive side of law is its content — not how it is put together or how it functions but what is in it or what it is about — that is, its subject matter. The fact that the U.S. Constitution contains a Bill of Rights is a formal feature. What the rights consist of (for example, the guarantees of free speech and religion) are substantive matters. The fact that this legal system includes crimes (acts declared to be prohibited and punishable by the state) is a formal feature. What the crimes are (for example, murder, arson, or libel) is a substantive matter. The fact that this legal system recognizes contracts, property, torts, or corporations is a formal feature of that system. What the law of contracts, property, torts, or corporations says is a substantive question. In Unit I we will concentrate on form, although we will study both form and substance in this course.

We will also consider a third aspect of form. It is the most basic aspect of the form of anything, namely, the logical or conceptual properties of that thing. The logical or conceptual properties of law are postulated and examined in philosophical theories of the nature of law as such. These theories are not concerned with the features of particular legal systems but with the essential elements of law as a concept, with the justification of law, and with its logical or necessary connection to morality. To approach law in this way is to recognize that at the most abstract and fundamental level law is an idea. In these materials we will examine law as an idea and also as a social institution. This focus should enable us to consider the interplay of necessary features of law with aspects of law that are incidental but still important to particular legal systems.

We will begin in Chapter One by examining the structure of a political system to consider what difference the structure of government makes to law and whether there are basic structural devices any political process would have to have in order to be a government at all or in order to be a legitimate government. Section 1 of Chapter Two focuses especially on the notion of process, narrowing our view to the judicial process in particular. What is it that makes a legal process legal — or, for that matter, what is it that makes it a process? Also ask yourself whether the distinction drawn here between a political process and a judicial process is really a useful one, and if it is, with what limits. Finally, Section 2 of Chapter Two considers the concept of law itself. What is law? What is the difference between law and coercion? What is the connection between law and power or authority or justice? These are all formal questions, the examination of which (whether answered or not) should provide us with a good foundation for studying the substantive issues raised in Units II and III.

CHAPTER ONE

The Nature of the Political Process

What exactly is a political process, and what does it have to do with law? In other words, why do we need to talk about it in this course? A political process has everything to do with law. Although the two can be separated in theory for convenience, they cannot be separated in fact. Think of a political process as surrounding law. It is the environment within which law functions, develops, and changes. It is the environment within which law is produced. We need to talk about political process because the (political) environment we have is bound to affect the law we have.

A political process includes the widest application of all branches and functions of government. It is the management of affairs of state. It is the exercise of rights and privileges relevant to the control of public policy, and it includes all organizations related to that purpose. For short, think of the political process as the conduct of government in its widest sense.

In this course we will use the U.S. government as our model of a political process. Using that model we can note that the most fundamental features of this system are the following: (1) It is constitutional; (2) it is organized around a doctrine of separated power; (3) state power is limited by a Bill of Rights; and (4) it is democratic. That is the form of government in the United States. It also sets out the basic political process. We are talking about a government that functions by majority rule, limited by individual rights guaranteed by a Constitution that also limits centralized government power by the device of checks and balances. Must any political process have these features? Obviously not. A political process might take many forms. A government might be a democracy (ruled by the majority), it might be an oligarchy (ruled by a few, such as a family or a central committee), or it might be a monarchy or a dictatorship (ruled by one). Any of these sources of power might be limited by a constitution or it might not. Any of these forms might or might not recognize individual rights. Given the possible combinations of even these most basic features of government, it is easy to see that political processes come in a wide variety of forms.

In this chapter we will consider the four basic elements of a political process set out in the last paragraph: the notion of a constitution, the doctrine of separated power, the idea of a right, and the form of a legislative process—especially democracy. Section 1 first examines what it means for a government to be constitutional, especially in the modern sense of that term. Next, we will look at the implications of organizing government power so that each branch of government serves as a check and a balance against the power of other branches. Section 2 considers the concept of a right and the theory of natural rights that strongly influenced the U.S. Constitution. In Section 3 we will study democracy, the idea of a legislative process, and the concept of representation. Overall we will want to consider the implications and consequences of having a political process with basic features such as these, and what happens to law if you change them.

Constitutional Government and the Rule of Law

In this section we will first consider what it means for a government to be constitutional. Strictly speaking, the constitution of anything is simply its composition, the way it is put together. The constitution of the human body, for example, is the totality of the physical structure and the working systems (nervous, circulatory, skeletal, and so on) that make it up. The original use of the term *constitutional* as applied to government referred to descriptions of its structure. Aristotle, being a good political scientist as well as a good philosopher, collected and catalogued many different state constitutions. Monarchy is one way a state may be constituted. Oligarchy is another.

Today, however, the idea of a constitutional government has a more specialized meaning. In the United States many people think of a constitution as a document — a piece of paper that sets out the most basic rules of government. This view may (and should) also include a tradition of legal development, the fundamental law of the land, which flows from that document, generally through the interpretation of a system of courts. In this view a constitutional government is a government founded on such a document and legal tradition.

That view is too narrow, however, since it excludes England (to name only one example), which is clearly a constitutional government. England has no single written document called the Constitution that sets out its basic structure and principle. Obviously, a single document like the U.S. Constitution is not a necessary condition for constitutional government. In fact, no written document is necessary. But then what is?

For a government to be constitutional in the modern sense of the term there must be some set of understandings, some standards, that are commonly recognized and accepted as basic or fundamental, or even as defining with regard to that government. That is, there is a set of organizational and operational principles and requirements that is so basic that it exceeds or transcends the power of any individual to change it. England's Magna Carta is a good beginning example.

The Magna Carta (or Great Charter) was a set of demands presented to King John in 1215 by a group of powerful merchants, nobles, and clergymen that in effect said that the king henceforth would be bound by the law — at least the law written in the Magna Carta. Since at the time John desperately needed the support of these individuals, he had to agree that he, even he, the great King of England, would forever comply with the agreement. From that day forward the power of every king of England was limited by that set of demands (and by others that followed over time). From that day on, England became a constitutional monarchy. Constitutional government, then, is government according to a set of settled, recognized principles, the power of which is superior to that of any individual.

That does not mean that no king could or ever would break the agreement. Laws, agreements, contracts, promises can always be broken or abused by individuals on occasion. We will discuss later the question whether a law that is constantly broken is still a law; but in this context it is clear that if the kings of England consistently ignored the Magna Carta, the charter would not exist. There would be no agreement, no contract, only a useless piece of paper with some empty words written on it. On the other hand, if there were no written charter but rather an oral agreement, known by all, recognized by all, and generally complied with and acknowledged, the charter would exist without any document. The important point is not that a constitution be written but that it be recognized as binding.

It is a conceptual property of law, contracts, agreements, promises, and certainly of constitutions that they must be recognized as binding. It does not follow, of course, that they cannot be broken. In fact, if they were not binding, there would be nothing to break. Thus the kings of England could and would break the charter from time to time. They could be outside the law. What they could not be, ever again, was above the law. Never again could an English king say, as James I said: "The law is whatever I say it is." A king might get away with doing whatever he wanted to do, at least for a while, but no king could legally do whatever he wanted to do, because certain features of law had been fixed by agreement, the power of which was recognized to exceed the power of any individual. That fundamental quality, that priority of power, is the special feature of modern constitutions with which we are concerned here. It is often called the *rule of law*.

We have just seen an illustration of the modern meaning of *constitutional government*. The term no longer refers to the composition of government, whatever it may happen to be. Constitutionalism in modern usage incorporates certain normative ideals, most centrally the notion of a rule of law. The first reading selection, from George Dargo's little book, traces the American experience and explains the American conception of constitutionalism and the commitment to a rule of law. Keep in mind that Dargo is examining the constitution of a particular government only. With Aristotle, in the next selection, we return to the origins of systematic political thought to examine the constitution of all government, or of government in general. This is a very different perspective.

Aristotle catalogues a number of different constitutions and considers their implications and justifications. He also puts the question whether a rule of men or a rule of law is the better form of government. The little excerpt from Edward S. Corwin gives the American answer to that question. But ask yourself why that should be the answer. Aristotle provides some arguments. At the end of this section are collected several constitutions and related documents. As you review these documents, consider the range of possible constitutions. What makes one better than another?

Since constitutional government is a rule of law, it limits the power of individuals. Constitutional principles are fundamental in the sense that they override or outrank any other legal consideration. They are important because they limit the power of particular men and women. Even an emperor is not above the law in a constitutional government. Thus one very important feature of a constitution in modern usage is that it necessarily limits power. That is a conceptual feature of political constitutions.

It is also obvious that some constitutions limit individual power much more than others. As Aristotle pointed out, it is perfectly possible for a constitution to vest all power in a hereditary monarchy. If it did, then one family could be exceedingly powerful, although limited by constitution. That family might have the power to do anything whatsoever except give away their power. So constitutional limits can be quite minimal. In fact, however, constitutions have often been used to limit power a great deal. They are particularly well suited to this purpose because constitutions are what specify the organization of offices and the distribution of power. That is another conceptual feature of constitutions. All constitutions do that. It is part of what it means to be a constitution. A constitution just is (in part) a specification of the organization of offices, powers, and duties of a government.

It is not a necessary feature of constitutions to divide power but only to distribute it in one way or another. The idea of dividing power, of balancing the power of one branch of government against another, is a particular substantive theory of good government that presupposes certain values. These values and presuppositions are reflected in the U.S. Constitution. The cornerstone of American constitutional government was an abiding distrust of centralized power. As summarized by Laurence Tribe, the vision of government held by the framers of the Constitution (although differing in detail) was a model of separated and divided power. Thus the framers of the U.S. Constitution set up the structure of government explicitly to divide and limit power as much as possible. The goal was to produce a relatively weak central government. What is the purpose of structuring government this way? What can be accomplished and at what cost?

Montesquieu articulated the liberal foundations which led to the conclusion that such a structure was a superior form of government. The value that is fundamental to this view is the value of political liberty. Are there any restrictions on this value? Do any other values compete with it? Could any other values win? Montesquieu offers a particular theory of how to reconcile individual rights with the general welfare. Notice that how government is structured tilts it in the direction of individual rights or the public interest. Both are important values. What kinds of arguments does Montesquieu utilize to support his conclusions about this issue? How do his arguments compare with those of Aristotle?

Consider the impact of these views on the political arguments presented in the Federalist Papers (at the end of this section). The purpose of the Federalist Papers was to promote support for the adoption of the Constitution. How are Montesquieu's ideas manifested in the body of the Constitution (see Appendix)? Study questions to help focus the reading specifically on the topic are given at the beginning of each selection. Take advantage of these "Notes and Questions." They function as a comprehensive, self-contained study guide.

Notes and Questions

GEORGE DARGO, from *Law in the New Republic*

1. We begin with an example, the beginning of a new nation, the United States of America. We can consider the events described by George Dargo—the revolution, the Declaration of Independence, the drafting of the federal Constitution—to be the founding of a new government and the start of a new legal system. However, there are important respects in which that is not true. How so? In what ways did the American legal system originate long before the Constitution was drafted? What sorts of restrictions did history, background, or custom (for example) place on the form of government or constitution that was possible in the United States in 1787?

2. Dargo points out that the American Revolution produced (and was concerned with) profound legal changes in some areas of U.S. law and virtually no change at all in others. To explain this he makes use of a commonly drawn distinction between public and private law. How does he explain this distinction—in what does it consist? Is it a conceptual distinction—does the concept of law have divisions or subcategories? Is it a functional distinction—does it refer to how law works? What sort of distinction is it? Would any legal system have to incorporate this distinction, or is it specific to a particular legal system? Whether it is a contingent or a necessary property of legal systems, it is clear that the distinction need not always manifest itself in the same way. For example, religion and control of the press were once considered matters of public law but are now considered matters of private conscience, and in fact are so guaranteed by the Constitution. What, if anything, is the significance of this distinction? Does it imply or promote certain values and retard others? Does it say anything about the form of government?

3. According to Dargo there was intense concern to set up this new government on the "right foundation"—that is, the right constitution or basic structure—not just any foundation would do.

Obviously the American colonists thought that the way a government is put together has enormous consequences. What difference might it make? In "Collected Documents" at the end of this section and the next one, as well as in the Appendix at the end of this book, there are several sample constitutions and related documents, such as bills of rights. Review them and consider what difference it would make which you choose as the foundation of government. For example, would you prefer the Pennsylvania or the New York Constitution? Why? In general and in particular what did the drafters want to guarantee in these constitutions? Are such guarantees possible? How?

4. Is it important for a constitution to be written? Is the U.S. Constitution, for example, likely to be more secure than the (unwritten) Constitution of England? If so, in what way? If not, what differences might a written constitution make? Why did the colonists agree that the Constitution should be written?

5. The U.S. Constitution is recognized as a "compromise document" in many ways. In what ways? Is this view compatible with the idea that there are "fixed principles of natural law which should be embodied in a written document" as Dargo tells us the colonists believed? If so, how? What was the fight between the liberals and the conservatives about in regard to the Constitution? Compare the constitutions of Pennsylvania and New York. What clash of values is implied in such disputes?

6. It is thought that one of the most important phrases in the Constitution is the supremacy clause. What is it, and what does it mean? If the clause were not there would it be necessary to assume it? What would a constitution (written or unwritten) amount to without such an assumption? Look at the Articles of Confederation (see "Collected Documents"). Does the document contain a supremacy clause? How does the notion of a supremacy clause relate constitutionalism to the ideal of a rule of law? Dargo says that the Constitution made the government of the United States a rule of law and not of men. What does that mean? Look at the Concord Resolutions (also in "Collected Documents"). Is it advocating a rule of law? Does it justify or explain the need for constitutional supremacy?

7. Notice the way the term *constitution* is used by Dargo   or for that matter by the colonists. This is the modern use of the term mentioned in the introduction to this section. Keep this use in mind for comparison with the use of the term in the Aristotle selection.

[From] *Law in the New Republic*

GEORGE DARGO

C H A P T E R   1

Law, the Revolution, and the Constitutional Movement

We begin with the Revolution. There are reasons why we should. The Revolution ushered in a period of extraordinary legal activity, which required the participation of a whole new generation of lawyers. At the outset they were not the best known, or the most experienced, or even the ablest lawyers, since many of these sided with the Loyalists and eventually left the country.[1] Nevertheless, the Revolution was very much a "lawyers' revolution." Many Patriot lawyers played important roles at the state and continental levels of government. And the attitudes, values, and institutional changes which emerged in the aftermath of the Revolution, and which continue to this day to animate American public life, were rooted in the legal traditions which were the common experience of that unique generation of American legal professionals.

But if the Revolution was a lawyers' revolution, and if it did cause significant legal change in America, the effect of those changes was uneven. They affected some legal institutions and not others, and some areas of American law more than others. One way of capturing the differentiation is to distinguish between public law and private law. The words "public" and "private" are generally used as opposites. "Private" means belonging to or concerning an individual person, company, or interest. "Public" pertains to the people as a whole—to the nation, state, or community at large. A law is private if it is in the interest of the individual, as distinguished from being for the benefit of the public. Public laws affect the community and all persons within the law's jurisdiction; private law is law that is enforced by individual actions on the basis of common-law doctrines of private rights.

Public law embraces those areas of law that spell out the powers and limitations of government (constitutional and administrative law), those wrongs that the state will prosecute and punish (criminal law), and the methods, processes, and procedures of the legal system itself (procedural law). Lawmaking by the agreement of private parties (contract law), laws that define injuries and wrongs of one party against another in the absence of contractual obligation (tort law), the body of law that establishes the rights, powers, and privileges as well as the duties, obligations, and responsibilities of those owning property (property law), and a host of other subjects (agency, landlord, and tenant law; family law; commercial law) are called private law.[2]

The American Revolution had a deep, abiding, and immediate impact on American public law. In terms of private law, however, its effects were less dramatic and direct. Thus while changes in American law and in the American legal system in the fifty years after the Revolution were profound, those changes cannot be traced directly to the Revolution itself. What is striking, in fact, is the strong continuity of private law in the revolutionary era. Private law was one of those social systems that resisted deep change.[3] To be sure, the law's evolution in the half-century following 1776 was very much the product of social forces that the Revolution had released. But the relationship between law and society is complex, and without more evidence than we now have, we cannot conclude that the American Revolution and the changing American legal system were directly connected in a relationship of cause and effect.

This uneven distribution of the reform impulse as between public and private law tells us something about the character of the Revolution and the rather narrow way Americans defined the liberties for which they fought. Their overwhelming desire, after all, was to contain and control political power and to protect private, local rights from governmental interference. The revolutionary generation wanted to circumscribe authority and to define precisely the legitimate functions of government. Consequently, constitutionalism stood at the very center of revolutionary agitation, and constitutional change was the most salient manifestation of the Revolution's effect on American law.[4] Viewing the Revolution retrospectively, the main legal event of the period was the gathering of the Philadelphia Convention of 1787 and the ratification conflict that followed. But for Americans living at the time, the federal structure and the powers of the central government, although important, were questions of far less moment than the constitutional foundations of those governments closest to the people — namely, the states.

On May 10, 1776, almost two months before the Second Continental Congress declared that the North American colonies (except for Canada) were independent from Great Britain, it resolved:

> that it be recommended to the respective assemblies and conventions of the United Colonies, where no governments sufficient to the exigencies of their affairs have been hitherto established, to adopt such government as shall, in the opinion of the representatives of the people, best conduce to the happiness and safety of their constituents in particular, and America in general.[5]

The resolution of May 10 contributed to the resulting agitation for constitutional change, but more likely it was itself a response to that agitation. In either case, from 1776 until nearly the end of the War of Independence most of the American states went through an intensive process of constitution making. Some states even experienced a series of constitutional "revisions" in the course of just a few years, as they experimented with various forms of government and different processes of constitutional adoption.[6]

So central was this preoccupation with constitution making, it even interfered at times with the war effort. For example, in 1777 the New York delegation to the Continental Congress, then meeting in Philadelphia, complained that

> tho' the Enemy is daily expected an astonishing Langour prevails, and the embodying a competent Force to oppose the meditated Invasion,

seems to be a distant Object. The Seat of this Disease is not an Indifference to the Cause. . . . The unhappy Dispute about [the] Constitution is the fatal Rock on which [Pennsylvanians] have split . . . which threatens them with Destruction. We ardently wish that in our own State the utmost Caution may be used to avoid a like Calamity. Every wise Man here wishes that the Establishment of new Forms of Government had been deferred.[7]

And Robert Morris, chief financial officer of the Confederation, reported to General Horatio Gates that the entire Maryland delegation had gone home in order to participate in the formation of a state constitution. "This seems to be the present business of all America, except the Army," he lamented.[8] As a Virginia delegate concluded regretfully: "Constitutions employ every pen."[9]

But if some members of the Continental Congress understandably saw things from the perspective of the military emergency, many other Americans viewed the constitution-making process much less casually. For them, this was what the Revolution was all about. If the results of independence were to be nothing more than the substitution of one form of oppressive government for another, then the effort was not worth making. Climactic moments in history are infrequent, but this was clearly one of them, and the moment had to be seized. An article in a Philadelphia newspaper printed on July 1, 1776, one day before independence was declared and three days before the Declaration of Independence was adopted, put it best:

> The affair now in view is the most important that ever was before America. In my opinion it is the most important that has been transacted in any nation for some centuries past. If our civil Government is well constructed, and well managed, America bids fair to be the most glorious state that has ever been on earth. We should now at the beginning *lay the foundation right.* . . . The plan of American Government, should, as much as possible, be formed to suit all the varieties of circumstances that people may be in. . . . For we may expect a variety of circumstances in a course of time, and we should be prepared for every condition.[10]

How to "lay the foundation right" was, however, a source of bitter dispute and continuing conflict.

The issues were many, some procedural and others substantive. On the procedural side, a much debated question was whether the state legislatures or the people directly, acting through special constitutional conventions, should draft constitutional instruments. The latter was a novel idea, and like most truly revolutionary notions, it was not immediately accepted. The Town Meeting of Concord, Massachusetts, stated the problem with penetrating clarity:

> [If] the same body that forms a Constitution have of consequence a power to alter it [then there is no security for liberty] because a Constitution alterable by the Supreme Legislature is no security at all to the subject against any encroachment of the governing part on any, or on all of their rights and privileges.[11]

If the legislature had the power to draft and adopt a constitution then there would be no true difference between an ordinary statute and the organic or fundamental law. The constitution had to be kept safe from legislative tampering and interference. The most effective way to achieve such a goal was to call into being a special body whose sole purpose was the adoption of a constitution. Once adopted the body would dissolve forever. A constitutional convention was not a continuing body but a special body organized for a special purpose.[12]

On substantive issues, such as the structure of government, the powers of the different governmental branches, and the relations between local and central authority, there was deep division between "radicals" who wanted to give maximum authority to the people and "conservatives" who preferred to limit popular sovereignty as much as possible.[13] Included on the radical agenda for constitutional change were the following: (1) the reduction of the role and power of "governors" to that of mere "executives"; (2) provision for legislative impeachment for "executive maladministration"; (3) frequent elections of representatives to the state legislatures; (4) the substitution of residency for property tests in setting voting requirements; (5) separation of the powers of the three functional branches of government to reduce executive influence; and (6) unicameralism in the legislative branch. The most extreme example of radical constitutionalism in action was the Pennsylvania Constitution of 1776, which completely eliminated a single chief executive, established a unicameral legislature, and set up a procedure for periodic revision of the framework of government.[14]

On the other hand, conservatives wanted to maintain property qualifications for voting and for officeholding; they wanted bicameral legislatures so that each branch would serve as a check on the other; and they preferred to increase the power of the executive to counteract the excesses of runaway popular legislatures. While radicals wanted the executives to be chosen by and responsible to the legislatures, conservatives preferred to have the executives elected on their own so that they would have an independent power base that would enable them to withstand legislative "encroachment."[15] Above all, conservatives advocated judicial review of legislative action.

The constitutional convention idea, while innovative and even revolutionary in concept, was also part of the conservative program. Putting the constitution-making process into the hands of the people was one way of keeping it from the legislatures. Conservatives played on fears of "legislative tyranny." Their program for combating it was to emphasize the distinction between "ordinary law" and "fundamental law"; to support that distinction by giving the people the power to declare the fundamental law in the form of a written constitution; and then to give the courts the function of preserving that distinction through the exercise of the power of judicial review.

The first suggestion that courts should exercise some power of review over legislative enactments came from the conservative camp. New York established a Council of Revision, consisting of the highest executive and judicial officers of the state, whose job it was to review the acts of the legislature.[16] The New York Constitution of 1777 — in which the constitutional powers of the governor were unusually broad — was, in fact, a victory for constitutional conservatism. As such, it served as a model for the Founding Fathers in the design of the office of the presidency.[17] The creation at the national level of a powerful chief executive chosen by a special electoral college, rather than by Congress or the state legislatures directly, can be fairly interpreted as a conservative triumph.

On some constitutional issues there was little disagreement between radicals and conservatives. All agreed that a written constitution was preferable to England's unwritten constitution. Americans believed that fixed principles of government were among the immutable "laws of nature."[18] The task of political theorists was to discover those fixed principles, while the task of political activists was to ground those principles in the constitution, the fundamental law of the state. If from an English perspective the strength of the English constitution was its fluidity and its responsiveness to political change, then from an American perspective the strength of American constitutionalism was the detachment of day-to-day politics from those timeless truths about man and government that it wished to preserve for all time.

These ideas were codified in constitutional provisions that defined the constitution as law. The Massachusetts Constitution of 1780 put it this way:

> This form of government shall be enrolled on parchment, and deposited in the Secretarys office, *and be a part of the laws of the land*; and printed copies thereof shall be prefixed to the book containing the laws of this Commonwealth, in all future editions of the said laws [emphasis added].[19]

The notion of written charters having the force and effect of law was not new to Americans. Ever since early colonial times, "charters," "compacts," "orders," "liberties," and "agreements" had been recognized as having legal force.[20] But if it was not a new idea, the Revolution gave it special force and powerful articulation. The use of written constitutions as law was, and remains, a uniquely American contribution to the development of modern government. The French, for example, drafted written constitutions during the French Revolution; but these were little more than frames of government, constitutional blueprints, and statements of political purpose—rather than enforceable legal tools. In America, constitutions had legal authority to which all other law had to conform. As declared by the Massachusetts Constitution:

> [F]ull power and authority are hereby given and granted to the said General Court, from time to time, to make, ordain, and establish, all manner of wholesome and reasonable orders, laws, statutes, and ordinances, directions and instructions, either with penalties or without; *so as the same be not repugnant or contrary to this Constitution* [emphasis added].[21]

Provisions of this kind were significant for two reasons. First, and most important, they made constitutional guarantees of personal liberty enforceable in the courts. In many states these were called bills of rights.[22] Second, they laid the basis for judicial review. While some would argue that "nonrepugnancy" clauses— such as the Massachusetts provision cited above—were not a justification for court review of legislative enactments, particularly in the absence of specific constitutional authorization, it was surely inevitable that high appellate courts would use the written constitution to monitor the decisions of lower courts within their jurisdictions. Thus while the broad reach of John Marshall's decision in *Marbury v. Madison*,[23] outraged many, who labeled it "judicial usurpation," some sort of special constitutional role was bound to be played by the courts in a system with a written constitution that was defined as law.[24]

In the end, the idea of a written constitution appealed to radicals and conservatives alike, although in different ways. Radicals liked it because it made legally enforceable such individual rights as religious freedom, security from unlawful arrest, and the right of peaceable assembly and petition. But conservatives also favored the idea because it secured the right to property and was a potential basis for the exercise of the power of judicial review, a power that state as well as federal courts began to exercise with increasing frequency in the decades following the Revolution. Contemporaries perceived the Pennsylvania constitution of 1776, with its unicameral legislature and its plural executive, as the most "radical" of the state constitutions. The New York constitution of 1777, on the other hand, was thought to be a model of "conservatism" because of the great power of the governor's office and the establishment of a special body, the Council of Revision, to review acts of the legislative branch. In fact, almost every state constitution contained some elements of both the "radical" and the "conservative" program. But this should not be surprising since state constitutions were often adopted only after hot political conflict and debate which usually resulted in some kind of compromise and accommodation.

The United States Constitution drafted and ratified by Federalists* (who were seen as "rich and well-born") and opposed by Antifederalists (who had an image of radicalism) contained within it some of the radical program: representation by population in the House, congressional control over military budgets, the power to impeach, the machinery for amendment, specific enumeration of congressional powers, the reservation of powers to the states, and, eventually, the adoption of the federal Bill of Rights showed the impact of radical thought at the federal level. But conservatives could also claim victories: a bicameral Congress, a powerful chief executive, an independent federal judiciary, the equality of the House and Senate, and a prohibition on state legislative impairment of private contractual obligations.

However, there was, also, in the federal Constitution an overriding concept on which both radicals and conservatives could agree, each for their own reasons. This was the supremacy clause, which can be thought of as the single most important provision of that great document:

> This Constitution, and the laws of the United States which shall be made in pursuance thereof, and all treaties made, or which shall be made, under the authority of the United States, shall be the *supreme law of the land*: And the Judges in every State shall be bound thereby, *anything in the Constitution or laws of any State to the contrary notwithstanding* [emphasis added].[25]

The supremacy clause was principally designed to give effect to the nationalism of men such as John Jay, Alexander Hamilton, Gouverneur Morris, and George Washington: to bind the states into an organic nation under one supreme law that would be applied by national (or "federal") courts. But in the context of the whole constitutional movement, state as well as federal, the supremacy clause has independent and additional significance. It is the element that most distinguished the Constitution of the United States from the Articles of Confederation adopted in 1781. In giving the Constitution the force of law, the framers created an instrument of government comparable to the state constitutions. This was no mere "league of friendship"[26] among the several states but a true government of awesome potentiality. In that respect its opponents, who feared the enhanced power of the central government, were right to clamor for limitations on the national authority—a clamor that led to the adoption of the federal Bill of Rights.[27] The supremacy clause made the guarantees codified in the Bill of Rights legally enforceable limitations first on Congress and later on government in general.

For all of its economy of statement, therefore, the United States Constitution is extraordinary in its scope. It bound the states as well as the national government into a union of law, and it made the government of the United States truly a "government of laws and not of men."

NOTES

1. A recent study of the American Loyalists concludes that while a majority of lawyers were Whig (i.e., Patriots), most of the leaders of the bar, the "giants of the law," remained loyal to the Crown. See Wallace Brown, *The King's Friends: The Composition and Motives of the American Loyalist Claimants* (Providence, R.I., 1965), p. 265. For a discussion of the impact of the Revolution upon the legal profession in one state see Gerard W. Gawalt, *The Promise of Power: The Emergence of the Legal Profession in Massachusetts, 1760–1840* (Westport, Conn., 1979).

2. Statutes of general application are public laws, but private bills—those passed at the petition of individuals—are not. While statutes that have systematized large areas of commercial law, such as the modern Uniform Commercial Code, are part of public law, the body of substantive law thus codified and the continuing interpretation and construction of the UCC is the result of the litigation of private parties and is, to that extent, still part of the private law.

3. As one noted legal historian has concluded with reference to New England: "The War of Independence had virtually no effect upon the system of private law administered in New England." Richard B. Morris,

---

*The term "federalist" was used in the 1780s to denote strong nationalistic proclivities while the term "antifederalist" referred to that political persuasion which would preserve the sovereignty of the states. These terms should not be confused with the Federalist Party and the Jeffersonian opposition which grew out of the policies of the Washington administration in the early 1790s.

"Legalism *versus* Revolutionary Doctrine in New England," *The New England Quarterly*, 4 (1931), 195–215, quote at p. 215. See also Stanley N. Katz, "Republicanism and the Law of Inheritance in the American Revolutionary Era," *Michigan Law Review*, 76 (1977), 1–29, which examines the modest impact of the Revolution on inheritance law.

4. Gordon S. Wood, *The Creation of the American Republic*, 1776–1787 (Chapel Hill, N.C., 1969), chaps. 4, 5, and 6.

5. Worthington C. Ford (ed.), *Journals of the Continental Congress*, 1774–1789 (Washington, D.C., 1904–1937), vol. 4, p. 342.

6. Willi Paul Adams, *The First American Constitutions: Republican Ideology and the Making of the State Constitutions in the Revolutionary Era* (Chapel Hill, N.C., 1980); Elisha P. Douglass, *Rebels and Democrats: The Struggle for Equal Political Rights and Majority Rule During the American Revolution* (Chicago, 1965).

7. Philip Livingston, James Duane, and William Duer to Abraham Ten Broeck, April 29, 1777, reprinted in E. C. Burnett (ed.), *Letters of Members of the Continental Congress* (Washington, D.C., 1921–1936), vol. 2, p. 344.

8. Morris to Gates, October 27, 1776, in ibid., p. 135.

9. F. L. Lee to Landon Carter, November 9, 1776, in ibid., p. 149.

10. *Pennsylvania Packer*, July 1, 1776 (emphasis added); Wood, *Creation of the American Republic*, pp. 127–132 et passim. (See Document 2.)

11. See Document 1.

12. While a minority of the states used the convention device either as part of the drafting process or as part of ratification, the federal Constitution of 1787 was both proposed and ratified by the convention method. Thus the process of federal constitution-making was truly innovative, even radical, in its time. Contemporary critics—and liberal historians—focused more upon the conservative substance of the Constitution than the manner of its adoption. See Richard Hofstadter, *The Progressive Historians: Turner, Beard, Parrington* (New York, 1968), chaps. 5–7; Charles A. Beard, *An Economic Interpretation of the Constitution of the United States* (New York, 1913); and Wood, *Creation of the American Republic*, chap. 12.

13. Adams, *First American Constitutions*, chaps. 6–13, and Douglass, *Rebels and Democrats*, passim.

14. Ibid., chap. 14.

15. Wood, *Creation of the American Republic*, chap. 11.

16. See Document 4.

17. Compare New York Constitution (1777), Arts. XVII and XVIII, and U.S. Constitution (1787), Art. II (Documents 4 and 6).

18. George Dargo, "Parties and the Transformation of the Constitutional Idea in Revolutionary Pennsylvania," in *Party and Political Opposition in Revolutionary America*, ed. Patricia U. Bonomi (New York, 1980), p. 110 et passim.

19. Massachusetts Constitution (1780), Chap. VI, Art. XI.

20. George Dargo, *Roots of the Republic: A New Perspective on Early American Constitutionalism* (New York, 1974), chap. 3.

21. Massachusetts Constitution (1780), Chap. I, Art. IV.

22. For example, Virginia Declaration of Rights (1776). (See Document 7.)

23. See Document 8.

24. For a discussion of judicial review and the intent of the framers, see Raoul Berger, *Congress v. The Supreme Court* (Cambridge, Mass., 1969), chap. 7.

25. U.S. Constitution (1787), Art. VI.

26. See Document 5.

27. Alphens T. Mason, *The States Rights Debate: Antifederalism and the Constitution* (Englewood Cliffs, N.J., 1964), pp. 1–7.

[From] "The 'Higher Law' Background of American Constitutional Law"

EDWARD S. CORWIN

On Rule of Law as Constitutional

The Reformation superseded an infallible Pope with an infallible Bible; the American Revolution replaced the sway of a king with that of a document. That such would be the outcome was not unforeseen from the first. In the same number of *Common Sense* which contained his electrifying proposal that America should declare her independence from Great Britain, Paine urged also a "Continental Conference," whose task he described as follows:

> The conferring members being met, let their business be to frame a Continental Charter, or Charter of the United Colonies; (answering to what is called the Magna Charta of England) fixing the number and manner of choosing members of congress and members of assembly . . . and drawing the line of business and jurisdiction between them: (always remembering, that our strength is continental, not provincial) securing freedom and property to all men . . . with such other matter as it is necessary for a charter to contain. . . . But where, say some, is the King of America? Yet that we may not appear to be detective even in earthly honors, let a day be solemnly set apart for proclaiming the charter; let it be brought forth placed in the divine law, the word of God; let a crown be placed thereon, by which the world may know, that so far as we approve of monarchy, that in America the law is King.[1]

This suggestion, which was to eventuate more than a decade later in the Philadelphia Convention, is not less interesting for its retrospection than it is for its prophecy.

In the words of the younger Adams, "the Constitution itself had been extorted from the grinding necessity of a reluctant nation";[2] yet hardly had it gone into operation than hostile criticism of its provisions not merely ceased but gave place to "an undiscriminating and almost blind worship of its principles"[3] — a worship which continued essentially unchallenged till the other day. Other creeds have waxed and waned, but "worship of the Constitution" has proceeded unabated.[4] It is true that the Abolitionists were accustomed to stigmatize the Constitution as "an agreement with Hell," but their shrill heresy only stirred the mass of Americans to renewed assertion of the national faith. Even Secession posed as loyalty to the *principles* of the Constitution and a protest against their violation, and in form at least the constitution of the Southern Confederacy was, with a few minor departures, a studied reproduction of the instrument of 1787. For by far the greater reach of its history, Bagehot's appraisal of the British monarchy is directly applicable to the Constitution: "The English Monarchy strengthens our government with the strength of religion."[5]

* * *

NOTES

1. PAINE, POLITICAL WRITINGS (1837) 45–46.
2. ADAMS, JUBILEE DISCOURSE ON THE CONSTITUTION (1839) 55.
3. WOODROW WILSON, CONGRESSIONAL GOVERNMENT (13th ed. 1898) 4.
4. On the whole subject, see 1 VON HOLST, CONSTITUTIONAL HISTORY (1877) c. 2; Schechter, *Early History of the Tradition of the Constitution* (1915) 9 AM. POL. SCI. REV. 707 *et seq.*
5. BAGEHOT, ENGLISH CONSTITUTION (2d ed. 1925) 39. "The monarchy by its religious sanction now confirms all our political order. . . . It gives . . . a vast strength to the entire constitution, by enlisting on its behalf the credulous obedience of enormous masses." *Ibid.* 43–44.

Notes and Questions

ARISTOTLE, from *Politics*

1. What, according to Aristotle, is the constitution of a state? Name some different possible constitutions. Notice the different ways Aristotle uses the term *constitutional*. How does his use differ from the modern usage? What is the difference between constitutional principle and laws, according to Aristotle? Is the distinction helpful? How does it compare to the distinction implied in the Concord Resolutions (see "Collected Documents")?

2. Aristotle says that different laws are appropriate to different constitutions. What does this mean? Is it true regarding all laws, or are some laws (for example, the protection of some values or some requirements of justice, such as protection of life by sanction for murder) so basic as to transcend constitutional differences? How different does a constitution have to be in order to affect the appropriateness of laws? Is the difference between the New York and Pennsylvania constitutions enough? The difference between the American and French constitutions? Between the American and the Chinese constitutions? Between the constitutions of Sparta and Athens?

3. All constitutions have three elements, Aristotle observes. What are they? These elements refer to the basic functions of government, do they not? Do modern constitutions include these three elements? Would any government have to include them? In other words, suppose one of these functions were not performed. Would you still have a legal system? Would you still have a state? Do modern constitutions include other elements as well—are there basic elements that Aristotle omitted or some government function that has become indispensable since Aristotle wrote? If so, what are they? What new category must be invented to classify them?

4. Aristotle differentiates among forms of government in terms of the distribution of power. What are the possible ways power can be distributed? Does Aristotle characterize any of these distributions as necessarily better than any others?

5. What makes a government (or constitution) good—or as Aristotle puts it, a "true form" or legitimate form of government? Notice that Aristotle assumes that government is basically good. Since human beings by nature are political animals and the purpose of government is the common good, a true form of government is naturally good. Bad government—especially government that serves the interest of the rulers at the expense of the ruled—is a perversion of government. Is this compatible with the assumption of the framers of the U.S. Constitution? Does anything follow about the best constitution from Aristotle's view?

6. After struggling with the distinction between rule of the few and rule of the many, Aristotle decides that the distinction between aristocracy and constitutional government is not really based on numbers but on whether the basis of the claim to rule is wealth (we would now say property) or free birth. Why should either of these be a ground for power? If the purpose of government is the common good, who would be in a good position to fulfill that goal? Why? Who would be likely to be able to determine what the common good is? What did the colonists think?

7. What is justice, according to Aristotle? In considering how justice relates to democracy and oligarchy, what does Aristotle conclude? Why does he think neither wealth nor free birth can be a sufficient ground for the claim to rule? Ultimately, he argues, the state exists to promote the good life. What does he mean by the good life?

8. Does Aristotle say the best man or the best law should rule? Why does he think so? Do you agree? Suppose we consider the worst man or the worst law—or the best chance of avoiding the

worst government. Would these considerations strengthen or weaken Aristotle's argument? Does it follow that a rule of law is always better than a rule of men?

9. Compare the way Aristotle talks about a rule of law with the way the colonists (according to Dargo) regard the Constitution. Are they different? What are the differences? What are the similarities?

10. A rule of man is a dictatorship, in terms of power. The danger is in getting a bad one. That risk is not of an inherent evil. It simply leads to the conclusion that on balance the risk of a bad dictator is not worth the benefit of a good one. But Aristotle argues that a rule of law is better for more reasons than this. What are they? What are the benefits of each?

[From] *Politics*

ARISTOTLE

On Constitutions

Book IV

C.1. . . . A constitution is the organization of offices in a state, and determines what is to be the governing body, and what is the end of each community. But laws are not to be confounded with the principles of the constitution; they are the rules according to which the magistrates should administer the state, and proceed against offenders. So that we must know the varieties, and the number of varieties, of each form of government, if only with a view to making laws. For the same laws cannot be equally suited to all oligarchies or to all democracies, since there is certainly more than one form both of democracy and of oligarchy.

* * *

C.14. Having thus gained an appropriate basis of discussion we will proceed to speak of the points which follow next in order. We will consider the subject not only in general but with reference to particular constitutions. All constitutions have three elements, concerning which the good lawgiver has to regard what is expedient for each constitution. When they are well-ordered, the constitution is well-ordered, and as they differ from one another, constitutions differ. There is (1) one element which deliberates about public affairs; secondly (2) that concerned with the magistracies—the question being, what they should be, over what they should exercise authority, and what should be the mode of electing to them; and thirdly (3) that which has judicial power.

The deliberative element has authority in matters of war and peace, in making and unmaking alliances; it passes laws, inflicts death, exile, confiscation, elects magistrates and audits their accounts. These powers must be assigned either all to all the citizens or all to some of them (for example, to one or more magistracies, or different causes to different magistracies), or some of them to all and others of them only to some. That all things should be decided by all is characteristic of democracy; this is the sort of equality which the people desire. But there are various ways in which all may share in the government; they may deliberate, not all in one body, but by turns, as in the constitution of Telecles the Milesian. There are other constitutions in which the boards of magistrates meet and deliberate, but come into office by turns, and are elected out of the tribes and the very smallest divisions of the state, until every one has obtained office in his turn. The citizens, on the other hand, are assembled only for the purposes of legislation, and to consult about the constitution, and to hear the edicts of the magistrates. In another variety of democracy the citizens form one assembly, but meet only to elect magistrates, to pass laws, to advise about war and peace, and to make scrutinies. Other matters are referred severally to special magistrates, who are elected by vote or by lot out of all the citizens. Or again, the citizens meet about election to offices and about scrutinies, and deliberate concerning war or alliances while other matters are administered by the magistrates, who, as far as is possible, are elected by vote. I am speaking of those magistracies in which special knowledge is required. A fourth form of democracy is when all the citizens meet to deliberate about everything, and the magistrates decide nothing, but only make the preliminary inquiries; and that is the way in which the last and worst form of democracy, corresponding, as we maintain, to the close family oligarchy and to tyranny, is at present administered. All these modes are democratical.

On the other hand, that some should deliberate about all is oligarchical. This again is a mode which, like the democratical, has many forms.

* * *

Book III

C.6. . . . we have next to consider whether there is only one form of government or many, and if many, what they are, and how many, and what are the differences between them.

A constitution is the arrangement of magistracies in a state, especially of the highest of all. The government is everywhere sovereign in the state, and the constitution is in fact the government. For example, in democracies the people are supreme, but in oligarchies, the few; and, therefore, we say that these two forms of government also are different; and so in other cases.

First, let us consider what is the purpose of a state, and how many forms of government there are by which human society is regulated. We have already said, in the first part of this treatise, when discussing household management and the rule of a master, that man is by nature a political animal. And therefore, men, even whey they do not

require one another's help, desire to live together; not but that they are also brought together by their common interests in proportion as they severally attain to any measure of well-being. This is certainly the chief end, both of individuals and of states. And also for the sake of mere life (in which there is possibly some noble element so long as the evils of existence do not greatly overbalance the good) mankind meet together and maintain the political community. And we all see that men cling to live even at the cost of enduring great misfortune, seeming to find in life a natural sweetness and happiness.

There is no difficulty in distinguishing the various kinds of authority; they have been often defined already in discussions outside the school. The rule of a master, although the slave by nature and the master by nature have in reality the same interests, is nevertheless exercised primarily with a view to the interest of the master, but accidentally considers the slave, since, if the slave perish, the rule of the master perishes with him. On the other hand, the government of a wife and children and of a household, which we have called household management, is exercised in the first instance for the good of the governed or for the common good of both parties, but essentially for the good of the governed, as we see to be the case in medicine, gymnastic, and the arts in general, which are only accidentally concerned with the good of the artists themselves. For there is no reason why the trainer may not sometimes practise gymnastics, and the helmsman is always one of the crew. The trainer or the helmsman considers the good of those committed to his care. but, when he is one of the persons taken care of, he accidentally participates in the advantage, for the helmsman is also a sailor, and the trainer becomes one of those in training. And so in politics: when the state is framed upon the principle of equality and likeness, the citizens think that they ought to hold office by turns. Formerly, as is natural every one would take his turn of service; and then again, somebody else would look after his interest, just as he, while in office, had looked after theirs. But nowadays, for the sake of the advantage which is to be gained from the public revenues and from office, men want to be always in office. One might imagine that the rulers, being sickly, were only kept in health while they continued in office; in that case we may be sure that they would be hunting after places. The conclusion is evident: that governments which have a regard to the common interest are constituted in accordance with strict principles of justice and are therefore true forms; but those which regard only the interest of the rulers are all defective and perverted forms, for they are despotic, whereas a state is a community of freemen.

C.7. Having determined these points, we have next to consider how many forms of government there are, and what they are; and in the first place what are the true forms, for when they are determined the perversions of them will at once be apparent. The words constitution and government have the same meaning, and the government, which is the supreme authority in states, must be in the hands of one, or of a few, or of the many. The true forms of government, therefore, are those in which the one, or the few, or the many, govern with a view to the common interest; but governments which rule with a view to the private interest, whether of the one, or of the few, or of the many, are perversions. For the members of a state, if they are truly citizens, ought to participate in its advantages. Of forms of government in which one rules, we call that which regards the common interests, kingship or royalty; that in which more than one, but not many, rule, aristocracy; and it is so called, either because the rulers are the best men, or because they have at heart the best interests of the state and of the citizens. But when the citizens at large administer the state for the common interest, the government is called by the generic name, — a constitution. And there is a reason for this use of language. One man or a few may excel in virtue; but as the number increases it becomes more difficult for them to attain perfection in every kind of virtue, though they may in military virtue, for this is found in the masses. Hence in a constitutional government the fightingmen have the supreme power, and those who possess arms are the citizens.

Of the above-mentioned forms, the perversions are as follows: — of royalty, tyranny; of aristocracy, oligarchy; of constitutional government, democracy. For tyranny is a kind of monarchy which has in view the interest of the monarch only; oligarchy has in view the interest of the wealthy; democracy, of the needy: none of them the common good of all.

C.8. But there are difficulties about these forms of government, and it will therefore be necessary to state a little more at length the nature of each of them. For he who would make a philosophical study of the various sciences, and does not regard practice only, ought not to overlook or omit anything, but to set forth the truth in every particular. Tyranny, as I was saying, is monarchy exercising the rule of a master over the political society; oligarchy is when men of property have the government in their hands; democracy, the opposite, when the indigent, and not the men of property, are the rulers. And here arises the first of our difficulties, and it relates to the distinction just drawn. For democracy is said to be the government of the many. But what if the many are men of property and have the power in their hands? In like manner oligarchy is said to be the government of the few; but what if the poor are fewer than the rich, and have the power in their hands because they are stronger? In these cases the distinction which we have drawn between these different forms of government would no longer hold good.

Suppose, once more, that we add wealth to the few and poverty to the many, and name the governments accordingly — an oligarchy is said to be that in which the few and the wealthy, and a democracy that in which the many and the poor are the rulers — there will still be a difficulty. For, if the only forms of government are the ones already mentioned, how shall we describe those other governments also just mentioned by us, in which the rich are the more numerous and the poor are the fewer, and both govern in their respective states?

The argument seems to show that, whether in oligarchies or in democracies, the number of the governing body, whether the greater number, as in a democracy, or the smaller number, as in an oligarchy, is an accident due to the fact that the rich everywhere are few, and the poor numerous. But if so, there is a misapprehension of the causes of the difference between them. For the real difference between democracy and oligarchy is poverty and wealth. Whatever men rule by reason of their wealth, whether they be few or many, that is an oligarchy, and where the poor rule, that is a democracy. But as a fact the rich are few and the poor many; for few are well-to-do, whereas freedom is enjoyed by all, and wealth and freedom are the grounds on which the oligarchical and democratical parties respectively claim power in the state.

C.9. Let us begin by considering the common definitions of oligarchy and democracy, and what is justice oligarchical and democratical. For all men cling to justice of some kind, but their conceptions are imperfect and they do not express the whole idea. For example, justice is thought by them to be, and is, equality, not, however, for all, but only for equals. And inequality is thought to be, and is, justice; neither is this for all, but only for unequals. When the persons are omitted, then men judge erroneously. The reason is that they are passing judgement on themselves, and most people are bad judges in their own case. And whereas justice implies a relation to persons as well as to things, and a just distribution, as I have already said in the *Ethics*, implies the same ratio between the persons and between the things, they agree about the equality of the things, but dispute about the equality of the persons, chiefly for the reason which I have just given, — because they are bad judges in their own affairs; and secondly, because both the parties to the argument are speaking of a limited and partial justice, but imagine themselves to be speaking of absolute justice. For the one party, if they are unequal in one respect, for example wealth, consider themselves to be unequal in all; and the other party, if they are equal in one respect, for example free birth, consider themselves to be equal in all. But they leave out the capital point. For if men met and associated out of regard to wealth only, their share in the state would be proportioned to their property, and the oligarchical doctrine would then seem to carry the day. It would not be just that he who paid one mina should have the same share of a hundred minae, whether of the principal or of the profits, as he who paid the remaining ninety-nine. But a state exists for the sake of a good life, and not for the sake of life only: if life only were the object,

slaves and brute animals might form a state, but they cannot, for they have no share in happiness or in a life of free choice. Nor does a state exist for the sake of alliance and security from injustice, nor yet for the sake of exchange and mutual intercourse; for then the Tyrrhenians and the Carthaginians, and all who have commercial treaties with one another, would be the citizens of one state. True, they have agreements about imports, and engagements that they will do no wrong to one another, and written articles of alliance. But there are no magistracies common to the contracting parties who will enforce their engagements; different states have each their own magistracies. Nor does one state take care that the citizens of the other are such as they ought to be, nor see that those who come under the terms of the treaty do no wrong or wickedness at all, but only that they do no injustice to one another. Whereas, those who care for good government take into consideration virtue and vice in states. Whence it may be further inferred that virtue must be the care of a state which is truly so called, and not merely enjoys the name: for without this end the community becomes a mere alliance which differs only in place from alliances of which the members live apart; and law is only a convention, "a surety to one another of justice," as the sophist Lycophron says, and has no real power to make the citizens good and just.

This is obvious; for suppose distinct places, such as Corinth and Megara, to be brought together so that their walls touched, still they would not be one city, not even if the citizens had the right to intermarry, which is one of the rights peculiarly characteristic of states. Again, if men dwelt at a distance from one another, but not so far off as to have no intercourse, and there were laws among them that they should not wrong each other in their exchanges, neither would this be a state. Let us suppose that one man is a carpenter, another a husbandman, another a shoemaker, and so on, and that their number is ten thousand: nevertheless, if they have nothing in common but exchange, alliance, and the like, that would not constitute a state. Why is this? Surely not because they are at a distance from one another: for even supposing that such a community were to meet in one place, but that each man had a house of his own, which was in a manner his state, and that they made alliance with one another, but only against evil-doers; still an accurate thinker would not deem this to be a state, if their intercourse with one another was of the same character after as before their union. It is clear then that a state is not a mere society, having a common place, established for the prevention of mutual crime and for the sake of exchange. These are conditions without which a state cannot exist; but all of them together do not constitute a state, which is a community of families and aggregations of families in well-being, for the sake of a perfect and self-sufficing life. Such a community can only be established among those who live in the same place and intermarry. Hence arise in cities family connections, brotherhoods, common sacrifices, amuse-ments which draw men together. But these are created by friendship, for the will to live together is friendship. The end of the state is the good life, and these are the means towards it. And the state is the union of families and villages in a perfect and self-sufficing life, by which we mean a happy and honourable life.

Our conclusion, then, is that political society exists for the sake of noble actions, and not of mere companionship. Hence they who contribute most to such a society have a greater share in it than those who have the same or a greater freedom or nobility of birth but are inferior to them in political virtue; or than those who exceed them in wealth but are surpassed by them in virtue.

From what has been said it will be clearly seen that all the partisans of different forms of government speak of a part of justice only.

On Rule of Law

Book III

C.10. There is also a doubt as to what is to be the supreme power in the state: — Is it the multitude? Or the wealthy? Or the good? Or the one best man? Or a tyrant? Any of these alternatives seems to involve disagreeable consequences. If the poor, for example, because they are more in number, divide among themselves the property of the rich — is not this unjust? No, by heaven (will be the reply), for the supreme authority justly willed it. But if this is not injustice, pray what is? Again, when in the first division all has been taken and the majority divide anew the property of the minority, is it not evident, if this goes on, that they will ruin the state? Yet surely, virtue is not the ruin of those who possess her, nor is justice destructive of a state; and therefore this law of confiscation clearly cannot be just. If it were, all the acts of a tyrant must of necessity be just; for he only coerces other men by superior power, just as the multitude coerce the rich. But is it just then that the few and the wealthy should be the rulers? And what if they, in like manner, rob and plunder the people — is this just? If so, the other case will likewise be just.

But there can be no doubt that all these things are wrong and unjust.

Then ought the good to rule and have supreme power? But in that case everybody else, being excluded from power, will be dishonoured. For the offices of a state are posts of honour; and if one set of men always hold them, the rest must be deprived of them. Then will it be well that the one best man should rule? Nay, that is still more oligarchical, for the number of those who are dishonoured is thereby increased. Some one may say that it is bad in any case for a man, subject as he is to all the accidents of human passion, to have the supreme power, rather than the law. But what if the law itself be democratical or oligarchical, how will that help us out of our difficulties? Not at all; the same consequences will follow.

C.11. Most of these questions may be reserved for another occasion.

* * *

The discussion of the first question shows nothing so clearly as that laws, when good, should be supreme; and that the magistrate or magistrates should regulate those matters only on which the laws are unable to speak with precision owing to the difficulty of any general principle embracing all particulars. But what are good laws has not yet been clearly explained; the old difficulty remains. The goodness or badness, justice or injustice, of laws varies of necessity with the constitutions of states. This, however, is clear, that the laws must be adapted to the constitutions. But if so, true forms of government will of necessity have just laws, and perverted forms of government will have unjust laws.

* * *

C.15. Of these forms we need only consider two, the Lacedaemonian and the absolute royalty; for most of the others lie in a region between them, having less power than the last, and more than the first. Thus the inquiry is reduced to two points; first, is it advantageous to the state that there should be a perpetual general, and if so, should the office be confined to one family, or open to the citizens in turn? Secondly, is it well that a single man should have the supreme power in all things? The first question falls under the head of laws rather than of constitutions; for perpetual generalship might equally exist under any form of government, so that this matter may be dismissed for the present. The other kind of royalty is a sort of constitution; this we have now to consider, and briefly to run over the difficulties involved in it. We will begin by inquiring whether it is more advantageous to be ruled by the best man or by the best laws.

The advocates of royalty maintain that the laws speak only in general terms, and cannot provide for circumstances; and that for any science to abide by written rules is absurd. In Egypt the physician is allowed to alter his treatment after the fourth day, but if sooner, he takes the risk. Hence it is clear that a government acting according to written laws is plainly not the best. Yet surely the ruler cannot dispense with the general principle which exists in law; and that is a better ruler which is free from passion than that in which it is innate. Whereas the law is passionless, passion must ever sway the heart of man. Yes, it may be replied, but then on the other hand an individual will be better able to deliberate in particular cases.

The best man, then, must legislate, and laws must be passed, but these laws will have no authority when they miss the mark, though in all other cases retaining their authority. But when the law cannot determine a point at all, or not well, should the one best man or should all decide? According to our present practice assemblies meet, sit in judgement, deliberate, and decide, and their judgements all relate to individual cases. Now any member of the assembly, taken separately, is certainly inferior to the wise man. But the state is made up of many individuals. And as a feast to which all the guests contribute is better than a banquet furnished by a single man, so a multitude is a better judge of many things than any individual.

Again, the many are more incorruptible than the few; they are like the greater quantity of water which is less easily corrupted than a little. The individual is liable to be overcome by anger or by some other passion, and then his judgement is necessarily perverted; but it is hardly to be supposed that a great number of persons would all get into a passion and go wrong at the same moment. Let us assume that they are the freemen, and that they never act in violation of the law, but fill up the gaps which the law is obliged to leave. Or, if such virtue is scarcely attainable by the multitude, we need only suppose that the majority are good men and good citizens, and ask which will be the more incorruptible, the one good ruler, or the many who are all good? Will not the many? But, you will say, there may be parties among them, whereas the one man is not divided against himself. To which we may answer that their character is as good as his. If we call the rule of many men, who are all of them good, aristocracy, and the rule of one man royalty, then aristocracy will be better for states than royalty, whether the government is supported by force or not, provided only that a number of men equal in virtue can be found.

The first governments were kingships, probably for this reason, because of old, when cities were small, men of eminent virtue were few. Further, they were made kings because they were benefactors, and benefits can only be bestowed by good men. But when many persons equal in merit arose, no longer enduring the pre-eminence of one, they desired to have a commonwealth, and set up a constitution. The ruling class soon deteriorated and enriched themselves out of the public treasury; riches became the path to honour, and so oligarchies naturally grew up. These passed into tyrannies and tyrannies into democracies; for love of gain in the ruling classes was always tending to diminish their number, and so to strengthen the masses, who in the end set upon their masters and established democracies. Since cities have increased in size, no other form of government appears to be any longer even easy to establish.

C.16. At this place in the discussion there impends the inquiry respecting the king who acts solely according to his own will; he has now to be considered. The so-called limited monarchy, or kingship according to law, as I have already remarked, is not a distinct form of government, for under all governments, as, for example, in a democracy or aristocracy, there may be a general holding office for life, and one person is often made supreme over the administration of a state. A magistracy of this kind exists at Epidamnus, and also at Opus, but in the latter city has a more limited power. Now, absolute monarchy, or the arbitrary rule of a sovereign over all the citizens in a city which consists of equals, is thought by some to be quite contrary to nature; it is argued that those who are by nature equals must have the same natural right and worth, and that for unequals to have an equal share, or for equals to have an unequal share, in the offices of state, is as bad as for different bodily constitutions to have the same food and clothing. Wherefore it is thought to be just that among equals every one be ruled as well as rule, and therefore that all should have their turn. We thus arrive at law; for an order of succession implies law. And the rule of the law, it is argued, is preferable to that of any individual. On the same principle, even if it be better for certain individuals to govern, they should be made only guardians and ministers of the law. For magistrates there must be — this is admitted; but then men say that to give authority to any one man when all are equal is unjust. Nay, there may indeed be cases which the law seems unable to determine, but in such cases can a man?

Nay, it will be replied, the law trains officers for this express purpose, and appoints them to determine matters which are left undecided by it, to the best of their judgement. Further, it permits them to make any amendment of the existing laws which experience suggests. Therefore he who bids the law rule may be deemed to bid God and Reason alone rule, but he who bids man rule adds an element of the beast; for desire is a wild beast, and passion perverts the minds of rulers, even when they are the best of men. The law is reason unaffected by desire. We are told that a patient should call in a physician; he will not get better if he is doctored out of a book. But the parallel of the arts is clearly not in point; for the physician does nothing contrary to rule from motives of friendship; he only cures a patient and takes a fee; whereas magistrates do many things from spite and partiality. And, indeed, if a man suspected the physician of being in league with his enemies to destroy him for a bribe, he would rather have recourse to the book. But certainly physicians, when they are sick, call in other physicians, and training-masters, when they are in training, other training-masters, as if they could not judge truly about their own case and might be influenced by their feelings. Hence it is evident that in seeking for justice men seek for the mean or neutral, for the law is the mean. Again, customary laws have more weight, and relate to more important matters, than written laws, and a man may be a safer ruler than the written law, but not safer than the customary law.

Again, it is by no means easy for one man to superintend many things; he will have to appoint a number of subordinates, and what difference does it make whether these subordinates always existed or were appointed by him because he needed them? If, as I said before, the good man has a right to rule because he is better, still two good men are better than one: this is the old saying —

two going together

and the prayer of Agamemnon —

would that I had ten such counsellors!

And at this day there are magistrates, for example judges, who have authority to decide some matters which the law is unable to determine, since no one doubts that the law would command and decide in the best manner whatever it could. But some things can, and other things cannot, be comprehended under the law, and this is the origin of the vexed question whether the best law or the best man should rule. For matters of detail about which men deliberate cannot be included in legislation. Nor does any one deny that the decision of such matters must be to man, but it is argued that there should be many judges, and not one only. For every ruler who has been trained by the law judges well; and it would surely seem strange that a person should see better with two eyes, or hear better with two ears, or act better with two hands or feet, than many with many; indeed, it is already the practice of kings to make to themselves many eyes and ears and hands and feet. For they make colleagues of those who are the friends of themselves and their governments. They must be friends of the monarch and of his government; if not his friends, they will not do what he wants; but friendship implies likeness and equality; and, therefore, if he thinks that his friends ought to rule, he must think that those who are equal to himself and like himself ought to rule equally with himself. These are the principal controversies relating to monarchy.

But may not all this be true in some cases and not in others? for there is by nature both a justice and an advantage appropriate to the rule of a master, another to kingly rule, another to constitutional rule; but there is none naturally appropriate to tyranny, or to any other perverted form of government; for these come into being contrary to nature. Now, to judge at least from what has been said, it is manifest that, where men are alike and equal, it is neither expedient nor just that one man should be lord of all, whether there are laws, or whether there are no laws, but he himself is in the place of law. Neither should a good man be lord over good men, nor a bad man over bad; nor, even if he excels in virtue, should he have a right to rule, unless in a particular case, at which I have already hinted, . . .

* * *

Notes and Questions

MONTESQUIEU, from *The Spirit of the Laws*

1. Notice that the fundamental value to be protected by the political device of checks and balances is liberty. What is liberty, according to Montesquieu, and why is a system of checks and balances necessary to protect it? What is Montesquieu's concept of political liberty, and how does it differ from security?

2. Since power (or law) is necessary to preserve order, but power is naturally abused by anyone who has it, the protection of freedom requires that power itself be used to check power. This is often called the *theory of checks and balances*. How does Montesquieu suggest that checks and balances should work in a political system? How should power be divided and balanced? What arguments does he give for his way of dividing power?

3. What actual government does Montesquieu take as a model of an ideal system of checks and balances? Are there any problems with his example? Can you think of other divisions of power that might work as well, or must the divisions be pretty much as Montesquieu sets them out?

4. Montesquieu argues for representative government, but also for the protection of an elite class. How? Can these two objectives be compatible? Why does he argue for this view? Can both of these objectives be justified? Is this another mechanism for separating power? Is protecting an elite class different from protecting any other minority?

5. Why does Montesquieu think that juries are important? Should the question of jury protec-

tion be a constitutional matter? Does the right to a jury trial protect liberty? How? Is this another limitation of power?

6. Are so many limitations on power really necessary, or was Montesquieu paranoid about power? What is the cost of all these divisions of power?

7. Does Montesquieu think that the structure of government makes a difference to the functioning of law? Or to the protection of individual freedom? Or to the abuse of power?

8. What implications does Montesquieu's theory have for reconciling individual rights or freedom with the general welfare or common good?

[From] *The Spirit of the Laws*
MONTESQUIEU

Book XI. Of the Laws Which Establish Political Liberty, with Regard to the Constitution

* * *

3. *In what Liberty consists.* It is true that in democracies the people seem to act as they please; but political liberty does not consist in an unlimited freedom. In governments, that is, in societies directed by laws, liberty can consist only in the power of doing what we ought to will, and in not being constrained to do what we ought not to will.

We must have continually present to our minds the difference between independence and liberty. Liberty is a right of doing whatever the laws permit, and if a citizen could do what they forbid he would be no longer possessed of liberty, because all his fellow-citizens would have the same power.

4. *The same Subject continued.* Democratic and aristocratic states are not in their own nature free. Political liberty is to be found only in moderate governments; and even in these it is not always found. It is there only when there is no abuse of power. But constant experience shows us that every man invested with power is apt to abuse it, and to carry his authority as far as it will go. Is it not strange, though true, to say that virtue itself has need of limits?

To prevent this abuse, it is necessary from the very nature of things that power should be a check to power. A government may be so constituted, as no man shall be compelled to do things to which the law does not oblige him, nor forced to abstain from things which the law permits.

5. *Of the End or View of different Governments.* Though all governments have the same general end, which is that of preservation, yet each has another particular object. Increase of dominion was the object of Rome; war, that of Sparta; religion, that of the Jewish laws; commerce, that of Marseilles; public tranquillity, that of the laws of China; navigation, that of the laws of Rhodes; natural liberty, that of the policy of the Savages; in general, the pleasures of the prince, that of despotic states; that of monarchies, the prince's and the kingdom's glory; the independence of individuals is the end aimed at by the laws of Poland, thence results the oppression of the whole.

One nation there is also in the world that has for the direct end of its constitution political liberty. We shall presently examine the principles on which this liberty is founded; if they are sound, liberty will appear in its highest perfection.

To discover political liberty in a constitution,

no great labour is requisite. If we are capable of seeing it where it exists, it is soon found, and we need not go far in search of it.

6. *Of the Constitution of England.* In every government there are three sorts of power: the legislative; the executive in respect to things dependent on the law of nations; and the executive in regard to matters that depend on the civil law.

By virtue of the first, the prince or magistrate enacts temporary or perpetual laws, and amends or abrogates those that been already enacted. By the second, he makes peace of war, sends or receives embassies, establishes the public security, and provides against invasions. By the third, he punishes criminals, or determines the disputes that arise between individuals. The latter we shall call the judiciary power, and the other simply the executive power of the state.

The political liberty of the subject is a tranquility of mind arising from the opinion each person has of his safety. In order to have this liberty, it is requisite the government be so constituted as one man need not be afraid of another.

When the legislative and executive powers are united in the same person, or in the same body of magistrates, there can be no liberty; because apprehensions may arise, lest the same monarch or senate should enact tyrannical laws, to execute them in a tyrannical manner.

Again, there is no liberty, if the judiciary power be not separated from the legislative and executive. Were it joined with the legislative, the life and liberty of the subject would be exposed to arbitrary control; for the judge would be then the legislator. Were it joined to the executive power, the judge might behave with violence and oppression.

There would be an end of everything, were the same man or the same body, whether of the nobles or of the people, to exercise those three powers, that of enacting laws, that of executing the public resolutions, and of trying the causes of individuals.

Most kingdoms in Europe enjoy a moderate government because the prince who is invested with the two first powers leaves the third to his subjects. In Turkey, where these three powers are united in the Sultan's person, the subjects groan under the most dreadful oppression.

In the republics of Italy, where these three powers are united, there is less liberty than in our monarchies. Hence their government is obliged to have recourse to as violent methods for its support as even that of the Turks; witness the state inquisitors, and the lion's mouth into which every informer may at all hours throw his written accusations.

In what a situation must the poor subject be in those republics! The same body of magistrates are possessed, as executors of the laws, of the whole power they have given themselves in quality of legislators. They may plunder the state by their general determinations; and as they have likewise the judiciary power in their hands, every private citizen may be ruined by their particular decisions.

The whole power is here united in one body; and though there is no external pomp that indicates a despotic sway, yet the people feel the effects of it every moment.

Hence it is that many of the princes of Europe, whose aim has been levelled at arbitrary power, have constantly set out with uniting in their own persons all the branches of magistracy, and all the great offices of state.

I allow indeed that the mere hereditary aristocracy of the Italian republics does not exactly answer to the despotic power of the Eastern princes. The number of magistrates sometimes moderates the power of the magistracy; the whole body of the nobles do not always concur in the same design; and different tribunals are erected, that temper each other. Thus at Venice the legislative power is in the *council*, the executive in the *pregadi*, and the judiciary in the *quarantia*. But the mischief is, that these different tribunals are composed of magistrates all belonging to the same body; which constitutes almost one and the same power.

The judiciary power ought not to be given to a standing senate; it should be exercised by persons taken from the body of the people at certain times of the year, and consistently with a form and manner prescribed by law, in order to erect a tribunal that should last only so long as necessity requires.

By this method the judicial power, so terrible to mankind, not being annexed to any particular state or profession, becomes, as it were, invisible. People have not then the judges continually present to their view; they fear the office, but not the magistrate.

In accusations of a deep and criminal nature, it is proper the person accused should have the privilege of choosing, in some measure, his judges, in concurrence with the law; or at least he should have a right to except against so great a number that the remaining part may be deemed his own choice.

The other two powers may be given rather to magistrates or permanent bodies, because they are not exercised on any private subject; one being no more than the general will of the state, and the other the execution of that general will.

But though the tribunals ought not to be fixed, the judgments ought; and to such a degree as to be ever conformable to the letter of the law. Were they to be the private opinion of the judge, people would then live in society, without exactly knowing the nature of their obligations.

The judges ought likewise to be of the same rank as the accused, or, in other words, his peers; to the end that he may not imagine he is fallen into the hands of persons inclined to treat him with rigour.

If the legislature leaves the executive power in possession of a right to imprison those subjects who can give security for their good behaviour, there is an end of liberty; unless they are taken up, in order to answer without delay to a capital crime, in which case they are really free, being subject only to the power of the law.

But should the legislature think itself in danger by some secret conspiracy against the state, or by a correspondence with a foreign enemy, it might authorise the executive power, for a short and limited time, to imprison suspected persons, who in that case would lose their liberty only for a while, to preserve it for ever.

And this is the only reasonable method that can be substituted to the tyrannical magistracy of the Ephori, and to the state inquisitors of Venice, who are also despotic.

As in a country of liberty, every man who is supposed a free agent ought to be his own governor; the legislative power should reside in the whole body of the people. But since this is impossible in large states, and in small ones is subject to many inconveniences, it is fit the peo-

ple should transact by their representatives what they cannot transact by themselves.

The inhabitants of a particular town are much better acquainted with its wants and interests than with those of other places; and are better judges of the capacity of their neighbours than of that of the rest of their countrymen. The members, therefore, of the legislature should not be chosen from the general body of the nation; but it is proper that in every considerable place a representative should be elected by the inhabitants.

The great advantage of representatives is, their capacity of discussing public affairs. For this the people collectively are extremely unfit, which is one of the chief inconveniences of a democracy.

It is not at all necessary that the representatives who have received a general instruction from their constituents should wait to be directed on each particular affair, as is practised in the diets of Germany. True it is that by this way of proceeding the speeches of the deputies might with greater propriety be called the voice of the nation; but, on the other hand, this would occasion infinite delays; would give each deputy a power of controlling the assembly; and, on the most urgent and pressing occasions, the wheels of government might be stopped by the caprice of a single person.

When the deputies, as Mr. Sidney well observes, represent a body of people, as in Holland, they ought to be accountable to their constituents; but it is a different thing in England, where they are deputed by boroughs.

All the inhabitants of the several districts ought to have a right of voting at the election of a representative, except such as are in so mean a situation as to be deemed to have no will of their own.

One great fault there was in most of the ancient republics, that the people had a right to active resolutions, such as require some execution, a thing of which they are absolutely incapable. They ought to have no share in the government but for the choosing of representatives, which is within their reach. For though few can tell the exact degree of men's capacities, yet there are none but are capable of knowing in general whether the person they choose is better qualified than most of his neighbours.

Neither ought the representative body to be chosen for the executive part of government, for which it is not so fit; but for the enacting of laws, or to see whether the laws in being are duly executed, a thing suited to their abilities, and which none indeed but themselves can properly perform.

In such a state there are always persons distinguished by their birth, riches, or honours; but were they to be confounded with the common people, and to have only the weight of a single voice like the rest, the common liberty would be their slavery, and they would have no interest in supporting it, as most of the popular resolutions would be against them. The share they have, therefore, in the legislature ought to be proportioned to their other advantages in the state; which happens only when they form a body that has a right to check the licentiousness of the people, as the people have a right to oppose any encroachment of theirs.

The legislative power is therefore committed to the body of the nobles, and to that which represents the people, each having their assemblies and deliberations apart, each their separate views and interests.

Of the three powers above mentioned, the judiciary is in some measure next to nothing: there remain, therefore, only two; and as these have need of a regulating power to moderate them, the part of the legislative body composed of the nobility is extremely proper for this purpose.

The body of the nobility ought to be hereditary. In the first place it is so in its own nature; and in the next there must be a considerable interest to preserve its privileges — privileges that in themselves are obnoxious to popular envy, and of course in a free state are always in danger.

But as a hereditary power might be tempted to pursue its own particular interests, and forget those of the people, it is proper that where a singular advantage may be gained by corrupting the nobility, as in the laws relating to the supplies, they should have no other share in the legislation than the power of rejecting, and not that of resolving.

By the *power of resolving* I mean the right of ordaining by their own authority, or of amending what has been ordained by others. By the *power of rejecting* I would be understood to mean the right of annulling a resolution taken by another; which was the power of the tribunes at Rome. And though the person possessed of the privilege of

rejecting may likewise have the right of approving, yet this approbation passes for no more than a declaration that he intends to make no use of his privilege of rejecting, and is derived from that very privilege.

The executive power ought to be in the hands of a monarch, because this branch of government, having need of despatch, is better administered by one than by many: on the other hand, whatever depends on the legislative power is oftentimes better regulated by many than by a single person.

But if there were no monarch, and the executive power should be committed to a certain number of persons selected from the legislative body, there would be an end then of liberty; by reason the two powers would be united, as the same persons would sometimes possess, and would be always able to possess, a share in both.

Were the legislative body to be a considerable time without meeting, this would likewise put an end to liberty. For of two things one would naturally follow: either that there would be no longer any legislative resolutions, and then the state would fall into anarchy; or that these resolutions would be taken by the executive power, which would render it absolute.

It would be needless for the legislative body to continue always assembled. This would be troublesome to the representatives, and, moreover, would cut out too much work for the executive power, so as to take off its attention to its office, and oblige it to think only of defending its own prerogatives, and the right it has to execute.

Again, were the legislative body to be always assembled, it might happen to be kept up only by filling the places of the deceased members with new representatives; and in that case, if the legislative body were once corrupted, the evil would be past all remedy. When different legislative bodies succeed one another, the people who have a bad opinion of that which is actually sitting may reasonably entertain some hopes of the next; but were it to be always the same body, the people upon seeing it once corrupted would no longer expect any good from its laws; and of course they would either become desperate or fall into a state of indolence.

The legislative body should not meet of itself. For a body is supposed to have no will but when it is met; and besides, were it not to meet unanimously, it would be impossible to determine which was really the legislative body; the part assembled, or the other. And if it had a right to prorogue itself, it might happen never to be prorogued; which would be extremely dangerous, in case it should ever attempt to encroach on the executive power. Besides, there are seasons, some more proper than others, for assembling the legislative body: it is fit, therefore, that the executive power should regulate the time of meeting, as well as the duration of those assemblies, according to the circumstances and exigencies of a state known to itself.

Were the executive power not to have a right of restraining the encroachments of the legislative body, the latter would become despotic; for as it might arrogate to itself what authority it pleased, it would soon destroy all the other powers.

But it is not proper, on the other hand, that the legislative power should have a right to stay the executive. For as the execution has its natural limits, it is useless to confine it; besides, the executive power is generally employed in momentary operations. The power, therefore, of the Roman tribunes was faulty, as it put a stop not only to the legislation, but likewise to the executive part of government; which was attended with infinite mischief.

But if the legislative power in a free state has no right to stay the executive, it has a right and ought to have the means of examining in what manner its laws have been executed; an advantage which this government has over that of Crete and Sparta, where the Cosmi and the Ephori gave no account of their administration.

But whatever may be the issue of that examination, the legislative body ought not to have a power of arraigning the person, nor, of course, the conduct, of him who is entrusted with the executive power. His person should be sacred, because as it is necessary for the good of the state to prevent the legislative body from rendering themselves arbitrary, the moment he is accused or tried there is an end of liberty.

In this case the state would be no longer a monarchy, but a kind of republic, though not a free government. But as the person entrusted with the executive power cannot abuse it without bad counsellors, and such as have the laws as ministers, though the laws protect them as subjects, these men may be examined and punished—an advantage which this government has over that of Gnidus, where the law allowed of no such thing as calling the Amymones[1] to an account, even after their administration;[2] and therefore the people could never obtain any satisfaction for the injuries done them.

Though, in general, the judiciary power ought not be united with any part of the legislative, yet this is liable to three exceptions, founded on the particular interest of the party accused.

The great are always obnoxious to popular envy; and were they to be judged by the people, they might be in danger from their judges, and would, moreover, be deprived of the privilege which the meanest subject is possessed of in a free state, of being tried by his peers. The nobility, for this reason, ought not to be cited before the ordinary courts of judicature, but before that part of the legislature which is composed of their own body.

It is possible that the law, which is clear-sighted in one sense, and blind in another, might, in some cases, be too severe. But as we have already observed, the national judges are no more than the mouth that pronounces the words of the law, mere passive beings, incapable of moderating either its force or rigour. That part, therefore, of the legislative body, which we have just now observed to be a necessary tribunal on another occasion, is also a necessary tribunal in this; it belongs to its supreme authority to moderate the law in favour of the law itself, by mitigating the sentence.

It might also happen that a subject entrusted with the administration of public affairs may infringe the rights of the people, and be guilty of crimes which the ordinary magistrates either could not or would not punish. But, in general, the legislative power cannot try causes: and much less can it try this particular case, where it represents the party aggrieved, which is the people. It can only, therefore, impeach. But before what court shall it bring its impeachment? Must it go and demean itself before the ordinary tribunals, which are its inferiors, and, being composed, moreover, of men who are chosen from the people as well as itself, will naturally be swayed by the authority of so powerful an accuser? No: in order to preserve the dignity of the people, and the security of the subject, the legislative part which represents the people must bring in its charge before the legislative part which represents the nobility, who have neither the same interests nor the same passions.

Here is an advantage which this government has over most of the ancient republics, where this abuse prevailed, that the people were at the same time both judge and accuser.

The executive power, pursuant of what has been already said, ought to have a share in the legislature by the power of rejecting, otherwise it would soon be stripped of its prerogative. But should the legislative power usurp a share of the executive, the latter would be equally undone.

If the prince were to have a part in the legislature by the power of resolving, liberty would be lost. But as it is necessary he should have a share in the legislature for the support of his own prerogative, this share must consist in the power of rejecting.

The change of government at Rome was owing to this, that neither the senate, who had one part of the executive power, nor the magistrates, who were entrusted with the other, had the right of rejecting, which was entirely lodged in the people.

Here then is the fundamental constitution of the government we are treating of. The legislative body being composed of two parts, they check one another by the mutual privilege of rejecting. They are both restrained by the executive power, as the executive is by the legislative.

These three powers should naturally form a state of repose or inaction. But as there is a necessity for movement in the course of human affairs, they are forced to move, but still in concert.

As the executive power has no other part in the legislative than the privilege of rejecting, it can have no share in the public debates. It is not even necessary that it should propose, because as it may always disapprove of the resolutions that shall be taken, it may likewise reject the decisions on those proposals which were made against its will.

In some ancient commonwealths, where public debates were carried on by the people in a body, it was natural for the executive power to propose and debate in conjunction with the people, otherwise their resolutions must have been attended with a strange confusion,.

Were the executive power to determine the raising of public money, otherwise than by giving its consent, liberty would be at an end; because it would become legislative in the most important point of legislation.

If the legislative power was to settle the subsidies, not from year to year, but for ever, it would run the risk of losing its liberty, because the executive power would be no longer dependent; and when once it was possessed of such a perpetual right, it would be a matter of indifference whether it held it of itself or of another. The same may be said if it should come to a resolution of entrusting, not an annual, but a perpetual command of the fleets and armies to the executive power.

To prevent the executive power from being able to oppress, it is requisite that the armies with which it is entrusted should consist of the people, and have the same spirit as the people, as was the case at Rome till the time of Marius. To obtain this end, there are only two ways, either that the persons employed in the army should have sufficient property to answer for their conduct to their fellow-subjects, and be enlisted only for a year, as was customary at Rome: or if there should be a standing army, composed chiefly of the most despicable part of the nation, the legislative power should have a right to disband them as soon as it pleased; the soldiers should live in common with the rest of the people; and no separate camp, barracks, or fortress should be suffered.

When once an army is established, it ought not to depend immediately on the legislative but on the executive, power; and this from the very nature of the thing, its business consisting more in action than in deliberation.

* * *

As all human things have an end, the state we are speaking of will lose its liberty, and perish. Have not Rome, Sparta, and Carthage perished? It will perish when the legislative power shall be more corrupt than the executive.

* * *

NOTES

1. These were magistrates chosen annually by the people. See Stephen of Byzantium.

2. It was lawful to accuse the Roman magistrates after the expiration of their several offices. See in Dionysius Halicarnassus, ix, the affair of Genutius the tribune.

Notes and Questions

LAURENCE TRIBE, from *American Constitutional Law*

1. Laurence Tribe's book, *American Constitutional Law*, is made up of a series of models that provide the theoretical rationale which is intended to explain constitutional analysis through the history of American law. Thus, according to Tribe, there is not one model of American law but several models, which have evolved through changes in legal analysis. The first model is the model of separated and divided power. Tribe calls this the central tenet of American constitutionalism. Is this claim supported by the structure of the constitution? What value is fundamental to this model? What else is presupposed by the model?

2. According to Tribe, it was assumed that human rights were best protected by inaction and indirection. What does this mean? How well does it correspond with accounts of colonial attitudes by Dargo or Corwin? What do you think of this rationale? What sorts of rights are best protected by inaction and indirection? Whose rights? Against whom? Would this rationale be as effective today as it was in the eighteenth century? Why or why not?

3. What two forms of division were instituted to protect freedom and rights from centralized power? Was the concern for the freedom and rights of individuals or of states? Why were two forms of division needed? What different functions do they serve?

4. Tribe concludes that in the last anaylsis rights were to be protected by "the preservation of boundaries between and among institutions" of government. There was great confidence or perhaps optimism about the effectiveness of good legal process, which could be guaranteed by properly structuring the system. From the perspective of 200 years of history, did that confidence prove to be misplaced? What two qualifications does Tribe place on his conclusion? Why should they be necessary?

[From] *American Constitutional Law*

LAURENCE TRIBE

Model I — Separated and Divided Power

§1–2. The Basic Pattern: Model I and the Roots of Models III and IV

That all lawful power derives from the people and must be held in check to preserve their freedom is the oldest and most central tenet of American constitutionalism. At the outset, only a small number of explicit substantive limitations on the exercise of governmental authority were thought essential; in the main, it was believed that personal freedom could be secured more effectively by decentralization than by express command. From the thought of seventeenth century English liberals, particularly as elaborated in eighteenth century France by Montesquieu, the Constitution's framers had derived the conviction that human rights could best be preserved by inaction and indirection — shielded behind the play of deliberately fragmented centers of countervailing power, in a vision almost Newtonian in its inspiration. In this first model, the centralized accumulation of power in any man or single group of men meant tyranny; the division and separation of powers, both vertically (along the axis of federal, state and local authority) and horizontally (along the axis of legislative, executive, and judicial authority) meant liberty. It was thus essential that no department, branch, or level of government be empowered to achieve dominance on its own. If the legislature would punish, it must enlist the cooperation of the other branches—the executive to prosecute, the judicial to try and convict. So too with each other center of governmental power: exercising the mix of functions delegated to it by the people in the social compact that was the Constitution, each power center would remain dependent upon the others for the final efficacy of its social designs.

Although exerting continuing influence to the present day, Model I played its most pervasive role from the era of the Marshall Court to the Civil War. While "kicking upstairs" those governmental powers, primarily over commerce, that the individual states could not be relied upon to exercise without undue parochialism or factionalism, Model I relied heavily upon the vitality and autonomy of the states in most other respects to furnish, in the words of the 46th Federalist, a "barrier against the enterprises of ambition." Interestingly, this reliance on state autonomy did not take the form of judicially declaring Acts of Congress *ultra vires** in the name of state sovereignty. On the contrary, every such challenge was defeated in the pre-Civil War Supreme Court, with the sole exception of *Dred Scott's* ill-fated invalidation of the Missouri compromise. Instead, reliance on state autonomy as a major source of individual rights and security in Model I took the indirect form of preserving state sovereignty by rejecting all but a handful of individual challenges to exercises of state authority said to violate the Constitution. Witness, for example, the refusal by the Supreme Court in 1833, and by the Senate nearly half a century earlier, to extend the Bill of Rights into a general charter of liberty against the states and municipalities.

In part, this refusal reflected a concession to state power as such, and a degree of ambivalence about the actual content of the personal freedom that merited protection. But also implicit in the refusal to extend the Bill of Rights against the states seems to have been a view that, just as the states were by and large adequately represented in the Congress, so individuals were likely for most purposes to be sufficiently represented in their own states, whose obliteration or serious erosion would leave individuals exposed to oppression by private violence and national tyranny alike. Thus it was largely through the preservation of boundaries between and among institutions in Model I that the rights of persons were to be secured.

Two qualifications must be noted. First, a Bill of Rights directed against federal abuses was thought necessary in addition to the separation and division of powers; although actual Bill-of-Rights invalidation of congressional legislation is a fairly recent phenomenon, institutional boundaries in the absence of such a list of liberties were not deemed quite sufficient to preserve individual rights. Indeed, two supplementary models—that of settled expectations (Model III, expressed through guarantees like those against contract impairment and uncompensated takings, and that of governmental regularity (Model IV, expressed through guarantees like those against ex post facto laws, bills of attainder, and procedurally arbitrary deprivations)—are directly traceable to the earliest decisions of the federal judiciary.* Built on the leanest of substantive premises that could be teased from the basic model of separated and divided powers, these additional models posited judicially enforceable guarantees for vested rights and for the interest in having government proceed in accord with settled rules of law. Although their independent significance was not to be demonstrated until many decades later, those two models plainly went beyond notions of checks and balances from the very beginning.

---

*Beyond the powers conferred by law—Ed.

*Models III and IV are discussed in Chapters 9 and 10 of Laurence Tribe's book, *American Constitutional Law* (1978)—Ed.

Second, although the effort was finally rejected in the Senate, the House was sufficiently persuaded by James Madison's fear of state and local oppression across a wide spectrum of issues to approve a constitutional amendment which would have provided that "no State shall infringe the equal rights of conscience, nor the freedom of speech or of the press, nor of the right of trial by jury in criminal cases. Not until well after the adoption of the fourteenth amendment itself some 79 years later was Madison's aim accomplished. For purposes of this introduction, it is noteworthy both that he came close to succeeding in 1789, and that it took a Civil War to make the difference.

Collected Documents

Notes and Questions

Concord Resolutions (1776)

1. The Concord Resolutions are a response to a proposal (or resolve) of the Massachusetts House of Representatives to draft a state constitution. Concord rejects this proposal. Why?

2. What are the presuppositions about law and constitutions in the Concord Resolutions? How does constitutional law differ from statutory law? What is the purpose of a constitution?

Concord Resolutions (1776)

At a meeting of the Inhabitants of the Town of Concord being free & twenty one years of age and upwards, met by adjournment on the twenty first Day of October 1776 to take into Consideration a Resolve of the Honorable House of Representatives of this State on the 17th of September Last the Town Resolved as followes—

Resolved 1st: That this State being at Present destitute of a Properly established form of Government, it is absolutely necessary that one should be immediately formed and established—

Resolved 2: That the Supreme Legislative, either in their Proper Capacity, or in Joint Committee, are by no means a Body proper to form & Establish a Constitution, or form of Government; for Reasons following. First Because we Conceive that a Constitution in its Proper Idea intends a System of Principles Established to Secure the Subject in the Possession & enjoyment of their Rights & Privileges, against any Encroachment of the Governing Part—2nd Because the Same Body that forms a Constitution have of Consequence a power to alter it. 3d—Because a Constitution alterable by the Supreme Legislative is no Security at all to the Subject against any Encroachment of the Governing part on any or on all of their Rights and privileges.

Resolved 3d. That it appears to this Town highly necessary & Expedient that a Convention, or Congress be immediately Chosen, to form & establish a Constitution, by the Inhabitants of the Respective Towns in this State, being free & of twenty one years of age, and upwards, in Proportion as the Representatives of this State formerly were Chosen; the Convention or Congress not to

Consist of a greater number then the House of assembly of this State heretofore might Consist of, Except that each Town & District Shall have the Liberty to Send one Representative, or otherwise as Shall appear meet to the Inhabitents of this State in General.

Resolved 4th. that when the Convention, or Congress have formed a Constitution they adjourn for a Short time, and Publish their Proposed Constitution for the Inspection and Remarks of the Inhabitents of this State.

Resolved 5ly. that the Honorable House of assembly of this State be Desired to Recommend it to the Inhabitents of the State to Proceed to Chuse a Convention or Congress for the Purpas abovesaid as soon as Possable.

A True Copy of the Proceeding of the Town of Concord at the General Town meeting above mentioned — attest Ephraim Wood, Jr., Town Clerk.[1]

NOTE

1. Massachusetts (State) Archives vol. 156, p. 167.

Notes and Questions

From Pennsylvania Constitution (1776)

1. The Pennsylvania Constitution of 1776 was generally considered the most radical state constitution of the time because it incorporated certain elements: a unicameral legislature, liberalized voting and officeholding requirements, frequent constitutional review, and replacement of the governor with a president and a council. What is the effect of such features? Why are they radical?

2. Compare the Pennsylvania Constitution with that of New York. What is the significance of the differences?

[From] Pennsylvania Constitution (1776)

Section 1. The commonwealth or state of Pennsylvania shall be governed hereafter by an assembly of the representatives of the freemen of the same, and a president and council, in manner and form following —

Sect. 2. The supreme legislative power shall be vested in a house of representatives of the freemen of the commonwealth or state of Pennsylvania.

Sect. 3. The supreme executive power shall be vested in a president and council.

Sect. 4. Courts of justice shall be established in the city of Philadelphia, and in every county of this state.

Sect. 5. The freemen of this commonwealth and their sons shall be trained and armed for its defence under such regulations, restrictions, and exceptions as the general assembly shall by law direct, preserving always to the people the right of choosing their colonel and all commissioned officers under that rank, in such manner and as often as by the said laws shall be directed.

Sect. 6. Every freeman of the full age of twenty-one years, having resided in this state for the space of one whole year next before the day of election for representatives, and paid public taxes during that time, shall enjoy the right of an elector: Provided always, that sons of freeholders of the age of twenty-one years shall be intitled to vote although they have not paid taxes.

Sect. 7. The house of representatives of the freemen of this commonwealth shall consist of persons most noted for wisdom and virtue, to be chosen by the freemen of every city and county of this commonwealth respectively. And no person shall be elected unless he has resided in the city or county for which he shall be chosen two years immediately before the said election; nor shall any member, while he continues such, hold any other office, except in the militia.

Sect. 8. No person shall be capable of being elected a member to serve in the house of representatives of the freemen of this commonwealth more than four years in seven.

* * *

Sect. 19. For the present the supreme executive council of this state shall consist of twelve persons. . . .

No member of the general assembly or delegate in congress, shall be chosen a member of the council. The president and vice-president shall be chosen annually by the joint ballot of the general assembly and council, of the members of the council. Any person having served as a counsellor for three successive years, shall be incapable of holding that office for four years afterwards. Every member of the council shall be a justice of the peace for the whole commonwealth, by virtue of his office.

In case new additional counties shall hereafter be erected in this state, county or counties shall elect a counsellor, and such county or counties shall be annexed to the next neighboring counties, and shall take rotation with such counties.

The council shall meet annually, at the same time and place with the general assembly.

The treasurer of the state, trustees of the loan office, naval officers, collectors of customs or excise, judge of the admiralty, attornies general, sheriffs, and prothonotaries, shall not be capable of a seat in the general assembly, executive council, or continental congress.

Sect. 20. The president, and in his absence the vice-president, with the council, five of whom shall be a quorum, shall have power to appoint and commissionate judges, naval officers, judge of the admiralty, attorney general and all other officers, civil and military, except such as are chosen by the general assembly or the people, agreeable to this frame of government, and the laws that may be made hereafter.

* * *

Sect. 47. In order that the freedom of the commonwealth may be preserved inviolate forever, there shall be chosen by ballot by the freemen in each city and county respectively, on the second Tuesday in October, in the year one thousand seven hundred and eighty-three, and on the second Tuesday in October, in every seventh year thereafter, two persons in each city and county of this state, to be called the COUNCIL OF CENSORS; who shall meet together on the second Monday of November next ensuing their election; the majority of whom shall be a quorum in every case, except as to calling a convention, in which two-thirds of the whole number elected shall agree: And whose duty it shall be to enquire whether the constitution has been preserved inviolate in every part; and whether the legislative and executive branches of government have performed their duty as guardians of the people, or assumed to themselves, or exercised other or greater powers than they are intitled to by the constitution: They are also to enquire whether the public taxes have been justly laid and collected in all parts of this commonwealth, in what manner the public monies have been disposed of, and whether the laws have been duly executed. For these purposes they shall have power to send for persons, papers, and records; they shall have authority to pass public censures, to order impeachments, and to recommend to the legislature the repealing such laws as appear to them to have been enacted contrary to the principles of the constitution. These powers they shall continue to have, for and during the space of one year from the day of their election and no longer: The said council of censors shall also have power to call a convention, to meet within two years after their sitting, if there appear to them an absolute necessity of amending any article of the constitution which may be defective, explaining such as may be thought not clearly expressed, and of adding such as are necessary for the preservation of the rights and happiness of the people: But the articles to be amended, and the amendments proposed, and such articles as are proposed to be added or abolished, shall be promulgated at least six months before the day appointed for the election of such convention, for the previous consideration of the people, that they may have an opportunity of instructing their delegates on the subject.

Passed in Convention the 28th day of September, 1776, and signed by their order.

Benj. Franklin, Prest.

* * *

Notes and Questions

From New York Constitution (1777)

1. These selections from the New York Constitution illustrates the relative power of the different branches. Where is the power concentrated? Is there a commitment to the separation of powers here?

2. The New York Constitution is considered very conservative. What features make it so? How does it compare with the Pennsylvania Constitution or the Articles of Confederation?

[From] New York Constitution (1777)

* * *

III. And whereas laws inconsistent with the spirit of this constitution, or with the public good, may be hastily and unadvisedly passed: Be it ordained, that the governor for the time being, the chancellor, and the judges of the supreme court, or any two of them, together with the governor, shall be, and hereby are, constituted a council to revise all bills about to be passed into laws by the legislature; and for that purpose shall assemble themselves from time to time, when the legislature shall be convened; for which, nevertheless, they shall not receive any salary or consideration, under any pretence whatever. And that all bills which have passed the senate and assembly shall, before they become laws, be presented to the said council for their revisal and consideration; and if, upon such revision and consideration, it should appear improper to the said council, or a majority of them, that the said bill should become a law of this State, that they return the same, together with their objections thereto in writing, to the senate or house of assembly (in whichsoever the same shall have originated) who shall enter the objection sent down by the council at large in their minutes, and proceed to reconsider the said bill. But if, after such reconsideration, two-thirds of the said senate or house of assembly shall, notwithstanding the said objections, agree to pass the same, it shall, together with the objections, be sent to the other branch of the legislature, where it shall also be reconsidered, and, if approved by two-thirds of the members present, shall be a law.

* * *

XVII. And this convention doth further, in the name and by the authority of the good people of this State, ordain, determine, and declare that the supreme executive power and authority of this State shall be vested in a governor; and that statedly, once in every three years, and as often as the seat of government shall become vacant, a wise and discreet freeholder of this State shall be, by ballot, elected governor, by the freeholders of this State, qualified, as before described, to elect senators; which elections shall be always held at the times and places of choosing representatives in assembly for each respective county; and that the person who hath the greatest number of votes within the said State shall be governor thereof.

XVIII. That the governor shall continue in office three years, and shall, by virtue of his office, be general and commander-in-chief of all the militia, and admiral of the navy of this State; that he shall have power to convene the assembly and senate on extraordinary occasions; to prorogue them from time to time, provided such prorogations shall not exceed sixty days in the space of any one year; and, at his discretion, to grant reprieves and pardons to persons convicted of crimes, other than treason or murder, in which he may suspend the execution of the sentence, until it shall be reported to the legislature at their subsequent meeting; and they shall either pardon or direct the execution of the criminal, or grant a further reprieve.

XIX. That it shall be the duty of the governor to inform the legislature, at every session, of the condition of the State, so far as may respect his department; to recommend such matters to their consideration as shall appear to him to concern its good government, welfare, and prosperity; to correspond with the Continental Congress, and other States; to transact all necessary business with the officers of government, civil and military; to take care that the laws are faithfully executed to the best of his ability; and to expedite all such measures as may be resolved upon by the legislature. . . .

XXIV. That all military officers be appointed during pleasure; that all commissioned officers, civil and military, be commissioned by the governor; and that the chancellor, the judges of the supreme court, and first judge of the county court in every county, hold their offices during good behavior or until they shall have respectively attained the age of sixty years.

Notes and Questions

From Articles of Confederation

1. The Articles of Confederation were, of course, the forerunner to the U.S. Constitution. What are the important differences between them? (See the U.S. Constitution in the Appendix.)

2. How, if at all, do the Articles differ from the state constitutions of New York and Pennsylvania?

[From] Articles of Confederation (1781)

Article I. The Stile of this Confederacy shall be "The United States of America."

Article II. Each state retains its sovereignty, freedom, and independence, and every Power, Jurisdiction and right, which is not by this confederation expressly delegated to the United States, in Congress assembled.

Article III. The said states hereby severally enter into a firm league of friendship with each other, for their common defence, the security of their Liberties, and their mutual and general welfare, binding themselves to assist each other, against all force offered to, or attacks made upon them, or any of them, on account of religion, sovereignty, trade, or any other pretence whatever.

Article IV. The better to secure and perpetuate mutual friendship and intercourse among the people of the different states in this union, the free inhabitants of each of these states, paupers, vagabonds and fugitives from justice excepted, shall be entitled to all privileges and immunities of free citizens in the several states; and the people of each state shall have free ingress and regress to and from any other state, and shall enjoy therein all the privileges of trade and commerce, subject to the same duties, impositions and restrictions as the inhabitants thereof respectively, provided that such restrictions shall not extend so far as to prevent the removal of property imported into any state, to any other state of which the Owner is an inhabitant; provided also that no imposition, duties or restrictions shall be laid by any state, on the property of the united states, or either of them.

If any Person guilty of, or charged with treason, felony, or other high misdemeanor in any state, shall flee from Justice, and be found in any of the united states, he shall, upon demand of the Governor or executive power, of the state from which he fled, he delivered up and removed to the state having jurisdiction of his offence.

Full faith and credit shall be given in each of these states to the records, acts and judicial proceedings of the courts and magistrates of every other state.

* * *

Notes and Questions

The Federalist 45, 50

1. The purpose of *The Federalist* 45 was to defend the proposed Constitution against the charge that it imposed a central government that was too strong; the claim was that state governments should be strong and the federal government weak. How does the author argue that, as proposed, the federal government will not overbalance state governments in terms of the new Constitution? Do you see anything wrong with the argument? In hindsight, the author's claim is clearly false. The federal government has grown progressively stronger, far outdistancing state power, has it not? Can you think of any defense that the author might offer? What changed?

2. It is also argued that the military power is not to be feared. Why not? Again, this position has not borne out over time. What happened? Remember that the original idea was to structure the government in such a way that the structure and process would limit and direct the range of possible effects. Do the false claims (very reasonably defended) in *The Federalist* 45 suggest that such effects cannot be controlled by such devices as procedural checks and balances, or can you offer some other explanation?

3. *The Federalist* 50 suggests ways to maintain a "just" (optimal, perhaps) balance of power. What are they? According to *The Federalist* 50, the American system of government protects freedom by several means. First, it combats government power in two ways. Second, it combats majority power in two ways. What are these ways? Are they effective? Why or why not?

The Federalist 45

JAMES MADISON

Federal and State Governments and the People

Resuming the subject of the last paper, I proceed to inquire whether the federal government or the State governments will have the advantage with regard to the predilection and support of the people. Notwithstanding the different modes in which they are appointed, we must consider both of them as substantially dependent on the great body of the citizens of the United States. I assume this position here as it respects the first, reserving the proofs for another place. The federal and State governments are in fact but different agents and trustees of the people, constituted with different powers, and designated for different purposes. The adversaries of the Constitution seem to have lost sight of the people altogether, in their reasonings on this subject, and to have viewed these different establishments, not only as mutual rivals and enemies, but as uncontrolled by any common superior, in their efforts to usurp the authorities of each other. These gentlemen must here be reminded of their error. They must be told, that the ultimate authority, wherever the derivative may be found, resides in the people alone, and that it will not depend merely on the comparative ambition or address of the different governments whether either, or which of them, will be able to enlarge its sphere of jurisdiction at the expense of the other. Truth, no less than decency, requires that the event in every case should be supposed to depend on the sentiments and sanction of their common constituents.

Many considerations, beside those suggested on a former occasion, seem to place it beyond doubt that the first and most natural attachment of the people will be to the governments of their respective States. Into the administration of these a greater number of individuals will expect to rise. From the gift of these, a greater number of offices and emoluments will flow. By the superintending care of these, all the more domestic and personal interests of the people will be regulated and provided for. With the affairs of these, the people will be more familiarly and minutely conversant; and with the members of these will a greater proportion of the people have the ties of personal acquaintaince and friendship and of family and party attachments; on the side of these, therefore, the popular bias may well be expected most strongly to incline.

Experience speaks the same language in this case. The federal administration, though hitherto very defective, in comparison with what may be hoped under a better system, had, during the war, and particularly while the independent fund of paper emissions was in credit, an activity and importance as great as it can well have in any future circumstances whatever. It was engaged, too, in a course of measures which had for their object the protection of everything that was dear, and the acquisition of everything that could be desirable to the people at large. It was, nevertheless, invariably found, after the transient enthusiasm for the early Congresses was over, that the attention and attachment of the people were turned anew to their own peculiar governments; that the federal council was at no time the idol of popular favor; and that opposition to proposed enlargements of its powers and importance was the side usually taken by the men, who wished to build their political consequence on the prepossessions of their fellow-citizens.

If, therefore, as has been elsewhere remarked, the people should in future become more partial to the federal than to the State governments, the change can only result from such manifest and irresistible proofs of a better administration as will overcome all their antecedent propensities; and in that case the people ought not surely to be precluded from giving most of their confidence where they may discover it to be the most due; but even in that case the State governments could have little to apprehend, because it is only within a certain sphere that the federal power can, in the nature of things, be advantageously administered.

The remaining points on which I propose to compare the federal and State governments are the disposition and the faculty they may respectively possess, to resist and frustrate the measures of each other.

It has been already proved that the members of the federal will be more dependent on the members of the State governments than the latter will be on the former. It has appeared also that the prepossessions of the people, on whom both will depend, will be more on the side of the State governments than of the federal government. So far as the disposition of each toward the other may be influenced by these causes, the State governments must clearly have the advantage; but in a distinct and very important point of view the advantage will lie on the same side. The prepossessions which the members themselves will carry into the federal government will generally be favorable to the States; while it will rarely happen that the members of the State governments will carry into the public councils a bias in favor of the general government. A local spirit will infallibly prevail much more in the members of Congress than a national spirit will prevail in the legislatures of the particular States. Everyone knows that a great proportion of the errors committed by the State legislatures proceeds from the disposition of the members to sacrifice the comprehensive and permanent interest of the State, to the particular and separate views of the counties or districts in which they reside; and if they do not sufficiently enlarge their policy to embrace the collective welfare of their particular State, how can it be imagined that they will make the aggregate prosperity of the Union, and the dignity and respectability of its government, the objects of their affections and consultations? For the same reason that the members of the State legislatures will be unlikely to attach themselves sufficiently to national objects, the members of the federal legislature will be likely to attach themselves too much to local objects. The States will be to the latter what counties and towns are to the former. Measures will too often be decided according to their probable effect, not on the national prosperity and happiness, but on the prejudices, interests, and pursuits of the governments and people of the individual States. What is the spirit that has in general characterized the proceedings of Congress? A perusal of their journals, as well as the candid acknowledgments of such as have had a seat in that assembly, will inform us that the members have but too frequently displayed the character rather of partisans of their respective States than of impartial guardians of a common interest; that where on one occasion improper sacrifices have been made of local considerations to the aggrandizement of the federal government, the great interests of the nation have suffered on a hundred, from an undue attention to the local prejudices, interests, and views of the particular States. I mean not by these reflections to insinuate that the new federal government will not embrace a more enlarged plan of policy than the existing government may have pursued; much less that its views will be as confined as those of the State legislatures; but only that it will partake sufficiently of the spirit of both, to be disinclined to invade the rights of the individual States or the prerogatives of their governments. The motives on the part of the State governments to augment their prerogatives by defalcations from the federal government will be overruled by no reciprocal predispositions in the members.

Were it admitted, however, that the federal government may feel an equal disposition with the State governments to extend its power beyond the due limits, the latter would still have the advantage in the means of defeating such encroachments. If an act of a particular State, though unfriendly to the national government, be generally popular in that State, and should not too grossly violate the oaths of the State officers; it is executed immediately and, of course, by means on the spot, and depending on the State alone. The opposition of the federal government, or the interposition of federal officers, would but inflame the zeal of all parties on the side of the State, and the evil could not be prevented or

repaired, if at all, without the employment of means which must always be resorted to with reluctance and difficulty. On the other hand, should an unwarrantable, measure of the federal government be unpopular in particular States, which would seldom fail to be the case, or even a warrantable measure be so, which may sometimes be the case, the means of opposition to it are powerful and at hand. The disquietude of the people; their repugnance and, perhaps, refusal to co-operate with the officers of the Union; the frowns of the executive magistracy of the State; the embarrassments created by legislative devices, which would often be added on such occasions — would oppose, in any State, difficulties not to be despised; would form, in a large State, very serious impediments; and where the sentiments of several adjoining States happened to be in unison, would present obstructions which the federal government would hardly be willing to encounter.

But ambitious encroachments of the federal government, on the authority of the State governments, would not excite the opposition of a single State or of a few States only; they would be signals of general alarm. Every government would espouse the common cause. A correspondence would be opened. Plans of resistance would be concerted. One spirit would animate and conduct the whole. The same combination, in short, would result from an apprehension of the federal as was produced by the dread of a foreign yoke; and unless the projected innovations should be voluntarily renounced, the same appeal to a trial of force would be made in the one case as was made in the other. But what degree of madness could ever derive the federal government to such an extremity? In the contest with Great Britain, one part of the empire was employed against the other. The more numerous part invaded the rights of the less numerous part. The attempt was unjust and unwise; but it was not in speculation absolutely chimerical. But what would be the contest in the case we are supposing? Who would be the parties? A few representatives of the people would be opposed to the people themselves; or rather one set of representatives would be contending against thirteen sets of representatives, with the whole body of their common constituents on the side of the latter.

The only refuge left for those who prophesy the downfall of the State governments is the visionary supposition that the federal government may previously accumulate a military force for the projects of ambition. The reasonings contained in these papers must have been employed to little purpose, indeed, if it could be necessary now to disprove the reality of this danger. That the people and the States should, for a sufficient period of time, elect an uninterrupted succession of men ready to betray both; that the traitors should, throughout this period, uniformly and systematically pursue some fixed plan for the extension of the military establishment; that the governments and the people of the States should silently and patiently behold the gathering storm, and continue to supply the materials, until it should be prepared to burst on their own heads — must appear to everyone more like the incoherent dreams of a delirious jealousy, or the misjudged exaggerations of a counterfeit zeal, than like the sober apprehensions of genuine patriotism. Extravagant as the supposition is, let it, however, be made. Let a regular army, fully equal to the reasources of the country, be formed; and let it be entirely at the devotion of the federal government; still it would not be going too far to say that the State governments, with the people on their side, would be able to repel the danger. The highest number to which, according to the best computation, a standing army can be carried in any country, does not exceed one hundredth part of the whole number of souls; or one twenty-fifth part of the number able to bear arms. This proportion would not yield, in the United States, an army of more than 25,000 or 30,000 men. To these would be opposed a militia amounting to near half a million of citizens with arms in their hands, officered by men chosen from among themselves, fighting for their common liberties, and united and conducted by governments possessing their affections and confidence. It may well be doubted whether a militia thus circumstanced could ever be conquered by such a proportion of regular troops. Those who are best acquainted with the late successful resistance of this country against the British arms, will be most inclined to deny the possibility of it. Beside the advantage of being armed, which the Americans possess over the people of almost every other nation, the existence of subordinate governments, to which the people are attached, and by which the militia officers are appointed, forms a barrier, against the enterprises of ambition, more insurmountable than any which a simple government of any form can admit of. Notwithstanding the military establishments in the several kingdoms of Europe, which are carried as far as the public resources will bear, the governments are afraid to trust the people with arms. And it is not certain that with this aid alone they would not be able to shake off their yokes. But were the people to possess the additional advantages of local governments chosen by themselves, who could collect the national will, and direct the national force; and of officers appointed out of the militia, by these governments, and attached both to them and to the militia, it may be affirmed with the greatest assurance that the throne of every tyranny in Europe would be speedily overturned in spite of the legions which surround it. Let us not insult the free and gallant citizens of America with the suspicion that they would be less able to defend the rights of which they would be in actual possession than the debased subjects of arbitrary power would be to rescue theirs from the hands of their oppressors. Let us rather no longer insult them with the supposition that they can ever reduce themselves to the necessity of making the experiment, by a blind and tame submission to the long train of insidious measures which must precede and produce it.

The argument under the present head may be put into a very concise form, which appears altogether conclusive. Either the mode in which the federal government is to be constructed will render it sufficiently dependent on the people, or it will not. On the first supposition, it will be restrained by that dependence from forming schemes obnoxious to their constituents. On the other supposition it will not possess the confidence of the people, and its schemes of usurpation will be easily defeated by the State governments, who will be supported by the people.

On summing up the considerations stated in this and the last paper, they seem to amount to the most convincing evidence that the powers proposed to be lodged in the federal government are as little formidable to those reserved to the individual States, as they are indispensably necessary to accomplish the purposes of the Union; and that all those alarms which have been sounded, of a meditated and consequential annihilation of the State governments, must, on the most favorable interpretation, be ascribed to the chimerical fears of the authors of them.

PUBLIUS

The Federalist 50

JAMES MADISON

On Maintaining a Just Partition of Power among the Necessary Departments

To what expedient, then, shall we finally resort, for maintaining in practice the necessary partition of power among the several departments, as laid down in the Constitution? The only answer that can be given is that as all these exterior provisions are found to be inadequate, the defect must be supplied, by so contriving the interior structure of the government as that its several constituent parts may, by their mutual relations, be the means of keeping each other in their proper places. Without presuming to undertake a full development of this important idea, I will hazard a few general observations, which may, perhaps, place it in a clearer light, and enable us to form a more correct judgment of the principles and structure of the government planned by the Convention.

In order to lay a due foundation for that separate and distinct exercise of the different powers of government which to a certain extent is admitted on all hands to be essential to the preservation of liberty, it is evident that each department should have a will of its own, and consequently should be so constituted that the members of each should have as little agency as possible in the appointment of the members of the others. Were this principle rigorously adhered to, it would require that all the appointments for the supreme executive, legislative, and judiciary magistracies should be drawn from the same fountain of authority, the people, through channels having no communication whatever with one another. Perhaps such a plan of constructing the several departments would be less difficult in practice than it may in contemplation appear. Some difficulties, however, and some additional expense would attend the execution of it. Some deviations, therefore, from the principle must be admitted. In the constitution of the judiciary department, in particular, it might be inexpedient to insist rigorously on the principle: First, because peculiar qualifications being essential in the members, the primary consideration ought to be to select that mode of choice which best secures these qualifications; secondly, because the permanent tenure by which the appointments are held in that department must soon destroy all sense of dependence on the authority conferring them.

It is equally evident that the members of each department should be as little dependent as possible on those of the others, for the emoluments annexed to their offices. Were the executive magistrate, or the judges not independent of the Legislature in this particular, their independence in every other would be merely nominal.

But the great security against a gradual concentration of the several powers in the same department consists in giving to those who

administer each department the necessary constitutional means and personal motives to resist
encroachments of the others. The provision for
defence must in this, as in all other cases, be
made commensurate to the danger of attack.
Ambition must be made to counteract ambition.
The interest of the man must be connected with
the constitutional rights of the place. It may be a
reflection on human nature that such devices
should be necessary to control the abuses of government. But what is government itself, but the
greatest of all reflections on human nature? If
men were angels, no government would be necessary. If angels were to govern men, neither external nor internal controls on government would be
necessary. In framing a government which is to
be administered by men over men, the great difficulty lies in this; you must first enable the government to control the governed; and in the next
place oblige it to control itself. A dependence on
the people is, no doubt, the primary control on the
government; but experience has taught mankind
the necessity of auxiliary precautions.

This policy of supplying, by opposite and rival
interests, the defect of better motives, might be
traced through the whole system of human
affairs, private as well as public. We see it particularly displayed in all the subordinate distributions of power, where the constant aim is to
divide and arrange the several offices in such a
manner as that each may be a check on the other;
that the private interest of every individual may
be a sentinel over the public rights. These inven-
tions of prudence cannot be less requisite in the
distribution of the supreme powers of the State.

But it is not possible to give to each department
an equal power of self-defence. In republican government, the legislative authority necessarily predominates. The remedy for this inconveniency is
to divide the legislature into different branches;
and to render them, by different modes of election
and different principles of action, as little connected with each other as the nature of their common functions and their common dependence on

the society will admit. It may even be necessary to
guard against dangerous encroachments by still
further precautions. As the weight of the legislative authority requires that it should be thus
divided, the weakness of the executive may
require, on the other hand, that it should be forti-
fied. An absolute negative on the legislature
appears at first view to be the natural defence with
which the executive magistrate should be armed.
But perhaps it would be neither altogether safe nor
alone sufficient. On ordinary occasions it might
not be exerted with the requisite firmness, and on
extraordinary occasions it might be perfidiously
abused. May not this defect of an absolute negative be supplied by some qualified connection
between this weaker department and the weaker
branch of the stronger department, by which the
latter may be led to support the constitutional
rights of the former, without being too much
detached from the rights of its own department?

If the principles on which these observations
are founded be just, as I persuade myself they are,
and they be applied as a criterion to the several
State constitutions, and to the federal Constitution,
it will be found that, if the latter does not perfectly
correspond with them, the former are infinitely
less able to bear such a test.

There are, moreover, two considerations particularly applicable to the federal system of
America, which place that system in a very interesting point of view:

First. In a single republic all the power surrendered by the people is submitted to the administration of a single government, and the usurpations are guarded against by a division of the
government into distinct and separate departments. In the compound republic of America, the
power surrendered by the people is first divided
between two distinct governments, and then the
portion allotted to each subdivided among distinct
and separate departments. Hence a double security arises to the rights of the people. The different governments will control each other, at the
same time that each will be controlled by itself.

SECTION 2

Constitutional Rights and Natural Law

Having set up the Constitution on a model of checks and balances to divide and limit the power of centralized government, American colonists decided that this still was not enough protection. The Constitution of the United States was amended to include a Bill of Rights. Why? What are the grounds for doing so? In *The "Higher Law" Background of American Constitutional Law*, Edward S. Corwin explains that (historically) the American Constitution was founded on the belief, prevalent at the time, that any justified government must meet certain fundamental requirements. These moral requirements include the notion that legitimate authority is derived from the consent of the governed and, thus, is limited to what rational persons would accept. No legitimate government can exceed these limits. It follows that certain rights are fundamental and are guaranteed to every individual. Corwin traces the development of these ideas through the history of Western thought.

One of the most profound influences on this tradition was the thinking of John Locke, especially as articulated in *Two Treatises on Civil Government*. In the first treatise (not included here) Locke attacks a proposed defense of the divine right of kings to rule. Once he has disposed of divine right as a ground for political authority, in the second treatise Locke sets out his own view on the grounds and limits of legitimate government. The basic idea is that all legitimate government is limited by the requirements of morality, which at that time were called moral law or natural law. Even if authority of government is derived from the consent of the governed, no rational human being would consent to the violation or elimination of his or her own rights. Government is therefore restricted by the individual rights that morality requires all human beings to grant all others. A modern way of putting this view might be to say that we cannot make what is wrong into what is right just by enacting a law that says the wrong thing is legal. Law and government are limited by morality, and in particular by the moral rights of all human beings. Through Locke these views became widely known and influential.

We need to consider the influence of these ideas on the documents that were drafted during the revolutionary period, such as the Declaration of Independence, the Virginia Declaration of Rights, and the Bill of Rights adopted as the first ten amendments to the U.S. Constitution. (See "Collected Documents" and the Appendix.) Notice also Hamilton's arguments in *The Federalist* 84 against the adoption of a bill of rights. Does Hamilton disagree with Locke?

Finally, in *Anarchical Fallacies* consider Jeremy Bentham's step-by-step rejection of the entire natural law point of view, particularly the French Declaration of Rights (see "Collected Documents"). Bentham, some people would say, refutes every argument advanced for natural law, at least as a foundation for legal documents or legal power. If his arguments are sound, how would Locke answer them?

The natural law tradition has profoundly influenced the development of government and law in Western civilization. At the same time, it has always been (and still is) an extremely controversial doctrine. The problem lies in determining the relationship between law and morality. This problem is discussed further in Chapter Two, but for now suffice it to note that natural law theory has greatly affected views on the place of individual rights in constitutional law. These rights, built into the basic structure of government, superseded the power of majority rule, legislative enactment, or executive order. Thus they represent further limits on government.

There are two sorts of questions to ask yourself about these fundamental constitutional rights. On the one hand, there are substantive questions, especially what should these rights be? Should all citizens (or all human beings) be guaranteed rights to free speech, free press, free medical care, free education? Basic rights differ dramatically from country to country. For example, the United States has a tradition of strong guarantees of basic liberties but not much in the way of rights to education or medical care. The USSR and China traditionally had strong guarantees of education and medical care but not much in the way of basic liberties. Is that acceptable, or should some rights be guaranteed to all? If some rights should be guaranteed to all human beings, the basis for such a claim will be some version of natural law (or objective morality).

The other set of questions is formal. Why should certain rights be constitutional, and which ones should they be? There is no structural reason for the rights in the U.S. Bill of Rights to be included in the Constitution, for example. The Constitution would not be structurally incomplete without them. Why then should they be there? The formal and substantive questions are not unrelated.

A major complaint about theories of natural rights is that they are unclear and ambiguous. Certainly this is one of Bentham's major objections in *Anarchical Fallacies*. A primary focus of contemporary theories of legal and moral rights, however, has been to clarify the concept. The essays that begin this section provide a clearer picture of the conceptual elements and distinguishing features of rights.

The brief selection from Lawrence Baker's "Individual Rights" introduces the conceptual analysis of rights by setting out some basic conceptual elements of the term in general, and by offering some helpful remarks about Wesley Hohfeld's famous analysis of legal rights in particular. Hohfeld's *Fundamental Legal Conceptions* is considered a classic in the analysis of legal rights. Hohfeld was concerned about the lack of precision with which the language of rights was used in legal discourse. In particular, the ambiguity of the term *right* in its broadest use made the term susceptible to mistake and abuse, he thought. In the interest of clarity Hohfeld distinguished eight legal concepts that, he suggested, might be considered the "lowest common denominators of the law." These are the most basic conceptions in legal analysis. They can be arranged by their logical relations to one another in terms of being opposites or correlatives as follows:

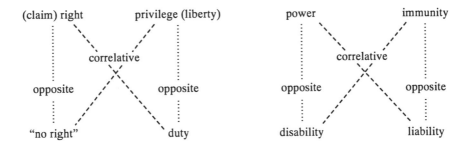

Understanding these conceptual relations facilitates understanding legal relations. The opposites are obvious. If you have a right, then it cannot be that you have "no right." If you have a privilege or liberty to do something, then you have no duty not to do it. If you have legal power over some legal relation, then you have no legal disability with regard to that relation. And if you are immune to some law, then you are not liable to it.

The correlatives are not as obvious, but are still logically necessary relations. If you have a right, then someone else has a duty to fulfill that right. If you have a liberty or privilege, then there is "no right" against you; that is, no one else has a right against your doing what you are at liberty to do. If you have a legal power, then someone else is liable to that power. And if you are immune to some law or authority, then it is disabled with regard to you.

Understanding these basic terms and relations can be immensely helpful. Not understanding them, as Hohfeld points out, can lead to some important confusions. Keep in mind one general point. The term *right* is regularly used in both a broad (sometimes called generic) and a narrow sense. The narrow sense is the one clarified by the eight relations in the illustration. In this sense right is sometimes called a claim-right by those wishing to be careful about their language. It is this narrow sense that logically and legally entails a correlative duty.

The broad sense of the term *right* encompasses all four terms at the top line of the squares, and some nonlegal senses as well. The term *right* is highly ambiguous, and whether it implies a duty, moral or legal, depends on which sense is being used. The problem is that it is very easy to slip from one sense to another, and so to think a duty is implied when it is not. The problem often occurs when *right* is used to mean *liberty* or, as Hohfeld calls it, *privilege*. For example, you have a right of free speech. That "right" is actually a liberty and an immunity. That means that you have no duty not to speak and that you are not liable to laws that restrict your speech in an absolute or unreasonable manner. It also means that others have no right that you not speak and that the government is under a disability (and thus has no power) to make laws unreasonably restricting your speech. As you can see, there is no correlative duty here. You may have the right to speak, but no one has, say, a duty to listen.

In the next essay Joel Feinberg analyzes the conceptual elements of moral (as opposed to legal) rights, explaining that human rights are a subset of moral rights and that natural rights are a subset of human rights. This is an important clarification for our study of legal rights, especially in terms of constitutional and civil rights. John Locke's essay formulates a theory of natural rights based on the old tradition of natural law. (See Chapter Two, Section 2, for further discussion of the natural law theory.) What conceptual philosophers such as Feinberg make clear (that Locke does not make clear) is that natural law is moral law, and natural rights are moral rights. Natural law theorists such as Locke merge the idea of moral and legal rights in the theory of natural rights. That lack of clarity is what Bentham, being a positivist, so strongly rejects. Bentham's idea of rights corresponds to Hohfeld's idea of legal rights, which has the advantage of clarity and precision. You should not conclude, however, that natural law is simply the result of sloppy thinking or that natural rights are simply the conflation of moral and legal rights. On the contrary, the dispute between all positivists such as Bentham and all natural law theorists such as Locke is much deeper than that. It is a dispute about the nature and justification of rights and law. As Becker points out, rights are not simply desires or needs or even claims. To have a right is to be entitled to something for some reason. Thus, rights, to be rights, must be justified by something. Similarly, law is not supposed to be the same thing as ordinary coercion. Law is supposed to be legitimate authority; that is, it is supposed to be justified by something. Natural law is one theory of what justifies law and rights and consequently of the nature of law and rights. According to natural law theorists, there are fundamental, objective moral requirements, ascertainable by human reason, that any legal system must meet in order to be legitimate or justified. Otherwise, law would be unjustified coercion, indistinguishable from assault or war. Locke characterizes these fundamental moral requirements as God-given individual rights, more basic than human law or government. Bentham, on the other hand, believes that all law and rights are conventional. They are the product of agreement, of social order, of government. There are no rights without law; there is no law without government. There is only power and chaos.

Feinberg's analysis helps to clarify this longstanding dispute about the nature and justification of law and rights by clarifying the terms in which it is discussed. Conceptual analysis cannot settle this dispute (which will be taken up in more detail in Chapter Two), but it can and does help to clarify the issues.

Notes and Questions

LAWRENCE BECKER, from "Individual Rights"

1. Lawrence Becker begins by pointing out that the term *right* is used in both a specialized and an unspecialized way. Explain this distinction. It is important to become familiar with this ambiguity in the term *right* since it is the source of much confusion and error. In the introduction to this section the unspecialized use of the term is called the *generic form*. Learn to recognize it.

2. Becker then briefly introduces the specialized distinctions among legal rights that were formulated by Wesley Hohfeld. These are discussed in more detail in the next article. Consider the argument about abortion rights that Becker uses to illustrate the importance of noticing Hohfeld's distinctions. What does Becker say is wrong with this argument? Do you see how the failure to recognize these distinctions can lead to serious error?

3. Becker also sets out several other crucial distinctions among rights. What is the difference between positive and negative rights? Between special and general rights? You will find further discussion of these concepts throughout this book. Special and general rights are of particular interest in the chapters on contract (Chapter Three), property (Chapter Four), and criminal law (Chapter Six). Positive and negative rights are of particular interest in Chapter Seven on civil rights to freedom and justice. See the introductions to these chapters for further discussion of these distinctions.

4. Becker argues that a general definition of the concept of a right must be so broad that it will not be very useful. Many philosophers do not agree with that assessment. Feinberg, for example, has analyzed rights as valid claims. More specifically, he argues that to say that X has a right to Y means that person X has a valid, or justified, claim against person Y to Z. That is, a right is always a right to something against someone. Feinberg's view is widely accepted, clear, and helpful. It vividly portrays certain important features of rights. But rights have also been analyzed as protected interests, as protected choices, as correlative benefits of duties, and as entitlements, among other things. Hence, Becker's conclusion that there is no single general theory of rights. However, even Becker recognizes that rights have certain common elements. What are those elements, according to Becker? Can you think of any common elements he omitted?

[From] "Individual Rights"

LAWRENCE C. BECKER

Types of Rights

What is right? Everyone agrees that there is no simple answer to that question because there are so many radically different types of rights. The word "right" is multiply ambiguous.

One important thing to get straight from the outset is the difference between the specialized and the unspecialized use of the term "right." In the unspecialized use, "I have a right to do it" may mean no more than "I am justified in doing it." A right in this sense is not a separate sort of moral consideration at all. It is simply any sort of consideration that is sufficient to justify a course of action. But here we are concerned with the other category — the specialized use of "right" — in which "I have a right to do it" means "I have a special sort of moral claim to do it." But what "special sort"? Again, there isn't just one.

Claim-Rights, Liberties, Powers and Immunities

Wesley Hohfeld, an American legal theorist working in the early part of this century, distinguished four sorts, and his distinctions are enormously useful. The idea is to think about what is on "the other side" of a right. If *you* have a right of some sort, what does that mean for my situation?

CLAIM-RIGHTS. One thing it might mean is that I have a duty to you. If you have a right not to be tortured, that means I have a duty not to do it. If you have a right to get pay for your work, your employer has a duty to pay for it. When rights correlate with duties in this way they are called claims, or claim-rights, or sometimes rights in the strict sense.

LIBERTIES. But sometimes there is not a duty on the other side. Sometimes there is just a kind of moral or legal vacuum. If you have a right to run in the race, that doesn't mean that the other runners have a duty to let you win. It simply means that they have no claim-right to the victory — no claim-right that you not win. Such rights are called liberties, or liberty-rights, or (less accurately) privileges. The United States Supreme Court has made it clear that a woman's legal right to an abortion is at present a liberty-right, not a claim-right. Women are simply at liberty to have abortions; no particular person has a duty to perform them, and states have no duty to pay for them.

POWERS. A third sort of right is a power. If you have the right to make a will, that means that you have the power to change some of the rights and duties of those around you. You can make me your executor, for example, which imposes duties on me. Or, as I would much prefer, you can make me your beneficiary. When you have a power, or power-right, people on the other side of it have a liability. They are, in effect, at your mercy.

IMMUNITIES. A fourth sort of right is an immunity. The other side of this is a disability or lack of power. If you have the right to remain silent, then I lack the power-right to make you speak.

Schematically, Hohfeld's distinctions look like this:

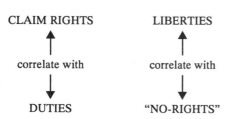

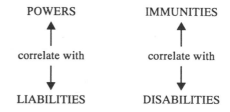

Careful attention to these distinctions is important. Rights are often compounds of two or more types, but until the elements of the compound have been identified, it is hard to make much progress in a moral argument about it.

Consider, for example, how you would deal with the following argument: "All rights, if they are genuine legal rights, have to be enforceable. If they are enforceable, that means the law can require people to respect them. If people are required to respect them, then duties are being imposed. So it is just a fraud to say in one breath that women have the right to have abortions and in the next breath to say that no one has a duty to provide or perform abortions. Either women have the right or they don't. If they do, then we have the duty to provide them."

There are several mistakes in this argument, but the fundamental one is its failure to see that the law might enforce (with appropriate duties) Hohfeldian "no-rights," liabilities and disabilities. The law might make sure, for example, that no one interferes with doctors who decide to perform abortions or women who decide to have them. The law might insist that hospitals permit staff doctors to schedule abortions in just the same way they schedule other elective surgery. The liberty-right to an abortion, then, would be buttressed by a duty on the part of hospitals not to put obstacles in the way. Doctors and their patients would then have correlative claim-rights against their hospitals, but those claim-rights would be for the enforcement of liberties.

Negative and Positive, General and Special Rights

Just two other distinctions are of crucial importance here. (For the moment I shall leave aside "natural," "conventional," "moral" and "legal" rights because those categories have to do with how a right is justified. Similarly, "human" rights, "women's" rights and so forth refer to scope — to those who are in the class of right-holders.)

One distinction is between *negative* and *positive rights*. Negative rights are rights to be free from interference. Criminal law defines many of these rights by imposing duties of restraint on people. We have duties to refrain from murder, mayhem, rape, pillage, and theft, and others have

the corresponding negative rights against us. Positive rights, on the other hand, are rights to assistance of some sort. Rights to food, to health care, and to an equal share of the world's resources would be positive rights. One of the most fundamental disagreements in political theory is between advocates of the minimal or "nightwatchman" state (who hold that the government has no business enforcing any [non-contractual] positive rights at all) and advocates of the welfare state (who insist that the government must enforce some positive rights).

The other important distinction is between general and special rights. In law, general rights are sometimes referred to as rights *in rem* — rights "against the world." Special rights are rights *in personam* — rights "against (specific) persons." My right not to be murdered is a general one: I have the right "against" everyone — against the world. But my right to compensation for my work is a special one. It comes from a special relationship between me and my employer. This distinction brings out the importance of identifying who is on the other side of a right. Until that is settled, it is hard to get very far with a moral argument about the right.

Getting a General Definition

Now with all that said, are we any closer to a general answer to the question of what a right is? Is there a general answer? Not a very useful one, I think. The various types of rights are different enough so that anything true of them all will be very general indeed. Wittgenstein liked to use the example of the problem of defining the concept of a game. There are so many different kinds of games that it is hard to find any interesting feature common to them all. Some are played alone (solitaire), and others are not. Some are played to win, and others are not (Spin the Bottle). Some are played just for fun; others are serious business for professionals. Some have fixed rules; others (like impromptu children's games) do not. And so on. Rights are a bit like that.

Even so, rights have a few common elements which are important. One is that rights are more than just norms, or expectations, or standards of conduct. They are rules which define the boundaries of what is "owed" to a specified group of people (the right holders) by another group (the right respecters). Consider the statement, "When Americans greet strangers, they typically smile and shake hands." Imagine this being given as a piece of advice to foreigners. Would it state a rule defining what is "owed" to strangers by Americans? No. It would merely define a general practice, or expectation. The statement, "Keep your promises," however, is quite different. It does state a ruling defining what is owed. And the people who are owed — that is, the promisees — are often said to have a right to what was promised.

This feature of rights accounts for two other general characteristics. One has to do with gratitude and indebtedness. When you respect my rights, you haven't done me a favor. I don't "owe" you anything for it — not even gratitude. (Though civility is not out of place.) . . . The other characteristic is that rights are supposed to be enforceable in a way that mere ideals or desires are not. If I simply want you to do something for me and you do not, that is too bad for me. Depending on the circumstance, it might not be good of you to refuse, but if all I have on my side is the fact that I want your help, I do not have any business twisting your arm for it. If I have a right to your help, however, and you refuse it, some sort of arm-twisting is presumably in order. I say some sort because of course the extent of it depends on the sort of right involved. If the right is a moral but not a legal one, verbal demands are frequently as far as one can go. But the general principle is important: If I have a right to it I can justifiably take steps to extract it from you if you fail to hand it over.

If rights are to be enforceable, however, they must be specific. They must indicate *who* has the right against whom, what the *content* of the right is, and what *kind of enforcement* is appropriate. Some claims of right are criticized on just this ground. What could "Everyone has a right to an education" mean? If it means that everyone has a right to go to school, then we can readily understand how it could be enforced. If it means more than that (say, for example, that the state has a duty to see to it that everyone actually learns calculus), could it be enforced at all? If it cannot be enforced, is it really a "right"?

Finally, there is *compensation*. The violation of rights — unlike other moral considerations — always at least raises a presumption that the victims should be compensated. If our desires conflict, and mine must be sacrificed, I am just unfortunate. But if my rights conflict with your desires, and for some reason my rights must (or just are) sacrificed, I am presumably "owed" something. Often this takes the form of compensation for my loss. Sometimes it merely means that I am owed an apology. But always, when rights are involved, a violation leaves unfinished business.

So to summarize: Rights are rules that define what is owed to some (the right holders) by others. Rights may be demanded and enforced. They are therefore part of our system of permissions and requirements.

Beyond that, because rights are so various, there is not much else one can usefully say about their general nature.

* * *

NOTE

1. W. N. Hohfeld, *Fundamental Legal Conceptions* (New Haven: Yale University Press, 1919).

Notes and Questions

WESLEY NEWCOMB HOHFELD, from *Fundamental Legal Conceptions*

1. Hohfeld's concern is to clarify the language of legal discourse, especially the language of rights. To do this, he distinguishes eight basic legal conceptions. What are they? How do they logically relate to one another? Why does Hohfeld think that explaining these relations provides a better understanding of these terms than a simple definition would? What do you think?

2. Explain the relation between a right and a duty. What does it mean to be correlative? How does this specify legal relations?

3. Notice that the terms *liberty* and *privilege* are interchangeable. What is the difference between a liberty or privilege and a right? Why is this difference important? What is the relation between a liberty or privilege and a duty? Between a privilege and no right?

4. The term *no right* was invented by Hohfeld because there was no term to represent this particular logical relation. Something had to fill the slot that was opposite to *right* and correlative to *privilege* or *liberty*, but there was no word. So Hohfeld adopted the phrase *no right* in order to serve that purpose. *No right* simply stands for the absence of a right.

5. The four terms so far encountered — *right*, *duty*, *privilege* (or *liberty*), and *no right* can be arranged in a square of opposition that illustrates the logical relations among them. This arrangement was set out in the introduction to this chapter; you may find it helpful to glance back at it.

6. What is a legal power? How does it relate to liability and disability? How, if at all, does it relate to a right? Remember that one of Hohfeld's complaints is that people (even lawyers) often say *right* when they mean *power*. He shows how understanding the difference clarifies, among other things, relations of agency and public service. How so?

7. The final relation is that of immunity and liability. What is an immunity? How does it relate to liability and disability? What is the difference between liability and disability? What is the difference between an immunity and a right? Notice that the terms *power*, *immunity*, *disability*, and *liability* can be arranged in a square of opposition analogous to that of the first four terms considered. As Hohfeld points out, "a power bears the same general contrast to an immunity that a right does to a privilege."

8. Remember that *right* is used in both a broad and a narrow sense. The broad sense merges all the distinctions we have just been studying. Try applying these distinctions to some of the documents and discussions presented in these materials and other important historical documents. For example, is the French Declaration of Rights talking about rights or liberties or immunities? How about the American Bill of Rights? It should make a difference, shouldn't it? Not all disputes can be solved this way, but some can, and the dispute that is left is clearer.

[From] *Fundamental Legal Conceptions*

WESLEY NEWCOMB HOHFELD

Fundamental Jural Relations Contrasted with One Another

One of the greatest hindrances to the clear understanding, the incisive statement, and the true solution of legal problems frequently arises from the express or tacit assumption that all legal relations may be reduced to "rights" and "duties," and that these latter categories are therefore adequate for the purpose of analyzing even the most complex legal interests, such as trusts, options, escrows, "future" interests, corporate interests, etc. Even if the difficulty related merely to inadequacy and ambiguity of terminology, its seriousness would nevertheless be worthy of definite recognition and persistent effort toward improvement; for in any closely reasoned problem, whether legal or non-legal, chameleon-hued words are a peril both to clear thought and to lucid expression. As a matter of fact, however, the above mentioned inadequacy and ambiguity of terms unfortunately reflect, all too often, corresponding paucity and confusion as regards actual legal conceptions. That this is so may appear in some measure from the discussion to follow.

The strictly fundamental legal relations are, after all, *sui generis;* and thus it is that attempts at formal definition are always unsatisfactory, if not altogether useless. Accordingly, the most promising line of procedure seems to consist in exhibiting all of the various relations in a scheme of "opposites" and "correlatives," and then proceeding to exemplify their individual scope and application in concrete cases. An effort will be made to pursue this method:

Jural Opposites

    right
    no-right
    privilege
    duty
    power
    disability
    immunity
    liability

Jural Correlatives

    right
    duty
    privilege
    no-right
    power
    liability
    immunity
    disability

RIGHTS AND DUTIES. As already intimated, the term "rights" tends to be used indiscriminately to cover what in a given case may be a privilege, a power, or an immunity, rather than a right in the strictest sense; and this looseness of usage is occasionally recognized by the authorities. As said by Mr. Justice Strong in *People v. Dikeman.*

The word "right" is defined by lexicographers to denote, among other things, *property, interest, power, prerogative, immunity, privilege* (Walker's Dict. word "Right"). In law it is most frequently applied to property in its restricted sense, but it is often used to designate *power, prerogative, and privilege.*

Recognition of this ambiguity is also found in the language of Mr. Justice Jackson, in *United States v. Patrick.*

The words "right" or "privilege" have, of course, a variety of meanings, according to the connection or context in which they are used. Their definition, as given by standard lexicographers, includes "that which one has a *legal claim to do,"* "*legal power,"* "*authority,"* "*immunity granted by authority,"* "the investiture with special or peculiar rights."

And, similarly, in the language of Mr. Justice Sneed, in *Lonas v. State.*

The state, then, is forbidden from making and enforcing any law which shall abridge the *privileges* and *immunities* of citizens of the United States. It is said that the words *rights, privileges* and *immunities* are abusively used, as if they were synonymous. The word *rights* is generic, common, embracing whatever may be lawfully claimed.

It is interesting to observe, also, that a tendency toward discrimination may be found in a number of important constitutional and statutory provisions. Just how accurate the distinctions in the mind of the draftsman may have been it is, of course, impossible to say.

Recognizing, as we must, the very broad and indiscriminate use of the term "right," what clue do we find, in ordinary legal discourse, toward limiting the word in question to a definite and appropriate meaning? That clue lies in the correlative "duty," for it is certain that even those who use the word and the conception "right" in the broadest possible way are accustomed to thinking of "duty" as the invariable correlative. As said in *Lake Shore & M. S. R. Co. v. Kurtz.*

A duty or a legal obligation is that which one ought or ought not to do. "Duty" and "right" are correlative terms. When a right is invaded, a duty is violated.

In other words, if X has a right against Y that he shall stay off the former's land, the correlative (and equivalent) is that Y is under a duty toward X to stay off the place. If, as seems desirable, we should seek a synonym for the term "right" in this limited and proper meaning, perhaps the word "claim" would prove the best. The latter has the advantage of being a monosyllable. In this connection, the language of Lord Watson in *Studd v. Cool* is instructive:

> Any words which in a settlement of movables would be recognized by the law of Scotland as sufficient to create a right or claim in favor of an executor . . . must receive effect if used with reference to lands in Scotland.

PRIVILEGES AND "NO-RIGHTS." As indicated in the above scheme of jural relations, a privilege is the opposite of a duty, and the correlative of a "no-right." In the example last put, whereas X has a *right* or *claim* that Y, the other man, should stay off the land, he himself has the *privilege* of entering on the land; or, in equivalent words, X does not have a duty to stay off. The privilege of entering is the negation of a duty to stay off. As indicated by this case, some caution is necessary at this point; for, always, when it is said that a given privilege is the mere negation of a *duty*, what is meant, of course, is a duty having a content or tenor precisely *opposite* to that of the privilege in question. Thus, if, for some special reason, X has contracted with Y to go on the former's own land, it is obvious that X has, as regards Y, both the privilege of entering and the *duty of entering*. The privilege is perfectly consistent with this sort of duty, — for the latter is of the *same* content or tenor as the privilege; — but it still holds good that, as regards Y, X's privilege of entering is the precise negation of a duty *to stay off*. Similarly, if A has not contracted with B to perform certain work for the latter, A's privilege of *not* doing so is the very negation of a duty of *doing* so. Here again the duty contrasted is of a content or tenor exactly opposite to that of the privilege.

Passing now to the question of "correlatives," it will be remembered, of course, that a duty is the invariable correlative of that legal relation which is most properly called a right or claim. That being so, if further evidence be needed as to the fundamental and important difference between a right (or claim) and a privilege, surely it is found in the fact that the correlative of the latter relation is a "no-right," there being no single term available to express the latter conception. Thus, the correlative of X's right that Y shall not enter on the land is Y's duty not to enter; but the correlative of X's privilege of entering himself is manifestly Y's "no-right" that X shall not enter.

In view of the considerations thus far emphasized, the importance of keeping the conception of a right (or claim) and the conception of a privilege quite distinct from each other seems evident; and, more than that, it is equally clear that there should be a separate term to represent the latter relation. No doubt, as already indicated, it is very common to use the term "right" indiscriminately, even when the relation designated is really that of privilege; and only too often this identity of terms has involved for the particular speaker or writer a confusion or blurring of ideas. Good instances of this may be found even in unexpected places. Thus Professor Holland, in his work on *Jurisprudence*, referring to a different and well-known sort of ambiguity inherent in the Latin "*Ius*," the German "*Recht*," the Italian "*Diritto*," and the French "*Droit*," — terms used to express "not only 'a right,' but also 'Law' in the abstract," — very aptly observes:

> If the expression of widely different ideas by one and the same term resulted only in the necessity for . . . clumsy paraphrases, or obviously inaccurate paraphrases, no great harm would be done; but unfortunately the identity of terms seems irresistibly to suggest an identity between the ideas expressed by them.

Curiously enough, however, in the very chapter where this appears, — the chapter on "Rights," — the notions of right, privilege and power seem to be blended, and that, too, although the learned author states that "the correlative of . . . legal right is legal duty," and that "these pairs of terms express . . . in each case the same state of facts viewed from opposite sides." While the whole chapter must be read in order to appreciate the seriousness of this lack of discrimination, a single passage must suffice by way of example:

> If . . . the power of the State will protect him in so carrying out his wishes, and will compel such acts or forbearances on the part of other people as may be necessary in order that his wishes

may be so carried out, then he has a "legal right" so to carry out his wishes.

The first part of this passage suggests privileges, the middle part rights (or claims), and the last part privileges.

* * *

On grounds already emphasized, it would seem that the line of reasoning pursued by Lord Lindley in the great case of *Quinn v. Leathem* is deserving of comment:

> The plaintiff had the ordinary *rights* of the British subject. He was *at liberty* to earn his living in his own way, provided he did not violate one special law prohibiting him from so doing, and provided he did not infringe the rights of other people. This *liberty* involved *the liberty* to deal with other persons who were willing to deal with him. *This liberty* is a *right* recognized by law; its *correlative* is the general *duty* of every one not to prevent the free exercise of this *liberty* except so far as his own liberty of action may justify him in so doing. But a person's *liberty* or *right* to deal with others is nugatory unless they are at liberty to deal with him if they choose to do so. Any interference with their liberty to deal with him affects him.

A "liberty" considered as a legal relation (or "right" in the loose and generic sense of that term) must mean, if it have any definite content at all, precisely the same thing as *privilege;* and certainly that is fair connotation of the term as used the first three times in the passage quoted. It is equally clear, as already indicated, that such a privilege or liberty to deal with others at will might very conceivably exist without any peculiar concomitant rights against "third parties" as regards certain kids of interference. Whether there should be such concomitant rights (or claims) is ultimately a question of justice and policy; and it should be considered, as such, on its merits. The only correlative logically implied by the privileges or liberties in question are the "no-rights" of "third parties." It would therefore be a *non sequitur* to conclude from the mere existence of such liberties that "third parties" are under a *duty* not to interfere, etc. Yet in the middle of the above passage from Lord Lindley's opinion there is a sudden and question-begging shift in the use of terms. First, the "liberty" in question is transmuted into a "right"; and then, possibly under the seductive influence of the latter word, it is assumed that the "correlative" must be "the general duty of every one not to prevent," etc.

* * *

POWERS AND LIABILITIES. As indicated in the preliminary scheme of jural relations, a legal power (as distinguished, of course, from a mental or physical power) is the opposite of legal disability, and the correlative of legal liability. But what is the intrinsic nature of a legal power as such? Is it possible to analyze the conception represented by this constantly employed and very important term of legal discourse? Too close an analysis might seem metaphysical rather than useful; so that what is here presented is intended only as an approximate explanation, sufficient for all practical purposes.

A change in a given legal relation may result (1) from some superadded fact or group of facts not under the volitional control of a human being (or human beings); or (2) from some superadded fact or groups of facts which are under the volitional control of one or more human beings. As regards the second class of cases, the person (or persons) whose volitional control is paramount may be said to have the (legal) power to effect the particular change of legal relations that is involved in the problem.

This second class of cases — powers in the technical sense — must now be further considered. The nearest synonym for any ordinary case seems to be (legal) "ability" — the latter being obviously the opposite of "inability," or "disability." The term "right," so frequently and loosely used in the present connection is an unfortunate term for the purpose, — a not unusual result being confusion of thought as well as ambiguity of expression. The term "capacity" is equally unfortunate; for, as we have already seen, when used with discrimination, this word denotes a particular group of operative facts, and not a legal relation of any kind.

Many examples of legal powers may readily be given. Thus, X, the owner of ordinary personal property "in a tangible object" has the power to extinguish his own legal interest (rights, powers, immunities, etc.) through that totality of operative facts known as abandonment; and — simultaneously and correlatively —

to create in other persons privileges and powers relating to the abandoned object, — e. g., the power to acquire title to the latter by appropriating it. *Similarly*, X has the power to transfer his interest to Y, — that is to extinguish his own interest and concomitantly create in Y a new and corresponding interest. So also X has the power to create contractual obligations of various kinds. Agency cases are likewise instructive. By the use of some *metaphorical* expression such as the Latin, *qui facit per alium, facit per se* the true nature of agency relations is only too frequently obscured. The creation of an agency relation involves, *inter alia*, the grant of legal powers to the so-called agent, and the creation of correlative liabilities in the principal. That is to say, one party, P, has the power to create agency powers in another party, A, — for example, the power to convey P's property, the power to impose (so called) contractual obligations on P, the power to "receive" title to property so that it shall vest in P, and so forth. In passing, it may be well to observe that the term "authority," so frequently used in agency cases, is very ambiguous and slippery in its connotation. Properly employed in the present connection, the word seems to be an abstract or qualitative term corresponding to the concrete "authorization," — the latter consisting of a particular group of operative facts taking place between the principal and the agent. All too often, however, the term in question is so used as to blend and confuse these operative facts, with the powers and privileges thereby created in the agent. A careful discrimination in these particulars would, it is submitted, go far toward clearing up certain problems in the law of agency.

* * *

In connection with the powers and liabilities created respectively by an ordinary offer and by an option, it is interesting to consider the liabilities of a person engaged in a "public calling"; for, as it seems, such a party's characteristic position is, one might almost say, intermediate between that of an ordinary contractual offerer and that of an option-giver. It has indeed been usual to assert that such a party is (generally speaking) under a present *duty* to all other parties; but this is believed to be erroneous. Thus,

Professor Wyman, in his work on *Public Service Companies*, says:

> The duty placed upon every one exercising a public calling is primarily a *duty* to serve every man who is a member of the public. . . . It is somewhat difficult to place this exceptional duty in our legal system. . . . The truth of the matter is that the obligation resting upon one who has undertaken the performance of public duty is *sui generis*.

It is submitted that the learned writer's difficulties arise primarily from a failure to see that the innkeeper, the common carrier and others similarly "holding out" are under present *liabilities* rather than present *duties*. Correlative to those liabilities are the respective powers of the various members of the public. Thus, for example, a traveling member of the public has the legal power, by making proper application and sufficient tender, to impose a duty on the innkeeper to receive him as a guest. For breach of the duty *thus* created an action would of course lie. It would therefore seem that the innkeeper is, to some extent, like one who had given an option to every traveling member of the public. He differs as regards net legal effect, only because he can extinguish his present liabilities and the correlative powers of the traveling members of the public *by going out of business*. Yet, on the other hand, his liabilities are more onerous than that of an ordinary contractual offerer, for he cannot extinguish his liabilities by any simple performance akin to revocation of offer.

As regards all the "legal powers" thus far considered, possibly some caution is necessary. If, for example, we consider the ordinary property owner's power of alienation, it is necessary to distinguish carefully between the *legal* power, the *physical* power to do the things necessary for the "exercise" of the legal power, and, finally, the *privilege* of doing these things — that is, if such privilege does really exist. It may or may not. Thus, if X, a landowner, has contracted with Y that the former will not alienate to Z, the acts of X necessary to exercise the power of alienating to Z are privileged as between X and every party other than Y; but, obviously, as between X and Y, the former has no privilege of doing the necessary acts; or conversely, he is under a duty to Y not to do what is necessary to exercise the power.

In view of what has already been said, very

little may suffice concerning a *liability* as such. The latter, as we have seen, is the correlative of power, and the opposite of immunity (or exemption). While no doubt the term "liability" is often loosely used as a synonym for "duty," or "obligation," it is believed, from an extensive survey of judicial precedents, that the connotation already adopted as most appropriate to the word in question is fully justified. A few cases tending to indicate this will not be noticed. In *McNeer v. McNeer*, Mr. Justice Magruder balanced the conceptions of power and liability as follows:

> So long as she lived, however, his interest in her land lacked those *elements of property*, such as *power of disposition* and *liability to sale on* execution which had formerly given it the character of a vested estate.

In *Booth v. Commonwealth*, the court had to construe a Virginia statute providing "that all free white male persons who are twenty-one years of age and not over sixty, shall be *liable* to serve as jurors, except as hereinafter provided." It is plain that this enactment imposed only a *liability* and not a *duty*. It is a liability to have a duty created. The latter would arise only when, in exercise of their powers, the parties litigant and the court officers had done what was necessary to impose a specific duty to perform the functions of a juror. The language of the court, by Moncure, J., is particularly apposite as indicating that liability is the opposite, or negative, of immunity (or exemption):

> The word both expressed and implied is "liable," which has a very different meaning from "qualified" . . . Its meaning is "bound" or "obliged." . . . A person exempt from serving on juries is not liable to serve, and a person not liable to serve is exempt from serving. The terms seem to be convertible.

* * *

IMMUNITIES AND DISABILITIES. As already brought out, immunity is the correlative of disability ("no-power"), and the opposite, or negation, of liability. Perhaps it will also be plain, from the preliminary outline and from the discussion down to this point, that a power bears the same general contrast to an immunity that a right does to a privilege. A right is one's affirmative claim against another, and a privilege is one's freedom from the right or claim of another. Similarly, a power is one's affirmative "control" over a given legal relation as against another; whereas an immunity is one's freedom from the legal power or "control" of another as regards some legal relation.

A few examples may serve to make this clear. X, a landowner, has, as we have seen, power to alienate to Y or to any other ordinary party. On the other hand, X has also various immunities as against Y, and all other ordinary parties. For Y is under a disability (i.e., has no power) so far as shifting the legal interest either to himself or to a third party is concerned; and what is true of Y applies similarly to every one else who has not by virtue of special operative facts acquired a power to alienate X's property. If, indeed, a sheriff has been duly empowered by a writ of execution to sell X's interest, that is a very different matter: correlative to such sheriff's power would be the *liability* of X, — the very opposite of immunity (or exemption). It is elementary, too, that as against the sheriff, X might be immune or exempt in relation to certain parcels of property, and be liable as to others. Similarly, if an agent has been duly appointed by X to sell a given piece of property, then, as to the latter, X has, in relation to such agent, a liability rather than an immunity.

For over a century there has been, in this country, a great deal of important litigation involving immunities from powers of taxation. If there be any lingering misgivings as to the "practical" importance of accuracy and discrimination in legal conceptions and legal terms, perhaps some of such doubts would be dispelled by considering the numerous cases on valuable taxation exemptions coming before the United States Supreme Court. Thus, in *Phoenix Ins. Co. v. Tennessee*, Mr. Justice Peckham expressed the view of the court as follows:

> In granting to the De Soto Company "all the rights, privileges, and immunities" of the Bluff City Company, all words are used which could be regarded as necessary to carry the exemption from taxation possessed by the Bluff City Company; while in the next following grant, that of the charter of the plaintiff in error, the word "immunity" is omitted. Is there any meaning to

be attached to that omission, and if so, what? We think some meaning is to be attached to it. The word "immunity" expresses more clearly and definitely an intention to include therein an exemption from taxation than does either of the other words. Exemption from taxation is more accurately described as an "immunity" than as a privilege, although it is not to be denied that the latter word may sometimes and under some circumstances include such exemptions.

In *Morgan v. Louisiana* there is an instructive discussion from the pen of Mr. Justice Field. In holding that on a foreclosure sale of the franchise and property of a railroad corporation an immunity from taxation did not pass to the purchaser, the learned judge said:

As has been often said by this court, the whole community is interested in retaining the power of taxation undiminished. . . . The exemption of the property of the company from taxation, and the exemption of its officers and servants from jury and military duty, were both intended for the benefit of the company, and its benefit alone. In their personal character they are analogous to exemptions from execution of certain property of debtors, made by laws of several of the states.

So far as immunities are concerned, the two judicial discussions last quoted concern respectively problems of interpretation and problems of alienability. In many other cases difficult constitutional questions have arisen as the result of statutes impairing or extending various kinds of immunities. Litigants have, from time to time, had occasion to appeal both to the clause against impairment of the obligation of contracts and to the provision against depriving a person of property without due process of law. This has been especially true as regards exemptions from taxation and exemptions from execution.

If a word may now be permitted with respect to mere terms as such, the first thing to note is that the word "right" is overworked in the field of immunities as elsewhere. As indicated, however, by the judicial expressions already quoted, the best synonym is, of course, the term "exemption." It is instructive to note, also, that the word "impunity" has a very similar connotation. This is made evident by the interesting discriminations of Lord Chancellor Finch in *Skelton v. Skelton*, a case decided in 1677:

But this I would be no means allow, that equity should enlarge the restraints of the disabilities introduced by act of parliament; and as to the granting of injunctions to stay waste, I took a distinction where tenant hath only *impunitatem*, and where he hath *jus in arboribus*. If the tenant have only a bare indemnity or *exemption* from an action (at law), if he committed waste, there it is fit he should be restrained by injunction from committing it.

In the latter part of the preceding discussion, eight conceptions of the law have been analyzed and compared in some detail, the purpose having been to exhibit not only their intrinsic meaning and scope, but also their relations to one another and the methods by which they are applied, in judicial reasoning, to the solution of concrete problems of litigation. Before concluding this branch of the discussion a general suggestion may be ventured as to the great practical importance of a clear appreciation of the distinctions and discriminations set forth. If a homely metaphor be permitted, these eight conceptions, — rights and duties, privileges and no-rights, powers and liabilities, immunities and disabilities, — seem to be what may be called "the lowest common denominators of the law." Ten fractions ($1/3$, $2/5$, etc.) may, superficially, seem so different from one another as to defy comparison. If, however, they are expressed in terms of their lowest common denominators ($5/15$, $6/15$, etc.), comparison becomes easy, and fundamental similarity may be discovered. The same thing is of course true as regards the lowest generic conceptions to which any and all "legal quantities" may be reduced.

Reverting, for example, to the subject of powers, it might be difficult at first glance to discover any essential and fundamental similarity between conditional sales of personality, escrow transactions, option agreements, agency relations, powers of appointment, etc. But if all these relations are reduced to their lowest generic terms, the conceptions of legal power and legal liability are seen to be dominantly, though not exclusively, applicable throughout the series. By such a process it becomes possible not only to discover essential similarities and illuminating analogies in the midst of what appears superficially to be infinite and hopeless variety, but also to discern common principles of justice and policy underlying the various jural problems involved. An indirect, yet very practical, consequence is that it frequently becomes feasible, by virtue of such analysis, to use as persuasive authorities judicial precedents that might otherwise seem altogether irrelevant. If this point be valid with respect to powers, it would seem to be equally so as regards all of the other basic conceptions of the law. In short, the deeper the analysis, the greater becomes one's perception of fundamental unity and harmony in the law.

Notes and Questions

JOEL FEINBERG, from *Social Philosophy*

1. What is the difference between being at liberty to do something and having a right to do it? What, according to Joel Feinberg, are the essential properties of legal claim-rights? What are the classifications of claim-rights that Feinberg sets out? How are claim-rights related to duties? What is the difference between a right and a claim?

2. In addition to those explicitly discussed by Feinberg, another important category of rights from the perspective of legal and political rights are civil rights. Civil rights are rights guaranteed to citizens by virtue of their citizenship. Clear cases of civil rights are institutional and legal; that is, they are publicly and officially recognized, and most often they are enacted and contained in public documents, such as the U.S. Constitution, or acts of Congress, such as the Civil Rights Act of 1965. But civil rights are also moral rights: They are claims about the moral entitlements of citizens to particular treatment by their own government or fellow citizens. To use *civil rights* in this sense is to make a particular kind of argument, using particular sorts of grounds. This multiple usage of terminology, while common, can be confusing. Feinberg's discussion helps to clarify the confusion. Consider his discussion of legal rights and human rights. Do you see why civil rights can fit into either category?

3. Feinberg classifies natural rights as a subcategory of human rights. This is because classical natural law theory assumed (as he notes) certain metaphysical and epistemological attributes of natural rights. That is, natural rights were considered to be a necessary part of the universal, objective moral order that was called natural law. And the nature of the rights could be known (that is, discovered) by the exercise of reason. Human rights, by contrast, are simply rights ascribed to all human beings. Many modern rights proponents prefer the more neutral foundation of human rights to the classical idea because the former embodies fewer controversial assumptions, or so it is thought. But as Feinberg points out, human rights theory has problems of its own. What are they?

4. How does Feinberg distinguish moral rights from legal rights? What senses of *moral right* does he set out? Human rights are a particular sort of moral right. What are the distinguishing features of a human right? Are they different from the features of a natural right?

5. Many of these categories overlap. Notice that once a human right is embodied in a document such as the U.S. Constitution, it is also a legal right or institutional right. It may also be a conventional right. What would make it so? Of what significance are these designations?

6. What are the grounds for thinking that there are human rights? Would the same grounds justify making human rights into civil rights (that is, enacted ones)? Would such civil rights be required of any just society? What sorts of rights would they be? If the ground were natural rights theory, would the rights be any different? Should they be?

[From] *Social Philosophy*

JOEL FEINBERG

C H A P T E R   6

Human Rights

1. Moral Rights

Legal and institutional rights are typically conferred by specific rules recorded in handbooks of regulations that can be observed and studied by the citizens or members subject to the rules. But not all rights are derived from such clearly visible laws and institutional regulations. On many occasions we assert that someone has a right to something even though we know there are no regulations or laws conferring such a right. Such talk clearly makes sense, so any theory of the nature of rights that cannot account for it is radically defective.

The term "moral rights" can be applied to all rights that are held to exist prior to, or independently of, any legal or institutional rules. Moral rights so conceived form a genus divisible into various species of rights having little in common except that they are not (necessarily) legal or institutional. The following are the main specific senses of "moral rights": (1) A *conventional right* is one derived from established customs and expectations, whether or not recognized by law (e.g., an old woman's right to a young man's seat on a subway train). (2) An *ideal right* is not necessarily an actual right of any kind, but is rather what *ought* to be a positive (institutional or conventional) right, and would be so in a better or ideal legal system or conventional code. (3) A *conscientious right* is a claim the recognition of which as valid is called for, not (necessarily) by actual or ideal rules or conventions, but rather by the principles of an enlightened individual conscience. (4) An *exercise right* is not, strictly speaking, a right at all, though it is so-called in popular usage; it is simply moral justification in the exercise of a right of some other kind, the latter right remaining in one's possession and unaffected by considerations bearing on the rightness

or wrongness of its exercising. When a person speaks of a moral right, he may be referring to a generically moral right not further specified, or to a right in one of these four specific senses; sometimes the context does not reveal which sense of "moral" is employed, and the possibility of equivocation is always present.

2. Human Rights

Among the rights that are commonly said to be moral in the generic sense (that is, independent of legal or other institutional recognition) are some also called "human rights." Human rights are sometimes understood to be ideal rights, sometimes conscientious rights, and sometimes both. In any case, they are held to be closely associated with actual claims. If a given human right is an ideal right, then human rightholders do or will have a claim against political legislators to convert (eventually) their "moral right" into a positive legal one. If the human right in question is a conscientious right, then it is an actual claim against private individuals for a certain kind of treatment—a claim that holds *now*, whatever the positive law may say about it.

I shall define "human rights" to be generically moral rights of a fundamentally important kind held equally by all human beings, unconditionally and unalterably. Whether these rights are "moral" in any of the more precise senses, I shall leave an open question to be settled by argument, not definition. Of course, it is also an open question whether there *are* any human rights and, if so, just what those rights are. All of the rights that have been characterized as "natural rights" in the leading manifestoes[1] can also be called human rights, but, as I shall be using the terms, not all human rights are also by definition natural rights. The theory of natural rights asserts not only that there are certain human rights, but also that these rights have certain further epistemic properties and a certain metaphysical status. In respect to questions of moral ontology and moral epistemology, the theory of human rights is neutral. Finally, it should be noticed that our definition includes the phrase "*all* human beings" but does not say "*only* human beings," so that a human right held by animals is not excluded by definition.

In addition to the characteristics mentioned in our definition, human rights have also been said to be "absolute." Sometimes this is simply a redundancy, another way of referring to the properties of universality and inalienability; but sometimes "absoluteness" is meant to refer to an additional characteristic, which in turn is subject to at least three interpretations. Human rights can be absolute, first, only in the sense that all rights are absolute, namely, unconditionally incumbent within the limits of their well-defined scope. Second, a human right might be held to be absolute in the sense that the rights to life, liberty, and the pursuit of happiness, as proclaimed in the Declaration of Independence, are most plausibly interpreted as absolute, namely, as "ideal directives" to relevant parties to "do their best" for the values involved. If the state has seriously considered Doe's right to his land, done its best to find alternative routes for a public road, and compensated Doe as generously as possible before expropriating him by eminent domain, it has faithfully discharged its duty of "due consideration" that is the correlative of his "right to property" conceived simply as an ideal directive. If a human right is absolute only in the sense in which an ideal directive is absolute, then it is satisfied whenever it is given the serious and respectful consideration it always deserves, even when that consideration is followed by a reluctant invasion of its corresponding interest.

The strongest and most interesting sense of "absolute" attributed to rights is that of being "absolutely exceptionless" not only within a limited scope but throughout a scope *itself* unlimited. The right to free speech would be absolute in this sense *if* it protected all speech without exception in all circumstances. In that case, the limits of the right would correspond with the limit of the form of conduct specified, and once these wide boundaries had been defined, no further boundary adjustments, incursions or encumbrances, legislative restrictions, or conditions for emergency suspensions would be permitted. For a human right to have this character it would have to be such that no conflicts with other human rights, either of the same or another type, would be possible.

Some formulations of human rights might be passed off as absolute in the strongest sense merely because they are so vaguely put. Some are formulated in conditional language ("a right to adequate nutrition *if* or *when* food is available") and then held to be absolute qua conditional. Other rights, put in glittering and general language ("a right to be treated like a human being," " a right to be treated like a person, not a thing") are safely held to be absolute because without detailed specification they yield few clear and uncontroversial injunctions. Others are formulated in language containing "standard-bearing terms" such as "reasonable," "proper," or "worthy," without any clue to the standards to be employed in applying these terms. Thus it is said that all men (like all animals) have a right not to be treated cruelly. So far, so good; there can be no exceptions to that right. But its "absoluteness" can be seen to be merely formal when one considers that cruel treatment is treatment that inflicts *unnecessary, unreasonable,* or *improper* suffering on its victim. The air of self-evidence and security beyond all controversy immediately disappears from this human right when men come to propose and debate precise standards of necessity, reasonableness, and propriety.

We should not despair, however, of finding explicit standards of (say) cruelty that will give human rights content and yet leave them plausible candidates for absoluteness in the strong sense. The right not to be *tortured*, for example, comes close to exhaustive definability in non-standard-bearing terms, and may be such that it cannot conflict with other rights, including other human rights, and can therefore be treated as categorical and exceptionless. If torture is still too vague a term, we can give exact empirical descriptions of the Chinese Water Torture, the Bamboo Fingernail Torture, and so on, and then claim that everyone has an absolutely exceptionless right in every conceivable circumstance not to be treated in any of those precisely described ways. Does this right pass the test of nonconflict with other rights?

Suppose a foreign tyrant of Caligulan character demands of our government that it seize certain political critics, imprison them, and slowly torture them to death, and threatens that unless that is done, his police will seize the members of our diplomatic staff in his country and torture *them* to death. At first sight this appears to be an authentic case of conflict between human rights, in that it would be impossible to do anything that would have as its consequence the fulfillment of everyone's right not to be tortured. What we should say about this blackmail situation if we wish to maintain that the right not to be tortured is nevertheless absolute (exceptionless and non-conflictable) is as follows. If the political critics in our grasp have a human right never to be tortured, then we have a categorical duty not to torture them. Thus, we ought not and will not torture them. We know, however, that this is likely to lead to the torture of the diplomatic hostages. We should therefore make every effort to dissuade Caligula, perhaps even through military pressure, not to carry out his threat. If Caligula nevertheless tortures his hostages, their rights have been infringed, but by Caligula, *not by us.*

All cases of apparent conflict of rights not to be tortured can be treated in this way. Whenever it is possible to honor all of them, the situation causing that impossibility is itself the voluntary creation of human beings. Nothing in nature itself can ever bring such a conflict into existence. A tyrant's threat is in this respect unlike a plague that renders it impossible for everybody to get enough to eat. It would be idle to claim that the right to enough food is an absolute, categorical right, exceptionless in every conceivable circumstance, because we cannot legislate over nature. But we can legislate for man (the argument continues), and this is a plausible way to do it: *No acts of torture anywhere at any time are ever to be permitted.* All human beings can thus be possessed of a right that is absolutely exceptionless. That we have no guarantee that some people somewhere won't violate it or try to force us to violate it is no argument against the "legislation" itself.

There is therefore no objection in principle to the idea of human rights that are absolute in the sense of being categorically exceptionless. It is another question as to whether there are such rights, and what they might be. The most plausible candidates, like the right not to be tortured, will be passive negative rights, that is, rights not to be done to by others in certain ways. It is more difficult to think of active negative rights (rights not to be interfered with) or positive rights (rights to be done to in certain ways) as absolute exceptionless. The positive rights to be given certain essentials — food, shelter, security, education — clearly depend upon the existence of an adequate supply, something that cannot be guaranteed categorically and universally.

If absoluteness in this strong sense is made part of the very meaning of the expression "human rights," then it would seem that there is a lamentable paucity of human rights, if any at all. Clarity will best be served, I think, if we keep "absoluteness" out of the definition of "human right." Two questions can then be kept separate: (1) Are there any human rights, i.e., generically moral, unforfeitable, irrevocable rights held equally and universally by human beings (at least)? (2) If so, are any of these rights absolute? We turn now to a consideration of the grounds for thinking that there are human rights, so defined.

3. Grounds for Equality

Despite its current popularity, the theory that there are rights held equally by all human beings continues to trouble philosophers. It is natural for them to imagine skeptics asking: "Why *all* human beings *equally*, and not only, or primarily, the deserving ones?" The skeptical question still has great force. To appreciate this we have only to consider that the theory of human rights requires that in certain basic ways we treat even congenital idiots and convicted mass murderers the same as everyone else.

To appreciate fully how revolutionary the idea of equal human rights was, recall how European society was organized during the centuries preceding the revolutionary period. The feudal system recognized distinct hereditary castes, each with its peculiar and irreducible legal status defined by elaborate sets of rights and duties. A legal *status* in the relevant sense differs from mere social roles like father, promiser, and farmer, in part because it is entirely hereditary and unmodifiable by voluntary arrangements. The rights men had as a matter of status were theirs as royalty, nobility, clergy, serfs, and so on; there was nothing "equal" about these status rights. Human rights, as a revolutionary idea, were associated with the idea of a single status society where the powers of the high and mighty were limited everywhere by the rights all persons derived from their "status" as human beings.

The single status society differs strikingly from a society with fixed hereditary caste distinctions as well as from a purely meritarian society in which *all* political rights are based on merit alone. Gregory Vlastos, in an important article,[2] has argued that the doctrine of universal equal human rights presupposes a concept of equal and universal human *worth* that is to be sharply distinguished from the idea of human merits. We grade persons according to their talents, skills, character and personality traits, and other rankable qualities, but in respect to "human worth" (by definition) all men must get equal grades. Indeed, "human worth" is not a "grading concept" at all. In this it differs from every kind of merit, including, of course, moral merit, in respect to which there are vast inequalities among persons. In a society based on human rights, at least some rights will belong irrevocably to fools and rogues as well as to everyone else. These are the rights, Vlastos suggests, that are based on the worth human beings have as individuals, quite apart from their valuable qualities.

*   *   *

"Human worth" itself is best understood to name no property in the way that "strength" names strength and "redness" redness. In attributing human worth to everyone we may be ascribing no property or set of qualities, but rather expressing an attitude — the attitude of respect — toward the humanity in each man's person. That attitude follows naturally from regarding everyone from the "human point of view," but it is not grounded on anything more ultimate than itself, and it is not demonstrably justifiable.

It can be argued further against skeptics that a world with equal human rights is a *more just*

world, a way of organizing society for which we would all opt if we were designing our institutions afresh in ignorance of the roles we might one day have to play in them. It is also a *less dangerous* world generally, and one with a *more elevated and civilized* tone. If none of this convinces the skeptic, we should turn our backs on him to examine more important problems.

4. Absolute and Nonabsolute Human Rights

In December 1948, the General Assembly of the United Nations adopted a Universal Declaration of Human Rights. Unlike the eighteenth-century manifestoes of natural rights, which were concerned almost exclusively with the individual's rights not to be interfered with by others, the U.N. Declaration endorses numerous basic positive rights to receive benefits and be provided with the means to satisfy basic human needs. Even the conception in the U.N. document of a basic need (in contrast to an unneeded but valuable commodity) reflected changes in the world's outlook and hopes since the eighteenth century. The U.N. Declaration contains the old-style negative rights, mostly pertaining to civic and political activities and criminal procedures, as well as the new "social and economic rights" that are correlated with the positive duties of others (usually of the state). Rights of the former kind impose duties upon private citizens and the state alike to keep hands off individuals in certain respects, to leave them alone.

Other articles, however, impose duties upon others that are so difficult that they may, under widely prevalent conditions of scarcity and conflict, be impossible for *anyone* to discharge. Articles 22–27, for example, state that "everyone, as a member of society . . . has the right to work, to free choice of employment . . . to protection against unemployment . . . to just and favorable remuneration . . . to rest and leisure . . . and periodic holidays with pay . . . to food, clothing, housing, and medical care . . . to education . . . to enjoy the arts and to share in scientific advancement and its benefits."[3] Now, as we have seen,[4] these positive (as opposed to negative) human rights are rights in an unusual new "manifesto sense," for, unlike all other claim-rights, they are not necessarily correlated with the duties of any assignable persons. The Declaration must therefore be interpreted to say that all men as such have a claim (that is, are in a position to make claim) to the goods therein mentioned, even if there should temporarily be no one in the corresponding position to be claimed against.

These social and economic human rights, therefore, are certainly not *absolute* rights, since easily imaginable and commonly actual circumstances can reduce them to mere claims. Moreover, these rights are clearly not nonconflictable. For example, where there are two persons for every job, there must be conflict between the claims of some workers to "free choice of employment," in the sense that if one worker's claim is recognized as valid, another's *must* be rejected.

Can any human rights plausibly be construed as absolutely exceptionless and therefore nonconflictable in principle, or must all rights in their very natures be vulnerable to legitimate invasion in some circumstances? The most plausible candidates for absoluteness are (some) *negative rights*; since they require no positive actions or contributions from others, they are less likely to be affected by conditions of scarcity. To say of a given negative right that it is nonconflictable is to say: (1) if conflicts occur with rights of other kinds, it must always win, and (2) no conflict is possible with other rights of its own kind. The right to speak freely is a plausible human right and is conferred by Article 19 of the U.N. Declaration, but it is certainly not nonconflictable in the sense defined above, for it cannot plausibly be said always and necessarily to win out whenever it conflicts with another's right to reputation, privacy, or safety. In theory, of course, we could consistently hold that the free expression right always overrides rights of other kinds, but then that right would fail to satisfy the second condition for non-conflictability, no matter how stubbornly we back it. The requirement that the right in question be incapable in principle of conflicting with another person's right of the *same* kind is the real stumbling block in the path of absoluteness. Consider an audience of hecklers exercising *their* "free speech" to shout down a speaker, or some scoundrel using his "free speech" to persuade others to cut out the tongue of his hated rival. In these cases, free speech must be limited

in its *own* interest. Similar examples can be provided, *mutatis mutandis*, for freedom of movement, free exercise of religion, the right to property, and to virtually all of the characteristically eighteenth-century rights of noninterference.

There remain at least three kinds of human rights that may very well be understood (without obvious absurdity) to be absolute and nonconflictable. Positive rights to "goods" that cannot ever, in the very nature of the case, be in scarce supply, are one possibility. Perhaps the right to a fair trial (really a package of positive and negative rights) or the right to equal protection of the law,[5] or "the right to equal consideration,"[6] fall into this category.

A second possibility is the negative right not to be treated inhumanely or cruelly, not to be tortured or treated barbarously. Whether we as legislators (actual or ideal) should confer such an absolute right on everyone is entirely up to us. There may be good policy reasons against it, but if we are convinced by the powerful policy and moral reasons in favor of it, we needn't be deterred by the fear of conflictability. As I argued in the previous section, we can *decide* without absurdity to let this right override rights of all *other* kinds, and there is nothing in nature to bring this right into conflict with other persons' rights of the *same* kind. Article 5 of the U.N. Declaration, which forbids "torture or . . . cruel, inhuman . . . treatment," may be conceived as conferring a human right in a very strong sense, namely one which is not only universal and inalienable, but also absolute. It is still not a human right in the very strongest sense — one that applies absolutely and unalterably to all and *only* humans — for it is presumably the one right that the higher animals have, if they have any rights at all.

A third possibility is the right not to be subjected to exploitation or degradation even when such subjection is utterly painless and therefore not cruel. It is possible to treat human beings with drugs, hypnosis, or other brainwashing techniques so that they become compliant tools in the hands of their manipulators, useful as means to their manipulators' ends, but with all serious purposes of their own totally obliterated. Once human beings are in this condition, they may have no notion that they are being exploited or degraded, having come to accept and internalize their exploiters' image of themselves as their own. In this state, human beings might be raised, as Swift suggested, for food, fattened up for a few years, and then slaughtered (humanely, of course); or they might be harnessed, like donkeys, to wagons or millstones. It would be good business as well as good morals to treat them kindly (so long as they are obedient), for that way one can get more labor out of them in the long run. Clearly, kindness and "humanity," while sufficient to satisfy the rights of animals, are not sufficient for human beings, who must therefore have ascribed to them another kind of right that we deliberately withhold from animals. That is a right to a higher kind of respect, an inviolate dignity, which as a broad category includes the negative rights not to be brainwashed, not to be made into a docile instrument for the purposes of others, and not to be converted into a domesticated animal. Rights in this category are probably the only ones that are human rights in the strongest sense: unalterable,

"absolute" (exceptionless and nonconflictable), and universally and *peculiarly* human.

NOTES

1. E.g., the American Declaration of Independence (1776), the Virginia Bill of Rights (1775), and the French Declaration of the Rights of Man and of Citizens (1789).

2. Gregory Vlastos, "Justice and Equality," in *Social Justice*, ed. Richard B. Brandt (Englewood Cliffs, N.J.: Prentice-Hall, Inc., 1962), pp. 31–72.

3. UNESCO, *Human Rights, a symposium* (London and New York: Allan Wingate, 1949).

4. *Supra*, pp. 66 f.

5. "Notice . . . that there is one ['natural'] right which . . . is to all intents and purposes an absolute right. That is the right to equal consideration — the right to be treated as the formula for justice provides. For this right is one which is the most basic of all, one which is under no conditions to be violated." Lucius Garvin, *A Modern Introduction to Ethics* (Boston: Houghton Mifflin Company, 1953), p. 491.

6. See *supra*, pp. 86–88.

Notes and Questions

EDWARD S. CORWIN, from "The 'Higher Law' Background of American Constitutional Law"

1. This selection traces the development of the idea of natural law through the history of Western thought to the time of the philosopher John Locke. Edward S. Corwin observes that every age has its distinctive "categories of thought." It is commonplace today to derive the authority of the American Constitution (and probably most other constitutions) from the idea of the consent of the people. This view corresponds nicely with the positivistic theory of law (considered in detail in Chapter Two). It implies, Corwin notes, two ideas. First, law is positive — that is, it is enacted or otherwise produced by human beings. Second, the highest authority or justification for such enactment is "the common consent of the people." This is now a very popular view, but it was not the predominant view of the seventeenth and eighteenth centuries. The predominant view of legal authority at that time was called *natural law*. As Corwin points out, natural law bases legal authority or legitimacy on the content and not the source of law. What are the features of natural law, as described by Corwin?

2. "True law," which corresponds to the requirements of natural justice, is not made but discovered. What does that mean? How should it be accomplished? Does any human authority guarantee it? What is the test for discerning whether a human authority (a king or a congress, for example) has made the positive law conform to the requirements of natural law? Is this test clear to you? What happens if the positive law does not meet these requirements?

3. Corwin explains the infusion of natural law ideas into the common law of England, from which American law is largely derived. How did the natural law idea manifest itself in the English legal experience at the time of Sir Edward Coke? What does it mean to say "the common law will control acts of parliament, and sometimes adjudge them to be utterly void?" When would this be justified? Do Coke's self-evident maxims provide such a justification? Would they provide justification for invalidating an act of Congress today? Remember, natural law is eternal, universal, and overriding.

4. What does Coke mean by fundamental law? Is it the same as natural law? Does it correspond to the colonial view of the Constitution? How is the distinction between natural law and fundamental law expressed in the Ninth Amendment to the U.S. Constitution?

5. What is the basis of legal obligation on the natural law view? Is this a plausible view of legal obligation?

[From] "The 'Higher Law' Background of American Constitutional Law"

EDWARD S. CORWIN

---

* * *

It is customary nowadays to ascribe the *legality* as well as the *supremacy* of the Constitution—the one is, in truth, but the obverse of the other—exclusively to the fact that, in its own phraseology, it was "ordained" by "the people of the United States." Two ideas are thus brought into play. One is the so-called "positive" conception of law as a general expression merely for the particular commands of a human lawgiver, as a series of acts of human will; the other is that the highest possible source of such commands, because the highest possible embodiment of human will is "the people."

* * *

The attribution of supremacy to the Constitution on the ground solely of its rootage in popular will represents, however, a comparatively late outgrowth of American constitutional theory. Earlier the supremacy accorded to constitutions was ascribed less to their putative source than to their supposed content, to their embodiment of an essential and unchanging justice. The theory of law thus invoked stands in direct contrast to the one just reviewed. *There are*, it is predicated, *certain principles of right and justice which are entitled to prevail of their own intrinsic excellence, altogether regardless of the attitude of those who wield the physical resources of the community. Such principles were made by no human hands; indeed, if they did not antedate deity itself, they still so express its nature as to bind and control it. They are external to all Will as such and interpenetrate all Reason as such. They are eternal and immutable. In relation to such principles, human laws are, when entitled to obedience save as to matters indifferent, merely a record or transcript, and their enactment an act not of will or power but one of discovery and declaration.* The Ninth Amendment of the Constitution of the United States, in stipulating that "the enumeration of certain rights in this Constitution shall not prejudice other rights not so enumerated," illustrates this theory perfectly except that the principles of transcendental justice have been here translated into terms of personal and private rights. The relation of such rights, nevertheless, to governmental power is the same as that of the principles from which they spring and which they reflect. They owe nothing to their recognition in the Constitution — such recognition was necessary if the Constitution was to be regarded as complete.

Thus the *legality* of the Constitution, its *supremacy*, and its claim to be worshipped, alike find common standing ground on the belief in a law superior to the will of human governors. Certain questions arise: Whence came this idea of a "higher law"? How has it been enabled to survive, and in what transformations? What special forms of it are of particular interest for the history of American constitutional law and theory? By what agencies and as a result of what causes was it brought to America and wrought into the American system of government? It is to these questions that the ensuing pages of this article are primarily addressed.

I

Words of Demosthenes attest the antiquity of the conception of law as a discovery: "Every law is a discovery, a gift of god, — a precept of wise men." Words of President Coolidge prove the persistence of the notion: "Men do not make laws. They do but discover them. . . . That state is most fortunate in its form of government which has the aptest instruments for the discovery of law." But not every pronouncement of even the most exalted human authority is necessarily law in this sense. This, too, was early asserted. A century before Demosthenes, Antigone's appeal against Creon's edict to the "unwritten and steadfast customs of the Gods" had already presented in immemorial usage as superior to human rule-making. A third stage in the argument is marked by Aristotle's advice to advocates in his *Rhetoric* that, when they had "no case according to the law of the land," they should "appeal to the law of nature," and, quoting the Antigone of Sophocles, argue that "an unjust law is not a law." The term law is, in other words, ambiguous. It may refer to a law of higher or a law of lower content; and, furthermore, some recourse should be available on the basis of the former against the latter.

But as Aristotle's own words show, the identification of higher law with custom did not

remain the final word on the subject. Before this idea could enter upon its universal career as one of the really great humanizing forces of history, the early conception of it had to undergo a development not dissimilar to that of the Hebrew conception of God, although, thanks to the Sophists and to their critic, Socrates, the process was immensely abbreviated. The discovery that custom was neither immutable nor invariable even among the Greek city states impelled the Sophists to the conclusion that justice was either merely "the interest of the strong," or at best a convention entered upon by men purely on considerations of expediency and terminable on like considerations. Ultimately, indeed, the two ideas boil down to the same thing, since it is possible to regard as convenient that which cannot maintain itself, while that which can do so will in the long run be shaped to the interests of its sustainers. Fortunately these were not the only possible solutions to the problem posed by the Sophists. Building on Socrates' analysis of Sophistic teaching and Plato's theory of Ideas, Aristotle advanced in his *Ethics* the concept of "natural justice." "Of political justice," he wrote, "part is natural, part legal — natural, that which everywhere has the same force and does not exist by people's thinking this or that; legal, that which is originally indifferent. . . ." That is to say, the essential ingredient of the justice which is enforced by the state is not of the state's own contrivance; it is a discovery from nature and a transcript of its constancy.

But practically what is the test of the presence of this ingredient in human laws and constitutions? By his conception of natural justice as universal, Aristotle is unavoidably led to identify the rational with the general in human laws. Putting the question in his *Politics* whether the rule of law or the rule of an individual is preferable, he answers his own inquiry in no uncertain terms. "To invest the law then with authority is, it seems, to invest God and reason only; to invest a man is to introduce a beast, as desire is something bestial, and even the best of men in authority are liable to be corrupted by passion. We may conclude then that the law is reason without passion and it is therefore preferable to any individual." Nearly two thousand years after Aristotle, the sense of this passage, condensed into Harrington's famous phrase, "a government of laws and not of men," was to find its way first into the Massachusetts constitution of 1780 and then into Chief Justice Marshall's opinion in *Marbury v. Madison*. The opposition which it discovers between the desire of the human governor and the reason of the laws lies, indeed, at the foundation of the American interpretation of the doctrine of the separation of powers and so of the entire American system of constitutional law.

It has been said of Plato that "he found philosophy a city of brick and left it a city of gold." The operation of the Stoic philosophy upon the concept of a higher law may be characterized similarly. While Aristotle's "natural justice" was conceived primarily as a norm and guide for law makers, the *Jus Naturale* of the Stoics was the way of happiness for all men. The supreme legislator was Nature herself; nor was the natural order the merely material one which modern science exploits. The concept which Stoicism stressed was that of a moral order, wherein man through his divinely given capacity of reason was directly participant with the gods themselves. Nature, human nature, and reason were one. The conception was, manifestly, an ethical, rather than a political or legal one, and for good cause. Stoicism arose on the ruins of the Greek city state. Plato's and Aristotle's belief that human felicity was to be achieved mainly by political means had proved illusory; and thrown back on his own resources, the Greek developed a new outlook, at once individualistic and cosmopolitan.

The restoration of the idea of natural law, enlarged and enriched by Stoicism, to the world's stock of legal and political ideas was accomplished by Cicero. In a passage of his *De Republica* which has descended to us through the writings of another (the preservative quality of a good style has rarely been so strikingly exemplified), Cicero sets forth his conception of natural law:

> True law is right reason, harmonious with nature, diffused among all, constant, eternal; a law which calls to duty by its commands and restrains from evil by its prohibitions. . . . It is a sacred obligation not to attempt to legislate in contradiction to this law; nor may it be derogated from nor abrogated. Indeed by neither the Senate nor the people can we be released from

this law; nor does it require any but ourself to be its expositor or interpreter. Nor is it one law at Rome and another at Athens; one now and another at a late time; but one eternal and unchangeable law binding all nations through all time. . . .

It is, however, in his *De Legibus* that Cicero makes his distinctive contribution. Identifying "right reason" with those qualities of human nature whereby "man is associated with the gods," he there assigns the binding quality of the civil law itself to its being in harmony with such universal attributes of human nature. In the natural endowment of man, and especially his social traits, "is to be found the true source of laws and rights," he asserts, and later says, "We are born for justice, and right is not the mere arbitrary construction of opinion but an institution of nature." Hence justice is not, as the Epicureans claim, mere utility, for "that which is established on account of utility may for utility's sake be overturned." There is, in short, discoverable in the permanent elements of human nature itself a durable justice which transcends expediency, and the positive law must embody this if it is to claim the allegiance of the human conscience.

* * *

III

It was the happy strategy of the Tudors to convert parliament from an outpost against the royal power into its active instrument. The result of this alliance for English constitutional ideas was momentous.

* * *

In consequence of the Tudor reformation, the joint work of king and Parliament, the concept of sovereignty in the sense of *potestas legibus soluta* became confined to that branch of his power which the king customarily exercised "by and with the advice and consent" of Parliament.

Yet to begin with, this characteristically English compromise was assailed from both sides. The Stuarts, not enjoying the cooperation of Parliament, sought to put themselves beyond the need of it by appealing to the doctrine of the divine right of kings. In answer, their Parliamentary opponents did not hesitate to challenge, in the name of the supremacy of the common law, the outstanding constitutional result of the Tudor reformation; and the foremost figure of this reaction was Sir Edward Coke.

* * *

While Coke as attorney general had shown himself conspicuously subservient to the royal interest, his clashes as judge with James I make a notable chapter in judicial history. His basic doctrine was "that the King hath no prerogative, but that which the law and the land follows," and that of this the judges and not the king were the authorized interpreters. The circumstances of his admonition to James that he had no right to judge as between subject and subject save through the ordinary courts proceeding without royal interference were reviewed above. Later he had cause to inform James that the latter could not by proclamation "make a thing unlawful which was permitted by the law before." On these occasions Coke had the support of his judicial brethren; but in the matter of the Commendams they deserted him to a man. The question put the judges was whether, in a case pending before them which the king thought "to concern him either in power or profit," they could be required to stay proceedings till the king could consult with them. All but Coke answered yes. Coke's answer was "that when that case should be, he would do that which should be fit for a judge to do." Shortly after he was removed from his chief justiceship.

For students of the origins of American constitutional law and theory, however, no judicial utterance of Coke's—few indeed in language—can surpass in interest and importance his so-called dictum in *Dr. Bonham's Case*, which was decided by the Court of Common Please in 1610. Holding that the London College of Physicians was not entitled, under the act of Parliament which it invoked in justification, to punish Bonham for practicing medicine in the city without its license, Coke said:

And it appears in our books, that in many cases, the common law will controul acts of parliament, and sometimes adjudge them to be utterly void: for when an act of parliament is against common right and reason, or repugnant, or impossible to be performed, the common law will controul it and adjudge such act as to be void.

In these words we have foreshadowed not merely the power which American courts today exercise in the disallowance of statutes on the ground of their conflict with the Constitution, but also that very test of "reasonableness" which is the ultimate flowering of this power. We must determine if we can to what extent Coke's own intention sanctions the modern application of his doctrine, and also to what extent the historical background of the dictum does so.

* * *

Reporting *Calvin's Case*, which was decided the same year, following argument by the chief legal lights of England, Coke says, by way of summary: "1. That ligeance or obedience of the subject to the Sovereign is due by the law of nature: 2. That this law of nature is part of the laws of England: 3. That the law of nature was before any judicial or municipal law in the world: 4. That the law of nature is immutable, and cannot be changed." He then recites in support of these propositions the following quaint argument:

The law of nature is that which God at the time of creation of the nature of man infused into his heart, for his preservation and direction; and this is *Lex aeterna*, the moral law, called also the law of nature. And by this law, written with the finger of God in the heart of man, were the people of God a long time governed before the law was written by Moses, who was the first reporter or writer of law in the world.

* * *

The receptive and candid attitude thus evinced toward natural law ideas, a fresh influx of which from the Continent was already setting in, is a matter of profound importance. In the great constitutional struggle with the Stuarts it enabled Coke to build upon Fortescue, and it enabled Locke to build upon Coke. It made allies of sixteenth century legalism and seventeenth century rationalism, and the alliance then struck has always remained, now more, now less vital, in American constitutional law and theory.

The question of the significance which Coke attached to "common rights and reason" can, however, be answered in much more definite terms. Let the reader's mind revert in this connection to those "maxims" which, according to Fortescue, "do not admit of proof by reason and argument" but bear with them their own evidence, and which, according to the same authority, constituted the very substance of the peculiar science of the judges. Coke yields very little to his predecessor in the reverence he pays to such "fundamental points of the common law." It was, moreover, just such a maxim that Coke found to be involved in *Bonham's Case*. The College of Physicians had, under color of authority from an act of Parliament, amerced Bonham and taken half the fine for themselves. Coke's comment is as follows: "The censors cannot be judges, ministers, and parties; judges to give sentence or judgment; ministers to make summons; and parties to have the moiety of the forfeiture, quia aliquis non debet esse judex in propria causa; imo iniquum est aliquem suae rei esse judicem." Thereupon follows the famous dictum.

"Common right and reason" is, in short, something fundamental, something permanent; it is higher law. And again it is relevant to note the ratification which Coke's doctrine received in American constitutional law and theory. With such axioms, traceable in many instances to the *Digest* and *Code* of Justinian, Coke's pages abound; and from his work many of them early found their way into American judicial decisions, sometimes as interpretative of the written constitution, sometimes as supplementary of it. Such a postulate is the doctrine that "a statute should have prospective, not retrospective operation." Another is the principle that "no one should be twice punished for the same offence." Another is the maxim that "every man's house is his own castle."

* * *

We are thus brought to the question of Coke's meaning when he speaks of "controuling" an act of Parliament and "adjudging such act to be void." When the Supreme Court of the United States pronounces an act of Congress "void," it ordinarily means void *ab initio*, because beyond the power of Congress to enact, and it furthermore generally implies that it would similarly dispose of any future act of the same tenor. Was Coke laying claim to any such sweeping power for the ordinary courts as against acts of Parliament?

One thing seems to be assured at the outset — Coke was not asserting simply a rule of statutory construction which owed its force to the assumed intention of Parliament as it would today,

although the statute involved in *Bonham's Case* was also construed from that point of view. As we have already seen, Coke was enforcing a rule of higher law deemed by him to be binding on Parliament and the ordinary courts alike. This also appears from his treatment of the precedents he adduces.

* * *

At the very least, therefore, we can assert that in *Bonham's Case* Coke deemed himself to be enforcing a rule of construction of statutes of higher intrinsic validity than any act of Parliament as such. Does this, on the other hand, necessarily signify that he regarded the ordinary courts as the *final* authoritative interpreters of such rule of construction? A contemporaneous critic of the dictum in *Bonham's Case* was Lord Chancellor Ellesmere, whose objection was couched in the following significant terms:

> He challenged not power for the Judges of this Court [King's Bench] to correct all misdemeanors as well extrajudicial as judicial, nor to have power to judge Statutes and acts of Parliament to be void, if they conceived them to be against common right and reason; but left to the King and Parliament to judge what was common right and reason. I speak not of impossibilities or direct repugnances.

The issue contemporaneously raised by the dictum, therefore, was not, as we should say today, between judicial power and legislative power; but between the law declaring power of the ordinary courts and the like power of "the High Court of Parliament."

* * *

In 1616 Coke, who had three years earlier been transferred from the Common Pleas to the King's Bench, was dismissed as judge altogether. Four years later he was elected to the House of Commons, and there at once assumed the leadership of the growing opposition to the Stuarts. In 1625 Charles succeeded James, and in 1627 occurred the arbitrary arrest by royal order of the Five Knights, giving rise in parliament to the great Inquest on the Liberties of the Subject, and eventually to the framing of the Petition of Right. In all these proceedings the leading role fell to Coke, and their general tendency is made clear in the quaint words of Sir Benjamin Rudyard, who expressed his great gratification to see "that good, old, decrepit law of Magna Charta, which hath been so long kept in and lain bed-rid as it were . . . walk abroad again." Coke's main objective was still the curbing of the royal prerogative, but the terms in which he expressed himself also assert the existence of constitutional limits to Parliament's power as well. Especially significant are his remarks on the clause "saving the sovereign power" of the king which was at first attached to the Petition by the Lords. The question arising, "what is Sovereign power," a member quoted Bodin to the effect "that is free from any conditions"; whereupon Coke arose and said:

> This is *magnum in parvo.* . . . I know that prerogative is a part of the law, but "Sovereign Power" is no parliamentary word. In my opinion it weakens Magna Charta, and all the statutes; for they are absolute without any saving of "Sovereign Power"; and should we now add it, we shall weaken the foundation law, and then the building must needs fall. Take heed what we yield unto: Magna Charta is such a fellow, that he will have no "Sovereign."

The words of Wentworth and Pym during the same debate were to like effect. The former said, "These laws are not acquainted with 'Sovereign Power'"; while Pym added that, far from being able to accord the king sovereign power, Parliament itself was "never possessed of it." Another noteworthy feature of the debate was the appearance in the course of it of the word "unconstitutional" in essentially its modern sense when used in political discussion.

In his *Institutes*, Coke, still the embattled commoner, completes his restoration of *Magna Carta* as the great muniment of English liberties. It is called "Magna Charta, not for the length or largeness of it . . . but . . . in respect of the great weightiness and weighty greatness of the matter contained in it; in a few words, being the fountain of all the fundamental laws of the realm." Declaratory of the common law, "this Statute of Magna Charta hath been confirmed above thirty times." Judgments and statutes against it "shall be void." Its benefits extend to all, even villains, they being freemen as to all save their own lords. And what are these benefits? Especially they are the benefits of the historical procedure of the

common law, the known processes of the ordinary courts, indictment by grand jury, trial by "law of the land," *habeas corpus*, security against monopoly, taxation by the consent of Parliament. Thus the vague concept of "common right and reason" is replaced with a "law fundamental" of definite content and traceable back to one particular document of ancient and glorious origin.

* * *

Coke's contributions to the beginnings of American constitutional law may be briefly summarized. First, in his dictum in *Bonham's Case* he furnished a form of word which, treated apart from his other ideas, as it was destined to be by a series of judges, commentators, and attorneys, became the most important single source of the notion of judicial review. This is true even though we of the present day can see that, in view of the universal subordination of the common law as such to statute law, judicial review grounded simply on "common right and reason" could not have survived. But, as if in anticipation of this difficulty, Coke came forward with his second contribution, the doctrine of a law fundamental, binding Parliament and king alike, a law, moreover, embodied to great extent in a particular document and having a verifiable content in the customary procedure of everyday institutions. From his version of *Magna Carta*, through the English Declaration and Bill of Rights of 1688 and 1689, to the Bills of Rights of our early American constitutions the line of descent is direct; and if American constitutional law during the last half century has tended increasingly to minimize the importance of procedural niceties and to return to the vaguer tests of "common right and reason," the intervening stage of strict law was nevertheless necessary. Lastly, Coke contributed the notion of Parliamentary supremacy *under* the law, which in time, with the differentiation of legislation and adjudication, became transmutable into the notion of *legislative* supremacy within a law subject to construction by the processes of adjudication.

IV

It has become a commonplace that every age has its own peculiar categories of thought; its speculations are carried on in a vocabulary which those who would be understood by it must adopt, and then adapt to their own special purposes. Nowadays intellectual discourse is apt to be cast in the mould of the evolutionary hypothesis. In the seventeenth and eighteenth centuries, the doctrine of natural law, with its diverse corollaries, furnished the basic postulates of theoretical speculation. For this there were several reasons; but our interest is naturally centered upon those which were especially operative in England.

The immense prestige of the natural law doctrine in the seventeenth and eighteenth centuries was due particularly to the work of two men, Grotius and Newton. In erecting the law of nations upon a natural law basis as a barrier against the current international anarchy, Grotius imparted to the latter a new solidity, as well as an immediate practicality such as it had never before been able to boast. Yet even more important was Grotius' revival of the Ciceronian idea of natural law, which served at one stroke to clear the concept from the theological implications which it had accumulated during the Middle Ages and from any suspicion of dependence on ecclesiastical and Papal interpretation. Once again natural law is defined as right reason; and is described as at once a law of, and a law to, God. God himself, Grotius asserted, could not make twice two other than four; nor would his rational nature fail to guide man even though there were no God, or though God lacked interest in human affairs. And at this point Newton enters the story. While modern science employs the term "natural law" in a sense that is alien and even hostile to its juristic use, the vast preponderance of deduction over observation in Newton's discoveries at first concealed this opposition. His demonstration that the force which brings the apple to the ground is the same force that holds the planets in their orbits, stirred his contemporaries with the picture of a universe which is pervaded with the same reason which shines in man and is accessible in all its parts to exploration by man. Between a universe "lapt in law" and the human mind all barriers were cast down. Inscrutable deity became scrutable nature. On this basis arose English deism, which, it has been wittily remarked, "deified Nature and denatured God." And one section of nature is human nature and its institutions. With Newton's

achievement at their back men turned confidently to the formulation of the inherently just and reasonable rules of social and political relationship. Entire systems were elaborated which purported to deduce with Euclidean precision the whole duty of man, both moral and legal, from a few agreed premises. It was the discredit into which such systems ultimately fell that revealed the disparity between the two uses of the term "natural law" of which we today are aware — or should be.

The revived Ciceronian conception of natural law, extended and deepened by Newtonian science, furnishes, therefore, the general background of credibility against which the contemporary political applications of natural law have to be projected. But these political applications also bring into requisition certain new elements — new, that is to say, in the combination in which they now appear. For it is always a question when theoretical notions are under consideration whether the term "new" is in strict propriety admissible. Systems fall apart and new systems are assembled from the wreckage. Any serious turn of events is apt to produce a fresh coruscation of ideas, elevating some and suppressing others; but the contents of the kaleidoscope remain throughout much the same. And never was this observation better borne out than by the political speculations of the sixteenth, seventeenth, and eighteenth centuries. These speculations contributed immensely to the shattering of the existing foundations of authority and in transferring authority to an entirely new basis. The particular ideas in which they dealt were, nevertheless, for the most part, far from novel. Not a few of them are identifiable, in embryo at least, among the writings of the ancients; and nearly all of them had been stated with varying degrees of clarity before the Reformation.

The conveyance of natural law ideas into American constitutional theory was the work preeminently — though by no means exclusively — of John Locke's *Second Treatise on Civil Government*, which appeared in 1690 as an apology for the Glorious Revolution. The outstanding feature of Locke's treatment of natural law is the almost complete dissolution which this concept undergoes through his handling into the natural rights of the individual; or — to employ Locke's own phrase, borrowed from the debates between Stuart adherents and Parliamentarians — into the rights of "life, liberty, and estate." The dissolving agency by which Locke brings this transformation about is the doctrine of the Social Compact, with its corollary notion of a State of Nature. Indeed, it is hardly an exaggeration to say that the only residuum which remains in the Lockian crucible from the original Ciceronian concept is the sanction which is claimed from natural law for the social compact, and at one point, he dispenses even with this. It thus becomes of interest to inquire whence Locke derived his intense preoccupation with rights, as well as the form in which he chose to express them.

* * *

Notes and Questions

JOHN LOCKE, from *The Second Treatise of Civil Government*

1. As Corwin pointed out, John Locke was a pivotal thinker in the history of the idea of natural law, transforming the idea of natural justice into the concept of individual rights. Locke's basic project was to understand and explain the justification and limitation of political power. What does he take political power to be? Is this a good definition? Why or why not? What supposed justification for political power does Locke reject? What is wrong with that justification? Notice that Locke assumes that justification is needed. Is it? If so, why?

2. After demolishing the divine right of kings to rule, Locke sets out to formulate better grounds (which include limits) of political power or government authority. To do this he uses a thought device called the *state of nature*. The idea is to imagine human beings in a state without the restrictions or influences of government power or law. What would the moral relations be in such a state? If we had only reason and human nature to guide us, and not custom or law, where would it lead? What does Locke say about this? What are the features of Locke's state of nature?

3. What, according to Locke, is a state of war? How does he distinguish a state of war from a state of nature? What problem does a state of war cause in a state of nature that is resolved in a society? Does this convince you that any rational human being would agree to live in a society? This is called a *social contract* (or a *social compact*) argument. It has long been popular as a justification for political authority. This argument supports the claim that the authority of government is derived from the consent of the governed. Why is such support necessary? Does it work?

4. According to Locke, even if political authority is derived from the consent of the governed, there are strict limits to that power. Why? Why can't the governed consent to whatever they want to? What are the limits, according to Locke? Do you agree, as a rational human being? If you agree, then you are agreeing that there are natural rights — rights based on the human moral order — that outweigh conventional rights (or rights by agreement). Would you eliminate some limits or add some? That is, do you agree with Locke's list of rights?

5. What reasons does Locke give as legitimate grounds for the dissolution of government? Are they good grounds? What reasons are given in the Declaration of Independence? (See Appendix.) Is this a natural law document? Does it use the rationale supplied by Locke? How else could you justify a revolution? To what other than natural rights could you appeal?

6. How does Locke try to reassure the faint of heart that such a view has no more tendency to produce revolution than any other view? Are you persuaded? Why or why not? Suppose Locke were right about natural rights but wrong about the revolutionary tendencies of the doctrine. Would it matter?

[From] *The Second Treatise of Civil Government*

JOHN LOCKE

C H A P T E R   1

1. It having been shown in the foregoing discourse:

(*1*) That Adam had not, either by natural right or fatherhood or by positive donation from God, any such authority over his children or dominion over the world as is pretended.

(*2*) That if he had, his heirs yet had no right to it.

(*3*) That if his heirs had, there being no law of nature nor positive law of God that determines which is the right heir in all cases that may arise, the right of succession, and consequently of bearing rule, could not have been certainly determined.

(*4*) That if even that had been determined, yet the knowledge of which is the eldest line of Adam's posterity being so long since utterly lost, that in the races of mankind and families of the world there remains not to one above another the least pretence to be the eldest house, and to have the right of inheritance.

All these premises having, as I think, been clearly made out, it is impossible that the rulers now on earth should make any benefit or derive any the least shadow of authority from that which is held to be the fountain of all power: Adam's private dominion and paternal jurisdiction; so that he that will not give just occasion to think that all government in the world is the product only of force and violence, and that men live together by no other rules but that of beasts, where the strongest carries it, and so lay a foundation for perpetual disorder and mischief, tumult, sedition, and rebellion — things that the followers of that hypothesis so loudly cry out against — must of necessity find out another rise of government, another original of political power, and another way of designing and knowing the persons that have it than what Sir Robert Filmer hath taught us.

2. To this purpose, I think it may not be amiss to set down what I take to be political power; that the power of a magistrate over a subject may be distinguished from that of a father over his children, a master over his servants, a husband over his wife, and a lord over his slave. All of which distinct powers happening sometimes together in the same man, if he be considered under these different relations, it may help us to distinguish these powers one from another, and show the difference betwixt a ruler of a commonwealth, a father of a family, and a captain of a galley.

3. Political power, then, I take to be a right of making laws with penalties of death and, consequently, all less penalties for the regulating and preserving of property, and of employing the force of the community in the execution of such laws, and in the defence of the commonwealth from foreign injury, and all this only for the public good.

C H A P T E R   2

Of the State of Nature

4. To understand political power right, and derive it from its original, we must consider what state all men are naturally in, and that is a state of perfect freedom to order their actions and dispose of their possessions and persons as they think fit, within the bounds of the law of nature, without asking leave or depending upon the will of any other man.

A state also of equality, wherein all the power and jurisdiction is reciprocal, no one having more than another; there being nothing more evident than that creatures of the same species and rank, promiscuously born to all the same advantages of nature and the use of the same faculties, should also be equal one amongst another without subordination or subjection; unless the lord and master of them all should, by any manifest declaration of his will, set one above another, and confer on him by an evident and clear appointment an undoubted right to dominion and sovereignty.

5. This equality of men by nature the judicious Hooker[1] looks upon as so evident in itself and beyond all questions that he makes it the foundation of that obligation to mutual love amongst men on which he builds the duties we owe one another, and from whence he derives the great maxims of justice and charity. His words are:

> The like natural inducement hath brought men to know that it is no less their duty to love other than themselves; for seeing those things which are equal must needs all have one measure; if I cannot but wish to receive good, even as much at every man's hands as any man can wish unto his own soul, how should I look to have any part of my desire herein satisfied unless myself be careful to satisfy the like desire, which is undoubtedly in other men, being of one and the same nature? To have anything offered them repugnant to this desire must needs in all respects grieve them as much as me; so that, if I do harm, I must look to suffer, there being no reason that others should show greater measure of love to me than they have by me showed unto them; my desire therefore to be loved of my equals in nature, as much as possibly may be, imposeth upon me a natural duty of bearing to them-ward fully the like affection; from which relation of equality between ourselves and them that are as ourselves, what several rules and canons natural reason hath drawn, for direction of life, no man is ignorant. (*Eccl. Pol. lib. i.*).

6. But though this be a state of liberty, yet it is not a state of licence; though man in that state have an uncontrollable liberty to dispose of his person or possessions, yet he has not liberty to destroy himself, or so much as any creature in his possession, but where some nobler use than its bare preservation calls for it. The state of nature has a law of nature to govern it which obliges every one; and reason, which is that law, teaches all mankind who will but consult it that, being all equal and independent, no one ought to

harm another in his life, health, liberty, or possessions; for men being all the workmanship of one omnipotent and infinitely wise Maker—all the servants of one sovereign master, sent into the world by his order, and about his business—they are his property whose workmanship they are, made to last during his, not one another's pleasure; and being furnished with like faculties, sharing all in one community of nature, there cannot be supposed any such subordination among us that may authorize us to destroy another, as if we were made for one another's uses as the inferior ranks of creatures are for ours. Every one, as he is bound to preserve himself and not to quit his station wilfully, so by the like reason, when his own preservation comes not in competition, ought he, as much as he can, to preserve the rest of mankind, and may not, unless it be to do justice to an offender, take away or impair the life, or what tends to the preservation of life: the liberty, health, limb, or goods of another.

7. And that all men may be restrained from invading others' rights and from doing hurt to one another, and the law of nature be observed which willeth the peace and preservation of all mankind, the execution of the law of nature is, in that state, put into every man's hands, whereby everyone has a right to punish the transgressors of that law to such a degree as may hinder its violation; for the law of nature would, as all other laws that concern men in this world, be in vain, if there were nobody that in the state of nature had a power to execute that law and thereby preserve the innocent and restrain offenders. And if any one in the state of nature may punish another for any evil he has done, every one may do so; for in that state of perfect equality where naturally there is no superiority or jurisdiction of one over another, what any may do in prosecution of that law, every one must needs have a right to do.

8. And thus in the state of nature one man comes by a power over another; but yet no absolute or arbitrary power to use a criminal, when he has got him in his hands, according to the passionate heats of boundless extravagancy of his own will; but only to retribute to him, so far as calm reason and conscience dictate, what is proportionate to his transgression, which is so

much as may serve for reparation and restraint; for these two are the only reasons why one man may lawfully do harm to another, which is that we call punishment. In transgressing the law of nature, the offender declares himself to live by another rule than that of reason and common equity, which is that measure God has set to the actions of men for their mutual security; and so he becomes dangerous to mankind, the tie which is to secure them from injury and violence being slighted and broken by him. Which being a trespass against the whole species and the peace and safety of it provided for by the law of nature, every man upon this score, by right he hath to preserve mankind in general, may restrain, or, where it is necessary, destroy things noxious to them, and so may bring such evil on any one who hath transgressed that law, as may make him repent the doing of it and thereby deter him, and by his example others, from doing the like mischief. And in this case, and upon this ground, *every man hath a right to punish the offender and be executioner of the law of nature.*

* * *

10. Besides the crime which consists in violating the law and varying from the right rule of reason, whereby a man so far becomes degenerate and declares himself to quit the principles of human nature and to be a noxious creature, there is commonly injury done to some person or other, and some other man receives damage by his transgression; in which case he who hath received any damage has, besides the right of punishment common to him with other men, a particular right to seek reparation from him that has done it; and any other person, who finds it just, may also join with him that is injured and assist him in recovering from the offender so much as may make satisfaction for the harm he has suffered.

11. From these two distinct rights — the one of punishing the crime for restraint and preventing the like offence, which right of punishing is in everybody; the other of taking reparation, which belongs only to the injured party — comes it to pass that the magistrate, who by being magistrate hath the common right of punishing put into his hands, can often, where the public good demands not the execution of the law, remit the punishment of criminal offences by his own authority, but yet cannot remit the satisfaction due to any private man for the damage he has received. That

he who has suffered the damage has a right to demand in his own name, and he alone can remit; the damnified person has this power of appropriating to himself the goods or service of the offender by right of self-preservation, as every man has a power to punish the crime to prevent its being committed again, by the right he has of preserving all mankind, and doing all reasonable things he can in order to that end; and thus it is that every man, in the state of nature, has a power to kill a murderer, both to deter others from doing the like injury, which no reparation can compensate, by the example of the punishment that attends it from everybody, and also to secure men from the attempts of a criminal who, having renounced reason — the common rule and measure God hath given to mankind — hath, by the unjust violence and slaughter he hath committed upon one, declared war against all mankind; and therefore may be destroyed as a lion or a tiger, one of those wild savage beasts with whom men can have no society nor security. And upon this is grounded that great law of nature, "Whoso sheddeth man's blood, by man shall his blood be shed." And Cain was so fully convinced that every one had a right to destroy such a criminal that, after the murder of his brother, he cries out, "Every one that findeth me, shall slay me;" so plain was it writ in the hearts of mankind.

12. By the same reason may a man in the state of nature punish the lesser breaches of that law. It will perhaps be demanded: with death? I answer: Each transgression may be punished to that degree and with so much severity as will suffice to make it an ill bargain to the offender, give him cause to repent, and terrify others from doing the like. Every offence that can be committed in the state of nature may in the state of nature be also punished equally, and as far forth as it may in a commonwealth; for though it would be beside my present purpose to enter here into the particulars of the law of nature, or its measures of punishment, yet it is certain there is such a law, and that, too, as intelligible and plain to a rational creature and a studier of that law as the positive laws of commonwealths, nay, possibly plainer, as much as reason is easier to be understood than the fancies and intricate contrivances of men, following contrary and hidden interests put into words; for so truly are a great part of the municipal laws of countries, which

are only so far right as they are founded on the law of nature, by which they are to be regulated and interpreted.

13. To this strange doctrine — viz., that in the state of nature every one has the executive power of the law of nature — I doubt not but it will be objected that it is unreasonable for men to be judges in their own cases, that self-love will make men partial to themselves and their friends, and, on the other side, that ill-nature, passion, and revenge will carry them too far in punishing others, and hence nothing but confusion and disorder will follow; and that therefore God hath certainly appointed government to restrain the partiality and violence of men. I easily grant that civil government is the proper remedy for the inconveniences of the state of nature, which must certainly be great where men may be judges in their own case; since it is easy to be imagined that he who was so unjust as to do his brother an injury will scarce be so just as to condemn himself for it; but I shall desire those who make this objection to remember that absolute monarchs are but men, and if government is to be the remedy of those evils which necessarily follow from men's being judges in their own cases, and the state of nature is therefore not to be endured, I desire to know what kind of government that is, and how much better it is than the state of nature, where one man commanding a multitude has the liberty to be judge in his own case, and may do to all his subjects whatever he pleases, without the least liberty to any one to question or control those who execute his pleasure, and in whatsoever he doth, whether led by reason, mistake, or passion, must be submitted to? Much better it is in the state of nature, wherein men are not bound to submit to the unjust will of another; and if he that judges, judges amiss in his own or any other case, he is answerable for it to the rest of mankind.

14. It is often asked as a mighty objection, "Where are or ever were there any men in such a state of nature?" To which it may suffice as an answer at present that, since all princes and rulers of independent governments all through the world are in a state of nature, it is plain the world never was, nor ever will be, without numbers of men in that state. I have named all governors of independent communities, whether they are, or are not, in league with others; for it is not every compact that puts an end to the state of nature between men, but only this one of agreeing together mutually to enter into one community and make one body politic; other promises and compacts men may make one with another and yet still be in the state of nature. The promises and bargains for truck, etc., between the two men in the desert island, mentioned by Garcilasso de la Vega, in his *History of Peru*, or between a Swiss and an Indian, in the woods of America, are binding to them, though they are perfectly in a state of nature in reference to one another; for truth and keeping of faith belongs to men as men, and not as members of society.

15. To those that say there were never any men in the state of nature, I will not only oppose the authority of the judicious Hooker, *Eccl. Pol.*, lib. i., sect. 10, where he says,

> The laws which have been hitherto mentioned, (*i. e.*, the laws of nature) do bind men absolutely, even as they are men, although they have never any settled fellowship, never any solemn agreement amongst themselves what to do, or not to do; but forasmuch as we are not by ourselves sufficient to furnish ourselves with competent store of things needful for such a life as our nature doth desire, a life fit for the dignity of man; therefore to supply those defects and imperfections which are in us, as living singly and solely by ourselves, we are naturally induced to seek communion and fellowship with others. This was the cause of men's uniting themselves at first in political societies.

But I, moreover, affirm that all men are naturally in that state and remain so till by their own consents they make themselves members of some politic society; and I doubt not in the sequel of this discourse to make it very clear

NOTE

1. "The judicious Hooker" (1554–1600) was the celebrated English ecclesiastic who defended the Reformation settlements and wrote the famous *Lawes of Ecclesiasticall Politie*, of which Books I to V appeared from 1594 to 1597, and Books VI to VIII were published posthumously in 1648. While defending the monarchy, he rested it on a doctrine of social contract. He was a precursor of Locke in that, while living in a monarchical government, he was not a defender of divine right, and took, on the whole, a constitutional position.

C H A P T E R   3

Of the State of War

16. The state of war is a state of enmity and destruction; and, therefore, declaring by word or action, not a passionate and hasty, but a sedate, settled design upon another man's life, puts him in a state of war with him against whom he has declared such an intention, and so has exposed his life to the other's power to be taken away by him, or anyone that joins with him in his defence and espouses his quarrel; it being reasonable and just I should have a right to destroy that which threatens me with destruction; for, by the fundamental law of nature, man being to be preserved as much as possible when all cannot be preserved, the safety of the innocent is to be preferred; and one may destroy a man who makes war upon him, or has discovered an enmity to his being, for the same reason that he may kill a wolf or a lion, because such men are not under the ties of the common law of reason, have no other rule but that of force and violence, and so may be treated as beasts of prey, those dangerous and noxious creatures that will be sure to destroy him whenever he falls into their power.

17. And hence it is that he who attempts to get another man into his absolute power does thereby put himself into a state of war with him, it being to be understood as a declaration of a design upon his life; for I have reason to conclude that he who would get me into his power without my consent would use me as he pleased when he got me there, and destroy me, too, when he had a fancy to it; for nobody can desire to have me in his absolute power unless it be to compel me by force to that which is against the right of my freedom, *i.e.,* make me a slave. To be free from such force is the only security of my preservation; and reason bids me look on him as an enemy to my preservation who would take away that freedom which is the fence to it; so that he who makes an attempt to enslave me thereby puts himself into a state of war with me. He that, in the state of nature, would take away the freedom that belongs to any one in that state, must necessarily be supposed to have a design to take away everything else, that freedom being the foundation of all the rest; as he that, in the

state of society, would take away the freedom belonging to those of that society or commonwealth, must be supposed to design to take away from them everything else, and so be looked on as in a state of war.

18. This makes it lawful for a man to kill a thief who has not in the least hurt him, nor declared any design upon his life any farther than, by the use of force, so to get him in his power as to take away his money, or what he pleases, from him; because, using force where he has no right to get me into his power, let his pretence be what it will, I have no reason to suppose that he who would take away my liberty would not, when he had me in his power, take away everything else. And therefore it is lawful for me to treat him as one who has put himself into a state of war with me, *i. e.,* kill him if I can; for to that hazard does he justly expose himself whoever introduces a state of war and is aggressor in it.

19. And here we have the plain difference between the state of nature and the state of war which, however some men have confounded, are as far distant as a state of peace, good-will, mutual assistance, and preservation, and a state of enmity, malice, violence, and mutual destruction are one from another. Men living together according to reason, without a common superior on earth with authority to judge between them, is properly the state of nature. But force, or a declared design of force, upon the person of another, where there is no common superior on earth to appeal to for relief, is the state of war; and it is the want of such an appeal gives a man the right of war even against an aggressor, though he be in society and a fellow-subject. Thus a thief, whom I cannot harm but by appeal to the law for having stolen all that I am worth, I may kill when he sets on me to rob me but of my horse or coat; because the law, which was made for my preservation, where it cannot interpose to secure my life from present force, which, if lost, is capable of no reparation, permits me my own defence and the right of war, a liberty to kill the aggressor, because the aggressor allows not time to appeal to our common judge, nor the decision

of the law, for remedy in a case where the mischief may be irreparable. Want of a common judge with authority puts all men in a state of nature; force without right upon a man's person makes a state of war both where there is, and is not, a common judge.

20. But when the actual force is over, the state of war ceases between those that are in society, and are equally on both sides subjected to the fair determination of the law; because then there lies open the remedy of appeal for the past injury and to prevent future harm. But where no such appeal is, as in the state of nature, for want of positive laws and judges with authority to appeal to, the state of war once begun continues with a right to the innocent party to destroy the other whenever he can, until the aggressor offers peace and desires reconciliation on such terms as may repair any wrongs he has already done, and secure the innocent for the future; nay, where an appeal to the law and constituted judges lies open, but the remedy is denied by a manifest perverting of justice and a barefaced wrestling of the laws to protect or indemnify the violence or injuries of some men, or party of men, there it is hard to imagine anything but a state of war; for wherever violence is used and injury done, though by hands appointed to administer justice, it is still violence and injury, however coloured with the name, pretences, or forms of law, the end whereof being to protect and redress the innocent by an unbiased application of it to all who are under it; wherever that is not bona fide done, war is made upon the sufferers, who having no appeal on earth to right them, they are left to the only remedy in such cases—an appeal to heaven.

21. To avoid this state of war—wherein there is no appeal but to heaven, and wherein every the least difference is apt to end, where there is no authority to decide between the contenders—is one great reason of men's putting themselves into society and quitting the state of nature; for where there is an authority, a power on earth from which relief can be had by appeal, there the continuance of the state of war is excluded, and the controversy is decided by that power. Had there been any such court, any superior jurisdiction on earth, to determine the right between Jephthah and the Ammonites, they had never come to a state of war; but we see he was forced to appeal to heaven: "The Lord the Judge," says he, "be judge this day between the children of Israel and the children of Ammon" (Judges xi.27.), and then prosecuting and relying on his appeal, he leads out his army to battle. And, therefore, in such controversies where the question is put, "Who shall be judge?" it cannot be meant, "who shall decide the controversy"; every one knows what Jephthah here tells us, that "the Lord the Judge" shall judge. Where there is no judge on earth, the appeal lies to God in heaven. That question then cannot mean: who shall judge whether another hath put himself in a state of war with me, and whether I may, as Jephthah did, appeal to heaven in it? Of that I myself can only be judge in my own conscience, as I will answer it at the great day to the supreme Judge of all men.

* * *

CHAPTER 11

Of the Extent of the Legislative Power

134. The great end of men's entering into society being the enjoyment of their properties in peace and safety, and the great instrument and means of that being the laws established in that society, the first and fundamental positive law of all commonwealths is the establishing of the legislative power; as the first and fundamental natural law which is to govern even the legislative itself is the preservation of the society and, as far as will consist with the public good, of every person in it. This legislative is not only the supreme power of the commonwealth, but sacred and unalterable in the hands where the community have once placed it; nor can any edict of anybody else, in what form soever conceived or by what power soever backed, have the force and obligation of a law which has not its sanction from that legislative which the public has chosen and appointed; for without this the law could not have that which is absolutely necessary to its

being a law: the consent of the society over whom nobody can have a power to make laws, but by their own consent and by authority received from them. And therefore all the obedience, which by the most solemn ties any one can be obliged to pay, ultimately terminates in this supreme power and is directed by those laws which it enacts; nor can any oaths to any foreign power whatsoever, or any domestic subordinate power, discharge any member of the society from his obedience to the legislative acting pursuant to their trust, nor oblige him to any obedience contrary to the laws so enacted, or farther than they do allow; it being ridiculous to imagine one can be tied ultimately to obey any power in the society which is not supreme.

135. Though the legislative, whether placed in one or more, whether it be always in being, or only by intervals, though it be the supreme power in every commonwealth; yet:

First, It is not, nor can possibly be, absolutely arbitrary over the lives and fortunes of the people; for it being but the joint power of every member of the society given up to that person or assembly which is legislator, it can be no more than those persons had in a state of nature before they entered into society and gave up to the community; for nobody can transfer to another more power than he has in himself; and nobody has an absolute arbitrary power over himself, or over any other, to destroy his own life, or take away the life or property of another. A man, as has been proved, cannot subject himself to the arbitrary power of another; and having in the state of nature no arbitrary power over the life, liberty, or possession of another, but only so much as the law of nature gave him for the preservation of himself and the rest of mankind, this is all he doth or can give up to the commonwealth, and by it to the legislative power, so that the legislative can have no more than this. Their power, in the utmost bounds of it, is limited to the public good of the society. It is a power that hath no other end but preservation, and therefore can never have a right to destroy, enslave, or designedly to impoverish the subjects. The obligations of the law of nature cease not in society but only in many cases are drawn closer and have by human laws known penalties annexed to them to enforce their observation. Thus the law of nature stands as an eternal

rule to all men, legislators as well as others. The rules that they make for other men's actions must, as well as their own and other men's actions, be conformable to the law of nature — to the will of God, of which that is a declaration — and the fundamental law of nature being the preservation of mankind, no human sanction can be good or valid against it.

136. Secondly, The legislative or supreme authority cannot assume to itself a power to rule by extemporary, arbitrary decrees, but is bound to dispense justice and to decide the rights of the subject by promulaged standing laws and known authorized judges. For the law of nature being unwritten, and so nowhere to be found but in the minds of men, they who through passion or interest shall miscite or misapply it, cannot so easily be convinced of their mistake where there is no established judge; and so it serves not, as it ought, to determine the rights and fence the properties of those that live under it, especially where every one is judge, interpreter, and executioner of it, too, and that in his own case; and he that has right on his side, having ordinarily but his own single strength, hath not force enough to defend himself from injuries, or to punish delinquents. To avoid these inconveniences which disorder men's properties in the state of nature, men unite into societies that they may have the united strength of the whole society to secure and defend their properties, and may have standing rules to bound it by which every one may know what is his. To this end it is that men give up all their natural power to the society which they enter into, and the community put the legislative power into such hands as they think fit with this trust, that they shall be governed by declared laws, or else their peace, quiet, and property will still be at the same uncertainty as it was in the state of nature.

* * *

138. Thirdly, The supreme power cannot take from any man part of his property without his own consent; for the preservation of property being the end of government and that for which men enter into society, it necessarily supposes and requires that the people should have property, without which they must be supposed to lose that, by entering into society, which was the end for which they entered into it — too gross an

absurdity for any man to own. Men, therefore, in society having property, they have such right to the goods which by the law of the community are theirs, that nobody hath a right to take their substance or any part of it from them without their own consent; without this, they have no property at all, for I have truly no property in that which another can by right take from me when he pleases, against my consent. Hence it is a mistake to think that the supreme or legislative power of any commonwealth can do what it will, and dispose of the estates of the subject arbitrarily, or take any part of them at pleasure.

* * *

140. It is true, governments cannot be supported without great charge, and it is fit every one who enjoys his share of the protection should pay out of his estate his proportion for the maintenance of it. But still it must be with his own consent — *i. e.*, the consent of the majority, giving it either by themselves or their representatives chosen by them. For if any one shall claim a power to lay and levy taxes on the people, by his own authority and without such consent of the people, he thereby invades the fundamental law of property and subverts the end of government; for what property have I in that which another may by right take, when he pleases, to himself?

141. Fourthly, The legislative cannot transfer the power of making laws to any other hands; for it being but a delegated power from the people, they who have it cannot pass it over to others. The people alone can appoint the form of the commonwealth, which is by constituting the legislative and appointing in whose hands that shall be. And when the people have said, we will sub-

mit to rules and be governed by laws made by such men, and in such forms, nobody else can say other men shall make laws for them; nor can the people be bound by any laws but such as are enacted by those whom they have chosen and authorized to make laws for them. The power of the legislative, being derived from the people by a positive voluntary grant and institution, can be no other than what that positive grant conveyed, which being only to make laws, and not to make legislators, the legislative can have no power to transfer their authority of making laws and place it in other hands.

142. These are the bounds which the trust that is put in them by society and the law of God and nature have set to the legislative power of every commonwealth, in all forms of government:

First, They are to govern by promulgated established laws, not to be varied in particular cases, but to have one rule for rich and poor, for the favourite at court and the countryman at plough.

Secondly, These laws also ought to be designed for no other end ultimately but the good of the people.

Thirdly, They must not raise taxes on the property of the people without the consent of the people, given by themselves or their deputies. And this properly concerns only such governments where the legislative is always in being, or at least where the people have not reserved any part of the legislative to deputies to be from time to time chosen by themselves.

Fourthly, The legislative neither must nor can transfer the power of making laws to anybody else, or place it anywhere but where the people have.

* * *

C H A P T E R   1 9

Of the Dissolution of Government

211. He that will with any clearness speak of the dissolution of government ought in the first place to distinguish between the dissolution of the society and the dissolution of the government. That which makes the community and brings men out of the loose state of nature into one politic society is the agreement which everybody has with the rest to incorporate and act as one

body, and so be one distinct commonwealth. The usual and almost only way whereby this union is dissolved is the inroad of foreign force making a conquest upon them; for in that case, not being able to maintain and support themselves as one entire and independent body, the union belonging to that body which consisted therein must necessarily cease, and so every one return to the state he was in before, with a liberty to shift for himself and provide for his own safety, as he thinks fit, in some other society. Whenever the society is dissolved, it is certain the government of that society cannot remain. Thus conquerors' swords often cut up governments by the roots and mangle societies to pieces, separating the subdued or scattered multitude from the protection of and dependence on that society which ought to have preserved them from violence. The world is too well instructed in, and too forward to allow of, this way of dissolving of governments to need any more to be said of it; and there wants not much argument to prove that where the society is dissolved, the government cannot remain — that being as impossible as for the frame of a house to subsist when the materials of it are scattered and dissipated by a whirlwind, or jumbled into a confused heap by an earthquake.

212. Besides this overturning from without, governments are dissolved from within.

First, When the legislative is altered. Civil society being a state of peace amongst those who are of it, from whom the state of war is excluded by the umpirage which they have provided in their legislative for the ending all differences that may arise amongst any of them, it is in their legislative that the members of a commonwealth are united and combined together into one coherent living body. This is the soul that gives form, life, and unity to the commonwealth; from hence the several members have their mutual influence, sympathy, and connexion; and, therefore, when the legislative is broken or dissolved, dissolution and death follows; for the essence and union of the society consisting in having one will, the legislative, when once established by the majority, has the declaring and, as it were, keeping of that will. The constitution of the legislative is the first and fundamental act of society, whereby provision is made for the continuation of their union under the direction of persons and bonds of laws made by persons authorized thereunto by the consent and appointment of the people, without which no one man or number of men amongst them can have authority of making laws that shall be binding to the rest. When any one or more shall take upon them to make laws, whom the people have not appointed so to do, they make laws without authority, which the people are not therefore bound to obey; by which means they come again to be out of subjection and may constitute to themselves a new legislative as they think best, being in full liberty to resist the force of those who without authority would impose anything upon them. Every one is at the disposure of his own will when those who had by the delegation of the society the declaring of the public will are excluded from it, and others usurp the place who have no such authority or delegation.

213. This being usually brought about by such in the commonwealth who misuse the power they have, it is hard to consider it aright, and know at whose door to lay it, without knowing the form of government in which it happens. Let us suppose then the legislative placed in the concurrence of three distinct persons:

(1) A single hereditary person having the constant supreme executive power, and with it the power of convoking and dissolving the other two within certain periods of time.

(2) An assembly of hereditary nobility.

(3) An assembly of representatives chosen *pro tempore* by the people. Such a form of government supposed, it is evident,

214. First, That when such a single person or prince sets up his own arbitrary will in place of the laws which are the will of the society declared by the legislative, then the legislative is changed; for that being in effect the legislative whose rules and laws are put in execution and required to be obeyed. When other laws are set up, and other rules pretended and enforced, than what the legislative constituted by the society have enacted, it is plain that the legislative is changed. Whoever introduces new laws, not being thereunto authorized by the fundamental appointment of the society, or subverts the old, disowns and overturns the power by which they were made, and so sets up a new legislative.

215. Secondly, When the prince hinders the legislative from assembling in its due time, or from acting freely pursuant to those ends for which it was constituted, the legislative is altered; for it is not a certain number of men, no, nor their meeting, unless they have also freedom of debating and leisure of perfecting what is for the good of the society, wherein the legislative consists. When these are taken away or altered so

as to deprive the society of the due exercise of their power, the legislative is truly altered; . . .

* * *

216. Thirdly, When, by the arbitrary power of the prince, the electors or ways of election are altered without the consent and contrary to the common interest of the people, there also the legislative is altered; for, if others than those whom the society hath authorized thereunto do choose, or in another way than what the society hath prescribed, those chosen are not the legislative appointed by the people.

217. Fourthly, The delivery also of the people into the subjection of a foreign power, either by the prince or by the legislative, is certainly a change of the legislative, and so a dissolution of the government; for the end why people entered into society being to be preserved one entire, free, independent society, to be governed by its own laws, this is lost whenever they are given up into the power of another.

* * *

219. There is one way more whereby such a government may be dissolved, and that is when he who has the supreme executive power neglects and abandons that charge, so that the laws already made can no longer be put in execution. This is demonstratively to reduce all to anarchy, and so effectually to dissolve the government; for laws not being made for themselves, but to be by their execution the bonds of the society, to keep every part of the body politic in its due place and function. When that totally ceases, the government visibly ceases, and the people become a confused multitude, without order or connexion. Where there is no longer the administration of justice for the securing of men's rights, nor any remaining power within the community to direct the force or provide for the necessities of the public, there certainly is no government left. Where the laws cannot be executed, it is all one as if there were no laws; and a government without laws is, I suppose, a mystery in politics, inconceivable to human capacity and inconsistent with human society.

220. In these and the like cases, when the government is dissolved, the people are at liberty to provide for themselves by erecting a new legislative, differing from the other by the change of persons or form, or both, as they shall find it most for their safety and good; for the society can never by the fault of another lose the native and original right it has to preserve itself, which can only be done by a settled legislative, and a fair and impartial execution of the laws made by it. But the state of mankind is not so miserable that they are not capable of using this remedy till it be too late to look for any. To tell people they may provide for themselves by erecting a new legislative, when by oppression, artifice, or being delivered over to a foreign power, their old one is gone, is only to tell them they may expect relief when it is too late and the evil is past cure. This is in effect no more than to bid them first be slaves, and then to take care of their liberty; and when their chains are on, tell them they may act like freemen. This, if barely so, is rather mockery than relief; and men can never be secure from tyranny if there be no means to escape it till they are perfectly under it; and therefore it is that they have not only a right to get out of it, but to prevent it.

221. There is, therefore, secondly, another way whereby governments are dissolved, and that is when the legislative or the prince, either of them, act contrary to their trust.

First, The legislative acts against the trust reposed in them when they endeavour to invade the property of the subject, and to make themselves or any part of the community masters or arbitrary disposers of the lives, liberties, or fortunes of the people.

222. The reason why men enter into society is the preservation of their property; and the end why they choose and authorize a legislative is that there may be laws made and rules set as guards and fences to the properties of all the members of the society, to limit the power and moderate the dominion of every part and member of the society; for since it can never be supposed to be the will of the society that the legislative should have a power to destroy that which every one designs to secure by entering into society, and for which the people submitted themselves to legislators of their own making. Whenever the legislators endeavour to take away and destroy the property of the people, or to reduce them to slavery under arbitrary power, they put themselves into a state of war with the people who are thereupon absolved from any fur-

ther obedience, and are left to the common refuge which God hath provided for all men against force and violence. Whensoever, therefore, the legislative shall transgress this fundamental rule of society, and either by ambition, fear, folly, or corruption, endeavour to grasp themselves, or put into the hands of any other, an absolute power over the lives, liberties, and estates of the people, by this breach of trust they forfeit the power the people had put into their hands for quite contrary ends, and it devolves to the people who have a right to resume their original liberty, and by the establishment of a new legislative, such as they shall think fit, provide for their own safety and security, which is the end for which they are in society. What I have said here concerning the legislative in general holds true also concerning the supreme executor, who having a double trust put in him — both to have a part in the legislative and the supreme execution of the law — acts against both when he goes about to set up his own arbitrary will as the law of the society. He acts also contrary to his trust when he either employs the force, treasure, and offices of the society to corrupt the representatives and gain them to his purposes, or openly pre-engages the electors and prescribes to their choice such whom he has by solicitations, threats, promises, or otherwise won to his designs, and employs them to bring in such who have promised beforehand what to vote and what to enact. Thus to regulate candidates and electors, and new-model the ways of election, what is it but to cut up the government by the roots, and poison the very fountain of public security? For the people, having reserved to themselves the choice of their representatives, as the fence to their properties, could do it for no other end but that they might always be freely chosen, and, so chosen, freely act and advise as the necessity of the commonwealth and the public good should upon examination and mature debate be judged to require. This, those who give their votes before they hear the debate, and have weighed the reasons on all sides, are not capable of doing. To prepare such an assembly as this, and endeavour to set up the declared abettors of his own will for the true representatives of the people and the lawmakers of the society, is certainly as great a breach of trust and as perfect a declaration of a design to subvert the government as is possible to be met with. To which if one shall add rewards and punishments visibly employed to the same end, and all the arts of perverted law made use of to take off and destroy all that stand in the way of such a design, and will not comply and consent to betray the liberties of their country, it will be past doubt what is doing. What power they ought to have in the society who thus employ it contrary to the trust that went along with it in it its first institution is easy to determine; and one cannot but see that he who has once attempted any such thing as this cannot any longer be trusted.

223. To this perhaps it will be said that the people being ignorant and always discontented, to lay the foundation of government in the unsteady opinion and uncertain humour of the people is to expose it to certain ruin; and no government will be able long to subsist, if the people may set up a new legislative whenever they take offence at the old one. To this I answer: Quite the contrary. People are not so easily got out of their old forms as some are apt to suggest. They are hardly to be prevailed with to amend the acknowledged faults in the frame they have been accustomed to. And if there be any original defects, or adventitious ones introduced by time or corruption, it is not an easy thing to get them changed, even when all the world sees there is an opportunity for it. This slowness and aversion in the people to quit their old constitutions has in the many revolutions which have been seen in this kingdom, in this and former ages, still kept us to, or after some interval of fruitless attempts still brought us back again to, our old legislative of king, lords, and commons; and whatever provocations have made the crown be taken from some of our princes' heads, they never carried the people so far as to place it in another line.

224. But it will be said this hypothesis lays a ferment for frequent rebellion. To which I answer:

First, No more than any other hypothesis; for when the people are made miserable, and find themselves exposed to the ill-usage of arbitrary power, cry up their governors as much as you will for sons of Jupiter, let them be sacred or divine, descended, or authorized from heaven, give them out for whom or what you please, the same will happen. The people generally ill-treated, and contrary to right, will be ready upon any occasion to ease themselves of a burden that sits heavy upon them. They will wish and seek for the opportunity, which in the change, weakness, and accidents of human affairs seldom delays long to offer itself. He must have lived but a little while in the world who has not seen examples of this in his time, and he must have read very little who cannot produce examples of it in all sorts of governments in the world.

225. Secondly, I answer, such revolutions happen not upon every little mismanagement in public affairs. Great mistakes in the ruling part, many wrong and inconvenient laws, and all the slips of human frailty will be born by the people without mutiny or murmur. But if a long train of abuses, prevarications, and artifices, all tending the same way, make the design visible to the people, and they cannot but feel what they lie under and see whither they are going, it is not to be wondered that they should then rouse themselves and endeavour to put the rule into such hands which may secure to them the ends for which government was at first erected.

* * *

Notes and Questions

JEREMY BENTHAM, from *Anarchical Fallacies*

1. Jeremy Bentham's *Anarchical Fallacies* is a pointed and detailed critique of the French Declaration of Rights of 1791. (See "Collected Documents.") Bentham offers two general arguments against the Declaration: (1) It is conceptually confused or meaningless; and (2) it is dangerous. On what grounds does Bentham argue that it is dangerous? Do you agree that justifying past insurrection encourages future insurrection? Does Locke answer this argument?

2. How does Bentham show that the language of the Declaration is "nonsense"? Do you agree that article 2, section 1, has no meaning definite enough to be law? Bentham claims that it is emotional rhetoric. Is it? Should emotional rhetoric be part of fundamental law? Does his argument apply to the U.S. Declaration of Independence? To the Bill of Rights?

3. Bentham argues that there are no rights prior to government. Rights owe their existence to government. An earlier philosopher, Thomas Hobbes (among other philosophers), also held this view. According to Hobbes, human life without government (that is, in a state of nature) would be anarchy, a war of all against all. There would be no rights, only the total freedom of anyone to do whatever he or she had the power, brute strength, or cunning to do. Rights are brought about by government monopoly of power. How would Locke respond? How would you?

4. How does Bentham respond to the idea of a social contract, or the authority of government being derived from the consent of the governed?

5. Why does Bentham argue that rights of liberty, property, security, and resistance to oppression cannot be imprescriptible? What does *imprescriptible* mean? Bentham's argument, as he states it, is undeniable. Can you think of an answer to it? Is there another way to state the argument so that it can be answered?

[From] *Anarchical Fallacies*

JEREMY BENTHAM

Preliminary Observations

The Declaration of Rights — I mean the paper published under that name by the French National Assembly in 1791 — assumes for its subject-matter a field of disquisition as unbounded in point of extent as it is important in its nature. But the more ample the extent given to any proposition or string of propositions, the more difficult it is to keep the import of it confined without deviation, within the bounds of truth and reason. If in the smallest corners of the field it ranges over, it fails of coinciding with the line of rigid rectitude, no sooner is the aberration pointed out, than (inasmuch as there is no medium between truth and falsehood) its pretensions to the appellation of a truism are gone, and whoever looks upon it must recognise it to be false and erroneous, — and if, as here, political conduct be the theme, so far as the error extends and fails of being detected, pernicious.

In a work of such extreme importance with a view to practice, and which throughout keeps practice so closely and immediately and professedly in view, a single error may be attended with the most fatal consequences. The more extensive the propositions, the more consummate will be the knowledge, the more exquisite the skill, indispensably requisite to confine them in all points within the pale of truth. The most consummate ability in the whole nation could not have been too much for the task — one may venture to say, it would not have been equal to it. But that, in the sanctioning of each proposition, the most consummate ability should happen to be vested in the heads of the sorry majority in whose hands the plenitude of power happened on that same occasion to be vested, in an event against which the chances are almost as infinity to one.

Here, then, is a radical and all-pervading error — the attempting to give to a work on such a subject the sanction of government; especially of such a government — a government composed of members so numerous, so unequal in talent, as well as discordant in inclinations and affections.

Had it been the work of a single hand, and that a private one, and in that character given to the world, every good effect would have been produced by it that could be produced by it when published as the work of government, without any of the bad effects which in case of the smallest error must result from it when given as the work of government.

The revolution, which threw the government into the hands of the penners and adopters of this declaration, having been the effect of insurrection, the grand object evidently is to justify the cause. But by justifying it, they invite it: in justifying past insurrection, they plant and cultivate a propensity to perpetual insurrection in time future; they sow the seeds of anarchy broad-cast: in justifying the demolition of existing authorities, they undermine all future ones, their own consequently in the number. Shallow and reckless vanity! — They imitate in their conduct the author of that fabled law, according to which the assassination of the prince upon the throne gave to the assassin a title to succeed him. *"People, behold your rights! If a single article of them be violated, insurrection is not your right only, but the most sacred of your duties."* Such is the constant language, for such is the professed object of this source and model of all laws — this self-consecrated oracle of all nations. . . .

. . . The great enemies of public peace are the selfish and dissocial passions: — necessary as they are — the one to the very existence of each individual, the other to his security. On the part of these affections, a deficiency in point of strength is never to be apprehended: all that is to be apprehended in respect of them, is to be apprehended on the side of their excess. Society is held together only by the sacrifices that men can be induced to make of the gratifications they demand: to obtain these sacrifices is the great difficulty, the great task of government. What has been the object, the perpetual and palpable object, of this declaration of pretended rights? To add as much force as possible to these passions, already but too strong, — to burst the cords that hold them in — to say to the selfish passions, there — everywhere — is your prey! — to the angry passions, there — everywhere — is your enemy.

Such is the morality of this celebrated manifesto, rendered famous by the same qualities that gave celebrity to the incendiary of the Ephesian temple.

The logic of it is of a piece with its morality: — a perpetual vein of nonsense, flowing from a perpetual abuse of words, — words having a variety of meanings, where words with single meanings were equally at hand — the same words used in a variety of meanings in the same page, — words used in meanings not their own, where proper words were equally at hand, — words and propositions of the most unbounded signification, turned loose without any of those exceptions or modifications which are so necessary on every occasion to reduce their import within the compass, not only of right reason, but even of the design in hand, of whatever nature it may be; — the same inaccuracy, the same inattention in the penning of this cluster of truths on which the fate of nations was to hang, as if it had been an oriental tale, or an allegory for a magazine: — state epigrams, instead of necessary distinctions, — figurative expressions preferred to simple ones, — sentimental conceits, as trite as they are unmeaning, preferred to apt and precise expressions, — frippery ornament preferred to the majestic simplicity of good sound sense, — and the acts of the senate loaded and disfigured by the tinsel of the playhouse. . . .

Article II

The end in view of every political association is the preservation of the natural and imprescriptible rights of man. These rights are liberty, property, security, and resistance to oppression.

SENTENCE 1. The end in view of every political association, is the preservation of the natural and imprescriptible rights of man.

More confusion — more nonsense, — and the nonsense, as usual, dangerous nonsense. The words can scarcely be said to have a meaning: but if they have, or rather if they had a meaning, these would be the propositions either asserted or implied: —

1. That there are such things anterior to the establishment of governments: for natural, as applied to rights, if it mean anything, is meant to stand in opposition to legal — to such rights as are acknowledged to owe their existence to government, and are consequently posterior in their date to the establishment of government.

2. That these rights *can not* be abrogated by government: for *can not* is implied in the form of the word imprescriptible, and the sense it wears when so applied, is the cutthroat sense above explained.

3. That the governments that exist derive their origin from formal associations, or what are now called *conventions:* associations entered into by a partnership contract, with all the members for partners, — entered into at a day prefixed, for a predetermined purpose, the formation of a new government where there was none before (for as to formal meetings holden under the control of an existing government, they are evidently out of question here) in which it seems again to be implied in the way of inference, though a necessary and an unavoidable inference, that all governments (that is, self-called governments, knots of persons exercising the powers of government) that have had any other origin than an association of the above description, are illegal, that is, no governments at all; resistance to them, and subversion of them, lawful and commendable; and so on.

Such are the notions implied in this first part of the article. How stands the truth of things? That there are no such things as natural rights — no such things as rights anterior to the establishment of government — no such things as natural rights opposed to, in contradistinction to, legal: that the expression is merely figurative; that when used, in the moment you attempt to give it a literal meaning it leads to error, and to that sort of error that leads to mischief — to the extremity of mischief.

We know what it is for men to live without government — and living without government, to live without rights: we know what it is for men to live without government, for we see instances of such a way of life — we see it in many savage nations, or rather races of mankind; for instance, among the savages of New South Wales, whose way of living is so well known to us: no habit of obedience, and thence no government — no government, and thence no laws — no laws, and thence no such things as rights — no security — no property: — liberty, as against regular control, the control of laws and government — perfect; but as against all irregular control, the mandates of stronger individuals, none. In this state, at a time earlier than the commencement of history — in this same state, judging from analogy, we, the inhabitants of the part of the globe we call Europe, were; — no government, consequently no rights; no rights, consequently no property — no legal security — no legal liberty: security not more than belongs to beasts — forecast and sense of insecurity keener — consequently in point of happiness below the level of the brutal race.

In proportion to the want of happiness resulting from the want of rights, a reason exists for wishing that there were such things as rights. But reasons for wishing there were such things as rights, are not rights; — a reason for wishing that a certain right were established, is not that right — want is not supply — hunger is not bread.

That which has no existence cannot be destroyed — that which cannot be destroyed cannot require anything to preserve it from destruction. *Natural rights* is simple nonsense: natural and imprescriptible rights, rhetorical nonsense, — nonsense upon stilts. But this rhetorical nonsense ends in the old strain of mischievous nonsense; for immediately a list of these pretended natural rights is given, and those are so expressed as to present to view legal rights. And of these rights, whatever they are, there is not, it seems, any one of which any government *can*, upon any occasion whatever, abrogate the smallest particle.

So much for terrorist language. What is the language of reason and plain sense upon this same subject? That in proportion as it is *right or proper*, i.e. advantageous to the society in question, that this or that right — a right to this or that effect — should be established and maintained, in that some proportion it is *wrong* that it should be abrogated: but that as there is no *right*, which ought not to be maintained so long as it is upon the whole advantageous to the society that it should be maintained, so there is no right which, when the abolition of it is advantageous to society, should not be abolished. To know whether it would be more for the advantage of society that this or that right should be maintained or abolished, the time at which the question about main-

taining or abolishing is proposed, must be given, and the circumstances under which it is proposed to maintain or abolish it; the right itself must be specifically described, not jumbled with an undistinguishable heap of others, under any such vague general terms as property, liberty, and the like.

One thing, in the midst of all this confusion, is but too plain. They know not of what they are talking under the name of natural rights, and yet they would have them imprescriptible — proof against all the power of the laws — pregnant with occasions summoning the members of the community to rise up in resistance against the laws. What, then, was their object in declaring the existence of imprescriptible rights, and without specifying a single one by any such mark as it could be known by? This and no other — to excite and keep up a spirit of resistance to all laws — a spirit of insurrection against all governments — against the governments of all other nations instantly, — against the government of their own nation — against the government they themselves were pretending to establish — even that, as soon as their own reign should be at an end. In us is the perfection of virtue and wisdom: in all mankind besides, the extremity of wickedness and folly. Our will shall consequently reign without control, and for ever: reign now we are living — reign after we are dead.

All nations — all future ages — shall be, for they are predestined to be, our slaves.

Future governments will not have honesty enough to be trusted with the determination of what rights shall be maintained, what abrogated — what laws kept in force, what repealed. Future subjects (I should say future citizens, for French government does not admit of subjects) will not have wit enough to be trusted with the choice whether to submit to the determination of the government of their time, or resist it. Governments, citizens — all to the end of time — all must be kept in chains.

Such are their maxims — such their premises — for it is by such premises only that the doctrine of imprescriptible rights and unrepeatable laws can be supported.

What is the real source of these imprescriptible rights — these unrepealable laws? Power turned blind by looking from its own height: self-conceit and tyranny exalted into insanity. No man was to have any other man for a servant, yet all men were forever to be their slaves. Making laws with imposture in their mouths, under pretence of declaring them — giving for laws anything that came uppermost, and these unrepeatable ones, on pretence of finding them ready made. Made by what? Not by a God — they allow of none; but by their goddess, Nature.

The origination of governments from a contact is a pure fiction, or in other words, a falsehood. It never has been known to be true in any instance; the allegation of it does mischief, by involving the subject in error and confusion, and is neither necessary nor useful to any good purpose.

All governments that we have any account of have been gradually established by habit, after having been formed by force; unless in the instance of governments formed by individuals who have been emancipated, or have emancipated themselves, from governments already formed, the governments under which they were born — a rare case, and from which nothing follows with regard to the rest. What signifies it how governments are formed? Is it the less proper — the less conducive to the happiness of society — that the happiness of society should be the one object kept in view by the members of the government in all their measures? is it the less the interest of men to be happy — less to be wished that they may be so — less the moral duty of their governors to make them so, as far as they can, at Mogadore than at Philadelphia?

Whence is it, but from government, that contracts derive their binding force? Contracts came from government, not government from contracts. It is from the habit of enforcing contracts, and seeing them enforced, that governments are chiefly indebted for whatever disposition they have to observe them.

SENTENCE 2. These rights [these imprescriptible as well as natural rights,] are liberty, property, security, and resistance to oppression.

Observe the extent of these pretended rights, each of them belonging to every man, and all of them without bounds. Unbounded liberty; that is, amongst other things, the liberty of doing or not doing on every occasion whatever each man pleases: — Unbounded property; that is, the right of doing with everything around him (with every

thing at least, if not with every person,) whatsoever he pleases; communicating that right to anybody, and withholding it from anybody: — Unbounded security; that is, security for such his liberty, for such his property, and for his person, against every defalcation that can be called for on any account in respect of any of them: — Unbounded resistance to oppression; that is, unbounded exercise of the faculty of guarding himself against whatever unpleasant circumstance may present itself to his imagination or his passions under that name. Nature, say some of the interpreters of the pretended law of nature — nature gave to each man a right to everything; which is, in effect, but another way of saying — nature has given no such right to anybody; for in regard to most rights, it is as true that what is every man's right is no man's right, as that what is every man's business is no man's business. Nature gave — gave to every man a right to everything: — be it so — true; and hence the necessity of human government and human laws, to give to every man his own right, without which no right whatsoever would amount to anything. Nature gave every man a right to everything before the existence of laws, and in default of laws. This nominal universality and real nonentity of right, set up provisionally by nature in default of laws, the French oracle lays hold of, and perpetuates it under the law and in spite of laws. These anarchical rights which nature has set out with, democratic art attempts to rivet down, and declares indefeasible.

Unbounded liberty — I must still say unbounded liberty; — for though the next article but one returns to the charge, and gives such a definition of liberty as seems intended to set bounds to it, yet in effect the limitation amounts to nothing; and when, as here, no warning is given of any exception in the texture of the general rule, every exception which turns up is, not a confirmation but a contradiction of the rule: — liberty, without any preannounced or intelligible bounds; and as to the other rights, they remain unbounded to the end: rights of man composed of a system of contradictions and impossibilities.

In vain would it be said, that though no bounds are here assigned to any of these rights, yet it is to be understood as taken for granted, and tacitly admitted and assumed, that they are to have bounds; viz. such bounds as it is understood will be set them by the laws. Vain, I say, would be this apology; for the supposition would be contradictory to the express declaration of the article itself, and would defeat the very object which the whole declaration has in view. It would be self-contradictory, because these rights are, in the same breath in which their existence is declared, declared to be imprescriptible; and imprescriptible, or, as we in England should say, indefeasible, means nothing unless it exclude the interference of the laws.

It would be not only inconsistent with itself, but inconsistent with the declared and sole object of the declaration, if it did not exclude the interference of the laws. It is against the laws themselves, and the laws only, that this declaration is levelled. It is for the hands of the legislator and all legislators, and none but legislators, that the shackles it provides are intended, — it is against the apprehended encroachments of legislators that the rights in question, the liberty and property, and so forth, are intended to be made secure, — it is to such encroachments, and damages, and dangers, that whatever security it professes to give has respect. Precious security for unbounded rights against legislators, if the extent of those rights in every direction were purposely left to depend upon the will and pleasure of those very legislators!

Nonsensical or nugatory, and in both cases mischievous: such is the alternative.

So much for all these pretended indefeasible rights in the lump: their inconsistency with each other, as well as the inconsistency of them in the character of indefeasible rights with the existence of government and all peaceable society, will appear still more plainly when we examine them one by one.

1. *Liberty*, then, is imprescriptible — incapable of being taken away — out of the power of any government ever to take away: liberty, — that is, every branch of liberty — every individual exercise of liberty; for no line is drawn — no distinction — no exception made. What these instructors as well as governors of mankind appear not to know, is, that all rights are made at the expense of liberty — all laws by which rights are created or confirmed. No right without a correspondent

obligation. Liberty, as against the coercion of the law, may, it is true, be given by the simple removal of the obligation by which that coercion was applied — by the simple repeal of the coercing law. But as again the coercion applicable by individual to individual, no liberty can be given to one man but in proportion as it is taken from another. All coercive laws, therefore (that is, all laws but constitutional laws, and laws repealing or modifying coercive laws,) and in particular all laws creative of liberty, are, as far as they go, abrogative of liberty. Not here and there a law only — not this or that possible law, but almost all laws, are therefore repugnant to these natural and imprescriptible rights: consequently null and void, calling for resistance and insurrection, and so on, as before.

Laws creative of rights of property are also struck at by the same anathema. How is property given? By restraining liberty; that is, by taking it away so far as is necessary for the purpose. How is your house made yours? By debarring every one else from the liberty of entering it without your leave.

2. *Property.* Property stands second on the list, — proprietary rights are in the number of the natural and imprescriptible rights of man — of the rights which a man is not indebted for to the laws, and which cannot be taken from him by the laws. Men — that is, every man (for a general expression given without exceptions is an universal one) has a right to property, to proprietary rights, a *right which* cannot be taken away from him by the laws. To proprietary rights. Good: but in relation to what subject? for as to proprietary rights — without a subject to which they are referable — without a subject in or in relation to which they can be exercised — they will hardly be of much value, they will hardly be worth taking care of, with so much solemnity. In vain would all the laws in the world have ascertained that I have a right to something. If this be all they have done for me — if there be no specific subject in relation to which my proprietary rights are established, I must either take what I want without right, or starve. As there is no such subject specified with relation to each man, or to any man (indeed how could there be?) the necessary inference (taking the passage literally) is, that every

man has all manner of proprietary rights with relation to every subject of property without exception: in a word, that every man has a right to every thing. Unfortunately, in most matters of property, what is every man's right is no man's right; so that the effect of this part of the oracle, if observed, would be, not to establish property, but to extinguish it—to render it impossible ever to be revived: and this is one of the rights declared to be imprescriptible.

It will probably be acknowledged, that according to this construction, the clause in question is equally ruinous and absurd:—and hence the inference may be, that this was not the construction—this was not the meaning in view. But by the same rule, every possible construction which the words employed can admit of, might be proved not to have been the meaning in view: nor is this clause a whit more absurd or ruinous than all that goes before it, and a great deal of what comes after it. And, in short, if this be not the meaning of it, what is? Give it a sense—give it any sense whatever,—it is mischievous:—to save it from that imputation, there is but one course to take, which is to acknowledge it to be nonsense.

Thus much would be clear, if anything were clear in it, that according to this clause, whatever proprietary rights, whatever property a man once has, no matter how, being imprescriptible, can never be taken away from him by any law: or of what use or meaning is the clause? So that the moment it is acknowledged in relation to any article, that such article is my property, no matter how or when it became so, that moment it is acknowledged that it can never be taken away from me: therefore, for example, all laws and all judgments, whereby anything is taken away from me without my free consent—all taxes, for example, and all fines—are void, and, as such, call for resistance and insurrection, and so forth, as before.

3. *Security*. Security stands the third on the list of these natural and imprescriptible rights which laws did not give, and which laws are not in any degree to be suffered to take away. Under the head of security, liberty might have been included, so likewise property: since security for liberty, or the enjoyment of liberty, may be spoken of as a branch of security:—security for property, or the enjoyment of proprietary rights, as another. Security for person is the branch that seems here to have been understood:—security for each man's person, as against all those hurtful or disagreeable impressions (exclusive of those which consist in the mere disturbance of the enjoyment of liberty,) by which a man is affected in his person; loss of life—loss of limbs—loss of the use of limbs—wounds, bruises, and the like. All laws are null and void, then, which on any account or in any manner seek to expose the person of any man to any risk—which appoint capital or other corporal punishment—which expose a man to personal hazard in the service of the military power against foreign enemies, or in that of the judicial power against delinquents:—all laws which, to preserve the country from pestilence, authorize the immediate execution of a suspected person, in the event of his transgressing certain bounds.

4. *Resistance to oppression.* Fourth and last in the list of natural and imprescriptible rights, resistance to oppression—meaning, I suppose, the right to resist oppression. What is oppression? Power misapplied to the prejudice of some individual. What is it that a man has in view when he speaks of oppression? Some exertion of power which he looks upon as misapplied to the prejudice of some individual—to the producing on the part of such individual some suffering, to which (whether as forbidden by the laws or otherwise) we conceive he ought not to have been subjected. But against everything that can come under the name of oppression, provision has been already made, in the manner we have seen, by the recognition of the three preceding rights; since no oppression can fall upon a man which is not an infringement of his rights in relation to liberty, rights in relation to property, or rights in relation to security, as above described. Where, then, is the difference?—to what purpose this fourth clause after the three first? To this purpose: the mischief they seek to prevent, the rights they seek to establish, are the same; the difference lies in the nature of the remedy endeavoured to be applied. To prevent the mischief in question, the endeavor of the three former clauses is, to tie the hand of the legislator and his subordinates, by the fear of nullity, and the

remote apprehension of general resistance and insurrection. The aim of this fourth clause is to raise the hand of the individual concerned to prevent the apprehended infraction of his rights at the moment when he looks upon it as about to take place.

Whenever you are about to be oppressed, you have a right to resist oppression: whenever you conceive yourself to be oppressed, conceive yourself to have a right to make resistance, and act accordingly. In proportion as a law of any kind—any act of power, supreme or subordinate, legislative, administrative, or judicial, is unpleasant to a man, especially if, in consideration of such its unpleasantness, his opinion is, that such act of power ought not to have been exercised,

he of course looks upon it as oppression: as often as anything of this sort happens to a man—as often as anything happens to a man to inflame his passions,—this article, for fear his passions should not be sufficiently inflamed of themselves, sets itself to work to blow the flame, and urges him to resistance. Submit not to any decree or other act of power, of the justice of which you are not yourself perfectly convinced. If a constable call upon you to serve in the militia, shoot the constable and not the enemy;—if the commander of a press-gang trouble you, push him into the sea—if a bailiff, throw him out of the window. If a judge sentence you to be imprisoned or put to death, have a dagger ready, and take a stroke first at the judge.

Collected Documents

Declaration of the Rights of Man and of Citizens (1789)[1]

The representatives of the people of France, formed into a National Assembly, considering that ignorance, neglect, or contempt of human rights, are the sole causes of public misfortunes and corruptions of Government, have resolved to set forth in a solemn declaration, these natural, imprescriptible, and inalienable rights: that this declaration being constantly present to the minds of the members of the body social, they may be for ever kept attentive to their rights and their duties; that the acts of the legislative and executive powers of government, being capable of being every moment compared with the end of political institutions, may be more respected; and also, that the future claims of the citizens, being directed by simple and incontestible principles, may always tend to the maintenance of the Constitution, and the general happiness.

For these reasons, the National Assembly doth recognise and declare, in the presence of the Supreme Being, and with the hope of his blessing and favour, the following *sacred* rights of men and of citizens:

I. Men are born, and always continue, free and equal in respect of their rights. Civil distinctions, therefore, can be founded only on public utility.

II. The end of all political associations, is the preservation of the natural and imprescriptible rights of man; and these rights are liberty, property, security, and resistance of oppression.

III. The nation is essentially the source of all sovereignty; nor can any individual, or any body of men, be entitled to any authority which is not expressly derived from it.

IV. Political liberty consists in the power of doing whatever does not injure another. The exercise of the natural rights of every man, has no other limits than those which are necessary to secure to every *other* man the free exercise of the same rights; and these limits are determinable only by the law.

V. The law ought to prohibit only actions hurtful to society. What is not prohibited by the law, should not be hindered; nor should any one be compelled to that which the law does not require.

VI. The law is an expression of the will of the

community. All citizens have a right to concur, either personally, or by their representatives, in its formation. It should be the same to all, whether it protects or punishes; and all being equal in its sight, are equally eligible to all honours, places, and employments, according to their different abilities, without any other distinction than that created by their virtues and talents.

VII. No man should be accused, arrested, or held in confinement, except in cases determined by the law, and according to the forms which it has prescribed. All who promote, solicit, execute, or cause to be executed, arbitrary orders, ought to be punished, and every citizen called upon, or apprehended by virtue of the law, ought immediately to obey, and renders himself culpable by resistance.

VIII. The law ought to impose no other penalties but such as are absolutely and evidently necessary; and no one ought to be punished, but in virtue of a law promulgated before the offence, and legally applied.

IX. Every man being presumed innocent till he has been convicted, whenever his detention becomes indispensable, all rigour to him, more than is necessary to secure his person, ought to be provided against by the law.

X. No man ought to be molested on account of his opinions, not even on account of his *religious* opinions, provided his avowal of them does not disturb the public order established by the law.

XI. The unrestrained communication of thoughts and opinions being one of the most precious rights of man, every citizen may speak, write, and publish freely, provided he is responsible for the abuse of this liberty, in cases determined by the law.

XII. A public force being necessary to give security to the rights of men and of citizens, that force is instituted for the benefit of the community and not for the particular benefit of the persons to whom it is intrusted.

XIII. A common contribution being necessary for the support of the public force, and for defraying the other expenses of government, it ought to be divided equally among the members of the community, according to their abilities.

NOTE

1. Prefixed to the French Constitution of 1791. The translation is by Thomas Paine as it appears in his *Rights of Man.*

Notes and Questions

1. Compare the Virginia Declaration of Rights with the French Declaration of the Rights of Man and of Citizens. How are they alike or different? Are both equally susceptible to Bentham's criticisms?

2. Compare the Virginia Declaration with the U.S. Bill of Rights or the U.N. Declaration of Rights. (See Appendix.) How are they alike or different? Do the same criticisms apply? Do they serve different functions?

Virginia Declaration of Rights (1776)

A Declaration of Rights Made by the Representatives of the Good People of Virginia, Assembled in Full and Free Convention; Which Rights Do Pertain to Them and Their Posterity, as the Basis and Foundation of Government

Sec. 1. That all men are by nature equally free and independent, and have certain inherent rights, of which, when they enter into a state of

society, they cannot by any compact deprive or divest their posterity; namely, the enjoyment of life and liberty, with the means of acquiring and possessing property, and pursuing and obtaining happiness and safety.

Sec. 2. That all power is vested in, and consequently derived from, the people; that magistrates are the trustees and servants, and at all times amenable to them.

Sec. 3. That government is, or ought to be instituted for the common benefit, protection, and security of the people, nation, or community; of all the various modes and forms of government, that is best which is capable of producing the greatest degree of happiness and safety, and is most effectually secured against the danger of maladministration; and that when any government shall be found inadequate or contrary to these purposes, a majority of the community hath an indubitable, unalienable and indefeasible right to reform, alter or abolish it, in such manner as shall be judged most conducive to the public weal.

Sec. 4. That no man, or set of men, are entitled to exclusive or separate emoluments or privileges from the community, but in consideration of publick services; which, not being descendible, neither ought the offices of magistrate, legislator or judge to be hereditary.

Sec. 5. That the legislative and executive powers of the state should be separate and distinct from the judiciary; and that the members of the two first may be restrained from oppression, by feeling and participating the burthens of the people, they should, at fixed periods, be reduced to a private station, return into that body from which they were originally taken, and the vacancies be supplied by frequent, certain, and regular elections, in which all, or any part of the former members to be again eligible or ineligible, as the laws shall direct.

Sec. 6. That elections of members to serve as representatives of the people in assembly, ought to be free; and that all men having sufficient evidence of permanent common interest with, and attachment to the community, have the right of suffrage, and cannot be taxed or deprived of their property for publick uses, without their own consent, or that of their representatives so elected, nor bound by any law to which they have not, in like manner, assented for the public good.

Sec. 7. That all power of suspending laws, or the execution of laws, by an authority without consent of the representatives of the people, is injurious to their rights, and ought not to be exercised.

Sec. 8. That in all capital or criminal prosecutions a man hath a right to demand the cause and nature of his accusation, to be confronted with the accusers and witnesses, to call for evidence in his favour, and to a speedy trial by an impartial jury of his vicinage, without whose unanimous consent he cannot be found guilty; nor can he be compelled to give evidence against himself; that no man be deprived of his liberty, except by the law of the land or the judgment of his peers.

Sec. 9. That excessive bail ought not to be required, nor excessive fines imposed, nor cruel and unusual punishments inflicted.

Sec. 10. That general warrants, whereby an officer or messenger may be commanded to search suspected places without evidence of a fact committed, or to seize any person or persons not named, or whose offence is not particularly described and supported by evidence, are grievous and oppressive, and ought not to be granted.

Sec. 11. That in controversies respecting property, and in suits between man and man, the ancient trial by jury is preferable to any other, and ought to be held sacred.

Sec. 12. That the freedom of the press is one of the great bulwarks of liberty, and can never be restrained but by despotick governments.

Sec. 13. That a well-regulated militia, composed of the body of the people trained to arms, is the proper, natural and safe defence of a free state; that standing armies in time of peace should be avoided as dangerous to liberty; and that in all cases the military should be under strict subordination to, and governed by, the civil power.

Sec. 14. That people have a right to uniform government; and, therefore, that no government separate from, or independent of the government of Virginia, ought to be erected or established within the limits thereof.

Sec. 15. That no free government, or the blessings of liberty, can be preserved to any people, but by a firm adherence to justice, moderation, temperance, frugality and virtue, and by frequent recurrence to fundamental principles.

Sec. 16. That religion, or the duty which we owe our Creator, and the manner of discharging it, can be directed only by reason and conviction, not by force or violence; and therefore all men are equally entitled to the free exercise of religion, according to the dictates of conscience; and that it is the mutual duty of all to practise Christian forbearance, love, and charity towards each other.

Notes and Questions

The Federalist 84

1. One of the great controversies regarding the adoption of the U.S. Constitution was whether it should contain a bill of rights. It was originally proposed (and adopted, strictly speaking) without one. (See the U.S. Constitution, Articles 1–7, in Appendix.) Alexander Hamilton is arguing that the Constitution should be adopted as proposed, with no amendment in the form of a bill of rights. Is he, like Bentham, arguing that there are no natural rights?

2. If there are no natural rights, why is it unnecessary to enumerate rights in the Constitution? Do you agree that the protections Hamilton lists from the body of the Constitution are adequate to protect basic civil rights? Do you agree that a bill of rights applies only to monarchies and not to republics? Why or why not?

3. Notice that Hamilton, in responding to the claim that the New York Constitution protects rights by incorporating the English statutory and common law, makes the same distinction between fundamental — or constitutional law — and ordinary law that Coke makes in the Corwin selection and that is also made in the Concord Resolutions. Do you see the significance of this distinction? Could it be used as an argument for or against putting a bill of rights in a constitution?

4. Why, according to Hamilton, would a written bill of rights be dangerous?

5. Do you agree that any statement of rights (such as freedom of the press) is necessarily so vague and so subject to interpretation as to rely on public opinion? Has the Bill of Rights been subject to interpretation? Has the interpretation been subject to the influence of public opinion? If so, does writing it into the Constitution make any difference?

6. Hamilton asserts that in the last analysis "the only solid basis of all our rights . . . must altogether depend on public opinion and on the general spirit of the people and of the government." He's right, isn't he? No government, whatever its structure or constitution, is immune to abuse, corruption, and apathy. Government is also subject to the general assumptions, attitudes, values, and beliefs held by the population at large. A constitution did not save communist sympathizers from Joseph McCarthy or Jews from Hitler. At the same time, Hamilton would have been the first to agree that some forms of government are more susceptible to abuse than others. Is it reasonable to expect a constitution to protect fundamental rights? What should we be able to expect from a constitution? From a government?

The Federalist 84
ALEXANDER HAMILTON

On Alleged Defects in the Constitution

In the course of the foregoing review of the Constitution I have taken notice of and endeavored to answer most of the objections which have appeared against it. There, however, remain a few which either did not fall naturally under any particular head or were forgotten in their proper places. These shall now be discussed; but as the subject has been drawn into great length, I shall so far consult brevity as to comprise all my observations on these miscellaneous points in a single paper.

The most considerable of the remaining objections is that the plan of the Convention contains no bill of rights. Among other answers given to this, it has been upon different occasions remarked that the constitutions of several of the States are in a similar predicament. I add that New York is of the number; and yet the opposers of the new system in this State who profess an unlimited admiration for its Constitution, are among the most intemperate partisans of a bill of rights. To justify their zeal in this matter, they allege two things: one is that though the Constitution of New York has no bill of rights prefixed to it, yet it contains in the body of it various provisions in favor of particular privileges and rights, which, in substance, amount to the same thing; the other is that the Constitution adopts, in their full extent, the common and statute law of Great Britain, by which many other rights, not expressed in it, are equally secured.

To the first I answer that the Constitution proposed by the Convention contains, as well as the Constitution of this State, a number of such provisions.

Independent of those which relate to the structure of the government, we find the following: Article I, section 3, clause 7, "Judgment in cases of impeachment shall not extend further than to removal from office, and disqualification to hold and enjoy any office of honor, trust, or profit under the United States; but the party convicted shall, nevertheless, be liable and subject to indictment, trial, judgment, and punishment according to law"; section 9 of the same article, clause 2, "The privilege of the writ of *habeas corpus* shall not be suspended, unless when in cases of rebellion or invasion the public safety may require it"; clause 3, "No bill of attainder or *ex post facto* law shall be passed"; clause 7, "No title of nobility shall be granted by the United States; and no person holding any office of profit or trust under them, shall, without the consent of the Congress, accept of any present, emolument, office, or title of any kind whatever, from any king, prince, or foreign State"; article 3, section 2, clause 3, "The trial of all crimes, except in cases of impeachment, shall be by jury; and such trial shall be held in the State where the said crimes shall have been committed; but when not committed within any State, the trial shall be at such place or places as the Congress may by law have directed"; section 3 of the same article, "Treason against the United States shall consist only in levying war against them, or in adhering to their enemies, giving them aid and comfort. No person shall be convicted of treason, unless on the testimony of two witnesses to the same overt act, or on confession in open court"; and clause 3 of the same section, "The Congress shall have power to declare the punishment of treason; but no attainder of treason shall work corruption of blood, or forfeiture, except during the life of the person attainted."

It may well be a question whether these are not, upon the whole, of equal importance with any which are to be found in the Constitution of this State. The establishment of the writ of *habeas corpus*, the prohibition of *ex post facto* laws, and of titles of nobility, to which we have no corresponding provisions in our Constitution, are, perhaps, greater securities to liberty and republicanism than any it contains. The creation of crimes after the commission of the fact, or, in other words, the subjecting of men to punishment for things which, when they were done, were breaches of no law, and the practice of arbitrary imprisonment, have been in all ages the favorite and most formidable instruments of tyranny. The observations of the judicious Blackstone in reference to the latter are well worthy of recital. "To bereave a man of life," says he, "or by violence to confiscate his estate without accusation or trial, would be so gross and notorious an act of despotism as must at once convey the alarm of tyranny throughout the whole nation; but confinement of the person, by secretly hurrying him to jail, where his sufferings are unknown or forgotten, is a less public, a less striking, and, therefore, a more dangerous engine of arbitrary government." And as a remedy for this fatal evil he is everywhere peculiarly emphatical in his encomiums on the *Habeas Corpus* Act, which in one place he calls "the bulwark of the British Constitution."

Nothing need be said to illustrate the importance of the prohibition of titles of nobility. This may truly be denominated the corner-stone of republican government; for so long as they are excluded there can never be serious danger that the government will be any other than that of the people.

To the second, that is, to the pretended establishment of the common and statute law by the Constitution, I answer that they are expressly made subject "to such alterations and provisions as the legislature shall from time to time make concerning the same." They are, therefore, at any moment liable to repeal by the ordinary legislative power, and, of course, have no constitutional sanction. The only use of the declaration was to recognize the ancient law, and to remove doubts which might have been occasioned by the Revolution. This consequently can be considered as no part of a declaration of rights; which under our constitutions must be intended as limitations of the power of the government itself.

It has been several times truly remarked that bills of rights are, in their origin, stipulations between kings and their subjects, abridgments of prerogative in favor of privilege, reservations of rights not surrendered to the prince. Such was Magna Charta, obtained by the barons, sword in hand, from King John. Such were the subsequent confirmations of that charter by succeeding

princes. Such was the Petition of Right assented to by Charles I, in the beginning of his reign. Such, also, was the Declaration of Right presented by the Lords and Commons to the Prince of Orange in 1688, and afterward thrown into the form of an act of Parliament called the Bill of Rights. It is evident, therefore, that, according to their primitive signification, they have no application to constitutions professedly founded upon the power of the people, and executed by their immediate representatives and servants. Here, in strictness, the people surrender nothing; and, as they retain everything, they have no need of particular reservations. "We, the people of the United States, to secure the blessings of liberty to ourselves and our posterity, do ordain and establish this Constitution for the United States of America." Here is a better recognition of popular rights than volumes of those aphorisms which make the principal figure in several of our State bills of rights, and which would sound much better in a treatise of ethics than in a constitution of government.

But a minute detail of particular rights is certainly far less applicable to a constitution like that under consideration, which is merely intended to regulate the general political interests of the nation, than to a constitution which has the regulation of every species of personal and private concerns. If, therefore, the loud clamors against the plan of the Convention on this score are well founded, no epithets of reprobation will be too strong for the Constitution of this State; but the truth is that both of them contain all which, in relation to their objects, is reasonably to be desired.

I go further, and affirm that bills of rights, in the sense and to the extent in which they are contended for, are not only unnecessary in the proposed Constitution, but would even be dangerous. They would contain various exceptions to powers not granted, and on this very account would afford a colorable pretext to claim more than were granted; for why declare that things shall not be done which there is no power to do? Why, for instance, should it be said that the liberty of the press shall not be restrained, when no power is given by which restrictions may be imposed? I will not contend that such a provision would confer a regulating power, but it is evident that it would furnish, to men disposed to usurp, a plausible pretence for claiming that power. They might urge with a semblance of reason that the Constitution ought not to be charged with the absurdity of providing against the abuse of an authority which was not given, and that the provision against restraining the liberty of the press afforded a clear implication that a power to prescribe proper regulations concerning it was intended to be vested in the national government. This may serve as a specimen of the numerous handles which would be given to the doctrine of constructive powers by the indulgence of an injudicious zeal for bills of rights.

On the subject of the liberty of the press, as much has been said, I cannot forbear adding a remark or two: in the first place I observe that there is not a syllable concerning it in the Constitution of this State; in the next, I contend that whatever has been said about it in that of any other State amounts to nothing. What signifies a declaration that "the liberty of the press shall be inviolably preserved"? What is the liberty of the press? Who can give it any definition which would not leave the utmost latitude for evasion? I hold it to be impracticable; and from this, I infer that its security, whatever fine declarations may be inserted in any constitution respecting it, must altogether depend on public opinion and on the general spirit of the people and of the government. And here, after all, as is intimated upon another occasion, must we seek for the only solid basis of all our rights.

There remains but one other view of this matter to conclude the point. The truth is, after all the declamation we have heard, that the Constitution is itself, in every rational sense, and to every useful purpose, a bill of rights. The several bills of rights in Great Britain form its Constitution, and, conversely, the constitution of each State is its bill of rights; and the proposed Constitution, if adopted, will be the bill of rights of the Union. Is it one object of a bill of rights to declare and specify the political privileges of the citizens in the structure and administration of the government? This is done in the most ample and precise manner in the plan of the Convention; comprehending various precautions for the public security, which are not to be found in any of the State constitutions. Is another object of a bill of rights to define certain immunities and modes of proceeding, which are relative to personal and private concerns? This we have seen has also been attended to, in a variety of cases, in the same plan. Adverting, therefore, to the substantial meaning of a bill of rights, it is absurd to allege that it is not found in the work of the Convention. It may be said that it does not go far enough, though it will not be easy to make this appear; but it can with no propriety be contended that there is no such thing. It certainly must be immaterial what mode is observed as to the order of declaring the rights of the citizens, if they are to be found in any part of the instrument which establishes the government; and, hence, it must be apparent that much of what has been said on this subject rests merely on verbal and nominal distinctions, entirely foreign from the substance of the thing.

* * *

SECTION 3

Democracy, Representation, and Legislative Process

We have been considering so far various constitutional limits on government or the political process. These constitutional features focus and constrain the political process so that it must function in certain ways and—more important—may not function in certain other ways. The constitutional features that we have considered so far at least have been aimed at structuring government so that it may not do certain things. That is, the nature of limits and setting limits are indeed major functions and properties of political constitutions.

But constitutions have positive features as well. For example, while constitutions limit power, they also delegate it. They may limit (indeed, may eliminate) offices, but they also authorize them. One of the most important and basic positive features of the constitution of government is to specify the official legislative process—that is, the authorized manner of making law. Aristotle and Montesquieu both discuss the legislative function of government. It is basic—a fundamental formal feature of both states and legal systems. There cannot be a state or a legal system without some means of performing the legislative function. The process may be very simple, for example, it might be the common recognition of the king's word as law. That is structurally a very simple process, but it is nevertheless a recognized way of making law. Try to imagine a legal system with *no* way of making law. If you can imagine anything at all, it is not a legal system. It might be a former legal system, or a potential legal system, but it is not a legal system. Furthermore, neither is it a state. The legislative function is fundamental to government; there is no government without it.

What, then, is the legislative function? It is the process of making or enacting law. There are innumerable ways in which that purpose can be accomplished, numerous forms and combinations of monarchies, aristocracies, oligarchies, dictatorships. Aristotle catalogued them rather well in "On Democracy," from *Politics*, the first selection in this section. We will consider only one legislative process here, namely, democracy. Keep in mind that there are many forms of democracy (we will consider only direct and representative here) and that democratic forms of government can be combined with other forms of government, such as in the parliamentary monarchies of England, Sweden, and other countries.

The most basic feature of democracy is commitment to an ideal of representation or participation in government. Aristotle's notion of democracy is participatory. The ideal behind it is the common self-government of equals. Of course, he has in mind a comparatively small group, more like the government of a small city than of a modern nation. Can Aristotle's ideas apply to vast countries and complex governments like that of the United States? In the second selection John Stuart Mill provides an answer to this question. Mill's solution (the common modern solution) is to move to representative democracy. Alexis de Tocqueville, however, in the third selection, sets out some apparent problems with American representative democracy, and in the last selection contemporary philosopher Robert Paul Wolff specifically attacks the solution of representative democracy. What do you think of his proposal for a modern direct democracy? Be prepared to explain why you agree or disagree with him.

Notes and Questions

ARISTOTLE, from *Politics*

1. Note first that Aristotle used the term *democracy* to refer to a perversion of government. (This point is discussed in Chapter One, Section 1.) Democracy, for Aristotle, refers to government of the many for the benefit of themselves rather than for the benefit of all. Any government that uses its power for the benefit of itself rather than for the common good is a perversion of government, according to Aristotle. Thus, he uses the phrase *constitutional government* to refer to government of the many for the benefit of all. Since *democracy* has come to mean this, and *constitutional government* has come to have a different meaning, we will use the term *democracy* in its modern sense. This is simply a terminological notation, but keep it in mind when you read Aristotle.

2. Aristotle was among the first to point out the virtues of democratic government. He offers several arguments in its favor. First, he argues that there may be a better chance of arriving at

good judgments by looking to the collective wisdom of the entire citizenry. What objection does this answer? Is it a realistic answer? Does it hold true today (if it ever did), when much government action requires judgment on technical issues which require special expertise to deal with? Do legislators have special expertise in technical matters? What sort of judgment is the collective wisdom good at?

3. Aristotle's second argument is a practical one. Democracy promotes harmony and reduces hostility. Why does he think so? Do you agree?

4. Next, Aristotle argues that democracy incorporates the necessary elements for good government, namely, wealth and freedom. Why would democracy do this more than any other form of government? Why is it good to do it? Furthermore, Aristotle argues that if education and virtue are added, justice and valor, which are necessary for the good life, will also be promoted. How is this addition connected to democracy, if at all? How would one add virtue to a political system or society? Perhaps by adding education? By creating the right environment? How would democracy do this better than other forms of government?

5. Aristotle also argues that the best government focuses on the middle class. What does he mean by this? Why is it good? Are we still talking about democracy here? What is the connection? Is the middle-class argument a derivative or an implication of the argument for democracy? Or is it an addition to democracy, but still dependent on it as a necessary condition for the good life? Or is it a completely separate issue?

[From] Politics

ARISTOTLE

On Democracy

Book III

* * *

C.11. . . . The principle that the multitude ought to be supreme rather than the few best is one that is maintained, and, though not free from difficulty, yet seems to contain an element of truth. For the many, of whom each individual is but an ordinary person, when they meet together may very likely be better than the few good, if regarded not individually but collectively, just as a feast to which many contribute is better than a dinner provided out of a single purse. For each individual among the many has a share of virtue and prudence, and when they meet together, they become in a manner one man, who has many feet, and hands, and senses; that is a figure of their mind and disposition. Hence the many are better judges than a single man of music and poetry; for some understand one part, and some another, and among them they understand the whole. There is a similar combination of qualities in good men, who differ from any individual of the many, as the beautiful are said to differ from those who are not beautiful, and works of art from realties, because in them the scattered elements are combined, although, if taken separately, the eye of one person or some other feature in another person would be fairer than in the picture. Whether this principle can apply to every democracy, and to all bodies of men, is not clear. Or rather, by heaven, in some cases it is impossible of application; for the argument would equally hold about brutes; and wherein, it will be asked, do some men differ from brutes? But there may be bodies of men about whom our statement is nevertheless true. And if so, the difficulty which has been already raised, and also another which is akin to it — viz. what power should be assigned to the mass of freemen and citizens, who are not rich and have no personal merit — are both solved. There is still a danger in allowing them to share the great offices of state, for their folly will lead them into error, and their dishonesty into crime. But there is a danger also in not letting them share, for a state in which many poor men are excluded from office will necessarily be full of enemies. The only way of escape is to assign to them some deliberative and judicial functions. For this reason Solon and certain other legislators give them the power of electing to offices, and of calling the magistrates to account, but they do not allow them to hold office singly. When they meet together their perceptions are quite good enough, and combined with the better class they are useful to the state (just as impure food when mixed with what is pure sometimes makes the entire mass more wholesome than a small quantity of the pure would be), but each individual, left to himself, forms an imperfect judgment. On the other hand the popular form of government involves certain difficulties. In the first place, it might be objected that he who can judge of the healing of a sick man would be one who could himself heal his disease, and make him whole — that is, in other words, the physician; and so in all professions and arts. As, then, the physician ought to be called to account by physicians, so ought men in general to be called to account by their peers. But physicians are of three kinds: — there is the ordinary practitioner, and there is the physician of the higher class, and thirdly the intelligent man who has studied the art: in all arts there is such a class; and we attribute the power of judging to them quite as much as to professors of the art. Secondly, does not the same principle apply to elections? For a right election can only be made by those who have knowledge; those who know geometry, for example, will choose a geometrician rightly, and those who know how to steer, a pilot; and, even if there be some occupations and arts in which private persons share in the ability to choose, they certainly cannot choose better than those who know. So that, according to this argument, neither the election of magistrates, nor the calling of them to account, should be entrusted to the many. Yet possibly these objections are to a great extent met by our old answer, that if the people are not utterly degraded, although individually they may be worse judges than those who have a special knowledge — as a body they are as good or better. Moreover, there are some arts whose products are not judged of solely, or best, by the artists themselves, namely those arts whose products are recognized even by those who do not possess the art; for example, the knowledge of the house is not limited to the builder only; the user, or, in other words, the master of the house will even be a better judge than the builder, just as the pilot will judge better of a rudder than the carpenter, and the guest will judge better of a feast than the cook.

This difficulty seems now to be sufficiently answered, but there is another akin to it. That inferior persons should have authority in greater matters than the good would appear to be a strange thing, yet the election and calling to account of the magistrates is the greatest of all. And these, as I was saying, are functions which in some states are assigned to the people, for the assembly is supreme in all such matters. Yet persons of any age, and having but a small property qualification, sit in the assembly and deliberate and judge, although for the great officers of state, such as treasurers and generals, a high qualification is required. This difficulty may be solved in the same manner as the preceding, and the present practice of democracies may be really defensible. For the power does not reside in the dicast, or senator, or ecclesiast, but in the court, and the senate, and the assembly, of which individual senators, or ecclesiasts, or dicasts, are only parts or members. And for this reason the many may claim to have a higher authority than the few; for the people, and the senate, and the courts consist of many persons, and their property collectively is greater than the property of one or of a few individuals holding great offices. But enough of this.

* * *

C.12. In all sciences and arts the end is a good, and the greatest good and in the highest degree a good in the most authoritative of all—this is the political science of which the good is justice, in other words, the common interest. All men think justice to be a sort of equality; and to a certain extent they agree in the philosophical distinctions which have been laid down by us about Ethics. For they admit that justice is a thing and has a relation to persons, and that equals ought to have equality. But there still remains a question: equality or inequality of what? here is a difficulty which calls for political speculation. For very likely some persons will say that offices of state ought to be unequally distributed according to superior excellence, in whatever respect, of the citizen, although there is no other difference between him and the rest of the community; for that those who differ in any one respect have different rights and claims. But, surely, if this is true, the complexion or height of a man, or any other advantage, will be a reason for his obtaining a greater share of political rights. The error here lies upon the surface, and may be illustrated from the other arts and sciences. When a number of flute-players are equal in their art, there is no reason why those of them who are better born should have better flutes given to them; for they will not play any better on the flute, and the superior instrument should be reserved for him who is the superior artist. If what I am saying is still obscure, it will be made clearer as we proceed. For if there were a superior flute-player who was far inferior in birth and beauty, although either of these may be a greater good than the art of flute-playing, and may excel flute-playing in a greater ratio than he excels the others in his art, still he ought to have the best flutes given to him, unless the advantages of wealth and birth contribute to excellence in flute-playing, which they do not. Moreover, upon this principle any good may be compared with any other. For if a given height may be measured against wealth and against freedom, height in general may be so measured. Thus if A excels in height more than B in virtue, even if virtue in general excels height still more, all goods will be commensurable; for if a certain amount is better than some other, it is clear that some other will be equal. But since no such comparison can be made, it is evident that there is good reason why in politics men do not

ground their claim to office on every sort of inequality any more than in the arts. For if some be slow, and others swift, that is no reason why the one should have little and the others much; it is in gymnastic contests that such excellence is rewarded. Whereas the rival claims of candidates for office can only be based on the possession of elements which enter into the composition of a state. And therefore the noble, or free-born, or rich, may with good reason claim office; for holders of offices must be freemen and tax-payers: a state can be no more composed entirely of poor men than entirely of slaves. But if wealth and freedom are necessary elements, justice and valour are equally so; for without the former qualities a state cannot exist at all, without the latter not well.

C.13. If the existence of the state is alone to be considered, then it would seem that all, or some at least, of these claims are just; but, if we take into account a good life, then, as I have already said, education and virtue have superior claims. As, however, those who are equal in one thing ought not to have an equal share in all, nor those who are unequal in one thing to have an unequal share in all, it is certain that all forms of government which rest on either of these principles are perversions. All men have a claim in a certain sense, as I have already admitted, but all have not an absolute claim. The rich claim because they have a greater share in the land, and land is the common element of the state; also they are generally more trustworthy in contracts. The free claim under the same title as the noble; for they are nearly akin. For the noble are citizens in a truer sense than the ignoble, and good birth is always valued in a man's own home and country. Another reason is, that those who are sprung from better ancestors are likely to be better men, for nobility is excellence of race. Virtue, too, may be truly said to have a claim, for justice has been acknowledged by us to be a social virtue, and it implies all others. Again, the many may urge their claim against the few; for, when taken collectively, and compared with the few, they are stronger and richer and better. But, what if the good, the rich, the noble, and the other classes who make up a state, are all living together in the same city, will there, or will there not, be any doubt who shall rule?—No doubt at all in determining who ought to rule in each of the above-mentioned forms of government. For states are characterized by differences in their governing bodies — one of them has a government of the rich, another of the virtuous, and so on. But a difficulty arises when all these elements coexist. How are we to decide? Suppose the virtuous to be very few in number: may we consider their numbers in relation to their duties and ask whether they are enough to administer the state, or so many as will make up a state? Objections may be urged against all the aspirants to political power. For those who found their claims on wealth or family might be thought to have no basis of justice; on this principle, if any one person were richer than all the rest, it is clear that he ought to be ruler of them. In like manner he who is very distinguished by his birth ought to have the superiority over all those who claim on the ground that they are freeborn. In an aristocracy, or government of the best, a like difficulty occurs about virtue; for if one citizen be better than the other members of the government, however good they may be, he too, upon the same principle of justice, should rule over them. And if the people are to be supreme because they are stronger than the few, then if one man, or more than one, but not a majority, is stronger than the many, they ought to rule, and not the many.

All these considerations appear to show that none of the principles on which men claim to rule and to hold all other men in subjection to them are strictly right. To those who claim to be masters of the government on the ground of their virtue or their wealth, the many might fairly answer that they themselves are often better and richer than the few — I do not say individually, but collectively. And another ingenious objection which is sometimes put forward may be met in a similar manner. Some persons doubt whether the legislator who desires to make the justest laws ought to legislate with a view to the good of the higher classes or of the many, when the case which we have mentioned occurs. Now what is just or right is to be interpreted in the sense of 'what is equal'; and that which is right in the sense of being equal is to be considered with reference to the advantage of the state, and the common good of the citizens. And a citizen is one who shares in governing and being governed. He

differs under different forms of government, but in the best state he is one who is able and willing to be governed and to govern with a view to the life of virtue.

* * *

Book IV

C.2. In our original discussion about governments we divided them into three true forms: kingly rule, aristocracy, and constitutional government, and three corresponding perversions — tyranny, oligarchy and democracy. Of kingly rule and of aristocracy we have already spoken, for the inquiry into the perfect state is the same thing with the discussion of the two forms thus named, since both imply a principle of virtue provided with external means. We have already determined in what aristocracy and kingly rule differ from one another, and when the latter should be established. In what follows we have to describe the so-called constitutional government, which bears the common name of all constitutions, and the other forms, tyranny, oligarchy, and democracy.

It is obvious which of the three perversions is the worst, and which is the next in badness. That which is the perversion of the first and most divine is necessarily the worst. And just as a royal rule, if not a mere name, must exist by virtue of some great personal superiority in the king, so tyranny, which is the worst of governments, is necessarily the farthest removed from a well-constituted form; oligarchy is little better, for it is a long way from aristocracy, and democracy is the most tolerable of the three.

A writer who preceded me has already made these distinctions, but his point of view is not the same as mine. For he lays down the principle that when all the constitutions are good (the oligarchy and the rest being virtuous), democracy is the worst, but the best when all are bad. Whereas we maintain that they are in any case defective, and that one oligarchy is not to be accounted better than another, but only less bad.

Not to pursue this question further at present, let us begin by determining (1) how many varieties of constitution there are (since of democracy and oligarchy there are several); (2) what constitution is the most generally acceptable, and what is eligible in the next degree after the perfect state; and besides this what other there is which is aristocratical and well-constituted, and at the same time adapted to states in general; (3) of the other forms of government to whom each is suited. For democracy may meet the needs of some better than oligarchy, and conversely. In the next place (4) we have to consider in what manner a man ought to proceed who desires to establish some one among these various forms, whether of democracy or of oligarchy; and lastly, (5) having briefly discussed these subjects to the best of our power, we will endeavour to ascertain the modes of ruin and preservation both of constitutions generally and of each separately, and to what causes they are to be attributed.

C.3. The reason why there are many forms of government is that every state contains many elements. In the first place we see that all states are made up of families, and in the multitude of citizens there must be some rich and some poor, and some in a middle condition; the rich are heavy-armed, and the poor not. Of the common people, some are husband-men, and some traders, and some artisans. There are also among the notables differences of wealth and property — for example, in the number of horses which they keep, for they cannot afford to keep them unless they are rich. And therefore in old times the cities whose strength lay in their cavalry were oligarchies, and they used cavalry in wars against their neighbours; as was the practice of the Eretrians and Chalcidians, and also of the Magnesians on the river Mæander, and of other peoples in Asia. Besides differences of wealth there are differences of rank and merit, and there are some other elements which were mentioned by us when in treating of aristocracy we enumerated the essentials of a state. Of these elements, sometimes all, sometimes the lesser and sometimes the greater number, have a share in the government. It is evident then that there must be many forms of government, differing in kind, since the parts of which they are composed differ from each other in kind. For a constitution is an organization of offices, which all the citizens distribute among themselves, according to the power which different classes possess, for example the rich or the poor, or according to some principle of equality which includes both. There must therefore be as many forms of government as there are modes of arranging the offices, according to the superiorities and the differences of the parts of the state.

There are generally thought to be two principal forms: as men say of the winds that there are but two — north and south, and that the rest of them are only variations of these, so of governments there are said to be only two forms — democracy and oligarchy. For aristocracy is considered to be a kind of oligarchy, as being the rule of a few, and the so-called constitutional government to be really a democracy, just as among the winds we make the west a variation of the north, and the east of the south wind. Similarly of musical modes there are said to be two kinds, the Dorian and the Phrygian; the other arrangements of the scale are comprehended under one or other of these two. About forms of government this is a very favourite notion. But in either case the better and more exact way is to distinguish, as I have done, the one or two which are true forms, and to regard the others as perversions, whether of the most perfectly attempered mode or of the best form of government: we may compare the severer and more overpowering modes to the oligarchical forms, and the more relaxed and gentler ones to the democratic.

* * *

C.11. We have now to inquire what is the best constitution for most states, and the best life for most men, neither assuming a standard of virtue which is above ordinary persons, nor an education which is exceptionally favoured by nature and circumstances, nor yet an ideal state which is an aspiration only, but having regard to the life in which the majority are able to share, and to the form of government which states in general can attain. As to those aristocracies, as they are called, of which we were just now speaking, they either lie beyond the possibilities of the greater number of states, or they approximate to the so-called constitutional government, and therefore need no separate discussion. And in fact the conclusion at which we arrive respecting all these forms rests upon the same grounds. For if what was said in the *Ethics* is true, that the happy life is the life according to virtue lived without impedient, and that virtue is a mean, then the life which is in a mean, and in a mean attainable by every one, must be the best. And the same principles of virtue and vice are characteristic of cities and of constitutions; for the constitution is in a figure the life of the city.

Now in all states there are three elements: one class is very rich, another very poor, and a third i[s] a mean. It is admitted that moderation and the mean are best, and therefore it will clearly be best to possess the gifts of fortune in moderation; for in that condition of life men are most ready to follow rational principle. But he who greatly excels in beauty, strength, birth, or wealth, or on the other hand who is very poor, or very weak, or very much disgraced, finds it difficult to follow rational principle. Of these two the one sort grow into violent and great criminals, the others into rogues and petty rascals. And two sorts of offences correspond to them, the one committed from violence, the other from roguery. Again, the middle class is least likely to shrink from rule, or to be overambitious for it; both of which are injuries to the state. Again, those who have too much of the goods of fortune, strength, wealth, friends, and the like, are neither willing nor able to submit to authority. The evil begins at home; for when they are boys, by reason of the luxury in which they are brought up, they never learn, even at school, the habit of obedience. On the other hand, the very poor, who are in the opposite extreme, are too degraded. So that the one class cannot obey, and can only rule despotically; the other knows not how to command and must be ruled like slaves. Thus arises a city, not of freemen, but of masters and slaves, the one despising, the other envying; and nothing can be more fatal to friendship and good fellowship in states than this: for good fellowship springs from friendship; when men are at enmity with one another, they would rather not even share the same path. But a city ought to be composed, as far as possible, of equals and similars; and these are generally the middle classes. Wherefore the city which is composed of middle-class citizens is necessarily best constituted in respect of the elements of which we say the fabric of the state naturally consists. And this is the class of citizens which is most secure in a state, for they do not, like the poor, covet their neighbours' goods; nor do others covet theirs, as

the poor covet the goods of the rich; and as they neither against others, nor are themselves plotted against, they pass through life safely. Wisely then did Phocylides pray, — 'Many things are best in the mean; I desire to be a middle condition in my city.'

Thus it is manifest that the best political community is formed by citizens of the middle class, and that those states are likely to be well-administered, in which the middle class is large, and stronger if possible than both the other classes, or at any rate than either singly; for the addition of the middle class turns the scale, and prevents either of the extremes from being dominant. Great then is the good fortune of a state in which the citizens have a moderate and sufficient property; for where some possess much, and the others nothing, there may arise an extreme democracy, or a pure oligarchy; or a tyranny may grow out of either extreme, — either out of the most rampant democracy, or out af an oligarchy; but it is not so likely to arise out of the middle constitutions and those akin to them. I will explain the reason of this hereafter, when I speak of the revolutions of states. The mean condition of states is clearly best, for no other is free from faction; and where the middle class is large, there are least likely to be factions and dissensions. For a similar reason large states are less liable to faction than small ones, because in them the middle class is large; whereas in small states it is easy to divide all the citizens into two classes who are either rich or poor, and to leave nothing in the middle. And democracies are safer and more permanent than oligarchies, because they have a middle class which is more numerous and has a greater share in the government; for when there is no middle class, and the poor greatly exceed in number, troubles arise, and the state soon comes to an end. A proof of the superiority of the middle class is that the best legislators have been of a middle condition; for example, Solon, as his own verses testify; and Lycurgus, for he was not a king; and Charondas and almost all legislators.

These considerations will help us to understand why most governments are either democratical or oligarchical. The reason is that the middle class is seldom numerous in them, and whichever party, whether the rich or the common people, transgresses the mean and predominates, draws the constitution its own way, and thus arises either oligarchy or democracy. There is another reason — the poor and the rich quarrel with one another, and whichever side gets the better, instead of establishing a just or popular government, regards political supremacy as the prize of victory, and the one party sets up a democracy and the other an oligarchy. Further, both the parties which had the supremacy in Hellas looked only to the interest of their own form of government, and established in states, the one, democracies, and the other, oligarchies; they thought of their own advantage, of the public not at all. For these reasons the middle form of government has rarely, if ever, existed, and among a very few only. One man alone of all who ever ruled in Hellas was induced to give this middle constitution to states. But it has now become a habit among the citizens of states, not even to care about equality; all men are seeking for dominion, or, if conquered, are willing to submit.

What then is the best form of government, and what makes it the best, is evident; and of other constitutions, since we say that there are many kinds of democracy and many of oligarchy, it is not difficult to see which has the first and which the second or any other place in the order of excellence, now that we have determined which is the best. For that which is nearest to the best must of necessity be better, and that which is further from it worse, if we are judging absolutely and not relatively to given conditions: I say 'relatively to given conditions', since a particular government may be preferable, but another form may be better for some people.

C.12. We have now to consider what and what kind of government is suitable to what and what kind of men. I may begin by assuming, as a general principle common to all governments, that the portion of the state which desires the permanence of the constitution ought to be stronger than that which desires the reverse. Now every city is composed of quality and quantity. By quality I mean freedom, wealth, education, good birth, and by quantity, superiority of numbers.

Quality may exist in one of the classes which make up the state, and quantity in the other. For example, the meanly-born may be more in number than the well-born, or the poor than the rich, yet they may not so much exceed in quantity as they fall short in quality; and therefore there must be a comparison of quantity and quality. Where the number of the poor is more than proportioned to the wealth of the rich, there will naturally be a democracy, varying in form with the sort of people who compose it in each case. If, for example, the husband-men exceed in number, the first form of democracy will then arise; if the artisans and labouring class, the last; and so with the intermediate forms. But where the rich and the notables exceed in quality more than they fall short in quantity, there obligarchy arises, similarly assuming various forms according to the kind of superiority possessed by the oligarchs.

The legislator should always include the middle class in his government; if he makes his laws oligarchical, to the middle class let him look; if he makes them democratical, he should equally by his laws try to attach this class to the state. There only can the government ever be stable where the middle class exceeds one or both of the others, and in that case there will be no fear that the rich will unite with the poor against the rulers. For neither of them will ever be willing to serve the other, and if they look for some form of government more suitable to both, they will find none better than this, for the rich and the poor will never consent to rule in turn, because they mistrust one another. The arbiter is always the one trusted, and he who is in the middle is an arbiter. The more perfect the admixture of the political elements, the more lasting will be the constitution. Many even of those who desire to form aristocratic governments make a mistake, not only in giving too much power to the rich, but in attempting to overreach the people. There comes a time when out of a false good there arises a true evil, since the encroachments of the rich are more destructive to the constitution than those of the people.

*   *   *

Notes and Questions

JOHN STUART MILL, from *Considerations on Representative Government*

1. What is the best form of government, according to Mill? That is, what should the best form of government accomplish? If we grant Mill his initial premise, does it lead to the conclusion that democracy is the best form of government? How does Mill argue that it does?

2. Do you agree that each person manages his or her own affairs or protects his or her own interests best? Why or why not? Would you rather defend your own rights or rely on someone else to do so? Would you like to have the choice of defending your own rights or getting someone else to do so, or would someone else be a better judge of that? Does it matter whether you apply this question to individuals or to the population at large? Who could manage your affairs better than you could or know your interests better than you do?

3. Why is it argued that the view that each individual should advance his own interests promotes universal selfishness? How does Mill answer this objection? What will combat selfishness?

4. What sort of character is needed for good government, according to Mill? Why should democratic government promote the right kind of character? Do you see any similarity between Mill's position and Aristotle's in "On Democracy"?

5. Essentially, Mill is arguing that participation in government builds character and protects individual interests better than any other form of government. If he is right about this, it follows that direct democracy is the best form of government. But does it follow that if direct democracy is not possible, then representative democracy is the next best form?

[From] *Considerations on Representative Government*
JOHN STUART MILL

There is no difficulty in showing that the ideally best form of government is that in which the sovereignty, or supreme controlling power in the last resort, is vested in the entire aggregate of the community, every citizen not only having a voice in the exercise of the ultimate sovereignty, but being, at least occasionally, called on to take an actual part in the government by the personal discharge of some public function, local or general.

To test this proposition, it has to be examined in reference to the two branches into which, as pointed out in the last chapter, the inquiry into the goodness of a government conveniently divides itself, namely, how far it promotes the good management of the affairs of society by means of the existing faculties, moral, intellectual, and active, of its various members, and what is its effect in improving or deteriorating those faculties.

The ideally best form of government, it is scarcely necessary to say, does not mean one which is practicable or eligible in all states of civilization, but the one which, in the circumstances in which it is practicable and eligible, is attended with the greatest amount of beneficial consequences, immediate and prospective. A completely popular government is the only polity which can make out any claim to this character.

It is pre-eminent in both the departments between which the excellence of a political Constitution is divided. It is both more favorable to present good government, and promotes a better and higher form of national character than any other polity whatsoever.

Its superiority in reference to present well-being rests upon two principles, of as universal truth and applicability as any general propositions which can be laid down respecting human affairs. The first is that the rights and interests of every or any person are only secure from being disregarded when the person interested is himself able, and habitually disposed, to stand up for them. The second is, that the general prosperity attains a greater height, and is more widely diffused, in proportion to the amount and variety of the personal energies enlisted in promoting it.

Putting these two propositions into a shape more special to their present application — human beings are only secure from evil at the hands of others in proportion as they have the power of being, and are, self-*protecting*; and they only achieve a high degree of success in their struggle with Nature in proportion as they are self-*dependent*, relying on what they themselves can do, either separately or in concert, rather than on what others do for them.

The former proposition — that each is the only safe guardian of his own rights and interests — is one of those elementary maxims of prudence which every person capable of conducting his own affairs implicitly acts upon wherever he himself is interested. Many, indeed, have a great dislike to it as a political doctrine, and are fond of holding it up to obloquy as a doctrine of universal selfishness. To which we may answer, that whenever it ceases to be true that mankind, as a rule, prefer themselves to others, and those nearest to them to those more remote, from that moment Communism is not only practicable, but the only defensible form of society, and will, when that time arrives, be assuredly carried into effect. For my own part, not believing in universal selfishness, I have no difficulty in admitting that Communism would even now be practicable among the *élite* of mankind, and may become so among the rest. But as this opinion is anything but popular with those defenders of existing institutions who find fault with the doctrine of the general predominance of self-interest, I am inclined to think they do in reality believe that most men consider themselves before other people. It is not, however, necessary to affirm even this much in order to support the claim of all to participate in the sovereign power. We need not suppose that when power resides in an exclusive class, that class will knowingly and deliberately sacrifice the other classes to themselves: it suffices that, in the absence of its natural defenders, the interest of the excluded is always in danger of being overlooked; and, when looked at, is seen with very different eyes from those of the persons whom it directly concerns. In this country, for example, what are called the working classes may be considered as excluded from all direct participation in the government. I do not believe that the classes who do participate in it have in general any intention of sacrificing the working classes to themselves. They once had that intention; witness the persevering attempts so long made to keep down wages by law. But in the present day their ordinary disposition is the very opposite: they willingly make considerable sacrifices especially of their pecuniary interest, for the benefit of the working classes, and err rather by too lavish and indiscriminating beneficence; nor do I believe that any rulers in history have been actuated by a more sincere desire to do their duty toward the poorer portion of their countrymen. Yet does Parliament, or almost any of the members composing it, ever for an instant look at any question with the eyes of a working man? When a subject arises in which the laborers as such have an interest, is it regarded from any point of view but that of the employers of labor? I do not say that the working men's view of these questioins is in general nearer to the truth than the other, but it is sometimes quite as near; and in any case it ought to be respectfully listened to, instead of being, as it is, not merely turned away from, but ignored. On the question of strikes, for instance, it is doubtful if there is so much as one among the leading members of either House who is not firmly convinced that the reason of the matter is unqualifiedly on the side of the masters, and that the men's view of it is simply absurd. Those who have studied the question know well how far this is from being the case, and in how different, and how infinitely less superficial a manner the point would have to be argued if the classes who strike were able to make themselves heard in Parliament.

It is an inherent condition of human affairs that no intention, however sincere, of protecting the interests of others can make it safe or salutary to tie up their own hands. Still more obviously true is it that by their own hands only can any positive and durable improvement of their circumstances in life be worked out. Through the joint influence of these two principles, all free communities have both been more exempt from social injustice and crime, and have attained more brilliant prosperity than any others, or than they themselves after they lost their freedom. Contrast the free states of the world, while their freedom lasted, with the contemporary subjects of monarchical or oligarchical despotism: the Greek cities with the Persian satrapies, the Italian republics, and the free towns of Flanders and Germany, with the feudal monarchies of Europe; Switzerland, Holland, and England with Austria or ante-revolutionary France. Their superior prosperity was too obvious ever to have been gainsaid; while their superiority in good government and social relations is proved by the prosperity, and is manifest besides in every page of history. If we compare, not one age with another, but the different governments which coexisted in the same age, no amount of disorder which exaggeration itself can pretend to have existed amidst the publicity of the free states can be compared for a moment with the contemptuous trampling upon the mass of the people which pervaded the whole life of the monarchical countries, or the disgusting individual tyranny which was of more than daily occurrence under the systems of plunder which they called fiscal arrangements, and in the secrecy of their frightful courts of justice.

It must be acknowledged that the benefits of freedom, so far as they have hitherto been enjoyed, were obtained by the extension of its privileges to a part only of the community, and that a government in which they are extended impartially to all is a desideratum still unrealized. But, though every approach to this has an inde-pendent value, and in many cases more than an approach could not, in the existing state of general improvement, be made, the participation of all in these benefits is the ideally perfect conception of free government. In proportion as any, no matter who, are excluded from it, the interests of the excluded are left without the guaranty accorded to the rest, and they themselves have less scope and encouragement than they might otherwise have to that exertion of their energies for the good of themselves and of the community, to which the general prosperity is always proportioned.

Thus stands the case as regards present well-being — the good management of the affairs of the existing generation. If we now pass to the influence of the form of government upon character, we shall find the superiority of popular government over every other to be, if possible, still more decided and indisputable.

This question really depends upon a still more fundamental one, viz., which of two common types of character, for the general good of humanity, it is most desirable should predominate — the active or the passive type; that which struggles against evils or that which endures them; that which bends to circumstances, or that which endeavors to make circumstances bend to itself.

The commonplaces of moralists and the general sympathies of mankind, are in favor of the passive type. Energetic characters may be admired, but the acquiescent and submissive are those which most men personally prefer. The passiveness of our neighbors increases our own sense of security, and plays into the hands of our willfulness. Passive characters, if we do not happen to need their activity, seem an obstruction the less in our own path. A contented character is not a dangerous rival. Yet nothing is more certain than that improvement in human affairs is wholly the work of the uncontented characters; and, moreover, that it is much easier for an active mind to acquire the virtues of patience, than for a passive one to assume those of energy. . . .

The striving, go-ahead character of England and the United States is only a fit subject of disapproving criticism on account of the very secondary objects on which it commonly expends its strength. In itself it is the foundation of the best hopes for the general improvement of mankind. It has been acutely remarked, that whenever anything goes amiss, the habitual impulse of French people is to say, "Il faut de la patience"; and of English people, "What a shame." The people who think it a shame when anything goes wrong — who rush to the conclusion that the evil could and ought to have been prevented, are those who, in the long run, do most to make the world better. If the desires are low placed, if they extend to little beyond physical comfort, and the show of riches, the immediate results of the energy will not be much more than the continual extension of man's power over material objects; but even this makes room, and prepares the mechanical appliances for the greatest intellectual and social achievements; and while the energy is there, some persons will apply it, and it will be applied more and more, to the perfecting not of outward circumstances alone, but of man's inward nature. Inactivity, unaspiringness, absence of desire, is a more fatal hindrance to improvement than any misdirection of energy, and is that through which alone, when existing in the mass, any very formidable misdirection by an energetic few becomes possible. It is this, mainly, which retains in a savage or semi-savage state the great majority of the human race.

Now there can be no kind of doubt that the passive type of character is favored by the government of one or a few, and the active self-helping type by that of the many. Irresponsible rulers need the quiescence of the ruled more than they need any activity but that which they can compel. Submissiveness to the prescriptions of men as necessities of nature is the lesson inculcated by all governments upon those who are wholly without participation in them. The will of superiors, and the law as the will of superiors, must be passively yielded to. But no men are mere instruments or materials in the hands of their rulers who have will, or spirit, or a spring of internal activity in the rest of their proceedings, and any manifestation of these qualities, instead of receiving encouragement from despots, has to get itself forgiven by them. Even when irresponsible rulers are not sufficiently conscious of dan-

ger from the mental activity of their subjects to be desirous of repressing it, the position itself is a repression. Endeavor is even more effectually restrained by the certainty of its impotence than by any positive discouragement. Between subjection to the will of others and the virtues of self-help and self-government, there is a natural incompatibility. This is more or less complete, according as the bondage is strained or relaxed. Rulers differ very much in the length to which they carry the control of the free agency of their subjects, or the suppression of it by managing their business for them. But the difference is in degree, not in principle; and the best despots often go the greatest lengths in chaining up the free agency of their subjects. A bad despot, when his own personal indulgences have been provided for, may sometimes be willing to let the people alone; but a good despot insists on doing them good by making them do their own business in a better way than they themselves know of. . . .

Very different is the state of the human faculties where a human being feels himself under no other external restraint than the necessities of nature, or mandates of society which he has his share in imposing, and which it is open to him, if he thinks them wrong, publicly to dissent from, and exert himself actively to get altered. No doubt, under a government partially popular, this freedom may be exercised even by those who are not partakers in the full privileges of citizenship; but it is a great additional stimulus to anyone's self-help and self-reliance when he starts from even ground, and has not to feel that his success depends on the impression he can make upon the sentiments and dispositions of a body of whom he is not one. It is a great discouragement to an individual, and a still greater one to a class, to be left out of the constitution; to be reduced to plead from outside the door to the arbiters of their destiny, not taken into consultation within. The maximum of the invigorating effect of freedom upon the character is only obtained when the person acted on either is, or is looking forward to become a citizen as fully privileged as any other. What is still more important than even this matter of feeling is the practical discipline which the character obtains from the occasional demand made upon the citizens to exercise, for a time and in their turn, some social function. It is not sufficiently considered how little there is in most men's ordinary life to give any largeness either to their conceptions or to their sentiments. Their work is a routine; not a labor of love, but of self-interest in the most elementary form, the satisfaction of daily wants; neither the thing done, nor the process of doing it, introduces the mind to thoughts or feelings extending beyond individuals; if instructive books are within their reach, there is no stimulus to read them; and in most cases, the individual has no access to any person of cultivation much superior to his own. Giving him something to do for the public supplies, in a measure, all these deficiencies. If circumstances allow the amount of public duty assigned him to be considerable, it makes him an educated man. Notwithstanding the defects of the social system and moral ideas of antiquity, the practice of the dicastery and the ecclesia raised the intellectual standard of an average Athenian citizen far beyond anything of which there is yet an example in any other mass of men, ancient or modern. The proofs of this are apparent in every page of our great historian of Greece; but we need scarcely look further than to the high quality of the addresses which their great orators deemed best calculated to act with effect on their understanding and will. A benefit of the same kind, though far less in degree, is produced on Englishmen of the lower middle class by their liability to be placed on juries and to serve parish offices, which, though it does not occur to so many, nor is so continuous, nor introduces them to so great a variety of elevated considerations as to admit of comparison with the public education which every citizen of Athens obtained from her democratic institutions, makes them nevertheless very different beings, in range of ideas and development of faculties, from those who have done nothing in their lives but drive a quill, or sell goods over a counter. Still more salutary is the moral part of the instruction afforded by the participation of the private citizen, if even rarely, in public functions. He is called upon, while so engaged, to weigh interests not his own; to be guided, in case of conflicting claims, by another rule than his private partialities; to apply, at every turn, principles and maxims which have for their reason of existence the general good; and he usually finds associated with him in the same work minds more familiarized than his own with these ideas and operations, whose study it will be to supply reason to his understanding, and stimulation to his feeling for the general good. He is made to feel himself one of the public, and whatever is their interest to be his interest. Where this school of public spirit does not exist, scarcely any sense is entertained that private persons, in no eminent social situation, owe any duties to society except to obey the laws and submit to the government. There is no unselfish sentiment of identification with the public. Every thought or feeling, either of interest or of duty, is absorbed in the individual and in the family. The man never thinks of any collective interest, of any objects to be pursued jointly with others, but only in competition with them, and in some measure at their expense. A neighbor, not being an ally or an associate, since he is never engaged in any common undertaking for joint benefit, is therefore only a rival. Thus even private morality suffers, while public is actually extinct. Were this the universal and only possible state of things, the utmost aspirations of the lawgiver or the moralist could only stretch to make the bulk of the community a flock of sheep innocently nibbling the grass side by side.

From these accumulated considerations, it is evident that the only government which can fully satisfy all the exigencies of the social state is one in which the whole people participate; that any participation, even in the smallest public function, is useful; that the participation should everywhere be as great as the general degree of improvement of the community will allow; and that nothing less can be ultimately desirable than the admission of all to a share in the sovereign power of the state. But since all cannot, in a community exceeding a single small town, participate personally in any but some very minor portions of the public business, it follows that the ideal type of a perfect government must be representative.

Notes and Questions

ALEXIS DE TOCQUEVILLE, from *Democracy in America*

1. Alexis de Tocqueville criticizes democracy, particularly in its American form. Its greatest danger, he argues, is that it is an unstable power — an irresistible but unstable power. Why? What is unstable about it?

2. His particular concern is what he calls the tyranny of the majority. He points out that the moral authority of majority rule must be based on the assumption that (a) wisdom increases with numbers or (b) the interest of the many is preferable to the interest of the few. Doesn't (a) sound like Aristotle's argument? Is it defensible? What does Tocqueville think? Is (b) a fair criticism of American democracy? Ours is a limited democracy, after all. Has American democracy done well at respecting and representing the interests of minorities? Does Tocqueville's argument show that absolute majority rule is no more likely to result in moral or just government than any other form of rule? Why isn't the interest of the many preferable to the interest of the few?

3. What arguments does Tocqueville give for limiting majority rule? Are they persuasive?

4. Why does he think that despite procedural limitations, the power of the majority is too strong in America? Does he think America is a free country? In what ways does he say it is not? Is he wrong in his observations? Is this a legal or a political problem? If it is a social or cultural problem, what does it have to do with democracy?

5. What is Tocqueville's view on the effect of democracy on character, both the character of officials and of the general population? How does it compare to Mill's or Aristotle's views? Is there any way these views can all be true?

6. Suppose Tocqueville's criticisms are right — they certainly are at least plausible. What do you conclude? Is he pointing to fatal flaws, or are these constructive criticisms that can lead to worthwhile corrections or adjustments, or to revisions of democratic theory or American government? What might be done to correct the problems Tocqueville points out?

[From] *Democracy in America*
ALEXIS DE TOCQUEVILLE

CHAPTER 12

Unlimited Power of the Majority in the United States and Its Consequences

The very essence of democratic government consists in the absolute sovereignty of the majority; for there is nothing in democratic states which is capable of resisting it. Most of the American constitutions have sought to increase this natural strength of the majority by artificial means.

The legislature is, of all political institutions, the one which is most easily swayed by the will of the majority. The Americans determined that the members of the legislature should be elected by the people *directly*, and for a *very brief term*, in order to subject them, not only to the general convictions, but even to the daily passions, of their constituents. The members of both houses are taken from the same classes in society, and nominated in the same manner; so that the movements of the legislative bodies are almost as rapid, and quite as irresistible, as those of a single assembly. It is to a legislature thus constituted, that almost all the authority of the government has been intrusted.

At the same time that the law increased the strength of those authorities which of themselves were strong, it enfeebled more and more those which were naturally weak. It deprived the representatives of the executive power of all stability and independence; and, by subjecting them completely to the caprices of the legislature, it robbed them of the slender influence which the nature of a democratic government might have allowed them to exercise. In several States, the judicial power was also submitted to the election of the majority; and in all of them, its existence was made to depend on the pleasure of the legislative authority, since the representatives were empowered annually to regulate the stipend of the judges.

Custom has done even more than law. A proceeding is becoming more and more general in the United States, which will, in the end, do away with the guaranties of representative government: it frequently happens that the voters, in electing a delegate, point out a certain line of conduct to him, and impose upon him certain positive obligations which he is pledged to fulfill. With the exception of the tumult, this comes to the same thing as if the majority itself held its deliberations in the market-place.

Several other circumstances concur to render the power of the majority in America not only preponderant, but irresistible. The moral authority of the majority is partly based upon the notion, that there is more intelligence and wisdom in a number of men united than in a single individual, and that the number of the legislators is more important than their quality. The theory of equality is thus applied to the intellects of men; and human pride is thus assailed in its last retreat by a doctrine which the minority hesitate to admit, and to which they will but slowly assent. Like all other powers, and perhaps more than any other, the authority of the many requires the sanction of time in order to appear legitimate. At first, it enforces obedience by constraint; and its laws are not *respected* until they have been long maintained.

The right of governing society, which the majority supposes itself to derive from its superior intelligence, was introduced into the United States by the first settlers; and this idea, which of itself would be sufficient to create a free nation, has now been amalgamated with the manners of the people and the minor incidents of social life.

The French, under the old monarchy, held it for a maxim that the king could do no wrong; and if he did do wrong, the blame was imputed to his advisers. This notion made obedience very easy; it enabled the subject to complain of the law, without ceasing to love and honor the lawgiver. The Americans entertain the same opinion with respect to the majority.

The moral power of the majority is founded upon yet another principle, which is, that the interests of the many are to be preferred to those of the few. It will readily be perceived that the respect here professed for the rights of the greater number must naturally increase or diminish according to the state of parties. When a nation is divided into several great irreconcilable interests, the privilege of the majority is often overlooked, because it is intolerable to comply with its demands.

If there existed in America a class of citizens whom the legislating majority sought to deprive of exclusive privileges which they had possessed for ages, and to bring down from an elevated station to the level of the multitude, it is probable that the minority would be less ready to submit to its laws. But as the United States were colonized by men holding equal rank, there is as yet no natural or permanent disagreement between the interests of its different inhabitants.

There are communities in which the members of the minority can never hope to draw over the majority to their side, because they must then give up the very point which is at issue between them. Thus, an aristocracy can never become a majority whilst it retains its exclusive privileges, and it cannot cede its privileges without ceasing to be an aristocracy.

In the United States, political questions cannot be taken up in so general and absolute a manner; and all parties are willing to recognize the rights of the majority, because they all hope at some time to be able to exercise them to their own advantage. The majority, therefore, in that country, exercise a prodigious actual authority, and a power of opinion which is nearly as great; no obstacles exist which can impede or even retard its progress, so as to make it heed the complaints of those whom it crushes upon its path. This state of things is harmful in itself, and dangerous for the future. . . .

Tyranny of the Majority

I hold it to be an impious and detestable maxim, that, politically speaking, the people have a right to do anything; and yet I have asserted that all authority originates in the will of the majority. Am I, then, in contradiction with myself?

A general law, which bears the name of justice, has been made and sanctioned, not only by a majority of this or that people, but by a majority of mankind. The rights of every people are therefore confined within the limits of what is just. A nation may be considered as a jury which is empowered to represent society at large, and to apply justice, which is its law. Ought such a jury, which represents society, to have more power than the society itself, whose laws it executes?

When I refuse to obey an unjust law, I do not contest the right of the majority to command, but I simply appeal from the sovereignty of the people to the sovereignty of mankind. Some have not feared to assert that a people can never outstep the boundaries of justice and reason in those affairs which are peculiarly its own; and that consequently full power may be given to the majority by which they are represented. But this is the language of a slave.

A majority taken collectively is only an individual, whose opinions, and frequently whose interests, are opposed to those of another individual, who is styled a minority. If it be admitted that a man possessing absolute power may misuse that power by wronging his adversaries, why should not a majority be liable to the same reproach? Men do not change their characters by uniting with each other; nor does their patience in the presence of obstacles increase with their strength. For my own part, I cannot believe it; the power to do everything, which I should refuse to one of my equals, I will never grant to any number of them.

I do not think, for the sake of preserving liberty, it is possible to combine several principles in the same government so as really to oppose them to one another. The form of government which is usually termed *mixed* has always appeared to me a mere chimera. Accurately speaking, there is no such thing as a *mixed government*, in the sense usually given to that word, because, in all communities, some one principle of action may be discovered which preponderates over the others. England, in the last century, — which has been especially cited as an example of this sort of government, — was essentially an aristocratic state, although it comprised some great elements of democracy; for the laws and customs of the country were such that the aristocracy would not but preponderate in the long run, and direct public affairs according to its own will. The error arose from seeing the interests of the nobles perpetually contending with those of the people, without considering the issue of the contest, which was really the important point. When a community actually has a mixed government, — that is to say, when it is equally divided between adverse principles, — it must either experience a revolution, or fall into anarchy.

I am therefore of opinion, that social power superior to all others must always be placed somewhere; but I think that liberty is endangered when this power finds no obstacle which can retard its course, and give it time to moderate its own vehemence.

Unlimited power is in itself a bad and dangerous thing. Human beings are not competent to exercise it with discretion. God alone can be omnipotent, because his wisdom and his justice are always equal to his power. There is no power on earth so worthy of honor in itself, or clothed with rights so sacred, that I would admit its uncontrolled and all-predominant authority. When I see that the right and the means of absolute command are conferred on any power whatever, be it called a people or a king, an aristocracy or a democracy, a monarchy or a republic, I say there is the germ of tyranny, and I seek to live elsewhere, under other laws.

In my opinion, the main evil of the present democratic institutions of the United States does not arise, as is often asserted in Europe, from their weakness, but from their irresistible strength. I am not so much alarmed at the excessive liberty which reigns in that country, as at the inadequate securities which one finds there against tyranny.

When an individual or a party is wronged in the United States, to whom can he apply for redress? If to public opinion, public opinion constitutes the majority; if to the legislature, it represents the majority, and implicitly obeys it; if to the executive power, it is appointed by the majority, and serves as a passive tool in its hands. The public force consists of the majority under arms; the jury is the majority invested with the right of hearing judicial cases; and in certain States, even the judges are elected by the majority. However iniquitous or absurd the measure of which you complain, you must submit to it as well as you can.

If, on the other hand, a legislative power could be so constituted as to represent the majority without necessarily being the slave of its passions, an executive so as to retain a proper share of authority, and a judiciary so as to remain independent of the other two powers, a government would be formed which would still be democratic, without incurring hardly any risk of tyranny.

I do not say that there is a frequent use of tyranny in America, at the present day; but I maintain that there is no sure barrier against it, and that the causes which mitigate the government there are to be found in the circumstances and the manners of the country, more than in its laws.

Effects of the Omnipotence of the Majority upon the Arbitrary Authority of American Public Officers

A distinction must be drawn between tyranny and arbitrary power. Tyranny may be exercised by means of the law itself, and in that case it is not arbitrary; arbitrary power may be exercised for the public good, in which case it is not tyrannical. Tyranny usually employs arbitrary means, but, if necessary, it can do without them.

In the United States, the omnipotence of the majority, which is favorable to the legal despotism of the legislature, likewise favors the arbitrary authority of the magistrate. The majority has absolute power both to make the law and to watch over its execution; and as it has equal authority over those who are in power, and the community at large, it considers public officers as its passive agents, and readily confides to them the task of carrying out its designs. The

details of their office, and the privileges which they are to enjoy, are rarely defined beforehand. It treats them as a master does his servants, since they are always at work in his sight, and he can direct or reprimand them at any instant.

In general, the American functionaries are far more independent within the sphere which is prescribed to them than the French civil officers. Sometimes, even, they are allowed by the popular authority to exceed those bounds; and as they are protected by the opinion, and backed by the power, of the majority, they dare do things which even a European, accustomed as he is to arbitrary power, is astonished at. By this means, habits are formed in the heart of a free country which may some day prove fatal to its liberties.

Power Exercised by the Majority in America upon Opinion

It is in the examination of the exercise of thought in the United States, that we clearly perceive how far the power of the majority surpasses all the powers with which we are acquainted in Europe. Thought is an invisible and subtle power, that mocks all the efforts of tyranny. At the present time, the most absolute monarchs in Europe cannot prevent certain opinions hostile to their authority from circulating in secret through their dominions, and even in their courts. It is not so in America; as long as the majority is still undecided, discussion is carried on; but as soon as its decision is irrevocably pronounced, every one is silent, and the friends as well as the opponents of the measure unite in assenting to its propriety. The reason of this is perfectly clear: no monarch is so absolute as to combine all the powers of society in his own hands, and to conquer all opposition, as a majority is able to do, which has the right both of making and of executing the laws.

The authority of a king is physical, and controls the actions of men without subduing their will. But the majority possesses a power which is physical and moral at the same time, which acts upon the will as much as upon the actions, and represses not only all contest, but all controversy.

I know of no country in which there is so little independence of mind and real freedom of discussion as in America. In any constitutional state in Europe, every sort of religious and political theory may be freely preached and disseminated; for there is no country in Europe so subdued by any single authority, as not to protect the man who raises his voice in the cause of truth from the consequences of his hardihood. If he is unfortunate enough to live under an absolute government, the people are often upon his side; if he inhabits a free country, he can, if necessary, find a shelter behind the throne. The aristocratic part of society supports him in some countries, and the democracy in others. But in a nation where democratic institutions exist, organized like those of the United States, there is but one authority, one element of strength and success, with nothing beyond it.

In America, the majority raises formidable barriers around the liberty of opinion: within these barriers, an author may write what he pleases; but woe to him if he goes beyond them. Not that he is in danger of an *auto-da-fé*, but he is exposed to continued obloquy and persecution. His political career is closed forever, since he has offended the only authority which is able to open it. Every sort of compensation, even that of celebrity, is refused to him. Before publishing his opinions, he imagined that he held them in common with others; but no sooner has he declared them, than he is loudly censured by his opponents, whilst those who think like him, without having the courage to speak out, abandon him in silence. He yields at length, overcome by the daily effort which he has to make, and subsides into silence, as if he felt remorse for having spoken the truth.

Fetters and headsmen were the coarse instruments which tyranny formerly employed; but the civilization of our age has perfected despotism itself, though it seemed to have nothing to learn. Monarchs had, so to speak, materialized oppression: the democratic republics of the present day have rendered it as entirely an affair of the mind, as the will which it is intended to coerce. Under the absolute sway of one man, the body was attacked in order to subdue the soul; but the soul escaped the blows which were directed against it, and rose proudly superior. Such is not the course adopted by tyranny in democratic republics; there the body is left free, and the soul is enslaved. The master no longer says, "You shall

think as I do, or you shall die"; but he says, "You are free to think differently from me, and to retain your life, your property, and all that you possess; but you are henceforth a stranger among your people. You may retain your civil rights, but they will be useless to you, for you will never be chosen by your fellow-citizens, if you solicit their votes; and they will affect to scorn you, if you ask for their esteem. You will remain among men, but you will be deprived of the rights of mankind. Your fellow-creatures will shun you like an impure being; and even those who believe in your innocence will abandon you, lest they should be shunned in their turn. Go in peace! I have given you your life, but it is an existence worse than death."

Absolute monarchies had dishonored despotism; let us beware lest democratic republics should reinstate it, and render it less odious and degrading in the eyes of the many, by making it still more onerous to the few.

Works have been published in the proudest nations of the Old World, expressly intended to censure the vices and the follies of the times: La Bruyère inhabited the palace of Louis XIV, when he composed his chapter upon the Great, and Molière criticised the courtiers in the pieces which were acted before the court. But the ruling power in the United States is not to be made game of. The smallest reproach irritates its sensibility, and the slightest joke which has any foundation in truth renders it indignant; from the forms of its language up to the solid virtues of its character, everything must be made the subject of encomium. No writer, whatever be his eminence, can escape paying this tribute of adulation to his fellow-citizens. The majority lives in the perpetual utterance of self-applause; and there are certain truths which the Americans can only learn from strangers or from experience.

If America has not as yet had any great writers, the reason is given in these facts; there can be no literary genius without freedom of opinion, and freedom of opinion does not exist in America. The Inquisition has never been able to prevent a vast number of anti-religious books from circulating in Spain. The empire of the majority succeeds much better in the United States, since it actually removes any wish to publish them.

Unbelievers are to be met with in America, but there is no public organ of infidelity. Attempts have been made by some governments to protect morality by prohibiting licentious books. In the United States, no one is punished for this sort of books, but no one is induced to write them; not because all the citizens are immaculate in conduct, but because the majority of the community is decent and orderly.

In this case the use of the power is unquestionably good; and I am discussing the nature of the power itself. This irresistible authority is a constant fact, and its judicious exercise is only an accident.

Effects of the Tyranny of the Majority upon the National Character of the Americans

The tendencies which I have just mentioned are as yet but slightly perceptible in political society; but they already exercise an unfavorable influence upon the national character of the Americans. I attribute the small number of distinguished men in political life to the ever-increasing despotism of the majority in the United States.

When the American Revolution broke out, they arose in great numbers; for public opinion then served, not to tyrannize over, but to direct the exertions of individuals. Those celebrated men, sharing the agitation of mind common at that period, had a grandeur peculiar to themselves, which was reflected back upon the nation, but was by no means borrowed from it.

In absolute governments, the great nobles who are nearest to the throne flatter the passions of the sovereign, and voluntarily truckle to his caprices. But the mass of the nation does not degrade itself by servitude; it often submits from weakness, from habit, or from ignorance, and sometimes from loyalty. Some nations have been known to sacrifice their own desires to those of the sovereign with pleasure and pride, thus exhibiting a sort of independence of mind in the very act of submission. These nations are miserable, but they are not degraded. There is a great difference between doing what one does not approve, and feigning to approve what one does; the one is the weakness of a feeble person, the other befits the temper of a lackey.

In free countries, where every one is more or less called upon to give his opinion on affairs of state, — in democratic republics, where public life is incessantly mingled with domestic affairs, where the sovereign authority is accessible on every side, and where its attention can always be attracted by vociferation, — more persons are to be met with who speculate upon its weaknesses, and live upon ministering to its passions, than in absolute monarchies. Not because men are naturally worse in these states than elsewhere, but the temptation is stronger and of easier access at the same time. The result is a more extensive debasement of character.

In that immense crowd which throngs the avenues to power in the United States, I found very few men who displayed that manly candor and masculine independence of opinion which frequently distinguished the Americans in former times, and which constitutes the leading feature in distinguished characters wheresoever they may be found. It seems, at first sight, as if all the minds of the Americans were formed upon one model, so accurately do they follow the same route. A stranger does, indeed, sometimes meet with Americans who dissent from the rigor of these formularies, — with men who deplore the defects of the laws, the mutability and the ignorance of democracy, — who even go so far as to observe the evil tendencies which impair the national character, and to point out such remedies as it might be possible to apply; but no one is there to hear them except yourself, and you, to whom these secret reflections are confided, are a stranger and a bird of passage. They are very ready to communicate truths which are useless to you, but they hold a different language in public. . . .

The Greatest Dangers of the American Republics Proceed from the Omnipotence of the Majority

Governments usually perish from impotence or from tyranny. In the former case, their power escapes from them; it is wrested from their grasp in the latter. Many observers who have witnessed the anarchy of democratic states, have imagined that the government of those states was naturally weak and impotent. The truth is, that, when war is once begun between parties, the government loses its control over society. But I do not think that a democratic power is naturally without force or resources; say, rather, that it is almost always by the abuse of its force, and the misemployment of its resources, that it becomes a failure. Anarchy is almost always produced by its tyranny or its mistakes, but not by its want of strength.

It is important not to confound stability with force, or the greatness of a thing with its duration. In democratic republics, the power which directs society is not stable; for it often changes hands, and assumes a new direction. But, whichever way it turns, its force is almost irresistible. The governments of the American republics appear to me to be as much centralized as those of the absolute monarchies of Europe, and more energetic than they are. I do not, therefore, imagine that they will perish from weakness.

If ever the free institutions of America are destroyed, that event may be attributed to the omnipotence of the majority, which may at some future time urge the minorities to desperation, and oblige them to have recourse to physical force. Anarchy will then be the result, but it will have been brought about by despotism.

Mr. Madison expresses the same opinion in the Federalist, No. 51. "It is of great importance in a republic, not only to guard the society against the oppression of its rulers, but to guard one part of the society against the injustice of the other part. Justice is the end of government. It is the end of civil society. It ever has been, and ever will be, pursued until it be obtained, or until lib- erty be lost in the pursuit. In a society, under the forms of which the stronger faction can readily unite and oppress the weaker, anarchy may as truly be said to reign as in a state of nature, where the weaker individual is not secured against the violence of the stronger: and as, in the latter state, even the stronger individuals are prompted by the uncertainty of their condition to submit to a government which may protect the weak as well as themselves, so, in the former state, will the more powerful factions be gradually induced by a like motive to wish for a government which will protect all parties, the weaker as well as the more powerful. It can be little doubted, that, if the State of Rhode Island was separated from the Confederacy and left to itself, the insecurity of right under the popular form of government within such narrow limits would be displayed by such reiterated oppressions of the factious majorities, that some power altogether independent of the people would soon be called for by the voice of the very factions whose misrule had proved the necessity of it."

Jefferson also said: "This executive power in our government is not the only, perhaps not even the principal, object of my solicitude. The tyranny of the legislature is really the danger most to be feared, and will continue to be so for many years to come. The tyranny of the executive power will come in its turn, but at a more distant period."

I am glad to cite the opinion of Jefferson upon this subject rather than that of any other, because I consider him the most powerful advocate democracy has ever had.

* * *

Notes and Questions

ROBERT PAUL WOLFF, from *In Defense of Anarchism*

1. The question that concerns Robert Paul Wolff is how can any government be justified. If individual autonomy is taken seriously — if we accept the proposition that autonomy consists in the right and obligation of self-legislation, and that this is a fundamental or overriding moral consideration in general — how can any person or group have legitimate power, or authority, over any other individual? Government power as coercion is easy enough to understand. If you disobey the law you will be put in jail or otherwise made to suffer. But government power as authority entails the right to obedience in some sense. To justify that right is a problem of political theory. Wolff argues that democracy is the only possible solution. Why?

2. How is the problem as posed by Wolff different from the problem as posed by Mill or Aristotle? For Mill or Aristotle is it impossible in principle for a monarchy or an aristocracy to be a legitimate form of government? For Wolff what does a government have to do to be legitimate? Is this a significant difference? Is there any reason to think that democracy would handle all these objectives best? Each philosopher gives arguments that it will. Are their respective arguments compatible?

3. Given his special objectives, what form of democracy is necessary, according to Wolff? Why? Can you think of an argument that would support another form of democracy in terms of respecting individual autonomy? Can representative democracy be a reasonable substitute, in Wolff's view? Why not?

4. What are the two kinds of agency that Wolff describes? Which kind is relevant to political decisions? Do you agree that individuals should make their own decisions? Why or why not?

5. Consider Wolff's proposal for a direct democracy. The idea is to remove the most common objection to direct democracy, namely, the practical argument that this form is not possible in anything but a small community. Suppose this were a real proposal—a referendum for constitutional revision to make the United States a direct democracy. Would you vote in favor of it? If not, why not? Are there theoretical (rather than practical) arguments for favoring a representative democracy over a direct form? What are they? Can you think of any that do not undermine the basic argument that supports democracy in the first place?

[From] *In Defense of Anarchism*
ROBERT PAUL WOLFF

CHAPTER 2
The Solution of Classical Democracy

1. Democracy Is the Only Feasible Solution

It is not necessary to argue at length the merits of all the various types of state which, since Plato, have been the standard fare of political philosophies. John Locke may have found it worthwhile to devote an entire treatise to Sir Robert Filmer's defense of the hereditary rights of kings, but today the belief in all forms of traditional authority is as weak as the arguments which can be given for it. There is only one form of political community which offers any hope of resolving the conflict between authority and autonomy, and that is democracy.

The argument runs thus: men cannot be free so long as they are subject to the will of others, whether one man (a monarch) or several (aristocrats). But if men rule themselves, if they are both law-givers and law-obeyers, then they can combine the benefits of government with the blessings of freedom. Rule *for* the people is merely benevolent slavery, but rule *by* the people is true freedom. Insofar as a man participates in the affairs of state, he is ruler as well as ruled. His obligation to submit to the laws stems not from the divine right of the monarch, nor from the hereditary authority of a noble class, but from the fact that he himself is the source of the laws which govern him. Therein lies the peculiar merit and moral claim of a democratic state.

Democracy attempts a natural extension of the duty of autonomy to the realm of collective action. Just as the truly responsible man gives laws to himself, and thereby binds himself to what he conceives to be right, so a society of responsible men can collectively bind themselves to laws collectively made, and thereby bind themselves to what they have together judged to be right. The government of a democratic state is then, strictly speaking, no more than a servant of the people as a whole, charged with the execution of laws which have been commonly agreed upon. In the words of Rousseau, "every person, while uniting himself with all, . . . obey[s] only himself and remain[s] as free as before" (*Social Contract*, Bk. I, Ch. 6).

Let us explore this proposal more closely. We shall begin with the simplest form of democratic state, which may be labeled *unanimous direct democracy*.

2. Unanimous Direct Democracy

There is, in theory, a solution to the problem which has been posed, and this fact is in itself quite important. However, the solution requires the imposition of impossibly restrictive conditions which make it applicable only to a rather bizarre variety of actual situations. The solution is a direct democracy — that is, a political community in which every person votes on every issue — governed by a rule of unanimity. Under unanimous direct democracy, every member of the society wills freely every law which is actually passed. Hence, he is only confronted as a citizen with laws to which he has consented. Since a man who is constrained only by the dictates of his own will is autonomous, it follows that under the directions of unanimous direct democracy, men can harmonize the duty of autonomy with the commands of authority.

It might be argued that even this limiting case is not genuine, since each man is obeying himself, and hence is not submitting to a legitimate authority. However, the case is really different from the prepolitical (or extrapolitical) case of self-determination, for the authority to which each citizen submits is not that of himself simply, but that of the entire community taken collectively. The laws are issued in the name of the sovereign, which is to say the total population of the community. The power which enforces the law (should there be any citizen who, having voted for a law, now resists its application to himself) is the power of all, gathered together into the police power of the state. By this means, the moral conflict between duty and interest which arises from time to time within each man is externalized, and the voice of duty now speaks with the authority of law. Each man, in a manner of speaking, encounters his better self in the form of the state, for its dictates are simply the laws which he has, after due deliberation, willed to be enacted.

Unanimous direct democracy is feasible only so long as there is substantial agreement among *all* the members of a community on the matters of major importance. Since by the rule of unanimity a single negative vote defeats any motion, the slightest disagreement over significant questions will bring the operations of the society to a halt. It will cease to function as a political community and fall into a condition of anarchy (or at least into a condition of non-legitimacy; a *de facto* government may of course emerge and take control). However, it should not be thought that unanimous direct democracy requires for its existence a perfect harmony of the interests or desires of the citizens. It is perfectly consistent with such a system that there be sharp, even violent, oppositions within the community, perhaps of an economic kind. The only necessity is that when the citizens come together to deliberate on the means for resolving such conflicts, they agree unanimously on the laws to be adopted.[1]

For example, a community may agree unanimously on some principles of compulsory arbitration by which economic conflicts are to be settled. An individual who has voted for these principles may then find himself personally disadvantaged by their application in a particular case. Thinking the principles fair, and knowing that he voted for them, he will (hopefully) acknowledge his moral obligation to accept their operation even though he would dearly like not to be subject to them. He will recognize the principles as his own, just as any of us who has committed himself to a moral principle will, uncomfortably to be sure, recognize its binding force upon him even when it is inconvenient. More precisely, this individual will have a moral obligation to obey the commands of the mediation board or arbitration council, *whatever it decides*, because the principles which guide it issue from his own will. Thus the board will have authority over him (i.e., a right to be obeyed) while he retains his moral autonomy.

Under what circumstances might a unanimous direct democracy actually function for a reasonable period of time without simply coming to a series of negative decisions? The answer, I think, is that there are two sorts of practical unanimous direct democracies. First, a community of persons inspired by some all-absorbing religious or secular ideal might find itself so completely in agreement on the goals of the community and the means for achieving them that decisions could be taken on all major questions by a method of consensus. Utopian communities in the nineteenth century and some of the Israeli kibbutzim in the twentieth are plausible instances of such a functioning unanimity. Eventually, the consensus dissolves and factions appear, but in some cases the unanimity has been preserved for a period of many years.

Second, a community of rationally self-interested individuals may discover that it can only reap the fruits of cooperation by maintaining unanimity. So long as each member of the community remains convinced that the benefits to him from cooperation — even under the conditions of compromise imposed by the need for unanimity — outweigh the benefits of severing his connection with the rest, the community will continue to function. For example, a classical laissez-faire economy ruled by the laws of the marketplace is supposedly endorsed by all the participants because each one recognizes *both* that he is better off in the system than out *and* that any relaxation of the ban against arrangements in restraint of trade would in the end do him more harm than good. So long as every businessman believes these two propositions, there will be unanimity on the laws of the system despite the cutthroat competition.[2]

As soon as disagreement arises on important questions, unanimity is destroyed and the state must either cease to be *de jure* or else discover some means for settling disputed issues which does not deprive any member of his autonomy.

Furthermore, when the society grows too large for convenience in calling regular assemblies, some way must be found to conduct the business of the state without condemning most of the citizens to the status of voiceless subjects. The traditional solutions in democratic theory to these familiar problems are of course majority rule and representation. Our next task, therefore, is to discover whether representative majoritarian democracy preserves the autonomy which men achieve under a unanimous direct democracy.

Since unanimous democracy can exist only under such limited conditions, it might be thought that there is very little point in discussing it at all. For two reasons, however, unanimous direct democracy has great theoretical importance. First, it *is* a genuine solution to the problem of autonomy and authority, and as we shall see, this makes it rather unusualy. More important still, unanimous direct democracy is the (frequently unexpressed) ideal which underlies a great deal of classical democratic theory. The devices of majoritarianism and representation are introduced in order to overcome obstacles which stand in the way of unanimity and direct democracy. Unanimity is clearly thought to be the method of making decisions which is most obviously legitimate; other forms are presented as compromises with this ideal, and the arguments in favor of them seek to show that the authority of a unanimous democracy is not fatally weakened by the necessity of using representation or majority rule. One evidence of the theoretical primacy of unanimous direct democracy is the fact that in all social contract theories, the original collective adoption of the social contract is always a unanimous decision made by everyone who can later be held accountable to the new state. Then the various compromise devices are introduced as practical measures, and their legitimacy is derived from the legitimacy of the original contract. The assumption that unanimity creates a *de jure* state is usually not even argued for with any vigor; it seems to most democratic theorists perfectly obvious.

3. Representative Democracy

Although the problem of disagreement is the more immediate, I shall deal first with the difficulties of assembly which lead — in democratic theory — to the device of a representative parliament.[3] There are two problems which are overcome by representation: first, the total citizenry may be too numerous to meet together in a chamber or open field; and second, the business of government may require a continuous attention and application which only the idle rich or the career politician can afford to give it.

We may distinguish a number of types of representation, ranging from the mere delegation of the right to vote a proxy to a complete turning over of all decision-making functions. The question to be answered is whether any of these forms of representation adequately preserve the autonomy which men exercise through decisions taken unanimously by the entire community. In short, should a responsible man commit himself to obey the laws made by his representatives?

The simplest sort of representation is strict agency. If I am unable to attend the assembly at which votes are taken, I may turn over my proxy to an agent with instructions as to how to vote. In that case, it is obvious that I am as obligated by the decisions of the assembly as though I had been physically present. The role of legal agent is too narrowly drawn, however, to serve as an adequate model for an elected representative. In practice, it is impossible for representatives to return to their districts before each vote in the assembly and canvass their constituents. The citizens may of course arm their representative with a list of their preferences on future votes, but many of the issues which come before the assembly may not have been raised in the community at the time the representative was chosen. Unless there is to be a recall election on the occasion of each unforeseen deliberation, the citizens will be forced to choose as their representative a man whose general "platform" and political bent suggests that he will, in the future, vote as they imagine they would themselves, on issues which neither the citizens nor the representative yet have in mind.

When matters have reached this degree of removal from direct democracy, we may seriously doubt whether the legitimacy of the original arrangement has been preserved. I have an obligation to obey the laws which I myself enact. I have as well an obligation to obey the laws which are enacted by my agent in strict accord with my instructions. But on what grounds can it be claimed that I have an obligation to obey the laws which are made in my name by a man who has no obligation to vote as I would, who indeed has no effective way of discovering what my preferences are on the measure before him? Even if the parliament is unanimous in its adoption of some new measure, that fact can only bind the deputies and not the general citizenry who are said to be represented by them.

It can be replied that my obligation rests upon my *promise* to obey, and that may in fact be true. But insofar as a promise of that sort is the sole ground of my duty to obey, I can no longer be said to be *autonomous*. I have ceased to be the author of the laws to which I submit and have become the (willing) subject of another person. Precisely the same answer must be given to the argument that good effects of some sort will result from my obeying the duly elected parliament. The moral distinction of representative government, if there is any, does not lie in the general good which it does, nor in the fact that its subjects have consented to be ruled by a parliament. Benevolent elective kingship of a sort which has existed in past societies can say as much. The special legitimacy and moral authority of representative government is thought to result from its being an expression of the will of the people whom it rules. Representative democracy is said not simply to be government *for* the people but also government (indirectly) *by* the people. I must obey what the parliament enacts, *whatever that may be*, because its will is my will, its decisions my decisions, and hence its authority merely the collected authority of myself and my fellow citizens. Now, a parliament whose deputies vote without specific mandate from their constituents is no more the expression of their will than is a dictatorship which rules with kindly intent but independently of its subjects. It does not matter that I am pleased with the outcome after the fact, nor even that my representative has voted as he imagines I would have liked him to. So long as I do not, either in person or through my agent, join in the enactment of the laws by which I am governed, I cannot justly claim to be autonomous.

Unfounded as is traditional representative

government's claim to the mantle of legitimacy, it seems impeccable in comparison with the claims of the form of "democratic" politics which actually exist in countries like the United States today. Since World War II, governments have increasingly divorced themselves in their decision-making from anything which could be called the will of the people. The complexity of the issues, the necessity of technical knowledge, and most important, the secrecy of everything having to do with national security, have conspired to attenuate the representative function of elected officials until a point has been reached which might be called political stewardship, or, after Plato, "elective guardianship." The President of the United States is merely pledged to serve the unspecified interests of his constituents in unspecified ways.

The right of such a system to the title of democracy is customarily defended by three arguments: first, the rulers are chosen by the people from a slate which includes at least two candidates for each office; second, the rulers are expected to act in what they conceive to be the interest of the people; and third, the people periodically have the opportunity to recall their rulers and select others. More generally, the system allows individuals to have some measurable influence on the ruling elite if they choose. The genealogy of the term "democracy" need not concern us. It suffices to note that the system of elective guardianship falls so far short of the ideal of autonomy and self-rule as not even to seem a distant deviation from it. Men cannot meaningfully be called free if their representatives vote independently of their wishes, or when laws are passed concerning issues which they are not able to understand. Nor can men be called free who are subject to secret decisions, based on secret data, having unannounced consequences for their well-being and their very lives.

Some while after John Kennedy was assassinated, several memoirs appeared recounting the inside story of the decisions to invade Cuba in 1961 and to risk a nuclear war by blockading Cuba in 1962. More recently, with the advent of the Nixon Administration, we have begun to learn something of the way in which President Johnson and his advisers committed this country to a massive land war in Vietnam. As this book is being prepared for publication, new decisions are being taken in secret which may involve the United States in the Laotian situation.

In none of these instances of major decisions is there the slightest relation between the real reasons determining official policy and the rationale given out for public consumption. In what way, it may be wondered, are Americans better off than those Russian subjects who were allowed, by Khrushchev's decision, to know a bit of the truth about Stalin?

Even those forms of representative government which approximate to genuine agency suffer from a curious and little-noted defect which robs electors of their freedom to determine the laws under which they shall live. The assumption which underlies the practice of representation is that the individual citizen has an opportunity, through his vote, to make his preference known. Leaving aside for the moment the problems connected with majority rule, and ignoring as well the derogations from legitimacy which result when issues are voted on in the parliament which were not canvassed during the election of deputies, the citizen who makes use of this ballot is, as it were, present in the chamber through the agency of his representative. But this assumes that at the time of the election, each man had a genuine opportunity to vote for a candidate who represented his point of view. He may find himself in the minority, of course, his candidate may lose. But at least he has had his chance to advance his preferences at the polls.

But if the number of issues under debate during the campaign is greater than one or two, and if there are — as there are sure to be — a number of plausible positions which might be taken on each issue, then the permutations of consistent alternative total "platforms" will be vastly greater than the number of candidates. Suppose, for example, that in an American election there are four issues: a farm bill, medical care for the aged, the extension of the draft, and civil rights. Simplifying the real world considerably, we can suppose that there are three alternative courses of action seriously being considered on the first issue, four on the second, two on the third, and three on the last. There are then $3 \times 4 \times 2 \times 3 = 72$ possible stands which a man might take on these four issues. For example, he might favor full parity, Kerr-Mills, discontinuation of the draft, and no civil rights bill; or free market on agricultural produce, no medicare at all, extension of the draft, and a strong civil rights bill; and so on. Now, in order to make sure that every voter has a *chance* of voting for what he believes, there would have to be 72 candidates, each holding one of the logically possible positions. If a citizen cannot even find a *candidate* whose views coincide with his own, then there is no possibility at all that he will send to the parliament a genuine *representative*. In practice, voters are offered a handful of candidates and must make compromises with their beliefs before they ever get to the polls. Under these circumstances, it is difficult to see what content there is to the platitude that elections manifest the will of the people.

The most biting rejection of representative democracy can be found in Rousseau's *Social Contract*. In opposition to such writers as Locke, Rousseau writes:

> Sovereignty cannot be represented for the same reason that it cannot be alienated; its essence is the general will, and that will must speak for itself or it does not exist: it is either itself or not itself: there is no intermediate possibility. The deputies of the people, therefore, are not and cannot be their representatives; they can only be their commissioners, and as such are not qualified to conclude anything definitively. No act of theirs can be a law, unless it has been ratified by the people in person; and without that ratification nothing is a law. The people of England deceive themselves when they fancy they are free; they are so, in fact, only during the election of members of parliament: for, as soon as a new one is elected, they are again in chains, and are nothing. And thus, by the use they make of their brief moments of liberty, they deserve to lose it (Bk. III, Ch. 15).

Appendix: A Proposal for Instant Direct Democracy

The practical impossibility of direct democracy is generally taken for granted in contemporary discussions of democratic theory, and it is accounted an unpleasantly utopian aspect of the philosophy of Rousseau, for example, that it assumes a community in which every citizen can vote directly on all the laws. Actually, the obstacles to direct democracy are merely technical, and we may therefore suppose that in this day of planned technological progress it is possible to solve them. The following proposal sketches one such solution. It is meant a good deal more than half in earnest, and I urge those readers who are prone to reject it out of hand to reflect on what that reaction reveals about their real attitude toward democracy.

I propose that in order to overcome the obstacles to direct democracy, a system of in-the-home voting machines be set up. In each dwelling, a device would be attached to the television set which would electronically record votes and transmit them to a computer in Washington. (Those homes without sets would be supplied by a federal subsidy. In practice this would not be very expensive, since only the very poor and the very intelligent lack sets at present.) In order to avoid fraudulent voting, the device could be rigged to record thumbprints. In that manner, each person would be able to vote only once, since the computer would automatically reject a duplicate vote. Each evening, at the time which is now devoted to news programs, there would be a nationwide all-stations show devoted to debate on the issues before the nation. Whatever bills were "before the Congress" (as we would now describe it) would be debated by representatives of alternative points of view. There would be background briefings on technically complex questions, as well as formal debates, question periods, and so forth. Committees of experts would be commissioned to gather data, make recommendations for new measures, and do the work of drafting legislation. One could institute the position of Public Dissenter in order to guarantee that dissident and unusual points of view were heard. Each Friday, after a week of debate and discussion, a voting session would be held. The measures would be put to the public, one by one, and the nation would record its preference instantaneously by means of the machines. Special arrangements might have to be made for those who could not be at their sets during the voting. (Perhaps voting sessions at various times during the preceding day and night.) Simple majority rule would prevail, as is now the case in the Congress.

The proposal is not perfect, of course, for there is a great difference between the passive role of

listener in a debate and the active role of participant. Nevertheless, it should be obvious that a
political community which conducted its business
by means of "instant direct democracy" would be
immeasurably closer to realizing the ideal of genuine democracy than we are in any so-called
democratic country today. The major objection
which would immediately be raised to the proposal, particularly by American political scientists, is that it would be too democratic! What
chaos would ensue! What anarchy would prevail!
The feckless masses, swung hither and yon by the
winds of opinion, would quickly reduce the great,
slow-moving, stable government of the United
States to disorganized shambles! Bills would be
passed or unpassed with the same casual irresponsibility which now governs the length of a
hemline or the popularity of a beer. Meretricious
arguments would delude the simple, well-mean-
ing, ignorant folk into voting for pie-in-the-sky
giveaways; foreign affairs would swing between
jingoist militarism and craven isolationism. Gone
would be the restraining hand of wisdom, knowledge, tradition, experience.

The likelihood of responses of this sort indicates the shallowness of most modern belief in
democracy. It is obvious that very few individuals really hold with *government by the people*,
though of course we are all willing to obliterate
ourselves and our enemies in its name. Nevertheless, the unbelievers are, in my opinion, probably
wrong as well as untrue to their professed faith.
The initial response to a system of instant direct
democracy would be chaotic, to be sure. But
very quickly, men would learn — what is now
manifestly not true — that their votes made a difference in the world, an immediate, visible difference. There is nothing which brings on a sense
of responsibility so fast as that awareness. America would see an immediate and invigorating rise
in interest in politics. It would hardly be necessary to launch expensive and frustrating campaigns to get out the vote. Politics would be on
the lips of every man, woman, and child, day
after day. As interest rose, a demand would be
created for more and better sources of news.
Even under the present system, in which very
few Americans have any sense of participation in
politics, news is so popular that quarter-hour programs are expanded to half an hour, and news

specials preempt prime television time. Can anyone deny that instant direct democracy would
generate a degree of interest and participation in
political affairs which is now considered impossible to achieve?

Under a system of genuine democracy the
voices of the many would drown out those of the
few. The poor, the uneducated, the frightened
who today are cared for by the state on occasion
but never included in the process of government
would weigh, man for man, as heavily as the
rich, the influential, the well-connected. Much
might be endangered that is worthwhile by such
a system, but at least social justice would flourish as it has never flourished before.

If we are willing to think daringly, then, the
practical obstacles to direct democracy can be
overcome. For the moment, we need not discuss
any further *whether* we wish to overcome them;
but since our investigation concerns the *possibility* of establishing a state in which the autonomy
of the individual is compatible with the authority
of the state, I think we can take it that the difficulties which in the past have led to unsatisfactory forms of representative democracy do not
constitute a serious theoretical problem.

NOTES

1. In recent years, a number of political philosophers
have explored the possibilities of decision by unanimity,
and it turns out that much more can be achieved than
one would expect. For example, John Rawls, in an influential and widely read essay, "Justice as Fairness," uses
certain models taken from bargaining theory to analyze
the conditions under which rational men with conflicting interests might arrive at unanimous agreement on
the procedural principles for resolving their disputes.
See Rawls in *Philosophy, Politics, and Society*, 2nd
series, eds. P. Laslett and W. Runciman.

2. Strictly speaking, this second example of a
viable unanimous community is imperfect, since there
is a significant difference between committing oneself
to a moral principle and calculating one's enlightened
self-interest. For an illuminating discussion of the
moral importance of committing oneself to a principle,
see Rawls, *op. cit.*

3. Needless to say, the origin of parliaments historically has nothing to do with this problem. It is rather
the other way around: first there were parliaments,
then there was universal suffrage.

Ideas for Class Projects, Papers, or Debates

1. Analyze the Concord Resolutions (Section 1, "Collected Documents"). What does it tell you about the rule of law and the difference between constitutional provisions and statutes?

2. Assume that you are a member of a constitutional convention. You have before you two proposals for the constitution of your new state. One is exactly like the Pennsylvania Constitution (Section 1, "Collected Documents") and the other is exactly like the New York Constitution (also Section 1). Take a position and argue for the adoption of one and against the adoption of the other.

3. Is it a violation of the separation of power for the executive branch of government to solicit private money or to redistribute money already allocated to general funds in order to continue a program or policy that Congress has stopped funding? Discuss this question in regard to funding the Contras in Nicaragua or the WIN program for training the unemployed on public assistance. Funds for both were initially awarded and then discontinued by Congress. (See U.S. Constitution, Articles 1 and 2, in the Appendix for the allocation of power to the executive and legislative branches of government.)

4. Apply Bentham's analysis to the Virginia Declaration (Section 2, "Collected Documents") or the U.S. Bill of Rights (Appendix). On the basis of your analysis argue that the document should (or should not) be adopted as part of the constitution of Virginia or the U.S. Constitution.

5. In the appendix to his article in Section 3, Robert Paul Wolff offers a proposal for direct democracy in a modern technological society. Avoiding discussion of possible technical problems, argue for or against this proposal.

• The foregoing ideas may be used as topics for papers (long or short) or as subjects of class debates or panel discussions (or some combination of these). A class may be divided into small groups or teams; it may be divided in half to represent the pro and con sides of the assigned issue; or it may be left as one large informal group with each individual arguing or presenting his or her position.

One very workable formula is the following. The topic is assigned one week before a scheduled class debate. During that week each student writes a short (2–3 page) position paper, which serves as a basis for his or her argument. The debate is informal, with each student getting a turn to participate either in the presentation of the original argument or in response to the arguments of others. The instructor acts as moderator to ensure that the discussion is spread evenly among the group. After the debate a vote may be taken on the best argument (although this step is often counterproductive and I now prefer not to do it), or the instructor may provide a synopsis of the discussion (which seems to work better). Copies of all position papers are turned in directly after the debate, clearly marked "final" if they are not intended (by the student) to be rewritten and "draft" if they will be rewritten. Any student who opts to rewrite the position paper in light of the discussion has one week to do so. This is just one suggestion; of course, many variations are possible.

Writing a Position Paper

The idea behind writing a position paper is not to cover a topic exhaustively or review everything that has ever been said on the subject. The purpose is rather to set out, explain, and defend a particular position in the light of a topic. A position paper is not primarily a research paper, although you need to do enough background research to know what you are talking about. The basic ingredient of a position paper is good critical analysis.

Good critical analysis requires a clear understanding of the question to be explored. It requires the ability to break the issue down into its basic elements. And it requires attention to the implications and presuppositions of (that is, what follows from and what is assumed by) taking a position on an issue. You need to understand what you are committing yourself to by taking a particular position and what others are committing themselves to by taking a different stance.

One handy approach to writing position papers that helps to ensure covering all the bases is to start by setting out your position as clearly and succinctly as you can. Next, give your reasons for taking that position rather than another one—or better yet, state the reasons why others should agree with you. Why is your position the best one? What positive arguments do you have to support it?

When writing a short paper, you do not need to list every argument you can think of. Instead, make a preliminary list of all the arguments that come to mind and look it over. Select two or three arguments that are the strongest (the one most central or crucial to the issue, the most persuasive, or the most creative). If you have one argument that meets all three of these criteria, use it. You can't do better than that. In general, and certainly in philosophy courses, it is better to develop one or two arguments fully than to list six or eight arguments and leave them undeveloped. Set out your argument step by step, and do not assume that a passing reference to any argument is sufficient because you are writing to your instructor, who probably knows the argument anyway. Your instructor cannot tell whether you understand the argument unless you present it precisely. Always write as though you are explaining your position to someone who never really thought about the issue before.

Next, list what you believe are the major objections to your position, and try to answer them. Controversial issues involve genuine conflicts, so there will always be objections. Both sides are bound to offer points worth listening to. Even if you are dogmatic, never underestimate your opponents or their arguments might take you by surprise, leaving you without an answer. Your best approach is to anticipate the strongest arguments that an opponent can make against you and answer them, or explain why these arguments are not as important as others might think—or at least why they are outweighed. Lawyers win cases with this strategy. Try to put yourself in your opponent's place so you can anticipate the arguments that might be made against you.

But there is another reason for looking for objections to your position, a better reason than the adversarial model suggests. Selecting a preliminary position and investigating its pros and cons is a very good way to examine all sides of an issue. You need not think that because you choose a position you must stick with it no matter what (which is not to say, either, that you should flip over every time you hear a new argument). Sticking with your initial position no matter what, in the face of any counterargument, no matter how good, is exactly what we call being dogmatic or closed-minded (or bullheaded). It is far better to be open-minded, to be willing to hear and genuinely consider what others have to say. Even though it takes more work and more courage, it is a more honest and intelligent approach. It is therefore entirely acceptable to start with a position, consider the arguments pro and con, and then qualify or change your position in light of what you have learned. In fact, this is precisely the main purpose of participating in an exercise like this.

Note too that it is perfectly all right to use other people's arguments in your paper as long as you give them credit. Even when you are not writing a research paper, it is always a good practice to cite your sources (at least informally). You should cite sources because people deserve to get credit for their work. And if you do not do it, you will look either ignorant or dishonest. Your instructor can assume only one of two things if you do not cite your sources: Either you do not know that you are using someone else's work without giving credit (in which case you are probably ignorant of assigned materials) or you do know you are using someone else's work but not giving credit (in which case you are cheating). Using other people's work without giving them credit is plagiarism, which is not only a stupid thing to engage in but an offense that carries strong penalties. It is surprising that anyone commits plagiarism considering you always look good (both knowledgeable and honest) if you give credit to the work of others, and you almost always look bad if you don't. This is especially true for students, since it is insulting to your instructor if you assume that he or she does not know the general literature pertaining to his or her course. So cite your sources if you use any. Overall, this is the general formula:

1. Set out your position clearly.
2. Defend your position with a few well-developed arguments.
3. Acknowledge objections to your position, and develop the best opposing argument.
4. Answer or respond to the objections.
5. Draw your conclusion.

Of course, many other formats are possible. The one given here is simple and generally effective, especially as a starting point if you are not yet used to writing a position paper. Writing such a paper can be fun and is an effective way to clarify your thinking about different issues.

CHAPTER TWO

The Nature of the Judicial Process and the Concept of Law

The judicial process is often contrasted with the political process. At least in theory, it is said that the political process is motivated by the subjective (but collective) preferences and desires of the people; it aims (ideally) at the common good and is subject to negotiation and compromise (unless one posits a society so homogeneous that all its citizens have identical interests). The judicial process, on the other hand, is not supposed to be based on subjective preferences (even collective ones); it is not aimed at promoting the common good (at least not directly); and it is not supposed to be a process of negotiation and compromise. The judicial process is supposed to be objective, rational, principled, and based on the vindication of legal rights as expressed in the law of the land. This clear division between the judicial and the political processes is a matter of great contention and is reflected in all the reading selections in this chapter. While one author claims that the court is a nonpolitical or apolitical body, another author claims that it is impossible for any institution or individual to be nonpolitical—or if it is possible for some institution or individual in some circumstance to be nonpolitical, it certainly is not possible for courts or judges to be so. Keep this dispute in mind as you proceed through the articles in this chapter, since the position one takes on an issue affects the description of how courts should function and what purpose they should serve.

From our discussion in Section 3 of Chapter One, it is clear that a legislative process—a means of law-making—is fundamental to a legal system. Is the legislative process more fundamental than the judicial process? Is the judicial function a derivative function? Consider the question another way: Would a legal system be a legal system without courts? Could we get along without them? Put this way we have an easy question, and the answer is no: not only no, but absolutely not. A legal system is impossible without courts—that is, without an official government organ to perform the judicial function. What would you have without courts? At most you would have a system of general rules that could not be applied in particular cases.

At least since Aristotle, it has been generally recognized that law includes three distinct functions: the executive, the legislative, and the judicial. Unfortunately, we do not have the space or time to discuss the executive function in this course. The executive function is to carry out the laws, to execute or administer them, especially in the thousands of everyday cases in which there is no dispute as to how or whether the law applies. It is concerned with the running of the affairs of state and may involve the most powerful offices a government has. However, the executive function is often considered to be of less intellectual interest than the legislative and judicial functions, at least in terms of clarifying the nature and process of law.

The conceptual centrality of the executive function might be questioned, but the legislative and judicial functions are clear and equal conceptual necessities of law. Law is at a minimum (1) general rules (2) applied in particular cases. If you eliminate either you eliminate law altogether. Try to imagine law without either of them. There may be more to law, but there cannot be less. So it is clear that a judicial process is an indispensable part of a legal system or even of the concept of law.

It is also clear (in theory) what part the judicial process plays. Courts (or judges) perform the function of applying law (the general rules) in particular cases of conflict. It is easy to see that the function (or process) or law-making (that is, legislation) is very different from that of law-apply-ing. As we have seen, the process of law-making is a prospective or forward-looking process of deliberation calculated to formulate general rules intended to promote the common good (at least in a legitimate government). The judicial process, on the other hand, is a retrospective or back-ward-looking process of analysis calculated to interpret general rules in terms of particular sets of facts. The important point is that in order to apply law it must be interpreted; that is, someone in authority must be able to say which rule applies to the particular case at hand, to what extent, with what qualifications, and why. Someone must be able to say what the general rule of law means to a particular person in a particular set of circumstances.

Sometimes that is very easy (in which case there will be no dispute in court), but other times it is extremely difficult. For example, suppose we have a law that says no vehicles are allowed in the park. If John drives his car in the park, we might have a very easy case. The judge (the authority on the law) may observe that there are no exceptions applicable to this case: John is an ordinary person, his car is an ordinary vehicle, there are no extenuating circumstances, and John definitely drove his car in the park. So the rule applies, and John is clearly guilty of violating it. But often cases are not so simple. Suppose John's case was an emergency; then he might have an excuse. Suppose John is not an ordinary person. Suppose he is a policeman, who drove his car in the park in the line of duty. Then John might be an exception to the rule. Or suppose John did not drive his car but his bicycle in the park. Is a bicycle a vehicle or not? Suppose no one ever designated exactly which places are parks or whether the grounds of public buildings are included in the intent of the ordinance. The rule or law may not answer these questions. In such cases the judge has the much more difficult task of interpreting the rule in order to apply it. It may be necessary to draw analogies to other laws or even to other sources of law in order to decide the case.

How a judge goes about interpreting the law depends on the system. In any system anywhere the basic function of a court is to interpret and apply law. Beyond that generalization, however, there are vast differences in judicial method. For example, most European countries are governed by *civil codes*, whereas Anglo-American countries are governed by a traditionally British legal process called *common law*. These legal processes are not (at least not necessarily) mandated by constitution. They may be customary or traditional, but they make a profound difference in how particular courts function. This chapter considers how the judicial process operates in a common law system that is part of a constitutional government which embodies a bill of rights and a doc-trine of separated power. As you read the materials in Sections 1 and 2, ask yourself what differ-ence the structure of government and the process of law make to the kinds of decisions available to judges.

There is another factor that influences the decisions of judges (consciously or unconsciously). How a judge decides a case is affected by the concept of law that the judge holds. Any judicial opinion reflects a more general view of what law is, how it should function, and what it should (or should not) do. This factor reflects the old philosophical question, What is law? That is the subject of Section 2 of this chapter.

What is law? You might wonder how a question like that would come up. Who would ask it, and why? What is it that the questioner would like to know? What would count as a good answer?

The question might come up in a number of different contexts, and the focus would be different in each of them. Oliver Wendell Holmes, Jr., offers one in his speech on the study of law. One fundamental feature of law is that it is mandatory, or, one might say, coercive. Law is, as Holmes put it, the expression of the public force. It is not a matter of voluntary participation. Therefore, all people have reason to want to know what the law is in order to avoid running afoul of it.

We can put the same point in positive terms as well. There are a great number of things people want or need to do, which are essentially legal actions. That is, either these actions are impossible without law, or law has greatly facilitated them and in effect has taken them over. For example, getting married, selling property, making a business contract, or writing a will are all legal trans- actions. Thus if you want to do any of these things (and innumerable others), you have a reason to want to understand the law. In these cases, if you do not comply with the law, no one will punish you, but you will fail to accomplish your purpose. If you and your true love stand under your favorite old oak tree and sing together "I Love You Truly," you will not thereby be married even if you both intend to signify that you are. If you want to get married, you have to follow the pub- licly recognized rules (the laws) — so you have good reason to want to know what they are.

Thus, the "man on the street," or any ordinary person might well ask, with regard to either of these — let's call them restrictive and enabling laws — what is the law? We would ask the question in order to comply with the law. We might want to comply because we think all people should, but more likely, we want to protect our self-interest. What is it that we want to know when we ask this question in this context? We want to know what the rules are that affect us in a particular sys- tem at a particular time and place. The question is a specific, empirical one about certain factual properties of a social institution, namely, a legal system. What would count as a good answer to that question would be whatever the relevant "law on the books," for example, the state statute, the criminal code, the municipal ordinance, or the recorded court opinion, says about the particu- lar matter in question.

So if we ask our question what is law from the perspective of someone who wants to comply with it, the answer is the law is a set of officially recognized rules, generally recorded in books or in some other way publicly accessible, which are not a matter of voluntary participation but rather are enforced by the public power. There is a philosophical theory associated with this perspective called *legal positivism*. Legal positivism is concerned with formulating a clear, accurate, value- neutral description of law. It says, very roughly, that law is a set of rules, derived from and backed by (or sanctioned by) the public power and accessible to public knowledge. Legal positivism con- centrates on describing law as it is. In a vast number of cases, this is as far as the question, what is law, goes. In a large number of other cases, however, the answer is not so clear.

What Holmes and others (especially lawyers and judges) who are on the cutting edge of law, in that they deal with it in the courts, realize and focus on is that what counts as a good answer to the question is often not so simple. There may be a general rule, say, a statute on drawing up wills, but whether the rule applies in a particular case may not be clear; or if the rule does apply, it may not be clear how it applies. So the question arises, what does law do about questionable cases? Can we explain such cases by referring to the rules on the books? To make matters worse, you might have a problem, say a conflict with a neighbor, that is obviously the kind of thing that law deals with — the kind of conflict that gets settled by law, but no one happens to have brought it up before. There is no applicable rule on the books. If there is no rule, is there no law? Does that mean that you cannot take your dispute to a court to be settled? What does law do about new cases? Obviously, these cases cannot be explained very well by reference to rules, at least not the kinds of rules we have been discussing so far.

Faced with problems like these, certain legal theorists decided that a better test of what is law is not what is on the books but what happens in the courts. The law on the books is subject to the interpretation of the courts, after all. In terms of practical application for the person who goes to court about any matter of dispute, the law is what the court says it is. The philosophical theory associated with these ideas is called *legal realism*. While legal positivism focuses on the legislative aspect of law and offers a good description of settled law or clear cases, legal realism concentrates on the courts and offers a helpful picture of the legal process in unsettled cases.

But these are still not the only perspectives from which to ask the question, What is law. Another important viewpoint is that of the evaluator. Most thoughtful people are evaluators at some time or another. An evaluator may be an ordinary citizen deciding on principle whether or not to obey a law — that is, the potential conscientious objector. He or she would be asking, What is law that I should obey it?

An evaluator might be an official deciding whether or not to enforce the law, especially where the law in question appears to be a bad law in general or seems to be misfiring — that is, working an injustice in a particular case. It could be a policeman deciding whether to arrest or a prosecutor deciding whether to prosecute. They are asking, What is law that I should enforce it?

An evaluator might be a judge deciding how to interpret law, asking wht factors to consider relevant to a particular decision, especially for a novel case or an uncertain one. Here the question is what is included in the law: What should I include as relevant considerations in a legal decision?

The basic question raised in instances like all of these is, What is the relevance of morality to law? Is sn unjust law fundamentally flawed? Is it so flawed that it is not enforceable? If it is not enforceable, is it law? Law was once thought of as the enforcement of what is right. Associated with this view is a very old philosophical tradition called *natural law*. All three of the philosophical theories of law we have considered are concerned with better understanding the essential nature of law. However, approaching our question from different perspectives, they raise different issues and provide different insights, as we shall see. Section 2 considers each of these theories as well as another general critique that might itself constitute a fourth theory of law.

SECTION 1

Judicial Review and the Common Law

We will begin by asking what is distinctive about the judicial function in a constitutional democracy limited by the separation of power doctrine and a bill of rights. Note that the word *function* is ambiguous. *Function* may mean purpose: What function or purpose is supposed to be served by the court? What is the court supposed to do? That is what we mean when we ask, What is the function of the court? *Function* may also mean process or working format. That is what we mean when we ask, How does the court function? How does the court work? This section addresses both questions: What is the purpose of a court and how does it function?

The questions are related. How a judge ought to function may depend on the purpose a court ought to serve. On the other hand, the purpose of a court may depend on what is possible, or on what it is reasonable to think is possible for a judge to do. If judges function by utilizing a form of legal reasoning that can objectively determine the outcome of particular cases in terms of general rules, then it may be reasonable to think that a court *could* be nonpolitical. The purpose we think a court should serve may depend on whether it is reasonable to think a court is political or nonpolitical — and that in turn may depend on how we think judicial reasoning functions.

We will look first at how a court functions. As we have already noted, one feature that distinguishes the judicial function from the legislative function is that a court operates in terms of individual cases. Both its purpose and its mode of operation are to settle conflicts by applying general rules or standards to particular disputes. The question is where these general rules or standards (that is, law) come from and how they are applied. In Anglo-American legal systems there are three sources of law: (1) Some law is *constitutional*, deriving from the constitution or basic organization of government itself or from court interpretations of the constitution in earlier cases. (2) Some law is *statutory*, arising from enactments of the legislature or court interpretations of legislative enactments in earlier cases. And (3) some law is *judge-made* law, consisting in the tradition of judicial opinions in prior cases, that is called the *common law*.

The common law system is one method of law-building — one sort of judicial process. In a common law system law is built gradually or grows by a process of accumulating all the individual decisions of courts and inferring the general rules from successive particular cases. The only way such a system can work, of course, is to have a rule of procedure which requires each judge to decide his or her case in a way most consistent with the most similar cases decided before it. This is called following *precedent*. Thus, common law rests fundamentally on the idea of following precedent — also called the rule of *stare decisis*. The rational ground for this rule is consistency. Reason requires that similar cases be understood and dealt with similarly. Otherwise nothing makes sense. In order to understand one another and reason accurately we must be consistent. So if law is to be a rational (rather than an irrational and arbitrary) process, judicial decisions must be consistent with one another. The pragmatic ground for the rule of precedent is predictability: Lawyers and citizens want to be able to assess their future behavior in terms of current decisions of the courts. The moral ground is procedural justice. It has long been reorganized that justice (as well as reason) requires that like cases be treated alike and different cases be treated differently in proportion to their differences. Of course, this is easier said than done. The first problem is to figure out which cases are relevantly similar. The second is to figure out what it means to treat them alike. The brief excerpts from Oliver Wendell Holmes, Jr., and Benjamin Cardozo that open this section represent the views of two of our greatest judges on the complexity and difficulty of solving these problems.

In the first main selection, Edward Levi explains the fundamental elements of legal reasoning (or more specifically judicial reasoning) in American common law. He describes the process as a moving classification system, by which he means that the law changes or evolves in the very process of being applied. Judicial decision making is a three-step process of reasoning by analogy, Levi argues. First, a judge must identify a prior case as being similar to the case at hand. Second, the rule of the prior case must be determined. And third, the rule of the prior case must be applied to the present case. This is what it means to follow precedent. This view of judicial decision making as a three-step process of analogical reasoning is widely accepted as an accurate general description of common law theory and a true picture of what most American judges think they are supposed to do when they decide cases.

But whether judges actually do reason in this way, whether it is even possible to draw legal conclusions in this way, is a matter of dispute. We might say that the theory describes clear cases correctly decided. Difficulties with the standard description of judicial reasoning are raised by legal scholar Julius Stone. Stone argues that particular judicial decisions are underdetermined by legal rules. In fact, judges are constantly making choices about what constitutes precedent, what the rule of the precedent case is, and how broadly or narrowly it should be construed. None of these choices are determined by pre-existing legal rules, Stone argues. Thus judges are constantly making policy decisions, the political nature of which are masked by the myth of judicial reasoning propagated by theories like Levi's. The articles by Levi and Stone represent a longstanding debate in legal philosophy that goes to the basic nature of law and judicial reasoning. This debate is reflected in all of the reading selections in this section and in Section 2 on the concept of law.

David Kairys extends the general debate set out for us by Levi and Stone specifically to constitutional interpretation. Kairys argues (like Stone) that there is no special form of reasoning that is distinctive of judges. Nor is there a special form of legal reasoning that yields determinate answers on the basis of precedent. He uses a series of constitutional decisions to show that the Supreme Court has not been bound by its own precedents, in much the same way that Stone uses the common law decisions. If Stone and Kairys are right, what does it tell us about how a judge should function or what purpose is reasonable for a court? How are the theories offered in this section by Levi, Bork, Schauer, Ely, or Minow affected? On the other hand, if Stone and Kairys are wrong about the nature of judicial reasoning, how are their examples to be accounted for? Other legal scholars have provided many other examples of courts not following their own precedents, and perhaps more important, of the indeterminacy of precedent itself. Yet the ideal of following precedent persists. Is it a myth? Or is the Stone/Kairys view overstated? Or is there another explanation?

In "Original Understanding," Robert Bork takes a position that is flatly incompatible with that of Stone and Kairys. Bork argues that a court is a nonpolitical body and as such must be neutral in three ways: in deriving, defining, and applying its principles of law. The only approach that can provide this neutrality in constitutional interpretation, according to Bork, is what he calls the philosophy of original understanding (also often called the *intent of the framers* or the *original intent doctrine*). The judicial philosophy of original intent holds that a judge should interpret the Constitution according to the principles intended by those who ratified it. Since only this view embodies the notion that judges are not entitled to change the law, Bork argues, only this view prevents courts from being naked organs of unchecked power.

Frederick Schauer, however, has a very different idea of what is required for principled constitutional interpretation. He agrees that judges should have limited power, but he disagrees that the way to limit judicial power is in terms of the intent of the framers. He believes what is needed is a theory of constitutional language. By building a constitutional theory on the words of the document, Schauer believes that a principled foundation can be provided for constitutional interpretation that will limit judicial power.

John Hart Ely offers different suggestions regarding the proper function of the court and the possibility of principled constitutional interpretation. He suggests that the purpose of the court is to protect the process of coordinating popular government with minority protection—in other words, to protect the process of representation. Ely is concerned to deal with what Bork has called the "Madisonian dilemma," the recognition that the central problem for any court interpreting the U.S. Constitution is the problem of balancing the right of majority rule with the protection of individual and minority rights.

The U.S. Constitution sets up a *limited* democracy, which takes seriously both the principle of majority rule and the opposing principle of minority protection. Understanding, explaining, and operating within the limits of these opposing principles is the central problem of the Supreme Court. Bork believes that the problem can be managed only by the doctrine of original understanding. Schauer thinks that the problem should be approached through the words of the document by developing a theory of constitutional language. Ely argues that the Constitution should be interpreted in light of a particular constitutional purpose: protecting the process of representation.

In the next selection Martha Minow reviews the Supreme Court term of 1986 as the basis of her analysis of constitutional interpretation. Like Ely, she is concerned about the process of representation, particularly for those who are least likely to be heard in the normal course of events. She points out that in a pluralistic society the courts are inevitably faced with "dilemmas of difference": conflicts that involve the clash of fundamental values. These dilemmas are made worse, she suggests, by unstated assumptions about what is normal and whose viewpoint matters. Unless judges come to understand that like all human beings their own perspective is partial, Minow argues, they will not be able to identify their own unexamined assumptions, which bias them against minorities or outsiders whose perspectives have been overlooked. Institutional arrangements define whose reality sets the norm. That norm is typically assumed uncritically by judges, and anyone outside it is thereby at a disadvantage. The value of impartiality requires judges to adopt mechanisms that will enable them to examine the norms they assume and to consider seriously voices that usually go unheard.

As you proceed through the materials of this chapter, ask yourself whether the function of the judiciary is political or not. Then ask yourself what difference that makes in what judges can do and should do. Is the judicial process determined by the particular system of government of which it is a part? Is the judicial process set by the political process or by judges themselves, or are there other limits or requirements implied in the very nature of courts? Ask yourself what really distinguishes a court from a legislture or a judicial process from a political process.

[From] *The Common Law*
OLIVER WENDELL HOLMES, JR.

Lecture I. Early Forms of Liability

The object of this book is to present a general view of the Common Law. To accomplish the task, other tools are needed besides logic. It is something to show that the consistency of a system requires a particular result, but it is not all. The life of the law has not been logic: it has been experience. The felt necessities of the time, the prevalent moral and political theories, intuitions of public policy, avowed or unconscious, even the prejudices which judges share with their fellow-men, have had a good deal more to do than the syllogism in determining the rules by which men should be governed. The law embodies the story of a nation's development through many centuries, and it cannot be dealt with as if it contained only the axioms and corollaries of a book of mathematics. In order to know what it is, we must know what it has been, and what it tends to become. We must alternately consult history and

existing theories of legislation. But the most difficult labor will be to understand the combination of the two into new products at every stage. The substance of the law at any given time pretty nearly corresponds, so far as it goes, with what is then understood to be convenient; but its form and machinery, and the degree to which it is able to work out desired results, depend very much upon its past. . . .

The foregoing history, apart from the purposes for which it has been given, well illustrates the paradox of form and substance in the development of law. In form its growth is logical. The official theory is that each new decision follows syllogistically from existing precedents. But just as the clavicle in the cat only tells of the existence of some earlier creature to which a collarbone was useful, precedents survive in the law long after the use they once served is at an end and the reason for them has been forgotten. The result of following them must often be failure and confusion from the merely logical point of view.

On the other hand, in substance the growth of the law is legislative. And this in a deeper sense than that what the courts declare to have always been the law is in fact new. It is legislative in its grounds. The very considerations which judges most rarely mention, and always with an apology, are the secret root from which the law draws all the juices of life. I mean, of course, considerations of what is expedient for the community concerned. Every important principle which is developed by litigation is in fact and at bottom the result of more or less definitely understood views of public policy; most generally, to be sure, under our practice and traditions, the unconscious result of instinctive preferences and inarticulate convictions, but none the less traceable to views of public policy in the last analysis. And as the law is administered by able and experienced men, who know too much to sacrifice good sense to a syllogism, it will be found that, when ancient rules maintain themselves in the way that has been and will be shown in this book, new reasons more fitted to the time have been found for them, and that they gradually receive a new content, and at last a new form, from the grounds to which they have been transplanted.

But hitherto this process has been largely unconscious. It is important, on that account, to bring to mind what the actual course of events has been. If it were only to insist on a more conscious recognition of the legislative function of the courts, as just explained, it would be useful, as we shall see more clearly further on.

What has been said will explain the failure of all theories which consider the law only from its formal side, whether they attempt to deduce the *corpus* from *a priori* postulates, or fall into the humbler error of supposing the science of the law to reside in the *elegantia juris*, or *logical* cohesion of part with part. The truth is, that the law is always approaching, and never reaching, consistency. It is forever adopting new principles from life at one end, and it always retains old ones from history at the other, which have not yet been absorbed or sloughed off. It will become entirely consistent only when it ceases to grow.

The study upon which we have been engaged is necessary both for the knowledge and for the revision of the law.

However much we may codify the law into a series of seemingly self-sufficient propositions, those propositions will be but a phase in a continuous growth. To understand their scope fully, to know how they will be dealt with by judges trained in the past which the law embodies, we must ourselves know something of that past. The history of what the law has been is necessary to the knowledge of what the law is.

[From] *Paradoxes of Legal Science*

BENJAMIN CARDOZO

Introduction — Rest and Motion — Stability and Progress

"They do things better with logarithms." The wail escapes me now and again after putting forth the best that is in me, I look upon the finished product, and cannot say that it is good. In these moments of disquietude, I figure to myself the peace of mind that must come, let us say, to the designer of a mighty bridge. The finished product of his work is there before his eyes with all the beauty and simplicity and inevitableness of truth. He is not harrowed by misgivings whether the towers and piers and cables will stand the stress and strain. His business is to know. If his bridge were to fall, he would go down with it in disgrace and ruin. Yet withal, he has never a fear. No mere experiment has he wrought, but a highway to carry men and women from shore to shore, to carry them secure and unafraid, though the floods rage and boil below.

So I cry out at times in rebellion, "why cannot I do as much, or at least something measurably as much, to bridge with my rules of law the torrents of life?" I have given my years to the task, and behind me are untold generations, the judges and lawgivers of old, who strove with a passion as burning. Code and commentary, manor-roll and year-book, treatise and law-report, reveal the processes of trial and error by which they struggled to attain the truth, enshrine their blunders and their triumphs for warning and example. All these memorials are mine; yet unwritten is my table of logarithms, the index of the power to which a precedent must be raised to produce the formula of justice. My bridges are experiments. I cannot span the tiniest stream in a region unexplored by judges or lawgivers before me, and go to rest in the secure belief that the span is wisely laid.

Let me not seem to cavil at the difficulties that learning can subdue. They are trying enough in all conscience, yet what industry can master, it would be weakness to lament. I am not thinking of the multitude of precedents and the labor of making them our own. The pangs that convulse are born of other trials. Diligence and memory and normal powers of reasoning may suffice to guide us truly in those fields where the judicial function is imitative or static, where known rules are to be applied to combinations of facts identical with present patterns, or, at worst, but slightly different. The travail comes when the judicial function is dynamic or creative. The rule must be announced for a novel situation where competituve analogies supply a hint or clew, but where precedents are lacking with authoritative commands.

I know the common answer to these and like laments. The law is not an exact science, we are told, and there the matter ends, if we are willing there to end it. One does not appease the rebellion of the intellect by the reaffirmance of the evil against which intellect rebels. Exactness may be impossible, but this is not enough to cause the mind to acquiesce in a predestined incoherence. Jurisprudence will be the gainer in the long run by fanning the fires of mental insurrection instead of smothering them with platitudes. "If science," says Whitehead, "is not to degenerate into a medley of *ad hoc* hypotheses, it must become philosophical and must enter upon a thorough criticism of its own foundations." We may say the like of law.

* * *

Notes and Questions

EDWARD LEVI, from *An Introduction to Legal Reasoning*

1. Edward Levi's model of legal reasoning is considered by many to be the definitive description of judicial reasoning in the American legal system. What is the pretense against which he is contrasting his model?

2. What is the basic pattern of legal reasoning, according to Levi? He identifies a three-step process that he considers to be implicit in the doctrine of precedent, or the rule of *stare decisis*. Recall that *stare decisis* is recognized as the cornerstone of Anglo-American law, as the everyday working rule of all judges in our system. What are the three steps Levi describes as implicit in the rule?

3. Levi sets out the fundamental problem of the working legal system as that of identifying common classifications. What is involved in this problem?

4. In what way is this system of reasoning questionable? Levi points out that apparently judicial reasoning in a common law system is a process "in which the classification changes as the classification is made. The rules change as the rules are applied." Can such a process be defended as a system of reason? How about as a system of justice? Does Levi successfully defend it?

5. What does Levi mean by the "law forum," and how (or why) is it supposed to handle the

imperfections of legal reasoning? What does it require? Do you agree that it provides for participation and fairness? Why does Levi think it does? Why is it the forum or process that makes a hearing fair rather than the impartiality of a judge? Suppose you were a litigant who lost because society was not yet ready to recognize your claim — for example, a black before segregation was outlawed or a woman banned from the workplace or the voting booth before women's rights were recognized. Would Levi's argument persuade you that your loss was fair after all since you did get to participate in the process and the process was changed eventually? Would it be reasonable to expect more? Is it fair to construe Levi's point this way? What else might he mean?

6. How does Levi describe the infusion and development of legal concepts into the legal system? If he is right about this process, does it support his thesis about judicial reasoning? Does it support his argument regarding the incorporation of common social ideas into law? Why should such a process make judges and lawyers uncomfortable?

[From] *An Introduction to Legal Reasoning*

EDWARD LEVI

I

This is an attempt to describe generally the process of legal reasoning in the field of case law and in the interpretation of statutes and of the Constitution. It is important that the mechanism of legal reasoning should not be concealed by its pretense. The pretense is that the law is a system of known rules applied by a judge; the pretense has long been under attack. In an important sense legal rules are never clear, and, if a rule had to be clear before it could be imposed, society would be impossible. The mechanism accepts the differences of view and ambiguities of words. It provides for the participation of the community in resolving the ambiguity by providing a forum for the discussion of policy in the gap of ambiguity. On serious controversial questions, it makes it possible to take the first step in the direction of what otherwise would be forbidden ends. The mechanism is indispensable to peace in a community.

The basic pattern of legal reasoning is reasoning by example.[1] It is reasoning from case to case. It is a three-step process described by the doctrine of precedent in which a proposition descriptive of the first case is made into a rule of law and then applied to a next similar situation. The steps are these: similarity is seen between cases; next the rule of law inherent in the first case is announced; then the rule of law is made applicable to the second case. This is a method of reasoning necessary for the law, but it has characteristics which under other circumstances might be considered imperfections.

These characteristics become evident if the legal process is approached as though it were a method of applying general rules of law to diverse facts — in short, as though the doctrine of precedent meant that general rules, once properly determined, remained unchanged, and then were applied, albeit imperfectly, in later cases. If this were the doctrine, it would be disturbing to find that the rules change from case to case and are remade with each case. Yet this change in the rules is the indispensable dynamic quality of law. It occurs because the scope of a rule of law, and therefore its meaning, depends upon a determination of what facts will be considered similar to those present when the rule was first announced. The finding of similarity or difference is the key step in the legal process.

The determination of similarity or difference is the function of each judge. Where case law is considered, and there is no statute, he is not bound by the statement of the rule of law made by the prior judge even in the controlling case. The statement is mere dictum, and this means that the judge in the present case may find irrelevant the existence or absence of facts which prior judges thought important. It is not what the prior judge intended that is of any importance; rather it is what the present judge, attempting to see the law as a fairly consistent whole, thinks should be the determining classification. In arriving at his result he will ignore what the past thought important; he will emphasize facts which prior judges would have thought made no difference. It is not alone that he could not see the law through the eyes of another, for he could at least try to do so. It is rather that the doctrine of dictum forces him to make his own decision.

Thus it cannot be said that the legal process is the application of known rules to diverse facts. Yet it is a system of rules; the rules are discovered in the process of determining similarity or difference. But if attention is directed toward the finding of similarity or difference, other peculiarities appear. The problem for the law is: When will it be just to treat different cases as though they were the same? A working legal system must therefore be willing to pick out key similarities and to reason from them to the justice of applying a common classification. The existence of some facts in common brings into play the general rule. If this is really reasoning, then by common standards, thought of in terms of closed systems, it is imperfect unless some overall rule has announced that this common and ascertainable similarity is to be decisive. But no such fixed prior rule exists. It could be suggested that reasoning is not involved at all; that is, that no new insight is arrived at through a comparison of cases. But reasoning appears to be involved; the conclusion is arrived at through a process and was not immediately apparent. It seems better to say there is reasoning, but it is imperfect.[2]

Therefore it appears that the kind of reasoning involved in the legal process is one in which the classification changes as the classification is made. The rules change as the rules are applied. More important, the rules arise out of a process which, while comparing fact situations, creates the rules and then applies them. But this kind of reasoning is open to the charge that it is classifying things as equal when they are somewhat different, justifying the classification by rules made up as the reasoning or classification proceeds. In a sense all reasoning is of this type, but there is an additional requirement which compels the legal process to be this way. Not only do new situations arise, but in addition peoples' wants change. The categories used in the legal process must be left ambiguous in order to permit the infusion of new ideas. And this is true even where legislation or a constitution is involved. The words used by the legislature or the constitutional convention must come to have new meanings. Furthermore, agreement on any other basis would be impossible. In this manner the laws come to express the ideas of the community and even when written in general terms, in statute or constitution, are molded for the specific case.

But attention must be paid to the process. A controversy as to whether the law is certain, unchanging, and expressed in rules, or uncertain, changing, and only a technique for deciding specific cases misses the point. It is both. Nor is it helpful to dispose of the process as a wonderful mystery possibly reflecting a higher law, by which the law can remain the same and yet change. The law forum is the most explicit demonstration of the mechanism required for a moving classification system. The folklore of law may choose to ignore the imperfections in legal reasoning,[3] but the law forum itself has taken care of them.

What does the law forum require? It requires the presentation of competing examples. The forum protects the parties and the community by making sure that the competing analogies are before the court. The rule which will be created arises out of a process in which if different things are to be treated as similar, at least the differences have been urged.[4] In this sense the parties as well as the court participate in the law-making. In this sense, also, lawyers represent more than the litigants.

Reasoning by example in the law is a key to many things. It indicates in part the hold which the law process has over the litigants. They have participated in the law-making. They are bound by something they helped to make. Moreover, the examples or analogies urged by the parties bring into the law the common ideas of the society. The ideas have their day in court, and they will have their day again. This is what makes the hearing fair, rather than any idea that the judge is completely impartial, for of course he cannot be completely so. Moreover, the hearing in a sense compels at least vicarious participation by all the citizens, for the rule which is made, even though ambiguous, will be law as to them.

Reasoning by example shows the decisive role which the common ideas of the society and the distinctions made by experts can have in shaping the law. The movement of common or expert concepts into the law may be followed. The concept is suggested in arguing difference or similarity in a brief, but it wins no approval from the court. The idea achieves standing in the society. It is suggested again to a court. The court this time reinterprets the prior case and in doing so adopts the rejected idea. In subsequent cases, the idea is given further definition and is tied to other ideas which have been accepted by courts. It is now no longer the idea which was commonly held in the society. It becomes modified in subsequent cases. Ideas first rejected but which gradually have won acceptance now push what has become a legal category out of the system or convert it into something which may be its opposite. The process is one in which the ideas of the community and of the social sciences, whether correct or not, as they win acceptance in the community, control legal decisions. Erroneous ideas, of course, have played an enormous part in shaping the law. An idea, adopted by a court, is in a superior position to influence conduct and opinion in the community; judges, after all, are rulers. And the adoption of an idea by a court reflects the power structure in the community. But reasoning by example will operate to change the idea after it has been adopted.

More reasoning by example brings into focus important similarity and difference in the interpretation of case law, statutes, and the constitution of a nation. There is a striking similarity. It is only folklore which holds that a statute if clearly written can be completely unambiguous and applied as intended to a specific case. Fortunately or otherwise, ambiguity is inevitable in both statute and constitution as well as with case law. Hence reasoning by example operates with all three. But there are important differences. What a court says is dictum, but what a legislature says is a statute. The reference of the reasoning changes. Interpretation of intention when dealing with a statute is the way of describing the attempt to compare cases on the basis of the standard thought to be common at the time the legislation was passed. While this is the attempt, it may not initially accomplish any different result than if the standard of the judge had been explicitly used. Nevertheless, the remarks of the judge are directed toward describing a category set up by the legislature. These remarks are different from ordinary dicta. They set the course of the statute, and later reasoning in subsequent cases is tied to them. As a consequence, courts are less free in applying a statute than in dealing with case law. The current rationale for this is the notion that the legislature has acquiesced by legislative silence in the prior, even though erroneous, interpretation of the court. But the change in reasoning where legislation is concerned seems an inevitable consequence of the division of function between court and legislature, and, paradoxically, a recognition also of the impossibility of determining legislative intent. The impairment of a court's freedom in interpreting legislation is reflected in frequent appeals to the constitution as a necessary justification for overruling cases even though these cases are thought to have interpreted the legislation erroneously.

Under the United States experience, contrary to what has sometimes been believed when a written constitution of a nation is involved, the court has greater freedom than it has with the application of a statute or case law. In case law, when a judge determines what the controlling similarity between the present and prior case is, the case is decided. The judge does not feel free to ignore the results of a great number of cases which he cannot explain under a remade rule. And in interpreting legislation, when the prior interpretation, even though erroneous, is determined after a comparison of facts to cover the case, the case is decided. But this is not true with a constitution. The constitution sets up the conflicting ideals of the community in certain ambiguous categories.[5] These categories bring along with them satellite concepts covering the areas of ambiguity. It is with a set of these satellite concepts that reasoning by example must work. But no satellite concept, no matter how well developed, can prevent the court from shifting its course, not only by realigning cases which impose certain restrictions, but by going beyond realignment back to the over-all ambiguous category written into the document. The constitution, in other words, permits the court to be inconsistent. The freedom is concealed either as a search for the intention of the framers or as a proper understanding of a living instrument, and sometimes as both. But this does not mean that reasoning by example has any less validity in this field.

II

It may be objected that this analysis of legal reasoning places too much emphasis on the comparison of cases and too little on the legal concepts which are created. It is true that similarity is seen in terms of a word, and inability to find a ready word to express similarity or difference may prevent change in the law. The words which have been found in the past are much spoken of, have acquired a dignity of their own, and to a considerable measure control results. As Judge Cardozo suggested in speaking of metaphors, the word starts out to free thought and ends by enslaving it.[6] The movement of concepts into and out of the law makes the point. If the society has begun to see certain significant similarities or differences, the comparison emerges with a word. When the word is finally accepted, it becomes a legal concept. Its meaning continues to change. But the comparison is not only between the instances which have been included under it and the actual case at hand, but also in terms of hypothetical instances which the word by itself suggests. Thus the connotation of the word for a time has a limiting influence — so much so that the reasoning may even appear to be simply deductive.

But it is not simply deductive. In the long run a circular motion can be seen. The first stage is the creation of the legal concept which is built up as cases are compared. The period is one in which the court fumbles for a phrase. Several phrases may be tried out; the misuse or misun-

derstanding of words itself may have an effect. The concept sounds like another, and the jump to the second is made. The second stage is the period when the concept is more or less fixed, although reasoning by example continues to classify items inside and out of the concept. The third stage is the breakdown of the concept, as reasoning by example has moved so far ahead as to make it clear that the suggestive influence of the word is no longer desired.

The process is likely to make judges and lawyers uncomfortable. It runs contrary to the pretense of the system. It seems inevitable, therefore, that as matters of kind vanish into matters of degree and then entirely new meanings turn up, there will be the attempt to escape to some overall rule which can be said to have always operated and which will make the reasoning look deductive. The rule will be useless. It will have to operate on a level where it has no meaning. Even when lip service is paid to it, care will be taken to say that it may be too wide or too narrow but that nevertheless it is a good rule. The statement of the rule is roughly analogous to the appeal to the meaning of a statute or of a constitution, but it has less of a function to perform. It is window dressing. Yet it can be very misleading. Particularly when a concept has broken down and reasoning by example is about to build another, textbook writers, well aware of the unreal aspect of old rules, will announce new ones, equally ambiguous and meaningless, forgetting that the legal process does not work with the rule but on a much lower level.

* * *

NOTES

1. "Clearly then to argue by example is neither like reasoning from part to whole, nor like reasoning from whole to part, but rather reasoning from part to part, when both particulars are subordinate to the same term and one of them is known. It differs from induction, because induction starting from all the particular cases proves . . . that the major term belongs to the middle and does not apply the syllogistic conclusion to the minor term, whereas argument by example does make this application and does not draw its proof from all the particular cases." Aristotle, *Analytica Priora* 69a (McKeon ed., 1941).

2. The logical fallacy is the fallacy of the undistributed middle or the fallacy of assuming the antecedent is true because the consequent has been affirmed.

3. "That the law can be obeyed even when it grows is often more than the legal profession itself can grasp." Cohen and Nagel, An Introduction to Logic and Scientific Method 371 (1934); see Stone, The Province and Function of Law 140–206 (1946).

4. The reasoning may take this form: A falls more appropriately in B than in C. It does so because A is more like D which is of B than it is like E which is of C. Since A is in B and B is in G (legal concept), then A is in G. But perhaps C is in G also. If so, then B is in a decisively different segment of G, because B is like H which is in G and has a different result from C.

5. Compare Myrdal, An American Dilemma, Ch. 1 (1944); Dicey, Law of the Constitution 126, 146 (9th ed., 1939).

6. Berkey v. Third Ave. Ry. Co., 244 N.Y. 84, 94, 155 N.E. 58, 61 (1926).

Notes and Questions

JULIUS STONE, from *Legal System and Lawyers' Reasonings*

1. The Anglo-American common law is an evolutionary process of law-building that produces a body of (judge-made) law constructed out of individual decisions (or rules) formulated for particular cases using the cement of precedent. This raises certain questions. What does it mean to follow the rule of precedent? Levi tries to answer this question by explaining how a judge's decision in the case before him is determined by the rule of a prior case that is relevantly similar. But this raises a second question. It cannot be that the rule of the precedent case *determines* the next case, for if it did the law could not grow. The question is, if precedent determines judicial decisions, that is, if later cases are determined by prior ones, how can the law ever change? This is the question raised by Julius Stone.

2. Stone focuses his attack on the theory of A. L. Goodhart, which is basically the same as that of Levi. Both rely on the possibility of formulating the "rule of the case" (often called the *ratio decidendi*), based on the holding or result of the case interpreted in light of the material (or relevant) facts of that case. The rule (or *ratio*) is the principle that is necessary to explain the holding in light of the facts. Why does Stone claim that every case in fact produces not one but many potential *ratios*? Why is that a problem?

3. Levi's (or Goodhart's) view also relies on the commonly drawn distinction between *holdings* and *dicta*, or that which is essential to decide the particular case and that which is not essential for the particular decision. Stone argues that the distinction (between *ratio decidendi* and *obiter dictum*) is sometimes quite meaningless. Why does he think so? Would Levi have to disagree? Can he answer Stone's criticisms?

4. Stone says that all major theories of *ratio decidendi* assume that there is a single best answer (a *ratio*) for every case. Is that a fair statement? He then uses *Donoghue* v. *Stevenson* to show why material facts do not yield one right answer. Why is this? Is Stone's demonstration convincing?

5. Can Levi save his theory by adverting to the "explicit or implicit assertions of the precedent court"? (What are implicit assertions?) Why does Stone think that this will not work?

6. What leeways of choice does Stone identify within the common law system of precedent? Are these legitimate avenues of choice for judges, according to Stone? What does he mean by "categories of illusory reference"? Does he persuade you that some legal categories are circular, indeterminate, or meaningless? What examples does he give? Are such categories avoidable?

7. It is widely agreed that Levi's method of determining the *ratio* is the best account available. If Stone's criticisms are apt, can Anglo-American legal method be defended? Should other factors be considered?

[From] *Legal System and Lawyers' Reasonings*

JULIUS STONE

CHAPTER 7

Categories of Illusory Reference in the Growth of the Common Law

* * *

§ 12. The System of Precedent Itself is Based on a Legal Category of Indeterminate or Concealed Multiple Reference, namely, "The *Ratio Decidendi* of a Case." The illusory nature of many supposed compulsions of logical consistency in the judicial process has also been stated in terms of the indeterminacy of the notion of *ratio decidendi* itself.[1] What appear to be judicial liberties with the distinction between *ratio decidendi* and *obiter dictum*, which sometimes make it quite meaningless, are in part at least a function of the inherent indeterminacy of the *ratio decidendi* itself, the two notions being complementary.

* * *

If the *ratio* of a case is deemed to turn on the facts in relation to the holding, and nine fact-elements (a)–(i) are to be found in the report, there may (so far as logical possibilities are concerned) be as many rival *rationes decidendi* as there are possible combinations of distinguishable facts in it. What is more, each of these fact-elements is usually itself capable of being stated at various levels of generality all of which embrace "the fact" in question in the precedent decision, but each of which may yield a different result in the different fact-situation of a later case. The range of fact-elements of *Donoghue* v. *Stevenson*, standing alone, might be over-simplified into a list somewhat as follows, each fact being itself stated at alternative levels.[2]

(a) *Fact as to the Agent of Harm.* Dead snails, *or* any snails, *or* any noxious physical foreign body, *or* any noxious foreign element, physical or not, *or* any noxious element.

(b) *Fact as to Vehicle of Harm.* An opaque bottle of ginger beer, *or* an opaque bottle of beverage, *or* any bottle of beverage, *or* any container of commodities for human consumption, *or* any container of any chattels for human use,

or any chattel whatsoever, *or* any thing (including land or buildings).[3]

(c) *Fact as to Defendant's Identity.* A manufacturer of goods nationally distributed through dispersed retailers, *or* any manufacturer, *or* any person working on the object for reward, *or* any person working on the object, *or* anyone dealing with the object.

(d) *Fact as to Potential Danger from Vehicle of Harm.* Object likely to become dangerous by negligence, *or* whether or not so.

(e) *Fact as to Injury to Plaintiff.* Physical personal injury, *or* nervous or physical personal injury, *or* any injury.

(f) *Fact as to Plaintiff's Identity.* A Scots widow, *or* a Scotswoman, *or* a woman, *or* any adult, *or* any human being, *or* any legal person.

(g) *Fact as to Plaintiff's Relation to Vehicle of Harm.* Donee of purchaser from retailer who bought directly from the defendant, *or* the purchaser from such retailer, *or* the purchaser from anyone, *or* any person related to such purchaser or donee, *or* other person, *or* any person into whose hands the object rightfully comes, *or* any person into whose hands it comes at all.

(h) *Fact as to Discoverability of Agent of Harm.* The noxious element being not discoverable by inspection of any intermediate party, *or* not so discoverable without destroying the saleability of the commodity, *or* not so discoverable by any such party who had a duty to inspect, *or* not so discoverable by any such party who could reasonably be expected *by the defendant* to inspect, *or* not discoverable by any such party who could reasonably be expected *by the court or a jury* to inspect.

(i) *Fact as to Time of Litigation.* The facts complained of were litigated in 1932, *or* any time before 1932, *or* at any time.

We are, it is recalled, first considering the question of "materiality" *apart from any view on that matter "explicitly" or "implicitly" manifest in the precedent court's opinion.* As to none of these facts (a)–(i), and as to none of the several alternative levels of statement of each of them, could it be said, taking the facts and holding of *Donoghue* v. *Stevenson* alone, that it was on its face not "material" (in a logical sense) to the holding in that case. Even as to the time of litigation, as to which we are most tempted to say that this at least must be "immaterial" on the face of it, we must be careful to avoid a *petitio principii.* Are we really prepared to assert with dogmatism that *Donoghue* v. *Stevenson* should have been, and would in fact have been, so decided in 1800? If not, it follows that *logically,* i. e., apart from any special indication that should be drawn from the precedent court's own attitude, the "*ratio*" of *Donoghue* v. *Stevenson* did not compel later courts to impose liability in any case where only some of the above possible "material" facts, and some levels of statement of them, were found. And another way of saying this is that (apart still from such special indication) a *ratio decidendi* drawn from a case by the "material facts" method can only be prescriptive or binding for a later case whose facts are "on all fours" *in every respect.* And since the italicised words must be taken seriously, this reduces the range of the binding *ratio decidendi* to vanishing point. Outside this range, the question always is whether in the later court's view the presence in the instant case of *some* of the fact-elements (a)–(i), at some of their alternative levels of generalised statement, is more relevant to the present decision, than is the absence of *the rest of them.* And this is not a question of the "materiality" of facts to the decision in the precedent case imposing itself on the later court. It is rather a question of the analogical relevance of the prior holding to the later case, requiring the later court to choose between possibilities presented by the precedent case.

At this point then, *before* we begin searching for the precedent court's assertion as to which facts and levels of statement of them are "material," it is correct to say that the questions: What single principle does a particular case establish? What is *the ratio decidendi* of this case as at the time of its decision? are strictly nonsensical. For they can only be answered by saying that there is no such single principle or *ratio* that can in terms

of the "material facts" test be binding in a later case.[4]

Does it then overcome this difficulty to define "materiality," as Professor Goodhart in effect does, in terms of the precedent court's explicit or implicit assertion as to which of facts (a)–(i) are material? Or to insist that the question, What are the "material facts" by which we determine the prescriptive *ratio* of a case? is always to be determined *according to the view of the precedent court,* and not according to the view of the later court or observer? Indeed, in his defence of his position in 1959[5] this distinction becomes almost its central bastion. Yet there will often be the gravest doubt as to what facts the precedent court "explicitly or implicitly" "determined" to be material. There will often be inconsistent indications from what is expressed or implicit, even in a one judge court. Such inconsistencies as between the concurring judgments in appellate courts are notoriously also a constant and fruitful source of legal uncertainty and change. The more important the issue and the instance of appeal the more likely are there to be multiple judgments and therefore multiple versions of the *ratio decidendi;* and this by any test. And there are other chronic sources of competing versions and indeterminacies later to be mentioned.

Professor Goodhart recognises some of these difficulties in distinguishing which of fact-elements (a)–(i) are "material," and in particular that this would involve some guesswork on the part of later courts in applying his system. In his latest exposition he urges that they nevertheless do not affect his "system" since they are due to "the subject-matter itself, and not to the system which is applied to it."[6] On the most favourable understanding of this, it appears to mean that the difficulties spring from deficiencies in articulation of the precedent court or in the report, or other characteristics which are of a more or less "accidental" nature. Even to this it would have to be said that the "accident-proneness" in the subject-matter makes the difficulties serious and constant.

Yet these are not the most crucial difficulties with Professor Goodhart's system. The crucial ones arise rather from the several alternative *levels of statement* of each "material fact" of the precedent case, ranging from the full unique concreteness of that actual case, through a series of widening generalisations. In this series only the unique concreteness is *firmly* anchored to the precedent court's view that a given Fact A is "material"; and *ex hypothesi* that level of unique concreteness can scarcely figure as a part of the binding *ratio* for other cases. By the same token the reach of the *ratio*, even after each "material fact" seen by the original court is identified, will vary with the level of generalisation at which "the fact-element" is stated. How then is the "correct" level of statement of each fact-element to be ascertained by the later court?

Is this question, too, to be referred back entirely to the "explicit" or "implicit" view of the precedent court, as to which is the "material" level of statement of each "material" fact? Are we to say that merely because the House in *Donoghue* v. *Stevenson* might have stated the material facts as to the agent and vehicle of harm in terms of snails and bottles of beverage, this concludes one way or another a later case as to defects in cartons of butter, or the wheels of automobiles? Is it reasonable to assume that courts using language appropriate to the case before them do, or could, address themselves in their choice of language to all the levels of generality at which each "material" fact (a)–(i) of the concrete case is capable of statement, not to speak of the possible combinations and variations of these facts, and the implications of all these for as yet unforeseen future cases? Yet unless it is reasonable it would reduce judgment in later cases to a kind of lottery (turning on the chance of words used) to say that the later holding is controlled by that level of generalised statement of the assumed "material fact" which is explicit in the precedent court's judgment. And to admit also that level which might be "implicit" in the former judgment would in most cases be merely to impute to the precedent court a choice of levels of generalised statement (and therefore of the reach of the *ratio* in the instant case) which must in reality be made by the instant later court.

If, on the other hand, Professor Goodhart's reference of the question of "materiality" back to the precedent court does not extend to the question, Which level of generalised statement of the "material fact" is determinative of the *ratio*?, the *impasse* of his system would become, if possible, even clearer, because more patent. Each "material fact" of a case would then have to be recognised as capable of statement in an often numerous range of more or less generalised versions, the range of the *ratio* varying with each version.

We here approach the very core of the difference between Professor Goodhart and the present writer concerning "the *ratio decidendi* of a case." However it be as to certain interesting ancillary points of debate between Professor Montrose and Mr. Simpson on matters collateral to this writer's position, both of them are agreed (and, it is believed, correctly) on two matters.[7] One is that Professor Goodhart's "system" of discovering the *ratio decidendi* neither *describes* adequately the actual process by which case law is built up, nor can it be the answer to the question, How do we discover "the *ratio decidendi* of a single case"?

For, once it is granted that "a material fact" of the precedent case can be stated at various levels of generality, each of which is correct for that case, any of these levels of statement is potentially a "material fact." Insofar as the *ratio decidendi* is determined by each "material fact," then what the precedent case yields must be a number of potentially binding *rationes* competing *inter se* to govern future cases of which the facts may fall within one level of generality, but not within another. An automobile in bad repair can be a noxious physical object, but no one can call it an opaque bottle containing a reputed snail.

Professor Goodhart in his latest statement finally agrees with the present view that "further decisions are frequently required" to determine the *ratio*, and he adopts Professor Paton's metaphor for these decisions as "plotting the points on a graph."[8] Clearly this implies that the searching of a single case cannot reveal only one single set of "material facts," nor only one binding *ratio decidendi*. It yields rather a range of alternative *rationes decidendi*[9] competing *inter se* to govern future fact situations; and, as among these, only future decisions will show which is binding. Moreover, we believe that most of the sources of uncertainty thus concealed are central and not merely marginal to the operation of precedent, so that the need for guesswork, which Professor Goodhart admits, also becomes central in the operation of his "system."

§ 13. Conspectus of Leeways for Judicial Choice Within the Common Law System of Precedent. It seems appropriate at this point to place the areas within which the exercise of judicial choice is compelled by the indeterminate nature of the *ratio decidendi*, along with other areas of such required judicial choice. Such a stocktaking, as it were, of the bearing of modern juristic thought on "the rule of *stare decisis*," may afford some at least of the answer to Lord Wright's question how the "perpetual process of change" in the common law (and above all its movement on appellate levels) is to be reconciled with "the rule of *stare decisis*." The main sources from which the leeways for judicial choice arise can now be seen to occupy a number of the principal "control centres" in the operation of a system of precedent. They include:

(a) Choices unavoidably arising from the nature of terms used in substantive rules, or from interrelations of rules.

(b) Choices unavoidably arising from competing methods of seeking "the *ratio decidendi* of a case."

(c) Choices unavoidably arising from the competing versions of the *ratio decidendi* of a particular case, when the "material facts" method is applied even to a single judge decision.

(d) Additional choices arising from the competing versions of the *ratio decidendi* of a particular case (by any test) when several judgments are given. (We may recall that at higher appellate levels the number of judges tends to increase, and with it the number of individual judgments.)

(e) The multiplication of available choices arising from the interplay of the above.

Each area of required judicial choice arising in the above several ways imports room for action of a later court uncoerced by a supposed single *ratio decidendi* of the earlier case. Each such area may present itself in a particular case. And while all of them may not necessarily be present in every important appellate case, more than one of them may be, and indeed, often are, present together. When this occurs the effect of the interaction of the several areas will be to increase the area of judicial choice, not merely in arithmetical but in geometrical proportions, by dint of the range of combinations and variations of the series of choices available in each area.

The duty of choice in the interpretation of a precedent containing in its language a "category of illusory reference" (as above described) will be further expanded if later courts resort to competing versions of the method of determining its *ratio*.[10] And even if later courts all choose one method of determining its *ratio*, the choices might still be greatly expanded because the later courts, despite their similarity of method, still reach (as we have seen they may) competing versions of the *ratio decidendi* of that particular precedent.[11] And, of course, there will often be superadded to such situations, especially where the precedent is a leading case decided at a high appellate level, the range of choices and of further combinations and variations of them, arising from varied rules "enunciated," or "material facts" explicitly or implicitly found, as a basis of the respective decisions in a multiplicity of appellate judgments in the single case.

In practice, then, the leeways available after an important leading decision tend to be vastly extended by interplay of different categories even within the single case, permitting the entry of judicial experience of life, and judicially recognised social values, into the common law of successive generations. And this interplay may become enormously complicated as the line of cases builds up in an area of social and economic pressure and uncertainty, such as that of the law of conspiracy, or the scope of freedom of interstate commerce under s. 92 of the Australian Constitution Act.[12] It is scarcely necessary to stress again the fact that more than one of the illusory categories may operate both independently and in interplay with each other in a single case.[13] And we have already remarked on the effects of the apparent convergence and overlapping of categories — for instance, of circular and indeterminate reference, and of indeterminate and meaningless reference.

We should, perhaps, examine somewhat more closely the apparent phenomenon that the *same legal category* sometimes seems susceptible of simultaneous analysis in terms of more than one of the illusory categories. In *The Province and Function of Law*, Lord Atkin's "neighbour" test for duty of care in *Donoghue* v. *Stevenson* was offered as an example of concealed circular reference, or (in the terminology which we there used) of concealed circuitous reference. This arose from an analysis which saw one main issue in the case to be "Was the Defendant negligent towards the Plaintiff?" (i. e., "Did he injure the Plaintiff by acting or omitting to act when he ought reasonably to have anticipated that the act or omission would cause injury to the Plaintiff?"). On this assumption, when Lord Atkin posed the further question "Did the Defendant have a duty of care towards the Plaintiff?" and proceeded in effect to translate it as "Was the Plaintiff his neighbour?" and this in turn as "Ought he reasonably to have had the plaintiff in contemplation as likely to be affected by the act or omission if he did not exercise care?" his answer merely restated the first of the above questions, which was a main issue. It was, in short, circular in relation to that issue.

In the present work we have thought it important, however, to add that a category of meaningless reference seems rather to be involved. For if we focus not on the main issue of liability for the tort of negligence, but on two of the several elements required therefor, namely, the failure to exercise reasonable care (negligence in the narrower sense), and the duty of care, then the assertion that negligence and duty of care must both be shown implies *that there may be cases of negligence where there was no duty of care*. It assumes, in other words, that there can be cases where the Defendant ought reasonably to have foreseen the injury, and yet also in which, despite this, the Defendant ought not so to have foreseen the injury. It assumes, in short, that the same facts can simultaneously constitute a position of reasonable foreseeability and also the negation of it; and it thus involves a flat self-contradiction and thereby a category of meaningless reference.

Furthermore, as we have seen, there lurk centrally within the meaningless category thus implied, the standards of "neighbour," and *"reasonable"* contemplation, both categories of indeterminate reference. These both add to the leeways, and confuse the analysis of them. And as if to crown the example, Lord Atkin's duty concept entered the field in 1932 as one of other competing versions of the duty element in "general neg-

ligence." It may be that it has gone far to establish itself as *the most* authoritative version. Yet the other versions are still not beyond judicial resort, as is clear from such cases as *Commissioner for Railways* v. *Cardy*[14] concerning specific classes of negligence as between parties in particular relations, for instance, occupiers of land and invitees, licensees, and trespassers respectively. On Fullagar J.'s view that the standard of care imported in such specific classes is an application of Lord Atkin's test to different sets of facts, Lord Atkin's test becomes a category of concealed multiple reference. And on any view, Lord Atkin's test and the specific tests for specific relationships are likely to be categories of competing reference in any given case. All these facinating complexities arise quite apart from the various understandings of Lord Atkin's test itself, when seen in the full context of the facts of the case and of his speech as a whole.[15]

Nor is all this pointed out from any love of pedantry or even casuistry.[16] The main problem we are addressing is, on the contrary, one of dramatic social and legal significance — to explain, in Lord Wright's words, "the perpetual process of change" within the framework of authority and *stare decisis*. The leeways created by a single illusory category free the judge of any simple tyranny of the precedent cases over his judgment between the litigants. But in what direction he assumes this freedom is also important for future cases, insofar as his successors then seek their own leeways within the category which he used. The more illusory categories are involved, and the more interplay there is among them, the more wide-ranging are the directions of freedom into which the leeways will allow the later judge to reach out for a just solution for the instant case. And, correspondingly, the less inhibited are we likely to find the judicial successor who may be "bound" by *"stare decisis"* to "follow" the earlier decision.

* * *

NOTES

1. Roscoe Pound and others have stressed that only a line of decisions gives even an approximation to a definite rule. The best short account from the present standpoint is in [F. S.] Cohen, *Ethical Systems [and Legal Ideals]* 33–40.

2. That the above break-up of alternative versions of "material" facts is not merely fanciful is shown both by the later history of *Donoghue* v. *Stevenson*, and in other areas of the law as well. See, e. g., the fantastic story of the versions of the *ratio* on the question whether buyer or seller is responsible for obtaining an export license, beginning with Scrutton L. J., in *H. O. Brandt* v. *H. N. Morris* (1917) 2 K.B. 784, through to *A. V. Pound* v. *M. W. Hardy* (1956) 1 All E.R. 639 (C.A.), (1956) A.C. 588 (H.L.), discussed in the stimulating Note by J. L. Montrose (1956) 19 *M.L.R.* 525. And see K. N. Llewellyn, *The Bramble Bush* (2 ed. 1951) 47–48.

3. See *Otto* v. *Bolton* (1936) 2 K.B. 46, 54–55 (principle held limited to chattels): *Candler* v. *Crane, Christmas and Co.* (1951) 2 K.B. 164 (C.A. disagreement *inter se* whether it could be extended to a non-physical agent of non-physical harm). *Cf.* as to the latter case and on the discriminatory rules which arise from the decisions to resort or not to the "neighbour" principle in a given situation, R. F. V. Heuston, "Donoghue v. Stevenson in Retrospect" (1957) 20 *M.L.R.* 1, at 18–19. And as this part of the MS. went to press, the H.L. in *Hedley Byrne and Co.* v. *Heller* (1963) 3 W.L.R. 101 finally resolved the disagreement in *Candler's Case* in favour of the then minority view extending the principle. . . .

4. The question whether a court is "bound" by a single precedent must remain largely meaningless, with respect, however earnestly it continues to be discussed by courts and text writers. See the remarkable collection of such discussions in W. H. D. Winder, "Precedent in Equity" (1941) 57 *L.Q.R.* 245, 263–79.

Wright, *Essays* 399, writes that the same set of facts rarely repeats itself and that "generally" a judge who feels that justice so requires can distinguish the instant facts from the authorities. *Cf.* [F.S.] Cohen, *Ethical Systems* 35–36: "Elementary logic teaches us that every legal decision (particular proposition) can be subsumed under an indefinite number of different general rules, just as an infinite number of different curves may be traced through any point or finite collection of points. Every decision is a choice between different rules which logically fit all past decisions but logically dictate conflicting results in the instant case. Logic provides the springboard but it does not guarantee the success of any particular jump."

5. A. L. Goodhart, "The *Ratio Decidendi* of a Case" (1959) 22 *M.L.R.* 117, at 123 [p. 943, *supra*].

6. Art. cited *supra* n. 5, at 124 [p. 944, *supra*].

7. See esp. A. W. B. Simpson, "The *Ratio Decidendi* . . ." (1958) 21 *M.L.R.* 155, 160; J. L. Montrose, "*Ratio Decidendi* and the House of Lords" (1957) 20 *id.* 124; *id.*, "The *Ratio Decidendi* . . ." (1957) 20 *id.* 587, 593–94.

8. (1959) 22 *M.L.R.* 117 at 124, following G. W.

Paton, *Jurisprudence* (2 ed. 1950) 161. The metaphor scarcely advances the real point, which had frequently been made long before Professor Paton's work.

9. The number of such alternatives is strictly a function of the permutations and combinations of fact-elements and levels of generality of statement of these. The number of permutations of *n* objects taken two at a time is n(n–1), taken three at a time is n(n–1)(n–2), taken all together is n(n–1) . . . 3.2.1. etc. If, for example, the total number of fact-elements and levels of generality of statement of these in *Donoghue* v. *Stevenson* were 6, the number of *logically possible* alternative *rationes* would be 720; if the former number were 10 the logically possible alternatives would be 3,628,800.

10. A court or writer who follows consistently either the "material facts" version of the *ratio*, or the "classical" version, would be limited only to the competing choices under each of those heads. In fact, however, courts and writers often feel free to shift from one of these versions of the *ratio* to the other, sometimes even in the same case. There is thus opened up further possible multiplication of choices by switching from one version of the facts to another within the "material facts" version of the *ratio decidendi*, from one version of the propounded reasons to another within the "classical" version of the *ratio decidendi*, and from any of the versions within either of these classes, to a version within the other class. Hart, [*The Concept of*] *Law* 138–144, has now restated the uncertainties in precedent theory and the resulting leeways, in terms of the "rules of recognition" of the criteria of validity of judicially made law.

11. A striking illustration is the history of the joint "advisory" remarks of the majority judges in the Second *Hughes & Vale Case* (1955) 93 C.L.R. 127. Within two years, in *Armstrong* v. *Victoria (No. 2)* (1957) 99 C.L.R. 28, they were in sufficient disagreement as to the import of those remarks, for one of them to consider dissenting from the later application of them. See Webb J. at 144. This also nicely points the limit value of joint opinions for avoiding uncertainties as to the *ratio*. And see *supra* n. 204. *Cf.* in the U.S. the tensions between Justices Jackson and Douglas as to the latter's later versions of earlier joint holdings as to *locus standi* of corporations within the equal protection and due process clauses. See *Wheeling Steel Corp.* v. *Glander* (1949) 69 Sup.Ct. Rep. 1291, esp. 1208 ff. [337 U.S. 502, 576 ff, 93 L.Ed. 1544, 1552 ff.]

12. Leeways under a constitution on which judges have the last word become politically crucial, and their work correspondingly heavy and hazardous. *Cf.* the periodic crises of the U.S. Supreme Court, on the latest of which (school desegregation) see for a brief account, P. A. Freund, "Storm over the American Supreme Court" (1958) 21 *M.L.R.* 345–358. And see

other literature cited Stone, *Social Dimensions [of Law and Justice]* Ch. 1, n. 150, Ch. 14, §§ 4–14, . . .

13. The H.Ct. in *Alford* v. *Magee* (1952) 85 C.L.R. 437 provided a classical display of the pathology of a branch of law, resulting from long interplay of a number of illusory categories unbroken by reconsideration of the merits of the solutions they provided. In present terminology the Court's analysis of the contributory negligence and last opportunity rules displayed *meaningless references* (e. g. 451–452, in relation to either way of defining contributory negligence); *competing references* (e. g. 453, between traditional common law liability, and "no liability without fault"); *concealed multiple references* (e. g. 455–460, esp. 459–460 in judicial versions of the "last opportunity rule"), and *indeterminate reference* (460–461, where precision in the rules is said to be unattainable).

14. (1960) 104 C.L.R. 274. The particular passage referred to in the judgment of Fullagar J. is at 204. See also the discussion in W. L. Morison, "Streamlining Liability to Trespassers" (1980) 34 *A.L.J.* 204.

15. In particular, Lord Atkin stated his test at the end of his opinion in a more concrete form (referring to "manufacturers" of "products" sold in the "form" intended "to reach the ultimate consumer" with "no reasonable possibility of intermediate inspection," etc., etc.) than the "neighbour" formulation. See (1932) A.C. 599. Some writers, indeed, e. g., Cross, *Precedent [in English Law]* 39, boldly exclude the "neighbour" formulation from the *ratio* of *Donoghue* v. *Stevenson*. And almost as if to provide material for the present thesis, Lord Atkin also included in his speech two contradictory warnings. One warning, on 583–84, was that it was dangerous to state "propositions of law in wider

terms than is necessary," and that "the actual decision alone should carry authority" with "proper weight, of course" to "the *dicta*" of the judges. The other, on 594–95, was against "seeking to confine the law to rigid and exclusive categories" and "not giving sufficient attention to the general principle which governs the whole law of negligence. . . ." And, for the incorrigible believer in the (single) *ratio decidendi* of a case, we add for full measure that the words "*proper weight*" and "*sufficient* attention" are both of them categories of indeterminate reference; and that Lord Atkin's opposition of "the decision" to "the *dicta*" at 583–84 can be understood in either of two very different competing versions. One would favour Goodhart's "material facts" theory for finding the *ratio*, as against the "classical" theory. The other would amount merely to a commonplace assertion that the *ratio decidendi* (however found) is more binding than mere *obiter dicta*. And this would be quite neutral as between theories of how to find the *ratio*.

16. The multiplicity of illusory references surrounding *Donoghue* v. *Stevenson* can in any case be matched elsewhere. *Cf.*, e. g., the multiple versions of "merchantable quality" in *Benjamin on Sale* (8 ed. 1950) 645, and *Grant* v. *Aust. Knitting Mills* (1936) A.C. 85. Benjamin's version is indeterminate, and may even become (as in *George Wills & Co. Ltd.* v. *Davids Pty Ltd.* (1957) 98 C.L.R. 77) circular in operation. And as Fullagar J. pointed out, in *Mraz* v. *R. (No. 1)* (1955) 93 C.L.R. 493, 510, 512–13, a direction in a rape case that, to convict, the jury must find not only rape but that the rape was "malicious," introduced circular, concealed multiple and meaningless references.

Notes and Questions

DAVID KAIRYS, from *The Politics of Law*

1. In this essay David Kairys advances a position that extends Stone's thesis on the indeterminacy of precedent in the common law to constitutional interpretation and so-called legal reasoning in general. Kairys claims that there is no such thing as legal reasoning. What does he mean?

2. According to Kairys, *stare decisis*, as a method of objective decision making that determines answers in legal cases, is a myth. What function does *stare decisis* (or precedent) really play in his view? He suggests that a review of the development of precedent supports his position. How?

3. Kairys uses a line of Supreme Court decisions regarding the example of free speech to illustrate his argument that courts are free to choose which precedents to follow and how to construe them. What are these cases about, and how do they support his position? Is Kairys right that the same precedent will often support both sides of an issue? Is this the case in *Hudgens*?

4. Kairys says that the constitutional cases he cites demonstrate a central deception of traditional jurisprudence. What is that central deception? Why does it tend to be invisible to those trained in law? Can the traditionalist answer his objections?

5. On what, according to Kairys, do judicial decisions ultimately depend? Because of this, what should the focus of judicial decision making be? Should law schools, judicial opinions, and law review articles be changed as well?

6. How does Kairys explain the fact that some areas of law are quite settled and predictable? In what sense does he recognize the significance of *stare decisis*? Does his view do it justice?

7. Is there any difference between law and politics, according to Kairys? What are the really important questions, ignored by judges, law teachers, and commentators, that we should be addressing rather than perpetuating the myth of objectivity (or neutrality) through *stare decisis* or precedent?

[From] *The Politics of Law*

DAVID KAIRYS

C H A P T E R   1

Legal Reasoning

The idealized model of the legal process discussed in the introduction is based on the notion that there is a distinctly legal mode of reasoning and analysis that leads to and determines "correct" rules, facts, and results in particular cases. The concept of legal reasoning is essential to the fundamental legitimizing claim of government by law, not people; it purports to distinguish legal analysis and expertise from the variety of social, political, and economic considerations and modes of analysis that, in a democratic society, would be more appropriately debated and determined by the people, not judges.

This chapter focuses on one of the basic elements or mechanisms of legal reasoning, *stare decisis*, which embodies the notion of judicial subservience to prior decisions or precedents. The notion is that judges are bound by and defer to precedents, thereby restricting their domain to law rather than politics.

If legal reasoning has any real meaning, *stare decisis*, applied by a skilled and fair legal mind, should lead to and require particular results in specific cases. But anyone familiar with the legal system knows that some precedents are followed

and some are not; thus, not all precedents are treated similarly or equally. Moreover, the meaning of a precedent and its significance to a new case are frequently unclear. The important questions, largely ignored by judges, law teachers, and commentators, are: How do courts decide which precedents to follow? How do they determine the significance of ambiguous precedents? Do precedents really matter at all? Why do lawyers spend so much time talking about them?

The Supreme Court's recent decisions concerning exercise of free-speech rights in privately owned shopping centers provide a good illustration. In *Amalgamated Food Employees Union Local 590* v. *Logan Valley Plaza* (1968),[1] the Court upheld the constitutional right of union members to picket a store involved in a labor dispute in the shopping center where it was located. The Court recognized that shopping centers have to a large extent replaced inner-city business districts. The best, and perhaps only, place to communicate with suburbanites is in shopping centers. Citing *Marsh* v. *Alabama* (1946),[2] in which First Amendment freedoms were held applicable to a "company town," the Court ruled that the interest in free speech outweighed the private-property interests of shopping-center owners.

However, only four years later, in *Lloyd* v. *Tanner* (1972),[3] the Court held that an antiwar activist had no right to distribute leaflets in a shopping center, even though this center regularly attracted political candidates by avowing that it provided the largest audience in the state. The majority opinion justified the decision by claiming to differentiate the facts involved from those in *Logan Valley* primarily on the ground that speech concerning a labor dispute relates more closely to the activities of a shopping center than does antiwar speech. (In legal parlance, this is called distinguishing a precedent.)

Then, in *Hudgens* v. *NLRB* (1976),[4] the Court announced that, contrary to explicit language in *Lloyd*, the Court had actually overruled *Logan Valley* in the *Lloyd* case. The Court said that to treat labor speech differently from antiwar speech would violate the norm that First Amendment freedoms do not depend on the content of the speech, a result that surely was not intended in *Lloyd*. Having rewritten *Lloyd*, the *Hudgens* court went on to say that it was bound by *Lloyd* (as rewritten) and to hold that union members involved in a labor dispute with a store located in a shopping center do not have a constitutional right to picket in that shopping center. The stated rationale for this complete turnabout, within only eight years, was *stare decisis*: "Our institutional duty is to follow until changed the law as it now is, not as some members of the Court might wish it to be."[5]

The Court offered no explanation of what happened to this "institutional duty" in *Lloyd*, since the *Lloyd* court would seem to have been bound by *Logan Valley* (which the *Hudgens* court held had decided the same issue decided in *Lloyd*). Nor did the Court explain how its duty to "follow until changed the law as it now is" binds it in any real sense, since even within the system of *stare decisis* it is understood that the Court can change the law or overrule, ignore, or rewrite prior decisions. The Supreme Court is never really *bound* by a precedent. Finally, the majority opinion in *Hudgens* castigated the dissenting justices for deciding cases on the basis of what they "might wish [the law] to be," but there is no indication of how the majority's decision-making process is

different. The majority simply outnumbered the minority.

There were ample precedents supporting each of the conflicting policies in *Hudgens*. Freedom of speech was favored over private property in *Marsh* (from an earlier period when First Amendment rights were being expanded) and in *Logan Valley* itself. Private property and the interests of suburbanites in isolation were favored in earlier cases and recently in *Lloyd*. This policy conflict clearly was not — and could not be — resolved by some objective or required application of *stare decisis* or any other legal principle.

Unstated and lost in the mire of contradictory precedents and justifications was the central point that none of these cases was or could be decided without ultimate reference to values and choices of a *political* nature. The various justifications and precedents emphasized in the opinions serve to mask these little-discussed but unavoidable social and political judgments. In 1968, a majority of the members of the Court resolved the conflict in favor of freedom of speech; in 1972, a majority retreated from that judgment; in 1976, a majority decided that property interests would prevail.

In short, these cases demonstrate a central deception of traditional jurisprudence: the majority claims for its social and political judgment not only the status of law (in the sense of binding authority), which it surely has, but also that its judgment is the product of distinctly legal reasoning, of a neutral, objective application of legal expertise. This latter claim, essential to the legitimacy and mystique of the courts, is false.

Stare decisis is so integral to legal thinking and education that it becomes internalized by people trained in the law, and its social role and ideological content become blurred and invisible. To see these aspects of and to understand *stare decisis*, it is helpful to separate the social role from the functional impact on the decision-making process.

Our legal norms are broadly and vaguely stated. They do not logically lead to particular results or rationales concerning most important or difficult issues.[6] A wide variety of interpretations, distinctions, and justifications are available; and judges have the authority and power to choose the issues they will address and to ignore constitutional provisions, statutes, precedents, evidence, and the best legal arguments.

Moreover, there are prior decisions similar or related by analogy to both sides of almost any difficult or important issue. This should not be surprising, since issues are difficult or important largely because there are significant policies, rooted in social reality and/or legal doctrine, supporting both sides. Each such policy, or a closely related policy, will have been favored or given high priority in some context and/or during some period. Usually the various relevant precedents will provide some support for both sides rather than lead to a particular law or result.

Indeed, often the same precedent will provide support for both sides. For example, suppose after *Hudgens* an antinuclear activist claimed the right to distribute leaflets and picket in a privately owned railroad terminal. The terminal's counsel would argue that *Hudgens* should be broadly construed as definitively resolving the issue of speech on private property that is open to the public. He or she would emphasize the physical and functional similarities of shopping centers and train terminals. On the other hand, the activist's counsel would urge that *Hudgens* be narrowly construed as applicable only to the particular problem of labor picketing and only to the shopping center involved in that case or, at most, to shopping centers generally. He or she would emphasize the differences between train terminals and shopping centers. Much of legal education consists of training students to make arguments and distinctions of this kind. Both sides would argue that *Hudgens*, properly construed (a phrase likely to be found in both briefs), supports each of them. The judge would then decide the case, citing *Hudgens* as support for his or her decision regardless of which side won. There is no *legal* explanation in any of this; the law has provided a falsely legitimizing justification for a decision that is ultimately social and political.

Thus, *stare decisis* neither leads to nor requires any particular results or rationales in specific cases. A wide variety of precedents and still wider variety of interpretations and distinctions are available from which to pick and choose. Social and political judgments about the substance, parties, and context of the case guide such choices, even when they are not the explicit or conscious basis of decision. In the shopping-center cases, justices who placed a preeminent value on freedom of speech found *Marsh* and *Logan Valley* precedents that should be followed, while justices who viewed property rights as more important placed considerable precedential weight on *Lloyd*.

Judicial decisions ultimately depend on judgments based on values and priorities that vary with particular judges (and even with the same judge, depending on the context) and are the result of a composite of social, political, institutional, experimental, and personal factors. The socially and legally important focus of judicial decision making — hidden by *stare decisis* and the notion of legal reasoning, and largely ignored in law schools, opinions, and law review articles — should be on the content, origins, and development of these values and priorities.

This does not mean that judicial values and priorities, or the results in particular cases, are random or wholly unpredictable. The shared backgrounds, socialization, and experience of our judges, which include law school and usually law practice, yield definite patterns in the ways they categorize, approach, and resolve social and political conflicts. Moreover, some rules and results are relatively uncontroversial and predictable in a particular historical context, not based on *stare decisis* or any other legal principle but because of widely shared social and political assumptions characteristic of that context.

While seeming to limit discretion and to require objective and rational analysis, *stare decisis* in fact provides and serves to disguise enormous discretion. This discretion is somewhat broader in the higher courts, but it exists at all levels. Lower courts have an added institutional concern, since their decisions can be reviewed, but they also have added discretion stemming from their relatively larger control over the facts and the credibility of witnesses.

Functionally, *stare decisis* is not a process of decision making or a mechanism that ensures continuity, predictability, rationality, or objectivity. Precedents are largely reduced to rationalizations, not factors meaningfully contributing to the result; they support rather than determine the principles and outcomes adopted by judges.

There are, however, difficult and important cases where *stare decisis* or continuity seems to have considerable significance. For example, it is widely believed (and I will here assume) that a majority of the Supreme Court would decide *Miranda* v. *Arizona*[7] differently now than it did in 1966, and yet the Court has not overruled *Miranda*. There are two major, alternative explanations.

First, if one regards *stare decisis* as a decision-making process and accepts traditional jurisprudence, the Court is bound by *Miranda*. I obviously reject this: the *Hudgens* court also should have been bound by *Logan Valley*, and there is no objective explanation for the difference based in legal reasoning.

Second, although a present majority may substantively favor overruling *Miranda*, based on a different social and political judgment concerning police conduct and the rights of criminal defendants, there is not a majority willing to do so for institutional and political reasons unrelated to the substance of the issue, to any "duty" to follow precedent, or to any legal decision-making process. Rather, their decision not to overrule is based on the likely public perception of and reaction to such a decision and the effect on the Court's power and legitimacy. Thus, hypothetically (and without consulting any law clerks), there may be six justices whose substantive judgment is to overrule *Miranda*, but perhaps two or more of these six will not so vote. The "constrained" justices are not and do not view themselves as substantively, analytically, or institutionally "bound"; their judgment is to overrule. However, if the Court overrules *Miranda*, a well-known symbol, the decision would be widely perceived as political — and therefore raise the spector of government by people, not law. In fact, such a decision would not be any more political than was *Miranda* itself (just a different politics and a different context). But the popular perception could create a serious crisis of legitimacy and undermine the Court's power.[8]

Stare decisis is integral to the popular conception of the judicial process and an important component of the ideology with which judicial power is justified and legitimized. This ideological role is perhaps easiest to see if one looks at the historical development of *stare decisis*.

Viewing *stare decisis* as a component of a neutral, objective, or quasi-scientific discipline, one would expect a progressive development and a general tendency toward reliance on precedent, or at least toward concrete, rational standards for determining when precedent will not be followed. However, it is clear that *stare decisis* has not developed this way. The meaning and importance of *stare decisis* are not fixed by or independent of social and historical circumstances, and there has been no long-term tendency toward refinement. Rather, *stare decisis* has conveniently fallen by the wayside in periods when the legitimacy and power of the courts stood to be enhanced by openly rejecting continuity in favor of politically popular change.

For example, in the early 1800s, long-established legal principles of property, exchange, and relations among people clashed with an evolving social commitment to economic development. Widespread construction of mills and dams, for instance, was inconsistent with established rights of downstream and upstream landowners (based on the earlier conception of land as a source of enjoyment in its natural state rather than as a productive asset). In this context, *stare decisis* was explicitly rejected by the courts; rather, the law was seen as an active promoter of socially desirable goals and conduct (*i.e.*, capitalist economic growth). After a basic substantive transformation was accomplished (circa 1850), the new legal values were consolidated and entrenched by limiting the effect of social concerns on the law and by the reemergence of legal formalism and *stare decisis*. However, the renewed deference to precedent, though often expressed in terms of principles derived from time immemorial, looked back only as far as the early 1800s to the recently transformed legal norms.[9]

In sum, *stare decisis*, while integral to the language of legal discourse and the mystique of legal reasoning, serves a primarily ideological rather than functional role. Nor is there any more validity to the notion of legal reasoning when the source of law is a statutory or constitutional provision or the language of an agreement. Courts determine the meaning and applicability of the pertinent language; similar arguments and distinctions are available; and the ultimate basis is a social and political judgment. Indeed, even the facts relevant to a particular controversy (largely reduced to uncontroversial givens in law schools) are not capable of determination by any distinctly legal or nonpolitical methodology. Law is simply politics by other means.

In a broader sense, the ideological role of concepts like legal reasoning is but one aspect of a larger social phenomenon. In many areas of our lives, essentially social and political judgments gain legitimacy from notions of expertise and analysis that falsely purport to be objective, neutral, and quasi-scientific. For example, cost-benefit analyses have been used to lend a false scientific gloss to people-made judgments about workplace safety standards that place profits above human life. If religion is the opiate of the masses, it seems that objectivity, expertise, and science have become the tranquilizers.

NOTES

1. 391 U.S. 308 (1968).
2. 326 U.S. 501 (1946).
3. 407 U.S. 551 (1972).
4. 424 U.S. 507 (1976). On remand, a statutory right to picket in the shopping center concerning the labor dispute was recognized. 230 NLRB 414 (1977).

5. 424 U.S. at 518.
6. There are, of course, cases and areas of the law where there is considerable clarity and predictability. For example, some aspects of the law of commercial transactions are quite detailed, thorough, and currently uncontroversial, and continuity has more meaning there.
7. 384 U.S. 436 (1966).
8. There is possibly a third major alternative: although *stare decisis* is not a determinate decision-making process in the sense that it requires or explains the unwillingness to overrule *Miranda*, justices may earnestly believe in it apart from the political calculation that characterizes the second alternative. However, unless a justice always follows precedent (which none do) or has objective standards for determining when he or she will do otherwise (which is impossible), his or her honest belief in *stare decisis* is but an unconscious variant of the second alternative. For example, former Justice Potter Stewart is widely thought to have an unusually deep belief in the importance of continuity, but he wrote the majority opinion in *Hudgens*. Various judges place different emphases on various values and factors, and although Justice Stewart has a strong commitment to continuity, institutional and political factors — not technical expertise or objective analysis — determine when and where he deviates from that commitment.
9. *See* M. Horwitz, *The Transformation of American Law, 1780–1860* (Harvard University Press: Cambridge, Mass., 1977).

Notes and Questions

ROBERT BORK, from *The Tempting of America*

1. In addition to the problem of determining precedents in common law, courts also have the tasks of statutory and constitutional interpretation. Constitutional theories are highly controversial, since the Constitution itself does not say how it should be interpreted, and many of its abstract phrases have no concrete meaning without an interpretation of some sort. The theory of "original understanding" or "original intent" is, according to Robert Bork, the only theory of constitutional interpretation that is "consonant with the design of the American Republic." Why does he think so?

2. While the theory of original understanding (or original intent) has been applied to constitutional interpretation for many years, Bork's recent discussion provides perhaps the clearest and most attractive formulation the theory has ever received. What are the basic features of this theory?

3. Bork explains that by "original understanding" he means the public understanding of the time, and not any particular ideas or intentions held by any particular individual or small group (such as the founding fathers). Why is this point important? What objection does it address?

4. Are there special problems with Bork's version of original intent? Two objections are often raised: How do we know what the public understanding was at the time of ratification? Why should we think that the public understanding one hundred or two hundred years ago is more important or relevant to constitutional interpretation than the public understanding today? For

example, what was the public understanding of cruel and unusual punishment two hundred years ago when stocks, public flogging, and public hanging were still practiced? And even if we can make a reasonable estimate of what the public understanding was then, why should it be controlling today?

5. The central problem for constitutional courts, according to Bork, is what he calls the "Madisonian dilemma" — the problem of balancing individual rights or minority protection against majority rule, when neither majority nor minority can be trusted with the power to define those boundaries. The Constitution, says Bork, entrusts this task (as it must, to be fair) to a nonpolitical institution — the federal courts. Are the federal courts nonpolitical, according to Levi? To Stone? What difference does it make whether the federal courts are nonpolitical? Bork says that the only theory which resolves the Madisonian dilemma is the theory of original intent. Why does he think so?

6. According to Bork, the courts must be neutral because it is not legitimate for judges to rewrite the law. This is true, he thinks, in three ways: the derivation, the definition, and the application of constitutional principles. What does he mean by that? How does he defend his view?

7. The argument between Bork and Stone or Kairys is that Stone and Kairys see neutrality as an illusion. Judges may wish that they could be neutral, but the fact is they are not and cannot be neutral. They are constantly making choices about the derivation, definition and application of constitutional principles; about which precedent to follow; about which facts matter; about what the rule of law should be; and about how generally to construe it. What is Bork's answer?

[From] *The Tempting of America*
ROBERT BORK

CHAPTER 7

The Original Understanding

What was once the dominant view of constitutional law — that a judge is to apply the Constitution according to the principles intended by those who ratified the document — is now very much out of favor among the theorists of the field. In the legal academies in particular, the philosophy of original understanding is usually viewed as thoroughly passé, probably reactionary, and certainly — the most dreaded indictment of all — "outside the mainstream." That fact says more about the lamentable state of the intellectual life of the law, however, than it does about the merits of the theory.

In truth, only the approach of original under-standing meets the criteria that any theory of constitutional adjudication must meet in order to possess democratic legitimacy. Only that approach is consonant with the design of the American Republic.

The Constitution as Law: Neutral Principles

When we speak of "law," we ordinarily refer to a rule that we have no right to change except through prescribed procedures. That statement assumes that the rule has a meaning independent of our own desires. Otherwise there would be no need to agree on procedures for changing the rule. Statutes, we agree, may be changed by amendment or repeal. The Constitution may be changed by amendment pursuant to the procedures set out in article V. It is a necessary implication of the prescribed procedures that neither statute nor Constitution should be changed by judges. Though that has been done often enough, it is in no sense proper.

What is the meaning of a rule that judges should not change? It is the meaning understood at the time of the law's enactment. Though I have written of the understanding of the ratifiers of the Constitution, since they enacted it and made it law, that is actually a shorthand formulation, because what the ratifiers understood themselves to be enacting must be taken to be what the public of that time would have understood the words to mean. It is important to be clear about this. The search is not for a subjective intention. If someone found a letter from George Washington to Martha telling her that what he meant by the power to lay taxes was not what other people meant, that would not change our reading of the Consitution in the slightest. Nor would the subjective intentions of all the members of a ratifying convention alter anything. When lawmakers use words, the law that results is what those words ordinarily mean. If Congress enacted a statute outlawing the sale of automatic rifles and did so in the Senate by a vote of 51 to 49, no court would overturn a conviction because two senators in the majority testified that they really had intended only to prohibit the *use* of such rifles. They said "sale" and "sale" it is. Thus, the common objection to the philosophy of original understanding — that Madison kept his notes of the convention at Philadelphia secret for many years — is off the mark. He knew that what mattered was public understanding, not subjective intentions. Madison himself said that what mattered was the intention of the ratifying conventions. His notes of the discussions at Philadelphia are merely evidence of what informed public men of the time thought the words of the Constitution meant. Since many of them were also delegates to the various state ratifying conventions, their understanding informed the debates in those conventions. As Professor Henry Monaghan of Columbia has said, what counts is what the public

understood.[1] Law is a public act. Secret reservations or intentions count for nothing. All that counts is how the words used in the Constitution would have been understood at the time. The original understanding is thus manifested in the words used and in secondary materials, such as debates at the conventions, public discussion, newspaper articles, dictionaries in use at the time, and the like. Almost no one would deny this; in fact almost everyone would find it obvious to the point of thinking it fatuous to state the matter — except in the case of the Constitution. Why our legal theorists make an exception for the Constitution is worth exploring.

The search for the intent of the lawmaker is the everyday procedure of lawyers and judges when they must apply a statute, a contract, a will, or the opinion of a court. To be sure, there are differences in the way we deal with different legal materials, which was the point of John Marshall's observation in *McCulloch* v. *Maryland* that "we must never forget, that it is *a constitution* we are expounding."[2] By that he meant that narrow, legalistic reasoning was not to be applied to the document's broad provisions, a document that could not, by its nature and uses, "partake of the prolixity of a legal code." But he also wrote there that it was intended that a provision receive a "fair and just interpretation," which means that the judge is to interpret what is in the text and not something else. And, it will be recalled, in *Marbury* v. *Madison* Marshall placed the judge's power to invalidate a legislative act upon the fact that the judge was applying the words of a written document.[3] Thus, questions of breadth of approach or of room for play in the joints aside, lawyers and judges should seek in the Constitution what they seek in other legal texts: the original meaning of the words.[4]

We would at once criticize a judge who undertook to rewrite a statute or the opinion of a superior court, and yet such judicial rewriting is often correctable by the legislature or the superior court, as the Supreme Court's rewriting of the Constitution is not. At first glance, it seems distinctly peculiar that there should be a great many academic theorists who explicitly defend departures from the understanding of those who ratified the Constitution while agreeing, at least in principle, that there should be no departure from the understanding of those who enacted a statute or joined a majority opinion. A moment's reflection suggests, however, that Supreme Court departures from the original meaning of the Constitution are advocated *precisely because* those departures are not correctable democratically. The point of the academic exercise is to be free of democracy in order to impose the values of an elite upon the rest of us.

If the Constitution is law, then presumably its meaning, like that of all other law, is the meaning the lawmakers were understood to have intended. If the Constitution is law, then presumably, like all other law, the meaning the lawmakers intended is as binding upon judges as it is upon legislatures and executives. There is no other sense in which the Constitution can be what article VI proclaims it to be: "Law."[5] It is here that the concept of neutral principles, which Wechsler said were essential if the Supreme Court was not to be a naked power organ, comes into play. Wechsler, it will be recalled, in expressing his difficulties with the decision in *Brown* v. *Board of Education*,[6] said that courts must choose principles which they are willing to apply neutrally, apply, that is, to all cases that may fairly be said to fall within them.[7] This is a safeguard against political judging. No judge will say openly that any particular group or political position is always entitled to win. He will announce a principle that decides the case at hand, and Wechsler had no difficulty with that if the judge is willing to apply the same principle in the next case, even if it means that a group favored by the first decision is disfavored by the second. That was precisely what Arthur M. Schlesinger, Jr., said that the Black–Douglas wing of the Court was unwilling to do. Instead, it pretended to enuciate principles but in fact warped them to vote for interest groups.[8]

The Court cannot, however, avoid being a naked power organ merely by practicing the neutral application of legal principle. The Court can act as a legal rather than a political institution only if it is neutral as well in the way it derives and defines the principles it applies. If the Court is free to choose any principle that it will subsequently apply neutrally, it is free to legislate just as a political body would. Its purported resolution of the Madisonian dilemma is spurious, because there is no way of saying that the correct spheres of freedom have been assigned to the majority and the minority. Similarly, if the Court is free to define the scope of the principle as it sees fit, it may, by manipulating the principle's breadth, make things come out the way it wishes on grounds that are not contained in the principle it purports to apply. Once again, the Madisonian dilemma is not resolved correctly but only according to the personal preferences of the Justices. The philosophy of original understanding is capable of supplying neutrality in all three respects — in deriving, defining, and applying principle.

Neutrality in the Derivation of Principle

When a judge finds his principle in the Constitution as originally understood, the problem of the neutral derivation of principle is solved. The judge accepts the ratifiers' definition of the appropriate ranges of majority and minority freedom. The Madisonian dilemma is resolved in the way that the founders resolved it, and the judge accepts the fact that he is bound by that resolution as law. He need not, and must not, make unguided value judgments of his own.

This means, of course, that a judge, no matter on what court he sits, may never create new constitutional rights or destroy old ones. Any time he does so, he violates not only the limits to his own authority but, and for that reason, also violates the rights of the legislature and the people. To put the matter another way, suppose that the United States, like the United Kingdom, had no written constitution and, therefore, no law to apply to strike down acts of the legislature. The U.S. judge, like the U.K. judge, could never properly invalidate a statute or an official action as unconstitutional. The very concept of unconstitutionality would be meaningless. The absence of a constitutional provision means the absence of a power of judicial review. But when a U.S. judge is given a set of constitutional provisions, then, as to anything not covered by those provisions, he is in the same position as the U.K. judge. He has no law to apply and is, quite properly, powerless. In the absence of law, a judge is a functionary without a function.

This is not to say, of course, that majorities

may not add to minority freedoms by statute, and indeed a great deal of the legislation that comes out of Congress and the state legislatures does just that. The only thing majorities may not do is invade the liberties the Constitution specifies. In this sense, the concept of original understanding builds in a bias toward individual freedom. Thus, the Supreme Court properly decided in *Brown* that the equal protection clause of the fourteenth amendment forbids racial segregation or discrimination by any arm of government, but, because the Constitution addresses only governmental action, the Court could not address the question of private discrimination. Congress did address it in the Civil Rights Act of 1964 and in subsequent legislation, enlarging minority freedoms beyond those mandated by the Constitution.

Neutrality in the Definition of Principle

The neutral definition of the principle derived from the historic Constitution is also crucial. The Constitution states its principles in majestic generalities that we know cannot be taken as sweepingly as the words alone might suggest. The first amendment states that "Congress shall make no law . . . abridging the freedom of speech,"[9] but no one has ever supposed that Congress could not make some speech unlawful or that it could not make all speech illegal in certain places, at certain times, and under certain circumstances. Justices Hugo Black and William O. Douglas often claimed to be first amendment absolutists, but even they would permit the punishment of speech if they thought it too closely "brigaded" with illegal action. From the beginning of the Republic to this day, no one has ever thought Congress could not forbid the preaching of mutiny on a ship of the Navy or disruptive proclamations in a courtroom.

But the question of neutral definition remains and is obviously closely related to neutral application. Neutral application can be gained by defining a principle so narrowly that it will fit only a few cases. Thus, to return to *Griswold,*[10] we can make neutral application possible by stating the principle to be that government may not prohibit the use of contraceptives by married couples. But that tactic raises doubts as to the definition of the principle. Why does it extend only to married couples? Why, out of all forms of sexual behavior, only to the use of contraceptives? Why, out of all forms of behavior in the home, only to sex? There may be answers, but if there are, they must be given.

Thus, once a principle is derived from the Constitution, its breadth or the level of generality at which it is stated becomes of crucial importance. The judge must not state the principle with so much generality that he transforms it. The difficulty in finding the proper level of generality has led some critics to claim that the application of the original understanding is actually impossible. That sounds fairly abstract, but an example will make clear both the point and the answer to it.

In speaking of my view that the fourteenth amendment's equal protection clause requires black equality, Dean Paul Brest said:

> The very adoption of such a principle, however, demands an arbitrary choice among levels of abstraction. Just what *is* "the general principle of equality that applies to all cases"? Is it the "core idea of *black* equality" that Bork finds in the original understanding (in which case Alan Bakke [a white who sued because a state medical school gave preference in admissions to other races] did not state a constiutionally cognizable claim), or a broader principle of "*racial* equality" (so that, depending on the precise content of the principle, Bakke might have a case after all), or is it a still broader principle of equality that encompasses discrimination on the basis of gender (or sexual orientation) as well? . . .
> . . . The fact is that all adjudication requires making choices among the levels of generality on which to articulate principles, and all such choices are inherently non-neutral. No form of constitutional decisionmaking can be salvaged if its legitimacy depends on satisfying Bork's requirements that principles be "neutrally derived, defined and applied."[11]

If Brest's point about the impossibility of choosing the level of generality upon neutral criteria is correct, we must either resign ourselves to a Court that is a "naked power organ" or require the Court to stop making "constitutional" decisions. But Brest's argument seems to me wrong, and I think a judge committed to original understanding can do what Brest says he cannot. We may use Brest's example to demonstrate the point.

The role of a judge committed to the philosophy of original understanding is not to "*choose a level of abstraction.*" Rather, it is to find the meaning of a text—a process which includes finding its degree of generality, which is part of its meaning—and to apply that text to a particular situation, which may be difficult if its meaning is unclear. With many if not most textual provisions, the level of generality which is part of their meaning is readily apparent. The problem is most difficult when dealing with the broadly stated provisions of the Bill of Rights. It is to the latter that we confine discussion here. In dealing with such provisions, a judge should state the principle at the level of generality that the text and historical evidence warrant. The equal protection clause was adopted in order to protect the freed slaves, but its language, being general, applies to all persons. As we might expect, and as Justice Miller found in the *Slaughter House Cases*,[12] the evidence of what the drafters, the Congress that proposed the clause, and the ratifiers understood themselves to be requiring is clearest in the case of race relations. It is there that we may begin in looking for evidence of the level of generality intended. Without meaning to suggest what the historical evidence in fact shows, let us assume we find that the ratifiers intended to guarantee that blacks should be treated by law no worse than whites, but that it is unclear whether whites were intended to be protected from discrimination in favor of blacks. On such evidence, the judge should protect only blacks from discrimination, and Alan Bakke would not have had a case. The reason is that the next higher level of generality above black equality, which is racial equality, is not shown to be a constitutional principle, and therefore there is nothing to be set against a current legislative majority's decision to favor blacks. Democratic choice must be accepted by the judge where the Constitution is silent. The test is the reasonableness of the distinction, and the level of generality chosen by the ratifiers determines that. If the evidence shows the ratifiers understood racial equality to have been the principle they were enacting, Bakke would have a case. In cases concerning gender and sexual orientation, however, interpretation is not additionally assisted by the presence of known inten-

tions. The general language of the clause, however, continues to subject such cases to the test of whether statutory distinctions are reasonable. Sexual differences obviously make some distinctions reasonable while others have no apparent basis. That has, in fact, been the rationale on which the law has developed. Society's treatment of sexual orientation is based upon moral perceptions, so that it would be difficult to say that the various moral balances struck are unreasonable.

Original understanding avoids the problem of the level of generality in equal protection analysis by finding the level of generality that interpretation of the words, structure, and history of the Constitution fairly supports. This is a solution generally applicable to all constitutional provisions as to which historical evidence exists. There is, therefore, a form of constitutional decisionmaking that satisfies the requirement that principle be neutrally defined.

To define a legal proposition or principle involves simultaneously stating its contents and its limits. When you state what *is* contained within the clause of the first amendment guarantee of the free exercise of religion, you necessarily state what is *not* contained within that clause. Because the first amendment guarantees freedom of speech, judges are required reasonably to define what is speech and what is its freedom. In doing these things, the judge necessarily decides that some things are not speech or are not abridgments of its freedom. As to things outside the proposition, the speech clause gives the judge no power to do anything. Because it is only the content of a clause that gives the judge any authority, where that content does not apply, he is without authority and is, for that reason, forbidden to act. The elected legislator or executive may act where not forbidden; his delegation of power from the people through an election is his authority. But the judge may act only where authorized and must do so in those cases; his commission is to apply the law. If a judge should say that the freedom of speech clause authorizes him to abolish the death penalty, we would unanimously say that he had exceeded the bounds of his lawful authority. The judge's performance is not improved if, following *Griswold* v. *Connecticut*, he adds four more inapplicable provisions to his list of claimed authorizations and claims that five inapplicable provisions give him the authority one alone did not. Where the law stops, the legislator may move on to create more; but where the law stops, the judge must stop.

Neutrality in the Application of Principle

The neutral or nonpolitical application of principle has been discussed in connection with Wechsler's discussion of the *Brown* decision.[13] It is a requirement, like the others, addressed to the judge's integrity. Having derived and defined the principle to be applied, he must apply it consistently and without regard to his sympathy or lack of sympathy with the parties before him. This does not mean that the judge will never change the principle he has derived and defined. Anybody who has dealt extensively with law knows that a new case may seem to fall within a principle as stated and yet not fall within the rationale underlying it. As new cases present new patterns, the principle will often be restated and redefined. There is nothing wrong with that; it is, in fact, highly desirable. But the judge must be clarifying his own reasoning and verbal formulations and not trimming to arrive at results desired on grounds extraneous to the Constitution. This requires a fair degree of sophistication and self-consicousness on the part of the judge. The only external discipline to which the judge is subject is the scrutiny of professional observers who will be able to tell over a period of time whether he is displaying intellectual integrity.

An example of the nonneutral application of principle in the service of a good cause is provided by *Shelley* v. *Kraemer*,[14] a 1948 decision of the Supreme Court striking down racially restrictive covenants. Property owners had signed agreements limiting occupancy to white persons. Despite the covenants, some whites sold to blacks, owners of other properties sued to enforce the convenants, and the state courts, applying common law rules, enjoined the blacks from taking possession.

The problem for the Supreme Court was that the Constitution restricts only action by the state, not actions by private individuals. There was no doubt that the racial restrictions would have violated the equal protection clause of the fourteenth amendment had they been enacted by the state legislature. But here state courts were not the source of the racial discrimination, they merely enforced private agreements according to the terms of those agreements. The Supreme Court nonetheless held that "there has been state action in these cases in the full and complete sense of the phrase."[15]

In a 1971 article in the Indiana Law Journal,[16] I pointed out the difficulty with *Shelley*, for which I was severely taken to task in my Senate hearings and elsewhere. That criticism consisted entirely of the observation that I had disapproved of a case that favored blacks and was therefore hostile to civil rights. Both the fact that many commentators had criticized *Shelley* and my approval of other cases that favored blacks were ignored. The implicit position taken by some senators and activist groups was that a judge must always rule for racial minorities. That is a position I reject, because it requires political judging. Members of racial minorities should win when the law, honestly applied, supports their claim and not when it does not. *Shelley* v. *Kraemer* rested upon a theory that cannot be honestly applied, and, in the event, has not been applied at all.

The Supreme Court in *Shelley* said that the decision of a state court under common law rules constitutes the action of the state and therefore is to be tested by the requirements of the Constitution. The racial discrimination involved was not the policy of the state courts but the desire of private individuals, which the courts enforced pursuant to normal, and neutral, rules of enforcing private agreements. The impossibility of applying the state action ruling of *Shelley* in a neutral fashion may easily be seen. Suppose that a guest in a house becomes abusive about political matters and is ejected by his host. The guest sues the host and the state courts hold that the property owner has a right to remove people from his home. The guest then appeals to the Supreme Court, pointing out that the state, through its courts, has upheld an abridgment of his right of free speech guaranteed by the first amendment and made applicable to the sates by the fourteenth. The guest cites *Shelley* to show that this is state action and therefore the case is constitutional. There is no way of escaping that conclusion except by importing into the rule of *Shelley* qualifications and limits that themselves have no foundation in the Constitution or the case. Whichever way it decided, the

Supreme Court would have to treat the case as one under the first amendment and displace state law with constitutional law.

It is necessary to remember that absolutely anything, from the significant to the frivolous, can be made the subject of a complaint filed in a state court. Whether the state court dismisses the suit out of hand or proceeds to the merits of the issue does not matter; any decision is, according to *Shelley*, state action and hence subject to constitutional scrutiny. That means that all private conduct may be made state conduct with the result that the Supreme Court will make the rules for all allowable or forbidden behavior by private individuals. That is not only a complete perversion of the Constitution of the United States, it makes the Supreme Court the supreme legislature. The result of the neutral application of the principle of *Shelley* v. *Kraemer* would be both revolutionary and preposterous. Clearly, it would not be applied neutrally, and it has not been, which means that it fails Wechsler's test.

Shelley was a political decision. As such, it should have been made by a legislature. It is clear that Congress had the power to outlaw racially restrictive covenants. Subsequently, in fact, in a case in which as Solicitor General I filed a brief supporting the result reached, the Supreme Court held that one of the post–Civil War civil rights acts did outlaw racial discrimination in private contracts.[17] That fact does not, however, make *Shelley* a proper constitutional decision, however much its result may be admired on moral grounds.

Judicial adherence to neutral principles, in the three senses just described, is a crucial element of the American doctrine of the separation of powers. Since the Court's invocation of the Constitution is final, the judiciary is the only branch of the government not subject to the ordinary checks and balances that pit the powers of the other branches against each other. If it is to be faithful to the constitutional design, therefore, the Court must check itself.

The Original Understanding of Original Understanding

The judicial role just described corresponds to the original understanding of the place of courts in our republican form of government. The political arrangements of that form of government are complex, its balances of power continually shifting, but one thing our constitutional orthodoxy does not countenance is a judiciary that decides for itself when and how it will make national policy, when and to what extent it will displace executives and legislators as our governors. The orthodoxy of our civil religion, which the Constitution has aptly been called, holds that we govern ourselves democratically, except on those occasions, few in number though crucially important, when the Constitution places a topic beyond the reach of majorities.

* * *

The interpretation of the Constitution according to the original understanding, then, is the only method that can preserve the Constitution, the separation of powers, and the liberties of the people. Only that approach can lead to what Felix Frankfurter called the "fulfillment of one of the greatest duties of a judge, the duty not to enlarge his authority. That the Court is not the maker of policy but is concerned solely with questions of ultimate power, is a tenet to which all Justices have subscribed. But the extent to which they have translated faith into works probably marks the deepest cleavage among the men who have sat on the Supreme Bench. . . . The conception of significant achievement on the Supreme Court has been too much identified with largeness of utterance, and too little governed by inquiry into the extent to which judges have fulfilled their professed role in the American constitutional system."[18]

Without adherence to the original understanding, even the actual Bill of Rights could be pared or eliminated. It is asserted nonetheless, and sometimes on high authority, that the judicial philosophy of original understanding is fatally defective in any number of respects. If that were so, if the Constitution cannot be law that binds judges, there would remain only one democratically legitimate solution: judicial supremacy, the power of courts to invalidate statutes and executive actions in the name of the Constitution, would have to be abandoned. For the choice would then be either rule by judges according to their own desires or rule by the people according to theirs. Under our form of government, under the entire history of the American people, the choice between an authoritarian judicial oligarchy and a representative democracy can have only one outcome. But this is a false statement of alternatives, for judicial interpretation of the Constitution according to its original understanding is entirely possible. When that course is followed, judges are not a dictatorial oligarchy but the guardians of our liberties. I turn next to the objections that have been raised to this conclusion.

NOTES

1. Monaghan, *Stare Decisis and Constitutional Adjudication*, 88 Colum. L. Rev. 723, 725–27 (1988) ("The relevant inquiry must focus on the *public* understanding of the language when the Constitution was developed. Hamilton put it well: 'whatever may have been the intention of the framers of a constitution, or of a law, that intention is to be sought for in the instrument itself, according to the usual & established rules of construction.'" [emphasis in original; footnotes omitted]).

2. 17 U.S. (4 Wheat.) 316, 407 (1819).

3. 5 U.S. (1 Cranch) 137, 177–79 (1803).

4. *See also* Scalia, *Originalism: The Lesser Evil*, 57 U. Cin. L. Rev. 849, 853 (1989) (It is a canard to interpret Marshall's observation in *McCulloch* as implying that our interpretation of the Constitution must change from age to age. "The real implication was quite the

opposite: Marshall was saying that the Constitution had to be interpreted generously because the powers conferred upon Congress under it had to be broad enough to serve not only the needs of the federal government originally discerned but also the needs that might arise in the future. If constitutional interpretation could be adjusted as changing circumstances required, a broad initial interpretation would have been unnecessary.").

5. U.S. CONST. art. VI.

6. 347 U.S. 483 (1954).

7. *See* Chapter 3, *supra*, at 78–84.

8. Schlesinger, *The Supreme Court: 1947*, FORTUNE, vol. 35, Jan. 1947, at 73, 201–02.

9. U.S. CONST. amend. I.

10. *Griswold* v. *Connecticut*, 381 U.S. 479 (1965).

11. Brest, *The Fundamental Rights Controversy: The Essential Contradictions of Normative Constitutional Scholarship*, 90 Yale L.J. 1063, 1091–92 (1981) (footnotes omitted).

12. *Slaughter-House Cases*, 83 U.S. (16 Wall.) 36 (1873).

13. *See* Chapter 3, *supra*, at 78–84.

14. 334 U.S. 1 (1948).

15. *Id.* at 19.

16. Bork, *Neutral Principles and Some First Amendment Problems*, 47 Ind. L.J. 1 (1971).

17. *Runyon* v. *McCrary*, 427 U.S. 160 (1976).

18. F. Frankfurter, *The Commerce Clause* 80–81 (1937).

Notes and Questions

FREDERICK SCHAUER, from "An Essay on Constitutional Language"

1. Frederick Schauer examines the meaning of the Constitution in terms of the words of the document itself. What is needed, he suggests, is a theory of constitutional language. The debate about adhering to or departing from the text of the Constitution is meaningless without a clear idea of what the text means or requires.

2. Citing H. L. A. Hart, Schauer notes that legal language has been recognized as different from ordinary language. In what sense is it different? What further differences does Schauer point out between constitutional language and other legal language? In what sense is the Constitution like an eloquently written manifesto? On the other hand, what are the similarities between constitutional language and other legal language?

3. Is constitutional language unique because of its presuppositions? What are the presuppositions of constitutional language? How helpful are they for grounding a theory of constitutional language? How important are they for establishing the context of meaning for constitutional interpretation?

4. What is the "intentional paradigm," according to Schauer? How does he compare it to using a code? Why is that a mistake? Is Schauer right that the "intent of the framers" theory fails to represent the authority of the text itself?

5. Do Schauer's criticisms hold against Bork's theory of original understanding? Is there any

difference between original understanding and original intent? Does Bork answer these objections? Can he?

6. Why does Schauer think that a constitutional theory should be built on the words of the Constitution? How does it help to recognize constitutional phrases as theory-laden? What does it mean? What makes a term in the Constitution theory-laden in the strong sense? What does that require?

7. What exactly is the difference between Schauer's theory of constitutional interpretation and Bork's? Try applying each theory to the cases following Chapters Three, Six, and Seven. Which is more helpful? Does either theory avoid or address the sorts of problems raised by Stone or Kairys? Is constitutional adjudication more or less determinate than common law precedent?

[From] "An Essay on Constitutional Language"

FREDERICK SCHAUER

Many contemporary constitutional scholars have explored the extent to which, if at all, judges should go "outside of" or "beyond" the constitutional text for decisional principles in constitutional cases.[1] Although the resulting discussions have been highly illuminating, I do not wish to deal directly with this controversy here. Rather, I propose to discuss what is logically a prior question. For before we can argue intelligently about whether to go outside of the text, we ought to explore the meaning of the words *inside* the text. Only then will we know what counts as going "outside," and until then, it is not clear that there even is an outside because "inside" and "outside" are relative terms.

We assume, perhaps too easily, that the language of the Constitution is neither the source of, nor the answer to, our problems, and we then head off into the forbidding jungles of history, political theory, moral philosophy, public policy, and what have you without any clear guide. An examination of the words in the Constitution has been merely the hors d'oeuvre, with high theory as the main course.

There is nothing unseemly about high theory in this sense. Nevertheless, we need to look at the words of the Constitution *as language*, and we need to examine closely some of our rarely questioned presuppositions about constitutional language. Although this examination logically is prior to any broader interpretation of the Constitution, it has received surprisingly little concentrated attention in the literature.[2]

Constitutional cogniscenti talk about "gaps," "great silences," "vague language," and "open texture" as if these were concepts of little controversy.[3] But what makes the requirement that the President be of "the Age of thirty five Years" specific and the requirement of "equal protection of the laws" vague? Why are there "loopholes" in the Internal Revenue Code, but not in the Constitution? In order to understand and to attempt to answer questions like these, we need a theory of constitutional language as much as we need theories of constitutional law.

The Constitution is, after all, a writing,[4] and at bottom we are interpreting the *words* of a written document. But how do we do this? What does it mean to "interpret" a constitutional provision? What do we mean when we say that a constitutional provision "means" something? How do we start such an analysis? These are hard and important questions, and we should not dismiss them as irrelevant philosophical speculation. Indeed, answers to these questions underlie any theory of constitutional adjudication, and this Essay attempts to bring some of these answers to the surface for closer inspection.

My intention here is not to offer a completely mature theory of constitutional language. Rather, I wish to explore the way in which the conventions of language affect constitutional theory. At the end of this Essay, I conclude that constitutional language acts as a significant restraint on constitutional decision, but I will not have developed a complete theory of constitutional language which directs any particular substantive outcomes. A complete theory will have to wait for another time.

I. On the Supposed Uniqueness of Constitutional Language

In his pioneering work on legal language, H.L.A. Hart argued that legal language is fundamentally different from ordinary language.[5] According to Hart, if one fails to recognize the unique context and the distinct presuppositions of legal discourse, then one commits the errors of formalism or conceptualism — giving to words in the abstract an aura of authority and of unique reference inconsistent with the view of language as an activity determined and governed by social rules. If, as Hart and his philosophical contemporaries supposed, meaning is use, then legal use ought to produce different meanings than a physicist's use, a sociologist's use, or the use of the man on the Clapham omnibus. And, just as legal language is different in kind from ordinary language, constitutional language may be different from other legal language. In fact, this hypothesis implicitly undergirds many different theories of constitutional interpretation.[6] The various theories of a "living" or "changeable" constitution each presuppose a view of the uniqueness of constitutional language, setting it off from the linguistic raw material with which lawyers normally deal.

There *seem* to be readily apparent differences between constitutional language and other legal language. Grandiloquent phrases like "freedom of speech," "equal protection of the laws," "due process of law," and "privileges and immunities of citizens of the United States" have few counterparts in the Internal Revenue Code or the Public Utility Holding Company Act of 1935. Indeed, many constitutional provisions are more than merely indeterminate. They have a powerful emotive component. The Constitution is more an eloquently written manifesto than it is a code, and in many ways we are much better for that. But the eloquence and emotive force of the document further reinforce the view that the Constitution's words are as different as they are special. To construe its language too literally or too much like the language in a conventional statute would be both unrealistic and inconsistent with its deeper purposes. In some ways, the Constitution is a metaphor.

Not unrelated to the Constitution's metaphorical quality is its permanence. Statutes are frequently amended, and the common law is continually changing, but the Constitution has a special sort of durability. Not only is amending the Constitution extremely difficult, but we also seem remarkably averse to doing so. Many have feared a constitutional convention because too much might be changed, even though such changes would still require ratification by the states. On the other hand, we certainly do not suspend Congress or the state legislatures for fear that they might legislate too much — however appealing that suggestion may at times seem.

Despite these important differences, we would be mistaken to view constitutional language as a wholly unique creature. The seemingly intentional openness of many constitutional terms, upon which most of the supposition about the uniqueness of constitutional language is based,[7] has counterparts in other areas of law, especially in American law. The generality of "equal protection of the laws" or "the freedom of speech" differs little from the language in Rule 10b-5 of the Securities and Exchange Commission, which prohibits the employment of "any device, scheme, or artifice to defraud."[8] Likewise, the fourth amendment's prohibition of "unreasonable" searches and seizures provides no more guidance than the Sherman Act's ban on "[e]very contract, combination . . . or conspiracy, in restraint of trade or commerce. . . ."[9] As a result, the task of the courts in putting flesh on the skeleton of the Constitution is not wholly different from the task that courts have undertaken in developing the elaborate structure of tests, rules, and standards that surround and govern the application of the securities laws, the antitrust laws, and many other statutory schemes.

If the openness of constitutional language does not provide its uniqueness, perhaps the notion of presupposition,[10] which undergirds Hart's argument in "Definition and Theory in Jurisprudence,"[11] can explain the uniqueness. Statements of law, or *in* law (as opposed to statements *about* law), presuppose the existence of a legal system, and particular statements of legal rules themselves contain presuppositions. Thus, the statement "the corporation is liable in damages" presupposes a body of law creating and defining a "corporation." But presupposition is hardly unique to law. When we use "home run" or "small slam," we presuppose the systems of baseball and bridge, respectively, and when we use "professor" or "hour examination," we similarly presuppose the existence of a college or university, which is in turn defined by a (probably looser) set of constitutive rules. Legal language is not special because it contains presuppositions, but rather because it alone contains presuppositions which relate to the existence of a legal system.

In this sense, then, constitutional language is unique because it, and no other language, presupposes the existence of a constitution, and incorporates those particular presuppositions which concern the role of a constitution in a given legal system. But this is not going to get us very far, because the presuppositions of constitutionalism are themselves both vague and contested. Unlike the specific terms of a general legal system, which, to some extent, relate to relatively uncontroversial presuppositions about the way the legal system operates, the terms of a constitution *themselves* determine the differences between the constitutional presuppositions and other legal presuppositions. Therefore, an initial search for constitutional uniqueness reduces itself to circularity because the presuppositions of a constitutional system are dependent on our view of the language of a constitution. Perhaps constitutional language *is* unique. But we cannot articulate the differences which make it unique simply by examining the presuppositions of constitutionalism. Rather, we must examine the *language* in order to discover the differences between the presuppositions embedded in that language and the presuppositions included in the language of statutes or the common law.

These observations on the presuppositional nature of constitutional language are neither interesting nor important enough to provide the touch-

stone for a theory of constitutional language. They show, however, that certain uses of language have distinct meanings because of the context in which they occur. When an entomologist talks about "bugs," when a physicist describes something as "solid," and when a logician refers to "implication," each uses those terms in a more technical and precise sense than the ordinary person uses them. We know this because we know something about the special context in which entomologists, physicists, and logicians speak. Similarly, the context in which lawyers talk determines their use of "real property" (which is not the opposite of "fake property") or "wrongful" (which refers to conduct that may have no moral counterpart in ordinary language). Unlike strictly technical legal terms, such as "habeas corpus," "demurrer," and "curtesy," which have no ordinary language meaning, the technical uses of "real property" and "wrongful" are parasitic on ordinary language. If this phenomenon occurs in conventional (non-constitutional) legal language, then the equally parasitic nature of certain constitutional terms, such as "equal protection of the laws," "free exercise of religion," and "search and seizure" should not surprise us. These are expressions derived from ordinary language, but their constitutional meaning in the context of constitutional adjudication diverges in important ways from the ordinary meaning that first generated each expression. The constitutional presuppositions of constitutional language may not establish the complete uniqueness of constitutional language, but they do emphasize the context from which the words take their meaning.

II. The Intentional Paradigm

Most discussion of constitutional language takes place within what I call the "intentional paradigm" — the assumption that any interpretation of the constitutional text must comport with the explicit, implicit, reconstructed, or fictionalized intentions of the drafters. In its crudest and least plausible version, the intentional paradigm focuses on the results that the drafters specifically had in mind.[12] Thus, because we can show that the drafters of the due process clauses of the fifth and fourteenth amendments intended to invalidate lengthy imprisonment without trial, we can be confident that we are correct in applying those provisions to that end.[13] Conversely, because we can fairly clearly infer that those same drafters did not intend to invalidate prejudgment real estate attachment for the purpose of securing a potential money judgment,[14] we can be equally confident that we are correct in refusing to apply the due process clause to invalidate prejudgment real estate attachment. Use of the same methodology would support the first amendment's application to prior restraints and at the same time justify excluding its application to obscenity, defamation, commercial speech, and blasphemy.[15]

The specific intention theories of constitutional interpretation, of which the writings of Raoul Berger represent the most extreme example,[16] are the least plausible of any of the theories discussed in this Essay. They are implausible precisely because they ignore the distinction between the meaning of a rule (such as a constitutional provision) and the instances of its application.[17]

When we draft any rule, we envision certain particular applications of that rule, certain cases where the rule will produce a particular outcome. We do not merely list these outcomes in a series of specific commands because we do not see those particular outcomes as exhaustive. They are only instances of a more general problem, and we analyze the problem to discover some underlying unity in the instances that we wish to treat. We then formulate the rule to deal with this general unitary problem. By formulating a rule in general terms, the rule extends, by the nature of language, further in time or space than those particular applications envisaged by the drafters of the rule.

This is a commonplace observation, and we can easily imagine examples of the distinction between meaning and instances of application in constitutional interpretation. For example, punishment by electric shocks to the genitalia falls plainly within the eighth amendment's prohibition of cruel and unusual punishments even though the drafters could not have imagined this particular procedure in 1791.

This much is relatively uncontroversial, but it does not take us very far because, at some point, the new applications are so different that the meaning has changed.[18] The "meaning" of a cruel and unusual punishment clause prohibiting only painful and humiliating punishment is different from one prohibiting capital punishment. The "meaning" of an equal protection clause prohibiting only racial discrimination is different from the meaning of an equal protection clause prohibiting discrimination on the basis of, say, gender, alienage, illegitimacy, or wealth. And the meaning of "the freedom of speech" that includes only political argument is different from the meaning of "the freedom of speech" that includes the right to advertise pharmaceutical prices or the right to display a "For Sale" sign on a front lawn.[19]

I am not contending that such shifts in constitutional meaning are constitutionally impermissible. I am saying only that they *are* shifts in meaning, and thus are neither explained nor justified by the distinction between the meaning of a rule and the instances of its application. For such explanation or justification we must look elsewhere.

The defects of the specific intention approach have been amply documented in the literature,[20] and there is little need for me to belabor these criticisms here. Intriguingly, however, even the most vehement critics of the specific intention approach still feel obliged to tether their arguments to some form of original intent. According to Laurence Tribe[21] and Ronald Dworkin,[22] for example, the extremely general language in the Constitution conclusively proves the drafters' intent that subsequent generations should work out their own theories applying such phrases as cruel and unusual punishment, due process of law, equal protection of the laws, and so on. John Hart Ely implicitly criticizes wide excursions from the text as a whole[23] but his argument is as revealing as it is interesting. Ely bases his deference to the text on the idea that the text constitutes *the best evidence* of the drafters' intent.[24] The text, for Ely as for the others, is still a way of bringing forward the intentions of the framers.

Those who argue within the framework of this "intentional paradigm" appear to operate on the model of the "convention" in the game of bridge. When bridge players reach a certain level of proficiency, they begin to use artificial conventions in bidding. These bids do not represent the intended contract, but rather aim at describing specific features of the bidder's hand or at asking questions about the partner's hand. The bids are in a *code* whose primary ordinary meaning ("clubs" means clubs) may be irrelevant to the specific contextual use. Most bridge players use simple conventions like Blackwood or Stayman, and more advanced players are likely to use complex systems containing a high percentage of so-called "artificial" bids. These systems and conventions are languages designed in part, like other languages, to convey information. But the important feature of a bridge convention (or indeed the notion of bidding at all) is that the use of conventions is derived from and directed towards one quite simple fact—in the game of bridge, you are not permitted to look at your partner's cards. If a player could look at his partner's hand before arriving at the final contract, he could dispense with every convention yet devised.

Many people understand constitutional language in much the same way as a bridge convention. Under the intentional paradigm, constitutional language exists only because we are unable to know the specific intentions (the cards) of the drafters. If we could ascertain the specific intention, or if we knew how the drafters would treat the constitutional problems of the present, we would have no need for constitutional language. To the extent that we know that intention, then the importance of the text is diminished *pro tanto*.[25]

This is not a useful model, for it fails to capture the sense in which a text is authoritative *as a text*. No amount of looking into the minds of the framers, or constructing fictionalized intentions at various levels of abstraction, can render the text less authoritative. The text is not only the starting point, but is also in some special way the finishing point as well. Constitutional language exists not only because the constitutional convention is not still sitting, nor because James Madison and his colleagues were not immortal. The text interposes itself between the intentions of the framers and the problems of the present, cutting off the range of permissible access and references to original intent, thereby reducing the extent to which original intent persists after the text's adoption. A theory of constitutional language is incomplete if it does not recognize the way in which a text is authoritative—the way in which we treat the Constitution, but not, for example, the Declaration of Independence or the Mayflower Compact, *as law*.

The authoritativeness of a text is by no means a peculiar feature of a written constitution.

Although constitutional law is exciting and popular at the moment, we should not forget our basic law school contracts principles. One such basic principle requires that the parties be held to the reasonable meaning of the terms they have used, regardless of their subjective intent at the time they used those words. And the considerations that led to acceptance of this "objective" theory of contracts are the same as those that generated other common law rules, for example the "plain meaning" rule in the common law of defamation.

What the analogy with contract law shows us, however, is not something about contracts, or even about law. The analogy illuminates, rather, something about language in general, of which the language of a written constitution and the language of a contract are subsets. In order to make sense of language, we presume that it represents the intentional acts of human beings. But there is a difference between the intention of a text and the human thoughts that accompanied the creation of that text. Although the authority of a text is derived in part from the intention that it be authoritative, a text can have purpose without reference to the psychological condition of its creator, as we see in the attempts of courts to derive purpose from statutes themselves. As one philosopher has put it, "[c]ommunication is a public, social affair and [the communicator] is not exempted from responsibility for aspects of his performance he failed to notice." Thus, "a speaker is not the sole arbiter over what import his utterances have,"[26] and our touchstone must be the rules of language rather than largely futile explorations into the mind of the communicator. So long as the distinction between "what he said" and "what he meant to say" is meaningful, then we must recognize that the conventions of language use are superior, in the hierarchy of interpretive tools, to the intentions of the speaker. This is even more true when the language used has an authoritative embodiment, as in a statute or in a written constitution.

The intentional paradigm implicitly confuses a language with a code (as in "morse code" rather than in "Uniform Commercial Code"). Codes, such as bridge conventions, are only one form of language, and it is wrong to assume that every language is a code. In theory, codes are dispensable, as the bridge example demonstrates, but language is not. Moreover, language operates only because *it* has meaning, quite apart from what the speaker may have *meant* to say. Perhaps meaning is use, but the intentions of the user do not determine exclusively, or even mainly, the use.

In arguing for greater attention to the Constitution as an authoritative text, I do not urge a literalist, conceptualist, or formalist approach to constitutional adjudication.[27] The view that the text can be interpreted as self-defining, or as ordinary language, or without reference to purpose does not follow from the proposition that the text is authoritative. In many instances, we can derive purpose from a text, and we can apply canons of interpretation peculiar to the nature of the Constitution itself. Working out the details of such a program is difficult, but it is a task that cannot be avoided if we are to develop a theory of constitutional interpretation that captures both the authoritativeness of the text and the necessity of contextual interpretation.

* * *

IV. Language and Theory

* * *

. . . Some words or terms, such as "anal-retentive personality" or "kinetic energy" or "wave function," can only be understood with reference to a theory. When we use terms such as these, we presuppose the existence of some theory, even though we do not explain the theory every time we use the terms. If theory-laden words can appear in non-legal texts, then similar terms ought to be able to appear in legal texts, and it seems promising to look at terms such as "the freedom of speech" and "equal protection of the laws" as such theory-laden words, except that here the use of the term precedes the development of the theory, rather than following after it.

If the use of the terms precedes the development of the theory, the terms themselves may have no meaning other than some ordinary language associations and some syntactic meaning. Notwithstanding this fact, they are still in a text which we take to be authoritative. Their irremovable presence in the text must then be authoritative. Their irremovable presence in the text must then be taken as a mandate for the development of a theory that will give content to the terms used. Significantly, the mandate does not derive from the personal intentions or states of the mind

of the drafters of the document. It derives from the conventions that govern language use, conventions that operate without regard to the intentions of the user. We argue unnecessarily and misleadingly when we argue that the use of such terms provides evidence of an original intent by the framers that the underlying theories be developed and changed, an intent we can assume from the failure to use more specific terminology. The constructed intent here is unnecessary, because the rules and conventions of language cut off the necessity and possibly even the permissibility of looking behind them into the mind of the speaker or writer.

Philosophers commonly argue that if a speaker says *p*, and *p* logically entails *q*, then the speaker is committed to *q* even if he had never thought of *q* and never would have intended to say *q*. A similar convention of language use appears applicable to the use of theory-laden terms. When a speaker uses a theory-laden term, the speaker is committed to the theory that may at any time surround the use of the term, even if the speaker did not intend that result. If, for example, I accuse someone of having an anal-retentive personality, my use of that term commits me to accusing him of having whatever an anal-retentive personality entails as a matter of psychiatric theory. And if I use terms such as "equal protection of the laws," that too commits me to having authorized the incorporation (and, if necessary, the creation) of a theory without which the term's meaning is incomplete.

Given that theories change, we can legitimately commit the user of theory-laden terminology to the possibility of change implicit in any theory. Thus, the users of theory-laden language such as "the freedom of speech" and "privileges and immunities of citizens of the United States" are committed to the theory whose construction they have authorized by their choice of words. Whether or not the user of those terms intended to be so committed does not matter. It's just part of the rules of the game. Theory-laden terms are incomplete, and the use of an incomplete term commits the user to the fact that the completion is going to come from somewhere else. The interpreter of the Constitution is thus, in some sense, like a musician working with a score that is not complete until it is interpreted; and in some sense like a trial lawyer who is expected to make the best case possible with the available evidence. An interpretation becomes an explication rather than an explanation,[28] and we can hope for no more.

Additionally, we can argue that all of ordinary language is theory-laden and indeed this is the assumption of much of Western metaphysics, embodied, for example, in the categories of Aristotle and Kant. But even if not all of ordinary language is theory-laden, it is fairly uncontroversial that at least much of it is. In some sense, the word "lunch" is theory-laden, at least as compared to "eating" or "placing organic matter in one's mouth for the purpose of introducing it into the digestive system." So, too, are terms like "time," "space," "hailing" a cab, "playing" a game, "sending" a letter, and "understanding" a book. We constantly use expressions which presuppose or incorporate theories that do more than identify a physical object or activity.

Thus, when we say that a term is theory-laden, we presuppose a particular point of view of the speaker with respect to which a term is theory-laden. I cannot explain to a person ignorant of baseball what a "home run" is without explaining a great deal of baseball, but it seems strange to describe "home run" as theory-laden when one baseball player is talking to another. Similarly, I cannot explain a "trick" to a non-bridge player without explaining at least the rudiments of the game of bridge, even though "trick" is not highly theory-laden in conversations between bridge players. But suppose that after a sequence of bidding I explain to my opponents at the bridge table that a particular bid was an "impossible negative." I must then explain a bidding system or theory known as "Precision," without which the term "impossible negative" cannot be understood.

We can clarify things by distinguishing between two forms of theory-ladenness. In the weaker sense, many of the terms of ordinary language are theory-laden. But in a stronger sense, terms are only theory-laden if they force us to go outside the domain of discourse in which they are used. Thus, "lunch" and "time" are theory-laden in the weaker sense but not in the stronger, because the theory that they presuppose is as much a part of ordinary language as is the language itself. But "straight flush" or "anal-retentive personality" or "habeas corpus," if used in ordinary conversation, are theory-laden in the

stronger sense because they presuppose theories outside the domain of ordinary discourse.

Therefore, we can say that terms are theory-laden in a strong sense only when they require us to go outside the context in which we are speaking. And that is why "habeaus corpus" may be theory-laden in ordinary language but not in law, as is even more true for terms like "pleading," "statute of limitations," or "appeal."

This distinction applies directly to constitutional language. The requirement that the President shall have attained "the Age of thirty-five years" is theory-laden in the weak sense because it presupposes a theory of determining age. It also presupposes the deeper idea of determining growth with reference to chronology. But it is not theory-laden in the strong sense because it is uncontroversially known to all participants speaking *within* the domain. A reference in the Constitution to "habeas corpus," or "Congress," or "amendment" is similar. But a term in the Constitution is theory-laden in the strong sense when it sends us outside the legal domain. "Freedom of speech" and "equal protection of the laws" are different from "habeas corpus" or "Congress," because they send us outside of the legal domain and into the moral or the political. That is also why the use of terminology that lacks meaning within the domain in which it is used can be said to commit the user to whatever meaning may appear in or be provided by another domain.

V. Language as a Constraint

Characterizing constitutional terms as theory-laden is problematic because the language then provides little if any guidance in our search for theory. Perhaps, therefore, a theory-authorizing view of constitutional language gives no weight to the text of the Constitution. Yet this view would mistakenly ignore the important asymmetry between positive and negative responses. Constitutional language can constrain the development of theory, or set the boundaries of theory-construction, without otherwise directing its development. Constitutional language can tell us when we have gone too far without telling us anything else. The statement that "It doesn't mean that" need not necessarily occasion the response "Then what does it mean?" I can know some of what a term does not mean without knowing what it does mean, just as I can tell you quite confidently that "the theory of relativity" does not mean "shirt collar" even though I have only the dimmest perception of what "the theory of relativity" does mean.

In this sense, we might do best to look at constitutional language as a frame without a picture, or, better yet, a blank canvas. We know when we have gone off the edge of the canvas even though the canvas itself gives us no guidance as to what to put on it.

But if language constitutes the frame, then how does it do that? The ordinary language associations of theory-laden terms do not explain the frame-like quality of the words, because we would not hesitate to extend freedom of speech to black armbands or oil paintings, although neither is "speech" in ordinary language. Furthermore, we would have little difficulty in holding universal tongue-boring to be a violation of the eighth amendment, although the universality would prevent a finding that the punishment was "unusual" in the ordinary language sense. We do, however, incorporate some very rough, pre-theoretical understandings into our sense of the limits of language. For example, it is probably largely pre-theoretical that castration as a punishment for jaywalking does not violate the principles of freedom of speech and that a fine of $1.00 for criticizing the President does not violate the prohibition on cruel and unusual punishment. But this helps very little in most real cases.

Perhaps, at best, we can only note the importance, as in all development of language, of moving in small steps. Highly theory-laden constitutional language is like the ship, imagined by the philosopher Neurath, which is to be rebuilt while afloat and therefore can only be rebuilt plank by plank. So long as the ship stays afloat during the process, it is no objection that the finished product bears little or no resemblance to the original. With constitutional language, so long as the enterprise stays afloat it is no objection that the current conception bears no close relation to the ordinary language meaning of the text. If we have moved in small steps from the original text, the enterprise stays afloat. The question, then, is not necessarily whether the putative move is justified by the text, but whether the move is justified by the last move.

In some ways, constitutional interpretation parallels some theories of literary criticism. In literary criticism, or indeed in any artistic interpretation, we do not demand *the* uniquely correct interpretation, but only *an* interpretation justified by the text. The paint or text underdetermines an interpretation (a theory) of an oil painting or a literary work in the same way that the text of the Constitution underdetermines a constitutional theory. The interpretation must be plausibly coherent with the painting or the text, but an interpretation cannot be uniquely derived from the text or painting alone. Therefore no one interpretation is uniquely acceptable, just as no constitutional theory is uniquely acceptable in terms of the text. Although non-textual sources may mandate a particular result, such a mandate is not the function of the language. The language limits, but does not command.

The analogy with literary criticism should not be pressed too far, because the literary critic has the freedom to select particularly important parts of his text for attention, a freedom not nearly as available in constitutional interpretation. But the analogy does effectively capture the relationship between flexibility and an authoritative text, a relationship that lies at the core of understanding the nature of constitutional adjudication.

Were this theory to be more fully developed, it might be said to be horizontally clause-bound, but not vertically clause-bound.[29] That is, it recognizes, as more free-wheeling theories do not, that the values specified in the text are more or less discrete, and that they have a textual preeminence over values not so specified. In this sense, it is horizontally clause-bound because each interpretation must derive originally from some particular portion of the text or from some justified interpretation of that portion of the text. It is vertically open because there is no limit on the source from which we can derive the full theory for the textually stated value, other than the intuitive, pre-theoretical limits placed on that theory by the language.

These discrete constitutional values are like a series of funnels, separate from each other, but open to receive anything of the right size that may be poured into them. Of course, if we extend the rims of the funnels too far, the funnels bump into each other, and the important conceptual separation becomes difficult to maintain. But that is a caution against the extremes, and not necessarily a crippling failure of the notion of conceptual separation. Courts must supply content to those theory-laden terms that send us outside the domain of legal knowledge and legal discourse. That content need not come from philosophy (as argued by Dworkin and Richards) or from history (as argued by Berger[30]) or from somewhere else. As I have argued in this Essay, the conventions of language demonstrate that Berger's extreme form of historical reference and even the more mild forms of historical interpretation are mistaken as a matter of textual derivation. Historical reference is neither mandated nor implicit in a permanently authoritative constitutional text. But although the text does not require a reference to history, it does not necessarily prohibit such reference. The text requires that we supply the theory, but there may be extra-textual, or extra-constitutional, reasons for constructing it from one source rather than from another. History is one possible source, but not the only possible source, and the same can be said for moral philosophy, or political policy, or any other source of values.

Conclusion

The Constitution has been written in a language, and a user of language must be taken to know and intend that the language is open to interpretation. Although a user of language has intentions that are relevant in determining what the user meant to say, the user has no power to veto the conventions of the language that have been used. Constitutional interpretations can change because the linguistic conventions and presuppositions change, even though the words remain the same. Thus, a fixed reference to history or original intent seems curious. Even historians expect to interpret the past anew for each generation, because perspective, and therefore meaning, is mutable. Of course, our craving for certainty may cause us to search for the immutable. This is most apparent in law, where the myth of certainty has a persistent appeal. But the law cannot be certain, in large part because language itself is not certain. What is unfortunate is that quixotic quests for certainty are likely to interfere with more fruitful

quests for an intelligent understanding of the causes and management of our uncertainty.

NOTES

1. The contemporary jargon draws a distinction between "interpretivism" and "noninterpretivism," but this is merely one characterization of an issue that predates the current labels. *See generally* J.H. ELY, DEMOCRACY AND DISTRUST 1–14 (1980); Brest, *The Misconceived Quest for the Original Understanding*, 60 B.U.L. REV. 204 (1980); Grey, *Do We Have an Unwritten Constitution?*, 27 STAN. L. REV. 703 (1975) [hereinafter cited as Grey, *Unwritten Constitution*]; Grey, *Origins of the Unwritten Constitution: Fundamental Law in American Revolutionary Thought*, 30 STAN. L. REV. 843 (1978) [hereinafter cited as Grey, *Origins*]; Linde, *Judges, Critics and the Realist Tradition*, 82 YALE L.J. 227 (1972); Monaghan, *Of "Liberty" and "Property,"* 62 CORNELL L. REV. 405 (1977); Monaghan, *The Constitution Goes to Harvard*, 13 HARV. C.R.-C.L. L. REV. 117 (1978) [hereinafter cited as Monaghan, *The Constitution*]; Perry, *Substantive Due Process Revisited: Reflections on (and Beyond) Recent Cases*, 71 Nw. U.L. REV. 417 (1976); Richards, *Human Rights as the Unwritten Constitution: The Problem of Change and Stability in Constitutional Interpretation*, 4 U. DAYTON L. REV. 295 (1979); *Constitutional Adjudication and Democratic Theory*, 56 N.Y.U. L. REV. 259 (1981); *Judicial Review versus Democracy*, 42 OHIO ST. L.J. 1 (1981).

2. One notable exception is Munzer & Nickel, *Does the Constitution Mean What It Always Meant?*, 77 COLUM. L. REV. 1029 (1977). *See also* Alexander, *Modern Equal Protection Theories: A Metatheoretical Taxonomy and Critique*, 42 OHIO ST. L.J. 3, 4–16 (1981); Smith, *Rights, Right Answers, and the Constructive Model of Morality*, 5 SOC. THEORY AND PRAC. 409, 421–25 (1980). Philosophy is at the moment having a good run in the constitutional arena but, with few exceptions, it is moral philosophy rather than the philosophy of language that is taken to be the most useful for constitutional inquiries. Given that we have a *written* constitution, this lack of attention from the perspective of the philosophy of language seems a bit surprising. Although not directed specifically towards constitutional interpretation, there has been some recent attention to legal language from a philosophical perspective. Moore, *The Semantics of Judging*, 54 S. CAL. L. REV. 151 (1981); Stone, *From a Language Perspective*, 90 YALE L.J. 1149 (1981).

3. In addition to the works cited *supra* note 1, see L. TRIBE, AMERICAN CONSTITUTIONAL LAW at iii (1978) ("[T]he Constitution is an intentionally incomplete,

often deliberately indeterminate structure for the participatory evolution of political ideals and governmental practices."); L. TRIBE, AMERICAN CONSTITUTIONAL LAW 2 (Supp. 1979) ("open-textured" provisions such as "equal protection" and "due process"; use of "broad terminology" in the Constitution). *See also* Baker v. Carr, 369 U.S. 186, 242 (1962) (Douglas, J., concurring) ("large gaps in the Constitution"); H.P. Hood & Sons, Inc. v. Du Mond, 336 U.S. 525, 535 (1949) (Jackson, J.) ("great silences of the Constitution"); Prudential Ins. Co. v. Benjamin, 328 U.S. 408, 413 (1946) ("great constitutional gaps").

4. Although it illustrates the focus both of this inquiry and of my conclusions, the phrase in the text is, at this stage, question-begging. For even if we note that the Constitution is written, what does this say about the constitution? This question can be expressed in terms of how much of the constitution is contained or captured in the (written) Constitution. It is this question that this essay is intended to address. Positing the question in this way suggests the Continental distinction between a material constitution and a formal constitution. *See* H. KELSEN, THE PURE THEORY OF LAW 222–24 (M. Knight trans. 2d ed. 1967).

5. Hart's original foray into the field was *The Ascription of Responsibility and Rights*, in LOGIC AND LANGUAGE (First Series) 145–66 (A. Flew ed. 1955). Hart's later repudiation of this strictly performative view of legal language (H.L.A. HART, PUNISHMENT AND RESPONSIBILITY v (1968)) was the result of the more complex, presupposition-oriented theory first put forth in Hart, *Definition and Theory in Jurisprudence*, 70 LAW Q. REV. 37 (1954) [hereinafter cited as Hart, *Definition and Theory*], and embellished in H.L.A. HART, THE CONCEPT OF LAW 13–17 (1961). *See also* Cohen, *Theory and Definition in Jurisprudence*, 29 PROC. ARISTOTELIAN SOC. (SUPP.) 213 (1955); Hart, *Theory and Definition in Jurisprudence*, 29 PROC. ARISTOTELIAN SOC. (SUPP.) 239 (1955). *See generally* N. MACCORMICK, H.L.A. HART (1981); Hacker, *Hart's Philosophy of Law*, and Baker, *Defeasibility and Meaning*, in LAW, MORALITY, AND SOCIETY: ESSAYS IN HONOUR OF H.L.A. HART 1, 26 (P. Hacker & J. Raz eds. 1977).

6. Thus, when John Marshall observed that "we must never forget that it is a *constitution* we are expounding," McCulloch v. Maryland, 17 U.S. (4 Wheat.) 316, 407 (1819), he was adopting the thesis discussed in the text, although *McCulloch* is significantly obscure in that Marshall did not explain in what way constitutional interpretation was unique. *See* Frankfurter, *John Marshall and the Judicial Function*, 69 HARV. L. REV. 217 (1955). For a sampling of the various theories that embody this view in one way or other, see C. BLACK, STRUCTURE AND RELATIONSHIP IN CONSTITUTIONAL LAW (1969); C. MILLER, THE SUPREME COURT AND THE USES OF HISTORY (1969); Llewellyn, *The Con-*

stitution as an Institution, 34 COLUM. L. REV. 1 (1934); Murphy, *The Art of Constitutional Interpretation: A Preliminary Showing*, in ESSAYS ON THE CONSTITUTION OF THE UNITED STATES 150 (M. Harmon ed. 1978).

7. *See supra* note 3. A pervasive problem in attempting to generalize about constitutional language is that constitutional language is hardly uniform in degree of generality, in purpose, or in historical origin. This recognition of the diversity of constitutional language is most prominently associated with Justice Frankfurter. *See, e.g.*, Malinski v. New York, 324 U.S. 401, 414–15 (1945). *See generally* H. THOMAS, FELIX FRANKFURTER: SCHOLAR ON THE BENCH 127–47 (1960).

8. 17 C.F.R. § 240.10b-5(a) (1981).

9. 15 U.S.C. § 1 (1976).

10. "When did you stop beating your wife?" contains a prototypical presupposition in that it presupposes, but does not assert, that you have a wife and that you have beaten her. Presuppositions are not asserted to be true or false, but undergird the thought and language of people. *See also* J. AUSTIN, WORDS, *supra* note 7, at 48–52; J. SEARLE, SPEECH ACTS (1969). *See generally* Strawson, *On Referring*, 59 MIND 320 (1950).

11. Hart, *Definition and Theory, supra* note 5, at 37. *See supra* note 5.

12. The nature of the ratification process makes the search for original intent in constitutional adjudication especially problematic. Are the states presumed to have ratified the intent of the drafters as well as the language those drafters wrote? What if legislative history from state legislatures shows that different states ratified for different reasons? What if the intent of the drafters is unavailable to the states? Given the nature of my conclusions, I need not attempt to answer these very troubling questions, but they cannot be avoided by any theory that is tied to original intent.

Even if we put the "whose intent?" question aside, we must still address two different questions. The first is "What results would the drafters have intended had they been confronted with the problems and context of today's world?" This question seems largely unanswerable, inviting the most speculative kind of historical psychoanalysis. This formulation of the issue has, however, attracted a substantial following. *See, e.g.*, L. LUSKY, BY WHAT RIGHT? 21 (1975); Murphy, Book Review, 87 YALE L.J. 1752, 1770 (1978).

The other question that could be asked is "What results did the drafters specifically intend?" This question is, at least, one that is possible to answer, although much of this Essay contends that it is still the wrong question. This question is at the heart of the much discussed theories of Raoul Berger. R. BERGER, GOVERNMENT BY JUDICIARY: THE TRANSFORMATION OF THE FOURTEENTH AMENDMENT (1977). The assumption that clear or unmistakable intent, as evidenced in historical documents, is the exact equivalent of a textual statement to that effect is central to Berger's thesis. *See, e.g., id.* at 368; Berger, *A Political Scientist as Constitutional Lawyer: A Reply to Louis Fisher*, 41 OHIO ST. L.J. 147, 162–63, 167 (1980). *See also* Oregon v. Mitchell, 400 U.S. 112, 203 (1970) (Harlan, J., concurring and dissenting in part); Harper v. Virginia Board of Elections, 383 U.S. 663, 677–78 (1966) (Black, J., dissenting); West Coast Hotel Co. v. Parrish, 300 U.S. 379, 402–03 (1937) (Sutherland, J., dissenting). Among current members of the Supreme Court, Justice Rehnquist most clearly subscribes to the view that original intent is dispositive. *See, e.g.,* Trimble v. Gordon, 430 U.S. 762, 777–86 (1977) (Rehnquist, J., dissenting); Sugarman v. Dougall, 413 U.S. 634, 649-64 (1973) (Rehnquist, J., dissenting in *Sugarman* and also in *In re* Griffiths, 413 U.S. 717 (1973)). Because, as should be apparent from all of this Essay, I disagree with Berger's assumption as to what is the proper question, I have no need to deal with the issue of whether Berger's own answers to his question are even correct. It is certainly not abundantly clear that they are. *See, e.g.,* Murphy, *supra*, at 1754–60.

13. *See* Palko v. Connecticut, 302 U.S. 319 (1937); Murray's Lessee v. Hoboken Land & Improvement Co., 59 U.S. (18 How.) 272 (1856).

14. *See* Sniadach v. Family Finance Corp., 395 U.S. 337, 344–51 (1969) (Black, J., dissenting); Ownbey v. Morgan, 256 U.S. 94 (1921).

15. Patterson v. Colorado, 205 U.S. 454 (1907), is the Supreme Court's most explicit statement of the now-repudiated "prior restraints only" interpretation of the first amendment. *Id.* at 462. For references to other historical exclusions, see, e.g., Roth v. United States, 354 U.S. 476 (1957); *Ex parte* Jackson, 96 U.S. 727 (1877); L. LEVY, LEGACY OF SUPPRESSION: FREEDOM OF SPEECH AND PRESS IN EARLY AMERICAN HISTORY (1960).

16. *See supra* note 12.

17. "The provisions of the Federal Constitution, undoubtedly, are pliable in the sense that in appropriate cases they have the capacity of bringing within their grasp every new condition which falls within their meaning. But, their *meaning* is changeless; it is only their *application* which is extensible." Home Bldg. & Loan Assn. v. Blaisdell, 290 U.S. 398, 451 (1934) (Sutherland, J., dissenting) (footnote omitted). *See also* Village of Euclid v. Ambler Realty Co., 272 U.S. 365, 387 (1926) (Sutherland, J.); 1 T. COOLEY, CONSTITUTIONAL LIMITATIONS 124 (8th ed. 1927).

18. *See* Munzer & Nickel, *supra* note 2, at 1–31. This seems to have been Justice Sutherland's point. *See supra* note 17.

Whether there is a shift in meaning may depend on why a particular provision is in the Constitution. The narrower the reason, the more likely it is that a new application will be beyond the scope of that reason and will therefore constitute a shift of meaning. Conversely, the broader the reason taken to justify the provision in the text, the more likely it is that subsequent applications will still be within the scope of that reason, and therefore not represent a change of meaning.

19. Linmark Associates, Inc. v. Township of Willingboro, 431 U.S. 85 (1977).

20. *See, e.g.,* Lusky, *"Government By Judiciary": What Price Legitimacy?*, 6 HASTINGS CONST. L.Q. 403 (1979); Munzer & Nickel, *supra* note 2, at 1030–33; Murphy, *supra* note 12; Nathanson, Book Review, 56 TEX. L. REV. 579 (1978); Perry, Book Review, 78 COLUM. L. REV. 685 (1978). Although it is possible that we have ignored the relevance of history and original intent, *see* Monaghan, *The Constitution, supra* note 1, at 117, it seems that we have more often succumbed to the error of ignoring Joseph Story's admonition that "Nothing but the text itself was adopted by the people." J. STORY, COMMENTARIES ON THE CONSTITUTION OF THE UNITED STATES 300 (4th ed. 1873).

21. *See supra* note 3.

22. R. DWORKIN *Taking Rights Seriously* (1980), at 133; Dworkin, *The Forum of Principle*, 56 N.Y.U. L. REV. 469 (1981).

23. J.H. ELY, *supra* note 1; Ely, *The Wages of Crying Wolf: A Comment on* Roe v. Wade, 82 YALE L.J. 920 (1973).

24. "[T]he most important datum bearing on what was intended is the constitutional language itself." J.H. ELY, *supra* note 1, at 16.

25. This is implicit in any view that treats "unmistakable intention" as being equivalent to text. *See supra* note 12. The difficult question occurs, however, when the text and the legislative history are in some way inconsistent. On this point, the canons of interpretation are not helpful, because one canon suggests that we look at the legislative history only when the text is unclear, and another says that we can look at legislative history to reject a textual statement inconsistent with that history. *Compare* Caminetti v. United States, 242 U.S. 470, 490 (1917), *with* United Steelworkers v. Weber, 443 U.S. 193, 201–02 (1979). *See generally,* Note, *Intent, Clear Statements, and the Common Law: Statutory Interpretation in the Supreme Court*, 95 HARV. L. REV. 892 (1982).

It is unfortunately common for commentators to conflate textual and historical approaches to constitutional interpretation. *See, e.g.,* Bork, *Neutral Principles and Some First Amendment Problems*, 47 IND. L.J. 1 (1971) at 8; Grey, *Unwritten Constitution, supra* note 1, at 712–13; Perry, *Interpretivism, Freedom of Expression, and Equal Protection*, 42 OHIO ST. L.J. 261, 280–81 (1981). The two approaches are, however, fundamentally different. *See* Bobbitt, *Constitutional Fate*, 58 TEX. L. REV. 695, 707 (1980). *See also* Alexander, *supra* note 2.

26. P. JONES, PHILOSOPHY AND THE NOVEL 183–84 (1975). The dispute between the "intentionalists" and the "anti-intentionalists" is prominent in contemporary philosophy of literary criticism. The dispute is described and fully documented in P. JUHL, INTERPRETATION: AN ESSAY IN THE PHILOSOPHY OF LITERARY CRITICISM (1980). Juhl himself is an intentionalist. There is much in the corpus of writing about literary interpretation that is of great importance to the constitutional theorist, both for intentionalists and anti-intentionalists like myself.

27. The term "literalism" is ambiguous, because it is unclear where the literal meaning of the term at issue comes from. In one sense, every textually oriented theory, including this one, is a version of literalism. But we more commonly equate literalism with the ordinary language definition of constitutional terms, or with the notion that the text provides clear answers to all of our problems. In this sense, literalism shares both the characteristics and the flaws of what we usually refer to as "formalism" or "conceptualism." *See* H.L.A. HART, *supra* note 5, at 126; J. STONE, THE PROVINCE AND FUNCTION OF LAW 149–65 (1946).

28. "*Explication,* when not simply a synonym for 'explanation,' is the process whereby a hitherto imprecise notion is given a formal definition, and so made suitable for use in formal work. The definition does not claim to be synonymous with the original notion, since it is avowedly making it more precise." A. LACEY, A DICTIONARY OF PHILOSOPHY 66 (1976). The idea of *explication* is usually attributed to Carnap. R. CARNAP, MEANING AND NECESSITY 7–8 (2d ed. 1956). I am using "explication" in a slightly looser sense. We explicate when we work out a theory, and when we explicate we put something in, rather than just pulling something out.

29. I draw the term "clause-bound" from J. H. ELY, *supra* note 1.

30. *See supra* note 12.

Notes and Questions

JOHN HART ELY, from *Democracy and Distrust*

1. Given the recognition of the authority of the courts to review the actions of other branches of government in light of compatibility with the Constitution, the question arises how this authority is to be legitimately exercised. Since the judicial power includes the authority to (a) interpret the Constitution and (b) invalidate legislation as incompatible with that interpretation, how the courts should interpret the Constitution has been a subject of enduring controversy. In terms of a general philosophy of constitutional adjudication, Ely points out that the dispute is polarized between those who favor a narrow or "interpretivist" approach and those who advocate a broad or "noninterpretivist" approach. How does Ely explain the difference? What is his response to these two approaches? What approach does he favor, and where does he place it in relation to interpretivist or noninterpretivist views?

2. Ely uses the Warren Court (generally) as a model of the approach he advocates, but he argues for a particular interpretation of the Warren Court approach that is not the traditional or usual characterization of that Court. What is Ely's picture of the Warren Court? What picture is he arguing against? How does he distinguish the Warren Court from the *Lochner* Court? (The Court that decided *Lochner* v. *New York* was notorious for blocking much progressive social legislation from about the turn of the century through the early 1930s. This case and related ones are considered in Chapter Three.)

3. The famous *Carolene Products* footnote is one of the most often quoted pieces of legal dicta in American history. Ely suggests that it foreshadows the approach he is advocating. In what way does it do so? How does Ely elaborate the *Carolene Products* rationale?

4. Ely concludes from his elaboration of the *Carolene Products* argument that a political theory of representative government is necessary to show consistency of competing ideals. To meet this need he formulates a theory of representative government. What are the essential elements of his theory? How does he attempt to fit the conflicting ideals of popular government and minority protection into a common duty of representation?

5. Next Ely offers three arguments for a "participation-oriented, representation-reinforcing approach" to judicial review. What are the three arguments? Do you find them persuasive? Why or why not?

[From] *Democracy and Distrust*

JOHN HART ELY

CHAPTER 4

Policing the Process of Representation: The Court as Referee

. . . An interpretivist approach — at least one that approaches constitutional provisions as self-contained units — proves on analysis incapable of keeping faith with the evident spirit of certain of the provisions. When we search for an external source of values with which to fill in the Constitution's open texture, however — one that will not simply end up constituting the Court a council of legislative revision — we search in vain. Despite the usual assumption that these are the only options, however, they are not, for value imposition is not the only possible response to the realization that we have a Constitution that needs filling in. A quite different approach is available, and to discern its outlines we need look no further than to the Warren Court.*

---

*As shall become clear soon enough, "activism" and "self-restraint" are categories that cut across interpretivism and noninterpretivism, virtually at right angles. "Strict constructionism" is a term that certainly might be used to designate something like interpretivism; unfortunately it has been used more often, perhaps most notably in recent years by President Nixon, to signal a quite different thing, a proclivity to reach constitutional judgments that will please political conservatives. The interpretivism-noninterpretivism dichotomy stirs a long-standing debate that pervades all of law, that between "positivism" and "natural law." Interpretivism *is* about the same thing as positivism, and natural law approaches are surely one form of noninterpretivism. But these older terms are just as well omitted here, since they have acquired baggage that can mislead.

That Court's reputation as "activist" or interventionist is deserved. A good deal of carping to the contrary notwithstanding, however, that is where its similarity to earlier interventionist Courts, in particular the early twentieth-century Court that decided *Lochner v. New York* and its progeny, ends. For all the while the commentators of the Warren era were talking about ways of discovering fundamental values, the Court itself was marching to a different drummer. The divergence wasn't entirely self-conscious, and the Court did lapse occasionally into the language of fundamental values: it would be surprising if the thinking of earlier Courts and the writings of the day's preeminent commentators hadn't taken some toll. The toll, however, was almost entirely rhetorical: the constitutional decisions of the Warren Court evidence a deep structure significantly different from the value-oriented approach favored by the academy.

Many of the Warren Court's most controversial decisions concerned criminal procedure or other questions of what judicial or administrative process is due before serious consequences may be visited upon individuals — process-oriented decisions in the most ordinary sense. But a concern with process in a broader sense — with the process by which the laws that govern society are made — animated its other decisions as well. Its unprecedented activism in the fields of political expression and association obviously fits this broader pattern. Other Courts had recognized the connection between such political activity and the proper functioning of the democratic process: the Warren Court was the first seriously to act upon it. That Court was also the first to move into, and once there seriously to occupy, the voter qualification and malapportionment areas. These were certainly interventionist decisions, but the interventionism was fueled not by a desire on the part of the Court to vindicate particular substantive values it had determined were important or fundamental, but rather by a desire to ensure that the political process—which is where such values *are* properly identified, weighed, and accommodated—was open to those of all viewpoints on something approaching an equal basis.

Finally there were the important decisions insisting on equal treatment for society's habitual unequals: notably racial minorities, but also aliens, "illegitimates," and poor people. But rather than announcing that good or value *X* was so important or fundamental it simply had to be provided or protected, the Court's message here was that insofar as political officials had chosen to provide or protect *X* for some people (generally people like themselves), they had better make sure that everyone was being similarly accommodated or be prepared to explain pretty convincingly why not. Whether these two broad concerns of the Warren Court—with clearing the channels of political change on the one hand, and with correcting certain kinds of discrimination against minorities on the other—fit together to form a coherent theory of representative government, or whether, as is sometimes suggested, they are actually inconsistent impulses, is a question I shall take up presently. But however that may be, it seems to be coming into focus that the pursuit of these "participational" goals of broadened access to the processes and bounty* of representative government, as opposed to the more traditional and academically popular insistence upon the provision of a series of particular substantive goods or values deemed fundamental, was what marked the work of the Warren Court.

Some condemn and others praise, but at least we're beginning to understand that something different from old-fashioned value imposition was for a time the order of the day.†

The Carolene Products Footnote

The Warren Court's approach was foreshadowed in a famous footnote in *United States v. Carolene Products Co.*, decided in 1938. Justice Stone's opinion for the Court upheld a federal statute prohibiting the interstate shipment of filled milk, on the ground that all it had to be was "rational" and it assuredly was that. Footnote four suggested, however, that mere rationality might not always be enough:

> There may be narrower scope for operation of the presumption of constitutionality when legislation appears on its face to be within a specific prohibition of the Constitution, such as those of the first ten amendments, which are deemed equally specific when held to be embraced within the Fourteenth . . .
>
> It is unnecessary to consider now whether legislation which restricts those political processes

---

†Participation itself can obviously be regarded as a value, but that doesn't collapse the two modes of review I am describing into one. As I am using the terms, value imposition refers to the designation of certain goods (rights or whatever) as so important that they must be insulated from whatever inhibition the political process might impose, whereas a participational orientation denotes a form of review that concerns itself with how decisions effecting value choices and distributing the resultant costs and benefits are made. I surely don't claim that the words have to be used thus. (There is even doubt that "participational" deserves to be recognized as a word at all.) I claim only that that is how I am using them, and that so used they are not synonyms.

If the objection is not that I have not distinguished two concepts but rather that one might well "value" certain decision procedures for their own sake, of course it is right: one might. And to one who insisted on that terminology, my point would be that the "values" the Court should pursue are "participational values" of the sort I have mentioned, since those are the "values" (1) with which our Constitution has preeminently and most successfully concerned itself, (2) whose "imposition" is not incompatible with, but on the contrary supports, the American system of representative democracy, and (3) that courts set apart from the political process are uniquely situated to "impose."

---

*The reference here should be understood as including exemptions or immunities from hurts (punishments, taxes, regulations, and so forth) along with benefits. It is thus to patterns of distribution generally.

which can ordinarily be expected to bring about repeal of undesirable legislation, is to be subjected to more exacting judicial scrutiny under the general prohibitions of the Fourteenth Amendment than are most other types of legislation . . .

Nor need we enquire whether similar considerations enter into the review of statutes directed at particular religious . . . or national . . . or racial minorities . . . ; whether prejudice against discrete and insular minorities may be a special condition, which tends seriously to curtail the operation of those political processes ordinarily to be relied upon to protect minorities, and which may call for a correspondingly more searching judicial inquiry.

The first paragraph is pure interpretivism: it says the Court should enforce the "specific" provisions of the Constitution. We've seen, though, that interpretivism is incomplete: there are provisions in the Constitution that call for more. The second and third paragraphs give us a version of what that more might be. Paragraph two suggests that it is an appropriate function of the Court to keep the machinery of democratic government running as it should, to make sure the channels of political participation and communication are kept open. Paragraph three suggests that the Court should also concern itself with what majorities do to minorities, particularly mentioning laws "directed at" religious, national, and racial minorities and those infected by prejudice against them.

For all its notoriety and influence, the *Carolene Products* footnote has not been adequately elaborated. Paragraph one has always seemed to some commentators not quite to go with the other two. Professor Lusky, who as Stone's law clerk was substantially responsible for the footnote, has recently revealed that the first paragraph was added at the request of Chief Justice Hughes. Any implied substantive criticism seems misplaced: positive law has its claims, even when it doesn't fit some grander theory. It's true, though, that paragraphs two and three are more interesting, and it is the relationship between those two paragraphs that has not been adequately elaborated. Popular control and egalitarianism are surely both ancient American ideals; indeed, dictionary definitions of "democracy" tend to incorporate both. Frequent conjunction is

not the same thing as consistency, however, and at least on the surface a principle of popular control suggests an ability on the part of a majority simply to outvote a minority and thus deprive its members of goods they desire. Borrowing Paul Freund's word, I have suggested that both *Carolene Products* themes are concerned with participation: they ask us to focus not on whether this or that substantive value is unusually important or fundamental, but rather on whether the opportunity to participate either in the political processes by which values are appropriately identified and accommodated, or in the accommodation those processes have reached, has been unduly constricted. But the fact that two concepts can fit under the same verbal umbrella isn't enough to render them consistent either, and a system of equal participation in the processes of government is by no means self-evidently linked to a system of presumptively equal participation in the benefits and costs that process generates; in many ways it seems calculated to produce just the opposite effect. To understand the ways these two sorts of participation join together in a coherent political theory, it is necessary to focus more insistently than I did in Chapter 1 on the American system of representative democracy.

Representative Government

It is a principle of general application that the exercise of a granted power to act in behalf of others involves the assumption toward them of a duty to exercise the power in their interest and behalf . . .

We think that the Railway Labor Act imposes upon the statutory representative of a craft at least as exacting a duty to protect equally the interests of the members of the craft as the Constitution imposes upon a legislature to give equal protection to the interests of those for whom it legislates.
— United States Supreme Court (1944)

Representative democracy is perhaps most obviously a system of government suited to situations in which it is for one reason or another impractical for the citizenry actually to show up and personally participate in the legislative process. But the concept of representation, as understood by our forebears, was richer than this. Prerevolutionary rhetoric posited a continuing conflict between the interests of "the rulers" on the one hand, and those of "the ruled" (or "the people") on the other. A solution was sought by building into the concept of representation the idea of an association of the interests of the two groups. Thus the representatives in the new government were visualized as "citizens," persons of unusual ability and character to be sure, but nonetheless "of" the people. Upon conclusion of their service, the vision continued, they would return to the body of the people and thus to the body of the ruled. In addition, even while in office, the idea was that they would live under the regime of the laws they passed and not exempt themselves from their operation: this obligation to include themselves among the ruled would ensure a community of interest and guard against oppressive legislation. The framers realized that even visions need enforcement mechanisms: "some force to oppose the insidious tendency of power to separate . . . the rulers from the ruled" was required. The principal force envisioned was the ballot: the people in their self-interest would choose representatives whose interests intertwined with theirs and by the critical reelection decision ensure that they stayed that way, in particular that the representatives did not shield themselves from the rigors of the laws they passed.

Actually it may not matter so much whether our representatives are treating themselves the way they treat the rest of us. Indeed it may be precisely because in some ways they treat themselves better, that they seem so desperately to want to be reelected. And it may be that desire for reelection, more than any community of interest, that is our insurance policy. If most of us feel we are being subjected to unreasonable treatment by our representatives, we retain the ability — irrespective of whether they are formally or informally insulating themselves — to turn them out of office. What the system, at least as described thus far, does *not* ensure is the effective protection of minorities whose interests differ from the interests of most of the rest of us. For if it is not the "many" who are being treated unreasonably but rather only some minority, the situation will not be so comfortably amenable to political correction. Indeed there may be political

pressures to *encourage* our representatives to pass laws that treat the majority coalition on whose continued support they depend in one way, and one or more minorities whose backing they don't need less favorably. Even assuming we were willing and able to give it teeth, a requirement that our representatives treat themselves as they treat most of the rest of us would be no guarantee whatever against unequal treatment for minorities.

This is not to say that the oppression of minorities was a development our forebears were prepared to accept as inevitable. The "republic" they envisioned was not some "winner-take-all" system in which the government pursued the interests of a privileged few or even of only those groups that could work themselves into some majority coalition, but rather — leaving slavery to one side, which of course is precisely what they did — one in which the representatives would govern in the interest of the whole people. Thus every citizen was said to be entitled to equivalent respect, and equality was a frequently mentioned republican concern. Its place in the Declaration of Independence, for example, could hardly be more prominent. When it came to describing the actual mechanics of republican government in the Constitution, however, this concern for equality got comparatively little explicit attention. This seems to have been largely because of an assumption of "pure" republican political and social theory that we have brushed but not yet stressed: that "the people" were an essentially homogeneous group whose interests did not vary significantly. Though most often articulated as if it were an existing reality, this was at best an ideal, and the fact that wealth redistribution of some form — ranging from fairly extreme to fairly modest proposals — figured in so much early republican theorizing, while doubtless partly explainable simply in terms of the perceived desirability of such a change, also was quite consciously connected to republicanism's political theory. To the extent that existing heterogeneity of interest was a function of wealth disparity, redistribution would reduce it. To the extent that the ideal of homogeneity could be achieved, legislation in the interest of most would necessarily be legislation in the interest of all, and extensive further attention to equality of treatment would be unnecessary.

The key assumption here, that everyone's interests are essentially identical, is obviously a hard one for our generation to swallow, and in fact we know perfectly well that many of our forebears were ambivalent about it too. Thus the document of 1789 and 1791, though at no point explicitly invoking the concept of equality, did strive by at least two strategies to protect the interests of minorities from the potentially destructive will of some majority coalition. The more obvious one may be the "list" strategy employed by the Bill of Rights, itemizing things that cannot be done to anyone, at least by the federal government (though even here the safeguards turn out to be mainly procedural). The original Constitution's more pervasive strategy, however, can be loosely styled a strategy of pluralism, one of structuring the government, and to a limited extent society generally, so that a variety of voices would be guaranteed their say and no majority coalition could dominate. As Madison — pointedly eschewing the ("Chapter 3") approach of setting up an undemocratic body to keep watch over the majority's values — put it in *Federalist* 51:

> It is of great importance in a republic not only to guard the society against the oppression of its rulers, but to guard one part of the society against the injustice of the other part . . . If a majority be united by a common interest, the rights of the minority will be insecure. There are but two methods of providing against this evil: the one by creating a will in the community independent of the majority . . . the other, by comprehending in the society so many separate descriptions of citizens as will render an unjust combination of a majority of the whole very improbable, if not impracticable. The first method prevails in all governments possessing an hereditary or self-appointed authority. This, at best, is but a precarious security; because a power independent of the society may as well espouse the unjust views of the major, as the rightful interests of the minor party, and may possibly be turned against both parties. The second method will be exemplified in the federal republic of the United States.

The crucial move from a confederation to a system with a stronger central government was so conceived. Madison has been conspicuously attacked for not understanding pluralist political theory, but in fact there is reason to suppose he understood it rather well. His theory, derived from David Hume and spelled out at length in *The Federalist*, was that although at a local level one "faction" might well have sufficient clout to be able to tyrannize others, in the national government no faction or interest group would constitute a majority capable of exercising control. The Constitution's various moves to break up and counterpoise governmental decision and enforcement authority, not only between the national government and the states but among the three departments of the national government as well, were of similar design.

It is a rightly renowned system, but it didn't take long to learn that from the standpoint of protecting minorities it was not enough. Whatever genuine faith had existed at the beginning that everyone's interests either were identical or were about to be rendered so, had run its course as the republic approached its fiftieth birthday. Significant economic differences remained a reality, and the fear of legislation hostile to the interests of the propertied and creditor classes — a fear that of course had materialized earlier, during the regime of the Articles of Confederation, and thus had importantly inspired the constitutional devices to which we have alluded — surely did not abate during the Jacksonian era, as the "many" began genuinely to exercise political power. The Pennsylvania Supreme Court summed it up thus in 1851:

> [W]hen, in the exercise of proper legislative powers, general laws are enacted, which bear or may bear on the whole community, if they are unjust and against the spirit of the constitution, the whole community will be interested to procure their repeal by a voice potential. And that is the great security for just and fair legislation.
>
> But when individuals are selected from the mass, and laws are enacted affecting their property, . . . who is to stand up for them, thus isolated from the mass, in injury and injustice, or where are they to seek relief from such acts of despotic power?

Also relevant was the persistence of the institution of slavery. So long as blacks could conveniently be regarded as subhuman, they provided no proof that some people were tyrannizing others. Once that assumption began to blur, there came into focus another reason for doubting that the protection of the many was necessarily the protection of all.

Simultaneously we came to recognize that the existing constitutional devices for protecting minorities were simply not sufficient. No finite list of entitlements can possibly cover all the ways majorities can tyrannize minorities, and the informal and more formal mechanisms of pluralism cannot always be counted on either. The fact that effective majorities can usually be described as clusters of cooperating minorities won't be much help when the cluster in question has sufficient power and perceived community of interest to advantage itself at the expense of a minority (or group of minorities) it is inclined to regard as different, and in such situations the fact that a number of agencies must concur, and others retain the right to squawk, isn't going to help much either. If, therefore, the republican ideal of government in the interest of the whole people was to be maintained, in an age when faith in the republican tenet that the people and their interests were essentially homogeneous was all but dead, a frontal assault on the problem of majority tyranny was needed. The existing theory of representation had to be extended so as to ensure not simply that the representative would not sever his interests from those of a majority of his constituency but also that he would not sever a majority coalition's interests from those of various minorities. Naturally that cannot mean that groups that constitute minorities of the population can never be treated less favorably than the rest, but it does preclude a refusal to *represent* them, the denial to minorities of what Professor Dworkin has called "equal concern and respect in the design and administration of the political institutions that govern them." The Fourteenth Amendment's Equal Protection Clause is obviously our Constitution's most dramatic embodiment of this ideal. Before that amendment was ratified, however, its theory was understood, and functioned as a component — even on occasion as a judicially enforceable component — of the concept of representation that had been at the core of our Constitution from the beginning.

It's ironic, but the old concept of "virtual representation" is helpful here. The actual term was anathema to our forefathers, since it was invoked to answer their cries of "taxation without representation." But the concept contained an insight that has survived in American political theory and in fact has informed our constitutional thinking from the beginning. The colonists' argument that it was wrong, even "unconstitutional," to tax us when we lacked the privilege of sending representatives to Parliament was answered on the British side by the argument that although the colonies didn't actually elect anyone, they were "virtually represented" in Parliament. Manchester was taxed, it was pointed out, without the privilege of sending representatives to Parliament; yet surely, the argument concluded, no one could deny that Manchester was represented. The colonists' answer, at least their principal one, took the form of a denial not of the concept's general sense, but rather of its applicability to our case. Thus Daniel Dulany responded:

> The security of the non-electors [of Manchester] against oppression is that their oppression will fall also upon the electors and the representatives . . . The electors, who are inseparably connected in their interests with the non-electors, may be justly deemed to be the representatives of the non-electors . . . and the members chosen, therefore, the representatives of both.

However,

> there is not that intimate and inseparable relation between the electors of Great Britain and the inhabitants of the colonies, which must inevitably involve both in the same taxation. On the contrary, not a single actual elector in England might be immediately affected by a taxation in America . . . Even acts oppressive and injurious to an extreme degree, might become popular in England, from the promise or expectation that the very measures which depressed the colonies, would give ease to the inhabitants of Great Britain.

Although the term understandably has not been revived, the protective device of guaranteeing "virtual representation" by tying the interests of those without political power to the interests of those with it, was one that importantly influenced both the drafting of our original Constitution and its subsequent interpretation. Article IV's Privileges and Immunities Clause was intended and has been interpreted to mean that state legislatures cannot by their various regulations treat out-of-staters less favorably than they treat locals. "It was designed to insure to a citizen of State A who ventures into State B the same privileges which the citizens of State B enjoy." Article IV conveys no set of substantive entitlements, but "simply" the guarantee that whatever entitlements those living in a state see fit to vote themselves will generally be extended to visitors. An ethical ideal of equality is certainly working here, but the reason inequalities against nonresidents and not others were singled out for prohibition in the original document is obvious: nonresidents are a paradigmatically powerless class politically. And their protection proceeds by what amounts to a system of virtual representation: by constitutionally tying the fate of outsiders to the fate of those possessing political power, the framers insured that their interests would be well looked after. The Commerce Clause of Article I, Section 8 provides simply that Congress shall have the power to regulate commerce among the states. But early on the Supreme Court gave this provision a self-operating dimension as well, one growing out of the same need to protect the politically powerless and proceeding by the same device of guaranteed virtual representation. Thus, for example, early in the nineteenth century the Court indicated that a state could not subject goods produced out of state to taxes it did not impose on goods produced locally. By thus constitutionally binding the interests of out-of-state manufacturers to those of local manufacturers represented in the legislature, it provided political insurance that the taxes imposed on the former would not rise to a prohibitive or even an unreasonable level.

These examples involve the protection of geographical outsiders, the literally voteless. But even the technically represented can find themselves functionally powerless and thus in need of a sort of "virtual representation" by those more powerful than they. From one perspective the claim of such groups to protection from the ruling majority is even more compelling than that of the out-of-stater: they are, after all, members of the community that is doing them in. From another, however, their claim seems weaker: they do have the vote, and it may not in the abstract seem unreasonable to expect them to wheel and deal as the rest of us (theoretically) do, yielding on issues about which they are comparatively indifferent and "scratching the other guy's back" in order to get him to scratch theirs. "[N]o group that is prepared to enter into the process and combine with others need remain permanently and completely out of power." Perhaps not "permanently and completely" if by that we mean forever, but certain groups that are technically enfranchised *have* found themselves for long stretches in a state of persistent inability to protect themselves from pervasive forms of discriminatory treatment. Such groups might just as well be disenfranchised.

The issues adumbrated here — relating to the conditions under which it is appropriate constitutionally to bind the interests of the majority to those of some minority with which no felt community of interests has naturally developed — obviously need a good deal more attention, and they shall receive it in Chapter 6. The point that is relevant here is that even before the enactment of the Equal Protection Clause, the Supreme Court was prepared at least under certain conditions to protect the interests of minorities that were not literally voteless by constitutionally tying their interests to those of groups that did possess political power — and what is the same thing, by intervening to protect such interests when it appeared that such a guarantee of "virtual representation" was not being provided. In the landmark case of *McCulloch v. Maryland*, decided in 1819, the Court invalidated a state tax on the operations of all banks (preeminently including the Bank of the United States) not chartered by the state legislature. Toward the end of Chief Justice Marshall's Court opinion, there appears a potentially battling qualification: "This opinion . . . does not extend to a tax paid by the real property of the bank, in common with the other real property within the state, nor to a tax imposed on the interest which the citizens of Maryland may hold in this institution, in common with other property of the same description throughout the state." What ever did he have in mind? It can't have been that he knew the sorts of property taxes mentioned were in fact less burdensome, for nothing in his opinion had indicated that the tax the Court was invalidating was in fact disabling or even burdensome. Indeed it was at the heart of his argument that no such showing was necessary: "the power to tax involves the power to destroy" and a little tax on bank operations was declared as impermissible as a big one. A tax on the land on which the local branch of the Bank of the United States sits also has the potential to destroy, however. *Either* tax, if it got out of hand — and there was no indication that either had — could destroy the Bank.

By now we should be in a position to spot the trick right away: it lies in Marshall's indication that the real estate tax would have to be "in common with the other real property within the state," the tax on any interest held by citizens "in common with other property of the same description throughout the state." The unity of interest with all Maryland property owners assured by this insistence on equal treatment would protect the Bank from serious disablement by taxes of this sort. The power to tax real or personal property *is* potentially the power to destroy. But people aren't lemmings, and while they may agree to disadvantage themselves somewhat in the service of some overriding social good, they aren't in the habit of destroying themselves en masse.

The tax in issue, on the operations of banks not chartered by the state, presented a different configuration of interests. Naturally the Bank of the United States didn't have a vote in the Maryland legislature, but no corporation did. The interests of organizations generally have to be protected by persons whose interests are tied up with theirs — officers, employees, stockholders — and in these respects there is no reason to suppose the Bank of the United States was more impoverished than any other organization. Thus the Bank was not voteless, at least not voteless in any sense that other corporations were not. Yet the tax on bank operations was invalidated, and the reason it was is quite obvious: this was a tax exclusively on banks, indeed exclusively on banks not chartered by the state. The Bank of the United States may have had a "vote" as effective as that of any other single corporation, but it was clear nonetheless that with regard to a tax on the operations of non-state-chartered banks it would find itself in a perpetually losing situation politically, since at best — though it appears even this was lacking — its only allies on this issue would be a couple of wildcat banks. Here too there is

reason to suppose that constitutional salvation would have been found only in a genuine guarantee of virtual representation — if, for example, the Bank's operations had been taxed only as part of a tax equally affecting all business operations in Maryland.

I certainly do not mean to suggest that *McCulloch* was a direct precursor of the *Carolene Products* footnote, generally heralding the special judicial protection of discrete and insular minorities: it is most unlikely that the Bank would have received this special solicitude had it not been a federal instrumentality. The Court's discussion is instructive nonetheless. It suggests by its reference to the property taxes the clear assumption of even that early day that representatives were expected to represent the entirety of their constituencies without arbitrarily severing disfavored minorities for comparatively unfavorable treatment. And it suggests by its invalidation of the bank operations tax its further assumption that at least in some situations judicial intervention becomes appropriate when the existing processes of representation seem inadequately fitted to the representation of minority interests, even minority interests that are not voteless. I do not suggest that these themes were very often made explicit before the Civil War, but the frequency of their invocation is not to the present point. Whatever may have been the case before, the Fourteenth Amendment quite plainly imposes a judicially enforceable duty of virtual representation of the sort I have been describing. My main point in using the examples has been to suggest a way in which what are sometimes characterized as two conflicting American ideals — the protection of popular government on the one hand, and the protection of minorities from denials of equal concern and respect on the other — in fact can be understood as arising from a common duty of representation. Once again, Madison said it early and well:

> I will add, as a fifth circumstance in the situation of the House of Representatives, restraining them from oppressive measures, that they can make no law which will not have its full operation on themselves and their friends, as well as on the great mass of society . . . If it be asked, what is to restrain the House of Representatives from making legal discriminations in favor of

themselves and a particular class of the society? I answer: the genius of the whole system; the nature of just and constitutional laws; and above all, the vigilant and manly spirit which actuates the people of America . . .

The remainder of this chapter will comprise three arguments in favor of a participation-oriented, representation-reinforcing approach to judicial review. The first will take longer than the others, since it will necessitate a tour, albeit brisk, of the Constitution itself. What this tour will reveal, contrary to the standard characterization of the Constitution as "an enduring but evolving statement of general values," is that in fact the selection and accommodation of substantive values is left almost entirely to the political process and instead the document is overwhelmingly concerned, on the one hand, with procedural fairness in the resolution of individual disputes (process writ small), and on the other, with what might capaciously be designated process writ large* — with ensuring broad participation in the processes and distributions of government. An argument by way of *ejusdem generis* seems particularly justified in this case, since the constitutional provisions for which we are attempting to identify modes of supplying content, such as the Ninth Amendment and the Privileges or Immunities Clause, seem to have been included in a "we must have missed something here, so let's trust our successors to add what we missed" spirit. On my more expansive days, therefore, I am tempted to claim that the mode of review developed here represents the ultimate interpretivism.† Our review will tell us something else that may be even more relevant to the issue

before us — that the few attempts the various framers *have* made to freeze substantive values by designating them for special protection in the document have been ill-fated, normally resulting in repeal, either officially or by interpretative pretense. This suggests a conclusion with important implications for the task of giving content to the document's more open-ended provisions, that preserving fundamental values is not an appropriate constitutional task.

The other two arguments are susceptible to briefer statement but are not less important. The first is that a representation-reinforcing approach to judicial review, unlike its rival value-protecting approach, is not inconsistent with, but on the contrary (and quite by design) entirely supportive of, the underlying premises of the American system of representative democracy. The second is that such an approach, again in contradistinction to its rival, involves tasks that courts, as experts on process and (more important) as political outsiders, can sensibly claim to be better qualified and situated to perform than political officials.

The Nature of the United States Constitution

In the United States the basic charter of the lawmaking process is found in a written constitution . . . [W]e should resist the temptation to clutter up that document with amendments relating to substantive matters . . . [Such attempts] involve the obvious unwisdom of trying to solve tomorrow's problems today. But their more insidious danger lies in the weakening effect they would have on the moral force of the Constitutional itself.

— Lon Fuller

---

*I don't mean to be hanging any of the argument on this characterization. It is true, however, that the approach I shall recommend is more thoroughgoingly process-oriented in elaboration than might be supposed even from the discussion thus far.

†As I've indicated, I don't think this terminological question is either entirely coherent or especially important. Obviously the approach recommended is neither "interpretivist" in the usual sense (of treating constitutional clauses as self-contained units) nor "noninterpretivist" in the usual sense (of seeking the principal stuff of constitutional judgment in one's rendition of society's fundamental values rather than in the document's broader themes). What counts is not whether it is

"really" a broad interpretivism or rather a position that does not fall entirely in either camp, but whether it is capable of keeping faith with the document's promise in a way I have argued that a clause-bound interpretivism is not, and capable at the same time of avoiding the objections to a value-laden form of noninterpretivism, objections rooted most importantly in democratic theory. In that regard the two arguments that close this chapter, those addressed explicitly to consistency with democratic theory and the relative institutional capacities of legislatures and courts, seem at least as important as the argument from the nature of the Constitution (which given the complexity of the document must be a qualified one in any event).

Many of our colonial forebears' complaints against British rule were phrased in "constitutional" terms. Seldom, however, was the claim one of deprivation of some treasured good or substantive right: the American colonists, at least the white males, were among the freest and best-off people in the history of the world, and by and large they knew it. "Constitutional" claims thus were often jurisdictional — that Parliament lacked authority, say, to regulate the colonies' "internal commerce" — the foundation for the claim being generally that we were not represented in Parliament. (Obviously the colonists weren't any crazier about being taxed than anyone else is, but what they damned as tyrannical was taxation *without representation*.) Or they were arguments of inequality: claims of entitlement to "the rights of Englishmen" had an occasional natural law flavor, but the more common meaning was that suggested by the words, a claim for equality of treatment with those living in England. Thus the colonists' "constitutional" arguments drew on the two participational themes we have been considering: that (1) their input into the process by which they were governed was insufficient, and that (partly as a consequence) (2) they were being denied what others were receiving. The American version of revolution, wrote Hannah Arendt, "actually proclaims no more than the necessity of civilized government for all mankind; the French version . . . proclaims the existence of rights independent of and outside the body public . . ."

The theme that justice and happiness are best assured not by trying to define them for all time, but rather by attending to the governmental processes by which their dimensions would be specified over time, carried over into our critical constitutional documents. Even our foremost "natural law" statement, the Declaration of Independence, after adverting to some admirable but assuredly open-ended goals — made more so by using "the pursuit of happiness" in place of the already broad Lockean reference to "property" — signals its appreciation of the critical role of (democratic) process:

> We hold these truths to be self-evident, that all men are created equal, that they are endowed by their creator with certain unalienable rights; that among these are life, liberty, and the pursuit of happiness; that *to secure these rights govern-ments are instituted among men, deriving their just powers from the consent of the governed . . .*

The Constitution, less surprisingly, begins on the same note, not one of trying to set forth some governing ideology — the values mentioned in the Preamble could hardly be more pliable — but rather one of ensuring a durable structure for the ongoing resolution of policy disputes:

> We the People of the United States, in Order to form a more perfect Union, establish Justice, insure domestic Tranquility, provide for the common defence, promote the general Welfare, and secure the Blessings of Liberty to ourselves and our Posterity, do ordain and establish this Constitution for the United States of America.

I don't suppose it will surprise anyone to learn that the body of the original Constitution is devoted almost entirely to structure, explaining who among the various actors — federal government, state government, Congress, executive, judiciary — has authority to do what, and going on to fill in a good bit of detail about how these persons are to be selected and to conduct their business. Even provisions that at first glance might seem primarily designed to assure or preclude certain substantive results seem on reflection to be principally concerned with process. Thus, for example, the provision that treason "shall consist only in levying War against [the United States], or in adhering to their Enemies, giving them Aid and Comfort," appears at least in substantial measure to have been a precursor of the First Amendment, reacting to the recognition that persons in power can disable their detractors by charging disagreement as treason. The prohibitions against granting titles of nobility seem rather plainly to have been designed to buttress the democratic ideal that all are equals in government. The Ex Post Facto and Bill of Attainder Clauses prove on analysis to be separation of powers provisions, enjoining the legislature to act prospectively and by general rule (just as the judiciary is implicitly enjoined by Article III to act retrospectively and by specific decree). And we have seen that the Privileges and Immunities Clause of Article IV, and at least in one aspect — the other being a grant of congressional power — the Commerce Clause as well, function as equality provisions, guaranteeing virtual representation to the politically powerless.

During most of this century the Obligation of Contracts Clause has not played a significant role. Powerful arguments have been made that the clause was intended importantly to limit the extent to which state governments could control the subjects and terms of private contracts. Early in the nineteenth century the Supreme Court rejected this broad interpretation, however, holding that the clause affected only the extent to which the legislature could alter or overrule the terms of contracts in existence at the time the statute was passed, and thus did not affect what legislation could say about future contracts. What's more, though there have been signs of stiffening in the past two years, the Court in general has not been very energetic about protecting existing contracts either, holding in essence that legislatures can alter them so long as they do so reasonably (which virtually denudes the clause of any independent function). It is tempting to conclude that the Court's long-standing interpretation of the clause as protecting only existing contracts reduces it to just another hedge against retroactive legislation and thus, like the Ex Post Facto Clause, essentially a separation of powers provision. That conclusion, however, is a little quick. Legislation effectively overruling the terms of an existing contract is not really "retroactive" in the ex post facto sense of attaching untoward consequences to an act performed before it was enacted; rather it refuses to recognize a prior act (the making of the contract) as a defense to or exemption from a legal regime the legislature now wishes to impose. Thus both interpretations of the clause recognize the existence of a contract as a special shield against legislative regulation of future behavior, though on the long-accepted narrow interpretation only contracts already in existence can serve thus.

At this point another temptation arises, to characterize the Contracts Clause as serving an institutional or "separation of powers" function of cordoning off an extragovernmental enclave, in this case an enclave of decision via contract, to serve as a counterpoise to governmental authority. The problem with this account is not that it does not fit, but rather that it will *always* fit: it is difficult to imagine any purported constitutional right that cannot be described as creating a private space where actions antithetical to the wishes of our elected representatives can be

taken. For this reason the account seems incapable of serving as a meaningful explanation (or as a basis from which broader constitutional themes can responsibly be extrapolated). Thus whichever interpretation of the clause was in fact intended, it is difficult to avoid the conclusion that in the Contracts Clause the framers and ratifiers meant to single out for special protection from the political processes—though note that in this case it is only the *state* political processes—a substantive value that is not wholly susceptible to convincing rationalization in terms of either the processes of government or procedure more narrowly conceived. On the broad and rejected interpretation, that value is contract, the ability to arrive at binding agreements. On the narrower and received interpretation, applying the clause only to contracts in existence at the time of the legislation—which I should reiterate is an interpretation the Court has not, at least until very recently, pursued very enthusiastically either—what is protected is a somewhat narrower reliance interest, an assurance that by entering into a contract one can render oneself immune from future shifts in the identity or thinking of one's elected representatives.

This needn't throw us into a tailspin: my claim is only that the original Constitution was principally, indeed I would say overwhelmingly, dedicated to concerns of process and structure and not to the identification and preservation of specific substantive values. Any claim that it was exclusively so conceived would be ridiculous (as would any comparable claim about any comparably complicated human undertaking). And indeed there are other provisions in the original document that seem almost entirely value-oriented, though my point, of course, is that they are few and far between.* Thus "corruption of blood" is forbidden as a punishment for treason. Punishing people for their parents' transgressions is outlawed as a substantively unfair outcome: it

---

*I realize that by stressing the few occasions on which values *were* singled out for protection I run the risk of conveying the impression that that is the character of much of the Constitution. My point of course is quite the opposite, but I'm not sufficiently sadistic to list all the provisions that are obviously concerned only with process. If you find yourself thinking I'm not making my case here, please read a few pages of the Constitution to assure yourself that I could.

just can't be done, irrespective of procedures and also irrespective of whether it is done to the children of all offenders. The federal government, along with the states, is precluded from taxing articles exported from any state. Here too an outcome is simply precluded; what might be styled a value, the economic value of free trade among the states, is protected. This short list, however, covers just about all the values protected in the original Constitution — save one. And a big one it was. Although an understandable squeamishness kept the word out of the document, *slavery* must be counted a substantive value to which the original Constitution meant to extend unusual protection from the ordinary legislative process, at least temporarily. Prior to 1808, Congress was forbidden to prohibit the slave trade into any state that wanted it, and the states were obliged to return escaping slaves to their "homes."

The idea of a bill of rights was not even brought up until close to the end of the Constitutional Convention, at which time it was rejected. The reason is not that the framers were unconcerned with liberty, but rather that by their lights a bill of rights did not belong in a constitution, at least not in the one they had drafted. As Hamilton explained in *Federalist* 84, "a minute detail of particular rights is certainly far less applicable to a Constitution like that under consideration, which is merely intended to regulate the general political interests of the nation . . ." Moreover, the very point of all that had been wrought had been, in large measure, to preserve the liberties of individuals. "The truth is, after all the declamations we have heard, that the Constitution is itself, in every rational sense, and to every useful purpose, *a Bill of Rights*." "The additional securities to republican government, to liberty, and to property, to be derived from the adoption of the plan under consideration, consist chiefly in the restraints which the preservation of the Union will impose on local factions . . . in the prevention of extensive military establishments . . . in the express guarantee of a republican form of government to each [state]; in the absolute and universal exclusion of titles of nobility . . ."

Of course a number of the state ratifying conventions remained apprehensive, and a bill of rights did emerge. Here too, however, the data are unruly. The expression-related provisions of

the First Amendment — "Congress shall make no law . . . abridging the freedom of speech, or of the press; or the right of the people peaceably to assemble, and to petition the Government for a redress of grievances" — were centrally intended to help make our governmental processes work, to ensure the open and informed discussion of political issues, and to check our government when it gets out of bounds. We can attribute other functions to freedom of expression, and some of them must have played a role, but the exercise has the smell of the lamp about it: the view that free expression per se, without regard to what it means to the process of government, is our preeminent right has a highly elitist cast. Positive law has its claims, and I am not suggesting that such other purposes as are plausibly attributable to the language should not be attributed: the amendment's language is not limited to political speech and it should not be so limited by construction (even assuming someone could come up with a determinate definition of "political"). But we are at present engaged in an exploration of what sort of document our forebears thought they were putting together, and in that regard the linking of the politically oriented protections of speech, press, assembly, and petition is highly informative.

The First Amendment's religious clauses — "Congress shall make no law respecting an establishment of religion, or prohibiting the free exercise thereof" — are a different matter. Obviously part of the point of combining these cross-cutting commands was to make sure the church and the government gave each other breathing space: the provision thus performs a structural or separation of powers function. But we must not infer that because one account fits the data it must be the only appropriate account, and here the obvious cannot be blinked: part of the explanation of the Free Exercise Clause has to be that for the framers religion was an important substantive value they wanted to put significantly beyond the reach of at least the federal legislature.

The Second Amendment, protecting "the right of the people to keep and bear Arms," seems (at least if that's all you read) calculated simply to set beyond congressional control another "important" value, the right to carry a gun. It hasn't been construed that way, however, and instead has been interpreted as protecting only the right of state governments to keep militias (National Guards) and to arm them. The rationalization for this narrow construction has ordinarily been historical, that the purpose the framers talked most about was maintaining state militias. However, a provision cannot responsibly be restricted to less than its language indicates simply because a particular purpose received more attention than others (and in fact that favored purpose of today's firearms enthusiasts, the right of *individual* self-protection, was mentioned more than a couple of times). Arguments can be right for the wrong reasons, however, and though the point is debatable, the conclusion here is probably correct. The Second Amendment has its own little preamble: "A well regulated Militia, being necessary to the security of a free State, the right of the people to keep and bear Arms, shall not be infringed." Thus here, as almost nowhere else, the framers and ratifiers apparently opted against leaving to the future the attribution of purposes, choosing instead explicitly to legislate the goal in terms of which the provision was to be interpreted.

The Third Amendment, undoubtedly another of your favorites, forbids the nonconsensual peacetime quartering of troops. Like the Establishment of Religion Clause, it grew largely out of fear of an undue influence, this time by the military: in that aspect it can be counted a "separation of powers" provision. Again, however, one cannot responsibly stop here. Other provisions provide for civilian control of the military, and although that is surely one of the purposes here, there is obviously something else at stake, a desire to protect the privacy of the home from prying government eyes, to say nothing of the annoyance of uninvited guests. Both process and value seem to be involved here.

Amendments five through eight tend to become relevant only during lawsuits, and we tend therefore to think of them as procedural — instrumental provisions calculated to enhance the fairness and efficiency of the litigation process. That's exactly what most of them are: the importance of the guarantees of grand juries, criminal and civil petit juries, information of the charge, the right of confrontation, compulsory process, and even the assistance of counsel inheres mainly in their tendency to ensure a reliable determination. Uncon-

cerned with the substance of government regulation, they refer instead to the ways in which regulations can be enforced against those they cover. Once again, however, that is not the whole story. The Fifth Amendment's privilege against self-incrimination surely has a lot to do with wanting to find the truth: coerced confessions are less likely to be reliable. But at least as interpreted, the privilege needs further rationalization than that; the argument runs that there is simply something immoral — though it has proved tricky pinning down exactly what it is — about the state's asking somebody whether he committed a crime and expecting him to answer. The same amendment's guarantee against double jeopardy gets complicated. Insofar as it forbids retrial after acquittal, it seems a largely procedural protection, designed to guard against the conviction of innocent persons. But insofar as it forbids additional prosecution after conviction or added punishment after sentence, it performs the quite different (and substantive) function, which obviously is present in the acquittal situation too, of guaranteeing a sense of repose, an assurance that at some definable point the defendant can assume the ordeal is over, its consequences known.

The Fourth Amendment provides: "The right of the people to be secure in their persons, houses, papers, and effects, against unreasonable searches and seizures, shall not be violated, and no Warrants shall issue, but upon probable cause, supported by Oath or affirmation, and particularly describing the place to be searched, and the persons or things to be seized." This provision most often becomes relevant when a criminal defendant tries to suppress evidence seized as the fruit of an illegal search or arrest, but it would be a mistake to infer from that that it is a purely procedural provision. In fact (as thus enforced by the exclusionary rule) it *thwarts* the procedural goal of accurately determining the facts, in order to serve one or more other goals felt to be more important. The standard line is that other, more important goal is privacy, and surely privacy is sometimes implicated. But the language of the amendment reaches further — so for that matter did the customs abuses we know had a lot to do with its inclusion — and when it is read in its entirety the notion of "privacy" proves inadequate as an explanation. The amendment covers seizures of goods and arrests ("seizures of the person") along with searches, and it does not distinguish public episodes from private: a completely open arrest or seizure of goods is as illegal as a search of a private area if it is effected without probable cause. It thus "protects individual privacy against certain kinds of governmental intrusion, but its protections go further, and often have nothing to do with privacy at all."

A major point of the amendment, obviously, was to keep the government from disrupting our lives without at least moderately convincing justification. That rationale intertwines with another — and the historic customs abuses are relevant here too — namely, a fear of official discretion. In deciding whose lives to disrupt in the ways the amendment indicates — that is, whom to search or arrest or whose goods to seize — law enforcement officials will necessarily have a good deal of low visibility discretion. In addition they are likely in such situations to be sensitive to social station and other factors that should not bear on the decision. The amendment thus requires not simply a certain quantum of probability but also when possible, via the warrant requirement, the judgment of a "neutral and detached magistrate." From this perspective, which obviously is only one of several, the Fourth Amendment can be seen as another harbinger of the Equal Protection Clause, concerned with avoiding indefensible inequities in treatment. The Eighth Amendment's ban on "cruel and unusual punishments" is even more obviously amenable to this account. Apparently part of the point was to outlaw certain understood and abhorred forms of torture, but the decision to use open-ended language can hardly have been inadvertent. It is possible that part of the point also was to ban punishments that were unusually severe in relation to the crimes for which they were being imposed. But much of it surely had to do with a realization that in the context of imposing penalties too there is tremendous potential for the arbitrary or invidious infliction of "unusually" severe punishments on persons of various classes other than "our own."

On first reading, the Fifth Amendment's requirement that private property not be taken for public use without just compensation may appear simply to mark the substantive value of private property for special protection from the political process (though, on the face of the document, from only the federal political process). Again, though, we must ask why. Because property was regarded as unusually important? That may be part of the explanation, but note that property is not shielded from condemnation by this provision. On the contrary, the amendment assumes that property will sometimes be taken and provides instead for compensation. Read through it thus emerges — and this account fits the historical situation like a glove — as yet another protection of the few against the many, "a limit on government's power to isolate particular individuals for sacrifice to the general good." Its point is to "spread the cost of operating the governmental apparatus throughout the society rather than imposing it upon some small segment of it." If we want a highway or a park we can have it, but we're all going to have to share the cost rather than imposing it on some isolated individual or group.*

With one important exception, the Reconstruction Amendments do not designate substantive values for protection from the political process. The Fourteenth Amendment's Due Process Clause, we have seen, is concerned with process writ small, the processes by which regulations are enforced against individuals. Its Privileges or Immunities Clause is quite inscrutable, indicating only that there should exist some set of constitutional entitlements not explicitly enumerated in the document: it is one of the provisions for which we are seeking guides to construction. The Equal Protection Clause is also unforthcoming with details, though it at least gives us a clue: by its explicit concern with equality among the persons within a state's jurisdiction it constitutes the document's clearest,

---

*This view of the clause is also of some assistance in deciding whether a given government action should be counted a taking in the first place as opposed to say, a regulation or a tax. In recent discussions of this issue the Court has begun to ask whether the measure under review singles out a minority for unusually harsh treatment or rather affects a class sufficiently generalized to have a fair shot at protecting itself politically. E.g., Penn Central Transp. Co. v. New York City. 438 U.S. 104, 132 (1978).

though not sole, recognition that technical access to the process may not always be sufficient to guarantee good-faith representation of all those putatively represented. The Fifteenth Amendment, forbidding abridgment of the right to vote on account of race, opens the process to persons who had previously been excluded and thus by another strategy seeks to enforce the representative's duty of equal concern and respect. The exception, of course, involves a value I have mentioned before, slavery. The Thirteenth Amendment can be forced into a "process" mold — slaves don't participate effectively in the political process — and it surely significantly reflects a concern with equality as well. Just as surely, however, it embodies a substantive judgment that human slavery is simply not morally tolerable. Thus at no point has the Constitution been neutral on this subject. Slavery was one of the few values the original document singled out for protection from the political branches; *non*-slavery is one of the few values it singles out for protection now.

What has happened to the Constitution in the second century of our nationhood, though ground less frequently plowed, is most instructive on the subject of what jobs we have learned our basic document is suited to. There were no amendments between 1870 and 1913, but there have been eleven since. Five of them have extended the franchise: the Seventeenth extends to all of us the right to vote for our Senators directly, the Twenty-Fourth abolishes the poll tax as a condition of voting in federal elections, the Nineteenth extends the vote to women, the Twenty-Third to residents of the District of Columbia, and the Twenty-Sixth to eighteen-year-olds. Extension of the franchise to groups previously excluded has therefore been the dominant theme of our constitutional development since the Fourteenth Amendment, and it pursues both of the broad constitutional themes we have observed from the beginning: the achievement of a political process open to all on an equal basis and a consequent enforcement of the representative's duty of equal concern and respect to minorities and majorities alike. Three other amendments — the Twentieth, Twenty-Second, and Twenty-Fifth — involve Presidential eligibility and succession. The Six-

teenth, permitting a federal income tax, adds another power to the list of those that had previously been assigned to the central government. That's it, save two, and indeed one of those two did place a substantive value beyond the reach of the political process. The amendment was the Eighteenth, and the value shielded was temperance. It was, of course, repealed fourteen years later by the Twenty-First Amendment, precisely, I suggest, because such attempts to freeze substantive values do not belong in a constitution. In 1919 temperance obviously seemed like a fundamental value; in 1933 it obviously did not.

What has happened to the Constitution's other value-enshrining provisions is similar, and similarly instructive. Some surely have survived, but typically because they are so obscure that they don't become issues (corruption of blood, quartering of troops) or so interlaced with procedural concerns they seem appropriate in a constitution (self-incrimination, double jeopardy). Those sufficiently conspicuous and precise to be controvertible have not survived. The most dramatic examples, of course, were slavery and prohibition. Both were removed by repeal, in one case a repeal requiring unprecedented carnage. Two other substantive values that at least arguably were placed beyond the reach of the political process by the Constitution have been "repealed" by judicial construction — the right of individuals to bear arms, and freedom to set contract terms without significant state regulation. Maybe in fact our forebears did not intend very seriously to protect those values, but the fact that the Court, in the face of what must be counted at least plausible contrary arguments, so readily read these values out of the Constitution is itself instructive of American expectations of a constitution. Finally, there is the value of religion, still protected by the Free Exercise Clause. Something different has happened here. In recent years that clause has functioned primarily to protect what must be counted as discrete and insular minorities, such as the Amish, Seventh Day Adventists, and Jehovah's Witnesses. Whatever the original conception of the Free Exercise Clause, its function during essentially all of its effective life has been one akin to the Equal Protection Clause and thus entirely appropriate to a constitution.

Don't get me wrong: our Constitution has always been substantially concerned with preserving liberty. If it weren't, it would hardly be worth fighting for. The question that is relevant to our inquiry here, however, is how that concern has been pursued. The principal answers to that, we have seen, are by a quite extensive set of procedural protections, and by a still more elaborate scheme designed to ensure that in the making of substantive choices the decision process will be open to all on something approaching an equal basis, with the decision-makers held to a duty to take into account the interests of all those their decisions affect. (Most often the document has proceeded on the assumption that assuring access is the best way of assuring that someone's interests will be considered, and so in fact it usually is. Other provisions, however — centrally but not exclusively the Equal Protection Clause — reflect a realization that access will not always be sufficient.) The general strategy has therefore not been to root in the document a set of substantive rights entitled to permanent protection. The Constitution has instead proceeded from the quite sensible assumption that an effective majority will not inordinately threaten its own rights, and has sought to assure that such a majority not systematically treat others less well than it treats itself — by structuring decision processes at all levels to try to ensure, first, that everyone's interests will be actually or virtually represented (usually both) at the point of substantive decision, and second, that the processes of individual application will not be manipulated so as to reintroduce in practice the sort of discrimination that is impermissible in theory. We have noted a few provisions that do not comfortably conform to this pattern. But they're an odd assortment, the understandable products of particular historical circumstances — guns, religion, contract, and so on — and in any event they are few and far between. To present them as a dominant theme of our constitutional document one would have to concentrate quite single-mindedly on hopping from stone to stone and averting one's eyes from the mainstream.

The American Constitution has thus by and large remained a constitution properly so called, concerned with constitutive questions. What has distinguished it, and indeed the United States itself, has been a process of government, not a governing ideology. Justice Linde has written: "As a charter of government a constitution must prescribe legitimate processes, not legitimate outcomes, if like ours (and unlike more ideological documents elsewhere) it is to serve many generations through changing times."

Democracy and Distrust

As I have tried to be scrupulous about indicating, the argument from the general contours of the Constitution is necessarily a qualified one. In fact the documentary dictation of particular substantive outcomes has been rare (and generally unsuccessful), but our Constitution is too complex a document to lie still for *any* pat characterization. Beyond that, the premise of the argument, that aids to construing the more open-ended provisions are appropriately found in the nature of the surrounding document, though it is a premise that seems to find acceptance on all sides, is not one with which it is impossible to disagree. Thus the two arguments that follow, each overtly normative, are if anything more important than the one I have just reviewed. The first is entirely obvious by now, that unlike an approach geared to the judicial imposition of "fundamental values," the representation-reinforcing orientation whose contours I have sketched and will develop further is not inconsistent with, but on the contrary is entirely supportive of, the American system of representative democracy. It recognizes the unacceptability of the claim that appointed and life-tenured judges are better reflectors of conventional values than elected representatives, devoting itself instead to policing the mechanisms by which the system seeks to ensure that our elected representatives will actually represent. There may be an illusion of circularity here: my approach is more consistent with representative democracy because that's the way it was planned. But of course it isn't any more circular than setting out to build an airplane and ending up with something that flies.

The final point worth serious mention is that (again unlike a fundamental-values approach) a representation-reinforcing approach assigns judges a role they are conspicuously well situated to fill.* My reference here is not principally to expertise. Lawyers *are* experts on process writ small, the processes by which facts are found and contending parties are allowed to present their claims. And to a degree they are experts on process writ larger, the processes by which issues of public policy are fairly determined: lawyers do seem genuinely to have a feel, indeed it is hard to see what other special value they have, for ways of insuring that everyone gets his or her fair say. But too much shouldn't be made of this. Others, particularly the fulltime participants, can also claim expertise on how the political process allocates voice and power. And of course many legislators are lawyers themselves. So the point isn't so much one of expertise as it is one of perspective.

The approach to constitutional adjudication recommended here is akin to what might be called an "antitrust" as opposed to a "regulatory" orientation to economic affairs — rather than dictate substantive results it intervenes only when the "market," in our case the political market, is systemically malfunctioning. (A referee analogy is also not far off: the referee is to intervene only when one team is gaining unfair advantage, not because the "wrong" team has scored.) Our government cannot fairly be said to be "malfunctioning" simply because it sometimes generates outcomes with which we disagree, however strongly (and claims that it is reaching results with which

"the people" really disagree — or would "if they understood" — are likely to be little more than self-deluding projections). In a representative democracy value determinations are to be made by our elected representatives, and if in fact most of us disapprove we can vote them out of office. Malfunction occurs when the *process* is undeserving of trust, when (1) the ins are choking off the channels of political change to ensure that they will stay in and the outs will stay out, or (2) though no one is actually denied a voice or a vote, representatives beholden to an effective majority are systematically disadvantaging some minority out of simple hostility or a prejudiced refusal to recognize commonalities of interest, and thereby denying that minority the protection afforded other groups by a representative system.

Obviously our elected representatives are the last persons we should trust with identification of either of these situations. Appointed judges, however, are comparative outsiders in our governmental system, and need worry about continuance in office only very obliquely. This does not give them some special pipeline to the genuine values of the American people: in fact it goes far to ensure that they won't have one. It does, however, put them in a position objectively to assess claims — though no one could suppose the evaluation won't be full of judgment calls — that either by clogging the channels of change or by acting as accessories to majority tyranny, our elected representatives in fact are not representing the interests of those whom the system presupposes they are.

Before embarking on his career-long quest for a satisfactory approach to constitutional adjudication, Alexander Bickel described the challenge thus:

> The search must be for a function . . . which is peculiarly suited to the capabilities of the courts; which will not likely be performed elsewhere if the courts do not assume it; which can be so exercised as to be acceptable in a society that generally shares Judge Hand's satisfaction in a "sense of common venture"; which will be effective when needed; and whose discharge by the courts will not lower the quality of the other departments' performance by denuding them of the dignity and burden of their own responsibility.

---

*For reasons that are currently obscure, I went through a period of worrying that the orientation here recommended might mean less protection for civil liberties. (Of course it would deny the opportunity to create rights out of whole cloth: that is much of its point and strength. What I had in mind was the possibility that the *same* freedoms might systematically come out thinner if derived from a participational orientation than they would if protected on the ground that they are "good.") Reflection has convinced me that just the opposite is true, that freedoms are more secure to the extent that they find foundation in the theory that supports our entire government, rather than gaining protection because the judge deciding the case thinks they're important. Cf. C. Black, *Structure and Relationship in Constitutional Law* 29–30 (1969). Indeed, the only remotely systematic "Carolene Products" Court we have had was also clearly the most protective of civil liberties.

As quoted, it's a remarkably appropriate set of specifications, one that fits the orientation suggested here precisely. Unfortunately, by adding one more specification (where I have put the elipsis) and thereby committing himself to a value orientation — "which might (indeed must) involve the making of policy, yet which differs from the legislative and executive functions" — he built in an inescapable contradiction and thereby ensured the failure of his enterprise.

Notes and Questions

MARTHA MINOW, from "Justice Engendered"

1. While no one disputes the ideal of neutrality as impartiality for judges in theory, there are divergent views about how or whether this state of mind can be attained in fact. While Stone argues that following precedent fails to determine cases, inevitably leaving leeways of discretion, Martha Minow is concerned with how that discretion gets used. She notes that particularly in certain areas courts are facing issues which require them to grapple with what she calls the problem of difference. What does she mean by the problem of difference? Is this a problem that arises only in pluralistic societies, or would any legal system face it? What would it take actually to eliminate it?

2. Minow is concerned with equal justice and judicial impartiality, particularly in cases involving disadvantaged groups of people, such as women and minorities, that fall outside the mainstream norms. She notes that every year courts face issues which turn on questions of difference among people. This problem of difference manifests itself in the form of (at least) three dilemmas. What are these dilemmas, and what makes them dilemmas rather than simply hard problems?

3. Minow then argues that there are (at least) five unstated assumptions about the nature of difference that underlie the dilemmas. What are these assumptions? Are they specific to judges, or do we all tend to make them? Do you recognize them in your own thinking?

4. These assumptions entrench the dominant view as "objective" and make departures from the status quo appear to be "special treatment." This, in fact, is what creates the dilemmas, so it would certainly be good judicial practice to avoid such assumptions. Why, according to Minow, is this so difficult, not only for judges but for everyone? She suggests three factors to explain the difficulty we all have in overcomming our reliance on common assumptions such as the five she discusses. What are these factors, and what can be done to combat them?

5. Noting that power is strongest when it is accepted, and thus invisible, Minow makes some suggestions for what she calls "engendering justice." What does she suggest?

6. Minow notes that legal authorities have shown a remarkable lack of ability to reshape categories for people who do not fit into them. But confronting such problems is necessary to move beyond current attutudes, assumptions, or stereotypes about differences. Courts, she argues, should provide a forum for competing views of reality. How does she suggest that this can be done? What legal mechanisms could be used? What legal mechanisms should be avoided? Are her suggestions realistic? If not, why not?

7. How would other theorists respond to Minow's thesis? Consider her position as compared to that of Bork, Schauer, or Ely. Where does it fall in the dispute among Kairys, Stone, and Levi? What does it imply about judicial reasoning?

[From] "Justice Engendered"

MARTHA MINOW

I. Introduction

A. What's the Difference?

The use of anesthesia in surgery spread quickly once discovered. Yet the nineteenth-century doctors who adopted anesthesia selected which patients needed it and which deserved it. Both the medical literature and actual medical practices distinguished people's need for pain-killers based on race, gender, ethnicity, age, temperament, personal habits, and economic class. Some people's pain was thought more serious than others; some people were thought to be hardy enough to withstand pain. Doctors believed that women, for example, needed painkillers more than men and that the rich and educated needed painkillers more than the poor and uneducated. How might we, today, evaluate these examples of discrimination? What differences between people should matter, and for what purposes?

The endless variety of our individualism means that we suffer different kinds of pain and may well experience pain differently. But when professionals use categories like gender, race, ethnicity, and class to presume real differences in people's pain and entitlement to help, I worry. I worry that unfairness will result under the guise of objectivity and neutrality. I worry that a difference assigned by someone with power over a more vulnerable person will become endowed with an apparent reality, despite powerful competing views. If no one can really know another's pain, who shall decide how to treat pain, and along what calculus? These are questions of justice, not science. These are questions of complexity, not justification for passivity, because failing to notice another's pain is an act with significance.

B. The Problem and the Argument

Each Term, the Supreme Court and the nation confront problems of difference in this heterogeneous society. The cases that present these prob-lems attract heightened media attention and reenact continuing struggles over the meanings of sub-group identity in a nation committed to an idea called equality. The drama of these cases reveals the enduring grip of "difference" in the public imagination, and the genuine social and economic conflicts over what particular differences come to mean over time. During the 1986 Term, litigators framed for the Court issues about the permissible legal meanings of difference in the lives of individuals, minority groups, and majority groups in cases involving gender, race, ethnicity, religion and handicap.

Uniting these questions is the dilemma of difference. The dilemma of difference has three versions . . .

* * *

I believe these dilemmas arise out of powerful unstated assumptions about whose point of view matters, and about what is given and what is mutable in the world. "Difference" is only meaningful as a comparison. I am no more different from you than you are from me. A short person is different only in relation to a tall one. Legal treatment of difference tends to take for granted an assumed point of comparison: women are compared to the unstated norm of men, "minority" races to whites, handicapped persons to the able-bodied, and "minority" religions to "majorities." Such assumptions work in part through the very structure of our language, which embeds the unstated points of comparison inside categories that bury their perspective and wrongly imply a natural fit with the world. The term "working mother," modifies the general category "mother," revealing that the general term carries some unstated common meanings (that is, a woman who cares for her children full-time without pay), which, even if unintended, must expressly be modified. Legal treatment of difference thus tends to treat as unproblematic the point of view from which difference is seen, assigned, or ignored, rather than acknowledging that the problem of difference can be described and understood from multiple points of view.

Noticing the unstated point of comparison and point of view used in assessments of difference does not eliminate the dilemma of difference; instead, more importantly, it links problems of difference to questions of vantage point. I will argue that what initially may seem to be an objective stance may appear partial from another point of view. Furthermore, what initially appears to be a fixed and objective difference may seem from another viewpoint like the subordination or exclusion of some people by others. Regardless of which perspective ultimately seems persuasive, the possibility of multiple viewpoints challenges the assumption of objectivity and shows how claims to knowledge bear the imprint of those making the claims.

Difference may seem salient not because of a trait intrinsic to the person but instead because the dominant institutional arrangements were designed without that trait in mind. Consider the difference between buildings built without considering the needs of people in wheelchairs and buildings that are accessible to people in wheelchairs. Institutional arrangements define whose reality is to be the norm and make what is known as different seem natural. By asking how power influences knowledge, we can address the question of whether difference was assigned as an expression of domination or as a remedy for past domination. In so doing, we can determine the risks of creating a new pattern of domination while remedying unequal power relationships.

The commitment to seek out and to appreciate a perspective other than one's own animates the reasoning of some Supreme Court Justices, some of the time. It is a difficult commitment to make and to fulfill. Aspects of language, social structure, and political culture steer in the opposite direction: toward assertions of absolute categories transcending human choice or perspective. It is not only that justice is created by, and defeated by, people who have genders, races, ethnicities, religions — people who are themselves situated in relation to the differences they discuss. It is also the case that justice is made by people who live in a world already made. Existing institutions and language already carve the world and already express and recreate attitudes

about what counts as a difference, and who or what is the relevant point of comparison. Once we see that any point of view, including one's own, *is* a point of view, we will realize that every difference we see is seen in relation to something already assumed as the starting point. Then we can expose for debate what the starting points should be. The task for judges is to identify vantage points, to learn how to adopt contrasting vantage points, and to decide which vantage points to embrace in given circumstances.

* * *

In Part II, I explore three versions of the dilemma of difference, illustrating how they arose in the contexts of religion, ethnicity, race, gender, and handicapping conditions in cases before the Supreme Court during the 1986 Term. Next, in Part III, I turn to the influence in these cases of unstated assumptions about points of reference and starting points for analysis, assumptions that are continually reinforced by established modes of thought, language, and patterns of legal reasoning.

In Part IV, I first identify how members of the Court periodically challenge these assumptions by seeking the perspective of individuals and groups unlike themselves. Unfortunately, the Justices are not always successful in their efforts. Feminist scholars have done much to reveal the persistence of these assumptions, particularly the assumption that men — their needs and experiences — are the standard for individual rights, and in Part IV I go on to develop and pursue this basic feminist insight. In so doing, I also explore ways in which some feminist analyses have recreated the problems they sought to address, elaborating the idea of "woman's experience," leaving unstated the race, ethnicity, religion, and bodily condition presumed in the identification of woman's point of view.

What, then, is to be done? In Part V, I urge the judiciary to make a perpetual commitment to approach questions of difference by seeking out unstated assumptions about difference and typically unheard points of view. There will not be a rule, a concept, a norm, or a test to apply to these problems. The very yearning for simple and clear solutions is part of the difference problem. The allure of this simplicity reflects our dangerous tendency to assign differences, to pretend that they are natural, and to use categorical solutions to cut off rather than to promote understanding. Instead of a new solution, I urge struggles over descriptions of reality. Litigation in the Supreme Court should be an opportunity to endow rival vantage points with the reality that power enables, to redescribe and remake the meanings of difference in a world that has treated only some vantage points on difference as legitimate.

Far from being unmanageable, this approach describes what happens already in the best practices of justice. Justice, in this view, is not abstract, universal, or neutral. Instead, justice is the quality of human engagement with multiple perspectives framed by, but not limited to, the relationships of power in which they are formed. Decisions, then, can and must be made. Despite the distortions sometimes injected by a language of objectivity and neutrality, the Supreme Court has "engendered" justice in many cases. These cases show the commitment in contemporary statutory and constitutional law to give equality meaning for people once thought to be "different" from those in charge. From the work of this Term, which is the last for Justice Powell, the first for Justice Scalia, and the first for Chief Justice Rehnquist as head of the Court, I hope to demonstrate how our common humanity wins when the Court struggles with our differences.

II. A Case of Differences

Arguments before the Supreme Court engage all three versions of the difference dilemma and cut across cases otherwise differentiated by doctrine and contexts. The dilemma arises in both equality and religion cases, and in statutory and constitutional contexts. This Section explicitly draws connections across these seemingly disparate cases and explores the dilemma in cases decided in the 1986 Term.

A. The Dilemma of Recreating Difference Both by Ignoring It and by Noticing It

California Federal Savings & Loan Association v. Guerra (CalFed) presented in classic form the dilemma of recreating difference through both noticing and ignoring it. Petitioners, a collection of employers, argued that a California statute mandating a qualified right to reinstatement following an unpaid pregnancy disability leave amounted to special preferential treatment, in violation of title VII's prohibition of discrimination on the basis of pregnancy. Writing an opinion announcing the judgment for the Court, Justice Marshall transformed the question presented by the plaintiffs: instead of asking whether the federal ban against discrimination on the basis of pregnancy precluded a state's decision to require special treatment for pregnancy, the majority asked whether the state could adopt a minimum protection for pregnant workers, while still permitting employers to avoid treating pregnant workers differently by extending similar benefits to nonpregnant workers. Framing the problem this way, the majority ruled that "Congress intended the PDA to be 'a floor beneath which pregnancy disability benefits may not drop — not a ceiling above which they may not rise.'" The majority acknowledged the risk that recognizing the difference of pregnancy could recreate its stigmatizing effects, but noted that "a State could not mandate special treatment of pregnant workers based on stereotypes or generalizations about their needs and abilities." Thus, despite the federal antidiscrimination requirement, the majority found that states could direct employers to take the sheer physical disability of the pregnancy difference into account, but not any stereotyped views associated with that difference. The majority gave two responses to the problem of difference: first, accommodating pregnant workers would secure a workplace that would equally enable both female and male employees to work and have a family; second, the federal and state statutes should be construed as inviting employers to provide the same benefits to men and women in comparable situations of disability.

Writing for the dissenters, Justice White maintained that the California statute required disability leave policies for pregnant workers even in the absence of similar policies for men. It thus violated the PDA, which "leaves no room for preferential treatment of pregnant workers." In the face of this conflict, the federal statute must preempt the state law. The commands of nondiscrimination prohibit taking differences into account, Justice White argued, regardless of the impact of this neglect on people with the difference. Justice White acknowledged the majority's argument that preferential treatment would revive nineteenth-century protective legislation, perpetuating sex-role stereotypes and "imped[ing] women in their efforts to take their rightful place in the workplace." For Justice White, however, such arguments were irrelevant, because the Court's role was restricted to interpreting congressional intent and thus would not permit consideration of the arguments about stereotyping. Yet, to some extent, the issue of stereotypes was unavoidable: the dilemma in the case, from one point of view, was whether women could secure a benefit that would eliminate a burden connected with their gender, without at the same time reactivating negative meanings about their gender.

In two other cases in the 1986 Term, the Court confronted the dilemma of recreating difference in situations in which individuals claimed to be members of minority races in order to obtain special legal protections. By claiming an identity in order to secure some benefit from it, the individuals faced the dilemma that they might fuel negative meanings of that identity, meanings beyond their control. Although racial identification under federal civil rights statutes provides a means of legal redress, it also runs the risk of recreating stigmatizing associations, thereby stimulating prejudice.

In *Saint Francis College v. Al-Khazraji*, a man from Iraq who had failed to secure tenure from his employer, a private college, brought a claim of racial discrimination under 42 U.S.C. section 1981. His case foundered, however, when the lower courts rejected his claim that his Arab identity constituted racial membership of the sort protected by the federal statute.

In *Shaare Tefila Congregation v. Cobb*, members of a Jewish congregation whose synagogue was defaced by private individuals alleged violations of the federal guarantee against interference with property rights on racial grounds. The difference dilemma appeared on the face of the complaint: the petitioners argued that Jews are not a racially distinct group, and yet they claimed that Jews should be entitled to protection against racial discrimination because others treat them as though they were distinct. The petitioners thus demonstrated their reluctance to have a difference

identified in a way that they themselves could not control, while simultaneously expressing their desire for protection against having that difference assigned to them by others. To gain this protection, the petitioners had to identify themselves through the very category they rejected as a definition of themselves. Both the district court and the court of appeals refused to allow the petitioners to be included in the protected group on the basis of the attitudes of others, without some proof of well-established traits internal to the group. The court of appeals reasoned:

> Although we sympathize with appellant's position, we conclude that it cannot support a claim of racial discrimination solely on the basis of defendants' perception of Jews as being members of a racially distinct group. To allow otherwise would permit charges of racial discrimination to arise out of nothing more than the subjective, irrational perceptions of defendants.

In contrast, one members of the appeals panel, dissenting on this point, argued: "Misperception lies at the heart of prejudice, and the animus formed of such ignorance sows malice and hatred wherever it operates without restriction."

Is the cause of individualized treatment advanced by allowing groups to claim legal protections by dint of group membership, however erroneously assigned by others? Conversely, may denying these claims of legal protection against assigned difference allow the Supreme Court to avoid addressing the dilemma and thereby reenact it? In both *Shaare Tefila* and *Saint Francis*, the Court asked only whether the legislators adopting the antidiscrimination legislation shortly after the Civil War viewed Jews and Arabs as distinct races. The Court answered the question affirmatively in both cases but based its conclusion on a review of the legislative histories and contemporaneous dictionaries and encyclopedias instead of tackling the difference dilemma directly.

The Court's historical test for membership in a minority race effectively revitalized not just categorical thinking in general, but the specific categorical thinking about race prevailing in the 1860's, despite considerable changes in scientific and moral understandings of the use of abstract categories to label people and solve problems.

Whether the issue is gender, religion, or race, reviving old sources for defining group difference may reinvigorate older attitudes about the meanings of group traits. Denying the presence of those traits, however, and their significance in society, deprives individuals of protection against discrimination due to outmoded or unsubstantiated conceptions of group difference.

B. Neutrality and Non-neutrality: The Dilemma of Government Embroilment in Difference

The dilemma of difference appears especially acute for a government committed to acting neutrally. Neutral means might not produce neutral results, given historic practices and social arrangements that have not been neutral. For example, securing neutrality toward religious differences is the explicit goal of both the first amendment's ban against the establishment of religion and its protection of the free exercise of religion. Thus, to be truly neutral, the government must walk a narrow path between promoting or endorsing religion and failing to make room for religious exercise. Accommodation of religious practices may look non-neutral, but failure to accommodate may also seem non-neutral by burdening the religious minority whose needs were not built into the structure of mainstream institutions.

The "Creation Science" case, *Edwards v. Aguillard*, question of how the government, in the form of public schools, can respect religious differences while remaining neutral toward them. In *Edwards*, parents and students claimed that a Louisiana statute requiring public schools to teach creation science whenever they taught the theory of evolution violated the establishment clause. Community members subscribing to fundamentalist religious beliefs, however, have argued that public school instruction in evolution alone is not neutral, because it gives a persuasive advantage to views that undermine their own religious beliefs. Relying on similar arguments, the state avowed a neutral, nonreligious purpose for its statute.

The majority, in an opinion by Justice Brennan, concluded that the legislation was actually intended to "provide persuasive advantage to a particular religious doctrine that rejects the factual basis of evolution in its entirety." By contrast, the dissenting opinion by Justice Scalia, which was joined by Chief Justice Rehnquist, expressly tangled with the neutrality problem, noting the difficult tensions between antiestablishment and free exercise concerns, and between neutrality through indifference and neutrality through accommodation. In the end, the dissent was moved by the state's attempt to avoid undermining the different views of fundamentalist Christian students, while the majority was persuaded that the statute gave an illegal preference to a particular religious view. For both sides, however, the central difficulty was how to find a neutral position between these two risks.

In a second case, *Hobbie v. Unemployment Appeals Commission*, the neutrality problem arose when the Court reviewed a state's decision to deny unemployment benefits to a woman under an apparently neutral scheme. Hobbie was discharged from her job when she refused to work during her religious Sabbath. The state argued that Hobbie's refusal to work amounted to misconduct related to her work and rendered her ineligible for unemployment benefits under a statute limiting compensation to persons who become "unemployed through no fault of their own.'" The Court rejected this emphasis on the cause of the conflict, because the "salient inquiry" was whether the denial of unemployment benefits unlawfully burdened Hobbie's free exercise right. The Court also rejected the state's claim that making unemployment benefits available to Hobbie would unconstitutionally establish religion by easing eligibility requirements for religious adherents. By requiring accommodation for free exercise, despite charges of establishing religion, the Court's solution thus framed a dilemma of neutrality: how can the government's means be neutral in a world that is not itself neutral?

A facially neutral state policy on unemployment compensation also figured in *Wimberly v. Labor & Industrial Relations Commission*. Wimberly had taken a pregnancy leave from her job with no guarantee of reinstatement, and upon her return the employer told her that there were no positions available. Her application for unemployment benefits was denied under a state law disqualifying applicants unless their reasons for leaving were directly attributable to the work or to the employer. Wimberly argued that a federal statute forbidding discrimination in unemployment compensation "solely on the basis of pregnancy or termination of pregnancy" required accommodation for women who leave work because of pregnancy.

The Supreme Court unanimously rejected Wimberly's claim that this denial of benefits contravened the federal statute. The Court found that the state had not singled out pregnancy as the reason for withholding unemployment benefits; instead, pregnancy fell within a broad class of reasons for unemployment unrelated to work or to the employer. The Court interpreted the federal statute to forbid discrimination but not to mandate preferential treatment. In the Court's eyes, then, it was neutral to have a general rule denying unemployment benefits to anyone unemployed for reasons unrelated to the workplace or the employer.

In essence, the Court interpreted the federal statutory scheme as granting discretion to state legislatures to define their own terms for disqualification from eligibility for benefits. Although many states provide unemployment benefits for women who leave their jobs because of pregnancy, subsuming it under terms like "good cause," along with other compelling personal reasons, injury, illness, or the federal ban against refusing benefits "solely on the basis of pregnancy" does not, according to the Court, compel such coverage. A state choosing to define its unemployment eligibility narrowly enough to disqualify not just those who leave work due to pregnancy, but also those who leave work for good cause, illness, or compelling personal reasons, may thus do so without violating federal law.

The Court in *Wimberly* rejected the argument that ignoring the difference of pregnancy produces illicit discrimination under an apparently neutral unemployment benefits rule. In *Hobbie*, on the other hand, the Court embraced the view that ignoring a religious difference produces illicit discrimination under an apparently neutral unemployment benefits rule. In both cases, the Court grappled with the dilemma of whether to give meaning to neutrality by recognizing or not recognizing difference.

C. Discretion and Formality: The Dilemma of Using Power to Differentiate

The Court's commitment to the rule of law often leads it to specify, in formal terms, the rules that govern the decisions of others. This practice can secure adherence to the goals of equality and neutrality by assuring that differences are not taken into account except in the manner explicitly specified by the Court. Although likely to promote accountability, this solution of formal rules has drawbacks. Making and enforcing specific rules engages the Court in the problem of reinvesting differences with significance by noticing them. Specifically requiring the Court to articulate permissible and impermissible uses of difference may enshrine categorical analysis and move further away from the ideal of treating persons as individuals. One way for the Court to resolve the difference dilemma is to grant or cede discretion to other decisionmakers. Then the problems from both noticing and ignoring difference, and from risking non-neutrality in means and results, are no longer problems for the Court, but instead matters within the discretion of other private or public decisionmakers. This approach simply moves the problem to another forum, allowing the decisionmaker with the discretion to take difference into account in an impermissible manner. The tension between formal, predictable rules and individualized judgments under discretionary standards thus assumes heightened significance in dilemmas of difference.

This dilemma of discretion and formality most vividly occupied the Court in *McCleskey v. Kemp*, in which the Court evaluated charges of racial discrimination in the administration of the death penalty in Georgia's criminal justice system. A statistical study of over 2000 murder cases in Georgia during the 1970's submitted by the defendant and assumed by the Court to be valid, demonstrated that the likelihood of a defendant's receiving the death sentence was correlated with the victim's race and, to a lesser extent, the defendant's race. According to the study, black defendants convicted of killing white victims "have the greatest likelihood of receiving the death penalty." Should the Court treat a sentencing "discrepancy that appears to correlate with race" as a defect requiring judicial constraints on prosecutorial and jury discretion, or as an unavoidable consequence of such discretion? In making this choice, the majority and the dissenters each latched onto opposing sides of the dilemma about discretion and formality.

Justice Powell, for the majority, began by asserting that the discretion of the jury is critical to the criminal justice system, and operates to the advantage of criminal defendants, because it permits individualized treatment rather than arbitrary application of rules. Because of the importance of discretion, unexplained racial discrepancies in the sentencing process should not be assumed to be invidious or unconstitutional. In the majority's view, recognizing claims such as McCleskey's would open the door "to claims based on unexplained discrepancies that correlate to membership in other minority groups, and even to gender" or physical appearance. This argument, perhaps meant in part to trivialize the dissent's objections by linking physical appearance with race, sex, and ethnicity, implied that discrepancies in criminal sentences are random and too numerous to control. Furthermore, in the majority's view, any attempt to channel discretion runs the risk of undermining it altogether: "it is difficult to imagine guidelines that would produce the predictability sought by the dissent without sacrificing the discretion essential to a humane and fair system of criminal justice."

Justice Brennan, in dissent, approached the problem of discretion and formality from the other direction. Like the majority, Justice Brennan asserted that imposition of the death penalty must be based on an "individualized moral inquiry." To Justice Brennan, however, the statistical correlation between death sentences and the race of defendants and victims showed that participants in the state criminal justice system had, in fact, considered race and produced judgments "completely at odds with [the] concern that an individual be evaluated as a unique human being." Justice Brennan argued that "[d]iscretion is a means, not an end" and that, under the circumstances, the Court must monitor the discretion of others. Justice Brennan also responded to the majority's fear of widespread challenges to all aspects of criminal sentencing: "Taken on its face, such a statement seems to suggest a fear of too much justice. . . . The

prospect that there may be more widespread abuse than McCleskey documents may be dismaying, but it does not justify complete abdication of our judicial role."

Justice Stevens, also in dissent, argued that there remains a middle road between forbidding the death penalty and ignoring, in the name of prosecutorial and jury discretion, the correlation between the death penalty and the defendant's and victim's races. He urged a specific rule: the class of defendants eligible for the death penalty should be narrowed to the category of cases, identified by the study, in which "prosecutors consistently seek, and juries consistently impose, the death penalty without regard to the race of the victim or the race of the offender."

For the majority in *McCleskey*, constricting prosecutorial and jury discretion would push toward so regulated a world that the criminal justice system would no longer produce particularized, individualized decisions about defendants. For the dissenters, the Court's acquiescence in unmonitored prosecutorial and jury discretion, in the face of sentencing disparities correlated with race, condoned and perpetuated racial discrimination and thereby allowed racial stereotyping to be substituted for individualized justice.

Debate among the Justices last Term in an entirely different context exposed a similar tension between rules and discretion. In *Corporation of the Presiding Bishop of the Church of Jesus Christ of Latter-Day Saints v. Amos (Presiding Bishop)*, the Court considered whether the federal statute exempting religious organizations from nondiscrimination requirements in their employment decisions arising out of nonprofit activities violated the establishment clause. The Court's majority endorsed the legislative grant of discretion to religious organizations, while rejecting the discharged engineer's claims that such state accommodation unconstitutionally promotes religion.

The opinions in the case clearly illustrate the dilemma of discretion. The majority reasoned that under the exemption the preference for religion was not exercised by the government, but rather by the church. Justice O'Connor, however, pointed out in her concurring opinion that allowing discretion to the private decisionmaker to use religion in his decisions inevitably engaged the government in that differentiation. The Court could not, simply by protecting the discretion of religious organizations, escape consideration of the tension between the constitutional command against promoting religion and the constitutional demand for free exercise of religion. Instead, Justice O'Connor argued, in distinguishing constitutional accommodation of religion from unconstitutional assistance to religious organizations, the Court must evaluate the message of the government's policy as perceived by an "objective observer."

Justice Brennan's separate opinion also treated this tension as unavoidable. Yet Justice Brennan focused on the risk that case-by-case review by the Court would chill the very freedom assured to religious organizations. He therefore endorsed a categorical exemption from the ban against religious discrimination in employment for the nonprofit activities of religious organizations, but argued for reserving judgment as to profitmaking activities. Like Justice Stevens in *McCleskey*, Justice Brennan searched for a formal rule that could preserve discretion for other decisionmakers while also implementing the Court's special commitment to protect individuals from categorical, discriminatory treatment.

D. The Dilemmas in Sum

Other cases before the Court have raised one or more aspects of the difference dilemma. The Court's voluntary affirmative action cases, during the 1986 Term and earlier, directly present dilemmas about recreating difference, risking non-neutral means to transform non-neutral ends, and choosing between rules and discretion in an effort to avoid categorical decisions. Decisions about handicapped persons also raise perplexing issues about when the Court should permit public and private decisionmakers to make the difference of handicap matter. The Court comes down one way or another in each case, but the splits between majority and minority views persist and recreate the dilemmas. The next Section argues that assumptions buried within the dilemmas make them seem more difficult than they need be. The task, then, is to articulate those assumptions and to evaluate the choices that remain for decisionmakers.

III. Behind and Beyond the Dilemma

The dilemma of difference appears unresolvable. The risk of non-neutrality—the risk of discrimination—accompanies efforts both to ignore and to recognize difference in equal treatment and special treatment; in color- or gender-blindness and in affirmative action; in governmental neutrality and in governmental preferences; and in decisionmakers' discretion and in formal constraints on discretion. Yet the dilemma is not as intractable as it seems. What makes it seem so difficult are unstated assumptions about the nature of difference. Once articulated and examined, these assumptions can take their proper place among other choices about how to treat difference. I will explore here the assumptions underlying the dilemma of difference, assumptions that usually go without saying.

First, we often assume that "differences" are intrinsic, rather than viewing them as expressions of comparisons between people. We are all different from one another in innumerable ways. Each of these differences is an implicit comparison we draw. And the comparisons themselves depend upon and reconfirm socially constructed meanings about what traits should matter for purposes of comparison.

Second, typically we adopt an unstated point of reference when assessing others. From the point of reference of this norm, we determine who is different and who is normal. Women are different in relation to the unstated male norm. Blacks, Mormons, Jews, and Arabs are different in relation to the unstated white, Christian norm. Handicapped persons are different in relation to the unstated norm of able-bodiedness, or, as some have described it, the vantage point of the "Temporarily Able Persons." The unstated point of comparison is not neutral, but particular, and not inevitable, but only seemingly so when left unstated. A notion of equality that demands disregarding a "difference" calls for assimilation to an unstated norm. To strip away difference, then, often is to remove or ignore a feature distinguishing an individual from a presumed norm—like a white, able-bodied Christian man—but leaving that norm in place as the measure for equal treatment.

Third, we treat the perspective of the person doing the seeing or judging as objective, rather than as subjective. Although a person's perspective does not collapse into his or her demographic characteristics, no one is free from perspective, and no one can see fully from another's point of view.

Fourth, we assume that the perspectives of those being judged are either irrelevant or are already taken into account through the perspective of the judge. That is, we regard a person's self-conception or world view as unimportant to our treatment of that person.

Finally, there is an assumption that the existing social and economic arrangements are natural and neutral. We presume that individuals are free to form their own preferences and act upon them. In this view, any departure from the status quo risks non-neutrality and interference with free choice.

These related assumptions, once made explicit, must contend with some contrary ones. Consider these alternative starting points. Difference is relational, not intrinsic. Who or what should be taken as the point of reference for defining differences is debatable. There is no single, superior perspective for judging questions of difference. No perspective asserted to produce "the truth" is objective, but rather will obscure the power of the person attributing a difference while excluding important competing perspectives. Social arrangements can be changed: maintaining the status quo is not neutral and cannot be justified by the claim that everyone has freely chosen it.

* * *

Discussion challenges the sheer power behind the usual practice of leaving [assumptions] unstated — the power that privileges unstated assumptions over alternative, competing views. Each of these assumptions bears the imprint of an historical association between power and the production of knowledge about the world. Thus, the characteristics and experiences of those people who have had power to construct legal rules and social arrangements also influence and reflect the dominant cultural expressions of what is different and what is normal.

* * *

IV. Perspectives on Perspectives

The difference dilemma seems paralyzing if framed by the unstated assumptions described in Part III. Those assumptions so entrench one point

of view as natural and orderly that any conscious decision to notice or to ignore difference breaks the illusion of a legal world free of perspective. The assumptions make it seem that departures from unstated norms violate commitments to neutrality. Yet adhering to the unstated norms undermines commitments to neutrality — and to equality. Is it possible to proceed differently, putting these assumptions into question?

I will suggest that it is possible, even if difficult, to move beyond the constricting assumptions. At times in the past Term, members of the Court have employed the most powerful device to expose and challenge the unstated assumptions: looking at an issue from another point of view. By asking how a member of a religious group might experience a seemingly neutral rule, or how a nonmember might experience the discretion of a religious group, Justices O'Connor, Brennan, and White made an effort in several cases to understand a different perspective. Justice Marshall and the majority in *CalFed* tried to assume the perspective of pregnant women by considering how treatment of pregnancy affects women's abilities to work outside the home while having a family. The dissenting Justices in *McCleskey* asked how defendants would react to the statistical disparity in capital sentencing by race, breaking out of the tendency to see the challenge only as a threat to the discretion and manageability of the criminal justice system. In *Saint Francis College, Shaare Tefila,* and *Arline,* members of the Court struggled over whose perspective should count for purposes of defining a race and a handicap, reaching conclusions that refused to take the usual answers for granted.

Efforts to adopt or imagine alternate perspectives are also reflected in opinions from previous Terms. For example, Justice Stevens assessed an equal protection challenge to a zoning restriction burdening mentally retarded people by expressing sensitivity to a point of view other than his own: "I cannot believe that a rational member of this disadvantaged class could ever approve of the discriminatory application of the city's ordinance in this case." Still earlier, Justice Douglas invited inquiry into the experience of non-English-speaking students sitting in a public school classroom conducted entirely in English. Similarly, litigants have sometimes tried to convince the Court to adopt their perspective. Justice Harlan's dissent in *Plessy v. Ferguson* may have been assisted by Homer Plessy's attorney, who had urged the Justices to imagine themselves in the shoes of a black person:

> Suppose a member of this court, nay, suppose every member of it, by some mysterious dispensation of providence should wake to-morrow with a black skin and curly hair . . . and in traveling through that portion of the country where the 'Jim Crow Car' abounds, should be ordered into it by the conductor. It is easy to imagine what would be the result. . . . What humiliation, what rage would then fill the judicial mind!

It may be ultimately impossible to take the perspective of another completely, but the effort to do so may help us recognize that our perspective is partial and that the status quo is not inevitable or ideal. After shaking free of these unstated assumptions and developing a sense of alternate perspectives, judges must then choose. The process of looking through other perspectives does not itself yield an answer but it may lead to an answer different from the one that the judge would otherwise have reached. Seen in this light, the dilemma is hard, but not impossible. . . .

* * *

V. Engendering Justice

The nineteenth-century American legal system recognized only three races: "white," "Negro," and "Indian." Californian authorities faced an influx of Chinese and Mexicans and were forced to confront the now complicated question of racial categorization. They solved the problem of categorizing Mexicans by defining them as "whites" and by according them the rights of free white persons. Chinese, however, were labeled "Indian" and denied the political and legal rights of white persons. Similarly, in 1922, a unanimous Supreme Court concluded that Japanese persons were not covered by a federal naturalization statute applicable to "free white persons," "aliens of African nativity," and "persons of African descent.

In retrospect, these results seem arbitrary. The legal authorities betrayed a striking inability to reshape their own categories for people who did not fit. Of course, it is impossible to know what

might have happened if some piece of history had been otherwise. Still, it is tempting to wonder: what if the California legal authorities had changed their racial scheme, rather than forcing the Chinese and Mexican applicants into it? The officials then might have noticed that nationality, not race, distinguished these groups. What if these officials and the Justices in 1922 had tried to take the point of view of the people they were labeling? Perhaps, from this vantage point, the Justices would have realized the need for reasons — beyond racial classification — for granting or withholding legal rights and privileges.

In this Foreword, I have argued that trying to take seriously the point of view of people labeled "different" is a way to move beyond current difficulties in the treatment of differences in our society. This last statement, like much of the article, is addressed to people in positions of sufficient power to label others "different" and to make choices about how to treat difference. If you have such power, you may realize the dilemma of difference: by taking another person's difference into account in awarding goods or distributing burdens, you risk reiterating the significance of that difference and, potentially, its stigma and stereotyping consequences. But if you do not take another person's difference into account — in a world that has made that difference matter — you may also recreate and reestablish both the difference and its negative implications. If you draft or enforce laws, you may worry that the effects of the laws will not be neutral whether you take difference into account or you ignore it. If you employ people, judge guilt or innocence, or make other decisions affecting lives, you may want and need the discretion to make an individualized assessment, free from any focus on categorical differences. But if that discretion is exercised without constraint, difference may be taken into account in a way that does not treat that person as an individual — and in a way that disguises this fact from view.

These dilemmas, I have argued, become less paralyzing if you try to break out of unstated assumptions and take the perspective of the person you have called "different." Once you do that, you may glimpse that your patterns for organizing the world are both arbitrary and foreclose their own reconsideration. You may find that the categories you take for granted do not well serve features you had not focused upon in the past. You may see an injury that you had not noticed, or take more seriously a harm that you had otherwise discounted. If you try to take the view of the other person, you will find that the "difference" you notice is part of the relationship or comparison you draw between that person and someone else, with reference to a norm, and you will then get the chance to examine the reference point you usually take for granted. Maybe you will conclude that the reference point itself should change. Employers do not have to treat pregnancy and parenthood as a disability, but instead as a part of the lives of valued workers. You may find that you had so much ignored the point of view of others that you did not realize that you were mistaking your point of view for reality. Perhaps you will find that the way things are is not the only way things could be — that changing the way you classify, evaluate, reward, and punish may make the differences you had noticed less significant, or even irrelevant to the way you run your life.

I have also argued, however, that we often forget how to take the perspective of another. We forget even that our point of view is not reality and that our conceptual schemes are simplifications, serving some interests and uses rather than others. We forget because our minds and probably our hearts cannot contain the whole world, and so we reduce the world to short-hand that we can handle. Our short-hand — because it is our short-hand — reflects what we thought we needed, where we stood, and who we are. We treat our divisions of the world as though they were real and universal. We do not see that they embody our early experiences of discovering how we are both the same as and different from our parents. We forget how we learned from them to encode the world into the same classifications they used to serve their own needs. We forget that things may appear frightful only because they are unfamiliar. We look at people we do not know, and think they are different from us in important ways. We forget that even if they are different, in a way that matters to them, too, they also have a view of reality, and ours is as different from theirs as theirs is from ours.

We think we know what is real, what differences are real, and what really matters, even though sometimes we realize that our perceptions and desires are influenced by others. Sometimes we realize that television, radio, classes we had in school, or the attitudes of people who matter to us affect our inclinations. Every time we wear an item of clothing that we now think is fashionable, but used to think was ugly, we brush up against the outside influences on what we think inside. Yet we think that we think independently. We forget that widely held beliefs may be the ones most influenced from the outside.

The more powerful we are, the less we may be able to see that the world coincides with our view precisely because we shaped it in accordance with those views. That is just one of our privileges. Another is that we are able to put and hear questions in ways that do not question ourselves. In contrast, the more marginal we feel from the world, from the groups we know, the more likely we are to glimpse a contrast between some people's perceptions of reality and our own. Yet we still may slip into the world view of the more powerful, because it is more likely to be validated. We prefer to have our perceptions validated; we need to feel acknowledged and confirmed. But when we fail to take the perspective of another, we deny that very acknowledgment and confirmation in return.

If we want to preserve justice, we need to develop a practice for more knowing judgments about problems of difference. We must stop seeking to get close to the "truth" and instead seek to get close to other people's truths. The question is, how do we do this? In this Section, I argue that we must persuade others as much as they must persuade us about the reality we should construct. Justice can be impartial only if judges acknowledge their own partiality. Justice depends on the possibility of conflicts among the values and perspectives that justice pursues. Courts, and especially the Supreme Court, provide a place for the contest over realities that govern us — if we open ourselves to the chance that a reality other than our own may matter. Justice can be engendered when we overcome our pretended indifference to difference and instead people our world with individuals who surprise one another about difference.

A. *Impartiality and Partial Truths*

It is a paradox. Only by admitting our partiality can we strive for impartiality. Impartiality is the guise partiality takes to seal bias against exposure. It looks neutral to apply a rule denying unemployment benefits to anyone who cannot fulfill the work schedule, but it is not neutral if the work schedule was devised with one religious Sabbath, and not another, in mind. The idea of impartiality implies human access to a view beyond human experience, a "God's eye" point of view. Not only do humans lack this inhuman perspective, but humans who claim it are untruthful, trying to exercise power to cut off conversation and debate. Doris Lessing argues that a single absolute truth would mean the end of human discourse, but that we are happily saved from that end because any truth, once uttered, becomes immediately one truth among many, subject to more discourse and dispute. If we treat other points of view as irritants in the way of our own vision, we are still hanging on to faulty certainty. Even if we admit the limits of our view, while treating those limits as gaps and leaving the rest in place, we preserve the pretense that our view is sufficiently rooted in reality to resist any real change prompted by another.

Acknowledging partiality may cure the pretense of impartiality. But unless we have less capacity to step outside our own skins than I think we do, we then have a choice of which partial view to advance or accept. Whose partial view should resolve conflicts over how to treat assertions of difference, whether assigned or claimed? Preferring the standpoint of an historically denigrated group can reveal truths obscured by the dominant view, but it can also reconfirm the underlying conceptual scheme of the dominant view by focusing on it. Similarly, the perspective of those who are labeled "different" may offer an important challenge to the view of those who imposed the label, but it is a corrective lens, another partial view, not absolute truth. We then fight over whether to prefer it. "Standpoint theories" may also deny the multiple experiences of members of the denigrated group and create a new claim of essentialism.

Instead of an impartial view, we should strive for the standpoint of someone who is committed to the moral relevance of contingent particulars. Put in personal terms, if I pretend to be impartial, I hide my partiality; however, if I embrace partiality, I risk ignoring you, your needs, and your alternate reality—or, conversely, embracing and appropriating your view into yet another rigid, partial view. I conclude that I must acknowledge and struggle against my partiality by making an effort to understand your reality and what it means for my own. I need to stop seeking certainty and acknowledge the complexity of our shared and colliding realities, as well as the tragic impossibility of all prevailing at once. It is this complexity that constitutes our reciprocal realities, and it is the conflict between our realities that constitutes us, whether we engage in it overtly or submerge it under a dominant view.

Moral action, then, takes place in a field of complexity, and we act ethically when we recognize what we give up as well as what we embrace. The solution is not to adopt and cling to some new standpoint, but instead to strive to become and remain open to perspectives and claims that challenge our own. Justice, like philosophy, ought

> to trust rather to the multitude and variety of its arguments than to the conclusiveness of any one. Its reasoning should not form a chain which is no stronger than its weakest link, but a cable whose fibers may be ever so slender, provided they are sufficiently numerous and intimately connected.

We who judge should remove the removal of ourselves when we either ignore or notice a difference. We can and should confront our involvement in and responsibility for what happens when we act in a reality we did not invent but still have latitude to discredit or affirm. We should have the humility and the courage to act in each situation anew, rather than applying what we presume to know already, as though each case were merely a repetition of an episode from the past.

* * *

Two exercises can help those who judge to glimpse the perspectives of others and to avoid a false impartiality. The first is to explore our own stereotypes, our own attitudes toward people we treat as different—and, indeed, our own categories for organizing the world. Audre Lorde put it powerfully: "I urge each one of us here to reach down into that deep place of knowledge inside herself and touch that terror and loathing of any difference that lives there. See whose face it wears. Then the personal as the political can begin to illuminate all our choices." This is a call for applying "strict scrutiny" not just to a defendant's reasons for burdening a protected minority group, but also to ourselves when we judge those reasons. It is a process that even we who see ourselves as victims of oppression need to undertake, for devices of oppression are buried within us. We must also examine and retool our methods of classification and consider how they save us from questioning our instincts, ourselves, and our existing social arrangements. Putting ourselves in the place of those who look different can push us to challenge our ignorance and fears and to investigate our usual categories for making sense of the world. This is an opportunity to enlarge judges' understanding and abilities to become better practitioners in the business of solving problems.

The second exercise is to search out differences and celebrate them, constructing new bases for connection. We can pursue the possibilities of difference behind seeming commonalities and seek out commonalities across difference, thereby confronting the ready association of sameness with equality and difference with inferiority. One route is to emphasize our common humanity, despite our different traits. Another tack is to disentangle difference from the allocation of benefits and burdens in society — a tack that may well require looking at difference to alter how people use it. The Court's effort to assure equality for women and men in the conjunction of work and family life in *CalFed* represents such an effort to disentangle institutional arrangements from the difference they create. A third approach to cherish difference and welcome anomaly. Still another is to understand that which initially seems strange and to learn about sense and reason from this exercise — just as philosophers, anthropologists, and psychologists have urged us to take seriously the self-conceptions and perceptions of others. In the process of trying to understand how another person understands, we may even remake our categories of understanding. Other persons may not even define "self" the same way we do, and glimpsing their "self-concepts" thus challenges us to step beyond our operating assumptions. A fur-

ther skill to practice is to recognize commonality in difference itself: in the relationships within which we construct difference and connect and distinguish ourselves from one another.

These exercises in taking the perspective of the other will deepen and broaden anyone's perspective. For judges, who debate the use of the coercive forces of the law in relation to issues of difference, these exercises are critical. Judges can and should act as representatives, standing in for others and symbolizing society itself. Judicial acts of representation must also be responsive to the demands of the people they govern, in order to secure apparent legitimacy and, ultimately, to remain effective. One judge explained that law's coercive power must be applied to assure "the viability of a pluralistic democracy," which "depends upon the willingness to accept all of the 'thems' as 'us.' Whether the moralistic or pragmatic, the structure of the Constitution rests on the foundational principle that successful self-governance can be achieved only through public institutions following egalitarian policies."

This exhortation — that we must take the perspective of another, while remembering that we cannot really know what another sees, and must put our own categories up for challenge, without ceding the definition of reality over to others — sounds quite complicated. What do we do with the sense of complexity?

B. Complexity, Passivity, and the Status Quo: The Problem of Deference

We are mistaken when we hold onto simple certainties. Yet complexity seems both overwhelming and incapacitating. By bearing into complexity rather than turning away from it, by listening to the variety of voices implicated in our problems, we may lose a sense of ready solutions and steady certainties. But clear answers have been false gods, paid homage to in the coinage of other people's opportunities, and also at cost to our own character. We harden ourselves when we treat our categories as though they were real, closing off responses to new facts and to challenges to how we live and think. Our certainties also leave unresolved conflicts among incompatible but deeply held values. In the face of complexity, "[t]he politics of difference can all too easily degenerate into the politics of 'mutual indifference . . .'" If we care about justice, the biggest mistake would be to respond to complexity with passivity. That response is not impartial; it favors the status quo, those benefited by it, and the conception of reality it fosters.

I. Forms of Passivity.—Four forms of judicial passivity may be tempting in the face of complexity: deference, intent requirements, reliance on apparent choices or concessions of the parties, and reliance on doctrine. I will consider each in turn.

Respect for other institutions and persons is a critical part of judging, but there are particular risks when the Court, while acknowledging the complexity of a problem of difference, defers to other branches or levels of government, to private actors, or even to the parties before the Court. One risk is that the Court will pretend that it has no power over or responsibility for what results. When the Court defers to Congress, the executive, a state government, or a private actor, the Justices are saying, let's not make a decision, let's leave it to others, or let's endorse the freedom or respect the power of others. It is surely important for the Justices to understand their relationship with other people or institutions with interests in a matter, but such understanding is quite different from ceding responsibility for what ensues. This principle is important for everybody, but especially for a judicial body, which has parties with genuine conflicts before it. As Frank Michelman put it, "attention [to other branches of government] cannot mean deference, or talismanic invocation of authority. The norm of justice to parties itself commands that no other norm should ever take a form that preempts questions or exempts from reason-giving."

Problems also arise when the Court takes on the second form of passivity: focusing on the intentions of the parties before it. When the Court demands evidence of intentional discrimination before upholding a plaintiff's charges, the Justices are deferring to and thereby entrenching the perspective of the defendant, thus rejecting the perspective of the plaintiff-victim. Asking only about the sincerity of the motive behind a statute whose effect is challenged is also an act that takes sides, defines which reality will govern, and avoids the real challenge of responding to the perspective of the plaintiff.

It is equally problematic for the Court, in a third form of passivity, to point to apparent choices made by plaintiffs, victims, or members of minority groups, as Justice Scalia did in *Johnson*, as a justification for holding against them. The Court may presume incorrectly that the choices are free and uncoerced, or the Court may wrongly attribute certain meanings to a choice. Similarly, judicial references to litigants' concessions during litigation, including during oral argument, are not without risk. Although the Court may be trying to take the perspective of others seriously, its reliance on litigants' concessions as the peg for a judicial decision may also be the Court's way of reducing the task of deciding on its own. Reliance on concessions of the lawyer may be especially troubling in cases involving the rights of minorities, because it is unclear for whom the lawyer speaks at that moment: the client, the cause, or others unrepresented there who will be affected in the future by the Court's ruling.

The fourth form of passivity is perhaps one of the most effective circumventions of responsibility: the Court's reliance on its own doctrinal boundaries and categories to resolve the cases before it. This Foreword has demonstrated that the difference dilemma poses similar problems in a wide variety of contexts, including cases involving religion, gender, race, and sexual preference. Yet when the Court takes the boundaries between doctrines as given, filling the doctrines with operative tests and lines of precedent, it obscures these potential similarities across contexts. By the time a case reaches an appellate court, the adversary process has so focused on specific issues of doctrinal disagreement that the competing arguments have come under one framework, not under competing theories. Legal analogy is typically inseparable from precedential reasoning, telescoping the creative potential of a search for surprising similarities into a narrow focus on prior rulings that could "control" the instant case. The Court's practice vividly demonstrates how fabricated categories can assume the status of immutable reality. Of course, law would be overwhelming without doctrinal categories and separate lines of precedent. Yet by holding to rigid categories, the Court denies the existence of tensions and portrays a false simplicity amid a rabbit warren of complexity. The Court's strict segregation of doctrines also cloisters lines of thought and insights, thereby restricting the Court's ability to use larger frames of judgment.

2. Avoiding Passivity. — Besides resisting tempting forms of passivity — which do not lessen judicial responsibility — the Court can and should challenge rigid patterns of thought. What if litigants argued more emphatically across contexts, and reminded members of the Court, "you have seen something like this before"? Litigants can help the Court to avoid the dangers of complacency and complexity by searching out analogies and developing unfamiliar perspectives. At the same time, litigants may gain a tactical advantage, because they may persuade a member of the Court of their point of view by analogizing to something the Justice has glimpsed elsewhere. This practice also has some support in epistemology. The difficulties each of us has in seeing around the bend of our own thought can be eased with the help of insights from others who are positioned differently. Given the relationship between knowledge and power, those with less privilege may well see better than those with more.

Surprisingly, traditional legal techniques actually provide fruitful starting points for avoiding passivity. One noted feature of the legal system that can be used to mount this challenge is analogical reasoning. The existence of encrusted practices and categories, however, frustrates the full use of these tools. Litigants and judges should search out unexpected analogies to scrape off barnacles of thought and to challenge views so settled that they are not thought to be views. This process may persuade particular judges, in particular cases, to see a different angle on a problem. It also holds promise as a method for finding surprising commonalities that can nudge us all to reassess well-established categories of thought.

The promise of reasoning by analogy is lost if it becomes an arid conceptualist enterprise. Yet when immersed in the particulars of a problem, we sometimes are able to think up analogies that break out of ill-fitting conceptual schemes. As one observer of creative processes in art, science, and philosophy has commented, "'in the history of human thinking the most fruitful develop-ments frequently take place at those points where two different lines of thought meet.'" By seeing something in a new light, seeing its similarity to something else once thought quite different, we are able to attribute different meanings and consequences to what we see. A glimpse of difference in one context may enable litigants and judges better to appreciate it in another context.

The adversarial process is another feature of the legal system that, with some modification, can be used to challenge judicial complacency. In fact, the values of thinking through analogies bear a striking similarity to the virtues of reasoning in dialogue. The dialogue form puts the student in a position to follow the connections and divergences in argument and invent for herself ways to think anew, rather than simply internalizing the monologue of inherited knowledge. Barbara Johnson notes that "[l]earning seems to take place most rapidly when the student must respond to the contradiction between *two* teachers. And what the student learns in the process is both the power of ambiguity and the non-innocence of ignorance." Similarly, dialogue in legal briefs and courtroom arguments can stretch the minds of listeners, especially if they are actively forming their own position and not simply picking between the ones before them.

The introduction of additional voices may enable adversary dialogue to expand beyond a stylized, either/or mode, prompting new and creative insights. Consequently, the Court can, and should, seek out alternative views in amicus briefs. Inventive approaches can bring the voices of those who are not present before the Court, as in the recent brief filed with the Court that collected the autobiographical accounts of men and women who believed their lives had been changed by the availability of legalized abortion. Similarly, the famous "Brandeis brief" in *Muller v. Oregon* marked a creative shift for the Court, introducing the use of vivid, factual detail as a way to break out of the formalist categories dominating the analysis. Seeking unusual perspectives enables justices to avail themselves of the "partial superiority" of other people's views and to reach for what is unfamiliar and perhaps suppressed under the dominant ways of seeing. Bringing in a wider variety of views can also make the so-called "counter-majoritarian" Court more "democratic."

Besides seeking out unfamiliar perspectives and analogies new to the law, all judges should also consider the human consequences of their decisions in difference cases, rather than insulating themselves in abstractions. Such engagement encourages the judge to fill in textual gaps based on his or her own experiences. It may seem paradoxical to urge those who judge to bring their own experiences to the problems before them, after identifying the dangerous ways in which we all confuse our own perceptions and interests for reality. In the process of personal reflection, however, the judge may stretch faculties for connection, while engaging in dialogue with the parties over their legal arguments and analogies. I petition all judges to open up to the chance that someone may move them — the experience will not tell them what to do, but it may give them a way outside of routinized categories to forge new approaches to the problem at hand.

This call to be open, to canvass personal experience, applies to all legal controversies, but it is especially important in the context of cases that present the dilemma of difference. Here the judicial mainstays of neutrality and distance prove most risky, for they blind judges to their own involvement in recreating the negative meanings of difference. Yet the dangers of making differences matter also argue against categorical solutions. By struggling to respond humanly to the dilemma in each particular context, the judge can supply the possibility of connection otherwise missing in the categorical treatments of difference.

C. Choosing among Divergent Demands

Urging judges to allow themselves to be moved by the arguments may seem misguided. A judge who identifies with every perspective may simply feel indecisive and overburdened. Would feeling the tugs in all directions render us powerless to choose? It may be just this fear that explains our attachment to simplifying categories, stereotypes, and fixed ways of thought. Some of us may fear being overwhelmed by the world, others fear being too moved by it, others fear being powerless before it. Challenging familiar categories and styles of reasoning may threaten the search for order, decisiveness, and manageability that maintain the predictability in our lives. But there are other ways to hold things together than the methods we have used in the past.

Some may aspire to a jurisprudence of individualism, never treating any individual as a member of a group. Yet, resonant as it is with many American traditions, individualization is a myth: because our language is shared and our categories communally invented, any word I use to describe your uniqueness draws you into the classes of people sharing your traits. Even if ultimately I produce enough words so that the intersection of all classes you belong in contains only one member — you — we understand this through a language of comparison with others. This language, however, seems to embroil us in the dilemma of difference.

What could we do instead? I believe we should welcome complexity and challenge complacency — and stop fearing that we will be unable to make judgments. We can and do make judgments all the time, in a way committed to making meaning, rather than recreating or ignoring difference. We make commitments when we make decisions; we reconfirm or remake current understandings by reflecting so deeply and particularly about a new situation that we challenge presumptive solutions. Instead of trying continually to fit people into categories, and to enforce or deny rights on that basis, we can and do make decisions by immersing in particulars to renew commitments to a fair world.

* * *

Thus, one reason we can still decide, amid powerfully competing claims, is that immersion in particulars does not require the relinquishment of general commitments. The struggle is not over the validity of principles and generalizations — it is over which ones should prevail in a given context. The choice from among principles, in turn, implicates choices about which differences, and which similarities, should matter. These are moral choices, choices about which voices should persuade those who judge.

Even when we understand them, some voices will lose. The fundamentalist Christians who supported the Balanced Treatment Act in Louisiana deserve respect and understanding: their view of the world may well be threatened by the curriculum taught to their children in the public schools. However, this is what the fight is about. Whose view of reality should prevail in public institutions? This deep conundrum involves the conflicts between the world view animating any rule for the entire society, and the world views of subgroups who will never share the dominant views. I am tempted to propose a seemingly "neutral" rule, such as a rule that judges interpreting the commitment to respect difference should make the choice that allows difference to flourish without imposing it on others. If exclusion of their world view from the biology curriculum creates an intolerable choice for the fundamentalists, they do and they must have the choice to establish their own educational institutions, and their own separate community. Yet this seemingly "neutral" position is a comfortable view for a nonfundamentalist like myself, who cannot appreciate the full impact of the evolution science curriculum as experienced by at least some fundamentalists. Rather than pretending to secure a permanent solution through a "neutral" rule, I must acknowledge the tragedy of non-neutrality — and admit that our very commitment to tolerance yields intolerance toward some views. If the fundamentalists lose in this case, they can continue to struggle to challenge the meaning of the commitment to separate church and state, and they may convince the rest of us in the next round. Although it may be little solace for the minority group, its challenge achieves something even when it loses, by reminding the nation of our commitment to diversity, and our inability, thus far, to achieve it fully.

Thus, choices from among competing commitments do not end after the Court announces its judgment. Continuing skepticism about the reality endorsed by the Court — or any source of governmental power — is the only guard against tyranny.

The continuing process of debate over deeply held but conflicting commitments is both the mechanism and the promise of our governmental system. Within that system, the Supreme Court's power depends upon persuasion. As Hannah Arendt wrote: "the thinking process which is active in judging something is not, like the thought process of pure reasoning, a dialogue between me and myself, but finds itself always and primarily, even if I am quite alone in making up my mind, in an anticipated communication with others with whom I know I must finally come to some agreement." The important question

is, with whom must you come to agreement? In a society of diversity with legacies of discrimination, within a polity committed to self-governance, the judiciary becomes a critical arena for demands of inclusion. I see the judicial arena as a forum for contests over competing realities. The question remains, however, whose definitions of realities will govern in a given case and over time.

Court judgments endow some perspectives, rather than others, with power. Judicial power is least accountable when judges leave unstated — and treat as a given — the perspective they select. Litigation before the Supreme Court sometimes highlights individuals who otherwise seldom imprint their perspective on the polity. In eliciting these perspectives, and accepting their challenge to the version of reality the justices otherwise would take for granted, the Court advances the fundamental constitutional commitment to require reasons before exercises of power, whether public or private. Growing from our history, wrought from many struggles, is the tradition we have invented, and it is a tradition that declares that the status quo cannot be immune from demands for justification. Litigation over the meanings of difference represents demands for such accountability. By asking how power influences knowledge, the Court can address whether a "difference" has been assigned through past domination or as a remedy for past domination. In this way, the Court can solicit information about contrasting views of reality without casting off the moorings of historical experience; and in this inquiry, the Court can assess the risk of creating new patterns of domination while remedying inequalities of the past. As we compete for power to give reality to our visions, we confront tragic limits in our abilities to make meaning together. Yet we must continue to seek a language to speak across conflicting affiliations.

We need settings in which to engage in the clash of realities that breaks us out of settled and complacent meanings and creates opportunities for insight and growth. This is the special burden and opportunity for the Court: to enact and preside over the dialogue through which we remake the normative endowment that shapes current understandings.

When the Court performs these roles, it engenders justice. Justice is engendered when judges admit the limitations of their own viewpoints, when judges reach beyond those limits by trying to see from contrasting perspectives, and when people seek to exercise power to nurture differences, not to assign and control them. Rather than securing an illusory universality and objectivity, law is a medium through which particular people can engage in the continuous work of making justice. The law "is part of a distinctive manner of imagining the real." Legal decisions engrave upon our culture the stories we tell to and about ourselves, the meanings that constitute the traditions we invent. Searching for words to describe realities too multiple and complex to be contained by their language, litigants and judges struggle over what will be revealed and what will be concealed in the inevitable partiality of human judgment. Through deliberate attention to our own partiality, we can begin to acknowledge the dangers of pretended impartiality. By taking differ-

ence into account, we can overcome our pretended indifference to difference, and people our worlds with those who can surprise and enrich one another. As we make audible, in official arenas, the struggles over which version of reality will secure power, we disrupt the silence of one perspective, imposed as if universal. Admitting the partiality of the perspective that temporarily gains official endorsement may embolden resistance to announced rules. But only by admitting that rules are resistible — and by justifying to the governed their calls for adherence — can justice be done in a democracy. "[I]t is only through the variety of relations constructed by the plurality of beings that truth can be known and community constructed." Then we constitute ourselves as members of conflicting communities with enough reciprocal regard to talk across differences. We engender mutual regard for pain we know and pain we do not understand.

SECTION 2

The Concept of Law

What is law? This is the most basic question that can be asked in this course. When we talk about a rule of law, what do we mean? When we talk about a legislature making and a judiciary interpreting law, what is the law to which we are referring?

The answer may seem obvious at first. Everybody knows what law is. The law is what makes us stop at stop signs and file our income taxes and pay our bills. The law is what protects us from murder or assault or burglary. If you want to know what law is just look around. You can't get through a day of your life without running into examples of it, even if you want to. All this is true, but it doesn't really tell us what law is. Asking about the nature of law is like asking about the nature of time or truth or beauty. Everybody knows what they are, too. Time is all around us. We measure our lives by it. But what is it? We can point to examples of truth and beauty, like children pointing to pictures of stars or clouds. But just because we can identify some examples doesn't mean that we can explain these concepts. And so, like other great ideas that have come to occupy the human mind, we ponder the nature of law, trying to understand its essential properties. What is important about it and what isn't?

In ancient times law was closely associated with morality. It was considered to be the enforcement of what was right. Ancient Jewish law is a good example of this view, as is ancient Greek and Roman law. Although by the time of Socrates the idea was already controversial, the prevalent view continued to be that law was the enforcement of right. Cicero, for example, regarded law as right reason. In the *Laws* he says, "Law [is] the mind and reason of the intelligent man, the standard by which Justice and Injustice are measured." This is the concept of law associated with the theory called natural law. We had a glimpse of this theory in Chapter One, and you may wish to review those materials now.

The greatest systematizer of natural law theory was the thirteenth-century philosopher and theologian St. Thomas Aquinas. According to Aquinas, law is "nothing else than an ordinance of reason for the common good, promulgated by him who has the care of the community." In the *Summa Theologica*, Aquinas lays out the basic priciples of classical natural law theory.

First, natural law is moral law. It is a set of fundamental, objective moral principles that are discoverable by reason. It is our moral conscience, what we know to be right or wrong, provided that we are thinking properly. Natural law is not merely convention or custom or agreement but the laws of morality that we discover in more or less the same way we discover the laws of logic or physics. Natural law is the morality required by right reason.

Second, the rules of human society (which Aquinas called *human law* and which today we often call *positive law*), in other words the laws on the books of any state, are valid only if they do not conflict with the demands of the natural law (or objective morality) — that is, valid law cannot be immoral. There are two interpretations of this point. The strong interpretation says that any unjust law is not a valid law at all; an unjust law is a contradiction in terms. The weak interpretation says only that a legal system to be valid must be more moral than not. To put it another way, a legal system is not legitimate unless, all things considered, it is for the common good.

Third, natural law in some way accords with human nature or is the fulfillment of human nature. This is why it was called the law of nature. (This third point has largely been discarded by modern natural law theorists, but the first two points remain central tenets even today.)

Despite skeptical attacks on it, this theory was the predominant view of law until well into the seventeenth century and has remained strong to this day. It has much to recommend it — primarily, it accounts for the authority of law and it provides guidelines (albeit vague ones) for leaders.

On the other hand, there are difficulties with natural law theory. It rests on some controversial assumptions. First, it assumes that morality is objective and that its objective moral requirements are knowable or discoverable by reason. The theory presupposes that human values are ultimately not contradictory. Finally, it appears to conflate law with morality, to confuse what law is with what law ought to be.

This final point was the focus of attack on natural law theory by nineteenth-century legal positivists. Legal positivism was first set out systematically by John Austin, an English law professor, in 1832. Austin, as a positivist, had two major objections to natural law theory.

First, he argued, there is a sharp distinction between law and morality, so that there is no necessary connection between the two. An unjust law is still a law: It is not a contradiction in terms; it makes perfectly good sense. An illegal law makes no sense; it is incoherent, unintelligible. But an immoral law is coherent, even if it is a bad thing. Furthermore, we can point to examples of immoral laws in any legal system. They are still laws. Thus, natural law theory provides an inaccurate description of law because it confuses what law is with what law ought to be. Law ought to be moral, but in fact it often is not.

Second, Austin states, law can and should be defined and described formally — that is, in terms of its form rather than its content. An accurate description can and should be value neutral. It need not and should not build values into law by placing moral content in the very definition. This is because such analytical moves make jurisprudential theory inaccurate. Law does not in fact have any particular content. Properly so called, however, laws can be identified in terms of their origin or source in the legal system. What makes a legal rule *legal* is not its moral content but its source in the system.

These two points are still the central tenets of legal positivism today, although the character of the formal definition of law has been the subject of considerable debate and change over time. According to Austin, law is the command of a sovereign. A command is the expression of a wish or desire coupled with the likelihood (or threat) of some evil (that is, a sanction) for the failure to comply. A sovereign is a person or body of persons who are habitually obeyed by the bulk of the population but who do not habitually obey anyone else. Legal duty flows from sovereign command, so that sovereign command entails a duty of obedience.

This theory enabled Austin to provide a value-neutral description of law, which distinguishes law from morality, identifies valid law in terms of its source in the legal system, and accounts for independent nations as distinct entities. The theory provides a conceptually clear description of many features of law, but it contains inadequacies. It does not capture the importance of rule and system in law. And it does not clearly distinguish law from coercion, which means that the theory cannot provide a good account of legal rights and legal obligations. Yet it is a powerful theory and remained prominent well into the twentieth century.

In the 1950s a law professor named H. L. A. Hart undertook to reformulate the positivist position by means of a theory that provides the definitive statement of positivism to this day. According to Hart, Austin was right that there is a sharp distinction between law and morality and that law should be defined formally by reference to its source in the legal system, but wrong that law is the command of a sovereign. Hart defined law as a system of rules promulgated according to an authorized set of procedures that are accepted and used by officials and obeyed by the bulk of the population. A mature legal system is a union of primary and secondary rules; primary rules are those that direct conduct (for example, forbid murder), and secondary rules are procedural directives that explain how to identify, change, or adjudicate all the rules of the system. Individual laws are valid because they are traceable to an authoritative source in the system. Legal obligation is accounted for by understanding the nature of rules. Individual laws are binding because they are valid. The system overall (or the ultimate rule of recognition, as Hart puts it) is binding because it is accepted.

This theory provides a certain explanation of the authority of law (that is, it distinguishes law from coercion) by including the idea of accepted rules that are recognized as binding. Yet it maintains the conceptual distinction between law and morality by offering a value-neutral definition of law in terms of its source or form. Hart's theory is a significant improvement over Austin's. It is exceedingly powerful, providing a clear explanation of many features of law, but it too has problems.

First, it is still not clear whether Hart can explain legitimate authority: Why is law entitled to be obeyed? This question is the centerpiece of the continuing debate between positivism and natural law, represented here in the articles by Hart (for positivism) and Ronald Dworkin (for natural law). Dworkin argues against positivism (which he calls *conventionalism*) and for an updated version of natural law (which he calls *naturalism*) by arguing that any good theory of law (or adjudication) must include the values of political morality. It is widely recognized, he points out, that people have rights beyond those recognized by positivist theory and, furthermore, that judges struggle to accommodate such rights. In doing so, Dworkin notes, judges use principles that cannot be characterized as the legal rules which form the centerpiece of Hart's theory. Positivism cannot account for any of these objections.

The second problem with positivism is that although Hart's theory is sophisticated and enlightening, it may not be an adequate description of law. Perhaps law cannot be accounted for entirely in terms of rules. There are other legal standards that do not appear to fit into the logic of rules. And the phenomena of judicial legislation and judicial discretion are not captured well by the positivist focus on rules. Law as a system of rules goes a long way toward capturing the generality of law, but it is not obvious that it can handle the particularity of law.

This second problem is the focus of a twentieth-century jurisprudential movement that is often called *legal realism*. The movement was largely made up of American and Scandinavian judges, law professors, and jurists who were involved in the working process of law. The realists objected to both positivism and natural law theory. Natural law theory, they complained, is too metaphysical, mysterious, and obscurantist. It violates the principle of simplicity. And positivism is formalistic, rigid, static, and overly abstract, but law in fact is fluid, functional, particular, and practical. Law is essentially a social function or phenomenon and should be studied as such — not by the use of logic and abstraction but by sociology and empirical observation.

Thus, the realists emphasize the process, flux, particularity, and uncertainty of law and look especially for a working definition, usually by looking to the function of the courts. How does law look to the lawyer or to the person on the street? Isn't law in essence a practical, social function? A good definition needs to be accessible and useful to people in terms of the function of law as they will encounter it. What, then, is the realist definition of law? There are many definitions, but a small sample should provide the general idea. Llewellyn said that law is what officials do about disputes. Oliver Wendell Holmes characterized law as a prediction of what judges will decide. According to Jerome Frank, law is (1) the specific decisions of judges (actual law) and (2) a prediction of future decisions (probable law). John Chipman Gray defined law as a body of rules laid down by judges according to which they decide legal consequences from facts. Alf Ross explained that valid law is an abstract set of norms that serves as a scheme of interpretation for legal phenomena, or court decisions.

From examples such as these a general picture emerges that exhibits certain salient features. First, legal realism is instrumentalist in approach: Law exists for a purpose; it is a functional process or institution and should be viewed as such. Second, the best theory of law is sociological, not conceptual, so the analytical focus is on the daily interactions of government officials, especially the courts. Third, adjudication, the most enlightening feature of law, is not a deductive process but an intuitive interpretation of data and/or a reflection of social convention. We are not rule governed so much as act governed. The key to understanding law lies in the study of the actions of judges.

From these features we can note that in its extreme form the realist view is that law is essentially what judges say it is, and law is valid because judges say it is (authority derives from the office). All other pronouncements of law (such as statutes, ordinances, and administrative regulations) are more properly considered sources of law (and are essentially predictions of court decisions). In its moderate form realism views law as a process of conflict resolution according to official authority (courts) within the general guidance of a set of recognized norms. John Chipman Gray's essay represents this theory in its most articulate, and moderate, form.

The great virtue of the realist theory is that it provides a dynamic picture of law as a functioning process made up of human beings making decisions in countless particular situations. But for all its emphasis on particularity, how well realism accounts for the generality of law is not clear. Perhaps some combination of the positivist and the realist descriptions of law is what is needed (if such a combination is possible). Furthermore, the realist, like the positivist, does not clearly meet the challenge of natural law.

So although great insights have illuminated the study of the nature of law over time, we are left with two abiding questions. First, what justifies the authority of law? What, if anything, makes state "coercion" legitimate state action? Second, how can we account for the application of general rules in particular cases when we know that particular cases are unique? How does that work, and what justifies it? Until we can answer these basic questions we cannot explain the essential nature of law. Each theory has contributed to our understanding, but none has yet supplied a satisfactory account. Each theory handles certain problems well and others poorly, and each offers insights into the problems of the other two.

The final essay in this section is a critique of all jurisprudence, or legal philosophy, from a feminist perspective. Janet Rifkin represents the new feminist jurisprudence, arguing that law in its present form is the systematic "legitimation" of inequality and, in particular, male dominance. Rifkin is concerned with the relation between law and patriarchy. Recognizing that law has always in fact been a symbol and vehicle of male authority, she inquires into the origin of patriarchy and whether there is a necessary connection between patriarchy and law. Rifkin views law as ideology, characterizing law as the assumption, expression, and enforcement of a particular picture of reality, or worldview. As such, law perpetuates the status quo, particularly male authority. Unless the ideology of law as male domination is challenged, she argues, patriarchy will be perpetuated, even if small inroads are made to correct particular inequalities between men and women.

Not all feminist legal scholarship is alike, but Rifkin's article is representative of a major concern of this scholarship—namely, the relation between law and patriarchy and/or the effect of each on the other. There are some analogies between feminist jurisprudence and legal realism. Both are radical critiques of law, and both focus on the concrete particularities of legal systems. Most important, both feminist jurisprudence and legal realism (especially the modern manifestation of legal realism called *critical legal studies*) argue for or assume that law is ideology, which is to say, law is inherently political. You will notice differences as well. Unlike Gray, Rifkin assumes the purpose of eliminating domination as the proper overriding goal of law. This might be more like a natural law view. Ask yourself whether the feminist critique fits within one of the other theories, whether it might be some combination of them, or whether it is itself a new theory of law.

Notes and Questions

H. L. A. HART, from *The Concept of Law*

1. H. L. A. Hart is the best-known contemporary proponent of the philosophical theory of law called *legal positivism*. His view incorporates the basic features of legal positivism, including: (1) Law and morality are clearly distinguishable. There is no necessary connection between the two. (2) Law is best defined formally—that is, by describing its formal features rather than its content. (3) Legal validity is determined by reference to a law's source in the legal system and not by its content. (4) Legal obligation means that one's case (or act) is covered by a law (or rule) that is recognized as valid. The thrust of all this is to supply a value-neutral definition of law in general. What is Hart's definition? How does he describe law? Is it a plausible description? Is it value neutral?

2. What are the two types of rules Hart describes? Could a legal system exist without both? Could there be a rule of law without both? Hart further divides secondary rules into three types. What are they? Are these distinctions fundamental—exactly how do these types of rules differ from one another? Can you account for constitutional rules using Hart's theory? Does Hart's theory help you understand the structure of a legal system?

3. How does Hart explain the idea of legal obligation? Does his view adequately explain why a law is binding? Does it explain why a law *should* be binding? What is the difference? What does *binding* mean—legally required or morally required? If *legally binding* simply means "subject to

legal penalty for disobedience" and does not include the idea that law *should* be obeyed, then what does legal obligation amount to? Can it be distinguished from coercion? Ask yourself, what *does* legal obligation amount to? How would Hart handle this question?

4. How exactly does Hart account for legal validity? Does this view correspond well with the American model of a legal system? Consider the several forms of government reviewed by Aristotle. Would Hart's view explain all of them? A conceptual theory of law should explain the fundamentals of any legal system.

5. Notice that Hart also explains the transition from a prelegal to a legal community. Is this a descriptive or a normative point? How does it correspond with the ideal of a rule of law? Would an absolute dictatorship be a legal system according to Hart? What limits would have to be placed on the dictator in order for his or her rule to qualify as a legal system? Would the limits be moral limits or some other kind?

[From] *The Concept of Law*

H. L. A. HART

A New Conception of Law

Law as the Union of Primary and Secondary Rules

A Fresh Start

In the last three chapters we have seen that, at various crucial points, the simple model of law as the sovereign's coercive orders failed to reproduce some of the salient features of a legal system. To demonstrate this, we did not find it necessary to invoke (as earlier critics have done) international law or primitive law which some may regard as disputable or borderline examples of law; instead we pointed to certain familiar features of municipal law in a modern state, and showed that these were either distorted or altogether unrepresented in this over-simple theory.

The main ways in which the theory failed are instructive enough to merit a second summary. First, it became clear that though of all the varieties of law, a criminal statute, forbidding or enjoining certain actions under penalty, most resembles orders backed by threats given by one person to others, such a statute nonetheless differs from such orders in the important respect that it commonly applies to those who enact it and not merely to others. Secondly, there are other varieties of law, notably those conferring legal powers to adjudicate or legislate (public powers) or to create or vary legal relations (private powers) which cannot, without absurdity, be construed as orders backed by threats. Thirdly, there are legal rules which differ from orders in their mode of origin, because they are not brought into being by anything analogous to explicit prescription. Finally, the analysis of law in terms of the sovereign, habitually obeyed and necessarily exempt from all legal limitation, failed to account for the continuity of legislative authority characteristic of a modern legal system, and the sovereign, person or persons could not be identified with either the electorate or the legislature of a modern state.

It will be recalled that in thus criticizing the conception of law as the sovereign's coercive orders we considered also a number of ancillary devices which were brought in at the cost of corrupting the primitive simplicity of the theory to rescue it from its difficulties. But these too failed.

One device, the notion of a *tacit* order, seemed to hāve no application to the complex actualities of a modern legal system, but only to very much simpler situations like that of a general who deliberately refrains from interfering with orders given by his subordinates. Other devices, such as that of treating power-conferring rules as mere fragments of rules imposing duties, or treating all rules as directed only to officials, distort the ways in which these are spoken of, thought of, and actually used in social life. This had no better claim to our assent than the theory that all the rules of a game are "really" directions to the umpire and the scorer. The device, designed to reconcile the self-binding character of legislation with the theory that a statute is an order given to *others*, was to distinguish the legislators acting in their official capacity, as *one* person ordering *others* who include themselves in their private capacities. This device, impeccable in itself, involved supplementing the theory with something it does not contain: this is the notion of a rule defining what must be done to legislate; for it is only in conforming with such a rule that legislators have an official capacity and a separate personality to be contrasted with themselves as private individuals.

The last three chapters are therefore the record of a failure and there is plainly need for a fresh start. Yet the failure is an instructive one, worth the detailed consideration we have given it, because at each point where the theory failed to fit the facts it was possible to see at least in outline why it was bound to fail and what is required for a better account. The root cause of failure is that the elements out of which the theory was constructed, viz. the ideas of orders, obedience, habits, and threats, do not include, and cannot by their combination yield, the idea of a rule, without which we cannot hope to elucidate even the most elementary forms of law. It is true that the idea of a rule is by no means a simple one: we have already seen in [a previous discussion] the need, if we are to do justice to the complexity of a legal system, to discriminate between two different though related types. Under rules of the one type, which may well be considered the basic or primary type, human beings are required to do or abstain from certain actions, whether they wish to or not. Rules of the other type are in a

sense parasitic upon or secondary to the first; for they provide that human beings may by doing or saying certain things introduce new rules of the primary type, extinguish or modify old ones, or in various ways determine their incidence or control their operations. Rules of the first type impose duties; rules of the second type confer powers, public or private. Rules of the first type concern actions involving physical movement or changes; rules of the second type provide for operations which lead not merely to physical movement or change, but to the creation or variation of duties or obligations.

We have already given some preliminary analysis of what is involved in the assertion that rules of these two types exist among a given social group, and in this chapter we shall not only carry this analysis a little farther but we shall make the general claim that in the combination of these two types of rule there lies what Austin wrongly claimed to have found in the notion of coercive orders, namely, "the key to the science of jurisprudence." We shall not indeed claim that wherever the word "law" is "properly" used this combination of primary and secondary rules is to be found; for it is clear that the diverse range of cases of which the word "law" is used are not linked by any such simple uniformity, but by less direct relations—often of analogy of either form or content to a central case. What we shall attempt to show, in this and the succeeding chapters, is that most of the features of law which have proved most perplexing and have both provoked and eluded the search for definition can best be rendered clear, if these two types of rule and the interplay between them are understood. We accord this union of elements a central place because of their explanatory power in elucidating the concepts that constitute the framework of legal thought. The justification for the use of the word "law" for a range of apparently heterogeneous cases is a secondary matter which can be undertaken when the central elements have been grasped.

The Idea of Obligation

It will be recalled that the theory of law as coercive orders, notwithstanding its errors, started from the perfectly correct appreciation of the fact that where there is law, there human conduct is made in some sense non-optional or obligatory. In choosing this starting-point the theory was well inspired, and in building up a new account of law in terms of the interplay of primary and secondary rules we too shall start from the same idea. It is, however, here, at this crucial first step, that we have perhaps most to learn from the theory's errors.

Let us recall the gunman situation. A orders B to hand over his money and threatens to shoot him if he does not comply. According to the theory of coercive orders this situation illustrates the notion of obligation or duty in general. Legal obligation is to be found in this situation writ large; A must be the sovereign habitually obeyed and the orders must be general, prescribing courses of conduct not single actions. The plausibility of the claim that the gunman situation displays the meaning of obligation lies in the fact that it is certainly one in which we would say that B, if he obeyed, was "obliged" to hand over his money. It is, however, equally certain that we should misdescribe the situation if we said, on these facts, that B "had an obligation" or a "duty" to hand over the money. So from the start it is clear that we need something else for an understanding of the idea of obligation. There is a difference, yet to be explained, between the assertion that someone *was obliged* to do something and the assertion that he *had an obligation* to do it. The first is often a statement about the beliefs and motives with which an action is done: B was obliged to hand over his money may simply mean, as it does in the gunman case, that he believed that some harm or other unpleasant consequences would befall him if he did not hand it over and he handed it over to avoid those consequences. In such cases the prospect of what would happen to the agent if he disobeyed has rendered something he would otherwise have preferred to have done (keep the money) less eligible.

Two further elements slightly complicate the elucidation of the notion of being obliged to do something. It seems clear that we should not think of B as obliged to hand over the money if the threatened harm was, according to common judgements, trivial in comparison with the disadvantage or serious consequences, either for B or for others, of complying with the orders, as it would be, for example, if A merely threatened to pinch B. Nor perhaps should we say that B was obliged, if there were no reasonable grounds for thinking that A could or would probably implement his threat of relatively serious harm. Yet, though such references to common judgments of comparative harm and reasonable estimates of likelihood, are implicit in this notion, the statement that a person was obliged to obey someone is, in the main, a psychological one referring to the beliefs and motives with which an action was done. But the statement that someone *had an obligation* to do something is of a very different type and there are many signs of this difference. Thus not only is it the case that the facts about B's action and his beliefs and motives in the gunman case, though sufficient to warrant the statement that B was obliged to hand over his purse, are *not sufficient* to warrant the statement that he had an obligation to do this; it is also the case that facts of this sort, i.e. facts about beliefs and motives, are *not necessary* for the truth of a statement that a person had an obligation to do something. Thus the statement that a person had an obligation, e.g. to tell the truth or report for military service, remains true even if he believed (reasonably or unreasonably) that he would never be found out and had nothing to fear from disobedience. Moreover, whereas the statement that he had this obligation is quite independent of the question whether or not he in fact reported for service, the statement that someone was obliged to do something, normally carries the implication that he actually did it.

Some theorists, Austin among them, seeing perhaps the general irrelevance of the person's beliefs, fears, and motives to the question whether he had an obligation to do something, have defined this notion not in terms of these subjective facts, but in terms of the *chance* or *likelihood* that the person having the obligation will suffer a punishment or "evil" at the hands of others in the event of disobedience. This, in effect, treats statements of obligation not as psychological statements but as predictions or assessments of chances of incurring punishment or "evil." To many later theorists this has appeared as a revelation, bringing down to earth an elusive notion and restating it in the same clear, hard, empirical terms as are used in science. It has, indeed, been accepted sometimes as the only alternative to metaphysical conceptions of obligation or duty as invisible objects mysteriously existing "above" or "behind" the world of ordinary, observable facts. But there are many reasons for rejecting this interpretation of statements of obligation as predictions, and it is not, in fact, the only alternative to obscure metaphysics.

The fundamental objection is that the predictive interpretation obscures the fact that, where rules exist, deviations from them are not merely grounds for a prediction that hostile reactions will follow or that a court will apply sanctions to those who break them, but are also a reason or justification for such reaction and for applying the sanctions. We have already drawn attention in [a previous discussion] to this neglect of the internal aspect of rules and we shall elaborate it later in this chapter.

There is, however, a second, simpler, objection to the predictive interpretation of obligation. If it were true that the statement that a person had an obligation meant that *he* was likely to suffer in the event of disobedience, it would be a contradiction to say that he had an obligation, e.g. to report for military service but that, owing to the fact that he had escaped from the jurisdiction, or had successfully bribed the police or the court, there was not the slightest chance of his being caught or made to suffer. In fact, there is no contradiction in saying this, and such statements are often made and understood.

It is, of course, true that in a normal legal system, where sanctions are exacted for a high proportion of offences, an offender usually runs a risk of punishment; so, usually the statement that a person has an obligation and the statement that he is likely to suffer for disobedience will both be true together. Indeed, the connexion between these two statements is somewhat stronger than this: at least in a municipal system it may well be true that, unless *in general* sanctions were likely to be exacted from offenders, there would be little or no point in making particular statements about a person's obligations. In this sense, such statements may be said to presuppose belief in the continued normal operation of the system of sanctions much as the statement "he is out" in cricket presupposes, though it does not assert, that players, umpire, and scorer will probably take the usual steps. Nonetheless, it is crucial for

the understanding of the idea of obligation to see that in individual cases the statement that a person has an obligation under some rule and the prediction that he is likely to suffer for disobedience may diverge.

It is clear that obligation is not to be found in the gunman situation, though the simpler notion of being obliged to do something may well be defined in the elements present there. To understand the general idea of obligation as a necessary preliminary to understanding it in its legal form, we must turn to a different social situation which, unlike the gunman situation, includes the existence of social rules; for this situation contributes to the meaning of the statement that a person has an obligation in two ways. First, the existence of such rules, making certain types of behaviour a standard, is the normal, though unstated, background or proper context for such a statement; and, secondly, the distinctive function of such statement is to apply such a general rule to a particular person by calling attention to the fact that his case falls under it. We have already seen in [a previous discussion] that there is involved in the existence of any social rules a combination of regular conduct with a distinctive attitude to that conduct as a standard. We have also seen the main ways in which these differ from mere social habits, and how the varied normative vocabulary ("ought," "must," "should") is used to draw attention to the standard and to deviations from it, and to formulate the demands, criticisms, or acknowledgements which may be based on it. Of this class of normative words the words "obligation" and "duty" form an important sub-class, carrying with them certain implications not usually present in the others. Hence, though a grasp of the elements generally differentiating social rules from mere habits is certainly indispensable for understanding the notion of obligation or duty, it is not sufficient by itself.

The statement that someone has or is under an obligation does indeed imply the existence of a rule; yet it is not always the case that where rules exist the standard of behaviour required by them is conceived of in terms of obligation. "He ought to have" and "He had an obligation to" are not always interchangeable expressions, even though they are alike in carrying an implicit reference to existing standards of conduct or are used in drawing conclusions in particular cases from a general rule. Rules of etiquette or correct speech are certainly rules: they are more than convergent habits or regularities of behaviour; they are taught and efforts are made to maintain them; they are used in criticizing our own and other people's behaviour in the characteristic normative vocabulary. "You ought to take your hat off," "It is wrong to say 'you was.'" But to use in connexion with rules of this kind the words "obligation" or "duty" would be misleading and not merely stylistically odd. It would misdescribe a social situation; for though the line separating rules of obligation from others is at points a vague one, yet the main rationale of the distinction is fairly clear.

Rules are conceived and spoken of as imposing obligations when the general demand for conformity is insistent and the social pressure brought to bear upon those who deviate or threaten to deviate is great. Such rules may be wholly customary in origin: there may be no centrally organized system of punishments for breach of the rules; the social pressure may take only the form of a general diffused hostile or critical reaction which may stop short of physical sanctions. It may be limited to verbal manifestations of disapproval or of appeals to the individuals' respect for the rule violated; it may depend heavily on the operation of feelings of shame, remorse, and guilt. When the pressure is of this last-mentioned kind we may be inclined to classify the rules as part of the morality of the social group and the obligation under the rules as moral obligation. Conversely, when physical sanctions are prominent or usual among the forms of pressure, even though these are neither closely defined nor administered by officials but are left to the community at large, we shall be inclined to classify the rules as a primitive or rudimentary form of law. We may, of course, find both these types of serious social pressure behind what is, in an obvious sense, the same rule of conduct; sometimes this may occur with no indication that one of them is peculiarly appropriate as primary and the other secondary, and then the question whether we are confronted with a rule of morality or rudimentary law may not be susceptible of an answer. But for the moment the possibility of drawing the line between law and morals need

not detain us. What is important is that the insistence on importance or *seriousness* of social pressure behind the rules is the primary factor determining whether they are thought of as giving rise to obligations.

Two other characteristics of obligation go naturally together with this primary one. The rules supported by this serious pressure are thought important because they are believed to be necessary to the maintenance of social life or some highly prized feature of it. Characteristically, rules so obviously essential as those which restrict the free use of violence are thought of in terms of obligation. So too rules which require honesty or truth or require the keeping of promises, or specify what is to be done by one who performs a distinctive role or function in the social group are thought of in terms of either "obligation" or perhaps more often "duty." Secondly, it is generally recognized that the conduct required by these rules may, while benefiting others, conflict with what the person who owes the duty may wish to do. Hence obligations and duties are thought of as characteristically involving sacrifice or renunciation, and the standing possibility of conflict between obligation or duty and interest is, in all societies, among the truisms of both the lawyer and the moralist.

The figure of a *bond* binding the person obligated, which is buried in the word "obligation," and the similar notion of a debt latent in the word "duty" are explicable in terms of these three factors, which distinguish rules of obligation or duty from other rules. In this figure, which haunts much legal thought, the social pressure appears as a chain binding those who have obligations so that they are not free to do what they want. The other end of the chain is sometimes held by the group of their official representatives, who insist on performance or exact the penalty: sometimes it is entrusted by the group to a private individual who may choose whether or not to insist on performance or its equivalent in value to him. The first situation typifies the duties or obligations of criminal law and the second those of civil law where we think of private individuals having rights correlative to the obligations.

Natural and perhaps illuminating though these figures or metaphors are, we must not allow them to trap us into a misleading conception of obligation as essentially consisting in some feeling of pressure or compulsion experienced by those who have obligations. The fact that rules of obligation are generally supported by serious social pressure does not entail that to have an obligation under the rules is to experience feelings of compulsion or pressure. Hence there is no contradiction in saying of some hardened swindler, and it may often be true, that he had an obligation to pay the rent but felt no pressure to pay when he made off without doing so. To *feel* obliged and to have an obligation are different though frequently concomitant things. To identify them would be one way of misinterpreting, in terms of psychological feelings, the important internal aspect of rules to which we drew attention in [a previous discussion].

Indeed, the internal aspect of rules is something to which we must again refer before we can dispose finally of the claims of the predictive theory. For an advocate of that theory may well ask why, if social pressure is so important a feature of rules of obligation, we are yet so concerned to stress the inadequacies of the predictive theory; for it gives this very feature a central place by defining obligation in terms of the likelihood that threatened punishment or hostile reaction will follow deviation from certain lines of conduct. The difference may seem slight between the analysis of a statement of obligation as a prediction, or assessment of the chances, of hostile reaction to deviation, and our own contention that though this statement presupposes a background in which deviations from rules are generally met by hostile reactions, yet its characteristic use is not to predict this but to say that a person's case falls under such a rule. In fact, however, this difference is not a slight one. Indeed, until its importance is grasped, we cannot properly understand the whole distinctive style of human thought, speech, and action which is involved in the existence of rules and which constitutes the normative structure of society.

The following contrast again in terms of the "internal" and "external" aspect of rules may serve to mark what gives this distinction its great importance for the understanding not only of law but of the structure of any society. When a social group has certain rules of conduct, this fact affords an opportunity for many closely related yet different kinds of assertion; for it is possible to be concerned with the rules, either merely as an observer who does not himself accept them, or as a member of the group which accepts and uses them as guides to conduct. We may call these respectively the "external" and the "internal points of view." Statements made from the external point of view may themselves be of different kinds. For the observer may, without accepting the rules himself, assert that the group accepts the rules, and thus may from outside refer to the way in which *they* are concerned with them from the internal point of view. But whatever the rules are, whether they are those of games, like chess or cricket, or moral or legal rules, we can if we choose occupy the position of an observer who does not even refer in this way to the internal point of view of the group. Such an observer is content merely to record the regularities of observable behaviour in which conformity with the rules partly consists and those further regularities, in the form of the hostile reaction, reproofs, or punishments, with which deviations from the rules are met. After a time the external observer may, on the basis of the regularities observed, correlate deviation with hostile reaction, and be able to predict with a fair measure of success, and to assess the chances that a deviation from the group's normal behaviour will meet with hostile reaction or punishment. Such knowledge may not only reveal much about the group, but might enable him to live among them without unpleasant consequences which would attend one who attempted to do so without such knowledge.

If, however, the observer really keeps austerely to this extreme external point of view and does not give any account of the manner in which members of the group who accept the rules view their own regular behaviour, his description of their life cannot be in terms of rules at all, and so not in the terms of the rule-dependent notions of obligation or duty. Instead, it will be in terms of observable regularities of conduct, predictions, probabilities, and signs. For such an observer, deviations by a member of the group from normal conduct will be a sign that hostile reaction is likely to follow, and nothing more. His view will be like the view of one who, having observed the working of a traffic signal in a busy street for some time, limits himself to saying that when the light turns red there is a high probability that the traffic will stop. He treats the light merely as a natural *sign that* people will behave in certain ways, as clouds are a *sign that* rain will come. In so doing he will miss out a whole dimension of the social life of those whom he is watching, since for them the red light is not merely a sign that others will stop: they look upon it as a *signal for* them to stop, and so a reason for stopping in conformity to rules which make stopping when the light is red a standard of behaviour and an obligation. To mention this is to bring into the account the way in which the group regards its own behaviour. It is to refer to the internal aspect of rules seen from their internal point of view.

The external point of view may very nearly reproduce the way in which the rules function in the lives of certain members of the group, namely those who reject its rules and are only concerned with them when and because they judge that unpleasant consequences are likely to follow violation. Their point of view will need for its expression, "I was obliged to do it," "I am likely to suffer for it if . . . ," "You will probably suffer for it if . . . ," "They will do that to you if. . . ." But they will not need forms of expression like "I had an obligation" or "You have an obligation" for these are required only by those who see their own and other persons' conduct from the internal point of view. What the external point of view, which limits itself to the observable regularities of behaviour, cannot reproduce is the way in which the rules function as rules in the lives of those who normally are the majority of society. These are the officials, lawyers, or private persons who use them, in one situation after another, as guides to the conduct of social life, as the basis for claims, demands, admissions, criticism, or punishment, viz., in all the familiar transactions of life according to rules. For them the violation of a rule is not merely a basis for the prediction that a hostile reaction will follow but a *reason* for hostility.

At any given moment the life of any society which lives by rules, legal or not, is likely to consist in a tension between those who, on the one hand, accept and voluntarily co-operate in maintaining the rules, and so see their own and other persons' behaviour in terms of the rules, and those who, on the other hand, reject the rules and attend to them only from the external point of view as a sign of possible punishment. One of the difficulties facing any legal theory anxious to do justice to the complexity of the facts is to remember the presence of both these points of view and not to define one of them out of existence. Perhaps all our criticisms of the predictive theory of obligation may be best summarized as the accusation that this is what it does to the internal aspect of obligatory rules.

The Elements of Law

It is, of course, possible to imagine a society without a legislature, courts or officials of any kind. Indeed, there are many studies of primitive communities which not only claim that this possibility is realized but depict in detail the life of a society where the only means of social control is that general attitude of the group towards its own standard modes of behaviour in terms of which we have characterized rules of obligation. A social structure of this kind is often referred to as one of "custom"; but we shall not use this term, because it often implies that the customary rules are very old and supported with less social pressure than other rules. To avoid these implications we shall refer to such a social structure as one of primary rules of obligation. If a society is to live by such primary rules alone, there are certain conditions which, granted a few of the most obvious truisms about human nature and the world we live in, must clearly be satisfied. The first of these conditions is that the rules must contain in some form restrictions on the free use of violence, theft, and deception to which human beings are tempted but which they must, in general, repress, if they are to coexist in close proximity to each other. Such rules are in fact always found in the primitive societies of which we have knowledge, together with a variety of others imposing on individuals various positive duties to perform services or make contributions to the common life. Secondly, though such a society may exhibit the tension, already described, between those who accept the rules and those who reject the rules except where fear of social pressure induces them to conform, it is plain that the latter cannot be more than a minority, if so loosely organized a society of persons, approximately equal in physical strength, is to endure: for otherwise those who reject the rules would have too little social pressure to fear. This too is confirmed by what we know of primitive communities where, though there are dissidents and malefactors, the majority live by the rules seen from the internal point of view.

More important for our present purpose is the following consideration. It is plain that only a small community closely knit by ties of kinship, common sentiment, and belief, and placed in a stable environment, could live successfully by such a régime of unofficial rules. In any other conditions such a simple form of social control must prove defective and will require supplementation in different ways. In the first place, the rules by which the group lives will not form a system, but will simply be a set of separate standards, without any identifying or common mark, except of course that they are the rules which a particular group of human beings accepts. They will in this respect resemble our own rules of etiquette. Hence if doubts arise as to what the rules are or as to the precise scope of some given rule, there will be no procedure for settling this doubt, either by reference to an authoritative text or to an official whose declarations on this point are authoritative. For, plainly, such a procedure and the acknowledgement of either authoritative text or persons involve the existence of rules of a type different from the rules of obligation or duty which *ex hypothesi* are all that the group has. This defect in the simple social structure of primary rules we may call its *uncertainty*.

A second defect is the *static* character of the rules. The only mode of change in the rules known to such a society will be the slow process of growth, whereby courses of conduct once thought optional become first habitual or usual, and then obligatory, and the converse process of decay, when deviations, once severely dealt with, are first tolerated and then pass unnoticed. There will be no means, in such a society, of deliberately adapting the rules to changing circumstances, either by eliminating old rules or introducing new ones: for, again, the possibility of doing this presupposes the existence of rules of a different type from the primary rules of obligation by which alone the society lives. In an extreme case the rules may be static in a more drastic sense. This, though never perhaps fully realized in any actual community, is worth considering because the remedy for it is something very characteristic of law. In this extreme case, not only would there be no way of deliberately changing the general rules, but the obligations which arise under the rules in particular cases could not be varied or modified by the deliberate choice of any individual. Each individual would simply have fixed obligations or duties to do or abstain from doing certain things. It might indeed very often be the case that others would benefit from the performance of these obligations; yet if there are only primary rules of obligation they would have no power to release those bound from performance or to transfer to others the benefits which would accrue from performance. For such operations of release or transfer create changes in the initial positions of individuals under the primary rules of obligation, and for these operations to be possible there must be rules of a sort different from the primary rules.

The third defect of this simple form of social life is the *inefficiency* of the diffuse social pressure by which the rules are maintained. Disputes as to whether an admitted rule has or has not been violated will always occur and will, in any but the smallest societies, continue interminably, if there is no agency specially empowered to ascertain finally, and authoritatively, the fact of violation. Lack of such final and authoritative determinations is to be distinguished from another weakness associated with it. This is the fact that punishments for violations of the rules, and other forms of social pressure involving physical effort or the use of force, are not administered by a special agency but are left to the individuals affected or to the group at large. It is obvious that the waste of time involved in the group's unorganized efforts to catch and punish offenders, and the smouldering vendettas which may result from self help in the absence of an official monopoly of "sanctions," may be serious. The history of law does, however, strongly suggest that the lack of official agencies to determine authoritatively the fact of violation of the rules is a much more serious defect; for many societies have remedies for this defect long before the other.

The remedy for each of these three main defects in this simplest form of social structure consists in supplementing the *primary* rules of obligation with *secondary* rules which are rules of a different kind. The introduction of the remedy for each defect might, in itself, be considered a step from the pre-legal into the legal world; since each remedy brings with it many elements that permeate law: certainly all three remedies together are enough to convert the régime of primary rules into what is indisputably a legal system. We shall consider in turn each of these remedies and show why law may most illuminatingly be characterized as a union of primary rules of obligation with such secondary rules. Before we do this, however, the following general points should be noted. Though the remedies consist in the introduction of rules which are certainly different from each other, as well as from the primary rules of obligation which they supplement, they have important features in common and are connected in various ways. Thus they may all be said to be on a different level from the primary rules, for they are all *about* such rules; in the sense that while primary rules are concerned with the actions that individuals must or must not do, these secondary rules are all concerned with the primary rules themselves. They specify the ways in which the primary rules may be conclusively ascertained, introduced, eliminated, varied, and the fact of their violation conclusively determined.

The simplest form of remedy for the *uncertainty* of the régime of primary rules is the introduction of what we shall call a "rule of recognition." This will specify some feature or features possession of which by a suggested rule is taken as a conclusive affirmative indication that it is a rule of the group to be supported by the social pressure it exerts. The existence of such a rule of recognition may take any of a huge variety of forms, simple or complex. It may, as in the early law of many societies, be no more than that an authoritative list or text of the rules is to be found in a written document or carved on some public monument. No doubt as a matter of history this step from the pre-legal to the legal may be accomplished in distinguishable stages, of which the first is the mere reduction to writing of hitherto unwritten rules. This is not itself the crucial step, though it is a very important one: what is crucial is the acknowledgement of reference to the writing or inscription as *authoritative*, i.e. as the *proper* way of disposing of doubts as to the existence of the rule. Where there is such an acknowledgement there is a very simple form of secondary rule: a rule for conclusive identification of the primary rules of obligation.

In a developed legal system the rules of recognition are of course more complex; instead of identifying rules exclusively by reference to a text or list they do so by reference to some general characteristic possessed by the primary rules. This may be the fact of their having been enacted by a specific body, or their long customary practice, or their relation to judicial decisions. Moreover, where more than one of such general characteristics are treated as identifying criteria, provision may be made for their possible conflict by their arrangement in an order of superiority, as by the common subordination of custom or precedent to statute, the latter being a "superior source" of law. Such complexity may make the rules of recognition in a modern legal system seem very different from the simple acceptance of an authoritative text: yet even in this simplest form, such a rule brings with it many elements distinctive of law. By providing an authoritative mark it introduces, although in embryonic form, the idea of a legal system: for the rules are now not just a discrete unconnected set but are, in a simple way, unified. Further, in the simple operation of identifying a given rule as possessing the required feature of being an item on an authoritative list of rules we have the germ of the idea of legal validity.

The remedy for the *static* quality of the régime of primary rules consists in the introduction of what we shall call "rules of change." The simplest form of such a rule is that which empowers an individual or body of persons to introduce new primary rules for the conduct of the life of the group, or of some class within it, and to eliminate old rules. As we have already argued in [a previous discussion] it is in terms of such a rule, and not in terms of orders backed by threats, that the ideas of legislative enactment and repeal are to be understood. Such rules of change may be very simple or very complex: the powers conferred may be unrestricted or limited in various ways: and the rules may, besides specifying the persons who are to legislate, define in more or less rigid terms the procedure to be followed in legislation. Plainly, there will be a very close connexion between the rules of change and the rules of recognition: for where the former exists the latter will necessarily incorporate a reference to legislation as an identifying feature of the rules, though it need not refer to all the details of procedure involved in legislation. Usually some official certificate or official copy will, under the rules of recognition, be taken as a sufficient proof of due enactment. Of course if there is a social structure so simple that the only "source of law" is legislation, the rule of recognition will simply specify enactment as the unique identifying mark or criterion of validity of the rules. This will be the case for example in the imaginary kingdom of Rex I depicted in [a previous discussion]: there the rule of recognition would simply be that whatever Rex I enacts is law.

We have already described in some detail the rules which confer on individuals power to vary their initial positions under the primary rules. Without such private power-conferring rules society would lack some of the chief amenities which law confers upon it. For the operations which these rules make possible are the making of wills, contracts, transfers of property, and many other voluntarily created structures of rights and duties which typify life under law, though of course an elementary form of power-conferring rule also underlies the moral institution of a promise. The kinship of these rules with the rules of change involved in the notion of legislation is clear, and as recent theory such as Kelsen's has shown, many of the features which puzzle us in the institutions of contract or property are clarified by thinking of the operations of making a contract or transferring property as the exercise of limited legislative powers by individuals.

The third supplement to the simple régime of primary rules, intended to remedy the *inefficiency* of its diffused social pressure, consists of secondary rules empowering individuals to make authoritative determinations of the question whether, on a particular occasion, a primary rule has been broken. The minimal form of adjudication consists in such determinations, and we shall call the secondary rules which confer the power to make them "rules of adjudication." Besides identifying the individuals who are to adjudicate, such rules will also define the procedure to be followed. Like the other secondary rules these are on a different level from the primary rules: though they may be reinforced by further rules imposing duties on judges to adjudicate, they do not impose duties but confer judicial powers and a special status on judicial declarations about the breach of obligations. Again these rules, like the other secondary rules, define a group of important legal concepts: in this case the concepts of judge or court, jurisdiction and judgment. Besides these resemblances to the other secondary rules, rules of adjudication have intimate connexions with them. Indeed, a system which has rules of adjudication is necessarily also committed to a rule of recognition of an elementary and imperfect sort. This is so because, if courts are empowered to make authoritative determinations of the fact that a rule has been broken, these cannot avoid being taken as authoritative determinations of what the rules are. So the rule which confers jurisdiction will also be a rule of recognition, identifying the primary rules through the judgments of the courts and these judgments will become a "source" of law. It is true that this form of rule of recognition, inseparable from the minimum form of jurisdiction, will be very imperfect. Unlike an authoritative text or a statute book, judgments may not be couched in general terms and their use as authoritative guides to the rules depends on a somewhat shaky inference from particular decisions, and the reliability of this must fluctuate both with the skill of the interpreter and the consistency of the judges.

It need hardly be said that in few legal systems are judicial powers confined to authoritative determinations of the fact of violation of the primary rules. Most systems have, after some delay, seen the advantages of further centralization of social pressure; and have partially prohibited the use of physical punishments or violent self help by private individuals. Instead they have supplemented the primary rules of obligation by further secondary rules, specifying or at least limiting the penalties for violation, and have conferred upon judges, where they have ascertained the fact of violation, the exclusive power to direct the application of penalties by other officials. These secondary rules provide the centralized official "sanctions" of the system.

If we stand back and consider the structure which has resulted from the combination of primary rules of obligation with the secondary rules of recognition, change and adjudication, it is plain that we have here not only the heart of a legal system, but a most powerful tool for the analysis of much that has puzzled both the jurist and the political theorist.

Not only are the specifically legal concepts with which the lawyer is professionally concerned, such as those of obligation and rights, validity and source of law, legislation and jurisdiction, and sanction, best elucidated in terms of this combination of elements. The concepts (which bestride both law and political theory) of the state, of authority, and of an official require a similar analysis if the obscurity which still lingers about them is to be dissipated. The reason why an analysis in these terms of primary and secondary rules has this explanatory power is not far to seek. Most of the obscurities and distortions surrounding legal and political concepts arise from the fact that these essentially involve reference to what we have called the internal point of view: the view of those who do not merely record and predict behavior conforming to rules, but *use* the rules as standards for the appraisal of their own and others' behaviour. This requires more detailed attention in the analysis of legal and political concepts than it has usually received. Under the simple régime of primary rules the internal point of view is manifested in its simplest form, in the use of those rules as the basis of criticism, and as the justification of demands for conformity, social pressure, and punishment. Reference to this most elementary manifestation of the internal point of view is required for the analysis of the basic concepts of obligation and duty. With the addition to the system of secondary rules, the range of what is said and done from the internal point of view is much extended and diversified. With this extension comes a whole set of new concepts and they demand a reference to the internal point of view for their analysis. These include the notions of legislation, jurisdiction, validity and, generally, of legal powers, private and public.

There is a constant pull towards an analysis of these in the terms of ordinary or "scientific," fact-stating or predictive discourse. But this can only reproduce their external aspect: to do justice to their distinctive, internal aspect we need to see the different ways in which the law-making operations of the legislator, the adjudication of a court, the exercise of private or official powers, and other "acts-in-the-law" are related to secondary rules.

In [a subsequent discussion] we shall show how the ideas of the validity of law and sources of law, and the truths latent among the errors of the doctrines of sovereignty may be rephrased and clarified in terms of rules of recognition. But we shall conclude this chapter with a warning: though the combination of primary and secondary rules merits, because it explains many aspects of law, the central place assigned to it, this cannot by itself illuminate every problem. The union of primary and secondary rules is at the centre of a legal system; but it is not the whole, and as we move away from the centre we shall have to accommodate, in ways indicated in later chapters, elements of a different character.

The Foundations of a Legal System

Rule of Recognition and Legal Validity

According to the theory criticized in [a previous discussion] the foundations of a legal system consist of the situation in which the majority of a social group habitually obey the orders backed by threats of the sovereign person or persons, who themselves habitually obey no one. This social situation is, for this theory, both a necessary and a sufficient condition of the existence of law. We have already exhibited in some detail the incapacity of this theory to account for some of the salient features of a modern municipal legal system: yet nonetheless, as its hold over the minds of many thinkers suggests, it does contain, though in a blurred and misleading form, certain truths about certain important aspects of law. These truths can, however, only be clearly presented, and their importance rightly assessed, in terms of the more complex social situation where a secondary rule of recognition is accepted and used for the identification of primary rules of obligation. It is this situation which deserves, if anything does, to be called the foundations of a legal system. In this chapter we shall discuss various elements of this situation which have received only partial or misleading expression in the theory of sovereignty and elsewhere.

Wherever such a rule of recognition is accepted both private persons and officials are provided with authoritative criteria for identifying primary rules of obligation. The criteria so provided may, as we have seen, take any one or more of a variety of forms: these include reference to an authoritative text; to legislative enactment; to customary practice; to general declarations of specified persons, or to past judicial decisions in particular cases. In a very simple system like the world of Rex I depicted in [a previous discussion], where only what he enacts is law and no legal limitations upon his legislative power are imposed by customary rule or constitutional document, the sole criterion for identifying the law will be a simple reference to fact of enactment by Rex I. The existence of this simple form of rule of recognition will be manifest in the general practice, on the part of officials or private persons, of identifying the rules by this criterion. In a modern legal system where there are a variety of "sources" of law, the rule of recognition is correspondingly more complex: the criteria for identifying the law are multiple and commonly include a written constitution, enactment by a legislature, and judicial precedents. In most cases, provision is made for possible conflict by ranking these criteria in an order of relative subordination and primacy. It is in this way that in our system "common law" is subordinate to "statute."

It is important to distinguish this relative *subordination* of one criterion to another from *derivation*, since some spurious support for the view that all law is essentially or "really" (even if only "tacitly") the product of legislation, has been gained from confusion of these two ideas. In our own system, custom and precedent are subordinate to legislation since customary and common law rules may be deprived of their status as law by statute. Yet they owe their status of law, precarious as this may be, not to a "tacit" exercise of legislative power but to the acceptance of a rule of recognition which accords them this independent though subordinate place. Again, as in the simple case, the existence of

such a complex rule of recognition with this hierarchical ordering of distinct criteria is manifested in the general practice of identifying the rules by such criteria.

In the day-to-day life of a legal system its rule of recognition is very seldom expressly formulated as a rule; though occasionally, courts in England may announce in general terms the relative place of one criterion of law in relation to another, as when they assert the supremacy of Acts of Parliament over other sources or suggested sources of law. For the most part the rule of recognition is not stated, but its existence is *shown* in the way in which particular rules are identified, either by courts or other officials or private persons or their advisers. There is, of course, a difference in the use made by courts of the criteria provided by the rule and the use of them by others: for when courts reach a particular conclusion on the footing that a particular rule has been correctly identified as law, what they say has a special authoritative status conferred on it by other rules. In this respect, as in many others, the rule of recognition of a legal system is like the scoring rule of a game. In the course of the game the general rule defining the activities which constitute scoring (runs, goals, &c.) is seldom formulated; instead it is *used* by officials and players in identifying the particular phases which count towards winning. Here too, the declarations of officials (umpire or scorer) have a special authoritative status attributed to them by other rules. Further, in both cases there is the possibility of a conflict between these authoritative applications of the rule and the general understanding of what the rule plainly requires according to its terms. This, as we shall see later, is a complication which must be catered for in any account of what it is for a system of rules of this sort to exist.

The use of unstated rules of recognition, by courts and others, in identifying particular rules of the system is characteristic of the internal point of view. Those who use them in this way thereby manifest their own acceptance of them as guiding rules and with this attitude there goes a characteristic vocabulary different from the natural expressions of the external point of view. Perhaps the simplest of these is the expression, "It is the law that . . . ," which we may find on the lips not only of judges, but of ordinary men living under a legal system, when they identify a given rule of the system. This, like the expression "Out" or "Goal," is the language of one assessing a situation by reference to rules which he in common with others acknowledges as appropriate for this purpose. This attitude of shared acceptance of rules is to be contrasted with that of an observer who records *ab extra* the fact that a social group accepts such rules but does not himself accept them. The natural expression of this external point of view is not "It is the law that . . ." but "In England they recognize as law . . . whatever the Queen in Parliament enacts. . . ." The first of these forms of expression we shall call an *internal statement* because it manifests the internal point of view and is naturally used by one who, accepting the rule of recognition and without stating the fact that it is accepted, applies the rule in recognizing some particular rule of the system as valid. The second form of expression we shall call an *external statement* because it is the natural language of an external observer of the system who, without himself accepting its rule of recognition, states the fact that others accept it.

If this use of an accepted rule of recognition in making internal statements is understood and carefully distinguished from an external statement of fact that the rule is accepted, many obscurities concerning the notion of legal "validity" disappear. For the word "valid" is most frequently, though not always, used, in just such internal statements, applying to a particular rule of a legal system, an unstated but accepted rule of recognition. To say that a given rule is valid is to recognize it as passing all the tests provided by the rule of recognition and so as a rule of the system. We can indeed simply say that the statement that a particular rule is valid means that it satisfies all the criteria provided by the rule of recognition. This is incorrect only to the extent that it might obscure the internal character of such statements; for, like the cricketers' "Out," these statements of validity normally apply to a particular case a rule of recognition accepted by the speaker and others, rather than expressly state that the rule is satisfied.

Some of the puzzles connected with the idea of legal validity are said to concern the relation between the validity and the "efficacy" of law. If by "efficacy" is meant that the fact that a rule of

law which requires certain behaviour is obeyed more often than not, it is plain that there is no necessary connexion between the validity of any particular rule and *its* efficacy, unless the rule of recognition of the system includes among its criteria, as some do, the provision (sometimes referred to as a rule of obsolescence) that no rule is to count as a rule of the system if it has long ceased to be efficacious.

From the inefficacy of a particular rule, which may or may not count against its validity, we must distinguish a general disregard of the rules of the system. This may be so complete in character and so protracted that we should say, in the case of a new system, that it had never established itself as the legal system of a given group, or, in the case of a once-established system, that it had ceased to be the legal system of the group. In either case, the normal context or background for making any internal statement in terms of the rules of the system is absent. In such cases it would be generally *pointless* either to assess the rights and duties of particular persons by reference to the primary rules of a system or to assess the validity of any of its rules by reference to its rules of recognition. To insist on applying a system of rules which had either never actually been effective or had been discarded would, except in special circumstances mentioned below, be as futile as to assess the progress of a game by reference to a scoring rule which had never been accepted or had been discarded.

One who makes an internal statement concerning the validity of a particular rule of a system may be said to *presuppose* the truth of the external statement of fact that the system is generally efficacious. For the normal use of internal statements is in such a context of general efficacy. It would however be wrong to say that statements of validity "mean" that the system is generally efficacious. For though it is normally pointless or idle to talk of the validity of a rule of a system which has never established itself or has been discarded, none the less it is not meaningless nor is it always pointless. One vivid way of teaching Roman Law is to speak *as if* the system were efficacious still and to discuss the validity of particular rules and solve problems in their terms; and one way of nursing hopes for the restoration of an old social order destroyed by revolution, and rejecting the new, is to cling to the criteria of legal validity of the old régime. This is implicitly done by the White Russian who still claims property under some rule of descent which was a valid rule of Tsarist Russia.

A grasp of the normal contextual connexion between the internal statement that a given rule of a system is valid and the external statement of fact that the system is generally efficacious, will help us see in its proper perspective the common theory that to assert the validity of a rule is to predict that it will be enforced by courts or some other official action taken. In many ways this theory is similar to the predictive analysis of obligation which we considered and rejected in [a previous discussion]. In both cases alike the motive for advancing this predictive theory is the conviction that only thus can metaphysical interpretations be avoided: that either a statement that a rule is valid must ascribe some mysterious property which cannot be detected by empirical means or it must be a prediction of future behaviour of officials. In both cases also the plausibility of the theory is due to the same important fact: that the truth of the external statement of fact, which an observer might record, that the system is generally efficacious and likely to continue so, is normally presupposed by anyone who accepts the rules and makes an internal statement of obligation or validity. The two are certainly very closely associated. Finally, in both cases alike the mistake of the theory is the same: it consists in neglecting the special character of the internal statement and treating it as an external statement about official action.

This mistake becomes immediately apparent when we consider how the judge's own statement that a particular rule is valid functions in judicial decision; for, though here too, in making such a statement, the judge presupposes but does not state the general efficacy of the system, he plainly is not concerned to predict his own or others' official action. His statement that a rule is valid is an internal statement recognizing that the rule satisfies the tests for identifying what is to count as law in his court, and constitutes not a prophecy of but part of the *reason* for his decision. There is indeed a more plausible case for saying that a statement that a rule is valid is a prediction when such a statement is made by a private person; for in the case of conflict between unofficial statements of validity or invalidity and that of a court in deciding a case, there is often good sense in saying that the former must then be withdrawn. Yet even here, as we shall see when we come . . . to investigate the significance of such conflicts between official declarations and the plain requirements of the rules, it may be dogmatic to assume that it is withdrawn as a statement now shown to be *wrong,* because it has falsely *predicted* what a court would say. For there are more reasons for withdrawing statements than the fact that they are wrong, and also more ways of being wrong than this allows.

The rule of recognition providing the criteria by which the validity of other rules of the system is assessed is in an important sense, which we shall try to clarify, an *ultimate* rule: and where, as is usual, there are several criteria ranked in order of relative subordination and primacy one of them is *supreme*. These ideas of the ultimacy of the rule of recognition and the supremacy of one of its criteria merit some attention. It is important to disentangle them from the theory, which we have rejected, that somewhere in every legal system, even though it lurks behind legal forms, there must be a sovereign legislative power which is legally unlimited.

Of these two ideas, supreme criterion and ultimate rule, the first is the easiest to define. We may say that a criterion of legal validity or source of law is supreme if rules identified by reference to it are still recognized as rules of the system, even if they conflict with rules identified by reference to the other criteria, whereas rules identified by reference to the latter are not so recognized if they conflict with the rules identified by reference to the supreme criterion. A similar explanation in comparative terms can be given of the notions of "superior" and "subordinate" criteria which we have already used. It is plain that the notions of a superior and a supreme criterion merely refer to a *relative* place on a scale and do not import any notion of legally *unlimited* legislative power. Yet "supreme" and "unlimited" are easy to confuse — at least in legal theory. One reason for this is that in the simpler forms of legal system the ideas of ultimate rule of recognition, supreme criterion, and legally unlimited legislature seem to converge. For where there is a legislature subject to no constitutional limitations and competent by its enactment to deprive all other rules of law emanating from other sources of their status as law, it is part of the rule of recognition in such a system that enactment by that legislature is the supreme criterion of validity. This is, according to constitutional theory, the position in the United Kingdom. But even systems like that of the United States in which there is no such legally unlimited legislature may perfectly well contain an ultimate rule of recognition which provides a set of criteria of validity, one of which is supreme. This will be so, where the legislative competence of the ordinary legislature is limited by a constitution which contains no amending power, or places some clauses outside the scope of that power. Here there is no legally unlimited legislature, even in the widest interpretation of "legislature"; but the system of course contains an ultimate rule of recognition and, in the clauses of its constitution, a supreme criterion of validity.

The sense in which the rule of recognition is the *ultimate* rule of a system is best understood if we pursue a very familiar chain of legal reasoning. If the question is raised whether some suggested rule is legally valid, we must, in order to answer the question, use a criterion of validity provided by some other rule. Is this purported by-law of the Oxfordshire County Council valid? Yes: because it was made in exercise of the powers conferred, and in accordance with the procedure specified, by a statutory order made by the Minister of Health. At this first stage the statutory order provides the criteria in terms of which the validity of the by-law is assessed. There may be no practical need to go farther; but there is a standing possibility of doing so. We may query the validity of the statutory order and assess its validity in terms of the statute empowering the minister to make such orders. Finally when the validity of the statute has been queried and assessed by reference to the rule that what the Queen in Parliament enacts is law, we are brought to a stop in inquiries concerning validity: for we have reached a rule which, like the intermediate statutory order and statute, provides criteria for the assessment of the validity of other rules; but it is also unlike them in that there is no rule providing criteria for the assessment of its own legal validity.

There are, indeed, many questions which we can raise about this ultimate rule. We can ask whether it is the practice of courts, legislatures, officials, or private citizens in England actually to use this rule as an ultimate rule of recognition. Or has our process of legal reasoning been an idle game with the criteria of validity of a system now discarded? We can ask whether it is a satisfactory form of legal system which has such a rule at its root. Does it produce more good than evil? Are there prudential reasons for supporting it? Is there a moral obligation to do so? These are plainly very important questions; but, equally plainly, when we ask them about the rule of recognition, we are no longer attempting to answer the same kind of question about it as those which we answered about other rules with its aid. When we move from saying that a particular enactment is valid, because it satisfies the rule that what the Queen in Parliament enacts is law, to saying that in England this last rule is used by courts, officials, and private persons as the ultimate rule of recognition, we have moved from an internal statement of law asserting the validity of a rule of the system to an external statement of fact which an observer of the system might make even if he did not accept it. So too when we move from the statement that a particular enactment is valid, to the statement that the rule of recognition of the system is an excellent one and the system based on it is one worthy of support, we have moved from a statement of legal validity to a statement of value.

Some writers, who have emphasized the legal ultimacy of the rule of recognition, have expressed this by saying that, whereas the legal validity of other rules of the system can be demonstrated by reference to it, its own validity cannot be demonstrated but is "assumed" or "postulated" or is a "hypothesis." This may, however, be seriously misleading. Statements of legal validity made about particular rules in the day-to-day life of a legal system whether by judges, lawyers, or ordinary citizens do indeed carry with them certain presuppositions. They are internal statements of law expressing the point of view of those who accept the rule of recognition of the system and, as such, leave unstated much that could be stated in external statements of fact about the system. What is thus left unstated forms the normal background or context of statements of legal validity and is thus said to be "presupposed" by them. But it is important to see precisely what these presupposed matters are, and not to obscure their character. They consist of two things. First, a person who seriously asserts the validity of some given rule of law, say a particular statute, himself makes use of a rule of recognition which he accepts as appropriate for identifying the law. Secondly, it is the case that this rule of recognition, in terms of which he assesses the validity of a particular statute, is not only accepted by him but is the rule of recognition actually accepted and employed in the general operation of the system. If the truth of this presupposition were doubted, it could be established by reference to actual practice: to the way in which courts identify what is to count as law, and to the general acceptance of or acquiescence in these identifications.

Neither of these two presuppositions are well described as "assumptions" of a "validity" which cannot be demonstrated. We only need the word "validity," and commonly only use it, to answer questions which arise *within* a system of rules where the status of a rule as a member of the system depends on its satisfying certain criteria provided by the rule of recognition. No such question can arise as to the validity of the very rule of recognition which provides the criteria; it can neither be valid nor invalid but is simply accepted as appropriate for use in this way. To express this simple fact by saying darkly that its validity is "assumed but cannot be demonstrated," is like saying that we assume, but can never demonstrate, that the standard metre bar in Paris which is the ultimate test of the correctness of all measurement in metres, is itself correct.

A more serious objection is that talk of the "assumption" that the ultimate rule of recognition is valid conceals the essentially factual character of the second presupposition which lies behind the lawyers' statements of validity. No doubt the practice of judges, officials, and others, in which the actual existence of a rule of recognition consists, is a complex matter. As we shall see later, there are certainly situations in which questions as to the precise content and scope of this kind of rule, and even as to its existence, may not admit of a clear or determinate answer. None the less it is important to distinguish "assuming the validity" from "presupposing the existence" of such a rule; if only because failure to do this obscures what is meant by the assertion that such a rule *exists*.

In the simple system of primary rules of obligation sketched in the last chapter, the assertion that a given rule existed could only be an external statement of fact such as an observer who did not accept the rules might make and verify by ascertaining whether or not, as a matter of fact, a given mode of behaviour was generally accepted as a standard and was accompanied by those features which, as we have seen, distinguish a social rule from mere convergent habits. It is in this way also that we should now interpret and verify the assertion that in England a rule — though not a legal one — exists that we must bare the head on entering a church. If such rules as these are found to exist in the actual practice of a social group, there is no separate question of their validity to be discussed though of course their value or desirability is open to question. Once their existence has been established as a fact we should only confuse matters by affirming or denying that they were valid or by saying that "we assumed" but could not show their validity. Where, on the other hand, as in a mature legal system, we have a system of rules which includes a rule of recognition so that the status of a rule as a member of the system now depends on whether it satisfies certain criteria provided by the rule of recognition, this brings with it a new application of the word "exist." The statement that a rule exists may now no longer be what it was in the simple case of customary rules — an external statement of the *fact* that a certain mode of behaviour was generally accepted as a standard in practice. It may now be an internal statement applying an accepted but unstated rule of recognition and meaning (roughly) no more than "valid given the systems criteria of validity." In this respect however, as in others a rule of recognition is unlike other rules of the system. The assertion that it exists can only be an external statement of fact. For whereas a subordinate rule of a system may be valid and in that sense "exist" even if it is generally disregarded, the rule of recognition exists only as a complex, but normally concordant, practice of the courts, officials, and private persons in identifying the law by reference to certain criteria. Its existence is a matter of fact.

Notes and Questions

RONALD A. DWORKIN, "'Natural' Law Revisited"

1. Ronald A. Dworkin acknowledges at the outset of his article that natural law has not been a popular theory in the twentieth century. The introduction to this section discusses some reasons why this is true. What are they? As you read this selection consider whether Dworkin meets these objections.

2. Dworkin notes that natural law recognizes a necessary connection between what law is and what law ought to be — that is, between law and morality. But the connection, he claims, is complex and not simply one of identity. So we must try to understand what the connection is. Dworkin explains this connection in the context of adjudication. What role do principles of political morality play in judicial decision making, according to Dworkin?

3. Dworkin says that judges should decide hard cases by finding the best fit with the best justification in principles of political morality for the legal structure as a whole or the area being considered. What does he mean by "hard cases?" What about easy cases? What does he mean by "best fit"? He illustrates his theory by comparing the judicial process to a "chain novel." Explain this illustration. Does it provide you with a clear picture of Dworkin's model of adjudication?

4. In practice, Dworkin says, judges will develop "working rules" that have two important features. What are these features? How are they related to one another? How would they work in hard cases? In easy cases? Is it now clear why many commentators call this a natural law theory? Do you think it should be?

5. The skeptical objection to natural law, and Dworkin's theory, is that it rests on an assumption of objective morality that yields by rational analysis a single right answer in legal cases. The skeptic argues that there is (at least often) no single right answer. Judges often disagree and use the same legal principles to arrive at contrary or even contradictory opinions. Pre-existing law, the skeptic claims, underdetermines results in particular cases, so judges are free to use their discretion. How does Dworkin answer this point? He recognizes that "global internal skepticism" is the greatest threat to his view, but he offers no argument against it except that he can't think of an argument to support it. Yet he admits that judges in fact disagree over both political morality and legal interpretation. Thus, he admits that no one can prove his side is objectively right. Why isn't that a foundation for skepticism?

"Natural" Law Revisited

RONALD A. DWORKIN

---

1. What Is Naturalism?

Everyone likes categories, and legal philosophers like them very much. So we spend a good deal of time, not all of it profitably, labeling ourselves and the theories of law we defend. One label, however, is particularly dreaded: no one wants to be called a natural lawyer. Natural law insists that what the law is depends in some way on what the law should be. This seems metaphysical or at least vaguely religious. In any case it seems plainly wrong. If some theory of law is shown to be a natural law theory, therefore, people can be excused if they do not attend to it much further.

In the past several years, I have tried to defend a theory about how judges should decide cases that some critics (though not all) say is a natural law theory and should be rejected for that reason. I have of course made the pious and familiar objection to this charge, that it is better to look at theories than labels. But since labels are so much a part of our common intellectual life it is almost as silly to flee as to hurl them. If the crude description of natural law I just gave is correct, that any theory which makes the content of law sometimes depend on the correct answer to some moral question is a natural law theory, then I am guilty of natural law. I am not now interested, I should add, in whether this crude characterization is historically correct, or whether it succeeds in distinguishing natural law from positivist theories of law. My present concern is rather this. Suppose this is natural law. What in the world is wrong with it?

A. Naturalism

I shall start by giving the picture of adjudication I want to defend a name, and it is a name which accepts the crude characterization. I shall call this picture naturalism. According to naturalism, judges should decide hard cases by interpreting the political structure of their community in the following, perhaps special way: by trying to find the best *justification* they can find, in principles of political morality, for the structure as a whole, from the most profound constitutional rules and arrangements to the details of, for example, the private law of tort or contract. Suppose the question arises for the first time, for example, whether and in what circumstances careless drivers are liable, not only for physical injuries to those whom they run down, but also for any emotional damage suffered by relatives of the victim who are watching. According to naturalism, judges should then ask the following questions of the history (including the contemporary history) of their political structure. Does the best possible justification of that history suppose a principle according to which people who are injured emotionally in this way have a right to recover damages in court? If so, what, more precisely, is that principle? Does it entail, for example, that only immediate relatives of the person physically injured have that right? Or only relatives on

the scene of the accident, who might themselves have suffered physical damage?

Of course a judge who is faced with these questions in an actual case cannot undertake anything like a full justification of all parts of the constitutional arrangement, statutory system and judicial precedents that make up his "law." I had to invent a mythical judge, called Hercules, with superhuman powers in order even to contemplate what a full justification of the entire system would be like.[1] Real judges can attempt only what we might call a partial justification of the law. They can try to justify, under some set of principles, those parts of the legal background which seem to them immediately relevant, like, for example, the prior judicial decisions about recovery for various sorts of damage in automobile accidents. Nevertheless it is useful to describe this as a partial justification – as a part of what Hercules himself would do – in order to emphasize that, according to this picture, a judge should regard the law he mines and studies as embedded in a much larger system, so that it is always relevant for him to expand his investigation by asking whether the conclusions he reaches are consistent with what he would have discovered had his study been wider.

It is obvious why this theory of adjudication invites the charge of natural law. It makes each judge's decision about the burden of past law depend on his judgment about the best political justification of that law, and this is of course a matter of political morality. Before I consider whether this provides a fatal defect in the theory, however, I must try to show how the theory might work in practice. It may help to look beyond law to other enterprises in which participants extend a discipline into the future by re-examining its past. This process is in fact characteristic of the general activity we call interpretation, which has a large place in literary criticism, history, philosophy and many other activities. Indeed, the picture of adjudication I have just sketched draws on a sense of what interpretation is like in these various activities, and I shall try to explicate the picture through an analogy to literary interpretation.[2] I shall, however, pursue that analogy in a special context designed to minimize some of the evident differences between law and literature, and so make the comparison more illuminating.

B. The Chain Novel

Imagine, then, that a group of novelists is engaged for a particular project. They draw lots to determine the order of play. The lowest number writes the opening chapter of a novel, which he then sends to the next number who is given the following assignment. He must add a chapter to that novel, which he must write so as to make the novel being constructed the best novel it can be. When he completes his chapter, he then sends the two chapters to the next novelist, who has the same assignment, and so forth. Now every novelist but the first has the responsibility of interpreting what has gone before in the sense of interpretation I described for a naturalist judge. Each novelist must decide what the characters are "really" like; what motives in fact guide them; what the point or theme of the developing novel is; how far some literary device or figure consciously or unconsciously used can be said to contribute to these, and therefore should be extended, refined, trimmed or dropped. He must decide all this in order to send the novel further in one direction rather than another. But all these decisions must be made, in accordance with the directions given, by asking which decisions make the continuing novel better as a novel.

Some novels have in fact been written in this way (including the soft-core pornographic novel NAKED CAME THE STRANGER) though for a debunking purpose, and certain parlor games, for rainy weekends in English country houses, have something of the same structure. But in this case the novelists are expected to take their responsibilities seriously, and to recognize the duty to create, so far as they can, a single unified novel rather than, for example, a series of independent short stories with characters bearing the same names. Perhaps this is an impossible assignment; perhaps the project is doomed to produce, not simply an impossibly bad novel, but no novel at all, because the best theory of art requires a single creator, or if more than one, that each have some control over the whole. (But what about legends and jokes? What about the Old Testament, or, on some theories, the ILIAD?) I need not push that question further, because I am interested only in the fact that the assignment makes sense, that each of the novelists in the chain can

have some sense of what he or she is asked to do, whatever misgivings each might have about the value or character of what will then be produced.

The crucial question each must face is this. What is the difference between continuing the novel in the best possible way, by writing plot and development that can be seen to flow from what has gone before, and starting a fresh novel with characters having the same names? Suppose you are a novelist well down the chain, and are handed several chapters which are, in fact, the first sections of the Dickens short novel, A CHRISTMAS CAROL. You consider these two interpretations of the central character: that Scrooge is irredeemably, inherently evil, and so an example of the degradation of which human nature is intrinsically capable, or that Scrooge is inherently good, but progressively corrupted by the false values and perverse demands of high capitalist society. The interpretation you adopt will obviously make an enormous difference in the way you continue the story. You aim, in accordance with your instructions, to make the continuing novel the best novel it can be; but you must nevertheless choose an interpretation that makes the novel a single work of art. So you will have to respect the text you have been given, and not choose an interpretation that you believe the text rules out. The picture that text gives of Scrooge's early life, for example, might be incompatible with the claim that he is inherently wicked. In that case you have no choice. If, on the other hand, the text is equally consistent with both interpretations, then you do have a choice. You will choose the interpretation that you believe makes the work more significant or otherwise better, and this will probably (though not inevitably) depend on whether you think people like Scrooge are in fact, in the real world, born bad or corrupted by capitalism.

Now consider a more complex case. Suppose the text does not absolutely rule out either interpretation, but is marginally less consistent with one, which is, however, the interpretation you would pick if they both fit equally well. Suppose you believe that the original sin interpretation (as we might call it) is much the more accurate depiction of human nature. But if you choose that interpretation you will have to regard certain incidents and attributions established in the text you were given as "mistakes." You must then ask yourself which interpretation makes the work of art better *on the whole*, recognizing, as you will, that a novel whose plot is inconsistent or otherwise lacks integrity is thereby flawed. You must ask whether the novel is still better as a novel, read as a study of original sin, even though it must now be regarded as containing some "mistakes" in plot, than it would be with fewer "mistakes" but a less revealing picture of human nature. You may never have reflected on that question before, but that is no reason why you may not do so now, and once you make up your mind you will believe that the correct interpretation of Scrooge's character is the interpretation that makes the novel better on the whole.

C. The Chain of Law

Naturalism is a theory of adjudication not of the interpretation of novels. But naturalism supposes that common law adjudication is a chain enterprise sharing many of the features of the story we invented. According to naturalism, a judge should decide fresh cases in the spirit of a novelist in the chain writing a fresh chapter. The judge must make creative decisions, but must try to make these decisions "going on as before" rather than by starting in a new direction as if writing on a clean slate. He must read through (or have some good idea through his legal training and experience) what other judges in the past have written, not simply to discover what these other judges have said, or their state of mind when they said it, but to reach an opinion about what they have collectively *done*, in the way that each of our novelists formed an opinion about the collective novel so far written. Of course, the best interpretation of past judicial decisions is the interpretation that shows these in the best light, not aesthetically but politically, as coming as close to the correct ideals of a just legal system as possible. Judges in the chain of law share with the chain novelists the imperative of interpretation, but they bring different standards of success — political rather than aesthetic — to bear on that enterprise.

The analogy shows, I hope, how far naturalism allows a judge's beliefs about the personal and political rights people have "naturally" — that is, apart from the law — to enter his judgments

about what the law requires. It does not instruct him to regard these beliefs as the only test of law. A judge's background and moral convictions will influence his decisions about what legal rights people have under the law. But the brute facts of legal history will nevertheless limit the role these convictions can play in those decisions. The same distinction we found in literary interpretation, between interpretation and ideal, holds here as well. An Agatha Christie mystery thriller cannot be interpreted as a philosophical novel about the meaning of death even by someone who believes that a successful philosophical novel would be a greater literary achievement than a successful mystery. It cannot be interpreted that way because, if it is, too much of the book must be seen as accidental, and too little as integrated, in plot, style and trope, with its alleged genre or point. Interpreted that way it becomes a shambles and so a failure rather than a success at anything at all. In the same way, a judge cannot plausibly discover, in a long and unbroken string of prior judicial decisions in favor of the manufacturers of defective products, any principle establishing strong consumers' rights. For that discovery would not show the history of judicial practice in a better light; on the contrary it would show it as the history of cynicism and inconsistency, perhaps of incoherence. A naturalist judge must show the facts of history in the best light he can, and this means that he must not show that history as unprincipled chaos.

Of course this responsibility, for judges as well as novelists, may best be fulfilled by a dramatic reinterpretation that both unifies what has gone before and gives it new meaning or point. This explains why a naturalist decision, though it is in this way tied to the past, may yet seem radical. A naturalist judge might find, in some principle that has not yet been recognized in judicial argument, a brilliantly unifying account of past decisions that shows them in a better light than ever before. American legal education celebrates dozens of such events in our own history. In the most famous single common law decision in American jurisprudence, for example, Cardozo reinterpreted a variety of cases to find, in these cases, the principle on which the modern law of negligence was built.[3]

Nevertheless the constraint, that a judge must continue the past and not invent a better past, will often have the consequence that a naturalist judge cannot reach decisions that he would otherwise, given his own political theory, want to reach. A judge who, as a matter of political conviction, believes in consumers' rights may nevertheless have to concede that the law of his jurisdiction has rejected this idea. It is in one way misleading to say, however, that he will be then forced to make decisions *at variance with* his political convictions. The principle that judges should decide consistently with principle, and that law should be coherent, is part of his convictions, and it is this principle that makes the decision he otherwise opposes necessary.

D. Interpretation in Practice

In this section I shall try to show how a self-conscious naturalist judge might construct a working approach to adjudication, and the role his background moral and political convictions would play in that working approach. When we imagined you to be a novelist in the chain novel, several pages ago, we considered how you would continue the first few chapters of A CHRISTMAS CAROL. We distinguished two dimensions of a successful interpretation. An interpretation must "fit" the data it interprets, in order not to show the novel as sloppy or incoherent, and it must also show that data in its best light, as serving as well as can be some proper ambition of novels. Just now, in noticing how a naturalist judge who believed in consumers' rights might nevertheless have to abandon the claim that consumers' rights are embedded in legal history, [*sic*] the same distinction between these two dimensions was relied upon. A naturalist judge would be forced to reject a politically attractive interpretation, we supposed, simply because he did not believe it fit the record well enough. If fit is indeed an independent dimension of success in interpretation, then any judge's working approach would include some tacit conception of what "fit" is, and of how well a particular interpretation must fit the record of judicial and other legal decisions in order to count as acceptable.

This helps us to explain why two naturalist judges might reach different interpretations of past judicial decisions about accidents, for example. They might hold different conceptions of "fit" or "best fit," so that, for instance, one thinks that an interpretation provides an acceptable fit only if it is supported by the opinions of judges in prior cases, while the other thinks it is sufficient, to satisfy the dimension of fit, that an interpretation fit the actual decisions these judges reached even if it finds no echo in their opinions. This difference might be enough to explain, for example, why one judge could accept an "economic" interpretation of the accident cases — that the point of negligence law is to reduce the overall social costs of accidents — while another judge, who also found that interpretation politically congenial, would feel bound by his beliefs about the requirement of fit to reject it.

At some point, however, this explanation of differences between two judges' theories of the same body of law would become strained and artificial. Suppose Judge X believes, for example, that pedestrians ought to look out for themselves, and have no business walking in areas in which drivers are known normally to exceed the legal speed limit. He might rely on this opinion in deciding that "our law recognizes no general right to recover whenever someone is injured by a speeding driver while walking on a highway where most drivers speed." If Judge Y reaches a different judgment about what the law is, because he believes that pedestrians should be entitled to assume that people will obey the law even when there is good evidence that they will not, then it would strain language to explain this difference by saying that these judges disagree about the way or the degree in which an interpretation of the law must fit past decisions. We would do better to say that these judges interpret the law differently, in this instance, because they bring different background theories of political morality to their interpretations, just as two art critics might disagree about the correct interpretation of impressionism because they bring different theories about the value of art to that exercise.

Any naturalist judge's working approach to interpretation will recognize this distinction between two "dimensions" of interpretations of the prior law, and so we might think of such a theory as falling into two parts. One part refines and develops the idea that an interpretation must fit the data it interprets. This part takes up positions on questions like the following. How many decisions (roughly) can an interpretation set aside as mistakes, and still count as an interpretation of the string of decisions that includes those "mistakes"? How far is an interpretation better if it is more consistent with later rather than earlier past decision? How far and in what way must a good interpretation fit the opinions judges write as well as the decisions they make? How far must it take account of popular morality contemporary with the decisions it offers to interpret? A second part of any judge's tacit theory of interpretation, however, will be quite independent of these "formal" issues. It will contain the substantive ideals of political morality on which he relies in deciding whether any putative interpretation is to be preferred because it shows legal practice to be better as a matter of substantive justice. Of course, if any working approach to interpretation has these two parts, then it must also have principles that combine or adjudicate between them.

This account of the main structure of a working theory of interpretation has heuristic appeal. It provides judges, and others who interpret the law, with a model they might use in identifying the approach they have been using, and self-consciously to inspect and improve that model. A thoughtful judge might establish for himself, for example, a rough "threshold" of fit which any interpretation of data must meet in order to be "acceptable" on the dimension of fit, and then suppose that if more than one interpretation of some part of the law meets this threshold, the choice among these should be made, not through further and more precise comparisons between the two along that dimension, but by choosing the interpretation which is "substantively" better, that is, which better promotes the political ideals he thinks correct. Such a judge might say, for example, that since both the foreseeability and the area-of-physical-risk interpretations rise above the threshold of fit with the emotional damage cases I mentioned earlier, foreseeability is better *as an interpretation* because it better accords with the "natural" rights of people injured in accidents.

The practical advantages of adopting such a threshold of fit are plain enough. A working theory need specify that threshold in only a rough and impressionistic way. If two interpretations both satisfy the threshold, then, as I said, a judge who uses such a theory need make no further comparisons along that dimension in order to establish which of them in fact supplies the "better" fit, and he may therefore avoid many of the difficult and perhaps arbitrary decisions about better fit that a theory without this feature might require him to make. But there are nevertheless evident dangers in taking the device too seriously, as other than a rule-of-thumb practical approach. A judge might be tricked into thinking that these two dimensions of interpretations are in some way deeply competitive with one another, that they represent the influence of two different and sometimes contradictory ambitions of adjudication.

He will then worry about those inevitable cases in which it is unclear whether some substantively attractive interpretation does indeed meet the threshold of fit. He will think that in such cases he must define that threshold, not impressionistically, as calling for a "decent" fit, but precisely, perhaps everything will then turn on whether that interpretation in fact just meets or just fails the crucial test. This rigid attitude toward the heuristic distinction would miss the point that any plausible theory of interpretation, in law as in literature, will call for some cross influence between the level of fit at which the threshold is fixed and the substantive issues involved. If an interpretation of some string of cases is far superior "substantively" it may be given the benefit of a less stringent test of fit for that reason.

For once again the underlying issue is simply one of comparing two pictures of the judicial past to see which offers a more attractive picture, from the standpoint of political morality, overall. The distinction between the dimensions of fit and substance is a rough distinction in service of that issue. The idea of a threshold of fit, and therefore of a lexical ordering between the two dimensions, is simply a working hypothesis, valuable so far as the impressionistic characterization of fit on which it depends is adequate, but which must be abandoned in favor of a more sophisticated and piecemeal analysis when the occasion demands.

Of course the moment when more sophisticated analysis becomes necessary, because the impressionistic distinction of the working theory no longer serves, is a moment of difficulty calling for fresh political judgments that may be hard to make. Suppose a judge faces, for the first time, the possibility of overruling a narrow rule followed for some time in his jurisdiction. Suppose, for example, that the courts have consistently held, since the issue was first raised, that lawyers may not be sued in negligence. Our judge believes that this rule is wrong and unjust, and that it is inconsistent in principle with the general rule allowing actions in negligence against other professional people like doctors and accountants. Suppose he can nevertheless find some putative principle, in which others find though he does not, which would justify the distinction the law has drawn. Like the principle, for example, that lawyers owe obligations to the courts or to abstract justice, it would be unfair to impose on the many legal obligation of due care to their clients. He must ask whether the best interpretation of the past includes *that* principle in spite of the fact that he himself would reject it.

Neither answer to this question will seem wholly attractive to him. If he holds that the law does include this putative principle, then this argument would present the law, including the past decisions about suits against lawyers as coherent; but he would then expose what he would believe to be a flaw in the substantive law. He would be supposing that the law includes a principle he believes is wrong, and therefore has no place in a just and wise system. If he decides that the law does not include the putative principle, on the other hand, then he can properly regard this entire line of cases about actions against lawyers as mistakes, and ignore or overrule them; but he then exposes a flaw in the record of a different sort, namely that past judges have acted in an unprincipled way, and a demerit in his own decision, that it treats the lawyer who loses the present case differently from how judges have treated other lawyers in the past. He must ask which is, in the end, the greater of these flaws; which way of reading the record shows it, in the last analysis, in the better and which in the worse light.

It would be absurd to suppose that all the lawyers and judges of any common law community share some set of convictions from which a single answer to that question could be deduced. Or even that many lawyers or judges would have ready at hand some convictions of their own

which could supply an answer without further ado. But it is nevertheless possible for any judge to confront issues like these in a principled way, and this is what naturalism demands of him. He must accept that in deciding one way rather than another about the force of a line of precedents, for example, he is developing a working theory of legal interpretation in one rather than another direction, and this must seem to him the right direction as a matter of political principle, not simply an appealing direction for the moment because he likes the answer it recommends in the immediate case before him. Of course there is, in this counsel, much room for deception, including self-deception. But in most cases it will be possible for judges to recognize when they have submitted some issue to the discipline this description requires and also to recognize when some other judge has not.

Let me recapitulate. Interpretation is not a mechanical process. Nevertheless, judges can form working styles of interpretation, adequate for routine cases, and ready for refinement when cases are not routine. These working styles will include what I called formal features. They will set out, impressionistically, an account of fit, and may characterize a threshold of fit an interpretation must achieve in order to be eligible. But they will also contain a substantive part, formed from the judge's background political morality, or rather that part of his background morality which has become articulate in the course of his career. Sometimes this heuristic distinction between fit and substantive justice, as dimensions of a successful interpretation, will itself seem problematic, and a judge will be forced to elaborate that distinction by reflecting further on the full set of the substantive and procedural political rights of citizens a just legal system must respect and serve. In this way any truly hard case develops as well as engages a judge's style of adjudication.

2. Is It Delusion?

A. Internal and External Scepticism

I have been describing naturalism as a theory about how judges should decide cases. It is of course a further question whether American (or any other) judges actually do decide cases that way. I shall not pursue that further question now. Instead, I want to consider certain arguments that I expect will be made against naturalism simply as a recommendation. In fact, many of the classical objections to "natural law" theories are objections to such theories as models, for rather than descriptions of, judicial practice. I shall begin with what might be called the sceptical attack.

I put my description of naturalism in what might be called a subjective mode. I described the question which, according to naturalism, judges should put to themselves, and answer from their own convictions. Someone is bound to object that, although each judge can answer these questions for himself, different judges will give different answers, and no single answer can be said to be *objectively* right. "There are as many different 'best' interpretations as there are interpreters, he will say, because no one can offer any argument in favor of one interpretation over another, except that it strikes him as the best, and it will strike some other interpreter as the worst. No doubt judges (as well as many other people) would deny this. They think their opinions can have some objective standing, that they can be either true or false. But this is delusion merely."

What response can naturalism, as I have described it, make to this sceptical challenge? We must begin by asking what kind of scepticism is in play. I have in mind a distinction which, once again, might be easier to state if we return to a literary analogy. Suppose we are studying Hamlet and the question is put by some critic whether, before the play begins, Hamlet and Ophelia have been lovers. This is a question of interpretation, and two critics who disagree might present arguments trying to show why the play is, all things considered, more valuable as a work of art on one or the other understanding about Hamlet and Ophelia. But plainly a third position is possible. Someone might argue that it makes no difference to the importance or value of the play which of these assumptions is made about the lovers, because the play's importance lies in a humanistic vision of life and fate, not in any detail of plot or character whose reading would be affected by either assumption. This third position argues that the right answer to this particular question of interpretation is only that there is no right answer; that there is no "best"

interpretation of the sexual relationship between Hamlet and Ophelia, only "different" interpretations, because neither interpretation would make the play more or less valuable as a work of art. This might strike you (it does me) as exactly the right position to take on this particular issue. It is, in a sense, a sceptical position, because it denies "truth" both to the proposition that Hamlet slept with Ophelia, and to the apparently contrary proposition that he did not. But if this is scepticism, it is what he might call *internal* scepticism. It does not challenge the idea that good arguments can in principle be found for one interpretation of Hamlet rather than another. On the contrary it *relies* on an interpretive argument — that the value of the play lies in a dimension that does not intersect the sexual question — in order to reach its "sceptical" position on that question.

Contrast the position of someone who says that no one interpretation of any work of art could ever succeed in showing it to be either really better or really worse, because there is not and cannot be any such thing as "value" in art at all. He means that there is something very wrong with the enterprise of interpretation (at least as I have described it) as a whole, not simply with particular issues or arguments within it. Of course he may have arguments for his position, or think he has; but these will not be arguments that, like the arguments of the internal sceptic, explicitly assume a positive theory of the value of art in general or of a particular work of art. They will be a priori, philosophical arguments attempting to show that the very idea of value in art is a deep mistake, that people who say they find a work of art "good" or "valuable" are not describing any objective property, but only expressing their own subjective reaction. This is *external* scepticism about art, and about interpretation in art.

B. The Threat of Scepticism

If a lawyer says that no one interpretation of the legal record can be "objectively" the correct interpretation, he might have external scepticism in mind. He might mean that if two judges disagree about the "correct" interpretation of the emotional damages cases, because they hold different theories of what a just law of negligence would be like, their disagreement is for that reason alone merely "subjective," and neither side can be "objectively" right. I cannot consider, in this essay, the various arguments that philosophers have offered for external scepticism about political morality. The best of these arguments rely on a general thesis of philosophy that might be called the "demonstrability hypothesis." This holds that no proposition can be true unless the means exist, at least in principle, to demonstrate its truth through arguments to everyone who understands the language and is rational. If the demonstrability hypothesis is correct, then external scepticism is right about a great many human enterprises and activities; perhaps about all of them, including the activities we call scientific. I know of no good reason to accept the demonstrability hypothesis (it is at least an embarrassment that this hypothesis cannot itself be demonstrated in the sense it requires) and I am not myself an external sceptic. But rather than pursue the question of the demonstrability hypothesis, I shall change the subject.

Suppose you are an external sceptic about justice and other aspects of political morality. What follows about the question of how judges should decide cases? About whether naturalism is better than other (more conservative or more radical) theories of adjudication? You might think it follows that you should take no further interest in these questions at all. If so, I have some sympathy with your view. After all, you believe, on what you take to be impressive philosophical grounds, that no way of deciding cases at law can really be thought to be any better than any other, and that no way of interpreting legal practice can be preferred to any other on rational grounds. The "correct" theory of what judges should do is only a matter of what judges feel like doing, or of what they believe will advance political causes to which they happen to be drawn. The "correct" interpretation of legal practice is only a matter of reading legal history so that it appeals to you, or so that you can use it in your own political interests. If you are convinced of these externally sceptical propositions, you might well do better to take up the interesting questions raised by certain sociologists of law — questions about the connection between judges'

economic class and the decisions they are likely to reach, for example. Or to take up the study of strategies for working your will on judges if you ever come to argue before them, or on other judges if you ever join the bench yourself. Your external scepticism might well persuade you to take up these "practical" questions and set aside the "theoretical" questions you have come to see as meaningless.

But it is worth noticing that philosophers who say they are external sceptics rarely draw that sort of practical conclusion for themselves. Most of them seem to take a rather different line, which I do not myself fully understand, but which can, I think, fairly be represented as follows. External scepticism is not a position within an enterprise, but about an enterprise. It does not tell us to stop making the kinds of arguments we are disposed to make and accept and act on within morality or politics, but only to change our beliefs about what we are doing when we act this way. Imagine that some chessplayers thought that chess was an "objective" battle between forces of light and darkness, so that when black won good had triumphed in some metaphysical sense. External sceptics about chess would reject this view, and think that chess was entertainment merely; but they would not thereupon cease playing chess or play it any differently from their deluded fellow players. So external sceptics about political morality will still have opinions and make arguments about justice; they will simply understand, in their philosophical moments, that when they do this they are not discovering timeless and objective truths.

If you are an external sceptic who takes this attitude, you will have driven a wedge between your external scepticism and any judgments you might make about how judges should decide cases, in general, or about what the best justification is of some part of the law, in particular. You will have your own opinions about these matters, which you will express in arguments or, if you are an academic lawyer, in law review articles or, if you are a judge, in your decisions. You may well come to believe that the best interpretation of the emotional damages cases shows them to be grounded in the principle of foreseeability, for example. When you retreat to your philosophical study, you will have a particular view about the opinions you expressed or exhibited while you were "playing the game." You will believe that your opinions about the best justification of the emotional damage cases were "merely" subjective opinions (whatever that means) with no basis in any "objective" reality. But this does not itself provide any argument in favor of *other* opinions about the best interpretation. In particular, it does not provide any argument in favor of the *internally* sceptical opinion that no interpretation of the accident cases is best.

Of course your external scepticism leaves you free to take up that internally sceptical position if you believe you have good internal arguments for it. Suppose you are trying to decide whether the best interpretation of the emotional damage cases lies in the principle that people in the area of physical risk may recover for emotional damage, or the broader principle that anyone whose emotional damage was foreseeable may recover. After the most diligent search and reflection asking yourself exactly the questions naturalism poses, you may find that the case for neither of these interpretations seems to you any stronger than the case for the other. I think this is very unlikely, but that is beside the present point, which is only that it is possible. You would be internally sceptical, in this way, about any uniquely "correct" interpretation of this group of cases; but you would have supplied an affirmative argument, beginning in your naturalistic theory, for that internally sceptical conclusion. It would not have mattered whether you were an external sceptic, who nevertheless "played the game" as a naturalist, or an external "believer" who thought that naturalism was stitched into the fabric of the universe. You would have reached the same internally sceptical conclusion, on these assumed beliefs and facts, in either case.

What is, then, the threat that external scepticism poses to naturalism? It is potentially very threatening indeed, not only to naturalism, but to all its rival theories of adjudication as well. It may persuade you to try to have nothing to do with morality or legal theory at all, though I do not think you will succeed in giving up these immensely important human activities. If this very great threat fails (as it seems to have failed for almost all external sceptics) then no influence remains. For in whatever spirit you do enter any

of these enterprises—however firmly your fingers may be crossed—the full range of positions within the enterprise is open to you on equal terms. If you end in some internally sceptical position of some sort, this will be because of the internal power of the arguments that drove you there, not because of your external sceptical credentials.

We must now consider another possibility. The sceptical attack upon naturalism may in fact consist, not in the external scepticism I have been discussing, but in some global form of internal scepticism. I just conceded the possibility that we might find reason for internal scepticism about the best interpretation of some particular body of law. Suppose we had reasons to be internally sceptical about the best interpretation of any and all parts of the law? It is hard to imagine the plausible arguments that would bring us to that conclusion, but not hard to imagine how someone with bizarre views might be brought to it. Suppose one holds that all morality rests on God's will, and had just decided that there is no God. Or he believes that only spontaneous and unreflective decisions can have moral value, and that no judicial decision can either be spontaneous or encourage spontaneity. These would be arguments not rejecting the idea or sense of morality, as in the case of external scepticism, but employing what the author takes to be the best conception of morality in service of a wholesale internally sceptical position. If this position were in fact the right view to take up about political morality, then it would always be wrong to suppose that one interpretation of past judicial decisions was better than another, at least in cases when both passed the threshold test of fit. Naturalism would therefore be a silly theory to recommend to judges. So the threat of external scepticism, it materializes, is in fact much greater than the threat of external scepticism. But (as the examples I chose may have suggested) I cannot think of any plausible arguments for global internal scepticism about political morality.

Of course, nothing in this short discussion disputes the claim, which is plainly true, that different judges hold different political moralities, and will therefore disagree about the best justification of the past. Or the claim, equally true, that there will be no way for any side in such disagreements to prove that it is right and its opponents wrong. The demonstrability thesis (as I said) argues from these undeniable facts to general external scepticism. But even if we reject that thesis, as I do, the bare fact of disagreement may be thought to support an independent challenge of naturalism, which does not depend on either external or internal scepticism. For it may be said that whether or not there is an objectively right answer to the question of justification, it is unfair that the answer of one judge be accepted as final when he has no way to prove, as against those who disagree, that his position is better. This is part of the argument from democracy to which we must now turn.

3. Is It Undemocratic?

So if we are to reject naturalism, in favor of some other positive theory of adjudication, this cannot be by virtue of any general appeal to external scepticism as a philosophical doctrine. We need arguments of substantive political morality showing why naturalism is unwise or unjust. In the remaining sections of the essay I shall consider certain arguments, that I have either heard or invented, to that effect. Of course arguments against naturalism must compare it, unfavorably, with some other theory, and arguments that might be effective in the context of one such comparison would be self-defeating in another.

I shall consider, first, the arguments that might be made against naturalism from the standpoint of what I believe is a more positive theory of adjudication, though nothing turns on whether this theory is properly called positivism. Someone might propose, as an alternative to naturalism, that judges should decide cases in the following way. First, they should identify the persons or institutions which are authorized to make law by the social conventions of their community. Next, they should check the record of history to see whether any such persons or institutions have laid down a rule of law whose language unambiguously covers the case at hand. If so, they should decide that case by applying that rule. If not—if history shows that no rule has been laid down deciding the case either way—then they should create the best rule for the

future, and apply it retrospectively. The rule they thus create would then become, for later judges, part of the record endorsed by convention, so that later judges facing the same issue could then find, in that decision, language settling the matter for them. We might call this theory of adjudication "conventionalism."

Some people are drawn to conventionalism, over naturalism, because they think the former is more democratic. It argues that people only have the rights, in court, that legislators and judges, whom convention recognizes to have legislative power, have already decided to give them. Naturalism, on the other hand, assigns judges the power to draw from judicial history rights that no official institution has ever sanctioned before, and to do so on no stronger argument than that the past is seen in a better light, according to the convictions of the judges, if these rights are presupposed. This seems the antithesis of what democracy requires.

But this argument mistakes the cases in which a conventionalist and a naturalist are likely to disagree. Conventionalist judges can dispose of cases at the first stage, by copying the decisions already made by elected officials, only in those cases in which some statute exactly in point unambiguously dictates a particular result. Any conscientious naturalist is very likely to make exactly the same decisions in those "simple" cases, so conventionalism cannot be more democratic because it decides these differently. The two styles of adjudication will normally recommend different decisions only when some fresh judicial judgment is required which goes beyond what the legislature has unarguably said, either because the statute in play is open to different interpretations, or because no particular statute is in play at all. But in these "hard" cases the difference between the two theories of adjudication cannot be that one defers to the legislature's judgment while the other challenges that judgment. Because, by hypothesis, there is no legislative judgment that can be treated in either of these ways. Conventionalism argues that the judge must, in these "hard" cases, choose the rule of decision which best promotes the good society as he conceives it. It is hardly more democratic for judges to rely on their own convictions about the best design of the future than to rely instead on their own convictions about the best interpretation of the past.

So the argument from democracy in favor of conventionalism over naturalism seems to come to nothing. But we should consider one possible counter-argument. I have been assuming that conventionalism and naturalism will designate the same cases as "easy," that is, as cases in which no fresh judgment is required by the judge. But perhaps a naturalist has more room than a conventionalist to deny that an apparently "easy" case really is. Consider the following example. Since naturalism encourages a judge to rely on his own convictions about which interpretation shows the past in the best light, it permits outrageous political convictions to generate outrageous judicial decisions. Suppose a naturalist judge believes that majority will is tyranny. He believes that our political institutions should be arranged so that statutes are enforced only when they have been enacted by a two-thirds vote. He acknowledges that he cannot apply this principle unless it provides an acceptable fit with past practice, but he sets the threshold of fit low enough, in perfect good faith, so as to be able conscientiously to claim that all counter-examples (all cases in which statutes passed by a bare majority have been enforced by the courts) are "mistakes."

This is no doubt possible. Nothing in the design of naturalism insures that a judge with silly or mad opinions will not be appointed; but nothing in the design of conventionalism insures that either; and conventionalism will not prevent him from reaching preposterous decisions once appointed. A conventionalist judge needs a concept of convention. He must decide, for example, whether it is a convention of our society that the Constitution should be followed, and nothing in the structure of conventionalism can insure that a judge will in fact reach the correct answer to that question. No theory of adjudication can guarantee that only sensible decisions will be reached by judges who embrace that theory. We can protect ourselves from madness or gross stupidity only by independent procedures governing how judges are to be appointed, how their decisions may be appealed and reversed, and how they may be removed from office if this should appear necessary.

But it may now be said that naturalism would encourage anti-democratic decisions from judges who hold, not mad, but plausible and even attractive political convictions, and who deploy perfectly sensible theories about how much of the past an interpretation must fit. For naturalism leaves no doctrine or practice immune from re-examination. We may use an earlier example as an illustration. Suppose a firm line of cases has rejected the idea that clients may sue lawyers who are negligent. Conventionalism is then committed (so it might be said) to continuing that doctrine until it is reversed by legislation, which seems the democratic solution. But naturalism encourages judges to put this line of cases in a wider context, and ask whether the rule refusing recovery against negligent lawyers would not itself be rejected by the best justification of the rest of the law, which allows recovery for negligent injury of almost every other kind. So a naturalist might be led to overrule these cases, which a conventionalist would leave for the legislature to review.

Indeed there is nothing in the theory of naturalism, as I described it, which would prevent an intelligent and sensible naturalist from taking the same line with certain statutes. Suppose an old statute makes blasphemy a crime and, though it has not been enforced in centuries, it is suddenly revived by a public prosecutor anxious to make a splash. A naturalist judge might well develop a theory of obsolescence, even though this had never been recognized in the jurisdiction before. He might say that the best interpretation of judicial practice as a whole yields the following qualification to the rule that statutes are always to be enforced. "Old statutes quite at variance with the spirit of the present time, which would not be enacted by a present legislature, and which have not been employed since ancient times, are unavailable as grounds of criminal prosecution." If prosecutors have not tried to revive old statutes in the fairly recent past, this qualification would be consistent with judicial practice, and it might plausibly be thought to show that practice in a better light, as both more rational and more closely tying what counts as valid legislation to the will of the people.

So both in the case of precedent and legislation a competent naturalist judge might find certain cases hard, and amenable to the command of imaginative reinterpretation, which a conventionalist must concede to be easy even when the obvious answer is unattractive. So perhaps naturalism would sometimes produce "novel" decisions by sensible judges that conventionalism would discourage. But is it right to say that naturalism is for this reason less "democratic." A minimally competent naturalist judge would begin his argument by recognizing, indeed, insisting, that our political system is a democracy; he would continue by arguing that democracy, properly understood, is best served by a coherent rather than an unprincipled private law of negligence, and by an institution of legislation that is sensitive rather than obdurate to changes in popular morality. So the disagreement between naturalism and conventionalism about which cases are really "easy" is not a disagreement between those who oppose and those who respect democracy; it is rather the more familiar disagreement about what democracy really is. When the disagreement is seen in this light, it is far from apparent that the naturalist has the worst of the argument. In the next section, I shall argue that naturalism respects, better than its rivals, a right that has seemed to many people crucial to the idea of democracy, which is the right each person has to be treated, by his government, as an equal.

4. Is It Crazy?

A. Instrumentalism

We must turn now to the arguments that might be made against naturalism, not from the standpoint of conventionalism, but from the different direction of a more radical theory I shall call instrumentalism. This theory encourages judges always to look to the future: to try to make the community as good and wise and just a community as it can be, with no essential regard to what it has been until now. Of course instrumentalist judges will differ, among themselves, about the correct model of the good community. Some will define this in almost exclusively economic terms. They will think that a rich community is for that reason a good community. Others will take a more utilitarian line, and emphasize the importance of general happiness over total wealth. But

still others will insist on the importance of personal and political rights, and will therefore provide, in their account of the good society, that certain fundamental interests of individuals, like liberty of conscience or a decent standard of living, be respected at the cost of general wealth or average happiness.

An instrumentalist judge will see himself or herself as an officer of government charged with contributing to the good society according to his or her conception of what that is. Of course a sensible instrumentalist judge will acknowledge the importance of institutional factors as either an obstacle or opportunity in this enterprise. He will understand, in particular, that the rules he fashions must work together with the rules provided by other institutions and other officials, so that he is constrained by what we might call consistency in strategy. If the legislature and other judges have laid down rules in the past that he is powerless to overrule, for example, he must not create rules of his own which, operating alongside those established rules, would produce chaos. For that would make the community worse not better off through his efforts. But instrumentalism denies that judges should be constrained by the past in any less pragmatic way than that. It denies, in particular, that they should also seek consistency in principle, by making their decisions conform to the best interpretation, as the naturalist conceives this, of the past. Naturalism insists that the past should be allowed to cast a shadow over the future beyond the pragmatic requirements of strategy. Instrumentalism condemns this as irrational.

In order to bring out the difference between the two theories, consider this situation. You think that it would be best, all things considered, if no one were ever allowed to recover damages for emotional injury. You think this because you believe that actions for emotional damage involve the risk of fraud, and force insurance premiums higher than the optimum for economic efficiency. Of course you think, as part of this view, that no one has what we might call a moral right that the law provide damages for emotional injuries. If you thought anyone did have such a right, then you would think that the good society should recognize that right and enforce it by producing the appropriate legislation even at the cost of efficiency. But since you think people have no such moral right you think that society would be better off, on the whole, if it provided no legal right to such damages.

Now suppose you are an instrumentalist judge faced with a suit by a mother who suffered emotional injury when she heard, on the telephone, that her son had been run down by a careless driver. You find, when you search the books, that the other judges of your jurisdiction have consistently awarded recovery for emotional damages to relatives who actually saw physical damage to someone they loved. Of course you think that all these decisions were wrong. You would be tempted to overrule the whole line of decisions if you could, but suppose this is beyond your power. The line might include decisions of the highest court of the state, for example, and you might be sitting in a lower court. You will nevertheless grasp the opportunity to limit the damage these cases do to the community's welfare, according to your convictions, by declaring that only relatives who actually saw the injury may recover for emotional damage. This will create no practical contradictions, or inconsistency in strategy.

What objection could there be to this instrumentalist solution to the problem, assuming as you do, that it conduces to a better state of affairs, on the whole, than the opposite decision? A naturalist might be led by his naturalism to the opposite decision, even if he shared your assumptions about the best state of affairs. He would be unable to find any principled distinction between seeing and hearing about an accident, and he would be forced to concede that the best justification of the past recognizes a judicial right to recover for emotional damage if that damage was reasonably forseeable. Of course he might try to show (as the naturalist judge in the example I considered earlier was able to show about actions in negligence against lawyers) that allowing recovery for emotional damage was inconsistent with some broader line of cases. But suppose he could not show this, as indeed he is unlikely to be able to do. He would then be forced to decide the present case for the plaintiff mother, therefore compounding the damage to the future. What could be the possible sense or other merit in that? This is the basis of the instrumentalist charge: that

insofar as naturalism requires different decisions from those an instrumentalist would reach, naturalism is crazy.

Naturalism seems to assume that in these circumstances it would be for some reason *unfair* to decide against her. But why? She has (by hypothesis) no moral right to a rule allowing her damages. On the contrary, the situation would be better if no one were ever required to pay damage for her sort of injury. The fact that our judicial process has made one mistake is no good argument for making that mistake more general. Of course a naturalist cannot say that it would be unfair to decide against the mother because most judges in the past have behaved as naturalists. It would beg the present question to say that this provides a reason why a judicial decision that offends naturalism is unfair. For the question at issue is whether it is unfair to reach a decision which offends the best interpretation of the past. If we want to sustain naturalism as against instrumentalism, we must argue that the fact that a given principle figures in the best justification of legal practice as a whole provides a reason for extending that principle into the future, and we must not rely on that very claim in making our case for it. But how can we then argue the case? What can we say to the instrumentalist who claims, reasonably enough, that two mistakes are worse than one?

B. The Political Order

The naturalist might begin his reply by noticing that the dispute now in play is wider than simply a dispute about how judges should decide cases. Naturalism assumes and instrumentalism denies that the members of a community can have rghts and duties against one another, and against the community as such, just by virtue of the political history of the community. That they can have rights and duties they would not have if that history had been different. But this is an idea familiar not only to lawyers but to our general political rhetoric. Politicians say that America is a democracy, and therefore that certain things ought and ought not to be done. Or that America respects the rule of law, and therefore that Congress should not enact certain laws.

We should give a name to the idea behind this

rhetoric. Let us say that the set of political rights people have just by virtue of the political history of their community constitutes the "political order" of the community. Naturalism recognizes that communities have political orders, and offers an account of what a political order is. A community's political order is provided by the principles assumed in the best interpretation (in the sense we have been using) of its concrete political structures, practices and decisions. Naturalism supposes that people have a right to have this order enforced, in court, on demand. It is not true that every rule of law a legislature or court adopts is part of the political order, properly understood. The best interpretation of the order as a whole may show this particular rule inconsistent with the rest, and so a "mistake" that should be ignored in stating what the order really is. But if it is indeed part of the genuine political order, properly understood, that people suffering emotional injury are entitled to damages against the tortfeasor, then someone who has suffered such damage is for that reason entitled to a judicial order to that effect.

Of course naturalism is a theory about *judicial* rights, that is, about the rights people have to win law suits. It takes no position about how far the political order furnishes or constrains the rights people have to particular legislation in their favor, or their rights to revolt or otherwise to establish a very different political order. If the political order includes a constitution which, properly interpreted, disables the legislature from changing the present order in certain ways, then people do have judicial rights, under this order, that the courts not enforce legislation which contradicts these commands. But naturalism, as such, leaves the legislature otherwise free to improve the present order, both in detail and, if appropriate, radically. The idea, that people have an abstract judicial right to the enforcement of the present order, imposes a kind of conservatism on politics; but this is a conservatism imposed on adjudication alone.

Instrumentalism challenges not simply naturalism's conception of a political order, but the concept of a political order itself. It denies the fact that political history that has taken a certain form can ever be the ground of a genuine right or duty at least against a court. This is the upshot of the instrumentalist's thesis that there are no judicial rights by virtue of the judicial past. He believes that a judge is never obliged, by the nature of the past, to work against the best solution for the future. The instrumentalist argues that the idea that judges are constrained in this way is irrational. Of course he recognizes each society has a distinctive political past, and concedes that most people believe their rights and duties are, at least in some ways, a function of the past. But the instrumentalist holds that this opinion is silly.

Now what arguments does a naturalist have available in reply? We might begin by considering one familiar argument a naturalist might be tempted to make, though only to reject it. Someone might argue that judges should never attempt to change the political order because this would require them to make judgments of political morality which ought to be left to the peoples' elected representatives. So judges should accept the popular idea of a political order, and enforce that order as history presents it to them, for that reason. This is like the (bad) argument we supposed a conventionalist might make against naturalism; in any case it is not an argument a naturalist can make against instrumentalism because, according to naturalism, a judge must make decisions of political morality in order to decide what the political order, properly construed, really is. We labored that point in our description of how a naturalist judge would go about deciding which interpretation of the past was the best interpretation. There is, for the naturalist, a crucial distinction between interpreting and improving the political order of the community, but these are both activities which engage the judge's moral sense.

For much the same reason the naturalist cannot use another familiar argument often made in favor of judicial conservatism. It is sometimes said that judges do great damage to social efficiency when they surprise litigants by changing established rules of law. Once again this is an argument that a conventionalist might be tempted to employ against naturalism. But it is unavailable to naturalism because nothing insures that a naturalist judge's interpretation of the past will not prove surprising. A naturalist is charged with discovering and enforcing the best interpretation of his community's political structure and past decisions, but the interpretation he believes best may be (as we saw in the example of Cardozo's decision in *McPherson v. Buick*) interpretation that has occurred to no one else. In any case, the argument is a bad argument against instrumentalism for a different reason. This argument supposes that a novel decision, such as an instrumentalist might make, will in fact be unwise, pragmatically, for the future. But if this is really so, then an instrumentalist is ready to take that into account in deciding which decision will be best for the future. We noticed that an instrumentalist will look to the past, not as a source of rights, but strategically, to discover whether his judgment will in fact have the beneficial effects on the future he supposes. If disregarding some established line of precedent will actually diminish efficiency, because it will discourage people from counting on established rules of law in planning their affairs, then this is exactly the kind of strategic consideration instrumentalism stands ready to acknowledge.

A naturalist must find his defense of naturalism — of his idea that the standing political order is a source of judicial rights — elsewhere. He must meet the instrumentalist's challenge directly, by showing why people can have genuine political rights just by virtue of the actual political history of their community, and why these rights hold with special force in litigation. Can we find such an argument for naturalism? We might begin by stipulating a general requirement of justice in government. Any government must treat its citizens as equals, as equally entitled to concern and respect. Of course this general requirement is very abstract. Different people — and different societies — will have different views of what it is to treat people as equals. But we can nevertheless speak of a general duty of government to treat its citizens this way, and derive from this two distinct and more concrete responsibilities. The first is the responsibility, in creating a political order, to respect whatever underlying moral and political rights citizens may have in the name of genuine equality. The second is the obligation to extend whatever political order it does create equally and consistently to everyone.

These obligations are distinct because they can be fulfilled or violated independently. A society may develop a conception of justice that we, as critics of that society, reject. In its pursuit of efficiency or other collective goals, it may violate rights we think people have as individuals, but it may nevertheless enforce that conception consistently and, in that sense, fairly, allowing to everyone the resources, opportunities, and protections each is entitled to have under the theory it has adopted. It may, on the other hand, put in place an admirable political order; it may adopt a general scheme of principles and institutions, which we, as critics, approve as exactly what justice requires; but it may nevertheless fail to enforce that scheme consistently, so that some people do not have the resources and opportunities the public order requires them to have.

Once we recognize both the fact and the independence of these two rights, we see how it is possible that a government might commit the following special form of injustice. It might deny to some people a right it has, but need not have, extended to others. But that is exactly what the instrumentalist judge I just imagined does in denying the mother her suit for emotional damages. In one sense the situation that follows his decision is an improvement over the situation that would have resulted had he decided for the mother. If he is right in thinking that allowing recovery for emotional damage is not required by morality, and that it is damaging to the economy, then there will be less "unnecessary" damage to economic efficiency. But the plaintiff mother in this case nevertheless has a complaint. Though she has no right to a legal regime under which people in her position recover damages, she does have a right that the legal regime in force be consistently applied to her. Otherwise society fails to give her justice according to its conception of what justice requires, and that is a failure to treat her with equal concern and respect. One of her political rights has been violated.

So the naturalist's approach to this case is correct, and the instrumentalist's wrong, because the former respects and the latter violates the plaintiff's right to be treated as an equal. This is enough to make out what I am presently most anxious to show: that instrumentalism is wrong in assuming that the political order cannot be an independent source of rights. Of course the case I supposed as an example made it easier to demonstrate that point; it is implausible to think that a negligent driver has a moral right *not* to have the law recognize emotional damages. So the defendant driver seemed to have no proper objection to a naturalist judge's decision in favor of the mother. We can easily imagine cases, however, in which even the best interpretation of the community's law would show that it failed to recognize a substantive right someone ought to have.

Suppose, for example, that someone sues for damages for invasion of privacy, but even the most sophisticated interpretation of the law of the community fails to reveal a principle sustaining any such right. Now the situation reveals a conflict (as we might put it) between the two rights that follow from the abstract right to justice. A naturalist judge, who denies the action, will have upheld the defendant's right to a consistent application of the public order, but failed to uphold the plaintiff's right to a better public order. Naturalism insists that the function of courts, at least in a political society meeting minimum standards of justice, is to address the former rather than the latter right. No doubt more argument is necessary (which I cannot supply here) to sustain that choice. Once the two rights are distinguished, however, and both recognized, that choice is not crazy. Naturalism is not, as the present objection supposed, irrational.

But what if the condition I just mentioned is not met? What if the best interpretation of the legal system (or some important part of it) shows it to be wicked? Suppose that the most sophisticated interpretation of our Constitution, at the time of the Fugitive Slave Acts, contained no principle in virtue of which slaves had a right to be free, so that even a naturalist judge would have had to recognize those unfortunate statutes as perfectly constitutional. An instrumentalist might well want to say that here, at least, instrumentalism would provide a better guide to decision, because it would advise the judge to ignore the constitutional structure, if he could get away with this, and find some way to thwart the Acts. But naturalism has the virtue, even in cases like this one, of bringing to the surface an issue of political morality that cannot be ignored.

Of course a constitutional structure that permits slavery is deeply defective. It violates people's first political right: the right to a public order that treats them as equals. The more difficult issue is this: is there any room, in this sorry picture, for the slaveholders' second right? Does the slaveholder whose slaves have escaped have any right, however weak, that the constitutional system be enforced on his behalf, as it is on behalf of the slaveowner who has managed to keep his slaves imprisoned at home? If you were a naturalist judge, you might think that he does. In that case you would have to decide the Fugitive Slave Cases for the slaveowners even though you despise them and deplore that constitution, and even though you privately work for a constitutional amendment or even for civil war. But you might also come to the opposite conclusion. You might think that no one can have any right, even a weak right, to the equal benefit of wicked laws. In that case you would decide against the slaveowners if you could, because the underlying reason for your concern with the past, which is people's abstract rights to institutional consistency, would have exhausted its power. It would not matter if you put your conclusion in the terminology of older natural law theories, and said that the Fugitive Slave Acts were not really law. Or if you used the language of modern positivism, and said that though they were law they were too evil to be enforced. For the important issue is not what you say but what you do, and, though naturalism does not in itself answer the difficult moral question I posed, it does tell you what consequences for your decision follow from the answer you give to that question.

C. The Two Ideals

Perhaps you will allow me a summary of this last part of my argument. Our political system admits of two ideals; it is imperfect in two ways. It stands in the shadow of an external ideal, which is the ideal of a perfectly just and effective system. This is the challenge it offers to legislation, and, beyond that, to the political will and sense of justice of the community which has the standing power to make it better, closer to the external ideal of what a political system should be. But unless it is a very bad political system it stands also in the shadow of a different, internal ideal, which is the ideal of itself made pure. This is the challenge it offers to adjudication: the challenge of making the standards that govern our collective lives articulate, coherent and effective. Naturalism insists on the difference between the two ideals, and makes that difference the nerve of the rule of law.

People will disagree about what the internal ideal of our order is like, perhaps just as much as they disagree about what external ideal our order should pursue. Indeed they will disagree about the former precisely because they disagree about the latter. So no one will have any guarantee that, if he should come to court, those who judge him according to naturalism will reach the result that he himself thought was the best interpretation of our order when he acted. That is inevitable in any community which recognizes what is plainly true: that people have rights beyond the rights conventionalism recognizes, that is, that they have rights beyond the strict and narrow limits within which everyone agrees what these rights are. But naturalism at least takes the actual political order, properly interpreted, as the common standard, so that citizens are encouraged to put to themselves the same questions that officials who adjudicate their disputes will ask in judging them. No doubt this practice will cause surprise and disappointment, even despair. No doubt it will produce injustice. Its virtue is that it seems less vulnerable, in all these respects, than available alternatives for bringing the rule of principle to an imperfect world.

We can, as a community, strive towards these two ideals at the same time, though through different institutions and practice. We embrace the two ideals as an agenda for sustained and continuing debate. We have no hope — and indeed no wish — that the debate will end. We understand that the decision of political officials must be accepted, from time to time. But we insist that this is only because someone's decisions must be accepted and not because these decisions come guaranteed for accuracy. We know that the quality of the debate is itself, quite apart from any agreement it might produce, something that makes ourselves and our community better. This is the image we should have of politics and of our lives in politics. Our courts play a distinct sovereign and indispensible role in this image. They are the forum of the second ideal.

NOTES

1. R. Dworkin, *Taking Rights Seriously* 105–130 (1977).

2. R. Dworkin, *Law and Interpretation*, CRITICAL INQUIRY (1982).

3. McPherson v. Buick, 217 N.Y. 382, 111 N.E. 1050 (N.Y. 1916).

Notes and Questions

JOHN CHIPMAN GRAY, from *The Nature and Sources of Law*

1. The John Chipman Gray selection represents a theoretical movement called *legal realism* that was prominent in the 1930s and 1940s and that has adherents today. This school of thought focuses on the function of courts as the key to understanding the nature of law. How does Gray define the law as a whole? Notice that he distinguishes "a law" from "The law." What is the significance of this distinction? He also argues that it is important to distinguish law from sources of law. Why does he think so? Does it help you to understand law better to make this distinction — for example, is there some problem that it clears up or some function it makes more understandable?

2. Gray provides a very nice summary of prominent competing theories. Do you recognize any of them? Hart's theory of law as rules is a later development of Austin's command theory of law. Both are forms of legal positivism. Would Gray's objections to Austin's theory hold up against Hart's version of positivism? The idea that judges are discoverers of the law is a natural law view. What are Gray's objections to it? Can a modern theory like Dworkin's handle these criticisms? Are the criticisms fair? We have not considered elsewhere in this book the theory that law is just the outward expression of the collective wisdom that lives in the consciousness of the people. This

theory has fallen out of favor and is no longer talked about. Does it seem less plausible than the other theories? How does Gray object to it? Can you think of any answers to his objections?

3. How does Gray affirmatively defend his theory? Is it a descriptive theory or a normative theory? Gray says that whoever has the final authority to interpret the law — the last person in the chain of command with the power to say the law means — is the law giver. Is that false? How well does it account for the problems raised in novel cases, cases of first instance (such as the famous case of *Griswold* v. *Connecticut*)? How well can you account for such problematic cases (in any legal system) if you reject Gray's thesis? What are the implications, if any, of this thesis for the idea of a rule of law?

4. What are the objections to the realist theory of law (in particular Gray's version)? Can Gray explain law that is never obeyed? Can he explain law that is never disobeyed? Are there other problems?

[From] *The Nature and Sources of Law*

JOHN CHIPMAN GRAY

CHAPTER 4

The Law

Definition of the Law

The Law of the State or of any organized body of men is composed of the rules which the courts, that is, the judicial organs of that body, lay down for the determination of legal rights and duties. The difference in this matter between contending schools of Jurisprudence arises largely from not distinguishing between the Law and the Sources of the Law. On the one hand, to affirm the existence of *nicht positivisches Recht*, that is, of Law which the courts do not follow, is declared to be an absurdity; and on the other hand, it is declared to be an absurdity to say that the Law of a great nation means the opinions of half-a-dozen old gentlemen, some of them, conceivably, of very limited intelligence.

The truth is, each party is looking at but one side of the shield. If those half-a-dozen old gentlemen form the highest judicial tribunal of a country, then no rule or principle which they refuse to follow is Law in that country. However

desirable, for instance, it may be that a man should be obliged to make gifts which he has promised to make, yet if the courts of a country will not compel him to keep his promise, it is not the Law of that country that promises to make a gift are binding. On the other hand, those six men seek the rules which they follow not in their own whims, but they derive them from sources often of the most general and permanent character, to which they are directed, by the organized body to which they belong, to apply themselves. I believe the definition of Law that I have given to be correct; but let us consider some other definitions of the Law which have prevailed and which still prevail.

Of the many definitions of the Law which have been given at various times and places, some are absolutely meaningless, and in others a spark of truth is distorted by a mist of rhetoric. But there are three theories which have commended themselves to accurate thinkers, which have had and which still have great acceptance, and which deserve examination. In all of them it is denied that the courts are the real authors of the Law, and it is contended that they are merely the mouthpieces which give it expression.

Law as the Command of the Sovereign

The *first* of these theories is that Law is made up of the commands of the sovereign. This is Austin's view. "Every Positive Law," he says, "obtaining in any community, is a creature of the Sovereign or State; having been established immediately by the monarch or supreme body, as exercising legislative or judicial functions; or having been established immediately by a subject individual or body, as exercising rights or powers of direct or judicial legislation, which the monarch or supreme body has expressly or tacitly conferred."

In a sense, this is true; the State can restrain its courts from following this or that rule; but it often leaves them free to follow what they think right; and it is certainly a forced expression to say that one commands things to be done, because he has power (which he does not exercise) to forbid their being done.

Mr. A. B., who wants a house, employs an architect, Mr. Y. Z., to build it for him. Mr. Y. Z. puts up a staircase in a certain way; in such a case, nine times out of ten, he puts it up in that way, because he always puts up staircases in that way, or because the books on construction say they ought to be so put up, or because his professional brethren put up their staircases in that fashion, or because he thinks to put it up so would be good building, or in good taste, or because it costs him less trouble than to put it up in some other way; he seldom thinks whether Mr. A. B. would like it in that way or not; and probably Mr. A. B. never thinks whether it could have been put up in any other fashion. Here it certainly seems strained to speak, as Austin would do, of the staircase as being the "creature" of Mr. A. B.; and yet Mr. A. B. need not have had his staircase put up in that way, and indeed need never have had any staircase or any house at all.

When an agent, servant, or official does acts as to which he has received no express orders from his principal, he may aim, or may be expected to aim, *directly* at the satisfaction of the principal, or he may not. Take an instance of the first,—a cook, in roasting meat or boiling eggs, has, or at any rate the ideal cook is expected to have, *directly* in view the wishes and tastes of her master. On the other hand, when a great painter is employed to cover a church wall with a picture, he is not expected to keep constantly in mind what will please the wardens and vestry; they are not to be in all his thoughts; if they are men of ordinary sense, they will not wish to be; he is to seek his inspiration elsewhere, and the picture when done is not the "creature" of the wardens and vestry; whereas, if the painter had adopted an opposite course, and had bent his whole energies to divining what he thought would please them best, he would have been their "tool," and the picture might not unfairly be described as their creature.

Now it is clear into which of these classes a judge falls. Where he has not received direct commands from the State, he does not consider, he is not expected to consider, *directly* what would please the State; his thoughts are directed to the questions—What have other judges held? What does Ulpian or Lord Coke say about the matter? What decision does *elegantia juris* or sound morals require?

It is often said by hedonistic moralists that, while happiness is the end of human life, it is best attained by not aiming directly at it; so it may be the end of a court, as of any other organ of a body, to carry out the wishes of that body, but it best reaches that object by not directly considering those wishes.

Austin's statement that the Law is entirely made up of commands directly or indirectly imposed by the State is correct, therefore, only on the theory that everything which the State does not forbid its judges to do, and which they in fact do, the State commands, although the judges are not animated by a direct desire to carry out the State's wishes, but by entirely different ones.

"A Law" and "The Law"

In this connection, the meaning of "Law," when preceded by the indefinite, is to be distinguished from that which it bears when preceded by the definite, article. Austin, indeed, defines the Law as being the aggregate of the rules established by political superiors; and Bentham says, "*Law, or the Law*, taken indefinitely, is an abstract and collective term; which, when it means anything, can mean neither more nor less than the sum total of a number of individual laws taken together." But this is not, I think, the ordinary meaning given to "the Law." *A* law ordinarily means a statute passed by the legislature of a State. "*The* Law" is the whole system of rules applied by the courts. The resemblance of the terms suggests the inference that the body of rules applied by the courts is composed wholly of the commands of the State; but to erect this suggestion into a demonstration, and say: — The system administered by the courts is "the Law," "the Law" consists of nothing but an aggregate of single laws, and all single laws are commands of the State, — is not justifiable.

It is to Sir Henry Maine that we owe the distinct pointing out that Austin's theory "is founded on a mere artifice of speech, and that it assumes courts of justice to act in a way and from motives of which they are quite unconscious. . . . Let it be understood that it is quite possible to make the theory fit in with such cases, but the process is a mere straining of language. It is carried on by taking words and propositions altogether out of the sphere of the ideas habitually associated with them."

Austin's theory was a natural reaction against the views which he found in possession of the field. Law had been defined as "the art of what is good and equitable"; "that which reason in such sort defines to be good that it must be done"; "the abstract expression of the general will existing in and for itself"; "the organic whole of the external conditions of the intellectual life." If Austin went too far in considering the Law as always proceeding from the State, he conferred a great benefit on Jurisprudence by bringing out clearly that the Law is at the mercy of the State.

Law in the Consciousness of the People

The *second* theory on the nature of Law is that the courts, in deciding cases, are, in truth, applying what has previously existed in the common consciousness of the people. Savigny is the ablest expounder of this theory. At the beginning of the *System des heutigen römischen Rechts*, he has set it forth thus: "It is in the common consciousness of the people that the positive law lives, and

hence we have to call it *Volksrecht*. . . . It is the *Volksgeist*, living and working in all the individuals in common, which begets the positive law, so that for the consciousness of each individual there is, not by chance but necessarily, one and the same law. . . . The form, in which the Law lives in the common consciousness of the people, is not that of abstract rule, but the living intuition of the institute of the Law in its organic connection. . . . When I say that the exercise of the *Volksrecht* in single cases must be considered as a means to become acquainted with it, an indirect acquaintance must be understood, necessary for those who look at it from the outside, without being themselves members of the community in which the *Volksrecht* has arisen and leads its continuous life. For the members of the community, no such inference from single cases of exercise is necessary, since their knowledge of it is direct and based on intuition."

Savigny is careful to discriminate between the common consciousness of the people and custom: "The foundation of the Law," he says, "has its existence, its reality, in the common consciousness of the people. This existence is invisible. How can we become acquainted with it? We become acquainted with it as it manifests itself in external acts, as it appears in practice, manners, and custom: by the unifromity of a continuous and continuing mode of action, we recognize that the belief of the people is its common root, and not mere chance. Thus, custom is the sign of positive law, not its foundation."

Opinions of Jurists

Savigny is confronted by a difficulty of the same kind as confronted Austin. The great bulk of the Law as it exists in any community is unknown to its rulers, and it is only by aid of the doctrine that what the sovereign permits he commands, that the Law can be considered as emanating from him; but equally, the great bulk of the Law is unknown to the people; how, then, can it be the product of their "common consciousness"? How can it be that of which they "feel the necessity as law"?

Take a simple instance, one out of thousands. By the law of Massachusetts, a contract by letter is not complete until the answer of acceptance is received. By the law of New York, it is complete when the answer is mailed. Is the common consciousness of the people of Massachusetts different on this point from that of the people of New York? Do the people of Massachusetts feel the necessity of one thing as law, and the people of New York feel the necessity of the precise opposite? In truth, not one in a hundred of the people of either State has the dimmest notion on the matter. If one of them has a notion, it is as likely as not to be contrary to the law of his State.

Savigny meets the difficulty thus: "The Law, originally the common property of the collected people, in consequence of the ramifying relations of real life, is so developed in its details that it can no more be mastered by the people generally. Then a separate class of legal experts is formed which, itself an element of the people, represents the community in this domain of thought. In the special consciousness of this class, the Law is only a continuation and peculiar development of the *Volksrecht*. The last leads, henceforth, a double life. In its fundamental principles it continues to live in the common consciousness of the people; the exact determination and the application to details is the special calling of the class of jurisconsults."

But the notion that the opinions of the jurisconsults are the developed opinions of the people is groundless. In the countries of the English Common Law, where the judges are the jurists whose opinions go to make up the Law, there would be less absurdity in considering them as expressing the opinions of the people; but on the Continent of Europe, in Germany for instance, it is difficult to think of the unofficial and undeterminate class of jurists, past and present, from whose writings so great a part of the Law has been derived, as expressing the opinions of the people. In their reasonings, it is not the opinions of the people of their respective countries, Prussia, or Schwartzburg-Sonderhausen, which guide their judgment. They may bow to the authority of statutes, but in the domain of Law which lies outside the statute, the notions of Law, if they exist and are discoverable, which they are mostly not, of the persons among whom they live, are the last things which they take into account. What they look to are the opinions of foreign lawyers, of Papinian, of Accursius, of Cujacius, or at the *elegantia juris*, or at "juristic necessity."

The jurists set forth the opinions of the people no more and no less than any other specially educated or trained class in a community set forth the opinions of that community, each in its own sphere. They in no other way set forth the *Volksgeist* in the domain of Law than educated physicians set forth the *Volksgeist* in the matter of medicine. It might be very desirable that the conceptions of the *Volksgeist* should be those of the most skilful of the community, but however desirable this might be, it is not the case. The *Volksgeist* carries a piece of sulphur in its waistcoat pocket to keep off rheumatism, and thinks that butchers cannot sit on juries.

Not only is popular opinion apart from professional opinion in Law as in other matters, but it has been at times positively hostile. Those who hold that jurists are the mouthpieces of the popular convictions in matters of law have never been able to deal satisfactorily with the reception of the Roman law in Germany, for that Law was brought in not only without the wishes, but against the wishes of the great mass of the people.

Judges as Discoverers of the Law

A *third* theory of the Law remains to consider. That theory is to this effect: The rules followed by the courts in deciding questions are not the expression of the State's commands, nor are they the expression of the common consciousness of the people, but, although what the judges rule is the Law, it is putting the cart before the horse to say that the Law is what the judges rule. The Law, indeed, is identical with the rules laid down by the judges, but those rules are laid down by the judges because they are the law, they are not the Law because they are laid down by the judges; or, as the late Mr. James C. Carter puts it, the judges are the discoverers, not the creators, of the Law. And this is the way that judges themselves are apt to speak of their functions.

Only What the Judges Lay Down Is Law

This theory concedes that the rules laid down by the judges correctly state the Law, but it denies that it is Law because they state it. Before considering the denial, let us look a moment at the concession. It is a proposition with which I think most Common-Law lawyers would agree. But we ought to be sure that our ideas are not colored by the theories or practice of the particular system of law with which we are familiar. In the Common Law, it is now generally recognized that the judges have had a main part in erecting the Law; that, as it now stands, it is largely based on the opinions of past generations of judges; but in the Civil Law, as we shall see hereafter, this has been true to a very limited extent. In other words, judicial precedents have been the chief material for building up the Common Law, but this has been far otherwise in the systems of the Continent of Europe. But granting all that is said by the Continental writers on the lack of influence of judicial precedents in their countries to be true, yet, although a past decision may not be a source of Law, a present decision is certainly an expression of what the Law now is. The courts of France to-day may, on the question whether a blank indorsement of a bill of exchange passes title, care little or nothing for the opinions formerly expressed by French judges on the point, but, nevertheless, the opinion of those courts to-day upon the question is the expression of the present Law of France, for it is in accordance with such opinion that the State will compel the inhabitants of France to regulate their conduct. To say that any doctrine which the courts of a country refuse to adopt is Law in that country, is to set up the idol of *nicht positivisches Recht*; and, therefore, it is true, in the Civil as well as in the Common Law, that the rules laid down by the courts of a country state the present Law correctly.

The great gain in its fundamental conceptions which Jurisprudence made during the last century was the recognition of the truth that the Law of a State or other organized body is not an ideal, but something which actually exists. It is not that which is in accordance with religion, or nature, or morality; it is not that which ought to be, but that which is. To fix this definitely in the Jurisprudence of the Common Law, is the feat that Austin accomplished. He may have been wrong in treating the Law of the State as being the command of the sovereign, but he was right in teaching that the rules for conduct laid down by the persons acting as judicial organs of the State, are the Law of the State, and that no rules not so laid down are the Law of the State.

The Germans have been singularly inappreciative of Bentham and Austin, and, as so often happens, the arrival at a sound result has been greatly hampered by nomenclature. Ethics is, in Continental thought, divided into two parts, one dealing with matters which can be enforced by external compulsion, and the other with those which cannot. The former of these is called *Rechtslehre*. According to Kant, Moral philosophy (*Metaphysik der Sitten*) is divisible into two parts: (1) the metaphysical principles of Jurisprudence (*Rechtslehre*), and (2) the metaphysical principles of ethics (*Tugendlehre*). Jurisprudence has for its subject-matter the aggregate of all the laws which it is possible to promulgate by external legislation. All duties are either duties of justice (*Rechtspflicht*) or duties of virtue (*Tugendpflicht*). The former are such as *admit* of external legislation; the latter are those for which such legislation is not possible. *Rechtslehre*, that is, deals not only with the rules which the State has actually imposed upon conduct, but also with all conduct which can be *potentially subjected* to such rules; and this has tended to obscure the distinction between the rules which have actually been laid down from those which might have been laid down. But of late years, the Germans, in their own way, have been coming round to Austin's view; and now the abler ones are abjuring all *"nicht positivisches Recht."*

Questions Not Previously Decided

To come, then, to the question whether the judges discover preëxisting Law, or whether the body of rules that they lay down is not the expression of preëxisting Law, but the Law itself. Let us take a concrete instance: On many matters which have come in question in various jurisdictions, there is no doctrine received *semper, ubique, et ab omnibus*. For instance, Henry Pitt has built a reservoir on his land, and has filled it with water; and, without any negligence on his part, either in the care or construction of his reservoir, it bursts, and the water, pouring forth, floods and damages the land of Pitt's neighbor, Thomas Underhill. Has Underhill a right to recover compensation from Pitt? In England, in the leading case of *Rylands* v. *Fletcher*, it was held that he could recover, and this decision has been followed in some of the United States—for instance, in Massachusetts; but in others, as, I believe, in New Jersey, the contrary is held.

Now, suppose that Pitt's reservoir is in one of the newer States, say Utah, and suppose, further, that the question has never arisen there before; that there is no statute, no decision, no custom on the subject; the court has to decide the case somehow; suppose it should follow *Rylands* v. *Fletcher* and should rule that in such cases the party injured can recover. The State, then, through its judicial organ, backed by the executive power of the State, would be recognizing the rights of persons injured by such accidents, and, therefore, the doctrine of *Rylands* v. *Fletcher* would be undoubtedly the present Law in Utah.

Suppose, again, that a similar state of facts arises in the adjoining State of Nevada, and that there also the question is presented for the first time, and that there is no statute, decision, or custom on the point; the Nevada court has to decide the case somehow; suppose it should decline to follow *Rylands* v. *Fletcher*, and should rule that in such cases the party injured is without remedy. Here the State of Nevada would refuse to recognize any right in the injured party and, therefore, it would unquestionably be the present Law in Nevada that persons injured by such an accident would have no right to compensation.

Let us now assume that the conditions and habits of life are the same in these two adjoining States; that being so, these contradictory doctrines cannot both conform to an ideal rule of Law, and let us, therefore, assume that an all-wise and all-good intelligence, considering the question, would think that one of these doctrines was right and the other wrong, according to the true standard of morality, whatever that may be. It matters not, for the purposes of the discussions, which of the two doctrines it is, but let us suppose that the intelligence aforesaid would approve *Rylands* v. *Fletcher*; that is, it would think the Law as established in Nevada by the decision of its court did not conform to the eternal principles of right.

The fact that the ideal theory of Law disapproved the Law as established in Nevada would not affect the present existence of that Law. However wrong intellectually or morally it might be, it would be the Law of that State to-day. But what was the Law in Nevada a week before a rule for decision of such questions was adopted by the courts of that State? Three views seem possible: *first*, that the Law was then ideally right, and contrary to the rule now declared and practised on; *second*, that the Law was then the same as is now declared practised; *third*, that there was then no Law on the matter.

The first theory seems untenable on any notion of discovery. A discoverer is a discoverer of that which is, — not of that which is not. The result of such a theory would be that when Underhill received the injury and brought his suit, he had an interest which would be protected by the State, and that it now turns out that he did not have it, — a contradiction in terms.

No Law Previous to Decision

We have thus to choose between the theory that the Law was at that time what it now is, and the theory that there was then no law at all on the subject. The latter is certainly the view of reason and common sense alike. There was, at the time in question, *ex hypothesi*, no statute, no precedent, no custom on the subject; of the inhabitants of the State not one out of a hundred had an opinion on the matter or had ever thought of it; of the few, if any, to whom the question had ever occurred, the opinions were, as likely as not, conflicting. To say that on this subject there was really Law existing in Nevada, seems only to show how strong a root legal fictions can strike into our mental processes.

When the element of long time is introduced, the absurdity of the view of Law preëxistent to its declaration is obvious. What was the Law in the time of Richard Coeur de Lion on the liability of a telegraph company to the persons to whom a message was sent? It may be said that though the Law can preëxist its declaration, it is conceded that the Law with regard to a natural force cannot exist before the discovery of the force. Let us take, then, a transaction which might have occurred in the eleventh century: A sale of chattels, a sending to the vendee, his insolvency, and an order by the vendor to the carrier not to deliver. What was the Law on stoppage *in transitu* in the time of William the Conqueror?

The difficulty of believing in preëxisting Law is still greater when there is a change in the decision of the courts. In Massachusetts it was held in 1849, by the Supreme Judicial Court, that if a man hired a horse in Boston on a Sunday to drive to Nahant, and drove instead to Nantasket, the keeper of the livery stable had no right to sue him in trover for the conversion of the horse. But in 1871 this decision was overruled, and the right was given to the stable-keeper. Now, did stable-keepers have such rights, say, in 1845? If they did, then the court in 1849 did not discover the Law. If they did not, then the court in 1871 did not discover the Law.

Courts Make Ex Post Facto *Law*

And this brings us to the reason why courts and jurists have so struggled to maintain the preëxistence of the Law, why the common run of writers speak of the judges as merely stating the Law, and why Mr. Carter, in an advance towards the truth, says of the judges that they are discoverers of the Law. That reason is the unwillingness to recognize the fact that the courts, with the consent of the State, have been constantly in the practice of applying in the decision of controversies, rules which were not in existence and were, therefore, not knowable by the parties when the causes of controversy occurred. It is the unwillingness to face the certain fact that courts are constantly making *ex post facto* Law.

The unwillingness is natural, particularly on the part of the courts, who do not desire to call attention to the fact that they are exercising a power which bears so unpopular a name, but it is not reasonable. Practically in its application to actual affairs, for most of the laity, the Law, except for a few crude notions of the equity involved in some of its general principles, is all *ex post facto*. When a man marries, or enters into a partnership, or buys a piece of land, or engages in any other transaction, he has the vaguest possible idea of the Law governing the situation, and with our complicated system of Jurisprudence, it is impossible it should be otherwise. If he delayed to make a contract or do an act until he understood exactly all the legal consequences it involved, the contract would never be made or the act done. Now the Law of which a man has no knowledge is the same to him as if it did not exist.

Again, the function of a judge is not mainly to declare the Law, but to maintain the peace by deciding controversies. Suppose a question comes up which has never been decided, — and such questions are more frequent than persons not lawyers generally suppose, — the judge must decide the case somehow; he will properly wish to decide it not on whim, but on principle, and he lays down some rule which meets acceptance with the courts, and future cases are decided in the same way. That rule is the Law, and yet the rights and duties of the parties were not known and were not knowable by them. That is the way parties are treated and have to be treated by the courts; it is solemn juggling to say that the Law, undiscovered and undiscoverable, and which is finally determined in opposite ways in two communities separated only by an artificial boundary, has existed in both communities from all eternity. I shall recur to this matter when we come to consider the topic of Judicial Precedents.

Law and the Natural Sciences

It may be said that there are reasons, based on the highest welfare of the human race, why the Law should be so or otherwise, and that it is one of the functions and duties of a judge to investigate those reasons; that he is an investigator as much as, in his sphere, was Sir Isaac Newton; that he may make mistakes, just as Newton did; and yet that truth is largely discovered by his means. But the difference between the judges and Sir Isaac is that a mistake by Sir Isaac in calculating the orbit of the earth would not send it spinning round the sun with an increased velocity; his answer to the problem would be simply wrong; while if the judges, in investigating the reasons on which the Law should be based, come to a wrong result, and give forth a rule which is discordant with the eternal verities, it is none the less Law. The planet can safely neglect Sir Isaac Newton, but the inhabitants thereof have got to obey the assumed pernicious and immoral rules which the courts are laying down, or they will be handed over to the sheriff.

Decisions as Conclusive Evidence of the Law

It is possible to state the facts in the terms of discovery by use of a device familiar enough in the Common Law. We may say that the rule has always existed, and that the opinions and consequent action of the judges are only conclusive evidence that such is the rule; but this is merely a form of words to hide the truth. Conclusive evidence is not evidence at all; it is something which takes the place of evidence and of the thing to be proved, as well. When we say that men are conclusively presumed to know the Criminal Law, we mean that men are to be punished for certain acts without regard to whether they know them to be against the Law or not; when we say that the registration of a deed is conclusive evidence against all the world, we mean that all the world are bound by a registered deed whether they know or not of its existence.

Rules of conduct laid down and applied by the courts of a country are coterminous with the Law of that country, and as the first change, so does the latter along with them. Bishop Hoadly has said: "Whoever hath an *absolute authority* to *interpret* any written or spoken laws, it is *he* who is truly the *Law-giver* to all intents and purposes, and not the person who first wrote or spoke them"; *a fortiori*, whoever hath an absolute authority not only to interpret the Law, but to say what the Law is, is truly the Law-giver. *Entia non multiplicanda*. There seems to be nothing gained by seeking to discover the sources, purposes, and relations of a mysterious entity called "The Law," and then to say this Law is exactly expressed in the rules by which the courts decide cases. It is better to consider directly the sources, purposes, and relations of the rules themselves, and to call the rules "The Law."

There is a feeling that makes one hesitate to accept the theory that the rules followed by the courts constitute the Law, in that it seems to be approaching the Law from the clinical or therapeutic side; that it is as if one were to define medicine as the science of the rules by which physicians diagnose and treat diseases; but the difference lies in this, that the physicians have not received from the ruler of the world any commission to decide what diseases are, to kill or to cure according to their opinion whether a sickness is mortal; whereas, this is exactly what the judges do with regard to the cases brought before them. If the judges of a country decide that it is Law that a man whose reservoir bursts must pay the damage, Law it is; but all the doctors in town may declare that a man has the yellow fever, and yet he may have only the German measles. If when a board of physicians pronounced that Titius had the colic, *ipso facto* Titius did have the colic, then I conceive the suggested definition of medicine would be unobjectionable.

To sum up. The State exists for the protection and forwarding of human interests, mainly through the medium of rights and duties. If every member of the State knew perfectly his own rights and duties, and the rights and duties of everybody else, the State would need no judicial organs; administrative organs would suffice. But there is no such universal knowledge. To determine, in actual life, what are the rights and duties of the State and of its citizens, the State needs and establishes judicial organs, the judges. To determine rights and duties, the judges settle what facts exist, and also lay down rules according to which they decide legal consequences from facts. These rules are law.

Notes and Questions

JANET RIFKIN, "Toward a Theory of Law and Patriarchy"

1. Janet Rifkin wants to understand the origin of patriarchy and, more important, why it is perpetuated. To do that she suggests a framework for examining the connection among culture, patriarchy, and law. The power of law as both symbol and vehicle of male authority is based on an ideology of law and an ideology of women, Rifkin claims. How does she explain the ideology of law? Law functions as a "hegemonic ideology," she says. What does that mean? Could law be otherwise?

2. What is the ideology — the official picture — of women in the eyes of the law, according to Rifkin? What is the nature of women according to law? How did this traditional picture mask real-

ity? Did the legal "protection" of women effectively require them to conform to the legal stereotype of women? What effect did that have economically and politically?

3. Is the ideology of women changing in law? In the past twenty years or so great efforts have been made in litigation and legislation to change the status of women. Rifkin says, "The reliance on litigation reflects the belief in law as a source of social change, while ignoring the ideological potential of law to mask social reality and block social change." What does she mean by that? Does the reaction to, say, abortion or affirmative action illustrate her point? If so, how?

4. What historical evidence does Rifkin give for her claim that patriarchal authority is the basis of culture itself? Assuming that the historical claim is correct, how would that affect the origin and nature of law? Even if, as a matter of historical fact, law has always been formulated by men, is there any reason to think that it would be any different if women had equally participated in its formulation? If so, what might be different, and why? Is law less likely to be universal if only one sex formulates it? Is it precluded from universality for that reason?

5. Rifkin argues that the image of maleness, and the male dominant paradigm of political power as objective, rational, and public, is also the image of law. Is there anything wrong with that image in itself? Is it, say, inaccurate, misleading, incomplete, flawed, unwholesome? Of course, the problem it causes for women is that the concomitant legal ideology of women — as subjective, irrational (or emotional), and private — excluded them from all public spheres of authority, especially, perhaps, political power and economic sufficiency. If the ideology of women could be changed (it is in fact slowly changing now) to include them in the public spheres equally (that is, if legal ideology as male authority could be changed), is there any further reason to change the image of law as objective, rational, and public?

6. How did capitalism make things worse for women, according to Rifkin? Is there anything about capitalism as such that should necessarily make things worse for women? Does capitalism have to be challenged to challenge the male dominant paradigm of law? How can it be challenged?

Toward a Theory of Law and Patriarchy

JANET RIFKIN

I. Ideology, Law and Power

The nature and meaning of patriarchal social order and of patriarchal culture has recently become the subject of intense scholarly questioning. Historians, literary scholars, political theorists, economists, anthropologists, sociologists, psychologists, and law teachers have been attempting through their respective disciplines, to understand the origin of patriarchy and the perpetuation of a patriarchal social order. By patriarchy, I mean any kind of group organization in which males hold dominant power and determine what part females shall and shall not play, and in which capabilities assigned to women are relegated generally to the mystical and aesthetic and excluded from the practical and political realms, these realms being regarded as separate and mutually exclusive.

Law plays a primarily and significant role in social order. The relationship between law and patriarchy, however, needs to be clarified and developed. I intend to suggest a theoretical framework in which the fundamental connections between culture, patriarchy and law can begin to become clearer. In this context, I will examine the cultural and anthropological origins of patriarchy: how law is a paradigm of maleness; how law and legal ideology under capitalism preserved, transformed and updated pre-existing patriarchal forms to serve the interests of the emerging bourgeoisie; and finally, why legal change does not lead to social reordering. I want to emphasize that my efforts are directed primarily toward developing a theoretical base from which many of these issues can be more exhaustively reviewed and studied in the future.

Law is powerful as both a symbol and a vehicle of male authority. This power is based both on an ideology of law and an ideology of women which is supported by law. One function of ideology is to mystify social reality and to block social change.[1] Law functions as a form of hegemonic ideology.[2] Thus, a court could rule that

> civil law, as well as nature herself, has always recognized a wide difference in the respective spheres and destinies of man and woman. Man is, or should be, woman's protector and defender. The natural and proper timidity and delicacy which belongs to the female sex evidently unfits it for many of the occupations of civil life.[3]

By the acceptance of this as a statement of reality, law is reinforced as a powerful ideological force of social cohesion and stability.

The ideology of law is also tied to its manifestation as a written set of formulations, principles and regulation. "Freezing ideas and information in words makes it possible to assess more coolly and rigorously the validity of an argument, . . . thus, 'reinforcing a certain kind and measure of [increased] rationality'."[4] The power of law as ideology is to mask or distort social reality in the name of tradition. Law, in relation to women, is seen as a measured and rational set of beliefs which at the same time asserts a mythological vision which is believed by many to present an accurate statement of the world.

A good example of this phenemonon is found in the suffragist movement of the early twentieth century. "Operating within the male-dominant paradigm, the form, language, and mode of Suffragist protest was set not so much by the objective conditions of female oppression as by their response to the idealizations and mystifications and legalities which rationalized continuance of the *status quo*."[5] Thus, the suffragist, in not challenging the ideology of law which supported an ideology of women, perpetuated mystifications which supported the status quo.

The power of legal ideology is so great that it often becomes hard to differentiate between legal principles and social customs. For example, American women have long worked outside the home in significant numbers. This fact of women's work in the labor market is constantly restricted by specific laws,[6] and is at odds with the basic legal ideology that females should be excluded from the public sphere of work. The legal ideology of these restrictions carries forward the basic message that women *are to be* at home. The legal ideology of women does not bend to accommodate the economic reality of working women.

In 1908, when a substantial number of American women were working,[7] the United States Supreme Court upheld a maximum hours law which applied to women only, reasoning that "her physical structure and a proper discharge of her maternal functions — having in view not merely her own health, but the well being of the race, justify legislation to protect her from the greed as well as the passion of man."[8] The ideological statement that women should be at home was couched in the context of the capitalist framework of competition for jobs. Economic competition between women and men was recognized, and in the name of protecting women, the hierarchical, male-dominated sex/gender system was reinforced. This reinforcement is supported by the ideological assertion that women are in need of greater protection than men.

The power of law as ideology continues into the present and may be examined in light of massive litigative efforts to change the status of women in contemporary society. The reliance on litigation reflects the belief in law as a source of social change, while ignoring the ideological power of law to mask social reality and block social change. Court battles about "women's issues" are waged and sometimes won with the result that a new body of rights is created and deployed in battle, but the basic sexual hierarchy is not changed. Although the hierarchy may be threatened in that each battle subjects the traditional law and legal ideology to examination and review, the litigation of "rights" never reaches the question of collective social organization.

In the area of the law of abortion, for instance, one sees that while the decisions[9] relating to contraception and abortion have been thought of in terms of the expansion of a woman's right to privacy and reproductive freedom, a challenge asserting a competing claim surfaces after every expression of an apparently broadened claim. Thus, after the decision in *Roe v. Wade* recognizing a limited constitutional right to abortion, cases were brought alleging that the rights of fathers were violated,[10] arguments were made that the rights of parents would be violated if minors had full rights to choose abortion[11] and laws and restrictions threatened doctors who performed abortions.[12]

Another significant example of this pattern is in the legal war over affirmative action, where there have been numerous lawsuits brought by individuals claiming that granting members of minority groups preference discriminates against members of the majority group.[13] Here the struggle is articulated as a battle between individuals competing for jobs and education. This focus ignores and obscures the more fundamental social and political questions of power which generate these lawsuits.

The crucial point is that these legal battles reflect anger and dissatisfaction which, in reality, potentially threaten the patriarchal hierarchy. The power of law is that by framing the issues as questions of law, claims of right, precedents and problems of constitutional interpretation, the effect is to divert potential public consciousness from an awareness of the deeper roots of the expressed dissatisfaction and anger. The ideology of law serves to mask the real social and political questions underlying these problems of law. At the same time, the paradigm of law which historically has been and continues to be the symbol of male authority is not only unchallenged but reinforced as a legitimate mechanism for resolving social conflict. In the end, patriarchy as a form of power and social order will not be eliminated unless the male power paradigm of law is challenged and transformed. In order to challenge the male paradigm of law, the origin of law as a form of male authority and power must be discovered and examined more thoroughly.

Although the relationship between women and the law has been the subject of a number of recent books, law school courses, undergraduate programs, and law review articles, few of these efforts have helped to elucidate the complexity of the relationship between law and patriarchal power. Similarly, the practice of law now includes "women's" litigation and women litigators. Litigation has resulted in challenges to statutory restrictions and common law practices in areas such as marriage and parenting, abortion, pregnancy disabilities, and equal employment benefits and opportunities. Nonetheless, these litigation efforts have not challenged the fundamental patriarchal social order. Litigation and other forms of formal legal relief, however, cannot lead to social changes, because in upholding and relying on the paradigm of law, the paradigm of patriarchy is upheld and reinforced.

The fact that little exploration of the connection between law and patriarchy has been done can be largely attributed to the fact that the study of law takes place primarily in the context of law school where the focus is exclusively on legal principles and case study. The study of law in law school is confined to a narrow doctrinal analysis of law and largely excludes an approach which examines the connections between law and social theory. For the most part, law school does not provide students with a framework of ideas to aid them in formulating personal values to help them explore the relationship between social values and law. Because traditional legal education ignores the cultural, political and social foundations of law, it is not possible, in the law school context, to illuminate the relationship of patriarchy and law.

II. Nature, Culture and Women

The efforts to find and explain the origins of patriarchy have led some scholars to examine mythology, fables and kinship bonds. Kate Millett, for example, in *Sexual Politics*, claims that "myth and kinship ties are the most lasting vestiges of that vast historical shift whereby patriarchy replaced whatever order preceded it and instituted that long government of male over female."[14] In this context, she turns to Aeschylus's Oresteia trilogy and its final play *The Eumenides*, in which he presents a confrontation between paternal authority and maternal order. In the first two plays, we have seen Clytemnestra, rebelling against the masculine authority of husband and King, kill Agamemnon upon his return from Troy, and her son Orestes revenge his father's death by killing her. In so doing, Orestes provokes the rage of the Furies, who accuse him of matricide. In the third play they put him on trial, assured that justice will be done. They are not prepared, however, for the emergence of the new form of patriarchal justice articulated by Athena, who says:

No mother gave me birth. Therefore, the father's claim
And male supremacy in all things, save to give
Myself in marriage, wins my whole heart's loyalty.
Therefore a woman's death, who killed her husband, is,
I judge, outweighed in grievousness by his. . . .15

Through Athena's deciding vote, Orestes is acquitted and his patrimony is reinforced. The Furies lament helplessly:

The old is trampled by the new!
Curse on you younger gods who override
The ancient laws . . .16

In this fable, law emerges as the symbol of patriarchal authority. The complex and fundamental connections, however, between law and patriarchy in a more general historical context have not been adequately developed, and these connections are essential to an understanding of political and social power.

In *The Elementary Structure of Kinship*,[17] Levi-Strauss, in analyzing the meaning of the universality of incest taboos, also analyzes the role of women in pre-state societies. He suggests that the concept of women as the property of men that is based in the universal notion of the exchange of women emerges as a fundamental tenet of culture. The origins of social order then are grounded on the conception of women as the property of men; the patriarchal social order is the basis of culture itself.

Levi-Strauss begins by asking where nature ends and culture begins. He suggests that the "absence of rules seems to provide the surest criterion for distinguishing a natural from a cultural process.[18] He finds that the incest taboo is a phenomenon which has the "distinctive characteristics both of nature and of its theoretical contradiction, culture. The prohibition of incest has the universality of bent and instinct and the coercive character of law and institution."[19] The rule against incest gives rise to rules of marriage, which although varying somewhat from group to group, are universally based on the taboo against incest. The rules of marriage also universally are based on the idea of exchange, and in particular, the exchange of women.[20] The exchange of women is a universal mode of culture, although not everywhere equally developed. Levi-Strauss asserts further that the incest taboo "is at once on the threshold of culture, in culture, and in one sense, . . . culture itself."[21] Since, as he shows, the exchange of women is integrally connected to the incest taboo, it can also be said that the exchange of women, as objects of male property, is also on the threshold of culture, in culture and is culture itself.

Levi-Strauss states that the role of exchange

in primitive society is essential because it embraces material objects, social values and women. But while in the case of merchandise this role has progressively diminished in importance in favour of other means of acquisition, as far as women are concerned, reciprocity has maintained its fundamental function, . . . because women are the most precious possession . . . [and] a natural stimulant.[22]

He asserts the universality of the exchange of women: "The inclusion of women in the number of reciprocal prestations from group to group and from tribe to tribe is such a general custom that a whole volume would not be sufficient to enumerate the instances of it."[23]

The notion of women as male property is then at the heart of cultural-social order. Matrimonial exchange is only a particular case of those forms of multiple exchanges embracing material goods, rights and persons:

The total relationship of exchange which constitutes marriage is not established between a man and a woman, . . . but between two groups of men, and the woman figures only as one of the objects in the exchange, not as one of the partners between whom the exchange takes place.[24]

Even where matrilinear descent is established, the woman is never more than the symbol of her lineage. And Levi-Strauss disposes of the myth of the "reign of women" which he says is "remembered only in mythology, [as] an age . . . when men had not resolved the antimony which is always likely to appear between their roles as takers of wives and givers of sisters, making them both the authors and victims of their exchanges."[25]

The origin of culture as reflected in kinship systems is universally based on the idea that women are the property of men to be exchanged between individuals or groups of males. Levi-Strauss sees a "masculinity of political authority"[26] when political power takes precedence over other forms of organization. Early political philosophy, as reflected by the writings of Aristotle, did not challenge this universal social fact. Aristotle, who developed a philosophy of politics and power, also saw political authority as masculine and saw women as nonparticipants in the political world.[27]

> Aristotle radically bifurcates public (political) from private (apolitical) realms. . . . Fully realized moral goodness and reason are attainable only through participation in public life, and this involvement is reserved to free, adult males. Women *share* in goodness and rationality in the limited sense appropriate to their confinement in a lesser association, the household. . . . Indeed, it can be said with no exaggeration that women in Aristotle's schema are *idiots* in the Greek sense of the word, that is, persons who do not participate in the *polis*.[28]

The political analysis of Aristotle upholds a male-dominant power paradigm which "serves to perpetuate an arbitrary bifurcation between that which is politics and that which is not. . . . Implicit within the paradigm is a concept of persons which admits into the privileges of full personhood . . . only those individuals who hold dual statuses as both public and private persons" — i.e., men.[29] The male-dominant paradigm of political power is also the paradigm of law. The historical image of maleness — objective, rational and public — is the dominant image of law.[30]

Law, in mythology, in culture and in philosophy, is the ultimate symbol of masculine authority and patriarchal society. The form of law is different in varying social groups, ranging from kinship bonds, custom, and the tribal rules in pre-state societies, to written codes in modern society. The point, however, is that law in state and non-state contexts is based on male authority and patriarchal social order.

III. Patriarchy, Law and Capitalism

In *Law and the Rise of Capitalism*, Michael Tigar and Madeline Levy show that the Thirteenth Century in England and in continental Europe "saw the creation and application of specific rules about contracts, property and procedure which strengthened the power of the rising bourgeoisie."[31] They show that these "rules were fashioned in the context of a legal ideology which identified freedom of action for businessmen with natural law and natural reason."[32]

In their study, however, Tigar and Levy do not examine the emerging law in relation to women. They do not discuss, for example, how the rise of capitalism profoundly changed the nature of work, the family, and the role of women. I maintain that law, which emerged "as a form of rationality appropriate to the social relations generated by the emergence of entrepreneurial capitalism,"[33] retained the pre-existing hierarchy of masculine authority and made more explicit the subordination of women to men by increasingly excluding women from working in trades and relegating them to the private world of the home, which itself also became more and more non-productive.

The feudal world, which was organized for war, was essentially a masculine world. Although laws and custom put wives under the power of their husbands, records indicate, nonetheless, participation by some noble women in social, political and legal activities. Women also demonstrated great productive capacity when society was organized on the basis of family and domestic industry. At the end of the Fourteenth Century, one-fourth of the cloth woven in York was produced by women. Laws, restrictive in some spheres, there encouraged women's economic participation. The Act of 1363, for example, declared that:

> [T]he intent of the king and of his council is that women, that is to say brewers, bakers, carders and spinners, and workers as well of wool as of linen-clothing . . . , and all other that do use and work all handiworks, may freely use and work as they have done before this time.[34]

This attitude began to change, however, during the next century as legal regulations promulgated by various guilds became increasingly restrictive of women's participation. Many of these laws reflected the blatant threat of competition to the male workers. In Bristol in 1461, it was complained that weavers employed their wives, daughters, and maidens "by the which many and divers of the king's liege people, likely men to do the king service in his wars and in the defence of this his land, and sufficiently learned in the said craft, goeth vagrant and unoccupied, and may not have their labour to their living."[35]

Sometimes a guild prohibited employment of women, though generally widows could work in their husband's craft. As late as 1726, the Baker's craft in Aberdeen which was distressed by the competition of women who used their own ovens and sold the produce themselves passed a law which mandated a severe fine to any freeman in the baking trade who allowed a woman to use his oven.[36] Other craft guilds were equally restrictive of women working in trades. Rachel Baxter, for example, was admitted to the tailor's craft provided "that she shall . . . have only the privilege of mantua-making, and no ways make stays, or import the same to sell from any other place . .. and it is hereby declared that thi [sic] presents to be no precedent to any woman in tyme coming."[37]

Thus, with the emergence of capitalism and through the power of legal regulation, women were affected in several fundamental ways: individual wages were substituted for family earnings, enabling men to organize themselves in the competition of the labor market without sharing with the women of their families all the benefits derived through their combination; the withdrawal of wage-earners from home life to work upon the premises of the masters and the prevention of the employment of the wage-earner's wife in her husband's occupation, and the rapid increase of wealth which allowed the upper class women to withdraw altogether from business.

Whereas the system of family industry united labor and capital in one person or family group, capitalism brought them into conflict and competition; men and women struggled with each other to secure work and wages. The keystone of the male journeymen's superior economic position in capitalism lay in their ability to restrict their own numbers by promulgating and enforcing laws which specifically limited numbers, imposed long apprenticeship programs and limited the number of apprentices.

The pre-existing patriarchal culture supported historically by kinship bonds and custom was transformed in capitalism through law in the service of new economic interest.

> [C]ustomary and traditional modes of conceptualizing bonds of obligation and duty were of diminishing relevance in bourgeois society, where people experienced a growing and radical separation between public life and private life. . . . [F]amily, and personal dependence begin to dissolve and crumble under the corrosive impact of the single universalist principles of social solidarity underlying capitalist social relations — *exchange*.[38]

The role of law in early capitalism was to help create a climate in which production for exchange could thrive. To accomplish this, law, always a symbol of male authority, fostered competition between women and men and severely limited female participation in the world of market production. Law became a primary and powerful tool of the rising bourgeoisie. Legal regulations were enacted which symbolized a continuation of the male authority of the past and which transformed and updated patriarchal society to serve new capitalistic interests. Laws were used increasingly to restrict women from working in trades, relegating them to the private world of the home. Thus, legal rules helped to create a social order where women were excluded from the public world of production exchange. And these new laws, justified in the name of the natural order, were accepted as an accurate vision of the world.

Conclusion

This discussion has suggested that there are fundamental connections between culture, patriarchy and law. The origins of culture, according to Levi-Strauss, are grounded in the conception of women as the property of men and that patriarchal social order is the basis of culture itself. Law emerges as the symbol of patriarchal authority in varying ways. With the emergence of capitalist society, law became a crucial, substantial and ideological mechanism which updated a pre-existing patriarchal social order to meet the needs of emerging capitalist interests. Through law women were relegated to the private world of the home and family and excluded from the public world of monetary exchange.

Although the recent litigation efforts to change the role of women in society have resulted in alleviating some oppressive practices, the paradigm of law as a symbol of male authority has not been challenged Indeed, the reliance on litigative and legislative strategies has reinforced the belief that the law-paradigm is a legitimate mechanism for resolving conflict and that it is a source of social change. As long as the male-dominant power paradigm of law remains unchallenged, the basic social hierarchy will not change. The struggle for sexual equality can be successful only if it challenges, rather than reifies, the male paradigm of law.

NOTES

1. Kellner, *Ideology, Marxism, and Advanced Capitalism*, 42 SOCIALIST REV. 38 (1978).
2. *Id.* at 49–50. "Ideology becomes hegemonic when it is widely accepted as describing 'the way things are,' inducing people to consent to their society and its way of life as natural, good, and just." *Id.*
3. Bradwell v. State, 83 U.S. (16 Wall.) 130, 141 (Bradley, J., concurring).
4. Kellner, *supra* note 10, at 45, quoting A. GOULDNER, THE DIALECTIC OF IDEOLOGY AND TECHNOLOGY 41 (1976).
5. Elshtain, *Moral Woman and Immoral Man: A Consideration of the Public-Private Split and its Political Ramifications*, 4 POL. & SOC'Y 453, 469 (1974).
6. *E.g.*, Muller v. Oregon, 208 U.S. 412 (1908); Goesart v. Cleary, 335 U.S. 464 (1948).
7. In 1900, 5,114,461 (20.4%) women aged fourteen years and over were gainfully employed out of a total female population in this age group of 25,024,415. By 1910, the number had increased to 7,788,826 out of 30,959,473 (25.2%). BUREAU OF THE CENSUS, UNITED STATES DEP'T OF COMMERCE, STATISTICAL ABSTRACT OF THE UNITED STATES 1944–45, at 134 (1945).
8. Muller v. Oregon, 208 U.S. 412, 422 (1908).
9. Roe v. Wade, 410 U.S. 113 (1973); Eisenstadt v. Baird, 405 U.S. 438 (1972); Griswold v. Conn., 381 U.S. 479 (1965).
10. Planned Parenthood of Cent. Missouri v. Danforth, 428 U.S. 52 (1976); Coe v. Gerstein, 376 F.Supp. 695 (S.D. Fla. 1973), *cert. denied*, 417 U.S. 279 (1974); Doe v. Rampton, 366 F.Supp. 189 (D. Utah), *vacated and remanded*, 410 U.S. 950 (1973); Coe v. General Hosp., No. 1477–71 (D.D.C. 1972); Doe v. Doe, 365 Mass. 556, 314 N.E.2d 128 (1974);

Jones v. Smith, 278 So.2d 339 (Fla. Dist. Ct. App. 1973), *cert. denied*, 415 U.S. 958 (1974).
11. Bellotti v. Baird, 99 S.Ct. 3035 (1979); Planned Parenthood of Cent. Missouri v. Danforth, 428 U.S. 52 (1976).
12. Colautti v. Franklin, 439 U.S. 463 (1979); Commonwealth v. Edelin, 359 N.E.2d 4 (Mass. 1976).
13. United Steelworkers v. Weber, 99 S.Ct. 2721 (1979); Regents of Univ. of California v. Bakke, 438 U.S. 265 (1978).
14. K. MILLETT, *supra*, Sexual Politics (1970).
15. AESCHYLUS, THE BUMENIDES 172, 11. 736–42, (P. Vellacott trans. 1956) in K. MILLETT, SEXUAL POLITICS, at 114.
16. *Id.* at 173, 11. 776–78.
17. C. LEVI STRAUSS, THE ELEMENTARY STRUCTURES OF KINSHIP (2d ed. J. Bell & J. von Stariner trans. 1969).
18. *Id.* at 8.
19. *Id.* at 10.
20. *Id.* at 62.
21. *Id.* at 12.
22. *Id.* at 62.
23. *Id.* at 63.
24. *Id.* at 115.
25. *Id.* at 118.
26. *Id.* at 116.
27. Elshtain, *supra* note 5, at 453. *See* ARISTOTLE, POLITICS 1127–30, 1194–97, 1.2, 13. 1252a–1253a, 1259b–1260b (R. McKeon ed. 1941).
28. *Id.* at 455 (emphasis in original).
29. *Id.* at 472.
30. *See* H. MELVILLE, BILLY BUDD, SAILOR III. ch. 21 (H. Hayford & M Sealts, Jr. eds. 1962). "However pitilessly that law may operate in any instances, we nevertheless adhere to it and administer it. . . . Ashore in a criminal case, will an upright judge allow himself off the bench to be waylaid by some tender kinswoman of the accused seeking to touch him with her tearful plea? Well, the heart here, sometimes the feminine in man, is as that piteous woman, and hard though it be, she must here be ruled out." *Id.*
31. M. TIGAR & M. LEVY, LAW AND THE BASE OF CAPITALISM 6 (1978).
32. *Id.*
33. Fraser, *The Legal Theory We Need Now*, 37 SOCIALIST REV. 147, 154 (1978).
34. E. LIPSON, I THE ECONOMIC HISTORY OF ENGLAND 359 (7th ed. 1937), at 361.
35. *Id.*
36. E. BAIN, MERCHANT AND CRAFT GUILDS 228 (1887).
37. *Id.* at 257.
38. Fraser, *supra* note 33, at 15–55 (emphasis in original).

Ideas for Class Projects, Papers, or Debates

1. Compare and contrast the view of Levi with the view of Stone on the nature of judicial reasoning. Explain which view is more plausible and why. If you think the two can be reconciled, explain how.

2. There is currently much dissatisfaction with the process of selecting Supreme Court Justices. If the reason for setting up the Supreme Court as a third and independent branch of government, and especially providing life tenure for Supreme Court Justices, was to produce independent thinking, uninfluenced by political considerations, on the part of the Justices, does appointment by the President undermine or fulfill this basic objective of the Constitution? Should the Constitution be amended to provide a different process of selection? If so, what should it be? Could the political nature of the selection be countered without constitutional amendment, by appointing a bipartisan committee or a committee of experts (say, other judges or law professors or lawyers) to assemble the list from which the President selects the final candidate?

3. What does it mean for judges to be impartial, and how is this task made more difficult in a pluralistic society? Explain how judges should handle the problem of difference in a diverse culture. Does impartiality require indifference to or accommodation of differences from the mainstream norm? To put it another way, is the accommodation of differences impartial treatment or special treatment? You may find the work of Minow or Ely helpful for this project.

4. Use the cases in Chapters Three, Six, and Seven to examine the theories of constitutional interpretation set out by Bork, Schauer, Minow, and Ely. For example:

   a. Compare the *Lochner* case in Chapter Three with the *Griswold* case in Chapter Seven. *Lochner* was ultimately reversed as illegitimate. *Griswold* stands. What would each theory say about these cases?
   b. Chapter Six offers three decisions on capital punishment as "cruel and unusual." Consider how each theory would interpret these cases.
   c. Chapter Seven provides lines of cases on free speech, privacy, racial discrimination, and inequality or poverty. Select one of these areas and explain how each theory would approach them.

5. Consider the first article, by Lon L. Fuller, from *The Morality of Law*. Pick a position and defend it. Explain what your position tells you about the nature of law.

6. Consider the next article, by Jerome Frank, from *Law and the Modern Mind*. Explain how positivism, legal realism, and natural law theory would handle this case. Pick one of these theories and defend it from the objections of the other two in light of this case.

• Following these questions you will find two short sections: "How to Read a Case" and "How to Evaluate a Theory," which you may find helpful in answering the questions in this chapter and many others throughout the rest of the course.

How to Read a Case

When you read a legal case you should ask yourself the following questions:

1. *What is the nature of the case*? In other words, what is the plaintiff (that is, the person who brought the complaint to court) asking the court to do? At the beginning of an opinion the judge generally states the form of action (such as assault, fraud, breach of contract), the type of proceeding (such as appeal from summary judgment or appeal from directed verdict; most of the cases we

will read will be appeals from verdicts of lower courts) and the type of relief sought (such as damages, injunctions, or criminal sanctions). Whenever you read a case, this kind of information is the first thing you need to know.

2. *Facts*. What happened, to whom, in what order, with what consequences? Specifically, what took place between the parties that led to a legal controversy? Be brief but complete about the relevant facts of the case.

3. *Issue*. What is the exact point in dispute? What exactly is the question around which the conflict revolves? The issue should be stated briefly and specifically in a form that can be answered yes or no ("Is the defendant liable?" is too broad). It is important to be able to state clearly what is at issue in a case. The court's decision will often depend on how the issue is formulated.

4. *Holding*. How does the court answer the question posed as the issue of the case? You should be able to state the holding or decision of the court by restating the issue with a yes or no appended to it.

5. *Rule*. What is the rule of law that justifies the holding of the case? The rule of law is sometimes called the *ratio decidendi*. Determining this rule is discussed in the articles by Levi and Stone in this section.

• Note that everything else in an opinion is called *dicta* and has no direct legal effect. As a matter of fact, *dicta* often finds its way into holdings eventually, but that is simply a matter of history and judicial discretion. No judge is legally bound by *dicta*, only by the holding of the case. Students need to learn to distinguish the two.

Try applying these five steps to the cases in this book.

How to Evaluate a Theory

Throughout this course you will be presented with a variety of theories intended to illuminate some area of law or perhaps the nature or concept of law itself. Many of these theories support competing values or start with conflicting assumptions and in general offer divergent views about law, society, and human nature that must be evaluated. You may find some criteria helpful in assessing and comparing these theories. The following are some commonly recognized principles for evaluating theories and some suggestions for using them.

1. *Explanatory Power*: The strength of a theory may be said to reside in its ability to explain some important area of human thought, some significant process, institution, or set of concepts. A powerful theory should have the ability to organize and explain its subject matter in a way that offers new insight and understanding. The opposite of a powerful theory is a *circular* or *question begging* theory. A circular theory assumes what it claims to prove, and so does not really explain anything, or at least not very much. You should keep in mind one caveat here. Even a circular theory can be helpful. That is because it is sometimes illuminating to state the same thing in different ways. So to the extent that a theory leads to insight, it is valuable, even if it does not accomplish what it claims to do. The real problem with circular theories is that they are misleading; they claim to prove something that they do not really establish because they assume what they claim to prove. But this will not be obvious. (If a theory is obviously circular it is simply uninteresting; no one will talk about it.) The fact that a theory is circular is something that has to be discovered. It will appear to offer a new explanation when actually it is saying the same thing in two different ways. When you evaluate the explanatory power of a theory, then, consider what the theory purports to explain. What does it claim to do? The more it claims to do the more powerful it is, pro-

vided it is not begging any questions. You should be very careful to determine its basic assumptions and how those assumptions are developed to lead to the theory's conclusions.

2. *Simplicity*: A theory should rest on intuitive foundational assumptions and should not import controversial assumptions to explain anything that could be explained without such assumptions. Simplicity here means there is nothing extra, nothing superfluous. Nothing should be assumed that doesn't have to be (the fewer assumptions, the better); and the less controversial the assumptions, the better. This is also often called elegance or theoretical elegance. Do not, however, confuse a simple (elegant) explanation with a simplistic one. The explanation of a complex subject matter must be as complex as the subject matter requires. It is not a virtue to leave something out that is necessary for a full explanation—that is being simplistic. The principle of simplicity says only that if each of two theories provides a complete explanation, all other things being equal, the simpler one is the better.

3. *Clarity*: A theory should be clear, not vague. Its terms should be well defined so that its implications can be determined and its conclusions evaluated. It should be assessable in the sense of being more or less verifiable or falsifiable. There should be some set of criteria that would count for it or against it. If nothing can count against a theory, the theory is not telling you anything. It has been said that it is a virtue of a theory, even if wrong, to be wrong clearly. Do not assume, however, that clear means formal or mathematical, especially in an area like legal and political philosophy. Aristotle said long ago that any subject should be approached only at the level of precision to which it is susceptible. And Oliver Wendell Holmes, Jr., said that the life of the law is experience and not logic. A theory should be as clear and unambiguous as possible, but that does not mean that if someone gives a list of precise stipulative definitions, which are then manipulated in a rigorous and elegant logical system, that the theory is necessarily better than one that explains an amorphous area of law in a way that reflects the vagueness which is unavoidable. A clear picture of a foggy day is a foggy picture, especially if what needs to be analyzed or represented is the fog. Logical analysis can sometimes make problems appear to disappear when in fact the problem is simply being defined out of view. A theory should be as clear, precise, and specific as possible, but it need not be formal in the sense of formal logic, and you should be careful to note how the clarity is achieved.

4. *Consistency*: A theory should not embody contradictory elements or have contradictory implications. The more powerful the theory, the harder it is to meet this requirement, especially with regard to implications. The strongest sort of counterexample that can be raised against a theory is one that exposes a contradiction in its own terms. If a theory is committed to contradictory propositions, any conclusion can be drawn from it, which is unhelpful. In political philosophy, theoretical contradictions may reflect actual contradictions in human life and thus be more accurate than theories that gloss over this problem. You will have to decide for yourself whether a theoretical contradiction reflects an unavoidable contradiction in human life or indicates that a theory is misformulating the issue, or both. Whatever the answer, self-contradiction is a serious theoretical problem.

5. *Defensible Implications*: In addition to counterexamples that expose self-contradiction, there can also be counterexamples that simply expose implications of a theory that are unacceptable or questionable on other grounds. These may be implications that run counter to widely shared assumptions or values or that undermine some other powerful theory, institution, or even worldview. This is a weaker form of argument than self-contradiction, but an important one, especially in theories about law and society. Keep in mind, on the other hand, that it is sometimes not an argument at all. That is, a theory may be specifically intended—or if not intended, one of its great-

est benefits may be — to challenge widely held assumptions, values, worldviews, and theories. The function of revolutionary theories is to change old attitudes or explanations. This criterion, then, is a two-edged sword. The more challenging a theory is, the more potentially powerful it is; but the more challenging it is, the better it has to be in order to overcome the values of the view that it is challenging. Not all good theories are challenging, however. Do not assume that a theory must be challenging to be good. Some theories are powerful and useful precisely because they are able to explain a subject in a way not seen before or to organize apparently disparate or contradictory items in a way that renders them connected and consistent.

It may seem to you at this point that these criteria are ambiguous, but they are not. What they are is qualified or limited. No legal or political criterion is absolute. Every one has qualifications attached to it that must be considered in a balanced evaluation. This simply reflects the fact that theories of law and society do not work quite like theories of mathematics or science (at least as far as we know). For the most part, you cannot expect logical proofs to provide you with yes or no answers that demonstrate or refute these theories once and for all. Instead, evaluation requires personal judgment by comparing the theories in terms of all the criteria, balanced against one another.

[From] *The Morality of Law*

LON L. FULLER

The Problem of the Grudge Informer

By a narrow margin you have been elected Minister of Justice of your country, a nation of some twenty million inhabitants. At the outset of your term of office you are confronted by a serious problem that will be described below. But first the background of this problem must be presented.

For many decades your country enjoyed a peaceful, constitutional and democratic government. However, some time ago it came upon bad times. Normal relations were disrupted by a deepening economic depression and by an increasing antagonism among various factional groups, formed along economic, political, and religious lines. The proverbial man on horseback appeared in the form of the Headman of a political party or society that called itself the Purple Shirts.

In a national election attended by much disorder the Headman was elected President of the Republic and his party obtained a majority of the seats in the General Assembly. The success of the party at the polls was partly brought about by a campaign of reckless promises and ingenious falsifications, and partly by the physical intimidation of night-riding Purple Shirts who frightened many people away from the polls who would have voted against the party.

When the Purple Shirts arrived in power they took no steps to repeal the ancient Constitution or any of its provisions. They also left intact the Civil and Criminal Codes and the Code of Procedure. No official action was taken to dismiss any government official or to remove any judge from the bench. Elections continued to be held at intervals and ballots were counted with apparent honesty. Nevertheless, the country lived under a reign of terror.

Judges who rendered decisions contrary to the wishes of the party were beaten and murdered. The accepted meaning of the Criminal Code was perverted to place political opponents in jail.

Secret statutes were passed, the contents of which were known only to the upper levels of the party hierarchy. Retroactive statutes were enacted which made acts criminal that were legally innocent when committed. No attention was paid by the government to the restraints of the Constitution, of antecedent laws, or even of its own laws. All opposing political parties were disbanded. Thousands of political opponents were put to death, either methodically in prisons or in sporadic night forays of terror. A general amnesty was declared in favor of persons under sentence for acts "committed in defending the fatherland against subversion." Under this amnesty a general liberation of all prisoners who were members of the Purple Shirt party was effected. No one not a member of the party was released under the amnesty.

The Purple Shirts as a matter of deliberate policy preserved an element of flexibility in their operations by acting at times through the party "in the streets," and by acting at other times through the apparatus of the state which they controlled. Choice between the two methods of proceeding was purely a matter of expediency. For example, when the inner circle of the party decided to ruin all the former Socialist-Republicans (whose party put up a last-ditch resistance to the new regime), a dispute arose as to the best way of confiscating their property. One faction, perhaps still influenced by prerevolutionary conceptions, wanted to accomplish this by a statute declaring their goods forfeited for criminal acts. Another wanted to do it by compelling the owners to deed their property over at the point of a bayonet. This group argued against the proposed statute on the ground that it would attract unfavorable comment abroad. The Headman decided in favor of direct action through the party to be followed by a secret statute ratifying the party's action and confirming the titles obtained by threats of physical violence.

The Purple Shirts have now been overthrown and a democratic and constitutional government restored. Some difficult problems have, however, been left behind by the deposed regime. These you and your associates in the new government must find some way of solving. One of these problems is that of the "grudge informer."

During the Purple Shirt regime a great many people worked off grudges by reporting their enemies to the party or to the government authorities. The activities reported were such things as the private expression of views critical of the government, listening to foreign radio broadcasts, associating with known wreckers and hooligans, hoarding more than the permitted amount of dried eggs, failing to report a loss of identification papers within five days, etcetera. As things then stood with the administration of justice, any of these acts, if proved, could lead to a sentence of death. In some cases this sentence was authorized by "emergency" statutes; in others it was imposed without statutory warrant, though by judges duly appointed to their offices.

After the overthrow of the Purple Shirts, a strong public demand grew up that these grudge informers be punished. The interim government, which preceded that with which you are associated, temporized on this matter. Meanwhile it has become a burning issue and a decision concerning it can no longer be postponed. Accordingly, your first act as Minister of Justice has been to address yourself to it. You have asked your five Deputies to give thought to the matter and to bring their recommendations to conference. At the conference the five Deputies speak in turn as follows:

FIRST DEPUTY. "It is perfectly clear to me that we can do nothing about these so-called grudge informers. The acts they reported were unlawful according to the rules of the government then in actual control of the nation's affairs. The sentences imposed on their victims were rendered in accordance with principles of law then obtaining. These principles differed from those familar to us in ways that we consider detestable. Nevertheless they were then the law of the land. One of the principal differences between that law and our own lies in the much wider discretion it accorded to the judge in criminal matters. This rule and its consequences are as much entitled to respect by us as the reform which the Purple Shirts introduced into the law of wills, whereby only two witnesses were required instead of three. It is immaterial that the rule granting the judge a more or less uncontrolled discretion in criminal cases was never formally enacted but was a matter of tacit acceptance. Exactly the same thing can be said of the opposite rule which we accept that restricts the judge's discretion narrowly. The difference between ourselves and the Purple Shirts is not that theirs was an unlawful government — a contradiction in terms — but lies rather in the field of ideology. No one has a greater abhorrence than I for Purple Shirtism. Yet the fundamental difference between our philosophy and theirs is that we permit and tolerate differences in viewpoint, while they attempted to impose their monolithic code on everyone. Our whole system of government assumes that law is a flexible thing, capable of expressing and effectuating many different aims. The cardinal point of our creed is that when an objective has been duly incorporated into a law or judicial decree it must be provisionally accepted even by those that hate it, who must await their chance at the polls, or in another litigation, to secure a legal recognition for their own aims. The Purple Shirts, on the other hand, simply disregarded laws that incorporated objectives of which they did not approve, not even considering it worth the effort involved to repeal them. If we now seek to unscramble the acts of the Purple Shirt regime, declaring this judgment invalid, that statute void, this sentence excessive, we shall be doing exactly the thing we most condemn in them. I recognize that it will take courage to carry through with the program I recommend and we shall have to resist strong pressures to public opinion. We shall also have to be prepared to prevent the people from taking the law into their own hands. In the long run, however, I believe the course I recommend is the only one that will insure the triumph of the conceptions of law and government in which we believe."

SECOND DEPUTY. "Curiously, I arrive at the same conclusion as my colleague, by an exactly opposite route. To me it seems absurd to call the Purple Shirt regime a lawful government. A legal system does not exist simply because policemen continue to patrol the streets and wear uniforms or because a constitution and code are left on the shelf unrepealed. A legal system presupposes laws that are known, or can be known, by those subject to them. It presupposes some uniformity of action and that like cases will be given like treatment. It presupposes the absence of some lawless power, like the Purple Shirt Party, standing above the government and able at any time to interfere with the administration of justice whenever it does not function according to the whims of that power. All of these presuppositions enter into the very conception of an order of law and have nothing to do with political and economic ideologies. In my opinion law in any ordinary sense of the word ceased to exist when the Purple Shirts came to power. During their regime we had, in effect, an interregnum in the rule of law. Instead of a government of laws we had a war of all against all conducted behind barred doors, in dark alleyways, in palace intrigues, and prison-yard conspiracies. The acts of these so-called grudge informers were just one phase of that war. For us to condemn these acts as criminal would involve as much incongruity as if we were to attempt to apply juristic conceptions to the struggle for existence that goes on in the jungle or beneath the surface of the sea. We must put this whole dark, lawless chapter of our history behind us like a bad dream. If we stir among its hatreds, we shall bring upon ourselves something of its evil spirit and risk infection from its miasmas. I therefore say with my colleague, let bygones be bygones. Let us do nothing about the so-called grudge informers. What they did do was neither lawful nor contrary to law, for they lived, not under a regime of law, but under one of anarchy and terror."

THIRD DEPUTY. "I have a profound suspicion of any kind of reasoning that proceeds by an 'either-or' alternative. I do not think we need to assume either, on the one hand, that in some manner the whole of the Purple Shirt regime was outside the realm of law, or, on the other, that all of its doings are entitled to full credence as the acts of a lawful government. My two colleagues have unwittingly delivered powerful arguments against these extreme assumptions by demonstrating that both of them lead to the same absurd conclusion, a conclusion that is ethically and politically impossible. If one reflects about the matter without emotion it becomes clear that we did not have during the Purple Shirt regime a 'war of all against all.' Under the surface much of what we call normal human life went on — marriages were contracted, goods were sold, wills were drafted and executed. This life was attended by the usual dislocations — automobile accidents, bankruptcies, unwitnessed wills, defamatory misprints in the newspapers. Much of this normal life and most of these equally normal dislocations of it were unaffected by the Purple Shirt ideology. The legal questions that arose in this area were handled by the courts much as they had been formerly and much as they are being handled today. It would invite an intolerable chaos if we were to declare everything that happened under the Purple Shirts to be without legal basis. On the other hand, we certainly cannot say that the murders committed in the streets by members of the party acting under orders from the Headman were lawful simply because the party had achieved control of the government and its chief had become President of the Republic. If we must condemn the criminal acts of the party and its members, it would seem absurd to uphold every act which happened to be canalized through the apparatus of a government that had become, in effect, the alter ego of the Purple Shirt Party. We must therefore, in this situation, as in most human affairs, discriminate. Where the Purple Shirt philosophy intruded itself and perverted the administration of justice from its normal aims and uses, there we must interfere. Among these perversions of justice I would count, for example, the case of a man who was in love with another man's wife and brought about the death of the husband by informing against him for a wholly trivial offense, that is, for not reporting a loss of his identification papers within five days. This informer was a murderer under the Criminal Code which was in effect at the time of his act and which the Purple Shirts had not repealed. He encompassed the death of one who stood in the way of his illicit passions and utilized the courts for the realization of his murderous intent. He knew that the courts were themselves the pliant instruments of whatever policy the Purple Shirts might for the moment consider expedient. There are other cases that are equally clear. I admit that there are also some that are less clear. We shall be embarrassed, for example, by the cases of mere busybodies who reported to the authorities everything that looked suspect. Some of these persons acted not from desire to get rid of those they accused, but with a desire to curry favor with the party, to divert suspicions (perhaps ill-found) raised against themselves, or through sheer officiousness. I don't know how these cases should be handled, and make no recommendation with regard to them. But the fact that these troublesome cases exist

should not deter us from acting at once in the cases that are clear, of which there are far too many to permit us to disregard them."

FOURTH DEPUTY. "Like my colleague I too distrust 'either-or' reasoning, but I think we need to reflect more than he has about where we are headed. This proposal to pick and choose among the acts of this deposed regime is thoroughly objectionable. It is, in fact, Purple Shirtism itself, pure and simple. We like this law, so let us enforce it. We like this judgment, let it stand. This law we don't like, therefore it never was a law at all. This governmental act we disapprove, let it be deemed a nullity. If we proceed this way, we take toward the laws and acts of the Purple Shirt government precisely the unprincipled attitude they took toward the laws and acts of the government they supplanted. We shall have chaos, with every judge and every prosecuting attorney a law unto himself. Instead of ending the abuses of the Purple Shirt regime, my colleague's proposal would perpetuate them. There is only one way of dealing with this problem that is compatible with our philosophy of law and government and that is to deal with it by duly enacted law, I mean, by a special statute directed toward it. Let us study this whole problem of the grudge informer, get all the relevant facts, and draft a comprehensive law dealing with it. We shall not then be twisting old laws to purposes for which they were never intended. We shall furthermore provide penalties appropriate to the offense and not treat every informer as a murderer simply because the one he informed against was ultimately executed. I admit that we shall encounter some difficult problems of draftsmanship. Among other things, we shall have to assign a definite legal meaning to 'grudge' and that will not be easy. We should not be deterred by these difficulties, however, from adopting the only course that will lead us out of a condition of lawless, personal rule."

FIFTH DEPUTY. "I find a considerable irony in the last proposal. It speaks of putting a definite end to the abuses of the Purple Shirtism, yet it proposes to do this by resorting to one of the most hated devices of the Purple Shirt regime, the ex post facto criminal statute. My colleague dreads the confusion that will result if we attempt without a statute to undo and redress 'wrong' acts of the departed order, while we uphold and enforce its 'right' acts. Yet he seems not to realize that his proposed statute is a wholly specious cure for this uncertainty. It is easy to make a plausible argument for an undrafted statute; we all agree it would be nice to have things down in black and white on paper. But just what would this statute provide? One of my colleagues speaks of someone who had failed for five days to report a loss of his identification papers. My colleague implies that the judicial sentence imposed for that offense, namely death, was so utterly disproportionate as to be clearly wrong. But we must remember that at that time the underground movement against the Purple Shirts was mounting in intensity and that the Purple Shirts were being harassed constantly by people with false identification papers. From their point of view they had a real problem, and the only objection we can make to their solution of it (other than the fact that we didn't want them to solve it) was that they acted with somewhat more rigor than the occasion seemed to demand. How will my colleague deal with this case in his statute, and with all of its cousins and second cousins? Will he deny the existence of any need for law and order under the Purple Shirt regime? I will not go further into the difficulties involved in drafting this proposed statute, since they are evident enough to anyone who reflects. I shall instead turn to my own solution. It has been said on very respectable authority that the main purpose of the criminal law is to give an outlet to the human instinct for revenge. There are times, and I believe this is one of them, when we should allow that instinct to express itself directly without the intervention of forms of law. This matter of the grudge informers is already in process of straightening itself out. One reads almost every day that a former lackey of the Purple Shirt regime has met his just reward in some unguarded spot. The people are quietly handling this thing in their own way and if we leave them alone, and instruct our public prosecutors to do the same, there will soon be no problem left for us to solve. There will be some disorders, of course, and a few innocent heads will be broken. But our government and our legal system will not be involved in the affair and we shall not find ourselves hopelessly bogged down in an attempt to unscramble all the deeds and misdeeds of the Purple Shirts."

As Minister of Justice which of these recommendations would you adopt?

[From] *Law and the Modern Mind*

JEROME FRANK

Legal Realism

We have talked much of the law. But what is "the law"? A complete definition would be impossible and even a working definition would exhaust the patience of the reader. But it may not be amiss to inquire what, in a rough sense, the law means to the average man of our times when he consults his lawyer.

The Jones family owned the Blue & Gray Taxi Company, a corporation incorporated in Kentucky. That company made a contract with the A. & B. Railroad Company, also a Kentucky corporation, by which it was agreed that the Blue & Gray Taxi Company was to have the exclusive privilege of soliciting taxi-cab business on and adjacent to the railroad company's depot.

A rival taxi-cab company, owned by the

Williams family, the Purple Taxi Company, began to ignore this contract; it solicited business and parked its taxi-cabs in places assigned by the railroad company to the Blue & Gray Company and sought in other ways to deprive the Blue & Gray Company of the benefits conferred on it by the agreement with the railroad.

The Jones family were angered; their profits derived from the Blue & Gray stock, which they owned, were threatened. They consulted their lawyer, a Louisville practitioner, and this, we may conjecture, is about what he told them: "I'm afraid your contract is not legally valid. I've examined several decisions of the highest court of Kentucky and they pretty clearly indicate that you can't get away with that kind of an agreement in this state. The Kentucky court holds such a contract to be bad as creating an unlawful monopoly. But I'll think the matter over. You come back tomorrow and I'll try meanwhile to find some way out."

So, next day, the Joneses returned. And this time their lawyer said he thought he had discovered how to get the contract sustained: "You see, it's this way. In most courts, except those of Kentucky and of a few other states, an agreement like this is perfectly good. But, unfortunately, as things now stand, you'll have to go into the Kentucky courts.

"If we can manage to get our case tried in the Federal court, there's a fair chance that we'll get a different result, because I think the Federal court will follow the majority rule and not the Kentucky rule. I'm not sure of that, but it's worth trying.

"So this is what we'll do. We'll form a new Blue & Gray Company in Tennessee. And your Kentucky Blue & Gray Company will transfer all its assets to the new Tennessee Blue & Gray Company. Then we'll have the railroad company execute a new contract with the new Tennessee Blue & Gray Company, and at the same time cancel the old contract and, soon after, dissolve the old Kentucky Blue & Gray Company."

"But," interrupted one of the Joneses, "what good will all that monkey-business do?"

The lawyer smiled broadly. "Just this," he replied with pride in his cleverness. "The A. & B. Railroad Company is organized in Kentucky. So is the Purple Taxi which we want to get at. The Federal court will treat these companies as if they were citizens of Kentucky. Now a corporation which is a citizen of Kentucky can't bring this kind of suit in the Federal court against other corporations which are also citizens of Kentucky. But if your company becomes a Tennessee corporation, it will be considered as if it were a citizen of Tennessee. Then your new Tennessee company can sue the other two in the Federal court, because the suit will be held to be one between citizens of different states. And that kind of suit, based on what we lawyers call 'diversity of citizenship,' can be brought in the Federal court by a corporation which organized in Tennessee against corporations which are citizens of another State, Kentucky. And the Federal court, as I said, ought to sustain your contract."

"That sounds pretty slick," said one of the Joneses admiringly. "Are you sure it will work?"

"No," answered the lawyer. "You can't ever be absolutely sure about such a plan. I can't find any case completely holding our way on all these facts. But I'm satisfied that's the law and that that's the way the Federal court ought to decide. I won't guarantee success. But I recommend trying out my suggestion."

His advice was followed. Shortly after the new Tennessee Blue & Gray Company was organized and had entered into the new contract, suit was brought by the Joneses' new Blue & Gray Corporation of Tennessee in the Federal District Court against the competing Purple Co. and the railroad company. In this suit, the Blue & Gray Taxi Company of Tennessee asked the court to prevent interference with the carrying out of its railroad contract.

As the Joneses' lawyer had hoped, the Federal court held, against the protest of the Purple Company's lawyer, first that such a suit could be brought in the Federal court and, second, that the contract was valid. Accordingly the court enjoined the Purple Company from interfering with the depot business of the Joneses' Blue & Gray Company. The Joneses were elated, for now their profits seemed once more assured.

But not for long. The other side appealed the case to the Federal Circuit Court of Appeals. And the Joneses' lawyer was somewhat worried that that court might reverse the lower Federal court. But it didn't and the Joneses again were happy.

Still the Purple Company persisted. It took the

case to the Supreme Court of the United States. That Court consists of nine judges. And the Joneses' lawyer couldn't be certain just how those judges would line up on all the questions involved. "Some new men on the bench, and you never can tell about Holmes and Brandeis. They're very erratic," was his comment.

When the United States Supreme Court gave its decision, it was found that six of the nine judges agreed with counsel for the Joneses. Three justices (Holmes, Brandeis and Stone) were of the contrary opinion. But the majority governs in the United States Supreme Court, and the Joneses' prosperity was at last firmly established.

Now what was "the law" for the Joneses, who owned the Blue & Gray Company, and the Williamses, who owned the Purple Company? The answer will depend on the date of the question. If asked before the new Tennessee company acquired the contract, it might have been said that it was almost surely "the law" that the Joneses would lose; for any suit involving the validity of that contract could then have been brought only in the Kentucky state court and the prior decisions of that court seemed adverse to such an agreement.

After the suggestion of the Joneses' lawyer was carried out and the new Tennessee corporation owned the contract, "the law" was more doubtful. Many lawyers would have agreed with the Joneses' lawyer that there was a good chance that the Jones family would be victorious if suit were brought in the Federal courts. But probably an equal number would have disagreed: they would have said that the formation of the new Tennessee company was a trick used to get out of the Kentucky courts and into the Federal court, a trick of which the Federal court would not approve. Or that, regardless of that question, the Federal court would follow the well-settled Kentucky rule as to the invalidity of such contracts as creating unlawful monopolies (especially because the use of Kentucky real estate was involved) and that therefore the Federal court would decide against the Joneses. "The law," at any time before the decision of the United States Supreme Court, was indeed unsettled.[1] No one could know what the court would decide. Would it follow the Kentucky cases? If so, the law was that no "rights" were conferred

by the contract. Would it refuse to follow the Kentucky cases? If so, rights were conferred by the contract. To speak of settled law governing that controversy, or of the fixed legal rights of those parties, as antedating the decision of the Supreme Court, is mere verbiage. If two more judges on that bench had agreed with Justices Holmes, Brandeis and Stone, the law and the rights of the parties would have been of a directly opposite kind.

After the decision, "the law" was fixed. There were no other courts to which an appeal could be directed. The judgment of the United States Supreme Court could not be disturbed and the legal "rights" of the Joneses and the Williamses were everlastingly established.

We may now venture a rough definition of law from the point of view of the average man: For any particular lay person, the law, with respect to any particular set of facts, is a decision of a court with respect to those facts so far as that decision affects that particular person. Until a court has passed on those facts no law on that subject is yet in existence. Prior to such a decision, the only law available is the opinion of lawyers as to the law relating to that person and to those facts. Such opinion is not actually law but only a guess as to what a court will decide.[2]

Law, then, as to any given situation is either (a) actual law, *i.e,* a specific past decision, as to that situation,[3] or (b) probable law, *i.e.,* a guess as to a specific future decision.

Usually when a client consults his lawyer about "the law," his purpose is to ascertain not what courts have actually decided in the past but what the courts will probably decide in the future. He asks, "Have I a right, as a stockholder of the American Taffy Company of Indiana, to look at the corporate books?" Or, "Do I have to pay an inheritance tax to the State of New York on bonds left me by my deceased wife, if our residence was in Ohio, but the bonds, at the time of her death, were in a safety deposit box in New York?" Or, "Is there a right of 'peaceful' picketing in a strike in the State of California?" Or, "If Jones sells me his Chicago shoe business and agrees not to compete for ten years, will the agreement be binding?" The answers (although they may run "There is such a right," "The law is that the property is not taxable," "Such picketing is unlawful," "The agreement is not legally binding") are in fact prophecies or predictions of judicial action.[4] It is from this point of view that the practice of law has been aptly termed an art of prediction.

Actual specific past *decisions*, and guesses as to actual specific future *decisions*. Is that how lawyers customarily define the law? Not at all.

NOTES

1. That is, it was unsettled whether the Williamses had the energy, patience and money to push an appeal. If not, then the decision of the lower Federal court was the actual settled law for the Jones and Williams families.

2. The United States Supreme Court has wittily been called the "court of ultimate conjecture."

3. That is, a past decision in a case which has arisen between the specific persons in question as to the specific facts in question. Even a past decision fixes the rights of the parties to the suit only to a limited extent. In other words, what a court has actually decided as between the parties may in part still be open to question by other courts and therefore may continue to be the subject of guesses.

4. The emphasis in this book on the conduct of judges is admittedly artificial. Lawyers and their clients are vitally concerned with the ways of all governmental officials and with the reactions of non-official persons to the ways of judges and other officials. There is a crying need in the training of lawyers for clear and unashamed recognition and study of all these phenomena as part of the legitimate business of lawyers.

But one job at a time. Inasmuch as the major portion of a lawyer's time is today devoted to predicting or bringing about decisions of judges, the law considered in this book is "court law." "Actual law" and "probable law" here discussed mean "actual or probable court law." This limitation, while artificial, is perhaps the more excusable because it roughly corresponds to the notion of the contemporary layman when consulting his lawyer.

Of course, any one can define "law" as he pleases. The word "law" is ambiguous and it might be well if we could abolish it. But until a substitute is invented, it seems not improper to apply it to that which is central in the work of the practising lawyer. *This book is primarily concerned with "law" as it affects the work of the practising lawyer and the needs of the clients who retain him.*

From that point of view, court law may roughly be defined as *specific past or future judicial decisions which are enforced or complied with.*

UNIT II

Private Law and Individual Interests

In Unit I we were concerned with the idea or concept of law, with the structure or form of a legal system, and with the nature or function of a legal process. We wanted to know what is fundamental to the very idea of law and to find out what makes a social institution a legal system. We wanted to understand what it is that makes a set of procedures a legal process. These are all formal questions — questions about the essential properties and distinguishing features that set out the fundamental nature of law. Before considering some examples of the substantive side of law, which we will do in this unit and the next, we need to make one further formal distinction. It is the distinction between public and private law.

Traditionally the distinction between public and private law is based on the distinction between public and private interests. "A law is private if it is in the interest of the individual, as distinguished from being for the benefit of the public." The quotation, from George Dargo's *Law in the New Republic* (1983), is a typical example of the most common way of drawing the distinction. It is, we might say, a useful shorthand.

In fact, as just described, this distinction is not as specific or clear as one might hope, is it? If you had no information other than what you read in the last paragraph, what areas of law would you put into each category and why? Is a business transaction private or public? Does it matter what kind of a transaction it is? How about a labor contract for a national labor union? How about a contract to build one house? A contract to build a dam across the Ohio River? What about other interactions? How about a punch in the nose? A plot to take over the municipal government of Happy Valley, North Dakota? A plot to take over an international corporation? Suppose your boss fires you because he thinks his customers do not have confidence in a black real estate agent? Should you have a cause of action to protect your private interests, or is this a public concern, or both? Is it clear which activities concern private interests and which affect the public at large? I expect that it is not. This is not to suggest that the distinction is not useful or legitimate, but we will need more than we have so far before we can use it.

What else do we need? First, it may help to recognize that any society can be viewed from two fundamentally different perspectives, each important in its own way. On the one hand, we can view a society as an aggregate of individuals — private citizens — each engaged in his or her own particular private interests and pursuits. Just for the sake of clarity we can imagine each of these individuals as isolated and unique from all others. Of course, every human being really is isolated and unique from everyone else in some important respects; but at the same time there is not just one individual in a society. There are a great many of us. And all of us either want to or have to interact in all sorts of ways with a great many other individuals. That is the perspective of private law: the perspective of individuals who want or need to interact with or transact business with one another. Studying law from this perspective is like studying a bee colony by studying the function of every individual bee as it interacts with other individual bees.

On the other hand, we can view a society as a whole, as a group or a culture. In that case we are not interested in the characteristics and functions of individuals but in the characteristics and functions of the group. By analogy, we would not study individual bees from this focus but from a view of the structure and development of the hive as a whole. Any society embodies certain commitments, values, traditions, institutions, beliefs, and assumptions that make it more than the sum of its parts. Imagine the difference between a hive of bees and a swarm of bees. A hive and a swarm may be comprised of the same bees, but a hive presupposes order. That is the perspective of public law.

Public law is focused not on the undertakings of individuals but on the needs and values of the group as a whole. It is concerned not with what distinguishes individuals but with what is common to them; not with what makes them unique but with what makes them alike. What are the needs and values that are shared? These are what the public law should protect and facilitate. Public law protects the common good, the public interest.

The tricky part is to determine exactly what the public interest is. We will deal with this issue in Unit III, but unless we at least clarify it here, we will be right back where we started in the first paragraph: Public law protects public interests and private law protects private interests, and we still do not know how to distinguish these interests.

Private interests are relatively easy to define. They are roughly whatever individuals value or have a stake in. For some purposes we will need to make some further qualifications, but for our present needs the important feature of private interests is that private individuals determine what these interests are for themselves. That's what makes these interests private rather than public. *Private* here means individual rather than, say, secret. So a private interest is basically what any individual determines as a value for himself or herself.

Public interest is more difficult to define, but as a starting point (until we get to Unit III) we can use a simple device: Consider *public* as roughly synonymous with *government* or *state*. Legally speaking, *public interest* is *state interest* as determined by *government officials* (such as judges, legislators, and public administrators). Government officials are the spokespersons of (legal) public decisions. Public decisions are made and declared by government. Public power is state power, or government power. Private law, then, is concerned with facilitating private interests, private decisions, and private power. Public law facilitates government decisions, protects state interests, and embodies state or government power.

George Dargo illustrates this process in the first reading selection. He points out that the American revolutionary generation that formulated the Constitution was suspicious of and concerned to limit public, or government, power. These people had had bad experiences with the English king and with governors from England and therefore wanted to limit sharply the power of government officials to make binding decisions about the lives of private citizens. They had much more confidence in the ability of individuals to make their own decisions and conduct their own transactions. They believed that human rights and freedom would be best protected by limiting the government's power to interfere with the activities of individuals. Thus, the commitment was to the use of private law wherever possible and to the use of public law only where necessary.

This objective resulted, as Dargo points out, in the *privatization* of areas of life that were previously considered matters of public concern. Religion was determined to be a matter of private conscience rather than public doctrine, so there would be no official, state church. The business of the press would be pursued by private individuals — entrepreneurs — so there would be no official, state newspaper. These are the clear cases which illustrate that views can change about how different areas of life should be regarded by the state and regulated by the law. In one time or place a matter may be considered private — the proper subject of individual decision making. In another time or place the same matter might be considered a public interest — an area of official policy — or we might say, more idealistically, a matter of common commitment. With public law, officially and legally, everyone is committed to the same thing: We all oppose murder and robbery; we all support the Constitution; and we all agree to use the same legal procedures to settle our differences. If we lived in a different time or place, we might also all agree by official policy to observe the same religion — or to any number of other things just so long as those things are matters of common commitment in terms of state policies binding on all.

In sum, private law protects private interests by empowering private parties to facilitate their private decisions. Public law protects the public interest by declaring and enforcing public policy as a common bond.

You may be wondering why we need any law at all in areas that we have decided are matters of private decision. To answer this question we need to keep in mind that law serves two fundamentally different purposes, as reflected in the distinction between public and private law. On the one hand, law restricts people from harming the public interest. On the other, it enables people to do things that otherwise they could not do, or could do only with great difficulty and risk. The purpose of private law is to enable people to do things they want to be able to do. All too often we forget the enabling side of law and think of law only as restrictive. Taking this perspective is understandable because there is a sense in which all laws (or rules) are restrictive. But this is a weak sense that we need to clarify and distinguish from the stronger sense of restriction best exemplified by criminal law.

As an illustration consider the rules of baseball. There is a sense in which the rules are restrictive — namely, they must be followed, *if you play.* This is the weak sense of restriction because it does not require you to play or prohibit you from playing. Whether you play or not is up to you. The rules simply tell you how to play if you want to. And this is by far the most important feature of the rules of baseball. The rules tell you how to play. They enable you to play. You could not play without them. In fact, no one could play without them, because in order to play everyone must play by the same rules. Otherwise there is chaos. That is the function of enabling rules and enabling laws, and it is a very important function. Society would fall apart without enabling laws. Think of all the things you could not do, or at least could not do without great difficulty or risk. How could you own property if law did not recognize and protect your rights to things? How could you get married or write a will or make a contract with a stranger? All sorts of business transactions would be out of the question. We could not possibly have mortgages or car loans or corporations or stocks and bonds or even money. All of these examples are legal devices that enable people to do what they want to be able to do. And these are the sorts of things that constitute private law. Without private law society would be primitive indeed.

At the same time, as Dargo's article illustrates, it is not always obvious which areas of life should be handled by private law. Since we are using American law as our model we should note that in nineteenth- and twentieth-century Anglo-American law, private law generally includes contracts, property, torts, commercial and corporate law, and family and agency law as major categories. Public law includes constitutional and administrative law, criminal law, and procedural law. In this volume we use contract, property, and tort law as examples of private law. Other areas might be chosen instead, but these three provide a core of what is currently taken to be private law. Since we cannot cover all areas of law in this course, the examples were chosen simply to provide an illustration of the area and an interesting complement or comparison with contrasting areas of public law. Tort law makes an interesting comparison with criminal law in general. The focus on freedom in contract law provides a provocative contrast with the development of civil liberties in constitutional law, especially the right to privacy. And the question of distributive justice in property law makes an interesting complement to questions of civil rights to equal protection in constitutional law.

We may sum up the basic features of public and private law as follows. Private law is concerned with and formulated to facilitate the transactions and interactions of individuals. (*Individual* here may also refer to a group, such as a business partnership or corporation, so long as the group is organized to promote some interest of its own choice or for its own benefit rather than for a purpose designated by a public, or government, body as a public interest.) Such law is initiated and used by private parties at their own expense for the purpose of protecting their individual interests. Public law is concerned with the organization and administration of government, legal procedures, and the identification and prohibition of public harms (crimes). It is initiated and used by public officials at public expense on behalf of the public at large or the people as a whole.

Keep in mind that the distinction between private interests and public interests does not refer to an objective state of affairs or to objective sets of characteristics. Making the distinction is not like distinguishing a tree from a rock. It involves value commitments about how areas of life ought to be viewed and handled. Dargo's discussion sets the private law model in historical perspective. What does the model reflect about the characteristics and commitments of the time he discusses? Have they changed? Do the changes matter? In particular, as we proceed through Units II and III, ask yourself what sorts of factors ought to be considered in deciding whether something is a private matter or a public concern. Indeed, you should ask yourself whether this distinction can really be made usefully. What purpose is served in making it?

As we move into Units II and III, we will be interested not so much in the form of law as in its content or substance. Remember from the introduction to Unit I the comparison between the study of law and the study of poetry. Poetry may be studied in terms of its form—grammatical structure, rhyme scheme, rhythm, meter, and so forth. Or it may be studied in terms of its content, or subject matter. We will now turn to the subject matter of law.

What does law deal with? What is it about? What does it do? These are simply different ways of asking the same question, and the question can be asked at different levels of abstraction. Obviously, we could be very specific about the content of any legal system. The more particular we get, the more it will be a matter of mere coincidence whether the particular feature has any significance for the understanding of law or legal process. For example, pick any country and you will find that its legal system has rules regarding property—that is, laws about what constitutes property, what property is, and what can be done with it. If we get a little more specific, very likely all legal systems have rules about how to dispose of property at death. If we get more specific, some legal systems will determine how wills must be written. Even more specifically, some will require three signatures on a will. Studying the top end of the continuum (what a legal system does about property) can tell us some interesting things about both the society and the law. The other end of the continuum (a requirement of three signatures on a will) is not likely to tell us anything interesting about either. Such particularities might be of historical interest and certainly are of practical importance, but they are not philosophically significant because they do not add to our understanding of law. Consequently, we will examine the content of law at a rather abstract and general level.

Law has many different subject matters. Its content is as varied as the needs of human beings. In this unit on private law we could discuss any kind of law that enables private parties to interact in ways that would be difficult or impossible without the enforcement of law. One particularly interesting area of private law is contract law, and to that we now turn.

[From] *Law in the New Republic*

GEORGE DARGO

CHAPTER 2

The Privatization of Public Law

The revolutionary generation's extraordinary preoccupation with the process of constitution making is not surprising. Fear of political excess was a central issue of the Revolution. The innovations in constitutional government at the state and national levels that emerged as a direct consequence of this concern represented the deepest, most long-lasting, and most important contribution that generation made—not only to America but to the political development of many new countries in the two centuries since 1776. The American colonial experience had taught that the exercise of public power, when unrestrained, was dangerous. Americans were more comfortable with private decision making, and they regarded the enhancement of private power as a necessary check on potential governmental abuse. This predilection resulted in the *privatization* of American law.

Privatization presupposes that all individuals are equal before the law, that the law is neutral, and that the good of all is best promoted by shifting power from public bodies to private (preferably individual) actors. In reality, however, all individuals are not equal in relation to law, and collective action by individuals with common interests is inevitable. Privatization makes some sense in a perfectly individualized and atomized society; but in one where competing interests and pluralistic groupings jockey for power, privatization tends to substitute new forms of unchecked authority for older ones.

The American revolutionaries had perceived the threat to liberty as largely a problem of public power, and the revolutionary generation had fashioned legal remedies to deal with that problem. But no similar sensitivity to the challenge of private power in its many guises existed at the time of the Revolution. Thus while privatization extended the reach of human freedom in some respects, in others it had the effect of desensitizing Americans to the dangers posed by a class system based on sharp inequalities of wealth and power. Such inequalities were already much in evidence by the end of the colonial period. Thereafter, in the century following the Revolution, the problem of power and its control shifted from the public to the private sector. Social and, later, industrial exploitation replaced political abuse as the major challenge of American liberalism. But the ideological cast of the Revolution remained so strong that it took a revolution in political theory at the beginning of the twentieth century to devise new remedies to meet the threat to individual freedom and human dignity that the concentration of unchecked economic power in private hands then presented.

Long overlooked by historians, the leading social issue of the Revolutionary period was slavery and agitation for its abolition. Privatization manifested itself in liberalized procedures for personal manumission. Slave codes in most colonies made emancipation exceedingly difficult even for masters who wished to manumit their slaves either by *inter vivos* gift or by testamentary bequest. After the Revolution, however, even in the South, slave laws were eased, and increasing numbers of blacks achieved freedom through private acts of manumission. Still, both in the North as well as the South, the law of slavery and freedom remained an area of primary concern to public law. But in the law of Church and State, in seditious libel law, and in criminal law privatization showed its effects with more dramatic force.

Church-State Law

The disestablishment of churches, a gradual and complex process in most of the original thirteen states, represented the fulfillment of a long-term tendency that had its beginnings in the colonial past. The notion that religion was a matter of public concern gradually gave way to a new attitude, which held that religious preference was a matter of private choice. Increasingly, Americans viewed the issue of religious belief, forms of religious practice, and differences over church governance as beyond the jurisdiction of public law. Rather, they conceived these to be problems of conscience to be resolved in the give-and-take of private religious controversy. This was the central meaning of the movement to disestablish official, state churches in most of the colonies and in the early states. Roger Williams, that passionate seventeenth-century religious dissenter, first invented the metaphor of the "wall of separation" between the "garden" of the church and the "wilderness" of the state; but it was Thomas Jefferson, the leading figure of the eighteenth-century American Enlightenment, who put it best:

> The legitimate powers of government extend to such acts only as are injurious to others. But it does me no injury for my neighbor to say there are twenty gods, *or no god*. It neither picks my pocket nor breaks my leg.

At the time of the Revolution, the question in most of the states was not whether there should be a single, established church such as the Congregational church in New England or the Anglican church in the South. The main issue was whether religion in general should be protected and supported by the state. While there was almost universal agreement that no single Christian church ought to occupy a favored position in public law, there was widespread disagreement over how far the separation of church and state should go. Organized religion was thought to be an essential pillar of society. The state's civic responsibility to support religion in some way was equal in importance to its duty to maintain public health and domestic security. Learned teachers and ministers of the gospel were necessary to keep people from vice and to protect the social order from decay.

The essential question was how to keep religion part of the fabric of society without re-creating a religious establishment in the manner of the discredited colonial regime. Virginia's was the most radical response to this dilemma. There, the old Anglican (now Episcopalian) establishment was closely identified with Loyalism. As a result, it did not have the kind of popular support that Congregationalism enjoyed in New England. Dissenter groups, Baptist and Presbyterians particularly, were located everywhere in Virginia, but their concentration in the western part of that state gave them a geographical base to mount an effective campaign of reform. Moreover, the leading political figures in Virginia, Thomas Jefferson and James Madison, were philosophically committed to complete separation of church and state. Consequently, there was a major confrontation in Virginia in the 1780s between separationists and those still anxious to maintain an alliance of church and state.

The two issues which brought that confrontation to a head were the incorporation of the Episcopal church and the so-called General Assessment Plan. The Church Incorporation Act of 1784 was a housekeeping measure whereby the property of the old Anglican establishment was put into the hands of reconstituted Episcopalian vestries. The vestries were democratized, church ministers were denied veto power over vestry decisions, and the commonwealth removed itself from further involvement in church governance. Nevertheless, deep opposition to the incorporation act persisted because it favored Episcopalian congregations over all others, and in 1786 the act providing for Episcopal incorporation was repealed.

Even more controversial than incorporation, however, was the plan to tax every citizen for the support of the religious minister of the taxpayer's choice. The plan was a compromise measure that would provide for religion in general without singling out a particular church for preferential treatment. Each taxpayer could designate the church that was to receive the monies he was assessed. In the final version of the plan, those taxpayers who had no religious affiliations could earmark the funds collected for the support of "seminaries of learning" within the county.

Dissenter groups were divided over the general assessment. Presbyterians sided with Episcopalians, but Baptists remained opposed to any kind of compulsory religious tax, even one from which they stood to benefit. A major campaign was mounted to defeat the assessment, and James Madison's famous *Memorial and Remonstrance*, which was widely circulated by his political allies in 1785, is generally credited with accomplishing its defeat in the fall of 1785. The opponents of the assessment plan, led by Jefferson and Madison, went on to consolidate their victory by enacting the Bill for Establishing Religious Freedom, which Jefferson had authored back in 1779. First presented to the Virginia legislature as part of the Revisal of the Laws (a general scheme of law reform), the Religious Freedom Bill was finally enacted into law in 1786. It was the most far-reaching statute of its kind. For all practical purposes, the act destroyed the vestiges of the old Anglican religious establishment in Virginia for all time.

Disestablishment was a movement that affected the entire country in the aftermath of the Revolution, but in Virginia disestablishment meant more than just local control. The whole thrust of the Madisonian attack on the general assessment plan was that religion was a matter for the private "conscience of every man." Separation of church and state, disestablishment, religious freedom, and the right of "conscience" — these were central themes in the religious and legal history of the postrevolutionary era. Modern, twentieth-century efforts to define "zones of privacy" owe much to the religious experience of the late eighteenth century. Religion was the first such zone, the first major sphere where public law was privatized.

The Law of the Press

Privatization also affected freedom of the press and the changing definition of seditious libel law in the 1790s and the early decades of the nineteenth century. In the eighteenth century, to criticize the government — or indeed anyone in authority — was a criminal offense. To do so was to invite prosecution and the possibility of fine or imprisonment. The only question to be decided by a jury in a seditious libel case was a question of *fact* — did the writer or printer accused of publishing the offensive material actually publish it? If the jury's answer to that question was yes, then the accused was guilty of the offense charged. The judge's role was to decide, as a matter of *law*, whether or not the material in question was

seditious. The fact that the offensive publication might be true was of no consequence.

As Sir William Blackstone put it in explaining the English view of this common law crime, "(I)t is immaterial . . . whether the matter of it be true or false, since the provocation, and not the falsity, is the thing to be punished criminally." As for the liberty of the press, said Blackstone, it "consists in laying no *previous* restraints upon publications, and not in freedom from censure for criminal matter when published." In short, a printer was free to publish without fear of "prior restraint" through censorship or licensing laws, but he had to expect to be penalized by fine or imprisonment should a court of law find the publication seditious.

The case of John Peter Zenger, publisher of the *New York Weekly Journal*, in 1735 is one of the landmarks in the development of press freedom in America. Zenger's acquittal represented an important change in seditious libel law, in that it established a precedent for the right of a jury to decide not only the fact of publication but the legal issue as well — that is, whether or not the material published was seditious. The Zenger case established that the truth of the statements contained in the suspect publication could be offered in evidence as a defense to the charge.

The Zenger case marked a breakthrough in the prevailing theory of seditious libel law. But not until the end of the century did Zengerian principles become firmly established in law. Ironically, it was the Sedition Act, passed in 1798 as part of a program of Federalist repression against the Jeffersonian opposition party, that codified these new legal doctrines by statute. The Sedition Act enlarged the role of the jury and allowed truth as a defense in libel actions. It soon became evident, however, that Zengerian principles no longer provided adequate protection against governmental repression. First, making truth a defense in a seditious libel case merely meant that seditious libel was no longer a strict liability crime. The Sedition Act made truth an "affirmative defense" which put the burden of proving truth upon the defendant. But how could charges of corruption, incompetence, or ineffectiveness, the normal subjects of political debate, be proved? Open, vigorous, and healthy political discourse simply does not lend itself to analysis on a true-false standard.

Political truth to one person is errant nonsense to another. Moreover, Federalist appointees to the new federal district courts were highly partisan and their jury charges in seditious libel cases were so pro-prosecution as to make guilty verdicts practically inevitable. As a result the federal government was able to win a significant number of well-publicized cases under the Sedition Act despite the act's liberalization of seditious libel law. Consequently, after 1798 liberal writers began to challenge the whole concept of seditious libel on the grounds that it was a remnant of British monarchism. Liberals attacked the Sedition Act as an affront to the First Amendment to the Constitution, and seditious libel as ill-suited to a republican system of government, where the rulers are answerable to the people. Criticism of the people's representatives could not be illegitimate in a free society. These bold attacks on the law of seditious libel reinforced an emerging acceptance of political parties as a legitimate feature of political life in a free society. Political parties were increasingly perceived as voluntary, private associations outside the realm of governmental interference. This "privatization" of political life was closely associated with the decline in seditious libel prosecutions and the liberalization of libel law with which the Sedition Act was so ironically connected.

The radical critique of seditious libel did not prevail immediately, however. On the state level, where all criminal libel cases occurred after expiration of the infamous federal Sedition Act, public prosecutors still sought convictions on the basis of the old Blackstonian common-law formulations. *Commonwealth v. Clap* is an example of such a conviction. The case involved an alleged libel against a minor public official. Defense counsel argued that since "every citizen may be considered as a candidate for public office," therefore everyone's character was "fair game" thus anticipating the modern constitutional doctrine of the "public figure." While Chief Justice Parsons of the Massachusetts Supreme Judicial Court was not prepared to go this far, he did distinguish between elected and appointed officials. In the case of elected officials, liberal rules — such as truth as a defense — would be permitted. But in the case of a libel against an appointed official, private reputation

would receive greater protection and truth would not be allowed. Since Clap had attacked an appointed official, the public auctioneer, the Court allowed his conviction to stand.

In a number of jurisdictions, most notably New York and Massachusetts, state legislatures enacted statutes that so changed the law of libel in the next several decades that criminal libel cases became a rarity after 1820, thereby indicating an overall decline in government interest in curbing subversive publications. This net reduction in official intervention in public discourse may be interpreted as another instance of the privatization theme that runs through much of American legal history in the postrevolutionary period. To be sure, civil libel remained a subject of continuing importance. Nevertheless, by the mid-nineteenth century, the days when prosecutors went after writers, publishers, and printers for their seditious utterances had passed. Not until the twentieth century has the United States government again made serious efforts to suppress freedom of the press. During the Vietnam War, for example, the government tried and failed to prevent *The New York Times* from publishing a documentary history of that war prepared by the Department of Defense. More recently the Central Intelligence Agency has successfully forced a former CIA agent to submit nonclassified material concerning the agency for prepublication review. In upholding this restriction on activity which in another context would clearly come under First Amendment protection, the Supreme Court has fashioned what dissenting Justice John Paul Stevens called a "drastic new . . . species of prior restraint on a citizen's right to criticize his government."

Moral Offenses

In the field of criminal law enforcement, prosecutors have wide discretion in deciding who is to be prosecuted, for which kinds of crime, and with what degree of vigor. In the postrevolutionary period, prosecutions for crimes against property and persons increased, whereas prosecutorial interest in offenses against morality — sexual offenses in particular — began to wane.

For example, prosecutions for fornication, in both secular courts and church courts, were very

Table 1. Premarital Pregnancy in America: First Births Occurring
in Less Than 6, 8½, and 9 Months After Marriage

	Less Than 6 Months		Under 8½ Months		Under 9 Months	
	%	N	%	N	%	N
−1680	3.3	511	6.8	511	8.1	663
1681–1720	6.7	445	14.1	518	12.1	1156
1721–1760	9.9	881	21.2	1146	22.5	1442
1761–1800	16.7	970	27.2	1266	33.0	1097
1801–1840	10.3	573	17.7	815	23.7	616
1841–1880	5.8	572	9.6	467	12.6	572
1881–1910	15.1	119	23.3	232	24.4	119

Source: Adapted from D.S. Smith and M.S. Hindus, "Premarital Pregnancy in America, 1640–1971: An Overview and Interpretation," *Journal of Interdisciplinary History*, 5 (1975), p. 561, by permission of the *Journal of Interdisciplinary History* and the M.I.T. Press, Cambridge, Mass. Copyright © 1975 by the Massachusetts Institute of Technology Press and the editors of the *Journal of Interdisciplinary History*.

high in the middle of the eighteenth century; but such prosecutions declined steadily in the 1780s and 1790s despite the fact that illicit fornication was still quite pervasive in America. The premarital pregnancy rate is one measure of this form of moral deviance after the Revolution. Table 1 demonstrates that premarital pregnancy remained high until about the middle of the nineteenth century. It shows the percentage of "first births" (i.e., first child born to a married couple) that occurred in less than 6 months, in less than 8½ months, and in less than 9 months of formal marriage. The figures clearly indicate a trend of increasing premarital pregnancy rates before 1800 and then a dramatic drop in those rates until 1880. Table 2 gives data on the disciplinary actions taken by Massachusetts churches between 1620 and 1840 in enforcing the law against illicit fornication.

The peak period of enforcement came in the decades preceding the Revolution, with a dramatic drop in the last years of the eighteenth century, precisely the time when the premarital pregnancy rate — as shown is Table 1 — was highest. While evidence derived from the numbers of cases appearing in church courts must be used with caution because of a steady decline in ecclesiastical disciplinary process in the postrevolutionary period, studies of prosecution patterns in the regular secular courts support similar conclusions. Clearly the decline in prosecutions was not due to a lower incidence of fornication. Rather, it suggests a dramatic drop in prosecutorial attention to sexual immorality even by church courts, which in turn suggests that society was beginning to recognize that certain forms of private behavior between consenting

Table 2. Fornication Cases in Massachusetts Churches (by County), 1620–1840

	1620–1689	1690–1729	1730–1769	1770–1809	1810–1840
Plymouth	4	9	64	29	3
Barnstable	6	5	71	10	0
Norfolk	3	25	90	20	2
Suffolk	28	41	30	11	2
Essex	15	67	120	36	1
Middlesex	1	30	134	44	0
Worcester	0	1	32	19	1
Hampshire	0	9	133	96	13
Berkshire	0	0	5	25	11
Total	57	187	679	290	31

Source: Derived from Emil Oberholzer, Jr., *Delinquent Saints: Disciplinary Action in the Early Congregational Churches of Massachusetts* (New York, 1956), pp. 254–255.

adults should no longer be the primary concern of the criminal law.

Criminal law reformers had begun to apply rationalistic and utilitarian measures to the social analysis of crime and punishment. Differentiating between public and private offenses was clearly part of this movement. The law remained nominally opposed to the same kinds of behavioral deviations as in the past. Statutes against adultery, fornication and bastardy were not repealed. Prosecutions for blasphemy continued into the 1830s. Nevertheless, these kinds of offenses were in areas that the law increasingly viewed as within the sphere of private life and, therefore, beyond the legitimate reach of the criminal process.

To freedom of conscience and freedom of political expression and association, then, must be added the growing freedom of sexual expression — another manifestation of the effects of legal privatization. In short, in sharp contrast with the colonial past, government in the postrevolutionary period was becoming less activist in seeking to monitor religious, political, and moral behavior.

CHAPTER THREE

The Nature of Contracts and the Value of Freedom

The law of contracts is often considered a paradigm of private law. There is no law requiring people to make contracts or prohibiting them from it. You may make a contract with anyone about anything you wish to just so long as the other party agrees and the activity is not prohibited by some other law (such as criminal law). Contract law does not tell you what you may or may not make contracts about but simply how to proceed if you want to make a legal agreement.

Why do we need law to tell us how to make agreements? In a sense, we don't. We can make agreements of any sort with each other and take our chances that each of us will keep the agreement. Given the frailties of human beings, however, there is a good chance that one party will back out of a bargain, leaving the other party with a loss. Most people feel rather insecure about this fact of human nature, and the more important the agreement, the longer it takes to fulfill it; and the less well acquainted the parties are with one another, the greater the insecurity becomes. In advanced societies where the agreement may be of crucial importance to the well-being or livelihood of many people, the terms of the agreement may span many years, and the parties may be total strangers, the risk of agreement without enforcement would be intolerable. Thus, contract law says: If you want to protect your agreements with the enforcement of law, follow these rules and your bargain will be recognized as a binding legal contract enforceable in a court of law. Complying with the rules of contract law, then, is rather like buying an insurance policy. It is not illegal not to, but most people do so because the risk is too great without legal protection.

Furthermore, the more people rely on such devices, the more it becomes impossible, in practice, not to conform. First, this is because others will not deal with you unless you agree to follow the rules that enable them to protect themselves. Second, following these rules becomes the established practice, and thus people reasonably expect that the rules are being followed, since they usually are, and the law tends to protect the reasonable expectations of people in general. You may therefore be held to the rules even if you thought you were not following them or never gave the rules a thought unless you explicitly rebut the reasonable assumptions generated by standard practice. In other words, a feature of standard practice — not just in contract law but in general — is that it tends to become the only game in town, so to speak. Consequently, in practice, it becomes very difficult not to play. But this is not because the law requires you to play. It is because there isn't anything else to play. Everybody plays the same game. It's the only game in town. Now, if you are ingenious, you can make up your own game. Most people are simply not creative enough to do this, but even if you are, no one else will know how to play. They all know how to play their game, and most people cannot imagine any other, so probably no one will play your game. But you break no law if you refuse to play their game. Contract law does not require you to make any contracts. What does, in practice, require you to make contracts are other people, other laws, and widespread standard practice.

If you do not follow the rules of contract, you do not break any law. What you really do is fail to make law. This is an important feature of contract law and of enabling law in general. Similarly, if you do not follow the rules for making wills, you do not break the law, but you fail to make a will.

Whatever you are trying to do, if you fail to comply with the law that enables you to do it, you will not thereby break the law; you will fail to accomplish your purpose. You may have a piece of paper with words on it, but it will not be a contract or a will or a mortgage or a marriage certificate, as you intended, because all of those instruments have to be recognized by law. To accomplish that you must follow the rules. If you follow the rules, you will succeed in making a legally binding contract. This is an important feature of contract law, but obviously it is not a distinctive one.

What is distinctive about contract law? What sets it apart from all other forms of law? It has long been said that the idea of a contract "results from the combination of two ideas: agreement and obligation. Contractual obligation is that form of obligation which springs from agreement" (see W.R. Anson, *Principles of the Law of Contracts*, 2d ed., 1882). This is only one view among many theories and definitions of contract. It is worth noting, however, that all are variations on a theme which incorporates some notion of agreement or consent coupled with the idea of special obligation and special rights. Consider the following examples.

RESTATEMENT OF CONTRACTS

Sec. 1.   Contract Defined. A contract is a promise or a set of promises for the breach of which the law gives a remedy, or the performance of which the law in some way recognizes a duty.

UNIFORM COMMERCIAL CODE

Sec. 1–201.   General Definitions: (11) "Contract" means the total obligation in law which results from the parties' agreement as affected by this Act and any other applicable rules of law. (Compare "Agreement.")

   (3)**"Agreed" or "Agreement"** means the bargain in fact as found in the language of the parties or in the course of dealing or usage of trade or course of performance or by implication from other circumstances. (Compare "Contract.")

A contract, then, is a legal device that establishes a set of special rights and obligations, or legal relations, between particular parties who are bound (only) because of the contract, or agreement. Contractual relations are thus distinguishable from legal relations based on other legal rules, such as rules of ownership or status or criminality. In none of these cases is agreement necessary for the existence of rights or obligations.

In the case of criminality the obligations are in no sense voluntary and cannot be changed in any way by agreement. Indeed, a contract to perform a crime is void. Furthermore, the rights and obligations involved are not special — that is, applicable only to particular individuals — but general — that is, applicable to all people. All people are obligated not to commit criminal acts against any other people, and all people have rights not to be victimized by crimes. But contractual rights and obligations apply only to the contracting parties, and the rights and obligations are whatever the parties specify.

Property ownership involves a cluster of rights set by common rules of acquisition and transfer and held by a particular party (the owner) against all others. It is often said that property rights (rights *in rem*) are rights "in the thing itself" held "against all the world." Obviously, these are quite unlike contract rights (which are rights *in personam*, "in the person," held against the contracting party only). Property rights can be altered by agreement, but that is incidental to property law. It simply shows that within the bundle of rights that comprise ownership is the right to make agreements about one's property. But a person could acquire, maintain, dispose of, or lose property without ever making an agreement about it.

Legal relations based on status may generate rights and obligations that are somewhat like contractual relations in that they may involve only particular parties, such as parent and child. That is, the rights and duties involved are special (like contract rights) rather than general (like rights against criminal acts). However, they are not generated by or based on agreement but rather on the position held—the status of the person involved. The best example is the parent-child relation, which clearly is not governed by agreement. Most forms of the status relation have tended to dissolve into contractual relations. Slavery, for example, was replaced by contractual employment. The contrast between contractual obligation and obligation based on status has often been taken to exemplify the distinction between freedom and bondage, between voluntarily assumed obligations and nonvoluntary ones. Thus, a foundation of agreement is precisely what distinguishes these two areas of law.

As a starting point, then, we will take as the distinguishing feature of contract the idea of special rights and duties generated by some notion of agreement. This at least appears to be a necessary conceptual condition as well as a distinguishing feature. All other areas of law seem to be describable without primary reference to the idea of agreement. But if we eliminate the notion of agreement (in any form, such as consent or promise), the idea of contract seems to disappear along with it. By and large the theoretical and philosophical problems arise (1) in characterizing these elements (what constitutes an agreement, what counts as consent) and in explaining (2) the justification and (3) the scope of obligation (why and when should an agreement or promise be legally binding?).

We start with the idea that a contract is a legally binding agreement. But what makes an agreement *binding?* What justifies contractual obligation? Consider the following example. Suppose you and I make a contract. You agree to landscape my yard, and in return I will pay you $500. You have virtually completed the job, but just as you are planting the last gingko tree I come to you and say, "Listen, I have decided that I don't really want my yard landscaped after all and certainly it's not worth $500 to me."

You say, "Now, wait a minute. We have an agreement about this!"

I say, "I know I agreed, but I changed my mind. I don't want it anymore."

You reply somewhat emphatically, "We have a contract, buster, and you can't just change your mind because you feel like it!"

"But why not?" I want to know. "I change my mind about all sorts of things all the time, and so do you. So why can't I change my mind about this?"

"Well, I'll tell you why," you articulate slowly while poking me in the shoulder with your finger, "because if you don't keep this agreement I will see you in court, that's why."

"Well," I whimper, a little offended, "I guess I understand that kind of language. Anyone understands brute force. But that's just like saying if you don't keep your agreement I'll beat you to a pulp. It certainly gives me an incentive to comply with your demand, but that's just coercion. Coercing someone to do what you want is hardly the same as persuading with reason. All I'm asking for is a legitimate reason for not changing my mind."

Taken back a little by all this, you reply with some confusion, "Look, the reason for being held to one's agreements is so obvious that it never occurred to me that it needed stating, even to someone like you."

"Well, if it's so obvious," I suggest, "why don't you indulge me and say what it is."

Now what are you going to say? What reasons are you going to give? As outrageous as this conversation may seem, the question is a legitimate one. It is a request for justification. We could put the question this way: Recognizing that you can take me to court in the scenario above, why should you be able to do so? Why should you be able to go to court, and if you do, why should you win? Why should anyone be bound by his or her agreements? What is it about an agreement that makes it binding? What elements must be present or absent? Another way to ask the same question is to ask what kind of agreement is or ought to be legally binding. Obviously, not all agreements are legally binding. If we agree to meet for dinner we are not legally bound. If you agree to let me go fishing with you, you are not legally bound. If your grandfather and I agree with each other that we will both give you $500 so that you can go to school, we are not legally bound. None of these situations is legally binding unless we further embroider the story. Many agreements, promises, and other voluntary transactions of that sort are not binding in law. So the question is, from among the vast array of agreements into which human beings might conceivably enter, which ones should be enforceable by law, and more important, why?

Clearly, the Restatement of Contracts definition given earlier will not help us. Nor will that in the Uniform Commercial Code. Those definitions presuppose that the distinction between legal and nonlegal agreements has already been made. Note that the Uniform Commercial Code and the Restatement of Contracts define contracts as agreements (or promises) *that are legally recognized.* But that is hardly helpful. Our question is, What makes an agreement a contract (that is, what makes it legally binding)? The Uniform Commercial Code and the Restatement definitions say that an agreement is a contract when it is legally recognized. But that just says that an agreement is legally binding when it is legally binding. Or more expansively, the definitions say that an agreement is legally binding when the law says it is. These are certainly true statements. In fact, they are tautologies—that is, statements which are true by definition, true in virtue of the meaning of the words in them. To say that what the law says is legally binding is in fact legally binding has to be true because that is just what *legally binding* means. So whereas these definitions are comprised of true statements, they are uninformative for our purposes. They don't tell us anything we did not already know. Consequently, we cannot use these definitions for what we want to find out.

What we need is a principle or a theory of justification. Is there a theory or guiding principle that explains what makes an agreement a contract? What is it exactly that generates contractual obligation? Several theories have been offered to explain this question. In Chapter Three we will consider three contemporary theories that provide rather different insights. Since there are three of them, it should be obvious that the theoretical rationale for the law of contracts is far from settled. As you study these three options, consider which one would provide you with the best explanation for why the law is right to compel me to pay you your $500. Furthermore, assess whether these theories are incompatible with one another or not. It may be that we need not choose only one but rather that some combination of two or all of them will provide the best justification of contractual obligation. On the other hand, you may find none of the theories satisfactory. Finally, keep in mind that contract law is complex, covering a wide range of social and economic circumstances. One theory may apply to certain aspects of contract law while other theories best capture other aspects. Again, consider whether that is acceptable or indicative of contradictions in the law—or both.

In the first selection Charles Fried defends the classical conception of contract as promise. The wide acceptance of this view is reflected in the Restatement definition. But as a principle that explains the idea of contractual obligation by distinguishing it from agreements which are not legally binding, the notion of a promise leaves much to be desired. Nevertheless, Fried argues that the idea of a promise-generating obligation, which is central to the liberal individualist tradition, is the operative and fundamental principle of contracts. Since no other principle, for example, reliance or receipt of benefits, holds up under scrutiny, Fried argues, the practice of promising must be taken as the foundation of contractual obligation. Since the doctrine of "consideration" apparently causes problems for this view, Fried confronts it specifically and directly. Is his approach adequate? Is his view on consideration a descriptive or a normative view?

Patrick S. Atiyah rejects the traditional view of contracts as the enforcement of promises, arguing that there is too much in the law which the traditional view does not and cannot capture. Atiyah focuses on the receipt of benefits and reliance as the sources of contractual obligation. He argues that these ideas provide a better explanation of the disposition of court cases, in fact. Is he also arguing that these ideas provide a better normative foundation for contract law? If so, why? In many ways Atiyah's and Fried's theories can be viewed as opposites, since Atiyah is arguing that the doctrine of consideration and not the notion of a promise accounts for contractual obligation. What normative arguments are there for selecting Atiyah's or Fried's view?

Max Radin presents a very different view, suggesting that no single principle can account for modern contract law. Radin's view is very much in the legal realist tradition and as such might be fairly considered a "nontheory" or "antitheory." That is, it is the denial that a systematic, conceptual theory is possible without distortion of the subject matter and the suggestion of a functional approach instead. Each of the theories presented here provides a different approach and perspective with its own set of assumptions. Each captures an important aspect of contract law. Use the criteria for evaluating theories in Chapter Two to make your overall assessments of these views.

Radin is concerned to place contract law within a social and historical context rather than to engage in conceptual analysis in the abstract. Law exists and functions in a society. But what is the relationship between society and contract law? What does the law of contracts imply about an economic and social system within which or with regard to which it functions? Does it imply a commitment to individual freedom? To growth and commerce?

Does it require some notion of a fair bargain? What would that include, and who should decide — the parties to the contract, the legislature, the courts? Some philosophers have argued that the only requirements for a fair bargain are that the parties be competent, uncoerced, and not defrauded. Others have argued that "background" fairness must be considered as well. That is, if parties are in positions of grossly (or perhaps moderately) unequal bargaining power (especially if that feature is inherent in the contractual situation or type of bargain), one party is placed at such a disadvantage that the contract cannot be fair. Eighteenth-century judges seemed to hold this position. Courts and legislatures have always recognized this view within limits. To do so is to limit individual freedom in the name of justice or the public interest. Balancing these values is not an easy task, and no principled way of doing so has yet been articulated. The selections in this chapter are intended to raise questions about the relationship between contract law and economic development.

Preceding Radin's contextual thesis are two brief historical selections. Henry Maine provides the classical account of the development of contract law. Maine is famous for the general contention that the development of modern society is marked by a gradual expansion of individual freedom, and that this development is reflected and facilitated (or even made possible) by the evolution of law from obligation based on status to obligation based on contract. In ancient societies, according to Maine, members received their responsibilities from the place they held, generally from the position into which they were born. A mark of a modern civilization is that individuals rather than families assume responsibility for transactions and that they assume it on the basis of consent rather than status. Does Maine assume, then, that the idea of contract is essentially individualistic? If so, is that a reasonable assumption? If not, what is meant by the notion of agreement?

M. E. Tigar and M. R. Levy trace the development of contract law during the transformation of feudal society by the industrial revolution. They contest the apparent claim of legal historians like

Maine of the power of contract law (or the individualistic ideals it was taken to embody) to transform social institutions. According to Tigar and Levy, the transformation runs the other way — from social (or economic) change to legal change, not from legal change to social change.

Fried and Maine represent the individualist view of contracts, whereas Atiyah, Tigar and Levy, and Radin represent challenges to that view from three different perspectives. The line of cases at the end of this chapter traces a piece of Supreme Court history that embodies this very debate.

The Supreme Court in the late nineteenth and early twentieth centuries developed a line of cases intended to protect the "freedom of contract." This line of cases had a profound impact on U.S. business and labor relations for at least thirty years until it was essentially abandoned as a judicial policy. In this famous (or infamous) period of Court history, the persistent efforts of the Court to protect the freedom of contract from government interference ultimately resulted in a serious conflict between the judiciary and the legislature. Attempts at progressive labor reform primarily through wage and hour legislation were repeatedly blocked by the Court. The U.S. Congress and state legislatures were up in arms over what they saw as judicial encroachment on legislative jurisdiction, and President Franklin D. Roosevelt was threatening to pack the Court with Justices more favorable to New Deal policy. Furthermore, the composition of the Court itself changed over the years, and internal dissent became strong and unrelenting. Then in *Nebbia* v. *New York* Justice Owen J. Roberts changed his vote, thereby reversing a judicial policy of some fifty years and eliminating a formerly recognized constitutional right protecting the freedom to contract without legislative interference.

These cases raise many issues while illustrating the development of a judicial doctrine. What went wrong with this doctrine? Why was the Court wrong to protect individuals from government interference? Was the Court wrong to assume liberty of contract as a fundamental value of the U.S. system of government? If so, why? Is the Court guilty of a conceptual error? Is its interpretation of the Constitution flawed? In what way? Is the reasoning invalid? Is this line of cases wrong from the beginning or at some later step? Where is the mistake? Does the Court assume an improper function? At what point? This line of cases has much to tell us about both the judicial process and the nature of contracts.

There are, in fact, traditional limits on the right to contract, which all theories try to accommodate in one way or another. The most standard of these are elements that concern the process of formation and performance of contracts, such as fraud, duress, or bad faith. These limits are defensible because they suggest a flaw in the contract itself. If deception or coercion is involved, then there never was any real agreement. The problem with these elements is not whether they should be limiting factors but rather in identifying what they encompass. What counts as fraud, coercion, or bad faith? These limits are required by any theory of contracts because not meeting them would violate both values of freedom and fairness. That is, fraud and coercion are unjust precisely because they violate the autonomy of their victim.

Other commonly used limits, however, are not free from controversy — for example, unconscionability and public policy. In Anglo-American law a contract can be declared void because it is against public policy or because it "shocks the conscience of the court." These limits go to the substance or content of the contract rather than to the process of formation or performance.

Unconscionability is typically aimed at the unequal bargaining power of the parties. It looks to agreements no reasonable person would make except in consequence of inexperience or of economic duress (such as poverty or emergency). In such cases it is assumed that someone is being taken advantage of because of the intrinsic unfairness of the bargaining situation. The contract is declared void as unconscionable, as grossly unfair.

Public policy, on the other hand, is not so concerned with the contractual parties as with the general welfare of society. If a contract is declared void because it is against public policy, that generally means that the act itself, which is the subject of the contract, is questionable or frowned upon. The contract is considered harmful to society in some way.

Both grounds — unconscionability and public policy — are controversial for several reasons. First, they empower a court to evaluate the substance of private agreements. Second, they are exceedingly open ended and consequently subject to abuse. Third, they necessarily involve the courts in imposing subjective value judgments on private individuals. Fourth, public policy judgments border on judicial legislation. Despite these reservations, both doctrines are widely accepted, are considered useful or even necessary in some circumstances, and have been used by courts for many years (whether or not with reasonable restraint depends upon one's point of view). Presumably there must be limits, but what should the limits be?

At the end of Chapter Three is a set of materials concerned specifically with the problem of surrogate mother contracts. The purpose of these articles is to raise the general question of when contracts should be declared void on grounds of public policy. To make a contract void as against public policy is to say with regard to a particular activity or transaction that we will not sanction this activity in the legal system because we do not think such activity should be engaged in. We might criminalize some such activities. On the other hand, we might not criminalize an activity but we will not recognize it; we will not back such activity with law. In such a case, if individuals want to engage in this activity, they must do so at their own risk. Such are the issues raised by surrogate mother contracts. Study the materials at the end of this section and decide whether the public interest demands that such contracts not be recognized, and if so, why. The question is, Why can't people make whatever agreements they wish? If all parties agree, why should society — or judges on behalf of society — limit the private arrangements of competent, consenting adults?

The question this raises is what are the proper limits of contract law? What should the outer boundaries be? There is a special relation between contract law and freedom in that contract law enables individuals to tailor their own law to their own needs. Contract law delegates legislative authority to individuals to bind themselves by their own agreements. You and I could make up our own law (our contract) that binds us and only us. But how free should contracts be? How far should individuals be allowed to go and still expect legal enforcement?

In fact, the scope of individual freedom is the central issue of this chapter and of contract law overall. The examination of this value provides a theme running through all the materials in this chapter. The right to contract is the recognized freedom to obligate oneself, thereby creating new legal relations. The question to ask yourself is why or how does that work? What is it about an agreement that generates obligation (and therefore also rights), and when should such self-imposed obligations (and rights) be enforced or sanctioned by society?

Notes and Questions

CHARLES FRIED, from *Contract as Promise*

1. Charles Fried wants to explain what justifies enforcing contracts. He points out that the classical liberal tradition has stood for individual freedom and respect for all persons. This respect for individual autonomy has been considered the foundation of moral responsibility by philosophers from Immanuel Kant in the seventeenth century to John Rawls in the twentieth. The rationale of this view is that each person should be free to pursue her own ends to the greatest extent possible,

so long as she recognizes an equal freedom on the part of all others. We all may use whatever we will to pursue our goals so long as we do not use another person. The great accomplishment of the discovery of contract or promise, Fried argues, is that it enables people to use one another — to enlist cooperation, without violating anyone's right to be respected as an individual. This was accomplished by enabling people to bind themselves by their own free will by their agreements. What value does Fried say is basic to this enterprise?

2. Given that the convention of promising is a significant social practice and a crucial mechanism for explaining the law of contracts, it is important to examine the nature of promising. Fried asks why a promise is binding. How can a simple communication turn a morally neutral statement into a moral requirement? He considers several possible answers. Can a prohibition against lying account for the binding force of a promise? Why or why not?

3. It is sometimes argued that promises must be kept because breaking them causes harm or unfair benefit. How does Fried view these arguments? Does the fact that a promise invites reliance provide the ground for its being binding? Why do some people think so? What does Fried think?

4. What does Fried mean by his observation that promises are conventional? What is the significance of that convention? Is this the ground that Fried has been looking for?

5. Even if it is the case that a single promise is binding because promises are always binding by convention, what justifies this convention, according to Fried? What value(s) are basic to and encouraged by this convention? Are other justifications possible for the convention of promising?

6. *Consideration* is a legal term that refers to the value exchanged in a contractual transaction. If I agree to wash your car every week for one year for $10 a week, the consideration — the value exchanged — is the service for the money. It has long been held in Anglo-American law that a contract without consideration will not be enforced. For example, if I promise to wash your car for a year for nothing, the contract is not enforceable because no value is exchanged. Virtually all legal systems distinguish "mere" promises from contracts in more or less this way, which poses a problem for Fried's theory of contract as promise. All promises are not enforced. Fried is well aware of this and proposes to undermine the objection by showing that the doctrine of consideration is neither necessary nor sufficient for contractual obligation. What examples does he give? Are they compelling? Is a promise necessary or sufficient for contractual obligation?

7. Fried also tries to show that the doctrine of consideration is internally inconsistent. What are the two inconsistent principles embodied in the doctrine, according to Fried? Does this inconsistency account for the inconsistent cases he cites? Could there be another explanation? Would eliminating the requirement of consideration eliminate these inconsistencies? Would that be a good thing?

8. Finally, Fried acknowledges that most legal systems distinguish gifts from bargains. But he suggests that they should not do so. Do you think charitable promises should be enforceable? Do you think they are essentially the same as contract obligations? If you think that they are different, do you have any ideas as to what accounts for the difference?

[From] *Contract as Promise*

CHARLES FRIED

C H A P T E R   2

Contract as Promise

It is a first principle of liberal political morality that we be secure in what is ours — so that our persons and property not be open to exploitation by others, and that from a sure foundation we may express our will and expend our powers in the world. By these powers we may create good things or low, useful articles or luxuries, things extraordinary or banal, and we will be judged accordingly — as saintly or mean, skillful or ordinary, industrious and fortunate or debased, friendly and kind or cold and inhuman. But whatever we accomplish and however that accomplishment is judged, morality requires that we respect the person and property of others, leaving them free to make their lives as we are left free to make ours. This is the liberal ideal. This is the ideal that distinguishes between the good, which is the domain of aspiration, and the right, which sets the terms and limits according to which we strive. This ideal makes what we achieve our own and our failures our responsibility too — however much or little we may choose to share our good fortune and however we may hope for help when we fail.

Everything must be available to us, for who can deny the human will the title to expand even into the remotest corner of the universe? And when we forbear to bend some external object to our use because of its natural preciousness we use it still, for it is to our judgment of its value that we respond, our own conception of the good that we pursue. Only other persons are not available to us in this way — they alone share our self-consciousness, our power of self-determination; thus to use them as if they were merely part of external nature is to poison the source of the moral power we enjoy. But others *are* part of the external world, and by denying ourselves access to their persons and powers, we drastically shrink the scope of our efficacy. So it was a cru-

cial moral discovery that free men may yet freely serve each others' purposes: the discovery that beyond the fear of reprisal or the hope of reciprocal favor, morality itself might be enlisted to assure not only that you respect me and mine but that you actively serve my purposes. When my confidence in your assistance derives from my conviction that you will do what is right (not just what is prudent), then I trust you, and trust becomes a powerful tool for our working our mutual wills in the world. So remarkable a tool is trust that in the end we pursue it for its own sake; we prefer doing things cooperatively when we might have relied on fear or interest or worked alone.

The device that gives trust its sharpest, most palpable form is promise. By promising we put in another man's hands a new power to accomplish his will, though only a moral power: What he sought to do alone he may now expect to do with our promised help, and to give him this new facility was our very purpose in promising. By promising we transform a choice that was morally neutral into one that is morally compelled. Morality, which must be permanent and beyond our particular will if the grounds for our willing are to be secure, is itself invoked, molded to allow us better to work that particular will. Morality then serves modest, humdrum ends: We make appointments, buy and sell, harnessing this loftiest of all forces.

What is a promise, that by my words I should make wrong what before was morally indifferent? A promise is a communication — usually verbal; it says something. But how can my saying something put a moral charge on a choice that before was morally neutral? Well, by my misleading you, or by lying. Is lying not the very paradigm of doing wrong by speaking? But this won't do, for a promise puts the moral charge on a *potential* act — the wrong is done later, when the promise is not kept — while a lie is a wrong committed at the time of its utterance. Both wrongs abuse trust, but in different ways. When I speak I commit myself to the truth of my utterance, but when I promise I commit myself to *act*, later. Though these two wrongs are thus quite distinct there has been a persistent tendency to run them together by treating a promise as a lie after all, but a particular kind of lie: a lie about one's intentions. Consider this case:

I. I sell you a house, retaining an adjacent vacant lot. At the time of our negotiations, I state that I intend to build a home for myself on that lot. What if several years later I sell the lot to a person who builds a gas station on it? What if I sell it only one month later? What if I am already negotiating for its sale as a gas station at the time I sell the house to you?

If I was already negotiating to sell the lot for a gas station at the time of my statement to you, I have wronged you. I have lied to you about the state of my intentions, and this is as much a lie as a lie about the state of the plumbing. If, however, I sell the lot many years later, I do you no wrong. There are no grounds for saying I lied about my intentions; I have just changed my mind. Now if I had *promised* to use the lot only as a residence, the situation would be different. Promising is more than just truthfully reporting my present intentions, for I may be free to change my mind, as I am not free to break my promise.

Let us take it as given here that lying is wrong and so that it is wrong to obtain benefits or cause harm by lying (including lying about one's intentions). It does not at all follow that to obtain a benefit or cause harm by breaking a promise is also wrong. That my act procures me a benefit or causes harm all by itself proves nothing. If I open a restaurant near your hotel and prosper as I draw your guests away from the standard hotel fare you offer, this benefit I draw from you places me under no obligation to you. I should make restitution only if I benefit *unjustly*, which I do if I deceive you — as when I lie to you about my intentions in example I. But where is the injustice if I honestly intend to keep my promise at the time of making it, and later change my mind? If we feel I owe you recompense in that case too, it cannot be because of the benefit I have obtained through my promise: We have seen that

benefit even at another's expense is not alone sufficient to require compensation. If I owe you a duty to return that benefit it must be because of the promise. It is the promise that makes my enrichment at your expense unjust, and not the enrichment that makes the promise binding. And thus neither the statement of intention nor the benefit explains why, if at all, a promise does any moral work.

A more common attempt to reduce the force of a promise to some other moral category invokes the harm you suffer in relying on my promise. My statement is like a pit I have dug in the road, into which you fall. I have harmed you and should make you whole. Thus the tort principle might be urged to bridge the gap in the argument between a statement of intention and a promise: I have a duty just because I could have foreseen (indeed it was my intention) that you would rely on my promise and that you would suffer harm when I broke it. And this wrong then not only sets the stage for compensation of the harm caused by the misplaced reliance, but also supplies the moral predicate for restitution of any benefits I may have extracted from you on the strength of my promise. But we still beg the question. If the promise is no more than a truthful statement of my intention, why am *I* responsible for harm that befalls you as a result of my change of heart? To be sure, it is not like a change in the weather — I might have kept to my original intention — but how does this distinguish the broken promise from any other statement of intention (or habit or prediction of future conduct) of mine of which you know and on which you choose to rely? Should your expectations of me limit my freedom of choice? If you rent the apartment next to mine because I play chamber music there, do I owe you more than an expression of regret when my friends and I decide to meet instead at the cellist's home? And in general, why should my liberty be constrained by the harm you would suffer from the disappointment of the expectations you choose to entertain about my choices?

Does it make a difference that when I promise you do not just happen to rely on me, that I communicate my intention to you and therefore can be taken to know that changing my mind may put you at risk? But then I might be aware that you would count on my keeping to my intentions even if I myself had not communicated those intentions to you. (*You* might have told me you were relying on me, or you might have overheard me telling some third person of my intentions.) It might be said that I become the agent of your reliance by telling you, and that this makes my responsibility clearer: After all, I can scarcely control all the ways in which you might learn of my intentions, but I *can* control whether or not I tell you of them. But we are still begging the question. If promising is no more than my telling you of my intentions, why do we both not know that I may yet change my mind? Perhaps, then, promising is like telling you of my intention and telling you that I don't intend to change my mind. But why can't I change my mind about the latter intention?

Perhaps the statement of intention in promising is binding because we not only foresee reliance, we invite it: We intend the promisee to rely on the promise. Yet even this will not do. If I invite reliance on my stated intention, then that is all I invite. Certainly I may hope and intend, in example I, that you buy my house on the basis of what I have told you, but why does that hope bind me to do more than state my intention honestly? And that intention and invitation are quite compatible with my later changing my mind. In every case, of course, I should weigh the harm I will do if I do change my mind. If I am a doctor and I know you will rely on me to be part of an outing on which someone may fall ill, I should certainly weigh the harm that may come about if that reliance is disappointed. Indeed I should weigh that harm even if you do not rely on me, but are foolish enough not to have made a provision for a doctor. Yet in none of these instances am I bound as I would be had I promised.

A promise invokes trust in my future actions, not merely in my present sincerity. We need to isolate an additional element, over and above benefit, reliance, and the communication of intention. That additional element must *commit* me, and commit me to more than the truth of some statement. That additional element has so far eluded our analysis.

It has eluded us, I believe, because there is a real puzzle about how we can commit ourselves to a course of conduct that absent our commitment is morally neutral. The invocation of benefit and reliance are attempts to explain the force of a promise in terms of two of its most usual effects, but the attempts fail because these effects depend on the prior assumption of the force of the commitment. The way out of the puzzle is to recognize the bootstrap quality of the argument: To have force in a *particular case* promises must be assumed to have force generally. Once that general assumption is made, the effects we intentionally produce by a particular promise may be morally attributed to us. This recognition is not as paradoxical as its abstract statement here may make it seem. It lies, after all, behind every conventional structure: games, institutions and practices, and most important, language.

Let us put to one side the question of how a convention comes into being, or of when and why we are morally bound to comply with its terms, while we look briefly at what a convention is and how it does its work. Take the classical example of a game. What the players do is defined by a system of rules—sometimes quite vague and informal, sometimes elaborate and codified. These rules apply only to the players—that is, to persons who invoke them. These rules are a human invention, and their consequences (castling, striking out, winning, losing) can be understood only in terms of the rules. The players may have a variety of motives for playing (profit, fun, maybe even duty to fellow players who need participants). A variety of judgments are applicable to the players—they may be deemed skillful, imaginative, bold, honest, or dishonest—but these judgments and motives too can be understood only in the context of the game. For instance, you can cheat only by breaking rules to which you pretend to conform.

This almost canonical invocation of the game example has often been misunderstood as somehow applying only to unserious matters, to play, so that it is said to trivialize the solemn objects (like law or promises) that it is used to explain. But this is a mistake, confusing the interests involved, the reasons for creating and invoking a particular convention, with the logical structure of conventions in general. Games are (often) played for fun, but other conventions—for instance religious rituals or legal procedures—may have most earnest ends, while still other conventions are quite general. To the last category belongs language. The conventional nature of language is too obvious to belabor. It is worth pointing out, however, that the various things we do with language — informing, reporting, promising, insulting, cheating, lying — all depend on the conventional structure's being firmly in place. You could not lie if there were not both understanding of the language you lied in and a general convention of using that language truthfully. This point holds irrespective of whether the institution of language has advanced the situation of mankind and of whether lying is sometimes, always, or never wrong.

Promising too is a very general convention — though less general than language, of course, since promising is itself a use of language. The convention of promising (like that of language) has a very general purpose under which we may bring an infinite set of particular purposes. In order that I be as free as possible, that my will have the greatest possible range consistent with the similar will of others, it is necessary that there be a way in which I may commit myself. It is necessary that I be able to make nonoptional a course of conduct that would otherwise be optional for me. By doing this I can facilitate the projects of others, because I can make it possible for those others to count on my future conduct, and thus those others can pursue more intricate, more far-reaching projects. If it is my purpose, my will that others be able to count on me in the pursuit of their endeavor, it is essential that I be able to deliver myself into their hands more firmly than where they simply predict my future course. Thus the possibility of commitment permits an act of generosity on my part, permits me to pursue a project whose content is that *you* be permitted to pursue *your* project. But of course this purely altruistic motive is not the only motive worth facilitating. More central to our concern is the situation where we facilitate each other's projects, where the gain is reciprocal. Schematically the situation looks like this:

> You want to accomplish purpose A and I want to accomplish purpose B. Neither of us can succeed without the cooperation of the other. Thus I want to be able to commit myself to help you achieve A so that you will commit yourself to help me achieve B.

Now if A and B are objects or actions that can be transferred simultaneously there is no need for commitment. As I hand over A you hand over B,

and we are both satisfied. But very few things are like that. We need a device to permit a trade over time: to allow me to do A for you when you need it, in the confident belief that you will do B for me when I need it. Your commitment puts your future performance into my hands in the present just as my commitment puts my future performance into your hands. A future exchange is transformed into a present exchange. And in order to accomplish this all we need is a conventional device which we both invoke, which you know I am invoking when I invoke it, which I know that you know I am invoking, and so on.

The only mystery about this is the mystery that surrounds increasing autonomy by providing means for restricting it. But really this is a pseudomystery. The restrictions involved in promising are restrictions undertaken just in order to increase one's options in the long run, and thus are perfectly consistent with the principle of autonomy — consistent with a respect for one's own autonomy and the autonomy of others. To be sure, in getting something for myself now by promising to do something for you in the future, I am mortgaging the interest of my future self in favor of my present self. How can I be sure my future self will approve?* This is a deep and difficult problem about which I say more later in this chapter. Suffice it to say here that unless one assumes the continuity of the self and the possibility of maintaining complex projects over time, not only the morality of promising but also any coherent picture of the person becomes impossible.

The Moral Obligation of Promise

Once I have invoked the institution of promising, why exactly is it wrong for me then to break my promise?

My argument so far does not answer that question. The institution of promising is a way for me to bind myself to another so that the other may expect a future performance, and binding myself in this way is something that I may want

---

*Note that this problem does not arise where I make a present sacrifice for a future benefit, since by hypothesis I am presently willing to make that sacrifice and in the future I only stand to gain.

to be able to do. But this by itself does not show that I am morally obligated to perform my promise at a later time if to do so proves inconvenient or costly. That there should be a system of currency also increases my options and is useful to me, but this does not show why I should not use counterfeit money if I can get away with it. In just the same way the usefulness of promising in general does not show why I should not take advantage of it in a particular case and yet fail to keep my promise. That the convention would cease to function in the long run, would cease to provide benefits if everyone felt free to violate it, is hardly an answer to the question of why I should keep a particular promise on a particular occasion.

David Lewis has shown that a convention that it would be in each person's interest to observe if everyone else observed it will be established and maintained without any special mechanisms of commitment or enforcement. Starting with simple conventions (for example that if a telephone conversation is disconnected, the person who initiated the call is the one who calls back) Lewis extends his argument to the case of language. Now promising is different, since (unlike language, where it is overwhelmingly in the interest of all that everyone comply with linguistic conventions, even when language is used to deceive) it will often be in the interest of the promisor *not* to conform to the convention when it comes time to render his performance. Therefore individual self-interest is not enough to sustain the convention, and some additional ground is needed to keep it from unraveling. There are two principal candidates: external sanctions and moral obligation.

David Hume sought to combine these two by proposing that the external sanction of public opprobrium, of loss of reputation for honesty, which society attaches to promise-breaking, is internalized, becomes instinctual, and accounts for the sense of the moral obligation of promise. Though Hume offers a possible anthropological or psychological account of how people feel about promises, his is not a satisfactory *moral* argument. Assume that I can get away with breaking my promise (the promisee is dead), and I am now asking why I should keep it anyway in the face of some personal inconvenience. Hume's account of obligation is more like an argument *against* my keeping the promise, for it tells me

how any feelings of obligation that I may harbor have come to lodge in my psyche and thus is the first step toward ridding me of such inconvenient prejudices.

Considerations of self-interest cannot supply the moral basis of my obligation to keep a promise. By an analogous argument neither can considerations of utility. For however sincerely and impartially I may apply the utilitarian injunction to consider at each step how I might increase the sum of happiness or utility in the world, it will allow me to break my promise whenever the balance of advantage (including, of course, my own advantage) tips in that direction. The possible damage to the institution of promising is only one factor in the calculation. Other factors are the alternative good I might do by breaking my promise, whether and by how many people the breach might be discovered, what the actual effect on confidence of such a breach would be. There is no a priori reason for believing that an individual's calculations will come out in favor of keeping the promise always, sometimes, or most of the time.

Rule-utilitarianism seeks to offer a way out of this conundrum. The individual's moral obligation is determined not by what the best action at a particular moment would be, but by the rule it would be best for him to follow. It has, I believe, been demonstrated that this position is incoherent: Either rule-utilitarianism requires that rules be followed in a particular case even where the result would not be best all things considered, and so the utilitarian aspect of rule-utilitarianism is abandoned; or the obligation to follow the rule is so qualified as to collapse into act-utilitarianism after all. There is, however, a version of rule-utilitarianism that makes a great deal of sense. In this version the utilitarian does not instruct us what our individual moral obligations are but rather instructs legislators what the best rules are. If legislation is our focus, then the contradictions of rule-utilitarianism do not arise, since we are instructing those whose decisions can *only* take the form of issuing rules. From that perspective there is obvious utility to rules establishing and enforcing promissory obligations. Since I am concerned now with the question of individual obligation, that is, moral obligation, this legislative perspective on the argument is not available to me.

The obligation to keep a promise is grounded not in arguments of utility but in respect for individual autonomy and in trust. Autonomy and trust are grounds for the institution of promising as well, but the argument for *individual* obligation is not the same. Individual obligation is only a step away, but that step must be taken. An individual is morally bound to keep his promises because he has intentionally invoked a convention whose function it is to give grounds — moral grounds — for another to expect the promised performance. To renege is to abuse a confidence he was free to invite or not, and which he intentionally did invite. To abuse that confidence now is like (but only *like*) lying: the abuse of a shared social institution that is intended to invoke the bonds of trust. A liar and a promise-breaker each *use* another person. In both speech and promising there is an invitation to the other to trust, to make himself vulnerable; the liar and the promise-breaker then abuse that trust. The obligation to keep a promise is thus similar to but more constraining than the obligation to tell the truth. To avoid lying you need only believe in the truth of what you say when you say it, but a promise binds into the future, well past the moment when the promise is made. There will, of course, be great social utility to a general regime of trust and confidence in promises and truthfulness. But this just shows that a regime of mutual respect allows men and women to accomplish what in a jungle of unrestrained self-interest could not be accomplished. If this advantage is to be firmly established, there must exist a ground for mutual confidence deeper than and independent of the social utility it permits.

The utilitarian counting the advantages affirms the general importance of enforcing *contracts*. The moralist of duty, however, sees *promising* as a device that free, moral individuals have fashioned on the premise of mutual trust, and which gathers its moral force from that premise. The moralist of duty thus posits a general obligation to keep promises, of which the obligation of contract will be only a special case — that special case in which certain promises have attained legal as well as moral force. But since a contract is first of all a promise, the contract must be kept because a promise must be kept.

To summarize: There exists a convention that defines the practice of promising and its entailments. This convention provides a way that a person may create expectations in others. By virtue of the basic Kantian principles of trust and respect, it is wrong to invoke that convention in order to make a promise, and then to break it.

What a Promise Is Worth

If I make a promise to you, I should do as I promise; and if I fail to keep my promise, it is fair that I should be made to hand over the equivalent of the promised performance. In contract doctrine this proposition appears as the expectation measure of damages for breach. The expectation standard gives the victim of a breach no more or less than he would have had had there been no breach — in other words, he gets the benefit of his bargain. Two alternative measures of damage, reliance and restitution, express the different notions that if a person has relied on a promise and been hurt, that hurt must be made good; and that if a contract-breaker has obtained goods or services, he must be made to pay a fair (just?) price for them. Consider three cases:

II-A. I enter your antique shop on a quiet afternoon and agree in writing to buy an expensive chest I see there, the price being about three times what you paid for it a short time ago. When I get home I repent of my decision, and within half an hour of my visit — before any other customer has come to your store — I telephone to say I no longer want the chest.

II-B. Same as above, except in the meantime you have waxed and polished the chest and had your delivery van bring it to my door.

II-C. Same as above, except I have the use of the chest for six months, while your shop is closed for renovations.

To require me to pay for the chest in case II-A (or, if you resell it, to pay any profit you lost, including lost business volume) is to give you your expectation, the benefit of your bargain. In II-B if all I must compensate is your effort I am reimbursing your reliance, and in II-C to force me to pay a fair price for the use I have had of the chest is to focus on making me pay for, restore, an actual benefit I have received.

The assault on the classical conception of contract, the concept I call contract as promise, has centered on the connection — taken as canonical for some hundred years — between contract law and expectation damages. To focus the attack on this connection is indeed strategic. As the critics recognize and as I have just stated, to the extent that contract is grounded in promise, it seems natural to measure relief by the expectation, that is, by the promise itself. If that link can be threatened, then contract itself may be grounded elsewhere than in promise, elsewhere than in the will of the parties. In his recent comprehensive treatise, *The Rise and Fall of Freedom of Contract*, Patrick Atiyah makes the connection between the recourse to expectation damages and the emerging enforceability of executory contracts — that is, contracts enforced, though no detriment has been suffered in reliance and no benefit has been conferred. (Case II-A is an example of an executory contract.) Before the nineteenth century, he argues, a contractual relation referred generally to one of a number of particular, community-sanctioned relations between persons who in the course of their dealings (as carriers, innkeepers, surgeons, merchants) relied on each other to their detriment or conferred benefits on each other. It was these detriments and benefits that had to be reimbursed, and an explicit promise — if there happened to be one — was important primarily to establish the reliance or to show that the benefit had been conferred in expectation of payment, not officiously or as a gift. All this, Atiyah writes, turned inside out when the promise itself came to be seen as the basis of obligation, so that neither benefit nor reliance any longer seemed necessary and the proper measure of the obligation was the promise itself, that is, the expectation. The promise principle was embraced as an expression of the principle of liberty — the will binding itself, to use Kantian language, rather than being bound by the norms of the collectivity — and the award of expectation damages followed as a natural concomitant of the promise principle.

The insistence on reliance or benefit is related to disputes about the nature of promising. As I have argued, reliance on a promise cannot alone explain its force: There is reliance because a promise is binding, and not the other way around. But if a person is bound by his promise and not by the harm the promisee may have suffered in reliance on it, then what he is bound to is just its performance. Put simply, I am bound to do what I promised you I would do — or I am bound to put you in as good a position as if I had done so. To bind me to do no more than to reimburse your reliance is to excuse me to that extent from the obligation I undertook. If your reliance is less than your expectation (in case II-A there is no reliance), then to that extent a reliance standard excuses me from the very obligation I undertook and so weakens the force of an obligation I chose to assume. Since by hypothesis I chose to assume the obligation in its stronger form (that is, to render the performance promised), the reliance rule indeed precludes me from incurring the very obligation I chose to undertake at the time of promising. The most compelling of the arguments for resisting this conclusion and for urging that we settle for reliance is the sense that it is sometimes harsh and ungenerous to insist on the full measure of expectancy. (This is part of Atiyah's thrust when he designates the expectation standard as an aspect of the rigid Victorian promissory morality.) The harshness comes about because in the event the promisor finds the obligation he assumed too burdensome.

This distress may be analyzed into three forms: (1) The promisor regrets having to pay for what he has bought (which may only have been the satisfaction of promising a gift or the thrill of buying a lottery ticket or stock option), though he would readily do the same thing again. I take it that this kind of regret merits no sympathy at all. Indeed if we gave in to it we would frustrate the promisor's ability to engage in his own continuing projects and so the promisor's plea is, strictly speaking, self-contradictory. (2) The promisor regrets his promise because he was mistaken about the nature of the burdens he was assuming — the purchaser in case II-A thought he would find the money for the antique but in fact his savings are depleted, or perhaps the chest is not as old nor as valuable as he had imagined, or his house has burned down and he no longer needs it. All of these regrets are based on mistaken assumptions about the facts as they are or as they turn out to be. As we shall see in chapter 5, the doctrines of mistake, frustration, and impossibility provide grounds for mitigating the effect of the promise principle without at all undermining it.

Finally there is the most troublesome ground of regret: (3) The promisor made no mistake about the facts or probabilities at all, but now that it has come time to perform he no longer values the promise as highly as when he made it. He regrets the promise because he regrets the value judgment that led him to make it. He concludes that the purchase of an expensive antique is an extravagance. Compassion may lead a promise to release an obligation in such a case, but he releases as an act of generosity, not as a duty, and certainly not because the promisor's repentance destroys the force of the original obligation. The intuitive reason for holding fast is that such repentance should be the promisor's own responsibility, not one he can shift onto others. It seems too easy a way of getting out of one's obligations. Yet our intuition does not depend on suspicions of insincerity alone. Rather we feel that holding people to their obligations is a way of taking them seriously and thus of giving the concept of sincerity itself serious content. Taking this intuition to a more abstract level, I would say that respect for others as free and rational requires taking seriously their capacity to determine their own values. I invoke again the distinction between the right and the good. The right defines the concept of the self as choosing its own conception of the good. Others must respect our capacity as free and rational persons to choose our own good, and that respect means allowing persons to take responsibility for the good they choose. And, of course, that choosing self is not an instantaneous self but one extended in time, so that to respect those determinations of the self is to respect their persistence over time. If we decline to take seriously the assumption of an obligation because we do not take seriously the promisor's prior conception of the good that led him to assume it, to that extent we do not take him seriously as a person. We infantilize him, as we do quite properly when we release the very young from the consequences of their choices.

Since contracts invoke and are invoked by promises, it is not surprising that the law came to impose on the promises it recognized the same incidents as morality demands. The connection between contract and the expectation principle is so palpable that there is reason to doubt that its legal recognition is a relatively recent invention. It is true that over the last two centuries citizens in the liberal democracies have become increasingly free to dispose of their talents, labor, and property as seems best to them. The freedom to bind oneself contractually to a future disposition is an important and striking example of this freedom (the freedom to make testamentary dispositions or to make whatever present use of one's effort or goods one desires are other examples), because in a promise one is taking responsibility not only for one's present self but for one's future self. But this does not argue that the promise principle itself is a novelty—surely Cicero's, Pufendorf's and Grotius's discussions of it show that it is not—but only that its use has expanded greatly over the years.

C H A P T E R   3

Consideration

It is a standard textbook proposition that in Anglo-American law a promise is not binding without consideration. Consideration is defined as something either given or promised in exchange for a promise. As it stands this proposition is too unqualified to be quite accurate. Into the nineteenth century a promise contained in a document bearing a seal was binding without consideration in most common law jurisdictions. In the last hundred years there has been a gradual movement to abolish the effect of the seal by legislation, while statutes in different jurisdictions have made a wide variety of particular promises binding without consideration: promises to keep an offer open, to release a debt, to modify an obligation, to pay for past favors. Nevertheless, the trend away from the seal as an anachronistic relic and the narrow, episodic nature of the statutory exceptions leaves the doctrine of consideration as very much the norm.

It is the doctrine of consideration that leads some to see contract as distinct from promise; it is consideration that leads people to say that promise may be all well and good as a ground of moral obligation, but the law is concerned with different and more serious business. What is this more serious business? One intuitive idea is that exchanges are enforced because one who welches on an exchange is a kind of cheat or thief: He has obtained a benefit and now refuses to pay for it. As we have seen in chapter 2, this intuitive sense does not fit the facts—at least in the many cases of executory contracts where the "cheat" has not yet received anything in exchange for his promise except the "victim's" own promise. Where you have given in exchange for my promise nothing more than your own return promise, it is a bootstrap argument to reason that you must be allowed to recover because I by my breach appropriate to myself a value without rendering the agreed-upon exchange. The only value I have received or you given is just your promise, and so I benefit at your expense only on the premise that your promise is enforceable. But that premise is inadmissible in an argument designed to show that promises are enforceable only so far as necessary to prevent one party from deriving a one-sided benefit. This is not to say that exchanges of promises are not truly exchanges, only that the prevention of unjust enrichment cannot be the basis for enforcing such promissory exchanges. An analogous argument obtains to block the suggestion that the doctrine of consideration shows that the law of contracts is concerned not to enforce promises but to compensate harm suffered through reliance.

Exactly what kind of challenge does the doctrine of consideration pose to my thesis of contract as promise? If consideration implies a basis other than promise for contractual obligation, what exactly is that basis? To answer these questions and thus take the measure of the challenge, we must examine the present doctrine in some detail. The doctrine comprises two propositions: (A) The consideration that in law promotes a mere promise into a contractual obligation is something, or the promise of something, given in exchange for the promise. (B) The law is not at all interested in the adequacy of the consideration. The goodness of the exchange is for the parties alone to judge—the law is concerned only that there *be* an exchange. Thus the classic conception seeks to affirm both exchange and freedom of contract. These two ideas turn out to be contradictory.

Consider first the leading case of *Hamer v. Sidway*:

> I. An uncle promises his nephew that he will pay him $5000 if the nephew will neither smoke nor drink until his twenty-first birthday. The nephew complies, but the uncle's executor refuses to pay, claiming the promise was made without consideration.

The court held that the nephew's forbearance was sufficient consideration, even if the nephew had benefited from this forbearance and indeed even if the nephew had had no desire to smoke or drink in that period. It was enough that he had the right to do so and did not exercise it. The law will not inquire into actual motives. This seems reasonable. Imagine a concert manager refusing to pay a pianist an agreed fee on the ground that the pianist would have been glad to perform for nothing. Such subjective inquiries are obviously objectionable. How then should we deal with this case:

> II. A father, wanting to assure his son of a gift but not having the funds in hand, promises to pay $5000 in return for a peppercorn or some other worthless object.

Such a promise, we are told, is unenforceable because the peppercorn is "a mere pretense." When the law says that there must be an exchange, it means just that and not a charade pretending to be an exchange. This too seems reasonable, but how can we decide that the exchange in this case is a charade without looking either at motive—which *Hamer* forbids us to do—or at the substance of the exchange, which the second of the two premises (B) stated at the outset of this section forbids?

The concept of exchange is highly abstract. Perhaps the inquiry would be advanced if we used the more evocative term "bargain," which is in fact traditionally used to explain consideration. To this we may add Holmes's suggestion that consideration does not necessarily require an actual bargain, but "reciprocal *conventional* inducement." This means either a real bargain *or* the kind of exchange that in general constitutes an actual bargain, though in a particular case the usual motive might be missing. People do not usually exchange large sums of money for peppercorns, but they regularly bargain about the terms of compensation for a musical performance. How else, after all, are pianists supposed to make a living? Thus the suggestion is that a transaction counts as a bargain either if it was so intended or if it belongs to a type of transactions that people generally bargain about. It looks as if the law can then go about its business of enforcing promissory exchanges without having to look at their substance — that is, allowing people the freedom to make whatever bargains seem best to them. If the doctrine of consideration did at least this the only question left to answer would be what there is about bargains that makes them among promises the privileged objects of legal recognition.

An examination of some cases shows, however, that this simple notion depending on the intuitive idea of bargain cannot account for all of the epicycles of the doctrine of consideration.

> III. An author promises his agent that the agent will have the exclusive right to deal with his manuscript during six months, in return for the agent's adding the manuscript to his list. The agent does not promise to make any effort at all to place the manuscript, but he does insist that without the exclusive right he will do nothing.

The common law holds that a promisor in the author's position is not bound, because the agent has given no consideration — he has promised nothing in return for the author's promise, nor paid for the exclusive privilege of considering the manuscript. Yet there is a bargain in the sense that the author has obtained something he wants — namely, the *chance* that this agent might peddle his manuscript — something he could not have obtained other than in return for his promise. And in general the common law has refused to admit the enforceability of options, unless the beneficiary has given or promised something of value for the option. Such arrangements are said to lack mutuality.

Lack of mutuality in only one ground for denying enforcement to arrangments that are bargains in fact. Here is another:

> IV. A widow promises to repay a debt owed by her deceased husband in return for the creditor bank's canceling the estate's debt. The husband's estate is without assets, and no part of the canceled debt could ever have been collected.

Is there not consideration for the widow's promise? Let us assume the widow knows that the released claim is worthless. Nevertheless she considers the prospect of clearing her husband's name worth exchanging for a promise to pay the debt. Is this not a bargain? We can even imagine the bank and the widow actually haggling about the details of the promise. Yet the court said that since the bank gave nothing of value, the widow's promise was unenforceable. The widow believed she was "buying" something of value to her, so this is not even a case of a pretended bargain. Perhaps the court found the transaction too far from the central paradigm of a bargain, too remote from the model of some standard commercial transaction; but if so, case III is hard to explain. Perhaps, then, the court had a sense that the widow was being put upon in a difficult situation; but such transactions have been held to lack consideration even where no widows are involved, while plenty of hard bargains made by distressed widows are enforced.

Consider this case:

> V. A small contractor borrows money from one of his craftsmen and becomes bankrupt without repaying it. Many years later, he makes an explicit written promise to pay this debt, even though it has long ago become unenforceable by reason of both the bankruptcy and the passage of time.

In this case courts typically do enforce the subsequent promise, using the puzzling rationale that the prior obligation is somehow sufficient to support a later promise — the passage of time and the bar of bankruptcy being held to be only formal defects which the subsequent promise removes. Whatever the substantive merit of allowing recovery in such cases, the stated explanation is obviously gibberish. To be consistent the courts would have to find that in such cases there was no bargain, any more than in the case of the widow, since one does not bargain for what one already has: the repentant contractor has already got clear of all obligation the money that he subsequently promises to repay. This notion that you cannot bargain for what you already have is illustrated in these so-called moral consideration cases:

> VI. A workman throws himself in the way of a falling object, saving his employer's life but suffering disabling injuries. The grateful employer promises a pension, which the employer's executors refuse to continue, on

the grounds that it was promised without consideration.

VII. A family nurses to health over a considerable period the adult son of a distant father. When the father learns of this kindness, he promises recompense but does not keep his promise.

In the second of these cases the court accepted the consequences of the bargain theory and refused enforcement. In the first that result was apparently too repellent to accept and the court granted enforcement—by a process of reasoning too strained to repeat. But the problem of promises about prior obligations may arise as well in contexts where not gratitude but calculation is the motive:

VIII. Architect threatens to abandon supervision of an industrial construction project at a crucial stage unless the desperate owner promises to pay an additonal fee.

IX. Builder discovers that the land on which he has contracted to build consists of a shallow crust of hard earth with swamp underneath. Completing the project would be far more costly than he had expected. Although the builder clearly accepted the risk of such a surprise, the owner promises to pay an additional sum on successful completion of the work.

X. Debtor is hard pressed and promises to pay creditor an already overdue debt in three monthly installments in return for creditor's promise to forgive the promised interest on the debt.

In each of these cases, the promisor later reneges. Owners in cases VIII and IX claim that they received nothing for their promises and so refuse the extra payment. In the first of these the defense succeeded and the architect did not recover; in the second the defense failed and builder recovered. The creditor in X later claims the interest on the debt on the ground that debtor paid nothing for creditor's promise to forgive the interest. The common law has regularly enforced the original debt in full against the debtor in spite of the creditor's promise of partial forgiveness.

The bargain theory of consideration not only fails to explain why this pattern of decisions is just; it does not offer *any* consistent set of principles from which all of these decisions would flow.

These cases particularly cannot be accounted for by the two guiding premises of the doctrine of consideration: (A) that only promises given as part of a bargain are enforceable; (B) that whether there is a bargain or not is a formal question only. As in the cases of the author and the widow (III and IV), so in each of these cases there has been a bargain in fact: The owners and creditor have promised something in return for an assurance or performance. The difference is that in cases VIII–X there is a unilateral modification of earlier bargains so that the promisors (the two owners and the creditor) make new promises, but get no more (creditor gets *less*) than they were entitled to under their old bargains. Nevertheless, new bargains have been made, and propositions A and B are satisfied.

The intuitive appeal of the decisions, at least in the two building cases, VIII and IX, may be easily explained. Architect has owner over a barrel: Their original bargain made owner depend on him, and the second bargain exploits the vulnerability created by the owner's trust in that original promise. The builder in IX, by contrast, has had a nasty surprise, though by the terms of the original deal the risk of such a surprise was his. Finally, case X may be one where debtor, like the builder, falls on unexpected difficulties, or it may be more like IX: exploitation of the creditor's unwillingness to suffer the expense and hazards of suing for his money.

The formal device to deal with these modification cases is the doctrine that consideration not only must be bargained for but must be "fresh"— that the promisor cannot, as it were, sell the same thing twice. So perhaps we might just add to A and B a new premise, A'; that what is given or promised in return for a promise must not be something that is already owed to the promisor. Never mind for a moment why we are adding this premise, ask only if now the courts can proceed formally—that is, in compliance with premise B—to decide which promises are to be enforced. This new theory of consideration (consisting now of three propositions) would certainly block the blackmailing architect in VIII, but only at the cost of blocking the quite reasonable accommodation between the builder and the owner in IX. And it offers no way to distinguish reasonable from extortionate compositions between debtors and creditors. (The common law does indeed fail to make that distinction, applying it indiscriminately to all debtor compositions.)

The rigors of this expanded theory might be mitigated if we treated a contract modification as if builder and owner in IX had cancelled their old contract and entered into a new one containing the desired additional compensation for builder. At the time of the modification each still owned the other some duty under the old contract (builder to build; owner to pay). Without looking at motives and content (premise B), we can treat the putative mutual release of these outstanding obligations as a bargain, and having done so the way is clear to the making of a new bargain on whatever terms the parties choose. Neat? Alas, it is not to be. For if the trick works in case IX where we want it to, it will work in VIII too, where we do not. If we exclude the trick in both, A′ bars too much; if we allow it in both, whatever we hoped to accomplish by A′ is circumvented. And if we allow it only where the purpose is "reasonable" or the new arrangement fair on its merits, we violate B. Indeed the situation is worse still: The trick will not work at all for any case like X, reasonable or not. At the time debtor and creditor contemplate a modification, the only outstanding obligation is the debtor's, so there can be no *mutual* release of obligations, no mutual bargain to tear up the old contract. (In a case like X the debtor would have to offer some actual fresh consideration.) But some cases like X will be as appealing as IX or as unappealing as VIII, yet none can be accommodated.

I conclude that the standard doctrine of consideration, which is illustrated by the preceding ten quite typical common law cases, does not pose a challenge to my conception of contract law as rooted in promise, for the simple reason that that doctrine is too internally inconsistent to offer an alternative at all. The matrix of the inconsistency is just the conjunction of propositions A and B. Proposition B affirms the liberal principle that the free arrangements of rational persons should be respected. Proposition A, by limiting the class of arrangements to bargains, holds that individual self-determination is not a sufficient ground of legal obligation, and so implies that collective policies may after all override individual judgments, frustrating the

projects of promisees after the fact and the potential projects of promisors. Proposition A is put forward as if it were neutral after all, leaving the parties their "freedom of contract." But there is a sense in which any promisor gets something for his promise, if only the satisfaction of being able to realize his purpose through the promise. Freedom of contract is freedom of promise, and, as my illustrations show, the intrusions of the standard doctrines of consideration can impose substantial if random restrictions on perfectly rational projects.

The anomalous character of the doctrine of consideration has been widely recognized. A variety of statutes abrogate some of its more annoying manifestations, such as the unenforceability of gratuitous options or of contract modifications. There have also been proposals for its virtual abolition.* Before commenting on these proposals briefly at the end of this chapter, I must turn to a perspective on the doctrine that rescues it from its gravest anomalies and does indeed pose a challenge to my view.

In a recent work, John Dawson compares the common law to French and German law and concludes that an impulse shared by all of these systems distinguishes gratuitous promises, that is, promises to make a gift, from true bargains. Another comparativist, Arthur von Mehren, writing in *The International Encyclopedia of Comparative Law*, also contrasts bargains to promises to make a gift, dubbing the latter economically "sterile." Dawson faults the common law not for making this distinction, but for assuming "a doctrinal overload" in using the doctrine of consideration to regulate or exclude promises that hold an offer open (options) and promises that modify or discharge existing arrangements. Dawson empha-

---

* The most striking of these are Samuel Williston's Model Written Obligations Act (in force only in Pennsylvania) and Lord Wright's call, as yet unanswered, in "Ought the Doctrine of Consideration to Be Abolished from the Common Law?," 49 *Harv. L. Rev.* 1225 (1936). Though he disapproves, Professor Atiyah quite correctly observes that these calls are the logical entailments of freedom of contract and the promise principle. Atiyah, *The Rise and Fall of Freedom of Contract* (Oxford, 1979), at 134–40, 440, 452–54, 687–90; and see Fried, review of Atiyah, 93 *Harv. L. Rev.* 1858, 1865–67 (1980).

sizes what he believes is the basic idea of the doctrine of consideration, the substantive, intuitive idea of bargain. Options and modifications fall under that notion because they are part of a "deal"; they are related to bargains. An option is the first step along the way to a bargain. Cases like VIII–X also occur as part of the bargaining process; modifications and discharges should be facilitated to keep that process flexible and serviceable. Substantive unfairness should be controlled not by the manipulation of formalities but by substantive inquiry under the aegis of the doctrines of duress and unconscionability.

This conception challenges my thesis that the basis of contract is promise by locating that basis now in a distinct collective policy, the furtherance of economic exchange. A promise may be necessary, on this view, but it is the largely commercial needs of the market that ground contract. As an explanation this is certainly more satisfying than the incoherent formalities of the common law doctrine, but it too fails on inspection. Neither Dawson's proposal nor French and German law limits contract to commercial transactions: Deals between private individuals selling or exchanging property in no recognized or customary market and family settlements of many sorts are everywhere recognized as binding. It could hardly be otherwise, for to deny a private individual the facility for, say, selling his car or his house to a friend, would lessen the free transferability of property and thus its value, while creating a wholly unjustifiable monopoly in some vaguely defined merchant class. So apparently at least these transactions are not economically "sterile." Rather it is agreed all around that the gift, the donative promise, is the villain of the piece, because of its "sterility." But why is my enforceable promise to sell my brother-in-law my automobile less sterile than my promise to give it to my nephew? The law recognizes the *completed* transaction (after I actually hand over or sign over the automobile), presumably in recognition of my right to do with my property as I choose. In a sense the completed transaction in both cases is quite fertile enough: It is an expression of my will, it increases my satisfaction in some broad sense, and it does so by increasing the satisfaction of my nephew or brother-in-law. Both actual transfers are useful just in the sense that any

freely chosen, significant act of mine is useful to me, and therefore is of net utility to society unless it harms someone else. Allowing people to *make* gifts (let us assume freely, deliberately, reasonably) serves social utility by serving individual liberty.* Given the preceding chapter's analysis of promise, there simply are no grounds for not extending that conclusion to *promises* to make gifts. I make a gift because it pleases me to do so. I promise to make a gift because I cannot or will not make a present transfer, but still wish to give you a (morally and legally) secure expectation.

I conclude that the life of contract is indeed promise, but this conclusion is not exactly a statement of positive law. There are too many gaps in the common law enforcement of promises to permit so bold a statement. My conclusion is rather that the doctrine of consideration offers no coherent alternative basis for the force of contracts, while still treating promise as necessary to it. Along the way to this conclusion I have made or implied a number of qualifications to my thesis. The promise must be freely made and not unfair. . . . It must also have been made rationally, deliberately. The promisor must have been serious enough that subsequent legal enforcement was an aspect of what he should have contemplated at the

---

* The objection might be raised that in the case of the promise to make a gift my account of the moral basis for promissory obligation does not hold: It is not obvious that a disappointed promisee, who has suffered no losses in reliance on the promise, is "used" or his confidence "abused" when he is not given a promised gift. And yet abuse there is. The promisor for reasons of his own has chosen to create in the promisee what is, by hypothesis, a firm expectation fixed in moral obligation. The promisee thinks he has something — a moral entitlement — which is what the promisor wants him to think he has. And now, having created this expectation, the promisor chooses to disappoint it. Consider an analogous case drawn from the morality of lying: I tell you that I have just heard you have been awarded the Nobel Prize in philosophy. One hour later, before you have had a chance to spend the prospective prize money or even to announce this fact, I tell you that the whole thing was a joke. I have lied to you. I have abused your confidence and used you. Now in both this case and the gift-promise case the harm may have been trivial and perhaps the wrong done rather marginal, but that is beside the point. In both instances for analogous reasons I have indeed wronged you.

time he promised.* Finally, certain promises, particularly those affecting the situation and expectations of various family members, may require substantive regulation because of the legitimate interests of third parties. In a classic article, "Consideration as Form," Lon Fuller argued that the doctrine of consideration serves several, often convergent policies. The law hesitates to enforce casual promises where promisor or promisee or both would be surprised to find the heavy machinery of the law imposed on what seemed an informal encounter. Requiring an exchange increases the chance that the parties had in contemplation serious business with serious consequences. Moreover, by requiring an exchange, the law allows contracts to be channeled into a number of predetermined types of arrangements, and the existence of these types itself alerts the parties to a conventional set of problems to be considered and a conventional set of answers to those problems. Finally, the requirement of an exchange might exclude the more dubious and meretricious kinds of gift in which strangers are promised the moon, to the prejudice of a spouse or children.

According to Fuller these are convergent reasons for requiring consideration, because none is either necessary or sufficient. There is the important category of family settlements, and surely these should not be denied enforceability indiscriminately. Furthermore, by using the correct forms it is possible to cast wholly novel transactions — transactions unsupported by the gloss of custom and experience — in an enforceable mold. Finally, the doctrine of consideration makes it possible to lend enforceability to arrangements that are trivial if not frivolous, so long as the forms are observed. And indeed, so long as the forms are observed, it is possible that a person who makes a promise will be legally bound even if he did not intend to be legally bound — if he intended only to promise and to take some value in exchange for his promise. Consideration in Fuller's view is like a rather awkward tool, which has the virtue of being able to pound nails, drive screws, pry open cans, although it does none of these things well and although each of them might be done much better by a specialized tool. (The archaic institution of the promise under seal might be compared for its ability to serve these useful ends with more or less convenience.)

The movement in the law rather suggests that we may have in the not too distant future a more candid set of principles to determine which promises should be enforceable in terms of the fairness of each type. We are moving in that direction as a result of decisions and statutes lending validity to types of promises whose legitimacy had been in doubt under the doctrine of consideration: option contracts, firm offers, compromises of debts, modification of contracts, and the whole domain of promissory estoppel. Secondly, we are moving in that direction as a result of a more open willingness to stigmatize certain promises as unfair or unconscionable and to deny enforcement on that ground rather than on the ground of insufficient consideration.

---

* This last qualification is captured in the law by the term "intention to create legal relations." The term as it stands is misleading. No one supposes that two merchants who make a deal must entertain some additional intention to create legal relations in order for that deal to be binding in law. On the other hand, given the consensual basis of contract as promise, the parties should in principle be free to *exclude* legal enforcement so long as this is not a fraudulent device to trap the unwary. See, e.g., Spooner v. Reserve Life Insurance, 47 Wash.2d 454, 287, P.2d 735 (1955). In a particular case it may be a difficult problem of interpretation whether such a purpose is fairly to be implied. In a particular case it will be a task for interpretation to determine whether legal enforcement would not do violence to the intention of the parties — as with so-called social promises.

Notes and Questions

PATRICK S. ATIYAH, from *Promises, Morals, and Law*

1. Patrick S. Atiyah recognizes that the theoretical rationale of the common law of contracts is the *prima facie* enforcement of promises. This rationale has been assumed in Anglo-American law since the eighteenth century. Similarly, the philosophical position has long been that promising is the paradigm of contract. He points out, however, that in early contract law the general obligation

of promises was never sufficient for legal obligation. What was the necessary condition for a legally binding contract, according to Atiyah? Does his view correspond to other historical accounts in this section (that is, by Maine, Tigar and Levy, and Radin)?

2. Atiyah suggests that if we look to the reasons for which promises are made we will find a set of rules that make up the doctrine of consideration. What are these rules?

3. Atiyah claims that if only some promises are enforced—which is in fact the case—then the doctrine of consideration says why and when this is so. How does he support his thesis? How would Fried respond?

4. Atiyah suggests that the doctrine of consideration now appears odd because of the prominence of the theoretical rationale of the doctrine of freedom of contract (or contract as promise, as Fried characterizes it). Atiyah claims, however, that in the past twenty years the theoretical rationale has been changing back to a more equitable view. What evidence does he give? Can you think of some reasons that might explain this change? Review the Supreme Court cases in the *Lochner* line at the end of this chapter. Do they suggest any explanations?

5. Atiyah argues that the principle requiring us to keep our promises is not nearly as strong in practice as the lip service given it might suggest. What support does he offer? Do you think he is right? If so, what follows? How would Fried respond to this point?

6. The central contention of Atiyah's thesis is that promising is the wrong paradigm for representing legal contracts, and in particular, the charitable promise is the wrong paradigm. Why are promises usually made, according to Atiyah? What do you think?

[From] *Promises, Morals, and Law*

PATRICK S. ATIYAH

CHAPTER 1

Promising in Law and Morals

Promissory and contractual obligations raise many issues of common interest to philosophers and lawyers. For lawyers, it goes without saying that the nature and extent of contractual liabilities are matters of enduring professional concern. But because the nature of their discipline makes them more immediately interested in practical questions, lawyers tend to adopt theories of liability without testing them too rigorously for consistency with positive law. And for many years now English lawyers, including even academic lawyers, have shown little interest in the underlying rationale of the law of contract. They generally take it to be axiomatic that this branch of the law is founded upon the prima-facie enforceability of promises, subject only to compliance with some simple legal rules. There has been virtually no disposition to inquire into the nature of promises, or to probe into the reasons for their legal enforceability. It is almost always taken for granted by lawyers that prima facie promises are morally binding and that this is at least one, if not itself a sufficient, ground of legal liability.

For their part, philosophers have found the nature of promissory obligation of absorbing interest. For many years, the morally binding nature of a promise has been thought one of the strongest refutations of utilitarianism, on the ground that breach of a promise would not normally be condoned even though it seemed likely to produce more happiness (or more good) than keeping it. On the other hand, if utilitarianism is rejected, the moral obligation to keep a promise has seemed to some philosophers to be puzzling in the extreme. How, it is asked, can a person create an obligation by the mere process of wishing to have one, or perhaps, declaring that he has one? To some, ethical theory has centred on the concept of duty, irrespective of consequences, and the nature of these duties is a matter for internal reflection or intuition. The obligation to keep a promise has been treated by some writers as a paradigm example of a duty which is readily recognized by this intuitive process. More recently, promising has figured prominently in the work of linguistic philosphers. Promising has been treated as an obvious illustration of a performative, a verb with the aid of which one can not merely say that one promises but actually *do* it. Yet another group of writers has used the rule that promises should be kept as a prime illustration of a constitutive rule; the 'practice of promising', it is said, is logically impossible without prior recognition of rules constituting the practice, and enabling obligations to be created by the mere act of promising. And there has, too, been controversy about whether it is possible to bridge the logical gap between 'is' and 'ought' by pointing to the binding nature of a promise.

With isolated and minor exceptions, most of this literature has, in recent years, proceeded in total disregard of the law. Just as the lawyer tends to think of the philosopher as an airy theorist having little contact with reality, so the philosopher tends to see the law as technical and abstruse, having little contact with morality. It was not always thus. Until Bentham and Austin wrought their work in setting apart legal and moral obligations, discussions of the nature and limits of promissory liability treated the two as though they were inextricably interwoven. In the works of the seventeenth-century Natural Lawyers, for example, positive law, natural law, and the moral law are all treated together in such a way as to suggest that it would be impossible to understand at least the latter two in isolation from each other. And even in the writings of moralists and philosophers in the British tradition, such as Hume and Paley,

there is a much greater awareness of, and reference to, the law as itself of profound relevance to the moral issues involved in the subject of promises. With the common lawyers, too, particularly in the early formative period of the development of modern contract law, there are signs that lawyers tended to fashion the law of contracts broadly in accord with what they took to be moral principles. They tended to create the law in the image of morality as they understood it. No doubt, as the Natural Lawyers made explicit, positive law did sometimes diverge from morality. But in its central doctrines and ideas, law and morality were largely congruent.

Now the importance of this lies in the fact that the English common law has never treated the mere fact that a promise has been made as even prima facie a sufficient condition for the creation of a legal obligation. Even in the latter half of the sixteenth century, when common lawyers began to build the modern law of contract on new foundations, it is quite plain that they rejected the notion that prima facie a promise created a legal obligation. To them, it was of vital importance to ask *why* a promise had been given. A promise made for a good reason — a good 'consideration' as it came to be said — was prima facie enforceable; a promise made without reason — or consideration — was prima facie not enforceable.

Very roughly, it could be said that a promise was only legally actionable if the promise was to do something which the promiser ought to have done anyway. As a matter of positive law, the doctrine of consideration crystallized in the reign of Elizabeth I into a number of rules which are still clearly recognizable by the modern common lawyer. First, if a person received a benefit at the hands of the promisee for which he promised to pay, the benefit was a sufficient consideration: in effect, the promise here was bought and paid for. Second, if the promisee acted to his detriment in reliance on the promise, so that the non-fulfilment of the promise would cause him actual pecuniary loss, the detriment was a sufficient consideration. And thirdly, if two parties exchanged mutual promises, each promise was a sufficient consideration for the other promise: here, as in the first case, an exchange of benefit was contemplated, though one party might be able to sue the other (for example where the latter's performance was due first) even though he had not himself yet performed, or even though the anticipated benefit turned out to be harmful rather than beneficial. Much has been written by modern lawyers and legal historians about this doctrine of consideration, but most of this literature has tended to take for granted the perspective of the modern lawyer who accepts the prima-facie binding nature of a simple promise. The doctrine of consideration has, therefore, often seemed in need of explanation; the assumption has nearly always been that the doctrine is somehow odd and perhaps unjust in rejecting the simple notion that prima facie a promise is binding. But in recent times it has been suggested that this is to read history through modern spectacles. The doctrine of consideration, it is now urged, was a profoundly moral doctrine, reflecting the belief of the early common lawyers, not merely that a promise *per se* should not be legally enforceable, but also that a promise *per se* was not necessarily morally binding. More acceptably to modern eyes, the doctrine of consideration itself showed what circumstances *were* conceived to render a promise morally binding, and hence legally deserving of protection. What has not so far been seriously canvassed is the possibility that the ideas underlying the doctrine of consideration are relevant also to the nature of a promise itself, the question whether a promise creates an obligation, the weight of that obligation, and, indeed, to the question whether a promise has ever been made at all.

I myself have written at length elsewhere suggesting that the common lawyers' approach to these questions underwent a complete metamorphosis between about 1600 and 1800. By the latter date, the common lawyers had largely come round to the modern viewpoint, that promises *per se* are morally binding, and that insofar as the doctrine of consideration fails to give effect to this moral ideal, it is an anomaly, a technicality, a curiosity of legal history. During the greater part of the nineteenth century, I have argued, the result of this change in attitude reflected itself in a large number of ways in the development of the law. Although the doctrine of consideration could not be overthrown — it was too firmly embedded in the law for that — it could be downgraded into a subordinate role. Lawyers came to place an increasing emphasis on the notion that the law of contract was designed to give full effect to the intention of the parties: the distinc-

tion between liability on a bare promise (or an exchange of bare promises) on the one hand, and liability on paid-for, or relied-upon promises, on the other hand, became much less important. Lawyers tended increasingly to ignore the reasons for which promises were given, and to assume that promises were always made with a view to creating a binding future commitment.

During this period, it may be said that the morality underlying the law of contract fell largely into line with the writings of utilitarians and other moralists. From Paley at one end of the period to Sidgwick at the other, moral discussion about the nature and extent of promissory liability was closely in accord with the moral ideals prevailing in the Courts. There remained, of course, the problem of the gratuitous unilateral promise, binding in morals, no doubt, but still not legally enforceable. But cases of this nature only rarely came before the Courts, and when they did, it was not difficult for judges to find some implied counter-promise, or some act of detrimental reliance, or some element of benefit to the promisor, and thus uphold the binding nature of the promise. For example, in the well-known case of *Shadwell* v. *Shadwell* an uncle promised his nephew (who was a barrister) £150 a year on hearing of the nephew's intended marriage. The Court decided that, on his marriage, the nephew acted to his detriment in the sense that he took upon himself the obligation of maintaining a wife, and that this rendered the promise legally enforceable.*

There were, of course, other legal rules (such as the requirement that certain legal contracts should be evidenced in writing) which sometimes compelled Courts to refuse legal validity to promises which would generally have been regarded as morally binding. Thus under the Statute of Frauds of 1677 (an Act which may well have been influenced by the then prevailing morality) various types of contract could not be

---

*Many modern lawyers consider the decision was wrong, precisely because there appears to have been no 'real' detriment or benefit, and the Court was thus enforcing a bare gratuitous promise. Interestingly, Byles J., who dissented, is known to have been out of sympathy with the prevailing adherence to freedom of contract ideology, see my *Freedom of Contract*, pp. 380–3.

enforced unless they had been partly performed, or were evidenced by some signed note or memorandum. In the mid-nineteenth century, judges made no secret of their dislike for this Statute, and to plead the Statute as a defence came to be thought a dishonourable and shabby thing to do.

Since the end of the last century, and, more particularly, in the past twenty or thirty years, there have been (I have argued) growing signs of a legal reversion to the moral ideals which were more in evidence before the nineteenth century. On the one hand, there are signs of an increasing reluctance to impose liability in wholly executory contracts, that is, on promises which have neither been paid for, nor relied upon. And on the other hand, there are many signs of an increasing tendency to regard the rendering of benefits and acts of justifiable reliance as more important grounds for the imposition of legal liability than bare mutual promises.

A good example of the former tendency can be found in the increasing stress on the legal doctrine of 'mitigation of damages', whereby the innocent party to a breach of contract cannot recover damages for a loss which he has, or even could have, avoided by taking reasonable steps following the breach. In *Lazenby Garages v. Wright*, for instance, the defendant contracted to buy a second-hand car from the plaintiffs, who were car dealers. Before the car was delivered or the price paid, the defendant refused to go through with the transaction, and the dealers resold the car to another customer at the same price. The Court held that the dealers could not claim damages as they had suffered no 'loss'. It will be seen that a decision of this kind, although it does not in terms deny the 'binding' nature of the contract, or of the defendant's promise, does in effect remove one of the chief legal consequences of holding a contract to be binding, viz. that it is enforceable by an award of damages. It is, therefore, possible that decisions of this character indicate increasing doubts about the desirability of holding such contracts to be binding, while they remain wholly unperformed and unrelied upon; and this in turn may suggest increasing doubts about whether such contracts (or promises) are even morally binding.

Even where contracts are created as a result of a clear agreement, a clear exchange of promises, there is a trend towards treating the consensual aspects of the arrangements as of less importance when once performance has begun, benefits have been rendered to one side, or acts of justifiable and detrimental reliance have begun on the other. To take one simple example, the 'small print', which is so commonly seen in written consumer transactions, is nowadays usually regarded as something which must give way before the consumer's actual expectations which are nearly always in contradiction to the small print. Yet the consumer will, by his signature on the document, have indicated that he assents to the terms contained in it (the document often says this, even though it may well not be read), so that, in one sense at least, the consumer's expectations are allowed to override the terms to which he has given at least a nominal agreement, or even a nominal promise.*

These are no doubt controversial suggestions. Not all lawyers would agree that (even in the limited ways I have argued) judges no longer believe in the sanctity of contract, or in upholding the morally binding nature of promises. Certainly it is true that judges do not say these things very loudly, if at all. It is only through their actual decisions and sometimes in their *obiter dicta*, that one can (as I have attempted to do) draw conclusions about the changing values which influence them. I have argued elsewhere that one of the reasons for this divergence between the theory and the practice of the law is to be found in the history of the subject. Modern contract theory is still largely based on the 'classical contract model', a model which was developed between 1770 and 1870, by which time the ideal of freedom of contract had reached its highest point in the Courts, though it was perhaps already in decline elsewhere. The classical model of contract grew up under the shadow of a number of intellectual movements which stressed the importance of free choice and consent as the origin of legal and moral obligation alike. It is unnecessary here to do more than point to the obvious sources of the legal ideal of freedom of contract — the classical economists, the

---

*And it is only now that judges would agree that such promises or agreements are only 'nominal'. Nineteenth-century judges generally found them real enough.

Benthamite utilitiarians, the radical politicians calling for democracy, and, perhaps more generally, liberalism and all that it stood for.

It is, therefore, a matter of no surprise to find that much contemporary philosophical writing concerning promises appears to be closely related to the classical model of contract theory. In both, one finds the same stress on free choice; in both one finds the promise or contract regarded as the paradigm way of creating obligations merely by declaring one's intention to be bound; in both one finds the same disregard for the distinction between paid-for or relied-upon promises or contracts, on the one hand, and wholly executory promises and contracts, on the other hand; in both one finds the same widespread use of the notion of 'implied' or 'tacit' promises and contracts to explain results otherwise difficult to reconcile with the theory; and in both one finds (I will argue) an apparent or overt belief in the sanctity of promises and contracts which is no longer to be found in the value systems of modern England, at least.

In this book I propose, therefore, to re-examine the nature and extent of promissory and contractual liability. This re-examination is conducted from the standpoint of a modern contracts

lawyer who rejects the classical model of contract as not reflecting contemporary law or legal values. My primary objectives are twofold. First, to see what light is thrown on the moral foundations of the law by examination of the principal philosophical theories concerning promises; and secondly, to see how well these theories themselves stand up to examination in the light both of the law itself and of the empirical data thrown up by any study of the law.

Preliminary Note on Terminology

It is well to make clear two points at the outset, as they affect the terminology used throughout this book. The first is that I do not believe that all promises are morally binding; accordingly, I use the term 'promise' without prejudging the question whether the promise creates an obligation. The second is that, where a promise does create an obligation, the reason for that may depend upon whether the promise was explicit or implied. There is thus, in my view, a fundamental distinction between explicit and implied promises, and when I use the word 'promise' without qualification, I normally mean an explicit promise.

C H A P T E R   6

The Practice of Promising

From time to time I have commented critically on the methodology of various writers who have sought answers to questions about the nature and sources of promissory obligation without any sociological inquiry into the institution of promising as it currently exists in a modern Western society. I have commented that this approach seems particularly odd when it comes from philosophers who argue that promises derive their binding force from the 'practice of promising', but make no attempt to inquire into the rules of this practice. In this chapter I propose to make some preliminary inquiry into the 'practice of promising' as it exists in modern England. This in no way professes to be a serious sociological study of promising; in particular, my data come mainly (though not exclusively) from the

Law Reports and are no doubt unrepresentative for that reason. This is conceded without reservations; but it remains true that much may be learnt about the morality of promising from some acquaintance with the law, and the legal treatment of promises. It is right to stress that, when people's interests are seriously affected by what they regard as a breach of a promise, they can and do have recourse to the Courts for justice; and although judges are not free to do justice precisely as they please, there is no doubt that in most cases of this nature, the justice which the Courts administer is very largely congruent with the moral sense of the community. Although it may differ from the sort of verdict often to be found in philosophical writings, this is, I believe, because lawyers and judges are more aware of the complexity and subtlety of the problems which are involved. The law is thus more sophisticated in its morality than many non-lawyers might think; it is difficult to substantiate this assertion without a substantial treatment of the law of contract and this is obviously not the place for that. But it is a place for a beginning to be made.

The Strength of the Promise-Keeping Principle

I want to begin by suggesting that the strength of the principle that promises must be kept is not nearly so great as seems to be assumed by many writers. Neither in the community at large, nor in the law, I suggest, is the principle accorded that sanctity which many philosophers still think is due to it. Historically, it is of course true that in the middle of the last century the sanctity of contract was widely regarded, by lawyers and others, as the keystone of the social and legal edifice. But the law has moved a long way since then, and this movement certainly appears to have been a response to changing social attitudes; philosophers who still write about the duty to keep promises with the high moral tone that one often finds (for example in Ross, Hare, Hart, Warnock, or Rawls) appear to be reflecting the moral attitudes of the last century rather than those of the present day. It is perhaps significant that a philosopher who has recently made a serious attempt to study the law of contract discovered somewhat to his surprise that in the law, 'the opprobrium attached to [promise breaking] is not often great'.

So far as the rules of law are concerned, it must be stressed that the sanctions for breach of promise, or (contract) are usually very mild by comparison with many of the sanctions at the law's disposal. It is very rare that the law provides for the *punishment* of the contract-breaker. Neither imprisonment nor fines are available as remedies for breach of contract, nor is it custom-

ary (except in certain limited categories) for Courts actually to order contracting parties to perform their contracts.* In the great majority of contractual actions the law merely provides for the payment of sums which are due, or for damages in default. And damages are almost invariably assessed on purely compensatory principles, that is to say, they are limited by the extent of the promisee's loss. They cannot include an element of 'exemplary' or 'punitive' damages such as are sometimes allowed in other kinds of actions. It is true (as we have seen) that the promisee's 'loss' is understood sufficiently widely to encompass his lost expectations, but that is normally the limit of the promisor's liability.

But this is not all, because (as I have also pointed out) where the promisee has not relied upon the promise, and no payment has been made to the promisor, so that the promisee's claim is purely for his loss of expectations, it will often happen that no damages are recoverable at all. If the promisee can obtain substitute performance elsewhere at no additional cost, he is expected, as a reasonable man, to do so, and not to insist upon performance by the promisor. This explains why, in cases like *Lazenby Garages* v. *Wright*, to which I referred earlier, a car dealer who is able to resell a car which the buyer has refused to take and pay for, may be unable to claim any damages at all. So in cases like this the sanction for breach of contract is, in fact, nil.

Moreover, empirical studies of business attitudes to contracts and contract-breaking, both in England and in the United States, suggest that business men in fact expect and tolerate a considerable amount of contract-breaking, at all events on matters which they do not regard as of fundamental importance. A leading American contracts scholar has recently been moved to say that 'it is perfectly clear that a great deal of promise breaking is tolerated and expected. Indeed, it is so widely tolerated that a realist would have to say that beneath the covers we are firmly committed to the desirability of promises being broken, not just occasionally but quite regularly'.

This kind of evidence may not tell us much about social attitudes to the morality of promising. But there is also evidence from other legal cases that public bodies, at least, appear to have less compunction about promise-breaking today

---

* In practice, contracts for the purchase and sale of houses, or land, are normally 'specifically enforceable' by order of the Court: failure to comply is punishable by imprisonment.

than perhaps they would have done a hundred years ago. Promises are frequently made by corporate bodies or other associations of people (such as Governments) as well as by individuals. And when there is a change in those who represent such bodies, personal moral scruples about promise keeping may be non-existent. Thus (for example) where a local council contracted (that is, promised) to sell council houses to certain tenants, and then, following an election, a new council took office pledged to a new policy, the new council declined to fulfil these contracts. They were sued by one tenant and put up a manifestly untenable defence; they appealed to the Court of Appeal where again, they strenuously defended on the flimsiest of grounds; and when they lost again, they sought leave to appeal to the House of Lords — unsuccessfully. And it is, perhaps, not irrelevant to remember also that in 1975 the Labour Government invited the people of Britain to decide, in the Common Market referendum, whether they wished to affirm or repudiate the treaty obligations solemnly entered into by their elected representatives only a few years earlier. One factor which played virtually no part in the public debates was that the country's representatives had actually signed the Treaty of Accession, and thus pledged the nation's word. The public debates treated the whole issue as though the question was one which arose *de novo*, and as though the merits of joining the Community were up for discussion.

When we turn to the actual rules of law for the 'enforcement' of promises, we also find (as I have previously mentioned) that there are different degrees of bindingness. As was stressed in a seminal article on the theory of contractual liability, 'the "binding" effect of a promise is a matter of degree, proceeding in an ascending scale which embraces, in order, the restitution, reliance and expectation interests'. If this sounds a little cryptic for those unacquainted with this legal terminology, all that it means is that the legal right of a promisee to obtain recompense for value actually rendered to the promisor ranks highest, that his right to be compensated for loss incurred through reliance on a promise, ranks second, and that his right to compensation for his disappointed expectations ranks lowest in the scale. Some philosophers have recognized that the

binding force of promises may vary in a similar sort of way, but the implications of this have not (I think) been properly grasped. At the lowest, recognition of these differing degrees of bindingness must involve acceptance that pure expectations are not generally thought deserving of a high degree of protection, and in some cases are not thought worthy of protection at all. On this view, the breach of a promise which has not been paid for or relied upon is a relatively venial wrong, and in some instances (for example where alternative arrangements can readily be made by the promisee), not of sufficient importance to warrant legal protection. But the point may involve deeper implications, as can be seen if we turn to examine some of the generally accepted justifications for breaking promises.

Justifications for Promise-Breaking

Few philosophers have attempted to analyse the circumstances in which a breach of promise may be found morally justifiable. When they discuss this question at all, it is usually in terms of trivial cases such as a social promise to meet or dine with a friend, which is broken because the promisor's son is taken ill. Now in law, by far the most important justification for breaking a promise is that a return promise has itself been broken in whole or in part. It is the breach by one party of his contractual duties which is the principal justification for breach by the second party of *his* duties. This was originally justified by lawyers at the end of the eighteenth century in the same way that they (and the Natural Lawyers) explained why promises induced by fraud or supervening events might be discharged; that is to say, they argued that it was 'impliedly' intended that the promises were conditional upon mutual performance. Thus if one party refused to perform, the other party's promise did not have to be performed, because he had not promised to perform in that event. It later came to be felt that this argument from 'implication' was too fanciful to explain the many difficult situations which had to be differentiated by law, and that other considerations explained the legal approach. In particular, judges were, and are, much influenced by the belief that it is *unjust* for a party to be compelled to perform a promise if he has not received (or may not receive) substantially the benefits that he has bargained for.

It thus seems that not only is the receipt of a benefit itself one of the principal grounds for holding a promise to be binding, not only that the duty to recompense for benefits is a strong source of legal obligation even in the absence of a promise; but also that the failure to receive an anticipated benefit is a strong ground for treating the duty to perform a promise as no longer binding. So here too there seems confirmation for the idea that perhaps it is not the promise itself which creates the obligation, so much as the accompanying incidents, such as the rendering of benefits, (or in other circumstances, acts of detrimental reliance).

Why Are Promises Made and Kept, or Broken?

The above discussion serves as a convenient link to some other questions which are little discussed in the philosophical writings about promises. Why do people make promises? Why do they keep them? Why do they break them? It is evident from the previous discussion that one common reason why people break promises is that a return promise has been, or is likely to be, broken by the promisee. And this itself is some indication of the fact that people who make promises very often — perhaps usually — do so because they want to get something from the promisee which they can only get by doing so. It seems too often to be assumed by philosophers that the paradigm of a promise is the charitable or wholly benevolent promise, the promise which involves no return at all. This is surely wrong. It is of course difficult to be sure, in the absence of empirical research, what are the most common types of promises, and why these are given, but it seems highly probable that they are promises given as the price of something the promisor wants. Promises of this kind do not confer an uncovenanted benefit on the promisee. On the contrary, it is the promisor who often benefits from such a promise, for it is a means of deferring a liability, rather than of creating an obligation. To take a simple illustration, a person wishes to buy goods but has not the cash to pay the price; he asks the seller to give him credit, that is to say, to accept a promise of payment in lieu of actual payment. In

a case of this nature, the buyer's obligation to pay the price surely derives from his purchase of the goods, rather than from his promise; and, as I have previously argued, the implication of a promise to pay the price may be the result, rather than the cause of holding the transaction to be a purchase. Of course, it must be clear that the transaction is not a gift (and that no doubt depends on the intentions and relationship of the parties), but once this possibility is ruled out, the voluntary acceptance or receipt of the goods by the buyer is the necessary and sufficient condition for his liability. An explicit promise alone is neither of these things. If the promise was given and the seller failed to deliver the goods, the buyer (as explained above) would not be bound to perform his promise; and if the buyer requested the seller to supply the goods and voluntarily accepted them when supplied, he would be liable to pay the price even in the absence of an explicit promise. No doubt it would be said that he had 'impliedly' promised, but it is not clear why the implication needs to be made, and the buyer's obligation to pay the price would exist even if he promised without any intention of keeping his promise.

Cases of this nature — that is the giving of promises in lieu of immediate performance of a duty — are very common indeed. But there are other similar cases where the promisor's duty is not deferred, and yet he makes the promise to obtain some benefit which he desires. Two parties enter into a contract on 1 January for the purchase and sale of a house on 1 February. Each promises something to the other because he wants what the other is willing to give. The case differs from that discussed in the previous paragraph because the performance of the two promises is intended to be simultaneous; neither party will perform before the other, and no credit is to be given. But this does not alter the fact that each promise is given because of what it brings; and this also is borne out by the rule that prima facie a failure by one party to perform will discharge the other. Thus many promises are given because the promisor expects to derive some benefit from the promise. But it may be possible to put the matter more generally: promises are given to induce people to act upon them. In the cases so far discussed, the action which the promisor wants is something beneficial to him.

In these cases, the promisor *wants* the promisee to act in reliance on the promise. But there may be cases in which the action will be of little or no benefit to him except in the trivial sense that if he wants it, it must be assumed that it will be *some* benefit to him. Because this case is conceptually wider than the previous one, it is the one which lawyers and philosophers have tended to concentrate upon. Action in reliance is more generally recognized as a 'consideration' in the law than conduct beneficial to the promisor; and a parallel is to be found in much philosophical writing. But it is important to appreciate that in a large proportion of cases, perhaps most cases, the action in reliance which the promisor seeks to induce the promisee to undertake, is something beneficial to the promisor, directly or indirectly.

Now it is apparent that where the promisor has not yet actually obtained what he wants at the time when performance of his promise is due, he will (unless he has changed his mind in the interim) normally be motivated to perform his promise for precisely the same reason that he originally gave it — namely, that he wants to induce the promisee to act in some way likely to be beneficial to him. Thus, in the example of the contract for the purchase and sale of the house, both parties will normally be motivated to perform their promises on the day set for performance for the same reason that they originally gave their promises, that is the seller wants money in preference to the house, and the buyer wants the house in preference to the money.

It should, I hope, be apparent now why it seems to me idle to discuss the source of the moral obligation to perform a promise without having some regard to the question *why* promises are given, and *why* they are (normally) performed. If we assume that promises are binding because of some inherent moral power, or even if we assume that they are binding because of the expectations they rouse, or that they are binding because of the existence of a practice of promising, we are in danger of overlooking that *most* promises are performed because it is in the interests of the promisor to perform. The legal and moral sanction thus turns out to be needed for some cases only; and (I would venture to guess) for a small minority of cases. It is needed for those cases where the promisor has obtained credit, or full performance of what he sought to

obtain by his promise; and it is needed for those cases where the promisor changes his mind after giving his promise, and before he performs it. Of course, even in these cases, it may be in the long-term interests of the promisor to perform. As many writers have observed, the loss of credit and trustworthiness which results from promise-breaking may make it in the long-term interests of the promisor to perform, even in the two situations I have mentioned.

The importance of this, I suggest, is that it should influence our view of the paradigm case. In much philosophical writing, it seems to be assumed that the paradigmatic case is of a promise which is wholly gratuitous and is given for charitable or benevolent purposes. It seems to me far more likely that the source of both legal and moral obligations concerning the binding force of promises is derived from the more common case where the promisor obtains, or expects to obtain, some advantage from his promise, and that cases of charitable and benevolent promises are the result of extrapolating from the common case.

The Intentions of the Promisor

I want now to draw attention to certain difficulties which arise concerning the intention of the promisor. There is, of course, the obvious and initial difficulty arising from promises which the promisor has no intention of performing. Are these to be called genuine promises? Those who believe that the essence of a promise is the intentional commitment, the intentional acceptance of an obligation, plainly have difficulty with the case of the fraudulent or dishonest promise. I have previously pointed out that there would in fact be no insuperable difficulty in arguing that the promisor in such a case is under a duty, not because he has promised, but because he has deceived. However, this is certainly not the legal approach. A lawyer would unhesitatingly say that a dishonest promise was a promise, and that the promisor is liable because he has promised, and not because he has deceived. Hence he is legally liable for disappointing the promisee's expectations, and not just for loss incurred in reliance. If the dishonest party had not made an apparent promise, but a dishonest statement of a different character, this would not be so. I think it probable that current English 'positive' morality would broadly agree with the law in regarding a dishonest promisor as bound because he had promised, and not because he had deceived, though obviously that point cannot be settled by general argument.

Nevertheless, the nature of the intention which a promisor must have — even leaving aside this particular problem — is a much more difficult question than seems to be generally assumed. One of the few writers to discuss this issue is Searle, who argues that a promisor must intend that his words 'will place him under an obligation' to do what he promises. Thus, he says, Mr Pickwick did not promise to marry Mrs Bardell because 'we know that he did not have the appropriate intention'. A lawyer's reaction to this would be that although *we* may know that he did not intend to marry Mrs Bardell, (because the author has told us) Mrs Bardell did not know this fact. And since, in everyday life, there is no benevolent author to tell us what other people's intentions are, we are in fact entitled to assume that their intentions are what they appear to be. The jury's verdict in *Bardell* v. *Pickwick* — if we can assume that they honestly thought that Mrs Bardell had reasonably construed Mr Pickwick's words as an offer of marriage — was thus sound in law. This may be thought to show that a promisor must at least intend to act in such a way as to make it reasonable to construe him as intending to promise, rather than that he should merely intentionally act. But the significance of this distinction depends on what 'reasonable construction' involves. It may involve merely implying a promise because the kind of conduct in question usually is accompanied by an intention voluntarily to assume an obligation. But it may, *per contra*, involve 'implying' a promise because the neutral, impartial judge thinks that in all the circumstances, an obligation ought to be imposed on the promisor.

No doubt Mr Pickwick's was an extreme case. But there is also no doubt that it is very common for the law to hold a person bound by a promise when he never intended to give one. Sometimes, as in Mr Pickwick's case, this may well be because the promisee has reasonably understood the words and conduct of the putative promisor as indicating that the promisor does mean to make a promise. Even here, of course, if no such intention is actually present, it is not self-evident what is the source of the obligation. Some moralists,

while agreeing that in such circumstances, a duty or obligation may rest on the promisor, would derive the duty from some other source than a promise. And it is perhaps significant also that some legal writers think that the law goes too far in protecting pure expectations when they are the result of a mistake or misunderstanding of this kind. If, for instance, the mistake is discovered before the promisee has acted on the promise, and before any payment has been rendered for it, it is not obviously just that the promise should still be held binding. In legal theory, the promise probably is still binding, but I think it fair to say that a Court would probably find that theory unpalatable, and would strive to avoid it if it could do so. But, in light of what has already been said in this book, this does not show a legal hankering after a subjective theory of liability. What it shows is that — here as elsewhere — the protection of those who have paid for, or relied upon promises, is generally accorded a much higher priority, than the protection of bare disappointed expectations.

It must now be noted that in the law there are many circumstances in which a promise is implied, not only where there is probably no intention to give one, but where it cannot even be said that the words and behaviour of the promisor, reasonably construed, would give rise to the inference that he intended to give one. A simple example arises in the law of sale, where a seller is often treated as 'impliedly' promising to supply goods of merchantable quality, goods fit for their purpose, and so on. Obligations of this kind appear to be imposed on sellers as an expression of the sense of justice arising from social policy; they appear to have little to do with the real intentions of most sellers.

Promises with Variable Content

I now want to say a little about a variety of other difficulties which experience with the law shows to be involved in the notion of intention in this particular sphere. Too many writers appear (at least in dealing with promises) to assume that the state of mind of a person who promises to do something is a relatively simple matter; whether he is honest or not, it seems to be widely assumed that sharp lines can be drawn between the person who intends to do something and the person who does not. Unfortunately this is not the case. There are many acutely difficult questions here. For example, a person may sign a written document which contains many printed clauses, and which purports to be a contract. Each clause may even begin by saying 'I hereby promise' or words to that effect. The promisor may, or may not read all or part of the document; he probably has some understanding of the general nature of the document, but it is unlikely that he knows in any detail what the clauses contain or what they mean or what is their legal result. I find it very difficult to say what this person's intentions are in relation to such matters. Lawyers have in the past tended to assume (with little articulated justification) that to sign a document is, in a sense, to indicate one's acceptance of all that it contains. The signer, by placing his signature at the foot of the document, *intends* to bind himself to all that it contains. He may thus be said to promise to do whatever the document requires him to do. But this conclusion creates great difficulties. Suppose the document contains some wholly unexpected and grossly unfair clause, such as has never been included in contracts of this nature, would it still be said that the signature amounts to a promise to do whatever the document requires? Or suppose that the document contains clauses which are today declared to be void by Act of Parliament, for the very purpose of protecting unwary customers who sign such documents without reading them? To the lawyer it matters little whether or not one says that the signer has promised to perform the void clause, because in either event, it is not binding. But to the moralist, it may matter whether we say, 'there is no promise here at all', or, 'there is a promise but the promisor is legally relieved from performance'. And surely the moralist needs to be aware of these problems. Can he really assert that clauses made void by Parliament under consumer protection legislation, are still morally binding and ought to be kept? But if such promises are not morally binding, while other promises (of whose content the promisor is equally ignorant) are binding, how can the explanation be sought in the intention of the promisor?

There are other difficulties. Contracts sometimes contain clauses under which one party may vary the duty of the other party. An example only too well known to many householders today, is the power of a building society to alter the terms of a mortgage by increasing the interest rate payable, after due notice given. Suppose a person has entered into a mortgage of this character, at an initial rate of 7 per cent, but ten years later finds himself paying 12 per cent. Would it be said that he has promised to pay 12 per cent? Or that he intended to pay 12 per cent? Certainly, he is legally bound to pay 12 per cent; he is treated as having contracted to pay for it, but it is not clear to me whether one would say that he had *promised* to pay it, still less that he *intended* to pay it. The reality would seem to be that he intentionally entered into a certain transaction and that one of the consequences of that transaction, to which he is committed, is that he is now bound to pay the higher interest rate.

Stronger cases can be found in the law. For example, a person joins a club or society, or takes shares in a company. The association (whatever its form) will have rules which bind the members, and the person joining will be bound by them, even though he does not read them or know anything about them. Thus far the case is no different from the one discussed earlier. But the rules of an association will almost always contain procedures for their own alteration, and frequently these procedures will envisage alteration by some majority vote of the members. Suppose that a person joins a tennis club with an annual subscription of £5; we may readily agree that he has promised to pay £5 a year, and that he fully intends to do so. But suppose now that the club, by majority vote, with our friend dissenting, increases the subscription to £10. Are we to say that, so long as he remains a member, he has promised to pay £10 annually; are we to say that when he joined he intended to pay whatever subscription was due, from time to time, as duly required by the club rules? Of course, a member may resign from a tennis club, and if he does not resign, we may say he must be 'assumed' to have acquiesced in the new subscription and so has impliedly promised to pay it. For most practical purposes this is no doubt legitimate enough; but what is not legitimate is to *equate* this person's state of mind with that of the man who says, 'I promise to pay £10'. Still more difficult cases can be found where the opportunity to escape the consequences of the new rule by resignation does not exist. For example, a member of a company who holds shares of class A is outvoted on a resolution which has the result of reducing the value of class A shares and increasing the value of class B shares. To 'resign' or sell his shares is no solution to this person's problems. The reduction in the value of his shares is already an accomplished fact. Is he bound by the result? Are we to say that, when he joined the company, he must be deemed to have accepted the consequences of any change duly passed by appropriate legal procedures?

Now all these cases raise questions as to the precise relationship which subsists between the intentions of the promisor and the content of the promise. These illustrations show that, in law at least, a person who enters into a transaction may be held bound by many consequences of the transaction even though he does not intend those consequences. Obligations of this kind surely cannot be justified by saying that the promisor 'intended' to assume them. The reality is that he intends to enter into a transaction, the consequences of which are imposed upon him by the law. It seems difficult to argue that, in principle, the moral solution to these cases differs from the legal solution. No doubt there may be moral dissent from some extreme legal cases; but it surely cannot be doubted that (for example) a mortgagor is morally, no less than legally, bound to pay the interest rate properly required of him, even though it is far higher than the one he originally promised to pay.

One further problem needs mention. In law, breach of a contract often has the result of making the promisor liable to pay damages. The way in which the damages are assessed often depends on a number of legal rules which may, in some situations, involve much complexity. If, in the cases discussed in the previous paragraphs, we are willing to say that all the consequences of the original contract, or promise, must be 'deemed' to have been covered by the promise, or by the promisor's intentions, are we now to say the same for the legal consequences? It would seem remarkably odd to say that a person who is guilty of a breach of contract must be deemed to have promised (and intended?) to pay damages for breach, as assessed by the Courts. Yet the total consequences of the promise are an elaborate mesh of the actual words used (particularly written words) and of the law. Some promises are read in by the law which are not explicitly stated; some promises which are explicitly stated are

struck out by the law as void; other promises are subject to legal interpretation which may alter their literal or prima-facie import; and the calculation of the damages, as I have said, may involve some complex legal rules.

Who Makes Promises, to Whom, and Who Is Bound by Them?

There are further sociological matters about the practice of promising on which the law provides some guidance; and here again, I believe, it will be found that some of the assumptions made in much philosophical writing are too simplistic, for lack of attention paid to these data. Let me begin with the question, Who makes promises? Philosophers nearly always assume that promises are only made by individual human beings. But this is not true. Promises are made by people acting collectively in all manner of institutional groups. Promises are made by companies, associations, schools, hospitals, universities, Governments, and many other institutions. This fact is relevant to the moral issues arising from promising for a number of obvious, and perhaps less obvious reasons. First, it makes it necessary to recognize that one person (the agent) can make a promise which binds another person (the principal), something which many philosophers seem reluctant to recognize. Second, it is much more difficult to attribute a 'real' intention to a collective group than to a single individual promisor. For one thing, the intentions of (say) the members of a Board or a Committee, acting on behalf of an institution, may not all be the same. For another thing, institutions often act through agents (in the legal sense) such as executives, directors, secretaries, and so forth. Agents sometimes commit their principals by promises which the principal (or superior agents) did not wish, or intend, to make. Legally, there are rules for determining when a principal can be bound by an agent who thus acts in excess of his authority, but there is no doubt that this is a common legal phenomenon. All this naturally strengthens the legal tendency to ignore 'real' intentions, and focus on apparent intentions—on what is said and done, rather than what was 'actually' intended.

A second reason why the nature of institutional promisors is often relevant to the moral issues is this. Institutions often have specified formal procedures for making decisions. Boards of directors, College Governing Bodies, Committees of various kinds, normally have formal meetings, and keep records of their decisions. When a body of this kind announces its intentions, or makes a decision which it then communicates to the persons concerned, the line between a mere statement of intent and a promise becomes somewhat blurred. A public announcement in the form 'The Committee [Board, Government, etc.] has decided . . .' is much closer to being a promise than a comparable statement by a private individual. Decisions of this character are usually more trustworthy than declarations of intent by a single individual, because the former are so much more difficult to change than the latter. An extreme example of this may, perhaps, be found in legislative procedures. There is a sense in which an Act of Parliament is a declaration of Parliament's will and intention that the persons concerned should behave in the manner laid down in the Act. In the British constitutional system, such a declaration of intent does not preclude Parliament from changing its mind tomorrow and repealing the first Act. But parliamentary procedure is a formal process, governed by many technical rules of procedure, and, in the majority of cases, taking several months to transform a Bill into an Act. It is, in the result, reasonable to assume that laws will remain unchanged, save at longish intervals (except of course after an election!), and the public are generally entitled to adjust their conduct on the assumption that they can rely upon the existing law. Indeed, we can go further, because it is reasonable to say that legislation tells the citizen how he must and also how he may behave. Those who adjust their behaviour in reliance on the legality of a course of conduct are entitled to feel aggrieved if they are not given adequate time to adjust to changes in the law. It would indeed not be wholly fanciful to suggest that the legislature, by laying down the lines of proscribed behaviour, is impliedly promising that those who do *not* cross the lines will not be subject to penalties. The implication of a promise in such a case arises from the nature of decision-making procedures, and the way in which Parliament declares its intent. It may, of course, be said that any such implied promise would be fictitious, but that depends upon the nature and purpose of implied promises. No doubt it would be fictitious to impute to Parliament any actual intent to assume a legal obligation not to change the law without adequate notice. But it would not be a fiction to argue that Parliament passes laws in order to tell citizens how to behave in various respects; and that if the citizen complies with these instructions, and assumes that if he observes the law he will not be subject to penalties, it would be morally wrong for Parliament to punish him. If we think that that would be morally wrong, it is because we think that people are justified in relying on the law as from time to time enacted, and that such reliance should be protected. So Parliament may well come under a moral obligation to respect such reliance. It seems to be largely a matter of taste whether we say that such an obligation derives from an 'implied promise'.

One final point may be made here about the parties to a promise. It is not uncommon in law for a promise to become binding on some third party, other than the promisor. For example, contractual promises may bind the executors of the promisor after his death; in effect the promisor's successors take his property burdened with his liabilities, and these liabilities include promissory, or at least contractual liabilities. Or, again, it is sometimes possible for an owner of a piece of land to burden the land with a promise (for example, not to build on it, or not to build certain types of property), and this promise will bind subsequent owners of the land provided that certain simple formalities as to registration have been complied with. Cases of this nature may be of some importance to the basis of promissory liability for the moralist as well as the lawyer. For one thing, they illustrate what is often thought to be an impossibility, namely that a promisor can promise that someone else will do something; but they also illustrate cases where it is plain that the liability of a person on a promise must be based on something other than his consent. The third party who succeeds to, or buys, property thus burdened with another's promises, will often know of the burden when he takes the property, and may in some sense be assumed to acquiesce in it; but this is not necessarily the case. The purchaser of land burdened with a registered covenant is bound by it even if he knew nothing of it at all: the onus is on him to discover it by searching the register. Of course, it can be said that the reasons for holding such a third party bound by a promise may be quite different from those affecting the promisor himself. But in practice it will usually be found that, in the absence of consent, there will be present one or both of the other two bases of contractual liability, viz. that the third party has derived some benefit, for which the promise is, in a broad sort of way, the *quid pro quo*; or alternatively that the promisee has acted upon the promise in such a way that it would seem unreasonable and unjust if the third party was not bound by it. So once again, it seems that the duty to recompense benefits and to compensate for losses incurred by actions in reliance may actually embrace liabilities thought to be promissory, and which certainly are promissory in origin.

Notes and Questions

HENRY MAINE, from *Ancient Law*

1. Henry Maine observes that social organization has changed a great deal from the time of ancient societies to the present day (or at least until 1864 when he was writing). In ancient societies the mode of social organization was patriarchal. Explain the basic features of the patriarchal theory of social organization, as Maine sets them out. What are the implications for the ability to contract? How do the features of ancient social organization contrast with those of modern social organization?

2. This difference in organization reflects a difference in thinking so profound that we may call it a different worldview. This worldview takes the family rather than the individual as its fundamental unit of obligation. As Maine points out, ancient law was framed for corporate action. What does he mean? In what way is a family (especially as viewed by ancient law) like a corporation? What are the implications and/or consequences of this different worldview for notions of responsibility, contractual interaction, guilt, and retribution, according to Maine?

3. Not only was the family the basis of obligation and responsibility in civil matters, it was in very early society the basis of law in general. Each family or tribe was its own nation. Maine observes that there was a significant change in social organization when locality rather than family became the basis of society. How would such a change affect law and the distribution of power?

4. Even after locality became the basis of society and law in many respects, social organization was still patriarchal, and the family was still the unit of obligation in many other respects, including contract law. It is suggested that this change of social structure from family to locality paved the way for the gradual change of contract law from a ceremonial process to its mature form. Describe this development as Maine relates it. How different is the early ceremony from the mature law of contracts? What ideas have been added or eliminated over time? Does the change reflect a change in the concept or purpose of contract? How does Maine account for the change?

5. Maine's most famous contention is that social progress is marked by a gradual move away from family obligation to individual obligation, and more specifically from obligation based on status (that is, birth or position) to obligation based on contract (that is, consent or agreement). What is the significance of this change? What, according to Maine, are its advantages? Does it have disadvantages?

6. Maine criticizes the ethnocentricity of scholarship in his own time. What does he mean by his claim that the supposition that a society cannot exist without a view of contracts like ours is wrong? How could a society function if its members did not basically believe in keeping their word and honoring their agreements? Does Maine make ethnocentric assumptions himself? Is individualism an incontrovertible advance over family obligation? Why or why not?

[From] *Ancient Law*

HENRY MAINE

CHAPTER 5

Primitive Society and Ancient Law

* * *

The effect of the evidence derived from comparative jurisprudence is to establish that view of the primeval condition of the human race which is known as the Patriarchal Theory.

* * *

The points which lie on the surface of the history are these: — The eldest male parent — the eldest ascendant — is absolutely supreme in his household. His dominion extends to life and death, and is as unqualified over his children and their houses as over his slaves; indeed the relations of sonship and serfdom appear to differ in little beyond the higher capacity which the child in blood possesses of becoming one day the head of a family himself. The flocks and herds of the children are the flocks and herds of the father, and the possessions of the parent, which he holds in a representative rather than in a proprietary character, are equally divided at his death among his descendants in the first degree, the eldest son sometimes receiving a double share under the name of birthright, but more generally endowed with no hereditary advantage beyond an honorary precedence.

* * *

When we go forward to the state of society in which these early legal conceptions show themselves as formed, we find that they still partake of the mystery and spontaneity which must have seemed to characterise a despotic father's commands, but that at the same time, inasmuch as they proceed from a sovereign, they presuppose a union of family groups in some wider organisation. The next question is, what is the nature of this union and the degree of intimacy which it involves? It is just here that archaic law renders us one of the greatest of its services and fills up a gap which otherwise could only have been bridged by conjecture. It is full, in all its provinces, of the clearest indications that society in primitive times was not what it is assumed to be at present, a collection of *individuals*. In fact, and in the view of the men who composed it, it was *an aggregation of families*. The contrast may be most forcibly expressed by saying that the *unit* of an ancient society was the Family, of a modern society the Individual. We must be prepared to find in ancient law all the consequences of this difference. It is so framed as to be adjusted to a system of small independent corporations. It is therefore scanty, because it is supplemented by the despotic commands of the heads of households. It is ceremonious, because the transactions to which it pays regard resemble international concerns much more than the quick play of intercourse between individuals. Above all it has a peculiarity of which the full importance cannot be shown at present. It takes a view of *life* wholly unlike any which appears in developed jurisprudence. Corporations *never die*, and accordingly primitive law considers the entities with which it deals, *i.e.* the patriarchal or family groups, as perpetual and inextinguishable. This view is closely allied to the peculiar aspect under which, in very ancient times, moral attributes present themselves. The moral elevation and moral debasement of the individual appear to be confounded with, or postponed to, the merits and offences of the group to which the individual belongs. If the community sins, its guilt is much more than the sum of the offences committed by its members; the crime is a corporate act, and extends in its consequences to many more persons than have shared in its actual perpetration. If, on the other hand, the individual is conspicuously guilty, it is his children, his kinsfolk, his tribesmen, or his fellow-citizens, who suffer with him, and sometimes for him. It thus happens that the ideas of moral responsibility and retribution often seem to be more clearly realised at very ancient than at more advanced periods, for, as the family group is immortal, and its liability to punishment indefinite, the primitive mind is not perplexed by the questions which become troublesome as soon as the individual is conceived as altogether separate from the group. One step in the transition from the ancient and simple view of the matter to the theological or metaphysical explanation of later days is marked by the early Greek notion of an inherited curse. The bequest received by his posterity from the original criminal was not a liability to punishment, but a liability to the commission of fresh offences which drew with them a condign retribution; and thus the responsibility of the family was reconciled with the newer phase of thought which limited the consequences of crime to the person of the actual delinquent.

It would be a very simple explanation of the origin of society if we could base a general conclusion on the hint furnished us by the Scriptural example already adverted to, and could suppose that communities began to exist wherever a family held together instead of separating at the death of its patriarchal chieftain. In most of the Greek states and in Rome there long remained the vestiges of an ascending series of groups out of which the State was at first constituted. The Family, House, and Tribe of the Romans may be taken as the type of them, and they are so described to us that we can scarcely help conceiving them as a system of concentric circles which have gradually expanded from the same point. The elementary group is the Family, connected by common subjection to the highest male ascendant. The aggregation of Families forms the Gens or House. The aggregation of Houses makes the Tribe. The aggregation of Tribes constitutes the Commonwealth. Are we at liberty to follow these indications, and to lay down that the commonwealth is a collection of persons united by common descent from the progenitor of an original family? Of this we may at least be certain, that all ancient societies regarded themselves as having proceeded from one original stock, and even laboured under an incapacity for comprehending any reason except this for their holding together in political union. The history of political ideas

begins, in fact, with the assumption that kinship in blood is the sole possible ground of community in political functions nor is there any of those subversions of feeling, which we term emphatically revolutions, so startling and so complete as the change which is accomplished when some other principle — such as that, for instance of *local contiguity* — establishes itself for the first time as the basis of common political action. It may be affirmed then of early commonwealths that their citizens considered all the groups in which they claimed membership to be founded on common lineage. What was obviously true of the Family was believed to be true, first of the House, next of the Tribe, lastly of the State. And yet we find that along with this belief, or, if we may use the word, this theory, each community preserved records or traditions which distinctly showed that the fundamental assumption was false. Whether we look to the Greek states, or to Rome, or to the Teutonic aristocracies in Ditmarsh which furnished Niebuhr with so many valuable illustrations, or to the Celtic clan associations, or to that strange social organisation of the Sclavonic Russians and Poles which has only lately attracted notice, everywhere we discover traces of passages in their history when men of alien descent were admitted to, and amalgamated with, the original brotherhood. Adverting to Rome singly, we perceive that the primary group, the Family, was being constantly adulterated by the practice of adoption, while stories seem to have been always current respecting the exotic extraction of one of the original Tribes and concerning a large addition to the Houses made by one of the early kings. The composition of the state uniformly assumed to be natural, was nevertheless known to be in great measure artificial. This conflict between belief or theory and notorious fact is at first sight extremely perplexing; but what it really illustrates is the efficiency with which Legal Fictions do their work in the infancy of society. The earliest and most extensively employed of legal fictions was that which permitted family relations to be created artificially, and there is none to which I conceive mankind to be more deeply indebted....

* * *

The movement of the progressive societies has been uniform in one respect. Through all its course it has been distinguished by the gradual dissolution of family dependency and the growth of individual obligation in its place. The individual is steadily substituted for the Family, as the unit of which civil laws take account. The advance has been accomplished at varying rates of celerity, and there are societies not absolutely stationary in which the collapse of the ancient organisation can only be perceived by careful study of the phenomena they present. But, whatever its pace, the change has not been subject to reaction or recoil, and apparent retardations will be found to have been occasioned through the absorption of archaic ideas and customs from some entirely foreign source. Nor is it difficult to see what is the tie between man and man which replaces by degrees those forms of reciprocity in rights and duties which have their origin in the Family. It is Contract. Starting, as from one terminus of history, from a condition of society in which all the relations of Persons are summed up in the relations of Family, we seem to have steadily moved towards a phase of social order in which all these relations arise from the free agreement of individuals. In Western Europe the progress achieved in this direction has been considerable. Thus the status of the Slave has disappeared — it has been superseded by the contractual relation of the servant to his master. The status of the Female under Tutelage, if the tutelage be understood of persons other than her husband, has also ceased to exist; from her coming of age to her marriage all the relations she may form are relations of contract. So too the status of the Son under Power has no true place in the law of modern European societies. If any civil obligation binds together the Parent and the child of full age, it is one to which only contract gives its legal validity. The apparent exceptions are exceptions of that stamp which illustrate the rule. The child before years of discretion, the orphan under guardianship, the adjudged lunatic, have all their capacities and incapacities regulated by the Law of Persons. But why? The reason is differently expressed in the conventional language of different systems, but in substance it is stated to the same effect by all. The great majority of Jurists are constant to the principle that the classes of persons just mentioned are subject to extrinsic control on the single ground that they do not possess the faculty of forming a judgment on their own interests; in other words, that they are wanting in the first essential of an engagement by Contract.

The word Status may be usefully employed to construct a formula expressing the law of progress thus indicated, which, whatever be its value, seems to me to be sufficiently ascertained. All the forms of Status taken notice of in the Law of Persons were derived from, and to some extent are still coloured by, the powers and privileges anciently residing in the Family. If then we employ Status, agreeably with the usage of the best writers, to signify these personal conditions only, and avoid applying the term to such conditions as are the immediate or remote result of agreement, we may say that the movement of the progressive societies has hitherto been a movement *from Status to Contract.*

Notes and Questions

M. E. TIGAR and M. R. LEVY, from *Law and the Rise of Capitalism*

1. M. E. Tigar and M. R. Levy trace the development of contract law in England through the industrial revolution. Their general thesis is that legal change occurs in response to social change and not the other way around. More specifically, they argue that the idea of individual free bargain embodied in contract law is insufficient alone to transform a feudal economic system into a capitalist one. Rather, the changes in law are a response to social and economic changes that create a need for new legal mechanisms. What evidence do Tigar and Levy give to support their thesis? How does their view compare with Maine's? Are the views compatible?

2. The authors note that in England between 1400 and 1600 there was a great deal of tension between the courts of law and the court of equity. The English legal system at that time was divided into two parts: the courts of law, which were concerned with applying rules of law (which were very

rigid and complex) and the court of equity, which was associated with the church and was concerned with substantive justice or fairness in particular cases, especially cases in which the rules of law seemed inadequate. Tigar and Levy explain how this organization of the courts worked. How did it help merchants? How did it enable Sir Thomas More (the chancellor of the court of equity) to put pressure on the courts of law to bring about legal reform? Why was legal reform needed?

3. When it was evident that legal reform was required in order to fill new economic and commercial needs, why didn't the courts of law simply adopt the law already developed in the special mercantile courts? What did the courts of law do instead? Explain what Lord Coke meant by "out of the old fields must come the new corn."

4. The value of this excerpt is that it illustrates the process of change in common law legal institutions, and specifically the incorporation of contract law into the common law of England, which was later adopted by the U.S. legal system. This process of incremental change through court decisions raises a special jurisprudential problem, one that was treated in in Chapter Two in the more general terms of judicial process and in the abstract terms of the concept of law itself. This is an issue raised by structural features of the common law process; consequently it will manifest itself in every substantive area of common law. The problem is how can law develop legitimately through the courts to meet changing social and economic needs while still following precedent. If judicial authority is derived from the meticulous following of precedent, how can law grow and change through the courts? Given the historical fact of changing needs, how can new interests be protected without betraying old ones? How can new ideas be included in the law without violating the reasonable expectation of the people that the courts will follow rules of law known in advance by all? How can procedural justice be reconciled with substantive justice?

[From] *Law and the Rise of Capitalism*

M. E. TIGAR AND M. R. LEVY

C H A P T E R   1 7

Contract — A Study of Law and Social Reality

The development of the contract law in England and on the Continent reveals the limitations of legal reform as a means of achieving fundamental social change. Bourgeois legal writers were fond of writing that the movement from feudalism to capitalism was achieved through the device of contract. As Sir Henry Maine wrote in the nineteenth century, the history of human progress is one of liberation from obligations based upon status and of their replacement by those based upon contract, or free bargain. In other words, the legal institution of contract was the motive force of the bourgeois revolution.

The statement, found in the writings of every bourgeois legal philosopher of that period, contains an important historical truth and a serious analytical falsehood. The historical truth is that a developed system of bourgeois social relations, such as came to maturity by 1800 in both England and France, had a well-developed theory of contract. The bonds uniting the different elements of such a society are almost exclusively bilateral and nominally consensual — that is to say, contractual. No longer, as in the feudal period, could landed property, its exploitation and defense, mediate the legal relations between people. Property became the relationship of *persona* and *res*. The contract — to work, to sell, even to live in marriage — took pride of place.

The analytical falsehood is the assertion that bourgeois social relations will come into being, regardless of material conditions, whenever the legal idea of free bargain is sufficiently developed. The law of contract did not burst into existence and become established on the basis of the self-evident justice of its principles. The field in which contracts operate is limited by the system of economic relations and this system is in turn determined by the level of technology, the strength of the opposing classes, and, in general, the state of development of the forces of production. Having access to a sophisticated theory of contract is no guarantee of the presence of the ensemble of forces needed to put it to work.

A high level of scholarship and legal science, therefore, was of no particular use to the bourgeoisie, for there was no way to create a unified national "common market" regulated by consistent principles of commercial law. Possession of a sophisticated theory of contract could not itself transform social relations. Transformation is a question of power, of appropriating and running a system of production.

In examining life in southern France in the 1200s and the 1300s, we saw how depopulation and economic stagnation led nascent bourgeois institutions to wither and die. Between 1400 and 1600, in the move toward a society dominated by the bourgeois class and governed in its interest, France and the Italian city-states, with their highly developed and sophisticated law of contract, were outdistanced by England, which began the period with a relatively backward system of contract law.

* * *

In sum, the presence in France and Italy of substantial groups of law-trained men and women in the service of the bourgeoisie was of no avail without a unified national market and a strong state apparatus wedded to bourgeois interests. These conditions existed in England: the legal ideology of the bourgeoisie there became the expressed justification for the exercise of state power on its behalf. King Henry's confiscation of Church land gave legal rights to a new group of landowners, reinforcing the position they already had by virtue of their entrepreneurship and mercantile activity. Here the law could be a battering ram, to take down the houses of "poor wretches." But law — those principles which made up the legal ideology of the old nobility — was also a shield for that class and for those who, owning property outside the cities, shared its problems. They too had to be brought into the system of bourgeois legal relations. At least those relations had to be integrated into the old common law and applied by the King's courts, which had been established to serve essentially feudal interests.

The common law, we have seen, was in its origins the law of "the land" — that is, of realty. Between approximately 1400 and 1600, it became the law of "the Land," of the country, and it incorporated principles developed in the merchant and maritime jurisdictions. In 1400, King's Bench and Common Pleas grudgingly admitted to only the most limited and rudimentary ideas of contract. Just after 1600, Sir Edward Coke — who became Attorney General in 1594 and Chief Justice of the Court of Common Pleas in 1606 and who was a prolific commentator on the law — declared the law merchant to be part of the common law, by which he meant that the common lawyers and common-law courts would thenceforth serve the interests of merchants.

This process is worth describing, for it was accomplished without overt violence to the landed class, whose interests were nominally protected, left to be dealt with more harshly at some future date. The fiction of uninterrupted tradition could, with some recasting of history, be maintained. "Let us now peruse our ancient authors," Coke wrote, "for out of the old fields must come the new corne."

Coke was not the first to venture the opinion that the common law had to be expanded. Thomas More, as Chancellor, had sought to coerce the common-law courts into changing by the liberal use of his power to issue injunctions directed to them. When the complaints of the common-law judges reached him, More invited all of them to dinner in the Council Chamber at Westminster. His son-in-law, William Roper, recounts that after dinner, when he had broken with them what complaints had heard of his injunctions and moreover showed them both the number of causes of every one of them, in order, so plainly that, upon full debating of those matters, they were all forced to confess that they, in like case, could have done no otherwise themselves. Then offered he this unto them, that if the Justices of every court (unto whom the reformation of the rigor of the law, by reason of their office, most especially appertained) would, upon reasonable considerations, by their own discretions (as they were, he thought, in conscience bound), mitigate and reform the rigor of the law themselves, there should from thenceforth by him no more injunctions be granted. Whereunto when they refused to condescend, then said he unto them, "Forasmuch as yourselves, my lords, drive me to that necessity for awarding out injunctions to relieve the people's injury, you cannot hereafter any more justly blame me."

It is a great pity that we do not know the precise terrain over which the argument between More and the common lawyers was waged. But we can surmise what at least some of the questions must have been.

To do this, we must first recall something of the setting within which the dispute took place. More, having been trained as a common lawyer at Lincoln's Inn and spent time at the bar, knew his opponents well. At that time a lawyer was trained not in university, but in the Inns of Court, lodging there for three years to receive formal training from the younger members of the bar and to learn by example and discussion from the older members. Judges of the common-law courts were drawn from the ranks of practicing lawyers. Sir John Fortescue's *De Laudibus Legum Anglie* (In Praise of the Laws of England), written about 1470, gives us a glimpse of the process. At the Inns, he wrote:

> there is in addition to the study of law a kind of academy of all the manners that the nobles learn. There they learn to sing and to practice all kinds of harmony. They are also taught there to dance and engage in passtimes that are proper for nobles.

Fortescue's picture is a bit idyllic, but certainly the Inns welcomed many sons of noble families who were not seeking to enter legal practice.

Legal education consisted of reading judges' opinions and reports of argued cases and partici-

pating in mock legal battles. But the most important subject of study was procedure and pleading: Thomas Littleton, author of a leading treatise on land law, *Of Tenures*, said to his son:

> It is one of the most honorable, laudable and profitable things in our law to have the science of well pleading in actions real and personal; and therefore I counsel thee especially to employ thy courage and care to learn this.

It was good advice. One could not proceed in the common-law courts without mastering a bewildering array of procedural devices, each of which required a written pleading in a precise form. Every common-law lawsuit was initiated with a writ. The only suits permitted were those in which the facts alleged could be fitted to the requirements of one of the available writs. The first writs were authorized soon after the Norman Conquest, as directions to a royal officer to bring in the defendant so that inquiry could be made about the right to possess a given piece of land. The writ system was elaborated to provide remedies in a broader range of actions, but it also retained a rigid format which required a prospective plaintiff to fit his case within a standard form. The development of the law was thus linked to the interpretation of the words of standard forms of initial pleading. If none of the authorized forms fit the facts of one's case, there was no remedy in the common-law courts. To abate the rigors of this system, lawyers pressed for creation of new writs — new "forms of action" — and indulged in sometimes spectacular feats of casuistry to adapt the facts to one of the available forms.

If the plaintiff of 1500 consulted a common lawyer complaining that a contract had been breached, the lawyer first turned to the writ of covenant. To sustain an action of covenant one had to allege and prove that there had been a formal contract reduced to writing and sealed. A simple, unsealed written agreement, much less an oral one, could not be enforced. To surmount this difficulty, many contracts were written in the form of bonds. One party would say that he owed the other a sum of money, but it would be stipulated that the bond was void upon the performance of certain conditions. If the conditions were not performed, the injured party could bring a writ of debt to collect.

Such roundabout ways of making and enforcing bargains did not appeal to merchants who had a large volume of business to transact and relied upon simple forms of contract. At first the merchants turned away from the common-law courts for the bulk of their legal business and sought royal assistance in creating parallel institutions which would fashion and apply a more hospitable law of contract. For example, they had recourse to the judicial jurisdiction of the Lord Chancellor — to More and his predecessors and successors — who had from about 1350 exercised judicial powers, based in theory upon the obligation of the Crown to administer "justice," irrespective of the rules of the common law. By 1500 there was a clearly defined core of such "equity" doctrine, grounded in the notion that the Chancellor would provide a remedy for injustice when the common law would not.

What were the sources of this doctrine? From its beginnings, equity jurisdiction was meant by the Crown to be used for mercantile causes, such as when the sovereign was bound by treaty to see that foreign merchants had an efficacious tribunal. It is likely indeed that the mercantile courts of the City of London, which also had cognizance of merchant matters, were responsible for much of the legal learning put into practice by the Chancellors. One detects also, in the Chancellors' jurisprudence, a continual absorption of canon-law and Roman-law principles. Notions of "justice" and "conscience," watchwords of basic equity theory, sound both of canonist concern with souls and of Roman-law ideas of contractual good faith. Under the Tudors this reception of Roman-canon principles was accelerated. In this respect, Thomas More was an ideal Chancellor, for he was probably unique in combining common-law experience, and knowledge of canon and Roman law, with a deep personal sense of justice and extensive familiarity with merchant affairs.

In theory, equity power was purely personal, in the sense that the litigant was commanded to do or refrain from doing a certain thing on pain of losing his soul. Should that not be enough, the Chancellor could lock up his body. A defendant brought before the court of equity might be ordered to carry out a contract for which the common-law courts provided no remedy; or he might be ordered to abandon a suit he had brought in the common-law courts if the Chancellor was convinced that the suit would result in a judgment which, though "lawful," would offend mercantile-law principles that had been basic to the original bargain between the parties. Such decisions created both the hostility More confronted at dinner in Westminister Hall and some unsubtle pressure for the common-law courts to modify the doctrine they applied.

Merchants also had tribunals specially created for their needs by treaty, by royal charter, by virtue of municipal privileges, or otherwise. Merchant and admiralty courts continued to function through the 1500s. Indeed, as the royal navy became more important to trade and warmaking, the admiralty jurisdiction was increased. A number of special courts were created to administer specific aspects of economic and land policy, and judges trained in civil law were appointed to them. (It has even been contended, with some justice, that England came close to adopting the Roman law as the basis of jurisprudence, as a kind of final ornament to the changes being wrought by the Tudor monarchs.)

Merchant causes could also be heard in courts established by royally chartered corporations of merchants, the corporation having a partial or total monopoly on a particular branch of trade. The Mercers are the most notable example, and in the 1400s a branch of the fellowship — those interested in exporting cloth, paticularly to the Low Countries — began to meet separately, as indicated by a 1443 mention in a royal charter of "des Aventurers del Mercery." From 1486 onward, the Merchant Adventurers among the Mercers took the lead among all exporters in organizing and controlling English trade to the Low Countries.

In form the Adventurers were a corporation under royal charter. They were presided over by a governor, apparently named by the king on nomination of the group. Henry VII sent John Pykering to be governor over "oure trusty and welbeloved subiettes the marchauntes adventerers" in the Low Countries, "at the desyre and nomination of the most partie of you resident in our said citie of London." The Adventurers had the right to hold their own courts and to impose sanctions on all those carrying on overseas trade in the region assigned to them. Their courts applied mercantile law. Their jurisdiction was assured in London by royal grant, and in other lands by treaty confirming their power over all English traders in a particular sovereignty. Thus, the royal chartered company with a monopoly, a model for later colonial enterprises, was combined with the earlier model of the consular court, which had existed since the Crusades. The importance attached to encouraging and protecting the Merchant Adventurers' trade is apparent in the obvious diplomatic effort expended on their behalf. It is likely that More's being given the "freedom" of the Mercers in 1509 was a reward for some of his efforts.

In sum, the wealthy bourgeois in the middle of the 1500s confronted great opportunities in trade and enterprise, provided he was willing to submit to the rules of a financial system run from London — a domination which caused some distress to Merchant Adventurers in the North. Contracts drawn under merchant law were enforceable in merchant courts, in chancery, and in admiralty. More and more, the principles of this continental import were being applied and studied. The common lawyers, from whose ranks the judges of the King's Bench and the Court of Common Pleas were drawn, knew that the portion of the legal system they administered was in danger of being reduced to insignificance as their clientele, the landed nobles or the gentry, declined in relative financial power. For its part, the bourgeoisie welcomed the opportunity to have access to the common-law courts, which were more independent of the Crown than some of the special tribunals established by the Tudor monarchs; alliance with the Crown was one thing; dependence on it quite another.

There was room, therefore, for an alliance of the common lawyers and the bourgeoisie, if only the lawyers could convince the forums where they practiced to be receptive to bourgeois legal principles. The closing years of the century saw the alliance begin to take shape, as the common-law courts moved toward a bourgeois theory of contract. In 1602, in *Slade's Case*, all the common-law judges, meeting in Exchequer Chamber, ruled that a contract for the sale of goods, though not under seal, could be sued upon in the common-law courts. It would have been simpler for the judges to adopt the merchant rule, but their respect for tradition required taking a different route.

The action of covenant, which could be brought only on a contract under seal, was clearly unsuited to merchant contracts. There was also the action of debt, for a written promise to pay money, but this had its own limitations. *Slade's Case* turns, therefore, on the reinterpretation of a third writ, that of *assumpsit*, and the judges were ratifying and making express a process of development in the use of this writ which had begun decades earlier. The common lawyers had begun to argue: suppose I agree with a contractor that he shall make me a house, and this agreement is under seal; if he does not make the house at all ("nonfeasance"), I have an action in covenant. If he makes it badly, and he has promised, even orally, to make it well, I am cheated because he has defaulted on an undertaking (an *assumpsit* which is dishonored by his "misfeasance"). The argument that violation of an undertaking to use care and skill, even one not under seal, could give rise to an action in *assumpsit* began to be used around 1400 in actions against carpenters, against veterinarians who agreed to cure animals, and in other similar circumstances. Rather than simply adopt the mercantile principle that a bargain must be kept, the common lawyers began to reinterpret the notions of fraud and deceit. Default on an *assumpsit* was cheating; once that notion was established, the road was open to adopting the essential elements of contract law.

In the 1500s the action in *assumpsit* was extended to cover certain debts. If there was a debt owing, and the debtor said he would pay it by a certain date, the creditor, according to developing doctrine, could sue on the debt or on the promise *(assumpsit)* to pay the pre-existing obligation. Hence, *indebitatus assumpsit*.

Slade's Case united and refined the doctrine. If A agrees to sell corn to B on a future day, and B to pay for it, this is an executory contract, i.e., one to be performed in the future. If A does not deliver, or if B does not pay, the defaulting party has violated his *assumpsit*. That is, as the judges declared, "every contract executory imports in itself an *assumpsit*." From old fields had come new corn.

Once the principle had been accepted, it became easier to admit the mercantile notion of contract through the front door. The King's Bench reaffirmed and expanded its custom of admiting evidence of merchant customs and empaneled a jury of merchants to establish them if necessary. To accommodate the claims of international traders, the common-law courts expanded their geographical jurisdiction: they permitted the plaintiff to plead that Amsterdam, or some other foreign city where a dispute had arisen, was "in the parish of St. Mary-le-Bow, in the Ward of Cheap" in the City of London, and then declined to permit the opposing party to deny the allegation.

The struggle of the common lawyers and judges to attract the business of the newly powerful merchants intensified in the late 1500s and persisted into the 1600s. The common-law judges, at the behest of the defendants who appeared before them, began to issue writs prohibiting the merchant or admiralty court from proceeding, or ordering the plaintiff to desist and come to them. The merchant jurisdictions, and especially admiralty—which enjoyed royal support—responded with writs and injunctions of their own. This struggle within the legal profession, at the expense of the litigants whose business was at stake, persisted into the 1600s.

The common lawyers' gradual assimilation of bourgeois law was one necessary condition of their alliance with the bourgeoisie which came to full fruition in the English Revolution of the mid-1600s. That alliance could not succeed unless the paper war of writs and injunctions could be settled to the advantage of the common lawyers, either through royal intervention or, as proved necessary, by some more violent means.

The alliance of the bourgeoisie and the common lawyers had a constitutional dimension as well, for the common-law courts were not the creatures of royal prerogative as were the merchant and admiralty tribunals and the other "special" jurisdictions. As we explain more fully in our discussion of the English Revolution, Sir Edward Coke was a major architect of the alliance's ideology. Magisterially, not to say outrageously, he recast English history and precedent. The old fields were the common-law reports, and perhaps Magna Carta, seen not as concessions extracted by some barons but as a charter of liberty. From Magna Carta could be deduced the notion that the King was limited by the "law of the land," a phrase used in that document most probably to refer to protection of baronial privilege, but capable of wider interpretation. From the old common-law reports came a recast legal system accepting of new principles, but resting on old traditions. This rewritten history of royal concession and judicial decision, as T.F.T. Plucknett has remarked, "limited Crown and Parliament indifferently."

The bourgeoisie bore no small responsibility for the creation of a monarchy with claims to absolute power, for its interests had been served by forceful Tudor policies. But having achieved a redistribution of land, and having profited from the breakup of village life, the bourgeoisie sought allies in a new struggle to restrain the power of the Crown to interfere with trade. The common lawyers proved ready to join such an alliance.

Notes and Questions

MAX RADIN, "Contract Obligation and the Human Will"

1. Writing in 1943, Max Radin defends the American legal shift from a laissez-faire individualist notion of freedom of contract to the acceptance of regulation in the public interest. The two sides of this theoretical debate are represented in modern form by Fried, who argues for a return to a laissez-faire or "subjective view" of contractual obligation, and Atiyah, who rejects the subjective view and offers an alternative explanation for the grounds of contractual obligation. Where does Radin fit into this debate? Notice that while he, like Atiyah, rejects the subjective view of contractual obligation, unlike Atiyah he gives a pragmatic and historical explanation rather than a theoretical justification for a particular view. Is Radin's view compatible with a future shift back to a laissez-faire view, or does he rule that out?

2. Radin picks up the historical threads spun by Maine and by Tigar and Levy, advancing the story to the 1940s. Like Tigar and Levy, he disputes Maine's thesis of social progress as progress from status-based obligation to contractual obligation, but he offers a different argument. What is Radin's objection to Maine's thesis?

3. Comparing contract with status in terms of compulsory (or nonvoluntary) obligation, Radin distinguishes two ways in which contractual obligation may be compulsory. What are they?

4. Responding to arguments that compulsory contracts are contradictions in terms as well as affronts to morality (which were made by defenders of laissez-faire economic individualism, particularly in arguments against wage and hour regulation and antitrust laws), Radin uses his distinction to show the many ways in which contracts have always been compulsory in one way or another, and thus that contractual obligation has never implied agreement without limits. What are the ways in which contracts are not now, and for many years have not been, the product of free choice?

5. Radin observes that (in 1943) 40 percent of the population was restricted by standardized contracts, set prices, set professional fees, and the collective negotiation of mass labor contracts in many fields. That figure is undoubtedly much higher today. Does that suggest that our sense of individual freedom about contracting is illusory? Does it show (as Radin intends) that the subjective or laissez-faire theory of contractual obligation is misleading or inapplicable to the real world? What does Radin conclude from his legal survey of contractual restrictions?

6. Radin points out that while economic regulations have increased, personal arrangements, such as divorce and marriage, have been deregulated. That is, personal relations are now more open than they once were to individualized contractual arrangements. And this trend has continued since 1943. For example, divorce is now widely available by mutual consent, as it was not when Radin wrote this article. Is it better for personal relations to be freely contractual, or are there benefits and drawbacks either way? Radin seems to suggest that increased freedom in personal relations makes up for or is more important than lesser freedom in economic relations. Do you agree? What are the differences between personal and economic arrangements that argue for or against their regulation?

7. Arguing for the restriction of monopolies, Radin points out that the founders of the American Constitution would have opposed de facto monopolies as much as they opposed guilds and royal grants. Why is that likely to be true? Or is it? What does Radin mean by "de facto" monopoly? His argument raises the point noted earlier by Dargo: Government power, unrestrained, is a danger to individual freedom. On the other hand, government power may be the only protection individuals have against powerful private corporations that can restrict individual freedom as much as any government can. Small government supports big business by default. What two areas does Radin claim are especially susceptible to restrictive monopoly? What do you think about his position?

8. The cases following this article trace the use of the subjective theory (which the Supreme Court and its commentators called the *freedom of contract doctrine*) from its beginning in the 1890s to its abandonment in the 1930s. Keep Radin's observations in mind as you read these cases.

Contract Obligation and the Human Will

MAX RADIN

A number of years ago, an ingenious legal mythologist invented the expression "meeting of the minds." It made a profound impression on hard-headed practical lawyers, although it was slightly ludicrous if the imagery was carried out in detail. The phrase is treated with cold contempt by Williston[1] in his monumental work on Contracts and this formal and authoritative repudiation has been enshrined in the summary of Williston on Contracts which is called the Restatement.[2] Whether "mutual assent" involving a *consensus ad idem* is anything more than a Latin translation of the "meeting of the minds" may perhaps be doubted,[3] but in any event, American and English lawyers in general reject what they call the "subjective" theory of contracts in favor of an "objective" theory.

The "subjective" theory as it was developed in nineteenth century Germany and France dealt with obligations in general. Its fullest statement is Ihering's,[4] who had much to say of the "primacy of the will." Men ought to be bound only when they deliberately chose to be and to the extent that they chose. Why this seemed a desirable ideal is not difficult to discover. It flattered the sense of individual self-sufficiency which was so large a part of the sense of freedom, as the eighteenth century had understood it and as Manchester had sought to effectuate it in the nineteenth century.

The nineteenth century created a formula to show that this system of legal self-determination was the goal of progress in society. It was contained in the famous phrase of Maine, "from status to contract."[5] Society grew, it was declared, out of a situation in which obligations and functions were determined by a man's status into one in which all obligations were created by free contract. The term "status" further suggested a sort of caste. Men found themselves in a definite status by birth or at any rate by forces they did not control.

Now, as a statement of historic fact, this famous generalization was never quite true.

There had never been a time in Western communities so far as our records go, when all social and economic functions were determined by status. There were certain relationships such as father and son, husband and wife, master and slave, guardian and ward, which were of far greater importance in ancient society than they are today. Slavery has practically disappeared, wardship has dwindled into insignificance,[6] and the family relationships have become loosened and substantially changed. On the economic side, however, freedom of selecting and limiting functions was more general in the centuries just before and just after the establishment of the Roman Empire than they became in the third and later centuries.[7] For some groups in society, the beginnings of the feudal system created a freedom of enterprise. Others sank into serfdom which again broke down in different degrees at different times and places. The rise of the guilds created a special status for the emerging economic function of commerce[8] and this status became a matter of free choice in England — in theory at least — at the beginning of the seventeenth century.

Indeed it is the transformation of the mercantile function from an incident of a status, that of guild membership, into a profession freely chosen by those who desired to enter it, which looms largest in the minds of those who have made excessive use of Maine's generalization. And, in the same way, the frequent statement that we are reversing the process at the present time needs considerable qualification. Those who make it have chiefly in mind the changes that have taken place in the relations of employer and employed. In the earlier stages of the industrial development created by mechanized production, this relationship was a personal one. It has to a large extent become a group relationship and many of the obligations involved have been regulated by law. If we like we can call it a status, but it is a different type of status from what is usually understood under that term, and is limited in its scope.

And if we turn to the most striking examples of status in ancient society, those which dealt with family relationship, it may be said that these have become less and less regulated at precisely the same time at which the employee-relationship has moved into the sphere of public regulation. While it is true that the marital relationship still retains more of the vestiges of an undoubted status, in many respects it has become much more nearly a contract relationship than ever before. In Europe this has happened rather suddenly, while in the United States, it was a somewhat gradual process. In this case also, the development has not been uniform. The status of husband and wife was a rigid one in ancient Rome. It developed into a loose contract arrangement in the late Republic and Empire. It became an undoubted status again under Christianity. It once more approximated a contract in England and the United States in certain Evangelical denominations, and the contract character has made considerable strides throughout the Western world, without regard to religious affiliations.

If we deal with the matter from the point of view of legal analysis, the essence of a status is that it involves a complex of legal relations, obligations, rights, privileges, powers, just as so many other legal transactions and situations do. In a status, however, we are prone to stress the obligations and the fact that they are imposed on us without our precious self-determination or that they cannot be shaken off or seriously modified by any act of the will.

And this brings us to the point in all discussions of externally imposed obligations, where a scholastic *distinguo* is important. The modern marital relationship is a special illustration. Persons became husband and wife by contract. That is not questioned even by the supporters of the sacramental theory of marriage. Indeed, it is expressly stressed under that theory. Anything that vitiates the contract, i.e. fraud, duress, incompetence, mental or physical, annuls or may be made to annul the marriage.

But once the marriage has been entered into, the complex of rights and duties which constitute the status are for the most part fixed,[9] not by the free agreement of the parties but by the fact of the status itself. Further, in many communities, South Carolina among American states, Italy among European, for example, no divorce is permitted even for cause. And in all the American states and several European states, no agreement[10] — that is to say, no contractual arrangement — can withdraw persons from this status.

There are, therefore, two things to consider when "compulsory" contracts or obligations are discussed. Is there any compulsion to make the contract? And, secondly, once made, are the terms of the contract the subject of an agreement or are they created by law in the case of every contract of that particular type?

The difficulties of a legal terminology that knows "obligation" only as a casual and late intruder into a system that developed a legal language without it, are never more apparent. The Roman law knew that obligations were frequently — in fact, generally — involuntary, and both Greek and Roman law originally found it hard to understand how a man could be bound by merely agreeing to be. After, however, a contractual obligation by mere agreement was well known and assigned to a sense of reason and justice which seemed a necessary background of civilized living, the same sense of reason — as embodied in the *ius gentium* — made it necessary to impose contract-like obligations on persons who had no intention of making a contract, but on the contrary intended to get rid of one.[11] The payment of money by mistake, the recovery of property that had improperly got into the hands of another were called obligations *quasi ex contractu*. The common law had to call them "implied contracts" and give specifically contractual remedies for them, until well into the nineteenth century.

The quasi-contract was not made by the agreement of the parties. Because of this — if this fact is a proper classificatory test — the kind of obligation that was solely a creation of statute or regulation was dumped into the same hamper.[12] The great majority of these statutory obligations, taxes, tolls, excises, fees, have almost no resemblance to a contract, but in many cases, contractual actions were and are allowed in order to recover them. In some of these cases, the compulsory character is complete. In others, as in fees for the conduct of certain businesses or professions, we have the same distinction as before. It is a matter of free choice whether a person will enter the profession. But if he chooses, he cannot bargain for the terms on which he will serve.

If we put aside these public obligations, is

there a free choice about the normal economic functions of a member of a given community? Is he quite free to decide both whether he will make any contracts at all and what contracts he will make? I think it must be clear that as a matter of fact, this is not the case. The vast majority of the persons in any given community must make contracts in order to live. They have a considerable latitude of choice in the large centres of population. But in smaller centres and in rural areas, that latitude does not exist. In a steel town or a mining town, the vast majority must work in these commodities or not work at all, which is another way of saying that they have no choice in the matter.

It is quite true that in the United States the population is probably more mobile than anywhere else, so that there are more opportunities for the free exercise of choice of economic function than is normally the case in modern states. This choice involves of course a freedom of selecting the contracts one wishes to make. But even in the United States this freedom is limited by the difficulties of migration, social, economic and personal. A very large portion do not really have it, and in any case soon lose it, since the opportunities offered by migration are in inverse proportion to the age of the migrant. And in any case, there is no choice about whether a contract is to be made or not. That is compulsory for nearly all of us.

The compulsion to make a contract may be for sale of commodities, for labor, for management, for the exercise of professional skill, for training in a profession. Those who have capital to invest, can utilize this investment in lieu of performing services. But the investment involves a contract and is predicated on the further making of contracts by the corporation in which the investment is made. If such contracts cannot be made, the capital will produce no income and the majority of investors depend on this return for their living.

Perhaps the only group in the community that are freed from the compulsion to make contracts are those whose capital is so large that they could live on it. Even these, however, must have their capital in the form of marketable securities or it will really have no value for them whatever and marketability means that there are persons ready to make contracts about them.

Not only is there a compulsion in the making

of the contract, but the terms of the contract are not as much the creation of the free consent of the contracting parties as we like to believe. Almost all the contracts that we must make to secure and maintain our living are type contracts. They are standardized as to performance and as to consideration for performance. The range of return from investments is limited and does not deviate very much at any given time. The fees for professional services vary but they are likely to be standardized in kind, at any rate within a given area. There are "market prices" for most commodities, and producers and distributors profess themselves glad to get the market price.

In the case of labor contracts, the rise and rapid spread of collective bargaining constitute one of the special grievances of those who deplore the passing of "free" contract in favor of the "compulsion" of the present system. There is no question that the only freedom here is the selection of the persons with whom the bargain can be made. That freedom does not exist when there are hiring halls. Nor does it really exist on the part of labor since the opportunities for working in any craft are sharply limited and may be ended by the employers at any time, by abandonment of the enterprise, by merger or any reorganization that requires retrenchment. Since this situation affects some forty per cent of the entire population, it will be seen that some element of economic compulsion exists both in the making of contracts and in the terms of the contracts made, for a considerable part of our society.

Freedom of contract is much more evident in the field of luxury goods and services, in art and in literature and in amusements generally. Bargaining has a wider range here, but for many of these cases "standard" contracts are fairly common. Publishers and dramatic producers have definitely established printed forms, which most of those who make such contracts sign almost as a matter of course. It would be difficult, as a matter of fact, to select any type of economic activity that involves a substantial number of persons, in which one could not tell in advance what the terms of the contract are likely to be which these persons are compelled to make.

So far the compulsory element is created by the economic organization of our society. Are there any contracts in which the compulsion is more formal and immediate, outside of those obligations arising out of public relations, which are not really contracts at all and scarcely arise to the dignity of a quasi-contract, except as a rather forced figure of speech?

There is first of all, the huge field of public services, those which distribute the utilities of gas, light and water and furnish transportation by land, sea and now by air. To this we may add those who furnish radio-communication, radio-entertainment and telegraph and telephone service. In all these cases, in relatively recent times, government control has supervened. Many of those who furnish these commodities may not select freely the persons with whom they will make contracts nor the terms on which they will make them. They may not, in all cases but radio, decide whether they will cease to make contracts at all. If they do cease, they forfeit their right to do business altogether. There is a standard bill of lading. Freight and passenger rates, rates for gas, electricity and water, are fixed either by statute or periodically set by a public commission.

Very frequently — quite generally in Europe — the state itself owns the facilities which render these services and the prospect of such state acquisition often appears as a threat to the private companies who furnish them in the United States. But while they are privately furnished here, the contracts involved are pretty well compelled, and the importance and extent of these contracts can scarcely be overstated.

In the same way, banking and insurance contracts are sharply supervised and regulated by statute and administrative regulations. The conditions under which such businesses may be conducted at all are onerous and can be met by relatively few persons. Once the privilege-right of conducting them is acquired, the manner in which they shall be carried on is limited. There is, however, a greater freedom here than in the field of utilities, about the persons with whom the banks will make contracts and to whom the insurance companies will issue policies.

A field in which a negative compulsion is becoming increasingly important is the regulation of business practices in the ordinary sale of commodities. Once more the "status to contract" formula is found quite ineffective as an historical description. After an almost complete freedom in ancient society, the Roman imperial law introduced restrictions as an outgrowth of market practice. In this the aedilician edict played a considerable part. Only some of these restrictions could be contracted away. Most of them formed integral parts of the contract of sale. On the other hand, the expansion of the defense of *dolus* ruled out a great many practices which in a freely competitive society would be legally, if not morally, unobjectionable.

To these limitations on the terms of the contract of sale, the Middle Ages added the drastic additional limitation of the persons who could sell. Selling was a prerogative of members of a guild. Or else it was a special privilege conferred on persons — often foreigners — who had paid for it. But the terms on which they could sell were sharply controlled by the guild itself. So far as some commodities were concerned, such as bread, ale and cloth, maximum prices were set, although the enforcement of these prices left much to be desired.[13]

Obviously compulsion in the kind of contract that could be made could scarcely go much further. From 1600 on, a rapid removal of these restrictions made the contract of sale the freest of contracts.[14] Even the warranties of the seller on which the later Roman law had insisted disappeared and with the exaltation of laissez-faire, practices of more than questionable morality were taken to be the very cachet of competitive business.

The movement against "unfair competition" brought back some of the restrictions which the guild-system had imposed on its privileged monopolists. And in very recent times — in the United States more than in Britain — "unfair competition" has become extended to include business practices that are unfair or even improper, so far as the buying public is concerned and not merely unfair toward competitors.[15] The terms of contracts of sale are not much modified by these regulations. But the methods of making them are restricted and that affects the terms of the contract, by exclusion of some terms previously quite common.

The commercial revolution of the seventeenth century in England was directed both against the vestiges of the guild system and the new monopolies which had proliferated under royal grants of the Tudors. Hatred of monopolies was the essense of liberty for the middle class groups who were most articulate during the American and French Revolutions. "Liberty" was as much liberty of contract as of the person.

It is scarcely doubtful that they would have regarded the de facto monopoly of huge combinations with as vigorous hostility as the open and legal monopolies by royal grant. Whatever may be the economic value or detriment of these concentrations of productive or distributive power, there can scarcely be any doubt that they limit the range of free contractual activity for all but a small number of persons. Even when there is no natural monopoly of the product itself, it is idle for any but this small number of persons to plan selling certain types of commodities except on terms set by the large industrial units.

This is especially the case in two groups of commodities. One is that in which a special market has been created by extensive advertising under a brand-name or label. The other is that in which technological advances have become the exclusive property of a few powerful bodies. Whether or not the control in this latter case has been acquired in violation of the Sherman Act, of the Clayton Act or of some other antimonopoly statutes, the net result in both cases must be that those who wish to deal in the products so advertised and so controlled, must do so on terms which they have no voice in fixing and no bargaining power to modify.

Those consequently who think of "compulsory contracts" as a recent monstrous innovation involving the reversal of a secular trend, have left out of account an entire economic and legal background because of their absorption in some special incident of it. The forces that have put restrictions on making certain contracts and have lifted these restrictions are of diverse origin. Some of them are derived from the vast extent of territory in the United States and the wide use of new methods of communication. Others are the result of rapid growth in complicated mechanical techniques. Still others are political and social in character. They do not operate uniformly and they do not indicate a fixed movement in any direction of historical growth.

If the present effort of the government to enforce the anti-monopoly laws is successful, especially the attacks on cartels and the present patent-licensing system, we may well see after the war a considerable extension of freedom in contractual relations in this field. But this may have no effect whatever on the movement toward greater supervision and control of employment contracts and toward an even more rigid control of transportation or communication contracts than is now the case.

The notion of an obligation which public authority will enforce is older than the notion of contract, although the term "obligation" itself is derived from the earliest type of contract. But this term, *obligatio*, had nothing to do with agreement. It derived its binding force from a ritual act which had a sort of magical efficacy.[16] It might be an oath, a libation, the use of a wand. In later Greek law, the writing itself was binding because it was a writing. In Roman law — apparently as early as the Twelve Tables[17] — a formal question and answer produced the binding *(ligatio)* for a definite purpose *(ob)* which only performance could untie *(solvere)*. In Medieval English law, the ritual required the impression on a wax seal, no matter how this was effected.

All this was unilateral. It required an act of the will in the sense that — except in the case of the English specialty — it was almost impossible to see how the act creating the obligation could be performed except by the obligor himself. To be sure his will might be coerced. To which the Roman retort was *coactus voluit tamen voluit*.[18] "He willed under compulsion, none the less he willed." It was in the main an exemplification of the "objective" theory to which most modern lawyers adhere. Equity, both in the Roman and the English systems, would give relief, but the obligation was in itself no less real, because the will was merely formally present. The court would need conviction that the expressed will did not correspond to the desires and intention of the person who expressed it.

It was the same with other denials of a real will when in a stipulation the promisor asserted he had not meant what he said. "The defendant will always deny he meant what he said," said Paul in the third century.[19] The enforcement of obligations was a matter of adjusting functions which had come into conflict. There was nothing sacred in the will as such, but there was a real advantage in a complicated society in giving a definite range within which intention and desire expressed in a certain way could determine the personal and property relations of the people involved.

Every society and every period circumscribe

this area in different ways. If the special development of the immediate present and the imminent future has created in certain fields many new situations in which the desire and intention of a contracting party have both in law and fact only a limited effect on the terms of the contract, this neither destroys the whole doctrine of contract obligation nor implies a complete regimentation of social life. We are not likely, in a highly organized community, to be free from economic compulsions. It is quite normal that the legal system will take them into account in deciding on what conditions it will enforce obligations which the obligor was compelled to assume.

If the term "compulsory" were not tinged with reproach there would be no paradox whatever in the idea of "compulsory contracts." The process of communal living "draws man together" *contrahere*, and it is during only a special period in our development that it has seemed important to stress the will as the basis of this drawing together. If it be true that the post-war community will impose an even larger number of economic restrictions than now exist, there may be a compensatory expansion of freedom of contract in non-economic fields. At any rate "contract" is an instrument, not a value in itself, while "freedom" is a thing intrinsically desirable. It does not quite follow that the two are always bound in an indissoluble union.

NOTES

1. WILLISTON, CONTRACTS (rev. ed. by Williston and Thompson 1936) § 22, p. 42. The term is called an "unfortunate survival" (*id.* at 42, n. 4), and in the Index, "a discredited formula" (*id.* at 8, 7540). It is, however, still used in cases (*id.* at 1, 42, n. 4), generally to call attention to the fact that it is not to be taken literally. *But cf.* Lemp Co. v. Secor, 21 Okl. 537, 541, 96 Pac. 636, 639; Warren v. New York Life Ins. Co., 37 F. Supp. 358, 361 (1941).

2. The exact words of Williston on Contracts frequently enough reappear in the Restatement of Contracts. But it is the arrangement of materials and the tone and attitude which make the similarity apparent. The use of the Restatement by many courts as though it had statutory effect has imported this masterpiece of dialectic into American law more fundamentally than has fallen to the lot of any other American treatise.

3. 1 WILLISTON 41, n. 2.

4. I IHERING, DER ZWECK IM RECHT 9–16, 266–267

(1893); I. HUSIK, LAW AS A MEANS TO AN END (Eng. tr. 1913) 3 *et seq.* The conflict between the *Vorstellungstheorie* and *Willenstheorie* in Germany has swept over the entire field of law and covers crimes and torts as well as contracts. *Cf.* Planck's edition of the B. G. B. (3d ed. 1903) I, pp. 41 *et seq.*; SCHOLLMEYER, RECHT DER SCHULDVERHÄLTNISSE (1900) commenting on B. G. B. § 277; PAUL OERTMANN, in his COMMENTARY ON THE B. G. B. § 276 (3d ed. 1910) Vol. II, p. 107, decides in favor of the Will-theory. Such statements as appear in OTTO WARNEYER'S COMMENTARY ON THE B. G. B. (1923) I, pp. 166–68, are indistinguishable from the English and American "objective" doctrine.

If the "objective" theory is really as fundamental in our system as is so often said, it is hard to see why "compulsory" contracts should seem abhorrent to the common lawyer, who so frequently boasts of his contempt for mere verbalism. All obligatory transactions are compulsory by the fact of being obligatory. And if a man is compelled to carry out what he never meant or what he did not quite understand — and that is implied in the "objective" theory — merely because his words or acts might reasonably be assumed to carry certain implications, we have something not very different from contracts made for parties by statutes or regulations.

5. The development of this idea occurs in ANCIENT LAW (Pollock's ed. 1930) c. 5, esp. 180–182. See further Pollock's note at 190-193. Maine undoubtedly thought of this as an absolute, a necessary and univocal movement. "The change has not been subject to reaction or recoil (*id.* at 180)." This is, of course, a piece of that Hegelian fetishism which has so befuddled most nineteenth century social and political theory. For a rational estimate of Maine and his importance, see Mr. K. Smellie's article in 10 ENCYC. SOC. SCI. 49–50.

6. As an example of contraction and expansion, it may be pointed out that wardship in the late Empire developed out of the need of providing social security for large classes of economically incompetent persons, and after a recession, grew into a wholly different thing in feudal law out of the special circumstances of feudal tenure. The disappearance of the determining factors in modern society has produced a corresponding decay of the institution.

7 *Cf.* Kornemann, *s. v. Collegium*, in PAULY-WISSOWA, REAL-ENZYKLOPÄDIE DES KLASS. ALTERTUMS. IV, 380, 479, esp. at 442–458, 477–479; WALTZING, ÉTUDE SUR LES CORP. II, 16–246.

8. The standard work on the guilds is GROSS, THE GILD MERCHANT (1890). *Cf.* Henri Pirenne's brief résumé in 7 ENCYC. SOC. SCI. 208–214, and the bibliography (at 223), and HANDLER, CASES AND OTHER MATERIALS ON TRADE REGULATION (1937) 34–58.

9. The formula for this is found in such enactments as that of the CALIFORNIA CIVIL CODES § 159. "A husband and wife cannot, by any contract with each other,

alter their legal relations, except as to property." The exception if we compare this section with BLACKSTONE, I, 599, is large enough, but it still is far from making the terms of the marriage purely contractual, in spite of "equal rights" statutes. *Cf.* 3 VERNIER, AMERICAN FAMILY LAWS (1935) 24–29.

10. Divorce by mutual consent is not permitted even in the laxest of American jurisdictions. To be sure, mutual consent is often covered by collusion between the parties. Many European countries, like Germany and Austria after the War of 1917–1918, permitted divorce by mutual consent, in some cases, however, limiting it to those whose religion did not forbid it.

11. JUST. INST. 3, 14, 1; 3, 27, 6. DIG. 44, 7, 5, 3 (Gaius).

12. Professor Keener, who restored quasi-contracts to its proper place among orthodox legal categories, meant it to be all-inclusive. So did Professor Corbin. See Corbin, *Quasi-Contractual Obligations* (1912) 21 YALE L. J. 533–554. Professor Woodward in his treatise on the subject, QUASI-CONTRACTS (1913), is inclined to confine the term to transactions involving unjust enrichment. In his definition of quasi-contracts as "paramount and irrecusable as distinguished from consensual or recusable obligations," he goes far toward creating a class of "compulsory" contracts. The term "irrecusable" is Dean Wigmore's. See Wigmore, *The Scope of the Contract-Concept* (1943) 43 COLUMBIA LAW REV. 569; *The Tripartite Division of Torts* (1894) 8 HARV. L. REV. 200–201. The quasi-contracts recognized by Corbin (*supra* at 537) include "statutory" and "official" obligations which are definitely in the class of compulsory contracts.

13. Control of prices in one way or another is fairly ancient. Vespasian fixed prices for certain luxury goods (*cf.* STATIUS, SILVAE 3, 3, 89 *et seq.* and Vollmer's note, *ibid*). Tiberius fixed the price of grain and subsidized the dealers to secure them against loss

(TACITUS, ANN. 2, 87). *Cf.* 5 FRANK, ECONOMIC SURVEY OF ANCIENT ROME 231, 267. The famous EDICT OF DIOCLETIAN of 301 A.D. is the most extensive attempt. The text of this edict is now best found in the edition of Miss E. R. Graser; 5 FRANK, *op. cit.* 307–421. A study of the edict's economic significance by the same editor is under way.

For the ASSIZES OF BREAD, ALE, CLOTH, FUEL, *etc.*, *cf.* LIPSON, AN INTRODUCTION TO THE ECONOMIC HISTORY OF ENGLAND 267–270. For texts of the statutes *cf.* 51 HENRY III, 1, repealed and restated in elaborate detail by 8 ANN. 19 (1 ST. OF REALM 199, 9 *id.* 248 ff.). The various statutes for regulating the sale of cloth run from 2 ED. III, 4 (1 *id.* 260) to 21 JAC. I, 28 (4 *id.* 2, 1235). The statute of fuel was issued under Edward VI, 7 ED. VI, 7 (4 *id.*, 171).

14. *Cf.* RADIN, MANNERS AND MORALS OF BUSINESS (1939) 150–153. This "commercial revolution" can almost be precisely dated by the petition of 1604.

15. For a study of unfair competition in its historical development compare Professor Handler's collection of CASES AND OTHER MATERIALS ON TRADE REGULATION (1937) 540–556, esp. the brief bibliography, p. 542, note 2.

16. I have set forth my reasons for recurring to this concept in the article on *Obligatio*, in PAULY-WISSOWA-KROLL, REAL-ENZYKLOPÄDIE DES KLASS. ALTERTUMS, XVII, 1717–1726. Only the exaggerated rationalism of the mid-nineteenth century would have rejected the obvious connection of the juristic *obligare* with the magical one. *Cf.* HUVELIN, LES TABLETTES MAGIQUES ET LE DROIT ROMAIN (1902).

17. De Zulueta, *The New Gaius*, 24 J. OF ROM. STUD. 198 *et seq*; 25 *id.* at 19 *et seq.* *Cf.* GAIUS, IV, 17a, 17b. (7th ed. Seckel-Kübler 1935).

18. DIG. 4, 21, 5, 6.

19. DIG. 45, 1, 83, 1. *Cf.* my HANDBOOK OF ROMAN LAW (1927) 175–176.

Notes and Questions

Cases on Freedom of Contract

1. This line of Supreme Court decisions is often called the *Lochner* line in reference to its most famous case. It represents a line of reasoning developed by the Court over a span of about fifty years. Through its decisions we will follow the reasoning of the Court from 1887 when the first ideas leading to the constitutional protection of the freedom to contract were developed until 1937 when the full-blown doctrine was rejected. The doctrine was called *substantive due process*. The idea was to determine the substantive meaning of the due process clause of the Fourteenth Amendment to the Constitution ("nor shall any state deprive any person of life, liberty, or property, without due process of law") by the gradual and incremental process of common law development. Since the notion of due process is abstract, the Court would rely on the common law to flesh out its meaning case by case over time. Doing this sort of thing is supposed to be one of the

great virtues of the common law system. Was the Court wrong to use this method on this particular problem? If so, why?

2. The first three cases, *Mugler* v. *Kansas; Chicago, Minneapolis, & St. Paul Railroad Co.* v. *Minnesota;* and *Allgeyer* v. *Louisiana,* illustrate the beginnings of the *Lochner* line. Notice that in *Mugler* the statute is upheld. Nevertheless, the groundwork for the doctrine of substantive due process is set in the dicta of this case. What does the Court say are the limits of legislative authority? We can see the doctrine solidifying in *Chicago,* where the Court holds a Minnesota statute fixing railroad rates to be an unconstitutional interference with property without due process of law. Do you see how this follows from *Mugler*? This is the way common law is supposed to work. Each case clarifies the doctrine a little more than the last. *Allgeyer* elaborates the doctrine further, applying it specifically to the freedom to contract. Does the Court's view in *Allgeyer* seem an unreasonable interpretation of the due process clause? It is indeed a strong commitment to the protection of individual freedom. Is that a mistake? Is the Court out of line here? If so, who, if anyone, should protect individual freedom?

3. *Lochner* v. *New York*, made famous by Oliver Wendell Holmes, Jr.'s eloquent dissenting opinion, follows and expands on the earlier freedom of contract cases. *Lochner* struck down a New York labor law that attempted to limit the working hours of bakers because, the Court says, such limitation of individual freedom is not within the police power (that is, there is no reason related to the public health, safety, or morals for such restriction). If this analysis is right, could we have any labor regulations? What's wrong with that? What did Holmes think was wrong with it? Given the way the Court sets up the issues, is there any way New York or any other state could defend its labor laws?

4. The *Muller* v. *Oregon* case was one of the few labor laws to survive this period of Court history. It is a tribute to the genius of Louis D. Brandeis, who defended the constitutionality of the Oregon law setting maximum hours for women working in laundries and factories. He did this by producing what is now known as the *Brandeis brief,* which was a copious collection of expert opinion gathered to support factual assertions crucial to the case. In this way Brandeis proved that the Oregon labor law was really a health law. This, of course, was not really its intent at all, but given the posture of the Court, was there any other way it could be defended? Unfortunately, this ploy could not work often. It could not, for example, save a law guaranteeing women a minimum wage, in the *Adkins* v. *Children's Hospital* case a few years later. Do you see why?

5. In *Coppage* v. *Kansas* the Court strikes down a Kansas statute that made "yellow dog" contracts illegal. Yellow dog contracts were those that required as one of the terms of the employment contract that the employee agree not to be a member of a labor union. At this point the Court is applying settled doctrine used for fifteen or twenty years. Does this case follow naturally from the earlier ones? Does it follow necessarily? Can you think of another opinion that would follow the earlier cases as well? Recognizing that the doctrine is harsh, is there anything wrong with the reasoning? If so, what? If the reasoning of the Court is correct, is there any way at all that working people — employees — can protect themselves from the power of big business?

6. In 1934, in *Nebbia* v. *New York* the Court reverses its policy on freedom of contract. (although it does not explicitly overrule any specific case). Notice the language of reversal. The former view of the Court is referred to as the *view of the appellant,* which, of course, it is. The argument is stated in full with conditions and exceptions. It is noted that no conditions or exceptions apply in this case. But then the argument is rejected by denying its first premise, which was the former view of the Court. The Court also refers to cases that predate its former view. Then the new policy is stated — quite a surprise to the unfortunate appellant, presumably. But then, this was

a time of crisis, with President Franklin D. Roosevelt threatening to pack the Court precisely because of its conservative stand on freedom of contract, so perhaps it was not such a surprise. On what grounds does the Court decide that price regulation is within the police power after all? Due process requires only that legislation not be arbitrary, discriminatory, or irrelevant to its purpose. What changed?

7. *West Coast Hotel* v. *Parrish* explicitly overrules *Adkins*, thereby removing any constitutional barrier to labor regulation. In doing so, the Court denies the constitutional protection for the freedom to contract (without legislative regulation), and it examines the nature of due process. What, according to this Court opinion, is required by due process? Do the arguments in *Nebbia* and *West Coast Hotel* seem more logical, reasonable, or persuasive than the arguments presented in the earlier cases? Do they clearly set out the flaw in the earlier reasoning? What do you think the flaw is?

8. Through all these cases there runs an issue of process and an issue of substance. Throughout this time period the opinions have been articulated as though they were logically determined by the terms of the Constitution (and the cases interpreting it). Is it reasonable to think that more than one interpretation is possible? If so, that may be a major problem with this line of cases. On the other hand, if several opinions are possible, what makes a decision right? Is that improper terminology? In terms of substance, how should a Court know when it is supposed to protect the freedom of individuals or minorities from the majority? Apparently, only sometimes. But when? Not when the minority is big business? Isn't that what all these cases are about? If so, why shouldn't big business be a protected minority?

Cases on Freedom of Contract

Mugler v. Kansas
123 U.S. 623 (1887)

Upholding a Kansas statute prohibiting the production and sale of intoxicating liquors, the Court noted that determining whether such a law should be passed is the proper domain of the legislature, but only within certain limits, namely, the protection of public health, safety, or morals. Any law must be reasonably related to one such purpose, and, the Court declared, deciding whether a statute met this standard of reasonableness was within its own authority. In this case, the Court continued, the statute did meet the standard, as a protection of the public health and morals.

"It belongs to that department to exert what are known as the police powers of the State, and to determine, primarily, what measures are appropriate or needful for the protection of the public morals, the public health, or the public safety.

"It does not at all follow that every statute enacted ostensibly for the promotion of these ends is to be accepted as a legitimate exertion of the police powers of the State. There are of necessity, limits beyond which legislation cannot rightfully go. . . . The courts are not bound by mere forms, nor are they to be misled by mere pretenses. They are at liberty — indeed, are under a solemn duty — to look at the substance of things, whenever they enter upon the inquiry whether the Legislature has transcended the limits of its authority. If, therefore, a statute purporting to have been enacted to protect the public health, the public morals, or the public safety, has no real or substantial relation to those objects, or is a palpable invasion of rights secured by the fundamental law, it is the duty of the courts to so adjudge, and thereby give effect to the Constitution." The Court went on to hold that facts "within the knowledge of all" and "established by statistics accessible to everyone" were sufficient to uphold the statute.

Chicago, Minneapolis, & St. Paul Railroad Co. v. Minnesota
134 U.S. 418 (1890)

Relying on the power it established but did not use in *Mugler*, the Court held unconstitutional a Minnesota statute authorizing a state commission to set railroad rates and denying any judicial review of these rates. Since the due process clause guarantees judicial review of any interference with property, the railroad companies were entitled to a hearing, the Court said, as to whether the rates set were "reasonable."

"The question of the reasonableness of a rate of charge for transportation by a railroad company, involving as it does the element of reasonableness both as regards the company and as regards the public, is eminently a question for judicial investigation, requiring due process of law for its determination. If the company is deprived of the power of charging reasonable rates for the use of its property, and such deprivation takes place in the absence of an investigation by judicial machinery, it is deprived of the lawful use of its property, and thus, in substance and effect, of the property itself, without due process of law and in violation of the Constitution of the United States; and in so far as it is thus deprived, while other persons are permitted to receive reasonable profits upon their invested capital, the company is deprived of the equal protection of the laws."

Allgeyer v. Louisiana
165 U.S. 578 (1897)

Using broad language to indicate the scope of the coverage of the due process clause, the Court declared it unconstitutional for Louisiana to prohibit a Louisiana resident from using the mails to contract with a New York firm to insure goods shipped from Louisiana to Europe. Any restriction of individual freedom, and especially the freedom to contract for private purposes, was unreasonable unless it protected the public health, safety, or morals.

The Court said: "The Supreme Court of Louisiana says that the act of writing within that State the letter of notification, was an act therein done to effect an insurance on property then in the State, in a marine insurance company which had not complied with its laws, and such act was, therefore, prohibited by the statute. As so construed we think the statute is a violation of the Fourteenth Amendment of the Federal Constitution, in that it deprives the defendants of their liberty without due process of law. The statute which forbids such act does not become due process of law, because it is inconsistent with the provisions of the Consti- tution of the Union. The liberty mentioned in that amendment means not only the right of the citizen to be free from the mere physical restraint of his person, as by incarceration, but the term is deemed to embrace the right of the citizen to be free in the enjoyment of all his faculties; to be free to use them in all lawful ways; to live and work where he will; to earn his livelihood by any lawful calling; to pursue any livelihood or avocation, and for that purpose to enter into all contracts which may be proper, necessary and essential to his carrying out to a successful conclusion the purposes above mentioned."

Lochner v. New York
198 U.S. 45 (1905)

Mr. Justice Peckham delivered the opinion of the Court.

The indictment, it will be seen, charges that the plaintiff in error violated the 110th section of article 8, chapter 415, of the Laws of 1897, known as the labor law of the state of New York, in that he wrongfully and unlawfully required and permitted an employee working for him to work more than sixty hours in one week. . . .

* * *

It is not an act merely fixing the number of hours which shall constitute a legal day's work, but an absolute prohibition upon the employer permitting, under any circumstances, more than ten hours' work to be done in his establishment. The employee may desire to earn the extra money which would arise from his working more than the prescribed time, but this statute forbids the employer from permitting the employee to earn it.

The statute necessarily interferes with the right of contract between the employer and employees, concerning the number of hours in which the latter may labor in the bakery of the employer. The general right to make a contract in relation to his business is part of the liberty of the individual protected by the 14th Amendment of the Federal Constitution. Allgeyer v. Louisiana, 165 U.S. 578. Under that provision no state can deprive any person of life, liberty, or property without due process of law. The right to purchase or to sell labor is part of the liberty protected by this amendment, unless there are circumstances which exclude the right. There are, however, certain powers, existing in the sovereignty of each state in the Union, somewhat vaguely termed police powers, the exact description and limitation of which have not been attempted by the courts. Those powers, broadly stated, and without, at present, any attempt at a more specific limitation, relate to the safety, health, morals, and general welfare of the public. Both property and liberty are held on such reasonable conditions as may be imposed by the governing power of the state in the exercise of those powers, and with such conditions the 14th Amendment was not designed to interfere. Mugler v. Kansas, 123 U.S. 623. . . .

* * *

Therefore, when the state, by its legislature, in the assumed exercise of its police powers, has passed an act which seriously limits the right to labor or the right of contract in regard to their means of livelihood between persons who are *sui juris* (both employer and employee), it becomes of great importance to determine which shall prevail, — the right of the individual to labor for such time as he may choose, or the right of the state to prevent the individual from laboring, or from entering into any contract to labor, beyond a certain time prescribed by the state.

This court has recognized the existence and upheld the exercise of the police powers of the states in many cases which might fairly be considered as border ones, and it has, in the course of its determination of questions regarding the asserted invalidity of such statutes, on the ground of their violation of the rights secured by the Federal Constitution, been guided by rules of a very liberal nature, the application of which has resulted, in numerous instances, in upholding the validity of state statutes thus assailed. Among the later cases where the state law has been upheld by this court is that of Holden v. Hardy, 169 U.S. 366. A provision in the act of the legislature of Utah was there under consideration, the act limiting the employment of workmen in all underground mines or workings, to eight hours per day, "except in cases of emergency, where life or property is in imminent danger." It also limited the hours of labor in smelting and other institutions for the reduction or refining of ores or metals to eight hours per day, except in like cases of emergency. The act was held to be a valid exercise of the police powers of the state. . . .

* * *

It must, of course, be conceded that there is a limit to the valid exercise of the police power by the state. . . .

* * *

In every case that comes before this court, therefore, where legislation of this character is concerned, and where the protection of the Federal Constitution is sought, the question necessarily arises: Is this a fair, reasonable, and appropriate exercise of the police power of the state, or is it an unreasonable, unnecessary, and arbitrary interference with the right of the individual to his personal liberty, or to enter into those contracts in relation to labor which may seem to him appropriate or necessary for the support of himself and his family? Of course the liberty of contract relating to labor includes both parties to it. The one has as much right to purchase as the other to sell labor.

This is not a question of substituting the judgment of the court for that of the legislature. If the act be within the power of the state it is valid, although the judgment of the court might be totally opposed to the enactment of such a law. But the question would still remain: Is it within the police power of the state? and that question must be answered by the court.

The question whether this act is valid as a labor law, pure and simple, may be dismissed in a few words. There is no reasonable ground for interfering with the liberty of persons or the right of free contract by determining the hours of labor, in the occupation of a baker. . . . Viewed in the light of a purely labor law with no reference whatever to the question of health, we think that a law like the one before us involves neither the safety, the morals, nor the welfare of the public, and that the interest of the public is not in the slightest degree affected by such an act. The law must be upheld, if at all, as a law pertaining to the health of the individual engaged in the occupation of a baker. . . .

* * *

We think the limit of the police power has been reached and passed in this case. There is, in our judgment, no reasonable foundation for holding this to be necessary or appropriate as a health law to safeguard the public health, or the health of the individuals who are following the trade of a baker. . . .

* * *

It is also urged, pursuing the same line of argument, that it is to the interest of the state that its population should be strong and robust, and therefore any legislation which may be said to tend to make people healthy must be valid as health laws, enacted under the police power. If this be a valid argument and a justification for this kind of legislation, it follows that the protection of the Federal Constitution from undue interference with liberty of person and freedom of contract is visionary, wherever the law is sought to be justified as a valid exercise of the police power. Scarcely any law but might find shelter under such assumptions, and conduct, properly so called, as well as contract, would come under the restrictive sway of the legislature. Not only the hours of employees, but the hours of employers, could be regulated, and doctors, lawyers, scientists, all professional men, as well as athletes and artisans, could be forbidden to fatigue their brains and bodies by prolonged hours of exercise, lest the fighting strength of the state be impaired. We mention these extreme cases because the contention is extreme. We do not believe in the soundness of the views which uphold this law. . . .

* * *

Statutes of the nature of that under review, limiting the hours in which grown and intelligent men may labor to earn their living, are mere meddlesome interferences with the rights of the individual, and they are not saved from condemnation by the claim that they are passed in the exercise of the police power and upon the subject of the health of the individual whose rights are interfered with, unless there be some fair ground, reasonable in and of itself, to say that there is material danger to the public health, or to the health of the employees, if the hours of labor are not curtailed. . . .

* * *

It is impossible, for us to shut our eyes to the fact that many of the laws of this character, while passed under what is claimed to be the police power for the purpose of protecting the public health or welfare, are, in reality, passed from other motives. We are justified in saying so when, from the character of the law and the subject upon which it legislates, it is apparent that the public health or welfare bears but the most remote relation to the law. The purpose of a statute must be determined from the natural and legal effect of the language employed; and whether it is or is not repugnant to the Constitution of the United States must be determined from the natural effect of such statutes when put into operation, and not from their proclaimed purpose. . . .

* * *

It is manifest to us that the limitation of the hours of labor as provided for in this section of the statute under which the indictment was found, and the plaintiff in error convicted, has no such direct relation to, and no such substantial effect upon, the health of the employee, as to justify us in regarding the section as really a health law. It seems to us that the real object and purpose were simply to regulate the hours of labor between the master and his employees (all being men, *sui juris*), in a private business, not dangerous in any degree to morals, or in any real and substantial degree to the health of the employees. Under such circumstances the freedom of master and employee to contract with each other in relation to their employment, and in defining the same, cannot be prohibited or interfered with, without violating the Federal Constitution.

The judgment of the Court of Appeals of New York, as well as that of the Supreme Court and of the County Court of Oneida County, must be reversed and the case remanded to the County Court for further proceedings not inconsistent with this opinion.

Reversed.

Mr. Justice Holmes dissenting:

I regret sincerely that I am unable to agree with the judgment in this case, and that I think it my duty to express my dissent.

This case is decided upon an economic theory which a large part of the country does not entertain. If it were a question whether I agreed with that theory, I should desire to study it further and long before making up my mind. But I do not conceive that to be my duty, because I strongly believe that my agreement or disagreement has nothing to do with the right of a majority to embody their opinions in law. It is settled by various decisions of this court that state constitutions and state laws may regulate life in many ways which we as legislators might think as injudicious, or if you like as tyrannical, as this, and which, equally with this, interfere with the liberty to contract. Sunday laws and usury laws are ancient examples. A more modern one is the prohibition of lotteries. The liberty of the citizen to do as he likes so long as he does not interfere with the liberty of others to do the same which has been a shibboleth for some well-known writers, is interfered with by school laws, by the Postoffice, by every state or municipal institution which takes his money for purposes though desirable, whether

he likes it or not. The 14th Amendment does not enact Mr. Herbert Spencer's Social Statics. The other day we sustained the Massachusetts vaccination law. Jacobson v. Massachusetts, 197 U.S. 11. United States and state statutes and decisions cutting down the liberty to contract by way of combination are familiar to this court. Northern Securities Co. v. United States, 193 U.S. 197. Two years ago we upheld the prohibition of sales of stock on margins, or for future delivery, in the Constitution of California. Otis v. Parker, 187 U.S. 606. The decision sustaining an eight-hour law for miners is still recent. Holden v. Hardy, 169 U.S. 366. Some of these laws embody convictions or prejudices which judges are likely to share. Some may not. But a Constitution is not intended to embody a particular economic theory, whether of paternalism and the organic relation of the citizen to the state or of *laissez faire*. It is made for people of fundamentally differing views, and the accident of our finding certain opinions natural and familiar, or novel, and even shocking, ought not to conclude our judgment upon the question whether statutes embodying them conflict with the Constitution of the United States.

General propositions do not decide concrete cases. The decision will depend on a judgment or intuition more subtle than any articulate major premise. But I think that the proposition just stated, if it is accepted, will carry us far toward the end. Every opinion tends to become a law. I think that the word "liberty," in the 14th Amendment, is perverted when it is held to prevent the natural outcome of a dominant opinion, unless it can be said that a rational and fair man necessarily would admit that the statute proposed would infringe fundamental principles as they have been understood by the traditions of our people and our law. It does not need research to show that no such sweeping condemnation can be passed upon the statute before us. A reasonable man might think it a proper measure on the score of health. Men whom I certainly could not pronounce unreasonable would uphold it as a first instalment of a general regulation of the hours of work. Whether in the latter aspect it would be open to the charge of inequality I think it unnecessary to discuss.

Mr. Justice Harlan (with whom Mr. Justice White and Mr. Justice Day concurred) also dissented.

Muller v. Oregon
208 U.S. 412 (1908)

Upholding an Oregon statute that forbids the employment of women in factories or laundries for more than ten hours a day, the Court distinguished *Lochner* on the factual basis of the physical differences between men and women. This factual difference, as supplied by the famous "brief" of Louis D. Brandeis, was relied on heavily by the Court in order to construe the Oregon law as a health regulation, thereby within the police powers.

"In patent cases counsel are apt to open the argument with a discussion of the state of the art. It may not be amiss, in the present case, before examining the constitutional question, to notice the course of legislation as well as expressions of opinion from other than judicial sources. In the brief filed by Mr. Louis D. Brandeis, for the defendant in error, is a very copious collection of all these matters, an epitome of which is found in the margin. . . .

* * *

"The legislation and opinions referred to in the margin may not be, technically speaking, authorities, and in them is little or no discussion of the constitutional question presented to us for determination, yet they are significant of a widespread belief that woman's physical structure, and the functions she performs in consequence thereof, justify special legislation restricting or qualifying the conditions under which she should be permitted to toil. Constitutional questions, it is true, are not settled by even a consensus of present public opinion, for it is the peculiar value of a written constitution that it places in unchanging form limitations upon legislative action, and thus gives a permanence and stability to popular government which otherwise would be lacking. At the same time, when a question of fact is debated and debatable, and the extent to which a special constitutional limitation goes is affected by the truth in respect to that fact, a widespread and long continued belief concerning it is worthy of consideration. We take judicial cognizance of all matters of general knowledge."

Coppage v. Kansas
236 U.S. 1 (1915)

Invalidating a Kansas law that would forbid so-called "yellow dog" contracts (contracts in which an employer requires an employee not to be a member of any labor union during his term of employment), the Court said:

"An interference with this liberty so serious as that now under consideration, and so disturbing of equality of right, must be deemed to be arbitrary, unless it be supportable as a reasonable exercise of the police power of the State. But, notwithstanding the strong general presumption in favor of the validity of state laws, we do not think the statute in question, as construed and applied in this case, can be sustained as a legitimate exercise of that power. . . .

* * *

"As to the interest of the employed, it is said by the Kansas Supreme Court (87 Kansas Rep., p. 759) to be a matter of common knowledge that 'employees, as a rule, are not financially able to be as independent in making contracts for the sale of their labor as are employers in making contracts of purchase thereof.' No doubt, wherever the right of private property exists, there must and will be inequalities of fortune; and thus it naturally happens that parties negotiating about a contract are not equally unhampered by circumstances. This applies to all contracts and not merely to that between employer and employee. Indeed a little reflection will show that wherever the right of private property and the right of free contract coexist each party when contracting is inevitably more or less influenced by the question whether he has much property, or little, or none; for the contract is made to the very end that each may gain something that he needs or desires more urgently than that which he proposes to give in exchange. And, since it is self-evident that, unless all things are held in common, some persons must have more property than others, it is from the nature of things impossible to uphold freedom of contract and the right of private property without at the same time recognizing as legitimate those inequalities of fortune that are the necessary result of the exercise of those rights. But the Fourteenth Amendment, in declaring that a State shall not 'deprive any person of life, liberty or property without due process of law,' gives to each of these an equal sanction; it recognizes 'liberty' and 'property' as coexistent human rights, and debars the States from any unwarranted interference with either.

"And since a State may not strike them down directly it is clear that it may not do so indirectly, as by declaring in effect that the public good requires the removal of those inequalities that are but the normal and inevitable result of their exercise, and then invoking the police power in order to remove the inequalities, without other object in view. The police power is broad, and not easily defined, but it cannot be given the wide scope that is here asserted for it, without in effect nullifying the constitutional guaranty."

JUSTICES DAY and HUGHES dissented.

Adkins v. *Children's Hospital*
261 U.S. 525 (1923)

Striking down an Act of Congress setting minimum wages for women and children in the District of Columbia by a vote of 5 to 3, the Court offered the following opinion:

"There is, of course, no such thing as absolute freedom of contract. It is subject to a great variety of restraints. But freedom of contract is, nevertheless, the general rule and restraint the exception; and the exercise of legislative authority to abridge it can be justified only by the existence of exceptional circumstances. Whether these circumstances exist in the present case constitutes the question to be answered."

* * *

"But the ancient inequality of the sexes, otherwise than physical, as suggested in the Muller Case has continued 'with diminishing intensity.' In view of the great — not to say revolutionary — changes which have taken place since that utterance, in the contractual, political and civil status of women, culminating in the Nineteenth Amendment, it is not unreasonable to say that these differences have now come almost, if not quite, to the vanishing point. In this aspect of the matter, while the physical differences must be recognized in appropriate cases, and legislation fixing hours or conditions of work may properly take them into account, we cannot accept the doctrine that women of mature age, *sui juris*, require or may be subjected to restrictions upon their liberty of contract which could not lawfully be imposed in the case of men under similar circumstances. . . .

* * *

"The relation between earnings and morals is not capable of standardization. It cannot be shown that well paid women safeguard their morals more carefully than those who are poorly paid. Morality rests upon other considerations than wages; and there is, certainly, no such prevalent connection between the two as to justify a broad attempt to adjust the latter with reference to the former. As a means of safeguarding morals the attempted classification, in our opinion, is without reasonable basis. No distinction can be made between women who work for others and those who do not; nor is there ground for distinction between women and men, for, certainly, if women require a minimum wage to preserve their morals, men require it to preserve their honesty. . . ."

* * *

"The feature of this statute which, perhaps more than any other, puts upon it the stamp of invalidity is that it exacts from the employer an arbitrary payment for a purpose and upon a basis having no causal connection with his business, or the contract or the work the employee engages to do. . . .

"A statute requiring an employer to pay in money, to pay at prescribed and regular intervals, to pay the value of the services rendered, even to pay with fair relation to the extent of the benefit obtained from the service, would be understandable. But a statute which prescribes payment without regard to any of these things and solely with relation to circumstances apart from the contract of employment, the business affected by it and the work done under it, is so clearly the product of a naked, arbitrary exercise of power that it cannot be allowed to stand under the Constitution of the United States."

CHIEF JUSTICE TAFT and JUSTICE SANFORD dissented. JUSTICE HOLMES wrote a separate dissenting opinion which included the following:

"I confess that I do not understand the principle on which the power to fix a minimum for the wages of women can be denied by those who admit the power to fix a maximum for their hours of work. I fully assent to the proposition that here as elsewhere the distinctions of the law are distinctions of degree, but I perceive no difference in the kind or degree of interference with liberty, the only matter with which we have any concern, between the one case and the other. The bargain is equally affected whichever half you regulate. Muller v. Oregon, I take it, is as good law today as it was in 1908. It will need more than the Nineteenth Amendment to convince me that there are no differences between men and women, or that legislation cannot take those differences into account. I should not hesitate to take them into account if I thought it necessary to sustain this act. . . . But after Bunting v. Oregon, 243 U.S. 426, I had supposed that it was not necessary, and that Lochner v. New York, 198 U.S. 45, would be allowed a deserved repose."

Nebbia v. *New York*
291 U.S. 502 (1934)

Reversing its policy on price regulation, the Court, (by a vote of 5 to 4), upheld a New York statute that set maximum and minimum prices for the sale of milk. The very long opinion was delivered by Justice Roberts:

* * *

"But we are told that because the law essays to control prices it denies due process. Notwithstanding the admitted power to correct existing economic ills by appropriate regulation of business, even though an indirect result may be a restriction of the freedom of contract or a modification of charges for services or the price of commodities, the appellant urges that direct fixation of prices is a type of regulation absolutely forbidden. His position is that the Fourteenth Amendment requires us to hold the challenged statute void for this reason alone. The argument runs that the public control of rates or prices is per se unreasonable and unconstitutional, save as applied to businesses affected with a public interest; that a business so affected is one in which property is devoted to an enterprise of a sort which the public itself might appropriately undertake, or one whose owner relies on a public grant or franchise for the right to conduct the business, or in which he is bound to serve all who apply; in short, such as is commonly called a public utility; or a business in its nature a monopoly. The milk industry, it is said, possesses none of these characteristics, and therefore, not being affected with a public interest, its charges may not be controlled by the state. Upon the soundness of this contention the appellant's case against the statute depends.

"We may as well say at once that the dairy industry is not, in the accepted sense of the phrase, a public utility. We think the appellant is also right in asserting that there is in this case no suggestion of any monopoly or monopolistic practice. It goes without saying that those engaged in the business are in no way dependent upon public grants or franchises for the privilege of conducting their activities. But if, as must be conceded, the industry is subject to regulation in the public interest, what constitutional principle bars the state from correcting existing maladjustments by legislation touching prices? We think there is no such principle. The due process clause makes no mention of sales or of prices any more than it speaks of business or contracts or buildings or other incidents of property. The thought seems nevertheless to have persisted that there is something peculiarly sacrosanct about the price one may charge for what he makes or sells, and that, however able to regulate other elements of manufacture or trade, with incidental effect upon price, the state is incapable of directly controlling the price itself. This view was negatived many years also. Munn v. Illinois, 94 U.S. 113. . . .

* * *

"It is clear that there is no closed class or category of businesses affected with a public interest, and the function of courts in the application of the Fifth and Fourteenth Amendments is to determine in each case whether circumstances vindicate the challenged regulation as a reasonable exertion of governmental authority or condemn it as arbitrary or discriminatory. Wolff Packing Co. v. Court of Industrial Relations, 262 U.S. 522, 535. The phrase 'affected with a public interest' can, in the nature of things, mean no more than that an industry, for adequate reason, is subject to control for the public good. In several of the decisions of this court wherein the expressions 'affected with a public interest,' and 'clothed with a public use,' have been brought forward as the criteria of the validity of price control, it has been admitted that they are not susceptible of definition and form an unsatisfactory test of the constitutionality of legislation directed at business practices or prices. These decisions must rest, finally, upon the basis that the requirements of due process were not met because the laws were found arbitrary, in their operation and effect. But there can be no doubt that upon proper occasion and by appropriate measures the state may regulate a business in any of its aspects, including the prices to be charged for the products or commodities it sells.

"So far as the requirement of due process is concerned, and in the absence of other constitutional restriction, a state is free to adopt whatever economic policy may reasonably be deemed to promote public welfare, and to enforce that policy by legislation adapted to its purpose. The courts are without authority either to declare such policy, or, when it is declared by the legislature, to override it. If the laws passed are seen to have a reasonable relation to a proper legislative purpose, and are neither arbitrary nor discriminatory, the requirements of due process are satisfied, and judicial determination to that effect renders a court functus officio. . . .

* * *

"With the wisdom of the policy adopted, with the adequacy or practicability of the law enacted to forward it, the courts are both incompetent and unauthorized to deal. The course of decision in this court exhibits a firm adherence to these principles. Times without number we have said that the Legislature is primarily the judge of the necessity of such an enactment, that every possible presumption is in favor of its validity, and that though the court may hold views inconsistent with the wisdom of the law, it may not be annulled unless palpably in excess of legislative power. . . .

* * *

"Price control, like any other form of regulation, is unconstitutional only if arbitrary, discriminatory, or demonstrably irrelevant to the policy the Legislature is free to adopt, and hence an unnecessary and unwarranted interference with individual liberty."

* * *

West Coast Hotel Co. v. Parrish
300 U.S. 379 (1937)

Mr. Chief Justice Hughes delivered the opinion of the Court, ending the doctrine of substantive due process:

This case presents the question of the constitutional validity of the minimum wage law of the State of Washington.

The Act . . . authorizes the fixing of minimum wages for women and minors. . . .

* * *

The appellant conducts a hotel. The appellee Elsie Parrish was employed as a chambermaid

and (with her husband) brought this suit to recover the difference between the wages paid her and the minimum wage fixed pursuant to the state law . . . The Supreme Court of the State . . . sustained the statute. . . .

The appellant relies upon the decision of this Court in Adkins v. Children's Hospital. . . .

* * *

[The violation of the due process clause alleged by the appellant] is deprivation of freedom of contract. What is this freedom? The Constitution does not speak of freedom of contract. It speaks of liberty and prohibits the deprivation of liberty without due process of law. . . . But the liberty safeguarded is liberty in a social organization which requires the protection of law against the evils which menace the health, safety, morals and welfare of the people. Liberty under the Constitution is thus necessarily subject to the restraints of due process, and regulation which is reasonable in relation to its subject and is adopted in the interests of the community is due process.

This essential limitation of liberty in general governs freedom of contract in particular. . . .

* * *

We think . . . that the decision in the *Adkins* Case was a departure from the true application of the principles governing the regulation by the state of the relation of employer and employed. . . .

With full recognition of the earnestness and vigor which characterize the prevailing opinion in the *Adkins* Case we find it impossible to reconcile that ruling with these well-considered declarations. What can be closer to the public interest than the health of women and their protection from unscrupulous and overreaching employers? And if the protection of women is a legitimate end of the exercise of state power, how can it be said that the requirement of the payment of a minimum wage fairly fixed in order to meet the very necessities of existence is not an admissible means to that end? . . .

* * *

There is an additional and compelling consideration which recent economic experience has brought into a strong light. The exploitation of a class of workers who are in an unequal position with respect to bargaining power and are thus relatively defenseless against the denial of a living wage is not only detrimental to their health and well being, but casts a direct burden for their support upon the community. What these workers lose in wages the taxpayers are called upon to pay. The bare cost of living must be met. We may take judicial notice of the unparalleled demands for relief which arose during the recent period of depression and still continue to an alarming extent despite the degree of economic recovery which has been achieved. It is unnecessary to cite official statistics to establish what is of common knowledge through the length and breadth of the land. While in the instant case no factual brief has been presented, there is no reason to doubt that the state of Washington has encountered the same social problem that is present elsewhere. . . .

* * *

Our conclusion is that the case of Adkins v. Children's Hospital, *supra*, should be, and it is, overruled.

JUSTICES SUTHERLAND, VAN DEVANTER, MCREYNOLDS and BUTLER dissented.

Ideas for Class Projects, Papers, or Debates

1. Compare the *Lochner* line of cases just given with the *Griswold* line of cases at the end of Section 2, Chapter Seven, "The Nature of Civil Rights." Explain why the right to freedom of contract cannot legitimately be found in the Constitution, but the right to privacy can. To put it a different way, explain the difference between the doctrine of substantive (economic) due process and the reasoning the Court used to develop the right to privacy. Alternatively, argue that the two cannot be distinguished, and anticipate the arguments of the opposing side.

2. Defend or attack the doctrine of consideration in contract law. If you choose to defend the doctrine, you may qualify it to any degree you deem appropriate, giving reasons for your qualifications. Anticipate and address opposing arguments.

3. Explain why mass contracts or standardized contracts are or are not "real" contracts. If you claim that they are not, explain the implications of your claim. If you claim that they are, explain what theory is needed to justify them.

4. Review the materials following this question. Then defend one of the following positions. As a matter of public policy (explaining which public policy), surrogate mother contracts should (a) be enforced; (b) not be enforced; (c) be illegal. Explain why the alternative you chose is better than the others.

Surrogate Mother Contracts

"A Legal, Moral, Social Nightmare"
TIME, SEPTEMBER 10, 1984

Society Seeks to Define the Problems of the Birth Revolution

Alexander Morgan Capron, a sandy-haired professor of law at Georgetown University, stood at a blackboard in a hearing room of Congress's Rayburn Office Building and began writing formulas: the symbols represented ten different ways of making babies. The fourth formula that he chalked up read X_M & Y_D by AI with Gestation M, meaning that a married woman is artificially inseminated by a male donor's sperm. The fifth formula X_D & Y_M by IVF with Gestation M, meant that the beginnings of life could be created through the uniting in a laboratory dish (in-vitro fertilization) of a woman's donated egg and a married man's sperm. Capron's final version — X_1 & Y_2 by IVF or Natural/AI w/embryo flushing with Gestation 3 and Social Parents 4 & 5 — outlined how a baby could theoretically have five different "parents."

One reason why Capron resorts to formulas is that biology is now creating concepts of birth and parenthood faster than the standard English vocabulary can define them. As Capron testified before a House science subcommittee early last month, "Many of the new reproductive possibilities remain so novel that terms are lacking to describe the human relationships they can create. For example, what does one call the woman who bears a child conceived from another woman's egg? I'm not even sure we know what to call the area under inquiry."

The answers are sometimes rich in emotional bias. "In some places, it's called 'unnatural reproduction'; in others, it's 'abnormal reproduction,'" says Lori Andrews, a research attorney for the American Bar Foundation and author of *New Conceptions*, a guide to the new reproductive techniques. "We prefer 'artificial' or 'alternative reproduction,'" she adds. As for the increasing number of children born by these methods, there is no standard term at all.

The linguistic confusion echoes in the laws and theories applied to these various new methods of having babies. To some experts it seems nonsensical for such children even to be born at a time when high birth rates and burgeoning populations represent one of the world's most challenging problems. There are other paradoxes: the new techniques of fertilization are becoming almost commonplace, but there are no federal laws to guard against the dangers of exploitation and manipulation; nor is there federal financing to provide research guidelines. The state and local laws that do exist — many of them outdated — have sprouted into thickets of illogicality and contradiction. About all they have in common are moralizing judgments and a squeamish avoidance of controversial details. "It's a legal, moral and social nightmare," says Doris J. Freed, head of the American Bar Association's family-law section committee on research. "It's going to take years of debate, legislation, trial and error to figure out how to deal with these problems." Or, as Samuel Gorovitz, a professor of philosophy at the University of Maryland, summarized it for the House subcommittee chaired by Congressman Albert Gore Jr., "We have a patchwork of laws and gaps, stigmas, deprivations, uncertainties, confusions and fears."

For example:

Artificial insemination by donor (AID), or a woman being inseminated by a donor's sperm, has been widely practiced since the 1960s and has led to about 250,000 births in the U.S. alone, but the law is only gradually accepting it. A New York court ruled in 1963 that a child born by AID was illegitimate even if the mother's husband consented; another New York court ruled the opposite a decade later. Now 25 states, including New York, have statutes governing AID babies, recognizing them as the legitimate children of the mother and her husband (providing that the husband has consented to the procedure). Elsewhere, all kinds of consequences remain unsettled, however. After a divorce, can a sterile husband deny financial responsibility for an AID baby? Conversely, can such a husband be denied visitation rights?

In-vitro fertilization (IVF) now accounts for about 100 babies in the U.S., but there are virtually no new laws to deal with this method of conception. In the wake of the 1973 U.S. Supreme Court decision legalizing abortion, however, many states passed laws forbidding or limiting "experimentation" with fetuses. Of the 25 such state laws, eleven specifically apply to embryos; doctors in some of these states fear that they might be prosecuted for carrying out IVF, particularly if the technique fails, as it does about four times out of five. And six states have laws that seem to forbid freezing an embryo, on the ground that this would constitute illegal experimentation.

Surrogate mothers have been bearing other people's children since the late 1970s, and the number of such births in the U.S. so far totals at least 100, perhaps 150, but the law here is even more ambiguous. No state has a statute specifically dealing with surrogates, but about a dozen have been considering measures ranging from permission to an outright ban. At least 24 states have old laws generally forbidding payment to a woman who gives a child up for adoption, as a surrogate mother is expected to do. Moreover, private contracts between prospective parents and surrogate mothers may not be legally binding. Thus, if a surrogate refuses to give up a baby, or if the would be parents refuse to accept it, the law offers no certain solution to the dispute.

These are only the basic complexities; the refinements are myriads. If a married couple can use a donor to help create a baby, for example, should a single woman who wants a child be allowed the same right? What about a lesbian, or a transexual or a homosexual male couple? If a surrogate mother contracts to bear another couple's child, does she have a right to smoke and drink in defiance of their wishes? Does she have a right to an abortion? And what of the baby born through such methods: Does it have a right to know its biological parents? Or even a right to inherit their property?

These are not idle flights of fancy. There have already been attempts by lesbians and transsexuals to acquire babies. And the varied fertility controversies that reach the courts are sometimes of a rending intensity. In New York City, for instance, a Florida couple named John and Doris Del Zio in 1973 became the first couple in the U.S. to attempt IVF. An infertility specialist removed an egg from Mrs. Del Zio, put it in a container and handed it to her husband, who raced across town in a taxi to deliver it to the Columbia-Presbyterian Medical Center. There, another doctor fertilized it with some of Del Zio's sperm and stored it in an incubator. The next day the hospital doctor was furiously scolded by his superior, Dr. Raymond Vande Wiele, who not only accused him of dangerous and unethical practices but also stopped the experiment entirely by unsealing the incubated container, thus killing the embryo. The couple sued the hospital and Vande Wiele and won $50,000 in damages. Yet when the hospital opened its own IVF program in 1983, Vande Wiele became its co-director.

In Michigan, Surrogate Mother Judy Stiver agreed to be artificially inseminated by Alexander Malahoff for $10,000. When the baby was born last year, it turned out to be microcephalic and mentally retarded. Malahoff insisted on blood tests that might show he was not the father. As a macabre touch, these test results were announced on Phil Donahue's TV show. They disclosed that Malahoff was indeed not the father; Stiver had had sexual intercourse with her husband at about the same time as the insemination. Now the baby is in the custody of the Stivers, and both sides are suing each other.

In Illinois, the first state to deal specifically with IVF, the legislature decided in 1979 to make any doctor who undertakes such a procedure the legal custodian of the embryo — and liable for possible prosecution under an 1877 law against child abuse. The result was that many Illinois doctors, though not specifically forbidden to perform IVF, refused to do so. The state attorney general said that most simple IVF procedures would not violate the law, so a number of doctors went ahead. Still, one couple, identified as John and Mary Smith, who have been married for nine years and have two adopted children, are challenging the Illinois attempt at regulation as unconstitutional. Their class action, due for trial in federal court in November, argues that such restrictions violate the fundamental right of "privacy," which the Supreme Court has proclaimed several times in its rulings on abortion, contraception and various aspects of procreation.

If the array of U.S. laws and regulations seems confusing, the legal wilderness abroad is totally bewildering. A group of West European justice ministers meeting in Strasbourg tried to work out some international policies on reproduction technology, but they gave up in despair. In Germany, where there are no laws either permitting or forbidding surrogate motherhood, a man in Bad Oeynhausen was fined $1,750 for advertising for a woman willing to gestate an embryo and then give the child up for adoption to a childless couple. Before he could find such a woman, he was fined because the law forbids any ads in connection with adoptions.

In Britain two years ago, Parliament established a 16-member committee of experts under Dame Mary Warnock to examine the social, ethical and legal implications of the new technology. Among its recommendations published in July: all clinics providing infertility services such as AID, IVF or egg donation should be licensed and regulated; research on embryos up to 14 days old could be permitted, also under license and regulation; but the use of surrogate mothers should be forbidden because such arrangements are "liable to moral objection." Critics on all sides did not hesitate to attack. A Roman Catholic spokesman called the practice of AID "morally unacceptable," while a newspaper columnist denounced restrictions on pregnancy as "ludicrously inconsistent." But unless such differences are settled, warned Sir John Peel, former president of the British Medical Association, society will confront "the brink of something almost like the atomic bomb."

The most striking illustration of Europe's legal confusion is the case of Corinne Parpalaix, 22, a secretary in the Marseille police department, whose husband died of cancer last year after depositing sperm in a sperm bank. Parpalaix asked for the sperm so that she could be impregnated with it, but the bank refused on the grounds that the dead man had left no instructions on what he wanted done. The press clucked; the church frowned; Parpalaix sued.

French law offered little guidance, and so the whole case rested on exquisitely philosophical arguments about what the dead man's frozen sperm really was. An organ transplant? An inheritable piece of property? State Prosecutor Yves Lesec, siding with the sperm bank, argued that it was part of the dead man's body, even though separated from that body. The dead man had a basic right to "physical integrity," the prosecutor concluded, saying in effect that his widow had no more right to his sperm than to his feet or ears. Not so, retorted Parpalaix's lawyer. The deposited sperm, he argued, implied a contract. Somewhat to the surprise of legal experts, the court last month agreed, ruling that this "secretion containing the seeds of life" should be given to Parpalaix. "I'll call him Thomas," she said of her prospective infant. "He'll be a pianist. That's what his father wanted."

There are elements of absurdity in such a controversy, and yet it derives quite directly from a broader question that is not absurd at all: When does human life begin? At the moment of conception, say many conservatives, both religious and secular. The Rev. Donald McCarthy, of the Pope John XXIII Medical-Moral Research and Education Center in St. Louis, argued sweepingly before the congressional hearings that there is "no evidence of a threshold, a starting point other than fertilization itself, for the beginning of human nature." This is a standard argument against abortion, but McCarthy used it to endow every new embryo with a panoply of civil rights. These included a right not to be frozen, a right not to be experimented on, a right not to be destroyed, even a right not to be created at all except as a consequence of "personal self-giving and conjugal love."

Neither current law nor current custom supports such an array of rights, however. On the contrary, a pregnant woman's right of decision is generally considered paramount, at least during the first three months. Even so, says Professor Maurice Mahoney of Yale's medical school, every embryo deserves a certain respect. "I see it as an individual human being," he says, "not with the same claims and rights as a newborn baby, but at least as an individual who calls upon me for some kind of protectiveness."

No case encapsulates all the ambiguities more dramatically than that of the late Mario and Elsa

Rios, a Los Angeles couple whose orphaned embryos now lie in a freezer in Melbourne, Australia. Doctors there had removed several of Mrs. Rios' eggs in 1981, then fertilized them with sperm from an anonymous donor. Some were implanted in Mrs. Rios, and the remaining two were frozen. "You must keep them for me," she said. The implant failed, and the couple later died in a plane crash in Chile. Australian laws grant no "rights" to the two frozen embryos, but though local officials are believed to have the authority to destroy them, they have refrained from doing so. A state committee of inquiry is supposed to issue a report on the whole subject of reproductive technology this week.

The creation of extra embryos raises a number of delicate problems. Aside from the question of whether they have a "right" to be implanted (most experts deny it), doctors say they are needed for research. Some even favor creating embryos deliberately for the sake of research. But what exactly is "research"? Ideally, it is some experimental treatment that will help the embryo itself. Some states — Minnesota, for example — prescribe that any experimentation must be known to be harmless. A number of authorities also believe that experimentation should be limited to the first 14 days after fertilization. There are scientists, however, who chafe at such restrictions on their research.

Beyond the argument about experimentation lies an even more touchy controversy: eugenics, the idea that the species can be improved through selective breeding. Now that it is possible to create human embryos by a process of selection among donor eggs ad sperm, is it desirable to leave that selection entirely to chance? In one sense, doctors are already applying eugenics when they screen donors for genetic defects, a standard practice that many feel should become a lot more standard. In another sense, they are engaging in eugenics when they select medical students as sperm donors, a procedure that one survey showed to be happening in 62% of artificial inseminations. Says George J. Annas, professor of health law at Boston University: "Physicians in all of these situations are . . . selecting what they consider 'superior' genes . . . They have chosen to reproduce themselves."

The institution that most nearly fulfills the dubious idea of selective breeding is the Repository for Germinal Choice, of Escondido, Calif., which announced at its opening in 1980 that it would use sperm donated by Nobel prizewinners. The repository has received the cooperation of only three such prizewinners and now relies on donors of less than Nobel stature, but Founder Robert Graham is as enthusiastic as ever. "We're proud of our results," says he of the repository's 15 children. "These kids will sail through schools. We are indicating how good human beings can have it."

Given a choice, most parents would probably prefer a bright child, but intelligence is hardly the only variable. Many sperm banks now offer prospective parents some options on what the collaborating donors look like, on the ground that it is preferable for the child to resemble its legal parents. From there it is only a short step before some parents try to choose blonds instead of brunets, or boys instead of girls. A German clinic in Essen claims that its sperm donors include "no fat men, no long ears, no hook noses . . ." "We can talk in impressive pseudoscientific terms about how we want to help society," says the Rev. Roger Shinn, professor of social ethics at New York's Union Theological Seminary, "but as long as genetic manipulation is the motive, what we would be doing is what Hitler intended to do."

There are also tricky questions posed by the financing of the new technology. Dr. John Buster of the UCLA School of Medicine has been working since 1979 to develop a technique of embryo transplants for women who are unable to conceive but able to carry a child to term. The husband's sperm is used to impregnate a woman artificially; the embryo is then flushed out and implanted in the man's wife. The first two babies to be produced by this method were born this year.

"We called the National Institutes of Health in 1980, and we were told that no money was available for this work," says Buster. "The people who make these decisions are politicians, and they have to make those decisions to remain in office. After all, infertility never killed anyone." So Buster made an alliance with Randolph Seed, a surgeon, and his brother Richard, a scientist who had experimented in cattle breeding. The Seed brothers' Chicago firm, Fertility and Genetics Research Inc., invested $500,000 in Buster's UCLA project, and they have applied for a patent on the process. Despite criticism of this arrangement by a number of doctors, Richard Seed declares, "This is a typical free-market activity. We have investors expecting to obtain a return on their money."

In such a free-for-all atmosphere, the courts have been increasingly forced to intervene. A typical case was *Syrkowski* vs. *Appleyard* in Michigan. George Syrkowski and his wife had contracted to pay Corinne Appleyard $10,000 to bear his child, but a state court refused to recognize him as the father. Detroit Circuit Court Judge Roman Gribbs ruled in 1981 that surrogate arrangements are not for a court to approve but are "matters of legislative concern." However, Michigan has no state laws regulating the hiring of surrogate mothers, an omission that Richard Fitzpatrick, a Democrat in the state legislature, has been trying to correct for three years. His latest attempt is a comprehensive proposal requiring that all births involving third parties be covered by contracts, and that the "societal parents" (*i.e.*, those who plan to rear the baby) have "all parental rights and responsibilities for a child, regardless of the condition of the child, conceived through a fertility technique." At the same time, another Michigan legislator has drafted a rival law making all surrogate parenting a crime punishable by up to 90 days in prison and a $10,000 fine for a first offense. Both legislators hope the issue will come to a vote this fall — presumably after Election Day.

Political caution about what voters want — together with the legal uncertainties about invasions of privacy — are likely to continue to inhibit government action in a field where some guidelines seem sorely needed. Congressman Gore, a Tennessean with four children aged eleven, seven, five and two, is keenly aware of the mixed feelings that the new technologies can arouse. Says he: "There is something unnatural, even violent, about a procedure that takes a newborn from its mother's arms and gives it to another by virtue of a contract. But I don't think I'm in favor of outlawing it. The touching search for children may justify a great many things that make others of us who are more fortunate uncomfortable."

A Surrogate's Story
TIME, SEPTEMBER 10, 1984

Valerie is a New Jersey mother of two boys, age two and three, whom she describes as "little monsters full of mischief." Her husband works as a truck driver, and money is tight. The family of four is living with her mother while they save for an apartment of their own. One day last March, Valerie, 23, who prefers to remain anonymous, saw the following advertisement in a local New Jersey paper. *Surrogate mother wanted. Couple unable to have child willing to pay $10,000 fee and expenses to woman to carry husband's child. Conception by artificial insemination. All replies strictly confidential.*

The advertisement made Valerie stop and think. "I had very easy pregnancies," she says, "and I didn't think it would be a problem for me to carry another child. I figured maybe I could help someone." And then there was the lure of the $10,000 fee. "The money could help pay for my children's education," she says, "or just generally to make their lives better."

The next day Valerie went for an interview at the Infertility Center of New York, a profit-making agency owned by Michigan Attorney Noel Keane, a pioneer in the controversial business of matching surrogate mothers with infertile parents. She was asked to fill out a five-page application, detailing her medical history and reasons for applying. Most applicants are "genuine, sincere, family-oriented women," says agency Administrator Donna Spiselman. The motives they list range from "I enjoy being pregnant" and an urge to "share maternal joy" to a need to alleviate guilt about a past abortion by bearing someone else's child. Valerie's application and her color photograph were added to 300 others kept in scrapbooks for prospective parents to peruse. Valerie was amazed when only a week later her application was selected, and she was asked to return to the agency to meet the couple.

Like most people who find their way to surrogate agencies, "Aaron" and "Mandy" (not their real names) had undergone years of treatment for infertility. Aaron, 36, a Yale-educated lawyer, and his advertising-executive wife, 30, had planned to have children soon after marrying in 1980. They bought a two-bedroom town house in Hoboken, N.J., in a neighborhood that Aaron describes as being "full of babies." But after three years of tests, it became painfully clear that there was little hope of having the child they longed for. They considered adoption, but were discouraged by the long waiting lists at American agencies and the expense and complexity of foreign adoptions. Then, to Aaron's surprise, Mandy suggested that they try a surrogate.

Their first choice from the Manhattan agency failed her mandatory psychological test, which found her to be too emotionally unstable. Valerie, who was Aaron and Mandy's second choice, passed without a hitch. A vivacious woman who is an avid reader, she more than met the couple's demands for a surrogate who was "reasonably pretty," did not smoke or drink heavily and had no family history of genetic disease. Says Aaron: "We were particularly pleased that she asked us questions to find out whether we really want this child."

At first, Valerie's husband had some reservations about the arrangement, but, she says, he ultimately supported it "100%." Valerie is not concerned about what her neighbors might think because the family is planning to move after the birth. Nor does she believe that her children will be troubled by the arrangement because, she says, they are too young to understand. And although her parents are being deprived of another grandchild, they have raised no objections.

For their part, Aaron and Mandy have agreed to pay Valerie $10,000 to be kept in an escrow account until the child is in their legal custody. In addition, they have paid an agency fee of $7,500 and are responsible for up to $4,000 in doctors' fees, lab tests, legal costs, maternity clothes and other expenses. In April, Valerie became pregnant after just one insemination with Aaron's sperm. Mandy says she was speechless with joy when she heard the news.

Relationships between surrogate mothers and their employers vary widely. At the National Center for Surrogate Parenting, an agency in Chevy Chase, Md., the two parties never meet. At the opposite extreme is the case of Marilyn Johnston, 31, of Detroit. Johnston and the couple who hired her became so close during her pregnancy that they named their daughter after her. She continues to make occasional visits to see the child she bore and says, "I feel like a loving aunt to her."

Not all surrogate arrangements work so well. Some women have refused to give up the child they carried for nine months. As a lawyer, Aaron is aware that the contract he signed with Valerie would not hold up in court, should she decide to back out of it. "But I'm a romantic," he says. "I have always felt that the real binding force was not paper but human commitment." Valerie, whose pregnancy is just beginning to show, says she is "conditioning" herself not to become too attached to the baby. "It is not my husband's child," she says, "so I don't have the feeling behind it as if it were ours." She does not plan to see the infant after it is born, but, she admits, "I might like to see a picture once in a while."

'Baby M' Contract Illegal, Court in New Jersey Rules
LEXINGTON (KENTUCKY) *HERALD-LEADER*,
FEBRUARY 4, 1988

TRENTON, N.J. — Paying a woman to have a baby amounts to illegal baby-selling, the state Supreme Court ruled yesterday in the landmark "Baby M" case. But it allowed Melissa Elizabeth Stern, the child at the center of the case, to remain with her father, William Stern, and his wife, Elizabeth.

The decision is legally binding only in New Jersey. But experts say it is likely to imperil the commercial practice of surrogate motherhood.

Because it is the nation's first ruling on surrogate parenthood by a state's highest court, it is also expected to offer guidance to legislators and lower-court judges grappling with the issue in other states.

"The unfortunate events that have unfolded illustrate that its unregulated use can bring suffering to all involved," the justices said.

The 7–0 opinion upheld the custody decision but overturned all other aspects of the ruling in the case last March by Superior Court Judge Harvey R. Sorkow. The ruling restored the parental rights of the baby's mother, Mary Beth Whitehead-Gould. That means she can seek a new custody hearing.

The justices also threw out Sorkow's order of almost a year ago allowing Elizabeth Stern to adopt the child, now 22 months old.

Having restored Mrs. Whitehead-Gould's parental rights, they also ordered a new court hearing to set rules for her visits with Melissa. She is now allowed to see the girl two hours a week in a Bergen County youth shelter in Hackensack.

"We thus restore the surrogate as the mother of the child," the court said. "She is not only the natural mother, but also the legal mother, and is not to be penalized one iota because of the surrogate contract."

The Sterns, through their attorney, expressed surprise at the decision. At a news conference in Livingston, N.J., the attorney, Gary N. Skoloff, said: "We were pleased that the Supreme Court affirmed the trial judge's decision on custody. We were not pleased that the Supreme Court reversed the trial court's decision on parental rights."

Mrs. Whitehead-Gould, who appeared at a news conference in Red Bank, N.J., said she had not expected to win custody of the child. But she said she was grateful that the court had reinstated her parental rights, "and that I'll be able to continue to see my daughter."

In its 95-page opinion, written by Chief Justice Robert N. Wilentz, the court found that the contract between the Sterns and Mrs. Whitehead-Gould violated the state's adoption laws because it involved a payment for the child. A $10,000 fee was specified in Mrs. Whitehead-Gould's February 1985 contract with the Sterns.

"This is the sale of a child, or, at the very least, the sale of a mother's right to her child, the only mitigating factor being that one of the purchasers is the father," the court said.

The court did not prohibit women from freely becoming surrogates as volunteers, as long as no money is paid directly to the surrogate mother and as long as she is allowed to revoke her decision to surrender the baby.

The court said a mother's parental rights could be ended only if she voluntarily surrendered her child to an approved adoption agency or if she was proved unfit because of abandonment or substantial neglect of the child.

The fact that Mrs. Whitehead-Gould originally agreed to provisions of the contract and signed it was irrelevant, the court said.

The justices said awarding custody to Stern was valid for the baby's "best interests."

"The Sterns promise a secure home, with an understanding relationship that allows nurturing and independent growth to develop together," Wilentz said.

Panel OKs Bill to Outlaw Surrogate Parenthood
LEXINGTON (KENTUCKY) *HERALD LEADER*,
FEBRUARY 4, 1988

FRANKFORT — A bill to outlaw surrogate parenthood for pay was approved by a Senate committee yesterday. But the doctor who pioneered the practice said the bill would not stop it.

Senate Bill 4, sponsored by Republican Joe Lane Travis of Glasgow, would declare the hiring of a woman to bear a child for another couple contrary to public policy.

The Kentucky Supreme Court ruled in February 1986 that surrogate parenthood was legal in the state because the General Assembly had not outlawed it.

Travis' bill, approved by the Judiciary-Civil Committee, would render void any contract involving artificial insemination that resulted in termination of parental rights. The bill, expected to go before the full Senate, would not impose a penalty for violations.

Dr. Richard Levin, who made national headlines with his Surrogate Parenting Associates Inc. in Louisville, said his contracts did not mention termination of parental rights and were never claimed to be enforceable.

He also said the committee was underestimating the determination of some infertile couples to have children.

In an interview later, Levin said his contracts between surrogates and the couples who hire them were merely "a statement of facts" and did not spell out legal rights.

CHAPTER FOUR

The Nature of Property and the Value of Justice

Like the law of contracts, property law is private law, concerned with facilitating the interactions of individuals. Property law enables individuals peacefully to acquire, keep, transfer, or dispose of virtually every kind of thing that has value. As with contracts, this would be difficult to accomplish without the guarantee of law. Presumably, without the protection of law, property would be reduced to little more than the possession of goods, and even possession would hardly be secure. On the other hand, some reformers and philosophers have argued that property law simply protects the status quo; that is, it protects the rich from the poor. Whether it must do that is open to question. It has been both argued and assumed that private property necessarily institutionalizes inequality. You may recall that assumption expressed in some of the contracts cases (especially *Coppage* v. *Kansas*) in Chapter Three. Whether property law should do that, whether it is justified in doing so, and to what extent are questions we will weigh in this chapter.

Property law is also common law. Property law developed through the common law system (at least in Anglo-American law). To find out what the law requires you must look to the opinions of the courts. In the United States the body of law has been summarized and explained in treatises and restatements, which are useful guides and aids to understanding. But the legal authority for property law is the body of court opinion that has accumulated over the years through the cases of the common law. It is important to note that this is in contrast to statutory law, such as criminal law. For one thing, this means that the requirements of property law are not determined by majority rule or by the elected representatives of the people, although, presumably, they could be if we took it upon ourselves to revise the law and make it statutory. What then justifies property law? Whatever justifies common law. Common law is not democratic, and it is not primarily concerned with the common good. Its focus, rather, is individual rights and transactions. Common law is, however, assumed to embody the general standards of the society and the moral views of right-thinking citizens. Decide for yourself how well it does this or whether there is a better way to do it. In any case, property law is a basic example of common law (as are contract and tort law).

What exactly is property? The idea of property is unreflectively associated with land or goods, in other words, with *things*. I say to you that my car, my house, or my land is my property, and quite naturally you think of the property as the car, the house, or the land itself. But, in fact, that notion is entirely inadequate to account for the law of property. Consider the sorts of things that can be property. Discoveries can be property. Businesses can be property. Reputations can be property. Ideas can be property. The idea for a song or a book or an invention can be property, particularly if it is copyrighted or patented.

Determining what that amounts to in law can be complicated. An idea for an invention, for example, must be considered a new and separate idea in order to qualify for a patent. But when is an idea new and when is it just a modification of an old idea? How different does an idea have to be to be considered new and separate? We will ignore these difficulties here, for even if we approach the issue simplistically, we will see that property is not a concrete object as such.

Suppose you write a song and you copyright it: You apply to the state for official recognition that the song is your property. What then do you have? You have a set of rights or entitlements attached to your song that no one else has or can obtain without your permission. You could, if you wanted to, keep the song for yourself and not let anyone else have it or use it, which is to say, see it or hear it. You could destroy the song if you decided you never wanted anyone to hear it. Or you could transfer some of your rights in the song to someone else, a publisher or a producer, say. In exchange for certain rights — such as the right to receive income from selling the song — a producer might undertake the expense of reproducing and marketing the song. Then both you and the producer would have certain property rights in the song.

After the song goes on sale, I go to the store and buy a copy of it. Now I own a copy of your song. My copy of the song is my property, and that means simply that I have certain rights that apply to my copy. I can use it, give it away, or burn it if I want to. But I cannot reproduce and sell the song without your permission. Why not? Because I do not own the song itself. You and your producer own that. I own only a copy. What is important about property, then, is not the thing itself so much as the relationships, or the rights and duties, that hold between the owner and everyone else with regard to that thing. Black's *Law Dictionary* defines property as

> that which belongs exclusively to one. In the strict legal sense, an aggregate of rights which are guaranteed and protected by the government. . . . The term is said to extend to every species of valuable right and interest. More specifically, ownership; the unrestricted and exclusive right to a thing; the right to dispose of a thing in every legal way, to possess it, to use it, and to exclude every one else from interfering with it. . . . The word is also commonly used to denote everything which is the subject of ownership, . . . everything that has an exchangeable value or which goes to make up wealth or estate. . . . Property embraces everything which is or may be the subject of ownership.

A number of theorists argue that property is entirely a legal concept. Without law there would be no property. Others claim that property is a moral notion that follows from certain conceptions of rights and justice. From either view it is clear that property has more to do with human rights, relationships, and interactions than with things in and of themselves. In the selections that follow we will examine the concept of property and consider what it has to do with distributive justice and rights.

As a starting point consider this basic proposition: Property is the object of ownership, or property is something one owns. That much, at least, should be agreeable to anyone, and it puts our inquiry into a certain framework. Namely, it focuses on the relationship between the owner and the thing owned.

But what does that statement mean? In the first selection, A. M. Honoré discusses the notion of ownership as such. If you own something, does that mean simply you have the right to use the item, to keep it from others, to give it away, to sell it, to destroy it, to bequeath it to your descendants? To be an owner must you have all these rights or only some? Does your answer vary depending on what the owned item is, on how you acquired it, or on whether anyone else has any of this item, or need any?

Another set of questions focuses on the justification of private property. What justifies the recognition of private property at all? Why have it? Why not hold all property in common? Private property, it can be argued, is a social institution that foments greed, selfishness, egotism, and alienation. That is not an implausible claim. Suppose it is true. What good is accomplished by private property that could offset such evils? Some philosophers and reformers have argued that private property should be abolished. Karl Marx and Henry George, among others, say that private property causes inequality, injustice, and social problems like poverty and unemployment. In the face of such criticism the institution of private property certainly requires justification.

John Locke sets out the classic justification for private property, which has been highly influential in Anglo-American law and politics. According to Locke, there is a natural right to private property that stands alongside natural rights to life and liberty. What does it mean to claim that something is a natural right? Is it an assumption or a conclusion? Is it the foundation or premise upon which argumentation is based, or is it the result or conclusion to which argumentation leads? Your answer might vary according to whose theory you are considering. What, if any, argument does Locke give for the claim that private property is a natural right? What follows from his view? According to Locke, any person is justified in acquiring private property so long as he leaves "as much and as good for others." This is often called the *Lockean proviso*. Would Locke's view work without it? If the Lockean proviso is taken seriously, what, if anything, follows from it for a modern society? Can Locke's theory justify private property in a modern world?

John Stuart Mill uses a different justification for private property, namely, a utilitarian one. According to Mill, private property is justified so long as the common good is promoted by its existence; or, to use a utilitarian slogan, it is justified if it produces the greatest good for the greatest number of people. Is this a more plausible justification for modern property law than the natural rights view? Does Mill's view provide better answers to the questions we raised about the possible ill effects of private property? He clearly does not address Locke's contentions. Indeed, the major objection to utilitarian theory is that it insufficiently protects individual rights. On the other hand, the benefit of a utilitarian approach is that it naturally accommodates the problem of balancing competing interests. Clearly, so long as human beings live together in societies, individual or private rights must be balanced, to some extent, against public needs. Is there any way a natural rights theory can handle this problem? Perhaps Locke's proviso does that. Is one view more effective than the other or more plausible or better justified? Mill argues for some stringent limits on rights of ownership. Are his arguments justified on utilitarian grounds? What are the major objections to his view? The cases at the end of the chapter present some modern problems generated by the conflict between private property rights and claims of public interest.

There are also deep philosophical divisions over what constitutes a just distribution of property. The problem is much like that encountered in the regulation or limitation of the right to contract. In a society committed to values of freedom and individualism on the one hand and equality and social welfare on the other, how are the two sides of this commitment equation to be balanced where the advancement or protection of one side will necessarily be at the expense of the other? There are several ways to deal with the problem. It is possible to deny the conflict by defining either value in such a way that it does not conflict with the other. Many philosophers have used this approach. Another way is to rank the values. If one is more fundamental than the other, the more basic value should be protected when the two conflict. A third possibility is to balance the two values in terms of a third consideration. The third consideration could be another value (such as justice or the common good) or a moral theory (such as utilitarianism or Kantianism) or a political or economic commitment (such as capitalism or socialism).

Marx provides the classical account of the communist approach. Notice the values implicit in his view. Although we do not have space here to consider the Marxist perspective in detail, we may note that Marxists are concerned with the injustice and demoralization arising from entrenched inequality that they believe results from a capitalistic economic system. The Marxist solution is a centrally planned economy based on the common ownership of the means of production. Marxism does not abolish all private property, but only the private ownership of the means of production.

Henry George suggests a solution to the problem of unequal property distribution that is quite different from the Marxist view. George argues that the problems of poverty and unemployment result from the private ownership of land, and he therefore proposes as a solution to both problems the common ownership of land. Both Marx and George were concerned with social problems that they believed were caused by certain forms of private property. Decide for yourself what the connection is between such problems of social injustice and the ownership of private property. If you decide there is a connection, then consider what, if anything, that implies about the institution of private ownership.

In the next selection Robert Nozick articulates a modern defense of the classical liberal — that is, the libertarian or Lockean — view of property that challenges any proposal to "redistribute" goods. There is no such thing as distributive justice, he argues, because in fact there is no unowned pot of wealth to be distributed. All property belongs to people. Therefore, theories, like those of Marx and of George, that advocate redistributing property according to a principle or pattern is supposed to promote good consequences are really advocating taking property away from people who own it and giving it to those who don't. But people have rights to keep what they own so long as they did not violate another person's right in acquiring their property. Redistribution of property, then, involves the violation of a basic natural right. Furthermore, Nozick argues, free enterprise and exchange will always produce inequality, so any system of redistribution of goods intended to equalize wealth will require the constant and continual interference of government in the private lives of citizens — in other words, the impairment of freedom. Thus, Nozick presents the basic conflict referred to earlier in this introduction. Like the Supreme Court in *Coppage* v. *Kansas*, he argues that equality can be promoted only at the expense of freedom. And since freedom is a fundamental right, equality cannot be promoted. Justice in the form of distribution is not at issue, Nozick contends.

Does Nozick's view justify the situation produced by the industrial revolution in eighteenth-century England that Marx objected to? Does it justify the situation produced by recession in the United States that George was addressing? If not, why not? If so, is that an objection to any part of Nozick's argument?

In the final selection, A. M. Honoré defends private property but argues against Nozick's view of it. The basic point of debate is whether justice in ownership can be evaluated by focusing on individual transactions alone or whether the inclusion of social considerations is necessary. What is the relationship between private property rights and economic equality? Can you be committed to both? Nozick says no. Honoré, however, argues that the possibility of such a commitment depends on the scope of the right. Is private property necessarily a total, exclusive, and indefeasible set of rights? Must it be all or nothing? Nozick assumes without argument that it is. But Honoré argues that such a position ignores the social benefits received from the group by all individuals in it. Once social benefits are recognized, he maintains, private property can be limited accordingly. Therefore, absolute and unqualified rights in private property cannot be assumed.

Furthermore, Honoré points out, legal systems have in fact always limited private property rights. Nozick ignores legal considerations such as lapse of title, eminent domain, and compulsory acquisition, which are and always have been part of the Western liberal legal tradition. Why reproduce some legal factors and not others? In particular, why select only those factors that protect private ownership and not those that limit it? Honoré raises many doubts about Nozick's particular conception of private property, but he defends the institution of private property in general. If Honoré, like Mill, is right, private property is justified, but it can be limited by other rights or values. Some of the writers in this chapter offer rationales for determining how these rights and values should be ordered. Assess their arguments as you consider the relation among freedom, social responsibility, economic inequality, and private property. These are the elements of distributive justice.

Notes and Questions

A. M. HONORÉ, "Ownership"

1. Property is something one owns. But what does it mean to own something? A. M. Honoré undertakes to analyze the elements of ownership, specifying first that it is the liberal concept of full ownership that he means to examine. How does he define the concept provisionally? What, if any, qualifications does he place on the universality of the concept? Do all cultures use the concept the same way? Do most?

2. Honoré points out first that the foundation of the very idea of property is the right of possession. What is the difference between the right of possession and mere possession? What are the two aspects of this right noted by Honoré? What legal remedies follow necessarily from the right?

3. The basic idea of exclusive or ultimate control implies the rest of the property rights set out by Honoré, in the sense that they follow naturally from the idea of exclusive control itself. What are these other rights or incidents of property? Notice that what Honoré calls the incident of transmissibility and the incident of the absence of term are also rights, as is the ultimate residuary character of property. You need to understand these different elements to understand the nature of property.

4. Despite the importance of the characteristic rights of property Honoré lists, the exact nature of these rights is hard to pin down. Certainly all of them together are sufficient for the liberal concept of full ownership. Yet it is not clear whether any of them are necessary conditions. For example, you could sell, lease, or even give away rights 1–4 and still be the owner of a certain piece of property so long as you kept right 5 or 11. Does ownership, then, come down to right 5 or 11, or both, perhaps? They are not without restriction. For example, you can own something and not have the right to destroy it, or in some societies, to bequeath it. What does that leave? Is there any element that is always necessary or sufficient for ownership?

5. If you want to narrow or shorten the list of basic elements, you might consider whether rights 6, 7, and 8 are contained within right 5 or 11. Are they simply further specifications of what it means to have the ultimate power of disposition or transfer? Do they really add anything new or simply spell out the right to capital and/or the residuary character of property? What is the relation, if any, between rights 5 and 11?

6. Notice that incidents 9 and 10 are not rights but limits. All property rights are limited. Honoré notes, both in this article and elsewhere, that for accuracy it is important to recognize the limits placed on property rights. Even though the liberal concept of full ownership is arguably the strongest concept of property in the world, Honoré points out, some libertarian writers have mistakenly characterized it as stronger than it is by failing to recognize the natural and traditional limits of the concept. What limits does Honoré mention in this article?

Ownership

A. M. HONORÉ

Ownership is one of the characteristic institutions of human society. A people to whom ownership was unknown, or who accorded it a minor place in their arrangements, who meant by *meum* and *tuum* no more than 'what I (or you) presently hold' would live in a world that is not our world. Yet to see why their world would be different, and to assess the plausibility of vaguely conceived schemes to replace 'ownership' by 'public administration', or of vaguely stated claims that the importance of ownership has declined or its character changed in the twentieth century, we need first to have a clear idea of what ownership is.

I propose, therefore, to begin by giving an account of the standard incidents of ownership: *i.e.* those legal rights, duties and other incidents which apply, in the ordinary case, to the person who has the greatest interest in a thing admitted by a mature legal system. To do so will be to analyse the concept of ownership, by which I mean the 'liberal' concept of 'full' individual ownership, rather than any more restricted notion to which the same label may be attached in certain contexts. . . .

If ownership is provisionally defined as the *greatest possible interest in a thing which a mature system of law recognizes*, then it follows that, since all mature systems admit the existence of 'interests' in 'things', all mature systems have, in a sense, a concept of ownership. Indeed, even primitive systems, like that of the Trobriand islanders, have rules by which certain persons, such as the 'owners' of canoes, have greater interests in certain things than anyone else.

For mature legal systems it is possible to make a larger claim. In them certain important legal incidents are found, which are common to different systems. If it were not so, 'He owns that umbrella', said in a purely English context, would mean something different from 'He owns that umbrella'. profferred as a translation of 'Ce parapluie est à lui'. Yet, as we know, they mean the same. There is indeed, a substantial similarity in the position of one who 'owns' an umbrella in England, France, Russia, China, and any other modern country one may care to mention. Everywhere the 'owner' can, in the simple uncomplicated case, in which no other person has an interest in the thing, use it, stop others using it, lend it, sell it or leave it by will. Nowhere may he use it to poke his neighbour in the ribs or to knock over his vase. Ownership, *dominium, propriété, Eigentum* and similar words stand not merely for the greatest interest in things in particular systems but for a type of interest with common features transcending particular systems. It must surely be important to know what these common features are?

* * *

I now list what appear to be the standard incidents of ownership. They may be regarded as necessary ingredients in the notion of ownership, in the sense that, if a system did not admit them, and did not provide for them to be united in a single person, we would conclude that it did not know the liberal concept of ownership, though it might still have a modified version of ownership, either of a primitive or sophisticated sort. But the listed incidents are not individually necessary, though they may be together sufficient, conditions for the person of inherence to be designated 'owner' of a particular thing in a given system. As we have seen, the use of 'owner' will extend to cases in which not all the listed incidents are present.

Ownership comprises the right to possess, the right to use, the right to manage, the right to the income of the thing, the right to the capital, the right to security, the rights or incidents of transmissibility and absence of term, the prohibition of harmful use, liability to execution, and the incident of residuarity: this makes eleven leading incidents. Obviously, there are alternative ways of classifying the incidents; moreover, it is fashionable to speak of ownership as if it were just a bundle of rights, in which case at least two items in the list would have to be omitted.

No doubt the concentration in the same person of the right (liberty) of using as one wishes, the right to exclude others, the power of alienating and an immunity from expropriation is a cardinal feature of the institution. Yet it would be a distortion — and one of which the eighteenth century, with its over-emphasis on subjective rights, was patently guilty — to speak as if this concentration of patiently garnered rights was the only legally or socially important characteristic of the owner's position. The present analysis, by emphasizing that the owner is subject to characteristic prohibitions and limitations, and that ownership comprises at least one important incident independent of the owner's choice, is an attempt to redress the balance.

(1) The Right to Possess

The right to possess, *viz.* to have exclusive physical control of a thing, or to have such control as the nature of the thing admits, is the foundation on which the whole superstructure of ownership rests. It may be divided into two aspects, the right (claim) to be put in exclusive control of a thing and the right to remain in control, *viz.* the claim that others should not without permission, interfere. Unless a legal system provides some rules and procedures for attaining these ends it cannot be said to protect ownership.

It is of the essence of the right to possess that it is *in rem* in the sense of availing against persons generally. This does not, of course, mean that an owner is necessarily entitled to exclude everyone from his property. We happily speak of the ownership of land, yet a largish number of officials have the right of entering on private land without the owner's consent, for some limited period and purpose. On the other hand, a general licence so to enter on the 'property' of others would put an end to the institution of landowning as we now know it.

The protection of the right to possess (still using 'possess' in the convenient, though over-simple, sense of 'have exclusive physical control') should be sharply marked off from the protection of mere present possession. To exclude others from what one presently holds is an instinct found in babies and even, as Holmes points out, in animals, of which the seal gives a striking example. To sustain this instinct by legal rules is to protect possession but not, as such, to protect the right to possess and so not to protect ownership. If dispossession without the possessor's consent is, in general, forbidden, the possessor is given a right *in rem* valid against persons generally, to remain undisturbed, but he has no *right to possess in rem* unless he is entitled to recover from persons generally what he has lost or had taken from him, and to obtain from them what is due to him but not yet handed over. . . .

* * *

To have worked out the notion of 'having a right to' as distinct from merely 'having', or, if that is too subjective a way of putting it, of rules allocating things to people as opposed to rules merely forbidding forcible taking, was a major intellectual achievement. Without it society would have been impossible. Yet the distinction is apt to be overlooked by English lawyers, who are accustomed to the rule that every adverse possession is a root of title, *i.e.* gives rise to a right to possess, or at least that '*de facto* possession is *prima facie* evidence of seisin in fee and right to possession'.

The owner, then, has characteristically a battery of remedies in order to obtain, keep and, if necessary, get back the thing owned. Remedies such as the actions for ejectment and wrongful detention and the *vindicatio* are designed to enable the plaintiff either to obtain or to get back a thing, or at least to put some pressure on the defendant to hand it over. Others, such as the actions for trespass to land and goods, the Roman possessory interdicts and their modern counterparts are primarily directed towards enabling a present possessor to keep possession. Few of the remedies mentioned are confined to the owner; most of them are available also to persons with a right to possess falling short of ownership, and some to mere possessors. Conversely, there will be cases in which they are not available to the owner, for instance because he has voluntarily parted with possession for a temporary purpose, as by hiring the thing out. The availability of such remedies is clearly not a necessary and sufficient condition of owning a thing; what is necessary, in order that there may be ownership of things at all, is that such remedies shall be available to the owner in the usual case in which no other person has a right to exclude him from the thing.

(2) The Right to Use

The present incident and the next two overlap. On a wide interpretation of 'use', management and income fall within use. On a narrow interpretation, 'use' refers to the owner's personal use and enjoyment of the thing owned. On this interpretation it excludes management and income.

The right (liberty) to use at one's discretion has rightly been recognized as a cardinal feature of ownership, and the fact that, as we shall see, certain limitations on use also fall within the standard incidents of ownership does not detract from its importance, since the standard limitations are, in general, rather precisely defined, while the permissible types of use constitute an open list.

(3) The Right to Manage

The right to manage is the right to decide how and by whom the thing owned shall be used. This right depends, legally, on a cluster of powers, chiefly powers of licensing acts which would otherwise be unlawful and powers of contracting: the power to admit others to one's land, to permit others to use one's things, to define the limits of such permission, and to contract effectively in regard to the use (in the literal sense) and exploitation of the thing owned. An owner may not merely sit in his own deck chair but may validly license others to sit in it, lend it, impose conditions on the borrower, direct how it is to be painted or cleaned, contract for it to be mended in a particular way. This is the sphere of management in relation to a simple object like a deck chair. When we consider more complex cases, like the ownership of a business, the complex of powers which make up the right to manage seems still more prominent. The power to direct how resources are to be used and exploited is one of the cardinal types of economic and political power; the owner's legal powers of management are one, but only one possible basis for it. Many observers have drawn attention to the growth of managerial power divorced from legal ownership; in such cases it may be that we should speak of split ownership or redefine our notion of the thing owned. This does not affect the fact that the right to manage is an important element in the notion of ownership; indeed, the fact that we feel doubts in these cases whether the 'legal owner' *really* owns is a testimony to its importance.

* * *

(4) The Right to the Income

To use or occupy a thing may be regarded as the simplest way of deriving an income from it, of enjoying it. It is, for instance, expressly contemplated by the English income tax legislation that the rent-free use or occupation of a house is a form of income, and only the inconvenience of assessing and collecting the tax presumably prevents the extension of this principle to movables.

Income in the more ordinary sense (fruits, rents, profits) may be thought of as a surrogate of use, a benefit derived from forgoing personal use of a thing and allowing others to use it for reward; as a reward for work done in exploiting the thing; or as the brute product of a thing, made by nature or by other persons. Obviously the line to be drawn between the earned and unearned income from a thing cannot be firmly drawn.

* * *

(5) The Right to the Capital

The right to the capital consists in the power to alienate the thing and the liberty to consume, waste or destroy the whole or part of it: clearly it has an important economic aspect. The latter liberty need not be regarded as unrestricted; but a general provision requiring things to be conserved in the public interest, so far as not consumed by use in the ordinary way, would perhaps be inconsistent with the liberal idea of ownership. . . .

An owner normally has both the power of disposition and the power of transferring title. Disposition on death is not permitted in many primitive societies but seems to form an essential element in the mature notion of ownership. The tenacity of the right of testation once it has been recognized is shown by the Soviet experience. The earliest writers were hostile to inheritance, but gradually Soviet law has come to admit that citizens may dispose freely of their 'personal property' on death, subject to limits not unlike those known elsewhere.

(6) The Right to Security

An important aspect of the owner's position is that he should be able to look forward to remaining owner indefinitely if he so chooses and he remains solvent. His right to do so may be called the right to security. Legally, this is in effect an immunity from expropriation, based on rules which provide that, apart from bankruptcy and execution for debt, the transmission of ownership is consensual.

However, a general right to security, availing against others, is consistent with the existence of a power to expropriate or divest in the state or public authorities. From the point of view of security of property, it is important that when expropriation takes place, adequate compensation should be paid; but a general power to expropriate subject to paying compensation would be fatal to the institution of ownership as we know it. Holmes' paradox, that where specific restitution of goods is not a normal remedy, expropriation and wrongful conversion are equivalent, obscures the vital distinction between acts which a legal system permits as rightful and those which it reprobates as wrongful: but if wrongful conversion were general and went unchecked, ownership as we know it would disappear, though damages were regularly paid.

In some systems, as (*semble*) English law, a private individual may destroy another's property without compensation when this is necessary in order to protect his own person or property from a greater danger. Such a rule is consistent with security of property only because of its exceptional character. Again, the state's (or local authority's) power of expropriation is usually limited to certain classes of thing and certain limited purposes. A general power to expropriate any property for any purpose would be inconsistent with the institution of ownership. If, under such a system, compensation were regularly paid, we might say either that ownership was not recognized in that system, or that money alone could be owned, 'money' here meaning a strictly fungible claim on the resources of the community. As we shall see, 'ownership' of such claims is not identical with the ownership of material objects and simple claims.

(7) The Incident of Transmissibility

It is often said that one of the main characteristics of the owner's interest is its 'duration'. In England, at least, the doctrine of estates made lawyers familiar with the notion of the 'duration' of an interest and Maitland, in a luminous metaphor, spoke of estates as 'projected upon the plane of time'.

Yet this notion is by no means as simple as it seems. What is called 'unlimited' duration (*perpétuité*) comprises at least two elements (i) that the interest can be transmitted to the holder's successors and so on *ad infinitum* (The fact that in medieval land law all interests were considered 'temporary' is one reason why the terminology of ownership failed to take root, with consequences which have endured long after the cause has disappeared); (ii) that it is not certain to determine at a future date. These two elements may be called 'transmissibility' and 'absence of term' respectively. We are here concerned with the former.

No one, as Austin points out, can enjoy a thing after he is dead (except vicariously) so that, in a sense, no interest can outlast death. But an interest which is transmissible to the holder's successors (persons designated by or closely related to the holder who obtain the property after him) is more valuable than one which stops with his death. This is so both because on alienation the alienee or, if transmissibility is generally recognized, the alienee's successors, are thereby enabled to enjoy the thing after the alienor's death so that a better price can be obtained for the thing, and because, even if alienation were not recognized, the present holder would by the very fact of transmissibility be dispensed *pro tanto* from making provision for his intestate heirs. Hence, for example, the moment when the tenant in fee acquired a heritable (though not yet fully alienable) right was a crucial moment in the evolution of the fee simple. Heritability by the state would not, of course, amount to transmissibility in the present sense: it is assumed that the transmission is in some sense *advantageous* to the transmitter.

Transmissibility can, of course, be admitted, yet stop short at the first, second or third generation of transmittees. The owner's interest is characterized by *indefinite* transmissibility, no limit being placed on the possible number of transmissions, though the nature of the thing may well limit the actual number.

In deference to the conventional view that the exercise of a right must depend on the choice of the holder, I have refrained from calling transmissibility a right. It is, however, clearly something in which the holder has an economic interest, and it may be that the notion of a right requires revision in order to take account of incidents not depending on the holder's choice which are nevertheless of value to him.

(8) The Incident of Absence of Term

This is the second part of what is vaguely called 'duration'. The rules of a legal system usually seem to provide for determinate, indeterminate and determinable interests. The first are certain to determine at a future date or on the occurrence of a future event which is certain to occur. In this class come leases for however long a term, copyrights, etc. Indeterminate interests are those, such as ownership and easements, to which no term is set. Should the holder live for ever, he would, in the ordinary way, be able to continue in the enjoyment of them for ever. Since human beings are mortal, he will in practice only be able to enjoy them for a limited period, after which the fate of his interest depends on its transmissibility. Again, since human beings are mortal, interests for life, whether of the holder or another, must be regarded as determinate. The notion of an indeterminate interest, in the full sense, therefore requires the notion of transmissibility, but if the latter were not recognized, there would still be value to the holder in the fact that his interest was not due to determine on a fixed date or on the occurrence of some contingency, like a general election, which is certain to occur sooner or later.

*   *   *

(9) The Prohibition of Harmful Use

An owner's liberty to use and manage the thing owned as he chooses is in mature systems of law, as in primitive systems, subject to the condition that uses harmful to other members of society are forbidden. There may, indeed, be much dispute over what is to count as 'harm' and to what extent give and take demands that minor inconvenience between neighbours shall be tolerated. Nevertheless, at least for material objects, one can always point to abuses which a legal system will not allow.

I may use my car freely but not in order to run my neighbour down, or to demolish his gate, or even to go on his land if he protests; nor may I drive uninsured. I may build on my land as I choose, but not in such a way that my building collapses on my neighbour's land. I may let off fireworks on Guy Fawkes night, but not in such a way as to set fire to my neighbour's house. These and similar limitations on the use of things are so familiar and so obviously essential to the existence of an orderly community that they are not often thought of as incidents of ownership; yet, without them 'ownership' would be a destructive force.

(10) Liability to Execution

Of a somewhat similar character is the liability of the owner's interest to be taken away from him for debt, either by execution of a judgment debt or on insolvency. Without such a general liability the growth of credit would be impeded and ownership would, again, be an instrument by which the owner could defraud his creditors. This incident, therefore, which may be called *executability*, seems to constitute one of the standard ingredients of the liberal idea of ownership.

*   *   *

(11) Residuary Character

A legal system might recognize interests in things less than ownership and might have a rule that, on the determination of such interests, the rights in question lapsed and could be exercised by no one, or by the first person to exercise them after their lapse. There might be leases and easements; yet, on their extinction, no one would be entitled to exercise rights similar to those of the former lessee or of the holder of the easement. This would be unlike any system known to us and I think we should be driven to say that in such a system the institution of ownership did not extend to any thing in which limited interests existed. In such things there would, paradoxically, be interests less than ownership but no ownership.

This fantasy is intended to bring out the point that it is characteristic of ownership that an owner has a residuary right in the thing owned. In practice, legal systems have rules providing that on the lapse of an interest rights, including liberties, analogous to the rights formerly vested in the holder of the interest, vest in or are exercisable by someone else, who may be said to acquire the 'corresponding rights'. Of course, the 'corresponding rights' are not the same rights as were formerly vested in the holder of the interest. The easement holder had a right to exclude the owner; now the owner has a right to exclude the easement holder. The latter right is not identical with, but corresponds to, the former.

It is true that corresponding rights do not always arise when an interest is determined. Sometimes, when ownership is abandoned, no corresponding right vests in another; the thing is simply *res derelicta*. Sometimes, on the other hand, when ownership is abandoned, a new ownership vests in the state, as is the case in South Africa when land has been abandoned.

It seems, however, a safe generalization that, whenever an interest less than ownership terminates, legal systems always provide for corresponding rights to vest in another. When easements terminate, the 'owner' can exercise the corresponding rights, and when bailments terminate, the same is true. It looks as if we have found a simple explanation of the usage we are investigating, but this turns out to be but another deceptive short cut. For it is not a sufficient condition of *A*'s being the owner of a thing that, on the determination of *B*'s interests in it, corresponding rights vest in or are exercisable by *A*. On the determination of a sub-lease, the rights in question become exercisable by the lessee, not by the 'owner' of the property.

Can we then say that the 'owner' is the ultimate residuary? When the sub-lessee's interest determines the lessee acquires the corresponding rights; but when the lessee's right determines the 'owner' acquires these rights. Hence the 'owner' appears to be identified as the ultimate residuary. The difficulty is that the series may be continued, for on the determination of the 'owner's' interest the state may acquire the corresponding rights; is the state's interest ownership or a mere expectancy?

A warning is here necessary. We are approaching the troubled waters of split ownership. Puzzles about the location of ownership are often generated by the fact that an ultimate residuary right is not coupled with present alienability or with the other standard incidents we have listed. . . .

We are of course here concerned not with the puzzles of split ownership but with simple cases in which the existence of *B*'s lesser interest in a thing is clearly consistent with *A*'s owning it. To explain the usage in such cases it is helpful to point out that it is a necessary but not sufficient condition of *A*'s being owner that, either immediately or ultimately, the extinction of other interests would enure for his benefit. In the end, it turns out that residuarity is merely one of the standard incidents of ownership, important no doubt, but not entitled to any special status.

* * *

Notes and Questions

JOHN LOCKE, from *Second Treatise of Civil Government*

1. John Locke's basic project here is to show how private property can be justified, even if we start with the basic assumption that all people intrinsically are, or at least originally were, equally entitled to the land and fruits of the earth. Or as Locke might have put it, we are all the children of God. Locke uses religious-sounding language, but all religious references can easily be translated into the language of objective morality. Do not be fooled by the style: That is the way people talked in seventeenth-century England. Nothing in Locke's argument depends on a religious claim. It relies only on reason. Three conditions have to be true for Locke to be right: (1) Morality is objective—that is, there is such a thing as right and wrong; (2) we can figure out what is moral, or right and wrong, by the use of reason; and (3) Locke's analysis is the one supported or compelled by reason.

2. You may recall from Chapter One that Locke begins his theory with a state of nature (an initial premise of natural equality); assumes natural rights to life, liberty, and property as requirements of reason (that is, laws of nature); and arrives (through reason) at a social contract that justifies government. All "property" in the state of nature is held in common. Yet, Locke notes, there must be some way for individuals to appropriate common goods to their own use or everything would be worthless. Apples on a tree are no good to me unless I can pick and eat them. To explain how this is justified without the common consent of all the world, Locke formulates what has been called the *labor theory of property*. How does labor justify ownership, according to Locke?

3. Locke argues that the same law of reason which justifies the acquisition of property also limits ownership. What is this rational limit to ownership? Would it affect ownership today? How would it affect such programs as farm subsidies for not growing crops? Locke also discusses another limit, now often called the *Lockean proviso*. No one can complain about someone else holding property, he says, so long as there is as much and as good left for others. Did he think that there was plenty of land left for everyone when he was writing? Could he make the same argument today? Note that Locke distinguishes land held in common by agreement, such as parks and forests, in populated, commercially developed countries from unclaimed land in undeveloped countries. Only unclaimed land can be gained by labor.

4. Locke tells a story about how land was first held in common, then appropriated by labor and divided by compact or agreement as it became more populated and civilized. And so, he concludes, we can see how private property in land can come about with justification. What kind of agreement is he talking about, individual agreements or treaties? If history were as he sketched it, would private property be justified in your opinion? How does Locke's account of land ownership compare to Mill's view in the next article? Does Locke's theory justify land acquisition by conquest?

5. An important addition to Locke's theory is the recognition of money or durable goods as valuable by agreement. Isn't he right that money is valuable only because we agree it is? Locke also claims that money changes the whole character of property, circumvents the spoilage limit, and greatly increases inequality. Is he right about that, too? Does the labor justification of property still work if the nature of property is so greatly changed?

[From] *Second Treatise of Civil Government*

JOHN LOCKE

C H A P T E R   5

Of Property

25. Whether we consider natural reason, which tells us that men being once born have a right to their preservation, and consequently to meat and drink and such other things as nature affords for their subsistence; or Revelation, which gives us an account of those grants God made of the world to Adam, and to Noah and his sons, 'tis very clear that God, as King David says, Psalm cxv. 16, "has given the earth to the children of men," given it to mankind in common. But this being supposed, it seems to some a very great difficulty how any one should ever come to have

a property in anything. I will not content myself to answer that if it be difficult to make out property upon a supposition that God gave the world to Adam and his posterity in common, it is impossible that any man but one universal monarch should have any property upon a supposition that God gave the world to Adam and his heirs in succession, exclusive of all the rest of his posterity, but I shall endeavour to show how men might come to have property in several parts of that which God gave to mankind in common, and that without any express compact of all the commoners.

26. God, who hath given the world to men in common, hath also given them reason to make use of it to the best advantage of life and convenience. The earth and all that therein is given to men for the support and comfort of their being. And though all the fruits it naturally produces, and beasts it feeds, belong to mankind in common, as they are produced by the spontaneous hand of nature; and nobody has originally a private dominion exclusive of the rest of mankind in any of them as they are thus in their natural state; yet being given for the use of men, there must of necessity be a means to appropriate them some way or other before they can be of any use or at all beneficial to any particular man. The fruit or venison which nourishes the wild Indian, who knows no enclosure, and is still a tenant in common, must be his, and so his, *i.e.*, a part of him, that another can no longer have any right to it, before it can do any good for the support of his life.

27. Though the earth and all inferior creatures be common to all men, yet every man has a property in his own person; this nobody has any right to but himself. The labour of his body and the work of his hands we may say are properly his. Whatsoever, then, he removes out of the state that nature hath provided and left it in, he hath mixed his labour with, and joined to it something that is his own, and thereby makes it his property. It being by him removed from the common state nature placed it in, it hath by this labour something annexed to it that excludes the common right of other men. For this labour being the unquestionable property of the labourer, no man but he can have a right to what that is once joined to, at least where there is enough, and as good left in common for others.

28. He that is nourished by the acorns he picked up under an oak, or the apples he gathered from the trees in the wood, has certainly appropriated them to himself. Nobody can deny but the nourishment is his. I ask, then, When did they begin to be his — when he digested, or when he ate, or when he boiled, or when he brought them home, or when he picked them up? And 'tis plain if the first gathering made them not his, nothing else could. That labour put a distinction between them and common; that added something to them more than Nature, the common mother of all, had done, and so they became his private right. And will any one say he had no right to those acorns or apples he thus appropriated, because he had not the consent of all mankind to make them his? Was it a robbery thus to assume to himself what belonged to all in common? If such a consent as that was necessary, man had starved, notwithstanding the plenty God had given him. We see in commons which remain so by compact that 'tis the taking any part of what is common and removing it out of the state nature leaves it in, which begins the property; without which the common is of no use. And the taking of this or that part does not depend on the express consent of all the commoners. Thus the grass my horse has bit, the turfs my servant has cut, and the ore I have dug in any place where I have a right to them in common with others, become my property without the assignation or consent of anybody. The labour that was mine removing them out of that common state they were in, hath fixed my property in them.

29. By making an explicit consent of every commoner necessary to any one's appropriating to himself any part of what is given in common, children or servants could not cut the meat which their father or master had provided for them in common without assigning to every one his peculiar part. Though the water running in the fountain be every one's, yet who can doubt but that in the pitcher is his only who drew it out? His labour hath taken it out of the hands of Nature, where it was common, and belonged equally to all her children, and hath thereby appropriated it to himself.

30. Thus this law of reason makes the deer that Indian's who hath killed it; 'tis allowed to be his goods who hath bestowed his labour upon it, though before it was the common right of every

one. And amongst those who are counted the civilised part of mankind, who have made and multiplied positive laws to determine property, this original law of nature, for the beginning of property in what was before common, still takes place; and by virtue thereof, what fish any one catches in the ocean, that great and still remaining common of mankind, or what ambergris any one takes up here, is, by the labour that removes it out of that common state nature left it in, made his property who takes that pains about it. And even amongst us, the hare that any one is hunting is thought his who pursues her during the chase. For being a beast that is still looked upon as common, and no man's private possession, whoever has employed so much labour about any of that kind as to find and pursue her has thereby removed her from the state of nature wherein she was common, and hath begun a property.

31. It will perhaps be objected to this, that if gathering the acorns, or other fruits of the earth, &c., makes a right to them, then any one may engross as much as he will. To which I answer, Not so. The same law of nature that does by this means give us property, does also bound that property too. "God has given us all things richly" (I Tim. vi. 17), is the voice of reason confirmed by inspiration. But how far has He given it to us? To enjoy. As much as any one can make use of to any advantage of life before it spoils, so much he may by his labour fix a property in, whatever is beyond this, is more than his share, and belongs to others. Nothing was made by God for man to spoil or destroy. And thus considering the plenty of natural provisions there was a long time in the world, and the few spenders, and to how small a part of that provision the industry of one man could extend itself, and engross it to the prejudice of others — especially keeping within the bounds, set by reason, or what might serve for his use — there could be then little room for quarrels or contention about property so established.

32. But the chief matter of property being now not the fruits of the earth, and the beasts that subsist on it, but the earth itself, as that which takes in and carries with it all the rest, I think it is plain that property in that, too, is acquired as the former. As much land as a man tills, plants improves, cultivates, and can use the product of, so much is his property. He by his labour does as it were enclosing it from the common. Nor will it invalidate his right to say, everybody else has an equal title to it; and therefore he cannot appropriate, he cannot enclose, without the consent of all his fellow-commoners, all mankind. God, when He gave the world in common to all mankind, commanded man also to labour, and the penury of his condition required it of him. God and his reason commanded him to subdue the earth, *i.e.*, improve it for the benefit of life, and therein lay out something upon it that was his own, his labour. He that, in obedience to this command of God, subdued, tilled, and sowed any part of it, thereby annexed to it something that was his property, which another had no title to, nor could without injury take from him.

33. Nor was this appropriation of any parcel of land, by improving it, any prejudice to any other man, since there was still enough and as good left; and more than the yet unprovided could use. So that in effect there was never the less left for others because of his enclosure for himself. For he that leaves as much as another can make use of, does as good as take nothing at all. Nobody could think himself injured by the drinking of another man, though he took a good draught, who had a whole river of the same water left him to quench his thirst; and the case of land and water, where there is enough of both, is perfectly the same.

34. God gave the world to men in common; but since He gave it them for their benefit, and the greatest conveniences of life they were capable to draw from it, it cannot be supposed He meant it should always remain common and uncultivated. He gave it to the use of the industrious and rational (and labour was to be his title to it), not to the fancy or covetousness of the quarrelsome and contentious. He that had as good left for his improvement as was already taken up, needed not complain, ought not to meddle with what was already improved by another's labour; if he did, it is plain he desired the benefit of another's pains, which he had no right to, and not the ground which God had given him in common with others to labour on, and whereof there was as good left as that already possessed, and more than he knew what to do with, or his industry could reach to.

35. It is true, in land that is common in England, or any other country where there is plenty of people under Government, who have money and commerce, no one can enclose or appropriate any part without the consent of all his fellow-

commoners: because this is left common by compact, *i.e.*, by the law of the land, which is not to be violated. And though it be common in respect to some men, it is not so to all mankind; but is the joint property of this country, or this parish. Besides, the remainder, after such enclosure, would not be as good to the rest of the commoners as the whole was, when they could all make use of the whole; whereas in the beginning and first peopling of the great common of the world it was quite otherwise. The law man was under was rather for appropriating. God commanded, and his wants forced him, to labour. That was his property, which could not be taken from him wherever he had fixed it. And hence subduing or cultivating the earth, and having dominion, we see are joined together. The one gave title to the other. So that God, by commanding to subdue, gave authority so far to appropriate. And the condition of human life, which requires labour and materials to work on, necessarily introduces private possessions.

36. The measure of property nature has well set by the extent of men's labour and the convenience of life. No man's labour could subdue or appropriate all; nor could his enjoyment consume more than a small part; so that it was impossible for any man, this way, to intrench upon the right of another, or acquire to himself a property to the prejudice of his neighbour, who would still have room for as good and as large a possession (after the other had taken out his) as before it was appropriated. Which measure did confine every man's possession to a very moderate proportion, and such as he might appropriate to himself without injury to anybody, in the first ages of the world, when men were more in danger to be lost by wandering from their company in the then vast wilderness of the earth than to be straitened for want of room to plant in. And the same measure may be allowed still without prejudice to anybody, as full as the world seems. For supposing a man or family in the state they were at first peopling of the world by the children of Adam or Noah; let him plant in some inland vacant places of America, we shall find that the possessions he could make himself, upon the measures we have given, would not be very large, nor, even to this day, prejudice the rest of mankind, or give them reason to complain or think themselves injured by this man's encroachment, though the race of men

have now spread themselves to all the corners of the world, and do infinitely exceed the small number that was at the beginning. Nay, the extent of ground is of so little value without labour, that I have heard it affirmed that in Spain itself a man may be permitted to plough, sow, and reap, without being disturbed, upon land he has no other title to but only his making use of it. But, on the contrary, the inhabitants think themselves beholden to him who by his industry on neglected and consequently waste land has increased the stock of corn which they wanted. But be this as it will, which I lay no stress on, this I dare boldly affirm — that the same rule of propriety, viz., that every man should have as much as he could make use of, would hold still in the world without straitening anybody, since there is land enough in the world to suffice double the inhabitants, had not the invention of money, and the tacit agreement of men to put a value on it, introduced (by consent) larger possessions and a right to them; which how it has done I shall by-and-bye show more at large.

37. This is certain, that in the beginning, before the desire of having more than man needed had altered the intrinsic value of things, which depends only on their usefulness to the life of man; or had agreed that a little piece of yellow metal which would keep without wasting or decay should be worth a great piece of flesh or a whole heap of corn, though men had a right to appropriate by their labour, each one to himself, as much of the things of nature as he could use, yet this could not be much, nor to the prejudice of others, where the same plenty was still left to those who would use the same industry.

Before the appropriation of land, he who gathered as much of the wild fruit, killed, caught, or tamed as many of the beasts as he could; he that so employed his pains about any of the spontaneous products of nature as any way to alter them from the state which nature put them in, by placing any of his labour on them, did thereby acquire a propriety in them. But if they perished in his possession without their due use; if the fruits rotted, or the venison putrified before he could spend it, he offended against the common law of nature, and was liable to be punished; he invaded his neighbour's share, for he had no right further than his use called for any of them and they might serve to afford him conveniences of life.

38. The same measures governed the possessions of land, too. Whatsoever he tilled and reaped, laid up, and made use of before it spoiled, that was his peculiar right; whatsoever he enclosed and could feed and make use of, the cattle and product was also his. But if either the grass of his enclosure rotted on the ground, or the fruit of his planting perished without gathering and laying up, this part of the earth, notwithstanding his enclosure, was still to be looked on as waste, and might be the possession of any other. Thus, at the beginning, Cain might take as much ground as he could till and make it his own land, and yet leave enough for Abel's sheep to feed on; a few acres would serve for both their possessions. But as families increased, and industry enlarged their stocks, their possessions enlarged with the need of them; but yet it was commonly without any fixed property in the ground they made use of, till they incorporated, settled themselves together, and built cities; and then, by consent, they came in time to set out the bounds of their distinct territories, and agree on limits between them and their neighbours, and, by laws within themselves, settled the properties of those of the same society. For we see that in that part of the world which was first inhabited, and therefore like to be the best peopled, even as low down as Abraham's time they wandered with their flocks and their herds, which were their substance, freely up and down; and this Abraham did in a country where he was a stranger: whence it is plain that at least a great part of the land lay in common; that the inhabitants valued it not, nor claimed property in any more than they made use of. But when there was not room enough in the same place for their herds to feed together, they by consent, as Abraham and Lot did (Gen. xiii. 5), separated and enlarged their pasture where it best liked them. And for the same reason Esau went from his father and his brother, and planted in Mount Seir (Gen. xxxvi. 6).

39. And thus, without supposing any private dominion and property in Adam over all the world, exclusive of all other men, which can no way be proved, nor any one's property be made out from it; but supposing the world given as it was to the children of men in common, we see how labour could make men distinct titles to several parcels of it for their private uses, wherein there could be no doubt of right, no room for quarrel.

40. Nor is it so strange, as perhaps before consideration it may appear, that the property of labour should be able to overbalance the community of land. For it is labour indeed that puts the difference of value on everything; and let any one consider what the difference is between an acre of land planted with tobacco or sugar, sown with wheat or barley and an acre of the same land lying in common without any husbandry upon it, and he will find that the improvement of labour makes the far greater part of the value. I think it will be but a very modest computation to say that of the products of the earth useful to the life of man nine-tenths are the effects of labour; nay, if we will rightly estimate things as they come to our use, and cast up the several expenses about them — what in them is purely owing to nature, and what to labour — we shall find that in most of them ninety-nine hundredths are wholly to be put on the account of labour.

41. There cannot be a clearer demonstration of anything than several nations of the Americans are of this, who are rich in land and poor in all the comforts of life, whom nature having furnished as liberally as any other people with the materials of plenty — i.e., a fruitful soil, apt to produce in abundance what might serve for food, raiment, and delight — yet, for want of improving it by labour, have not one-hundreth part of the conveniences we enjoy. And a king of a large and fruitful territory there, feeds, lodges, and is clad worse than a day-labourer in England.

42. To make this a little clearer, let us but trace some of the ordinary provisions of life through their several progresses before they come to our use, and see how much they receive of their value from human industry. Bread, wine, and cloth are things of daily use and great plenty; yet, notwithstanding, acorns, water, and leaves or skins, must be our bread, drink, and clothing, did not labour furnish us with these more useful commodities. For whatever bread is more worth than acorns, wine than water, and cloth or silk than leaves, skins, or moss, that is wholly owing to labour and industry: the one of these being the food and raiment which unassisted nature furnishes us with; the other, provisions which our industry and pains prepare for us; which how much they exceed the other in value when any-

one hath computed, he will then see how much labour makes the far greatest part of the value of things we enjoy in this world. And the ground which produces the materials is scarce to be reckoned in as any, or at most but a very small, part of it; so little that even amongst us land that is left wholly to nature, that hath no improvement of pasturage, tillage, or planting, is called, as indeed it is, "waste," and we shall find the benefit of it amount to little more than nothing.

43. An acre of land that bears here twenty bushels of wheat, and another in America which, with the same husbandry, would do the like, are without doubt of the same natural intrinsic value; but yet the benefit mankind receives from the one in a year is worth £5, and from the other possibly not worth a penny, if all the profit an Indian received from it were to be valued and sold here; at least, I may truly say, not one-thousandth. 'Tis labour, then, which puts the greatest part of value upon land, without which it would scarcely be worth anything; 'tis to that we owe the greatest part of all its useful products, for all that the straw, bran, bread, of that acre of wheat is more worth than the product of an acre of as good land which lies waste, is all the effect of labour. For 'tis not barely the ploughman's pains, the reaper's and thresher's toil, and the baker's sweat, is to be counted into the bread we eat; the labour of those who broke the oxen, who dug and wrought the iron and stones, who felled and framed the timber employed about the plough, mill, oven, or any other utensils, which are a vast number, requisite to this corn, from its sowing, to its being made bread, must all be charged on the account of labour, and received as an effect of that. Nature and the earth furnished only the almost worthless materials as in themselves. 'Twould be a strange catalogue of things that industry provided, and made use of about every loaf of bread before it came to our use, if we could trace them — iron, wood, leather, bark, timber, stone, bricks, coals, lime, cloth, dyeing drugs, pitch, tar, masts, ropes, and all the materials made use of in the ship that brought any of the commodities made use of by any of the workmen to any part of the work, all which it would be almost impossible — at least, too long — to reckon up.

44. From all which it is evident that, though the things of nature are given in common, yet man, by being master of himself and proprietor of his own person and the actions or labour of it, had still in himself the great foundation of property; and that which made up the great part of what he applied to the support or comfort of his being, when invention and arts had improved the conveniences of life was perfectly his own, and did not belong in common to others.

45. Thus labour, in the beginning, gave a right of property, wherever any one was pleased to employ it upon what was common, which remained a long while the far greater part, and is yet more than mankind makes use of. Men at first, for the most part, contented themselves with what unassisted nature offered to their necessities; and though afterwards, in some parts of the world (where the increase of people and stock, with the use of money, had made land scarce, and so of some value), the several communities settled the bounds of their distinct territories, and, by laws within themselves, regulated the properties of the private men of their society, and so, by compact and agreement, settled the property which labour and industry began — and the leagues that have been made between several state and kingdoms, either expressly or tacitly disowning all claim and right to the land in the other's possession, have, by common consent, given up their pretences to their natural common right, which originally they had to those countries; and so have, by positive agreement, settled a property amongst themselves in distinct parts of the world — yet there are still great tracts of ground to be found which, the inhabitants thereof not having joined with the rest of mankind in the consent of the use of their common money, lie waste, and are more than the people who dwell on it do or can make use of, and so still lie in common; though this can scarce happen amongst that part of mankind that have consented to the use of money.

46. The greatest part of things really useful to the life of man, and such as the necessity of subsisting made the first commoners of the world look after, as it doth the Americans now, are generally things of short duration, such as, if they are not consumed by use, will decay and perish of themselves: gold, silver, and diamonds are things that fancy or agreement have put the value on more than real use and the necessary support of life. Now, of those good things which nature hath provided in common, every one hath a right, as hath been said, to as much as he could use, and had a

property in all he could effect with his labour — all that his industry could extend to, to alter from the state nature had put it in, was his. He that gathered a hundred bushels of acorns or apples had thereby a property in them; they were his goods as soon as gathered. He was only to look that he used them before they spoiled, else he took more than his share, and robbed others; and, indeed, it was a foolish thing, as well as dishonest, to hoard up more than he could make use of. If he gave away a part to anybody else, so that it perished not uselessly in his possession, these he also made use of; and if he also bartered away plums that would have rotted in a week, for nuts that would last good for his eating a whole year, he did no injury; he wasted not the common stock, destroyed no part of the portion of goods that belonged to others, so long as nothing perished uselessly in his hands. Again, if he would give his nuts for a piece of metal, pleased with its colour, or exchange his sheep for shells, or wool for a sparkling pebble or a diamond, and keep those by him all his life, he invaded not the right of others, he might heap up as much of these durable things as he pleased, the exceeding of the bounds of his just property not lying in the largeness of his possessions, but the perishing of anything uselessly in it.

47. And thus came in the use of money — some lasting thing that men might keep without spoiling, and that, by mutual consent, men would take in exchange for the truly useful but perishable supports of life.

48. And as different degrees of industry were apt to give men possessions in different proportions, so this invention of money gave them the opportunity to continue and enlarge them; for supposing an island, separate from all possible commerce with the rest of the world, wherein there were but a hundred families — but there were sheep, horses, and cows, with other useful animals, wholesome fruits, and land enough for corn for a hundred thousand times as many, but nothing in the island, either because of its commonness or perishableness, fit to supply the place of money — what reason could any one have there to enlarge his possessions beyond the use of his family and a plentiful supply to its consumption, either in what their own industry produced, or they could barter for like perishable useful commodities with others? Where there is not something both lasting and scarce, and so

valuable to be hoarded up, there men will not be apt to enlarge their possessions of land were it never so rich, never so free for them to take; for I ask, what would a man value ten thousand or a hundred thousand acres of excellent land, ready cultivated, and well stocked too with cattle, in the middle of the inland parts of America, where he had no hopes of commerce with other parts of the world, to draw money to him by the sale of the product? It would not be worth the enclosing, and we should see him give up again to the wild common nature whatever was more than would supply the conveniences of life to be had there for him and his family.

49. Thus in the beginning all the world was America and more so than that is now, for no such thing as money was anywhere known. Find out something that hath the use and value of money amongst his neighbours, you shall see the same man will begin presently to enlarge his possessions.

50. But since gold and silver, being little useful to the life of man in proportion to food, raiment, and carriage has its value only from the consent of men, whereof labour yet makes, in great part, the measure, it is plain that the consent of men have agreed to a disproportionate and unequal possession of the earth — I mean out of the bounds of society and compact; for in governments the laws regulate it; they having, by consent, found out and agreed in a way how a man may rightfully and without injury possess more than he himself can make use of by receiving gold and silver, which may continue long in a man's possession, without decaying for the overplus, and agreeing those metals should have a value.

51. And thus, I think, it is very easy to conceive without any difficulty how labour could at first begin a title of property in the common things of nature, and how the spending it upon our uses bounded it; so that there could then be no reason of quarrelling about title, nor any doubt about the largeness of possession it gave. Right and conveniency went together; for as a man had a right to all he could employ his labour upon, so he had no temptation to labour for more than he could make use of. This left no room for controversy about the title, nor for encroachment on the right of others; what portion a man carved to himself was easily seen, and it was useless, as well as dishonest, to carve himself too much, or take more than he needed.

Notes and Questions

JOHN STUART MILL, from *Principles of Political Economy*

1. John Stuart Mill's description of the history of private property in land is very different from Locke's. He argues that the origin of property provides no justification for the institution as it stands, yet he contends the system should be maintained once it is long established. Why?

2. Many people object to the institution of private property altogether, Mill notes. What two classes of objectors does he name? He suggests that although these alternative economic schemes may have defects, they are not without plausibility. Using communism as an example of an alternative economy, Mill argues that a communistic system is as defensible and practical as private property. What grounds does he give?

3. Mill's next question is, What are the implications and boundaries of the concept of property? This is rather like the question Honoré asked, but Mill approaches it a little differently. He sets out the foundation of ownership as Locke did, on the basis of labor. But for Mill labor is not the only consideration; we must also account for capital. How does he do that? How does Mill answer the objection that heirs profit from the work of others and not their own labor? How does he respond to the objection to competition?

4. Mill argues that the concept of property also includes the right of title by prescription after a certain lapse of time. How does he support this position? How does he limit it? How can this position be reconciled with justice? Mill recognizes that for a legitimate claim to die after a lapse of time may seem unjust. Do his limits help address this injustice?

5. Mill notes that while bequest is implied in the concept of property, inheritance is not. What conclusions does he draw from this idea? He further argues that even bequest should be limited. On what grounds?

6. Unlike Locke, Mill distinguishes the ownership of land from the ownership of goods or the products of labor. According to Mill, property in land should be sharply limited. Why? What is the only justification for land ownership?

7. Some things, Mill notes, should not be property at all. What does he name as things unfit for ownership? Do you find any principle that explains which things should not be owned and why?

[From] *Principles of Political Economy*

JOHN STUART MILL

Private property, as an institution, did not owe its origin to any of those considerations of utility, which plead for the maintenance of it when established. Enough is known of rude ages, both from history and from analogous states of society in our own time, to show, that tribunals (which always precede laws) were originally established, not to determine rights, but to repress violence and terminate quarrels. With this object chiefly in view, they naturally enough gave legal effect to first occupancy, by treating as the aggressor the person who first commenced violence, by turning, or attempting to turn, another out of possession. The preservation of the peace, which was the original object of civil government, was thus attained; while by confirming, to those who already possessed it, even what was not the fruit of personal exertion, a guarantee was incidentally given to them and others that they would be protected in what was so. . . .

* * *

The assailants of the principle of individual property may be divided into two classes: those whose scheme implies absolute equality in the distribution of the physical means of life and enjoyment, and those who admit inequality, but grounded on some principle, or supposed principle, of justice or general expediency, and not, like so many of the existing social inequalities, dependent on accident alone.

* * *

Whatever may be the merits or defects of these various schemes, they cannot be truly said to be impracticable. No reasonable person can doubt that a village community, composed of a few thousand inhabitants cultivating in joint ownership the same extent of land which at present feeds the number of people, and producing by combined labour and the most improved processes the manufactured articles which they required, could raise an amount of productions sufficient to maintain them in comfort; and would find the means of obtaining, and if need be, exacting, the quantity of labour necessary for this purpose, from every member of the association who was capable of work.

The objection ordinarily made to a system of community of property and equal distribution of the produce, that each person would be incessantly occupied in evading his fair share of the work, points, undoubtedly, to a real difficulty. But those who urge this objection, forget to how great an extent the same difficulty exists under the system on which nine-tenths of the business of society is now conducted. The objection supposes, that honest and efficient labour is only to be had from those who are themselves individually to reap the benefit of their own exertions. But how small a part of all the labour performed in England, from the lowest paid to the highest, is done by persons working for their own benefit. From the Irish reaper or hodman to the chief justice or the minister of state, nearly all the work of society is remunerated by day wages or fixed salaries. A factory operative has less personal interest in his work than a member of a Communist association, since he is not, like him, working for a partnership of which he is himself a member. It will no doubt be said, that though the labourers themselves have not, in most cases, a personal interest in their work, they are watched and superintended, and their labour directed, and the mental part of the labour performed, by persons who have. Even this, however, is far from being universally the fact. In all public, and many of the largest and most successful private undertakings, not only the labours of detail but the control and superintendence are entrusted to salaried officers. And though the "master's eye," when the master is vigilant and intelligent, is of proverbial value, it must be remembered that in a Socialist farm or manufactory, each labourer would be under the eye not of one master, but of the whole community. In the extreme case of obstinate perseverance in not performing the due share of work, the community would have the same resources which society now has for compelling conformity to the necessary conditions of the association. Dismissal, the only remedy at present, is no remedy when any other labourer who may be engaged does no better than his predecessor: the power of dismissal only enables an employer to obtain from his workmen the customary amount of labour, but that customary labour may be of any degree of inefficiency. Even the labourer who loses his employment by idleness or negligence, has nothing worse to suffer, in the most unfavourable case, than the discipline of a workhouse, and if the desire to avoid this be a sufficient motive in the one system, it would be sufficient in the other. . . .

* * *

. . . [Further,] mankind are capable of a far greater amount of public spirit than the present age is accustomed to suppose possible. History bears witness to the success with which large bodies of human beings may be trained to feel the public interest their own. And no soil could be more favourable to the growth of such a feeling, than a Communist association, since all the ambition, and the bodily and mental activity, which are now exerted in the pursuit of separate and self-regarding interests, would require another sphere of employment, and would naturally find it in the pursuit of the general benefit of the community. The same cause, so often assigned in explanation of the devotion of the Catholic priest or monk to the interest of his order—that he has no interest apart from it — would, under Communism, attach the citizen to the community. And independently of the public motive, every member of the association would be amenable to the most universal, and one of the strongest, of personal motives, that of public opinion. The force of this motive in deterring from any act or omission positively reproved by the community, no one is likely to deny; but the power also of emulation, in exciting to the most strenuous exertions for the sake of the approbation and admiration of others, is borne witness to by experience in every situation in which human beings publicly compete with one another, even if it be in things frivolous, or from which the public derive no benefit. A contest, who can do most for the common good, is not the kind of competition which Socialists repudiate. To what extent, therefore, the energy of labour would be diminished by Communism, or whether in the long run it would be diminished at all, must be considered for the present an undecided question. . . .

* * *

If . . . the choice were to be made between Communism with all its chances, and the present state of society with all its sufferings and injustices; if the institution of private property necessarily carried with it as a consequence, that the produce of labour should be apportioned as we now see it, almost in an inverse ratio to the labour — the largest portions to those who have never worked at all, the next largest to those whose work is almost nominal, and so in a descending scale, the remuneration dwindles as the work grows harder and more disagreeable, until the most-fatiguing and exhausting bodily labour cannot count with certainty on being able to earn even the necessaries of life; if this, or Communism, were the alternative, all the difficulties, great or small, of Communism, would be but as dust in the balance. But to make the comparison applicable, we must compare Communism at its best, with the régime of individual property, not as it is, but as it might be made. The principle of private property has never yet had a fair trial in any country; and less so, perhaps, in this country than in some others. The social arrangements of modern Europe commenced from a distribution of property which was the result, not of just partition, or acquisition by industry, but of conquest and violence: and notwithstanding what industry has been doing for many centuries to modify the work of force, the system still retains many and large traces of its origin. The laws of property have never yet conformed to the principles on which the justification of private property rests. They have made property of things which never ought to be property, and absolute property where only a qualified property ought to exist. They have not held the balance fairly between human beings, but have heaped impediments upon some, to give advantage to others; they have purposely fostered inequalities, and prevented all from starting fair in the race. . . .

* * *

It is next to be considered, what is included in the idea of private property, and by what considerations the application of the principle should be bounded.

The institution of property, when limited to its essential elements, consists in the recognition, in each person, of a right to the exclusive disposal of what he or she have produced by their own exertions, or received either by gift or by fair agreement, without force or fraud, from those who produced it. The foundation of the whole is, the right of producers to what they themselves have produced. It may be objected, therefore, to the institution as it now exists, that it recognises rights of property in individuals over things which they have not produced. For example (it may be said) the operatives in a manufactory create, by their labour and skill, the whole produce; yet, instead of its belonging to them, the law gives them only their stipulated hire, and transfers the produce to some one who has merely supplied the funds, without perhaps contributing anything to the work itself, even in the form of superintendence. The answer to this is, that the labour of manufacture is only one of the conditions which must combine for the production of the commodity. The labour cannot be carried on without materials and machinery, nor without a stock of necessaries provided in advance, to maintain the labourers during the production. All these things are the fruits of previous labour. If the labourers were possessed of them, they would not need to divide the produce with any one; but while they have them not, an equivalent must be given to those who have, both for the antecedent labour, and for the abstinence by which the produce of that labour, instead of being expended on indulgences, has been reserved for this use. The capital may not have been, and in most cases was not, created by the labour and abstinence of the present possessor; but it was created by the labour and abstinence of some former person, who may indeed have been wrongfully dispossessed of it, but who, in the present age of the world, much more probably transferred his claims to the present capitalist by gift or voluntary contract: and the abstinence at least must have been continued by each successive owner, down to the present. If it be said, as it may with truth, that those who have inherited the savings of others have an advantage which they have in no way deserved, over the industrious whose predecessors have not left them anything; I not only admit, but strenuously contend, that this unearned advantage should be curtailed, as much as is consistent with justice to those who thought fit to dispose of their savings by giving them to their descendants. But while it is true that the labourers are at a disadvantage compared with those whose predecessors have saved, it is also true that the labourers are far better off than if those predecessors had not saved. They share in the advantage, though not to an equal extent with the inheritors. The terms of co-operation between present labour and the fruits of past labour and saving, are a subject for adjustment between the two parties. Each is necessary to the other. The capitalist can do nothing without labourers, nor the labourers without capital. If the labourers compete for employment, the capitalists on their part compete for labour, to the full extent of the circulating capital of the country. Competition is often spoken of as if it were necessarily a cause of misery and degradation to the labouring class; as if high wages were not precisely as much a product of competition as low wages. The remuneration of labour is as much the result of the law of competition in the United States, as it is in Ireland, and much more completely so than in England.

The right of property includes, then, the freedom of acquiring by contract. The right of each to what he has produced, implies a right to what has been produced by others, if obtained by their free consent; since the producers must either have given it from good will, or exchanged it for what they esteemed an equivalent, and to prevent them from doing so would be to infringe their right of property in the product of their own industry.

Before proceeding to consider the things which the principle of individual property does not include, we must specify one more thing which it does include: and this is that a title, after a certain period, should be given by prescription. According to the fundamental idea of property, indeed, nothing ought to be treated as such, which has been acquired by force or fraud, or appropriated in ignorance of a prior title vested in some other person; but it is necessary to the security of rightful possessors, that they should not be molested by charges of wrongful acquisition, when by the lapse of time witnesses must have perished or been lost sight of, and the real character of the transaction can no longer be cleared up. Possession which has not been legally questioned within a moderate number of years, ought to be, as by the laws of all nations it is, a complete title. Even when the acquisition was wrongful, the dispossession, after a generation has elapsed, of the probably *bond fide* possessors, by the revival of a claim which had been long dormant, would generally be a greater injustice, and almost always a greater private and public mischief, than leaving the original wrong without atonement. It may seem hard that a claim, originally just, should be defeated by mere lapse of time; but there is a time after which, (even looking at the individual case, and without regard to the general effect on the security of possessors,) the balance of hardship turns the other way. With the injustices of men, as with the convulsions and disasters of nature, the longer they remain unrepaired, the greater become the obstacles to repairing them, arising from the aftergrowths which would have to be torn up or broken through. In no human transactions, not even in the simplest and clearest, does it follow that a thing is fit to be done now, because it was fit to be done sixty years ago. It is scarcely needful to remark, that these reasons for not disturbing acts of injustice of old date, cannot apply to unjust systems or institutions; since a bad law or usage is not one bad act, in the remote past, but a perpetual repetition of bad acts, as long as the law or usage lasts.

Such, then, being the essentials of private property, it is now to be considered, to what extent the forms in which the institution has existed in different states of society, or still exists, are necessary consequences of its principle, or are recommended by the reasons on which it is grounded.

Nothing is implied in property but the right of each to his (or her) own faculties, to what he can produce by them, and to whatever he can get for them in a fair market: together with his right to give this to any other person if he chooses, and the right of that other to receive and enjoy it.

It follows, therefore, that although the right of bequest, or gift after death, forms part of the idea of private property, the right of inheritance, as distinguished from bequest, does not. That the property of persons who have made no disposition of it during their lifetime, should pass first to their children, and failing them, to the nearest relations, may be a proper arrangement or not, but is no consequence of the principle of private property. Although there belong to the decision of such questions many considerations besides those of political economy, it is not foreign to the plan of this work to suggest, for the judgment of thinkers, the view of them which most recommends itself to the writer's mind. . . .

Whether the power of bequest should itself be subject to limitation is an ulterior question of great importance. Unlike inheritance *ab intestato*, bequest is one of the attributes of property: the ownership of a thing cannot be looked upon as complete without the power of bestowing it, at death or during life, at the owner's pleasure: and all the reasons, which recommend that private property should exist, recommend *pro tanto* this extension of it. But property is only a means to an end, not itself the end. Like all other proprietary rights, and even in a greater degree than most, the power of bequest may be so exercised as to conflict with the permanent interests of the human race. It does so, when, not content with bequeathing an estate to A, the testator prescribes that on A's death it shall pass to his eldest son, and to that son's son, and so on for ever. No doubt, persons have occasionally exerted themselves more strenuously to acquire a fortune from the hope of founding a family in perpetuity; but the mischiefs to society of such perpetuities outweigh the value of this incentive to exertion, and the incentives in the case of those who have the opportunity of making large fortunes are strong enough without it. A similar abuse of the power of bequest is committed when a person who does the meritorious act of leaving property for public uses, attempts to prescribe the details of its application in perpetuity; when in founding a place of education (for instance) he dictates, for ever, what doctrines shall be taught. It being impossible that any one should know what doctrines will be fit to be taught after he has been dead for centuries, the law ought not to give effect to such dispositions of property, unless subject to the perpetual revision (after a certain interval has elapsed) of a fitting authority. . . .

* * *

The next point to be considered is, whether the reasons on which the institution of property rests, are applicable to all things in which a right of exclusive ownership is at present recognized; and if not, on what other grounds the recognition is defensible.

The essential principle of property being to assure to all persons what they have produced by their labour and accumulated by their abstinence, this principle cannot apply to what is not the produce of labour, the raw material of the earth. If the land derived its productive power wholly from nature, and not at all from industry, or if there were any means of discriminating what is derived from each source, it not only would not be necessary, but it would be the height of injustice, to let the gift of nature be engrossed by individuals. The use of the land in agriculture must indeed, for the time being, be of necessity exclusive; the same person who has ploughed and sown must be permitted to reap: but the land might be occupied for one season only, as among the ancient Germans; or might be periodically redivided as population increased: or the State might be the universal landlord, and the cultivators tenants under it, either on lease or at will.

But though land is not the produce of industry, most of its valuable qualities are so. Labour is not only requisite for using, but almost equally so for fashioning, the instrument. Considerable labour is often required at the commencement, to clear the land for cultivation. In many cases, even when cleared, its productiveness is wholly the effect of labour and art. . . .

* * *

. . . Cultivation also requires buildings and fences, which are wholly the produce of labour. The fruits of this industry cannot be reaped in a short period. The labour and outlay are immediate, the benefit is spread over many years, perhaps over all future time. A holder will not incur this labour and outlay when strangers and not himself will be benefited by it. If he undertakes such improvements, he must have a sufficient period before him in which to profit by them; and he is in no way so sure of having always a sufficient period as when his tenure is perpetual. . . .

* * *

These are the reasons which form the justification in an economical point of view, of property in land. It is seen, that they are only valid, in so far as the proprietor of land is its improver. Whenever, in any country, the proprietor, generally speaking, ceases to be the improver, political economy has nothing to say in defence of landed property, as there established. In no sound theory of private property was it ever contemplated that the proprietor of land should be merely a sinecurist quartered on it. . . .

* * *

When the "sacredness of property" is talked of, it should always be remembered, that any such sacredness does not belong in the same degree to landed property. No man made the land. It is the original inheritance of the whole species. Its appropriation is wholly a question of general expediency. When private property in land is not expedient, it is unjust. It is no hardship to any one, to be excluded from what others have produced: they were not bound to produce it for his use, and he loses nothing by not sharing in what otherwise would not have existed at all. But is some hardship to be born into the world and to find all nature's gifts previously engrossed, and no place left for the new-comer. To reconcile people to this, after they have once admitted into their minds the idea that any moral rights belong to them as human beings, it will always be necessary to convince them that the exclusive appropriation is good for mankind on the whole, themselves included. But this is what no sane human being could be persuaded of, if the relation between the landowner and the cultivator were the same everywhere as it has been in Ireland.

Landed property is felt, even by those most tenacious of its rights, to be a different thing from other property; and where the bulk of the community have been disinherited of their share of it, and it has become the exclusive attribute of a small minority, men have generally tried to reconcile it, at least in theory, to their sense of justice, by endeavouring to attach duties to it, and erecting it into a sort of magistracy, either moral or legal. But if the state is at liberty to treat the possessors of land as public functionaries, it is only going one step further to say, that it is at liberty to discard them. The claim of the landowners to the land is altogether subordinate to the general policy of the state. The principle of property gives them no right to the land, but only a right to compensation for whatever portion of their interest in the land it may be the policy of the state to deprive them of. To that, their claim is indefeasible. It is due to landowners, and to owners of any property whatever, recognized as such by the state, that they should not be dispossessed of it without receiving its pecuniary value, or an annual income equal to what they derived from it. This is due on the general principles on which property rests. If the land was bought with the produce of the labor and abstinence of themselves or their ancestors, compensation is due to them on that ground; even if otherwise, it is still due on the ground of prescription. Nor can it ever be necessary for accomplishing an object by which the community altogether will gain, that a particular portion of the community should be immolated. When the property is of a kind to which peculiar affections attach themselves, the compensation ought to exceed a bare pecuniary equivalent. But, subject to this proviso, the state is at liberty to deal with landed property as the general interests of the community may require, even to the extent, if it so happen, of doing with the whole, what is done with a part whenever a bill is passed for a railroad or a new street. The community has too much at stake in the proper cultivation of the land, and in the conditions annexed to the occupancy of it, to leave these things to the discretion of a class of persons called landlords, when they have shown themselves unfit for the trust. . . .

To me it seems almost an axiom that property in land should be interpreted strictly, and that the balance in all cases of doubt should incline against the proprietor. The reverse is the case with property in moveables, and in all things the product of labour: over these, the owner's power both of use and of exclusion should be absolute, except where positive evil to others would result from it; but in the case of land, no exclusive right should be permitted in any individual, which cannot be shown to be productive of positive good. To be allowed any exclusive right at all, over a portion of the common inheritance, while there are others who have no portion, is already a privilege. No quantity of moveable goods which a person can acquire by his labour, prevents others from acquiring the like by the same means; but from the very nature of the case, whoever owns land, keeps others out of the enjoyment of it. The privilege, or monopoly, is only defensible as a necessary evil; it becomes an injustice when carried to any point to which the compensating good does not follow it.

For instance, the exclusive right to the land for purposes of cultivation does not imply an exclusive right to it for purposes of access; and no such right ought to be recognized, except to the extent necessary to protect the produce against damage, and the owner's privacy against invasion. The pretension of two Dukes to shut up a part of the Highlands, and exclude the rest of mankind from many square miles of mountain scenery to prevent disturbance to wild animals, is an abuse; it exceeds the legitimate bounds of the right of landed property. When land is not intended to be cultivated, no good reason can in general be given for its being private property at all; and if any one is permitted to call it his, he ought to know that he holds it by sufferance of the community, and on an implied condition that his ownership, since it cannot possibly do them any good, at least shall not deprive them of any, which they could have derived from the land if it had been unappropriated. Even in the case of cultivated land, a man whom, though only one among millions, the law permits to hold thousands of acres as his single share, is not entitled to think that all this is given to him to use and abuse, and deal with as if it concerned nobody but himself. The rents or profits which he can obtain from it are at his sole disposal; but with regard to the land, in everything which he does with it, and in everything which he abstains from doing, he is morally bound, and should whenever the case admits be legally compelled, to make his interest and pleasure consistent with the public good. The species at large still retains, of its orig-

inal claim to the soil of the planet which it inhabits, as much as is compatible with the purposes for which it has parted with the remainder.

Besides property in the produce of labour, and property in land, there are other things which are or have been subjects of property, in which no proprietary rights ought to exist at all. But as the civilized world has in general made up its mind on most of these, there is no necessity for dwelling on them in this place. At the head of them, is property in human beings. It is almost superfluous to observe, that this institution can have no place in any society even pretending to be founded on justice, or on fellowship between human creatures. But, iniquitous as it is, yet when the state has expressly legalized it, and human beings, for generations, have been bought, sold, and inherited under sanction of law, it is another wrong, in abolishing the property, not to make full compensation. . . . Other examples of property which ought not to have been created, are properties in public trusts; such as judicial offices under the old French régime, and the heritable jurisdictions which, in countries not wholly emerged from feudality, pass with the land. Our own country affords, as cases in point, that of a commission in the army, and of an advowson, or right of nomination to an ecclesiastical benefice. A property is also sometimes created in a right of taxing the public; in a monopoly, for instance, or other exclusive privilege. These abuses prevail most in semibarbarous countries; but are not without example in the most civilized. In France there are several important trades and professions, including notaries, attorneys, brokers, appraisers, printers, even bakers, and (until lately) butchers, of which the numbers are limited by law. The *brevet* or privilege of one of the permitted number consequently brings a high price in the market. In these cases, compensation probably could not with justice be refused, on the abolition of the privilege. There are other cases in which this would be more doubtful. The question would turn upon what, in the peculiar circumstances, was sufficient to constitute prescription; and whether the legal recognition which the abuse had obtained, was sufficient to constitute it an institution, or amounted only to an occasional license. It would be absurd to claim compensation for losses caused by changes in a tariff, a thing confessedly variable from year to year; or for monopolies like those granted to individuals by Queen Elizabeth, favours of a despotic authority, which the power that gave was competent at any time to recall.

So much on the institution of property, a subject of which, for the purposes of political economy, it was indispensable to treat, but on which we could not usefully confine ourselves to economical considerations. We have now to inquire on what principles and with what results the distribution of the produce of land and labour is effected, under the relations which this institution creates among the different members of the community.

Notes and Questions

HENRY GEORGE, from *Progress and Poverty*

1. The brief excerpts from Henry George and Karl Marx broaden Mill's questions and offer a quick look at two proposals to limit private property. George, taking Mill's position on restricted land ownership a step further, would abolish the ownership of land. He offers two arguments to support his view. His theoretical argument, like Mill's, is that the labor theory of property does not justify the ownership of land itself. Why not?

2. George's second argument is practical or, from a utilitarian view, moral. He maintains that private land ownership causes bad consequences. What are these bad consequences, and what evidence does George give that private land ownership causes them? Do you see any flaw in his argument? Is his argument as persuasive today as it might have been in the nineteenth century? How would George handle the objection that justice forbids confiscating private land without compensation? How does Mill respond to that objection?

KARL MARX, from *Capital*

1. Karl Marx was concerned with the deplorable working conditions that prevailed during the industrial revolution when owners of capital received huge benefits while laborers were brutally exploited. Like George, he focuses on the bad consequences of certain economic institutions and the distribution of property. How does he propose that property should be distributed?

2. It is interesting to note that Locke, Mill, George, and Marx, despite enormous theoretical differences, all justify property ownership by labor. If labor is what justifies ownership, why should ownership alone generate profit? Why should people profit from what they have rather than what they do?

[From] *Progress and Poverty*

HENRY GEORGE

[The] strange and unnatural spectacle of large numbers of willing men who cannot find employment is enough to suggest the true cause [of poverty] to whosoever can think consecutively. For, though custom has dulled us to it, it *is* a strange and unnatural thing that men who wish to labor, in order to satisfy their wants, cannot find the opportunity — as, since labor is that which produces wealth, the man who seeks to exchange labor for food, clothing, or any other form of wealth, is like one who proposes to give bullion for coin, or wheat for flour. We talk about the supply of labor and the demand for labor, but, evidently, these are only relative terms. The supply of labor is everywhere the same—two hands always come into the world with one mouth, twenty-one boys to every twenty girls; and the demand for labor must always exist as long as men want things which labor alone can procure. We talk about the "want of work," but, evidently, it is not work that is short while want continues; evidently, the supply of labor cannot be too great, nor the demand for labor too small, when people suffer for the lack of things that labor produces. The real trouble must be that supply is somehow prevented from satisfying demand, that somewhere there is an obstacle which prevents labor from producing the things that laborers want. . . .

Now, what is necessary to enable labor to produce these things, is land. When we speak of labor creating wealth, we speak metaphorically. Man creates nothing. The whole human race, were they to labor forever, could not create the tiniest mote that floats in a sunbeam—could not make this rolling sphere one atom heavier or one atom lighter. In producing wealth, labor, with the aid of natural forces, but works up, into the forms desired, pre-existing matter, and, to produce wealth, must, therefore, have access to this matter and to these forces—that is to say, to land. The land is the source of all wealth. It is the mine from which must be drawn the ore that labor fashions. It is the substance to which labor gives the form. And, hence, when labor cannot satisfy its wants, may we not with certainty infer that it can be from no other cause than that labor is denied access to land? . . .

Now, why is it that . . . unemployed labor cannot employ itself upon the land? Not that the land is all in use. Though all the symptoms that in older countries are taken as showing a redundancy of population are beginning to manifest themselves in San Francisco, it is idle to talk of redundancy of population in a State that with greater natural resources than France has not yet a million of people. Within a few miles of San Francisco is unused land enough to give employment to every man who wants it. I do not mean to say that every unemployed man could turn farmer or build himself a house, if he had the

land; but that enough could and would do so to give employment to the rest. What is it, then, that prevents labor from employing itself on this land? Simply, that it has been monopolized. . . .

There is but one way to remove an evil—and that is, to remove its cause. Poverty deepens as wealth increases, and wages are forced down while productive power grows, because land, which is the source of all wealth and the field of all labor, is monopolized. To extirpate poverty, to make wages what justice commands they should be, the full earnings of the laborer, we must therefore substitute for the individual ownership of land a common ownership. Nothing else will go to the cause of the evil.

This, then, is the remedy for the unjust and unequal distribution of wealth apparent in modern civilization, and for all the evils which flow from it:

We must make land common property.

* * *

When it is proposed to abolish private property in land the first question that will arise is that of justice. . . .

What constitutes the rightful basis of property? What is it that enables a man justly to say of a thing, "It is mine!" From what springs the sentiment which acknowledges his exclusive right as against all the world? Is it not, primarily, the right of a man to himself, to the use of his own powers, to the enjoyment of the fruits of his own exertions? Is it not this individual right, which springs from and is testified to by the natural facts of individual organization—the fact that each particular pair of hands obey a particular brain and are related to a particular stomach; the fact that each man is a definite, coherent, independent whole—which alone justifies individual ownership? As a man belongs to himself, so his labor when put in concrete form belongs to him.

And for this reason, that which a man makes or produces is his own, as against all the world—to enjoy or to destroy, to use, to exchange, or to give. No one else can rightfully claim it, and his exclusive right to it involves no wrong to any one else. Thus there is to everything produced by human exertion a clear and indisputable title to exclusive possession and enjoyment, which is perfectly consistent with justice, as it descends from the original producer, in whom it vested by natural law. The pen with which I am writing is justly mine. No other human being can rightfully lay claim to it, for in me is the title of the producers who made it. It has become mine, because transferred to me by the stationer, to whom it was transferred by the importer, who obtained the exclusive right to it by transfer from the manufacturer, in whom, by the same process of purchase, vested the rights of those who dug the material from the ground and shaped it into a pen. Thus, my exclusive right of ownership in the pen springs from the natural right of the individual to the use of his own faculties.

Now, this is not only the original source from which all ideas of exclusive ownership arise — as is evident from the natural tendency of the mind to revert to it when the idea of exclusive ownership is questioned, and the manner in which social relations develop — but it is necessarily the only source. There can be to the ownership of anything no rightful title which is not derived from the title of the producer and does not rest upon the natural right of the man to himself. There can be no other rightful title, because (1st) there is no other natural right from which any other title can be derived, and (2d) because the recognition of any other title is inconsistent with and destructive of this.

For (1st) what other right exists from which the right to the exclusive possession of anything can be derived, save the right of a man to himself? With what other power is man by nature clothed, save the power of exerting his own faculties? How can he in any other way act upon or affect material things or other men? Paralyze the motor nerves, and your man has no more external influence or power than a log or stone. From what else, then, can the right of possessing and controlling things be derived? If it spring not from man himself, from what can it spring? Nature acknowledges no ownership or control in man save as the result of exertion. In no other way can her treasures be drawn forth, her powers directed, or her forces utilized or controlled. She makes no discriminations among men, but is to all absolutely impartial. She knows no distinction between master and slave, king and subject, saint and sinner. All men to her stand upon an equal footing and have equal rights. She recognizes no claim but that of labor, and recognizes that with-

out respect to the claimant. . . . Hence, as nature gives only to labor, the exertion of labor in production is the only title to exclusive possession.

(2d) This right of ownership that springs from labor excludes the possibility of any other right of ownership. If a man be rightfully entitled to the produce of his labor, then no one can be rightfully entitled to the ownership of anything which is not the produce of his labor, or the labor of some one else from whom the right has passed to him. If production give to the producer the right to exclusive possession and enjoyment, there can rightfully be no exclusive possession and enjoyment of anything not the production of labor, and the recognition of private property in land is a wrong. For the right to the produce of labor cannot be enjoyed without the right to the free use of the opportunities offered by nature, and to admit the right of property in these is to deny the right of property in the produce of labor. When nonproducers can claim as rent a portion of the wealth created by producers, the right of the producers to the fruits of their labor is to that extent denied.

There is no escape from this position. To affirm that a man can rightfully claim exclusive ownership in his own labor when embodied in material things, is to deny that any one can rightfully claim exclusive ownership in land. To affirm the rightfulness of property in land, is to affirm a claim which has no warrant in nature, as against a claim founded in the organization of man and the laws of the material universe. . . .

Whatever may be said for the institution of private property in land, it is therefore plain that it cannot be defended on the score of justice.

The equal right of all men to the use of land is as clear as their equal right to breathe the air — it is a right proclaimed by the fact of their existence. For we cannot suppose that some men have a right to be in this world and others no right. . . .

* * *

The right to exclusive ownership of anything of human production is clear. No matter how many the hands through which it has passed, there was, at the beginning of the line, human labor — some one who, having procured or produced it by his exertions, had to it a clear title as against all the rest of mankind, and which could justly pass from one to another by sale or gift.

But at the end of what string of conveyances or grants can be shown or supposed a like title to any part of the material universe? To improvements, such an original title can be shown; but it is a title only to the improvements, and not to the land itself. If I clear a forest, drain a swamp, or fill a morass, all I can justly claim is the value given by these exertions. They give me no right to the land itself, no claim other than to my equal share with every other member of the community in the value which is added to it by the growth of the community.

But it will be said: There are improvements which in time become indistinguishable from the land itself! Very well; then the title to the improvements becomes blended with the title to the land; the individual right is lost in the common right. It is the greater that swallows up the less, not the less that swallows up the greater. Nature does not proceed from man, but man from nature, and it is into the bosom of nature that he and all his works must return again.

Yet, it will be said: As every man has a right to the use and enjoyment of nature, the man who is using land must be permitted the exclusive right to its use in order that he may get the full benefit of his labor. But there is no difficulty in determining where the individual right ends and the common right begins. A delicate and exact test is supplied by value and with its aid there is no difficulty, no matter how dense population may become, in determining and securing the exact rights of each, the equal rights of all. . . .

* * *

As for the deduction of a complete and exclusive individual right to land from priority of occupation, that is, if possible, the most absurd ground on which landownership can be defended. Priority of occupation give exclusive and perpetual title to the surface of a globe on which, in the order of nature, countless generations succeed each other! Had the men of the last generation any better right to the use of this world than we of this? or the men of a hundred years ago? or of a thousand years ago? Had the mound builders, or the cave dwellers, the contemporaries of the mastodon and the three-toed horse, or the generations still further back, who, in dim aeons that we can think of only as geologic periods, followed each other on the earth we now tenant for our little day?

Has the first comer at a banquet the right to turn back all the chairs and claim that none of the other guests shall partake of the food provided, except as they make terms with him? Does the first man who presents a ticket at the door of a theater, and passes in, acquire by his priority the right to shut the doors and have the performance go on for him alone? Does the first passenger who enters a railroad car obtain the right to scatter his baggage over all the seats and compel the passengers who come in after him to stand up?

The cases are perfectly analogous. We arrive and we depart, guests at a banquet continually spread, spectators and participants in an entertainment where there is room for all who come; passengers from station to station, on an orb that whirls through space — our rights to take and possess cannot be exclusive; they must be bounded everywhere by the equal rights of others. Just as the passenger in a railroad car may spread himself and his baggage over as many seats as he pleases, until other passengers come in, so may a settler take and use as much land as he chooses, until it is needed by others — a fact which is shown by the land acquiring a value — when his right must be curtailed by the equal rights of the others, and no priority of appropriation can give a right which will bar these equal rights of others. If this were not the case, then by priority of appropriation one man could acquire and could transmit to whom he pleased, not merely the exclusive right to 160 acres, or to 640 acres, but to a whole township, a whole state, a whole continent.

And to this manifest absurdity does the recognition of individual right to land come when carried to its ultimate — that any one human being, could he concentrate in himself the individual rights to the land of any country, could expel therefrom all the rest of its inhabitants; and could he thus concentrate the individual rights to the whole surface of the globe, he alone of all the teeming population of the earth would have the right to live. . . .

* * *

The examination through which we have passed has proved conclusively that private property in land cannot be justified on the ground of utility — that, on the contrary, it is the great cause to which are to be traced the poverty, misery, and degradation, the social disease and the political weakness which are showing themselves so menacingly amid advancing civilization. Expediency, therefore, joins justice in demanding that we abolish it.

When expediency thus joins justice in demanding that we abolish an institution that has no broader base or stronger ground than a mere municipal regulation, what reason can there be for hesitation?

The consideration that seems to cause hesitation, even on the part of those who see clearly that land by right is common property, is the idea that having permitted land to be treated as private property for so long, we should in abolishing it be doing a wrong to those who have been suffered to base their calculations upon its permanence; that having permitted land to be held as rightful property, we should by the resumption of common rights be doing injustice to those who have purchased it with what was unquestionably their rightful property. Thus, it is held that if we abolish private property in land, justice requires that we should fully compensate those who now possess it, as the British Government, in abolishing the purchase and sale of military commissions, felt itself bound to compensate those who held commissions which they had purchased in the belief that they could sell them again, or as in abolishing slavery in the British West Indies $100,000,000 was paid the slaveholders. . . .

It is this idea that suggests the proposition, which finds advocates in Great Britain, that the government shall purchase at its market price the individual proprietorship of the land of the country, and it was this idea which led John Stuart Mill, although clearly perceiving the essential injustice of private property in land, to advocate, not a full resumption of the land, but only a resumption of accruing advantages in the future. His plan was that a fair and even liberal estimate should be made of the market value of all the land in the kingdom, and that future additions to that value, not due to the improvements of the proprietor, should be taken by the state.

To say nothing of the practical difficulties which such cumbrous plans involve, in the extension of the functions of government which they would require and the corruption they would beget, their inherent and essential defect lies in the impossibility of bridging over by any compromise the radical difference between

wrong and right. Just in proportion as the interests of the landholders are conserved, just in that proportion must general interests and general rights be disregarded, and if landholders are to lose nothing of their special privileges, the people at large can gain nothing. To buy up individual property rights would merely be to give the landholders in another form a claim of the same kind and amount that their possession of land now gives them; it would be to raise for them by taxation the same proportion of the earnings of labor and capital that they are now enabled to appropriate in rent. Their unjust advantage would be preserved and the unjust disadvantage of the non-landholders would be continued. . . .

* * *

Such inefficient and impracticable schemes may do to talk about, where any proposition more efficacious would not at present be entertained, and their discussion is a hopeful sign, as it shows the entrance of the thin end of the wedge of truth. Justice in men's mouths is cringingly humble when she first begins a protest against a time-honored wrong, and we of the English-speaking nations still wear the collar of the Saxon thrall, and have been educated to look upon the "vested rights" of landowners with all the superstitious reverence that ancient Egyptians looked upon the crocodile. But when the times are ripe for them, ideas grow, even though insignificant in their first appearance. One day, the Third Estate covered their heads when the king put on his hat. A little while thereafter, and the head of a son of St. Louis rolled from the scaffold. The antislavery movement in the United States commenced with talk of compensating owners, but when four millions of slaves were emancipated, the owners got no compensation, nor did they clamor for any. And by the time the people of any such country as England or the United States are sufficiently aroused to the injustice and disadvantages of individual ownership of land to induce them to attempt its nationalization, they will be sufficiently aroused to nationalize it in a much more direct and easy way than by purchase. They will not trouble themselves about compensating the proprietors of land.

Nor is it right that there should be any concern about the proprietors of land. That such a man as

John Stuart Mill should have attached so much importance to the compensation of landowners as to have urged the confiscation merely of the future increase in rent, is explainable only by his acquiescence in the current doctrines that wages are drawn from capital and that population constantly tends to press upon subsistence. These blinded him as to the full effects of the private appropriation of land. He saw that "the claim of the landholder is altogether subordinate to the general policy of the state." and that "when private property in land is not expedient, it is unjust," but, entangled in the toils of the Malthusian doctrine, he attributed, as he expressly states in a paragraph I have previously quoted, the want and suffering that he saw around him to "the niggardliness of nature, not to the injustice of man," and thus to him the nationalization of land seemed comparatively a little thing, that could accomplish nothing toward the eradication of pauperism and the abolition of want—ends that could be reached only as men learned to repress a natural instinct. Great as he was and pure as he was—warm heart and noble mind—he yet never saw the true harmony of economic laws, nor realized how from this one great fundamental wrong flow want and misery, and vice and shame. Else he could never have written this sentence: "This land of Ireland, the land of every country, belongs to the people of the country. The individuals called landowners have no right in morality and justice to anything but the rent, or compensation for its salable value."

In the name of the Prophet—figs! If the land of any country belong to the people of that country, what right, in morality and justice, have the individuals called landowners to the rent? If the land belong to the people, why in the name of morality and justice should the people pay its salable value for their own?

Herbert Spencer says: "Had we to deal with the parties who originally robbed the human race of its heritage, we might make short work of the matter." Why not make short work of the matter anyhow? For this robbery is not like the robbery of a horse or a sum of money, that ceases with the act. It is a fresh and continuous robbery, that goes on every day and every hour. It is not from the produce of the past that rent is drawn; it is from the produce of the present. It is a toll levied

upon labor constantly and continuously. Every blow of the hammer, every stroke of the pick, every thrust of the shuttle, every throb of the steam engine, pays it tribute. It levies upon the earnings of the men who, deep under ground, risk their lives, and of those who over white surges hang to reeling masts; it claims the just reward of the capitalist and the fruits of the inventor's patient effort; it takes little children from play and from school, and compels them to work before their bones are hard or their muscles are firm; it robs the shivering of warmth; the hungry, of food; the sick, of medicine; the anxious, of peace. It debases, and embrutes, and embitters. It crowds families of eight and ten into a single squalid room; it herds like swine agricultural gangs of boys and girls; it fills the gin palace and groggery with those who have no comfort in their homes; it makes lads who might be useful men candidates for prisons and penitentiaries; it fills brothels with girls who might have known the pure joy of motherhood; it sends greed and all evil passions prowling through society as a hard winter drives the wolves to the abodes of men; it darkens faith in the human soul, and across the reflection of a just and merciful Creator draws the veil of a hard, and blind, and cruel fate!

It is not merely a robbery in the past; it is a robbery in the present—a robbery that deprives of their birthright the infants that are now coming into the world! Why should we hesitate about making short work of such a system? Because I was robbed yesterday, and the day before, and the day before that, is it any reason that I should suffer myself to be robbed today and tomorrow? any reason that I should conclude that the robber has acquired a vested right to rob me? ...

* * *

Try the case of the landholders by the maxims of the common law by which the rights of man and man are determined. The common law we are told is the perfection of reason, and certainly the landowners cannot complain of its decision, for it has been built up by and for landowners. Now what does the law allow to the innocent possessor when the land for which he paid his money is adjudged rightfully to belong to another? Nothing at all. That he purchased in good faith gives him no right or claim whatever.

The law does not concern itself with the "intricate question of compensation" to the innocent purchaser. . . . And not only this, it takes from him all the improvements that he has in good faith made upon the land. You may have paid a high price for land, making every exertion to see that the title is good; you may have held it in undisturbed possession for years without thought or hint of an adverse claimant; made it fruitful by your toil or erected upon it a costly building of greater value than the land itself, or a modest home in which you hope, surrounded by the fig trees you have planted and the vines you have dressed, to pass your declining days; yet if Quirk, Gammon & Snap can mouse out a technical flaw in your parchments or hunt up some forgotten heir who never dreamed of his rights, not merely the land, but all your improvements, may be taken away from you. And not merely that. According to the common law, when you have surrendered the land and given up your improvements, you may be called upon to account for the profits you derived from the land during the time you had it.

Now if we apply to this case of The People *vs.* The Landowners the same maxims of justice that have been formulated by landowners into law, and are applied every day in English and American courts to disputes between man and man, we shall not only not think of giving the landholders any compensation for the land, but shall take all the improvements and whatever else they may have as well.

But I do not propose, and I do not suppose that any one else will propose, to go so far. It is sufficient if the people resume the ownership of the land. Let the landowners retain their improvements and personal property in secure possession.

And in this measure of justice would be no oppression, no injury to any class. The great cause of the present unequal distribution of wealth, with the suffering, degradation, and waste that it entails, would be swept away. Even landholders would share in the general gain. The gain of even the large landholders would be a real one. The gain of the small landholders would be enormous. For in welcoming Justice, men welcome the handmaid of Love. Peace and Plenty follow in her train, bringing their good gifts, not to some, but to all.

[From] *Capital*

KARL MARX

[P]rimitive accumulation plays in Political Economy about the same part as original sin in theology. Adam bit the apple, and thereupon sin fell on the human race. Its origin is supposed to be explained when it is told as an anecdote of the past. In times long gone by there were two sorts of people; one, the diligent, intelligent, and, above all, frugal élite; the other, lazy rascals, spending their substance, and more, in riotous living. The legend of theological original sin tells us certainly how man came to be condemned to eat his bread in the sweat of his brow; but the history of economic original sin reveals to us that there are people to whom this is by no means essential. Never mind! Thus it came to pass that the former sort accumulated wealth, and the latter sort had at last nothing to sell except their own skins. And from this original sin dates the poverty of the great majority that, despite all its labour, has up to now nothing to sell but itself, and the wealth of the few that increases constantly although they have long ceased to work. Such insipid childishness is every day preached to us in the defence of property. M. Thiers, *e.g.*, had the assurance to repeat it with all the solemnity of a statesman, to the French people, once so *spirituel*. But as soon as the question of property crops up, it becomes a sacred duty to proclaim the intellectual food of the infant as the one thing fit for all ages and for all stages of development. In actual history it is notorious that conquest, enslavement, robbery, murder, briefly force, play the great part. In the tender annals of Political Economy, the idyllic reigns from time immemorial. Right and "labour" were from all time the sole means of enrichment, the present year of course always excepted. As a matter of fact, the methods of primitive accumulation are anything but idyllic.

* * *

The capitalist system presupposes the complete separation of the labourers from all property in the means by which they can realise their labour. As soon as capitalist production is once on its own legs, it not only maintains this separation, but reproduces it on a continually extending scale. The process, therefore, that clears the way for the capitalist system, can be none other than the process which takes away from the labourer the possession of his means of production; a process that transforms, on the one hand, the social means of subsistence and of production into capital, on the other, the immediate producers into wage-labourers. The so-called primitive accumulation, therefore, is nothing else than the historical process of divorcing the producer from the means of production.

* * *

What does the primitive accumulation of capital, *i.e.*, its historical genesis, resolve itself into? In so far as it is not immediate transformation of slaves and serfs into wage-labourers, and therefore a mere change of form, it only means the expropriation of the immediate producers, *i.e.*, the dissolution of private property based on the labour of its owner. Private property, as the antithesis to social, collective property, exists only where the means of labour and the external conditions of labour belong to private individuals. But according as these private individuals are labourers or not labourers, private property has a different character. The numberless shades, that it at first sight presents, correspond to the intermediate stages lying between these two extremes. The private property of the labourer in his means of production is the foundation of petty industry, whether agricultural, manufacturing or both; petty industry, again, is an essential condition for the development of social production and of the free individuality of the labourer himself. Of course, this petty mode of production exists also under slavery, serfdom, and other states of dependence. But it flourishes, it lets loose its whole energy, it attains its adequate classical form, only where the labourer is the private owner of his own means of labour set in action by himself: the peasant of the land which he cultivates, the artizan of the tool which he handles as a virtuoso. This mode of production pre-supposes parcelling of the soil, and scattering of the other means of production. As it excludes the concentration of these means of production, so also it excludes cooperation, division of labour within each separate process of production, the control over, and the productive application of the forces of Nature by society, and the free development of the social productive powers. It is compatible only with a system of production, and a society, moving within narrow and more or less primitive bounds. To perpetuate it would be, as Pecqueur rightly says, "to decree universal mediocrity." At a certain stage of development it brings forth the material agencies for its own dissolution. From that moment new forces and new passions spring up in the bosom of society; but the old social organization fetters them and keeps them down. It must be annihilated; it is annihilated. Its annihilation, the transformation of the individualised and scattered means of production into socially concentrated ones, of the pigmy property of the many into the huge property of the few, the expropriation of the great mass of the people from the soil, from the means of subsistence, and from the means of labour, this fearful and painful expropriation of the mass of the people forms the prelude to the history of capital. It comprises a series of forcible methods, of which we have passed in review only those that have been epoch-making as methods of the primitive accumulation of capital. The expropriation of the immediate producers was accomplished with merciless Vandalism, and under the stimulus of passions the most infamous, the most sordid, the pettiest, the most meanly odious. Self-earned private property, that is based, so to say, on the fusing together of the isolated, independent labouring-individual with the conditions of his labour, is supplanted by capitalistic private property, which rests on exploitation of the nominally free labour of others, *i.e.*, on wages-labour.

As soon as this process of transformation has sufficiently decomposed the old society from top to bottom, as soon as the labourers are turned into proletarians, their means of labour into capital, as soon as the capitalist mode of production stands on its own feet, then the further socialisation of labour and further transformation of the land and other means of production into socially exploited and, therefore, common means of production, as well as the further expropriation of private proprietors, takes a new form. That which is now to be expropriated is no longer the labourer working for himself, but the capitalist exploiting many labourers. This expropriation is accomplished by the action of the immanent laws of capitalistic production itself, by the centralisation of capital. One capitalist always kills many. Hand in hand with this centralisation, or this expropriation of many capitalists by few, develop, on an ever extending scale, the co-operative form of the labour-process, the conscious technical application of science, the methodical cultivation of the soil, the transformation of the instruments of labour into instruments of labour only usable in common, the economising of all means of production by their use as the means of production of combined, socialised labour, the entanglement of all peoples in the net of the world-market, and this, the international character of the capitalistic régime. Along with the constantly diminishing number of the magnates of capital, who usurp and monopolise all advantages of this process of transformation, grows the mass of misery, oppression, slavery, degradation, exploitation; but with this too grows the revolt of the working-class, a class always increasing in numbers, and disciplined, united, organised by the very mechanism of the process of capitalist production itself. The monopoly of capital becomes a fetter upon the mode of production, which has sprung up and flourished along with, and under it. Centralisation of the means of production and socialisation of labour at last reach a point where they become incompatible with their capitalist integument. This integument is burst

asunder. The knell of capitalist private property sounds. The expropriators are expropriated.

The capitalist mode of appropriation, the result of the capitalist mode of production, produces capitalist private property. This is the first negation of individual private property, as founded on the labour of the proprietor. But capitalist production begets, with the inexorability of a law of Nature, its own negation. It is the negation of negation. This does not re-establish private property for the producer, but gives him individual property based on the acquisitions of the capitalist era: *i.e.*, on cooperation and the possession in common of the land and of the means of production.

The transformation of scattered private property, arising from individual labour, into capitalist private property is, naturally, a process, incomparably more protracted, violent, and difficult, than the transformation of capitalistic private property, already practically resting on socialized production, into socialised property. In the former case, we had the expropriation of the mass of the people by a few usurpers; in the latter, we have the expropriation of a few usurpers by the mass of the people.[1]

NOTE

1. The advance of industry, whose involuntary promoter is the bourgeoisie, replaces the isolation of the labourers, due to compensation, by their revolutionary combination, due to association. The development of Modern Industry, therefore, cuts from under its feet, the very foundation on which the bourgeoisie produces and appropriates products. What the bourgeoisie, therefore, produces, above all, are its own grave-diggers. Its fall and the victory of the proletariat are equally inevitable . . . Of all the classes, that stand face to face with the bourgeoisie to-day, the proletariat alone is a really revolutionary class. The other classes perish and disappear in the face of Modern Industry, the proletariat is its special and essential product . . . The lower middle-classes, the small manufacturers, the shopkeepers, the artisan, the peasant, all these fight against the bourgeoisie, to save from extinction their existence as fractions of the middle-class . . . they are reactionary, for they try to roll back the wheel of history. Karl Marx und Friedrich Engels, "Manifest der Kommunistischen Partei," London, 1848, pp. 9, 11.

Notes and Questions

ROBERT NOZICK, from *Anarchy, State, and Utopia*

1. Robert Nozick defends liberal individualism and private ownership using his own development of Lockean natural rights theory. Ownership is justified, according to Nozick, if it is (a) justly acquired or (b) justly transferred and (c) not subject to the principle of rectification. Explain these three principles.

2. Nozick discusses the distinction between historical and end-state or patterned theories of property distribution. How does a patterned theory of distribution work? Do you agree with Nozick that F. A. Hayek's theory is a patterned theory? How does Nozick's own historical theory work?

3. Nozick argues that freedom upsets patterns. Thus, any patterned theory of distribution will require constant interference. How does the Wilt Chamberlain example show that this is true? What does this point amount to?

4. Nozick claims that taxation is equal to forced labor. How does he argue for this claim?

5. How does Nozick explain Locke's theory of acquisition as he is using it? Does his use depart significantly from Locke's own? If so, in what way?

6. Does Locke's proviso still hold, according to Nozick? What are the two interpretations he offers for it? Which does he defend and why? Reasonably interpreted, should Locke's proviso have a great impact on Nozick's theory of property?

[From] *Anarchy, State, and Utopia*

ROBERT NOZICK

The subject of justice in holdings consists of three major topics. The first is the *original acquisition of holdings*, the appropriation of unheld things. This includes the issues of how unheld things may come to be held, the process, or processes, by which unheld things may come to be held, the things that may come to be held by these processes, the extent of what comes to be held by a particular process, and so on. We shall refer to the complicated truth about this topic, which we shall not formulate here, as the principle of justice in acquisition. The second topic concerns the *transfer of holdings* from one person to another. By what processes may a person transfer holdings to another? How may a person acquire a holding from another who holds it? Under this topic come general descriptions of voluntary exchange, and gift and (on the other hand) fraud, as well as reference to particular conventional details fixed upon in a given society. The complicated truth about this subject (with placeholders for conventional details) we shall call the principle of justice in transfer. (And we shall suppose it also includes principles governing how a person may divest himself of a holding, passing it into an unheld state.)

If the world were wholly just, the following inductive definition would exhaustively cover the subject of justice in holdings.

1. A person who acquires a holding in accordance with the principle of justice in acquisition is entitled to that holding.

2. A person who acquires a holding in accordance with the principle of justice in transfer,

from someone else entitled to the holding, is entitled to the holding.

3. No one is entitled to a holding except by (repeated) applications of 1 and 2.

The complete principle of distributive justice would say simply that a distribution is just if everyone is entitled to the holdings they possess under the distribution.

A distribution is just if it arises from another just distribution by legitimate means. The legitimate means of moving from one distribution to another are specified by the principle of justice in transfer. The legitimate first "moves" are specified by the principle of justice in acquisition.[1] Whatever arises from a just situation by just steps is itself just. The means of change specified by the principle of justice in transfer preserve justice. As correct rules of inference are truth-preserving, and any conclusion deduced via repeated application of such rules from only true premises is itself true, so the means of transition from one situation to another specified by the principle of justice in transfer are justice-preserving, and any situation actually arising from repeated transitions in accordance with the principle from a just situation is itself just. The parallel between justice-preserving transformations and truth-preserving transformations illuminates where it fails as well as where it holds. That a conclusion could have been deduced by truth-preserving means from premises that are true suffices to show its truth. That from a just situation a situation *could* have arisen via justice-preserving means does *not* suffice to show its justice. The fact that a thief's victims voluntarily *could* have presented him with gifts does not entitle the thief to his ill-gotten gains. Justice in holdings is historical; it depends upon what actually has happened. We shall return to this point later.

Not all actual situations are generated in accordance with the two principles of justice in holdings: the principle of justice in acquisition and the principle of justice in transfer. Some people steal from others, or defraud them, or enslave them, seizing their product and preventing them from living as they choose, or forcibly exclude others from competing in exchanges. None of these are permissible modes of transition from one situation to another. And some persons acquire holdings by means not sanctioned by the principle of justice in acquisition. The existence of past injustice (previous violations of the first two principles of justice in holdings) raises the third major topic under justice in holdings: the rectification of injustice in holdings. If past injustice has shaped present holdings in various ways, some identifiable and some not, what now, if anything, ought to be done to rectify these injustices? What obligations do the performers of injustice have toward those whose position is worse than it would have been had the injustice not been done? Or, than it would have been had compensation been paid promptly? How, if at all, do things change if the beneficiaries and those made worse off are not the direct parties in the act of injustice, but, for example, their descendants? Is an injustice done to someone whose holding was itself based upon an unrectified injustice? How far back must one go in wiping clean the historical slate of injustices? What may victims of injustice permissibly do in order to rectify the injustices being done to them, including the many injustices done by persons acting through their government? I do not know of a thorough or theoretically sophisticated treatment of such issues.[2] Idealizing greatly, let us suppose theoretical investigation will produce a principle of rectification. This principle uses historical information about previous situations and injustices done in them (as defined by the first two principles of justice and rights against interference), and information about the actual course of events that flowed from these injustices, until the present, and it yields a description (or descriptions) of holdings in the society. The principle of rectification presumably will make use of its best estimate of subjunctive information about what would have occurred (or a probability distribution over what might have occurred, using the expected value) if the injustice had not taken place. If the actual description of holdings turns out not to be one of the descriptions yielded by the principle, then one of the descriptions yielded must be realized.[3]

The general outlines of the theory of justice in holdings are that the holdings of a person are just if he is entitled to them by the principles of justice in acquisition and transfer, or by the principle of rectification of injustice (as specified by the first two principles). If each person's holdings are just, then the total set (distribution) of holdings is just. To turn these general outlines into a specific theory we would have to specify the details of each of the three principles of justice in holdings: the principle of acquisition of holdings, the principle of transfer of holdings, and the principle of rectification of violations of the first two principles. I shall not attempt that task here. (Locke's principle of justice in acquisition is discussed below.)

Historical Principles and End-Result Principles

The general outlines of the entitlement theory illuminate the nature and defects of other conceptions of distributive justice. The entitlement theory of justice in distribution is *historical*; whether a distribution is just depends upon how it came about. In contrast, *current time-slice principles* of justice hold that the justice of a distribution is determined by how things are distributed (who has what) as judged by some *structural* principle(s) of just distribution. A utilitarian who judges between any two distributions by seeing which has the greater sum of utility and, if the sums tie, applies some fixed equality criterion to choose the more equal distribution, would hold a current time-slice principle of justice. As would someone who had a fixed schedule of trade-offs between the sum of happiness and equality. According to a current time-slice principle, all that needs to be looked at, in judging the justice of a distribution, is who ends up with what; in comparing any two distributions one need look only at the matrix presenting the distributions. No further information need be fed into a principle of justice. It is a consequence of such principles of justice that any two structurally identical distributions are equally just. (Two distributions are structurally identical if they present the same profile, but perhaps have different persons occupying the particular slots. My having ten and your having five, and my having five and your having ten are structurally identical distributions.) Welfare economics is the theory of current time-slice principles of justice. The subject is conceived as operating on matrices representing only current information about distribution.

This, as well as some of the usual conditions (for example, the choice of distribution is invariant under relabeling of columns), guarantees that welfare economics will be a current time-slice theory, with all of its inadequacies.

Most persons do not accept current time-slice principles as constituting the whole story about distributive shares. They think it relevant in assessing the justice of a situation to consider not only the distribution it embodies, but also how that distribution came about. If some persons are in prison for murder or war crimes, we do not say that to assess the justice of the distribution in the society we must look only at what this person has, and that person has, and that person has, . . . at the current time. We think it relevant to ask whether someone did something so that he *deserved* to be punished, deserved to have a lower share. Most will agree to the relevance of further information with regard to punishments and penalties. Consider also desired things. One traditional socialist view is that workers are entitled to the product and full fruits of their labor; they have earned it; a distribution is unjust if it does not give the workers what they are entitled to. Such entitlements are based upon some past history. No socialist holding this view would find it comforting to be told that because the actual distribution A happens to coincide structurally with the one he desires D, A therefore is no less just than D; it differs only in that the "parasitic" owners of capital receive under A what the workers are entitled to under D, namely very little. This socialist rightly, in my view, holds onto the notions of earning, producing, entitlement, desert, and so forth, and he rejects current time-slice principles that look only to the structure of the resulting set of holdings. (The set of holdings resulting from what? Isn't it implausible that how holdings are produced and come to exist has no effect at all on who should hold what?) His mistake lies in his view of what entitlements arise out of what sorts of productive processes.

We construe the position we discuss too narrowly by speaking of *current* time-slice principles. Nothing is changed if structural principles operate upon a time sequence of current time-slice profiles and, for example, give someone more now to counterbalance the less he has had earlier. A utilitarian or an egalitarian or any mixture of the two over time will inherit the difficulties of his more myopic comrades. He is not helped by the fact that *some* of the information others consider relevant in assessing a distribution is reflected, unrecoverably, in past matrices. Henceforth, we shall refer to such unhistorical principles of distributive justice including the current time-slice principles, as *end-result principles* or *end-state principles*

In contrast to end-result principles of justice, *historical principles* of justice hold that past circumstances or actions of people can create differential entitlement or differential deserts to things. An injustice can be worked by moving from one distribution to another structurally identical one, for the second, in profile the same, may violate people's entitlements or deserts; it may not fit the actual history.

Patterning

The entitlement principles of justice in holdings that we have sketched are historical principles of justice. To better understand their precise character, we shall distinguish them from another subclass of the historical principles. Consider as an example, the principle of distribution according to moral merit. This principle requires that total distributive shares vary directly with moral merit; no person should have a greater share than anyone whose moral merit is greater. (If more merit could be not merely ordered but measured on an interval or ratio scale stronger principles could be formulated.) Or consider the principle that results by substituting "usefulness to society" for "moral merit" in the previous principle. Or instead of "distribute according to moral merit," or "distribute according to usefulness to society," we might consider "distribute according to the weighted sum of moral merit, usefulness to society, and need," with the weights of the different dimensions equal. Let us call a principle of distribution *patterned* if it specified that a distribution is to vary along with some natural dimension, weighted sum of natural dimensions, or lexicographic ordering of natural dimensions. And let us say a distribution is patterned if it accords with some patterned principle. (I speak of natural dimensions, admittedly without a general criterion for them, because for any set of

holdings some artificial dimensions can be gimmicked up to vary along with the distribution of the set.) The principle of distribution in accordance with moral merit is a patterned historical principle, which specifies a patterned distribution. "Distribute according to I.Q." is a patterned principle that looks to information not contained in distributional matrices. It is not historical, however, in that it does not look to any past actions creating differential entitlements to evaluate a distribution; it requires only distributional matrices whose columns are labeled by I.Q. scores. The distribution in a society, however, may be composed of such simple patterned distributions, without itself being simply patterned. Different sectors may operate different patterns, or some combination of patterns may operate in different proportions across a society. A distribution composed in this manner, from a small number of patterned distributions, we also shall term "patterned." And we extend the use of "pattern" to include the overall designs put forth by combinations of end-state principles.

Almost every suggested principle of distributive justice is patterned: to each according to his moral merit, or needs, or marginal product, or how hard he tries, or the weighted sum of the foregoing, and so on. The principle of entitlement we have sketched is *not* patterned.[4] There is no one natural dimension or weighted sum or combination of a small number of natural dimensions that yields the distributions generated in accordance with the principle of entitlement. The set of holdings that results when some persons receive their marginal products, others win at gambling, others receive a share of their mate's income, others receive gifts from foundations, others receive interest on loans, others receive gifts from admirers, others receive returns on investment, others make for themselves much of what they have, others find things, and so on, will not be patterned. Heavy strands of patterns will run through it; significant portions of the variance in holdings will be accounted for by pattern-variables. If most people most of the time choose to transfer some of their entitlements to others only in exchange for something from them, then a large part of what many people hold will vary with what they held that others wanted. More details are provided by the theory of marginal productivity. But gifts to relatives, charitable donations, bequests to children, and the like, are not best conceived, in the first instance, in this manner. Ignoring the strands of pattern, let us suppose for the moment that a distribution actually arrived at by the operation of the principle of entitlement is random with respect to any pattern. Though the resulting set of holdings will be unpatterned, it will not be incomprehensible, for it can be seen as arising from the operation of a small number of principles. These principles specify how an initial distribution may arise (the principle of acquisition of holdings) and how distributions may be transformed into others (the principle of transfer of holdings). The process whereby the set of holdings is generated will be intelligible, though the set of holdings itself that results from this process will be unpatterned.

The writings of F. A. Hayek focus less than is usually done upon what patterning distributive justice requires. Hayek argues that we cannot know enough about each person's situation to distribute to each according to his moral merit (but would justice demand we do so if we did have this knowledge?); and he goes on to say, "our objection is against all attempts to impress upon society a deliberately chosen pattern of distribution, whether it be an order of equality or of inequality."[5] However, Hayek concludes that in a free society there will be distribution in accordance with value rather than moral merit; that is, in accordance with the perceived value of a person's actions and services to others. Despite his rejection of a patterned conception of distributive justice, Hayek himself suggests a pattern he thinks justifiable: distribution in accordance with the perceived benefits given to others, leaving room for the complaint that a free society does not realize exactly this pattern. Stating this patterned strand of a free capitalist society more precisely, we get "To each according to how much he benefits others who have the resources for benefitting those who benefit them." This will seem arbitrary unless some acceptable initial set of holdings is specified, or unless it is held that the operation of the system over time washes out any significant effects from the initial set of holdings. As an example of the latter, if almost anyone would have bought a car from Henry Ford, the supposition that it was an arbitrary matter who held the money then (and so bought) would not place Henry Ford's earnings under a cloud. In any event, *his* coming to hold it is not arbitrary. Distribution according to benefits to others *is* a major patterned strand in a free capitalist society, as Hayek correctly points out, but it is only a strand and does not constitute the whole pattern of a system of entitlements (namely, inheritance, gifts for arbitrary reasons, charity, and so on) or a standard that one should insist a society fit. Will people tolerate for long a system yielding distributions that they believe are unpatterned?[6] No doubt people will not long accept a distribution they believe is *unjust*. People want their society to be and to look just. But must the look of justice reside in a resulting pattern rather than in the underlying generating principles? We are in no position to conclude that the inhabitants of a society embodying an entitlement conception of justice in holdings will find it unacceptable. Still, it must be granted that were people's reasons for transferring some of their holdings to others always irrational or arbitrary, we would find this disturbing. (Suppose people always determined what holdings they would transfer, and to whom, by using a random device.) We feel more comfortable upholding the justice of an entitlement system if most of the transfers under it are done for reasons. This does not mean necessarily that all deserve what holdings they receive. It means only that there is a purpose or point to someone's transferring a holding to one person rather than to another; that usually we can see what the transferrer thinks he's gaining, what cause he thinks he's serving, what goals he thinks he's helping to achieve, and so forth. Since in a capitalist society people often transfer holdings to others in accordance with how much they perceive these others benefiting them, the fabric constituted by the individual transactions and transfers is largely reasonable and intelligible.[7] (Gifts to loved ones, bequests to children, charity to the needy also are nonarbitrary components of the fabric.) In stressing the large strand of distribution in accordance with benefit to others, Hayek shows the point of many transfers, and so shows that the system of transfer of entitlements is not just spinning its gears aimlessly. The system of entitlements is defensible when constituted by the individual aims of individual transactions. No overarching aim is needed, no distributional pattern is required.

To think that the task of a theory of distributive justice is to fill in the blank in "to each according to his ____ " is to be predisposed to search for a pattern; and the separate treatment of "from each according to his ____ " treats production and distribution as two separate and independent issues. On an entitlement view these are *not* two separate questions. Whoever makes something, having bought or contracted for all other held resources used in the process (transferring some of his holdings for these cooperating factors), is entitled to it. The situation is *not* one of something's getting made, and there being an open question of who is to get it. Things come into the world already attached to people having entitlements over them. From the point of view of the historical entitlement conception of justice in holdings, those who start afresh to complete "to each according to his ____ " treat objects as if they appeared from nowhere, out of nothing. A complete theory of justice might cover this limit case as well; perhaps here is a use for the usual conceptions of distributive justice.[8]

So entrenched are maxims of the usual form that perhaps we should present the entitlement conception as a competitor. Ignoring acquisition and rectification, we might say:

> From each according to what he chooses to do, to each according to what he makes for himself (perhaps with the contracted aid of others) and what others choose to do for him and choose to give him of what they've been given previously (under this maxim) and haven't yet expended or transferred.

This, the discerning reader will have noticed, has its defects as a slogan. So as a summary and great simplification (and not as a maxim with any independent meaning) we have:

> From each as they choose, to each as they are chosen.

How Liberty Upsets Patterns

It is not clear how those holding alternative conceptions of distributive justice can reject the entitlement conception of justice in holdings. For suppose a distribution favored by one of these nonentitlement conceptions is realized. Let us suppose it is your favorite one and let us call this distribution D_1; perhaps everyone has an equal share, perhaps shares vary in accordance with

some dimension you treasure. Now suppose that Wilt Chamberlain is greatly in demand by basketball teams, being a great gate attraction. (Also suppose contracts run only for a year, with players being free agents.) He signs the following sort of contract with a team: In each home game, twenty-five cents from the price of each ticket of admission goes to him. (We ignore the question of whether he is "gouging" the owners, letting them look out for themselves.) The season starts, and people cheerfully attend his team's games; they buy their tickets, each time dropping a separate twenty-five cents of their admission price into a special box with Chamberlain's name on it. They are excited about seeing him play; it is worth the total admission price to them. Let us suppose that in one season one million persons attend his home games, and Wilt Chamberlain winds up with $250,000, a much larger sum than the average income and larger even than anyone else has. Is he entitled to this income? Is this new distribution D_2 unjust? If so, why? There is *no* question about whether each of the people was entitled to the control over the resources they held in D_1; because that was the distribution (your favorite) that (for the purposes of argument) we assumed was acceptable. Each of these persons *chose* to give twenty-five cents of their money to Chamberlain. They could have spent it on going to the movies, or on candy bars, or on copies of *Dissent* magazine, or of *Monthly Review*. But they all, at least one million of them, converged on giving it to Wilt Chamberlain in exchange for watching him play basketball. If D_1 was a just distribution, and people voluntarily moved from it to D_2, transferring parts of their shares they were given under D_1 (what was it for if not to do something with?), isn't D_2 also just? if the people were entitled to dispose of the resources to which they were entitled (under D_1), didn't this include their being entitled to give it to, or exchange it with, Wilt Chamberlain? Can anyone else complain on grounds of justice? Each other person already has his legitimate share under D_1. Under D_1 there is nothing that anyone has that anyone else has a claim of justice against. After someone transfers something to Wilt Chamberlain, third parties *still* have their legitimate shares; *their* shares are not changed. By what process could such a transfer among two persons give rise to a legitimate claim of distributive justice on a portion of what was transferred, by a third party who had no claim of justice on any holding of the others *before* the transfers?[9] To cut off objections irrelevant here, we might imagine the exchanges occurring in a socialist society, after hours. After playing whatever basketball he does in his daily work, or doing whatever other daily work he does, Wilt Chamberlain decides to put in *overtime* to earn additional money. (First his work quota is set; he works time over that.) Or imagine it is a skilled juggler people like to see, who puts on shows after hours.

Why might someone work overtime in a society in which it is assumed their needs are satisfied? Perhaps because they care about things other than needs. I like to write in books that I read, and to have easy access to books for browsing at odd hours. It would be very pleasant and convenient to have the resources of Widener Library in my back yard. No society, I assume, will provide such resources close to each person who would like them as part of his regular allotment (under D_1). Thus, persons either must do without some extra things that they want, or be allowed to do something extra to get some of these things. On what basis could the inequalities that would eventuate be forbidden? Notice also that small factories would spring up in a socialist society, unless forbidden. I melt down some of my personal possessions (under D_1) and build a machine out of the material. I offer you, and others, a philosophy lecture once a week in exchange for your cranking the handle on my machine, whose products I exchange for yet other things, and so on. (The raw materials used by the machine are given to me by others who possess them under D_1, in exchange for hearing lectures.) Each person might participate to gain things over and above their allotment under D_1. Some persons even might want to leave their job in socialist industry and work full time in this private sector. . . . Here I wish merely to note how private property even in means of production would occur in a socialist society that did not forbid people to use as they wished some of the resources they are given under the socialist distribution D_1.[10] The socialist society would have to forbid capitalist acts between consenting adults.

The general point illustrated by the Wilt Chamberlain example and the example of the entrepreneur in a socialist society is that no end-state principle or distributional patterned principle of justice can be continuously realized without continuous interference with people's lives. Any favored pattern would be transformed into one unfavored by the principle, by people choosing to act in various ways; for example, by people exchanging goods and services with other people, or giving things to other people, things the transferrers are entitled to under the favored distributional pattern. To maintain a pattern one must either continually interfere to stop people from transferring resources as they wish to, or continually (or periodically) interfere to take from some persons resources that others for some reason chose to transfer to them. (But if some time limit is to be set on how long people may keep resources others voluntarily transfer to them, why let them keep these resources for *any* period of time? Why not have immediate confiscation?) It might be objected that all persons voluntarily will choose to refrain from actions which would upset the pattern. This presupposes unrealistically (1) that all will most want to maintain the pattern (are those who don't, to be "reeducated" or forced to undergo "self-criticism"?), (2) that each can gather enough information about his own actions and the ongoing activities of others to discover which of his actions will upset the pattern, and (3) that diverse and far-flung persons can coordinate their actions to dovetail into the pattern. Compare the manner in which the market is neutral among persons' desires, as it reflects and transmits widely scattered information via prices, and coordinates persons' activities.

It puts things perhaps a bit too strongly to say that every patterned (or end-state) principle is liable to be thwarted by the voluntary actions of the individual parties transferring some of their shares they receive under the principle. For perhaps some *very* weak patterns are not so thwarted. Any distributional pattern with any egalitarian component is overturnable by the voluntary actions of individual persons over time; as is every patterned condition with sufficient content so as actually to have been proposed as presenting the central core of distributive justice. Still, given the possibility that some weak conditions or patterns may not be unstable in this way, it would be better to formulate an explicit description of the kind of interesting and contentful patterns under discussion, and to prove a theorem about their instability. Since the weaker the patterning, the more likely it is that the entitlement system itself satisfies it, a plausible conjecture is that any patterning either is unstable or is satisfied by the entitlement system.

*   *   *

Redistribution and Property Rights

Apparently, patterned principles allow people to choose to expend upon themselves, but not upon others, those resources they are entitled to (or rather, receive) under some favored distributional pattern D_1. For if each of several persons chooses to expend some of his D_1 resources upon one other person, then that other person will receive more than his D_1 share, disturbing the favored distributional pattern. Maintaining a distributional pattern is individualism with a vengeance! Patterned distributional principles do not give people what entitlement principles do, only better distributed. For they do not give the right to choose what to do with what one has; they do not give the right to choose to pursue an end involving (instrinsically, or as a means) the enhancement of another's position. To such views, families are disturbing; for within a family occur transfers that upset the favored distributional pattern. Either families themselves become units to which distribution takes place, the column occupiers (on what rationale?), or loving behavior is forbidden. We should note in passing the ambivalent position of radicals toward the family. Its loving relationships are seen as a model to be emulated and extended across the whole society, at the same time that it is denounced as a suffocating institution to be broken and condemned as a focus of parochial concerns that interfere with achieving radical goals. Need we say that it is not appropriate to enforce across the wider society the relationships of love and care appropriate within a family, relationships which are voluntarily undertaken? Incidentally, love is an interesting instance of another relationship that is historical, in that (like justice) it depends upon what actually occurred. An adult may come to love another because of the other's characteristics; but it is the other person, and not the characteristics, that is loved. The love is not transferrable to someone else with the same characteristics, even to one who "scores" higher for these characteristics. And the love endures through changes of the characteristics that gave rise to it. One loves the particular person one actually encountered. Why love is historical, attaching to persons in this way and not to characteristics, is an interesting and puzzling question.

Proponents of patterned principles of distributive justice focus upon criteria for determining who is to receive holdings; they consider the reasons for which someone should have something, and also the total picture of holdings. Whether or not it is better to give than to receive, proponents of patterned principles ignore giving altogether. In considering the distribution of goods, income, and so forth, their theories are theories of recipient justice; they completely ignore any right a person might have to give something to someone. Even in exchanges where each party is simultaneously giver and recipient, patterned principles of justice focus only upon the recipient role and its supposed rights. Thus discussions tend to focus on whether people (should) have a right to inherit, rather than on whether people (should) have a right to bequeath or on whether persons who have a right to hold also have a right to choose that others hold in their place. I lack a good explanation of why the usual theories of distributive justice are so recipient oriented; ignoring givers and transferrers and their rights is of a piece with ignoring producers and their entitlements. But why is it *all* ignored?

Patterned principles of distributive justice necessitate redistributive activities. The likelihood is small that any actual freely-arrived-at set of holdings fits a given pattern; and the likelihood is nil that it will continue to fit the pattern as people exchange and give. From the point of view of an entitlement theory, redistribution is a serious matter indeed, involving, as it does, the violation of people's rights. (An exception is those takings that fall under the principle of the rectification of injustices.) From other points of view, also, it is serious.

Taxation of earnings from labor is on a par with forced labor.[11] Some persons find this claim obviously true: taking the earnings of n hours labor is like taking n hours from the person; it is like forcing the person to work n hours for another's purpose. Others find the claim absurd.

But even these, *if* they object to forced labor, would oppose forcing unemployed hippies to work for the benefit of the needy. And they would also object to forcing each person to work five extra hours each week for the benefit of the needy. But a system that takes five hours' wages in taxes does not seem to them like one that forces someone to work five hours, since it offers the person forced a wider range of choice in activities than does taxation in kind with the particular labor specified. (But we can imagine a gradation of systems of forced labor, from one that specifies a particular activity, to one that gives a choice among two activities, to . . . ; and so on up.) Furthermore, people envisage a system with something like a proportional tax on everything above the amount necessary for basic needs. Some think this does not force someone to work extra hours, since there is no fixed number of extra hours he is forced to work, and since he can avoid the tax entirely by earning only enough to cover his basic needs. This is a very uncharacteristic view of forcing for those who *also* think people are forced to do something *whenever* the alternatives they face are considerably worse. However, *neither* view is correct. The fact that others intentionally intervene, in violation of a side constraint against aggression, to threaten force to limit the alternatives, in this case to paying taxes or (presumably the worse alternative) bare subsistence, makes the taxation system one of forced labor and distinguishes it from other cases of limited choices which are not forcings.

The man who chooses to work longer to gain an income more than sufficient for his basic needs prefers some extra goods or services to the leisure and activities he could perform during the possible nonworking hours; whereas the man who chooses not to work the extra time prefers the leisure activities to the extra goods or services he could acquire by working more. Given this, if it would be illegitimate for a tax system to seize some of a man's leisure (forced labor) for the purpose of serving the needy, how can it be legitimate for a tax system to seize some of a man's goods for that purpose? Why should we treat the man whose happiness requires certain material goods or services differently from the man whose preferences and desires make such goods unnecessary for his happiness? Why should the man

who prefers seeing a movie (and who has to earn money for a ticket) be open to the required call to aid the needy, while the person who prefers looking at a sunset (and hence need earn no extra money) is not? Indeed, isn't it surprising that redistributionists choose to ignore the man whose pleasures are so easily attainable without extra labor, while adding yet another burden to the poor unfortunate who must work for his pleasures? If anything, one would have expected the reverse. Why is the person with the nonmaterial or nonconsumption desire allowed to proceed unimpeded to his most favored feasible alternative, whereas the man whose pleasures or desires involve material things and who must work for extra money (thereby serving whomever considers his activities valuable enough to pay him) is constrained in what he can realize? Perhaps there is no difference in principle. And perhaps some think the answer concerns merely administrative convenience. (These questions and issues will not disturb those who think that forced labor to serve the needy or to realize some favored-end-state pattern is acceptable.) In a fuller discussion we would have (and want) to extend our argument to include interest, entrepreneurial profits, and so on. Those who doubt that this extension can be carried through, and who draw the line here at taxation of income from labor, will have to state rather complicated patterned *historical* principles of distributive justice, since end-state principles would not distinguish *sources* of income in any way. It is enough for now to get away from end-state principles and to make clear how various patterned principles are dependent upon particular views about the sources or the illegitimacy or the lesser legitimacy of profits, interest, and so on; which particular views may well be mistaken.

What sort of right over others does a legally institutionalized end-state pattern give one? The central core of the notion of a property right in X, relative to which other parts of the notion are to be explained, is the right to determine what shall be done with X; the right to choose which of the constrained set of options concerning X shall be realized or attempted. The constraints are set by other principles or laws operating in the society; in our theory, by the Lockean rights people possess (under the minimal state). My property rights in my knife allow me to leave it where I will, but not in your chest. I may choose which of the acceptable options involving the knife is to be realized. This notion of property helps us to understand why earlier theorists spoke of people as having property in themselves and their labor. They viewed each person as having a right to decide what would become of himself and what he would do, and as having a right to reap the benefits of what he did.

This right of selecting the alternative to be realized from the constrained set of alternatives may be held by an *individual* or by a *group* with some procedure for reaching a joint decision; or the right may be passed back and forth, so that one year I decide what's to become of *X*, and the next year you do (with the alternative of destruction, perhaps, being excluded). Or, during the same time period, some types of decisions about *X* may be made by me, and others by you. And so on. We lack an adequate, fruitful, analytical apparatus for classifying the *types* of constraints on the set of options among which choices are to be made, and the *types* of ways decision powers can be held, divided, and amalgamated. A *theory* of property would, among other things, contain such a classification of constraints and decision modes, and from a small number of principles would follow a host of interesting statements about the *consequences* and effects of certain combinations of constraints and modes of decision.

When end-result principles of distributive justice are built into the legal structure of a society, they (as do most patterned principles) give each citizen an enforceable claim to some portion of the total social product; that is, to some portion of the sum total of the individually and jointly made products. This total product is produced by individuals laboring, using means of production others have saved to bring into existence, by people organizing production or creating means to produce new things or things in a new way. It is on this batch of individual activities that patterned distributional principles give each individual an enforceable claim. Each person has a claim to the activities and the products of other persons, independently of whether the other persons enter into particular relationships that give rise to these claims, and independently of whether they voluntarily take these claims upon themselves, in charity or in exchange for something.

Whether it is done through taxation on wages or on wages over a certain amount, or through

seizure of profits, or through there being a big *social pot* so that it's not clear what's coming from where and what's going where, patterned principles of distributive justice involve appropriating the actions of other persons. Seizing the results of someone's labor is equivalent to seizing hours from him and directing him to carry on various activities. If people force you to do certain work, or unrewarded work, for a certain period of time, they decide what you are to do and what purposes your work is to serve apart from your decisions. This process whereby they take this decision from you makes them a *part-owner* of you; it gives them a property right in you. Just as having such partial control and power of decision, by right, over an animal or inanimate object would be to have a property right in it.

End-state and most patterned principles of distributive justice institute (partial) ownership by others of people and their actions and labor. These principles involve a shift from the classical liberals' notion of self-ownership to a notion of (partial) property rights in *other* people.

Considerations such as these confront end-state and other patterned conceptions of justice with the question of whether the actions necessary to achieve the selected pattern don't themselves violate moral side constraints. Any view holding that there are moral side constraints on actions, that not all moral considerations can be built into end states that are to be achieved, . . . must face the possibility that some of its goals are not achievable by any morally permissible available means. An entitlement theorist will face such conflicts in a society that deviates from the principles of justice for the generation of holdings, if and only if the only actions available to realize the principles themselves violate some moral constraints. Since deviation from the first two principles of justice (in acquisition and transfer) will involve other persons' direct and aggressive intervention to violate rights, and since moral constraints will not exclude defensive or retributive action in such cases, the entitlement theorist's problem rarely will be pressing. And whatever difficulties he has in applying the principle of rectification to persons who did not themselves violate the first two principles are difficulties in balancing the conflicting considerations so as correctly to formulate the complex principle of rectification itself; he will not violate moral side constraints by applying the principle. Proponents of patterned conceptions of justice, however, often will face head-on clashes (and poignant ones if they cherish each party to the clash) between moral side constraints on how individuals may be treated and their patterned conception of justice that presents an end-state or other pattern that *must* be realized.

May a person emigrate from a nation that has institutionalized some end-state or patterned distributional principle? For some principles (for example, Hayek's) emigration presents no theoretical problem. But for others it is a tricky matter. Consider a nation having a compulsory scheme of minimal social provision to aid the neediest (or one organized so as to maximize the position of the worst-off group); no one may opt out of participating in it. (None may say, "Don't compel me to contribute to others and don't provide for me via this compulsory mechanism if I am in need.") Everyone above a certain level is forced to contribute to aid the needy. But if emigration from the country were allowed, anyone could choose to move to another country that did not have compulsory social provision but otherwise was (as much as possible) identical. In such a case, the person's *only* motive for leaving would be to avoid participating in the compulsory scheme of social provision. And if he does leave, the needy in his initial country will receive no (compelled) help from him. What rationale yields the result that the person be permitted to emigrate, yet forbidden to stay and opt out of the compulsory scheme of social provision? If providing for the needy is of overriding importance, this does militate against allowing internal opting out; but it also speaks against allowing external emigration. (Would it also support, to some extent, the kidnapping of persons living in a place without compulsory social provision, who could be forced to make a contribution to the needy in your community?) Perhaps the crucial component of the position that allows emigration solely to avoid certain arrangements, while not allowing anyone internally to opt out of them, is a concern for fraternal feelings within the country. "We don't want anyone here who doesn't contribute, who doesn't care enough about the others to contribute." That concern, in this case, would have to be tied to the view that forced aid-

ing tends to produce fraternal feelings between the aided and the aider (or perhaps merely to the view that the knowledge that someone or other voluntarily is not aiding produces unfraternal feelings).

Locke's Theory of Acquisition

Before we turn to consider other theories of justice in detail, we must introduce an additional bit of complexity into the structure of the entitlement theory. This is best approached by considering Locke's attempt to specify a principle of justice in acquisition. Locke views property rights in an unowned object as originating through someone's mixing his labor with it. This gives rise to many questions. What are the boundaries of what labor is mixed with? If a private astronaut clears a place on Mars, has he mixed his labor with (so that he comes to own) the whole planet, the whole uninhabited universe, or just a particular plot? Which plot does an act bring under ownership? The minimal (possibly disconnected) area such that an act decreases entropy in that area, and not elsewhere? Can virgin land (for the purposes of ecological investigation by high-flying airplane) come under ownership by a Lockean process? Building a fence around a territory presumably would make one the owner of only the fence (and the land immediately underneath it).

Why does mixing one's labor with something make one the owner of it? Perhaps because one owns one's labor, and so one comes to own a previously unowned thing that becomes permeated with what one owns. Ownership seeps over into the rest. But why isn't mixing what I own with what I don't own a way of losing what I own rather than a way of gaining what I don't? If I own a can of tomato juice and spill it in the sea so that its molecules (made radioactive, so I can check this) mingle evenly throughout the sea, do I thereby come to own the sea, or have I foolishly dissipated my tomato juice? Perhaps the idea, instead, is that laboring on something improves it and makes it more valuable; and anyone is entitled to own a thing whose value he has created. (Reinforcing this, perhaps, is the view that laboring is unpleasant. If some people made things effortlessly, as the cartoon characters in *The Yellow Submarine* trail flowers in their wake, would they have lesser claim to their own products whose making didn't *cost* them anything?) Ignore the fact that laboring on something may make it less valuable (spraying pink enamel paint on a piece of driftwood that you have found). Why should one's entitlement extend to the whole object rather than just to the *added value* one's labor has produced? (Such reference to value might also serve to delimit the extent of ownership; for example, substitute "increases the value of" for "decreases entropy in" in the above entropy criterion.) No workable or coherent value-added property scheme has yet been devised, and any such scheme presumably would fall to objections (similar to those) that fell the theory of Henry George.

It will be implausible to view improving an object as giving full ownership to it, if the stock of unowned objects that might be improved is limited. For an object's coming under one person's ownership changes the situation of all others. Whereas previously they were at liberty (in Hohfeld's sense) to use the object, they now no longer are. This change in the situation of others (by removing their liberty to act on a previously unowned object) need not worsen their situation. If I appropriate a grain of sand from Coney Island, no one else may now do as they will with *that* grain of sand. But there are plenty of other grains of sand left for them to do the same with. Or if not grains of sand, then other things. Alternatively, the things I do with the grain of sand I appropriate might improve the position of others, counterbalancing their loss of the liberty to use that grain. The crucial point is whether appropriation of an unowned object worsens the situation of others.

Locke's proviso that there be "enough and as good left in common for others" (sect. 27) is meant to ensure that the situation of others is not worsened. (If this proviso is met is there any motivation for his further condition of nonwaste?) It is often said that this proviso once held but now no longer does. But there appears to be an argument for the conclusion that if the proviso no longer holds, then it cannot even have held so as to yield permanent and inheritable property rights. Consider the first person Z for whom there is not enough and as good left to appropriate. The last person Y to appropriate left Z without his previous liberty to act on an object, and

so worsened Z's situation. So Y's appropriation is not allowed under Locke's proviso. Therefore the next to last person X to appropriate left Y in a worse position, for X's act ended permissible appropriation. Therefore X's appropriation wasn't permissible. But then the appropriator two from last, W, ended permissible appropriation and so, since it worsened X's position, W's appropriation wasn't permissible. And so on back to the first person A to appropriate a permanent property right.

This argument, however, proceeds too quickly. Someone may be made worse off by another's appropriation in two ways: first, by losing the opportunity to improve his situation by a particular appropriation or any one; and second, by no longer being able to use freely (without appropriation) what he previously could. A *stringent* requirement that another not be made worse off by an appropriation would exclude the first way if nothing else counterbalances the diminution in opportunity, as well as the second. A *weaker* requirement would exclude the second way, though not the first. With the weaker requirement, we cannot zip back so quickly from Z to A, as in the above argument; for though person Z can no longer *appropriate*, there may remain some for him to *use* as before. In this case Y's appropriation would not violate the weaker Lockean condition. (With less remaining that people are at liberty to use, users might face more inconvenience, crowding, and so on; in that way the situation of others might be worsened, unless appropriation stopped far short of such a point.) It is arguable that no one legitimately can complain if the weaker provision is satisfied. However, since this is less clear than in the case of the more stringent proviso, Locke may have intended this stringent proviso by "enough and as good" remaining, and perhaps he meant the nonwaste condition to delay the end point from which the argument zips back.

Is the situation of persons who are unable to appropriate (there being no more accessible and useful unowned objects) worsened by a system allowing appropriation and permanent property? Here enter the various familiar social considerations favoring private property: it increases the social product by putting means of production in the hands of those who can use them most efficiently (profitably); experimentation is encouraged, because with separate persons controlling resources, there is no one person or small group whom someone with a new idea must convince to try it out; private property enables people to decide on the pattern and types of risks they wish to bear, leading to specialized types of risk bearing; private property protects future persons by leading some to hold back resources from current consumption for future markets; it provides alternate sources of employment for unpopular persons who don't have to convince any one person or small group to hire them, and so on. These considerations enter a Lockean theory to support the claim that appropriation of private property satisfies the intent behind the "enough and as good left over" proviso, *not* as a utilitarian justification of property. They enter to rebut the claim that because the proviso is violated no natural right to private property can arise by a Lockean process. The difficulty in working such an argument to show that the proviso is satisfied is in fixing the appropriate baseline for comparison. Lockean appropriation makes people no worse off than they would be *how*? This question of fixing the baseline needs more detailed investigation than we are able to give it here. It would be desirable to have an estimate of the general economic importance of original appropriation in order to see how much leeway there is for differing theories of appropriation and of the location of the baseline. Perhaps this importance can be measured by the percentage of all income that is based upon untransformed raw materials and given resources (rather than upon human actions), mainly rental income representing the unimproved value of land, and the price of raw material *in situ*, and by the percentage of current wealth which represents such income in the past.[12]

We should note that it is not only persons favoring *private* property who need a theory of how property rights legitimately originate. Those believing in collective property, for example those believing that a group of persons living in an area jointly own the territory, or its mineral resources, also must provide a theory of how such property rights arise; they must show why the persons living there have rights to determine what is done with the land and resources there

that persons living elsewhere don't have (with regard to the same land and resources).

The Proviso

Whether or not Locke's particular theory of appropriation can be spelled out so as to handle various difficulties, I assume that any adequate theory of justice in acquisition will contain a proviso similar to the weaker of the ones we have attributed to Locke. A process normally giving rise to a permanent bequeathable property right in a previously unowned thing will not do so if the position of others no longer at liberty to use the thing is thereby worsened. It is important to specify *this* particular mode of worsening the situation of others, for the proviso does not encompass other modes. It does not include the worsening due to more limited opportunities to appropriate (the first way above, corresponding to the more stringent condition), and it does not include how I "worsen" a seller's position if I appropriate materials to make some of what he is selling, and then enter into competition with him. Someone whose appropriation otherwise would violate the proviso still may appropriate provided he compensates the others so that their situation is not thereby worsened; unless he does compensate these others, his appropriation will violate the proviso of the principle of justice in acquisition and will be an illegitimate one.[13] A theory of appropriation incorporating this Lockean proviso will handle correctly the cases (objections to the theory lacking the proviso) where someone appropriates the total supply of something necessary for life.[14]

A theory which includes this proviso in its principle of justice in acquisition must also contain a more complex principle of justice in transfer. Some reflection of the proviso about appropriation constrains later actions. If my appropriating all of a certain substance violates the Lockean proviso, then so does my appropriating some and purchasing all the rest from others who obtained it without otherwise violating the Lockean proviso. If the proviso excludes someone's appropriating all the drinkable water in the world, it also excludes his purchasing it all. (More weakly, and messily, it may exclude his charging certain prices for some of his supply.) This proviso (almost?) never will come into effect; the more someone acquires of a scarce substance which others want, the higher the price of the rest will go, and the more difficult it will become for him to acquire it all. But still, we can imagine, at least, that something like this occurs: someone makes simultaneous secret bids to the separate owners of a substance, each of whom sells assuming he can easily purchase more from the other owners; or some natural catastrophe destroys all of the supply of something except that in one person's possession. The total supply could not be permissibly appropriated by one person at the beginning. His later acquisition of it all does not show that the original appropriation violated the proviso (even by a reverse argument similar to the one above that tried to zip back from *Z* to *A*). Rather, it is the combination of the original appropriation *plus* all the later transfers and actions that violates the Lockean proviso.

Each owner's title to his holding includes the historical shadow of the Lockean proviso on appropriation. This excludes his transferring it into an agglomeration that does violate the Lockean proviso and excludes his using it in a way, in coordination with others or independently of them, so as to violate the proviso by making the situation of others worse than their baseline situation. Once it is known that someone's ownership runs afoul of the Lockean proviso, there are stringent limits on what he may do with (what it is difficult any longer unreservedly to call) "his property." Thus a person may not appropriate the only water hole in a desert and charge what he will. Nor may he charge what he will if he possesses one, and unfortunately it happens that all the water holes in the desert dry up, except for his. This unfortunate circumstance, admittedly no fault of his, brings into operation the Lockean proviso and limits his property rights.[15] Similarly, an owner's property right in the only island in an area does not allow him to order a castaway from a shipwreck off his island as a trespasser, for this would violate the Lockean proviso.

Notice that the theory does not say that owners do have these rights, but that the rights are overridden to avoid some catastrophe. (Overridden rights do not disappear; they leave a trace of a sort absent in the cases under discussion.) There is no such external (and *ad hoc*?) overriding. Consideration internal to the theory of property itself, to its theory of acquisition and appropriation, provide the means for handling such

cases. The results, however, may be coextensive with some condition about catastrophe, since the baseline for comparison is so low as compared to the productiveness of a society with private appropriation that the question of the Lockean proviso being violated arises only in the case of catastrophe (or a desert-island situation).

The fact that someone owns the total supply of something necessary for others to stay alive does *not* entail that his (or anyone's) appropriation of anything left some people (immediately or later) in a situation worse than the baseline one. A medical researcher who synthesizes a new substance that effectively treats a certain disease and who refuses to sell except on his terms does not worsen the situation of others by depriving them of whatever he has appropriated. The others easily can possess the same materials he appropriated; the researcher's appropriation or purchase of chemicals didn't make those chemicals scarce in a way so as to violate the Lockean proviso. Nor would someone else's purchasing the total supply of the synthesized substance from the medical researcher. The fact that the medical researcher uses easily available chemicals to synthesize the drug no more violates the Lockean proviso than does the fact that the only surgeon able to perform a particular operation eats easily obtainable food in order to stay alive and to have the energy to work. This shows that the Lockean proviso is not an "end-state principle"; it focuses on a particular way that appropriative actions affect others, and not on the structure of the situation that results.[16]

Intermediate between someone who takes all of the public supply and someone who makes the total supply out of easily obtainable substances is someone who appropriates the total supply of something in a way that does not deprive the others of it. For example, someone finds a new substance in an out-of-the-way place. He discovers that it effectively treats a certain disease and appropriates the total supply. He does not worsen the situation of others; if he did not stumble upon the substance no one else would have, and the others would remain without it. However, as time passes, the likelihood increases that others would have come across the substance; upon this fact might be based a limit to his property right in the substance so that others are not below their baseline position; for example, its bequest might be limited. The theme of someone worsening another's situation by depriving him of something he otherwise would posses may also illuminate the example of patents. An inventor's patent does not deprive others of an object which would not exist if not for the inventor. Yet patents would have this effect on others who independently invent the object. Therefore, these independent inventors, upon whom the burden of proving independent discovery may rest, should not be excluded from utilizing their own invention as they wish (including selling it to others). Furthermore, a known inventor drastically lessens the chances of actual independent invention. For persons who know of an invention usually will not try to reinvent it, and the notion of independent discovery here would be murky at best. Yet we may assume that in the absence of the original invention, sometime later someone else would have come up with it. This suggests placing a time limit on patents, as a rough rule of thumb to approximate how long it would have taken, in the absence of knowledge of the invention, for independent discovery.

I believe that the free operation of a market system will not actually run afoul of the Lockean proviso. (Recall that crucial to our story in Part I of how a protective agency becomes dominant and a *de facto* monopoly is the fact that it wields force in situations of conflict, and is not merely in competition, with other agencies. A similar tale cannot be told about other businesses.) If this is correct, the proviso will not play a very important role in the activities of protective agencies and will not provide a significant opportunity for future state action. Indeed, were it not for the effects of previous *illegitimate* state action, people would not think the possibility of the proviso's being violated as of more interest than any other logical possibility. (Here I make an empirical historical claim; as does someone who disagrees with this.) This completes our indication of the complication in the entitlement theory introduced by the Lockean proviso.

NOTES

1. Applications of the principle of justice in acquisition may also occur as part of the move from one distribution to another. You may find an unheld thing now and appropriate it. Acquisitions also are to be understood as included when, to simplify, I speak only of transitions by transfers.

2. See, however, the useful book by Boris Bittker, *The Case for Black Reparations* (New York: Random House, 1973).

3. If the principle of rectification of violations of the first two principles yields more than one description of holdings, then some choice must be made as to which of these is to be realized. Perhaps the sort of considerations about distributive justice and equality that I argue against play a legitimate role in *this* subsidiary choice. Similarly, there may be room for such considerations in deciding which otherwise arbitrary features a statute will embody, when such features are unavoidable because other considerations do not specify a precise line; yet a line must be drawn.

4. One might try to squeeze a patterned conception of distributive justice into the framework of the entitlement conception, by formulating a gimmicky obligatory "principle of transfer" that would lead to the pattern. For example, the principle that if one has more than the mean income one must transfer everything one holds above the mean to persons below the mean so as to bring them up to (but not over) the mean. We can formulate a criterion for a "principle of transfer" to rule out such obligatory transfers, or we can say that no correct principle of transfer, no principle of transfer in a free society will be like this. The former is probably the better course, though the latter also is true.

Alternatively, one might think to make the entitlement conception instantiate a pattern, by using matrix entries that express the relative strength of a person's entitlements as measured by some real-valued function. But even if the limitation to natural dimensions failed to exclude this function, the resulting edifice would *not* capture our system of entitlements to *particular* things.

5. F. A. Hayek, *The Constitution of Liberty* (Chicago: University of Chicago Press, 1960), p. 87.

6 This question does not imply that they will tolerate any and every patterned distribution. In discussing Hayek's views, Irving Kristol has recently speculated that people will not long tolerate a system that yields distributions patterned in accordance with value rather than merit. ("'When Virtue Loses All Her Loveliness—Some Reflections on Capitalism and The Free Society,'" *The Public Interest*, Fall 1970, pp. 3–15.) Kristol, following some remarks of Hayek's, equates the merit system with justice. Since some case can be made for the external standard of distribution in accordance with benefit to others, we ask about a weaker (and therefore more plausible) hypothesis.

7. We certainly benefit because great economic incentives operate to get others to spend much time and energy to figure out how to serve us by providing things we will want to pay for. It is not mere paradox monger-

ing to wonder whether capitalism should be criticized for most rewarding and hence encouraging, not individualists like Thoreau who go about their own lives, but people who are occupied with serving others and winning them as customers. But to defend capitalism one need not think businessmen are the finest human types. (I do not mean to join here the general maligning of businessmen, either.) Those who think the finest should acquire the most can try to convince their fellows to transfer resources in accordance with *that* principle.

8. Varying situations continuously from that limit situation to our own would force us to make explicit the underlying rationale of entitlements and to consider whether entitlement considerations lexicographically precede the considerations of the usual theories of distributive justice, so that the *slightest* strand of entitlement outweighs the considerations of the usual theories of distributive justice.

9. Might not a transfer have instrumental effects on a third party, changing his feasible options? (But what if the two parties to the transfer independently had used their holdings in this fashion?) I discuss this question below, but note here that this question concedes the point for distributions of ultimate intrinsic noninstrumental goods (pure utility experiences, so to speak) that are transferrable. It also might be objected that the transfer might make a third party more envious because it worsens his position relative to someone else. I find it incomprehensible how this can be thought to involve a claim of justice. On envy, see [*Anarchy, State, and Utopia,*] Chapter 8.

Here and elsewhere in this chapter, a theory which incorporates elements of pure procedural justice might find what I say acceptable, *if* kept in its proper place; that is, if background institutions exist to ensure the satisfaction of certain conditions on distributive shares. But if these institutions are not themselves the sum or invisible-hand result of people's voluntary (nonaggressive) actions, the constraints they impose require justification. At no point does *our* argument assume any background institutions more extensive than those of the minimal night-watchman state, a state limited to protecting persons against murder, assault, theft, fraud, and so forth.

10. See the selection from John Henry MacKay's novel, *The Anarchists*, reprinted in Leonard Krimmerman and Lewis Perry, eds., *Patterns of Anarchy* (New York: Doubleday Anchor Books, 1966), in which an individualist anarchist presses upon a communist anarchist the following question: "Would you, in the system of society which you call 'free Communism' prevent individuals from exchanging their labor among themselves by means of their own medium of exchange? And further: Would you prevent them from occupying land for the purpose of personal use?" The novel continues: "[the] question was not to be escaped. If he answered 'Yes!' he admitted that society had the right

of control over the individual and threw overboard the autonomy of the individual which he had always zealously defended; if on the other hand, he answered 'No!' he admitted the right of private property which he had just denied so emphatically. . . . Then he answered 'In Anarchy any number of men must have the right of forming a voluntary association, and so realizing their ideas in practice. Nor can I understand how any one could justly be driven from the land and house which he uses and occupies . . . every serious man must declare himself: for Socialism, and thereby for force and against liberty, or for Anarchism, and thereby for liberty and against force.'" In contrast, we find Noam Chomsky writing, "Any consistent anarchist must oppose private ownership of the means of production," "the consistent anarchist then . . . will be a socialist . . . of a particular sort." Introduction to Daniel Guerin, *Anarchism: From Theory to Practice* (New York: Monthly Review Press, 1970), pages xiii, xv.

11. I am unsure as to whether the arguments I present below show that such taxation merely *is* forced labor; so that "Is on a par with" means "is one kind of." Or alternatively, whether the arguments emphasize the great similarities between such taxation and forced labor, to show it is plausible and illuminating to view such taxation in the light of forced labor. This latter approach would remind one of how John Wisdom conceives of the claims of metaphysicians.

12. I have not seen a precise estimate. David Friedman, *The Machinery of Freedom* (New York: Harper & Row, 1973), pp. xiv, xv, discusses this issue and suggests 5 percent of U.S. national income as an upper limit for the first two factors mentioned. However, he does not attempt to estimate the percentage of current wealth which is based upon such income in the past. (The vague notion of "based upon" merely indicates a topic needing investigation.)

13. Fourier held that since the process of civilization had deprived the members of society of certain liberties (to gather, pasture, engage in the chase), a socially guaranteed minimum provision for persons was justified as compensation for the loss (Alexander Gray, *The Socialist Tradition* [New York: Harper & Row, 1968], p. 188). But this puts the point too strongly. This compensation would be due those persons, if any, for whom the process of civilization was a *net loss*, for whom the benefits of civilization did not counterbalance being deprived of these particular liberties.

14. For example, Rashdall's case of someone who comes upon the only water in the desert several miles ahead of others who also will come to it and appropriates it all. Hastings Rashdall, "The Philosophical Theory of Property," in *Property, Its Duties and Rights* (London: MacMillan, 1915).

We should note Ayn Rand's theory of property rights ("Man's Rights" in *The Virtue of Selfishness*

[New York: New American Library, 1964], p. 94), wherein these follow from the right to life, since people need physical things to live. But a right to life is not a right to whatever one needs to live; other people may have rights over these other things (see [*Anarchy, State, and Utopia,*] Chapter 3). At most, a right to life would be a right to have or strive for whatever one needs to live, provided that having it does not violate anyone else's rights. With regard to material things, the question is whether having it does not violate any right of others. (Would appropriation of all unowned things do so? Would appropriating the water hole in Rashdall's example?) Since special considerations (such as the Lockean proviso) may enter with regard to material property, one *first* needs a theory of property rights before one can apply any supposed right to life (as amended above). Therefore the right to life cannot provide the foundation for a theory of property rights.

15. The situation would be different if his water hole didn't dry up, due to special precautions he took to prevent this. Compare our discussion of the case in the text with Hayek, *The Constitution of Liberty*, p. 136; and also with Ronald Hamowy, "Hayek's Concept of Freedom; A Critique," *New Individualist Review*, April 1961, pp. 28–31.

16. Does the principle of compensation ([*Anarchy, State, and Utopia,*] Chapter 4) introduce patterning considerations? Though it requires compensation for the disadvantages imposed by those seeking security from risks, it is not a patterned principle. For it seeks to remove only those disadvantages which prohibitions inflict on those who might present risks to others, not all disadvantages. It specifies an obligation on those who impose the prohibition, which stems from their own particular acts, to remove a particular complaint those prohibited may make against them.

Notes and Questions

A. M. HONORÉ, "Property, Title and Redistribution"

1. A. M. Honoré defends private property but opposes Nozick's view of it. The basic question, he says, is the relation between private property and economic equality. Can one be committed to both? Nozick says no, as does the Court in the case of *Coppage* v. *Kansas* (see Chapter Three, "Cases on Freedom of Contract"). Since life, liberty, and property are equal rights, according to Nozick, taking property is equivalent to taking freedom. But Honoré objects that Nozick assumes, without argument, the extensive Western, liberal concept of ownership. If ownership is total, exclusive, and indefeasible, as the Western, liberal tradition assumes, then the initial acquisition is crucial, as Nozick assumes. But this view ignores the social benefits received from the group that enables property ownership in the first place, Honoré argues. If social considerations are included, that can limit the scope of ownership rights, so total, exclusive, indefeasible property rights cannot be assumed. How might Nozick answer this objection?

2. Furthermore, Honoré points out, Nozick also ignores legal considerations such as lapse of title, eminent domain, and compulsory acquisition, which are part of the Western, liberal legal tradition. Why reproduce some legal factors and not others? Especially, why select only those factors that protect private ownership and not those that limit it? Can Nozick respond?

3. Third, Honoré argues, Nozick ignores historical change and social context. Given his acceptance of the *Lockean proviso*, can Nozick consistently ignore changing circumstances? How does he answer this challenge? Does he succeed? Can he respond to Honoré's fishhook example? This is about what it means to say that a person is "worse off." Nozick would have to say that persons without the fishhook are no worse off than they would have been had the fishhook not been invented. Honoré would say that those without the fishhook are worse off than they would be if they had it. Which is the better view?

4. Like Mill, Honoré argues that historically no acquisitions are just in the long view, since all are products of conquest or fraud, and thus Nozick's view has no application outside utopia. Is this a fair criticism? Is it a reasonable view of property? Must Nozick consider acquisition this broadly? Why or why not? If he does not, what does his principle of rectification amount to?

5. Honoré points out that concepts of property other than the extensive notion that Nozick assumes are not only conceivable but actually exist and appear to be defensible. This is because a system of property may exist for different purposes. What different purposes might be served by different systems of property? What, if anything, follows about Nozick's concept of property?

Property, Title and Redistribution

A. M. HONORÉ

This discussion paper is concerned with the relationship between the institution of private property and the notion of economic equality. Is it inconsistent, or morally obtuse to recognize the value of the institution and at the same time to argue that each member of a society is entitled to an equal or approximately equal standard of living? I shall be particularly concerned with the argument of *R. Nozick*, in *Anarchy, State and Utopia*[1] to the effect that under a system of "just entitlements" such as he specifies there is no room to admit that the state has the right or duty to redistribute benefits so as to secure an equal or more equal spread, because "the particular rights over things fill the space of rights, leaving no room for general rights to be in a certain material condition."[2] Though *Nozick's* "just entitlements"[3] are not confined to titles to property I shall so confine myself. Rights of a more personal character could in theory be the subjects of redistribution and indeed *Nozick* discusses the case for transplanting organs from A to B in order to correct physical maldistribution of parts of the body.[4] Fascinating as such speculations may be, the physical and technical difficulties involved in such a programme would be stupendous and the moral objections to the invasion of people's bodies for whatever purpose are much stronger than they are when what is proposed is to tax or, in some cases, to expropriate. Nor can one concede the argument that the redistribution of part of what A has earned to B goes beyond the invasion of property rights and amounts to a system of forced labour[5] by which A is compelled to work part of his day for B, so that redistribution of property is really an invasion of the status and freedom of the person taxed or expropriated. This

is no more compelling than the Marxist argument that a wage-earner whose surplus product is appropriated by the employer is a sort of wage slave. The objection to this is not that the income-earner freely works under a system in which he knows that part of what he produces will be appropriated by his employer or transferred to other people by means of taxes. He may have no choice, if he is to earn a living, but to accept a system which he dislikes. The argument is open to attack rather because it rests on the morally questionable view that a person is entitled to keep exclusively and indefinitely for himself whatever he makes or produces. This would be true of a man working in complete isolation; no serious argument has been advanced to show that it is true of a social being.

Nozick's argument depends on accepting this questionable view. Against those who favour a principle of social justice by which things are to be distributed according to need, desert, the principle of equal claims or the like, he argues that the just allocation is the historically justifiable one. This can be ascertained, in relation to any given item of property, by asking whether the holder acquired it by a just title or derived his title justly from another who so held it, either originally or by derivation from such a just acquirer. Consequently just distribution depends on just acquisition and transfer, and redistribution is confined to those instances in which the original acquisition or the subsequent transmission of the property was unjust.

All therefore turns on what count as just principles of acquisition and transfer of title. According to *Nozick* —

1. a person who acquires a holding in accordance with the principle of justice in acquisition is entitled to that holding
2. a person who acquires a holding in accordance with the principle of justice in transfer from some one else entitled to the holding is entitled to the holding
3. no one is entitled to a holding except by (repeated) applications of 1 and 2

The complete principle of distributive justice would say simply that a distribution is just if everyone is entitled to the holdings they possess under the distribution.

What is presupposed by this set of rules for tracing title is apparently only that the principles of acquisition and transfer should be morally respectable. For acquisition something like *Locke's* theory of property is understood.[6] Transfers in a free society will be consensual. But that is only the appearance. What *Nozick* additionally presupposes, without seeking to justify, is that the interest acquired and transmitted is the ownership of property as conceived in western society on the model of Roman law.[7] He is assuming, first, that the acquirer obtains an exclusive right to the thing acquired, that he is entitled, having cleared the land, made the tool etc. to deny access and use to everyone else. Secondly he is supposing that the right acquired is of indefinite duration. The man who has made the clearing can remain there for his lifetime. He is not obliged to move on after 30 many years, and leave the fruits of his labour to another, nor does he lose his right by leaving. Thirdly the right is supposed to be transmissible inter vivos and on death, so that it can be sold, given, inherited, mortgaged and the like again without limit of time. Under such a system of property law, of course, the initial acquisition is decisive. Once A has cleared the land his neighbours, friends, associates and, if it comes to that, his family are obliged to look on while he enjoys and transmits his "entitlement" to whomsoever he chooses, irrespective of the fact that in a wider context they, along with him, form part of a single group[8] which is dedicated, among other objects, to the preservation of all. This system of property law, whatever its economic merits, is not self-evidently just. If the interest acquired (western type ownership) is greater than can be morally justified, then however just the methods by which A acquires the thing in question and transfers it to X, the distribution of property under which the thing is allocated to X is not thereby saved from criticism. Indeed, quite the contrary. If the interest awarded to owners under the system is greater than can reasonably be justified on moral, as opposed to economic grounds, any distribution of property will be inherently unjust. Hence the intervention of the state will be needed if justice is to be done.

There is no doubt that the *Nozick* rules about just acquisition, transfer and distribution reproduce in outline western systems of property law based on the liberal conception of ownership. According to these notions, ownership is a permanent, exclusive and transmissible interest in property. But this type of property system is neither the only conceivable system, nor the easiest to justify from a moral point of view, nor does it predominate in those societies which are closest to a "state of nature."

In so far as the *Nozick* principles are meant to reproduce western property law they are incomplete in that they omit provision for lapse of title and for compulsory acquisition. Lapse of title is not perhaps of great moral importance, but it is worth noting that legal rules about limitation of actions and prescription embody the idea that an owner who neglects his property may be deprived of it. The acquirer (squatter or the like) obtains it by a sort of private expropriation. More important is expropriation by the state or public authority. It is not at all clear why the parts of western property law favourable to the private owner should be reproduced in the system of entitlements to the exclusion of those which favour the claims of the community. The latter, after all, balance the former. The individualistic bias of property law is corrected by the admission of state claims to tax and expropriate.

Aside from the omission of rules about lapse and compulsory acquisition one may note that *Nozick's* principles rest on the assumption that whether a justification exists for acquiring or transferring property can be decided in abstraction from the historical and social context. A just acquisition in 1066 or 1620 remains a just root of title in 1975. If this were really so one would have to say either that the acquisition of slaves is seen in retrospect always to have been unjust and that the state would have been justified in intervening in a slave-owning society to correct the injustice, or that the descendants of slave-owners are entitled to own the descendants of freed slaves. So with colonies, *mutatis mutandis*. Are we to say that as a result of the post-war movement to free colonies we now see that the acquisition of colonies, apparently valid at the time in international law and morality, was always wrong and that the international society would have been justified, had it been so minded, in intervening even in the nineteenth century to free the existing colonies and prevent further acquisitions? If so, how can we be sure that there are not equally unjustified forms of property ownership in present-day society which in fact justify state intervention in a redistributive sense? And how can we be sure in any future society that these objectionable forms of acquisition are not present? In which case, outside Utopia, the thesis advanced by *Nozick* has no application. But if the acquisition of slaves and colonies was initially just, surely some provision should be made in his system for the redistribution of entitlements when the moral basis on which they originally rested has become eviscerated. These instances would count morally as cases of lapse of title owing to changing views of right and wrong. Legally they would furnish examples of just expropriation. There would have to be a further exception in *Nozick's* system to cater for changing conditions of fact. Suppose, apart from any question of the justification for colonies, that in the nineteenth century Metropolitania occupied a deserted tract which it proceeded to colonize, building roads and irrigating the land. As a result a numerous indigenous population crowded in from the neighbouring areas. These people now claim to be free and to decide their own destinies. Whether or not colonization is in general thought a permissible form of "entitlement" the changed situation must surely change one's moral evaluation of Metropolitania's title to the formerly deserted tract. So with the Mayflowerite who bagged a large stretch of unoccupied land in 1620. If the situation is now that irrespective of title the tracts in question are occupied by people who have nowhere else to live surely the moral basis of the title of the Mayflowerite's successors must at least be open to debate. Once there was more than enough to go round, now there is not. And is the case very different if the thousands without property

instead of occupying the colonies or tracts in question crowd the periphery and make claims on the unused resources inside: All this is intended to make the simple point that it is obtuse to suppose that the justification for acquiring or transmitting property could be settled once and for all at the date of acquisition or transfer. Legally it may be so, subject to the rules of lapse and expropriation. This is because of the need to frame rules of law in such a way as to ensure certainty of title. They are meant however to be applied in a context in which social and moral criticism may be directed against their operation and in which their defects may be corrected by legislation or similar means. Apart from positive law, can it seriously be maintained that the rules about what constitutes a just acquisition or transfer both express unchanging verities and, in their application to the facts of a given acquisition or transfer, are exempt from reassessment in the light of changed circumstances?

Systems of property law which diverge from the orthodox western type based on liberal conceptions of ownership are conceivable, morally defensible and have actually obtained in certain societies. To begin with the conceivable, let us take an imaginary case. Suppose that, in a "state of nature" a group of people live near a river and subsist on fish, which they catch by hand, and berries. There is great difficulty in catching fish by hand. Berries are however fairly plentiful. There are bits of metal lying around and I discover how to make one of them into a fishhook. With this invention I quadruple my catch of fish. My neighbours cannot discover the knack and I decline to tell them. They press me to lend them the fishhook or to give them lessons in acquiring the technique. I have however acquired western notions of property law and Lockean ideas about entitlement, I point out that I have a just title to the fishhook, since according to *Nozick's* version of *Locke* they are no worse off as a result of my invention. I am therefore entitled to the exclusive, permanent and transmissible use of the fishhook. My neighbors may try their hands at finding out how to make one, of course, but if they fail they may look forward to eating berries and from time to time a bit of fish while I and those persons whom I choose to invite to a meal propose to enjoy ourselves with daily delicacies. If they object that this is unfair I shall point out (though the relevance is not obvious) that they are not actually starving. Nor am I monopolizing materials. There are other pieces of metal lying around. They are no worse off than they were before or than they would have been without my find (in fact they *are* worse off, relatively to me). As to the parrot cry that they protect me and my family from marauders, wild animals and the like, so that I ought to share my good fortune with them, I reply that they have not grasped what is implied by a system of just entitlements. Are they saying that I am not entitled to the fishhook?

One of my brighter neighbours might well answer me as follows. "I do not deny that you have a right to the fishhook. As you say you made it and you invented the system of using it to catch fish. But it does not follow that, as you assert, your right to it is exclusive, permanent and transmissible. Your views seem to be coloured by reading books about sophisticated societies. In those societies men are dedicated to increasing production, come what may, and in order to achieve that they accept institutions which to us seem very unfair. We are simple people used to sharing our fortunes and misfortunes. We recognize that you have a right to the fishhook but not that the right has the unlimited content which you assign to it. You ought to allow each of us to use it in turn. Naturally as the maker and inventor you are entitled to a greater share in the use than the rest of us individually, and if you like to call that share 'ownership' we shall not object. But please stop looking up the definition of 'ownership' in foreign books. These notions will only disrupt our way of life."

The point my neighbour is making is that a system of private property can be inherently distributive. In the system envisaged there is an "owner" in the sense of a person whose right to the use of the thing is greater than that of others, who has a residual claim if others do not want to use the thing, and in whom powers of management will be vested. He will be responsible for lending the fishhook out, it will be returned to him each evening, he will keep it in repair. But these powers of use, management and reversion fall short of western conception of ownership. In such a system the redistributive power of the state will be unnecessary unless the members of the group fail to keep the rules. For the rules themselves ensure an even distribution of prop-

erty, subject to the recognition of desert and choice — recognition which is not allowed to subvert the principle of sharing.

Is the projected system of property law obviously unjust? How does it compare with western notions of ownership? From the point of view of justice, though perhaps not of economic efficiency, it seems to compare rather favourably. It is designed to give effect to the interdependence of the members of the group and to recognize overtly that they cannot survive in isolation. It rejects the notion that I do no harm to a member of my group if as a result of my effort I am better off, and he is no worse off than he would otherwise be. That notion, which is common to the outlook of *Nozick* and *Rawls*, however much they otherwise differ, rests on the assumption that a person who is *comparatively* worse off is not worse off. But he is, and the precise wrong he suffers is that of being treated as an unequal by the more fortunate member or members of the group.

The fruits of an invention which raises production have therefore, in the projected system, to be shared, either by a system of compulsory loan or, in a weaker version, by a system of surplus sharing, under which what an owner "has in excess of his needs or is not using must be made available to other members of his group."[9]

The sort of system envisaged is unlikely to survive the division of labour, viz. specialisation. The members of the group other than the inventor are likely to feel that he can fish better than they and that they would do well to get him to fish for them. But then they must pay him. At first perhaps the payment is a fraction of the catch. Later the inventor is bemused by the idea that he is entitled to the whole product of his invention. So he argues that his neighbours owe him the whole of his catch and, if they want any of it, must pay in some other way, as by repairing his hut. As he has possession on his side his views may prevail. We slide insensibly, therefore, from a participatory to an exclusive system of property law, and it is difficult to keep alive, in a society of economic specialisation, the notion that each participates in a common enterprise. The remedy for this is not, or is only to a minor extent, a return to rotatory labour. It is rather that the community as a whole, the state, must act as the surrogate of the participatory principles. The inventor of the fishhook will have to be taxed. In that way the economic advantages of specialisation can be combined with a just, or juster distribution of the benefits derived from it. The tax will be used to give the other members of the group benefits corresponding to their former rights to use the fishhook.

There is no point in attempting to work out in detail what a participatory system of property law would be like. The idea is easy to grasp. If such a system is morally sound, then it follows that in a western-type system the intervention of the state, so far from being, as *Nozick* thinks, ruled out except in peripheral instances, (initially unjust acquisitions, subsequently unjust transfers) is essential in order to achieve justice in distribution.[10] Whether one says that this is because in a western-type system all the holdings are unjust (because they are holdings of an unjust sort of property interest) or that they were initially just but that their permanent retention cannot be justified, is debatable: the former seems more appealing. In any event either *Nozick's* conclusion is empty because the premises are never fulfilled, or if the premises are fulfilled, they do not lead to the conclusions which they seem to lead.

If it is accepted that the sort of property system described is conceivable and morally defensible, that is sufficient to rebut the argument which denies a redistributive function to the state. It is not irrelevant, however, to draw attention to the fact that among the variety of property arrangements found in simple societies there are some which approximate to the distributive arrangement outlined. Among other things this will serve to rebut any argument that I am relying on a gimmicky obligatory principle of transfer.[11] A convenient outline of the variety of such property systems is to be found in *M. J. Herskowitz'* work.[12] They are of course multifold: apart from arrangements which resemble the western institution of ownership there are to be found types of group (e.g. family or clan) ownership, public ownership, rotating individual use (e.g. of fishing grounds) and also the sort of arrangement here envisaged, namely what may be called private ownership subject to compulsory loan or sharing. Thus among the Bushmen[13] "all kinds of food are private property" and "one who takes without the permission of the owner is liable to punishment for theft" but "one who shoots a buck or discovers a terrain where vegetable food is to be gathered is nevertheless expected to share with those who have nothing," so that "all available food, though from the point of view of customary law privately owned, is actually distributed among the members of a given group." The dividing is done by the owner and the skin, sinews etc. belong to him to deal with as he pleases. Among the Indians of the Pacific North-West[14] a man is said to have "owned" an economically important tract and this "ownership" was expressed by his "giving permission" to his fellows to exploit the locality each season but "no instance was ever heard of an 'owner' refusing to give the necessary permission. Such a thing is inconceivable." The individual "ownership" is a sort of stewardship or ownership in trust carrying with it management and the right to use but not excluding the right of others to a similar use. Among certain tribes of Hottentots[15] a person who dug a waterhole or opened a spring made this his property and all who wished to use it had to have his permission, but he was under an obligation to see that no stranger or stranger's stock was denied access to it. Among the Tswana[16] where the chief allocates (and in that sense "owns") the land he will allot cattle-posts to individuals, but not exclusively. The allocee, whose position is closest to that of the private owner, "must share with a number of other people the pastures of the place where his cattle-post is situated, although no one else may bring his cattle there without permission." Yet occupation does give a certain prior right. "If a man builds a hut and so indicates that it is not merely for temporary use, he established a form of lien over the place, and can return to it at any time."

There are also examples of what I have termed surplus sharing, which give effect to the principle that what a person has in excess of his needs, or is not using must be made available to other members of the group. Among the Eskimos the principle that "personal possession is conditioned by actual use of the property" comes into play. A fox-trap lying idle may be taken by anyone who will use it. In Greenland a man already owning a tent or large boat does not inherit another, since it is assumed that one person can never use more than one possession of this type. "Though what a person uses is generally acknowledged to be his alone any excess must be at the disposal of those who need it and can make good use of it."[17]

These examples show that there is nothing unnatural about distributive property arrangements in a simple society. The mechanism, or one of the possible mechanisms by which such arrangements are secured, is that of what it seems preferable to call private ownership subject to a trust or a duty to permit sharing. The "ownership" is not of course ownership of the classical western type, but neither is it "primitive communism." Its essential feature is that the titles to acquisition are much the same as in modern societies — finding, invention, occupation, making and the like — and the types of transfer — sale, gift, inheritance — are not necessarily dissimilar, but the type of interest acquired and transmitted is different. The principle of sharing is written into the delineation of interests of property.

There is no special reason to think that our moral consciousness is superior to that of simple societies. So if compulsory sharing commends itself to some of them it should not be dismissed out of hand for societies in which the division of labour has made those simple arrangements out of date: but in these, given the weakened social cohesion which the division of labour introduces, the central authority (the state) is needed to see that sharing takes place.

NOTES

1. Oxford 1974.
2. Nozick p. 238.

3. Nozick pp. 150–182.
4. Nozick p. 206.
5. Nozick pp. 169 f, arguing that redistributive arrangements give B a sort of Property right in A. This mistake stems from the Lockean argument that we own ourselves and *hence* what we make etc. If human beings are free they cannot own themselves; their relationship to themselves and their bodies is more like one of "sovereignty" which cannot be alienated or foregone, though it can be restricted by (lawful) contract or treaty.
6. Nozick pp. 174 ff.
7. For an analysis see Honoré, "Ownership," in: Guest, *Oxford Essays in Jurisprudence* (London 1961).
8. For an analysis see Honoré ARSP 61 (1975) 161.
9. Herskowitz, below n. 12, p. 372.
10. Nozick, pp. 174 ff. However one interprets Locke's requirement that the acquirer must leave enough and as good in common for others (Second Treatise sec. 27) the intention behind it is not satisfied unless entitlements are adjusted from time to time according to what *then* remains for others.
11. Nozick p. 157.
12. M. J. Herskowitz, *Economic Anthropology* (New York 1952), part IV. Property.
13. Herskowitz, pp. 321–2, citing L. Schapera, *The Khosian Peoples of South Africa, Bushmen and Hottentots* (London 1930) p. 148.
14. Herskowitz pp. 332–3, citing P. Drucker "Rank, Wealth and Kinship in Northwest Coast Society," *Amer. Anth.* 41 (1939) p. 59.
15. Herskowitz pp. 343–4, citing Schapera, above n. 13, at pp. 286–291.
16. Herskowitz p. 344, citing L. Schapera and A. J. H. Goodwin "Work and Wealth" in *The Bantu-Speaking Tribes of South Africa* (ed. L. Schapera) pp. 156–7.
17. Herskowitz pp. 373–4 citing K. Birket-Smith, *The Eskimos* (London 1936) pp. 148–151.

Ideas for Class Projects, Papers, or Debates

1. As Honoré notes, while the Western, liberal concept of property is very broad, it is not without limits. Zoning restrictions are among the most common justified by the public interest. Look at the cases of *Euclid* v. *Ambler Realty Co.* and *Belle Terre* v. *Boraas*. *Euclid* simply says that residential zoning is a legitimate public interest. It also illustrates how much an individual property owner can lose from a simple zoning change. Consider the arguments presented for restrictive zoning in *Belle Terre*. Support or oppose the Court's decision in the case.

2. The case of *State* v. *Shack* presents a conflict between the right to exclusive control of one's property — presumably a very basic element of ownership itself — and the civil right to access to legal counsel and medical treatment. Explain the Court's decision in the case and why it is or is not justified.

3. Should taxpayers have to pay for privately owned historical landmarks? What restrictions on private property are justified for the preservation of our cultural heritage? In historical districts building and remodeling are strictly regulated by the city even though the property is privately owned. What justifies such restrictions, and how far should they be allowed to extend? Single landmarks may be restricted as well. Review the *Penn Central* case and support or oppose the Court's decision.

4. Control of population growth is a serious modern problem. In *Construction Industry Ass'n of Sonoma County* v. *City of Petaluma* the city has imposed severe restrictions on the use of private property at the outskirts of the city so as to maintain a greenbelt around the town. The Construction Association, as well as some property owners, object to this limitation of use. This is a severe limit, but also a very important public interest. Review the case and defend one side or the other.

• You may wish to consult "How to Read a Case" at the end of Chapter Two for general help with understanding and analyzing legal cases in general. Remember that some of the selections here are small excerpts from cases, intended to illustrate developments in legal thinking in the area. Since you do not have entire cases, you may not have all the information you need to analyze every selection fully. You do have enough information to analyze most of the cases included in this chapter.

Cases on Property

Euclid v. Ambler Realty Co.
272 U.S. 365 (1926)

Plaintiff brought suit in a federal district court to enjoin the enforcement of a comprehensive zoning ordinance as applied to a piece of property owned by him. He alleged that his land was vacant and had been held for years for the purpose of selling and developing it for industrial uses; that for such uses it had a market value of about $10,000 per acre; that the effect of the ordinance, in limiting the land to residential uses was to reduce its market value to about $2,500 per acre. The injunction was granted and the Supreme Court reversed.

JUSTICE SUTHERLAND, speaking for the Court, said, in part:

"The ordinance now under review, and all similar laws and regulations, must find their justification in some aspect of the police power, asserted for the public welfare. The line which in this field separates the legitimate from the illegit-

imate assumption of power is not capable of precise delimitation. It varies with circumstances and conditions. A regulatory zoning ordinance, which would be clearly valid as applied to the great cities, might be clearly invalid as applied to rural communities. In solving doubts, the maxim *sic utere tuo ut alienum non laedas*, which lies at the foundation of so much of the common law of nuisances, ordinarily will furnish a fairly helpful clew. And the law of nuisances, likewise, may be consulted, not for the purpose of controlling, but for the helpful aid of its analogies in the process of ascertaining the scope of, the power. Thus the question whether the power exists to forbid the erection of a building of a particular kind or for a particular use, like the question whether a particular thing is a nuisance, is to be determined, not by an abstract consideration of the building or of the thing considered apart, but by considering it in connection with the circumstances and the locality. . . . A nuisance may be merely a right thing in the wrong place, — like a pig in the parlor instead of the barnyard. If the validity of the legislative classification for zoning purposes be fairly debatable, the legislative judgment must be allowed to control. . . .

"There is no serious difference of opinion in respect of the validity of laws and regulations fixing the height of buildings within reasonable limits, the character of materials and methods of construction, and the adjoining area which must be left open, in order to minimize the danger of fire or collapse, the evils of overcrowding, and the like, and excluding from residential sections offensive trades industries and structures likely to create nuisances. . . .

* * *

". . . The serious question in the case arises over the provisions of the ordinance excluding from residential districts, apartment houses, business houses, retail stores and shops, and other like establishments. This question involves the validity of what is really the crux of the more recent zoning legislation, namely, the creation and maintenance of residential districts, from which business and trade of every sort, including hotels and apartment houses, are excluded. Upon that question this Court has not thus far spoken. The decisions of the state courts are numerous and conflicting; but those which broadly sustain the power greatly outnumber those which deny altogether or narrowly limit it; and it is very apparent that there is a constantly increasing tendency in the direction of the broader view. We shall not attempt to review these decisions at length, but content ourselves with citing a few as illustrative of all. . . .

* * *

"The matter of zoning has received much attention at the hands of commissions and experts, and the results of their investigations have been set forth in comprehensive reports. These reports, which bear every evidence of painstaking consideration, concur in the view that the segregation of residential, business, and industrial buildings will make it easier to provide fire apparatus suitable for the character and intensity of the development in each section; that it will increase the safety and security of home life; greatly tend to prevent street accidents, especially to children, by reducing the traffic and resulting confusion in residential sections; decrease noise and other conditions which pro-

duce or intensify nervous disorders; preserve a more favorable environment in which to rear children, etc. . . .

* * *

"If these reasons, thus summarized, do not demonstrate the wisdom or sound policy in all respects of those restrictions which we have indicated as pertinent to the inquiry, at least, the reasons are sufficiently cogent to preclude us from saying, as it must be said before the ordinance can be declared unconstitutional, that such provisions are clearly arbitrary and unreasonable, having no substantial relation to the public health, safety, morals, or general welfare. . . .

"It is true that when, if ever, the provisions set forth in the ordinance in tedious and minute detail, come to be concretely applied to particular premises, including those of the appellee, or to particular conditions, or to be considered in connection with specific complaints, some of them, or even many of them, may be found to be clearly arbitrary and unreasonable. . . ."

* * *

Village of Belle Terre v. *Boraas*
416 U.S. 1 (1974)

Mr. Justice Douglas delivered the opinion of the Court.

Belle Terre is a village on Long Island's north shore of about 220 homes inhabited by 700 people. Its total land area is less than one square mile. It has restricted land use to one-family dwellings excluding lodging houses, boarding houses, fraternity houses, or multiple dwelling houses. The word "Family" as used in the ordinance means, "One or more persons related by blood, adoption, or marriage, living and cooking together as a single housekeeping unit, exclusive of household servants. A number of persons but not exceeding two (2) living and cooking together as a single housekeeping unit though not related by blood, adoption, or marriage shall be deemed to constitute a family."

Appellees (Dickmans) are owners of a house in the village and leased it in December, 1971 for a term of 18 months to Michael Truman. Later Bruce Boraas became a colessee. Then Anne Parish moved into the house along with three others. These six are students at nearby State University at Stony Brook and none is related to the other by blood, adoption, or marriage. When the village served the Dickmans with an "Order to Remedy Violations" of the ordinance, the owners plus three tenants thereupon brought this action under 42 U.S.C. § 1983 for an injunction declaring the ordinance unconstitutional. The District Court held the ordinance constitutional and the Court of Appeals reversed, one judge dissenting. 2 Cir., 476 F.2d 806. The case is here by appeal, 28 U.S.C. § 1254(2); and we noted probable jurisdiction, 414 U.S. 907.

This case brings to this Court a different phase of local zoning regulations than we have previously reviewed. Village of Euclid v. Ambler Realty Co., 272 U.S. 365, involved a zoning ordinance classifying land use in a given area into six categories. . . .

* * *

The main thrust of the case in the mind of the Court was in the exclusion of industries and apartments and as respects that it commented on the desire to keep residential areas free of "disturbing noises"; "increased traffic"; the hazard of "moving and parked automobiles"; the "depriving children of the privilege of quiet and open spaces for play, enjoyed by those in more favored localities." . . . The ordinance was sanctioned because the validity of the legislative classification was "fairly debatable" and therefore could not be said to be wholly arbitrary. . . .

Our decision in Berman v. Parker, 348 U.S. 26, sustained a land use project in the District of Columbia against a land owner's claim that the taking violated the Due Process Clause and the Just Compensation Clause of the Fifth Amendment. The essence of the argument against the law was, while taking property for ridding an area of slums was permissible, taking it "merely to develop a better balanced, more attractive community" was not, 348 U.S., at 31. We refused to limit the concept of public welfare that may be enhanced by zoning regulations. . . .

If the ordinance segregated one area only for one race, it would immediately be suspect under the reasoning of Buchanan v. Warley, 245 U.S. 60, where the Court invalidated a city ordinance barring a Black from acquiring real property in a white residential area by reason of an 1866 Act of Congress, 14 Stat. 27, 42 U.S.C. § 1982 and an 1870 Act, 16 Stat. 144, both enforcing the Fourteenth Amendment. . . .

* * *

The present ordinance is challenged on several grounds: that it interferes with a person's right to travel; that it interferes with the right to migrate to and settle within a State; that it bars people who are uncongenial to the present residents; that the ordinance expresses the social preferences of the residents for groups that will be congenial to them; that social homogenity is not a legitimate interest of government; that the restriction of those whom the neighbors do not like trenches on the newcomers' rights of privacy; that it is of no rightful concern to villagers whether the residents are married or unmarried; that the ordinance is antithetical to the Nation's experience, ideology and self-perception as an open, egalitarian, and integrated society.[4]

We find none of these reasons in the record before us. It is not aimed at transients. Cf. Shapiro v. Thompson, 394 U.S. 618. It involves no procedural disparity inflicted on some but not on others such as was presented by Griffin v. Illinois, 351 U.S. 12. It involves no "fundamental" right guaranteed by the Constitution, such as voting, Harper v. Virginia State Board, 383 U.S. 663; the right of association, NAACP v. Alabama ex rel. Patterson, 357 U.S. 449; the right of access to the courts, NAACP v. Button, 371 U.S. 415; or any rights of privacy, cf. Griswold v. Connecticut, 381 U.S. 479; Eisenstadt v. Baird, 405 U.S. 438, 453–454. We deal with economic and social legislation where legislatures have historically drawn lines which we respect against the charge of violation of the Equal Protection Clause if the law be "reasonable, not arbitrary" (quoting F. S. Royster Guano Co. v. Virginia, 253 U.S. 412, 415) and bears "a rational relationship to a [permissible] state objective." Reed v. Reed, 404 U.S. 71, 76.

It is said, however, that if two unmarried people can constitute a "family," there is no reason why three or four may not. But every line drawn by a legislature leaves some out that might well have been included.[5] That exercise of discretion, however, is a legislative not a judicial function.

It is said that the Belle Terre ordinance reeks with an animosity to unmarried couples who live together. There is no evidence so support it; and the provision of the ordinance bringing within the definition of a "family" two unmarried people belies the charge.

The ordinance places no ban on other forms of

association, for a "family" may, so far as the ordinance is concerned, entertain whomever they like.

The regimes of boarding houses, fraternity houses, and the like present urban problems. More people occupy a given space; more cars rather continuously pass by; more cars are parked; noise travels with crowds.

A quiet place where yards are wide, people few, and motor vehicles restricted are legitimate guidelines in a land use project addressed to family needs. This goal is a permissible one within *Berman v. Parker, supra.* The police power is not confined to elimination of filth, stench, and unhealthy places. It is ample to lay out zones where family values, youth values, and the blessings of quiet seclusion, and clean air make the area a sanctuary for people.

* * *

Reversed.

NOTES

4. Many references in the development of this thesis are made to Turner, The Frontier in American History (1920), with emphasis on his theory that "democracy is born of free land." Id., 32.

5. Mr. Justice Holmes made the point a half century ago.

"When a legal distinction is determined, as no one doubts that it may be, between night and day, childhood and maturity, or any other extremes, a point has to be fixed or a line has to be drawn, or gradually picked out by successive decisions, to mark where the change takes place. Looked at by itself without regard to the necessity behind it the line or point seems arbitrary. It might as well or nearly as well be a little more to one side or the other. But when it is seen that a line or point there must be, and that there is no mathematical or logical way of fixing it precisely, the decision of the legislature must be accepted unless we can say that it is very wide of any reasonable mark." Louisville Gas & Electric Co. v. Coleman, 277 U.S. 32, 41 (dissenting).

State of New Jersey v. Peter K. Shack and Frank Tejeras
Supreme Court of New Jersey.
58 N.J. 297, 277 A.2d 369 (1971)

WEINTRAUB, C. J. Defendants entered upon private property to aid migrant farmworkers employed and housed there. Having refused to depart upon the demand of the owner, defendants were charged with violating N.J.S.A. 2A:170–31 which provides that "[a]ny person who trespasses on any lands . . . after being forbidden so to trespass by the owner . . . is a disorderly person and shall be punished by a fine of not more than \$50." Defendants were convicted in the Municipal Court of Deerfield Township and again on appeal in the County Court of Cumberland County on a trial *de novo.* R. 3:23–8(a). We certified their further appeal before argument in the Appellate Division. . . .

* * *

Complainant, Tedesco, a farmer, employs migrant workers for his seasonal needs. As part of their compensation, these workers are housed at a camp on his property.

Defendant Tejeras is a staff attorney with the Farm Workers Division of the Southwest Citizens Organization for Proverty Elimination, known by the acronym SCOPE, a nonprofit corporation funded by the Office of Economic Opportunity pursuant to an act of Congress, 42 U.S.C.A. §§ 2861–2864. The role of SCOPE includes providing for the "health services of the migrant farm worker."

Defendant Shack is a staff attorney with the Farm Workers Division of Camden Regional Legal Services, Inc., known as "CRLS," also a nonprofit corporation funded by the Office of Economic Opportunity pursuant to an act of Congress, 42 U.S.C.A. § 2809(a)(3). The mission of CRLS includes legal advice and representation for these workers.

Differences had developed between Tedesco and these defendants prior to the events which led to the trespass charges now before us. Hence when defendant Tejeras wanted to go upon Tedesco's farm to find a migrant worker who needed medical aid for the removal of 28 sutures, he called upon defendant Shack for his help with respect to the legalities involved. Shack, too, had a mission to perform on Tedesco's farm; he wanted to discuss a legal problem with another migrant worker there employed and housed. Defendants arranged to go to the farm together. Shack carried literature to inform the migrant farmworkers of the assistance available to them under federal statutes, but no mention seems to have been made of that literature when Shack was later confronted by Tedesco.

Defendants entered upon Tedesco's property

and as they neared the camp site where the farm-workers were housed, they were confronted by Tedesco who inquired of their purpose. Tejeras and Shack stated their missions. In response, Tedesco offered to find the injured worker, and as to the worker who needed legal advice, Tedesco also offered to locate the man but insisted that the consultation would have to take place in Tedesco's office and in his presence. Defendants declined, saying they had the right to see the men in the privacy of their living quarters and without Tedesco's supervision. Tedesco thereupon summoned a State Trooper who, how-ever, refused to remove defendants except upon Tedesco's written complaint. Tedesco then exe-cuted the formal complaints charging violations of the trespass statute.

I

The constitutionality of the trespass statute, as applied here, is challenged on several scores.

It is urged that the First Amendment rights of the defendants and of the migrant farmworkers were thereby offended. Reliance is placed on Marsh v. Alabama, 326 U.S. 501, 66 S.Ct. 276, 90 L.Ed. 265 (1946), where it was held that free speech was assured by the First Amendment in a company-owned town which was open to the pub-lic generally and was indistinguishable from any other town except for the fact that the title to the property was vested in a private corporation. . . .

Defendants also maintain that the application of the trespass statute to them is barred by the Supremacy Clause of the United States Constitu-tion, Art. VI, cl. 2, and this on the premise that the application of the trespass statute would defeat the purpose of the federal statutes, under which SCOPE and CRLS are funded, to reach and aid the migrant farmworker. . . .

The brief of New Jersey State Office of Legal Services, *amicus curiae*, asserts the workers' Sixth Amendment right to counsel in criminal matters is involved and suggests also that a right to counsel in civil matters is a "penumbra" right emanating from the whole Bill of Rights under the thinking of Griswold v. Connecticut, . . .

* * *

These constitutional claims are not established by any definitive holding. We think it unneces-sary to explore their validity. The reason is that we are satisfied that under our State law the own-ership of real property does not include the right to bar access to governmental services available to migrant workers and hence there was no tres-pass within the meaning of the penal statute. . . .

* * *

II

Property rights serve human values. They are recognized to that end, and are limited by it. Title to real property cannot include dominion over the destiny of persons the owner permits to come upon the premises. Their well-being must remain the paramount concern of a system of law. Indeed the needs of the occupants may be so imperative and their strength so weak, that the law will deny the occupants the power to con-tract away what is deemed essential to their health, welfare, or dignity.

Here we are concerned with a highly disad-vantaged segment of our society. . . .

* * *

The migrant farmworkers are a community within but apart from the local scene. They are rootless and isolated. Although the need for their labors is evident, they are unorganized and with-out economic or political power. It is their plight alone that summoned government to their aid. In response, Congress provided under Title III-B of the Economic Opportunity Act of 1964 (42 U.S.C.A. § 2701 et seq.) for "assistance for migrant and other seasonally employed farm-workers and their families." Section 2861 stated "the purpose of this part is to assist migrant and seasonal farmworkers and their families to improve their living conditions and develop skills necessary for a productive and self-suffi-cient life in an increasingly complex and techno-logical society." . . .

* * *

These ends would not be gained if the intended beneficiaries could be insulated from efforts to reach them. It is in this framework that we must decide whether the camp operator's rights in his lands may stand between the migrant workers and those who would aid them. The key to that aid is communication. Since the migrant workers are outside the mainstream of the communities in which they are housed and are unaware of their rights and opportunities and of the services available to them, they can be reached only by positive efforts tailored to that end. . . .

* * *

A man's right in his real property of course is not absolute. It was a maxim of the common law that one should so use his property as not to injure the rights of others. Broom, Legal Maxims (10th ed. Kersley 1939), p. 238; 39 Words and Phrases, "Sic Utere Tuo ut Alienum Non Laedas," p. 335. Although hardly a precise solvent of actual controversies, the maxim does express the inevitable proposition that rights are relative and there must be an accommodation when they meet. Hence it has long been true that necessity, private or public, may justify entry upon the lands of another. . . .

* * *

The subject is not static. As pointed out in 5 Powell, Real Property (Rohan 1970) § 745, pp. 493–494, while society will protect the owner in his permissible interests in land, yet

". . . [S]uch an owner must expect to find the absoluteness of his property rights curtailed by the organs of society, for the promotion of the best interests of others for whom these organs also operate as protective agencies. The necessity for such curtailments is greater in a modern industrialized and urbanized society than it was in the relatively simple American society of fifty, 100, or 200 years ago. The current balance between individualism and dominance of the social interest depends not only upon political and social ideologies, but also upon the physical and social facts of the time and place under discussion."

* * *

This process involves not only the accommodation between the right of the owner and the interests of the general public in his use of his property, but involves also an accommodation between the right of the owner and the right of individuals who are parties with him in consensual transactions relating to the use of the property. Accordingly substantial alterations have been made as between a landlord and his tenant. . . .

* * *

We see no profit in trying to decide upon a conventional category and then forcing the present subject into it. That approach would be artificial and distorting. The quest is for a fair adjustment of the competing needs of the parties, in the light of the realities of the relationship between the migrant worker and the operator of the housing facility.

Thus approaching the case, we find it unthinkable that the farmer-employer can assert a right to isolate the migrant worker in any respect significant for the worker's well-being. The farmer, of course, is entitled to pursue his farming activities without interference, and this defendants readily concede. But we see no legitimate need for a right in the farmer to deny the worker the opportunity for aid available from federal, State, or local services, or from recognized charitable groups seeking to assist him. Hence representatives of these agencies and organizations may enter upon the premises to seek out the worker at his living quarters. So, too, the migrant worker must be allowed to receive visitors there of his own choice, so long as there is no behavior hurtful to others, and members of the press may not be denied reasonable access to workers who do not object to seeing them.

It is not our purpose to open the employer's premises to the general public if in fact the employer himself has not done so. We do not say, for example, that solicitors or peddlers of all kinds may enter on their own; we may assume for the present that the employer may regulate their entry or bar them, at least if the employer's purpose is not to gain a commercial advantage for himself or if the regulation does not deprive the migrant worker of practical access to things he needs.

And we are mindful of the employer's interest in his own and in his employees' security. Hence he may reasonably require a visitor to identify himself, and also to state his general purpose if the migrant worker has not already informed him that the visitor is expected. But the employer may not deny the worker his privacy or interfere with his opportunity to live with dignity and to enjoy associations customary among our citizens. These rights are too fundamental to be denied on the basis of an interest in real property and too fragile to be left to the unequal bargaining strength of the parties.

It follows that defendants here invaded no possessory right of the farmer-employer. Their conduct was therefore beyond the reach of the trespass statute. The judgments are accordingly reversed and the matters remanded to the County Court with directions to enter judgments of acquittal.

Penn Central Transportation Co.
v. City of New York
438 U.S. 104 (1978)

Brennan, J., delivered the opinion of the Court, in which Stewart, White, Marshall, Blackmun, and Powell, JJ., joined. Rehnquist, J., filed a dissenting opinion, in which Burger, C.J., and Stevens, J., joined.

Mr. Justice Brennan delivered the opinion of the Court.

This case involves the application of New York City's Landmark Preservation Law to Grand Central Terminal (Terminal). The Terminal, which is owned by the Penn Central Transportation Company and its affiliates (Penn Central), is one of New York City's most famous buildings. Opened in 1913, it is regarded not only as providing an ingenious engineering solution to the problems presented by urban railroad stations, but also as a magnificent example of the French Beaux Arts style. . . .

*   *   *

II

The issues presented by appellants are (1) whether the restrictions imposed by New York City's law upon appellants' exploitation of the Terminal site effect a "taking" of appellants' property for a public use within the meaning of the Fifth Amendment, which of course is made applicable to the States through the Fourteenth Amendment, see Chicago B. & Q. R. Co. v. Chicago, 166 U.S. 226, 239, 17 S.Ct. 581, 585, 41 L.Ed. 979 (1897) and, (2) if so, whether the transferable development rights afforded appellants constitute "just compensation" within the meaning of the Fifth Amendment. We need only address the question whether a "taking" has occurred. . . .

*   *   *

B

In contending that the New York City law has "taken" their property in violation of the Fifth and Fourteenth Amendments, appellants make a series of arguments, which, while tailored to the facts of this case, essentially urge that any substantial restriction imposed pursuant to a landmark law must be accompanied by just compensation if it is to be constitutional. . . .

They first observe that the air space above the Terminal is a valuable property interest, citing United States v. Causby, supra. They urge that the Landmarks Law has deprived them of any gainful use of their "air rights" above the Terminal and that, irrespective of the value of the remainder of their parcel, the city has "taken" their right to this superadjacent air space, thus entitling them to "just compensation" measured by the fair market value of these air rights.

Apart from our own disagreement with appellants' characterization of the effect of the New York law, see infra, the submission that appellants may establish a "taking" simply by showing that they have been denied the ability to exploit a property interest that they heretofore had believed was available for development is quite simply untenable. . . .

*   *   *

. . . In deciding whether a particular governmental action has effected a taking, this Court focuses rather both on the character of the action and on the nature and extent of the interference with rights in the parcel as a whole, here, the city tax block designated as the "landmark site."

Secondly, appellants, focusing on the character and impact of the New York City law, argue that it effects a "taking" because its operation has significantly diminished the value of the Terminal site. Appellants concede that the decisions sustaining other land use regulations, which, like the New York law, are reasonably related to the promotion of the general welfare, uniformly reject the proposition that diminution in property value, standing alone, can establish a taking, see Euclid v. Ambler Realty Co., supra (75% diminution in value caused by zoning law); Hadacheck v. Sebastian, supra, (87 1/2% diminution in value); . . .

*   *   *

. . . Appellants argue that New York City's regulation of individual landmarks is fundamentally different from zoning or from historic district legislation because the controls imposed by New York City's law apply only to individuals who own selected properties.

Stated baldly, appellants' position appears to be that the only means of ensuring that selected owners are not singled out to endure financial hardship for no reason is to hold that any restriction imposed on individual landmarks pursuant to the New York scheme is a "taking" requiring the payment of "just compensation." Agreement with this argument would of course invalidate not just New York City's law, but all comparable landmark legislation in the Nation. We find no merit in it. . . .

*   *   *

Equally without merit is the related argument that the decision to designate a structure as a landmark "is inevitably arbitrary or at least subjective because it basically is a matter of taste," Reply Brief of Appellant 22, thus unavoidably singling out individual landowners for disparate and unfair treatment. . . .

*   *   *

. . . A landmark owner has a right to judicial review of any Commission decision, and, quite simply, there is no basis whatsoever for a conclusion that courts will have any greater difficulty identifying arbitrary or discriminatory action in the context of landmark regulation than in the context of classic zoning or indeed in any other context.

Next, appellants observe that New York City's law differs from zoning laws and historic district ordinances in that the Landmarks Law does not impose identical or similar restrictions on all structures located in particular physical communities. It follows, they argue, that New York City's law is inherently incapable of producing the fair and equitable distribution of benefits and burdens of governmental action which is characteristic of zoning laws and historic district legislation and which they maintain is a constitutional requirement if "just compensation" is not to be afforded. It is of course true that the Landmarks Law has a more severe impact on some landowners than on others, but that in itself does not mean that the law effects a "taking." Legislation designed to promote the general welfare commonly burdens some more than others. The owners of the brickyard in *Hadacheck*, of the cedar trees in Miller v. Schoene, and of the gravel and sand mine in Goldblatt v. Hempstead, were uniquely burdened by the legislation sustained in those cases. Similarly, zoning laws often impact more severely on some property owners than others but have not been held to be invalid on

that account. For example, the property owner in *Euclid* who wished to use his property for industrial purposes was affected far more severely by the ordinance than his neighbors who wished to use their land for residences. . . .

*   *   *

Appellants' final broad-based attack would have us treat the law as an instance, like that in United States v. Causby, supra, in which Government, acting in an enterprise capacity, has appropriated part of their property for some strictly governmental purpose. Apart from the fact that *Causby* was a case of invasion of airspace that destroyed the use of the farm beneath and this New York City law has in no wise impaired the present use of the Terminal, the Landmarks Law neither exploits appellants' parcel for city purposes nor facilitates nor arises from any entrepreneurial operations of the city. The situation is not remotely like that in *Causby* when the airspace above the Terminal was in the flight pattern for military aircraft. The Landmarks Law's effect is simply to prohibit appellants or anyone else from occupying portions of the airspace above the Terminal, while permitting appellants to use the remainder of the parcel in a gainful fashion. This is no more an appropriation of property by Government for its own uses than is a zoning law prohibiting, for "aesthetic" reasons, two or more adult theatres within a specified area, see Young v. American Mini Theatres, Inc., supra, or a safety regulation prohibiting excavations below a certain level. See Goldblatt v. City of Hempstead, supra. . . .

*   *   *

Unlike the governmental acts in *Goldblatt, Miller, Causby, Griggs*, and *Hadacheck*, the New York City law does not interfere in any way with the present uses of the Terminal. . . .

Appellants, moreover, exaggerate the effect of the Act on its ability to make use of the air rights above the Terminal in two respects. First, it simply cannot be maintained, on this record, that appellants have been prohibited from occupying *any* portion of the airspace above the Terminal. . . . Since appellants have not sought approval for the construction of a smaller structure, we do not know that appellants will be denied any use of any portion of the airspace above the Terminal.

Second, to the extent appellants have been denied the right to build above the Terminal, it is not literally accurate to say that they have been denied *all* use of even those pre-existing air rights. Their ability to use these rights has not been abrogated; they are made transferable to at least eight parcels in the vicinity of the Terminal . . .

* * *

On this record we conclude that the application of New York City's Landmarks Preservation Law has not effected a "taking" of appellants' property. The restrictions imposed are substantially related to the promotion of the general welfare and not only permit reasonable beneficial use of the landmark site but afford appellants opportunities further to enhance not only the Terminal site proper but also other properties.

Affirmed.

Mr. Justice Rehnquist, with whom the Chief Justice and Mr. Justice Stevens join, dissenting.

Of the over one million buildings and structures in the city of New York, appellees have singled out 400 for designation as official Landmarks.[1] The owner of a building might initially be pleased that his property has been chosen by a distinguished committee of architects, historians and city planners for such a singular distinction. But he may well discover, as appellant Penn Central Transportation Co. did here, that the Landmark designation imposes upon him a substantial cost, with little or no offsetting benefit except for the honor of the designation. The question in this case is whether the cost associated with the city of New York's desire to preserve a limited number of "landmarks" within its borders must be borne by all of its taxpayers or whether it can instead be imposed entirely on the owners of the individual properties.

Only in the most superficial sense of the word can this case be said to involve "zoning."[2]

NOTES

1. A large percentage of the designated landmarks are public structures (such as the Brooklyn Bridge, City Hall, the Statue of Liberty and the Municipal Asphalt Plant) and thus do not raise Fifth Amendment taking questions. See Landmarks Preservation Commission of the City of New York, Landmarks and Historic Districts (1977) and January 10, 1978 Supplement). Although the Court refers to the New York ordinance as a *comprehensive* program to preserve *historic* landmarks, ante, at 107, the ordinance is not limited to historic buildings and gives little guidance to the Landmarks Preservation Commission in its selection of landmark sites. Section 207–1.0(n) of the Landmarks Preservation Law requires only that the selected landmark be at least 30 years old and possess "a special character or special historical or aesthetic interest or value as part of the development, heritage or cultural characteristics of the city, state or nation."

2. Even the New York Court of Appeals conceded that "[t]his is not a zoning case. . . . Zoning restrictions operate to advance a comprehensive community plan for the common good. Each property owner in the zone is both benefited and restricted from exploitation, presumably without discrimination except for permitted continuing non-conforming uses. The restrictions may be designed to maintain the general character of the area, or to assure orderly development, objectives inuring to the benefit of all, which property owners acting individually would find difficult or impossible to achieve. . . .

"Nor does this case involve landmark regulation of a historic district. [In historic districting, as in traditional zoning] owners although burdened by the restrictions also benefit, to some extent, from the furtherance of a general community plan. . . .'"

Construction Industry Ass'n of Sonoma County v. The City of Petaluma
U.S. Court of Appeals, Ninth Circuit
522 F.2d 897 (1975)

Choy, Circuit Judge: The City of Petaluma (the City) appeals from a district court decision voiding as unconstitutional certain aspects of its five-year housing and zoning plan. We reverse.

Statement of Facts

The City is located in southern Sonoma County, about 40 miles north of San Francisco. In the 1950's and 1960's, Petaluma was a relatively self-sufficient town. It experienced a steady population growth from 10,315 in 1950 to 24,870 in 1970. Eventually, the City was drawn into the Bay Area metropolitan housing market as people working in San Francisco and San Rafael became willing to commute longer distances to secure relatively inexpensive housing available there. By

November 1972, according to unofficial figures, Petaluma's population was at 30,500, a dramatic increase of almost 25 per cent in little over two years. . . .

* * *

To correct the imbalance between single-family and multi-family dwellings, curb the sprawl of the City on the east, and retard the accelerating growth of the City, the Council in 1972 adopted several resolutions, which collectively are called the "Petaluma Plan" (the Plan).

The Plan, on its face limited to a five-year period (1972–1977) fixes a housing development growth rate not to exceed 500 dwelling units per year. . . .

* * *

The Plan also positions a 200 foot wide "greenbelt" around the City, to serve as a boundary for urban expansion for at least five years, and with respect to the east and north sides of the City, for perhaps ten to fifteen years. . . .

* * *

Purpose of the Plan

The purpose of the Plan is much disputed in this case. According to general statements in the Plan itself, the Plan was devised to ensure that "development in the next five years, will take place in a reasonable, orderly, attractive manner, rather than in a completely haphazard and unattractive manner." The controversial 500-unit limitation on residential development-units was adopted by the City "[i]n order to protect its small town character and surrounding open space." The other features of the Plan were designed to encourage an east-west balance in development, to provide for variety in densities and building types and wide ranges in prices and rents, to ensure infilling of close-in vacant areas, and to prevent the sprawl of the City to the east and north. The Construction Industry Association of Sonoma County (the Association) argues and the district court found, however, that the Plan was primarily enacted "to limit Petaluma's demographic and market growth rate in housing and in the immigration of new residents." Construction Industry Assn. v. City of Petaluma, 375 F. Supp. 574, 576 (N.D.Cal.1974).

Market Demand and Effect of the Plan

In 1970 and 1971, housing permits were allotted at the rate of 1000 annually, and there was no indication that without some governmental control on growth consumer demand would subside or even remain at the 1000-unit per year level. Thus, if Petaluma had imposed a flat 500-unit limitation on *all* residential housing, the effect of the Plan would clearly be to retard to a substantial degree the natural growth rate of the City. Petaluma, however, did not apply the 500-unit limitation across the board, but instead exempted all projects of four units or less. . . .

* * *

Substantive Due Process

Appellees claim that the Plan is arbitrary and unreasonable and, thus, violative of the due process clause of the Fourteenth Amendment. According to appellees, the Plan is nothing more than an exclusionary zoning device,[1] designed solely to insulate Petaluma from the urban complex in which it finds itself. The Association and the Landowners reject, as falling outside the scope of any legitimate governmental interest, the City's avowed purposes in implementing the Plan — the preservation of Petaluma's small town character and the avoidance of the social and environmental problems caused by an uncontrolled growth rate.

In attacking the validity of the Plan, appellees rely heavily on the district court's finding that the express purpose and the actual effect of the Plan is to exclude substantial numbers of people who would otherwise elect to move to the City. 375 F.Supp. at 581. The existence of an exclusionary purpose and effect reflects, however, only *one* side of the zoning regulation. Practically all zoning restrictions have as a purpose and effect the *exclusion* of some activity or type of structure or a certain density of inhabitants. And in reviewing the reasonableness of a zoning ordinance, our inquiry does not terminate with a finding that it is for an exclusionary purpose.[2] We must determine further whether the *exclusion* bears any rational relationship to a *legitimate state interest*. If it does not, then the zoning regulation is invalid. If, on the other hand, a legiti-

mate state interest is furthered by the zoning regulation, we must defer to the legislative act.
Being neither a super legislature nor a zoning
board of appeal, a federal court is without
authority to weigh and reappraise the factors
considered or ignored by the legislative body in
passing the challenged zoning regulation. The
reasonableness, not the wisdom, of the Petaluma
Plan is at issue in this suit.

It is well settled that zoning regulations "must
find their justification in some aspect of the
police power, asserted for the public welfare."
Village of Euclid v. Ambler Realty Co., 272 U.S.
365, 387, 47. . . .

In determining whether the City's interest in
preserving its small town character and in avoiding uncontrolled and rapid growth falls within
the broad concept of "public welfare," we are
considerably assisted by two recent cases. *Belle
Terre*, supra, and Ybarra v. City of Town of Los
Altos Hills, 503 F.2d 250 (9th Cir. 1974), each of
which upheld as not unreasonable a zoning regulation much more restrictive than the Petaluma
Plan, are dispositive of the due process issue in
this case. . . .

Both the Belle Terre ordinance and the Los
Altos Hills regulation had the purpose and effect
of permanently restricting growth; nonetheless,
the court in each case upheld the particular law
before it on the ground that the regulation served
a legitimate governmental interest falling within
the concept of the public welfare: the preservation
of quiet family neighborhoods (Belle Terre) and
the preservation of a rural environment (Los
Altos Hills). Even less restrictive or exclusionary
than the above zoning ordinances is the Petaluma
Plan which, unlike those ordinances, does not
freeze the population at present or near-present
levels. Further, unlike the Los Altos Hills ordinance and the various zoning regulations struck
down by state courts in recent years, the Petaluma
Plan does not have the undesirable effect of
walling out any particular income class nor any
racial minority group.

Although we assume that some persons desirous
of living in Petaluma will be excluded under the
housing permit limitation and that, thus, the Plan
may frustrate some legitimate regional housing
needs, the Plan is not arbitrary or unreasonable.
We agree with appellees that unlike the situation in

the past most municipalities today are neither isolated nor wholly independent from neighboring
municipalities and that, consequently, unilateral
land use decisions by one local entity affect the
needs and resources of an entire region. See, e.g.,
Golden v. Planning Board of Town of Ramapo, 30
N.Y.2d 359, 334 N.Y.S.2d 138, 285 N.E.2d 291,
appeal dismissed, 409 U.S. 1003, 93 S.Ct. 436, 34
L.Ed.2d 294 (1972); National Land & Investment
Co. v. Kohn, 419 Pa. 504, 215 A.2d 597 (1965);
Note, Phased Zoning: Regulation of the Tempo
and Sequence of Land Development, 26
Stan.L.Rev. 585, 605 (1974). It does not necessarily follow, however, that the *due process* rights of
builders and landowners are violated merely
because a local entity exercises in its own self-
interest the police power lawfully delegated to it by
the state. See *Belle Terre*, supra; *Los Altos Hills*,
supra. If the present system of delegated zoning
power does not effectively serve the state interest
in furthering the general welfare of the region or
entire state, it is the state legislature's and not the
federal courts' role to intervene and adjust the system. As stated supra, the federal court is not a
super zoning board and should not be called on to
mark the point at which legitimate local interests in
promoting the welfare of the community are outweighed by legitimate regional interests.

We conclude therefore that under *Belle Terre*
and *Los Altos Hills* the concept of the public welfare is sufficiently broad to uphold Petaluma's
desire to preserve its small town character, its
open spaces and low density of population, and
to grow at an orderly and deliberate pace.

Reversed.

NOTES

1. "Exclusionary zoning" is a phrase popularly
used to describe suburban zoning regulations which
have the effect, if not also the purpose, of preventing
the migration of low and middle-income persons.
Since a large percentage of racial minorities fall with
in the low and middle income brackets, exclusionary
zoning regulations may also effectively wall out racial
minorities.

Most court challenges to and comment upon so-
called exclusionary zoning focus on such traditional
zoning devices as height limitations, minimum square
footage and minimum lot size requirements, and the
prohibition of multi-family dwellings or mobile homes.

The Petaluma Plan is unique in that although it assertedly slows the growth rate it replaces the past pattern of single-family detached homes with an assortment of housing units, varying in price and design.

2. Our inquiry here is not unlike that involved in a case alleging denial of equal protection of the laws. The mere showing of some discrimination by the state is not sufficient to prove an invasion of one's constitutional rights. Most legislation to some extent discriminates between various classes of persons, business enterprises, or other entities. However, absent a suspect classification or invasion of fundamental rights, equal protection rights are violated only where the classification does not bear a rational relationship to a legitimate state interest. See Ybarra v. City of Town of Los Altos Hills, 503 F.2d 250, 254 (9th Cir. 1974).

CHAPTER FIVE

The Nature of Tort Law and Personal Responsibility

Basically, tort law is about injury, damage, or loss and what to do about it. In daily interactions people inflict damage on one another in all sorts of ways for all sorts of reasons. People suffer injury from car accidents, defective products, fights, muggings, vandalism, slanderous statements, invasions of privacy, hazardous working conditions, and careless hunters, to give just a few examples. Someone has to bear the cost of medical expenses, pain and suffering, loss of reputation, business, income, and damaged property. Tort law addresses the question of who should bear these losses. When damage occurs, who should pay for it? The answer assumed in tort law is that the wrongdoer rather than the victim should bear the cost of damage. Thus tort law enables victims to shift their losses to the wrongdoer who caused the loss. How does it do that?

Tort law functions in precisely the same way we have described private law. It focuses on the interactions of private individuals with one another (not with the state or the public as a whole), and it works by enabling the victim, the injured party, to initiate a lawsuit to recover compensation for damages from the party at fault. If the victim does not initiate action on her own behalf, nothing will happen, and she bears her own loss. It is up to the victim to use the law to protect herself if she wants to. Tort actions are considered private matters. The state has no interest in these individual disputes other than to provide fair and efficient procedures that enable individuals to interact and defend themselves. Tort law is private law. As you study the materials in this chapter consider whether it ought to be. Is this the best way to handle these sorts of disputes?

Tort law is also common law. A tort offense is a common law offense. Like contract law and property law, tort law developed through the common law system in successive court decisions. Legal authority for tort law resides in the body of court opinion that has accumulated over the years through the cases of the common law. This contrasts, for example, with the criminal law and civil rights law, which are statutory (or constitutional).

Tort law is essentially about interpersonal responsibility — or perhaps it would be better to say it is about interpersonal *ir*responsibility. Generally speaking, in the law of torts, a person is held *responsible* for harm or damage he wrongfully causes others. What does this statement mean? Suppose we are talking about you. What would it mean to say "you are *responsible* for X"? The problem is that there could be a number of different meanings, because the term *responsibility* has a number of different senses. H. L. A. Hart tells a story that illustrates these differences.

> As a captain of the ship, X was responsible for the safety of his passengers and crew. But on his last voyage he got drunk every night and was responsible for the loss of the ship with all aboard. It was rumoured that he was insane, but the doctors considered that he was responsible for his actions. Throughout the voyage he behaved quite irresponsibly, and various incidents in his career showed that he was not a responsible person. He always maintained that the exceptional winter storms were responsible for the loss of the ship, but in the legal proceedings brought against him he was found criminally responsible for his negligent conduct, and in separate civil proceedings he was held legally responsible for the loss of life and property. He is still alive and he is morally responsible for the deaths of many women and children.

Hart reduces this morass of ambiguity to four useful classifications, which he calls: (1) role-responsibility, (2) causal-responsibility, (3) liability-responsibility, and (4) capacity-responsibility.

These classifications do not cover all possible uses of the term, but they should serve our purposes quite well. All of them are relevant to responsibility in tort law.

Consider first the simplest notion of liability-responsibility. What does this mean? "You are liable for X" at the simplest level just means you have to pay for X. But responsibility means much more than that. In fact, we often say, "You are liable (to pay) for X because you were responsible for X." What does this mean? Using Hart's categories, we can spell it out. The statement might mean (1) it was your duty or role to take care of X and you didn't do it. Or it might mean (2) you caused X. Or it might mean (3) X is your fault. It might mean all of the above, and in addition it also always means (4) you are a competent person with the capacity to control your mind and body and to distinguish right from wrong. Obviously, responsibility is a complex notion, but that is what tort law is about. Furthermore, it is one of the most fundamental and essential elements of all human relationships. We often avoid talking about responsibility because it is burdensome, but personal relations on even the smallest, most intimate level are impossible without some sense of responsibility on the part of the individuals involved. To that extent, the study of responsibility in tort law is also the study of a basic element of personal relations and human life.

To return to the simple level of liability (which is a useful starting point) the question we want to examine in this chapter is why (on what grounds) *should* someone be required to pay for X? To approach this question it will be helpful to consider more carefully each of the senses of responsibility distinguished by Hart. All of them are involved in tort law. We will look first at the idea of obligation (or community standards of care), which corresponds generally to Hart's notion of role-responsibility.

In addition, there are two basic questions to keep in mind throughout this chapter: a conceptual question and a substantive question. The conceptual question is, What does it mean to be responsible? What do we mean when we use the language of responsibility? If we are not clear about our concepts, then we will make foolish mistakes. Hart's categories help us clarify the concept of responsibility. The second question is substantive: What are our responsibilities to one another? To whom are we responsible, for what, and why? Providing answers to these questions is the primary focus of tort law.

As Dan B. Dobbs explains in the first selection, torts are "wrongs" of a certain sort. Specifically, they are wrongs that are recognized by law as grounds for lawsuit. That is a handy, functional definition which enables us to identify what a legal system calls a tort, but what we want to examine is why something *should* be called a tort. Just what is it that makes these "wrongs" wrong? Causing harm is not enough in itself, for a person can cause harm without doing wrong. You are prohibited from causing me harm by throwing a rock though the window of my grocery store (that is a wrong, so you are liable for the damage), but you are not prohibited from driving me out of business by opening your own grocery store across the street that is able to undercut my prices (which is not a wrong, so you are not liable for the damage). Obviously, all harms are not wrongs. And the size of the harm is not decisive, since losing my business is a much greater harm than losing my window. Furthermore, the history of property law tells us that our legal system as late as the nineteenth century recognized competitive injury as a wrong in the sense that it was considered an actionable injury to property. Thus, something may be a (legal) wrong at one time and not at another. One way to account for this is to recognize that standards of responsibility change with time and circumstances.

But that doesn't help much at this point. We still need to know what makes a harm a wrong. What makes a harm a wrong (in tort law) is the violation of a duty. In every tort action there is a legal duty owed to the plaintiff that has been breached by the defendant with resulting damage to the plaintiff. I am under a duty not to throw a rock through your window or otherwise vandalize your property. I am not under a duty not to compete with you in business. Therefore, I am responsible to you for damage caused in the former case but not in the latter. Some basic duties are very clear, such as duties not to commit violent crimes (including vandalism) against one another, and these duties change very little over time or place. Other duties are not so obvious—for example, the idea of competitive injury—so attitudes about them can vary with place or time. At one time it may be felt that I am wrong to move in and undercut my neighbor's business. At another time it is considered fair play, the challenge of the market. At the former time I am considered responsible (that is, both blameworthy and liable to pay) for injuring my neighbor's business; at a later time I am not. Thus, standards of responsibility can and do change.

In this chapter we will examine first the nature of this standard of responsibility. What is it? Where does it come from? What are its origin and justification? How is it determined? How are people supposed to know what it is? The duty enforced by tort law is not a special duty that arises from any special agreement. We need not consent to this duty in order to have it. The duty does not originate in legislation or in contract. Thus, it is not justified by majority rule or by individual consent.

The duty, at least in our legal system, is a common law duty. How we describe and justify it will depend in part on our theory of law. From a positivist or legal realist view, the legal duty originates in the courts. It is determined by judges and is justified by valid legal rules and/or by the authority of the office. The natural law theory views the duty as a moral standard, discovered and articulated by courts as a legal reflection of the objective moral responsibility human beings owe one another universally or in a particular society. All theories recognize that the common law is intended to embody commonly held attitudes and assumptions of society. Tort law is assumed to embody commonly held attitudes about responsibility for personal injuries. The standard is a standard of reasonableness or "due care." Everyone is assumed to know what this standard requires, first, because the standard is commonly held and, second, because it is simply the minimal standard of careful behavior that any reasonable person would hold. Consequently, according to the traditional justification, the court is justified in judging any person liable who violates this standard.

In clear cases this position is easily supported. Suppose I am in a bad mood on my birthday—I hate birthdays—so I sock you in the jaw, knocking out three teeth to improve my mood. I am liable for your dental bill—at least—and I cannot defend myself by claiming that no one ever told me about a standard that prohibits socking an occasional person in the jaw. Everyone knows that you can't do that. Some standards are commonly held. Any reasonable person knows these standards and generally agrees with them, even if we sometimes break them.

Many cases, however, are not so obvious, especially cases of negligence. Thus, we will use negligence law to examine this standard of responsibility that every reasonable person is assumed to know. Using Dobbs's article, we will review the general features of tort law as a whole to provide us with a general background.

In the next selection William Prosser sets out the elements of a cause of action for negligence. We are interested in the first two elements here: (1) There is a duty to exercise reasonable care in one's activities so as not to subject others to unreasonable risks of harm, and (2) a negligent party is one who has violated that standard of care with regard to the person injured. The failure to meet this standard—the violation of this duty—is what makes the harm wrongful. And what is this standard? Traditionally, it is the standard of care that would have been exercised by a reasonable, prudent person in similar circumstances. Who is this reasonable, prudent person? It is not the average individual, who is, after all, sometimes careless. On the other hand, neither is it a hero or a saint. Extraordinary behavior is not demanded, but reasonable behavior is always required. As Prosser explains, the reasonable, prudent person is "a personification of a community ideal of reasonable behavior, determined by the jury's social judgment." This reasonable, prudent person is an "ordinary" person, with "ordinary" characteristics and no special talents, but one who is always careful.

And how would a reasonable, prudent person calculate the risks associated with her behavior? As Prosser points out, all human behavior involves some risk. This risk is not necessarily unreasonable; indeed, some risk is unavoidable. The first consideration for the reasonable person, then, is the level of probability that some harm will result from her conduct. What consequences are probable? Probability alone is not enough, however, since any person is expected to be more careful if serious risk is involved. The probability of harm, then, must be weighed in terms of the gravity of the possible consequences. But even this is not enough, for the probability and gravity of the harm on the one hand must be balanced against the social value of the activity in question, as well as the possible alternatives. Greater risk is tolerated for greater value.

For example, speeding and driving on the wrong side of the road create unreasonable risks in ordinary circumstances; that is, the probability of causing harm is high, and the probability that the harm will be serious is also high. However, we allow emergency vehicles to do such things because the social value of saving lives is considered worth the risk, so long as all possible precautions are taken and no better alternatives are available. So, in general, to evaluate reasonableness we must balance the probability and magnitude of the risk against the necessity and social value of the activity. This balancing provides a standard for assessing negligence, or irresponsibility. The thing to notice about this standard is that it does not involve hard-line rules of conduct. Instead, it is a formula that requires judgment in application. In a negligence case the court asks the jury to imagine what a reasonable, prudent person would have done in similar circumstances and then to measure the behavior of the defendant against this ideal standard.

This standard of care is illustrated and discussed in one of the most famous of all tort cases, *Palsgraf* v. *Long Island Railroad Co.* Many issues are raised in this case, but we are interested here in what it can tell us about the standard of care or duty owed to others. What does *Palsgraf* tell us about the nature of negligence? Ask yourself whether anyone was negligent to Mrs. Palsgraf. If not, why should the railroad be liable for damages? What sort of a duty does a railroad owe its passengers, anyway? Is it the same or different from the duty one individual owes another, namely, ordinary care? Are there different standards of care? Does a railroad owe more than an ordinary private person?

We, of course, cannot explore in depth the problems of this standard in tort law, but ask yourself whether there is some customary standard of ordinary care that everyone knows intuitively because we are all immersed in it as members of a community. In some vague sense the answer is clearly yes, but how can we assess this vague, general standard accurately in particular cases? How can we articulate it precisely, and if we cannot, then how can we justify holding others to it? The *Palsgraf* case provides us with a good picture of the court struggling to articulate the nature, or more specifically the extent, of the standard of reasonable care. What is the scope of this duty? How careful does a reasonable person have to be? As you will see, Judge Cardozo's opinion on this matter differs sharply from that of Judge Andrews. Cardozo's opinion represents the majority view, which is to say that it is the law. Cardozo's view limits the scope of liability for negligence. Consider for yourself whether this is a better view of interpersonal responsibility than Andrews' view, and if so, why.

Palsgraf is followed by a brief excerpt from the *Polemis* case. *Polemis* actually preceded *Palsgraf* in time, but its focus is not on duty. The *Polemis* case introduces us to another sense of responsibility that is central to tort law, namely, causal responsibility. Consider the following statement: "The long dry spell was responsible for widespread crop damage." This use of *respon-*

sible for simply means *caused* when it is applied to an inaminate object or nonhuman being. But the meaning is not so clear when applied to humans. H. L. A. Hart argues that at least when we use the term in the past tense ("Disraeli was responsible for the defeat of the government") the statement may be a straightforward, causal description of past events. But to say that some person *is* responsible for some disaster he in fact caused imports a claim of blameworthiness—Hart's liability-responsibility. Understanding the connection between causation and liability is much more difficult than most people assume.

In tort law as it presently stands, a person is liable for injury only if his negligent or intentional action caused harm or damage. This raises two questions that are a major focus of this chapter: (1) What is causation, especially for legal purposes, and (2) What is the connection between causation and liability? Discovering what it means to say that someone caused harm turns out to be one of the most formidable tasks ever undertaken in law.

In "Causation and Responsibility" H. L. A. Hart and A. M. Honoré set out the problems involved in understanding causation for legal purposes. The basic problem is how to trace the connection between cause and effect. In law this is called determining *cause-in-fact* or *but-for cause*. The first point we need to recognize in doing this is that the common idea of a "causal chain" is misleading as a description of most causal events. Hart and Honoré suggest that we think of the causal relation as a network or cone rather than as a single chain. Many factors are relevant to a comprehensive explanation of the necessary conditions of any given outcome, and judgments have to be made about which relevant factors to count as causes.

For example, suppose sparks from a cigarette set fire to a trash basket full of paper, which in turn ignites nearby curtains in an office. Then, due to faulty wiring the sprinkler system fails to operate and the office building burns to the ground. All the factors just mentioned are relevant to the outcome, but judgments have to be made for legal purposes about which factors are causal factors and which are merely normal conditions. For example, are you the cause of the fire if you merely filled the wastebasket full of paper and set it under the curtains? The fire would not have occurred without these conditions.

By using such examples Hart and Honoré demonstrate that our ordinary causal judgments in law and in daily life are not nearly as clear-cut as we tend to believe, nor are they simple descriptions. On the contrary, determining causation involves much more personal judgment than most people assume. As Hart and Honoré point out, how you trace causal connections, how you characterize cause and effect, depends on your reason for doing so. Causal language is used for different purposes.

One major purpose is explanatory. The scientific use of causal language is intended to illuminate or explain our world in a general and principled way. Scientists formulate causal explanations to help us understand why things happen the way they do. For example, we know that fire is caused by certain combinations of oxygen, heat, and combustible material. Science provides us with a causal explanation for the occurrence of fire. But, as has often been remarked, the law is not interested in what causes fire but in what caused *that* fire. Thus, explaining that oxygen, heat, and combustible material were present in proper proportions is simply the wrong causal explanation for the legal context because it does not serve the legal purpose. The legal purpose for causal language is quite different from the scientific purpose. The purpose of causal language in law—as in morals—is to enable us to ascribe responsibility or blame for some harmful event.

The second question of particular interest in the legal context is, What is the connection between causation and responsibility or liability? Given all the factors that should be recognized as causally relevant to an outcome, how do you pick out those that are significant enough to found a claim that the actor caused the outcome and therefore should be held liable for it? The fact that Henry Ford made it possible for the common man to own an automobile does not make Ford the cause of air pollution in major U.S. cities even if there would be no urban air pollution but for the widespread use of automobiles. This is the problem of distinguishing "proximate" or "legal" cause from what we have called a general causal network, which, as we have seen, in law is called *but-for-cause* or *cause-in-fact*. This also returns us to the problem of determining the scope of liability.

Remember that negligence is conduct which creates an unreasonable risk of causing harm. Suppose there is negligent conduct but that the consequences which follow are surprising, unforeseeable. (A cook negligently places rat poison on the same shelf with flour and sugar above the stove. The poison explodes and injures someone.) Or suppose that the consequences extend much farther than anyone could have anticipated. (Mrs. O'Leary sets her lantern too close to her cow. The cow kicks it over, starting a fire that burns down most of Chicago.) For which consequences or how much damage should a negligent actor be liable? The courts have attempted to define the scope of liability for causing harm in such cases. This is called determining *legal cause* or *proximate cause*. Ask yourself at this point whether the issue is any longer really a question of causation. Many legal commentators hold that limiting liability by means of the doctrine of proximate cause is really a policy matter that has nothing to do with causation.

This issue is illustrated in the excerpt from the famous *Polemis* case. This case provides us with an alternative point of view about the scope of liability for causing harm. Is it compatible with Hart and Honoré's analysis? The *Polemis* test states that if an actor is negligent, he is responsible for any consequences that directly flow from his conduct. Would Mrs. O'Leary be responsible for rebuilding Chicago on this test? Would the railroad be liable to Mrs. Palsgraf? Look again at the opinions of Cardozo and Andrews in *Palsgraf*. Is Andrews' view like the view held in *Polemis*? Whether we frame it in terms of duty or causation, the issue here is the scope or extent of responsibility for damage. Does framing the issue in terms of causation clarify it?

Obviously, there are major difficulties associated with figuring out what causation is and how it must be related to an outcome in order to form the basis of an ascription of responsibility for that outcome. The question Douglas Husak raises is whether, after all, causation ought always to be considered necessary for legal responsibility. Does the notion of causation really afford the best explanation of legal doctrines that we have? Furthermore, does it always provide legal outcomes that are just? Husak is concerned not with acts that cause harm but with omissions that fail to prevent harm. He proposes as an alternative foundation for responsibility the idea of being in control of a situation. Does his proposal help us avoid any of our causal problems?

The final question we want to consider is the nature and significance of fault in tort law. This idea is analogous to the fullest sense of Hart's notion of liability-responsibility. The vast majority of cases in tort law require that the defendant be guilty of some fault in order to be held responsible for harm or damage. Tort law is a fault-based system. So to say that a harm is a wrong is to say (in part) that the defendant (the tortfeasor) is at fault, is blameworthy, for causing the harm. Thus, the justification for holding you liable to pay for X is that it is your fault that X happened. But what is fault? The dictionary defines fault as shortcoming, wrongdoing, error, or defect (among other things). To be at fault, then, is to be in the wrong.

Fault is associated with a very strong notion of responsibility, or liability, that generally includes certain assumptions about the personal capacities and mental state or attitude of the actor. It assumes that the actor was a competent person in control of mind and body and with the capacity to distinguish right from wrong. A severely retarded, senile, or insane person cannot be held responsible. Such individuals are not considered to be at fault because they are not in control, or do not understand what they are doing. These are the minimal conditions for the notions of responsibility and fault to apply at all, and this is true in both law and morals.

Once the minimal conditions are met a person is considered responsible for his or her actions and, therefore, at fault when those actions are blameworthy. The level or degree of fault is determined by reference to many factors, primary among them the mental state or attitude of the actor. We will focus next on these mental states and their connection to fault.

One factor that is widely recognized as relevant to fault is the intention of the actor. As a beginning concept you may find it helpful to think of intention as what the actor thinks he is doing. For legal purposes, what a person intends is what the person thinks he is doing. For example, a car runs off the road onto a sidewalk, killing a pedestrian. What did the driver intend? Case 1: the driver intended to avoid an oncoming truck. Case 2: the driver intended to kill the pedestrian, who was an old enemy. Case 3: the driver intended to frighten the pedestrian but not to hit him. Case 4: the driver thought he was driving a tank in Vietnam and intended to kill a Vietcong soldier. For any event there could be any number of intentional explanations, but in any case the intention is what the actor thinks he is doing, and the intention makes a difference in our assessment of fault and responsibility for the consequences of the action. Thus, it is important to understand this concept clearly.

The brief selection by Jeremy Bentham provides the classic account that explains and illustrates the many elements of intention. Bentham also traces the equally complex connection between intention and consciousness; and finally he explains the important distinction between intention and motive. As a shorthand statement you may find it useful to note that while intention is what a person thinks he is doing, motive is his reason for doing it.

In addition to intention and motive, both tort law and criminal law base liability in part on the mental state (or *mens rea*) of the actor. The standard view is that there are different levels or degrees of blameworthiness associated with different mental states. Intentional or purposeful action is considered the most culpable. (For example, you start a fire for the purpose of killing your bedridden grandfather so as to collect on his will.) Acting "with knowledge" is considered almost, but not quite, as culpable as purposeful action. (You start a fire to collect on your own insurance, knowing that your bedridden grandfather will be killed, but not for the purpose of killing him.) Reckless action is not considered quite as blameworthy as acting with knowledge. (You start a fire knowing that there is some risk that your invalid grandfather may be killed.) Finally, negligent action is considered the least blameworthy. (You start a fire not realizing that your grandfather may be killed, although any reasonable person would have thought of this risk.) Distinctions among these different mental states are considered in Chapter Six on criminal law. You may wish to consult the selections by Jerome Hall and Herbert Packer, as well as the excerpt from the Model Penal Code, for more detail about these mental elements that the law associates with fault.

The remaining question is, What makes one mental state more culpable than another? Why is malicious action more blameworthy than indifference or carelessness? Why is hatred worse than apathy? Bentham, being a good utilitarian, answers that intentional action is more likely to cause harm or mischief. But is that true? In our machine age much more harm is caused by accident than by intentional action. Is there some other reason to consider intentional harm worse than accidental?

Finally, Fowler Harper and Fleming James raise the more basic question whether fault is the best way to handle losses due to certain accidents at all. Tort law is costly and inefficient in many ways. Harper and James point out that the main objectives in dealing with automobile accidents are the promotion of safety and the compensation of victims. A primary function of tort law is to shift losses from blameless victims to wrongdoers who cause harm. Another way to distribute losses is to spread them among a large group of people so that they can be absorbed and carried over time. This is the concept behind insurance plans. Harper and James suggest that pooling or spreading losses may be more efficient and fair in the case of automobile accidents, especially where fault may become a very tenuous idea.

The point is that in many automobile accidents the person at fault has committed some minor infraction, such as overlooking a stop sign, which we have all committed at one time or another. So we know that this person is no more faulty than the rest of us, but he or she may be liable for enormous damages. Fault becomes almost a technicality, a hook on which to catch a pocket. All people are a little careless now and then. Such accidents could happen to any of us. Therefore, liability for many auto accidents begins to look like bad luck rather than fault. But the cost of damages from auto accidents is a huge problem that must be dealt with. If no other arrangements are made, then victims must pay for their own losses. Hence, Harper and James suggest that we pool our losses by spreading them over the whole population of drivers.

Notice, however, that all accidents could be treated the same way. Any losses at all, even from intentional torts, could be treated the same way. This idea raises some very basic questions about tort law and individual responsibility.

The basic question here is how far tort law should go. When is it best to treat an accident as part of a social problem rather than as an individual problem? Remember that tort law is not concerned with social responsibility. The fault system of tort law reflects a commitment to individual responsibility, embodying the idea that anyone who wrongfully causes damage should pay for it. Isn't that what responsibility is all about? People who oppose ideas like that proposed by Harper and James are afraid that such an approach will erode our sense of individual responsibility. The question is, How far does individual responsibility extend?

Notes and Questions

DAN B. DOBBS, from *Torts and Compensation*

1. Dan B. Dobbs sets out the basic features of American tort law. A tort, he explains, is a "wrong" that is recognized as the basis for a lawsuit. Although torts and crimes often overlap — that is, they apply to the same human actions — they also differ in important ways. What are the ways in which they differ? What is the purpose of tort law as opposed to criminal law?

2. What are the three bases of liability in tort law? Notice that most torts are based on some notion of fault, or blameworthiness, either intentional or negligent. It is this fault that makes the causing of harm a "wrong" and thereby actionable at law. Understanding the notion of fault is a focus of this chapter.

3. Tort law is only one way of dealing with the cost of injuries. Since it is expensive and inefficient, some reformers have advocated alternatives for dealing with at least some injury problems. What are some of these alternatives? What are their advantages and disadvantages?

4. Dobbs points out that tort law emphasizes accountability. What does he mean by this? How is it that this focus on accountability also implies freedom? What is the conflicting concern?

5. The basic problem inherent in the conflict between individual accountability and social concern is the following. If individuals must be strictly responsible for themselves, many injuries would be left uncompensated and consequently many people would lack help when they badly need it. This may even harm society as a whole. On the other hand, having people be compensated for injury even if the injury is their own fault appears to undermine the idea of being responsible for oneself. Keep this problem in mind as you study the materials in this chapter.

[From] *Torts and Compensation*

DAN B. DOBBS

C H A P T E R   1

Introduction

§1. What Is Torts About?

a. What Is Tort Law?

Torts, roughly speaking, are "wrongs," recognized by law as grounds for a lawsuit. These wrongs include an intentional punch in the nose and also a negligent car wreck. They include medical malpractice and some environmental pollution. Other torts include such wrongs as libel or slander, fraud, and interference with contract. The list is very long.

In all these cases the defendant's wrong results in harm to another person (or corporation), a harm the law is willing to say constitutes a legal injury. The injured person is said to have a "cause of action" or claim against the person who committed the tort and caused the harm. This claim can be pursued in court. These are the claims adjudicated in the cases in this casebook.

TORTS AND CRIMES. Some torts are also crimes. The punch in the nose is a tort called battery, but it may also be a crime. It would be possible that a defendant who attacked the plaintiff would be prosecuted criminally and sentenced to jail or given a fine and that he would also be held liable to the plaintiff for the tort. The two fields of law often overlap and often serve similar purposes. However, they are not identical. Criminal prosecutions are aimed at vindicating public interests, not private harms. For this reason, some acts that cause no harm at all to individuals might be crimes. For example, a state might make it a crime to shoot a gun at a person, even if the person is not hurt and even if the person is wholly unaware of the shooting. The public interest in suppressing violence might justify such a rule. But if the individual who was the intended victim was not in fact hurt and not even in apprehension of danger, there is no reason to say this crime is also a tort for which the individual could sue.

TORT DAMAGES. What is characteristic of the tort claim, then, is that a person is, in the eyes of the law, harmed. Occasionally such a person sues for an injunction, a court order forbidding the tortious conduct. Usually, however, the tort is a single act and the plaintiff only sues for damages as compensation for the harm already done. Most of the attention in this book is devoted to torts that cause physical injury to persons or to property, often with accompanying emotional harm. It is a good idea to see immediately the general kinds of damages a plaintiff can recover when there is physical injury to an individual.

The *amount* of damages to be recovered by an injured plaintiff may vary from case to case, depending on how serious the injury is. But the *measure* of damages for compensation is the same, regardless how the injury came about. The injured plaintiff is entitled to recover:

1. Loss of earning capacity (or wage loss).
2. Reasonable medical expenses.
3. A payment for pain and suffering, including mental pain and suffering.

The law generally provides for one and only one legal action, and for this reason the plaintiff recovers not only the damages already suffered, but also all future expected damages. For example, a plaintiff who is paralyzed as the result of a tort will probably be unable to work as productively in the future, and will also have future medical expenses and future pain. He will be entitled to recover under all three heads.

In cases of especially bad conduct by the defendant, the plaintiff may also be permitted to recover punitive or exemplary damages, as a kind of punishment or example. Although such damages serve a purpose of criminal law, the individual plaintiff is allowed to recover these damages in special cases.

As you might suspect, there is a good deal more to the law of damages than is outlined here. . . . It is important to understand at the beginning, however, that damages recovered in tort cases may range from trivial or nominal to sums of several million dollars. Even an injury that sounds on the surface like a moderate one may result in a jury verdict of $50,000 or $100,000. When large sums of money are awarded, the most usual reason is that the jury has been influenced by the claim of "pain," which cannot be quantified. Much turns, then, on the seriousness of the injury and the persuasiveness of the lawyers and, unavoidably, on the sympathies of any particular jury for any particular plaintiff.

BASES OF LIABILITY IN TORT. Tort law is distinguished from criminal law partly because its purposes are compensatory rather than punitive. But there are some other distinctions. One of these is that crimes almost always involve some kind of intent, often an intent to cause harm or to do something people in general consider to be wrong. Some torts are also like this, but not all of them. The law of torts has recognized three distinct bases of tort liability:

1. *Intent.* For example, an intentional striking of another person.
2. *Negligence.* For example, driving too fast or failing to keep a proper lookout with a resulting collision.
3. *Strict liability.* For example, selling a consumer product that is "defective" and causes harm, even though the seller acted with reasonable care. This is sometimes called liability without fault and it may be imposed whenever it is thought that the defendant's activity, whatever it is, should "pay its own way," even though the defendant is guilty of no fault.

Roughly speaking, these three bases of liability will be considered in the order just given.

Although there are cases in which courts have consciously imposed liability upon a defendant who is said not to be at fault, in the great majority of cases judges have said the defendant must be guilty of some kind of fault before he can be held responsible. Fault may be defined in ways that will seem peculiar at times, but fault, according to the prevailing orthodoxy, is required in some degree. As we will see shortly in more detail, this fault usually appears as "intent," or as "negligence"—both terms that will require some considerable definition.

b. Economic and Dignitary Torts

Tort law is not limited to cases of *physical* injury. Some legally recognized injuries involve pure economic harm—that is, harm that costs the plaintiff money without causing him physical injury. Other injuries recognized by law involve "dignitary" harm—that is, harm that neither costs money nor causes physical injury, but may cause emotional harm or demean the plaintiff as a human being.

For example, it may be a tort to say that the plaintiff has a venereal disease, or to lie about the existence of termites in a house being sold, or to discharge the plaintiff from employment for highly improper reasons. The accusation of venereal disease may not cause any economic harm, but even if it does not, it denigrates the plaintiff as a human being (or so the law has said) and may involve emotional distress. The lie about the termites may cause the house buyer pure economic harm, since the house will require repairs or will be worth less because of the termites. The wrongful discharge of the plaintiff from employment will cause economic harm, and, given that improper reasons were behind the discharge, may also cause emotional harm to the plaintiff, as where the plaintiff is discharged because of race or gender. In none of these cases is there physical injury; yet all these cases are torts.

These economic and dignitary torts are often quite different from physical injury torts. For instance, most of the "pocketbook" torts involve some form of communication between people and therefore they involve, at least potentially, the First Amendment's protection for free speech. Because of such differences—of which the free speech concern is only one—it is useful to separate the economic and many of the dignitary torts for consideration late in the course, devoting the first and largest part of the course to torts that involve physical injury to person or property, or at least to acts that risk such injuries.

c. Physical Injury and the Law

Though physical injury is not the exclusive concern of tort law, it is a major one. Injury is also a very large social problem and society responds to that problem in a number of different ways, of which tort law is only one. This book attempts to consider both the tort-law response to the injury problem and some of the other responses — and possibilities.

Injury is a problem most obviously for the injured person, who may suffer a complete disruption of life, loss of income, excruciating pain, continuous medical costs, and a loss of emotional give and take with those around him. These are grounds enough for treating injury seriously, but the loss does not stop with the injured person. Those immediately around such a person usually also suffer. For example, a serious injury may disrupt a marriage or deprive it of its emotional or sexual content. It may also disrupt the larger family, too, and children of a seriously injured person appear at times to engage in antisocial activities, the least of which is vandalism. The radiating effects of injury may lessen the children's chances of adequate education, which in turn will have future disruptive effects on society at large.

Society at large suffers many costs from injury. There are something like 200,000 deaths a year from injury in the United States, and literally millions of disabling injuries from accidents in work, home and automobiles. The costs of these injuries is almost beyond grasp. Lost production, medical costs, loss of wages, and property damage runs to many billions. The radiating costs and their distribution to the non-injured also pose a problem. For example, if injury is uncompensated, public assistance may be required or creditors may go unpaid. If compensation is provided to an injured person, insurance rates may rise. Injury is costly to everyone in society. It is thus not merely an individual problem but also a social problem.

Tort law deals with physical injury mostly in terms of right and wrong. If the injury was wrongfully caused, the wrongdoer — tortfeasor, he is called — must pay compensation. But if the defendant caused harm without committing a legal wrong, or if he has a defense, he will pay nothing and the injury will go uncompensated, no matter how horrible or permanent it is. Each case is judged on its own merits with careful investigation of the facts, professional supervision of inferences to be drawn from the facts and professional application of legal rules, many of which are complex or difficult. This investment in each case is so great that it is likely to improve the chances of doing justice. On the other hand, given the millions of injuries, it is costly. Furthermore, it leaves many injured persons uncompensated. If injury itself is not merely an individual problem, uncompensated injury presents a social concern.

This concern has led many reformers to seek alternatives to tort law, not for all purposes, but for purposes of physical injury cases. Several schemes have been developed for providing compensation on a more massive — and procedurally more efficient — basis than tort law provides. One of these, workers' compensation, provides that when a worker is injured "on the job," he or she will be entitled to certain benefits. These benefits do not include any recovery for pain or suffering, but do cover most medical and most wage loss, at least in the average case. The worker is deprived of a tort action as well as a claim for pain and suffering. In exchange for this loss, however, the worker has the assurance that when injury comes, there will be compensation — an assurance tort law definitely does not give.

Another possible method of handling the injury problem is to respond in a massive way to serious but not to minor injury. It would be possible, for example, to say that if one is permanently disabled by an injury, that is equivalent to an early, forced retirement and the injured person should be entitled to his or her retirement fund. This, in effect, is the rule for social security disability payments.

Still other possibilities include the idea that each person should be compelled to provide for himself a certain minimum insurance protection against some of the more serious risks, such as automobile injury, and that, to the extent that protection is required, no tort action should be permitted at all. This is the essence of the "basic protection" or "no-fault auto plan," now in force in about half the states in some form or another.

These alternatives to the tort method of dealing with injury have several points in common.

They envision very little room for factual dispute since they do not turn on "fault," or wrongdoing. They also contemplate *no* payment for pain and suffering damages—one of the mainstays of tort litigation—but seek instead to be sure that all persons within the scope of coverage are assured of recovering actual out-of-pocket losses.

All of these means of dealing with injury are a part of this course, to be considered after the tort system of dealing with injury is first mastered. The tort system, as we will see, is complicated, bristling with puzzles and issues. This system, with its long trials, detailed examination of facts, careful analysis of arguments, is very expensive compared to some of the alternatives. Yet it has its advantages.

d. Freedom, Accountability and Social Responsibility

The tort system of dealing with injury emphasizes individual accountability—at least in theory and episodically. The defendant who has done "wrong" is liable to those whom he injures, and is thus held accountable. Just as important, the plaintiff is also accountable—if he causes his own injury he will not be allowed to recover damages from the defendant. Like most statements in this introduction, this one will be qualified at various places in these materials, but the thrust of it is correct. Although accountability is a complex idea—and so is "wrongdoing," by the way—the law of torts seeks to make it meaningful in these cases, and thus appeals to a strong moral sense.

The law of torts also protects the freedom of individuals to act as they please so long as they are not legal wrongdoers. As already indicated, there are some cases in which one commits a legal wrong even though one is not in any way morally at fault, and some commentators believe that this strict liability approach is or should be quite prevalent. The courts and the orthodox commentators, however, have traditionally taken the view for the last 130 years or so that liability for tort turns on a finding that the defendant was at fault in some important sense. One who is *not* at fault is not to be held liable in tort even if he causes an injury. This is the freedom side of the accountability coin, and of course it has its own appeal.

Against the strong historical preference in this country for letting each person work out his or her own destiny, holding each accountable for wrongs but free to act in the absence of wrongs, there is also a strong thread of social concern. For example, when it became apparent in the 19th century that railroad workers were injured in great numbers and that other people generally were not, the Congress enacted a statute requiring railroads in interstate commerce to provide certain safety equipment to protect workers. Conceivably the railroads were not negligent by standards of the times in failing to provide safety appliances; workers could have been expected to be "accountable" for their own safety. Yet the Congress acted, imposing on railroads an expense not imposed on everyone else. Similarly today some reformers have felt that tort law is not sufficient protection for large numbers of people who are injured in automobile accidents.

There is a great deal of conflict here. If people who are injured are allowed to recover even though they themselves are at fault, the idea of accountability is sacrificed. Yet if millions of injuries go uncompensated, society as a whole may suffer. This conflict furnishes one of the great themes of the modern course in tort law. Is accountability a goal we can achieve at all? If it is, can we hope to achieve both accountability and a reasonable degree of concern for what is "good for us all"?

The conflict just described can be described in other terms. Philosophers could talk in terms of a conflict between Kantian notions of right-and-wrong and the Utilitarian notions of doing, not what is right for right's sake, but doing what is best for the society as a whole. Economists can cast the issues in terms of efficiency, in the narrow economic sense. But for the moment it is sufficient to see that, whatever the terms, tort law today represents only *one* of the ways of dealing with physical injury.

As we proceed with the course, then, tort law should be evaluated. Does it seek and does it achieve accountability? Is it efficient? Might alternatives be better? The generation of lawyers represented in part by those now in law school will have much to say about the future of tort law and other solutions to the problem of injury.

* * *

Notes and Questions

WILLIAM PROSSER, from *The Law of Torts*

1. As Dobbs explained in the last selection, there are different grounds for liability in tort law. Liability may be based on intentional harm, on negligent harm, or on strict liability for harm, or harm without fault. William Prosser discusses only one of these grounds, the basis of negligence. How does Prosser define negligence?

2. Prosser sets out four elements of the cause of action based on negligence. The elements of a cause of action are the factors a plaintiff must prove in order to win his or her lawsuit. What are these elements?

3. Notice that, according to Prosser, negligence is conduct of a certain sort. What sort of conduct is it? Negligence is not a state of mind, although it is often associated with a state of mind. With what mental attitude is it generally associated? What does this imply about the intention or knowledge of the actor about the consequences of his action?

4. In order to be liable for negligence, the damage must be the result of an unreasonable risk caused by the defendant. But a number of factors must be considered to determine whether a risk is reasonable. Prosser explains the general formula courts have developed for assessing risk. What is this balancing test, according to Prosser? Does it seem to cover all the relevant considerations? Can you think of a simpler test? Is this a good way to decide what behavior is reasonable?

5. The theory of negligence presupposes what lawyers call an objective standard or community standard of behavior. All people need to be held to the same standard, but at the same time relevant differences should be taken into account. Fairness demands at least this much, but it is not easily accomplished, since these two requirements appear to clash. To try to meet these competing interests courts use a model or ideal, asking what a reasonable, prudent person in similar circumstances would do? Answering this question is the crux of negligence law. What are the attributes of the "reasonable, prudent person," according to Prosser? Do you agree? Is it reasonable to hold all people to this standard?

6. The courts deal with physical and mental attributes differently. Can you think of any justification for making allowances for physical but not mental handicaps?

7. Can children be negligent? Certainly at a very young age a child cannot understand the consequences of his actions and so cannot be held negligent. At what age can a child be expected to be responsible? How have the courts dealt with this problem? How would you deal with it?

8. How much is it reasonable to expect any person to know? Suppose a person has limited experience, or a bad memory. Suppose someone doesn't think well in an emergency. Is it fair to hold all people to the same standard? If so, how can such a standard be devised? On what is it based? Is there a common base of knowledge? If there is not, what could the foundation for negligence be? Is it fair to hold professionals or others with superior skill or knowledge to a higher standard?

[From] *The Law of Torts*

WILLIAM PROSSER

Negligence: Standard of Conduct

Elements of Cause of Action

Negligence, as we shall see, is simply one kind of conduct. But a cause of action founded upon negligence, from which liability will follow, requires more than conduct. The traditional formula for the elements necessary to such a cause of action may be stated briefly as follows:

1. A duty, or obligation, recognized by the law, requiring the person to conform to a certain standard of conduct, for the protection of others against unreasonable risks.

2. A failure on the person's part to conform to the standard required: a breach of the duty. These two elements go to make up what the courts usually have called negligence; but the term quite frequently is applied to the second alone. Thus it may be said that the defendant was negligent, but is not liable because he was under no duty to the plaintiff not to be.

3. A reasonably close causal connection between the conduct and the resulting injury. This is what is commonly known as "legal cause," or "proximate cause," and which includes the notion of cause in fact.

4. Actual loss or damage resulting to the interests of another. Since the action for negligence developed chiefly out of the old form of action on the case, it retained the rule of that action, that proof of damage was an essential part of the plaintiff's case. Nominal damages, to vindicate a technical right, cannot be recovered in a negligence action, where no actual loss has occurred. The threat of future harm, not yet realized, is not enough. Negligent conduct in itself is not such an interference with the interests of the world at large that there is any right to complain of it, or to be free from it, except in the case of some individual whose interests have suffered.

* * *

Unreasonable Risk

Negligence is a matter or risk—that is to say, of recognizable danger of injury. It has been defined as "conduct which involves an unreasonably great risk of causing damage," or, more fully, conduct "which falls below the standard established by law for the protection of others against unreasonable risk of harm." "Negligence is conduct, and not a state of mind." In most instances, it is caused by heedlessness or inadvertence, by which the negligent party is unaware of the results which may follow from his act. But it may also arise where the negligent party has considered the possible consequences carefully, and has exercised his own best judgment. The almost universal use of the phrase "due care" to describe conduct which is not negligent should not obscure the fact that the essence of negligence is not necessarily the absence of solicitude for those who may be adversely affected by one's actions but is instead behavior which should be recognized as involving unreasonable danger to others.

The standard of conduct imposed by the law is an external one, based upon what society demands generally of its members, rather than upon the actor's personal morality or individual sense of right and wrong. A failure to conform to the standard is negligence, therefore, even if it is due to clumsiness, stupidity, forgetfulness, an excitable temperament, or even sheer ignorance. An honest blunder, or a mistaken belief that no damage will result, may absolve the actor from moral blame, but the harm to others is still as great, and the actor's individual standards must give way in this area of the law to those of the public. In other words, society may require of a person not to be awkward or a fool.

It is helpful to an understanding of the negligence concept to distinguish it from intent. In negligence, the actor does not desire to bring about the consequences which follow, nor does he know that they are substantially certain to occur, or believe that they will. There is merely a risk of such consequences, sufficiently great to lead a reasonable person in his position to anticipate them, and to guard against them. If an automobile driver runs down a person in the street before him, with the desire to hit the person, or with the belief that he is certain to do so, it is an intentional battery; but if he has no such desire or belief, but merely acts unreasonably in failing to guard against a risk which he should appreciate, it is negligence. As the probability of injury to another, apparent from the facts within the acting party's knowledge, becomes greater, his conduct takes on more of the attributes of intent, until it approaches and finally becomes indistinguishable from that substantial certainty of harm that underlies intent. Such intermediate mental states, based upon a recognizably great probability of harm, may still properly be classed as "negligence," but are commonly called "reckless," "wanton," or even "willful." They are dealt with, in many respects, as if the harm were intended, so that they become in effect a hybrid between intent and negligence, occupying a sort of penumbra between the two. . . .

Negligence already has been defined as conduct which falls below a standard established by the law for the protection of others against unreasonable risk of harm. The idea of risk in this context necessarily involves a recognizable danger, based upon some knowledge of the existing facts, and some reasonable belief that harm may possibly follow. Risk, for this purpose, may then be defined as a danger which is apparent, or should be apparent, to one in the position of the actor. The actor's conduct must be judged in the light of the possibilities apparent to him at the time, and not by looking backward "with the wisdom born of the event." The standard is one of conduct, rather than of consequences. It is not enough that everyone can see now that the risk was great, if it was not apparent when the conduct occurred.

In the light of the recognizable risk, the conduct, to be negligent, must be unreasonable. Nearly all human acts, of course, carry some recognizable but remote possibility of harm to another. No person so much as rides a horse without some chance of a runaway, or drives a car without the risk of a broken steering gear or a heart attack. But these are not unreasonable risks. Those against which the actor is required to take precautions are those which society, in general, considers sufficiently great to demand preventive measures. No person can be expected to guard against harm from events which are not reasonably to be anticipated at all, or are so unlikely to occur that the risk, although recognizable, would commonly be disregarded. An unprecedented frost or flood, the robbery of a customer in the parking lot of a bank, a child picking up a plank with a nail in it and dropping it on his foot, a pedestrian tripping on a slight imperfection in the sidewalk, a workman being struck by lightning, — all of these things have happened, and will occur again; but they may not be so likely to do so on any particular occasion as to make it necessary to burden the freedom of human action with precautions against them. Such events are, in a sense, "unavoidable accidents," for which there is no liability.

On the other hand, if the risk is an appreciable one, and the possible consequences are serious, the question is not one of mathematical probability alone. The odds may be a thousand to one that no train will arrive at the very moment that an automobile is crossing a railway track, but the risk of death is nevertheless sufficiently serious to require the driver to look for the train and the train to signal its approach. It may be highly improbable that lightning will strike at any given place or time; but the possibility is there, and it may require precautions for the protection of inflammables. As the gravity of the possible harm increases, the apparent likelihood of its occurrence need be correspondingly less to generate a duty of precaution.

Against this probability, and gravity, of the risk, must be balanced in every case the utility of the type of conduct in question. The problem is whether "the game is worth the candle." While many risks are caused by simple carelessness, many other risks may reasonably be run, with the full approval of the community. To avert the risks created by heedlessness or inadvertence, the actor must only pay attention to his conduct and surroundings, a burden ordinarily considered a small and necessary price for living among one's fellows. Yet when a person's actions are deliberative, and are undertaken to promote a chosen goal, the negligence issue becomes more complex. Chief among the factors which must be considered is the social value of the interest which the actor is seeking to advance. A person may be justified in dashing into the path of a train to save the life of a child, where it would be arrant folly to save a hat. A railway will be permitted, or even required, to blow a whistle to warn travelers at a crossing, although it is likely to frighten horses on the highway; it may be negligence to blow the same whistle without the same occasion for warning. The public interest will justify the use of dangerous machinery, so long as the benefits outweigh the risk, and a railroad may reasonably be constructed near a highway, even at the expense of some danger to those who use it.

Consideration must also be given to any alternative course open to the actor. Whether it is reasonable to travel a dangerous road may depend upon the disadvantages of another route. While mere inconvenience or cost are often insufficient in themselves to justify proceeding in the face of danger, they will justify taking some risks which are not too extreme. A county will not be required, at a ruinous expense, to build a bridge which will be safe against any accident that might be anticipated; but the converse is also true, and where it can cheaply and easily post a warning, it may be required to do so. A railroad need not do without a turntable because there is some chance that children will play on it and be hurt; but it is quite another matter to keep it locked

The alternative dangers and advantages to the person or property of the actor himself and to others must be thrown into the scale, and a balance struck in which all of these elements are weighed.

It thus is fundamental that the standard of conduct which is the basis of the law of negligence is usually determined upon a risk-benefit form of analysis: by balancing the risk, in the light of the social value of the interest threatened, and the probability and extent of the harm, against the value of the interest which the actor is seeking to protect, and the expedience of the course pursued. For this reason, it is usually very difficult, and often simply not possible, to reduce negligence to any definite rules; it is "relative to the need and the occasion," and conduct which would be proper under some circumstances becomes negligence under others.

The Reasonable Person

The whole theory of negligence presupposes some uniform standard of behavior. Yet the infinite variety of situations which may arise makes it impossible to fix definite rules in advance for all conceivable human conduct. The utmost that can be done is to devise something in the nature of a formula, the application of which in each particular case must be left to the jury, or to the court. The standard of conduct which the community demands must be an external and objective one, rather than the individual judgment, good or bad, of the particular actor; and it must be, so far as possible, the same for all persons, since the law can have no favorites. At the same time, it must make proper allowance for the risk apparent to the actor, for his capacity to meet it, and for the circumstances under which he must act.

The courts have dealt with this very difficult problem by creating a fictitious person, who never has existed on land or sea: the "reasonable man of ordinary prudence."

Sometimes he is described as a reasonable person, or a person of ordinary prudence, or a person of reasonable prudence, or some other blend of reason and caution. It is evident that all such phrases are intended to mean very much the same thing. The actor is required to do what such an ideal individual would be supposed to do in his place. A model of all proper qualities, with only those human shortcomings and weaknesses which the community will tolerate on the occasion, "this excellent but odious character stands like a monument in our Courts of Justice, vainly appealing to his fellow-citizens to order their lives after his own example."

The courts have gone to unusual pains to emphasize the abstract and hypothetical character of this mythical person. He is not to be identified with any ordinary individual, who might occasionally do unreasonable things; he is a prudent and careful person, who is always up to standard. Nor is it proper to identify him with any member of the very jury which is to apply the standard; he is rather a personification of a community ideal of reasonable behavior, determined by the jury's social judgment.

The conduct of the reasonable person will vary with the situation with which he is confronted. The jury must therefore be instructed to take the circumstances into account; negligence is a failure to do what the reasonable person would do "under the same or similar circumstances." Under the latitude of this phrase, the courts have made allowance not only for the external facts, but sometimes for certain characteristics of the actor himself, and have applied, in some respects, a more or less subjective standard. Depending on the context, therefore, the reasonable person standard may, in fact, combine in varying measure both objective and subjective ingredients.

Physical Attributes

As to his physical characteristics, the reasonable person may be said to be identical with the actor. The person who is blind or deaf, or lame, or is otherwise physically disabled, is entitled to live in the world and to have allowance made by others for his disability, and the person cannot be required to do the impossible by conforming to physical standards which he cannot meet. Similar allowance has been made for the weaknesses of old age. At the same time, the conduct of the handicapped individual must be reasonable in the light of the person's knowledge of his infirmity, which is treated merely as one of the circumstances under which the person acts. A blind man may be negligent in going into a place of known danger, just as one who knows that he is subject to epileptic fits, or is about to fall asleep, may be negligent in driving a car. It is sometimes said that a blind man must use a greater degree of care than one who can see; but it is now generally agreed that the more accurate way to state the rule is that he must take the precautions, be they more or less, which the ordinary reasonable person would take if he were blind. Under the latter formulation, the standard remains essentially the same, but has added flexibility for taking the actor's physical deficiencies into account.

Mental Capacity

As to mental peculiarities of the actor, the standard remains of necessity an external one. "The law," says Mr. Justice Holmes in a much quoted passage, "takes no account of the infinite varieties of temperament, intellect, and education which make the internal character of a given act so dif-

ferent in different men. It does not attempt to see men as God sees them, for more than one sufficient reason." The fact that the individual is a congenital fool, cursed with inbuilt bad judgment, or that in the particular instance the person "did not stop to think," or that the person is merely a stupid ox, or of an excitable temperament which causes him to lose his head and get "rattled," obviously cannot be allowed to protect him from liability. Apart from the very obvious difficulties of proof as to what went on in the person's head, it may be no bad policy to hold a fool according to his folly. The harm to his neighbors is quite as great, and may be greater, than if the person exhibited a modicum of brains; and if the person is to live in the community, he must learn to conform to its standards or pay for what he breaks. As to all such mental deficiency of a minor nature, no allowance is made; the standard of reasonable conduct is applied, and "it is not enough that the defendant did the best he knew how."

As for more severe mental disabilities, including total insanity, where the actor entirely lacks the capacity to comprehend a risk or avoid an accident, one might expect a relaxation of the standard similar to the physical disability rule. Yet, for a variety of reasons, the law has developed the other way, holding the mentally deranged or insane defendant accountable for his negligence as if the person were a normal, prudent person. Against the apparent injustice of making persons responsible according to a standard they cannot meet, several rationales have been offered to support the decision to hold mentally deranged defendants accountable for their negligence and certain other torts, including the difficulty of distinguishing true incapacity from mere bad judgment, the belief that the custodians of incompetents will be encouraged by the rule to watch them more closely and keep them under control, and the perceived sense of fairness, even in the absence of moral blame, of a rule requiring mental defectives who live among the rest of society to conform to the general standards of conduct or pay their innocent victims for the damage they cause.

Similar to the cases involving sudden illness or unconsciousness, there is some sentiment for treating a sudden delerium or loss of mental faculties as a "circumstance" depriving the actor of control over his conduct, thus shielding him from liability, provided that the lapse was unforeseeable.

In the case of mentally defective or insane plaintiffs, where the issue involves the contributory or comparative fault of such persons, the policy arguments outlined above lose much of their force. In particular, the question shifts from which of two innocents should bear the loss to whether a negligent defendant should pay for the loss he has partially caused to a mentally incapacitated person incapable of properly looking after himself. Because of the obviously different equities in this situation, the great majority of courts in the contributory negligence context apply a lower standard of care and consider the plaintiff's incapacity as only one of the "circumstances" to be considered in judging the quality of his conduct.

Whether intoxication is to be regarded as a physical or a mental disability depends on how the accident occurs. On either basis, it is common enough; and it is uniformly held that voluntary or negligent intoxication cannot serve as an excuse for acts done in that condition which would otherwise be negligent. One who so becomes intoxicated is held thereafter to the same standard as if he were a sober person. One good reason is that an excuse based on such intoxication would be far too common and too easy to assert; another is that drunkenness is so antisocial that one who indulges in it ought to be held to the consequences. Yet intoxication is not negligence in itself, and it must be shown to have caused the actor's behavior to have deviated from that of a reasonable person and to have caused the plaintiff's injury.

Children

As to one very important group of individuals, it has been necessary, as a practical matter, to depart to a considerable extent from the objective standard of capacity. Children, although they are generally liable for their torts, obviously cannot, in all instances, be held to the same standard as adults, because they often cannot in fact meet it, nor are they generally expected to. It is feasible and appropriate to apply a special standard to them, because "their normal condition is one of incapacity and the state of their progress toward maturity is reasonably capable of determination," and because there is a sufficient basis of community experience, on the part of those who have been children or dealt with them, to permit the jury to apply a special standard.

Nevertheless, the capacities of children vary greatly, not only with age, but also with individuals of the same age; and it follows that no very definite statement can be made as to just what standard is to be applied to them. To a great extent it must necessarily be a subjective one. The standard which is ordinarily applied, and which is customarily given to the jury, is to measure the child's conduct against what would be reasonable to expect of a "child of like age, intelligence and experience." There is something of an individual standard: the capacity of the particular child to appreciate the risk and form a reasonable judgment must be taken into account. This means that more will be required of a child of superior skill or intelligence for his age, and less of one who is mentally backward, which is precisely what the courts have refused to do in the case of an adult. But the standard is still not entirely subjective, and if the conclusion is that the conduct of the child was unreasonable in view of his estimated capacity, the child may still be found negligent, even as a matter of law.

Most courts have attempted to fix a minimum age, below which the child is held to be incapable of all negligence. Although other limits have been set, those most commonly accepted are taken over from the arbitrary rules of the criminal law, as to the age at which children are capable of crime. Below the age of seven, about a dozen states hold that the child is arbitrarily considered incapable of any intelligence. Between seven and fourteen, a number of courts hold that the child is presumed to be incapable, but may be shown to be capable; and that, from fourteen to majority, he is presumed to be capable, but that the contrary may be shown. These multiples of seven are derived originally from the Bible, which is a poor reason for such arbitrary limits; and the analogy of the criminal law is certainly of dubious value where neither crime nor intent is in question. Other courts have rejected any such fixed and arbitrary rules of delimitation, and have held that children well under the age of seven can be capable of some negligent conduct. Undoubtedly there is an irreducible minimum, probably somewhere in the neighborhood of four years of age, but it arguably ought not to be fixed by rules laid down in advance without regard to the particular case.

As the age decreases, there are simply fewer possibilities of negligence, until finally, at some indeterminate point, there are none at all. There is even more reason to say that there is no arbitrary maximum age, beyond which a minor is to be held to the same standard as an adult.

The great bulk of the decisions in which all these questions have been considered have involved the contributory negligence of child plaintiffs. It has been contended that where the child is a defendant no allowance should be made for the child's age, and he should in all cases be treated like an adult, for the reason that in practice children do not pay judgments against them for injuries inflicted, and such payment comes, if at all, from an adult, or from insurance paid for by an adult. Whether this is universally true may perhaps be questioned; but however that may be, the case law has not sustained this point of view. Instead, the courts have developed the more limited rule, which is now quite generally accepted, that whenever a child, whether as plaintiff or as defendant, engages in an activity which is normally one for adults only, such as driving an automobile or flying an airplane, the public interest and the public safety require that any consequences due to the child's own incapacity shall fall upon him rather than the innocent victim, and that the child must be held to the adult standard, without any allowance for his age. This position has been rapidly gaining ground in recent years, and is now the rule in half the states.

There are a few decisions indicating that a similar allowance is to be made at the other end of the scale, for persons at the extreme of life whose mental or physical faculties have been impaired by age but the cases are few and the policy issues have yet to be thoroughly explored.

Knowledge

One of the most difficult questions in connection with negligence is that of what the actor may be required to know. Knowledge has been defined as belief in the existence of a fact, which coincides with the truth. It rests upon perception of the actor's surroundings, memory of what has gone before, and a power to correlate the two with previous experience. So far as perception is concerned, it seems clear that, unless his attention is legitimately distracted, the actor must give to his surroundings the attention which a standard reasonable person would consider necessary under the circumstances, and that he must use such senses as he has to discover what is readily apparent. He may be negligent in failing to look, or in failing to observe what is visible when he does look. As to memory, a person is required to fix in his mind those matters which would make such an impression upon the standard person, and, unless he is startled, or his attention is distracted for some sufficient reason, to bear them in mind, at least for a reasonable length of time. The real difficulty lies with the question of experience. The late Henry T. Terry came to the conclusion that "there are no facts whatever which every person in the community is absolutely bound at his peril to know." It seems clear, however, that there are certain things which every adult with a minimum of intelligence must necessarily have learned: the law of gravity, the fact that fire burns and water will drown, that inflammable objects will catch fire, that a loose board will tip when it is trod on, the ordinary features of the weather to which he is accustomed, and similar phenomena of nature. A person must know in addition a few elementary facts about himself: the amount of space he occupies, the principles of balance and leverage as applied to his own body, the effects of his weight, and, to the extent that it is reasonable to demand it of him, the limits of his own strength, as well as some elementary rules of health.

But beyond this, it seems clear that any individual who has led a normal existence will have learned much more: the traits of common animals, the normal habits, capacities and reactions of other human beings, including their propensities toward negligence and crime, the danger involved in explosives, inflammable liquids, electricity, moving machinery, slippery surfaces and firearms, that worn tires will blow out, and many other risks of life. Such an individual will not be excused when the individual denies knowledge of the risk; and to this extent, at least, there is a minimum standard of knowledge, based upon what is common to the community.

The few cases which have considered the question have held that when an abnormal individual who lacks the experience common to the particular community comes into it, as in the case of the old lady from the city who comes to the farm without ever having learned that a bull is a dangerous beast, the standard of ordinary knowledge will still be applied, and it is the individual who must conform to the community, rather than vice versa.

Above this minimum, once it is determined, the individual will not be held to knowledge of risks which are not known or apparent to him. A person may, however, know enough to be conscious of his own ignorance, and of possible danger into which it may lead him; and if that is the case, as where a layman attempts to give medical treatment, or one enters a strange dark passage, or an automobile driver proceeds with a mysterious wobble in his front wheels, or traverses a strange town without an attempt to discover the meaning of unfamiliar purple traffic lights which suddenly confront him, the person may be found negligent in proceeding in the face of known ignorance.

He may, furthermore, be engaged in an activity, or stand in a relation to others, which imposes upon him an obligation to investigate and find out, so that the person becomes liable not so much for being ignorant as for remaining ignorant; and this obligation may require a person to know at least enough to conduct an intelligent inquiry as to what he does not know. The occupier of premises who invites business visitors to enter, the manufacturer of goods to be sold to the public, the carrier who undertakes to transport passengers, all are charged with the duty of the affirmative action which would be taken by a reasonable person in their position to discover dangers of which they may not be informed. As scientific knowledge advances, and more and more effective tests become available, what was excusable ignorance yesterday becomes negligent ignorance today.

Superior Knowledge, Skill and Intelligence; Professional Malpractice

Thus far the question has been one of a minimum standard, below which the individual will not be permitted to fall. But if a person in fact has knowledge, skill, or even intelligence superior to that of the ordinary person, the law will demand of that person conduct consistent with it. Experienced milk haulers, hockey coaches, expert skiers, construction inspectors, and doctors must all use care which is reasonable in light of their superior learning and experience, and any special skills, knowledge or training they may personally have over and above what is normally possessed by persons in the field.

Professional persons in general, and those who undertake any work calling for special skill, are required not only to exercise reasonable care in what they do, but also to possess a standard minimum of special knowledge and ability. Most of the decided cases have dealt with surgeons and other doctors, but the same is undoubtedly true of dentists, pharmacists, psychiatrists, veterinarians, lawyers, architects and engineers, accountants, abstractors of title, and many other professions and skilled trades. Since, allowing for the inevitable differences in the work done, the principles applied to all of these appear to be quite similar, and since the medical cases are by far the most numerous, it will be convenient to talk only of doctors.

A doctor may, although he seldom does, contract to cure a patient, or to accomplish a particular result, in which case the doctor may be liable for breach of contract when he does not succeed. In the absence of such an express agreement, the doctor does not warrant or insure either a correct diagnosis or a successful course of treatment, and the doctor will not be liable for an honest mistake of judgment, where the proper course is open to reasonable doubt. But by undertaking to render medical services, even though gratuitously, a doctor will ordinarily be understood to hold himself out as having standard professional skill and knowledge. The formula under which this usually is put to the jury is that the doctor must have and use the knowledge, skill and care ordinarily possessed and employed by members of the profession in good standing; and a doctor will be liable if harm results because he does not have them. Sometimes this is called the skill of the "average" member of the profession; but this is clearly misleading, since only those in good professional standing are to be considered; and of these it is not the middle but the minimum common skill which is to be looked to. If the defendant represents himself as having greater skill than this, as where the doctor holds himself out as a specialist, the standard is modified accordingly.

The courts have been compelled to recognize that there are areas in which even experts will disagree. Where there are different schools of medical thought, and alternative methods of acceptable treatment, it is held that the dispute cannot be settled by the law, and the doctor is entitled to be judged according to the tenets of the school the doctor professes to follow. This does not mean, however, that any quack, charlatan or crackpot can set himself up as a "school," and so apply his individual ideas without liability. A "school" must be a recognized one within definite principles, and it must be the line of thought of a respectable minority of the profession. In addition, there are minimum requirements of skill and knowledge, which anyone who holds himself out as competent to treat human ailments is required to have, regardless of his personal views on medical subjects. Furthermore, the physician is required to exercise reasonable care in ascertaining the operational facts upon which his diagnosis is based, and will be liable if he fails to do so.

Formerly it was generally held that allowance must be made for the type of community in which the physician carries on his practice, and for the fact, for example, that a country doctor could not be expected to have the equipment, facilities, libraries, contacts, opportunities for learning, or experience afforded by large cities. Since the standard of the "same" locality was obviously too narrow, this was commonly stated as that of "similar localities," thus including other towns of the same general type. Improved facilities of communication, travel, availability of medical literature, and the like, have led some courts to abandon a fixed locality rule in favor of treating the community as merely one factor to be taken into account in applying the general professional standard. In other jurisdictions the "locality rule" has been discarded outright, and a general national standard applied in all cases, especially in the case of medical specialists.

Since juries composed of laymen are normally incompetent to pass judgment on questions of medical science or technique, it has been held in the great majority of malpractice cases that there can be no finding of negligence in the absence of expert testimony to support it. The well known reluctance of doctors to testify against one another, which has been mentioned now and then

in the decisions, may make this difficult or impossible to obtain, especially in a jurisdiction with a narrow locality rule, and so in some instances effectively deprive the plaintiff of any remedy for a real and grievous wrong. In recent years, however, at least some doctors appear to have become more willing to testify for plaintiffs, especially in cases where the evidence of medical negligence appears quite clear. Where the matter is regarded as within the common knowledge of laymen, as where the surgeon saws off the wrong leg, or there is injury to a part of the body not within the operative field, it is often held that the jury may infer negligence without the aid of any expert.

The cumulative effect of all of these rules has meant that the standard of conduct becomes one of "good medical practice," which is to say, what is customary and usual in the profession.

It has been pointed out often enough that this gives the medical profession, and also the others, the privilege, which is usually emphatically denied to other groups, of setting their own legal standards of conduct, merely by adopting their own practices. It is sometimes said that this is because the physician has impliedly represented that he will follow customary methods, and so has undertaken to do so. Another explanation, perhaps more valid, is the healthy respect which the courts have had for the learning of a fellow profession, and their reluctance to overburden it with liability based on uneducated judgment. It seems clear, in any case, that the result is closely tied in with the layman's ignorance of medical matters and the necessity of expert testimony, since, when the jury are considered competent to do so, they are permitted to find that a practice generally followed by the medical profession is negligent. This has frequently been done in the cases of sponges left in the patient's abdomen after an operation, where the task of keeping track of them has been delegated by the surgeon to a nurse. Although this was, and perhaps still is, universal practice, it has still been found to be negligent.

A rapidly growing form of medical malpractice litigation involves the doctrine of "informed consent," which concerns the duty of the physician or surgeon to inform the patient of the risks involved in treatment or surgery. The earliest cases treated this as a matter of vitiating the consent, so that there was liability for battery. Beginning around 1960, however, it began to be recognized that the matter was really one of the standard of professional conduct, and so negligence has now generally displaced battery as the basis for liability.

* * *

The late 1960's and early 1970's witnessed a tremendous increase in the level of medical malpractice litigation, in the size of damage awards in such suits, and in the cost of medical malpractice insurance therefor. As a result of this "medical malpractice crisis," most states passed some form of legislation affecting this type of litigation in one way or another. Among the many different types of provisions of such statutes are: various changes in statutes of limitations; creation of medical malpractice pre-litigation screening panels, composed of some combination of doctors, lawyers, judges and laymen; limitations on actual or punitive damages; modification of the collateral source rule; changes in the Good Samaritan statutes; setting arbitration guidelines; requirements of writings for warranty actions; regulation or elimination of contingent fees; and various changes in the burden of proof, the standard of care, the informed consent doctrine, and the rules of evidence. As a result of such legislative modifications to the common law of medical malpractice, the statute books must carefully be consulted in every case.

Notes and Questions

Palsgraf v. Long Island Railroad Company

1. The question raised in *Palsgraf* is what is the scope of liability for negligence. If we assume that a person has been negligent in some way or other, for what consequences should he or she be held responsible? *Palsgraf* provides two very different views regarding this question. Before considering these views familiarize yourself with the facts of the case. What happened? Who was negligent? What did he do? To whom?

2. Judge Benjamin Cardozo provides the opinion that was adopted by the court. He argues in general that negligence is relative — if you are negligent, you must be negligent *to someone*. You must have violated somebody's right not to be harmed in that way. Negligence in the abstract, or "in the air," as he says, if it makes sense at all, cannot be actionable. Consequently, Palsgraf cannot make the railroad pay for her injuries, at least not in a tort action. Why not? Was anyone negligent *to her*? Do you think negligence in the abstract makes any sense?

3. Cardozo argues that what makes Palsgraf's claim sound plausible is the ambiguity of the term *wrong*. A wrong may be the violation of a right, but it may also be any antisocial conduct. But, Cardozo argues, Palsgraf must show that her rights were violated, not merely that someone did something wrong to someone or other. She cannot derive her claim from the violation of someone else's rights. Were Palsgraf's rights violated? In what way?

4. Judge Andrews disagrees with Cardozo's position. He points out — rightly — that the result in the case depends on one's theory of the nature of negligence. All agree that negligence is conduct that unreasonably risks the rights of others. The first theory says that there is no negligence unless the right risked is the right of the plaintiff. The second theory says that if conduct unreasonably threatens the safety of others, the perpetrator is liable for any direct consequences. Andrews believes that the first theory is too narrow. Is it? How far should responsibility go?

5. Is the second theory too oppressive? Theory two is limited not by the scope of the negligence but by a doctrine called *proximate cause*. The selection by Hart and Honoré on causation and responsibility discusses this doctrine. For now notice that proximate cause is a matter of public policy, which limits liability at a certain point largely for pragmatic reasons. Consider Andrews' explanation of this doctrine. Does it seem more helpful or accurate or reasonable than limiting the scope of negligence? What reasons can you think of for or against either theory?

6. Andrews argues that Palsgraf's claim is not a derivative one. Since everyone owes reasonable care to all the world, Palsgraf can sue on the violation of her own right. How so? What is that right? Do you agree that everyone has a duty to everyone else to exercise reasonable care? Cardozo says that view blurs the distinction between torts and crimes: Crimes are wrongs to the general public; torts are wrongs to particular individuals. Is the distinction important?

Palsgraf v. Long Island Railroad Company

248 N.Y. 339, 162 N.E. 99 (1928)

CARDOZO, Ch. J. Plaintiff was standing on a platform of defendant's railroad after buying a ticket to go to Rockaway Beach. A train stopped at the station, bound for another place. Two men ran forward to catch it. One of the men reached the platform of the car without mishap, though the train was already moving. The other man, carrying a package, jumped aboard the car, but seemed unsteady as if about to fall. A guard on the car, who had held the door open, reached forward to help him in, and another guard on the platform pushed him from behind. In this act, the package was dislodged, and fell upon the rails. It was a package of small size, about fifteen inches long, and was covered by a newspaper. In fact it contained fireworks, but there was nothing in its appearance to give notice of its contents. The fireworks when they fell exploded. The shock of the explosion threw down some scales at the other end of the platform, many feet away. The scales struck the plaintiff, causing injuries for which she sues.

The conduct of the defendant's guard, if a wrong in its relation to the holder of the package, was not a wrong in its relation to the plaintiff, standing far away. Relatively to her it was not negligence at all. Nothing in the situation gave notice that the falling package had in it the potency of peril to persons thus removed. Negligence is not actionable unless it involves the invasion of a legally protected interest, the violation of a right. "Proof of negligence in the air, so to speak, will not do" (Pollock, *Torts*, 11th ed., p. 455; *Martin* v. *Herzog*, 228 N.Y. 164, 170; cf. Salmond, *Torts*, 6th ed., p. 24). "Negligence is the absence of care, according to the circumstances" (Willies, J., in *Vaughan* v. *Taff Vale Ry. Co.*, 5 H. & N. 679, 688 . . .). The plaintiff as she stood upon the platform of the station might claim to be protected against intentional invasion of her bodily security. Such invasion is not charged. She might claim to be protected against unintentional invasion by conduct involving in the thought of reasonable men an unreasonable hazard that such invasion would ensue. These, from the point of view of the law, were the bounds of her immunity, with perhaps some rare exceptions, survivals for the most part of ancient forms of liability, where conduct is held to be at the peril of the actor (*Sullivan* v. *Dunham*, 161 N.Y. 290). If no hazard was apparent to the eye of ordinary vigilance, an act innocent and harmless, at least to outward seeming, with reference to her, did not take to itself the quality of a tort because it happened to be a wrong, though apparently not one involving the risk of bodily insecurity, with reference to someone else. "In every instance, before negligence can be predicated of a given act, back of the act must be sought and found a duty to the individual complaining, the observance of which would have averted or avoided the injury" (McSherry, C. J., in *W. Va. Central R. Co.* v. *State*, 96 Md. 652, 666 . . .). The plaintiff sues in her own right for a wrong personal to her, and not as the vicarious beneficiary of a breach of duty to another.

A different conclusion will involve us, and swiftly too, in a maze of contradictions. A guard stumbles over a package which has been left upon a platform. It seems to be a bundle of newspapers. It turns out to be a can of dynamite. To the eye of ordinary vigilance, the bundle is abandoned waste, which may be kicked or trod on with impunity. Is a passenger at the other end of the platform protected by the law against the unsuspected hazard concealed beneath the waste? If not, is the result to be any different, so far as the distant passenger is concerned, when the guard stumbles over a valise which a truckman or a porter has left upon the walk? The passenger far away, if the victim of a wrong at all, has a cause of action, not derivative, but original and primary. His claim to be protected against invasion of his bodily security is neither greater nor less because the act resulting in the invasion is a wrong to another far removed. In this case, the rights that are said to have been violated, the interests said to have been invaded, are not even of the same order. The man was not injured in his person nor even put in danger. The purpose of the act, as well as its effect, was to make his person safe. If there was a wrong to him at all, which may very well be doubted, it was a wrong to a property interest only, the safety of his package. Out of this wrong to property, which threatened injury to nothing else, there has passed, we are told, to the plaintiff by derivation or succession a right of action for the invasion of an interest of another order, the right to bodily security. The diversity of interests emphasizes the futility of the effort to build the plaintiff's right upon the basis of a wrong to someone else. The gain is one of emphasis, for a like result would follow if the interests were the same. Even then, the orbit of the danger as disclosed to the eye of reasonable vigilance would be the orbit of the duty. One who jostles one's neighbor in a crowd does not invade the rights of others standing at the outer fringe when the unintended contact casts a bomb upon the ground. The wrongdoer as to them is the man who carries the bomb, not the one who explodes it without suspicion of the danger. Life will have to be made over, and human nature transformed, before prevision so extravagant can be accepted as the norm of conduct, the customary standard to which behavior must conform.

The argument for the plaintiff is built upon the shifting meanings of such words as "wrong" and "wrongful," and shares their instability. What the plaintiff must show is "a wrong" to herself, i.e., a violation of her own right, and not merely a wrong to someone else, nor conduct "wrongful" because

unsocial, but not "a wrong" to anyone. We are told that one who drives at reckless speed through a crowded city street is guilty of a negligent act and, therefore, of a wrongful one irrespective of the consequences. Negligent the act is, and wrongful in the sense that it is unsocial, but wrongful and unsocial in relation to other travelers, only because the eye of vigilance perceives the risk of damage. If the same act were to be committed on a speedway or a race course, it would lose its wrongful quality. The risk reasonably to be perceived defines the duty to be obeyed, and risk imports relation; it is risk to another or to others within the range of apprehension. . . . This does not mean, of course, that one who launches a destructive force is always relieved of liability if the force, though known to be destructive, pursues an unexpected path. "It was not necessary that the defendant should have had notice of the particular method in which an accident would occur, if the possibility of an accident was clear to the ordinarily prudent eye" (*Munsey* v. *Webb*, 231 U.S. 150, 156; *Condran* v. *Park & Tilford*, 213 N.Y. 341, 345; *Robert* v. *U.S.E.F. Corp.*, 240 N.Y. 474, 477). Some acts, such as shooting, are so imminently dangerous to anyone who may come within reach of the missile, however unexpectedly, as to impose a duty of prevision not far from that of an insurer. Even today, and much oftener in earlier stages of the law, one acts sometimes at one's peril. . . . Under this head, it may be, fall certain cases of what is known as transferred intent, an act willfully dangerous to A resulting by misadventure in injury to B. . . . These cases aside, wrong is defined in terms of the natural or probable, at least when unintentional (*Parrot* v. *Wells-Fargo Co. (The Nitro-Glycerine Case)*, 15 Wall. (U.S.) 524). The range of reasonable apprehension is at times a question for the court, and at times, if varying inferences are possible, a question for the jury. Here, by concession, there was nothing in the situation to suggest to the most cautious mind that the parcel wrapped in newspaper would spread wreckage through the station. If the guard had thrown it down knowingly and willfully, he would not have threatened the plaintiff's safety, so far as appearances could warn him. His conduct would not have involved, even then, an unreasonable probability of invasion of her bodily security. Liability can be no greater where the act is inadvertent.

Negligence, like risk, is thus a term of relation. Negligence in the abstract, apart from things related, is surely not a tort, if indeed it is understandable at all. . . . Negligence is not a tort unless it results in the commission of a wrong, and the commission of a wrong imports the violation of a right, in this case, we are told, the right to be protected against interference with one's bodily security. But bodily security is protected, not against all forms of interference or aggression, but only against some. One who seeks redress at law does not make out a cause of action by showing without more that there has been damage to his person. If the harm was not willful, he must show that the act as to him had possibilities of danger so many and apparent as to entitle him to be protected against the doing of it though the harm was unintended. Affront to personality is still the keynote of the wrong. Confirmation of this view will be found in the history and development of the action on the case. Negligence as a basis of civil liability was unknown to medieval law (8 Holdsworth, *History of English Law*, p. 449; Street, *Foundations of Legal Liability*, vol. 1, pp. 189, 190). For damage to the person, the sole remedy was trespass, and trespass did not lie in the absence of aggression, and that direct and personal (Holdsworth, *op. cit.*, p. 453; Street, *op. cit.*, vol. 3, pp. 258, 260, vol. 1, pp. 71, 74). Liability for other damage, as where a servant without orders from the master does or omits something to the damage of another, is a plant of later growth (Holdsworth, *op. cit.*, pp. 450, 457; Wigmore, *Responsibility for Tortious Acts*, vol. 3, *Essays in Anglo-American Legal History*, pp. 520, 523, 526, 533). When it emerged out of the legal soil, it was thought of as a variant of trespass, an offshoot of the parent stock. This appears in the form of action, which was known as trespass on the case (Holdsworth, *op. cit.*, p. 449; cf. *Scott v. Shepard*, 2 Wm. Black, 892; Green, *Rationale of Proximate Cause*, p. 19). The victim does not sue derivatively, or by right of subrogation, to vindicate an interest invaded in the person of another. Thus to view his cause of action is to ignore the fundamental difference between tort and crime (Holland, *Jurisprudence*, 12th ed., p. 328). He sues for breach of a duty owing to himself.

The law of causation, remote or proximate, is thus foreign to the case before us. The question

of liability is always anterior to the question of the measure of the consequences that go with liability. If there is no tort to be redressed, there is no occasion to consider what damage might be recovered if there were a finding of a tort. We may assume, without deciding, that negligence, not at large or in the abstract, but in relation to the plaintiff, would entail liability for any and all consequences, however novel or extraordinary (*Bird v. St. Paul F. & M. Ins. Co.*, 224, N.Y. 47, 54; *Ehrgott v. Mayer*, etc., of N.Y., 96 N.Y. 264; *Smith v. London & S.W. Ry. Co.*, L.R. 6 C.P. 14; 1 Beven, *Negligence*, p. 106; Street, *op. cit.* vol. 1, p. 90; Green, *Rationale of Proximate Cause*, pp. 88, 118; ct. *Matter of Polemis*, L.R. 1921, 3 K.B. 560; 44 *Law Quarterly Review*, 142). There is room for argument that a distinction is to be drawn according to the diversity of interests invaded by the act, as where conduct negligent in that it threatens an insignificant invasion of an interest in property results in an unforeseeable invasion of an interest of another order, as, e.g., one of bodily security. Perhaps other distinctions may be necessary. We do not go into the question now. The consequences to be followed must first be rooted in a wrong.

The judgement of the Appellate Division and that of the Trial Term should be reserved and the complaint dismissed, with costs in all courts.

ANDREWS, J. (dissenting). Assisting a passenger to board a train, the defendant's servant negligently knocked a package from his arms. It fell between the platform and the cars. Of its contents the servant knew and could know nothing. A violent explosion followed. The concussion broke some scales standing a considerable distance away. In falling they injured the plaintiff, an intending passenger.

Upon these facts may she recover the damages she has suffered in an action brought against the master? The result we shall reach depends upon our theory as to the nature of negligence. Is it a relative concept — the breach of some duty owing to a particular person or to particular persons? Or where there is an act which unreasonably threatens the safety of others, is the doer liable for all its proximate consequences, even where they result in injury to one who would generally be thought to be outside the radius of danger? This is not a mere dispute as to words. We might not believe that to the average mind the dropping of the bundle would seem to involve the probability of harm to the plaintiff standing many feet away whatever might be the case as to the owner or to one so near as to be likely to be struck by its fall. If, however, we adopt the second hypothesis we have to inquire only as to the relation between cause and effect. We deal in terms of proximate cause, not to negligence.

Negligence may be defined roughly as an act or omission which unreasonably does or may affect the rights of others, or which unreasonably fails to protect oneself from the dangers resulting from such acts. Here I confine myself to the first branch of the definition. Nor do I comment on the word "unreasonable." For present purposes it sufficiently describes that average of conduct that society requires of its members.

There must be both the act or the omission, and the right. It is the act itself, not the intent of the actor, that is important. (*Hover* v. *Barkhoof*, 44 N.Y. 113; *Metz* v. *Connecticut Co.*, 217 N.Y. 475.) In criminal law both the intent and the result are to be considered. Intent again is material in tort actions, where punitive damages are sought, dependent on actual malice — not on merely reckless conduct. But there neither insanity nor infancy lessens responsibility. (*Williams* v. *Hays*, 143 N.Y. 442.)

As has been said, except in cases of contributory negligence, there must be rights which are or may be affected. Often though injury has occurred, no rights of him who suffers have been touched. A licensee or trespasser upon my land has no claim to affirmative care on my part that the land be made safe. (*Meiers* v. *Koch Brewery*, 229 N.Y. 10.) Where a railroad is required to fence its tracks against cattle, no man's rights are injured should be wander upon the road because such fense is absent. (*Di Caprio* v. *N.Y.C.R.R.*, 231 N.Y. 94.) An unborn child may not demand immunity from personal harm. (*Drobner* v. *Peters*, 232 N.Y. 220).

But we are told that "there is no negligence unless there is in the particular case a legal duty to take care, and this duty must be one which is owed to the plaintiff himself and not merely to others." (Salmond, *Torts*, 6th ed., p. 24.) This, I think too narrow a conception. Where there is the unreasonable act, and some right that may be affected there is negligence whether damage does or does not result. That is immaterial. Should we

drive down Broadway at a reckless speed, we are negligent whether we strike an approaching car or miss it by an inch. The act itself is wrongful. It is a wrong not only to those who happen to be within the radius of danger but to all who might have been there — a wrong to the public at large. Such is the language of the street. Such the language of the courts when speaking of contributory negligence. Such again and again their language in speaking of the duty of some defendant and discussing proximate cause in cases where such a discussion is wholly irrelevant on any other theory. (*Perry* v. *Rochester Line Co.*, 219 N.Y. 60.) As was said by Mr. Justice Holmes many years ago, "the measure of the defendant's duty in determining whether a wrong has been committed is one thing, the measure of liability when a wrong has been committed is another." (*Spade* v. *Lynn & Boston R.R. Co.*, 172 Mass. 488.) Due care is a duty imposed on each one of us to protect society from unnecessary danger, not to protect A, B, or C alone.

It may well be that there is no such thing as negligence in the abstract. "Proof of negligence in the air, so to speak, will not do." In an empty world negligence would not exist. It does involve a relationship between man and his fellows. But not merely a relationship between man and those whom he might reasonably expect his act would injure. Rather, a relationship between him and those whom he does in fact injure. If his act has a tendency to harm someone, it harms him a mile away as surely as it does those on the scene. We now permit children to recover for the negligent killing of the father. It was never prevented on the theory that no duty was owing to them. A husband may be compensated for the loss of his wife's services. To say that the wrongdoer was negligent as to the husband as well as to the wife is merely an attempt to fit facts to theory. An insurance company paying a fire loss recovers its payment of the negligent incendiary. We speak of subrogation — of suing in the right of the insured. Behind the cloud of words is the fact they hide, that the act, wrongful as to the insured, has also injured the company. Even if it be true that the fault of father, wife, or insured will prevent recovery, it is because we consider the original negligence not the proximate cause of the injury. . . .

In the well-known *Polemis* Case (1921, 3 K.B.

560), Scrutton, L. J., said that the dropping of a plank was negligent for it might injure "workman or cargo or ship." Because of either possibility the owner of the vessel was to be made good for his loss. The act being wrongful, the doer was liable for its proximate results. Criticized and explained as this statement may have been, I think it states the law as it should be and as it is. . . .

The proposition is this. Everyone owes to the world at large the duty of refraining from those acts that may unreasonably threaten the safety of others. Such an act occurs. Not only is he wronged to whom harm might reasonably be expected to result, but he also who is in fact injured, even if he be outside what would generally be thought the danger zone. There needs be duty due the one complaining but this is not a duty to a particular individual because as to him harm might be expected. Harm to someone being the natural result of the act, not only that one alone, but all those in fact injured may complain. We have never, I think, held otherwise. Indeed in the *Di Caprio* case we said that a breach of a general ordinance defining the degree of care to be exercised in one's calling is evidence of negligence as to everyone. We did not limit this statement to those who might be expected to be exposed to danger. Unreasonable risk being taken, its consequences are not confined to those who might probably be hurt.

If this be so, we do not have a plaintiff suing by "derivation or succession." Her action is original and primary. Her claim is for a breach of duty to herself — not that she is subrogated to any right of action of the owner of the parcel or of a passenger standing at the scene of the explosion.

The right to recover damages rests on additional considerations. The plaintiff's rights must be injured, and this injury must be caused by the negligence. We build a dam, but are negligent as to its foundations. Breaking, it injures property down stream. We are not liable if all this happened because of some reason other than the insecure foundation. But when injuries do result from our unlawful act we are liable for the consequences. It does not matter that they are unusual, unexpected, unforeseen, and unforeseeable. But there is one limitation. The damages must be so connected with the negligence that the latter may be said to be the proximate cause of the former.

These two words have never been given an inclusive definition. What is a cause in a legal sense, still more, what is a proximate cause, depend in each case upon many considerations, as does the existence of negligence itself. Any philosophical doctrine of causation does not help us. A boy throws a stone into a pond. The ripples spread. The water level rises. The history of that pond is altered to all eternity. It will be altered by other causes also. Yet it will be forever the resultant of all causes combined. Each one will have an influence. How great only omniscience can say. You may speak of a chain, or if you please, a net. An analogy is of little aid. Each cause brings about future events. Without each the future would not be the same. Each is proximate in the sense it is essential. But that is not what we mean by the word. Nor on the other hand do we mean sole cause. There is no such thing.

Should analogy be thought helpful, however, I prefer that of a stream. The spring, starting on its journey, is joined by tributary after tributary. The river, reaching the ocean, comes from a hundred sources. No man may say whence any drop of water is derived. Yet for a time distinction may be possible. Into the clear creek, brown swamp water flows from the left. Later, from the right comes water stained by its clay bed. The three may remain for a space, sharply divided. But at last, inevitably no trace of separation remains. They are so commingled that all distinction is lost.

As we have said, we cannot trace the effect of an act to the end, if end there is. Again, however, we may trace it part of the way. A murder at Sarajevo may be the necessary antecedent to an assassination in London twenty years hence. An overturned lantern may burn all Chicago. We may follow the fire from the shed to the last building. We rightly say the fire started by the lantern caused its destruction.

A cause, but not the proximate cause. What we do mean by the word "proximate" is that because of convenience, of public policy, of a rough sense of justice, the law arbitrarily declines to trace a series of events beyond a certain point. This is not logic. It is practical politics. Take our rule as to fires. Sparks from my burning haystack set on fire my house and my neighbor's. I may recover from a negligent railroad. He may not. Yet the wrongful act as directly harmed the one as the other. We may regret that the line was drawn just where it was, but drawn somewhere it had to be. We said the act of the railroad was not the proximate cause of our neighbor's fire. Cause it surely was. The words we used were simply indicative of our notions of public policy. Other courts think differently. But somewhere they reach the point where they cannot say the stream comes from any one source.

Take the illustration given in an unpublished manuscript by a distinguished and helpful writer on the law of torts. A chauffeur negligently collides with another car which is filled with dynamite, although he could not know it. An explosion follows. A, walking on the sidewalk nearby, is killed. B, sitting in a window of a building opposite, is cut by flying glass. C, likewise sitting in a window a block away, is similarly injured. And a further illustration. A nursemaid, ten blocks away, startled by the noise, involuntarily drops a baby from her arms to the walk. We are told that C may not recover while A may. As to B it is a question for court or jury. We will all agree that the baby might not. Because, we are again told, the chauffeur had no reason to believe his conduct involved any risk of injuring either C or the baby. As to them he was not negligent.

But the chauffeur, being negligent in risking the collision, his belief that the scope of the harm he might do would be limited is immaterial. His act unreasonably jeopardized the safety of anyone who might be affected by it. C's injury and that of the baby were directly traceable to the collision. Without that, the injury would not have happened. C had the right to sit in his office, secure from such dangers. The baby was entitled to use the sidewalk with reasonable safety.

The true theory is, it seems to me, that the injury to C, if in truth he is to be denied recovery, and the injury to the baby is that their several injuries were not the proximate result of the negligence. And here not what the chauffeur had reason to believe would be the result of his conduct, but what the prudent would foresee, may have a bearing. May have some bearing, for the problem of proximate cause is not to be solved by any one consideration.

It is all a question of expediency. There are no fixed rules to govern our judgment. There are simply matters of which we may take account. We have in a somewhat different connection spoken of "the stream of events." We have asked whether that stream was deflected—whether it was forced into new and unexpected channels. (*Donnelly* v. *Piercy Contracting Co.,* 222 N.Y. 210.) This is rather rhetoric than law. There is in truth little to guide us other than common sense.

There are some hints that may help us. The proximate cause, involved as it may be with many other causes, must be, at the least, something without which the event would not happen. The court must ask itself whether there was a natural and continuous sequence between cause and effect. Was the one a substantial factor in producing the other? Was there a direct connection between them, without too many intervening causes? Is the effect of cause on result not too attenuated? Is the cause likely, in the usual judgment of mankind, to produce the result? Or by the exercise of prudent foresight could the result be foreseen? Is the result too remote from the cause, and here we consider remoteness in time and space. . . . Clearly we must so consider, for the greater the distance either in time or space, the more surely do other causes intervene to effect the result. When a lantern is overturned the firing of a shed is a fairly direct consequence. Many things contribute to the spread of the conflagration—the force of the wind, the direction and width of streets, the character of intervening structures, other factors. We draw an uncertain and wavering line, but draw it we must as best we can.

Once again, it is all a question of fair judgment, always keeping in mind the fact that we endeavor to make a rule in each case that will be practical and in keeping with the general understanding of mankind.

Here another question must be answered. In the case supposed it is said, and said correctly, that the chauffeur is liable for the direct effect of the explosion although he had no reason to suppose it would follow a collision. "The fact that the injury occurred in a different manner than that which might have been expected does not prevent the chauffeur's negligence from being in law the cause of the injury." But the natural results of a negligent act—the results which a prudent man would or should foresee—do have a bearing upon the decision as to proximate cause. We have said so repeatedly. What should be foreseen? No human foresight would suggest that a collision itself might injure one a block away. On the contrary, given an explosion, such a possibility might be reasonably expected. I think the direct connection, the foresight of which the courts speak, assumes prevision of the explosion, for the immediate results of which, at least, the chauffeur is responsible.

It may be said this is unjust. Why? In fairness he should make good every injury flowing from his negligence. Not because of tenderness toward him we say he need not answer for all that follows his wrong. We look back to the catastrophe, the fire kindled by the spark, or the explosion. We trace the consequences — not indefinitely, but to a certain point. And to aid us in fixing that point we ask what might ordinarily be expected to follow the fire or the explosion.

This last suggestion is the factor which must determine the case before us. The act upon which defendant's liability rests is knocking an apparently harmless package onto the platform. The act was negligent. For its proximate consequences the defendant is liable. If its contents were broken, to the owner; if it fell upon and crushed a passenger's foot, then to him. If it exploded and injured one in the immediate vicinity, to him also as to A in the illustration. Mrs. Palsgraf was standing some distance away. How far cannot be told from the record — apparently twenty-five or thirty feet. Perhaps less. Except for the explosion, she would not have been injured. We are told by the appellant in his brief "it cannot be denied that the explosion was the direct cause of the plaintiff's injuries." So it was a substantial factor in producing the result — there was here a natural and continuous sequence — direct connection. The only intervening cause was that instead of blowing her to the ground the concussion smashed the weighing machine which in turn fell upon her. There was no remoteness in time, little in space. And surely, given such an explosion as here, it needed no great foresight to predict that the natural result would be to injure one on the platform at no greater distance from its scene than was the plaintiff. Just how no one might be able to predict. Whether by flying fragments, by broken glass, by wreckage of machines or structures no one could say. But injury in some form was most probable.

Under these circumstances I cannot say as a matter of law that the plaintiff's injuries were not the proximate result of the negligence. That is all we have before us. The court refused to so charge. No request was made to submit the matter to the jury as a question of fact, even would that have been proper upon the record before us.

The judgment appealed from should be affirmed, with costs.

POUND, LEHMAN and KELLOGG, JJ., concur with CARDOZO, Ch. J.; ANDREWS, J., dissents in opinion in which CRANE and O'BRIEN, JJ., concur.

Judgment reversed, etc.

Notes and Questions

In Re Arbitration between Polemis and Furness, Withy & Co., Limited

1. What are the facts in this case — what exactly happened?

2. Presumably, anyone would agree that it would be negligent to knock a heavy plank into the hold of a ship, but this is because the plank would be likely to hit someone or something, not because it would be likely to cause a fire. Does it matter whether the actual consequences are reasonably foreseeable so long as the actor was negligent in some way? What does the court say in *Polemis*? What do you say? Is it fair to hold a negligent actor responsible for any consequences, no matter how unlikely? If not, is it fair to require the victim (who did nothing wrong) to bear the entire loss?

3. In an analogous case a cook placed a canister of rat poison on a shelf above the stove, along with flour, sugar, and other edible substances. This action was clearly negligent, since the rat poison could have been mistaken for one of the edible items. Instead was that the rat poison unforeseeably exploded as a result of the heat of the stove, injuring a delivery person. Should the cook — or the restaurant — be liable for the unforeseeable injury? Who should carry the loss?

4. Compare the opinions in *Polemis* with those in *Palsgraf*. What reasons are given for extending or limiting the negligent party's liability in each case? As a matter of fact, one reason Cardozo characterized the issue in *Palsgraf* as a matter of duty was to avoid a rule of direct cause much like that set out in *Polemis*. Later the direct cause test was itself abandoned by the courts. Do you think it should have been? Which opinion provides the clearest analysis of the connection between causation and liability?

In Re Arbitration between Polemis and Furness, Withy & Co., Limited

[1921] 3 K.B. 560 (C.A. 1921).

[Polemis and his partner owned a ship, which they chartered or leased to Furness, Withy & Company. While it was in possession of Furness, Withy, it was destroyed by fire. The ship at the time was in Casablanca, Morocco, with a cargo of cases of benzine and/or petrol in the No. 1 hold. Some of these cases had leaked on the voyage and there was "petrol vapour" in the hold. Arab stevedores employed by the charterers had placed some heavy planks across the hatchway. A sling dislodged one of these and it fell into the hold. "The fall was instantly followed by a rush of flames, and the result was the total destruction of the ship." The owners claimed damages for loss of the ship and the claim was submitted to arbitration. The arbitrator found expressly that the "causing of the spark couldn't reasonably have been anticipated." The arbitrator awarded damages to the owner and the award was affirmed by the trial judge. The charterers appeal. Summary from Dobbs, *Torts and compensation* (1985).

BANKES, L.J.

These findings are, no doubt, intended to raise the question whether the view taken, or said to have been taken, by Pollock, C.B., [ ], or the view taken by Channell, B., and Blackburn, J., in Smith v. London and South Western Rail. Co. (3) (L.R. 6 C.P. at p.21), is the correct one. Assuming the Chief Baron to have been correctly reported in the EXCHEQUER REPORTS, the

difference between the two views is this. According to the one view, the consequences which may reasonably be expected to result from a particular act are material only in reference to the question whether the act is or is not a negligent act; according to the other view, those consequences are the test whether the damages resulting from the act, assuming it to be negligent, are or are not too remote to be recoverable.

In the present case the arbitrators have found as a fact that the falling of the plank was due to the negligence of the defendants' servants. The fire appears to me to have been directly caused by the falling of the plank. In these circumstances I consider that it is immaterial that the causing of the spark by the falling of the plank could not have been reasonably anticipated. The charterers' junior counsel sought to draw a distinction between the anticipation of the extent of damage resulting from a negligent act, and the anticipation of the type of damage resulting from such an act. He admitted that it could not lie in the mouth of a person whose negligent act had caused damage to say that he could not reasonably have foreseen the extent of the damage, but he contended that the negligent person was entitled to rely upon the fact that he could not reasonably have anticipated the type of damage which resulted from his negligent act. I do not think that the distinction can be admitted. Given the breach of duty which constitutes the negligence, and given the damage as a direct result of that negligence, the anticipations of the person whose negligent act has produced the damage appear to me to be irrelevant. I consider that the damages claimed are not too remote.

WARRINGTON, L.J. . . . . The presence or absence of reasonable anticipation of damage determines the legal quality of the act as negligent or innocent. If it be thus determined to be negligent, then the question whether particular damages are recoverable depends only on the answer to the question whether they are the direct consequences of the act. . . .

SCRUTTON, L.J. . . . . To determine whether an act is negligent, it is relevant to determine whether any reasonable person would foresee that the act would cause damage; if he would not, the act is not negligent. But if the act would or might probably cause damage, the fact that the damage it in fact causes is not the exact kind of damage one would expect is immaterial, so long as the dam-

age is in fact caused sufficiently directly by the negligent act, and not by the operation of independent causes having no connection with the negligent act, except that they could not avoid its results. Once the act is negligent, the fact that its exact operation was not foreseen is immaterial. . . . In the present case it was negligent in discharging cargo to knock down the planks of the temporary staging, for they might easily cause some damage either to workmen, or cargo, or the ship. The fact that they did directly produce an unexpected result, a spark in an atmosphere of petrol vapour which caused a fire, does not relieve the person who was negligent from the damage which his negligent act directly caused. For these reasons the experienced arbitrators and the judge appealed from came, in my opinion, to a correct decision, and the appeal must be dismissed with costs.

Appeal dismissed.

Notes and Questions

H. L. A. HART and A. M. HONORÉ, from *Causation in the Law*

1. In tort law a person is responsible for damage he or she causes wrongfully. But what does it mean to say that a person *causes* damage? Explaining the meaning of *cause* is more difficult than it appears. Everybody has an ordinary notion of what a cause is, but what is it? Hart and Honoré argue that to designate a person as a cause, at least in the present tense, is to ascribe blame or responsibility to that person for the event. Note that ordinary assumptions are the other way around. If Fred caused X, then Fred is responsible for X — not if Fred is responsible for X then Fred caused X. Why do Hart and Honoré argue that it is the other way around?

2. The basic problem is how to trace the connection between cause and effect. How we trace this connection will depend on the reason for tracing it. When tracing the connections between human action and consequences we employ a number of concepts that restrict what counts as a consequence. What are these restrictions, according to Hart and Honoré?

3. A second problem is how to distinguish a cause from a condition. Hart and Honoré suggest that we think of the causal relation as a network or cone rather than as a single chain. If we start with the effect at the point of the cone and trace the connections back to the causes, we will have to make choices about which relevant factors to count as causes since many factors will be relevant. We will have to make judgments about what factors constitute normal conditions and which elements should be considered merely conditions rather than causes. Look at the examples Hart and Honoré provide. Can you give general reasons for designating an event to be a condition or a cause?

4. Hart and Honoré also note that causal chains are considered to be broken by intervening, superseding, or extraneous causes. This premise is regularly accepted. What is a superseding, intervening, or extraneous cause? Is there any way to distinguish these from conditions?

5. Human intervention regularly breaks the chain. Why should this be true? How do Hart and Honoré explain it? What qualifications are there on this generalization?

[From] *Causation in the Law*

H. L. A. HART AND A. M. HONORÉ

Causation and Responsibility

I. Responsibility in Law and Morals

We have so far traced the outline of a variety of causal concepts the diversity of which is to be seen in such familiar examples of the use of causal language as the following: "The explosion of gas caused the building to collapse," "He made him hand over his money by threatening to shoot," "The consequence of leaving the car unlocked was that it was stolen," "The strike was the cause of the drop in profits."

The main structure of these different forms of causal connection is plain enough, and there are many situations constantly recurring in ordinary life to which they have a clear application; yet it is also true that like many other fundamental notions these have aspects which are vague or indeterminate; they involve the weighing of matters of degree, or the plausibility of hypothetical speculations, for which no exact criteria can be laid down. Hence their application, outside the safe area of simple examples, calls for judgment and is something over which judgments often differ. Even the type of case which is most familiar, and most nearly approximates to Mill's model for "cause and effect," where causal connection between a physical event and some earlier initiating event or human action is traced through a series of physical events, involves an implicit judgment on such imprecise issues as the *normal* condition of the thing concerned and the *abnormality* of what is identified as the cause. Very often, in particular where an omission to take common precautions is asserted to be the cause of some disaster, a speculation as to what *would have* happened had the precaution been taken is involved. Though arguments one way or another over such hypothetical issues may certainly be rational and have more or less "weight," there is a sense in which they cannot be conclusive. When such areas of dispute are reached, the decision whether to describe the facts of a case in the terms of some given form of causal connection will be influenced very much by factors connected with the context and purpose of making the causal statement.

Hitherto we have discussed only one principal purpose for which causal language is used: i.e. when an explanation is sought or provided of some puzzling or unusual occurrence. But as well as this explanatory context, in which we are concerned with what *has* happened, there are many others. Our deliberations about our own conduct often take the form of an inquiry as to the future consequences of alternative actions; here causal connections are *ex hypothesi* bounded by the horizon of the foreseeable. But even if we confine ourselves to causal statements about the past there are still different contexts and purposes to be discriminated. Thus it would be wrong to think of the historian as using causal notions only when he is explaining. The movement of his thought is not always from the later problematic event to something earlier which explains it and in using causal language he is not always engaged in diagnosis. His thought very often takes the contrary direction; for in addition to providing explanations (answers to the question "why?") he is also concerned to trace the outcome, the results, or the consequences of the human actions and omissions which are his usual starting-points, though he may also work out the "effects" of natural events. So he will discuss the consequences of a king's policy or the effects of the Black Death. This is so because the narrative of history is scarcely ever a narrative of brute sequence, but is an account of the roles played by certain factors and especially by human agents. History is written to satisfy not only the need for explanation, but also the desire to identify and assess contributions made by historical figures to changes of importance; to triumphs and disasters, and to human happiness or suffering. This assessment involves tracing "consequences," "effects," or "results," and these are more frequently referred to than "causes" which has a primarily diagnostic or explanatory ring. In one sense of "responsibility" the historian determines the responsibility of human beings for certain types of change; and sometimes he does this with an eye to praising or blaming or passing other forms of moral judgement. But this need not be so; the historian, though concerned to trace the consequences of human action, need not be a moralist.

In the moral judgments of ordinary life, we have occasion to blame people because they have caused harm to others, and also, if less frequently, to insist that morally they are bound to compensate those to whom they have caused harm. These are the moral analogues of more precise legal conceptions; for, in all legal systems, liability to be punished or to make compensation frequently depends on whether actions (or omissions) have caused harm. Moral blame is not of course confined to such cases of causing harm. We blame a man who cheats or lies or breaks promises, even if no one has suffered in the particular case: this has its legal counterpart in the punishment of abortive attempts to commit crimes, and of offences constituted by the unlawful possession of certain kinds of weapons, drugs, or materials, for example, for counterfeiting currency. When the occurrence of harm is an essential part of the ground for blame the connection of the person blamed with the harm may take any of the forms of causal connection we have examined. His action may have initiated a series of physical events dependent on each other and culminating in injury to persons or property, as in wounding and killing. These simple forms are the paradigms for the lawyer's talk of harm "directly" caused. But we blame people also for harm which arises from or is the consequence of their neglect of common precautions; we do this even if harm would not have come about without the intervention of another human being deliberately exploiting the opportunities provided by neglect. The main legal analogue here is liability for "negligence." The wish of many lawyers to talk in this branch of the law of harm being "within the risk of" rather than "caused by" the negligent conduct manifests appreciation of the fact that a different form of relationship is involved in saying that harm is the consequence, on the one hand, of an explosion and, on the other, of a failure to lock the door by which a thief has entered. Again, we blame people for the harm which we say is the consequence of their influence over others, either exerted by non-rational means or in one of the ways we have designated "interpersonal transactions." To such grounds for responsibility there correspond many important legal conceptions: the instigation of crimes ("commanding" or "procuring") constitutes an important ground of criminal responsibility and the concepts of enticement and of inducement (by threats or misrepresentation) are an element in many civil wrongs as well as in criminal offences.

The law, however, especially in matters of compensation, goes far beyond these causal grounds for responsibility in such doctrines as the vicarious responsibility of a master for his servant's civil wrongs and that of the responsibility of an occupier of property for injuries suffered by passers-by from defects of which the occupier had no knowledge and which he had no opportunity to repair. There is a recognition, perhaps diminishing, of this non-causal ground of responsibility outside the law; responsibility is sometimes admitted by one person or group of persons, even if no precaution has been neglected by them, for harm done by persons related to them in a special way, either by family ties or as members of the same social or political association. Responsibility may be simply "placed" by moral opinion on one person for what others do. The simplest case of such vicarious moral responsibility is that of a parent for damage done by a child; its more complex (and more debatable) form is the moral responsibility of one generation of a nation to make compensation for their predecessors' wrong, such as the Germans admitted in payment of compensation to Israel.

At this point it is necessary to issue a caveat about the meaning of the expression "responsible" if only to avoid prejudicing a question about the character of *legal* determinations of causal connection. . . . Usually in discussion of the law and occasionally in morals, to say that someone is responsible for some harm means that in accordance with legal rules or moral principles it is at least permissible, if not mandatory, to blame or punish or exact compensation from him. In this use the expression "responsible for" does not refer to a factual connection between the person held responsible and the harm but simply to his liability under the rules to be blamed, punished, or made to pay. The expressions "answerable for" or "liable for" are practically synonymous with "responsible for" in *this* use, in which there is no implication that the person held responsible actually *did* or *caused* the harm. In this sense a master is (in English law) responsible for the damage done by his servants acting within the scope of their authority and a parent (in French and German law) for that done by his children; it is in this sense that a guarantor or surety is responsible for the debts or the good behaviour of other persons and an insurer for losses sustained by the insured. Very often, however, especially in discussion of morals, to say that someone is responsible for some harm is to assert (*inter alia*) that he *did* the harm or *caused* it, though such a statement is perhaps rarely confined to this for it usually also carries with it the implication that it is at least permissible to blame or punish him. This double use of the expression no doubt arises from the important fact that doing or causing harm constitutes not only the most usual but the primary type of ground for holding persons responsible in the first sense. We still speak of inanimate or natural causes such as storms, floods, germs, or the failure of electricity supply as "responsible for" disasters; this mode of expression, now taken only to mean that they caused the disasters, no doubt originated in the belief that all that happens is the work of spirits when it is not that of men. Its survival in the modern world is perhaps some testimony to the primacy of causal connection as an element in responsibility and to the intimate connection between the two notions.

We shall consider later an apparent paradox which interprets in a different way the relationship between cause and responsibility. Much modern though on causation in the law rests on the contention that the statement that someone has caused harm either means no more than that the harm would not have happened without ("but for") his action or where (as in normal legal usage and in all ordinary speech), it apparently means more than this, it is a disguised way of asserting the "normative" judgment that he is responsible in the first sense, i.e. that it is proper or just to blame or punish him or make him pay. On this view to say that a person caused harm is not

really, though ostensibly it is, to give a *ground* or *reason* for holding him responsible in the first sense; for we are only in a position to say that he has caused harm when we have decided that he is responsible. Pending consideration of the theories of legal causation which exploit this point of view we shall use the expression "responsible for" only in the first of the two ways explained, i.e. without any implication as to the type of factual connection between the person held responsible and the harm; and we shall provisionally, though without prejudicing the issue, treat statements that a person caused harm as one sort of non-tautologous ground or reason for saying that he is responsible in this sense.

If we may provisionally take what in ordinary life we say and do at its face value, it seems that there coexist in ordinary thought, apart from the law though mirrored in it, several different types of connection between a person's action and eventual harm which render him responsible for it; and in both law and morals the various forms of causal connection between act or omission and harm are the most obvious and least disputable reasons for holding anyone responsible. Yet, in order to understand the extent to which the causal notions of ordinary thought are used in the law, we must bear in mind the many factors which must differentiate moral from legal responsibility in spite of their partial correspondence. The law is not only not bound to follow the moral patterns of attribution of responsibility but, even when it does, it must take into account, in a way which the private moral judgment need not and does not, the general social consequences which are attached to its judgments of responsibility; for they are of a gravity quite different from those attached to moral censure. The use of the legal sanctions of imprisonment, or enforced monetary compensation against individuals, has such formidable repercusions on the general life of society that the fact that individuals have a type of connection with harm which is adequate for moral censure or claims for compensation is only *one* of the factors which the law must consider, in defining the kinds of connection between actions and harm for which it will hold individuals legally responsible. Always to follow the private moral judgment here would be far too expensive for the law: not only in the crude sense that it would entail a vast machinery of courts and officials, but in the more important sense that it would inhibit or discourage too many other valuable activities of society. To limit the *types* of harm which the law will recognize is not enough; even if the types of harm are limited it would still be too much for any society to punish or exact compensation from individuals whenever their connection with harm of such types would justify moral censure. Conversely, social needs may require that compensation should be paid and even (though less obviously) that punishment be inflicted where no such connection between the person held responsible and the harm exists.

So causing harm of a legally recognized sort or being connected with such harm in any of the ways that justify moral blame, though vitally important and perhaps basic in a legal system, is not and should not be either always necessary or always sufficient for legal responsibility. All legal systems in response either to tradition or to social needs both extend responsibility and cut it off in ways which diverge from the simpler principles of moral blame. In England a man is not guilty of murder if the victim of his attack does not die within a year and day. In New York a person who negligently starts a fire is liable to pay only for the first of several houses which it destroys. These limitations imposed by legal policy are *prima facie* distinguishable from limitations due to the frequent requirement of legal rules that responsibility be limited to harm caused by wrongdoing. Yet a whole school of thought maintains that this distinction does not exist or is not worth drawing.

Apart from this, morality can properly leave certain things vague into which a legal system must attempt to import some degree of precision. Outside the law nothing requires us, when we find the case too complex or too strange, to say whether any and, if so, which of the morally significant types of connection between a person's action and harm exists; we can simply say the case is too difficult for us to pass judgment, at least where moral condemnation of others is concerned. No doubt we evade less easily our questions about our own connection with harm, and the great novelists have often described, sometimes in language very like the lawyers, how the conscience may be still tortured by uncertainties as to the *character* of a part in the production of

harm, even when all the facts are known. The fact that there is no precise system of punishments or rewards for common sense to administer, and so there are no "forms of action" or "pleadings" to define precise heads of responsibility for harm, means that the principles which guide common-sense attributions of responsibility give precise answers only in relatively simple types of case.

II. Tracing Consequences

"To consequences no limit can be set": "Every event which would not have happened if an earlier event had not happened is the consequence of that earlier event." These two propositions are not equivalent in meaning and are not equally or in the same way at variance with ordinary thought. They have, however, both been urged sometimes in the same breath by the legal theorist and the philosopher: they are indeed sometimes said by lawyers to be "the philosophical doctrine" of causation. It is perhaps not difficult even for the layman to accept the first proposition as a truth about certain physical events; an explosion may cause a flash of light which will be propagated as far as the outer nebulae; its effects or consequences continue indefinitely. It is, however, a different matter to accept the view that whenever a man is murdered with a gun his death was the consequence of (still less an "effect" of or "caused by") the manufacture of the bullet. The first tells a perhaps unfamiliar tale about unfamiliar events; the second introduces an unfamiliar, though, of course, a possible way of speaking about familiar events. It is not that this unrestricted use of "consequence" is unintelligible or never found; it is indeed used to refer to bizarre or fortuitous connections or coincidences: but the point is that the various causal notions employed for the purposes of explanation, attribution of responsibility, or the assessment of contributions to the course of history carry with them implicit limits which are similar in these different employments.

It is, then, the second proposition, defining consequence in terms of "necessary condition," with which theorists are really concerned. This proposition is the corollary of the view that, if we look into the past of any given event, there is an infinite number of events, each of which is a necessary condition of the given event and so, as much as any other, is its cause. This is the "cone" of causation, so called because, since any event has a number of simultaneous conditions, the series fans out as we go back in time. The justification, indeed only partial, for calling this "the philosophical doctrine" of causation is that it resembles Mill's doctrine that "we have no right to give the name of cause to one of the conditions exclusive of the others of them." It differs from Mill's view in taking the essence of causation to be "necessary condition" and not "the sum total" of the sufficient conditions of an event.

Legal theorists have developed this account of cause and consequence to show what is "factual," "objective," or "scientific" in these notions: this they call "cause in fact" and it is usually stressed as a preliminary to the doctrine that any more restricted application of these terms in the law represents nothing in the facts or in the meaning of causation, but expresses fluctuating legal policy or sentiments of what is just or convenient. Moral philosophers have insisted in somewhat similar terms that the consequences of human action are "infinite": this they have urged as an objection against the Utilitarian doctrine that the rightness of a morally right action depends on whether its consequences are better than those of any alternative action in the circumstances. "We should have to trace as far as possible the consequences not only for the persons affected directly but also for those indirectly affected and to these no limit can be set." Hence, so the argument runs, we cannot either inductively establish the Utilitarian doctrine that right acts are "optimific" or use it in particular cases to discover what is right. Yet, however vulnerable at other points Utilitarianism may be as an account of moral judgment, this objection seems to rest on a mistake as to the sense of "consequence." The Utilitarian assertion that the rightness of an action depends on its consequences is not the same as the assertion that it depends on all those later occurrences which would not have happened had the action not been done, to which indeed "no limit can be set." It is important to see that the issue here is not the linguistic one whether the word "consequence" would be understood if used in this way. The point is that, though we could, we do not think in this way in tracing connections between human actions and events. Instead, whenever we are con-

cerned with such connections, whether for the purpose of explaining a puzzling occurrence, assessing responsibility, or giving an intelligible historical narrative, we employ a set of concepts restricting in various ways what counts as a consequence. These restrictions colour *all* our thinking in causal terms; when we find them in the law we are not finding something invented by or peculiar to the law, though of course it is for the law to say when and how far it will use them and, where they are vague, to supplement them.

No short account can be given of the limits thus placed on "consequences" because these limits vary, intelligibly, with the variety of causal connection asserted. Thus we may be tempted by the generalization that consequences must always be something intended or foreseen or at least foreseeable with ordinary care: but counterexamples spring up from many types of context where causal statements are made. If smoking is shown to cause lung cancer this discovery will permit us to describe past as well as future cases of cancer as the effect or consequence of smoking even though no one foresaw or had reasonable grounds to suspect this in the past. What is common and commonly appreciated and hence foreseeable certainly controls the scope of consequences in certain varieties of causal statement but not in all. Again the voluntary intervention of a second person very often constitutes the limit. If a guest sits down at a table laid with knife and fork and plunges the knife into his hostess's breast, her death is not in any context other than a contrived one thought of as caused by, or the effect or result of the waiter's action in laying the table; nor would it be linked with this action as its consequence for any of the purposes, explanatory or attributive, for which we employ causal notions. Yet as we have seen there are many other types of case where a voluntary action or the harm it does are naturally treated to the consequence of to some prior neglect of precaution. Finally, we may think that a simple answer is already supplied by Hume and Mill's doctrine that causal connection rests on general laws asserting regular connection; yet, even in the type of case to which this important doctrine applies, reference to it alone will not solve our problem. For we often trace a causal connection between an antecedent and a consequent which themselves very rarely go together: we do this when the case can be broken down into intermediate stages, which themselves exemplify different generalizations, as when we find that the fall of a tile was the cause of someone's death, rare though this be. Here our problem reappears in the form of the question: When can generalizations be combined in this way?

We shall examine first the central type of case where the problem is of this last-mentioned form. Here the gist of the causal connection lies in the general connection with each other of the successive states; and is not dependent on the special notions of one person providing another with reasons or exceptional opportunities for actions. This form of causal connection may exist between actions and events, and between purely physical events, and it is in such cases that the words "cause" and "causing" used of the antecedent action or event have their most obvious application. It is convenient to refer to cases of the first type where the consequence is harm as cases of "causing harm," and to refer to cases where harm is the consequence of one person providing another with reasons or opportunities for doing harm as cases of "inducing" or "occasioning" harmful acts. In cases of the first type a voluntary act, or a conjunction of events amounting to a coincidence, operates as a limit in the sense that events subsequent to these are not attributed to the antecedent action or event as its consequence even though they would not have happened without it. Often such a limiting action or coincidence is thought of and described as "intervening": and lawyers speak of them as "superseding" or "extraneous" causes "breaking the chain of causation." To see what these metaphors rest on (and in part obscure) and how such factors operate as a limit we shall consider the detail of three simple cases.

(i) A forest fire breaks out, and later investigation shows that shortly before the outbreak *A* had flung away a lighted cigarette into the bracken at the edge of the forest, the bracken caught fire, a light breeze got up, and fanned the flames in the direction of the forest. If, on discovering these facts, we hesitate before saying that *A*'s action caused the forest fire this would be to consider the alternative hypothesis that in spite of appearances the fire only succeeded *A*'s action in point of time, that the bracken flickered out harmlessly and the forest fire was caused by something else.

To dispose of this it may be necessary to examine in further detail the process of events between the ignition of the bracken and the outbreak of fire in the forest and to show that these exemplified certain types of continuous change. If this is shown, there is no longer any room for doubt: *A*'s action *was* the cause of the fire, whether he intended it or not. This seems and is the simplest of cases. Yet it is important to notice that even in applying our general knowledge to a case as simple as this, indeed in regarding it as simple, we make an implicit use of a distinction between types of factor which constitute a limit in tracing consequences and those which we regard as mere circumstances "through" which we trace them. For the breeze which sprang up after *A* dropped the cigarette, and without which the fire would not have spread to the forest, was not only subsequent to his action but entirely independent of it: it was, however, a common recurrent feature of the environment, and, as such, it is thought of not as an "intervening" force but as merely part of the circumstances in which the cause "operates." The decision so to regard it is implicitly taken when we combine our knowledge of the successive stages of the process and assert the connection.

It is easy here to be misled by the natural metaphor of a causal "chain," which may lead us to think that the causal process consists of a series of single events each of which is dependent upon (would not have occurred without) its predecessor in the "chain" and so is dependent upon the initiating action or event. In truth in any causal process we have at each phase not single events but complex sets of conditions, and among these conditions are some which are not only subsequent to, but independent of the initiating action or event. Some of these independent conditions, such as the evening breeze in the example chosen, we classify as mere conditions in or on which the cause operates; others we speak of as "interventions" or "causes." To decide how such independent elements shall be classified is also to decide how we shall combine our knowledge of the different general connections which the successive stages exemplify, and it is important to see that nothing *in* this knowledge itself can resolve this point. We may have to go to science for the relevant general knowledge before we can assert with proper confidence that *A*'s action did cause the fire, but science, though it tells us that an air current was required, is silent on the difference between a current in the form of an evening breeze and one produced by someone who deliberately fanned the flames as they were flickering out in the bracken. Yet an air current in this deliberately induced form is not a "condition" or "mere circumstance" through which we can trace the consequence; its presence would force us to revise the assertion that *A* caused the fire. Conversely if science helped us to identify as a necessary factor in producing the fire some condition or element of which we had previously been totally ignorant, e.g. the persistence of oxygen, this would leave our original judgment undisturbed if this factor were a common or pervasive feature of the environment or of the thing in question. There is thus indeed an important sense in which it is true that the distinction between cause and conditions is not a "scientific" one. It is not determined by laws or generalizations concerning connections between events.

When we have assembled all our knowledge of the factors involved in the fire, the residual question which we then confront (the attributive question) may be typified as follows: Here is *A*'s action, here is the fire: can the fire be attributed to *A*'s action as its consequence given that there is also this third factor (the breeze or *B*'s intervention) without which the fire would not have happened? It is plain that, both in raising questions of this kind and in answering them, ordinary thought is powerfully influenced by the analogy between the straightforward cases of causal attribution (where the elements required for the production of harm in addition to the initiating action are all "normal" conditions) and even simpler cases of responsibility which we do not ordinarily describe in causal language at all but the simple transitive verbs of action. These are the cases of the direct manipulation of objects involving changes in them or their position: cases where we say "He pushed it," "He broke it," "He bent it." The cases which we do confidently describe in causal language ("The fire was caused by his carelessness," "He caused a fire") are cases where no other human action or abnormal occurrence is required for the production of the effect, but only normal conditions. Such cases appear as mere long-range or less direct versions or extensions of the most obvious and fundamental case of all for the attribution of responsibility: the case where we can simply say "He did it." Conversely in attaching importance to thus causing harm as a distinct ground of responsibility and in taking certain kinds of factor (whether human interventions or abnormal occurrences), without which the initiating action would not have led to harm, to preclude the description of the case in simple causal terms, common sense is affected by the fact that here, because of the manner in which the harm eventuates, the outcome cannot be represented as a mere extension of the initiating action; the analogy with the fundamental case for responsibility ("He did it") has broken down.

When we understand the power exerted over our ordinary thought by the conception that causing harm is a mere extension of the primary case of doing harm, the interrelated metaphors which seem natural to lawyers and laymen, in describing various aspects of causal connection, fall into place and we can discuss their factual basis. The persistent notion that some kinds of event required in addition to the initiating action for the production of harm "break the chain of causation" is intelligible, if we remember that though such events actually *complete* the *explanation* of the harm (and so *make* rather than *break* the causal explanation) they do, unlike mere normal conditions, break the *analogy* with cases of simple actions. The same analogy accounts for the description of these factors as "new actions" (*novus actus*) or "new causes," "superseding," "extraneous," "intervening forces": and for the description of the initiating action when "the chain of causation" is broken as "no longer operative," "having worn out," *functus officio*. So too when the "chain" is held not to be "broken" the initiating action is said to be still "potent," "continuing," "contributing," "operative," and the mere conditions held insufficient to break the chain are "part of the background," "circumstances in which the cause operates," "the stage set," "part of the history."

(ii) *A* throws a lighted cigarette into the bracken which catches fire. Just as the flames are about to flicker out, *B*, who is not acting in concert with *A*, deliberately pours petrol on them. The fire spreads and burns down the forest. *A*'s action, whether or not he intended the forest fire, was not the cause of the fire: *B*'s was.

The voluntary intervention of a second human

agent, as in this case, is a paradigm among those factors which preclude the assimilation in causal judgments of the first agent's connection with the eventual harm to the case of simple direct manipulation. Such an intervention displaces the prior action's title to be called the cause and, in the persistent metaphors found in the law, it "reduces" the earlier action and its immediate effects to the level of "mere circumstances" or "part of the history." *B* in this case was not an "instrument" through which *A* worked or a victim of the circumstances *A* has created. He has, on the contrary, freely exploited the circumstances and brought about the fire without the co-operation of any further agent or any chance coincidence. Compared with this the claim of *A*'s action to be ranked the cause of the fire fails. That this and not the moral appraisal of the two actions is the point of comparison seems clear. If *A* and *B* both intended to set the forest on fire, and this destruction is accepted as something wrong or wicked, their moral wickedness, judged by the criterion of intention, is the same. Yet the causal judgment differentiates between them. If their moral guilt is judged by the outcome, this judgment though it would differentiate between them cannot be the source of the causal judgment; for it presupposes it. The difference just is that *B* has caused the harm and *A* has not. Again, if we appraise these actions as good or bad from different points of view, this leaves the causal judgments unchanged. *A* may be a soldier of one side anxious to burn down the enemy's hideout: *B* may be an enemy soldier who has decided that his side is too iniquitous to defend. Whatever is the moral judgment passed on these actions by different speakers it would remain true that *A* had not caused the fire and *B* had.

There are, as we have said, situations in which a voluntary action would not be thought of as an intervention precluding causal connection in this way. These are the cases discussed further below where an opportunity commonly exploited for harmful actions is negligently provided, or one person intentionally provides another with the means, the opportunity, or a certain type of reason for wrongdoing. Except in such cases a voluntary intervention is a limit past which consequences are not traced. By contrast, actions which in any of a variety of different ways are

less than fully voluntary are assimilated to the means by which or the circumstances in which the earlier action brings about the consequences. Such actions are not the outcome of an informed choice made without pressure from others, and the different ways in which human action may fall short in this respect range from defective muscular control, through lack of consciousness or knowledge, to the vaguer notions of duress and of predicaments, created by the first agent for the second, in which there is no "fair" choice.

In considering examples of such actions and their bearing on causal judgments there are three dangers to avoid. It would be folly to think that in tracing connections through such actions instead of regarding them, like voluntary interventions, as a limit, ordinary thought has clearly separated out their non-voluntary aspect from others by which they are often accompanied. Thus even in the crude case where *A* lets off a gun (intentionally or not) and startles *B*, so that he makes an involuntary movement of his arm which breaks a glass, the commonness of such a reaction as much as its compulsive character may influence the judgment that *A*'s action was the cause of the damage.

Secondly we must not impute to ordinary thought all the fine discriminations that could be made and in fact are to be found in a legal system, or an equal willingness to supply answers to complex questions in causal terms. Where there is no precise system of punishment, compensation or reward to administer, ordinary men will not often have faced such questions as whether the injuries suffered by a motorist who collides with another in swerving to avoid a child are consequences attributable to the neglect of the child's parents in allowing it to wander on to the road. Such questions courts have to answer and in such cases common judgments provide only a general, though still an important indication of what are the relevant factors.

Thirdly, though very frequently non-voluntary actions are assimilated to mere conditions or means by which the first agent brings about the consequences, the assimilation is never quite complete. This is manifested by the general avoidance of many causal locutions which are appropriate when the consequences are traced (as in the first case) through purely physical events.

Thus even in the case in which the second agent's role is hardly an "action" at all, e.g. where *A* hits *B*, who staggers against a glass window and breaks it, we should say that *A*'s blow made *B* stagger and break the glass, rather than that *A*'s blow caused the glass to break, though in any explanatory or attributive context the case would be *summarized* by saying that *A*'s action was the cause of the *damage*.

In the last two cases where *B*'s movements are involuntary in the sense that they are not part of any action which he chose or intended to do, their connection with *A*'s action would be described by saying that *A*'s blow *made B* stagger or *caused* him to stagger or that the noise of *A*'s shot *made* him jump. This would be true, whether *A* intended or expected *B* to react in this way or not, and the naturalness of treating *A*'s action as the cause of the ultimate damage is due to the causal character of this part of the process involving *B*'s action. The same is, however, true where *B*'s actions are not involuntary movements but *A* is considered to have made or caused *B* to do them by less crude means. This is the case if, for example, *A* uses threats or exploits his authority over *B* to make *B* do something, e.g. knock down a door. At least where *A*'s threats are serious harm, or *B*'s act was unquestionably within *A*'s authority to order, he too has made or forced or (in formal quasi-legal parlance) "caused" *B* to act.

Outside the area of such cases, where *B*'s will would be said either not to be involved at all, or to be overborne by *A*, are cases where *A*'s act creates a predicament for *B* *narrowing* the area of choice so that he has either to inflict some harm on himself or others, or sacrifice some important interest or duty. Such cases resemble coercion in that *A* narrows the area of *B*'s choice but differ from it in that this predicament need not be intentionally created. *A* sets a house on fire (intentionally or unintentionally): *B* to save himself has to jump from a height involving certain injury, or to save a child rushes in and is seriously burned. Here, of course, *B*'s movements are not involuntary; the "necessity" of his action is here of a different order. His action is the outcome of a choice between two evils forced on him by *A*'s action. In such cases, when *B*'s injuries are thought of as the consequence of

the fire, the implicit judgment is made that his action was the lesser of two evils and in this sense a "reasonable" one which he was obliged to make to avoid the greater evil. This is often paradoxically, though understandably, described by saying that here the agent "had no choice" but to do what he did. Such judgments involve a comparison of the importance of the respective interests sacrificed and preserved, and the final assertion that *A*'s action was the cause of the injuries rests on evaluations about which men may differ.

Finally, the ground for treating some harm which would not have occurred without *B*'s action as the consequence of *A*'s action may be that *B* acted in ignorance of or under a mistake as to some feature of the situation created by *A*. Poisoning offers perhaps the simplest example of the bearing on causal judgments of actions which are less than voluntary in this Aristotelian sense. If *A* intending *B*'s death deliberately poisons *B*'s food and *B*, knowing this, deliberately takes the poison and dies, *A* has not, unless he coerced *B* into eating the poisoned food, caused *B*'s death: if, however, *B* does not know the food to be poisoned, eats it, and dies, *A* has caused his death, even if he put the poison in unwittingly. Of course only the roughest judgments are passed in causal terms in such cases outside law courts, where fine degrees of "appreciation" or "reckless shutting of the eyes" may have to be discriminated from "full knowledge." Yet, rough as these are, they indicate clearly enough the controlling principles.

Though in the foregoing cases *A*'s initiating action might often be described as "the cause" of the ultimate harm, this linguistic fact is of subordinate importance to the fact that, for whatever purpose, explanatory, descriptive, or evaluative, consequences of an action are traced, discriminations are made (except in the cases discussed later) between free voluntary interventions and less than voluntary reactions to the first action or the circumstances created by it.

(iii) The analogy with single simple actions which guides the tracing of consequences may be broken by certain kinds of conjunctions of physical events. *A* hits *B* who falls to the ground stunned and bruised by the blow; at that moment a tree crashes to the ground and kills *B*. *A* has certainly caused *B*'s bruises but not his death: for though the fall of the tree was, like the evening breeze in our earlier example, independent of and subsequent to the initiating action, it would be differentiated from the breeze in any description in causal terms of the connection of *B*'s death with *A*'s action. It is to be noticed that this is not a matter which turns on the intention with which *A* struck *B*. Even if *A* hit *B* inadvertently or accidentally his blow would still be the cause of *B*'s bruises: he would have caused them, though unintentionally. Conversely even if *A* had intended his blow to kill, this would have been an attempt to kill but still not the cause of *B*'s death, unless *A* knew that the tree was about to fall just at that moment. On this legal and ordinary judgments would be found to agree; and most legal systems would distinguish for the purposes of punishment an attempt with a fatal upshot, issuing by such chance or anomalous events, from "causing death" — the terms in which the offenses of murder and manslaughter are usually defined.

Similarly the causal description of the case does not turn on the moral appraisal of *A*'s action or the wish to punish it. *A* may be a robber and a murderer and *B* a saint guarding the place *A* hoped to plunder. Or *B* may be a murderer and *A* a hero who has forced his way into *B*'s retreat. In both cases the causal judgment is the same. *A* had caused the minor injuries but not *B*'s death, though he tried to kill him. *A* may indeed be praised or blamed but not for causing *B*'s death. However intimate the connection between responsibility and causation, it does not determine causal judgments in this simple way. Nor does the causal judgment turn on a refusal to attribute grave consequences to actions which normally have less serious results. Had *A*'s blow killed *B* outright and the tree, falling on his body, merely smashed his watch we should still treat the coincidental character of the fall of the tree as determining the form of causal statement. We should then recognize *A*'s blow as the cause of *B*'s death but not the breaking of the watch.

The connection between *A*'s action and *B*'s death in the first case would naturally be described in the language of *coincidence*. "It was a coincidence: it just happened that, at the very moment when *A* knocked *B* down, a tree crashed at the very place where he fell and killed him." The common legal metaphor would describe the fall of the tree as an "extraneous" cause. This, however, is dangerously misleading, as an analysis of the notion of coincidence will show. It suggests merely an event which is subsequent to and independent of some other contingency, and of course the fall of the tree has both these features in relation to *A*'s blow. Yet in these respects the fall of the tree does not differ from the evening breeze in the earlier case where we found no difficulty in tracing causal connection. The full elucidation of the notion of a coincidence is a complex matter for, though it is very important as a limit in tracing consequences, causal questions are not the only ones to which the notion is relevant. The following are its most general characteristics. We speak of a coincidence whenever the conjunction of two or more events in certain spatial or temporal relations (1) is very unlikely by ordinary standards and (2) is for some reason significant or important, provided (3) that they occur without human contrivance and (4) are independent of each other. It is therefore a coincidence if two persons known to each other in London meet without design in Paris on their way to separate independently chosen destinations; or if two persons living in different places independently decide to write a book on the same subject. The first is a coincidence of time and place ("It just happened that we were at the same place at the same time"), and the second a coincidence of time only ("It just happened that they both decided to write on the subject at the same time").

Use of this general notion is made in the special case when the conjunction of two or more events occurs in temporal and/or spatial relationships which are significant, because, as our general knowledge of causal processes shows, this conjunction is required for the production of some given further event. In the language of Mill's idealized model, they form a necessary part of a complex set of jointly sufficient conditions. In the present case the fall of the tree just as *B* was struck down within its range satisfies the four criteria for a coincidence which we have enumerated. First, though neither event was of a very rare or exceptional kind, their conjunction would be rated very unlikely judged by the standards of ordinary experience. Secondly, this conjunction was causally significant for it was a necessary part of the process terminating in *B*'s death. Thirdly, this conjunction was not consciously designed by *A*; had he known of the impending fall of the tree and hit *B* with the intention that he should fall within its range *B*'s death would not have been the result of any coincidence. *A* would certainly have caused it. The common-sense principle that a contrived conjunction cannot be a coincidence is the element of truth in the legal maxim (too broadly stated even for legal purposes) that an intended consequence cannot be too "remote." Fourthly, each member of the conjunction in this case was independent of the other; whereas if *B* had fallen against the tree with an impact sufficient to bring it down on him, this sequence of physical events, though freakish in its way, would not be a coincidence and in most contexts of ordinary life, as in the law, the course of events would be summarized by saying that in this case, unlike that of the coincidence, *A*'s act was the cause of *B*'s death, since each stage is the effect of the preceding stage. Thus, the blow forced the victim against the tree, the effect of this was to make the tree fall and the fall of the tree killed the victim.

One further criterion in addition to these four must be satisfied if a conjunction of events is to rank as a coincidence and as a limit when the consequences of the action are traced. This further criterion again shows the strength of the influence which the analogy with the case of the simple manipulation of things exerts over thought in causal terms. An abnormal *condition* existing at the time of a human intervention is distinguished both by ordinary thought and, with a striking consistency, by most legal systems from an abnormal event or conjunction of events subsequent to that intervention; the former, unlike the latter, are not ranked as coincidences or "extraneous" causes when the consequences of the intervention come to be traced. Thus *A* innocently gives *B* a tap over the head of a normally quite harmless character, but because *B* is then suffering from some rare disease the tap has, as we say, "fatal results." In this case *A* has caused *B*'s death though unintentionally. The scope of the principle which thus distinguishes contemporaneous abnormal conditions from subsequent events is unclear; but at least where a human being initiates some physical change in a thing, animal, or person, abnormal physical

states of the object affected, existing at the time, are ranked as part of the circumstances in which the cause "operates." In the familiar controlling imagery these are part of "the stage already set" before the "intervention."

Judgments about coincidences, though we often agree in making them, depend in two related ways on issues incapable of precise formulation. One of these is patent, the other latent but equally important. Just how unlikely must a conjunction be to rank as a coincidence, and in the light of what knowledge is likelihood to be assessed? The only answer is: "very unlikely in the light of the knowledge available to ordinary men." It is, of course, the indeterminacies of such standards, implicit in causal judgments, that make them inveterately disputable, and call for the exercise of discretion or choice by courts. The second and latent indeterminacy of these judgments depends on the fact that the things or events to which they relate do not have pinned to them some uniquely correct description always to be used in assessing likelihood. It is an important pervasive feature of all our empirical judgments that there is a constant possibility of more or less specific description of any event or thing with which they are concerned. The tree might be described not simply as a "tree" but as a "rotten tree" or as a "fir tree" or a "tree sixty feet tall." So too its fall might be described not as a "fall" but as a fall of a specified distance at a specified velocity. The likelihood of conjunctions framed in these different terms would be differently assessed. The criteria of appropriate description like the standard of likelihood are supplied by consideration of common knowledge. Even if the scientist knew the tree to be rotten and could have predicted its fall with accuracy, this would not change the judgment that its fall at the time when *B* was struck down within its range was a coincidence; nor would it make the description "rotten tree" appropriate for the assessment of the chances involved in this judgment. There are other controls over the choice of description derived from the degree of specificity of our interests in the final outcome of the causal process. We are concerned with the fall of an object sufficient to cause "death" by impact and the precise force or direction which may account for the detail of the wounds is irrelevant here.

Opportunities and Reasons

OPPORTUNITIES. The discrimination of voluntary interventions as a limit is no longer made when the case, owing to the commonness or appreciable risk of such harmful intervention, can be brought within the scope of the notion of providing an opportunity, known to be commonly exploited for doing harm. Here the limiting principles are different. When A leaves the house unlocked the range of consequences to be attributed to this neglect, as in any other case where precautions are omitted, depends primarily on the way in which such opportunities are commonly exploited. An alternative formulation of this idea is that a subsequent intervention would fall within the scope of consequences if the likelihood of its occurring is one of the reasons for holding A's omission to be negligent.

It is on these lines that we would distinguish between the entry of a thief and of a murderer; the opportunity provided is believed to be sufficiently commonly exploited by thieves to make it usual and often morally or legally obligatory not to provide it. Here, in attributing consequences to prior actions, causal judgments are directly controlled by the notion of the risk created by them. Neglect of such precautions is both unusual and reprehensible. For these reasons it would be hard to separate the two ways in which such neglect deviates from the "norm." Despite this, no simple identification can be made of the notion of responsibility with the causal connection which is a ground for it. This is so because the provision of an opportunity commonly taken by others is ranked as the cause of the outcome independently of the wish to praise or blame. The causal judgment may be made simply to assess a contribution to some outcome. Thus, whether we think well or ill of the use made of railways, we would still claim that the greater mobility of the population in the nineteenth century was a consequence of their introduction.

It is obvious that the question whether any given intervention is a sufficiently common exploitation of the opportunity provided to come within the risk is again a matter on which judgments may differ, though they often agree. The courts, and perhaps ordinary thought also, often describe those that are sufficiently common as "natural" consequences of the neglect. They have in these terms discriminated the entry of a thief from the entry of a man who burnt the house down, and refused to treat the destruction of the house as a "natural" consequence of the neglect.

We discuss later . . . the argument that this easily intelligible concept of "harm within the risk," overriding as it does the distinctions between voluntary interventions and others, should be used as the general test for determining what subsequent harm should be attributed for legal purposes to prior action. The merits of this proposal to refashion the law along these simple lines are perhaps considerable, yet consequences of actions are in fact often traced both in the law and apart from it in other ways which depend on the discrimination of voluntary interventions from others. We distinguish, after all, as differing though related grounds of responsibility, causing harm by one's own action and providing opportunities for others to do harm, where the guiding analogy with the simple manipulation of things, which underlies causal thought, is less close. When, as in the examples discussed above, we trace consequences through the non-voluntary interventions of others our concern is to show that certain stages of the process have a certain type of connection with the preceding stages, and not, as when the notion of risk is applied, to show that the ultimate outcome is connected in some general way with the initiating action. Thus, when A's shot makes B start and break a glass it is the causal relationship described by the expression "made B start" that we have in mind and not the likelihood that on hearing a shot someone may break a glass. Causal connection may be traced in such cases though the initiating action and the final outcome are not contingencies that commonly go together.

Apart from these conceptual reasons for distinguishing these related grounds for responsibility, it is clear that both in the law . . . and apart from it we constantly treat harm as caused by a person's action though it does not fall "within the risk." If, when B broke the glass in the example given above, a splinter flew into C's eye, blinding him, A's action is indeed the cause of C's injury though we may not always blame him for so unusual a consequence.

REASONS. In certain varieties of interpersonal transactions, unlike the case of coercion, the second action is quite voluntary. A may not threaten

B but may bribe or advise or persuade him to do something. Here, *A* does not "cause" or "make" *B* do anything: the strongest words we should use are perhaps that he "induced" or "procured" *B*'s act. Yet the law and moral principles alike may treat one person as responsible for the harm which another free agent has done "in consequence" of the advice or the inducements which the first has offered. In such cases the limits concern the range of those actions done by *B* which are to rank as the consequence of *A*'s words or deeds. In general this question depends on *A*'s intentions or on the "plan of action" he puts before *B*. If *A* advises or bribes *B* to break in and steal from an empty house and *B* does so, he acts in consequence of *A*'s advice or bribe. If he deliberately burns down the house this would not be treated as the consequence of *A*'s bribe or advice, legally or otherwise, though it may in some sense be true that the burning would not have taken place without the advice or bribe. Nice questions may arise, which the courts have to settle, where *B* diverges from the detail of the plan of action put before him by *A*.

Notes and Questions

DOUGLAS N. HUSAK, "Omissions, Causation and Liability"

1. Special problems for the doctrine of causation are raised by omissions. It is obvious that causing harm is relevant to being liable for it, but what is the relation of omission to liability? The standard view in Anglo-American law is that people should not be held responsible for omissions in general. Douglas N. Husak lists the usual reasons given for this opposition. What are they?

2. Husak sets out what he calls the *causal argument*. What is it? He points out that the usual attack on the causal argument is aimed at countering the second premise: Omissions are not causes. Can you think of any good reasons to say that an omission is or is not a cause? Why is omission more problematic than action in this regard?

3. Husak takes a different tack by disputing the first premise of the argument, which he calls the *causal assumption*: no liability without cause. What general arguments does he give for rejecting this assumption? What argument might an opponent give for keeping the assumption?

4. Husak sets out three objections to his view — three arguments that favor the causal assumption. What are they, and how does he address them? Are his answers adequate? Why or why not?

5. What is Husak's proposal for an alternative to the causal assumption? How does he support this proposal? Can you think of deficiencies with it?

Omissions, Causation and Liability

DOUGLAS N. HUSAK

Critics of Anglo-American law have lamented for some time that our legal system fails to go as far as others in imposing criminal (or civil) liability for failures to avert harm.[1] The duty not to harm is owed to all persons alike, but the duty to avert harm is owed only to a narrowly defined class of persons.[2] This asymmetry requires explanation, especially in the light of legal consequences which some commentators have described as "shocking in the extreme" and "revolting to any moral sense."[3] A defendant rents a canoe to an intoxicated plaintiff, who overturns it. The defendant is an excellent swimmer, but sits passively on the dock, boat and rope at hand, smoking a cigarette and watching the plaintiff drown. In *Osterlind v. Hill*,[4] the court found no liability. One would expect powerful arguments in support of such a disappointing legal result.[5] In this paper I shall discuss *one* such argument that is especially pervasive in legal and philosophical literature, and shall conclude that it is unconvincing. But before this argument is reconstructed and attacked, it may be helpful to identify a factor that has contributed to some confusion on this topic.

Despite their implausibility, extremist positions on both sides of this controversy have attracted surprising support among commentators. Those who favour restricting liability for omissions to a few carefully limited circumstances sometimes dismiss apparent counterexamples with the tired apology that legal duty must occasionally fall short of moral obligation.[6] Those who regard cases of failing to avert harm as *equally* blameworthy as cases of actively harming[7] are embarrassed in their attempt to explain why no legal system has gone so far as to impose comparably severe punishments. The beginning of wisdom on this issue is to distinguish the question of whether liability should be imposed *at all* from the question of *how much* liability should be imposed. Unfortunately, even those commentators who seem on the verge of recognizing this distinction have not always remained attentive to it. George Fletcher observes that "we should keep in mind two questions: the first is determining that there is a duty and the second is pinpointing the scope of that duty."[8] Yet his subsequent discussion apparently ignores the implications of this distinction by maintaining that "the duty to avert death is based on the moral assumption that in the particular situation, the failure to avert death is *equivalent* to killing."[9] No reason is offered to explain why a duty to avert harm should be countenanced in only those circumstances in which the failure to avert harm is of blameworthiness *equal* to that of the act of causing harm. Why not impose a duty to assist in cases in which a breach of such duty would *not* be as dreadful as an act of harming? To a large extent, the fixation in contemporary philosophical literature on the question of whether liability should be *as great* for harmful omissions as for harmful actions distracts attention from the more fundamental issue of whether

there should be liability for harmful omissions *at all*. If one is arguing against the claim that liability should not be enlarged in cases of failure to avert harm, one should not simultaneously draw inferences about the extent of such liability.[10]

Before addressing the particular argument to be considered, it is appropriate briefly to place the issue of liability for omissions in a broader context. Recurrent in the literature are at least four reasons for opposing liability for omissions: (1) *actus reus* is a general requirement for criminal liability that is not satisfied by imposing liability for omissions, since omissions are not acts;[11] (2) liability for omissions is a greater deprivation of liberty than liability for positive acts, since agents who are prohibited from performing some act are allowed a greater number of permissible options than agents who are required to perform some positive act;[12] (3) no one has formulated an acceptable rule specifying precisely which omissions should give rise to liability that precludes a descent down the slippery slope to all sorts of absurd consequences;[13] (4) causation is a necessary condition of liability for harm, and one does not cause harm one merely fails to avert.[14] A more comprehensive treatment than that provided here would address each of these arguments, preferably by sorting them into two kinds: those that attempt to demonstrate why it is objectionable to convert an acknowledged moral obligation into a legal duty, and those that allege that, intuitions notwithstanding, one is seldom under a moral obligation to avert harm.[15] In the remainder of this paper, I shall focus on the last of the above arguments. Do the "facts" of causation provide any reason not to impose liability for harmful omissions to an extent greater than that currently recognized in most Anglo-American jurisdictions?

Expressed syllogistically, the argument to be discussed (henceforth called the *causal argument* is as follows:

(1) No one should be held liable for harm he has not caused.

(2) A failure to avert harm is not a cause of harm.

(3) Therefore no one should be held liable for harm he has failed to avert.

Premise (1) of this argument will be called the *causal assumption*, premise (2) will be called the *principle of causal efficacy*.

What is noteworthy in the relevant literature is that commentators who have been unconvinced by the causal argument have attacked the principle of causal efficacy much more frequently than the causal assumption. Many such critics have flooded the literature with analyses of causation according to which omissions as well as actions are capable of causing states of affairs.[16] Nearly all of these accounts propose a counterfactual analysis of causation, according to which one condition that must be satisfied before an act or omission *x* can be said to cause event *y* would not have occurred but for *x*. Such analyses purport to offer straightforward explanations of how omissions as well as acts can cause harm since, e.g., there is no reasonable doubt that the canoeist in *Osterlind* would not have drowned but for the failure of the defendant to try to rescue him. Cases of causal overdetermination, which have traditionally embarrassed counterfactual analyses of causation,[17] are sometimes dismissed as of no "immediate concern."[18]

I shall here propose no criticisms of the principle of causal efficacy. Instead, let us consider the fact that the burden of formulating an analysis of causation that is incompatible with the principle of causal efficacy is borne only by those critics of the causal argument who subscribe to the causal assumption. If there is no compelling reason to retain the causal assumption, the truth of the principle of causal efficacy should not disturb those who favor an enlargement of liability for harmful omissions. It will not persuade proponents of the causal argument to abandon the causal assumption on the ground that well-established legal practices (e.g., strict liability, vicarious liability, etc.) seem to have dispensed with it already. For adherents of the causal assumption can be expected to employ it as the basis of an objection to these controversial forms of liability.

A more telling criticism of the causal assumption (when used in the context of the causal argument) is that it precludes the imposition of liability in even those few circumstances in which it is currently recognized in law. It is simply unacceptable to all parties to the controversy to permit a mother to sit passively by and allow her infant to bleed to death after he has accidentally injured himself. In the face of such examples, defenders of the causal assumption are less than convincing. In a disingenuous footnote, Richard Epstein, unshaken in his confidence in the causal argument, writes: "I put aside here all those cases in which there are special relationships between the plaintiff and the defendants: parent and child, invitor and invitee, and the like."[19] It is best, after all, to "put aside" those objections to which one cannot respond.

An alternative strategy that at least acknowledges the importance of the difficulty attempts to analyse cases such as that of the bleeding infant as instances of an act of killing rather than as instances of an omission of letting die.[20] This tactic should quickly convince you that you no longer understand the distinction between acts and omissions. It will not do to recharacterize any apparent omission in which it seems clear that liability is properly imposed as an instance of acting. One might as well dissolve the problem by claiming that *Osterlind* involves positive action. What are sorely needed at this point are theoretical analyses of the concepts of acting and omitting.[21] However this elusive distinction is ultimately drawn, it would be surprising if it coincided with considered opinions about when behaviour should or should not give rise to liability. If such a coincidence obtained, there would be adequate grounds for suspecting that normative considerations had been smuggled into the respective analyses of acting and omitting. But if such normative considerations were indeed part of the analyses, the claim that omissions should not give rise to liability is in danger of becoming a tautology.[22] One might hope for a non-normative criterion to distinguish acts from omissions. Such a criterion could then be employed to test the substantive hypothesis that behaviour categorized as action rather than as omission gives rise to greater obligations. The claim that behaviour involves an omission rather than a positive act is typically put forward as *a reason* for exempting the agent from liability. If omissions are (in part) *defined* as behaviour involving fewer obligations than positive acts, the categorization of behaviour[23] cannot serve as such a (non-circular) reason, since the categorization already incorporates the normative conclusion. On this account, the conclusion of the causal argument is trivial and uninteresting. The fact that arguments (e.g., the causal argument) are constructed to support this conclusion is evidence that its defenders do not regard it as a logical truth.

It seems plausible to suppose that strong utilitarian arguments can be marshalled against the causal assumption. If the enforcement of sanctions for violations of law exerts any influence on human behaviour, the imposition of liability for failure to avert harm that one has not caused can be expected to result in a net reduction of harm. But this claim cannot be adequately defended here. Instead, it is profitable to examine what might be said on behalf of the causal assumption. This project requires a willingness to construct arguments for one's adversaries, for those who adopt the causal assumption generally exhibit a curious reluctance to argue for it. In the light of the fact that the causal assumption has gone virtually unchallenged in the long history of legal theory,[24] the results of this inquiry are disappointing. I shall assess three arguments.

(1) One clue to the appeal of the causal assumption is contained in the various labels under which causation is described by legal theorists. The counterfactual sense of causation typically said to constitute a necessary (though not a sufficient) condition for liability is characterized alternatively in the literature as "cause in fact," "scientific cause," or "cause in the philosophical sense."[25] Legal theorists who employ these labels seem undisturbed by the nearly universal resistance to this analysis of causation among both scientists and philosophers. But there is little difficulty in accounting for the attraction of allegedly "scientific," "objective," or "factual" principles which establish limits on the scope of behavior for which one can be held liable. One can thereby suppose that judgements of liability are not *entirely* normative. Both legal and nonlegal minds continue to be influenced by a "positivistic" bias that maintains that normative questions are inherently insoluble. It is reasonable to suspect that the causal assumption will be found appealing to the extent that one holds such a bias.

It hardly needs to be pointed out that this first basis for believing the causal assumption is without merit. The defects of this argument can be identified without defending a controversial theory according to which normative questions are as susceptible to rational solution as non-normative issues. A more direct response is as follows. Even if the counterfactual analysis of causation employed in Anglo-American law were "scientifically" accurate, the decision to *use* such an analysis to establish the limits of personal liability would remain a normative one. Surely no nonnormative *fact* of the matter tells us it is unjust to hold persons liable for harm they have not caused. Questions of liability *are* normative, despite the unfortunate tendency to pretend otherwise.

(2) A second possible basis for retaining the causal assumption is derived from the resistance of our legal system to apportion blame and liability. Many of the situations in which it is tempting to hold agent A liable for harm he has not caused are cases in which some agent B has unquestionably acted to cause the harm. Fletcher's treatment hazards the "experimental thesis" that (analogous to the law of accessories) liability for omissions is a branch of *derivative* liability.[26] Liability is said to be derivative when there exists some other, primary offence from which liability can be derived. It is no doubt true that a convincing argument that B has acted to cause a harm often makes us less inclined to hold A liable. But why? Perhaps there is a tendency to suppose that if B is held liable to the fullest extent of the law for the harm that is caused when C is pushed in a lake and drowned, we had better attribute no liability for the death to A, who merely watched the act. If the reluctance of our legal system to apportion liability requires that either A or B be held totally responsible for the death (in the absence of complicity), the relevant question becomes this: who is *more* liable for the harm — A or B? Surely greater liability attaches to B, hence it might be thought that there is none left over for A.

One version of this strategy has recently been advanced by Elazar Weinryb. He invokes the causal assumption to "shed grave doubts on the appropriateness of holding someone responsible for the harm he omits to prevent."[27] His defence of the principle of causal efficacy is detailed and plausible, but, characteristically, the causal assumption is supported almost as an afterthought. The reasoning in favour of the causal assumption is that "our idea of responsibility requires that it should be uniquely ascribed," and "in many situations causation is the only means by which we can satisfy the uniqueness requirement."[28]

This basis for retaining the causal assumption can be rejected without addressing the complex issues involved in apportionments of blame. In the first place, many of the cases in which it seems appropriate to impose liability for omissions are situations in which no other agent has acted to cause the harm. Hence Fletcher's "experiment" of treating liability for omissions as a kind of derivative liability is of limited application at best. It would not, for example, alter the legal result in *Osterlind*. More to the point, the failure to avert harm is easily conceptualized as an offence distinct from the act of causing harm. Hence questions about how blame might be apportioned for a *single* offence need not even arise.[29] Thus even if Weinryb is correct that "our idea of responsibility" necessitates that it be "uniquely ascribed" — a very debatable contention — there is no barrier to holding persons who fail to avert harm liable for offences distinct from that of actively causing harm.

(3) Finally, the causal assumption might be indirectly defended by the familiar process of criticizing alternative proposals to limit liability. Surely *some* general principles must limit the scope of events for which one may be held liable, and one should not be too quick to reject a plausible candidate for this role until a more suitable replacement can be found.

A radical response to this defence might question the *a priori* conviction that general principles to limit liability *must* exist. But the above challenge is better met by defending an alternative to causation. Clearly this project cannot be undertaken in detail here. But a tentative hypothesis is that our feelings about liability are better accommodated by supposing that agents should be held liable for only those states of affairs over which they have *control*. I shall not develop this suggestion[30] beyond pointing out that, whatever 'control' means, it seems reasonable to believe that the defendant in *Osterlind* had control over the fate of the canoeist — hence his failure to *cause* the drowning creates no obstacle to liability.

Thus no compelling arguments in favour of the causal assumption can be reconstructed from legal or philosophical literature. Considering the counter-intuitive implications of that premise, I suggest that it should be abandoned. Against this background, it is fair to point out that not all legal theorists have accepted it. Hart and Honoré, in perhaps the most comprehensive examination of the connection between causation and liability, explicitly reject the causal assumption. They write:

So causing harm of a legally recognized sort or being connected with such harm in any of the ways that justify moral blame, though vitally important and perhaps basic in a legal system, is not and should not be either always necessary or always sufficient for legal responsibility.[31]

Given this repudiation, why write an entire book on the connection between causation and legal responsibility? The answer, according to Hart and Honoré, consists in what I shall call the *causal relevance principle*, which they express as follows: "We shall provisionally . . . treat statements that a person caused harm as one sort of non-tautologous ground or reason for saying that he is responsible."[32]

Is the causal relevance principle true? Whether proposition p is a reason for believing proposition q is notoriously difficult to assess. One way to defend this principle would consist in providing an example in which the substantive issue is whether agent A or B is more appropriately held liable for some harm x. Suppose that a person felt relatively confident that A was a better candidate for liability than B, but was unclear about whether the action of A caused x. Suppose at some later time he became convinced (on independent grounds) of an analysis of causation that identified the action of B as the cause of x. Should this new conviction provide him with a reason to reexamine his earlier belief that A was a better candidate for liability than B? It is not clear why it would. If his original basis for holding A liable did not depend on a belief that A's action was the cause of x, it is not obvious why this conclusion should be undermined by an argument showing that A's action was *not* the cause of x. It is unclear whether any example corresponds to this description. The description merely suggests a test by which the truth of the causal relevance principle might be assessed.

Nonetheless, one cannot fail to be impressed by the strong positive correlation between cases in which the action of A causes harm x and cases in which A is properly held liable for x. Does this correlation establish the causal relevance principle? However this question might be answered, the proposition 'A's action caused harm x' (p) is not the *best* reason for believing the proposition 'A is responsible for harm x' (q). p fails to be the best reason for believing q when there is some other proposition r that correlates more strongly with q in the sense that (1) q is true when r is true but p is false; and (2) q is false when r is false but p is true. The proposition '*A* has control over whether or not harm x occurs' satisfies these conditions when substituted for 'r.' Perhaps the plausibility of the causal relevance principle can be explained by the fortunate fact that we have control over most of the harm we cause and no control over most of the harm we do not cause. But in those cases in which we have *no* control over the harm we *cause* (e.g., we injure someone while experiencing an epileptic seizure), we certainly are exempt from liability. It would seem that such an exemption is out of the question in the opposite case in which we *have* control over the harm we do *not* cause. Any example to support this contention is question-begging, but cases such as *Osterlind* seem to provide perfectly good illustrations.[33]

NOTES

1. This lament is historically associated with Bentham. See Bentham, *An Introduction to the Principles of Morale and Legislation*, ed. Burns and Hart (London, 1970), p. 293. For surveys see Note, "The Failure to Rescue: A Comparative Survey," *Col. L.R.*, 52 (1952), p. 631; and Feldbrugge, "Good and Bad Samaritans: A Comparative Survey of Criminal Law Provisions Concerning Failure to Rescue," *American Journal of Comparative Law*, 14 (1966), p. 631. See also Rudzinski, "The Duty to Rescue: A Comparative Analysis," in *The Good Samaritan and the Law*, ed. Ratcliffe (New York, 1966).

2. *Jones v. U.S.*, 308 F.2d 307 (D.C. Cir., 1962), perhaps the leading case in this area, purports to follow *People v. Beardsley*, 150 Mich. 206, 113 N.W. 1128 (1907) in describing "four situations in which the failure to act may constitute breach of a legal duty": "First, where a statute imposes a duty of care for another; second, where one stands in a certain status relationship to another; third, where one has assumed a contractual duty to care for another; and fourth, where one has voluntarily assumed the care of another and so secluded the helpless person as to prevent others from rendering aid." For interesting critical commentary on these conditions, see Fletcher, *Rethinking Criminal Law* (Boston, 1978), pp. 611–8.

3. Prosser, *Law of Torts*, 4th ed. (St. Paul, 1971), pp. 340–1.

4. 2b3 Mass. 73, 160 N.E. 301 (1928).

5. Criticism of such legal results is not directed primarily to the judiciary, which (insofar as criminal lia-

bility is concerned) cannot create new law without violating the maxim *nulla poena sine lege*. My remarks are addressed to the legislature, which did not recognize liability in the first place — and did not rectify the "oversight" subsequent to cases such as *Osterlind*.

6. See, e.g., the statement of Judge Carpenter in *Buch v. Amory Mfg. Co.*, 69 N.II. 257, 44 Atl. 809 (1897). See also Minor, "The Moral Obligation as a Basis of Liability," *Va.L.R.*, 9 (1923), p. 420. I describe such a rationale as a "tired apology" because, in the absence of further argument, it can be used to resist conforming *any* legal result with the conclusion of moral reasoning. It offers no *reason* for the disparity, when surely there is a *prima facie* case in favour of such a conformity.

7. See, e.g., Rachels, "Active and Passive Euthanasia," *New England Journal of Medicine*, 292 (1975), p. 78.

8. Fletcher, *supra* note 2, pp. 615–6.

9. *Ib.*, p. 621 (my italics). Earlier Fletcher writes (p. 611): "The general theoretical basis for recognizing a duty to avert harm is that in the context of the relationship and under the particular circumstances, the failure to avert harm is as egregious a wrong as causing the particular harm."

10. Those who are reluctant to recognize *any* liability before they are confident about *how much* liability to impose might profit from a study of the state of confusion among legal systems concerning how much to punish (1) persons who attempt crimes, and (2) persons who are accessories to criminal activity. No system exempts such persons from punishment altogether, though the issues of how to compare their liability with (1) those who complete crimes, and (2) perpetrators of criminal activity, are topics of considerable disagreement.

11. This argument combines the *actus reus* requirement (see *Robinson v. California*, 370 U.S. 660 (1962)) with an analysis according to which omissions cannot be acts, since acts consist of bodily movements (see M.P.C. §1.14(2); Restatement (Second) of Torts §2; and Holmes, *The Common Law* (Boston, 1881), p. 54).

12. See the discussions in Kleinig, "Good Samaritanism," *Philosophy and Public Affairs*, 5 (1976), p. 382; Bohlen, "The Moral Duty to Aid Others as a Basis of Tort Liability," *U.Pa.L.R.*, 56 (1908), p. 217; Fletcher, *supra* note 2, pp. 602–6; and Rawls, *A Theory of Justice* (Cambridge, 1971), pp. 60 and 195–257.

13. Prosser, *supra* note 3, p. 341, discusses "the difficulties of setting any standards of unselfish service to fellow men, and of making any workable rule to cover possible situations where fifty people might fail to rescue one." Others have offered similar criticism that an alleged duty of rescue would be *non-dischargeable*. See Trammel, "Saving Life and Taking Life," *Journal of Philosophy*, 62 (1975), p. 131.

14. Fletcher, *supra* note 2, p. 423; Epstein, "A Theory of Strict Liability," *J. Leg. Studies*, 2 (1973), p.

151; and Weinryb, "Omissions and Responsibility," *Philosophical Quarterly*, 30 (1980), p. 1.

15. Some commentators have blurred this distinction. Epstein, *supra* note 14, p. 201, seems to rest his critique of Good Samaritan legislation on the difficulty of translating moral obligations into legal duties: "It may well be that the conduct of individuals who do not aid fellow men is under some circumstances outrageous, but it does not follow that a legal system that does not enforce a duty to aid is outrageous as well." But elsewhere he claims to have moral reservations about an alleged duty to rescue: "The common law position on the Good Samaritan problem is in the end consistent with both moral and economic principles" (p. 200).

16. See, e.g., D'Arcy, *Human Acts* (Oxford, 1963); Casey, ed., *Morality and Moral Reasoning* (London, 1971); and Harris, "The Marxist Conception of Violence," *Philosophy and Public Affairs*, 3 (1974), p. 192.

17. See Bunzl, "Causal Overdetermination," *Journal of Philosophy*, 76 (1979), p. 134.

18. Fletcher, *supra* note 2, p. 589, note 6.

17. Epstein, *supra* note 14, p. 189, note 91. Fletcher also favours "leaving aside" such cases (p. 601).

20. Foot has maintained that some cases of "letting die" can be described as instances of causing death. See her "Euthanasia," *Philosophy and Public Affairs*, 6 (1977), p. 85.

21. See references in note 16; and Brand, "The Language of Not Doing," *American Philosophical Quarterly*, 8 (1971), p. 49; Chisholm, *Person and Object* (La Salle, 1976); Thomson, *Acts and Other Events* (Ithaca, 1977); and Davis, *Theory of Action* (1979).

22. See my "Killing, Letting Die and Euthanasia," *Journal of Medical Ethics*, 5 (1979), p. 200.

23. Here and elsewhere I use "behaviour" as a generic term including both acts and omissions. I prefer this to the term "conduct" employed, e.g., in M.P.C. §1.13(5).

24. Nearly every treatise on criminal law or torts includes causation as one of the necessary conditions of liability.

25. Some of these labels are discussed in LaFave and Scott, *Criminal Law* (St. Paul, 1972), §35.

26. Fletcher, *supra* note 2, pp. 581 ff.

27. Weinryb, *supra* note 14, p. 3.

28. *Op. cit.*, p. 9.

29. Treating the failure to rescue as an offence distinct from an act of causing harm helps make sense of cases such as *Jones v. State*, 220 Ind. 384, 43 N.E. 2d 1017 (1942), in which the defendant was held guilty of murder after he failed to rescue a woman who had fallen into a creek after he had raped her.

30. The notion of control plays a central role in Hart's rejection of the doctrine of the double effect in criminal law. See "Intention and Punishment," in his *Punishment and Responsibility* (Oxford, 1968), p. 113.

31. Hart and Honoré, *Causation in the Law* (London, 1959), p. 63.

32. *Op. cit.*, p. 62.

33. I wish to thank Michael Zimmerman for a number of helpful suggestions about how this paper might be improved.

Notes and Questions

JEREMY BENTHAM, from *An Introduction to the Principles of Morals and Legislation*

1. Jeremy Bentham is concerned overall to explain what makes an act culpable. One factor that may contribute to the culpability of an act is the intent of the actor. Bentham analyzes how intention is connected to the production of an act or event. What are the objects of intention or will, according to Bentham? How are these objects connected to one another, and how is intention connected to both of them? If an act is intentional must its consequences be? What about vice versa?

2. Next, Bentham considers how consciousness or understanding relates to the production of an act or event. He points out that a person may be aware, or unaware, of either the existence or the materiality — that is, the importance — of circumstances. What difference does this make?

3. Finally, Bentham considers the connection between intentionality and consciousness. If an act is intentional and the circumstances clear to consciousness, are the consequences intentional, according to Bentham? Do you agree?

4. It is often said that a heedless, or negligent, person may cause harm but act with good intention. According to Bentham, these statements are inaccurate. What does he think people really mean when they speak this way? What is the difference between intention and motive?

5. It is generally thought that negligence is the least culpable mental state. Why? Many people

argue that punishment is inappropriate with regard to negligence, but Bentham argues that it may be rational. Do his arguments persuade you? Are the same arguments more or less relevant to tort law? Even if liability does not promote careful behavior, is tort liability appropriate when punishment is not? Why? What is tort liability supposed to accomplish?

[From] *An Introduction to the Principles of Morals and Legislation*
JEREMY BENTHAM

Intentions and Motives

1. So much with regard to the two first of the articles upon which the evil tendency of an action may depend: viz., the act itself, and the general assemblage of the circumstances with which it may have been accompanied. We come now to consider the ways in which the particular circumstance of intention may be concerned in it.

2. First, then, the intention or will may regard either of two objects: (1) The act itself: or (2) Its consequences. Of these objects, that which the intention regards may be styled *intentional*. If it regards the act, then the act may be said to be intentional:[1] if the consequences, so then also may the consequences. If it regards both the act and consequences, the whole action may be said to be intentional. Whichever of those articles is not the object of the intention, may of course be said to be *unintentional*.

3. The act may very easily be intentional without the consequences; and often is so. Thus, you may intend to touch a man without intending to hurt him: and yet, as the consequences turn out, you may chance to hurt him.

4. The consequences of an act may also be intentional, without the act's being intentional throughout; that is, without its being intentional in every stage of it: but this is not so frequent a case as the former. You intend to hurt a man, suppose, by running against him, and pushing him down: and you run toward him accordingly: but a second man coming in on a sudden between you and the first man, before you can stop yourself, you run against the second man, and by him push down the first.

5. But the consequences of an act cannot be intentional, without the act's being itself intentional in at least the first stage. If the act be not intentional in the first stage, it is no act of yours: there is accordingly no intention on your part to produce the consequences: that is to say, the individual consequences. All there can have been on your part is a distant intention to produce other consequences of the same nature, by some act of yours, at a future time: or else, without any intention, a bare *wish* to see such event take place. The second man, suppose, runs of his own accord against the first, and pushes him down. You had intentions of doing a thing of the same nature: viz., To run against him, and push him down yourself; but you had done nothing in pursuance of those intentions: the individual consequences therefore of the act, which the second man performed in pushing down the first, cannot be said to have been on your part intentional.[2]

6. Second. A consequence, when it is intentional, may either be *directly* so, or only *obliquely*. It may be said to be directly or lineally intentional, when the prospect of producing it constituted one of the links in the chain of causes by which the person was determined to do the act. It may be said to be obliquely or collaterally intentional, when, although the consequence was in contemplation, and appeared likely to ensure in case of the act's being performed, yet the prospect of producing such consequence did not constitute a link in the aforesaid chain.

7. Third. An incident, which is directly intentional, may either be *ultimately* so, or only *mediately*. It may be said to be ultimately intentional, when it stands last of all exterior events in the

aforesaid chain of motives; insomuch that the prospect of the production of such incident, could there be a certainty of its taking place, would be sufficient to determine the will, without the prospect of its producing any other. It may be said to be mediately intentional, and no more, when there is some other incident, the prospect of producing which forms a subsequent link in the same chain: insomuch that the prospect of producing the former would not have operated as a motive, but for the tendency which it seemed to have toward the production of the latter.

8. Fourth. When an incident is directly intentional, it may either be *exclusively* so, or *inexclusively*. It may be said to be exclusively intentional, when no other but that very individual incident would have answered the purpose, insomuch that no other incident had any share in determining the will to the act in question. It may be said to have been inexclusively intentional, when there was some other incident, the prospect of which was acting upon the will at the same time.

9. Fifth. When an incident is inexclusively intentional, it may be either conjunctively so, *dis*junctively, or *indiscriminately*. It may be said to be conjunctively intentional with regard to such other incident, when the intention is to produce both: disjunctively, when the intention is to produce either the one or the other indifferently, but not both: indiscriminately, when the intention is indifferently to produce either the one or the other, or both, as it may happen.

10. Sixth. When two incidents are disjunctively intentional they may be so with or without *preference*. They may be said to be so with preference, when the intention is, that one of them in particular should happen rather than the other: without preference, when the intention is equally fulfilled, whichever of them happens.[3]

11. One example will make all this clear. William II, King of England, being out on a stag-hunting, received from Sir Walter Tyrrel a wound, of which he died. Let us take this case, and diversify it with a variety of suppositions, correspondent to the distinctions just laid down.

1. First then, Tyrrel did not so much as entertain a thought of the king's death: or, if he did, looked upon it as an event of which there was no danger. In either of these cases the incident of his killing the king was altogether unintentional.

2. He saw a stag running that way, and he saw the king riding that way at the same time: what he aimed at was to kill the stag: he did not wish to kill the king: at the same time he saw that if he shot, it was as likely he should kill the king as the stag: yet for all that he shot, and killed the king accordingly. In this case the incident of his killing the king was intentional, but obliquely so.

3. He killed the king on account of the hatred he bore him, and for no other reason than the pleasure of destroying him. In this case the accident of the king's death was not only directly but ultimately intentional.

4. He killed the king, intending fully so to do; not for any hatred he bore him, but for the sake of plundering him when dead. In this case the incident of the king's death was directly intentional, but not ultimately: it was mediately intentional.

5. He intended neither more nor less than to kill the king. He had no other aim nor wish. In this case it was exclusively as well as directly intentional: exclusively, to wit, with regard to every other material incident.

6. Sir Walter shot the king in the right leg, as he was plucking a thorn out of it with his left hand. His intention was, by shooting the arrow into his leg through his hand, to cripple him in both those limbs at the same time. In this case, the incident of the king's being shot in the leg was intentional: and that conjunctively with another which did not happen; viz., his being shot in the hand.

7. The intention of Tyrrel was to shoot the king either in the hand or in the leg, but not in both; and rather in the hand than in the leg. In this case the intention of shooting in the hand was disjunctively concurrent, with regard to the other incident, and that with preference.

8. His intention was to shoot the king either in the leg or the hand, whichever might happen: but not in both. In this case the intention was inexclusive, but disjunctively so: yet that, however, without preference.

9. His intention was to shoot the king either in the leg or the hand, or in both, as it might happen. In this case the intention was indiscriminately concurrent, with respect to the two incidents.

* * *

12. It is to be observed that an act may be unintentional in any stage or stages of it, though intentional in the preceding: and, on the other hand, it may be intentional in any stage or stages of it, and yet unintentional in the succeeding. But whether it be intentional or no in any preceding stage is immaterial, with respect to the consequences, so it be unintentional in the last. The only point, with respect to which it is material, is the proof. The more stages the act is unintentional in, the more apparent it will commonly be that it was unintentional with respect to the last. If a man, intending to strike you on the cheek, strikes you in the eye, and puts it out, it will probably be difficult for him to prove that it was not his intention to strike you in the eye. It will probably be easier, if his intention was really not to strike you, or even not to strike at all.

13. It is frequent to hear men speak of a good intention, of a bad intention; of the goodness and badness of a man's intention: a circumstance on which great stress is generally laid. It is indeed of no small importance, when properly understood: but the import of it is to the last degree ambiguous and obscure. Strictly speaking, nothing can be said to be good or bad, but either in itself; which is the case only with pain or pleasure: or on account of its effects; which is the case only with things that are the causes or preventatives of pain and pleasure. But in a figurative and less proper way of speech, a thing may also be styled good or bad, in consideration of its cause. Now the effects of an intention to do such or such an act, are the same objects which we have been speaking of under the appellation of its *consequences*: and the causes of intention are called *motives*. A man's intention then on any occasion may be styled good or bad with reference either to the consequences of the act, or with reference to his motives. If it be deemed good or bad in any sense, it must be either because it is deemed to be productive of good or of bad consequences, or because it deemed to originate from a good or from a bad motive. But the goodness or badness of the consequences depend upon the circumstances. Now the circumstances are no objects of the intention. A man intends the act: and by his intention produces the act: but as to the circumstances, he does not intend them: he does not,

inasmuch as they are circumstances of it, produce them. If by accident there be a few which he has been instrumental in producing, it has been by former intentions, directed to former acts, productive of those circumstances as the consequences: at the time in question he takes them as he finds them. Acts, with their consequences, are objects of the will as well as of the understanding: circumstances, as such, are objects of the understanding only. All he can do with these, as such, is to know or not to know them: in other words, to be conscious of them, or not conscious. To the title of Consciousness belongs what is to be said of the goodness or badness of a man's intention, as resulting from the consequences of the act: and to the head of Motives, which is to be said of his intention, as resulting from the motive.

NOTES

1. On this occasion the words *voluntary* and *involuntary* are commonly employed. These however, I purposely abstain from, on account of the extreme ambiguity of their signification. By a voluntary act is meant sometimes, any act, in the performance of which the will has had any concern at all; in this sense it is synonymous to *intentional*: sometimes such acts only, in the production of which the will has been determined by motives not of a painful nature; in this sense it is synonymous to unconstrained, or *uncoerced*: sometimes such acts only, in the production of which the will has been determined by motives which, whether of the pleasurable or painful kind, occurred to a man himself, without being suggested by anybody else; in this sense it is synonymous to *spontaneous*. The sense of the word involuntary does not correspond completely to that of the word voluntary. Involuntary is used in opposition to intentional; and to unconstrained: but not to spontaneous. It might be of use to confine the signification of the words voluntary and involuntary to one single and very narrow case, which will be mentioned in the next note.

2. To render the analysis here given of the possible states of the mind in point of intentionality absolutely complete, it must be pushed to such a farther degree of minuteness, as to some eyes will be apt to appear trifling. On this account it seemed advisable to discard what follows from the text to a place where anyone who thinks proper may pass by it. An act of the body, when of a positive kind, is a motion: now in motion there are always three articles to be considered: 1. The

quantity of matter that moves: 2. The direction in which it moves: and 3. The velocity with which it moves. Correspondent to these three articles, are so many modes of intentionality, with regard to an act, considered as being only in its first stage. To be completely unintentional, it must be unintentional with respect to every one of these three particulars. This is the case with those acts which alone are properly termed *involuntary*: acts, in the performance of which the will has no sort of share: such as the contraction of the heart and arteries. . . .

3. There is a difference between the case where an incident is altogether unintentional, and that in which, it being disjunctively intentional with reference to another, the preference is in favor of the other. In the first case, it is not the intention of the party that the incident in question should happen at all: in the latter case, the intention is rather that the other should happen, but if that cannot be, then that this in question should happen rather than that neither should, and that both, at any rate, should not happen.

All these are distinctions to be attended to in the use of the particle *or*: a particle of very ambiguous import, and of great importance in legislation.

Notes and Questions

FOWLER HARPER and FLEMING JAMES, from *The Law of Torts*

1. Tort law is one way of dealing with accidents and intentional harm by and large by basing compensation on fault. The person to blame pays for the damage. Fowler Harper and Fleming James challenge the idea of handling accidents with a fault-based system. They consider the implications of studies on the causes of accidents for the fault principle of liability in light of the objectives of an accident liability system. What are the four objectives they consider?

2. The first objective is the moral requirement of fairness. It seems fair for the person at fault to pay for damage. But Harper and James point out that modern studies deny the importance of moral shortcomings in causing accidents. Why is this, and what do Harper and James conclude?

3. The second objective of an accident liability system is to compensate victims. The problem is that this objective appears to conflict with the first. If it is true that many accidents occur without fault, then many victims will go uncompensated. Historically, each objective has been limited by the other. The basic question is who should carry the loss. What do Harper and James suggest?

4. The third objective is to deter dangerous conduct and promote safety. It has long been argued that liability for fault promotes careful behavior (compare Bentham) and corresponds to worthwhile notions of responsibility. But according to Harper and James, recent studies indicate that strict liability — particularly, insurance — systems work better. What explanation is there for this? What is the context of these studies? Is it reasonable to transfer the results of studies of industrial safety to individual activities such as driving cars? If not, are there other reasons for applying strict liability — that is, no fault insurance — to such situations? When?

5. What are some of the alternatives to tort liability proposed by Harper and James? Does the nature of the scheme suggest its application? Some commentators argue that it undermines individual accountability to introduce such social or socialized solutions to these problems. How would Harper and James answer such claims?

[From] *The Law of Torts*

FOWLER HARPER AND FLEMING JAMES

Accidents, Fault, and Social Insurance

* * *

. . . We have seen above the sort of studies that have recently been made concerning the causes of accidents, and the findings concerning accident proneness. It will be well at this time to examine some of the possible implications of these studies and their conclusions for the fault principle of liability. This of course should be done in the light of the possible objectives which a rational system of accident liability should serve. These, we have noted, are: (1) the moral objective; (2) compensation of accident victims; (3) prevention of accidents and promotion of safety; (4) avoidance of undue collateral disadvantages such as the overburdening of desirable activity. Possible implications of the recent studies for the fault principle will be treated under these heads.

1. *The moral objective.* The fault principle is sought to be justified in part by the inherent fairness of imposing liability on him who has been guilty of some personal moral shortcoming (here generally negligence) and of shielding from liability the man who has been free from blame. This is a kind of moral objective — an attempt to equate legal liability to the culpability of the individual participants in the accident. Of course, the legal standard of conduct is largely external and does not take into account the actor's personal equation with the result that legal fault does not entirely coincide with moral fault. But apologists of the present system justify it on the ground that by and large the two do coincide. The tendency of the recent studies, however, has been to cut down the importance of personal moral shortcoming as a factor in causing accidents and to do so in many cases where the "layman's common sense" would find something to blame. To be sure, personal fault is not entirely ruled out, but the scope of personal blameworthiness has been very drastically narrowed. This means either one of two things. If liability continues to be broadly imposed for substandard conduct the system will be ever harder to justify on any notion of its general correspondence with personal blame. If, on the other hand, the fault principle is carried to its logical conclusion (so that liability is imposed only where there is personal blame) liability will become more and more restricted and the cost of more and more accidents will be thrown on the victims. What has been said does not at all necessarily lead to the conclusion that accident law should abandon a moral objective. It does show that the existing system as presently administered largely lacks the moral justification which is often claimed for it. But the conclusion to be drawn from this showing is not that the fault basis should be perpetuated without regard to morals, but rather that other and broader moral considerations call for an entirely different system of liability (namely a wise distribution of accident losses over society, without regard to fault, as under workmen's compensation laws).

* * *

2. *Compensation of accident victims.* The present system recognizes this too as one of its objectives and awards compensatory damages whenever that may be done without offending its premises as to morality, as by making a blameless man pay damages, or as to expediency, as by unduly inhibiting desirable conduct. But we have just seen how the recent studies have narrowed the sphere of culpability and how this would cause a great restriction of liability if many accident-prone but morally blameless people are not to be held liable. This would mean, in turn, that a greatly increased number of victims would go uncompensated. The recent studies thus emphasize sharply the essential conflict between refining the fault principle and compensating accident victims. Of course, as we shall see, the existing rules are now and could continue to be administered so as to *conceal* this dilemma, e.g., by the use of an external standard of conduct for defendants; but this goes a long way toward an aban-

donment of the moral justification of the fault principle.

That does not, of course, end the matter, for even if personal culpability should be disregarded altogether, the present system could perhaps be justified on the ground of expediency. The claims of the injured innocent are meritorious and will be satisfied where the injury is caused by *unreasonably dangerous* conduct, for such conduct, by hypothesis, involves danger out of proportion to its social worth. But the exaction of compensation from one whose conduct is *not unreasonably dangerous* would impose an undue burden on desirable, affirmative activity which would be out of proportion to the benefit conferred on victims. The line which separates these two kinds of conduct, then, is the expedient one to draw between liability and nonliability for injury, since it combines a considerable incentive toward safety and a minimum of interference with desirable enterprise. In view of this possible contention, let us see what implications the recent studies have for the argument from expediency.

3. *The deterrence of conduct which causes accidents.* The fault principle is sought to be justified in part on the ground that it does not burden all affirmative activity but only that which is unreasonably dangerous thereby combining a considerable incentive toward safety with a minimum of interference with desirable enterprises. Now it is clear that the results of the recent studies will themselves tend to promote safety and reduce accidents under *any* system of liability. The question is whether the tendency to do so will be greater if the fault principle is retained, or if the principle of strict liability is substituted for it. We believe that the tendency would be stronger under a system of strict liability.

In the first place the recent studies emphasize the extent to which large units (such as transportation companies, the government, insurance companies, and the like) are in a strategic position to reduce accidents; and conversely, they emphasize the relatively insignificant part which the individual's conscious free choice or will plays in causing or preventing many types of accidents. This is shown in several ways. For one thing the studies themselves have been undertaken or pushed by such large units. Then, their results have been put into practical operation by large enterprises or groups and to a considerable

extent this is inevitable because the tests and findings have maximum validity when applied on a broad statistical basis. On the other hand the individual is often unaware of the fact he is accident-prone, or of the factors which lead to his accident proneness, or of the kind of training or treatment or precaution that his case requires. Indeed, as we have seen, the individual may be quite helpless to prevent some of his own accident-producing behavior (such as that which is compulsive), so that it would be altogether idle to expect the fear of paying damages to deter it.

Secondly, a system of absolute liability tends to increase the pressure toward accident prevention on large groups and enterprises, where we have seen it will do the most good, rather than on the individual, where it will do relatively little good. This is so for three reasons: (a) large units are involved in many accidents and appear often as defendants, rarely as claimants; (b) even where the accident is caused by an individual while acting for himself, in his aspect as potential defendant he is increasingly becoming covered by liability insurance, so that the pressure of increased liability is put in the first instance on the insurance company; (c) the abolition of the defense of contributory negligence — which usually accompanies a shift to absolute liability — clearly adds a further incentive to safety on the part of perennial defendants, and if there is a corresponding loss of incentive (which is not at all clear) it is on the part of the individuals who are potential accident victims.

Since the large business or governmental unit is in a far better position to reduce accidents than is the isolated individual, and since absolute liability puts added pressure to reduce accidents on the large unit, it follows that absolute liability will be a greater spur to safety than a system of less strict liability. "If the law requires a perfect score in result, the actor is more likely to strive for that than if the law requires only the ordinary precautions to be taken."[1] Available facts substantiate theory rather dramatically. Not only were the recent studies themselves undertaken by large units, but they were in the main undertaken because of the increased liability put upon such units by workmen's compensation acts. Moreover, the drop in the industrial fatality rate since the passage of those acts has been truly remarkable — it was cut in half between the two wars.

4. *Avoidance of undue collateral disadvantages such as the overburdening of desirable activity.* Perhaps the heaviest artillery which the proponents of the fault principle can muster is the contention that any stricter rule of liability will discourage affirmative activity and unduly fetter desirable enterprise. If this were true, it would constitute a pragmatic objection to a scheme of absolute liability which would certainly deserve serious consideration. But like so many appeals to practical common sense this one probably rests on no solid foundation of fact but simply on a bald assertion of plausible error. If a system of absolute liability involves fixed limitations on the amount to be recovered, as in the case of workmen's compensation, it may actually cost little or no more than a system where liability is for negligence as determined by a jury without limitation on the amount. In any event there is small reason to claim that the advent of workmen's compensation has had any effect in checking the phenomenal advances in applied science and industry which have taken place since that time. On the contrary, there is good reason to believe that any pressure which the stricter liability has exerted has spurred the businessman's ingenuity to find new devices and new ways of doing things which have at the same time cut down accidents and also increased productive efficiency. The coupling of these results will not be merely sporadic and accidental. Aside from any question of civil liability, accidents are costly to employers and disrupt production, and on the whole the cost of devices and techniques for avoiding them will be more than offset by the elimination of this waste and disruption. The recent studies show that the type of behavior which produces accidents is often inefficient behavior from the point of view of production, even where it does not actually succeed in bringing about an accident; and they illustrate how effective efforts toward safety may serve the end of productivity as well. More broadly they illustrate how the fear of greater accident liability tends not to discourage but actually to foster the most useful kind of productive activity.

* * *

. . . Beginning with workmen's compensation in 1910 and getting great impetus from the depression of the 1930's, social insurance legislation has grown apace in America. Such legislation is based on a faith that the general welfare is best served by protecting individuals from the consequences of pecuniary loss through such vicissitudes of life as accident, old age, sickness, and unemployment. The chief pecuniary losses are destruction of earning power and the expenses of medical care and cure and rehabilitation. Under these schemes, such losses are met (or partly met) without regard to questions of personal fault in causing them and are distributed over a wide segment of society. So much all this legislation has in common, but beyond this there are differences. The broadest possible scheme would largely disregard the source of loss and distribute its cost either by general taxation or by tax contributions levied at a flat rate upon a very large group (e.g., all employers). The philosophy of workmen's compensation, on the other hand, is that losses should be allocated to the enterprise that creates the hazards that cause the losses, and ultimately distributed among those who consume its products. Under such a system there is room for private insurance, and most of our states permit it to be handled that way. Still a third type of scheme seeks to distribute its costs among its beneficiaries, much as voluntary accident or health insurance does. And these variant notions are often found in combination. The trend in England has been toward the more socialized type of contributory system, that in this country toward the more individualized type, at least in fields which lend themselves to such treatment, e.g., workmen's compensation and unemployment compensation.

§13.2. *Comparison with fault principle.* Where this principle finds expression in a system which puts initial liability on the individual members of a group engaged in a risk-creating enterprise, it suggests similarities to the older liability for trespass. In both there is strict liability without regard to fault. Jeremiah Smith called workmen's compensation acts "a distinct reversion to earlier conceptions that he who causes harm, however innocently, is, as its author, bound to make it good."[2] On the other hand social insurance certainly rejects the limitations of the fault principle and it has for that reason been condemned as "offending the sense of justice."[3] The truth is that social insurance, even in its typically American individualized form, is a fundamentally different thing from either trespass or negligence. Formerly tort liability under either principle was looked on as shifting a loss that had already occurred from one individual to another—generally from the person who suffered it to the person who caused it.

It is against the background of this way of looking at things that nearly all of our conventional reasoning about the objectives of tort law has developed and that nearly all of our conclusions have been drawn and our rules formulated. But society has no interest in the mere shifting of a loss between individuals just for the sake of shifting it. The loss, by hypothesis, has already happened. A has been killed, or his leg broken or his automobile smashed up. If the only question is whether B shall be made to pay for this loss, any good that may come to society from having compensation made to one of its members is exactly offset by the harm caused by taking that amount away from another of its members. In that view of the problem there had to be some additional reason for a defendant to compensate a plaintiff for his injury before society would compel compensation. As we have seen, these reasons might be (1) a feeling of what is fair or just; (2) a desire to discourage dangerous conduct, or of course a combination of both. Now the trespass principle probably represents a fairly primitive sense of fairness, and the negligence principle embodies the morality of individualism and laissez faire. But in each case matters of fairness or deterrence were all considered on the assumption that plaintiff and defendant were alone involved and that what happened between them was the real issue—that tort liability was paid for out of the defendant's own pocketbook. This focused attention on the moral quality of the conduct of the individual participants in the accident. As the earlier, mechanical imputation of blame to any injurious activity gave way, the result came to be the general principle of no liability without fault as we know it today.

There is however an altogether different approach to tort law. Human failures in a machine age cause a large and fairly regular—though probably reducible—toll of life, limb, and property. The most important aspect of these failures is not their moral quality; frequently they involve little or nothing in the way of personal moral shortcoming. The really important problems they pose are, rather, those of accident prevention and concern

for the welfare of the victims. According to the view we are discussing, the problem of decreasing the accident toll can best be solved through the pressure of safety regulations with penal and licensing sanctions, and of self-interest in avoiding the host of nonlegal disadvantages that flow from accidents. But when this is all done, human losses remain. It is the principal job of tort law today to deal with these losses. They fall initially on people who as a class can ill afford them, and this fact brings great hardship upon the victims themselves and causes unfortunate repercussions to society as a whole. The best and most efficient way to deal with accident loss, therefore, is to assure accident victims of substantial compensation, and to distribute the losses involved over society as a whole or some very large segment of it. Such a basis for administering losses is what we have called social insurance.

This at once brings in an important new element. For while no social good may come from the mere shifting of a loss, society does benefit from the wide and regular distribution of losses, taken alone. The administration of losses in this way may entirely change evaluations of what is fair. If a certain type of loss is the more or less inevitable by-product of a desirable but dangerous form of activity it may well be just to distribute such losses among all the beneficiaries of the activity though it would be unjust to visit them severally upon those individuals who had happened to be the faultless instruments causing them.

Another difference between social insurance and older notions of liability concerns the assurance of compensation wherever there is liability. This is an integral part of the newer concept; formerly it was considered quite outside the scope of tort law.

To sum up: a scheme of social insurance involves (1) liability without fault (within the field of its operation), (2) an assurance that the amount of compensation theoretically due under the system will in fact be paid, and (3) a wide, regular and equitable distribution of losses under the system.

* * *

§13.5. *Effect of liability insurance on accident prevention.* There is another way in which the fact of widely held insurance may have affected the practical operation of tort law. One of the traditional objectives of tort law has been to deter unreasonably dangerous conduct and to promote the taking of reasonable precautions. If an individual actor must pay for the cost of his carelessness out of his own pocket, the way in which this works is pretty plain to be seen. But how does insurance affect this? In what types of situations, if any, does it dilute the deterrent effect of liability upon the individual? Does this dilution tend to foster irresponsibility, or are there countervailing forces brought into play which promote accident prevention—perhaps even more than the fear of individual liability would do? In this inquiry one thing should be kept constantly in mind. Accident prevention is not the only aim of tort law, and tort liability is not the only incentive to accident prevention. If anything leads to more adequate care of injured people and their dependents, it may be justified on that ground alone. Those aspects of tort law in operation which lead to the compensation and wide distribution of losses should be judged favorably, and extended, unless they actually bring about an increase in the accident rate. What then are the factors in the present situation which make for care or for carelessness?

In the first place it is obvious that fear of legal liability is not the only thing that spurs a man on to be careful. There are many situations, for instance, where one's negligence is likely to bring physical injury upon himself, as well as upon others. This is true of some of the commonest cases, such as driving an automobile, where the individual takes an active part in the situation at the time it is dangerous. In other types of situations, to be sure, a man's negligent conduct carries no real threat of bodily harm to himself either because of the nature of the case or because the man is acting through an agent. And, of course, a corporation cannot suffer this kind of injury. Even where the fear of personal bodily harm is absent, however, there are incentives to care. Accidents disrupt the normal processes of individual or business life. They often destroy valuable property. They are apt to cost money in collateral ways, quite apart from any question of possible damages. They may create bad public relations, or bad labor relations. Sometimes they threaten injury to a member of the family, or to a productive employee. And sometimes they involve the threat of criminal liability. Then, too,

the simply humanitarian impulses furnish at least some people with a motive to take precautions for the safety of others. Another thing should be noted. In situations of employment, agency, and the like, there are usually two sets of incentives at work: for the employer, those last mentioned; for the employee, the risk of personal injury and also the fear of discipline for a job badly done.

The factors referred to above operate quite independently of liability for civil damages. But the fear of such damages may afford some additional incentive to be careful, and the next questions are whether liability insurance appreciably dilutes this effect and whether it promotes or detracts from safety in other ways. The direct evidence on the first point is worth little. No doubt the protection given by insurance makes some individuals callous and every now and then a man will admit as much in his own case. But no one has measured how widespread such a reaction is. There are, however, certain facts which can be known and which shed considerable light on the net effect which the institution of liability insurance has on the matter of accident prevention. They are as follows:

(1) Insurance has made direct contributions to the work of accident prevention. The wide combination of risks has brought together large aggregations of capital. This has put the insurance companies in a strategic position effectively to carry out programs to promote safety. . . . Some such companies and organizations have very extensive technical and engineering staffs which devote all their time in well-directed and expert efforts along this line. This is the sort of service that only the largest industrial concerns could perform at all effectively if they had to do it for themselves. It includes analysis of past accidents generally, and of specific current accidents, to determine whether they disclose defects in supervision, equipment, or in the habits or states of mind of workers. It also includes inspection of equipment and survey of operations to discover in advance defects, practices, personal factors, and the like, which are dangerous, and the working out of devices, rules, and arrangements which will minimize the danger. In some lines of insurance, the amount of money spent on accident prevention exceeds the amount paid for losses.

The insurance companies and organizations

have also cooperated actively with other groups engaged in safety promotion, and have contributed materially to the education of the general public along this line.

(2) Insurance companies can and do adjust their rates and select their risks so as to furnish an incentive toward safety. Over-all rates in any field reflect over-all losses. And the latter are, of course, very much affected by the accident rate (among other factors). Probably there is a rather vague general realization of this relationship and it may afford some slight motive to be careful, but the effect of any individual's conduct on the general rate structure is so little that the motive can hardly be strong.

There are several ways, however, in which rating practices have rewarded or penalized individual assureds for their own safety records. Large risks are being increasingly written on an experience basis so that the rate for each more or less reflects the loss experience encountered on that risk itself. And before the war there was in wide use one form or another of a safe-driver reward plan for individual automobile owners. These have been pretty generally abandoned, largely it seems because of the administrative difficulties they entailed. But in this and other fields, companies do exert an influence for safety by rejecting risks which have had bad experience or accepting them only at higher premiums.

(3) Great strides toward safety have been made in many fields where insurance is widely held. This is notably true in the case of elevators, boilers, and machinery. Here, as one writer puts it, "the [insurance] rates have long been based largely upon the cost of accident prevention. The result of that work is a degree of safety little short of phenomenal."[4] And industrial accidents generally have sharply declined in the course of a generation. During the first World War there were in this country some 36,000 industrial fatalities a year. During the last war, although output was stepped up as never before, annual industrial deaths were held to about 17,000. In the field of aviation, some of the pioneer safety work has been claimed by insurance companies.

Automobile accidents, on the other hand, continue to occur at an alarming rate. Probably here, in the case of the individual car owner at any rate, the insurance companies have less effective leverage to implement their safety campaigns than in the case of larger risks where many operations are under the control of a single insured whose premiums vary with his loss experience. On the other hand, motor accident statistics contain no indication that the presence of insurance makes accident rates go up. Indeed, accident records are better on the whole in states where there is a relatively high proportion of insured owners.

The foregoing facts point to the following inferences: (1) in many fields the practical operation of liability insurance has been definitely to promote safety rather than foster carelessness, (2) in fields such as automobile and personal liability insurance the insurance companies have less effective means at their disposal to promote safety and their success in doing so is less readily demonstrable. On the other hand, there is no significant evidence to show that insurance protection leads to increased carelessness. And the insurance companies are engaging in these fields too in efforts to promote safety which in the long run will probably have material effect. All in all, therefore, it is safe to conclude that the benefits of social insurance which come even under the present law through the operation of liability insurance are not offset by any encouragement of irresponsibility. On the contrary, there has probably been some concomitant net gain in accident prevention. Moreover, there is no reason to expect any threat to safety from further extensions of the insurance principle in the field of accidents. It is clear that the liability-without-fault aspect of social insurance (if considered alone) will be a greater incentive to safety on the part of potential defendants than a system of liability for negligence only. In this connection it should be noted that the recent studies of safety were spurred to a considerable extent by the absolute liability provisions of workmen's compensation laws.

NOTES

1 Seavey, "Speculations as to 'Respondent Superior,'" in Harv. Legal Essays, pp. 433, 447 (1934) . . .

2. Sequel to Workmen's Compensation Acts, 27 Harv. L. Rev. 235, 246 (1914).

3. Holmes, *The Common Law* (1881), p. 96.

4. Sawyer, Retooling Casualty Insurance, 45 Best's Ins. News, No. 9, p. 37 (Fire & Cas. ed. 1945).

Ideas for Class Projects, Papers, or Debates

1. How careful must we be toward one another? What does due care require? What would a reasonable, prudent person do? Compare Judge Andrews' opinion with Judge Cardozo's in the *Palsgraf* case as to the nature of duty in negligence. Defend one opinion and answer the objections raised by the other.

2. Evaluate the *Polemis* case on causation and liability for negligence. As an alternative consider the rat poison case set out in the Notes and Questions for *Polemis*. In either case should the negligent party be held liable? Why or why not?

3. Should tort law recognize liability for the failure to aid in an emergency? Review the article on Good Samaritan statutes following these questions. Suppose that your state adopted the model statute on the last page of the article. You, as a state judge, have the discretion to decide whether to recognize liability for the failure to assist. You may decide (a) never to recognize such liability or (b) sometimes to recognize it. If you decide never to allow it, explain why. If you decide sometimes to allow it, explain when or on what grounds.

4. Does a person's mental state determine the level of fault? For example, is intentional action worse than recklessness? A few years ago the Ford Motor Company continued making Pintos with defective gas tanks, knowing that a certain number of people would be killed as a result of the defect, but certainly not intending this result. Suppose there are two executive officers of the Ford Motor Company. Executive Officer Q made the decision to proceed with the manufacture of defective cars, knowing that a significant number of people would be killed, but also knowing that the decision could not be traced to any individual within the corporation. Executive Officer P ordered a hit man to eliminate a competitor for a highly lucrative position, knowing that the order could not be traced. As a result of Q's order many people will be killed. P orders only one killing. Q is reckless. P is a murderer. Who is more blameworthy, and why?

5. Should tort law be sharply restricted? Some people feel that tort liability is out of control, especially for personal injury and malpractice, where million dollar lawsuits have exacerbated the rising cost of medicine and insurance. It is claimed that we are facing a litigation crisis. Would it be better to eliminate liability for ordinary negligence in these two areas (personal injury and malpractice), moving to systems like those suggested by Harper and James and limiting tort liability to gross (or extreme) negligence or wanton disregard? Why or why not?

[From] *Statutes Establishing a Duty to Report Crimes or Render Assistance to Strangers: Making Apathy Criminal*

SUSAN J. HOFFMAN

III. Statutes Imposing a Duty to Render Assistance

Vermont was the first state to enact legislation establishing a duty to rescue strangers in peril.[1] The statute requires:

A person who knows that another is exposed to grave physical harm shall, to the extent that the same can be rendered without danger or peril to himself or without interference with important duties to others, give reasonable assistance to the exposed person unless that assistance or care is being provided by others.[2]

Minnesota recently adopted a statute which is basically similar to this provision.[3] In contrast to this limited amount of legislation in the United States, many European countries have criminal statutes imposing a duty of rescue.[4] Thus, a complete analysis of the problems involved with such legislation should make reference to the European statutes as well as the American laws.

A. Statutory Requirements

As with the crime reporting legislation, vagueness is a central problem in statutes that impose a duty to render assistance. Persons must have fair notice of what acts or omissions are prohibited under the law. With the Vermont and Minnesota statutes, the meanings of many elements of the offense are uncertain.

A statute should clearly state what type of danger an individual must be in before a duty of rescue arises. The Vermont and Minnesota statutes are not sufficiently definite as to this matter, simply providing that the person must be "exposed to grave physical harm." Arguably, an alcoholic unconscious in the gutter is exposed to such harm, but probably no one would contend that the drafters of the statute intended it to apply in this kind of situation.

More definite guidelines must be established. For example, some European statutes provide that the responsibility of rescue only exists when there is "sudden and imminent danger to human life."[5] In addition to this language, the term "involuntary" should be included, so that the fortuitous nature of the circumstances would be emphasized.

Additionally, American statutes do not adequately specify the immediacy and degree of risk which will abrogate the duty to aid others. They state that rescue is excused where action would cause "danger or peril to himself [the potential rescuer] or interfere with important duties owed to others."[6] Since the possibility of peril to the rescuer is present in most emergencies, more guidance should be given as to the nature of the risk. In European countries, the degree of risk necessary to relieve the potential rescuer of any duty ranges from an extreme of only danger to the individual's life, to serious danger to him or others, to the other extreme allowing non-compliance with the statute when any risk to the rescuer is involved.[7]

The Minnesota statute also requires that the person be "at the scene of an emergency" before he must render aid. Such a negative definition is frankly useless, as it does nothing to state what is the "scene of an emergency," but merely what is not.

A statute imposing a duty to render assistance should also describe the standard under which a rescuer's actions shall be judged. Both the Vermont and Minnesota statutes use the standard that rescuers must give "reasonable assistance." The Minnesota statute elaborates on this point by stating that reasonable assistance "may include obtaining or attempting to obtain aid from law enforcement or medical personnel." In the European countries, the form of assistance required ranges from personal intervention or obtaining help from others, to only personal intervention, to statutes giving the potential rescuer a choice of giving aid or immediately notifying the proper authorities.[8]

Although a statute using a reasonableness standard is susceptible to varying interpretations, this aspect should withstand a vagueness claim because a more specific statement is not possible. The action required is not capable of exact guidelines, because it will depend upon the infinite range of possible factual circumstances. Additionally, as has been pointed out, this is no more vague than the concept of negligence under tort law, based on what the "reasonable man" would have done in that situation.

A statute of this type should also state who is required to render aid. Both the Vermont and Minnesota statutes limit the offense by requiring knowledge that the endangered person is exposed to grave physical harm. Thus, as with crime reporting statutes, ignorance of the circumstances establishing the duty should be a defense. Vermont imposes the additional statutory requirement that violation of the statute must be willful.

Other defenses are also recognized by the existing statutes. Both cite danger to the potential rescuer as a defense. The Vermont statute also excuses the duty to give assistance when it would interfere with "important duties owed to others" or if "that assistance or care is being provided by others." Other viable common law defenses include mistake, lack of capacity, and impossibility. Since the omissions are prohibited under the statutes without regard to a specific result, there can be no defense predicated on lack of causation.

Finally, both the Vermont and Minnesota laws have provisions limiting the civil liability of rescuers. According to Vermont scholars, this was inserted because of the medical community's fear of malpractice suits. Most states, including Kentucky,[9] have similar enactments, usually restricting liability when aid is given by certain qualified members of the medical profession — the so-called good Samaritan statutes.

B. Civil Versus Criminal Liability

Although the language contained in the Minnesota and Vermont provisions is almost identical, there is a fundamental difference: whereas the Vermont statute is criminal,[10] the Minnesota statute is civil. However, both laws are inadequate because such a statute should contain both civil and criminal elements.[11]

A criminal statute is "the core of any regulatory pattern. It can state the legislature's command most clearly, and its penalties can be keyed more closely than damages to the gravity of the offense." For these reasons, the failure to rescue others in danger should constitute — at least in part — a public wrong.[12] A civil statute giving rise to civil liability is an incomplete remedy.

However, a statute without any civil component would also be lacking.[13] There are some persuasive arguments against imposing civil liability;[14] but the possibility of a monetary award is a powerful incentive for an individual to bring charges in an area where prosecutors may be reluctant to do so. Additionally, civil liability can provide an essential deterrent to violation and necessary compensation to victims.

Vermont's criminal statute is silent as to the possibility of resulting tort liability. However, courts could use such a criminal statute as a statement of legislative policy to adopt a civil duty. This has been done in numerous cases which were brought under the European criminal statutes. Ideally, a statute should not be totally silent as to the propriety of civil liability, because courts may conclude that they have no discretion in the matter. Thus, an appropriate provision could state that the legislature expresses no opinion as to the desirability of civil liability, and that expansion in this area is solely within the discretion of the courts.

C. Effectiveness

Even if duty to aid statutes are enacted, there is no guarantee that, as a practical matter, they can be effective enough to accomplish results. Although initially the Vermont statute was viewed as landmark legislation, one commentator has noted that since the statute's enactment in 1967, there has been only one decision construing it, and no prosecutions under it. However, numerous prosecutions have been reported under the European statutes. It is thus possible that a statute establishing a duty to render assistance to others in danger could be effective, if prosecutorial reluctance could be overcome.

The unjustifiably low penalties under the Vermont and Minnesota statutes may contribute to a lack of enforcement. The maximum sanction under both is a $100 fine. Such a meager penalty could be viewed as evidence that the legislature itself does not take the offense seriously. A higher fine, combined with a possible prison term, would give a statute more force and emphasize to prosecutors that the legislature is concerned enough to back the offense with substantial penalties.

Additionally, if more states pass criminal statutes, the power of these laws, as both statements and shapers of public opinion, will probably convince prosecutors to consider statutory violations more worthy of enforcement. The Rhode Island experience is encouraging in this regard, as the state instituted a prosecution within months of enacting the crime reporting statute.

D. Policy Considerations

The basic problem with offenses establishing a duty of rescue is whether the advantage to be gained in the prevention of crime and apprehension of dangerous persons outweighs the threat to individual freedom posed by the imposition of the duty. It is contended that morality cannot be legislated, and that attempting to do so will deprive rescue of its altruistic nature. It is further contended that the responsibility for keeping peace should be exclusively in the police force,[15] and that such a duty would violate privacy interests by encouraging "officious intermeddling." On the other hand, it has been argued that individualistic concerns must be subordinated to laws for the common benefit, that the practical difficulties of such a statute are no more serious than in other areas of the law, and that a legal duty would promote rescue efforts.

These are the policy arguments which the Kentucky legislature would have to confront in deciding whether to enact a statute imposing some duty to render assistance to strangers. To gain some indication of what citizens in Lexington, Kentucky, might think about this issue, a question was submitted for the non-scientific poll at a local television station. The question was: "Should persons who see a crime be required to report it to the police?" The response rate was 47.9% "yes" and 52.1% "no." Of course, the survey lacks reliability, but it is interesting to note.

Conclusion

If Kentucky were to consider enacting a crime reporting statute or a statute establishing a duty to render assistance to persons in danger, the primary concern would be to draft the laws carefully enough to avoid constitutional attack under the void for vagueness doctrine. A crime reporting statute should contain a knowledge requirement and should also state with particularity the following: (1) the crimes which give rise to the duty to report; (2) the persons who are subject to the duty; (3) the time period within which witnesses must report the crime; (4) the order of prosecution; (5) the consequences of witness cooperation; (6) the available defenses; and (7) the exceptions to the statute based upon privileged communications. Additionally, the statute should not leave the decision to prosecute to the victim's discretion.

A model crime reporting statute might read as follows:

(1) Any person, who knows or has reason to know that a murder, rape, kidnapping, robbery or arson has been or is being committed, must notify law enforcement authorities within 24 hours of learning that such crime has been committed.

    (a) In a prosecution under (1) of this statute, the witness may be tried before the trial of the accused felon.

    (b) For purposes of the reporting requirement under (1), a victim of rape shall not be considered a witness.

    (c) Voluntary testimony for the state by any person violating the reporting duty under (1) in any prosecution against the accused felon shall authorize the court to waive his or her penalty under (f).

    (d) Any person making a good faith report pursuant to this statute shall be exempt from civil liability for acts which do not constitute gross negligence.

    (e) Compliance with (1) is not required in the following cases: [here list all applicable defenses and privileges].

    (f) Violation of the reporting requirement in (1) is punishable by a fine of up to $1,000 and/or one year imprisonment.

In connection with a statute establishing a duty to render assistance, the legislation should specifically state: (1) when the duty arises; (2) what degree of risk will abrogate the duty; (3) what action is required; (4) who must give aid; and (5) any statutory defenses.

A model statute requiring aid to others in peril might state:

(1) A person who knows that another is involuntarily in sudden and imminent danger of serious bodily harm or death shall, to the extent that assistance can be rendered without risk of serious bodily injury or death to himself or herself, give reasonable assistance to the endangered person unless that reasonable assistance or care is being provided by others.

    (a) [here insert good Samaritan provision].

    (b) Violation of the duty in (1) is punishable by a fine of up to $1,000 and/or one year imprisonment.

(2) The legislature expresses no opinion as to the desirability of civil liability arising from the criminal statute contained in (1), and expansion in this area is solely within the discretion of the courts.

NOTES

1. *See* VT. STAT. ANN., tit. 12, § 519 (1972 & Supp. 1982) [hereinafter cited as VSA].
2. VSA tit. 12, § 519(a).
3. The statute provides:
Any person at the scene of an emergency who knows that another person is exposed to or has suffered grave physical harm shall, to the extent that he can do so without danger or peril to himself or others, give reasonable assistance to the exposed person. Reasonable assistance may include obtaining or attempting to obtain aid from law enforcement or medical personnel.

MINN. STAT. ANN. § 604.05(1) (West 1984) [hereinafter cited as MSA]. Violation of the statute is a petty misdemeanor, which is defined as "a petty offense which is prohibited by statute, which does not constitute a crime and for which a sentence of a fine of not more than $100 may be imposed." MSA § 609.02(4)(a).

4. For excellent discussions of the duty to rescue under European legal systems, see Dawson, *Rewards for the Rescue of Human Life*, in THE GOOD SAMARITAN AND THE LAW 63 (J. Ratcliffe ed. 1966); Feldbrugge, *Good and Bad Samaritans: A Comparative Survey of Criminal Law Provisions Concerning Failure to Rescue*, 14 AM. J. COMP. L. 630 (1965–66); Linden, *Rescuers and Good Samaritans*, 10 ALBERTA L. REV. 89 (1972); Rudzinski, *The Duty to Rescue: A Comparative Analysis*, in THE GOOD SAMARITAN AND THE LAW 91 (J. Ratcliffe ed. 1966); Tunc, *supra* note 44, at 43; Note, *The Failure to Rescue: A Comparative Study*, 52 COLUM. L. REV. 631 (1952); Note, *Stalking the Good Samaritan: Communists, Capitalists and the Duty to Rescue,* 1976 UTAH L. REV. 529.

5. *See* Rudzinski, *supra* note 4, at 96. The Netherlands, Norway, Denmark, Poland and Czechoslovakia limit the duty of rescue to such cases. Other countries, including Germany, France, Belgium, Italy, Turkey and Hungary, extend the duty to "any serious danger to bodily integrity and health." *Id.* at 98. Portugal limits the rescue obligation to third party attack. *Id.* at 99.

6. *See, e.g.,* MSA § 604.05(1); VSA tit. 12, § 519(a).

7. Rudzinski explains that in Rumania only the risk of life to the potential rescuer excuses his duty, while in Norway, Denmark, Germany, Russia and Belgium, the duty is abrogated by "serious (or special) danger or sacrifice to the person of the potential rescuer or other persons." Rudzinski, *supra* note 4, at 105. "In Portugal and France intervention is obligatory only when no risk for the rescuer is involved; in Portugal he apparently need not even risk his property." *Id.* at 106.

8. "The Netherlands, France and Belgium explicitly require either personal intervention or the obtaining of help from other persons." In Italy, Turkey, Rumania and Russia "the law expressly formulates an alternative duty either to render help *or* to inform immediately the proper authority." Rudzinski, *supra* note 4, at 107–08.

9. The Kentucky Good Samaritan statute provides that certain health professionals are exempt from civil liability for acts performed at the scene of an emergency, unless such acts "constitute willful or wanton misconduct." *See* KRS § 411.148 (1974 & 1982 Supp.). An opinion of the Kentucky Attorney General states, "KRS 411.148, the 'Good Samaritan Act' is in violation of Ky. Const. § 54 to the extent that it limits the liability of persons named therein for death or physical injuries caused by negligent medical treatment rendered without remuneration or the expectation of it." 79 Ky. Op. Att'y Gen. 535 (Oct. 17, 1979). . . .

10. After a lengthy discussion of whether the Vermont statute is civil or criminal, one Vermont scholar concludes that the statute is criminal in view of the penalty and the legislative history. *See* Note, *supra* note 1, at 167–70.

11. Certain consequences are associated with a statute's civil or criminal characterization. A civil statute will not afford a violator the constitutional due process rights of a criminal defendant. . . . Further, the civil/criminal distinction can have a significant impact on the way a complaint is brought. . . .

12. All of the European statutes establishing a duty to rescue are criminal in nature. *See* authorities cited in note 4 *supra*.

13. *But see* D'Amato, *The "Bad Samaritan" Paradigm*, 70 NW. U.L. REV. 798 (1975–76) (noting the "ease of proof under the criminal statute" and the "greater sense of duty it would create" as opposed to civil liability). D'Amato has argued forcefully in favor of a criminal statute imposing a duty of rescue, but against resulting civil liability. He states: (1) such a duty derives not from a personal obligation, but because of interdependence of members of society; (2) the state is "vindicating a public wrong in addition to the victim's private injury"; (3) there is a "universal self-interested basis for criminal legislation" because all citizens can envision themselves in the role of a victim; and (4) prosecutorial discretion safeguards arbitrary and unfair prosecutions. *Id.* at 804–10.

14. D'Amato, *supra* note 13 at 808 ("[I]mposing tort liability gives a monetary reward to risk takers and penalizes risk avoiders."). D'Amato also argues: (1) tort liability has no deterrent effect on judgment proof persons; (2) tort liability is subject to abuse; (3) no moral reason justifies subjecting persons to liability who did not create the risk of injury; and (4) "tort liability would operate as an uneven penalty." *Id.* at 808–09.

15. *See* THE GOOD SAMARITAN AND THE LAW at ix, xiv (J. Ratcliffe ed. 1966) ("Are we to encourage the ordinary citizen to take direct action in the prevention of crime or the apprehension of criminals, after centuries of social development clearly pointing toward the elimination of vigilante action and the concentration of the responsibility for keeping the peace in the hands of public officials?"). For discussion of the police attitude toward Good Samaritans, see Goldstein, *Citizen Cooperation: The Perspective of the Police*, in THE GOOD SAMARITAN AND THE LAW 199, 206–07 (J. Ratcliffe ed. 1966) (refers to failure to cooperate in investigations and prosecutions, and concludes that "[w]e have allowed barriers to develop in our criminal justice system that frustrate the efforts of those city dwellers who do sense a responsibility to cooperate.").

UNIT III

Public Law and the Public Interest

Public law pertains to the people as a whole—to the nation, state, or community at large. As we have seen, law is private if it is initiated and pursued by private parties at their own expense and for their own private ends. It is public if it is initiated and used by public officials at public expense for public benefit.

Placing an area of life in the domain of public law assumes, with regard to that area, an external or public value, a value shared by the community at large. Using recognized law as a guide, we can note that public law includes those areas of law that set out the powers and limits of government (that is, constitutional and administrative law), the prohibitions that the state will enforce at public expense (criminal law), and the methods, processes, and procedures of the legal system itself (that is, procedural law). None of these areas is controversial or hard to justify in the abstract. That is, anyone but an anarchist would agree that a society needs some common law setting out the organization and administration of government, the legal procedures people will use, and the acts prohibited and punished as crimes. The controversy arises over what should fall within these categories. It is obvious that we must have some legal procedures, but not obvious what the procedures should be. It is clear that government must have a constitution—it must be organized and administered in some way, but it is far from clear what should be part of the constitution or how the government should be organized and administered. Certainly any society must protect itself by prohibiting some acts as crimes, but which acts is not so certain.

The question is, What should be assumed or undertaken as a public value and what should be reserved for individual decision making, and how is that reflected in law? Religion, as noted earlier in the Dargo selection, is an example of an area of life that was considered a public matter, a shared and crucial community value. It is now viewed as a matter of individual conscience in this society. In many countries, however, a particular religion is still considered a public value. An official or state church is far from obsolete.

The press is another area that was shifted in this country from the public to the private domain. As with religion, in many other societies the press is controlled or operated by the state for the avowed purpose of protecting the public interest. The press in these countries is a public resource for advancing and protecting public values of many sorts. We may ask again what sorts of factors make an area of life appropriate for public or private control.

In recent years abortion has been a highly polarized issue in precisely this regard. One side feels that abortion is a public matter (in its most extreme form, the crime of murder) that should be regulated by government on behalf of the people. The other side feels that abortion is a private matter that should be decided by individuals or families without government interference. Such examples illustrate that it makes quite a difference how an area of life is regarded. If an area is regarded as a private matter, it will be handled very differently than if it is viewed as a matter of public interest.

The justification for private law is largely pragmatic: People need it to transact their business and to protect their interests. Using tort law as an example, it is clear that victims of intentional or negligent harm could not easily make wrongdoers assume the responsibility for losses they caused if the law did not back up the claims of victims. The justification is the same in all other areas of private law: Contracts would be high-risk undertakings, property would dissolve into possession, corporations would be impossible, and so forth. So the justification for private law is that it is needed in order to enable private individuals to protect themselves and to promote their private interests.

But what is the justification for public law? The most likely candidate for a justification is that public law is necessary to protect the public interest. But what is the public interest? What are the common values to which we are all committed? What goals should be pursued at public expense? Who should decide, and on what grounds?

In Unit II on private law we adopted the pragmatic device of thinking about the public interest in terms of the state interest as determined by government officials. This approach, as we have seen, can be useful for certain purposes. It points to the fact that the public interest is the common good or the welfare of the community at large, as opposed to that of any subgroup, minority, or special interest. The state interest is the interest of the whole. Furthermore, it reminds us of the practical fact that decisions regarding the public interest are made by government officials: administrators, legislators, and judges. Very seldom — only in cases of popular vote on referendums — would the people as a whole directly make a decision of public policy.

This answers, at least on a superficial level, one of our questions: Who determines the public interest? Government officials decide what is in the public interest. In a representative democracy they are supposed to do this as representatives of the people. Of course, we have already examined the problem of understanding what constitutes representation. Whatever else may be involved, representation must include the promotion of the public interest or the common good.

In fact, all governments are justified, if at all, as necessary to promote and protect the common good. As Aristotle pointed out, no government can be justified as promoting the good of the governors, even if that is what it does in fact. Kings, dictators, or central committees must promote the common good to be legitimate. But that still leaves us with the question, What is the common good or the public interest?

As a starting point we can note that the public interest is not self-evident, although it is often treated as though it were. On the other hand, it is not totally a matter of subjective preference either. To claim that something is in the public interest is not just the same as to say, "I like it." Criteria must be met that substantiate the claim. Such a claim can be supported or disputed. We can make the claim and be wrong about it. So, although we use the term *public interest* to commend, it is not simply an expression of personal preference. But we should not expect a single, all-inclusive, once-for-all-time answer either. Determining the public interest will always be a subject of controversy.

We have established one starting point, and that is that the public interest refers to the community at large. The term *public* in this context refers to the whole, to the entire society or piece of society that is relevant to the issue being decided. This is clearly the meaning of the term *public*. Yet the meaning of the phrase *public interest* is difficult to pin down.

In fact, some scholars have given up on the usefulness of the phrase altogether, concluding that it has no clear, accurate meaning. While it is a useful rhetorical device in politics and a powerful tool of propaganda, according to this disillusioned view, the phrase ought to be abandoned by scholars and political scientists who aspire to anything approaching accuracy. But others have argued that while the concept may be a difficult one, it is not devoid of meaning. It has been pointed out that the term is used as a general commendation for a given public policy (in this sense rather like the term *good*), but in addition it performs a function that can affect the choice of policies and the political process itself. Why is that? It is because the term *public interest* does mean something. It means common good or general welfare, as opposed to private, special-interest, or personal welfare. Thus, a politics of public interest signals a commitment to the community at large and assumes that certain interests are common to the well-being of the whole community. But is this just fallacious thinking? Are there any interests that are common to all individuals, especially in a pluralistic society? And if there are, what are they?

It has been claimed that there are no genuine common interests. There are, however, arguments against this extreme position. Presumably, no one would support a program of universal self-annihilation. No one in the United States, for example, could rationally agree that the President should signal the military to use our nuclear weapons to devastate the entire surface of our country with all its artifacts and inhabitants, including the military. (Somebody might be happy with this plan, but not the inhabitants of the United States.) Why not? Presumably such a plan would be against everybody's interest. There is, then, a common interest in opposing common self-destruction. Thus, at least one counterexample can easily be found, and perhaps others as well.

Can anyone seriously claim that it is not a common interest to prevent violent acts such as murder, robbery, rape, or assault? Someone might say that preventing murder is not in the interest of the murderer. But in fact it is. Insofar as a murderer could also be the victim of a murder, then it is in his interest that murder be prevented.

The same kind of argument is sometimes made about freedom and justice before the law (or nondiscrimination). That is, freedom and justice are values often put forward as obviously in the public interest. But in response it is sometimes argued that although it may be in my own interest to be free, it would be even more in my interest if I were free and all the rest of you were my slaves. Similarly, justice is fine but privilege is better. Injustice is opposed to your interest only if it works against you. If it works in your favor it is called a special advantage. Thus, justice and freedom are not common interests, because the powerful and privileged do better without them.

But there are problems with this argument as well. First, it is not obviously true that the powerful and privileged would do better, any more than it is clear that the murderer would do better without laws against murder. Eroding commitment to such basic values as freedom and justice sets up highly unstable circumstances that tend to disintegrate to everyone's disadvantage. A Hobbesian war of all against all knocks out the strong along with the weak sooner or later. Therefore basic values of freedom, justice, and security cannot be flaunted openly.

The special advantage argument, then, can be maintained only by secret rule breakers, by deception. The general commitment to basic values is still a common interest even for the rule breakers. And once you allow special advantage, there is the nasty problem of making sure that you are among the advantaged rather than the disadvantaged.

A second problem with the special-advantage argument is that it fails to take account of the fact that something might be against an individual's interest and still be in the public interest. As a murderer it is not in my interest to have laws against murder enforced against me, but as a member of the public it is in my interest to have such laws. As a homeowner it is not in my personal interest to have a highway built that requires the condemnation of my property, but as a member of the public it is in my interest to have highways built — it may even be in my interest to have that particular highway built. Even if a policy or particular decision works against some individual or small group — whether advantaged or disadvantaged — it is not for that reason against the public interest. Public interest is calculated from the viewpoint of the community at large.

It appears, therefore, that so long as we are talking about abstract, general values — freedom, justice, security, unity, prosperity — these are common interests, and the public law is intended to protect them. The real question is not whether these values are in the public interest. Anyone who denies that has a difficult burden of proof to support. Rather, the real question is how these values (and thus the public interest) are best promoted and coordinated.

Governments, or individuals, for that matter, cannot promote a value as such. They promote or prohibit actions or policies on the basis of value judgments about those actions or policies. Sometimes the connections between actions (or policies) and values are clear, making goals clear. For example, violent actions clearly impede the value of security. Consider the reaction of people in a neighborhood in which violence is common: Fear and insecurity become prevalent. Thus, preventing violent crime becomes a clear goal.

Even where the goal is clear, how best to pursue the goal may not be so clear. The reason is that, first, there is usually more than one way to pursue any goal, and, second, pursuing one goal (or value) often impairs another. A curfew may reduce crime and thereby promote security, but it also restricts freedom. Higher taxes for more police may reduce crime, but higher taxes reduce the general welfare and potential revenue for other purposes. Higher taxes for better education, training, and jobs might more effectively reduce crime in the long run but not help much in the short run. There are always costs and alternatives. So how to pursue a goal may not be clear even when the goal is clear.

Worse than that, the connections between values and actions or policies are not always clear at all, so the goal itself may not be clear. Furthermore, every goal pursued leaves another undone. Every choice excludes other possible choices, and it is far from obvious how to rank competing goals or competing values. Many theories have been directed to these questions.

Utilitarians have perhaps done the most work on the idea of the public interest, since it is central to their theory of morality. According to utilitarian theory, a morally good act is one that promotes the greatest good for the greatest number of people (in other words, one that is in the common good or public interest), and it is held that the common good is the aggregate of all individual goods. On this basis a number of rather complex economic and noneconomic theories have been worked out on how to determine whether a policy is in the public interest.

The basic theory, however, is a controversial one in many ways, two of which we should note here. First, is the public interest merely the aggregate of all individual interests, or is there something more to it? Can public interest be determined by calculating the sum of all individual interests? It is not clear that this can be done, and even if it can, it is not clear whether important basic values would be preserved this way.

Second, supposing we can determine what the public interest is, how does it relate to individual justice and rights? A great deal of ink has been spilled trying to articulate the relation between the public interest and individual justice. Both values are crucial for a legitimate society, and yet they seem to conflict with one another. How should these two values be understood and correlated or ranked?

Chapter Six employs the law of crime and punishment to examine these issues and some important theories that deal with them. The criminal law is often taken to be a paradigm of public law. It is law that is utilized by public officials at public expense for the public good, yet it is intimately concerned with the requirements of justice. This should also provide a very clear contrast with the private law of torts. See if you can distinguish the fundamental elements and defining features of each.

Chapter Seven considers civil rights as a point of contrast from several directions. Civil rights law contrasts with criminal law in that it provides a guarantee of rights and freedoms rather than prohibitions and restrictions. Civil rights often restrict the state so as to protect individuals, rather than empowering the state to restrict individuals. Public law can do either in the interest of the public good. You will also see a contrast in the protection of freedom and justice offered by the private law of contracts and property, as opposed to the civil rights protection of free speech, privacy, and equal treatment (or equal protection of the law). Finally, interesting comparisons can be made regarding the development of law, court history, and models of adjudication, especially as between contract and privacy law. These issues raise basic questions about the nature and function of courts in public as opposed to private law adjudication. The article by Abram Chayes that follows this introduction lays out these issues, providing the background for our examination of public law. The question is, What are courts supposed to do?

In recent years a variety of social problems have presented themselves for resolution. Environmental issues, education, prison reform, consumer protection, discrimination in many areas of life, social services, and public assistance are just a few. How should such problems be approached? All of them raise issues of structure, process, procedure, and role for all branches of government, and in particular for courts.

The Chayes article discusses the problems raised for a court when it attempts to deal with problems that are apparently public in nature. Chayes contrasts the traditional model of adjudication with a public law model, which he claims is a more accurate description of the actual judicial function, at least a great deal of the time. Is Chayes's view radical? What problem does it raise? Should we revise our views of the proper function of the courts? Or should we deal with modern social problems in a different way? What factors must you consider in order to decide? The Chayes article provides a backdrop for all the issues raised in this unit, by providing a new model of adjudication for public law.

[From] "The Role of the Judge in Public Law Litigation"
ABRAM CHAYES

I. The Received Tradition

The traditional conception of adjudication reflected the late nineteenth century vision of society, which assumed that the major social and economic arrangements would result from the activities of autonomous individuals. In such a setting, the courts could be seen as an adjunct to private ordering, whose primary function was the resolution of disputes about the fair implications of individual interactions. The basic conceptions governing legal liability were "intention" and "fault." Intentional arrangements, not in conflict with more or less universal attitudes like opposition to force or fraud, were entitled to be respected, and other private activities to be protected unless culpable. Government regulatory action was presumptively suspect, and was tested by what was in form a common law action against the offending official in his private person. The predominating influence of the private law model can be seen even in constitutional litigation, which, from its first appearance in *Marbury v. Madison*, was understood as an outgrowth of the judicial duty to decide otherwise-existing private disputes.

Litigation also performed another important function—clarification of the law to guide future private actions. This understanding of the legal system, together with the common law doctrine of stare decisis, focussed professional and scholarly concern on adjudication at the appellate level, for only there did the process reach beyond the immediate parties to achieve a wider import through the elaboration of generally applicable legal rules. So, in the academic debate about the judicial function, the protagonist was the appellate judge (not, interestingly enough, the appellate *court*), and the spotlight of teaching, writing, and analysis was almost exclusively on appellate decisions. In practice, the circle was even more narrowly confined to the decisions of the United States Supreme Court, the English high courts (though decreasingly so in recent years), and a few "influential" federal and state appellate judges. As to this tiny handful of decisions subjected to critical scrutiny, the criterion for evaluation was primarily the technical skill of the opinion in disposing of the case adequately within the framework of precedent and other doctrinal materials, so as to achieve an increasingly more systematic and refined articulation of the governing legal rules.

In contrast to the appellate court, to which the motive power in the system was allocated, the functions of the trial judge were curiously neglected in the traditional model. Presumably, the trial judge, like the multitude of private persons who were supposed to order their affairs with reference to appellate pronouncements, would be governed by those decisions in disposing smoothly and expeditiously of the mine-run of cases. But if only by negative implication, the traditional conception of adjudication carried with it a set of strong notions about the role of the trial judge. In general he was passive. He was to decide only those issues identified by the parties, in accordance with the rules established by the appellate courts, or, infrequently, the legislature.

Passivity was not limited to the law aspects of the case. It was strikingly manifested in the limited involvement of the judge in factfinding. Indeed, the sharp distinction that Anglo-American law draws between factfinding and law declaration is itself remarkable. In the developed common law system, these were not only regarded as analytically distinct processes, but each was assigned to a different tribunal for performance. The jury found the facts. The judge was a neutral umpire, charged with little or no responsibility for the factual aspects of the case or for shaping and organizing the litigation for trial.

Because the immediate impact of the judgment was confined to the parties, the traditional model was relatively relaxed about the accuracy of its factfinding. If the facts were not assumed as stated in the pleadings or on the view most favorable to one of the parties or determined on the basis of burdens or presumptions, they were remitted to a kind of black box, the jury. True, some of the law of evidence reflects an active suspicion of the jury. And if the evidence adduced would not "rationally" support a finding for one party or the other, the case could be taken from the jury. But the limits of rationality are inevitably commodious. Even law application, unless there was a special verdict (never much favored in this country), was left to the jury's relatively untrammeled discretion. Indeed, one of the virtues of the jury was thought to be its exercise of a rough-hewn equity, deviating from the dictates of the law where justice or changing community mores required.

The emphasis on systematic statement of liability rules involved a corresponding disregard of the problems of relief. There was, to be sure, a good deal of discussion of measure of damages, as a corollary to the analysis of substantive rights and duties. Similarly, the question of the availability of specific performance and other equitable remedies came in for a share of attention. But the discussion was carried forward within the accepted framework that compensatory money damages was the usual form of relief. Prospective relief was highly exceptional in the traditional model and was largely remitted to the discretion of the trial judge.

So in theory. But from another perspective, it seems remarkable that the system—and for the most part its critics as well—could attach so much importance to uniformity and consistency of doctrinal statement in appellate opinions, while at the same time displaying an almost complete lack of curiosity about actual uniformity of decision in the vast bulk of cases heard. The realist analysis, which demonstrated the painful inevitability of choice for appellate judges on questions of law, was equally applicable at the trial level. The uncertainties introduced by remitting factfinding and fact characterization to the jury were also ignored. Such factors as differences among potential litigants in practical access to the system or in the availability of litigating resources were not even perceived as problems. Although it was well that particular disputes should be fairly settled, there was comfort in the thought that the consequences of the settlement would be confined to the individuals involved. And since the parties controlled the litigating process, it was not unfair to cast the burden of any malfunction upon them.

Besides its inherent plausibility in the nine-teenth century American setting, the traditional model of adjudication answered a number of important political and intellectual needs. The conception of litigation as a private contest between private parties with only minimal judicial intrusion confirmed the general view of government powers as stringently limited. The emphasis on the appellate function, conceived as an exercise in deduction from a few embracing principles themselves induced from the data of the cases, supplied the demand of the new legal academics for an intellectual discipline comparable to that of their faculty colleagues in the sciences, and for a body of teachable materials. For practitioners and judges, the same conception provided a professional methodology that could be self-consciously employed. Most importantly, the formulation operated to legitimate the increasingly visible political consequences of the actions of a judiciary that was not politically accountable in the usual sense.

II. The Public Law Litigation Model

Sometime after 1875, the private law theory of civil adjudication became increasingly precarious in the face of a growing body of legislation designed explicitly to modify and regulate basic social and economic arrangements. At the same time, the scientific and deductive character of judicial lawmaking came under attack, as the political consequences of judicial review of that legislation became urgent.

These developments are well known and have become an accepted part of our political and intellectual history. I want to address in somewhat greater detail the correlative changes that have occurred in the procedural structure of the lawsuit. Most discussion of these procedural developments, while recognizing that change has been far-reaching, proceeds on the assumption that the new devices are no more than piecemeal "reforms" aimed at improving the functional characteristics or the efficiency of litigation conducted essentially in the traditional mode. I suggest, however, that these developments are interrelated as members of a recognizable, if changing, system and that taken together they display a new model of judicial action and the judicial role, both of which depart sharply from received conceptions.

A. *The Demise of the Bipolar Structure*

Joinder of parties, which was strictly limited at common law, was verbally liberalized under the codes to conform with the approach of equity calling for joinder of all parties having an "interest" in the controversy. The codes, however, did not at first produce much freedom of joinder. Instead, the courts defined the concept of "interest" narrowly to exclude those without an independent legal right to the remedy to be given in the main dispute. The definition itself illustrates the continuing power of the traditional model. The limited interpretation of the joinder provisions ultimately fell before the banners of "rationality" and "efficiency." But the important point is that the narrow joinder rule could be perceived as irrational or inefficient only because of a growing sense that the effects of the litigation were not really confined to the persons at either end of the right-remedy axis.

The familiar story of the attempted liberalization of pleadings under the codes is not dissimilar. Sweeping away the convolutions of the forms of action did not lead to the hoped-for elimination of technicality and formality in pleading. The immediate response was the construction of cause-of-action rules that turned out to be almost as intricate as the forms themselves. The power of the right-remedy connection was at work here too, but so also was the late nineteenth century impulse toward systemization, which tended to focus attention on accurate statement of legal theory. The proponents of "efficiency" argued for a more informal and flexible approach, to the end that the courts should not have to rehear the same complex of events. This argument ultimately shifted the focus of the lawsuit from legal theory to factual context — the "transaction or occurrence" from which the action arose. This in — turn made it easier to view the set of events in dispute as giving rise to a range of legal consequences all of which ought to be considered together.

This more open-ended view of the subject matter of the litigation fed back upon party questions and especially intervention. Here, too, the sharp constraints dictated by the right-remedy nexus give way. And if the right to participate in litigation is no longer determined by one's claim to relief at the hands of another party or one's potential liability to satisfy the claim, it becomes hard to draw the line determining those who may participate so as to eliminate anyone who is or might be significantly (a weasel word) affected by the outcome — and the latest revision of the Federal Rules of Civil Procedure has more or less abandoned the attempt.

The question of the right to intervene is inevitably linked to the question of standing to initiate litigation in the first place. The standing issue could hardly arise at common law or under early code pleading rules, that is, under the traditional model. There the question of plaintiff's standing merged with the legal merits: On the facts pleaded, does this particular plaintiff have a right to the particular relief sought from the particular defendant from whom he is seeking it? With the erosion of the tight structural integration of the lawsuit, the pressure to expand the circle of potential plaintiffs has been inexorable. Today, the Supreme Court is struggling manfully, but with questionable success, to establish a formula for delimiting who may sue that stops short of "anybody who might be significantly affected by the situation he seeks to litigate."

"Anybody" — even "almost anybody" — can be a lot of people, particularly where the matters in issue are not relatively individualized private transactions or encounters. Thus, the stage is set for the class action, which is discussed at length in the remainder of this issue. Whatever the resolution of the current controversies surrounding class actions, I think it unlikely that the class action will ever be taught to behave in accordance with the precepts of the traditional model of adjudication. The class suit is a reflection of our growing awareness that a host of important public and private interactions — perhaps the most important in defining the conditions and opportunities of life for most people — are conducted on a routine or bureaucratized basis and can no longer be visualized as bilateral transactions between private individuals. From another angle, the class action responds to the proliferation of more or less well-organized groups in our society and the tendency to perceive interests as group interests, at least in very important aspects.

The emergence of the group as the real subject or object of the litigation not only transforms the party problem, but raises far-reaching new questions. How far can the group be extended and homogenized? To what extent and by what methods will we permit the presentation of views diverging from that of the group representative? When the judgment treads on numerous — perhaps innumerable — absentees, can the traditional doctrines of finality and preclusion hold? And in the absence of a particular client, capable of concretely defining his own interest, can we rely on the assumptions of the adversary system as a guide to the conduct and duty of the lawyer?

These questions are brought into sharp focus by the class action device. But it would be a mistake to think that they are confined to that procedural setting. The class action is only one mechanism for presenting group interests for adjudication, and the same basic questions will arise in a number of more familiar litigating contexts. Indeed, it may not be too much to say that they are pervasive in the new model.

B. The Triumph of Equity

One of the most striking procedural developments of this century is the increasing importance of equitable relief. it is perhaps too soon to reverse the traditional maxim to read that money damages will be awarded only when no suitable form of specific relief can be devised. But surely, the old sense of equitable remedies as "extraordinary" has faded.

I am not concerned here with specific performance — the compelled transfer of a piece of land or a unique thing. This remedy is structurally little different from traditional money-damages. It is a one-time, one-way transfer requiring for its enforcement no continuing involvement of the court. Injunctive relief, however, is different in kind, even when it takes the form of a simple negative order. Such an order is a presently operative prohibition, enforceable by contempt, and it is a much greater constraint on activity than the risk of future liability implicit in the damage remedy. Moreover, the injunction is continuing. Over time, the parties may resort to the court for enforcement or modification of the original order in light of changing circumstances. Finally, by issuing the injunction, the court takes public responsibility for any consequences of its decree that may adversely affect strangers to the action.

Beyond these differences, the prospective character of the relief introduces large elements of contingency and prediction into the proceedings. Instead of a dispute retrospectively oriented toward the consequences of a closed set of events, the court has a controversy about future probabilities. Equitable doctrine, naturally enough, given the intrusiveness of the injunction and the contingent nature of the harm, calls for a balancing of the interests of the parties. And if the immediate parties' interests were to be weighed and evaluated, it was not too difficult to proceed to a consideration of other interests that might be affected by the order.

The comparative evaluation of the competing interests of plaintiff and defendant required by the remedial approach of equity often discloses alternatives to a winner-takes-all decision. An arrangement might be fashioned that could safeguard at least partially the interests of both parties, and perhaps even of others as well. And to the extent such an arrangement is possible, equity seems to require it. Negative orders directed to one of the parties — even though pregnant with affirmative implications — are often not adequate to this end. And so the historic power of equity to order affirmative action gradually freed itself from the encrustation of nineteenth century restraints. The result has often been a decree embodying an affirmative regime to govern the range of activities in litigation and having the force of law for those represented before the court.

At this point, right and remedy are pretty thoroughly disconnected. The form of relief does not flow ineluctably from the liability determination, but is fashioned ad hoc. In the process, moreover, right and remedy have been to some extent transmuted. The liability determination is not simply a pronouncement of the legal consequences of past events, but to some extent a prediction of what is likely to be in the future. And relief is not a terminal, compensatory transfer, but an effort to devise a program to contain future consequences in a way that accommodates the range of interests involved.

The interests of absentees, recognized to some extent by equity's balancing of the public interest in individual suits for injunction, become more pressing as social and economic activity is increasingly organized through large aggregates of people. An order nominally addressed to an individual litigant—the labor injunction is an early example—has obvious and visible impact on persons not individually before the court. Nor must the form of the action be equitable: A suit against an individual to collect a tax, if it results in a determination of the constitutional invalidity of the taxing statute, has the same result for absentees as a grant or denial of an injunction. Statutory construction, for example of welfare or housing legislation, may have a similar extended impact, again even if the relief is not equitable in form. Officials will almost inevitably act in accordance with the judicial interpretation in the countless similar situations cast up by a sprawling bureaucratic program. We may call this a *stare decisis* effect, but it is quite different from the traditional image of autonomous adjustment of individual private transactions in response to judicial decisions. In cases of this kind, the fundamental conception of litigation as a mechanism for private dispute settlement is no longer viable. The argument is about whether or how a government policy or program shall be carried out.

Recognition of the policy functions of litigation feeds the already intense pressure against limitations on standing, as well as against the other traditional limitations on justiciability—political question, ripeness, mootness and the like. At the same time, the breadth of interests that may be affected by public law litigation raises questions about the adequacy of the representation afforded by a plaintiff whose interest is narrowly traditional.

Again, as in private litigation, the screw gets another turn when simple prohibitory orders are inadequate to provide relief. If a mental patient complains that he has been denied a right to treatment, it will not do to order the superintendent to "cease to deny" it. So with segregation in education, discrimination in hiring, apportionment of legislative districts, environmental management. And the list could be extended. If judicial intervention is invoked on the basis of congressional enactment, the going assumption is that the statute embodies an affirmative regulatory objective. Even when the suit is premised on constitutional provisions, traditionally regarded as constraining government power, there is an increasing tendency to treat them as embodying affirmative values, to be fostered and encouraged by judicial

action. In either case, if litigation discloses that the relevant purposes or values have been frustrated, the relief that seems to be called for is often an affirmative program to implement them. And courts, recognizing the undeniable presence of competing interests, many of them unrepresented by the litigants, are increasingly faced with the difficult problem of shaping relief to give due weight to the concerns of the unrepresented.

C. The Changing Character of Factfinding

The traditional model of adjudication was primarily concerned with assessing the consequences for the parties of specific past instances of conduct. This retrospective orientation is often inapposite in public law litigation, where the lawsuit generally seeks to enjoin future or threatened action, or to modify a course of conduct presently in train or a condition presently existing. In the former situation, the question whether threatened action will materialize, in what circumstances, and with what consequences can, in the nature of things, be answered only by an educated guess. In the latter case, the inquiry is only secondarily concerned with how the condition came about, and even less with the subjective attitudes of the actors, since positive regulatory goals are ordinarily defined without reference to such matters. Indeed, in dealing with the actions of large political or corporate aggregates, notions of will, intention, or fault increasingly become only metaphors.

In the remedial phases of public law litigation, factfinding is even more clearly prospective. As emphasized above, the contours of relief are not derived logically from the substantive wrong adjudged, as in the traditional model. The elaboration of a decree is largely a discretionary process within which the trial judge is called upon to assess and appraise the consequences of alternative programs that might correct the substantive fault. In both the liability and remedial phases, the relevant inquiry is largely the same: How can the policies of a public law best be served in a concrete case?

In public law litigation then, factfinding is principally concerned with "legislative" rather than "adjudicative" fact. And "fact evaluation" is perhaps a more accurate term than "factfinding." The whole process begins to look like the traditional description of legislation: Attention is drawn to a "mischief," existing or threatened, and the activity of the parties and court is directed to the development of on-going measures designed to cure that mischief. Indeed, if, as is often the case, the decree sets up an affirmative regime governing the activities in controversy for the indefinite future and having binding force for persons within its ambit, then it is not very much of a stretch to see it as, *pro tanto*, a legislative act.

Given these consequences, the casual attitude of the traditional model toward factfinding is no longer tolerable. The extended impact of the judgment demands a more visibly reliable and credible procedure for establishing and evaluating the fact elements in the litigation, and one that more explicitly recognizes the complex and continuous interplay between fact evaluation and legal consequence. The major response to the new requirements has been to place the responsibility for factfinding increasingly on the trial judge. The shift was in large part accomplished as a function of the growth of equitable business in the federal courts, for historically the chancellor was trier of fact in suits in equity. But on the "law side" also, despite the Supreme Court's expansion of the federal right to jury trial, there has been a pronounced decline in the exercise of the right, apart, perhaps, from personal injury cases.

The courts, it seems, continue to rely primarily on the litigants to produce and develop factual materials, but a number of factors make it impossible to leave the organization of the trial exclusively in their hands. With the diffusion of the party structure, fact issues are no longer sharply drawn in a confrontation between two adversaries, one asserting the affirmative and the other the negative. The litigation is often extraordinarily complex and extended in time, with a continuous and intricate interplay between factual and legal elements. It is hardly feasible and, absent a jury, unnecessary to set aside a contiguous block of time for a "trial stage" at which all significant factual issues will be presented. The scope of the fact investigation and the sheer volume of factual material that can be exhumed by the discovery process pose enormous problems of organization and assimilation. All these factors thrust the trial judge into an active role in shaping, organizing and facilitating the litigation. We may not yet have reached the investigative judge of the continental systems, but we have left the passive arbiter of the traditional model a long way behind.

D. The Decree

The centerpiece of the emerging public law model is the decree. It differs in almost every relevant characteristic from relief in the traditional model of adjudication, not the least in that it is the centerpiece. The decree seeks to adjust future behavior, not to compensate for past wrong. It is deliberately fashioned rather than logically deduced from the nature of the legal harm suffered. It provides for a complex, ongoing regime of performance rather than a simple, one-shot, one-way transfer. Finally, it prolongs and deepens, rather than terminates, the court's involvement with the dispute.

The decree is also an order of the court, signed by the judge and issued under his responsibility (itself a shift from the classical money judgment). But it cannot be supposed that the judge, at least in a case of any complexity, composes it out of his own head. How then is the relief formulated?

The reports provide little guidance on this question. Let me nonetheless suggest a prototype that I think finds some support in the available materials. The court will ask the parties to agree on an order or it will ask one party to prepare a draft. In the first case, a negotiation is stipulated. In the second, the dynamic leads almost inevitably in that direction. The draftsman understands that his proposed decree will be subject to comment and objection by the other side and that it must be approved by the court. He is therefore likely to submit it to his opponents in advance to see whether differences cannot be resolved. Even if the court itself should prepare the initial draft of the order, some form of negotiation will almost inevitably ensue upon submission of the draft to the parties for comment.

The negotiating process ought to minimize the need for judicial resolution of remedial issues. Each party recognizes that it must make some response to the demands of the other party, for issues left unresolved will be submitted to the court, a recourse that is always chancy and may result in a solution less acceptable than might be reached by horse-trading. Moreover, it will generally be advantageous to the demanding party to reach a solution through accommodation rather than through a judicial fiat that may be performed "in a literally compliant but substantively grudging and unsatisfactory way." Thus, the formulation of the decree in public law litigation introduces a good deal of party control over the practical outcome. Indeed, relief by way of order after a determination on the merits tends to converge with relief through a consent decree or voluntary settlement. And this in turn mitigates a major theoretical objection to affirmative relief—the danger of intruding on an elaborate and organic network of interparty relationships.

Nevertheless it cannot be supposed that this process will relieve the court entirely of responsibility for fashioning the remedy. The parties may fail to agree. Or the agreement reached may fail to comport with the requirements of substantive law as the judge sees them. Or the interests of absentees may be inadequately accommodated. In these situations, the judge will not, as in the traditional model, be able to derive his responses directly from the liability determination, since, as we have seen, the substantive law will point out only the general direction to be pursued and a few salient landmarks to be sought out or avoided. How then is the judge to prescribe an appropriate remedy?

If the parties are simply in disagreement, it seems plausible to suppose that the judge's choice among proposals advanced by the *quondam* negotiators will be governed by his appraisal of their good faith in seeking a way to implement the constitutional or statutory command as he has construed it. The interest in a decree that will be voluntarily obeyed can be promoted by enforcing a regime of good faith bargaining among the parties. Without detailed knowledge of the negotiations, however, any attempt to enforce such a regime can rest on little more than an uneasy base of intuition and impression. Where a proposed decree is agreed among the parties, but is inadequate because the interests shared by the litigants do not span the range that the court thinks must be taken into account, resubmission for further negotiation may not cure this fundamental defect. Here too, the judge will be unable to fill the gap without a detailed understanding of the issues at stake in the bargaining among the parties.

For these reasons, the judge will often find himself a personal participant in the negotiations on relief. But this course has obvious disadvantages, not least in its inroads on the judge's time and his pretentions to disinterestedness. To avoid these problems, judges have increasingly resorted to outside help—masters, amici, experts, panels, advisory committees—for information and evaluation of proposals for relief. These outside sources commonly find themselves exercising mediating and even adjudicatory functions among the parties. They may put forward their own remedial suggestions, whether at the request of the judge or otherwise.

Once an ongoing remedial regime is established, the same procedure may be repeated in connection with the implementation and enforcement of the decree. Compliance problems may be brought to the court for resolution and, if necessary, further remediation. Again, the court will often have no alternative but to resort to its own sources of information and evaluation.

I suggested above that a judicial decree establishing an ongoing affirmative regime of conduct is *pro tanto* a legislative act. But in actively shaping and monitoring the decree, mediating between the parties, developing his own sources of expertise and information, the trial judge has passed beyond even the role of legislator and has become a policy planner and manager.

E. A Morphology of Public Law Litigation

The public law litigation model portrayed in this paper reverses many of the crucial characteristics and assumptions of the traditional concept of adjudication:

(1) The scope of the lawsuit is not exogenously given but is shaped primarily by the court and parties.

(2) The party structure is not rigidly bilateral but sprawling and amorphous.

(3) The fact inquiry is not historical and adjudicative but predictive and legislative.

(4) Relief is not conceived as compensation for past wrong in a form logically derived from the substantive liability and confined in its impact to the immediate parties; instead, it is forward looking, fashioned ad hoc on flexible

and broadly remedial lines, often having important consequences for many persons including absentees.

(5) The remedy is not imposed but negotiated.

(6) The decree does not terminate judicial involvement in the affair: its administration requires the continuing participation of the court.

(7) The judge is not passive, his function limited to analysis and statement of governing legal rules; he is active, with responsibility not only for credible fact evaluation but for organizing and shaping the litigation to ensure a just and viable outcome.

(8) The subject matter of the lawsuit is not a dispute between private individuals about private rights, but a grievance about the operation of public policy.

In fact, one might say that, from the perspective of the traditional model, the proceeding is recognizable as a lawsuit only because it takes place in a courtroom before an official called a judge. But that is surely too sensational in tone. All of the procedural mechanisms outlined above were historically familiar in equity practice. It is not surprising that they should be adopted and strengthened as the importance of equity has grown in modern times.

We have yet to ask how pervasive is the new model. Is it, as was traditional equity, a supplementary weapon in the judicial armory, destined at best for a subordinate role? Is it a temporary, add-on phenomenon, more extensive perhaps, but not more significant than the railroad reorganization functions that the courts assumed (or were given) in other times? Or can we say that the new form has already or is likely to become the dominant form of litigation in the federal courts, either in terms of judicial resources applied to such cases, or in its impact on society and on attitudes toward the judicial role and function?

The question is not wholly quantitative, but certainly it has a quantitative dimension. A crude index for the new model in federal civil litigation is the well-known shift from diversity to federal question cases in the federal courts. Since most of the features I have discussed derive from the fact that public law provides the basis of the action, it seems plausible that litigation in the new model would increase concomitantly with the predominance of federal question jurisdiction. But the quantitative analysis is in patent need of much further development.

On the other hand, qualitatively — that is, in terms of the importance and interest of the cases and their impact on the public perception of the legal system — it seems abundantly clear that public law litigation is of massive and growing significance. The cases that are the focus of professional debate, law review and academic comment, and journalistic attention are overwhelmingly, I think, new model cases. It could hardly be otherwise, since, by hypothesis, these cases involve currently agitated questions of public policy, and their immediate consequences are to a considerable extent generalized.

I would, I think, go further and argue that just as the traditional concept reflected and related to a system in which social and economic arrangements were remitted to autonomous private action, so the new model reflects and relates to a regulatory system where these arrangements are the product of positive enactment. In such a system, enforcement and application of law is necessarily implementation of regulatory policy. Litigation inevitably becomes an explicitly political forum and the court a visible arm of the political process.

CHAPTER SIX

The Nature of Crime and Punishment

Perhaps the clearest and most obvious example of public law is criminal law. As a beginning we will consider the nature of criminal law by making some comparisons with tort law. In the U.S. legal system tort law has its basis in the common law — its origin is in the courts — whereas criminal law is statutory — its origin is in the legislature. This is not a necessary feature of tort or criminal law (they could, for example, be the other way around), but the origin or basis of any area of law is important. Criminal law was once common law in the Anglo-American system, but it came to be felt that criminal law ought to be statutory because it should be clearly specified, defined, and public. That is, it was felt that since no person should be condemned and punished for an act unless it was clear in advance that the act was prohibited, then statutory enactment was probably a better way to establish criminal prohibitions. In the criminal law, then, the courts are confined: Their discretion is limited by legislative enactment that specifies crimes and punishments.

Another important difference between tort law and criminal law is that tort law is private law while criminal law is public law. The differences that characterize this distinction have already been discussed, but the question remains whether these are necessary features. Is tort law necessarily private law and criminal law necessarily public law? This can become a very ticklish question. Presumably, the aim of tort law could be advanced and pursued by government officials at public expense and for public benefit, since its basic purpose would still be the compensation of victims by those responsible for damage. To this extent, then, it seems at least theoretically or conceptually possible that tort law could be conducted as public law. At the same time we would have to recognize how profound such a change would be. Many people would say that a change so great as to eliminate individual lawsuits would basically dissolve tort law into a different system, such as an insurance system.

And what about criminal law? Could criminal law be private law? In one respect it could. Individual cases in the criminal law (particular criminal offenses) could conceivably be initiated and pursued by private individuals (victims or insurance companies) at private expense for their own benefit (or vindication). Randy Barnett's innovative restitution model of criminal justice in Section 3 of this chapter proposes just such an approach to problems of punishment. But that is not all there is to criminal law. By definition a crime is, after all, a public wrong. Penal statutes are public prohibitions. All this assumes some common interest or public value that is being protected for the benefit and well-being of society at large. In this very fundamental respect criminal law is intrinsically public. Thus, although tort law could theoretically be public, we can see that the private vindication of private interests is a natural combination. On the other hand, criminal law is fundamentally public; it could not be private law without fundamentally changing its essential nature.

That leads us to a final significant difference between tort law and criminal law. The purpose of tort law is to enable victims of intentional or negligent harm or damage to compel compensation from the person who wrongfully inflicted the damage. In other words, tort law enables victims to shift their losses to the person who caused the losses. Tort law does not prohibit anything. It merely enables victims to hold people responsible for the consequences of what they do, in the sense of having to pay for damage that they cause.

Criminal law, however, is essentially prohibitive, restrictive, and coercive in that its primary purpose is to tell people what they must or must not do. The purpose of criminal law is not to compensate victims or deal with loss or damage but to regulate behavior, and this general purpose may be directed toward any number of ends. To what end should behavior be regulated by the state? At the most basic level, it has always been widely assumed that social behavior should be regulated to maintain order, peace, and security and thereby prevent fear, disorder, and disturbance. This is a bare minimum, not only for a legal system but for a society to exist. Without a minimal level of order and security there is no society at all but only war or anarchy.

Virtually all legal systems go beyond this notion of minimal protection to the more general idea that criminal law should regulate what is thought to be antisocial behavior — acts that undermine public values and the integrity of the community. The problem with the more expanded notion of criminal regulation is that antisocial behavior is a vague concept. What one person or group sees as antisocial another sees as patriotic; what one views as deviant another considers creative. And it is undeniable that any benefit bought by criminal prohibition is always bought at the expense of freedom. Every regulation or prohibition necessarily restricts freedom. That's just what regulation is: the restriction of freedom.

Furthermore, promoting the public interest is frequently in competition with the protection of individual rights and the requirements of justice. These are not contradictories, as are freedom and regulation, so that one necessarily precludes the other, but the relation between the public interest and individual justice is a difficult and uneasy one. How they fit together is not at all obvious, and it appears that they often impair one another. Both are crucial to any legitimate society, but it is not clear how they should be ranked.

These considerations raise certain basic questions that are fundamental to the study of the nature of criminal law: (1) What are the values that a society is entitled to protect as a public commitment by outlawing contrary behavior? (2) How can these basic values, such as security and property, that comprise the public interest be balanced against the equally important value of personal freedom? (3) How can the protection of the public interest be made compatible with the protection of individual rights or, in other words, the requirements of justice?

Questions (1) and (2) are addressed in Section 1 on the justification of criminal prohibition. Questions (2) and (3) are discussed in Section 2 on criminal responsibility and in Section 3 on punishment.

Remember that, strictly speaking, a crime is an act prohibited by the criminal law (the penal statutes of a society) because it is viewed as a public wrong. That is, a crime is defined as an offense against the public at large. It is important to remember this, and it is easy to forget it because, of course, the immediate damage done by any particular crime is almost always damage to an individual, the victim of the crime. The person most obviously hurt by an assault or a rape or a burglary is the person who was assaulted or raped or burglarized. The damage to society is much less obvious, but it is this idea of public harm that we must keep in mind in this chapter. To keep this idea clear recall the contrast drawn between criminal law and tort law. The purpose of tort law is to vindicate private interests. The purpose of criminal law is to protect the public welfare. If someone commits a tort, the response is the requirement of compensation. The tortfeasor is required to compensate the victim. If someone commits a crime, the response is punishment. But what is punishment? Traditionally, legal punishment is defined as

1. The intentional infliction
2. of something normally undesirable
3. by an authorized agent
4. on the perpetrator of a crime
5. because he or she committed a crime.

Each element of the definition is significant. First, punishment is intentional. If Arthur robs a bank and is accidentally run over by a car as he runs out the bank entrance, his injury is not punishment. Karma does not count as legal punishment, nor does accident or incidental suffering. Legal punishment is intentional, purposeful, state action.

Second, punishment must be something normally considered undesirable. If it were desirable, it would be a reward. But even if an unusual person, a masochist, say, finds his punishment to his liking, that does not undermine the general definition. So long as punishment is something normally considered undesirable, it qualifies as punishment.

Third, legal punishment must be inflicted by an authorized agent of the people as a whole. A lynch mob will not do as legal punishment, nor will a blood feud. This point is important, since in some circumstances authorization is the only thing that distinguishes punishment from crime. Authorization is the first step toward legitimacy. From where does this authorization come? In a democracy it is obtained through the representatives of the people. In any government it represents the power structure. More important, in any rule of law, authorized punishment is the manifestation of legal procedures agreed upon in advance of the commission of the crime.

Fourth and fifth, legal punishment can be inflicted only against someone who has committed a crime, precisely because the individual committed a crime. An innocent person cannot be sacrificed for the good of society under the heading of punishment. Punishment must be a response to a particular criminal act. In this way a particular punishment is always tied to a particular crime.

There are two major philosophical problems concerned with punishment: the problem of justification and the problem of alternatives. We will consider each of them here. The problem of justifying punishment involves an old and ongoing debate between two classical philosophical theories: the utilitarian and the retributive. These theories are discussed and evaluated by Richard B. Brandt, Edmund L. Pincoffs, and Jeffrie G. Murphy in Section 3 of this chapter. The problem of devising alternatives to punishment is a more recent concern. Two such proposals are considered in the selections by Karl Menninger and Randy E. Barnett.

SECTION 1

What Justifies Criminal Prohibitions?

To declare something a crime is to declare it a public harm or a public wrong. When is it reasonable or justifiable to label something a public wrong? Just what does that mean? To declare X a public harm assumes, first, that certain behavior impairs or undermines the common good or society as a whole. Second, it assumes that society is entitled to protect itself by prohibiting such behavior. The basic question is, When is a society justified in prohibiting activities or restricting individual freedom for the protection of itself—for the welfare of the community?

John Stuart Mill gives the classical liberal answer to this question in his famous essay "On Liberty." According to Mill, a society is justified in restricting the freedom of one individual only to prevent him from inflicting harm on another individual or on society. No society, of course, has ever allowed this level of freedom for its citizens. That is, all societies restrict individual freedom for reasons other than the prevention of harm. Furthermore, there is a great deal of dispute over what constitutes harm. One society might consider a free press or political dissent to be harmful, but another might not. Some states think polygamy is harmful, but others do not. Some societies consider pornography harmful, while others do not. Thus, while it is widely agreed that a state may restrict freedom to prevent harm, Mill's view raises two sets of issues. One is what counts as harm, especially public harm? The other is what besides harm (if anything) can justify interference with personal freedom?

In the second selection John Kleinig seeks to provide a clearer notion of criminal or public harm. After working through the meaning of harm as the impairment of basic and significant interests, Kleinig attempts to isolate the distinguishing features of public harm. Since a crime must be a distinguishable harm to society, he argues that a public harm must be that which erodes the trust that is necessary to maintain a social life which respects basic interests. In the course of his analysis Kleinig discusses a point also noted by Mill as one of great significance. Great care must be taken in the definition of public harm as an entity separate from individual harm, for such a concept can be and is regularly used or misused for totalitarian purposes. We must be constantly aware that the value sacrificed for the public interest is individual freedom. To protect this value public harm must be narrowly defined.

In the next selection Lawrence Friedman relates the history of the growth and development of the criminal law in this country in the last century. It is interesting to note that the number of acts declared criminal has steadily grown, and we will consider how well this comports with Mill's harm principle. Friedman observes that, at least until recently, violent crime has actually decreased, although other crime has increased because more acts have been declared criminal. What principles are needed to justify the various acts declared criminal, as cited by Friedman? Certainly more than the harm principle will be needed. This raises our second question: What other than protection from harm can the state use to justify restricting individual freedom with the threat of criminal sanction?

In his four-volume work *The Moral Limits of the Criminal Law,* Joel Feinberg provides the following summary of principles that have been proposed throughout history as justifications for limiting freedom. You may find them useful in evaluating arguments for the justification of criminal prohibitions.

DEFINITIONS OF LIBERTY LIMITING PRINCIPLES

1. *The Harm Principle:* It is always a good reason in support of penal legislation that it would probably be effective in preventing (eliminating, reducing) harm to persons other than the actor (the one prohibited from acting) and there is probably no other means that is equally effective at no greater cost to other values.

2. *The Offense Principle:* It is always a good reason in support of a proposed criminal prohibition that it is probably necessary to prevent serious offense to persons other than the actor and would probably be an effective means to that end if enacted.

3. *The Liberal Position* (on the moral limits of the criminal law): The harm and offense principles, duly clarified and qualified, between them exhaust the class of good reasons for criminal prohibitions. (The "extreme liberal position" is that only the harm principle states a good reason. . . .)

4. *Legal Paternalism* (a view excluded by the liberal position): It is always a good reason in support of a prohibition that it is probably necessary to prevent harm (physical, psychological, or economic) to the actor himself.

5. *Legal Moralism* (in the usual narrow sense): It can be morally legitimate to prohibit conduct on the ground that it is inherently immoral, even though it causes neither harm nor offense to the actor or to others.

6. *Moralistic Legal Paternalism* (where paternalism and moralism overlap via the dubious notion of a "moral harm"): It is always a good reason in support of a proposed prohibition that it is probably necessary to prevent moral harm (as opposed to physical, psychological, or economic harm) to the actor himself. (Moral harm

is "harm to one's character," "becoming a worse person," as opposed to harm to one's body, psyche, or purse.)

7. *Legal Moralism* (in the broad sense): It can be morally legitimate for the state to prohibit certain types of action that cause neither harm nor offense to anyone, on the grounds that such actions constitute or cause evils of other ("free-floating") kinds.

8. *The Benefit-to-Others Principle:* It is always a morally relevant reason in support of a proposed prohibition that it is probably necessary for the production of some benefit for persons other than the person who is prohibited.

9. *Benefit-Conferring Legal Paternalism:* It is always a morally relevant reason in support of a criminal prohibition that it is probably necessary to benefit the very person who is prohibited.

10. *Perfectionism* (Moral Benefit Theories): It is always a good reason in support of a proposed prohibition that it is probably necessary for the improvement (elevation, perfection) of the character

    a. of citizens generally, or certain citizens other than the person whose liberty is limited (the Moralistic Benefit-to-Others Principle), or

    b. of the very person whose liberty is limited (Moralistic Benefit-Conferring Legal Paternalism).*

To test these principles consider the last article in this section. Here Louis B. Schwartz offers several justifications for criminal offenses that are not harms to the community, at least not as Mill uses the term *harm*. Defending the "morals provisions" of the Model Penal Code, Schwartz argues that there can be justifications for restricting individual liberty even when no harm is at issue. Are his arguments persuasive? Why should liberty supersede important community values anyway? Mill gave one answer, but is it sufficient? If not, does Schwartz provide adequate criteria for deciding when community values should override individual freedom?

Notes and Questions

JOHN STUART MILL, from *On Liberty*

1. The subject of John Stuart Mill's famous treatise is "the nature and limits of the power which can be legitimately exercised by society over the individual." Mill offers "one very simple principle" for determining when society may restrict individual freedom. It is often called the *harm principle.* What is the harm principle, and what are the different ways Mill formulates it?

2. Does Mill think that society is ever justified in restricting an individual for his own good or his own protection? Why or why not?

3. What qualifications does Mill place on the application of his principle? Are these qualifications justified? On what grounds?

4. The ultimate ethical principle to which Mill appeals for justification of his harm principle is the principle of utility — that is, the principle which holds that the fundamental moral requirement is to promote the greatest good for the greatest number of people. How can protecting individual freedom by restricting state power or the power of the majority promote the greatest good for the greatest number, or the common good? How does Mill attempt to show that this is the case?

5. What are some of the examples that Mill gives of immoral restrictions on individual free-

---

* From J. Feinberg, *The Moral Limits of the Criminal Law*, Vol. 1, *Harm to Others* (New York: Oxford University Press, 1984), at pp. 26–27.

dom? Do you agree that these are morally illegitimate restrictions? Do you agree that we human beings are always susceptible to intolerance? Do you think Mormons should be able to practice polygamy if they believe in it? If not, why not?

6. Crucial to Mill's argument is the distinction between self-regarding and other-regarding conduct. Is this a legitimate distinction? What does Mill mean by self-regarding conduct?

[From] *On Liberty*

JOHN STUART MILL

The object of this Essay is to assert one very simple principle, as entitled to govern absolutely the dealings of society with the individual in the way of compulsion and control, whether the means used be physical force in the form of legal penalties, or the moral coercion of public opinion. That principle is, that the sole end for which mankind are warranted, individually or collectively, in interfering with the liberty of action of any of their number, is self-protection. That the only purpose for which power can be rightfully exercised over any member of a civilized community, against his will, is to prevent harm to others. His own good, either physical or moral, is not a sufficient warrant. He cannot rightfully be compelled to do or forbear because it will be better for him to do so, because it will make him happier, because, in the opinions of others, to do so would be wise, or even right. There are good reasons for remonstrating with him, or reasoning with him, or persuading him, or entreating him, but not for compelling him, or visiting him with any evil, in case he do otherwise. To justify that, the conduct from which it is desired to deter him must be calculated to produce evil to some one else. The only part of the conduct of any one, for which he is amenable to society, is that which concerns others. In the part which merely concerns himself, his independence is, of right, absolute. Over himself, over his own body and mind, the individual is sovereign.

It is, perhaps, hardly necessary to say that this doctrine is meant to apply only to human beings in the maturity of their faculties. We are not speaking of children, or of young persons below the age which the law may fix as that of manhood or womanhood. Those who are still in a state to require being taken care of by others, must be protected against their own actions as well as against external injury. For the same reason, we may leave out of consideration those backward states of society in which the race itself may be considered as in its nonage. The early difficulties in the way of spontaneous progress are so great, that there is seldom any choice of means for overcoming them; and a ruler full of the spirit of improvement is warranted in the use of any expedients that will attain an end, perhaps otherwise unattainable. Despotism is a legitimate mode of government in dealing with barbarians, provided the end be their improvement, and the means justified by actually effecting that end. Liberty, as a principle, has no application to any state of things anterior to the time when mankind have become capable of being improved by free and equal discussion. Until then, there is nothing for them but implicit obedience to an Akbar or a Charlemagne, if they are so fortunate as to find one. But as soon as mankind have attained the capacity of being guided to their own improvement by conviction or persuasion (a period long since reached in all nations with whom we need here concern ourselves), compulsion, either in the direct form or in that of pains and penalties for non-compliance, is no longer admissible as a means to their own good, and justifiable only for the security of others.

It is proper to state that I forgo any advantage which could be derived to my argument from the idea of abstract right, as a thing independent of utility. I regard utility as the ultimate appeal on all ethical questions; but it must be utility in the largest sense, grounded on the permanent interests of man as a progressive being. Those interests, I contend, authorize the subjection of individual spontaneity to external control, only in respect to those actions of each, which concern the interest of other people. If any one does an act hurtful to others, there is a *primâ facie* case for punishing him, by law, or, where legal penalties are not safely applicable, by general disapprobation. There are also many positive acts for the benefit of others, which he may rightfully be compelled to perform; such as, to give evidence in a court of justice; to bear his fair share in the common defence, or in any other joint work necessary to the interest of the society of which he enjoys the protection; and to perform certain acts of individual beneficence, such as saving a fellow creature's life, or interposing to protect the defenceless against ill-usage, things which whenever it is obviously a man's duty to do, he may rightfully be made responsible to society for not doing. A person may cause evil to others not only by his actions but by his inaction, and in either case he is justly accountable to them for the injury. The latter case, it is true, requires a much more cautious exercise of compulsion than the former. To make any one answerable for doing evil to others, is the rule; to make him answerable for not preventing evil, is, comparatively speaking, the exception. Yet there are many cases clear enough and grave enough to justify that exception. In all things which regard the external relations of the individual, he is *de jure* amenable to those whose interests are concerned, and if need be, to society as their protector. There are often good reasons for not holding him to the responsibility; but these reasons must arise from the special expediencies of the case: either because it is a kind of case in which he is on the whole likely to act better, when left to his own discretion, than when controlled in any way in which society have it in their power to control him; or because the attempt to exercise control would produce other evils, greater than those which it would prevent. When such reasons as these preclude the enforcement of responsibility, the conscience of the agent himself should step into the vacant judgment-seat, and protect those interests of others which have no external protection; judging himself all the more rigidly, because the case does not admit of his being made accountable to the judgment of his fellow-creatures.

But there is a sphere of action in which society, as distinguished from the individual, has, if any, only an indirect interest; comprehending all that portion of a person's life and conduct which affects only himself, or, if it also affects others, only with their free, voluntary, and undeceived consent and participation. When I say only himself, I mean directly, and in the first instance: for whatever affects himself, may affect others *through* himself; and the objection which may be grounded on this contingency, will receive consideration in the sequel. This, then, is the appropriate region of human liberty. It comprises, first, the inward domain of consciousness; demanding liberty of conscience, in the most comprehensive sense; liberty of thought and feeling; absolute freedom of opinion and sentiment on all subjects, practical or speculative, scientific, moral, or theological. The liberty of expressing and publishing opinions may seem to fall under a different principle, since it belongs to that part of the conduct of an individual which concerns other people; but, being almost of as much importance as the liberty of thought itself, and resting in great part on the same reasons, is practically inseparable from it. Secondly, the principle requires liberty of tastes and pursuits; of framing the plan of our life to suit our own character; of doing as we like, subject to such consequences as may follow; without impediment from our fellow-creatures, so long as what we do does not harm them, even though they should think our conduct foolish, perverse, or wrong. Thirdly, from this liberty of each individual, follows the liberty, within the same limits, of combination among individuals; freedom to unite, for any purpose not involving harm to others: the persons combining being supposed to be of full age, and not forced or deceived.

No society in which these liberties are not, on the whole, respected, is free, whatever may be its form of government; and none is completely free in which they do not exist absolute and unqualified. The only freedom which deserves the name, is that of pursuing our own good in our own way, so long as we do not attempt to deprive others of theirs, or impede their efforts to obtain it. Each is the proper guardian of his own health, whether bodily, or mental and spiritual. Mankind are greater gainers by suffering each other to live as seems good to themselves, than by compelling each to live as seems good to the rest . . .

We have now recognized the necessity to the mental well-being of mankind (on which all their other well-being depends) of freedom of opinion, and freedom of the expression of opinion, on four distinct grounds; which we will now briefly recapitulate.

First, if any opinion is compelled to silence, that opinion may, for aught we can certainly know, be true. To deny this is to assume our own infallibility.

Secondly, though the silenced opinion be an error, it may, and very commonly does, contain a portion of truth; and since the general or prevailing opinion on any subject is rarely or never the whole truth, it is only by the collision of adverse opinions that the remainder of the truth has any chance of being supplied.

Thirdly, even if the received opinion be not only true, but the whole truth; unless it is suffered to be, and actually is vigorously and earnestly contested, it will, by most of those who receive it, be held in the manner of a prejudice, with little comprehension or feeling of its rational grounds. And not only this, but, fourthly, the meaning of the doctrine itself will be in danger of being lost, or enfeebled, and deprived of its vital effect on the character and conduct: the dogma becoming a mere formal profession, inefficacious for good, but cumbering the ground, and preventing the growth of any real and heartfelt conviction from reason or personal experience . . .

Of the Limits to the Authority of Society over the Individual

What, then, is the rightful limit to the sovereignty of the individual over himself? Where does the authority of society begin? How much of human life should be assigned to individuality, and how much to society?

Each will receive its proper share, if each has that which more particularly concerns it. To individuality should belong the part of life in which it is chiefly the individual that is interested; to society, the part which chiefly interests society.

Though society is not founded on a contract, and though no good purpose is answered by inventing a contract in order to deduce social obligations from it, every one who receives the protection of society owes a return for the benefit, and the fact of living in society renders it indispensable that each should be bound to observe a certain line of conduct towards the rest. This conduct consists, first, in not injuring the interests of one another; or rather certain interests, which, either by express legal provision or by tacit understanding, ought to be considered as rights; and secondly, in each person's bearing his share (to be fixed on some equitable principle) of the labors and sacrifices incurred for defending the society or its members from injury and molestation. These conditions society is justified in enforcing, at all costs to those who endeavor to withhold fulfillment. Nor is this all that society may do. The acts of an individual may be hurtful to others, or wanting in due consideration for their welfare, without going the length of violating any of their constituted rights. The offender may then be justly punished by opinion, though not by law. As soon as any part of a person's conduct affects prejudicially the interests of others, society has jurisdiction over it, and the question whether the general welfare will or will not be promoted by interfering with it, becomes open to discussion. But there is no room for entertaining any such question when a person's conduct affects the interests of no persons besides himself, or needs not affect them unless they like (all the persons concerned being of full age, and the ordinary amount of understanding). In all such cases there should be perfect freedom, legal and social, to do the action and stand the consequences.

It would be a great misunderstanding of this doctrine, to suppose that it is one of selfish indifference, which pretends that human beings have no business with each other's conduct in life, and that they should not concern themselves about the well-doing or well-being of one another, unless their own interest is involved. Instead of any diminution, there is need of a great increase of disinterested exertion to promote the good of others. But disinterested benevolence can find other instruments to persuade people to their good, than whips and scourges, either of the literal or the metaphorical sort. I am the last person to undervalue the self-regarding virtues; they are only second in importance, if even second, to the social. It is equally the business of education to cultivate both. But even education works by conviction and persuasion as well as by compulsion, and it is by the former only that, when the period of education is past, the self-regarding virtues should be inculcated. Human beings owe to each other help to distinguish the better from the worse, and encouragement to choose the former and avoid the latter. They should be forever stimulating each other to increased exercise of their higher faculties, and increased direction of their feelings and aims towards wise instead of foolish, elevating instead of degrading, objects and contemplations. But neither one person, nor any number of persons, is warranted in saying to another human creature of ripe years, that he shall not do with his life for his own benefit what he chooses to do with it. He is the person most interested in his own well-being: the interest which any other person, except in cases of strong personal attachment, can have in it, is trifling, compared with that which he himself has; the interest which society has in him individually (except as to his conduct to others) is fractional, and altogether indirect: while, with respect to his own feelings and circumstances, the most ordinary man or woman has means of knowledge immeasurably surpassing those that can be possessed by anyone else. The interference of society to overrule his judgment and purposes in what only regards himself, must be grounded on general presumptions; which may be altogether wrong, and even if right, are as likely as not to be misapplied to individual cases, by persons no better acquainted with the circumstances of such cases than those are who look at them merely from without. In this department, therefore, of human affairs, Individuality has its proper field of action. In the conduct of human beings towards one another, it is necessary that general rules should for the most part be observed, in order that people may know what they have to expect; but in each person's own concerns, his individual spontaneity is entitled to free exercise. Considerations to aid his judgment, exhortations to strengthen his will, may be offered to him, even obtruded on him, by others; but he, himself, is the final judge. All errors which he is likely to commit against advice and warning, are far outweighed by the evil of allowing others to constrain him to what they deem his good.

I do not mean that the feelings with which a person is regarded by others, ought not to be in any way affected by his self-regarding qualities or deficiencies. This is neither possible nor desirable. If he is eminent in any of the qualities which conduce to his own good, he is, so far, a proper object of admiration. He is so much the nearer to the ideal perfection of human nature. If he is grossly deficient in those qualities, a sentiment the opposite of admiration will follow. There is a degree of folly, and a degree of what may be called (though the phrase is not unobjectionable) lowness or depravation of taste, which, though it cannot justify doing harm to the person who manifests it, renders him necessarily and properly a subject of distaste, or, in extreme cases, even of contempt: a person would not have the opposite qualities in due strength without entertaining these feelings. Though doing no wrong to anyone, a person may so act as to compel us to judge him, and feel to him, as a fool, or as a being of an inferior order: and since this judgment and feeling are a fact which he would prefer to avoid, it is doing him a service to warn him of it beforehand, as of any other disagreeable consequence to which he exposes himself. It would be well, indeed, if this good office were much more freely rendered than the common notions of politeness at present permit, and if one person could honestly point out to another that he thinks him in fault, without being considered unmannerly or presuming. We have a right, also, in various ways, to act upon our unfavorable opinion of any one, not to the oppression of his individuality, but in the exercise of ours. We are not bound, for example, to seek his society; we have a right to avoid it (though not to parade the avoidance), for we have a right to choose the society most acceptable to us. We have a right, and it may be our duty to caution others against him, if we think his example or conversation likely to have a pernicious effect on those with whom he associates. We may give others a preference over him in optional good offices, except those which tend to his improvement. In these various modes a person may suffer very severe penalties at the hands of others, for faults which directly concern only himself; but he suffers these penalties only in so far as they are the natural, and, as it were, the spontaneous consequences of the faults themselves, not because they are purposely inflicted on him for the sake of punishment. A person who shows rashness, obstinacy, self-conceit — who cannot live within moderate means — who cannot restrain himself from hurtful indulgences — who pursues animal pleasures at the expense of those of feelings and intellect — must expect to be lowered in the opinion of others, and to have a less share of their favorable sentiments, but of this he has no right to complain, unless he has merited their favor by special excellence in his social relations, and has thus established a title to their good offices, which is not affected by his demerits towards himself.

What I contend for is, that the inconveniences which are strictly inseparable from the unfavorable judgment of others, are the only ones to which a person should ever be subjected for that portion of his conduct and character which concerns his own good, but which does not affect the interests of others in their relations with him. Acts injurious to others require a totally different treatment. Encroachment on their rights; infliction on them of any loss or damage not justified by his own rights; falsehood or duplicity in dealing with them; unfair or ungenerous use of advantages over them; even selfish abstinence from defending them against injury — these are fit objects of moral reprobation, and, in grave cases, of moral retribution and punishment. And not only these acts, but the dispositions which lead to them, are properly immoral, and fit subjects of disapprobation which may rise to abhorrence. Cruelty of disposition; malice and ill-nature; that most anti-social and odious of all passions, envy; dissimulation and insincerity; irascibility on insufficient cause, and resentment disproportioned to the provocation; the love of domineering over others; the desire to engross more than one's share of advantages (the πλεονεξία of the Greeks); the pride which derives gratification from the abasement of others; the egotism which thinks self and its concerns more important than everything else, and decides all doubtful questions in his own favor — these are moral vices, and constitute a bad and odious moral character: unlike the self-regarding faults previously mentioned, which are not properly immoralities, and to whatever pitch they may be carried, do not constitute wickedness. They may be proofs of any amount of folly, or want of personal dignity and self-respect; but they are only a subject or

moral reprobation when they involve a breach of duty to others, for whose sake the individual is bound to have care for himself. What are called duties to ourselves are not socially obligatory, unless circumstances render them at the same time duties to others. The term duty to oneself, when it means anything more than prudence, means self-respect or self-development; and for none of these is any one accountable to his fellow-creatures, because for none of them is it for the good of mankind that he be held accountable to them.

The distinction between the loss of consideration which a person may rightly incur by defect of prudence or of personal dignity, and the reprobation which is due to him for an offence against the rights of others, is not a merely nominal distinction. It makes a vast difference both in our feelings and in our conduct towards him, whether he displeases us in things in which we think we have a right to control him, or in things in which we know that we have not. If he displeases us, we may express our distaste, and we may stand aloof from a person as well as from a thing that displeases us; but we shall not therefore feel called on to make his life uncomfortable. We shall reflect that he already bears, or will bear, the whole penalty of his error; if he spoils his life by mismanagement, we shall not, for that reason, desire to spoil it still further: instead of wishing to punish him, we shall rather endeavor to alleviate his punishment, by showing him how he may avoid or cure the evils his conduct tends to bring upon him. He may be to us an object of pity, perhaps of dislike, but not of anger or resentment; we shall not treat him like an enemy of society: the worst we shall think ourselves justified in doing is leaving him to himself, if we do not interfere benevolently by showing interest or concern for him. It is far otherwise if he has infringed the rules necessary for the protection of his fellow-creatures, individually or collectively. The evil consequences of his acts do not then fall on himself, but on others; and society, as the protector of all its members, must retaliate on him; must inflict pain on him for the express purpose of punishment, and must take care that it be sufficiently severe. In the one case, he is an offender at our bar, and we are called on not only to sit in judgment on him, but, in one shape or another, to execute our own sentence: in the other case, it is not our part to inflict any suffering on him, except what may incidentally follow from our using the same liberty in the regulation of our own affairs, which we allow to him in his.

The distinction here pointed out between the part of a person's life which concerns only himself, and that which concerns others, many persons will refuse to admit. How (it may be asked) can any part of the conduct of a member of society be a matter of indifference to the other members? No person is an entirely isolated being; it is impossible for a person to do anything seriously or permanently hurtful to himself, without mischief reaching at least to his near connections, and often far beyond them. If he injures his property, he does harm to those who directly or indirectly derived support from it, and usually diminishes, by a greater or less amount, the general resources of the community. If he deteriorates his bodily or mental faculties, he not only brings evil upon all who depended on him for any portion of their happiness, but disqualifies himself for rendering the services which he owes to his fellow-creatures generally; perhaps becomes a burden on their affection or benevolence; and if such conduct were very frequent, hardly any offence that is committed would detract more from the general sum of good. Finally, if by his vices or follies a person does no direct harm to others, he is nevertheless (it may be said) injurious by his example; and ought to be compelled to control himself, for the sake of those whom the sight or knowledge of his conduct might corrupt or mislead.

And even (it will be added) if the consequences of misconduct could be confined to the vicious or thoughtless individual, ought society to abandon to their own guidance those who are manifestly unfit for it? If protection against themselves is confessedly due to children and persons under age, is not society equally bound to afford it to persons of mature years who are equally incapable of self-government? If gambling, or drunkenness, or incontinence, or idleness, or uncleanliness, are as injurious to happiness, and as great a hindrance to improvement, as many or most of the acts prohibited by law, why (it may be asked) should not law, so far as is consistent with practicability and social convenience, endeavor to repress these also? And as a supplement to the unavoidable imperfections of law,

ought not opinion at least to organize a powerful police against these vices, and visit rigidly with social penalties those who are known to practise them? There is no question here (it may be said) about restricting individuality, or impeding the trial of new and original experiments in living. The only things it is sought to prevent are things which have been tried and condemned from the beginning of the world until now; things which experience has shown not to be useful or suitable to any person's individuality. There must be some length of time and amount of experience, after which a moral or prudential truth may be regarded as established: and it is merely desired to prevent generation after generation from falling over the same precipice which has been fatal to their predecessors.

I fully admit that the mischief which a person does to himself, may seriously affect, both through their sympathies and their interests, those nearly connected with him, and in a minor degree, society at large. When, by conduct of this sort, a person is led to violate a distinct and assignable obligation to any other person or persons, the case is taken out of the self-regarding class, and becomes amenable to moral disapprobation in the proper sense of the term. If, for example, a man, through intemperance or extravagance, becomes unable to pay his debts, or, having undertaken the moral responsibility of a family, becomes from the same cause incapable of supporting or educating them, he is deservedly reprobated, and might be justly punished; but it is for the breach of duty to his family or creditors, not for the extravagance. If the resources which ought to have been devoted to them, had been diverted from them for the most prudent investment, the moral culpability would have been the same. George Barnwell murdered his uncle to get money for his mistress, but if he had done it to set himself up in business, he would equally have been hanged. Again, in the frequent case of a man who causes grief to his family by addiction to bad habits, he deserves reproach for his unkindness or ingratitude; but so he may for cultivating habits not in themselves vicious, if they are painful to those with whom he passes his life, or who from personal ties are dependent on him for their comfort. Whoever fails in the consideration generally due to the interests and feelings of others, not being compelled by some more imperative duty, or justified by allowable self-preference, is a subject of moral disapprobation for that failure, but not for the cause of it, nor for the errors, merely personal to himself, which may have remotely led to it. In like manner, when a person disables himself, by conduct purely self-regarding, from the performance of some definite duty incumbent on him to the public, he is guilty of a social offence. No person ought to be punished simply for being drunk; but a soldier or a policeman should be punished for being drunk on duty. Whenever, in short, there is a definite damage, or a definite risk of damage, either to an individual or to the public, the case is taken out of the province of liberty, and placed in that of morality or law.

But with regard to the merely contingent, or, as it may be called, constructive injury which a person causes to society, by conduct which neither violates any specific duty to the public, nor occasions perceptible hurt to any assignable individual except himself; the inconvenience is one which society can afford to bear, for the sake of the greater good of human freedom. If grown persons are to be punished for not taking proper care of themselves, I would rather it were for their own sake, than under pretence of preventing them from impairing their capacity of rendering to society benefits which society does not pretend it has a right to exact. But I cannot consent to argue the point as if society had no means of bringing its weaker members up to its ordinary standard of rational conduct, except waiting till they do something irrational, and then punishing them, legally or morally, for it. Society has had absolute power over them during all the early portion of their existence: it has had the whole period of childhood and nonage in which to try whether it could make them capable of rational conduct in life. The existing generation is master both of the training and the entire circumstances of the generation to come; it cannot indeed make them perfectly wise and good, because it is itself so lamentably deficient in goodness and wisdom; and its best efforts are not always, in individual cases, its most successful ones; but it is perfectly well able to make the rising generation, as a whole, as good as, and a little better than, itself. If society lets any considerable number of its members grow up mere

children, incapable of being acted on by rational consideration of distant motives, society has itself to blame for the consequences. Armed not only with all the powers of education, but with the ascendency which the authority of a received opinion always exercises over the minds who are least fitted to judge for themselves; and aided by the *natural* penalties which cannot be prevented from falling on those who incur the distaste or the contempt of those who know them; let not society pretend that it needs, besides all this, the power to issue commands and enforce obedience in the personal concerns of individuals, in which, on all principles of justice and policy, the decision ought to rest with those who are to abide the consequences. Nor is there anything which tends more to discredit and frustrate the better means of influencing conduct, than a resort to the worse. If there be among those whom it is attempted to coerce into prudence or temperance, any of the material of which vigorous and independent characters are made, they will infallibly rebel against the yoke. No such person will ever feel that others have a right to control him in his concerns, such as they have to prevent him from injuring them in theirs; and it easily comes to be considered a mark of spirit and courage to fly in the face of such usurped authority, and do with ostentation the exact opposite of what it enjoins; as in the fashion of grossness which succeeded, in the time of Charles II, to the fanatical moral intolerance of the Puritans. With respect to what is said of the necessity of protecting society from the bad example set to others by the vicious or the self-indulgent; it is true that bad example may have a pernicious effect, especially the example of doing wrong to others with impunity to the wrongdoer. But we are now speaking of conduct which, while it does no wrong to others, is supposed to do great harm to the agent himself: and I do not see how those who believe this, can think otherwise than that the example, on the whole, must be more salutary than hurtful, since, if it displays the misconduct, it displays also the painful or degrading consequences which, if the conduct is justly censured, must be supposed to be in all or most cases attendant on it.

But the strongest of all the arguments against the interference of the public with purely personal conduct, is that when it does interfere, the odds are that it interferes wrongly, and in the wrong place. On questions of social morality, of duty to others, the opinion of the public, that is, of an overruling majority, though often wrong, is likely to be still oftener right; because on such questions they are only required to judge of their own interests; of the manner in which some mode of conduct, if allowed to be practised, would affect themselves. But the opinion of a similar majority, imposed as a law on the minority, on questions of self-regarding conduct, is quite as likely to be wrong as right; for in these cases public opinion means, at the best, some people's opinion of what is good or bad for other people; while very often it does not even mean that; the public, with the most perfect indifference, passing over the pleasure or convenience of those whose conduct they censure, and considering only their own preference. There are many who consider as an injury to themselves any conduct which they have a distaste for, and resent it as an outrage to their feelings; as a religious bigot, when charged with disregarding the religious feelings of others, has been known to retort that they disregard his feelings, by persisting in their abominable worship or creed. But there is no parity between the feeling of a person for his own opinion, and the feeling of another who is offended at his holding it; no more than between the desire of a thief to take a purse, and the desire of the right owner to keep it. And a person's taste is as much his own peculiar concern as his opinion or his purse. It is easy for any one to imagine an ideal public, which leaves the freedom and choice of individuals in all uncertain matters undisturbed, and only requires them to abstain from modes of conduct which universal experience has condemned. But where has there been seen a public which set any such limit to its censorship? or when does the public trouble itself about universal experience? In its interferences with personal conduct it is seldom thinking of anything but the enormity of acting or feeling differently from itself; and this standard of judgment, thinly disguised, is held up to mankind as the dictate of religion and philosophy, by nine tenths of all moralists and speculative writers. These teach that things are right because they are right; because we feel them to be so. They tell us to search in our own minds and hearts for laws of conduct binding on ourselves and on all others.

What can the poor public do but apply these instructions, and make their own personal feelings of good and evil, if they are tolerably unanimous in them, obligatory on all the world?

The evil here pointed out is not one which exists only in theory; and it may perhaps be expected that I should specify the instances in which the public of this age and country improperly invests its own preferences with the character of moral laws. I am not writing an essay on the aberrations of existing moral feeling. That is too weighty a subject to be discussed parenthetically, and by way of illustration. Yet examples are necessary, to show that the principle I maintain is of serious and practical moment, and that I am not endeavoring to erect a barrier against imaginary evils. And it is not difficult to show, by abundant instances, that to extend the bounds of what may be called moral police, until it encroaches on the most unquestionably legitimate liberty of the individual, is one of the most universal of all human propensities.

As a first instance, consider the antipathies which men cherish on no better grounds than that persons whose religious opinions are different from theirs, do not practise their religious observances, especially their religious abstinences. To cite a rather trivial example, nothing in the creed or practice of Christians does more to envenom the hatred of Mahomedans against them, than the fact of their eating pork. There are few acts which Christians and Europeans regard with more unaffected disgust, than Mussulmans regard this particular mode of satisfying hunger. It is, in the first place, an offence against their religion; but this circumstance by no means explains either the degree or the kind of their repugnance; for wine also is forbidden by their religion, and to partake of it is by all Mussulmans accounted wrong, but not disgusting. Their aversion to the flesh of the "unclean beast" is, on the contrary, of that peculiar character, resembling an instinctive antipathy, which the idea of uncleanness, when once it thoroughly sinks into the feelings, seems always to excite even in those whose personal habits are anything but scrupulously cleanly, and of which the sentiment of religious impurity, so intense in the Hindoos, is a remarkable example. Suppose now that in a people, of whom the majority were Mussulmans, that majority should insist upon not permitting pork to be eaten within the limits of the country. This would be nothing new in Mahomedan countries.* Would it be a legitimate exercise of the moral authority of public opinion? and if not, why not? The practice is really revolting to such a public. They also sincerely think that it is forbidden and abhorred by the Deity. Neither could the prohibition be censured as religious persecution. It might be religious in its origin, but it would not be persecution for religion, since nobody's religion makes it a duty to eat pork. The only tenable ground of condemnation would be, that with the personal tastes and self-regarding concerns of individuals the public has no business to interfere.

To come somewhat nearer home: the majority of Spaniards consider it a gross impiety, offensive in the highest degree to the Supreme Being, to worship him in any other manner than the Roman Catholic; and no other public worship is lawful on Spanish soil. The people of all Southern Europe look upon a married clergy as not only irreligious, but unchaste, indecent, gross, disgusting. What do Protestants think of these perfectly sincere feelings, and of the attempt to enforce them against non-Catholics? Yet, if mankind are justified in interfering with each other's liberty in things which do not concern the interests of others, on what principle is it possible consistently to exclude these cases? or who can blame people for desiring to suppress what they regard as a scandal in the sight of God and man? No stronger case can be shown for prohibiting anything which is regarded as a personal immorality, than is made out for suppressing these practices in the eyes of those who regard them as impieties; and unless we are willing to adopt the logic of persecutors, and to say that we may persecute others because we are right, and that they must not persecute us because they are wrong, we must be aware of admitting a principle of which we should resent as a gross injustice the application to ourselves.

The preceding instances may be objected to, although unreasonably, as drawn from contingencies impossible among us: opinion, in this country, not being likely to enforce abstinence from meats, or to interfere with people for worshipping, and for either marrying or not marrying, according to their creed or inclination. The next example, however, shall be taken from an interference with liberty which we have by no means passed all danger of. Wherever the puritans have been sufficiently powerful, as in New England, and in Great Britain at the time of the Commonwealth, they have endeavored, with considerable success, to put down all public, and nearly all private, amusements: especially music, dancing, public games, or other assemblages for purposes of diversion, and the theatre. There are still in this country large bodies of persons by whose notions of morality and religion these recreations are condemned; and those persons belonging chiefly to the middle class, who are the ascendant power in the present social and political condition of the kingdom, it is by no means impossible that persons of these sentiments may at some time or other command a majority in Parliament. How will the remaining portion of the community like to have the amusements that shall be permitted to them regulated by the religious and moral sentiments of the stricter Calvinists and Methodists? Would they not, with considerable peremptoriness, desire these intrusively pious members of society to mind their own business? This is precisely what should be said to every government and every public, who have the pretension that no person shall enjoy any pleasure which they think wrong. But if the principle of the pretension be admitted, no one can reasonably object to its being acted on in the sense of the majority, or other preponderating power in the country; and all persons must be ready to conform to the idea of a Christian commonwealth, as understood by the early settlers in New England, if a religious profession similar to theirs should ever succeed in regaining its lost ground, as religions supposed to be declining have so often been known to do.

---

* The case of the Bombay Parsees is a curious instance in point. When this industrious and enterprising tribe, the descendants of the Persian fire-worshippers, flying from their native country before the Caliphs, arrived in Western India, they were admitted to toleration by the Hindoo sovereigns, on condition of not eating beef. When those regions afterwards fell under the dominion of Mahomedan conquerors, the Parsees obtained from them a continuance of indulgence, on condition of refraining from pork. What was at first obedience to authority became a second nature, and the Parsees to this day abstain both from beef and pork. Though not required by their religion, the double abstinence has had time to grow into a custom of their tribe; and custom, in the East, is a religion.

To imagine other contingency, perhaps more likely to be realized than the one last mentioned. There is confessedly a strong tendency in the modern world towards a democratic constitution of society, accompanied or not by popular political institutions. It is affirmed that in the country where this tendency is most completely realized — where both society and the government are most democratic — the United States — the feeling of the majority, to whom any appearance of a more showy or costly style of living than they can hope to rival is disagreeable, operates as a tolerably effectual sumptuary law, and that in many parts of the Union it is really difficult for a person possessing a very large income, to find any mode of spending it, which will not incur popular disapprobation. Though such statements as these are doubtless much exaggerated as a representation of existing facts, the state of things they describe is not only a conceivable and possible, but a probable result of democratic feeling, combined with the notion that the public has a right to a veto on the manner in which individuals shall spend their incomes. We have only further to suppose a considerable diffusion of Socialist opinions, and it may become infamous in the eyes of the majority to possess more property than some very small amount, or any income not earned by manual labor. Opinions similar in principle to these, already prevail widely among the artisan class, and weigh oppressively on those who are amenable to the opinion chiefly of that class, namely, its own members. It is known that the bad workmen who form the majority of the operatives in many branches of industry, are decidedly of opinion that bad workmen ought to receive the same wages as good, and that no one ought to be allowed, through piecework or otherwise, to earn by superior skill or industry more than others can without it. And they employ a moral police, which occasionally becomes a physical one, to deter skillful workmen from receiving and employers from giving, a larger remuneration for a more useful service. If the public have any jurisdiction over private concerns, I cannot see that these people are in fault, or that any individual's particular public can be blamed for asserting the same authority over his individual conduct, which the general public asserts over people in general.

But, without dwelling upon suppositious cases, there are, in our own day, gross usurpations upon the liberty of private life actually practised, and still greater ones threatened with some expectation of success, and opinions proposed which assert an unlimited right in the public not only to prohibit by law everything which it thinks wrong, but in order to get at what it thinks wrong, to prohibit any number of things which it admits to be innocent.

Under the name of preventing intemperance, the people of one English colony, and of nearly half the United States, have been interdicted by law from making any use whatever of fermented drinks, except for medical purposes: for prohibition of their sale is in fact, as it is intended to be, prohibition of their use. And though the impracticability of executing the law has caused its repeal in several of the States which had adopted it, including the one from which it derives its name, an attempt has notwithstanding been commenced, and is prosecuted with considerable zeal by many of the professed philanthropists, to agitate for a similar law in this country. The association, or "Alliance" as it terms itself, which has been formed for this purpose, has acquired some notoriety through the publicity given to a correspondence between its Secretary and one of the very few English public men who hold that a politician's opinions ought to be founded on principles. Lord Stanley's share in this correspondence is calculated to strengthen the hopes already built on him, by those who know how rare such qualities as are manifested in some of his public appearances, unhappily are among those who figure in political life. The organ of the Alliance, who would "deeply deplore the recognition of any principle which could be wrested to justify bigotry and persecution," undertakes to point out the "broad and impassable barrier" which divides such principles from those of the association. "All matters relating to thought, opinion, conscience, appear to me," he says, "to be without the sphere of legislation; all pertaining to social act, habit, relation, subject only to a discretionary power vested in the State itself, and not in the individual, to be within it." No mention is made of a third class, different from either of these, viz., acts and habits which are not social, but individual; although it is to this class, surely, that the act of drinking fermented liquors belongs. Selling fermented liquors, however, is trading, and trading is a social act. But the infringement complained of is not on the liberty of the seller, but on that of the buyer and consumer; since the State might just as well forbid him to drink wine, as purposely make it impossible for him to obtain it. The Secretary, however, says, "I claim, as a citizen, a right to legislate whenever my social rights are invaded by the social act of another." And now for the definition of these "social rights." "If anything invades my social rights, certainly the traffic in strong drink does. It destroys my primary right of security, by constantly creating and stimulating social disorder. It invades my right of equality, by deriving a profit from the creation of a misery, I am taxed to support. It impedes my right to free moral and intellectual development, by surrounding my path with dangers, and by weakening and demoralizing society, from which I have a right to claim mutual aid and intercourse." A theory of "social rights," the like of which probably never before found its way into distinct language — being nothing short of this — that it is the absolute social right of every individual, that every other individual shall act in every respect exactly as he ought; that whosoever fails thereof in the smallest particular, violates my social right, and entitles me to demand from the legislature the removal of the grievance. So monstrous a principle is far more dangerous than any single interference with liberty; there is no violation of liberty which it would not justify; it acknowledges no right to any freedom whatever, except perhaps to that of holding opinions in secret, without ever disclosing them: for the moment an opinion which I consider noxious, passes any one's lips, it invades all the "social rights" attributed to me by the Alliance. The doctrine ascribes to all mankind a vested interest in each other's moral, intellectual, and even physical perfection, to be defined by each claimant according to his own standard.

Another important example of illegitimate interference with the rightful liberty of the individual, not simply threatened, but long since carried into triumphant effect, is Sabbatarian legislation. Without doubt, abstinence on one day in the week, so far as the exigencies of life permit, from the usual daily occupation, though in no respect religiously binding on any except Jews, it is a highly beneficial custom. And inasmuch as this custom cannot be observed without a general consent to that effect among the industrious classes, therefore, in so far as some persons by working may impose the same necessity on others, it may be allowable and right that the law should guarantee to each, the observance by others of the custom, by suspending the greater operations of industry on a particular day. But this justification, grounded on the direct interest which others have in each individual's observance of the practice, does not apply to the self-chosen occupations in which a person may think fit to employ his leisure; nor does it hold good, in the smallest degree, for legal restrictions on amusements. It is true that the amusement of some is the day's work of others; but the pleasure, not to say the useful recreation, of many, is worth the labor of a few, provided the occupation is freely chosen, and can be freely resigned. The operatives are perfectly right in thinking that if all worked on Sunday seven days' work would have to be given for six days' wages: but so long as the great mass of employments are suspended, the small number who for the enjoyment of others must still work, obtain a proportional increase of earnings; and they are not obliged to follow those occupations, if they prefer leisure to emolument. If a further remedy is sought, it might be found in the establishment by custom of a holiday on some other day of the week for those particular classes of persons. The only ground, therefore, on which restrictions on Sunday amusements can be defended, must be that they are religiously wrong; a motive of legislation which never can be too earnestly protested again. "Deorum injuriae Diis curae." It remains to be proved that society or any of its officers holds a commission from on high to avenge any supposed offence to Omnipotence, which is not also a wrong to our fellow-creatures. The notion that it is one man's duty that another should be religious, was the foundation of all the religious persecutions ever perpetrated, and if admitted, would fully justify them. Though the feeling which breaks out in the repeated attempts to stop railway travelling on Sunday, in the resistance to the opening of Museums, and the like, has not the cruelty of the old persecutors, the state of mind indicated by it is fundamentally the same. It is a determination not to tolerate others in doing what is permitted by their religion, because it is not permitted by the persecutor's religion. It is a belief that God not only abominates the act of the misbeliever, but will not hold us guiltless if we leave him unmolested.

I cannot refrain from adding to these examples of the little account commonly made of human liberty, the language of downright persecution which breaks out from the press of this country, whenever it feels called on to notice the remarkable phenomenon of Mormonism. Much might be said on the unexpected and instructive fact, that an alleged new revelation, and a religion founded on it, the product of palpable imposture, not even supported by the *prestige* of extraordinary qualities in its founder, is believed by hundreds of thousands, and has been made the foundation of a society, in the age of newspapers, railways, and the electric telegraph. What here concerns us is, that this religion, like other and better religions, has its martyrs; that its prophet and founder was, for his teaching, put to death by a mob; that others of its adherents lost their lives by the same lawless violence; that they were forcibly expelled, in a body, from the country in which they first grew up; while, now that they have been chased into a solitary recess in the midst of a desert, many of this country openly declare that it would be right (only that it is not convenient) to send an expedition against them, and compel them by force to conform to the opinion of other people. The article of the Mormonite doctrine which is the chief provocative to the antipathy which thus breaks through the ordinary restraints of religious tolerance, is its sanction of polygamy; which, though permitted to Mahomedans, and Hindoos, and Chinese, seems to excite unquenchable animosity when practised by persons who speak English, and profess to be a kind of Christians. No one has a deeper disapprobation than I have of this Mormon institution; both for other reasons, and because, far from being in any way countenanced by the principle of liberty, it is a direct infraction of that principle, being a mere riveting of the chains of one half of the community, and an emancipation of the other from reciprocity of obligation towards them. Still, it must be remembered that this relation is as much voluntary on the part of the women concerned in it, and who may be deemed the sufferers by it, as is the case with any other form of the marriage institution; and however surprising this fact may appear, it has its explanation in the common ideas and customs of the world, which teaching women to think marriage the one thing needful, make it intelligible that many a woman should prefer being one of several wives, to not being a wife at all. Other countries are not asked to recognize such unions, or release any portion of their inhabitants from their own laws on the score of Mormonite opinions. But when the dissentients have conceded to the hostile sentiments of others, far more than could justly be demanded; when they have left the countries to which their doctrines were unacceptable, and established themselves in a remote corner of the earth, which they have been the first to render habitable to human beings; it is difficult to see on what principles but those of tyranny they can be prevented from living there under what laws they please, provided they commit no aggression on other nations, and allow perfect freedom of departure to those who are dissatisfied with their ways. A recent writer, in some respects of considerable merit, proposes (to use his own words) not a crusade, but a *civilizade*, against this polygamous community, to put an end to what seems to him a retrograde step in civilization. It also appears so to me, but I am not aware that any community has a right to force another to be civilized. So long as the sufferers by the bad law do not invoke assistance from other communities, I cannot admit that persons entirely unconnected with them ought to step in and require that a condition of things with which all who are directly interested appear to be satisfied, should be put an end to because it is a scandal to persons some thousands of miles distant, who have no part or concern in it. Let them send missionaries, if they please, to preach against it; and let them, by any fair means (of which silencing the teachers is not one), oppose the progress of similar doctrines among their own people. If civilization has got the better of barbarism when barbarism had the world to itself, it is too much to profess to be afraid lest barbarism, after having been fairly got under, should revive and conquer civilization. A civilization that can thus succumb to its vanquished enemy must first have become so degenerate, that neither its appointed priests and teachers, nor anybody else, has the capacity, or will take the trouble, to stand up for it. If this be so, the sooner such a civilization receives notice to quit, the better. It can only go on from bad to worse, until destroyed and regenerated (like the Western Empire) by energetic barbarians.

Notes and Questions

JOHN KLEINIG, from "Crime and the Concept of Harm"

1. A crime is often defined as a public harm. As John Kleinig points out, while it is often claimed that harm to others is the only clear basis for criminal sanction, the concept of harm itself is notoriously fuzzy and susceptible to wide-ranging manipulation. Obviously, it would be valuable to have a clear analysis of the meaning of *harm*. Kleinig begins by distinguishing four traditions in the historical development of the concept. What are they, and why does he distinguish them?

2. Kleinig suggests that we analyze the concept of harm as "interference with or the invasion of a person's interests." What does Kleinig mean by an *interest?*

3. An interest must be suitably qualified if it is to serve as a tool for analyzing the meaning of harm. What qualifications does Kleinig reject, and why? What qualification does he ultimately accept? What arguments does he offer to support his position?

4. Kleinig draws a clear connection between our political-moral rights and our welfare interests. How, according to Kleinig, does the analysis of harm as the impairment of welfare interests help us to understand the violation of rights?

5. The next question to ask is what sorts of harms are, or should be, criminal harms. One way to ask this question is to ask what the difference is between crimes and torts, since both involve harms. What does Kleinig suggest?

6. Kleinig argues that a harm suitable for criminal action is one which includes a distinguishable harm to society. How does he think a harm to society should be understood? How does he support his position?

[From] "Crime and the Concept of Harm"

JOHN KLEINIG

It is frequently claimed that only harm (to others) provides a suitably non-partisan base for justifiable legal interference. Nevertheless, harm remains "the most underdeveloped concept in our criminal law."[1] It has been taken for granted that we know what it is, and that we can recognize it when it occurs. Yet even the most cursory reflection shows that harm is conceptually foggy, susceptible to fictional applications, and subject to ideologizing.[2] In this paper I develop a reasonably precise account of harm, and make some suggestions towards a theory of criminal harm.

I

As a heuristic device, I want to distinguish four "traditions" in the historical development of the concept of harm. Failure to make these distinctions is largely responsible for the confusion and vagueness which surround the concept. Though the first of these traditions is now almost defunct, the remaining three still coexist (even in the same writer).

TRADITION 1. The Old English "hearm," from which "harm" derives, referred to a psychologically defined phenomenon. Its primary meaning was grief or sorrow. Harm was necessarily *experienced*. To cause another harm was to cause him mental anguish or pain. A development of this tradition extended its reference to what was *sensed*. It thus came to include physical pain, suffering and hurt. Traces of this psychological sense still linger, though in an admittedly subdued fashion.

TRADITION 2. Grief and sorrow are not normally felt "out of the blue." We grieve or sorrow over some loss. "Harm" thus came to refer not only to the grief or sorrow, but also to the loss which had occasioned it. Typically, that loss was felt, but as the second tradition developed this no longer became necessary. A person could suffer harms of which he had no knowledge, either at the time he suffered them, or ever. Thus, while it remained true that what one didn't know couldn't hurt, it might harm. A man can harm his son's chances in life by the way in which he conducts his own, even though the son may not realize the harm done to him. Similarly, a person's reputation may be harmed by malicious and untruthful gossip, even though it is many years before the defamed person learns of this.[3] Within this tradition "harm" was and is sometimes extended even to inanimate objects, though the philosophical assumptions underlying such an extension are questionable.

TRADITION 3. This tradition involves a narrowing of the previous one. Here harm is seen as a moral notion: only acts are harmful; only people do harm. Thus, if a tree, weakened by termites, topples onto my leg, breaking it, the leg will be said to suffer damage or injury, but not harm. I have "come to grief," but not "come to harm." I come to harm only at someone else's hands. Who harms me wrongs me. Though later, this tradition exercises a fairly strong influence in contemporary usage. One reason, no doubt, is its baptism in J. S. Mill's "harm principle" (though Mill was hardly consistent in his use of "harm"). Another is its increasing use in legal discussion: "harm" has taken over the role once served by "injury" (*injuria*).

TRADITION 4. In law, harm has come to be understood as the violation of a legally protected interest.[4] This represents both a legalization and an extension of the third tradition. Some legal harms do not involve any harm as understood within the third tradition. The harm postulated is a legal fiction designed to provide a unified rationale for legal interference. If *X* trespasses on *Y*'s land he has done *Y* harm insofar as he has violated *Y*'s legally protected interest in the exclusive use and enjoyment of his land. The harm does not consist in any (wilful) damage to *Y*'s property, but simply in "depriving" *Y* of his exclusive use and enjoyment of it. Again, despite the frequently made claims that "harm is the tort signature"[5] and that where no harm is done no compensation is due, in cases of defamation it is necessary to show only that a statement was calculated to bring someone into "hatred, contempt or ridicule." A fictional harm is made the basis for "damages."

In attempting to provide an analysis of harm, there is some small advantage in developing the account implicit in the second tradition. The first is now too peripheral to cast much light on our current understanding, and the third and fourth can be viewed as specialized adaptations of the second tradition.

There is not much mileage to be gained by explicating harm in terms of loss, damage, or injury. These are synonyms lacking analytical power. More promising are certain legal writings which characterize harm as *interference with or the invasion of a person's interests*. This requires some modification, but its reference to *interests* illuminates a central feature of harm. "Interest," however, is ambiguous, and a number of uses need to be disentangled before the foregoing account can be made perspicuous. I shall distinguish three uses.

(i) One use of "interest," generally capturable in expressions of the form "*X* is interested in *Y*," refers to an inclination to pay attention to something: "Are you interested in seeing my slides of Japan?"; "School holds no interest for her." We speak here of interest being aroused or excited, dampened or suppressed, of it waxing and waning. It is a psychological phenomenon. A person lacking interest in this sense is said to be *un*interested.

It is improbable that harm is to be understood as interference with a person's interests, in this first sense. Were that to be the case, a person would always be aware of any harm done to him. It would also reduce and misrepresent our catalogue of harms. To interfere with your interest in skiing, it will not be enough if I break your legs, steal your equipment and burn your books on skiing, for your interest in skiing may continue unabated. All I have succeeded in doing is to interfere with your ability to pursue your interest, which is another matter. Moreover, even where someone does succeed in interfering with a psychological interest, the result is not necessarily characterizable as a harm. If, whenever I express an interest in strawberries and cream, my wife harangues me on calories, cholesterol and coronaries, I may find myself losing interest in strawberries and cream. But the "invasion" of my interest may have been all to the good.

(ii) More plausibly related to harm are the interests generally expressible in statements of the form "*X* has an interest in *Y*." Legal writers sometimes explicate this sense of "interest" as "anything which is the object of human desire."[6] But while it would be unusual (though not impossible) to have an interest in something which was not an object of desire, some objects of desire are only dubiously interest in this sense. Taking a fourth bowl of strawberries and cream may be the object of my desire, but it would dilute the notion of an interest too much to speak of this as an interest of mine.

Here, my interests are restricted to those projects (my own or others') in which I have some stake. To have a stake in something is to stand to gain or lose from it, because of some investment of energy or goods in it or some project affected by it, or because its outcome affects me advantageously or otherwise. Interests in the second sense are not logically tied to interest in the first sense, though they may not be completely unrelated at a conceptual level. The correct drafting of my aunt's will may be to my advantage, yet hold no interest for me. I may be *un*interested without being *dis*interested.

In considering whether harm is fruitfully analyzed in terms of interests (in the second sense), attention may be focused on the variable assessments to which they are subject. They may be saintly, morally indifferent, foolish, or satanic; they may be of profound significance, run-of-the-mill, or trivial. This might be thought to render implausible any attempt to analyze harm as interference with someone's (unqualified) interests. Consider the following cases:

(a) I advise my aunt on the drafting of her final will, which includes me as its chief beneficiary, but my (supposedly dispossessed) cousin successfully challenges its validity, and the money goes to him as the sole beneficiary of her last valid will.

(b) A millionaire is short-changed by his paper boy.

(c) A crime boss invests large amounts of money and energy in the successful outcome of a bank robbery, but his attempt is foiled, and he is gaoled.

In none of these cases would we normally consider the subject character to have been harmed. Yet there has been an interference with or invasion of his interest. To understand why this is so in case (a), we need to note the variable relations between harm and benefit. Depending on initial conditions, harm and benefit may be either contraries or contradictories. If I am a diabetic, my regular insulin injections will be beneficial to me. Removal of this benefit will be harmful. Here harm and non-benefit are to all intents equivalent. This is not so in the following circumstances: a new Foundation is set up to finance research projects. I apply but do not qualify for a grant. Had I received one, I would have benefited, but (other things being equal) my failure to benefit was not harmful. In the first case non-benefit is associated with a genuine diminution of welfare, whereas this is not so in the second. Case (a) parallels the latter. Unless I was of necessity financially dependent on my aunt before her death, my failure to benefit from her estate is not likely to diminish my welfare. The disappointment of my expectations would not normally suffice. This distinction between harmful and non-harmful non-benefit will be sharpened up at a later point. At present it should be enough to recognize that such a distinction exists, and that this is why in case (a) interference with the interest I had in my aunt's will does not constitute a harm.

Case (b) may seem to involve a real loss, but the loss is so trivial that calling it a harm is like using a sledgehammer to drive in a pin. Nevertheless, this sort of case bothers Feinberg, who feels constrained to distinguish between "being in a harmful condition" and "undergoing a change in one's condition in a harmful direction." Despite this, and because he analyzes harm as an invaded interest, he stipulates (for "clarity and convenience") that undergoing a change in one's condition in a harmful direction be considered a harm, and therefore that harm is done in case (b). He acknowledges, however, that in any ranking of harms, "being in a harmful condition" should be weighted more heavily than "undergoing a change in one's condition in a harmful direction."[7] I think Feinberg's account is too heavily influenced by the fourth tradition. The initial distinction seems reasonable enough. But the question which then needs to be asked is: At what point does a change in one's condition in a harmful direction constitute being in a harmful "condition"? It may be impossible to give an answer in terms of dollars and cents, but we should be able to provide general criteria against which losses can be assessed.[8]

Case (c) is more difficult, partly because our intuitions concerning its description may differ. Though *I* would find it puzzling to say that the crime boss had been harmed, some others would not. Laurence Stern, for example, speaks quite unselfconsciously of "deserved harm," and would presumably see (c) as a case of that.[9] My explanation for this is that our descriptions of this case may reflect the influence of either the second or the third tradition. For this reason (c) cannot be used as a clear counter-example to the account of harm under consideration. Since the rights of the crime boss have not been violated, it might be claimed, no harm was done to him. An expansion of this point will be provided later.

Despite its suggested irrelevance, case (c) has led some writers to suggest qualifications to the kinds of interests which may be harmed, consistent with the general boundaries of the second tradition. It will strengthen our later analysis if we see why some of these qualifications do not work. One suggestion is that harm is to be understood as interference with a person's *morally good* interests. But this is obviously too strong. If the neck of a two-years-old child is broken, it is unequivocally harmed, but it is quite unclear whether there are any morally good interests that are interfered with.

A slightly more plausible suggestion is that harm is interference with or the invasion of a person's *socially valuable* interests. This places great importance on the way in which the rather vague notion of social value is understood. But even if this hurdle is surmounted, the analysis would not be satisfactory. Robinson Crusoe could have been harmed by wild animals, falling branches, and visiting cannibals. It would be disingenuous to claim that the interests affected by these events could or should be viewed as socially valuable. Their value to *him* would seem

to be more relevant in assessing whether their frustration constituted a harm.

A third suggestion is that harm is constituted by the invasion of a person's *legitimate* interests. But how are we to understand legitimacy? There is a danger that it will collapse into something like "socially valuable" or "morally good." Perhaps we can avoid this by interpreting legitimate interests as those interests which are exclusively the person's own business. This may be explicated further as those interests whose pursuit does not interfere with the interests of others. But this will not do as a general account of harm. First of all, it involves an excessive narrowing down of candidate interests, since there are few of our interests whose pursuit does not involve some restriction on the ability of others to pursue their interests. Secondly, suppose that stamp collecting is *X*'s major interest. Most of his spare time and money is spent improving his collection. *X* has planned to spend the evening sorting out a new batch of stamps, but unexpectedly *Y*, who is a dreadful bore, visits him and ruins his plans. *X*'s stamp-collecting, we can assume, is legitimate in the requisite sense. But it would be overdramatic to claim that *Y* had harmed *X*. Thirdly, even interferences with a person's illegitimate interest may be harmful if they are severe enough. Suppose that the only food in the vicinity of a starving man belongs to someone else who also needs it. He attempts to steal it, but is prevented from doing so by the owner's dog, which savages him, and he dies. His interest in stealing the food is illegitimate, but he is harmed nevertheless.

The foregoing accounts are correct in their recognition that if harm is to be analyzed in terms of interests, the interests must be suitably qualified. I want now to suggest that the necessary qualification picks out a group of interests which is so distinctive that we frequently use special locutions to refer to them.

(iii) We sometimes use expressions of the form "*Y* is in *X*'s interests." Here a person's interests and his desires may well be in conflict. Indeed, a frequent use of such expressions is to draw attention to the fact that what a person desires—even what he has an interest in—is not in his interests. Exercise may be in a person's interests, though the thought may irk him; and he may desperately want to secure hard drugs, though this will not be in his interests. Normally, people have an interest in what is in their interests. However, they do not always behave rationally or with sufficient knowledge of the consequences of their actions, and they may acquire wants or stakes in projects which are contrary to their interests. And just occasionally, they may knowingly and reasonably accord certain interests such importance that they will be prepared to jeopardize that which is said to be in their interests.

The interests of which we are now speaking are appropriately referred to as *welfare* interests. The notion of welfare is complex, but, I believe, of central importance for an understanding of harm. Its explication is made more difficult by its common confusion with well-being and happiness (as is in the *Shorter O.E.D.*). In what follows I shall attempt to piece together the main outlines of the welfare jigsaw, concentrating on individual welfare.

In its central use, "welfare" is, to use von Wright's phrase, a "privative term."[10] A privative term is one whose opposite is logically primary. It is defined as the absence of those qualities which are constitutive of its opposite. "Healthy" is privative in this sense. Good health is not so much an "abundance" of health as an absence of disease, bodily malfunction, and psychological disturbance. Underlying privative notions is some conception of normalcy.[11] Good health is the norm; it is disease and ill-health which call for explanation. When our organs and faculties are functioning normally, we do not generally see any need to seek a cause (which is, of course, not to say that we cannot give an explanation for good health). Similarly with welfare. A being fares well when it does not fare ill. Welfare, like (good) health, is a functional norm in terms of which a being's performance can be measured. Unlike health, it provides an "across-the board" assessment. In this respect it is like well-being, though it differs from the latter in other respects. A being's welfare consists, most generally, in the absence of defects and irregularities with respect to some conception of its normal functioning. In the case of animals (and perhaps plants), welfare is largely a matter of the absence of disease and deformity. Unless we have bred or developed them for some specific purposes, our criteria for normalcy have no ulterior reference.

When we come to human welfare the notion is much richer. Here welfare has regard not only to some conception of normal biological functioning, but also to those characteristically human ulterior interests (interests as stakes). We do not view (mature) human beings simply as biological organisms, but also as purposing, self-reflective and moral agents. And in their case our criteria for normal functioning go beyond (though include) the welfare requirements of animals and plants. Human beings have a well-being and happiness beyond their welfare, and for which their welfare is a prerequisite. Thus Rescher correctly notes that human welfare is "a matter of 'well-being' not in its global totality, but in its 'basic requisites,' its indispensable foundations."[12] But he fails to pay adequate attention to its presupposition of some conception of normal functioning. Human welfare is a foundational matter, but the height of the foundation is determined by some conception of normal functioning. Those who fail to clear the foundations are said to be deprived or defective, or to fare ill.

Welfare interests, in their foundational aspect, are those interests which are indispensable to the pursuit and fulfilment of characteristically human interests, whatever those interests might be.[13] Being foundational, their satisfaction is not to be identified with a person's happiness or well-being so much as the conditions which make happiness and well-being possible. Nor is their satisfaction a guarantee of happiness. It is to be seen as an opportunity for happiness rather than its sufficient condition. A person may fail to exercise the opportunities given to him, or he may abuse them, or he may have competing interests which effectively frustrate the attainment of well-being and happiness.

A specification of human welfare interests is not easy to provide with complete confidence, but insofar as they represent, in general, the preconditions for the pursuit or fulfilment of whatever specific projects we have, they tend to be fairly uniform. Obvious candidates are bodily and mental health, normal intellectual development, adequate material security, stable and non-superficial interpersonal relationships, and a fair degree of liberty.[14] Of course, there will be differences between individuals with respect to the *specific details* of their welfare interests — what is essential to one person's bodily health may be detrimental to another's — though even here the differences ought not to obscure the considerable convergences of people's welfare interests. Perhaps institutionalized welfare programmes overestimate the extent of convergence, but convergence there is.

Built into the above specification of welfare interests is reference to some standard of normalcy. This standard is likely to differ from one society to another, where conditions, resources, and opportunities differ. Although this does not preclude the possibility of some objective welfare standard appropriate to all human beings, it is far from clear what such a standard should be. The welfare requirements in a highly technologized urban society will vary significantly from those in a simple agrarian society, and unless we can confidently claim that one is better than the other, we will vainly search for universally applicable criteria of normalcy. Further, in a society which is rich in resources, the available options will tend to be increased, and so the level of welfare which constitutes the standard below which people should not fall tends to be raised.

Insofar as welfare interests are understood as those interests which are indispensable to people's pursuit of their varied ulterior interests, there is some case for claiming that a person may not be the best judge of his own welfare. He may be more concerned for his welfare than anyone else, and he may be in a better position than anyone else to judge of those things in which he has an interest, but with respect to what is in his interests there is not the same uncompromising dependence on subjective factors. As Rescher points out, a person is likely to be more concerned for his physical health than his doctor, but his doctor is likely to be a better judge of what is necessary for his bodily welfare. The determination of welfare interests is a matter of judgment and some expertise, and though a person's own feelings and interests are not to be left out of account, they are not decisive.[15] This may not be as true where the satisfaction of one welfare interest may jeopardize other welfare interests (a dilemma posed by certain surgical procedures), for then a judgment needs to be made by the person concerned as to those interests which he considers most important to the ulterior interests he has, and the extent to which he wishes to jeopardize or enhance them.

Even so, there is a tendency for each welfare interest to be of importance as a condition for total well-being or the pursuit of our significant and enduring interests. Thus the extent of our welfare is most accurately determined, not by some averaging of welfare interests, but by that respect in which we are least well-off. Rescher likens welfare to a chain whose strength is determined by its weakest link. There are few, if any, trade-offs which compensate for weaknesses.[16] No doubt the chain metaphor is too strong, but it is helpful in emphasizing the respect in which welfare interests are the indispensable conditions for well-being or the pursuit or fulfilment of all our significant interests.

We are now in a better position to understand our common concept(s) of harm.

Welfare interests function as the differentia of those interests whose frustration may be harmful. They are non-trivial; interference with them usually amounts to more than a failure to benefit; they are valued by virtue of their relation to their possessor, and not on some social recognition. Welfare interests thus reflect and at the same time sharpen up a key feature in the second tradition of understanding harm. This is not meant to imply that harm is done only when welfare interests are *directly* interfered with. Frequently people invest so much in their ulterior interests that interference with them will have the consequence of jeopardizing their welfare. Thus a disappointed suitor may sink into a personality-scarring depression.

At this point it might seem plausible to explicate harm as interference with or the invasion of a person's welfare interests. But this will not quite do. For one thing, harm may be done to animals as well as people. Any being which possesses welfare interests may have harm done to it.[17]

More importantly, the language of interference and invasion is not wholly satisfactory. In the legal definitions, the terms "interference" and "invasion" are clearly intended to indicate human agency. However, the second tradition allows for the occurrence of naturally produced harms. That, perhaps, is not excluded by the terms "interference" and "invasion." Storms may interfere with the T.V. reception; holidays may interfere with my work schedule; and a disease invade my system. But the problem is not simply one of depersonification. An interference is something which comes between, as a result of which the attainment or achievement of some norm, end, or purpose, is retarded, impeded, or thwarted. "Invasion" is a military term, and refers to a forcible or hostile intrusion or encroachment onto the territory (interests) of another. It is possible to interfere with or invade the welfare interests of another without causing harm. This is because there is more to harm, vulgarly understood (i.e., as in the second tradition), than an interposition or crossing of boundaries. Suppose that a young child, *X*, is abducted, but is rescued not long after. At the time it may be said: "*X* was found unharmed," the implication being that *X* suffered no *bodily* harm. Later on it may also be said: "*X* was not harmed by the experience," by which it is at least implied that *X* suffered no *psychological* harm. Being a young child, we may also suppose that *X*'s abduction did not lead to the thwarting of any significant projects. Now, if we think of harm simply as *interference* with welfare interests, then *X* was most certainly harmed in being abducted. But harm normally involves more than mere interference; it implies *impairment*. To impair something is to make it worse or cause it to deteriorate. Impairment is thus an interference which has substantial deleterious effects. This is not to imply that what is impaired cannot be restored, any more than that which is damaged cannot be repaired. But restoration is not constituted solely by the removal of the interference.[18] A stab wound does not disappear when the knife is withdrawn. When harm is done, there is always a wound, or at least a weal, and there is often a scar. It may go with time, but take time it will.

The element of impairment gives a further reason for the frequent interchangeability of "harm" and "injury." In our (now) most common use of the term, "injury" refers to actual physical damage. An injured hand or leg is one which has been tangibly damaged — a broken bone, a rupture of the flesh, a bruising, or something of that order. Injuries may heal, but they tend to take time. This temporal element provides the basis for an extension of the term to cover relatively lasting damage done to a person's feelings, personality, reputation, or relationships.

Harm, understood as *the impairment of a being's welfare interests*, may be self-inflicted (a further reason for thinking that "invasion," at least, is unsatisfactory). Such inflictions will only rarely be deliberate, though they may be voluntary either in the sense that a person may knowingly risk harming himself in the prosecution of some interest which he holds dear, or in the (more contentious) sense that he may enter upon some course of action in ignorance of its unavoidably harmful outcome. Deliberately self-inflicted harm may give rise to a presumption of non-voluntariness, though like all presumptions this can be overridden. A person might engage in an act of self-immolation to draw attention to what he reasonably believes to be overridingly important social and political injustices.

The move from the second to the third tradition is accomplished most easily if we make some brief remarks about rights. The nature, presuppositions, and justification of politico-moral rights continue to be in dispute, and all I can hope to do here is to outline a position.[19] Whatever else we say about them, politico-moral rights are understood to be practical considerations of great weight. This is so whether we see them, with Dworkin, as moral claims which cannot be outweighed by considerations of social utility,[20] or, as I would prefer to see them, as moral claims whose enforcement would be appropriate. There is, with respect to rights, a "special congruity in the use of force, or the threat of force."[21] The reason for this "special congruity" is the importance of the treatment they are designed to secure. This can be seen if we look at the background conditions of rights in a little more detail. To qualify as a right-holder, it is commonly accepted that a being must possess interests, for it is only of a possessor of interests that something can be claimed as *its due*. This raises again the problem of the ambiguity in "interest." In the view of some writers, these interests must be rational in the sense of being conscious projects (i.e., things we have an interest in). But this seems to me to be too strong unless it is understood as the capacity to be disposed to form conscious plans and projects. An infant, I would think, has a right to have its linguistic and other intellectual capacities developed well before it is able consciously to desire that this be done. The only *actual* interests that need be presupposed are welfare interests, though it is possible to argue that unless these welfare interests also function as preconditions for the pursuit of ulterior interests which the being has, or will come to have in the ordinary course of events, then it will not qualify as a possible right-holder.[22] It is with welfare interests that rights are primarily concerned. Indeed, I would go so far as to suggest that our politico-moral rights are, in the first instance, to the components of our welfare. Other rights that we might claim, though not derivable from judgments of welfare, can be justified only by reference to our welfare rights. This does not mean that it is automatically permissible to interfere in the lives of those who have ignored their welfare. In this sort of case there is often a concrete conflict between a person's right to self-determination and one of his other welfare interests, and before we interfere we must weigh the two interests. No such conflict arises, however, if the person who has jeopardized his welfare lacks the capacity for self-control.

Within the third tradition, harm is characteristically explicated as *the violation of a being's rights*. If the foregoing remarks on rights are roughly correct, it should not be difficult to see the rationale behind this analysis. If we begin with an understanding of harm as the impairment of some being's welfare interests, and allow that our primary rights are to the components of our welfare, then culpable harm will involve the violation of some being's rights. As we noted at the beginning, this is one reason why "harm" and "injury" are so often used inter-changeably. "Injury," like "harm," belongs to two traditions. But unlike harm, its meaning seems to have shifted in the opposite direction. In its original sense, "injury" (*injuria*) was something "contrary to right." To do someone an injury was to do him a wrong, i.e. to violate his rights. But this use of "injury" is now almost confined to certain legal contexts, and our more common use is as I suggested earlier.

The notion of a violation is ambiguous. It may refer to a *mere transgression* of (in this context) someone's welfare interests. Or it can be understood more strongly to be a *damaging infringement* of their welfare interests. Certainly the latter accords with the understanding of harm found in the third tradition. It is much less clear whether the former — often regarded as peccadilloes — are to be thought of as harms. From our explication of harm as it has developed in the second tradition, there is reason for thinking that

the mere transgression of some being's rights would not represent a harm done to that being. However, the growth of the fourth tradition has tended to pull in the opposite direction. There harm is frequently understood as any encroachment on legally protected interests. This is a point at which the third tradition remains vague.

The fourth tradition, is, as suggested earlier, a legalizing of the third. But it is not just that. It has gained a momentum of its own, enabling the extension of "harm" to cover any violation of legal rights. Though there are moderating factors (e.g. the judicial doctrine of *de minimis non curat lex*), this has not stopped harm from becoming, in some cases, simply a legal fiction. Serious moral questions concerning the legitimacy of some legal interferences are raised by this extension. Fraying the links between the impairment of welfare interests and judicial harm jeopardizes the moral basis for such interferences.[23]

II

The moral questions which arise because of the fictional extensions of legal harm are multiplied when we consider some of the distinctions which are made within the law between different kinds of harm, in particular between criminal and tortious harms. I shall now attempt to develop and defend a concept of criminable harm as including though not being exhausted by a distinguishable "harm to society."

The distinction between crimes and torts is, to say the least, unclear. Most commonly, it is said that tort actions are initiated by private individuals and directed towards compensation, whereas criminal actions are initiated by the crown, state or people and have punishment in view. But practice does not conform to this neat division. Not only are some criminal actions initiated by private individuals, but some punishments are at least partially compensatory, and for some torts punitive damages are exacted. The orthodox distinction is frequently said to reflect a fundamental difference in the harms involved. Whereas tortious harms are "private" criminal harms are "public."[24]

But this way of differentiating criminal and civil harms is not without its difficulties: "*All* wrongs are in their *remote* consequences *generally* mischievous," Austin observed. "*All* offences affect the community, and all offences affect individuals."[25] Austin's criticism is not obviously correct. In the case of offences against public administration, no apparent harm may be caused to individuals. But neither is his criticism without force. The doctrine that "no man is an island" is at its strongest when the effects of other-regarding harmful acts are in view.

We meet the distinction between individual and social harm again in discussions of the harmfulness of attempts. According to Austin, attempts are "perfectly innocuous."[26] Livingston, on the other hand, claimed that "every attempt, although it fail . . . of itself, is an injury." The explanation for their divergence is to be found in the distinction between individual and social harm. Attempts, although they may not result in any measurable harm to any assignable individual, nevertheless produce "a disturbance of society" (May), "sufficient social harm to be deemed criminal" (Hitchler), or "social harm" (Curran). More recently, Lawrence Becker has argued that the punishment of attempts is justified by their "social volatility," their creation of social instability.[27] I think Becker is on the right track, though he goes too far in suggesting that it is the social harm actually produced by attempts rather than their threatening (dangerous) character which warrants their punishment. Both aspects need to be taken into account.

To make some sense of the notion of social as distinguished from individual harm, we cannot wholly avoid the muddied waters of the "individual-society" dispute. At the same time we need to keep in mind the moral problem posed by including as a ground for punishing individuals the fact that their acts have constituted some distinguishable harm to society. The moral problem is well exemplified in the 1926 Criminal Code of the RSFSR, which understands by crime "any act which is directed against the Soviet regime, or which violates the order of things established by the workers' and peasants' authority for the period of transition to a Communist regime" (art. 6). Here the idea of harm to particular individuals seems to require explication in terms of harm to the state. Yet without tacit reliance on some conception of the importance of the state (regime) to the welfare of individuals, it is difficult to see what justification could be given for criminalizing social harms.[28]

The sense of "society" which is in view is that which refers to any enduring group of individuals (whose membership may change over a period of time), who jointly recognize certain obligations to each other, and engage in a measure of deliberate co-operation. This is a fairly formal account. For a society to come into being and to persist, certain minimum obligations and purposes of co-operation will have to be recognized. Classical writers have included among these: severe restraints on the use of violence, and a degree of mutual aid, the keeping of promises, honesty, and fairness. For present purposes these can be accepted without elaboration or discussion.

The continued existence of society of any worthwhile kind will depend on the general maintenance of a fair measure of *trust* between its members. Trust is perhaps the most important ingredient in the social glue, and helps to explain why the classical catalogue of minimum social obligations has included those we have just enumerated.

Trust involves more than a prediction that others will act in a way which respects our welfare and interests. We may be able to predict accurately that this will be the case without trusting them. Our prediction may be based on a close investigation of their prior behaviour and the pressures to which they continue to be subject. Trust is paradigmly a relation, and involves a reliance, in the absence of direct evidence, that others will act in ways which reflect our welfare and interests. Thus trust is frequently shown by taking others at their word. This need not be irrational or unreasonable. It is reasonable if the credentials of the person in whom trust is placed are first checked, or at least recognized. Even though this is no guarantee against misplaced trust, it serves to distinguish it from gullibility.

I shall argue that harm to society is to be understood as the erosion of these relationships of trust. But to make this more plausible, and to accommodate the moral problem we have previously mentioned, I need to comment on the relation between individuals and society.

Individuals are in important respects *social* beings. For one thing, they are materially dependent on the existence and perseverance of certain social relations. Unlike most other animals, human beings are for a fairly long period dependent on others for the supply of their welfare interests. This goes far beyond the provision of physical needs such as food and drink, and protection from injury, but encompasses as well the development of linguistic, rational and emotional capacities. With maturity, the character of this dependence changes, but it does not entirely disappear. Most of us still rely on others for the production of food and drink, and for protection from injury, and although we might possibly fend for ourselves in these respects, doing so would involve a radical curtailment of the interests we now have and count significant. More likely, however, our welfare would be considerably diminished, and we would not have recourse to the remedies which are instituted in highly developed social relationships — medical care, welfare services, security arrangements, and so on. As well, it is within the context of continuing social relations that our linguistic, rational and emotional capacities are maintained and continue to develop.

But more than this, our very concept of an individual has regard to social factors. Moral agency, for example, is generally taken as fairly central to our conception of the individual person. Yet it is very difficult to explicate the notion of moral agency without presupposing man-in-society. Restricted to purely self-regarding behaviour, the notion of moral agency becomes thin indeed. In addition, many of our characteristically human interests are essentially social. Take, for example, our interests in friendship, love and co-operation. These are so important as to constitute welfare interests. Yet only in a general context of trust can they possibly be satisfied. Indeed, the attitude of trust itself, insofar as it expresses a positive relationship with others, has come to be valued for its own sake.

It is a common fact of experience that not everyone is to be trusted. To the extent that this is so, social relations are eroded. Most of us can tolerate some breaches of trust. Nevertheless, some breaches are more erosive than others, and to minimise them we reallocate resources (often scarce) to security or remedies. This is in one sense wasteful and frustrating, and may even be damaging to our welfare. If we think of what it costs to maintain security services, police, criminal courts and defence establishments (even placing the best possible construction on their purposes), we get an inkling of how the erosion of trust in society has also eaten into our material resources. But it does more than this. Our personalities also suffer. We become suspicious, impersonal, nervous, defensive, and frustrated. Our lives become cramped and unfulfilled. One has only to look at the sorry state of those who feel that they cannot trust anybody, to see how damaging the fracture of social relationships can be, even when they are still far from total breakdown.

The foregoing account helps us to understand what lies behind the traditional view of crime as involving harm to society. Society is not constituted by a constellation of atomistic individuals. Because individuals are social beings, harming a person also rends or at least warps the fabric which is integral to our personhood. Thus inchoate crimes, even though they may not impair the welfare of an assignable individual, are not without their social consequences. Of course, many criminal attempts are unsuccessful because the criminal is apprehended in the course of his offence, or is thwarted by security measures. In other words, they are unsuccessful only because our trust has already been eroded, and we have re-allocated valuable resources to security measures. Unsuccessful attempts give little cause for comfort. In consequence we become even more wary, increase security, buy another lock, hesitate before going somewhere, and so on. And if this reaches a certain level, the conditions for our own welfare deteriorate, and our ability to prosecute our interests diminishes.

Offences against public administration (e.g. bribery of officials, avoidance of customs duty, and the failure to submit, or falsification of, taxation returns) are a little more difficult to deal with, because of the somewhat problematic relations between the maintenance of social relationships and the observance of certain institutional arrangements. The latter may be geared to the maintenance of a particular social *status quo*, and have little to do with the protection and promotion of social co-operation. Even so, offences against public administration generally manifest personal traits which are incompatible with relations of trust. Bribery and deception, even where unfair advantage is not obtained, and even in the case of pointless or unjust laws, will tend to weaken the social fabric. It is socially less erosive though probably more damaging to a particular kind of institutional framework, if pointless or unjust administrative regulations are openly challenged or opposed.

Criminable harm, therefore, is not to be determined solely by reference to the impairment of the welfare interests of assignable individuals, but also by having regard to the social consequences of acts. It is this which helps legitimate the punishing authority of government and suggests certain limitations on that authority. Harm to society, though distinguishable from harm to individuals, is rooted in, and justifiably interfered with by reference to the latter.[29]

NOTES

1. G. O. W. Mueller, "Criminal Theory: An Appraisal of Jerome Hall's Studies in Jurisprudence and Criminal Theory," *Indiana Law Journal,* vol. 34 (1959), p. 220.

2. For example, in art. 7 of the Criminal Code of the RSFSR (1960), harm is explicated as "a socially dangerous act . . . which infringes the Soviet social or state system, the socialist system of economy, socialist property, the person, or the political, labour, property or other rights of citizens. . . ."

3. For a more detailed discussion of this point, see Joel Feinberg, *Social Philosophy* (Englewood Cliffs, N.J. 1973), pp. 27f.

4. See Albin Eser, "The Principle of 'Harm' in the Concept of Crime: A Comparative Analysis of Criminally Protected Legal Interests," *Duquesne University Law Review,* vol. 4 (1966), pp. 345–417.

5. W.A. Seavey, "Principles of Torts," *Harvard Law Review,* vol. 56 (1942), p. 73.

6. American Law Institute, *Restatement of the Law of Torts* (Philadelphia, 1934), Ch. I, sec. i.

7. Feinberg, *op. cit.*, pp. 30–31.

8. Feinberg does in fact offer an answer just prior to the distinction we have been discussing. Where the change results in *a need being unmet*, then one will be in "a harmful condition." Though he rejects this, I think his suggestion is roughly correct. But it does raise certain problems about the nature of needs, which can be avoided. See A.R. White, "Needs and Wants," *Proceedings of the Philosophy of Education Society of Great Britain,* vol. 8 (1974), pp. 150–180.

9. Laurence Stern, "Deserved Punishment, Deserved Harm, Deserved Blame," *Philosophy,* vol. 45 (1970), pp. 317–329.

10. G.H. von Wright, *The Varieties of Goodness* (London, 1963), pp. 55ff. With other aspects of von Wright's account of welfare I am not in agreement.

11. See, on this, Christopher Boorse, "On the Distinction Between Disease and Illness," *Philosophy and Public Affairs,* vol. 5 (1975), pp. 49–68.

12. Nicholas Rescher, *Welfare: the Social Issues in Philosophical Perspective* (Pittsburgh, 1972), p. 4.

13. This is not intended to suggest that there are no limits at all to the range of ulterior interests whose prerequisites are to be denominated "welfare interests." Welfare interests are those necessary to the functioning of people as purposing, self-reflective and responsible agents (normally) in a particular social context. We may also need to limit the ulterior interests by adding the Millian rider: "within the limits imposed by the rights and interests of others," but I am unsure of this.

14. A detailed classification of components is given in Rescher, *op. cit.*, pp. 12–13.

15. For an extended discussion, see *ibid.*, pp. 15–22.

16. *Ibid.*, p. 5.

17. On the interests of animals, see Joel Feinberg, "The Rights of Animals and Unborn Generations" in W.T. Blackstone (ed.), *Philosophy and Environmental Crisis* (Athens, Ga., 1974), pp. 43–68.

18. Cf. the difference between harm and offence.

19. I have discussed these ideas in a little more detail in "Mill, Children and Rights," *Educational Philosophy and Theory,* vol. 7 (1976), pp. 1–16.

20. Ronald Dworkin, "Taking Rights Seriously," *New York Review of Books*, vol. 15 (17 December, 1970), pp. 23–31.

21. H. L. A. Hart, "Are there any Natural Rights?", *The Philosophical Review*, vol. 64 (1955), p. 178.

22. However, I remain unsure about this. This is presumably one reason why the question of "animal rights" is so troublesome. Though animals have welfare interests, it is unclear whether the norm by reference to which these welfare interests are determined includes the formation and prosecution of ulterior interest. It is, moreover, problematic to speak of animals *in general* in this regard.

23. Not that harm constitutes the only basis for legitimate legal interferences. Nevertheless, an onus is placed on those who support interference with acts which are only fictionally harmful to provide some independent moral basis.

24. William Blackstone, *Commentaries on the Laws of England*, fifth edition (Oxford, 1773), vol. IV: "Of Public Wrongs," sec. 5.

25. Quoted in Jerome Hall, *General Principles of Criminal Law*, second edition (Indianapolis, 1960), p. 241.

26. This quotation, and those that follow, is taken from Hall, *ibid.*, p. 218.

27. Lawrence C. Becker, "Criminal Attempt and the Theory of Crimes," *Philosophy and Public Affairs*, vol. 3 (1974), pp. 262–294.

28. Even in the 1960 Code, people are citizens with "persons," not persons who are also citizens.

29. Interchanges with Joel Feinberg have contributed substantially to my thinking on this topic. An earlier draft benefited from the criticisms of Michael Bayles, Hyman Gross, Andrew von Hirsch and Robert Young.

Notes and Questions

LAWRENCE FRIEDMAN, from *A History of American Law*

1. Notice that federal criminal law was codified very early in the American system. That is, it was taken out of the domain of the common law courts and placed strictly within the jurisdiction of the legislature. What were the reasons for this? State criminal law was codified soon after. Were the reasons the same? Why don't these reasons apply to any law — for example, tort law?

2. Even if laws are codified, interpretation is still open to judges. According to Lawrence Friedman, the procedural protections in American law were much greater in theory than in fact. What examples does he give of majority power operating outside the law? What examples does he give of the uneven application of procedural protections? How well does this information fit with the high hopes for good legal process and constitutional protection expressed by the revolutionary generation and set out in Chapter One of this book?

3. Friedman compares treason under early English law with treason under American law, setting out some striking differences. He points out that any totalitarian state has difficulty distinguishing ordinary crime from treason. Why is that so? What is the difference between ordinary crime and treason? How did the U.S. Constitution radically restrict the crime of treason? This restriction suggests that despite deficiencies and abuses, good legal processes are still extremely valuable.

4. Friedman provides an array of examples that illustrate the growth and change of criminal law and the sorts of acts that have been criminalized over the years. He notes that American criminal law has moved from the prohibition of sin to the protection of private property as its major focus. Does this shift reflect a change in American values? Does it reflect a change in the purpose, or the perceived purpose, of the criminal law? What are some of the examples given of economic regulation and of the regulation of morals? Can you give good reasons for making these actions criminal? Obviously, American law has not embraced Mill's argument in *On Liberty*. What principles are needed to justify these restrictions of individual freedom?

5. Keep these examples of crimes in mind when you read the article by Louis Schwartz defending the "morals offenses" of the Model Penal Code. How many of Friedman's examples of crimes can be justified by Schwartz's arguments? Is this cause for relief or alarm?

[From] *A History of American Law*

LAWRENCE FRIEDMAN

Crime and Punishment . . .

* * *

The strength of the idea of checks and balances was also one of the factors that impelled penal law toward codification. To build up the power of citizen against state, rules of criminal law had to be open and knowable. The criminal law therefore tended to become highly codified. Codification, as the Puritan magistrates found, can be looked at as a means of controlling authorities. The same theory was behind codification of penal law in Europe, after the shock waves of the French Revolution.

The common law was supposed to rest on the community's moral consensus, refined by the collective mind of the judges. Courts had invented and elaborated doctrines of crime at common law, just as they had elaborated other sorts of doctrine. But the common-law crime was potentially an instrument of oppression. Common-law decisions were in a sense retroactive; and judges were less subject to public control than legislators. Statutory rules, on the other hand, were prospective only; and they were enacted by the people's representatives. The way the king's judges had behaved, in England and in the colonies, made it easy to disapprove of the power of judges to invent and define new crimes. There were instances on record where the concept was used in this country, too. In *Kanavan's case* (Maine, 1821), the defendant dropped the dead body of a child into the Kennebec River. No statute covered the case explicitly; but the highest court of Maine affirmed the man's conviction. An appeal court in Tennessee sustained an indictment for "eavesdropping" in 1808. But the concept of the common-law crime was in retreat during the whole of the 19th century.

There were special reasons to object to the idea of a *federal* common-law crime. The concept was completely and early exploded. The case was *United States* v. *Hudson and Goodwin* (1812); defendants were indicted for "a libel on the President and Congress of the United States, contained in the Connecticut Courant of the 7th of May, 1806, charging them with having in secret voted $2,000,000 as a present to Bonaparte, for leave to make a treaty with Spain." No statute covered such an "offense" against the federal government. The Supreme Court held that no federal court was "vested with jurisdiction over any particular act done by an individual in supposed violation of the peace and dignity of the sovereign power. The legislative authority of the Union must first make an act a crime, affix a punishment to it, and declare the court that shall have jurisdiction of the offense." If federal prosecutors and judges could define crimes for themselves and punish them, enormous (and in this instance, unwelcome) power would accrue to the central government.

Codification was only a partial curb on the power of the judges. Judges lost power to invent new crimes; but the common law still *defined* the precise meaning and application of old crimes, like rape or theft. The strong, sometimes freewheeling power of judges to interpret the laws remained. The judges developed and used *canons of construction* — rules of interpretation — that maximized their discretion and authority. One such canon declared that penal statutes had to be narrowly construed, that is, limited to the smallest possible compass their language would bear. The canon made some sense; otherwise, retroactive, judge-made criminal law could be brought in through the back door, so to speak. Only those acts ought to be crimes which were plainly so labeled. Courts should not widen the coverage of a penal law beyond the unvarnished meaning of its words. Criminal law had to be known and knowable, without subtlety and artifice:

> The law to bind (the prisoner) should first be *prescribed;* that is, not only willed by the legislature, but should also be announced, and clearly and plainly published, that every citizen, if he would, could learn its meaning and know the measure of its punishment.

This was said by counsel at the trial of one Timothy Heely of New York, charged with stealing a lottery ticket. The statute made it a crime to steal a "public security." The court agreed with counsel that a state lottery ticket was not a public security, and let Heely go. The canon of strict construction, in theory, expressed the humble role of judges, subordinate to the people and their elected representatives. But there was no short-run control over whether courts used the canon or avoided it. Hence its application was in fact if not theory a matter of discretion. And what was or was not a strict or narrow construction was itself a difficult question, which gave still more discretion to the courts.

The Substantive Law of Crimes

In English law, treason had been a complex, protean concept, used to suppress all sorts of persons or groups defined as enemies of state. It was treason to levy war on the kingdom; it was treason, too, to violate the king's (unmarried) eldest daughter. It was treason to alter or clip coins; or to color "any silver current coin . . . to make it resemble a gold one." When war broke out, the colonists seized this terrible weapon for themselves. New York, for example, passed a fire-breathing law in 1781: anyone who preached, taught, spoke, wrote, or printed that the king had or ought to have dominion over New York thereby committed a "Felony without Benefit of Clergy," punishable by death or by banishment. When the war ended, passions cooled. Maryland, Massachusetts, New York, Pennsylvania and Vermont all provided, in their early constitutions, that the legislatures had no power to attaint any person of treason. The federal Constitution radically restricted this king of crimes: it defined its content, once and for all, and hedged treason trials about with procedural safeguards. Treason against the United States "shall consist only in levying War against them, or in adhering to their Enemies, giving them Aid and Comfort. No Person shall be convicted of Treason unless on the testimony of two Witnesses to the same overt Act, or on Confession in open Court.

Treason was a special crime, with unusual political significance. The shrinking law of treason mirrored a prevailing theory of criminal law. A total state, even a semitotal state, has trouble distinguishing between treason and ordinary crime. In the Soviet Union, for example, it is a crime against the state, severely punished, to deal in currency, or to steal factory property (which is all state-owned). The United States took a strikingly different path. It shrank the concept of state crime to an almost irreducible minimum. The men who drafted penal codes were willing to accept a lot of slippage in enforcement, to protect the innocent, and (even more) to keep the government in check. No doubt much of this liberality was only on paper. The Sedition Law of 1798, passed by a nervous, partisan federal government, showed that historical fears were not groundless. But the theory helped determine how government was structured, and what resources government was given to do its job.

Not that the criminal law was not important in the United States. By any measure, the *number* of acts defined as criminal grew steadily from 1776 to 1847, despite the decline in the use of the common-law crime. The classic crimes (theft, murder, rape, arson) remained on the books. There were great numbers of economic crimes, and laws defining public morality; and new ones were constantly added. The revised statutes of Indiana of 1831 — a fair sample — made it a crime to allow epsom salts "to remain unenclosed and exposed to the stock, cattle or horses of the neighborhood." It was a crime in Indiana to "alter the mark or brand" of domestic animals; to sell retail liquor without a license; to ferry a person across a creek or river for money, within two miles of any licensed ferry. It was a crime, too, to keep "either of the gaming tables called A.B.C., or E.O. Tables, billiard table, roulette, spanish needle, shuffle board, [and] faro bank." It was an offense, punishable by fine, to "vend any merchandize which may not be the product of the United States, without having a license." Profane swearing was a crime; so was "open and notorious adultery or fornication." Major statutes often included, as a final clause, a provision punishing violation or frustration of the policy expressed.

One usually thinks of a crime as an act which offends some deep-seated moral sense. But crime can also be neutrally defined, as any behavior punished at public expense and through criminal process. An unpaid seller, or a person who slips on the ice, sues the buyer or landowner at his own expense, and on his own initiative. The costs of punishing a murderer are socialized, partly because violence is thought to be a danger to everyone, not only the victim's little circle of family and friends. Murder was once privately enforced. But private justice was not always effective, and when it was, it escalated the letting of blood. Regulatory and economic crimes are enforced at public expense and initiative, but for rather different reasons. If a man sells ten baskets of defective strawberries to ten different people, it would not pay any one buyer to sue the seller. The lawsuit would eat up far more money than could possibly be recovered. If the sheriff and district attorney — public servants, paid by the state — had the power to enforce the rules, they might deter the seller's behavior far more effectively. This is quite apart from whether or not selling spoiled strawberries is considered especially immoral or not. Criminal process, then, can act as a kind of crude, undifferentiated administrative agency. This (largely inarticulate) conception was one of the reasons for the flowering of the regulatory crime. Economic crimes never gave trial courts much work. They never captured the imagination of the public. Criminal provisions of regulatory laws were not always even *meant* to be rigorously enforced. They were meant more as a last resort, as a threat to persistent and flagrant violators. When administrative justice developed in later generations, some of these "crimes" actually disappeared from the books.

The *relative* rise of the economic crime, on the statute books, was probably an external sign of a real change in the center of gravity of the criminal law. If crime was sin — fornication, blasphemy — before the Revolution, it gradually shifted to concern for protection of private property and furtherance of the community's economic business. William E. Nelson's research, in Massachusetts, supports this notion. Nelson found that prosecutions for fornication, Sunday violation, and the like declined after 1780; prosecutions for theft, on the other hand, rose. By 1800, more than forty per cent of all prosecutions in seven counties studied were for theft; only seven per cent for offenses against morality. The criminal "was no longer envisioned as a sinner against God, but rather as one who preyed upon the property of his fellow citizens." From this attitude, however, it was a short step to the instrumental use of criminal law, the use of criminal law, in other words, as a means of fostering economic growth.

* * *

The Two Faces of Criminal Law

At one time, most lawyers were generalists, and handled criminal matters along with civil suits. Even so prestigious and prominent a business lawyer as Alexander Hamilton did criminal work. In the West, and in small towns generally, criminal law remained a staple of the practice. Later in the century, the bar in major cities became more specialized. There developed both professional criminals and a professional criminal bar. It was not necessarily a dignified bar; and it lacked the prestige of the bar that served big business. Some small-scale lawyers eked out a living by gathering crumbs of practice in the lower criminal courts. A few big-city lawyers made a more handsome, and sometimes less honorable, living. In New York, the "magnificent shyster," William F. Howe, flourished between 1875 and 1900. He was a member of the infamous firm of Howe and Hummel; he defended hundreds of madams, pickpockets, forgers, as

well as the most notorious murderers of his day. Howe's specialty was gilded courtroom oratory, judiciously backed up by perjury, bribery, and blackmail.

The leaders and money-makers of the criminal bar were always flamboyant, though not always unscrupulous. Howe and Hummel were not afraid to advertise their wares. Over their "shabby but conspicuous offices . . . hung not the modest shingle of a firm of counsellors-at-law but a sign thirty or forty feet long and three or four feet high . . . illuminated at night." The organized bar gradually stamped out the practice of openly asking for business through advertisements and illuminated signs. A criminal lawyer had no retainer business, and few repeats. This left word of mouth one of the few ways he could build a practice. This fact made the criminal bar, if anything, more flamboyant than otherwise, since it had to have publicity or die.

The criminal law itself, quite naturally, underwent considerable change in the later 19th century. It became and remained by and large a matter of statute. The concept of the common-law crime, as we have seen, had been wiped out in federal law. The common-law crime decayed on the state level, too. As of 1900, most states still *technically* recognized the possibility of a common-law crime. But some states had statutes that specifically abolished the concept. These statutes stated bluntly that all crimes were listed in the penal code, and nothing else was a crime. In some states, the courts *construed* their penal codes as (silently) abolishing common-law crime. Where the concept survived, it was hardly ever used; the penal codes were in fact complete and exclusive.

The living law was somewhat more complicated. The New York penal code (passed in 1881) provided that "no act . . . shall be deemed criminal or punishable, except as prescribed or authorized by this Code, or by some statute of this state not repealed by it." This was plain abolition. Yet the penal code had a sweeping catch-all clause: "A person, who willfully and wrongly commits any act, which seriously injures the person or property of another, or which disturbs or endangers the public peace or health, or which openly outrages public decency or is injurious to public morals . . . is guilty of a misdemeanor." Obviously, prosecutors and courts could have almost as much power under this language as under the reign of common-law crime. In fact, the section was probably little used, as little as the concept of common-law crime, in those states which retained it.

In *Hackney* v. *State* (1856), an Indiana case, Hackney, the defendant, had been arrested for maintaining a "public nuisance"; this consisted of "keeping a ten-pin alley, and procuring for gain certain disorderly persons to meet there, rolling balls night and day, cursing, quarreling, drinking, and making great noises." Indiana had abolished the common-law crime. There was no statute on the books which said anything specific about tenpin alleys, but maintaining a public nuisance was a statutory misdemeanor. The question was, what was a nuisance? There was a body of common-law decisions, defining nuisance; the court explicitly denied that these cases were relevant. The common law was not to be used, even as a source of interpretation. Instead, the court turned to an Indiana statute, which defined "nuisance" as anything "injurious to health, or indecent, or offensive to the senses." This, said the court, could cover Hackney's conduct; they affirmed his conviction by the lower court.

The New York statute, and the *Hackney* case, raise the suspicion that there was more to the death of the common-law crime than meets the eye. What died was the overt, unabashed power of courts to pull out new crimes from the folkways. It was killed by that pervasive feature in American legal culture, horror of uncontrolled power. Lawmakers believed that courts should be guided — ruled — by the words of objective law, enacted by the people's representatives; nothing else should be a crime. But at the same time, the courts found covert substitutes for their lost jurisdiction. First, they benefited from vague general clauses, like the one in the New York Penal Code. Indeed, a camouflaged power was more suitable to the courts, more soothing, more protective, than a naked power at common law. Second, they allowed themselves more amplitude in interpreting the law. They rejected the extremist language of *Hackney*, about common-law interpretation. But they retained the flair for "interpretation of statutes" that *Hackney* signified. There was an old maxim that courts had a duty to construe penal statutes narrowly. Courts constantly referred to this maxim; yet even this

helped judges elbow their way into power. It was the judges who decided, after all, what was narrow and what was wide.

As we have seen, countervailing power, one of the great themes of American history, was particularly strong in criminal justice. Trial judge, appellate judge, jury, legislature stood in uneasy balance. The Constitution, the Bill of Rights, and the 14th amendment struck some sort of balance between federal and state power. At least in legal theory, criminal trials were hedged about by many safeguards. A stern law of evidence, juries, and meticulous attention to procedure were thought to be essential, to protect the life and liberty of the citizen. And the "hypertrophy" of procedure was, as we saw, at its most extreme in appeals from criminal trials.

The picture that emerged was one of precision, rigidity, care. Crimes were only those acts clearly engraved in the statute books. Laws were to be strictly construed. There was no margin for error at the trial. Probably no field of law, however, was quite so two-faced. The ideal picture of criminal justice must be contrasted with the real criminal law, parts of which were blunt, merciless, and swift, other parts of which simply ignored whole kingdoms of crime. It was true that most appeals from criminal cases succeeded; but few were appealed — one half of one per cent of total prosecutions in Chippewa County, Wisconsin; only five per cent of the cases before the Wisconsin supreme court were criminal appeals. It was an aspect of living law that the safeguards did not safeguard everybody; it was also an aspect of living law that many more were arrested than convicted, and that in the view of some the law was too soft, rather than too hard. The regular criminal law had many irregular helpers. The Ku Klux Klan rode in the South, from 1867 to the early 1870's; it burned and pillaged, and punished blacks and whites who transgressed against the Klan's concept of a proper social order. In the slums and tenderloins of big cities, street gangs, prostitutes, and thieves were mostly left to run their own underworld, enforce their own rules, govern their own society. Force was the only kind of law that ever penetrated this jungle. Alexander S. Williams, of the New York police force, became famous in the 1870's, because he "invoked the gospel of the nightstick," and organized "a strong arm squad." Patrolling the Gas

House District, Williams "clubbed the thugs with or without provocation." Charges were preferred against Williams no less than eighteen times; but the board of police commissioners "invariably acquitted" him. He justified his "furious clubbing" by the observation that "there is more law in the end of a policeman's nightstick than in a decision of the Supreme Court."

The vigilantes of the West, those self-help groups, were in some ways following an old American tradition. The first American vigilantes, the South Carolina regulators, appeared in 1767. But the movement really flourished after 1850. As we have seen, the most famous, and the models for the rest, were the two Vigilance Committees of San Francisco (1851 and 1856). Vigilante justice cropped up throughout California; in Colorado, Nevada, Oregon, Texas, and Montana; and generally in the West. "Swift and terrible retribution is the only preventive of crime, while society is organizing in the far West," wrote Thomas J. Dimsdale, chronicler of the Montana vigilantes, in 1865. All told, there were hundreds of vigilante movements. One hundred and forty-one of them took at least one human life. The total death toll has been put at 729. Virtually all of these were in the West, and before 1900. Texas was the bloodiest vigilante state; and the peak decade was the 1860's

The vigilantes were not the only groups that engaged in private criminal justice. Claims clubs in the Middle West, and miners' courts in the sparse, bleak reaches of the far West, constructed their own version of property law and punished offenders. Later in the century, "Judge Lynch" presided at an all too frequent court in the South and the border states. Mobs, in the 1890's, tortured, hanged, and sometimes burned alive black men accused of assault, murder, or rape. They sometimes snatched their victims from jail, furious at delay. Lynch mobs and vigilantes had their own sense of mission. Some of them, hungry for legitimacy, parodied the regular written law; they had their own "judges" and "juries," their own quick and summary trials. They punished crimes without names or without remedies, and enforced public policy as they saw it. They were responses to the absence of law and order (as in Montana), the disorganization of a defeated society (as in the South), or the feebleness or venality of regular government. They also were a much cheaper

form of punishment than tax-fed trials and long prison sentences. A newspaper writer, after a vigilante lynching in Golden, Colorado, in 1879, reported that "the popular verdict seemed to be that the hanging was not only well merited, but a positive gain for the county, saving at least five or six thousand dollars."

The Southern lynch mobs were the most savage and the least excusable of all the self-help groups. Their law and order was naked racism, no more. Their real complaint against law was that the courts were too careful and too slow; that some guilty prisoners went free; and that the lesson for the rest of the blacks was not sharp enough. The Western vigilantes, on the other hand, have become almost folk heroes; it is usual to regard them with sympathy, or as a necessary evil, or even as a form of popular democracy. The historian Hubert H. Bancroft praised the vigilance committees lavishly. Indeed, he loved all forms of Western justice. Vigilance, he wrote, is an "expression of power on the part of the people in the absence or impotence of law." It is "the exercise informally of their rightful power by a people wholly in sympathy with existing forms of law." It is "the keen knife in the hands of a skilful surgeon, removing the putrefaction with the least possible injury to the body politic." The San Francisco Committee of 1856, for example, was just such a surgeon: "Never before in the history of human progress have we seen, under a popular form of government, a city-full rise as one man, summoned by almighty conscience, attend at the bedside of sick law . . . and perform a speedy and almost bloodless cure." It was certainly true that public opinion was not overly severe on the "beloved rough-necks"; many who joined the vigilantes were leaders of their communities, or became prominent in later life; they found that a vigilante past was no disgrace, no impediment.

Under some conditions, self-help law can make a persuasive case. The Donner party, in 1846, tried, convicted, and banished a man named James Reed, who had killed John Snyder in a fight. The travelers were months away from Missouri — in Mexican territory, in fact — and hundreds of miles from any court, or judge, or arm of any state. The ideology of self-help was strong, too, in the 19th century; and government was stingy. It is no surprise, then, that a Wisconsin law of 1861 authorized the "organization of societies for mutual protection against larcenies of live stock." The societies were given power to choose "riders" who might "exercise all the powers of constables in the arrest and detention of criminals." A similar law in Pennsylvania in 1869 incorporated the "Spring Valley Police Company of Crawford County," a "company for the recovery of stolen horses or other property." Its members were to have the same power of arrest and detention as policemen of Philadelphia. The anti-horsethief movement arose "spontaneously" after the Revolutionary War. From the 1850's on, the societies sought, and got, legislative authorization. They lasted until better public police and the automobile put them out of business. In their heyday, they had more than 100,000 members.

Private law enforcement was an attractive idea. A statute of 1865, in Pennsylvania, gave railroads the power to employ their own police. An act of 1866 extended this law to any "colliery, furnace or rolling-mill," thus creating the "coal and iron police." The state here authorized "a veritable private army," at the request of "powerful interests." These private police — they existed in other states, as well — became anathema to the unions. They were "toughs," strikebreakers, "necessarily the enemy of organized labor." But it was not until the 1930's that they were finally abolished in Pennsylvania.

The Statute Law of Crimes

Over the years, the criminal codes, like the dollar, became markedly inflated. Traditional crimes — treason, murder, burglary, arson, and rape — stayed on the books; and new crimes, some of which seem quite unnecessary, were added. Roscoe Pound found fifty crimes in 1822 in the Rhode Island penal code. The number had grown to 128 crimes by 1872. The revised statutes of Indiana of 1881 contained more than three hundred sections under the general heading of crimes. Instead of one section about embezzlement, there were many: embezzlement of public funds, embezzlement by officers (the crime committed when "any County Treasurer, County Auditor, Sheriff, Clerk, or Receiver of any Court, Township Trustee, Justice of the Peace, Mayor of a city, Constable, Marshal of any city or incor-

porated town," or any other officers and agents of local government, failed to turn over or account for funds in their trust), embezzlement by employees, by "lawyers and collectors," by railroad employees, by "innkeepers and carriers," by bailees (a "storage, forwarding, or commission merchant, carrier, warehouseman, factor, auctioneer, or his clerk, agent or employee"), by agricultural tenants, by treasurers (of state or local government), by city officials, or by fiduciaries (secs. 1942–52). A separate section of the code punished anyone who "maliciously or mischievously" injured "any telegraph-pole or telephone-pole" (sec. 1956). There were great numbers of new economic or regulatory crimes, some quite trivial: shooting prairie hens or prairie chickens out of season, selling grain seed that harbors seeds of Canada thistle, swindling an underwriter, selling coal by false weight (secs. 2107, 2121, 2138, 2202). Whoever "stretches or places any net . . . across any creek emptying into the Ohio river in this State . . . in order to prevent the ingress of fish . . . or their egress," was guilty of a crime, and liable to pay between $5 and $20 for each day the obstruction continued (sec. 2118). It was a crime to sell skimmed milk in Indiana; to dam up a stream and produce stagnant water; to sell "diseased or corrupted or unwholesome provisions" (secs. 2067, 2069, 2071). There were also many sections, regulating public morality, against gambling, "bunkosteering," selling liquor on Sunday, pimping, adultery, public indecency. It was a crime to "entice" any "female of previous chaste character . . . to a house of ill-fame," for the "purpose of prostitution" (sec. 1993); dealing in obscene literature was also proscribed. It was a crime to sell or advertise "any secret drug or nostrum purporting to be for the exclusive use of females, or which cautions females against their use when in a condition of pregnancy; or . . . any drug for preventing conception or for procuring abortion or miscarriage" (sec. 1998). In addition, the code referred, in the section on crimes, to more than ninety other statutory sections, scattered elsewhere in the revised statutes, which also imposed criminal sanctions for this or that conduct. These were tacked on to a wide variety of statutes — on maliciously killing or injuring a "registered and tagged dog" (sec. 2649), on selling intoxicating liquors to inmates of the Soldiers' Home (sec. 2834), on violations of provisions of the "Dentistry Act" (sec. 4254), on sale of commercial fertilizers not "labeled with the State Chemist's analysis . . . or . . . labeled with a false or inaccurate analysis" (sec. 4897), and on violations of the Public Warehouse Act (sec. 6549).

What was true in Indiana was true in the other states as well. The steady growth of statutory crimes continued. Few were ever repealed; fresh ones were constantly added. In 1891 it became a misdemeanor in Indiana to "wilfully wear the badges or buttonaire [*sic*] of the Grand Army of the Republic" or other veterans groups, unless one was "entitled to use or wear the same" under the rules and regulations of the organization. Another law required road supervisors or "Gravel Road Superintendents" to cut hedges along the highways; failure to do so was an offense, and was punishable by fine. It became a felony in that year for officers of public institutions to "purchase, sell, barter or give away to any other officer . . . or to appropriate to his or their own use any of the slops or offal of any of the said public institutions." Railroads had to employ flagmen at railroad crossings; for failure to comply, money penalties were prescribed. About a dozen more distinct items of behavior became criminal, in 1891, and other, older crime laws were amended.

In every state, every extension of governmental power, every new form of regulation brought in a new batch of criminal law. Every important statute, governing railroads, banks, and corporations, or the marketing of milk, cheese, fruit, or coal; or concerning taxation, or elections and voting, or licensing an occupation, trailed along with it at the end a sentence or two imposing criminal sanctions on violators. No doubt many of these stern laws were not criminally enforced at all; violators were rarely or never tried; appeals and reported cases practically did not exist. The full discussion of these statutes belongs more to the story of government regulation of business than to criminal justice.

These regulatory crimes should not, however, be written off completely. The multiplication of economic crimes did not mean, necessarily, that people looked on sharp business behavior with more and more sense of moral outrage. It meant, rather, a decision to socialize responsibility for enforcing certain parts of the law. This process began long before the Civil War. Crimes are,

among other things, wrongful acts punished wholly at the expense of the state, and largely on the state's initiative. The states, and the federal government, were invoking criminal law in one of its historic functions—a low-level, low-paid administrative aid. In New York, in 1898, an amendment to the penal code made it a misdemeanor to sell articles as "sterling silver," unless they consisted of 925/1000ths of pure silver. If a silver merchant sold a coffee pot or creamer to a housewife, and cheated her, it had long been true that she had the right to bring an action against him. But nine times out of ten, the cost of the lawsuit, compared to the dollars at stake, hardly merited the trouble. In a criminal action, enforcement and punishment were entirely at public expense. The enforcing officials, of course, were only the usual array of policemen, district attorneys, and judges. They were not specialists in regulatory crimes, and rarely bothered with them. Criminality was often only a halfway stage on the road to administrative law—to professional, specialized policing of some area of economic life.

The Indiana statutes, as we have seen, retained the letter of the law on many old crimes against morality and public decency. In most states, some of these were only fitfully enforced; others were dead letters. But aspects of public morality remained controversial, and engendered new outbursts of law. Liquor control was a constant fountain of law. In 1887, six states were legally dry: Iowa, Kansas, Maine, New Hampshire, Rhode Island, and Vermont. The temperance movement fought hard, had many triumphs, endured many defeats, before its last and most famous victory, national prohibition, in 1920. Joseph Gusfield has argued that the point of the liquor laws lay less in their real effect—less in whether or not people drank—than in whether the law, the official norm, allowed them to drink. The struggle, in short, was symbolic, not instrumental. The issue was: whose norms were dominant, whose should be labeled right and true: those of old-line, middle-class, rural Protestant America, or those of Catholics, immigrants, the working class, dwellers in cities, who drank without shame? Whether these newcomers drank more or less than old Americans mattered less than their attitude toward drink.

Much about this thesis is attractive: neat parallels can be drawn to other areas of struggle over law. Divorce, for example, comes easily to mind. Another instructive case was the battle over the lottery. Once widely used by government to raise money for new courthouses, internal improvements, and the like, the lottery was battered by successive abolition movements; by the time of the Civil War legal lotteries existed only in Delaware and Kentucky; there was a postwar revival, but in 1895, the federal government outlawed interstate traffic in lotteries; and this was the death blow. The death of the lottery can be explained in symbolic, normative terms. But in many of these legal struggles, morality laws had clear instrumental uses. The sleepy old Sunday laws came to life because unions wanted them enforced; unions wanted a shorter work week, and Sunday laws were a useful instrument. The ministers and preachers acted as willing accomplices; labor and religion here formed an odd but understandable coalition. In Philadelphia, for example, the barber's union formed a Sunday closing committee. The committee ran a campaign against barbers who would not co-operate; 239 of these were arrested in the two-year period starting December 1898. In New York City, in the 1890's, when Theodore Roosevelt was president of the police board, and vigorously enforced the laws forcing saloons to close on Sundays, the bakers and barbers also demanded enforcement for their trades, though with mediocre results. Connecticut passed a tightened Sunday law in 1897; the statute increased the fines that could be imposed for violation, and lengthened the hours of the ban. Between twelve o'clock Saturday night and twelve o'clock Sunday night all shops, warehouses, and factories had to stay closed. The law was, basically, labor legislation; but pure morality also mixed in; sports, too, were forbidden on Sunday.

It would be a mistake, too, to assume that unenforceable laws were uniformly unenforced. A symbol loses power when it is only a symbol and nothing more. The evidence suggests that blue laws and liquor laws came intermittently to life, for particular reasons in particular places. Francis Laurent has collected figures for the flow of court business in the lower courts of Chippewa County, Wisconsin. Between 1855 and 1894, sex-law prosecutions were extremely rare but not extinct. There were five cases of incest, nine of adultery, four of fornication, one of lewd and lascivious behavior. Fifteen accusation of prostitution were brought, all within one decade. There were sixty-one prosecutions for violation of liquor-control laws; fifty occurred in one year, 1871. It is hard to resist the conclusion that laws against immorality were used selectively, though not at random. They were used to "get" somebody or were invoked against some unusually flagrant or unlucky offender. One wonders who the one man was, who, alone in a forty-year period, was officially lewd and lascivious. What had he done, and how was he caught? The figures also suggest that laws came to life on the occasion of a crackdown. But a crackdown was most likely to occur after scandal or when a strong organization, like the Women's Christian Temperance Union, with a firm political base, expressed a moral position. Arrests for drunkenness were high in the 19th century, and rose dramatically between 1860 and 1900, at least in one jurisdiction, Massachusetts, where the matter has been carefully studied.

Notes and Questions

LOUIS B. SCHWARTZ, "Morals Offenses and the Model Penal Code"

1. Penalizing offenses because they are harmful to others is the clearest justification we have for criminal sanctions. In fact, virtually all legal systems penalize many actions for reasons other than harm to others. Some laws restrict people from harming themselves, for example, by taking drugs or alcohol. Others require conformity to moral or religious norms. Obviously, the justification for such laws must be different from those based on the harm principle. Louis B. Schwartz offers some such justifications in his attempt to defend the Model Penal Code approach to morals offenses. To do this he first makes clear what morals offenses are. What are they? What distinguishes morals offenses from other offenses?

2. Two major grounds could be used to justify restricting behavior that is considered immoral but is not harmful to others. One is that society is entitled to restrict, or protect itself from, conduct that is grossly offensive to others. The other is that society is entitled to guide or regulate the moral conduct of its members. These principles lead to quite different conclusions about appropriate restrictions on individual conduct. Which does Schwartz suggest as the motivation of the Model Penal Code restrictions or of most morals legislation?

3. Schwartz notes that although there is no evidence that society as a whole is harmed by the existence of immoral behavior, the language of legislators and others suggests that the majority does think that it is being harmed. Furthermore, he points out that we must recognize that the majority will protect itself from such perceived harm. Of course, that is not a justification, is it? Does it justify Schwartz's point that recognizing these realities, we can better protect minorities by adopting a moderate model, such as the Model Penal Code, rather than chance much more restrictive legislation by individual states? What kind of an argument is that?

4. Schwartz does offer a justification for some restrictive legislation—namely, that citizens may legitimately demand state protection from psychological as well as physical harm. Do you agree? What are some examples of laws that are intended to protect persons from psychological harm? Is it a legitimate extension to protect ordinary sensitivities to deviant behavior? When? By what standards should deviant behavior be judged?

5. Schwartz seems to suggest that it may often, perhaps usually, be better to regulate behavior indirectly by regulating commerce. Why does he think so? Do you agree?

6. Schwartz considers specifically three sections of the Model Penal Code. The first is flagrant affronts and penalization of private immorality. What is a flagrant affront? What examples does Schwartz give? Can private immorality be prohibited as a flagrant affront? If so, how?

7. Next, Schwartz discusses the regulation of obscenity. What is the Model Penal Code approach? What justifies it? Is it strong enough or too strong? Why or why not?

8. The final consideration is prostitution. Schwartz points out that the question was whether to penalize all promiscuous intercourse (even if not for hire) or, on the other hand, to penalize none at all (even if for hire). What arguments are there for or against either position? What does Schwartz suggest?

Morals Offenses and the Model Penal Code

LOUIS B. SCHWARTZ

What are the "offenses against morals"? One thinks first of the sexual offenses, adultery, fornication, sodomy, incest, and prostitution, and then, by easy extension, of such sex-related offenses as bigamy, abortion, open lewdness, and obscenity. But if one pauses to reflect on what sets these apart from offenses "against the person," or "against property," or "against public administration," it becomes evident that sexual offenses do not involve violation of moral principles in any peculiar sense. Virtually the entire penal code expresses the community's ideas of morality, or at least of the most egregious immoralities. To steal, to kill, to swear falsely in legal proceedings—these are certainly condemned as much by moral and religious as by secular standards. It also becomes evident that not all sexual behavior commonly condemned by prevailing American penal laws can be subsumed under universal moral precepts. This is certainly the case as to laws regulating contraception and abortion. But it is also true of such relatively uncontroversial (in the Western World) "morals" offenses as bigamy and polygamy; plural marriage arrangements approved by great religions of the majority of mankind can hardly be condemned out-of-hand as "immoralities."

What truly distinguishes the offenses commonly thought of as "against morals" is not their relation to morality but the absence of ordinary justification for punishment by a nontheocratic state. The ordinary justification for secular penal controls is preservation of public order. The king's peace must not be disturbed, or, to put the matter in the language of our time, public security must be preserved. Individuals must be able to go about their lawful pursuits without fear of attack, plunder, or other harm. This is an interest that only organized law enforcement can effectively safeguard. If individuals had to protect themselves by restricting their movements to avoid dangerous persons or neighborhoods, or by restricting their investments for fear of violent dispossession, or by employing personal bodyguards and armed private police, the economy would suffer, the body politic would be rent by conflict of private armies, and men would still walk in fear.

No such results impend from the commission of "morals offenses." One has only to stroll along certain streets in Amsterdam to see that prostitution may be permitted to flourish openly without impairing personal security, economic prosperity, or indeed the general moral tone of a most respected nation of the Western World. Tangible interests are not threatened by a neighbor's rash decision to marry two wives or (to vary the case for readers who may see this as economic suicide) by a lady's decision to be supported by two husbands, assuming that the arrangement is by agreement of all parties directly involved. An obscene show, the predilection of two deviate males for each other, or the marriage of first cousins — all these leave nonparticipants perfectly free to pursue their own goals without fear or obstacle. The same can be said of certain nonsexual offenses, which I shall accordingly treat in this paper as "morals offenses": cruelty to animals, desecration of a flag or other generally venerated symbol, and mistreatment of a human corpse. What the dominant lawmaking groups appear to be seeking by means of morals legislation is not security and freedom in their own affairs but restraint of conduct by others that is regarded as offensive.

Accordingly, Professor Louis Henkin has suggested[1] that morals legislation may contravene constitutional provisions designed to protect liberty, especially the liberty to do as one pleases without legal constraints based solely on religious beliefs. There is wisdom in his warning, and it is the purpose of this article to review in the light of that warning some of the Model Penal Code[2] sections that venture into the difficult area of morals legislation. Preliminarily, I offer some general observations on the point of view that necessarily governed the American Law Institute as a group of would-be lawmakers. We were sensitive, I hope, to the supreme value of individual liberty, but aware also that neither legislatures nor courts will soon accept a radical change in the boundary between permissible social controls and constitutionally protected nonconformity.

I. Considerations in Appraising Morals Legislation

The first proposition I would emphasize is that a statute appearing to express nothing but religious or moral ideas is often defensible on secular grounds.[3] Perhaps an unrestricted flow of obscenity *will* encourage illicit sexuality or violent assaults on women, as some proponents of the ban believe. Perhaps polygamy and polyandry as well as adultery are condemnable on Benthamite grounds. Perhaps tolerance of homosexuality *will* undermine the courage and discipline of our citizen militia, notwithstanding contrary indications drawn from the history of ancient Greece. The evidence is hopelessly inconclusive. Professor Henkin and I may believe that those who legislate morals are minding other people's business, not their own, but the great majority of people believe that morals of "bad" people do, at least in the long run, threaten the security of the "good" people. Thus, *they* believe that it is their own business they are minding. And that belief is not demonstrably false, any more than it is demonstrably true. It is hard to deny people the right to legislate on the basis of their beliefs not demonstrably erroneous, especially if these beliefs are strongly held by a very large majority. The majority cannot be expected to abandon a credo and its associated sensitivities, however irrational, in deference to a minority's skepticism.

The argument of the preceding paragraph does not mean that all laws designed to enforce morality are acceptable or constitutionally valid if enough people entertain a baseless belief in their social utility. The point is rather that recognizing irrational elements in the controversy over morals legislation, we ought to focus on other elements, about which rational debate and agreement are possible. For example, one can examine side effects of the effort to enforce morality by penal law. One can inquire whether enforcement will be so difficult that the offense will seldom be prosecuted and, therefore, risk of punishment will not in fact operate as a deterrent. One can ask whether the rare prosecutions for sexual derelictions are arbitrarily selected, or facilitate private blackmail or police discriminations more often than general compliance with legal norms. Are police forces, prosecution resources, and court time being wastefully diverted from the central insecurities of our metropolitan life — robbery, burglary, rape, assault, and governmental corruption?

A second proposition that must be considered in appraising morals legislation is that citizens may legitimately demand of the state protection of their psychological as well as their physical integrity. No one challenges this when the protection takes the form of penal laws guarding against fear caused by threat or menace. This is probably because these are regarded as incipient physical attacks. Criminal libel laws are clearly designed to protect against psychic pain;[4] so also are disorderly conduct laws insofar as they ban loud noises, offensive odors, and tumultuous behavior disturbing the peace. In fact, laws against murder, rape, arson, robbery, burglary, and other violent felonies afford not so much protection against direct attack — that can be done only by self-defense or by having a policeman on hand at the scene of the crime — as psychological security and comfort stemming from the knowledge that the probabilities of attack are lessened by the prospect of punishment and, perhaps, from the knowledge that an attacker will be condignly treated by society.

If, then, penal law frequently or typically protects us from psychic aggression, there is basis for the popular expectation that it will protect us also from blasphemy against a cherished religion, outrage to patriotic sentiments, blatant pornography, open lewdness affronting our sensibilities in the area of sexual mores, or stinging aspersions against race or nationality. Psychiatrists might tell us that the insecurities stirred by these psychic aggressions are deeper and more acute than those involved in crimes of physical violence. Physical violence is, after all, a phenomenon that occurs largely in the domain of the ego; we can rationally measure the danger and its likelihood, and our countermeasures can be proportioned to the threat. But who can measure the dark turbulences of the unconscious when sex, race, religion or patriotism (that extension of father-reverence) is the concern?

If unanimity of strongly held moral views is approached in a community, the rebel puts himself, as it were, outside the society when he arraigns himself against those views. Society owes debt to martyrs, madmen, criminals, and professors who occasionally call into question its fundamental assumptions, but the community cannot be expected to make their first protests respectable or even tolerated by law. It is entirely understandable and in a sense proper that blasphemy should have been criminal in Puritan Massachusetts, and that cow slaughter in a Hindu state, hog-raising in a theocratic Jewish or Moslem state, or abortion in a ninety-nine per cent Catholic state should be criminal. I do not mean to suggest a particular percentage test of substantial unanimity. It is rather a matter of when an ancient and unquestioned tenet has become seriously debatable in a given community. This may happen when it is discovered that a substantial, although inarticulate, segment of the population has drifted away from the old belief. It may happen when smaller numbers of articulate opinion-makers launch an open attack on the old ethic. When this kind of a beach-head has been established in the hostile country of traditional faith, then, and only then, can we expect constitutional principles to restrain the fifty-one per cent majority from suppressing the public flouting of deeply held moral views.

Some may find in all this an encouragement or approval of excessive conservatism. Societies, it seems, are by this argument morally entitled to use force to hold back the development of new ways of thought. I do not mean it so. Rather, I see this tendency to enforce old moralities as an inherent characteristic of organized societies, and I refrain from making moral judgments on group behavior that I regard as inevitable. If I must make a moral judgment, it is in favor of the individual visionaries who are willing to pay the personal cost to challenge the old moral order. There is a morality in some lawbreaking, even when we cannot condemn the law itself as immoral, for it enables conservative societies to begin the re-examination of even the most cherished principles.

Needless to say, recognizing the legitimacy of the demand for protection against psychic discomfort does not imply indiscriminate approval of laws intended to give such protection. Giving full recognition to that demand, we may still find that other considerations are the controlling ones. Can we satisfy the demand without impairing other vital interests? How can we protect religious feelings without "establishing" religion or impairing the free exercise of proselytizing faiths? How can we protect racial sensibilities without exacerbating race hatreds and erecting a government censorship of discussion?[5] How shall we prevent pain and disgust to many who are deeply offended by portrayal of sensuality without stultifying our artists and writers?

A third aspect of morals legislation that will enter into the calculations of the rational legislator is that some protection against offensive immorality may be achieved as a by-product of legislation that aims directly at something other than immorality. We may be uneasy about attempting to regulate private sexual behavior, but we will not be so hesitant in prohibiting the commercialization of vice. This is a lesser intrusion on freedom of choice in personal relations. It presents a more realistic target for police activity. And conceptually such regulation presents itself as a ban on a form of economic activity rather than a regulation of morals. It is not the least of the advantages of this approach that it preserves to some extent the communal disapproval of illicit sexuality, thus partially satisfying those who would really prefer outright regulation of morality. So also, we may be reluctant to penalize blasphemy or sacrilege, but feel compelled to penalize the mischievous or zealous blasphemer who purposely disrupts a religious meeting or procession with utterances designed to outrage the sensibilities of the group and thus provoke a riot.[6] Reasonable rules for the maintenance of public peace incidentally afford a measure of protection against offensive irreligion. Qualms about public "establishment" of religion must yield to the fact that the alternative would be to permit a kind of violent private interference with freedom to conduct religious ceremonies.

It remains to apply the foregoing analysis to selected provisions of the Model Penal Code.

II. The Model Penal Code Approach

A. Flagrant Affronts and Penalization of Private Immorality

The Model Penal Code does not penalize the sexual sins, fornication, adultery, sodomy or other illicit sexual activity not involving violence or imposition upon children, mental incompetents, wards, or other dependents. This decision to keep penal law out of the area of private sexual relations approaches Professor Henkin's suggestion that private morality be immune from secular regulation. The Comments in Tentative Draft No. 4 declared:

> The Code does not attempt to use the power of the state to enforce purely moral or religious standards. We deem it inappropriate for the government to attempt to control behavior that has no substantial significance except as to the morality of the actor. Such matters are best left to religious, educational and other social influences. Apart from the question of constitutionality which might be raised against legislation avowedly commanding adherence to a particular religious or moral tenet, it must be recognized, as a practical matter, that in a heterogeneous community such as ours, different individuals and groups have widely divergent views of the seriousness of various moral derelictions.[7]

Although this passage expresses doubt as to the constitutionality of state regulation of morals, it does so in a context of "widely divergent views of the seriousness of various moral derelictions." Thus, it does not exclude the use of penal sanctions to protect a "moral consensus" against flagrant breach. The Kinsey studies and others are cited to show that sexual derelictions are widespread and that the incidence of sexual dereliction varies among social groups. The Comments proceed to discuss various secular goals that might be served by penalizing illicit sexual relations, such as promoting the stability of marriage, preventing illegitimacy and disease, or forestalling private violence against seducers. The judgment is made that there is no reliable basis for believing that penal laws substantially contribute to these goals. Punishment of private vice is rejected on this ground as well as on grounds of difficulty of enforcement and the potential for blackmail and other abuse of rarely enforced criminal statutes.[8] The discussion with regard to homosexual offenses follows a similar course.[9]

The Code does, however, penalize "open lewdness" — "any lewd act which [the actor] . . . knows is likely to be observed by others who would be affronted or alarmed."[10] The idea that "flagrant affront to commonly held notions of morality" might have to be differentiated from other sorts of immorality appeared in the first discussions of the Institute's policy on sexual offenses, in connection with a draft that would have penalized "open and notorious" illicit relations.[11] Eventually, however, the decision was against establishing a penal offense in which guilt would depend on the level of gossip to which the moral transgression gave rise. Guilt under the open lewdness section turns on the likelihood that the lewd act itself will be observed by others who would be affronted.

Since the Code accepts the propriety of penalizing behavior that affects others only in flagrantly affronting commonly held notions of morality, the question arises whether such repression of offensive immorality need be confined to acts done in public where others may observe and be outraged. People may be deeply offended upon learning of private debauchery. The Code seems ready at times to protect against this type of "psychological assault," at other times not. Section 250.10 penalizes mistreatment of a corpse "in a way that [the actor] . . . knows would outrage ordinary family sensibilities," although the actor may have taken every precaution for secrecy. Section 250.11 penalizes cruel treatment of an animal in private as well as in public. On the other hand, desecration of the national flag or other object of public veneration, an offense under section 250.9, is not committed unless others are likely to "observe or discover." And solicitation of deviate sexual relations is penalized only when the actor "loiters in or near any public place" for the purpose of such solicitation.[12] The Comments make it clear that the target of this legislation is not private immorality but a kind of public "nuisance" caused by congregation of homosexuals offensively flaunting their deviance from general norms of behavior.[13]

As I search for the principle of discrimination between the morals offenses made punishable only when committed openly and those punishable even when committed in secrecy, I find nothing but differences in the intensity of the aversion with which the different kinds of behavior are regarded. It was the intuition of the draftsman and his fellow lawmakers in the Institute that disrespectful behavior to a corpse and cruelty to animals were more intolerable affronts to ordinary feelings than disrespectful behavior to a flag. Therefore, in the former cases, but not the latter, we overcome our general reluctance to extend penal controls of immorality to private behavior that disquiets people solely because they learn that things of this sort are going on.

Other possible explanations do not satisfy me. For example, it explains nothing to say that we wish to "protect" the corpse or the mistreated dog, but not the flag itself. The legislation on its face seeks to deter mistreatment of all three. All three cases involve interests beyond, and merely represented by, the thing that is immediately "protected." It is not the mistreated dog who is the ultimate object of concern; his owner is entirely free to kill him (though not "cruelly") without interference from other dog owners. Our concern is for the feelings of other human beings, a large proportion of whom, although accustomed to the slaughter of animals for food, readily identify themselves with a tortured dog or horse and respond with great sensitivity to its sufferings. The desire to protect a corpse from degradation is not a deference to this remnant of a human being — the dead have no legal rights and no legislative lobby — but a protection of the feelings of the living. So also in the case of the flag, our concern is not for the bright bit of cloth but for what it symbolizes, a cluster of patriotic emotions. I submit that legislative tolerance for private flag desecration is explicable by the greater difficulty an ordinary man has in identifying with a country and all else that a flag symbolizes as compared with the ease in identifying with a corpse or a warm-blooded domestic animal. This is only an elaborate way of saying that he does not feel the first desecration as keenly as the others. Perhaps also, in the case of the flag, an element of tolerance is present for the right of political dissent when it goes no further than private disrespect for the symbol of authority.[14]

A penal code's treatment of private homosexual relations presents the crucial test of a legislator's views on whether a state may legitimately protect people from "psychological assault" by repressing not merely overt affront to consensus morals but also the most secret violation of that moral code. As is often wise in legislative affairs, the Model Penal Code avoids a clear issue of principle. The decision against penalizing deviate sexuality is rested not merely on the idea of immunity from regulation of private morality, but on a consideration of practical difficulties and evils in attempting to use the penal law in this way.[15] The Comments note that existing laws dealing with homosexual relations are nullified in practice, except in cases of violence, corruption of children, or public solicitation. Capricious selection of a few cases for prosecution, among millions of infractions, is unfair and chiefly benefits extortioners and seekers of private vengeance. The existence of the criminal law prevents some deviates from seeking psychiatric aid. Furthermore, the pursuit of homosexuals involves policemen in degrading entrapment practices, and diverts attention and effort that could be employed more usefully against the crimes of violent aggression, fraud, and government corruption, which are the overriding concerns of our metropolitan civilization.

If state legislators are not persuaded by such arguments to repeal the laws against private deviate sexual relations among adults, the constitutional issue will ultimately have to faced by the courts. When that time comes, one of the important questions will be whether homosexuality is in fact the subject of a "consensus." If not, that is, if a substantial body of public opinion regards homosexuals' private activity with indifference, or if homosexuals succeed in securing recognition as a considerable minority having otherwise "respectable" status, this issue of private morality

may soon be held to be beyond resolution by vote of fifty-one per cent of the legislators.[16] As to the status of homosexuality in this country, it is significant that the Supreme Court has reversed an obscenity conviction involving a magazine that was avowedly published by, for, and about homosexuals and that carried on a ceaseless campaign against the repressive laws.[17] The much smaller group of American polygamists have yet to break out of the class of idiosyncratic heretic-martyrs[18] by bidding for public approval in the same group-conscious way.

B. The Obscenity Provisions

The obscenity provisions of the Model Penal Code best illustrate Code's preference for an obligue approach to morals offenses, that is, the effort to express the moral impulses of the community in a penal prohibition that is nevertheless pointed at and limited to something else than sin. In this case the target is not the "sin of obscenity," but primarily a disapproved form of economic activity—commercial exploitation of the widespread weakness for titillation by pornography. This is apparent not only from the narrow definition of "obscene" in section 251.4 of the Case, but even more from the narrow definition of the forbidden behavior; only sale, advertising, or public exhibition are forbidden, and noncommercial dissemination within a restricted circle of personal associates is expressly exempt.[19]

Section 251.4 defines obscenity as material whose "predominant appeal is to prurient interest. . . ."[20] The emphasis is on the "appeal" of the material, rather than its "effect," an emphasis designed explicitly to reject prevailing definitions of obscenity that stress the "effect."[21] This effect is traditionally identified as a tendency to cause "sexually impure and lustful thoughts" or to "corrupt or deprave."[22] The Comments on section 251.4 take the position that repression of sexual thoughts and desires is not a practicable or legitimate legislative goal. Too many instigations to sexual desire exist in a society like ours, which approves much eroticism in literature, movies, and advertising, to suppose that any conceivable repression of pornography would substantially diminish the volume of such impulses. Moreover, "thoughts and desires not manifested in overt antisocial behavior are generally regarded as the exclusive concern of the individual and his spiritual advisors."[23] The Comments, rejecting also the test of tendency to corrupt or deprave, point out that corruption or depravity are attributes of character inappropriate for secular punishment when they do not lead to misconduct, and there is a paucity of evidence linking obscenity to misbehavior.[24]

The meretricious "appeal" of a book or picture is essentially a question of the attractiveness of the merchandise from a certain point of view: what makes it sell. Thus, the prohibition of obscenity takes on an aspect of regulation of unfair business or competitive practices. Just as merchants may be prohibited from selling their wares by appeal to the public's weakness for gambling,[25] so they may be restrained from purveying books, movies, or other commercial exhibition by exploiting the well-nigh universal weakness for a look behind the curtain of modesty. This same philosophy of obscenity control is evidenced by the Code provision outlawing advertising appeals that attempt to sell material "whether or not obscene, by representing or suggesting that it is obscene."[26] Moreover, the requirement under section 251.4 that the material go "substantially beyond customary limits of candor" serves to exclude from criminality the sorts of appeal to eroticism that, being prevalent, can hardly give a particular purveyor a commercial advantage.

It is important to recognize that material may predominantly "appeal" to prurient interest notwithstanding that ordinary adults may actually respond to the material with feelings of aversion or disgust. Section 251.4 explicitly encompasses material dealing with excretory functions as well as sex, which the customer is likely to find *both* repugnant and "shameful" and yet attractive in a morbid, compelling way. Not recognizing that material may be repellent and appealing at the same time, two distinguished commentators on the Code's obscenity provisions have criticized the "appeal" formula, asserting that "hard core pornography," concededly the main category we are trying to repress, has no appeal for "ordinary adults," who instead would be merely repelled by the material.[27] Common experience suggests the contrary. It is well known that policemen, lawyers, and judges involved in obscenity cases not infrequently regale their fellows with viewings of the criminal material. Moreover, a poll conducted by this author among his fellow law professors — "mature" and, for the present purposes, "ordinary" adults — evoked uniformly affirmative answers to the following question: "Would you look inside a book that you had been certainly informed has grossly obscene hard-core pornography if you were absolutely sure that no one else would ever learn that you had looked?" It is not an answer to this bit of amateur sociological research to say that people would look "out of curiosity." It is precisely such shameful curiosity to which "appeal" is made by the obscene, as the word "appeal" is used in section 251.4.

Lockhart and McClure, the two commentators referred to above, prefer a "variable obscenity" concept over the Institute's "constant obscenity" concept. Under the "constant obscenity" concept, material is normally judged by reference to "ordinary adults."[28] The "variable obscenity" concept always takes account of the nature of the contemplated audience; material would be obscene if it is "primarily directed to an audience of the sexually immature for the purpose of satisfying their craving for erotic fantasy."[29] The preference for "variable obscenity" rests not only on the mistaken view that hard-core pornography does not appeal to ordinary adults, but also on the ground that this concept facilitates the accomplishment of several ancillary legislative goals, namely, exempting transactions in "obscene" materials by persons with scholarly, scientific, or other legitimate interests in the obscene and prohibiting the advertising of material "not intrinsically pornographic as if it were hard-core pornography."[30] The Code accomplishes these results by explicit exemption for justifiable transactions in the obscene and by specific prohibition of suggestive advertising.[31] This still seems to me the better way to draft a criminal statute.

The Code's exemption for justifiable dealing in obscene material provides a workable criterion of public gain in permitting defined categories of transactions. It requires no analysis of the psyche of customers to see whether they are sexually immature or given to unusual craving for erotic fantasy. It makes no impractical demand on the sophistication of policemen, magistrates, customs officers, or jurymen. The semantics of the variable obscenity concept assumes without basis that the Kinsey researchers were immune to the prurient appeal of the materials with which they worked.[32] Would it not be a safe psychiatric guess that some persons are drawn into research of this sort precisely to satisfy in a socially approved way the craving that Lockhart and McClure deplore? In any event, it seems a confusing distortion of language to say that a pornographic picture is not obscene as respects the blasé [sexually mature?] shopkeeper who stocks it, the policeman who confiscates it, or the Model Penal Code reporter who appraises it.

As for the prohibition against suggestive advertising, this is certainly handled more effectively by explicitly declaring the advertisement criminal without regard to the "obscene" character of the material advertised than by the circumlocution that an advertisement is itself to be regarded as obscene if it appeals to the cravings of the sexually immature. That kind of test will prove more than a little troublesome for the advertising departments of some respectable literary journals.

If the gist of section 251.4 is, as suggested above, commercial exploitation of the weakness for obscenity, the question arises whether the definition of the offense should not be formulated in terms of "pandering to an interest in obscenity," that is, "exploiting such an interest primarily for pecuniary gain. . . ."[33] This proposal, made by Professor Henry Hart, a member of the Criminal Law Advisory Committee, was rejected because of the indefiniteness of "exploiting . . . primarily for pecuniary gain," and because it would clearly authorize a bookseller, for example, to procure any sort of hard-core pornography upon the unsolicited order of a customer. "Exploiting . . . primarily for pecuniary gain" is not a formula apt for guiding either judicial interpretation or merchants' behavior. It is not clear what the prosecution would have to prove beyond sale of the objectionable item. Would advertising or an excessive profit convert sale into "exploitation"? Would the formula leave a bookseller free to enjoy a gradually expanding trade in obscenity so long as he kept his merchandise discreetly under the counter and let word-of-mouth publicize the availability of his tidbits? Despite these difficulties, it may well be that the Code section on obscenity has a constitutional infirmity of the sort that concerned Professor Henkin insofar as the section restricts the freedom

of an adult to buy, and thus to read, whatever he pleases. This problem might be met by framing an appropriate exemption for such transactions to be added to those now set forth in subsection (3).

The rejection of the Hart "pandering" formulation highlights another aspect of section 251.4, namely, its applicability to a class of completely noncommercial transactions that could not conceivably be regarded as "pandering." This ban on certain noncommercial disseminations results from the fact that subsection (2) forbids every dissemination except those exempted by subsection (3), and subsection (3) exempts noncommercial dissemination only if it is limited to "personal associates of the actor." Thus, a general distribution or exhibition of obscenity is prohibited even though no one is making money from it: a zealot for sex education may not give away pamphlets at the schoolyard gates containing illustrations of people engaged in erotic practices; a rich homosexual may not use a billboard on Times Square to promulgate to the general populace the techniques and pleasures of sodomy. Plainly, this is not the economic regulation to which I have previously tried to assimilate the Code's anti-obscenity regulations. But equally, it is not merely sin-control of the sort that evoked Professor Henkin's constitutional doubts. Instead, the community is merely saying: "Sin, if you must, in private. Do not flaunt your immoralities where they will grieve and shock others. If we do not impose our morals upon you, neither must you impose yours upon us, undermining the restraints we seek to cultivate through family, church, and school." The interest being protected is not, directly or exclusively, the souls of those who might be depraved or corrupted by the obscenity, but the right of parents to shape the moral notions of their children, and the right of the general public not to be subjected to violent psychological affront.

C. Prostitution

The prostitution provisions of the Model Penal Code, like the obscenity provisions, reflect the policy of penalizing not sin but commercial exploitation of a human weakness, or serious affront to public sensibilities. The salient features of section 251.2 are as follows. Sexual activity is penalized only when carried on as a business or for hire. The section covers any form of sexual gratification. "Promoters" of prostitution—that is, procurers, pimps, keepers of houses of prostitution—are penalized more severely than the prostitutes. The patron of the prostitute is subject to prosecution for a "violation" only, that is, he may be fined but not jailed, and the offense is, by definition, not a "crime." Dependents of a prostitute are not declared to be criminals by virtue of the fact that they live off the proceeds of prostitution, as under many present laws, but the circumstance of being supported by a prostitute is made presumptive evidence that the person supported is engaged in pimping or some other form of commercial exploitation of prostitution.

The main issues in the evolution of the Institute's position on prostitution were, on the one hand, whether to penalize all "promiscuous" intercourse even if not for hire or, on the other hand, whether even intercourse for hire should be immune from prosecution when it is carried on discreetly out of the public view. Those who favored extending the criminal law to promiscuous noncommercial sexuality did so on secular, not moral, grounds. They pointed to the danger that promiscuous amateurs would be carriers of venereal disease, and they argued that law enforcement against hire-prostitution would be facilitated if the law, proceeding on the basis that most promiscuity is accompanied by hire, dispensed with proof of actual hire. Others doubted the utility or propriety of the law's intervening in private sexual relations on the basis of a vague and moralistic judgment of promiscuity; and these doubts prevailed.

It was more strenuously contended that the Model Penal Code should, following the English pattern, penalize prostitution only when it manifests itself in annoying public solicitation.[34] This position was defeated principally by the argument that "call-houses" were an important cog in the financial machine of the underworld, linked to narcotics peddling and other "rackets." I find more interesting and persuasive the parallel between this problem of the discreet exploitation of sex and the suggestion in the obscenity and context that discreet sale of obscene books to patrons who request them might not constitute "pandering." Both distinctions present the difficulty of drawing an administrable line between aggressive merchandising and passive willingness to make profits by catering to a taste for spicy life or literature.

Other provisions of section 251.2 also demonstrate its basic orientation against undesirable commerce rather than sin. The grading of offenses under the section ranges from the classification of the patron's guilt as a noncriminal "violation," through the "petty misdemeanor" classification (thirty-day maximum imprisonment) for the prostitute herself, and the "misdemeanor" classification (one year maximum) for minor participation in the promotion of prostitution, to the "third degree felony" classification (five year maximum) for owning or managing a prostitution business, bringing about an association between a prostitute and a house of prostitution, or recruiting persons into prostitution. Clearly, from the point of view of the sinfulness of illicit sexual relations, the patron's guilt is equal to that of the prostitute, but it is the seller rather than the sinful customer who is labelled a criminal. And the higher the rank in the selling organization, the graver the penalty—a significant departure from the normal assimilation of accessorial guilt to that of the principal offender. This emphasis on the businessman in sex is underscored by the fact that the higher penalties applicable to him do not depend on whether he is the instigator of the relationship; if a prostitute persuades someone to manage her illicit business or to accept her in a house of prostitution, it is he, not she, who incurs the higher penalty.

In one respect, the Code's provisions against illicit sexual activity depart from the regulation of commerce. Section 251.3 makes it a petty misdemeanor to loiter "in or near any public place for the purpose of soliciting or being solicited to engage in deviate sexual relations." This extension is explained as follows in the accompanying status note:

> [T]he main objective is to suppress the open flouting of prevailing moral standards as a sort of nuisance in public thoroughfares and parks. In the case of females, suppression of professionals is likely to accomplish that objective. In the case of males, there is a greater likelihood that non-professional homosexuals will congregate and behave in a manner grossly offensive to other users of public facilities.

The situation is analogous to that of noncommercial dissemination of obscenity by billboard publication or indiscriminate gratuitous distribution of pornography. In a community in which assemblages of "available" women evoke the same degree of violent resentment as assemblages of homosexuals, it would be consistent with this analysis to make public loitering to solicit illicit heterosexual relations an offense regardless of proof of "hire." On the other hand, the legislator may well decide that even in such a community it is not worth risking the possibility of arbitrary police intrusion into dance halls, taverns, corner drug stores, and similar resorts of unattached adolescents, on suspicion that some of the girls are promiscuous, though not prostitutes in the hire sense . . .

NOTES

1. See Henkin, *Morals and the Constitution: The Sin of Obscenity*, 63 Colum. L. Rev. 391 (1963), to which the present article is a companion piece. Controversy on the role of the state in the enforcement of morals has recently reached a new pitch of intensity. See Hart, *Law, Liberty, and Morality* (1963); Devlin, *The Enforcement of Morals* (1959); Devlin, *Law, Democracy, and Morality*, 110 U. Pa. L. Rev. 635 (1962). I shall not attempt to judge this debate, cf. Rostow, *The Sovereign Prerogative* 45–80 (1962), and I leave it to others to align the present essay with one or another of the sides. The recent controversy traverses much the same ground as was surveyed in the nineteenth century. See Mill *On Liberty* (1859); Stephen, *Liberty, Equality, Fraternity* (1873).

2. The Model Penal Code is hereinafter cited as MPC. Unless other wise indicated, all citations are to the 1962 Official Draft.

3. See McGowan v. Maryland, 366 U.S. 420 (1961). The Supreme Court upheld the constitutionality of a law requiring business establishments to close on Sunday, on the ground that such regulation serves the secular goal of providing a common day of rest and recreation, notwithstanding that the statute proscribed profanation of "the Lord's day."

4. The Model Penal Code does not make libel a criminal offense. But this decision rests upon a judgment that the penal law is not a useful or safe instrument for repressing defamation; by no means is it suggested that the hurt experienced by one who is libelled is an inappropriate concern of government. See MPC § 250.7, comment 2 (Tent. Draft No. 13, 1961).

5. See MPC § 250.7 & comments 1–4 (Tent. Draft No. 13, 1961) ("Fomenting Group Hatred"). The section was not included in the Official Draft of 1962.

6. See MPC §§ 250.8, 250.3 & comment (Tent. Draft No. 13, 1961).

7. MPC § 207.1, comment at 207 (Tent. Draft No. 4, 1955).

8. MPC § 207.1, comment at 205–10 (Tent. Draft No. 4, 1955).

9. MPC § 207.5, comment at 278–79 (Tent. Draft No. 4, 1955). "No harm to the secular interests of the community is involved in atypical sex practice in private between consenting adult partners. This area of private morals is the distinctive concern of spiritual authorities. . . . [T]here is the fundamental question of the protection to which every individual is entitled against state interference in his personal affairs when he is not hurting others." MPC § 207.5, comment at 277–78 (Tent. Draft No. 4, 1955).

10. MPC § 251.1; *cf.* MPC § 213.5, which penalizes exposure of the genitals for the purpose of arousing or gratifying sexual desire in circumstances likely to cause affront or alarm. This later offense carries a heavier penalty than open lewdness, "since the behavior amounts to, or at least is often taken as, threatening sexual aggression." MPC § 213.4 & 251.1, comment at 82 (Tent. Draft No. 13, 1961).

11. MPC § 207.1 & comment at 209 (Tent. Draft No. 4, 1955).

12. MPC § 251.3; see text accompanying note 35 *infra*.

13. MPC § 251.3, status note at 237.

14. Not all legislatures are so restrained. See, e.g., Pa. Stat. Ann. tit. 18, § 4211 (1945) ("publicly or privately mutilates, defaces, defiles or tramples upon, or casts contempt either by words or act upon, any such flag"). Query as to the constitutionality of this effort to repress a private expression of political disaffection.

15. MPC § 207.5, comment 278–79 (Tent. Draft No. 4, 1955).

16. *Cf.* Robinson v. California, 371 U.S. 905 (1962) (invalidating statute that penalized addiction to narcotics).

17. One, Inc. v. Oleson, 355 U.S. 371 (1958), *reversing* 241 F.2d 772 (9th Cir. 1957). On the "homosexual community" see Helmer, *New York's "Middle-class" Homosexuals*, Harper's, March 1963, p. 85 (evidencing current nonshocked attitude toward this minority group).

18. See Cleveland v. United States, 329 U.S. 14 (1946); Reynolds v. United States, 98 U.S. 145 (1878).

19. MPC § 251.4(2), (3).

20. (1) *Obscene Defined.* Material is obscene if, considered as a whole, its predominant appeal is to prurient interest, that is, a shameful or morbid interest, in nudity, sex or excretion, and if in addition it goes substantially beyond customary limits of candor in describing or representing such matters. Predominant appeal shall be judged with reference to ordinary

adults unless it appears from the character of the material or the circumstances of its dissemination to be designed for children or other specially susceptible audience. . . . MPC § 251.4(1).

21. See MPC § 207.10, comment 6 at 19, 29 (Tent. Draft No. 6, 1957) (§ 207.10 was subsequently renumbered § 251.4).

22. See MPC § 207.10, comment 6 at 19 n.21, 21 (Tent. Draft No. 6, 1957).

23. MPC § 207.10, comment 6 at 20 (Tent. Draft No. 6, 1957).

24. MPC § 207.10, comment 6 at 22–28 (Tent. Draft No. 6, 1957).

25. See FTC v. R. F. Keppel & Brother, 291 U.S. 304 (1934) (sale of penny candy by device of awarding prizes to lucky purchasers of some pieces). The opinion of the Court declares that Section 5 of the Federal Trade Commission Act, proscribing unfair methods of competition, "does not authorize business men," *ibid.* p. 313, but that the Commission may prevent exploitation of consumers by the enticement of gambling, as well as imposition upon competitors by use of a morally obnoxious selling appeal.

26. MPC § 251.4(2)(e). Equivalent provisions appear in some state laws. E.g., N.Y. Pen. Law § 1141.

There is some doubt whether federal obscenity laws reach such advertising. See Manual Enterprises, Inc. v. Day, 370 U.S. 478. 491 (1962). *But* see United States v. Hornick, 229 F.2d 120, 121 (3d Cir. 1956).

27. See Lockhart & McClure, *Censorship of Obscenity: The Developing Constitutional Standards*, 45 Minn. L. Rev. 72–73 (1960).

28. The Model Penal Code employs the "variable obscenity" concept in part, since § 251.4(1) provides that "appeal" shall be judged with reference to the susceptibilities of children or other specially susceptible audience when it appears that the material is designed for or directed to such an audience.

29. Lockhart & McClure, *supra* note 27, at 79.

30. *Ibid.*

31. MPC § 251.4(2)(e), (3)(a).

32. *Cf.* United States v. 31 Photographs, 156 F.Supp. 350 (S.D.N.Y. 1957), in which, absent a statutory exemption, the court was compelled to rely on variable obscenity in order to sanction import of obscene pictures by the [Kinsey] Institute for Sex Research.

33. MPC § 207.10(1) (Tent. Draft No. 6, 1957) (alternative).

34. See Street Offenses Act, 1959, 7 & 8 Eliz. 2, c. 57.

SECTION 2

Criminal Responsibility and the Meaning of Guilt

Section 1 considered the nature of crime in general. A crime is an act prohibited and sanctioned by society as a public wrong — as an offense against the people. We can discover what these crimes are by looking to the penal statutes, the official list of prohibited acts of any given society. But how do we identify a particular crime, an actual offense? Suppose we know that murder is a crime. We look it up in the statutes and see that it is prohibited and punished by the state as a public offense. No one is allowed to commit murder. Anyone who does is liable to punishment by the state on behalf of the people. Suppose we also know that John Doe killed his brother. We saw him do it. How do we know whether John Doe is guilty of murder?

What does it mean to be guilty of a crime? The first thing it means is (1) there is some act that society has officially prohibited on pain of criminal saction — that is, a certain act is a crime; and (2) the accused person committed the prohibited act. But this is only the first step. We know that people sometimes commit prohibited acts, but are not found guilty of committing a crime. That is, they are not held responsible for their act for one reason or another. How do we decide whether John Doe is responsible for his act? To say that a person is guilty (rather than simply that he has been declared guilty) means, in part, that he did in fact commit the prohibited act. But that's not all it means.

What else has to be true in order to say that the person who committed the act is guilty of committing a crime? This question raises the same issues of personal fault and responsibility discussed in the materials on tort law. What did John Doe, the wrongdoer, intend? Was the act intentional or accidental? Was John Doe in control of himself? Did he understand what he was doing? What influenced his behavior? Was there any justification or excuse? Ask yourself whether the concept of fault or responsibility is the same in criminal law as in tort law. To be guilty of a crime is to be responsible for it. The basic question of this section, then, is when should a person be held criminally responsible?

In the first selection Richard B. Brandt sets out the traditional principles of criminal responsibility, helpfully comparing them to principles of moral blameworthiness. Brandt explains that a person is guilty of a crime if he committed a penal offense without justification or excuse. He also lays out the kinds of justifications and excuses that are recognized in law and explains how they work. It is, as Brandt says, crucial to the understanding of criminal responsibility to understand the nature and function of justification and excuse.

Following Brandt's essay is a short excerpt from Lawrence Friedman's book tracing the development of the *mens rea* condition, or mental element, in the criminal law. In the Anglo-American and most other legal systems a person is not guilty of a crime unless he or she had a "guilty mind." *Mens rea* means *guilty* or *evil mind*. In the example even if John Doe killed his brother, he is not guilty of murder unless he was in one of the appropriate mental states (those states identified by law) when he did it. We discussed in Chapter Five these mental states and the degrees of fault associated with them in tort law. Here we include an excerpt from the Model Penal Code, which gives the *mens rea* conditions for the criminal law. The Model Penal Code provides that "a person is not guilty of an offense unless he acted purposely, knowingly, recklessly, or negligently, as the law may require, with respect to each material element of the offense." If John Doe pushed his brother out a window for the purpose of killing him, John's mental state carries with it the highest level of responsibility. If John pushed his brother knowing he would fall out of the window and be killed, but not for the purpose of killing him, then John is almost but not quite as culpable as if he purposely killed him. If John pushed his brother knowing there was a substantial risk his brother would fall out of the window and be killed, then John is not as blameworthy as if he knew his brother would be killed. If John pushed his brother not realizing that his brother might fall out of the window and be killed, when any reasonable person would have recognized this risk, then John was negligent, but not as guilty as if he had recklessly taken a known risk. This is the way the categories are set up in the criminal law. The mental state of an actor directly affects the level of guilt with which he is charged. Consider for yourself what justifies this hierarchy of guilt.

Next, Jerome Hall discusses the connection between mental states (*mens rea* conditions) and personal fault, particularly in terms of the distinction between intention and motive. The basic question raised by Hall is, Should motive be considered a significant element of the criminal or other law, and if so, in what capacity? It is clear that motive is relevant to evaluating moral blameworthiness. Should it also be considered in respect to legal guilt? Hall thinks not, and his discussion explaining why helps to clarify further the elements of criminal guilt or responsibility.

Herbert Packer, in the final selection, asks whether strict liability can be justified in a criminal context. What is strict liability? Strict liability, as Packer points out, means that a claim of mistake will not be allowed as a defense against culpability for an act. Strict liability eliminates the consideration of a person's mental state (the guilty mind or *mens rea* requirement) as a material element of guilt or responsibility. Packer's main question is, Should mistake always be considered in criminal law? Is strict liability harder to justify for criminal offenses? Packer argues that it is. As he sees it, the criminal law has fallen into the use of strict liability for some offenses, but this can never be justified. Dividing the strict liability offenses into four categories, Packer considers the implications of each, arguing that the stigma and punishment associated with criminal offenses always require the defense of *mens rea*. According to Packer, no one should be convicted of a crime unless he or she has a guilty mind.

You may find it useful to look back at the Harper and James article in Chapter Five. These authors review the considerations that support adopting strict liability for tort damages from accidents. Do the considerations set out by Harper and James have any application in a criminal context? Are there considerations in criminal matters that have no application in torts? Ask yourself why. Reviewing these considerations should help to clarify the essential elements of both tort law and criminal law and the differences between them.

Notes and Questions

RICHARD B. BRANDT, from *Ethical Theory*

1. How does Richard Brandt define a *crime*, and how is it related to punishment and pardon? How does he amend his initial vague definition?

2. Brandt draws an analogy between the moral concept of prima facie obligations and the legal combination of crime plus defense. What is this analogy, and why does he draw it?

3. Brandt notes that there are different kinds of defenses. There is the defense of justification and the defense of excuse. What is the difference between them? What examples of justification does Brandt give?

4. There are also two kinds of excuses. What are they, and what is the significance of the difference? What are some of the examples given of each? Do the examples illuminate the difference?

5. In addition to justification and excuse, there are also certain relevant considerations that are grounds for reducing the severity of a sentence. What are some examples of these considerations? Can you explain the difference between them and excuses or justifications?

6. Brandt points out that legal excuses give content to the mental elements, often called *mens rea*, required in the law. What observation does he say can be made about the identity of this mental element?

7. There are two major exceptions to the mental element requirement. What are they? Are they significant, according to Brandt? Can they be explained or made consistent with the *mens rea* requirement?

8. Brandt outlines a number of important distinctions between the nature of legal and moral obligations and excuses. What are they? One question to be asked is whether legal liability can be justified where it diverges from the requirements of moral blameworthiness. What does Brandt have to say about this question?

[From] *Ethical Theory*

RICHARD B. BRANDT

The Principles of Criminal Law

In order to get before us concretely the ideas and practices of which we wish to discover the "ethical foundations," let us review the main concepts and principles of criminal law. Unfortunately there is controversy among judges and professors of law about what these concepts and principles are, and about whether they should be changed; our brief survey must necessarily ignore such differences of opinion and other subtleties, in large part.

The central feature of the system of criminal

justice in the United States is the existence of laws, statutory or common, requiring that persons be caused pain or loss by the state if a judicial process has found them guilty of a crime. It is difficult to explain in general what constitutes a crime, but we can, for a start, say that criminal action always includes overt behavior which causes or threatens a "public harm," that is, some effects considered to be harmful to the community as a whole. The law provides different penalties for different offenses, the more severe ones attaching to those crimes considered in some sense more serious. For most offenses the law does not specify an exact penalty for a particular type of offense, but only a range of permitted penalties; the judge must then select some penalty within the permitted range which strikes him as appropriate, everything considered. The executive department of the government, however, has the power to reduce a sentence or pardon a criminal altogether for any reasons which strike it as proper; but it does not have the power to increase the penalty set by the judge. Various boards established by the executive department may pardon or parole, or make recommendations for such actions. Theoretically juries decide only a factual question: whether the accused acted in a way defined by the law as criminal; but practically they often refuse to convict, when they regard the penalty prescribed by law for a certain offense as markedly out of line with the moral merits of the case. In some instances juries may make recommendations about the severity of sentences.

In order to get a deeper understanding of what it is to commit a certain crime, it is helpful to draw an analogy between legal and moral concepts. Let us recall the relations between prima facie obligation, over-all obligation, and blameworthiness. In general we incline to think that, for instance, if a person has promised to do something, he has a prima facie obligation to do that thing. Sometimes, however, he will not have an over-all obligation to do this, on account of the weight of conflicting obligations, such as obligation to avoid serious injury to other persons, or to give important assistance in case of need. A prima facie obligation to keep a promise, then, does not imply an over-all obligation to keep it. Moreover, failure to keep a promise, even if one is over-all obligated to keep it, does not necessarily imply moral blameworthiness.

This is obvious if we are talking of *objective* obligation, for a person can be objectively obligated to do something when he does not know that he is; a man of perfect character may fail to perform his objective obligations. But it is true even of subjective obligation — for instance, if a man because of confused moral thinking believes he is obligated to do what he is subjectively obligated not to do.

Corresponding roughly to objective prima facie obligations are the law's prohibitions of certain kinds of conduct. The law aims to prevent certain kinds of overt behavior, and sometimes the law states, in a preamble preceding clauses prescribing punishment, what kind of conduct it is aiming to prevent. For instance, it may say that "No company shall sell, . . . or offer for sale . . . any security of its own issue until it shall have . . . secured . . . a permit authorizing it to do so." (California Corporate Securities Act, Cal. Stats. 1917, p. 673.) But the law recognizes that conduct of the sort it aims to prevent in general may sometimes be justified; and therefore it permits, as defense against a criminal charge, a showing that the accused's action was justified (that in the special circumstances the agent did what the law does not really want to prevent). For instance, the law forbids killing another person; but it is prepared to accept the defense that the killing was in self-defense. Roughly, a defense of justification is analogous to a showing, in morals, that although one had a prima facie obligation not to do so-and-so, in the total circumstances doing this was the right thing. Moreover, just as infraction of overall obligation does not imply blameworthiness in morals, so the commission of some act the law intends to prevent is not necessarily criminally culpable, even if it cannot be justified in the foregoing sense. Just as there may be excuses in morals for doing what one ought not, so there are excuses in law. It is useful to distinguish three kinds of excuses in law: (a) excuses which completely exculpate, wholly free from taint of crime, (b) excuses which mitigate in the sense of reducing the crime to one of the types which the law regards as less serious (e.g., reducing from murder in the first degree to involuntary manslaughter), and (c) considerations which are properly viewed by the judge as calling for the selection of a lower penalty from among those permitted by law.

We can now see more clearly what it is to have committed some specific crime, for instance, murder in the first degree. It is (1) to have behaved in some overt way which the law aims to prevent, here to have caused the death of someone, (2) to be unable to show a legally acceptable justification of one's act, and (3) to be unable to offer an excuse of the above types (a) or (b). In a carefully written penal code, the crime of murder in the first degree will be carefully described so that one will not have committed it unless all these conditions are satisfied. To commit a certain crime, then, is to behave in a certain way, and be unable to offer one of these defenses.

It will illuminate the relation between legal liability to punishment and moral excuses and blameworthiness, to review the major types of defense. We begin with the major *justifications*. (1) An act, otherwise subject to punishment, is not a crime if done in reasonable self-defense against unlawful attack, by a soldier in execution of lawful orders, in order to prevent treason or a felony (at least one done with violence), or in the service of public welfare (as destruction of property in order to prevent flood damage or to bring a forest fire under control). (2) An act, otherwise subject to punishment, is not a crime if performed because someone threatened the agent with loss of life or personal injury, in such circumstances as would intimidate a person of ordinary firmness. This justification, however, is ordinarily not accepted for homicide. (3) One may perform a forbidden act with impunity if, in case one does not, the result one causes and worse will in all probability happen anyway. For instance, one judge has indicated that a seaman is not liable for putting persons out of an overcrowded lifeboat in a storm if otherwise the boat would sink, provided the selection of the unfortunates is made in a reasonable manner. (For a contrary opinion, see *Regina* v. *Dudley and Stephens*.) This is one sense in which "necessity knows no law."

Let us now survey the *excuses which exculpate*. (4) A person is usually exculpated if he causes a harm the law seeks to prevent, by accident, for instance, if he causes the death of someone, but unforeseeably, despite all reasonable precautions. However, such accidental harm is sometimes punished; in many situations in which the defendant is committing an unlawful act when the accident happens, he is treated as if he intended to cause the accident. (5) A man is exculpated if because of an innocent mistake in belief about facts he performs an unlawful act which would have been lawful had the facts been as he thought they were. For instance, it is lawful to shoot a person who has broken into one's house at night for the purpose of theft; and if a person shoots his wife or servant on account of a genuine and innocent supposition that the person fired at is a burglar, he is exonerated. (6) If a person is physically compelled to perform an unlawful act, e.g., if the hands of a stronger person held and guided his dagger, he is thought not to have performed that act at all, and will not be prosecuted. (7) The law excuses a man for doing what it is impossible not to do. It may forbid a car standing in a certain place, but if a car stands there because traffic is jammed and the car cannot be moved, the act is not subject to punishment. (8) A person under seven years of age cannot commit a crime; and he is not guilty of a crime if under fourteen unless malicious intent is established — although he may be subject to treatment under rules for juveniles. (9) A person is excused if he performed an otherwise unlawful act while walking in his sleep. Insanity is also an excuse if the defendant's mental disease or defect is such that he did "not know the nature and quality of the act he was doing; or, if he did know it, that he did not know he was doing what was wrong." (*The Queen* v. *M'Naghten*.) (10) Theoretically a person is excused from guilt if he performs an unlawful act because of involuntary intoxication — even though in practice courts are often reluctant to admit that intoxication is "involuntary."

There are also *mitigating* excuses, which reduce the seriousness of the crime. (11) In the case of homicide, a showing that the act was done impulsively often affects the degree of guilt. Premeditation is commonly necessary for first degree murder. If one kills in the heat of passion, without forethought, he is guilty only of second degree murder. Furthermore, if such heat of passion is brought about by legally recognized provocation — such as finding one's wife in the act of adultery — the defendant may be guilty only of manslaughter. (12) Voluntary intoxication may reduce the degree of crime, but it will not exculpate, on the ground that intoxication is itself an immoral act which cannot be used as a shield for wrong conduct.

Finally, judges regularly take into account various considerations as grounds for reducing the severity of a sentence: such as severe temptation, neurotic constitution, previous lack of opportunities in life, evidence indicating that the culprit is not a menace to society, the convicted person's state of health, probable serious affects of a harsh sentence on his family. Judges sometimes make a sentence *more* severe when they think the outrage of the community requires it — if the law would be brought disrespect by a mild sentence.

The excuses (nos. four to twelve) are of interest because they give practical content to the "mental element" or "guilty mind" (*mens rea*) which the law holds must be present in order for a person to be guilty of a crime on account of his overt behavior. In view of these excuses, is there any general statement possible about the identity of this mental element? There are several things we can say. (1) It must have been possible for the accused to have behaved, as a result of different decisions or volitions, in a way that was lawful (a requirement of excuses nos. six and seven). (2) The agent must have been aware to some degree that the events which the law proscribes would flow from his bodily behavior — or at any rate that they might, that his behavior was *risking* such consequences. (3) The agent must have been aware that it is wrong to produce such consequences, *or* that it is unlawful, *or* at least that society generally regards the production of such consequences as wrong. In general, all these three conditions are required. There are two major exceptions: the so-called "public welfare" or "strict liability" offenses, where *intent* in the sense of (2) is not required at all; and the rule which imputes intent to commit offenses which in fact were accidental, to persons engaged in committing some other wrong intentionally. These exceptions are regarded by many as simply illogical elements in the law, which are without justification.

These conditions required for legal guilt are not exactly identical with those required for moral reprehensibility, the latter requiring that an act show *defect of character*. Moral guilt usually

goes with legal guilt, but not necessarily. In practice, imputation of legal guilt is likely to be even more closely conformed to imputation of moral guilt than theory allows; for an unlawful act which is clearly consistent with moral character may not be prosecuted, or if prosecuted the jury may refuse to bring in a verdict of guilty.

How nearly is there a parallel between degree of moral reprehensibility of an act and seriousness of the act as a crime? We must expect some divergencies. The law, for instance, cannot concern itself with minor matters. Again, the law must be drawn in terms of relatively precise general rules, so that its administration does not place an intolerable burden of discretion on the officials charged with its application. Further, the law must be so phrased that available evidence can answer questions about its applicability; it is unfortunate if application of the law must turn on decisions about fact which are necessarily speculative.

At some points moral reprehensibility is more severe than the law. The law condemns only for overt behavior (including attempts) which is in some way publicly undesirable; it never condemns a man for his motives alone, or for his thoughts or feelings. Again, there are morally indefensible injuries of other persons (for instance, refusal to repay borrowed money) which, although they are actionable in civil suits, are not crimes and not punishable in criminal law. Again, there are many minor offenses that are morally wrong but legally are not prohibited. Further, the law automatically excuses offenses in persons under a certain age; moral judgments are more flexible and individual.

At other points, however, the law is more severe. (1) For instance, it is an axiom of the law that "ignorance of the law excuses nobody." And, we can add, it is no excuse to believe that it is morally right to do what the law forbids. Now, to some extent the same principles obtain in moral judgments: we would think it odd if anyone tried to excuse murder or rape on the ground that he did not believe the act to be wrong. Nevertheless, within a certain range, absence of belief that an act is wrong (or positive belief that it is a duty) serves as an excuse in morals; we hardly condemn a Mormon for practising polygamy, and we partly if not wholly excuse a Christian Scientist who refuses to take an ill child to the hospital.

The law, however, does not regard the absence of belief that an act was unlawful as an excuse. Part of the reason for this is that the law in major part is enforcing moral rules that are well known and that are respected as right by the vast majority. (This class of cases, however, does not include many regulations that a moral person could hardly be expected to observe as a part of moral behavior, for example, peculiar traffic regulations in a small town. It is not clear that there is any moral justification for the law's refusing to accept ignorance as an excuse, in these cases where law fails to coincide with morals and where a man of character could hardly be expected to know the law.) There is also reason for not permitting conscientious objection to the law as an excuse: the law cannot permit a man to set up his own conscience as the law of the land, since if it did law enforcement could probably not proceed at all, or at least only under great handicaps. So, both the Mormon and the Christian Scientist may go to jail on serious charges.

An even more striking difference (2) between law and moral judgment is the existence of "strict liability." There is a class of infractions of law that are *not excused by demonstrable lack of intent*, any infraction of these laws is liable to punishment even if it was unforeseeable, inadvertent, and practically impossible to prevent. Thus, a butcher who sells diseased meat innocently and without any negligence, and even on the advice of experts about the quality of his meat, may incur a prison sentence. In general, a highly conscientious and law-abiding man might, through no moral fault whatever, infringe one of these laws and be subject to serious penalty. Moral condemnation certainly does not follow the law at this point.

Finally (3) some excuses that exculpate in morals only mitigate in law. In morals, whenever the circumstances are such that a man of character might be expected to do what the defendant did, he is exonerated. This is not so in law. Suppose a person imbibes a cocktail for the first time, not knowing that one drink will affect him so much that he will thoughtlessly accept another, and then be drunk. Suppose as a result of the first drink (and the second), he becomes drunk. Suppose further that this man has no reason to think that, even if he became drunk, he

would be belligerent—beyond the vague awareness that some people do become belligerent when drunk. And suppose that, after becoming drunk, this person actually attacks a man and kills him. In law this can be a very serious offense; but in morals it is difficult to believe that the act is not blameless, as far as the homicide is concerned. The man *will* be morally to blame if, knowing what he did, he permits himself to become drunk again. But his drunken action was not rationally foreseeable. (It is a different matter if a man drinks, knowing that he is going to drive a car immediately after doing so.) Similarly, the rule that homicide is automatically manslaughter if the agent was committing a misdemeanor, or murder in the first degree if he was committing a felony, is by no means followed by moral judgment; perhaps in most cases the assumption of intent is reasonable, but it is not necessarily so in all cases.

It is often said that the law takes no account of *motives*, but only of the *intent* to perform a specific act. We have already noted that in practice this is not quite true. But we should also notice that, if we have a clear idea of what a *motive* is (namely, that for a person to have a certain motive is for him to be inclined or disinclined to perform a certain act by his belief that doing so will have a certain property or consequence), we can construe "intent" and *mens rea* as facts about a person's motives. Clearly, if a person intentionally performs a prohibited act, he thereby shows that he was *not motivated sufficiently* to avoid that act, and this fact is as much a fact about his motives as any other. What is true is that the law takes this fact about one's motives as very decisive for the legal culpability of one's act. But other motives also play an important role. One can, if one likes, construe justifying exculpations as based on a consideration of motives: for instance, one might say that the law recognizes the fact that the motive of saving oneself or one's children from death, or saving many from the destruction of a forest fire, is a good and sufficient justification for performing an unlawful act. Moreover, a showing of good motives or strong temptations may, although not exculpating from legal liability, result in a suspended or very light sentence (and, of course, may induce a jury not to convict at all—witness cases in which juries have refused to convict persons who practiced euthanasia under circumstances approved by the jury but against the law).

One might inquire whether any examination of the "ethical foundations" of the law can show that we are obligated to support and maintain the law at those points where it diverges from judgments of moral culpability. The answer is that it can, on matters where the law is less severe than morals (except for some of the artificial distinctions between crimes and torts — damages actionable in civil suits). It can because there is no alternative for law which is not excessively expensive and burdensome, or which would not introduce objectionably speculative elements into legal procedure. But, on some matters where the law is more severe than moral judgment, it cannot be shown that we ought to support the maintenance of present legal principles. It is quite true that (except for matters like traffic reg-

ulations where legal restrictions do not correspond with accepted judgments of moral obligation) it is impossible to accept ignorance of the law, or conscientious disagreement with the law, as an excuse. The law cannot cease to protect what it sets out to protect because some do not agree or are unaware. But the other practices of the law that morals cannot follow appear to be morally unjustified, and there is no obligation to defend them; on the contrary, there is an obligation to do what one can to get them changed. It is sometimes thought that a utilitarian foundation of the law can justify these discrepancies as necessary evils in the service of the public good. However, this is not true: it is only utilitarian theory applied on the basis of false factual premises that has such consequences, and it has not been shown that we maximize net expectable utility by continuing with these legal practices.

Notes and Questions

LAWRENCE FRIEDMAN, from *A History of American Law*

1. Notice that the consideration of mental states and even more so the evaluation of insanity are comparatively recent events in the law. Since 1843 the M'Naghten rule has been the dominant definition of legal insanity. What is the M'Naghten rule? Does it make sense? What other tests are used? Can you think of a better way to handle criminal responsibility when competence is at issue?

2. Lawrence Friedman points out that the criminal law is not consistent in its application of mental states for the evaluation of responsibility. Many economic crimes do not require a "guilty mind." Why not? Can you think of any justification for this? Keep this in mind as you read the article by Herbert Packer. He will have much to say about this issue.

3. Can intent apply to corporations? Should it? Does this cause any special problems for the criminal law?

4. Friedman notes that some criminal statutes reverse the presumption of innocence. What examples does he give? Do they seem reasonable? Actually this is not uncommon. Consider tax law or traffic violations. There is no presumption of innocence. Should there be? The presumption of innocence is a very basic principle of criminal justice in a free society. It is discussed in all the articles in this section.

[From] *A History of American Law*

LAWRENCE FRIEDMAN

Crime, Crime Rates, Insanity, the Guilty Mind

The criminal law, legitimate and illegitimate, assumes that there is a reality, called crime, on which law operates. Obviously, in one sense, a society chooses for itself how much crime it wants. When an act is declared criminal, all its actors are committing crime. In 1900, there was vastly more criminal law on the books than in 1850 or 1800, hence in this sense probably vastly more crime. But those who worry about the crime rate are usually concerned, not with economic crime, but with the classic crimes of violence and social disruption, murder, robbery, assault. These are enforced much more systematically and with greater use of public resources than other kinds of crime. The definitions of these crimes remained more or less constant during the century; or at least constant enough for meaningful comparisons, if only the figures were at hand.

Some facts are known about crime in the real world, in the 19th century. What evidence there is suggests that the crime rate for serious crimes, at least since 1860, gradually declined. There was proportionately *less* violence, murder, assault in the 1970's than a century before. Roger Lane's research, for 19th-century Massachusetts, saw a marked falling-off in jail commitments, from 333 per 100,000 population to 163, between 1860 and 1960. The social investment in crime-fighting increased; so, too, did the worry and the tumult. The basic reason may be that violent crime, particularly in the cities, becomes less tolerable the more society is one and interconnected. The city is the heart of modern society; society is governed from the city; the economy depends on city life. The city is the place where people are most interdependent; where they are most confronted with strangers, and where their lives, property, and health are most at hazard. The more a society is urban, industrial, and interdependent, the more there is division of labor in the economy, the less the society can tolerate violent crime. Crime is bad for business, and bad for the social order. The

city civilizes and tames, to a certain extent; for this reason violence has diminished. But by the same token crime has not gone down fast enough; the public demand for law and order more than keeps pace with the supply.

The violent crimes were also the crimes of mystery and drama; the crimes that provided raw material for novels, poems, and plays; the crimes par excellence, as the public thought of them. Pamphlets, trial transcripts, last words of condemned men were part of American popular culture. There were hundreds of these fugitive writings: John Erpenstein, who gave his wife a bread-and-butter sandwich, liberally sprinkled with arsenic, was credited with writing the "Life, Trial, Execution and Dying Confession of John Erpenstein, Convicted of Poisoning His Wife, and Executed in Newark, N.J., on March 30, 1852. Written by himself and translated from the German." Professor John W. Webster murdered Dr. George Parkman, in the Harvard Medical School, in 1849; publishers rushed many versions of the background and trial of this sensational crime into print. The Fall River tragedy — the murder of Lizzie Borden's parents in 1892 — has enlivened American literature ever since.

It was this type of crime, too, which evoked the raw hatred that could mold a mob and lead a man to be lynched. It was this type of crime in which trial by jury was frequent, and in which the jury was free to apply its "unwritten laws"; in which justice was, in theory, tailored to the individual case. Here, too, were the cases in which the defense of insanity was invoked. Juries, to be sure, probably went their own way; they excused men for insanity, or did not excuse, in accordance with their own moral code and common sense, rather than the science of their time. But those scientific notions had at least a marginal and indirect effect. And in the 19th century, almost for the first time, lawyers and doctors engaged in a grand and continuing debate about the meaning of criminal responsibility, and the scope of the insanity defense.

The dominant definition of legal insanity was the so-called M'Naghten rule, named after a mad Englishman, for whose case the rule was first announced, in 1843. Simply put, a defendant could not be excused from responsibility unless he was "labouring under such a defect of reason . . . as not to know the nature and quality of the act he was doing; or . . . that he did not know what he was doing was wrong." This "right or wrong" test was a pleasing platitude: it seemed to soothe the moral sense of the legal community; in any event it won rapid acceptance. In a few American states, this "right or wrong" test was supplemented by another, the "irresistible impulse" or "wild beast" test. If a man, said Chief Justice John F. Dillon of Iowa in 1868, knew that his act was wrong, but "was driven to it by an uncontrollable and irresistible impulse, arising, not from natural passion, but from an insane condition of the mind," he was not be be held responsible. The idea of irresistible impulse strikes the modern ear as somewhat romantic, not to say medically absurd; but the wild-beast test was broader than the M'Naghten test alone; and some of the best psychiatrists of the day believed in irresistible impulse. A third rule stood all by itself in New Hampshire. This was Chief Justice Charles Doe's rule, enunciated in *State* v. *Pike* (1869). Here the test was no test at all: the question to be answered in each case was, whether the criminal act was the "offspring or product of mental disease. . . ." Neither delusion, nor knowledge of right and wrong was, as a matter of law, a test of mental disease. Rather, all symptoms and "all tests of mental disease" were "purely questions of fact," within the province and power of the jury alone, to determine and decide.

Arguments over these various "tests" were really arguments over the form of stereotyped instructions, to be read to the jury. What distinguished the tests was the degree of autonomy they (apparently) gave to the jury. Whether the jury listened, or cared, or understood is another question. In a few great cases, the tests acted as a dark and bloody battleground for war between contending schools of psychiatry. Most notable was the weird trial of Charles Guiteau, who murdered President Garfield in 1881. Guiteau's behavior, before and after (and during) the trial, was bizarre, to say the least; but probably no test,

however worded, could have persuaded the jury not to send the President's killer to the gallows.

It would not be totally wrong to interpret the debate as evidence of moral sensitivity among those concerned with the criminal law—at least a horror of putting incompetent people to death. But, as we have seen, the criminal law was a two-edged sword. The other edge was the regulatory edge, and here, if anything, moral coloring faded away. The criminal law was both more and less than the moral steward of society. Small economic crimes—shooting a deer out of season—did not require a guilty and dangerous mind like murder and rape. To get a felony conviction, for crimes against property, the prosecution at common law had to show a specific intent to act illegally. Injury to property was not a crime unless it was malicious; there "had to be a definite motive of hatred, revenge, or cruelty, as well as an intent to cause the injury." In the 19th century, this requirement loosened. It was the behavior that was dangerous, not just the mind of the actor; the behavior had to be stamped out. "The demand for protection of the wealth of the country . . . has led to liability for intentional but nonmalicious injury to property." Motive or attitude was secondary. In the New York penal code of 1881, the fact that a defendant "intended to restore the property stolen or embezzled, is no ground of defense, or of mitigation of punishment." The code made it a crime to destroy or injure property "unlawfully or wilfully" (sec. 654). Similarly, "metaphysical difficulties" about whether a corporation could form an "intent" to commit a crime were brushed aside; originally, a corporation could not be indicted at all; and as late as the 1850's scattered cases held that corporations were criminally liable only for acts or omissions that did not require a criminal "intent." It was still theoretically true in 1900 that a corporation could not be convicted of rape or treason; but most cases that tried and convicted corporations arose under statutes on economic crime— creating a nuisance, charging too much interest, breaking the Sabbath, or, as in one case, "permitting gaming upon its fairgrounds."

For some crimes, the presumption of innocence or regularity—the principle that the state must specifically prove that a man was guilty or an action irregular, overcoming the presumption that no wrong had been done—was turned topsy-turvy by statute. The object was to toughen the regulatory blade of the criminal law. In the New York penal code, the "insolvency of a moneyed corporation" was "deemed fraudulent" unless "its affairs appear, upon investigation, to have been administered fairly, legally, and with . . . care and diligence" (sec. 604). In Indiana, under a law of 1891, a prima-facie case of "intent to defraud" the depositor was made out, when a bank failed or suspended within thirty days of accepting a deposit. There was no-nonsense toughness in liquor statutes, too. Dry states outlawed the sale of hard liquor; but it was not easy to catch violators red-handed. So, in New Hampshire it was *"prima facie* evidence" of violation of liquor laws if the defendant "exposed" any bottles with liquor labels "in the windows of, or upon the shelves within his place of business," or if his store had a "sign, placard, or other advertisement" for liquor, or if he possessed coupon receipts showing he had paid his federal tax as a dealer or wholesaler in liquor, or if a person delivered liquor "in or from any store, shop, warehouse, steamboat . . . or any shanty or tent . . . or any dwelling-house . . . if any part . . . be used as a public eating-house, grocery, or other place of common resort." In Iowa, possession of liquor, "except in a private dwelling house," created a presumption of guilt.

* * *

[From] Model Penal Code

Section 2.02. General Requirements of Culpability

(1) Minimum requirements of culpability. Except as provided in Section 2.05, a person is not guilty of an offense unless he acted purposely, knowingly, recklessly, or negligently, as the law may require, with respect to each material element of the offense.

(2) Kinds of culpability defined.

    (a) *Purposely.*

    A person acts purposely with respect to a material element of an offense when:

      (1) if the element involves the nature of his conduct or a result thereof, it is his conscious object to engage in conduct of that nature or to cause such a result; and

      (2) if the element involves the attendant circumstances, he knows of the existence of such circumstances.

    (b) *Knowingly.*

    A person acts knowingly with respect to a material element of an offense when:

      (1) if the element involves the nature of his conduct or the attendant circum-
stances, he knows that his conduct is of that nature or he knows of the existence of such circumstances; and

      (2) if the element involves a result of his conduct, he knows that his conduct will necessarily cause such a result.

    (c) *Recklessly.*

    A person acts recklessly with respect to a material element of an offense when he consciously disregards a substantial and unjustifiable risk that the material element exists or will result from his conduct. The risk must be of such a nature and degree that, considering the nature and purpose of the actor's conduct and the circumstances known to him, its disregard involves culpability of high degree. [Alternative: its disregard involves a gross deviation from proper standards of conduct.]

    (d) *Negligently.*

    A person acts negligently with respect to a material element of an offense when he should be aware of a substantial and unjustifiable risk that the material element exists or will result from his conduct. The risk must be of such a nature and degree that the actor's failure to perceive it, considering the nature and purpose of his conduct, the circumstances known to him and the care that would be exercised by a reasonable person in his situation, involves substantial culpability. [Alternative: considering the nature and purpose of his conduct and the circumstances known to him, involves a substantial deviation from the standard of care that would be exercised by a reasonable man in his situation.]

* * *

(6) Requirement of purpose satisfied if purpose is conditional.

When a particular purpose is an element of an offense, the element is established although such purpose is conditional, unless the condition negatives the harm or evil sought to be prevented by the law defining the offense.

(7) Requirement of knowledge satisfied by knowledge of substantial probability.

When knowledge of the existence of a particular fact is an element of an offense, such knowledge is established if a person is aware of a substantial probability of its existence, unless he actually believes that it does not exist.

(8) Requirement of willfulness satisfied by acting knowingly.

A requirement that an offense be committed willfully is satisfied if a person acts knowingly with respect to the material elements of the offense, unless a purpose to impose further requirements plainly appears

(9) Knowledge of illegality not an element of offenses.

Knowledge that conduct constitutes an offense or of the existence, meaning, or application of the law determining the elements of an offense is not an element of such offense, unless the definition of the offense or the Code plainly so provides.

(10) Culpability as determinant of grade of offense.

When the grade or degree of an offense depends on whether the offense is committed purposely, knowingly, recklessly, or negligently, its grade or degree shall be the lowest for which the determinative kind of culpability is established with respect to any material element of the offense.

* * *

Comments

Section 2.02. General Requirements of Culpability

This section attempts the extremely difficult task of articulating the general *mens rea* requirements for the establishment of liability.

1. The approach is based upon the view that clear analysis requires that the question of the kind of culpability required to establish the commission of an offense be faced separately with respect to each material element of the crime; and that, as indicated in section 1.14, the concept of "material element" include the facts that negative defenses on the merits as well as the facts included in the definition of the crime.

The reason for this treatment is best stated by suggesting an example. Given a charge of murder, the prosecution normally must prove intent to kill (or at least to cause serious bodily injury) to establish the required culpability with respect to that element of the crime that involves the result of the defendant's conduct. But if self-defense is claimed as a defense, it is enough to show that the defendant's belief in the necessity of his conduct to save himself did not rest upon reasonable grounds. As to the first element, in short, purpose or knowledge is required; as to the second negligence appears to be sufficient. Failure to face the question separately with respect to each of these ingredients of the offense results in obvious confusion.

A second illustration is afforded by the law of rape. A purpose to effect the sexual relation is most certainly required. But other circumstances also are essential to establish the commission of the crime. The victim must not have been married to the defendant and her consent to sexual relations would, of course, preclude the crime. Must the defendant's purpose have encompassed the facts that he was not the husband of the victim and that she opposed his will? These are certainly entirely different questions. Recklessness, for example, on these points may be sufficient although purpose is required with respect to the sexual result which is an element of the offense.

Under the draft, therefore, the problem of the kind of culpability that is required for conviction must be faced separately with respect to each material element of the offense, although the answer may in many cases be the same with respect to each such element.

2. The draft acknowledges four different kinds of culpability: purpose, knowledge, recklessness, and negligence. It also recognizes that the material elements of offenses vary in that they may involve (1) the nature of the forbidden conduct or (2) the attendant circumstances or (3) the result of conduct. With respect to each of these three types of elements, the draft attempts to define each of the kinds of culpability that may arise. The resulting distinctions are, we think, both necessary and sufficient for the general purposes of penal legislation.

The purpose of articulating these distinctions in detail is, of course, to promote the clarity of definitions of specific crimes and to dispel the obscurity with which the culpability requirement is often treated when such concepts as "general criminal intent," "*mens rea*," "presumed intent," "malice," "willfulness," "scienter" and the like must be employed. . . .

3. In defining the kinds of culpability, a narrow distinction is drawn between acting purposely and knowingly, one of the elements of ambiguity in legal usage of "intent." . . . Knowledge that the requisite external circumstances exist is a common element in both conceptions. But action is not purposive with respect to the nature or the result of the actor's conduct unless it was his conscious object to perform an action of that nature or to cause such a result. The distinction is no doubt inconsequential for most purposes of liability; acting knowingly is ordinarily sufficient. But there are areas where the discrimination is required and is made under existing law, using the awkward concept of "specific intent." This is true in treason, for example, in so far as a purpose to aid the enemy is an ingredient of the offense (see Haupt v. United States, 330 U.S. 631, 641 [1947]) and in attempts and conspiracy, where a true purpose to effect the criminal result is requisite for liability. See, e.g., Dennis v. United States, 341 U.S. 494, 499–500 (1951); Hartzel v. United States, 322 U.S. 680 (1944).

The distinction also has utility in differentiating among grades of an offense for purposes of sentence, e.g., in the case of homicide.

A broader discrimination is perceived between acting either purposely or knowingly and acting recklessly. As we use the term, recklessness involves conscious risk creation. It resembles acting knowingly in that a state of awareness is involved but the awareness is of risk, that is, of probability rather than certainty; the matter is contingent from the actor's point of view. Whether the risk relates to the nature of the actor's conduct or to the existence of the requisite attendant circumstances or to the result that may ensue is immaterial; the concept is the same. The draft requires, however, that the risk thus consciously disregarded by the actor be "substantial" and "unjustifiable"; even substantial risks may be created without recklessness when the actor seeks to serve a proper purpose, as when a surgeon performs an operation which he knows is very likely to be fatal but reasonably thinks the patient has no other, safer chance. Accordingly, to aid the ultimate determination, the draft points expressly to the factors to be weighed in judgment: the nature and degree of the risk disregarded by the actor, the nature and purpose of his conduct, and the circumstances known to him in acting.

Some principle must be articulated, however, to indicate what final judgment is demanded after everything is weighed. There is no way to state this value-judgment that does not beg the question in the last analysis; the point is that the jury must evaluate the conduct and determine whether it should be condemned. The draft, therefore, proposes that this difficulty be accepted frankly and the jury asked if the defendant's conduct involved "culpability of high degree." The alternative suggested asks if it "involves a gross deviation from proper standards of conduct." This formulation is designed to avoid the difficulty inherent in defining culpability in terms of culpability, but the accomplishment seems hardly more than verbal; it does not really avoid the tautology or beg the question less. It may, however, be a better way to put the issue to a jury, especially as some of the conduct to which the section must apply may not involve great moral culpability, even when the defendant acted purposely or knowingly, as in the violation of some minor regulatory measure.

The fourth kind of culpability is negligence. It

is distinguished from acting purposely, knowingly, or recklessly in that it does not involve a state of awareness. It is the case where the actor creates inadvertently a risk of which he ought to be aware, considering its nature and degree, the nature and the purpose of his conduct, and the care that would be exercised by a reasonable person in his situation. Again, however, it is quite impossible to avoid tautological articulation of the final question. The tribunal must evaluate the actor's failure of perception and determine whether, under all the circumstances, it was serious enough to be condemned. Whether that finding is verbalized as "substantial culpability," as the draft proposes or as "substantial deviation from the standard of care that would be exercised by a reasonable man under the circumstances," as the alternative would put it, presents the same problem here as in the case of recklessness. The jury must find fault and find it was substantial; that is all that either formulation says or, we believe, that can be said in legislative terms.

A further point merits attention: the draft invites consideration of the "care that would be exercised by a reasonable person in his [i.e., the actor's] situation." There is an inevitable ambiguity in "situation." If the actor were blind or if he had just suffered a blow or experienced a heart attack, these would certainly be facts to be considered, as they would be under present law. But the heredity, intelligence, or temperament of the actor would not now be held material in judging negligence; and could not be without depriving the criterion of all its objectivity. . . .

Of the four kinds of culpability defined, there is, of course, least to be said for treating negligence as a sufficient basis for imposing criminal liability. Since the actor is inadvertent by hypothesis, it has been argued that the "threat of punishment for negligence must pass him by, because he does not realize that it is addressed to him." . . . So, too, it has been urged that education or corrective treatment, not punishment, is the proper social method for dealing with persons with inadequate awareness, since what is implied is not a moral defect. . . . We think, however, that this is to oversimplify the issue. Knowledge that conviction and sentence, not to speak of punishment, may follow conduct that inadvertently creates improper risk supplies men with an additional motive to take care before acting, to use their faculties, and draw on their experience in gauging the potentialities of contemplated conduct. To some extent, at least, this motive may promote awareness and thus be effective as a measure of control. Certainly legislators act on this assumption in a host of situations and it seems to us dogmatic to assert that they are wholly wrong. Accordingly, we think that negligence, as here defined, cannot be wholly rejected as a ground of culpability which may suffice for purposes of penal law, though we agree that it should not be generally deemed sufficient in the definition of specific crimes, and that it often will be right to differentiate such conduct for the purposes of sentence. The content of the concept must, therefore, be treated at this stage.

Notes and Questions

JEROME HALL, from *General Principles of the Criminal Law*

1. Jerome Hall discusses the distinction between intention (*mens rea*) and motive. What is this distinction? Is there any correspondence between right or wrong intentions and good or bad motives?

2. Hall says, "That an action was motivated excludes accident and negligence." Why is this? How does it compare with Bentham's discussion of motive and intention in Chapter Five on torts?

3. What do inquiries about motives tell us? What kinds of evaluations can be made from knowing a person's motives? Can intentions be inferred from motives? Can motives be inferred from intentions?

4. Hall observes that in assessing moral culpability or personal guilt, both *mens rea* and motive must be considered. Why is this? How does it differ from assessing legal guilt?

5. Hall recognizes that hard cases are produced when legal harms are perpetrated from good motives. Such motives would certainly be relevant to moral evaluation of the culpability of the actor. Does he conclude that law ought to include motives as a material element in the assessment of guilt? Why or why not?

6. The logic of the criminal law presupposes an objective moral standard "expressed in the principles of *mens rea*." How does Hall support this claim? Is he right? If he is right, is this a reasonable presupposition? Does he think that it is?

7. Hall admits that there are many cases in which the offenders act according to their conscience. What are some examples he cites, and how should they be dealt with?

8. Preceding this article is a copy of the *mens rea* conditions set out in the Model Penal Code. You may wish to refer to them here to see the language used to describe these mental elements. They are often included in the definitions of many crimes, especially serious offenses, thereby allowing for degrees of guilt in the definition itself.

[From] *General Principles of the Criminal Law*

JEROME HALL

Mens Rea and Personal Guilt

To facilitate following the course of this discussion, an outline of a pertinent means-end situation may be suggestive. The most common of human experiences is the direction of conduct toward the attainment of goals. Such conduct involves (a) an end sought; (b) deliberate functioning to reach that end, which manifests the *intentionality* of the conduct; and (c) the reasons or grounds for the end-seeking, i.e., its *motivation*. The ethical distinction relevant to such action is that between "good" and "right," and their opposites. This distinction is very old; it is probably the most important one in ethics and, as will appear, it is fundamental in penal liability. If we examine a person's conduct with a view to assessing its moral significance, we can distinguish these two basic components, e.g., a man who gives property to an orphan asylum does right, but if he did that because he hated his heirs, his motive was bad. On the other hand, a motive may be good, although the act done is wrong, e.g., Jean Valjean. Finally, a good motive may coincide with a right act — which, of course, represents the ideal.

It must be emphasized that the distinction between goodness (or badness) of motive and the rightness (or wrongness) of what is done does not imply an actual bifurcation in the relevant conduct. Every act that is morally significant is motivated as well as intentional. We are, in fact, concerned with a unified process, a course of action which always, at every step and at each moment, involves both motive and intentionality. This is true even though it may also be true that motive precedes intention. If we do not recognize this or if we lose sight of it, we are apt to relegate motive to a prior and concluded area or, for some other reason, we are apt to concentrate on one of the essential components of action. In sum, the above distinction is analytical. It implies the necessity of viewing morally significant conduct from two perspectives, i.e., with reference to the goodness or badness of the motive and the rightness ("fitness") or wrongness of what was done.

* * *

In sum, motive in penal law is distinguished from intention (*mens rea*) and from the scientific sense of "cause." The former distinction is clarified if ulterior intention is ascribed to an objective or end, while motive retains its personal subjective meaning as a ground or reason of action. . . . That an action was motivated excludes accident and negligence and implies intention. An intention is thus descriptive of a mode of conduct that is contrasted with accident and inadvertent movement. A motive answers the question why, neither in terms of causation nor in those of a further ulterior objective, but in terms that give a reason which is the subject of an ethical appraisal. For when we ask questions about a person's motives, we are asking for data relevant to evaluation of his character or at least of the morality of a particular act. Given a motive, a relevant intention can be inferred. But the converse does not apply; i.e., one may be positive that certain conduct was intentional without knowing any motive for it. All of this conforms to the preponderant ethical-legal meaning of motive and to its exclusion from the scope of *mens rea*.

"*Mens Rea*" and Personal Guilt

Moral culpability, i.e., personal guilt, includes both *mens rea* and motivation. For example, D kills T; all agree that what he did is morally wrong. But the appraisal of D's moral culpability must also take account of his motive: was D acting from cupidity, knowing he was named the chief beneficiary of T's will? Or was the motive his love for his sick wife, who needed an operation? Just as we cannot pass an adequate moral judgment if we know only what harm has been committed but not the motive for committing it, so, too, we cannot properly estimate conduct solely on the basis of its motivation—we need to know also what was done. It is necessary to unite these judgments in a single evaluation to determine the moral culpability of the actor.

Difficult problems concern harms perpetrated from laudable motives, e.g., theft of food for a hungry family, actions inspired by religious convictions, certain cases of euthanasia, some political crimes, and the like. The relevant moral judgment implied in the penal law is absolute: no matter how good the actor's motive, since he voluntarily (*mens rea*) committed a penal harm he is to some degree morally culpable—"sufficiently" so to warrant at least control under pro-

bation. The legal restriction of the *substantive* law to that aspect of the actor's guilt has not been understood by criminologists and psychiatrists who assert that the law is not interested in an offender's motives; but it also raises serious questions for lawyers.

Even if it is granted that a point is reached in some cases where no harm was committed, nay, that a benefit was conferred, e.g., in the assassination of a brutal tyrant, such marginal cases cannot be made the sound basis for incorporating motive as an essential element in the definition of crimes. Instead, it should be recognized that the preservation of the objective meaning of the principle of *mens rea* as well as of the attendant principle of legality has its price. For it is impossible to forbid any class of harms without including rare marginal instances where a maximum of good motivation combines with the minimum of the proscribed harm, or even no harm at all, so that the final estimate is that the value protected by the rule was not impaired in that instance. When cases involving this type of problem recur, e.g., infanticide by mothers shortly after birth, which were formerly within the definition of murder, it is possible to construct a new crime by defining a separate class in terms which accord with the objective meaning of *mens rea* and harm, i.e., in terms which do not refer to motivation. The exercise of official discretion even to the point of forgoing prosecution or suspending sentence, e.g., as regards a Jean Valjean, is the "safety valve" which preserves the principles of *mens rea* and legality in the vast majority of cases. What needs emphasis is that there is an extremely important difference between the preservation of the legality and ethical significance of the principle of *mens rea* by allocating questions of motivation to administration and the depreciation of both penal law and its ethical significance by making the relevant rules vague, if motive is made material.

Despite the doubts raised by marginal cases, the logic of the substantive law excludes the possibility that there can ever be a violation of a penal law that is not a legal harm. The parallel ethical rationale implies equally that there can never be such action that is not immoral. Legal liability in the marginal cases does not therefore imply that the penal law is amoral, that it seeks mere outward conformity. It implies that it is based on an objective ethics, expressed in the principle of *mens rea* and, accordingly, that conscience may err. The premise is that the morality of a sound body of penal law is objective in the sense that it may be validly opposed to individual opinion. In extreme cases of impaired conscience, the M'Naghten Rules exclude liability; and in many others, where the motives were good, mitigation makes its greatest appeal. Holmes emphasized the fact that penal law disregards the defendant's ethical insensitivity and lack of education; and we shall later discuss his theory. It may be noted here that in view of the simple valuations expressed in penal law, these factors should not be exaggerated—it does not require a college education or extraordinary sensitivity to understand that it is wrong to kill, rape, or rob. Recent anthropological studies stressing universal values regarding homicide, treason, incest, theft, and so on, are also relevant. At the same time, one who defends the objective morality of the modern principle of *mens rea* must postulate a sound, spontaneously constructed penal law, the product of experience and inquiry functioning freely over many centuries; and this premise encounters difficulty in some parts of every actual legal system.

There are cases which trouble those who are concerned that actual guilt be the essential condition of penal liability. Sometimes organic disabilities are evident and there are other impairments which are not fully recognized in current legal rules, e.g., regarding addiction to alcohol and narcotics. Cultural differences sometimes engender attitudes which strongly oppose those represented in the penal law. For example, in certain Latin-American countries the sexual mores of the dominant minority are imposed by penal law upon the Indian population which for centuries approved the conduct that the code condemns as a serious crime. A neighborhood group of delinquents who respect each other's possessions and may be courageous and self-sacrificing think it is quite proper, perhaps praiseworthy, to take property from the automobiles of the "rich." So, too, occasional visitors from other countries find in some important respects a different criminal code. There are Mormons in the United States who believe they are obeying a divine injunction as well as an onerous social obligation when they contract multiple marriages. There are other religious minorities, e.g., Jehovah's Witnesses and Christian Scientists, who also encounter difficulty with prevalent opinion and penal law. There are conscientious objectors and political rebels. And, finally, we must recall the ethically insensitive, thoughtless persons, Shaw's "sick consciences," sometimes members of criminal or juvenile gangs, who often do not share the values of the majority. In sum, there are undoubtedly many cases of violence, theft, bigamy, political subversion, and so on, where the offenders acted in accordance with their conscience.

With reference to some of these offenders, it is pertinent to observe that penal law has an educational function to perform. But if it be granted that some of these offenders are not only well motivated but also enlightened, what can be done in their behalf that is compatible with the preservation of legality? Occasionally, a court takes cognizance of the standards of the community from which the defendant comes, as did an English court in *Wilson v. Inyang*; but while this can always be done in fixing the sentence, its recognition as a defense in substantive law would raise serious difficulties. A radical solution of the problem of justice in such cases might suggest the abandonment of the entire penal law. If that is excluded, there is no escape from the alternative that a functioning legal order must cleave to the objective meaning of the principle of *mens rea* (the constant premise being a sound, freely constructed penal law); and this undoubtedly falls far short of perfect justice. Mitigation is, of course, very much in order in such cases, but full exculpation would not only contradict the values of penal law, it would also undermine the foundation of a legal order. This is the difficult problem which confronts officials who wish to preserve legality and also dispense justice. The tensions are insistent and they sometimes lead to the enactment of provisions which are at odds with the principle of legality.

This is the tendency of provisions to the effect that if a negligent or an ignorant harm-doer "could" have acted with due care or "could" have known he was at fault, the conditions of just punishment are satisfied. In support of these provisions it is urged that they apply the test of actual fault, i.e., they exculpate if the defendant lacked such competence. But this is a very dubious claim, and it may well be the case that, instead of achieving that result, the actual effect is the imposition of a verbally disguised objective liability, aggravated by the concomitant depreciation of legality. If the requirement is competence to know the law, the ethical force of such provisions is illusory. For example, if sitting on a park bench is punishable by ten years' imprisonment, can it be successfully maintained that the fact that an offender could have discovered that there was such a law justifies the punishment or indeed any liability? With reference to Muslims, Mormons, Christian Scientists, Jehovah's Witnesses, and political and other rebels, what is pertinent is not that they could have known the law but that they espouse a different code of morals. So, too, it does not seem persuasive to argue that they "could" have known what was ethically right.

"Capacity," as that is determined by officials interpreting such vague provisions as that noted above, probably means the competence to form correct valuations, which are assumed to be those represented in the penal code. If that assumption is sound, it is only the intrusion of substantive incompatibility when sanctions are imposed because an offender "could" have known, and so on, or when there is exculpation on the ground that, though normal, he "could not" have known, etc. What is compatible with objectively moral penal law is the enforcement of it, mitigated by discretion and the occasional use of the "safety valve" to effect complete exculpation. The fact that this must be the over-all conclusion does not exclude the most enlightened individualization that is compatible with legality, e.g., the definition of crimes to reflect objective differences such as first offenders and habitual ones, a wide choice of sanctions, and the humane administration of penal-correctional institutions.

The need to exclude motive from the scope of *mens rea* may be further seen in the consequences of a contrary rule. Suppose it were enacted that criminal conduct required proof not only of the intentional or reckless doing of a forbidden act but also of a bad motive. The result would be that the judge and jury would hear evidence about *why* the defendant did the act; and they would be required to find not only what his motives actually were but also to evaluate them. Now, although motives are not always the dark unknowables they are sometimes believed to be, it is also true that it is often very difficult and sometimes impossible to discover them—a criminal sometimes refuses to talk and nothing may be known about him. Even in the usual run of less-difficult cases, a detailed case-history of the defendant's past life may be needed if reliable knowledge of his motivation is to be discovered. In some cases, a very long time would be required to complete the investigation; in others the results would be quite negative—the true motivation is sometimes concealed from the actor himself who rationalizes his conduct in terms of what he mistakenly believes his motives were. But suppose that in a majority of the cases the motives could be established with reasonable assurance. The equally difficult task remains—to evaluate them. In doing this, the actor's own estimate could hardly be accepted even if he had undoubtedly followed his conscience—unless one is prepared to hold that every fanatic has *carte blanche* to wreak whatever harm he wishes to inflict. Moreover, if a court could exculpate because it found that the harm-doer's motives were good, it would also be empowered to refuse exculpation because it thought his motives bad. These are among the reasons for excluding motive from the definition of *mens rea* and holding it not essential in criminal conduct.

Notes and Questions

HERBERT PACKER, from *The Limits of the Criminal Sanction*

1. The overall question that concerns Herbert Packer in this selection is whether *mistake* should always be considered as an excusing condition in a criminal action. He argues that a correct rationale or justification for criminal law does require this consideration, and he suggests that the gradual infusion of strict liability—that is, liability without fault—into the criminal law marks an erosion of value. What values are sacrificed if we allow criminal liability without fault? What would be promoted by doing so?

2. Packer cites the case of *United States* v. *Dotterweich* as an example of the erosion he is talking about. What does the court decide in this case? What alternative does Packer suggest? Would it be better? Why or why not?

3. Packer then considers four categories of cases that do not recognize mistake as an excuse. What are they? Can you fit Packer's examples of Dan, Evan, Frank, George, and Harry into these categories? Notice that his first three examples, Arthur, Barry, and Charlie, clearly do not fit into these categories. What kinds of mistakes do they involve? (You may find it helpful here to refer to the Brandt article in this section if you have not read it yet.)

4. The first category Packer considers is called *basic offense*. What is a basic offense? What is the rationale for excluding a defense of mistake for such offenses? How does Packer respond? How would you?

5. Next, Packer examines the offense of *criminal negligence*. Negligence in tort law was considered in Chapter Five. Are there special problems with criminal negligence that are not also problems in tort law? What problem does Packer find with criminal negligence? What does he conclude about it? Do you agree?

6. *Ignorance of the law* is Packer's next target. It is a well-known maxim that ignorance of the law is no excuse. What justification can be given for such a doctrine? What limits are implied in this justification? What is Packer's view?

7. Packer's final category is *public welfare offenses*. These offenses, he points out, are comparatively recent exceptions to the *mens rea* requirement. What are they? How, if at all, can they be justified? What does Packer say about them?

[From] *The Limits of the Criminal Sanction*

HERBERT PACKER

Strict Liability

When we leave the area of the dilemmatic choice, which comprises what is technically known as the law of justification and excuse, "mistake" becomes the operational signal for invoking a vast range of excuses. Indeed, the idea of mistake underlies the whole question of *mens rea* or the mental element, with the dubious exception of the insanity defense (which, as I shall argue subsequently, is most usefully viewed as something other than a problem of *mens rea*). When we say that a person, whose conduct in other respects fits the definition of a criminal offense, lacked the requisite *mens rea*, what we mean is that he made a mistake about some matter of fact or value that constituted a material element of the offense.

A few examples will show that the question of mistake pervades the entire criminal law. Arthur is charged with homicide and claims that he thought the man he shot at was really a deer. Barry is charged with stealing a raincoat that he claims he thought was really abandoned property. Charlie is charged with possessing heroin; he says he thought the white powder in the packet was talcum powder. Dan is charged with bigamy; he says that he thought his first wife had divorced him. Evan is charged with statutory rape; he claims the girl told him she was over the age of consent. Frank is charged with selling adulterated drugs; he says that so far as he knew the drugs conformed to requirements. George is charged with failing to file his income tax return; he says that he didn't know about the income tax. Harry is charged with carrying a concealed weapon; he claims he didn't know it was against the law to do so.

Under existing law Arthur, Barry, and probably Charlie will be listened to. That is, the trier of fact will decide whether each of them really did make the mistake he claims to have made. If it is believed that he did and (ordinarily) if the mistake is thought to be "reasonable," no crime has been committed. As recently as fifteen years ago Dan's mistake was simply ignored; however, he might be excused in some jurisdictions today if his claim is believed. Evan is probably out of luck, although there is a developing trend in his favor. Frank, George, and Harry might just as well save their breath; their exculpatory claim of mistake will not be listened to.

If all this seems confusing and arbitrary, that is only because it is confusing and arbitrary. Traditional criminal law has fallen into the deliberate, and on occasion inadvertent, use of strict liability or liability without fault. For our purposes strict liability can be defined as the refusal to pay attention to a claim of mistake. In a behavioral-utilitarian view of the criminal law there is, as we have seen, good reason to ignore the defense of mistake. But if the preventive goal of criminal law is to be limited by the negative implication of the retributive position, as we have concluded it should, then mistakes must be considered and, if found relevant and believable, accepted as excuses.

The story of how traditional law slipped into an easy reliance on strict liability, to the detriment of its essential doctrinal content, need not concern us here. However, it may be instructive to consider one famous case in which the Supreme Court of the United States contributed to the erosion of *mens rea*, because it shows that important values may be sacrificed as easily through inadvertence as through design. The narrow issue in *United States* v. *Dotterweich* was whether the president of a company that shipped misbranded or adulterated products in interstate commerce was a "person" who had done so under the Food, Drug, and Cosmetic Act, notwithstanding the fact that he had nothing to do with the shipment. Buffalo Pharmacal Company, a drug wholesaler, purchased drugs from manufacturers, repackaged them under its own label, and shipped them on order to physi-

cians. Dotterweich and the company were prosecuted for two interstate shipments alleged to be adulterated or misbranded. The first consisted of a cascara compound that conformed to specifications but whose label included reference to an ingredient that had, a short time before, been dropped from the National Formulary. One infers that the old labels were still being used. The other shipment was of digitalis tablets that were less potent than their label indicated. The company did not manufacture these tablets, but merely repackaged them under its own label. So far as appears, there was no way short of conducting a chemical analysis of the tablets for their seller to know that they were not what their label declared them to be. The jury found Dotterweich guilty but for "some unexplainable reason" disagreed as to the company's guilt. Dotterweich was sentenced to pay a fine and to "probation for 60 days." Under the statute he could have been sentenced to a year's imprisonment. The court of appeals reversed, on the ground that the statute should not be read as applying to an individual agent of the principal (here the company), since only the principal was in a position to exculpate itself by obtaining a guaranty of nonadulteration from its supplier. Since there appeared to be no statutory basis for distinguishing between a high corporate agent, like Dotterweich, who might have obtained such a guaranty, and a shipping clerk or other menial employee who might have actually made the forbidden shipment and who would not necessarily be covered by the statutory provision protecting people who obtained a guaranty, a divided court of appeals concluded that Dotterweich's conviction could not stand.

It will be noticed that the answer to the question whether this was indeed a "forbidden shipment" was dealt with rather cursorily. The court of appeals held merely that "intention to violate the statute" was not an element of the offense. The shipments in question were illegal under the statute, and that was that. Whether Dotterweich (or anyone else) had failed to take reasonable precautions was not put to the jury. Negligence as a possible mode of culpability was overlooked.

The court of appeals opinion had at least the merit of keeping separate two questions that it would confound analysis to blur: first, whether whoever was responsible for the shipment could be held criminally liable, notwithstanding the absence of culpability on his part (the issue of "strict liability"); and second, whether Dotterweich could be held criminally liable, notwithstanding his own lack of connection with the shipment (the issue of "vicarious liability"). It is obvious that the second issue is dependent on the first; if no one committed a crime, there was no crime for which Dotterweich could have been held vicariously liable. The underlying issue was whether the statute imposed strict liability.

The opinion for the Court, by Mr. Justice Frankfurter, did not make the essential distinction between the issues of strict and vicarious liability. It is not paraphrasing unfairly to say that the Court held that since the liability was strict it was also vicarious. But the premise that the Act dispensed with *mens rea* and imposed strict liability was assumed rather than examined:

> The prosecution to which Dotterweich was subjected is based on a now familiar type of legislation whereby penalties serve as effective means of regulation. Such legislation dispenses with the conventional requirement for criminal conduct — awareness of some wrong-doing. In the interest of the larger good it puts the burden of acting at hazard upon a person otherwise innocent but standing in responsible relations to a public danger. *United States* v. *Balint*, 258 U.S. 250. And so it is clear that shipments like those now in issue are "punished by the statute if the article is misbranded [or adulterated], and that the article may be misbranded [or adulterated] without any conscious fraud at all." It was natural enough to throw this risk on shippers with regard to the identity of their wares. . . .

It is well to note that this offhand passage is precisely all that the opinion had to say on the *mens rea* issue, despite the fact that this was the first time the Supreme Court had before it the construction of the mental element in this important federal criminal statute. It is also well to note the primitive and rigid view of *mens rea* that the quoted passage reflects. "Conscious fraud" and "awareness of some wrongdoing" are impossibly high standards, the opinion seems to say, and that leaves only strict liability. Did the company or its responsible agents behave recklessly or negligently with respect to the possibility that these shipments were not up to standard? Perhaps it was inexcusably careless not to have destroyed the old cascara labels and prepared

new ones. Perhaps not. But could not the lower courts have been told that this question should be submitted to the jury? The case posed an obvious opportunity for framing a more discriminating set of standards for the mental element, but the opportunity was forgone.

Next, let us consider the areas in which the minimal doctrinal content of the criminal law has been eroded. There are four categories to be considered in determining how responsive the traditional common law has been to the notion of *mens rea*. These may be characterized as:

(1) Basic offenses dispensing in whole or in part with *mens rea*.

(2) Negligence as a mode of culpability.

(3) The barrier of *ignorantia legis*.

(4) Public welfare offenses.

BASIC OFFENSES. The usual examples are sexual offenses, notably "statutory rape" and bigamy. These are universally regarded, in their traditional manifestations, as examples of strict liability in the criminal law. They serve as the basis for an assertion that might otherwise seem surprising, that there is no adequate operational distinction between offenses that dispense entirely with *mens rea* and offenses that dispense with *mens rea* only partially, or with respect to only one material element of the offense. Indeed, there is no such thing as a "strict liability" offense except as a partial rather than a complete discarding of *mens rea*, for there is always some element of any offense with respect to which a mental element is attached. In both the statutory rape and bigamy situations, it is the exclusion of *mens rea* with respect to the "circumstance" element of the offense that results in the imposition of strict liability: in the case of statutory rape, the circumstance that the girl is under the age of consent; in the case of bigamy, the circumstance that one or both of the parties is not legally free to remarry. Although there is an encouraging trend of contrary decisions in the bigamy field, it probably remains the majority rule in this country that a good-faith belief that one is legally free to remarry is not a defense to a charge of bigamy. Indeed, this view apparently has constitutional sanction. In the area of statutory rape, the strength of the traditional strict liability view has not been appreciably diminished.

These examples are familiar ones. It might perhaps be thought that they represent rather unusual exceptions to a generally pervasive principle of applicability of *mens rea*. Actually, the contrary is true. Two conspicuous examples arise in the area of homicide. Both the felony-murder and the misdemeanor-manslaughter rules, insofar as they have independent force and are not simply instances of the more general operation of homicide doctrines, reflect the imposition of strict liability as to the homicidal result. If a robber is automatically to be held for the death of an accomplice who is shot by their intended victim, or if a person commits a battery that leads to the unforeseen and reasonably unforeseeable result of the victim's death, liability for the homicide rests upon the refusal to consider *mens rea* as to the result.

The standard rejoinder to the argument that strict liability is being imposed in such a situation is that habitually given in the sex-offense cases. It comes down to the assertion that, since the underlying conduct is "wrongful," the actor must take all the consequences of that conduct, whether or not he foresaw or desired them. But it begs the question to assert that one who has intercourse with an underage girl, even though he is ignorant of her age, is to be held for statutory rape because his underlying conduct is "wrongful." The question is whether he should be held for an offense to whose elements he did not advert as well as for an offense to whose elements he did advert. The fact that various limitations have been worked out to prevent some of the most absurd consequences of rigid adherence to this "at peril" notion should not distract attention from its incompatibility with the spirit of *mens rea*.

NEGLIGENCE. If a man purposely or recklessly brings about a forbidden harm, we have no hesitation in saying that he had the requisite *mens rea* with respect to his conduct. But if he negligently brings about the forbidden harm, a different problem is presented. Negligence is not readily transformable into a state of mind. It is, by definition, the absence of a state of mind. Negligence is, in short, an extension rather than an example of the idea of *mens rea* in the traditional sense.

There are those who argue that negligence as a mode of culpability has no place in the criminal law, because the threat of punishment for causing harms inadvertently must be either inefficacious or unjust or both. Whatever the merits of this philosophic position, it is plain that negligence has a very strong foothold in the criminal law. It finds its most explicit formulation in the statutes penalizing negligent homicide in the driving of an automobile. But its hold on the criminal law is far more pervasive than this. Negligence suffices as a mode of culpability whenever the question asked with respect to the actor's perception is not whether he knew but whether he should have known. In the case of homicide, the difference between negligent inadvertence to the risk of death and conscious advertence to that risk is, very roughly speaking, the dividing line between manslaughter and murder. But beyond this, murder itself is sometimes treated as an offense that may be committed negligently, either by applying an external standard to the actor's perception of the risk or by applying an external standard to his perception of the basis for some excuse, such as self-defense. To the extent that we subject persons to liability for this most serious of offenses on the basis of an external standard, we are retreating very far from a doctrinal purist's stance. But even if murder by negligence is rejected as anomalous, we must face the challenge that negligence as a mode of culpability cannot be reconciled with the principle of *mens rea*.

It has been suggested that negligence has closer affinities with strict liability than it has with those modes of culpability that reflect subjective awareness on the part of the actor. However, there are important differences between a legislative determination that all instances of a certain kind of conduct are unacceptable and a jury's determination that a particular instance of such conduct falls below a previously established community standard. The decisive difference is that the legislature cannot and does not foresee the infinite variation of circumstance that may affect the jury's view of a particular case. If there is an issue of fault for the jury to adjudicate, the line between subjective and objective fault—between "he knew" and "he should have known"—is a very shadowy one. Often, a judgment that "he knew" will simply reflect an inference from "he should have known." Conversely, a judgment that "he should have known" may contain the further unarticulated statement: "and we think he probably did know but we aren't sure enough to say so." There simply isn't a definite line between imputations of subjective awareness and those of objective fault: They are points on a continuum. The jury's opportunity to make an individualized determination of fault may focus indifferently upon one or the other. Putting the issue in this light, it seems plausible for the criminal law to employ a negligence standard on occasion, although not as a matter of course, without being charged with having abandoned the substance of *mens rea*. To put it another way, it seems to me proper to view negligence as an extension of rather than a departure from the values associated with the *mens rea* concept.

IGNORANTIA LEGIS. The principle that ignorance of the law is no excuse is deeply embedded in our criminal law. If the criminal law faithfully reflected prevalent community standards of minimally acceptable conduct, there would be no difficulty in reconciling the principle *ignorantia legis* with the requirements of *mens rea*. Yet, the proliferation of minor sumptuary and regulatory offenses, many of them penalizing conduct under circumstances in which the fact of illegality can scarcely be known to a first offender, creates a sharp problem. Sometimes a legislature specifies that awareness of the law's requirement is a necessary ingredient of guilt. More often it does not. Courts rarely remedy the deficiency by fashioning a doctrine that distinguishes sensibly between innocent and guilty conduct in contravention of an esoteric legal proscription.

It has been suggested by the framers of the Model Penal Code that a limited defense should be available to persons accused of crime if they can show a good-faith belief that their conduct does not legally constitute an offense, owing to lack of publication or reasonable availability of the enactment. It is not entirely clear how broad this defense is meant to be. I should like to read it as establishing a negligence standard for the defense of ignorance or mistake of law. If read (or expanded) in this way, the proposal would go a long way toward resolving the *ignorantia legis* paradox. If we assume that an actor is unblameworthy in failing to know that his conduct violates a particular enactment (a condition that will ordinarily obtain only if either he or the enact-

ment is a stranger to prevailing standards in the relevant community), then criminal punishment is objectionable for precisely those reasons that obtain in respect to strict liability.

PUBLIC WELFARE OFFENSES. Ever since Francis B. Sayre gave the phrase currency, this category of offenses has been treated by commentators as the main "exception" to the principle of *mens rea* and by courts as a convenient pigeonhole for any crime construed to dispense with *mens rea*. Perhaps the principal significance of the public welfare offenses lies in their open flouting of *mens rea*, as opposed to the more covert erosions that have gone on in the main body of the criminal law. Despite the enormous body of judge-made law that affirms dispensing with the mental element in violations of food and drug relations, liquor regulations, traffic rules, and the like, few courts have explicitly considered and avowed the propriety of applying distinctively "criminal" sanctions to minor infractions. On the contrary, these offenses have been treated as something different from traditional criminal law, as a kind of hybrid category to which the odium and hence the safeguards of the criminal process do not attach. However limited in application the departure from *mens rea* may be in this category of offenses, it cannot be doubted that acceptance of this departure has been a powerful brake on the development of a general theory of *mens rea* in the criminal law.

This discussion of the "exceptions" to *mens rea* is intended to suggest that in every one of the cases enumerated at the beginning of this section the defense of "mistake" should be entertained and, if found warranted by the facts, accepted. This conclusion follows, however, only if what we are confronted with is a case in which the criminal sanction is fully appropriate. Here we are touching on a major thesis of this book, namely, that the criminal sanction should not be applied to trivial infractions such as minor traffic offenses, to cite perhaps the most conspicuous example of current misuse. The culpability issue highlights this point. Treating every kind of conduct that the legislature unthinkingly labels as criminal with the full doctrinal apparatus of culpability would place an intolerable burden on the courts. Yet our principles compel us to entertain *mens rea* defenses whenever the consequences of a criminal conviction are severe, whenever we are using the full force of the criminal sanction. A line must be drawn that does not depend simply upon the fortuitous use of the label "criminal." Labels aside, the combination of stigma and loss of liberty involved in a conditional or absolute sentence of imprisonment sets that sanction apart from anything else the law imposes.

When the law permits that degree of severity, the defendant should be entitled to litigate the issue of culpability by raising the kinds of defenses we have been considering. If the burden on the courts is thought to be too great, a less severe sanction than imprisonment should be the maximum provided for. The legislature ought not to be allowed to have it both ways.

SECTION 3

Punishment: Justification and Alternatives

Since punishment is the infliction of something undesirable — usually the deprivation of liberty (by imprisonment or probation) or property (by fine) in the United States, but sometimes the requirement of labor, and occasionally death — such infliction requires justification. Two major theories attempt to justify legal punishment, namely, theories of utility and retribution.

Utilitarian justifications of punishment are forward looking: They focus on promoting the public welfare in the future. The most often heard utilitarian justification of punishment is the idea of deterrence: Punishment is justified because it deters crime and thereby protects the public welfare. Certainly all members of society are better off with less crime. Other utilitarian justifications of punishment are self-protection, rehabilitation of criminals, and reinforcement of community values. All of these are goals that might be accomplished by punishment for criminal acts. If these goals are achieved, then the public welfare is promoted and punishment is justified so long as the benefits outweigh the costs. Thus, the utilitarian theory attempts to justify punishment by reference to the good that can be accomplished by means of it.

Retributive theories, on the other hand, are backward looking. They focus on a past event — the crime at issue in the particular case. Retributive views consider what justice requires, how the criminal deserves to be treated. Punishment is justified, according to a retributivist, because and only because a criminal deserves it.

The first selection, by Lawrence Friedman, traces the history of punishment in the American system. As will be evident, the development of humane practices of punishment has been slow and painful.

In the second article, Richard Brandt contrasts the utilitarian and retributive theories of punishment. He defends the utilitarian theory by showing that the objections to retributive theory count strongly against it, but that objections to utilitarian theory can be answered. Consider whether Brandt satisfactorily answers the objections he raises.

Next, Edmund Pincoffs' discussion is analogous to Brandt's, but from the perspective of the retributivist. Pincoffs also considers objections to both theories, but defends the retributive theory. The virtue of both Brandt's and Pincoffs' accounts is their clear articulation of the theories and objections. Ask yourself whether either of them succeeds in providing an exhaustive justification of punishment.

Some theorists — for example, John Rawls and Stanley Benn — have argued that we must distinguish the institution or general practice of punishment from particular cases. Utilitarian theory, it is suggested, provides the best account of the general institution of punishment, whereas retributive theory offers the best justification of punishment in particular cases. If these philosophers are right, both theories are needed to account for different aspects of punishment.

In the next selection Jeffrie G. Murphy argues that the retributive theory provides the only acceptable justification of punishment because it is the only theory that takes seriously the rights of individual human beings. After making this argument, however, Murphy considers whether the retributive theory can apply to any society that is less than just. This article raises the troubling question of whether, in an unjust world, punishment can be justified by any theory.

Punishment for criminal acts is probably the oldest legal action taken by human societies against certain individuals. Forms of punishment have been varied and often brutal, but over the years have been gradually reformed. At one time a criminal could be mutilated (and still can be in some Middle Eastern and Asian countries) for certain crimes. A person could lose a finger, a hand, an eye, or a tongue. As punishment a criminal could be tortured or humiliated or beaten or branded or exiled or killed. How could these legal actions be justified? Murphy demonstrates how difficult it is to justify punishment by determining either the requirements of justice or the requirements of utility. How much punishment is enough? Which punishment fits which crime? Over the years most penalties have been eliminated as inhumane, until for the most part only imprisonment and fine are left — as well as the enduring controversy over the death penalty.

Some people have argued that punishment of any kind cannot be justified. It is not clear that punishment deters crime, nor is it clear how such a claim could be supported. There is little evidence that punishment itself reforms criminals and even less that punishment rehabilitates them. Determining what an individual criminal deserves turns out to be an impossible task. The requirements of justice are far from clear, especially if the background conditions of a criminal's life are considered as excusing or mitigating conditions.

In "The Crime of Punishment" Karl Menninger argues that punishment is a relic of barbaric times when little was known of human psychology and motivation. Menninger believes that the institution of punishment should be discarded in favor of treatment and rehabilitation. Such an approach, he argues, would be more humane to criminals and more effective in protecting the public.

Finally, Randy Barnett argues for a restitution model of criminal justice, suggesting that in some cases at least the best approach to crime is to require the criminal to repay the victim. This proposal has attractive features. The approach has been used with some success in certain juvenile cases, although its general application appears questionable.

Consider the advantages and deficiencies of these alternative approaches to punishment. Some people have argued that they are best used in conjunction with a punishment system. The real value of considering these options is to refine our ideas about the notion of punishment. What are its purposes, justifications, and limits?

Notes and Questions

LAWRENCE FRIEDMAN, from *A History of American Law*

1. Lawrence Friedman provides us with the unhappy picture of American prisons, as well as with some history of the practice of punishment in the United States. Corporal punishment, such as whipping and flogging, was abolished by 1900 in this country. What was wrong with corporal punishment, especially for the crime of assault? Don't you think many criminals would prefer it to imprisonment? Why should it be abolished? Because it is unjust? Inhumane? Ineffective as a deterrent? What does the rejection of corporal punishment tell us about the purpose and justification of punishment?

2. Apparently prisons have always tended to be abominable and overflowing. That is certainly their history. But in recent years some prison systems (for example, in Arizona) have been declared "cruel and unusual" punishment because of overcrowded and brutal conditions. In many states convicts receive probation or early parole simply because prisons are overcrowded. The supply of prisons never seems to meet the demand. Does Friedman provide any explanation? Can we justify imprisoning people in bad conditions? How bad?

3. Despite bad general conditions many reform attempts have been made — some of them successful. What examples does Friedman give? What are the major obstacles to prison reform?

4. Probation has also been introduced as an alternative to punishment, especially for first offenders. What is the rationale behind probation? Does it accord with justice? With the utilitarian view?

5. Treating juvenile offenders separately from adults is another fairly modern reform. Why should juveniles be treated separately on a utilitarian theory? On a retributive theory?

6. Forced labor is still a form of punishment in some jurisdictions. Is there anything wrong in principle with forced labor as punishment? If it can be justified at all, what limits must be imposed?

7. Ironically, some reformers have proposed work as a means of rehabilitation. If work is offered as part of a rehabilitation and training program, is it then a benefit rather than a punishment? Could such a program be required? Would it still be a benefit rather than a punishment? Is it clear that we can distinguish the two? Is it important? What must be kept in mind to keep the distinction clear?

[From] *A History of American Law*

LAWRENCE FRIEDMAN

The Crime of Punishment: The American Prison

The typical jail of 1776 was a corrupt, inefficient institution — a warehouse for the dregs of society. Men and women were thrown into common cell rooms. Administration was totally unprofessional. Dirt and ordure were everywhere. Discipline was lax; yet brutality went unchecked. The new wave of theory about crime included new theories of punishment. Prison, it was agreed by penologists, should act to reform the criminal. As prisons were constituted, they could hardly be expected to improve the inmate in any way. To do the job, radical new structures were needed. In 1790, the Walnut Street prison, in Philadelphia, was remodeled as a showplace for an enlightened policy. Its chief novelty was a "penitentiary House" (the name is significant) containing sixteen solitary or separate cells:

Each cell was 8 feet long, 6 feet wide, and 10 feet high, had two doors, an outer wooden one, and an inside iron door. . . . Each cell had a large leaden pipe that led to the sewer, and thus formed a very primitive kind of a closet. The window of the cell was secured by blinds and wire, to prevent anything being passed in or out.

Some convicts in the prison worked in shops during the day; but the convicts in the solitary cells did no work at all. This lonely asceticism would presumably lead the prisoners of Walnut Street to rethink their lives, and meditate on self-improvement.

In New York, the north wing of Auburn prison was remodeled in 1821 to conform to advanced principles of penology. In the Auburn system, the prisoners worked together during the daytime, and slept in solitary cells at night. The Cherry Hill prison in Philadelphia (1829) was another innovation in prison styles. Cherry Hill was built in the form of a grim fortress, surrounded by walls of medieval strength. Great stone arms radiated out of a central core. Each arm contained a number of individual cells connected to tiny walled courtyards, one to a cell. The prisoners lived in cell and courtyard, utterly alone, night and day. Sometimes they wore masks. Through peepholes, the prisoners could listen to religious services. In both Auburn and Cherry Hill, absolute silence was imposed on the prisoner—a punishment more inhumane than the flogging and branding that the penitentiary supposedly supplanted.

Charles Dickens visited Cherry Hill on his American tour, and was horrified. "Those who devised this system of Prison Discipline," he remarked, "and those benevolent gentlemen who carry it into execution, do not know what it is that they are doing." This "dreadful punishment" inflicts "immense . . . torture and agony" on the prisoners. It was a "slow and daily tampering with the mysteries of the brain . . . immeasurably worse than any torture of the body." The silence, Dickens felt, was "awful. . . . Over the head and face of every prisoner who comes into this melancholy house, a black hood is drawn; and in this dark shroud . . . he is led to the cell. . . . He is a man buried alive." Many prisoners were indeed reclaimed from a life of crime; they went insane in their cells. Administration also quickly degenerated. In a few years, strait jackets, iron gags, and savage beatings were a way of life at Cherry Hill.

What went wrong? There was no lack of theory; there was no lack of detail in inventing plans. The laws were models of specificity. When Massachusetts converted its state prison to the Auburn system in 1828, its statute carefully provided that

> each convict shall be allowed, for his yearly clothing, one pair of thick pantaloons, one thick jacket, one pair of thin pantaloons, one thin jacket, two pairs of shoes, two pair of socks, three shirts, and two blankets, all of a coarse kind.

The daily ration was part of the law, down to an allowance of "two ounces of black pepper" per hundred rations. The pepper ration could not guarantee good government behind stone walls.

Society in the 19th century, fearful of moral failure, committed to a dour theory of deterrence, intensely suspicious of power, yet governed by interest blocs, factions, markets and political smallholders, could not devise a humane prison system, let alone carry one out. What little vigor and talent was available expended itself on theory, on legislation and, occasionally, on administration at the apex of the system. The central problem was administrative failure: not enough talent, and money, and care, to make the ideal real. This was the vice from top to bottom. Local jails—county and city—were scandals; and what is more, archaic scandals. The great new prisons were wrecked in the war between the aims of reformers and the anarchic indifference of everybody else. The real power in the country did not belong to reformers. It belonged to the rest of the public: people who wanted criminals safely behind bars, out of sight. It was, indeed, this interest that explains why prison reform was possible at all. Before the Walnut Street reforms in Philadelphia in 1790, the good citizens of the city had to suffer the sight of shaven-headed men working the streets, heavily guarded, in "infamous dress . . . begging and insulting the inhabitants, collecting crowds of idle boys, and holding with them the most indecent and improper conversations." Reform at least got convicts off the streets. The men of Walnut Street lived like monks, out of sight and out of mind.

Once prisoners were removed from their midst, the public lost interest, in both senses of that word. Prisons, like poorhouses and insane asylums, continued to serve primarily as storage bins for deviants. Beatings and strait jackets, like the well-meant cruelty of solitary confinement, were visited on a class of men who had no reason to expect good treatment from the world, no hope of changing that world, and no power to do so. Their interests were represented by proxies in the outside world, and their fate was determined by the strength and persistence—never great—of those proxies who stood for reform.

* * *

In the age of Judge Lynch, it might seem strange to speak of how punishment was humanized. But social movements are not required to be even or consistent. The use of capital punishment declined in the last half of the 19th century. Wisconsin entered statehood without any death penalty at all. Michigan abolished it in 1882, except for treason; Maine eliminated the death penalty completely in 1887, and practically speaking, it was absent in Rhode Island too. Corporal punishment (whipping and flogging) survived in few states — in Delaware, as a kind of abominable relic. Elsewhere, even in the South, its legitimacy was slowly sapped. Though whipping was still legal in South Carolina up to the Civil War, a "cloud of disapproval" made public whipping of whites a rare event. By 1900, except for convicts, whipping was almost extinct in the South. Death itself was somewhat modernized when the so-called "electrical chair" appeared in New York in 1888, to replace the hangman's noose. Basically, the two common modes of punishment were fine and imprisonment. By and large, fines were prescribed as punishment for economic crimes. Thieves and rapists went to jail. But allowable sentences, and sentencing behavior, differed drastically, without apparent rhyme or reason, in the various states.

Sentencing was humanized in one way, however. In 1841, a bootmaker named John Augustus began to frequent the Boston criminal courts. In August 1811, his heart was touched by the case of a "ragged and wretched looking" drunk who was, Augustus felt, "not yet past all hope of reformation." Augustus heard the man swear he would never touch another drop, if only "he could be saved from the House of Correction." Augustus stepped up, went bail for the man, and brought him back to court three weeks later, "a sober man." The judge, impressed as always by repentance, waived imprisonment. From this point on, Augustus began to act as a private angel and guardian of men convicted of crime. He bailed almost 2,000 convicts until his death in 1859. Other Bostonians had helped him out or given him money; now some of these carried on his work after his death. In 1878, a Massachusetts statute provided for the appointment of a paid probation officer, in the Boston criminal courts. A further law authorized a statewide system in 1891. Between 1897 and 1900, Missouri, Vermont, Rhode Island, and New Jersey also enacted probation laws; Illinois and Minnesota provided for juvenile probation. But the movement was still clearly in its infancy.

The 19th century also began to experiment with suspended sentences, indeterminate sentences, and parole. (Governors in many states also continued to make liberal use of the pardon.) A judge had always had the power to suspend a sentence, if he felt for some reason that the trial had miscarried. But could judges suspend sentences wholesale, after trials that were scrupulously fair, simply to give the defendant a second chance? The question was litigated in a New York case in 1894. The defendant, John Attridge, a "clerk in a mercantile firm," had helped himself to his employer's money. He pleaded guilty at the trial. Attridge was young and well-liked; there were a number of "mitigating circumstances." "Numerous respectable citizens" of Monroe County petitioned the court for suspended sentence. Two out of three of the judges agreed to suspend; and the highest court in the state affirmed their decision, on appeal. The power to suspend sentence, said the appeal court, was "inherent" in criminal courts.

Indeterminate sentence and parole were bound up with the latest episode in penal reform. The idea for this reform stemmed from the "Cincinnati Declaration" of the first meeting of the American Prison Association. Reform was put into practice at the Elmira "reformatory" in New York (1870). By law, all of the inmates of Elmira were to be young offenders, between the ages of sixteen and thirty, and "not known to have been previously sentenced to a State prison," in New York or elsewhere. They were to be given indeterminate sentences, that is, sentences of variable (and unpredictable) length. In prison, the prisoners were to learn trades; and, of course, the prison would furnish programs of religious and moral uplift. The prisoners were divided into several "classes"; those who behaved and showed progress were to be moved into a better class; for bad behavior, a prisoner moved down. The best prisoners, in the highest class, were eligible for parole.

Elmira was not an unqualified success by any means. Originally, it had been a maximum-security prison, surrounded by a grim high wall. Despite remodeling and good intentions, Elmira was essentially "founded on custody and security, not on rehabilitation." Within ten years, "it was just another prison." The other copies of Elmira in the 19th century (there were only a few of these) shared its defects. They suffered from "neglect, legislative starvation, perfunctory obedience to or complete neglect" of the theory of earning higher grades, and "commercialization of inmate industry—all to the tune of taxpayers' protests that reformatories were 'country clubs' or 'military academies' or 'private schools.'"

The Elmira idea had been thought especially good for young offenders. Many penologists believed that juveniles should not be treated the same as adult offenders. Legislatures ultimately agreed. As early as 1825, New York set up a "House of Refuge" for juveniles. A few states tried modified forms of probation for young people in trouble. A New York law of 1884 provided that when a person under sixteen was convicted of a crime, the judge might, in his discretion, put him in care of some suitable person or institution, instead of prescribing prison or fine. Laws in Massachusetts, and later in Rhode Island (1898), authorized separate trials of children's cases. Indiana, in a series of statutes beginning in 1889, established a Board of Children's Guardians for densely populated townships. The board had the right to petition the circuit court for custody and control of a child under fifteen. Custody might last until the child came of age. The board was empowered to act when it had "probable cause to believe" that the child was "abandoned, neglected or cruelly treated" at home, or had been sent out to beg on the streets, or was truant, or "in idle and vicious association," or if the parents of the child were "in constant habits of drunkenness and blasphemy, or of low and gross debauchery," or if the child was "known by language and life to be vicious or incorrigible."

Despite these halting moves, children in every state could still be arrested, detained, tried, and sent to prison or reformatory. There were 2,029 minors in jail in Massachusetts in 1870; 231 of these were under fifteen. The first true juvenile court was established in 1899 in Cook County, Illinois (Chicago). Under the governing statute, circuit-court judges of Cook County were to designate one special judge to hear all juvenile cases. He would sit in a separate court room, and keep separate records; his court was to be called "the juvenile court." The court had jurisdiction over dependent and neglected children, as well as over delinquents. In this way, the law extended its power over young people—mostly lower class—who had been beyond the reach of prior law, and who had committed no crimes. This reform had

the backing of the "child-savers" of the nineteenth century. Its paternalism, middle-class bias, and absence of due process make it seem less progressive after seventy years than it did to the good people of its day.

By any theory, Elmira and the juvenile court were landmarks; they were not typical of the everyday world of corrections. Elmira, though a failure, at least had high aspirations. Ordinary prisons, state and local, were starved for funds, filthy, sometimes debauched. Many prison jobs were held by ward heelers, appointed to pay off political debts. With dreary regularity, commissions reported bad news about local prisons—a dark chorus of complaints. Prisoners were whipped, starved and tortured in prisons all over the country, though not in all prisons at all times. The county jails of New Jersey were described as a disgrace in 1867. Young, old, men and women were heaped together, subjected to "dirt, vermin, offensive air and darkness." At the state prison, on the other hand, in a perversion of the penitentiary idea, the prisoner lived in a cell measuring $7^{1}/_{2} \times 12$ feet—with one to four cellmates; or alone in a newer cell only four feet—with one to four cellmates; or alone in a newer cell only four feet wide and seven feet long. In this case, he lived and ate "in a room the size of a small bathroom, with a noisome bucket for a toilet and a cot narrower than a bathtub." To bathe, "occasionally," there was a "bathhouse in the yard, which was closed in bad weather." In Illinois, the Cook County jail, inspected in 1869, was also "filthy and full of vermin." The county jails were "moral plague spots"; they made "great criminals out of little ones."

Somehow reforms never took hold; or were perverted in practice. The fact is that convicts, like paupers and blacks, were at the very bottom of American society; powerless, their wants and needs had no American priority. On the other hand, middle-class society had a definite program, even though it was not openly expressed. People detested crime, and were afraid of it. They wanted criminals punished, and severely; even more, they wanted bad people kept out of sight and circulation. Depite the rhetoric, the evidence of what men did shows that they considered it more important to warehouse, quarantine, and guard the "criminal class" than to cure them of their criminal habits. People were inclined to be skeptical, moreover, whether it was possible to make these criminals over. For a long time, criminal anthropologists had explored the idea that the tendency toward crime was inherited along with other inherited traits and that the criminal was a definite physical or mental type. "Intellectually and morally, criminals are for the most part weak," wrote Frederick Howard Wines, in 1895. This weakness showed itself in "inattention, lack of imagination or the power of representation, defective memory, lack of foresight, and general aversion to mental exertion." A rich literature, dating from the 18th century, taught the physical signs of criminal personality: "The prominence of the criminal ear has been especially noted. Prisoners are said to have wrinkled faces; male prisoners have often scanty beards; many hairy women are found in prison. Red-haired men and women do not seem to be given to the commission of crime. . . . Convicts have long arms, pigeon-breasts, and stooping shoulders." Criminals, it was commonly observed, did not blush.

The man on the street did not know these "facts"; but he had his own common sense, no doubt, to guide him. He no doubt *knew* that the criminal was another breed; that such people had to be removed from the society of respectable men, for the safety of the public. In the late 19th century, too, there was new interest in the question of eugenics. Concern for purity of morals joined hands with concern for purity of the blood. It is probably not too farfetched to suspect that these attitudes reinforced the central tendency of the law of corrections, which was to quarantine the bad. What went on inside prison walls was of much less concern so long as these walls were impermeable.

Yet, paradoxically, public unconcern sometimes was its own undoing. Legislatures (responding, no doubt, to what they felt was public opinion) invariably starved the prisons for funds. Jails were jam-packed, sometimes far beyond their capacity. Poor conditions inside the walls frustrated any hope of rehabilitating the men, and may in the long run have stimulated social disorder. Sometimes, too, the prisons were so crowded that the state made wholesale use of pardon and parole. This happened in New Jersey in the late 19th century, because the ordinary outflow of prisoners "did not clear the prison fast enough."

That prisoners ought to do useful work was a firm tenet of two very different groups — reformers, who wanted prisoners to improve themselves, and greedy officials, who wanted to cut costs and raise prison income. Convicts commonly made many products, including brushes, brooms, chairs, boots, and shoes. But organized labor was a sworn and deadly enemy of convict labor. The prisons were hotbeds of what unions saw as unfair competition. Manufacturers whose work force earned nonconvict wages had the same economic interest, in this case, as their workers. Labor and management united to fight against the labor of convicts. The Illinois constitution was amended in 1886 to make it "unlawful . . . to let by contract . . . the labor of any convict." Michigan provided that "no mechanical trade shall hereafter be taught to convicts in the State prison . . . except the manufacture of those articles of which the chief supply for home consumption is imported from other States or countries." Some states ruled that convict-made goods had to be specially marked. A Pennsylvania statute, passed in 1883, required these goods to be branded "convict made," in "plain English lettering . . . by casting, burning, pressing or other such process," in such a way that the brand "may not be defaced," and the brand had to be put "in all cases . . . upon the most conspicuous place upon such article, or the box . . . containing the same." States tried to divert prison labor into channels that did not offend their major interest groups. In Minnesota, beginning in 1891, statutes directed the state prison to acquire equipment and machinery "for the manufacture of twines known as hardfiber twines." Prison-made binding twine would be sold to farmers, "in quantities necessary for their own use." In this way, prison power would help farmers fight what they considered one of the worst of the trusts, the National Cordage Company.

Southern prisons were particularly disgraceful; and the campaign against prison labor made less headway there. In the South, convicts were still hired out on the contract system. Florida statutes specifically authorized the commissioner of agriculture (with the approval of the board of commissioners of state institutions) to "enter into contract . . . for the labor, maintenance and custody of . . . prisoners." No labor was to be done on Sunday, or "before sunrise or after sunset on any day." The contracts could provide for "surrendering the control and custody of the prisoners to the person . . . contracting for their labor." In Georgia, under the code of 1895, a person convicted of a misdemeanor could be sentenced "to work in the chaingang." These infamous gangs worked for counties and cities, often on the public roads. The law empowered the "authorities of any county or municipal corporation" using the gang to "appoint a whipping-boss for such convicts"; the boss was not to use his whip except "in cases where it is reasonably necessary to enforce discipline or compel work or labor by the convict."

The Southern lease system was only an exaggerated form of the national attitude toward corrections. It was heartless, in essence; it was designed to make the tax burden light. Indeed, criminal farming could bring in revenue to the state. In some places, large lessees subleased convicts in small or large gangs. The prisons of the South were "great rolling cages that followed construction camps and railroad building, hastily built stockades deep in forest or swamp or mining fields, or windowless log forts in turpentine flats."

The only protests of substance came from organized labor. In 1883, the Tennesseee Coal, Iron, and Railroad Company hired the thirteen hundred convicts of the Tennessee penitentiary. They used the convicts partly as a lever to force free workers to agree to stiff terms of employment. In 1891, free miners set the convicts loose at the Tennessee Coal Mine Company, and burned down the stockades. The next year miners battled the militia in Anderson County, over the issue of convict labor. The lease system was finally abolished, in Tennessee, after this period of lobbying with fire and with blood.

Notes and Questions

RICHARD B. BRANDT, from *Ethical Theory*

1. Why, according to Richard Brandt, does punishment require justification?

2. Brandt explains that the theory or principle of utility holds that actions should be guided by their tendency to promote "expectable utility" — that is, the general welfare or the greatest happiness for the greatest number. This principle can justify punishment if it is combined with certain "facts" or true assumptions about the effects of punishment. What are these "facts"?

3. Brandt follows Bentham on the question of how much to punish. What is Bentham's formula? Do you see any problems with it?

4. Bentham recognizes six excuses for not punishing at all. What are they, and why does he recognize them? Does Brandt agree?

5. Brandt considers several major objections to the utilitarian theory of punishment. The first is a denial of two of the basic "factual" assumptions made by utilitarians. Namely, it is argued that punishment does not deter crime, and it does not reform criminals — at least there is no evidence that it does. How does Brandt respond?

6. Another objection is that utilitarians, if they are consistent with their theory, should allow no excuses, since that would be a greater deterrence of crime. How does Brandt attempt to answer this claim?

7. The most serious objection to utilitarian theory is that it appears to justify the punishment of innocent people so long as it promotes the common good. What is Brandt's response to this serious charge?

8. Next, Brandt considers some objections to the retributive theory of punishment, which is the major alternative view. What, in general, is the retributive theory, and how does Brandt deal with it?

9. What does Brandt conclude about the relative merits of the utilitarian and the retributive theories for justifying punishment?

[From] *Ethical Theory*

RICHARD B. BRANDT

The ethical foundations of the institution and principles of criminal justice require examination just as do the ethical foundations of systems of economic distribution. In fact, the two problems are so similar that it is helpful to view either one in the light of conclusions reached about the other. It is no accident that the two are spoken of as problems of "justice," for the institution of criminal justice is essentially a mode of allocating welfare (or "illfare," if we prefer). Also, just as an economic return can be regarded as a reward for past services, the punishment of criminals can be regarded as punishment for past disservices. Moreover, just as a major reason for differences in economic reward is to provide motivation for promoting the public welfare by industrious effort, so a major reason for a system of punishment for criminals is to give motivation for not harming the public by crime. The two topics, then, are very similar; but they are also sufficiently different to require separate discussion.

What is meant by an "examination of the ethical foundations of the institution and principles of criminal justice"? The job of such an examination is *not* to provide a moral blessing for the status quo, for the system of criminal justice as it actually is in the United States, or in the Commonwealth of Pennsylvania. (It would be impossible to do this for all states of the U.S.A. together, or for all the Western nations, for the legal systems of different political units differ in important particulars.) Rather, it is to identify the more important valid ethical principles that are relevant to the institution of criminal justice and to furnish a model of their use in criticism or justification of important features of this institution.

The broad questions to be kept in the forefront of discussion are the following: (1) What justifies anyone in inflicting pain or loss on an individual on account of his past acts? (2) Is there a valid general principle about the punishments proper for various acts? (Possibly there should be no close connection between offense and penalty; perhaps punishment should be suited to the individual needs of the criminal, and not to his crime.) (3) What kinds of defense should excuse from punishment? An answer to these questions would comprise prescriptions for the broad outlines of an ideal system of criminal justice.

In our discussion of "distributive justice," we decided that "to act unjustly" means the same as "to treat unequally, in some matter that involves the distribution of things that are good or bad, except as the inequality is required by moral considerations (principles) with substantial weight in the circumstances." If this definition of "act unjustly" is correct, then there are two distinct ways in which there can be injustice in the treatment of criminals. First, criminals are *punished* whereas noncriminals are not. Punishment, however, is *unequal* treatment, in a matter that involves distribution of things good or bad. Therefore, if punishment is to be just, it must be shown that the unequal treatment is required by moral principles of weight. Thus, one thing that must be done in order to show that the practice of punishing criminals is not unjust, is to show that there are moral principles that require it. But second, the *procedures of applying* the principles directing unequal treatment for criminals may themselves operate unequally. One man gets a "fair" trial and another does not. There can be inequality in the chances given people to escape the application of legal sanctions in their case. Part of treating people "justly," then, is providing legal devices so that everyone has an equal hearing: scrupulous adherence to the rules of evidence, opportunity for appeal to higher courts for remedy of deviation from standard rules in the lower courts, and so on. We shall not here consider details about how legal institutions should be devised in order to secure equal application of the law; that is a specialized inquiry that departs too far from the main problems of ethical principle. It is a part of "justice," however. Indeed, we may view "criminal justice" as having two main aspects: just laws for the punishment of offenders and procedures insuring just application of these laws by the courts and other judicial machinery.

The existence of just laws directing certain punishments for certain offenses, then, is not the whole of justice for the criminal, but we shall concentrate on identifying such laws. . . .

1. The Utilitarian Theory

Historically there has been a cleavage of opinion about the kind of general ethical principles required for coherence with our concrete justified beliefs about criminal justice. Many writers have thought that a utilitarian principle is adequate. Others have though that some nonutilitarian principle, or more than one, is necessary. Most of the latter writers (formalists) have espoused some form of *retributive* principle — that is, a principle roughly to the effect that a wrongdoer should be punished approximately in correspondence with either the moral reprehensibility of his offense or with the magnitude of his breach or of the public harm he commits.

It is convenient to begin with the utilitarian theory. . . . The essence of the rule-utilitarian theory, we recall, is that our actions, whether legislative or otherwise, should be guided by a set of prescriptions, the conscientious following of which by all would have maximum net expectable utility. As a result, the utilitarian is not, just as such, committed to any particular view about how antisocial behavior should be treated by society — or even to the view that society should do anything at all about immoral conduct. It is only the utilitarian principle *combined* with statements about the kind of laws and practices which will maximize expectable utility that has such consequences. Therefore, utilitarians are free to differ from one another about the character of an ideal system of criminal justice; some utilitarians think that the system prevalent in Great Britain and the United States essentially corresponds to the ideal, but others think that the only system that can be justified is markedly different from the actual systems in these Western countries. We shall concentrate our discussion, however, on the more traditional line of utilitarian thought which holds that roughly the actual system of criminal law, say in the United States, is morally justifiable, and we shall follow roughly the classic exposition of the reasoning

given by Jeremy Bentham[1] — but modifying this freely when we feel amendment is called for. At the end of the chapter we shall look briefly at a different view.

Traditional utilitarian thinking about criminal justice has found the rationale of the practice, in the United States, for example, in three main facts. (Those who disagree think the first two of these "facts" happen not to be the case.) (1) People who are tempted to misbehave, to trample on the rights of others, to sacrifice public welfare for personal gain, can usually be deterred from misconduct by fear of punishment, such as death, imprisonment, or fine. (2) Imprisonment or fine will teach malefactors a lesson; their characters may be improved, and at any rate a personal experience of punishment will make them less likely to misbehave again. (3) Imprisonment will certainly have the result of physically preventing past malefactors from misbehaving, during the period of their incarceration.

In view of these suppositions, traditional utilitarian thinking has concluded that having laws forbidding certain kinds of behavior on pain of punishment, and having machinery for the fair enforcement of these laws, is justified by the fact that it maximizes expectable utility. Misconduct is not to be punished just for its own sake; malefactors must be punished for their past acts, according to law, as a way of maximizing expectable utility.

The utilitarian principle, of course, has implications for decisions about the severity of punishment to be administered. Punishment is itself an evil, and hence should be avoided where this is consistent with the public good. Punishment should have precisely such a degree of severity (not more or less) that the probable disutility of greater severity just balances the probable gain in utility (less crime because of the more serious threat). The cost, in other words, should be counted along with the value of what is bought; and we should buy protection up to the point where the cost is greater than the protection is worth. How severe will such punishment be? Jeremy Bentham had many sensible things to say about this. Punishment, he said, must be severe enough so that it is to no one's advantage to commit an offense even if he receives the punishment; a fine of $10 for bank robbery would give no security at all. Further, since many criminals will be undetected, we must make the penalty heavy enough in comparison with the prospective gain from crime, that a prospective criminal will consider the risk hardly worth it, even considering that it is not certain he will be punished at all. Again, the more serious offenses should carry the heavier penalties, not only because the greater disutility justifies the use of heavier penalties in order to prevent them, but also because criminals should be motivated to commit a less serious rather than a more serious offense. Bentham thought the prescribed penalties should allow for some variation at the discretion of the judge, so that the actual suffering caused should roughly be the same in all cases; thus, a heavier fine will be imposed on a rich man than on a poor man.

Bentham also argued that the goal of maximum utility requires that certain facts should *excuse* from culpability, for the reason that punishment in such cases "must be inefficacious." He listed as such (1) the fact that the relevant law was passed only after the act of the accused, (2) that the law had not been made public, (3) that the criminal was an infant, insane, or was intoxicated, (4) that the crime was done under physical compulsion, (5) that the agent was ignorant of the probable consequences of his act or was acting on the basis of an innocent misapprehension of the facts, such that the act the agent thought he was performing was a lawful one, and (6) that the motivation to commit the offense was so strong that no threat of law could prevent the crime. Bentham also thought that punishment should be remitted if the crime was a collective one and the number of the guilty so large that great suffering would be caused by its imposition, or if the offender held an important post and his services were important for the public, or if the public or foreign powers would be offended by the punishment; but we shall ignore this part of his view.

Bentham's account of the logic of legal "defenses" needs amendment. What he should have argued is that *not* punishing in certain types of cases (cases where such defenses as those just indicated can be offered) reduces the amount of suffering imposed by law and the insecurity of everybody, and that failure to impose punishment in these types of cases will cause only a negligible increase in the incidence of crime.

How satisfactory is this theory of criminal justice? Does it have any implications that are far from being acceptable when compared with concrete justified convictions about what practices are morally right?[2]

Many criminologists would argue that Bentham was mistaken in his facts: The deterrence value of threat of punishment, they say, is much less than he imagined, and criminals are seldom reformed by spending time in prison. If these contentions are correct, then the ideal rules for society's treatment of malefactors are very different from what Bentham thought, and from what actual practice is today in the United States. To say all this, however, is not to show that the utilitarian *principle* is incorrect, for in view of these facts presumably the attitudes of a "qualified" person would not be favorable to criminal justice as practiced today. Utilitarian theory might still be correct, but its implications would be different from what Bentham thought—and they might coincide with justified ethical judgments. We shall return to this.

The whole utilitarian approach, however, has been criticized on the grounds that it ought not in consistency to approve of *any* excuses from criminal liability.[3] Or at least, it should do so only after careful empirical inquiries. It is not obvious, it is argued, that we increase net expectable utility by permitting such defenses. At the, least, the utilitarian is committed to defend the concept of "strict liability." Why? Because we could get a more strongly deterrent effect if everyone knew that *all behavior* of a certain sort would be punished, irrespective of mistaken supposals of fact, compulsion, and so on. The critics admit that knowledge that all behavior of a certain sort will be punished will hardly deter from crime the insane, persons acting under compulsion, persons acting under erroneous beliefs about facts, and others, but, as Professor Hart points out, it does not follow from this that general knowledge that certain acts will always be punished will not be salutary.

The utilitarian, however, has a solid defense against charges of this sort. We must bear in mind (as the critics do not) that the utilitarian principle, *taken by itself, implies nothing whatever* about whether a system of law should excuse persons on the basis of certain defenses.

What the utilitarian does say is that, when we *combine* the principle of utilitarianism with *true* propositions about a certain thing or situation, then we shall come out with true statements about obligations. The utilitarian is certainly not committed to saying that one will derive true propositions about obligations if one starts with *false* propositions about fact or about what will maximize welfare, or with no such propositions at all. Therefore the criticism sometimes made (for example, by Hart), that utilitarian theory does not render it "obviously" or "necessarily" the case that the recognized excuses from criminal liability should be accepted as excusing from punishment, is beside the point. Moreover, in fact the utilitarian can properly claim that we do have excellent reason for believing that the general public would be no better motivated to avoid criminal offenses than it now is, if the insane and others were also punished along with intentional wrongdoers. Indeed, he may reasonably claim that the example of punishment of these individuals could only have a hardening effect — like public executions. Furthermore, the utilitarian can point out that abolition of the standard exculpating excuses would lead to serious insecurity. Imagine the pleasure of driving an automobile if one knew one could be executed for running down a child whom it was absolutely impossible to avoid striking! One certainly does not maximize expectable utility by eliminating the traditional excuses. In general, then, the utilitarian theory is not threatened by its implications about exculpating excuses.

It might also be objected against utilitarianism that it cannot recognize the validity of *mitigating* excuses. Would not consequences be better if the distinction between premeditated and impulsive acts were abolished? The utilitarian can reply that people who commit impulsive crimes, in the heat of anger, do not give thought to legal penalties; they would not be deterred by a stricter law. Moreover, such a person is unlikely to repeat his crime, so that a mild sentence saves an essentially good man for society.[4]

Sometimes it is objected to utilitarianism that it must view imprisonment for crime as morally no different from quarantine. This, it is said, shows that the utilitarian theory must be mistaken, since actually there is a vast moral difference between being quarantined and being imprisoned for crime. *Why* is it supposed utilitarian theory must view imprisonment as a kind of quarantine? The answer is that utilitarianism looks to the future; the treatment it prescribes for individuals is treatment with an eye to maximizing net expectable utility. The leper is quarantined because otherwise he will expose others to disease. The criminal is imprisoned because otherwise he, or others who are not deterred by the threat of punishment, will expose the public to crime. Both the convicted criminal and the leper are making contributions to the public good. So, quarantine and imprisonment are essentially personal sacrifices for the public welfare, if we think of punishment as the utilitarian does. But in fact, the argument goes on, we feel there is a vast difference. The public is obligated to do what is possible to make the leper comfortable, to make his necessary sacrifice as easy for him and his family as possible. But we feel no obligation to make imprisonment as comfortable as possible.

Again the utilitarian has a reply. He can say that people cannot help contracting leprosy, but they can avoid committing crimes — and the very discomforts and harshness of prison life are deterring factors. If prison life were made attractive, there might be more criminals — not to mention the indolent who would commit a crime in order to enjoy the benefits of public support. Furthermore, the utilitarian can say, why should we feel that we "ought to make it up to" a quarantined leper? At least partly because it is useful to encourage willingness to make such sacrifices. But we do not at all wish to encourage the criminal to make his "sacrifice"; rather, we wish him not to commit his crimes. There is all the difference between the kind of treatment justified on utilitarian grounds for a person who may have to make a sacrifice for the public welfare through no fault of his own, and for a person who is required to make a sacrifice because he has selfishly and deliberately trampled on the rights of others, in clear view of the fact that if he is apprehended society must make an example of him. There are all sorts of utilitarian reasons for being kindly to persons of the former type, and stern with people of the latter type.

Another popular objection to the utilitarian theory is that the utilitarian must approve of prosecutors or judges occasionally withholding evidence known to them, for the sake of convicting an innocent man, if the public welfare really is served by so doing. Critics of the theory would not deny that there *can* be circumstances where the dangers are so severe that such action is called for; they only say that utilitarianism calls for it all too frequently. Is this criticism justified? Clearly, the utilitarian is not committed to advocating that a provision should be written into the *law* so as to permit punishment of persons for crimes they did not commit if to do so would serve the public good. Any such provision would be a shattering blow to public confidence and security. The question is only whether there should be an informal moral rule to the same effect, for the guidance of judges and prosecutors. Will the rule-utilitarian necessarily be committed to far too sweeping a moral rule on this point? We must recall that he is not in the position of the act-utilitarian, who must say that an innocent man must be punished if in *his particular case* the public welfare would be served by his punishment. The rule-utilitarian rather asserts only that an innocent man should be punished if he falls within a class of cases such that net expectable utility is maximized if *all* members of the class are punished, taking into account the possible disastrous effects on public confidence if it is generally known that judges and prosecutors are guided by such a rule. . . . When we take these considerations into account, it is not obvious that the rule-utilitarian is committed to action that we are justifiably convinced is immoral.[5]

In recent years, some philosophers have sought to rescue the utilitarian from his supposed difficulty of being committed to advocate the punishment of innocent men, by a verbal point. Their argument is that it is *logically* guaranteed that only a guilty man may be *punished.* "Punishment," it is said, like "reward" and "forgive," has a backward reference; we properly speak of "punishing *for.* . . ." and if we inflict suffering on someone for the sake of utility and irrespective of guilt for some offense, it is a misuse of the word "punishment" to speak of such a person as being punished.[6] It is not clear, however, that anything is accomplished by this verbal move. If these writers are correct, then it is self-contradictory to say "innocent men may be punished for

the sake of the public good," and no one can say that utilitarian theory commits one to uttering such a self-contradiction. But it may still be that utilitarian theory commits one to advocating that prosecutors suppress evidence on certain occasions, that judges aid in conducting unfair trials and pronounce sentences out of line with custom for a particular type of case in times of public danger, and, in short, that innocent men be *locked up* or *executed* — only not *"punished"* — for the sake of the public welfare. So, if there is a difficulty here at all for the utilitarian theory, the verbal maneuver of these philosophers seem not to remove it.

Everything considered, the utilitarian theory seems to be in much less dire distress, in respect of its implications for criminal justice, than has sometimes been supposed. It does not seem possible to show that in any important way its implications are clearly in conflict with our valid convictions about what is right. The worst that can be said is that utilitarian theory does not in a clear-cut way definitely require us to espouse some practices we are inclined to espouse. But to this the utilitarian may make two replies. First, that there is reason to think our ordinary convictions about punishment for crime ought to be thoroughly re-examined in important respects. Second, the utilitarian may reply that if we consider our convictions about the punishments we should administer *as a parent* — and this is the point where our moral opinions are least likely to be affected by the sheer weight of tradition — we shall find that we think according to the principles of rule-utilitarianism. Parents do regard their punishment of their children as justified only in view of the future good of the child, and in order to make life in the home tolerable and in order to distribute jobs and sacrifices equally.

2. The Retributive Theory of Criminal Justice

Any system of basic principles that contains nonutilitarian principles relevant to the treatment of criminals may be called a "retributive" theory of criminal justice. However, it seems better to reserve the term "retributive theory" for a theory that asserts that it is a basic principle of ethics roughly that pain or loss should be caused to persons who have done wrong, with a severity corresponding with the moral gravity of their deed — and of course the "gravity" of the deed not being defined to accord exactly with the utilitarian theory about how severely wrongdoers should be made to suffer. In saying that such a principle is a "basic" principle of ethics, proponents of the retributive theory deny the possibility of deriving this principle from any principle directing to do good, that is, from any kind of utilitarian principle. . . .

The traditional retributive principle is perhaps best stated today in a way suggested by Ross' formalist system, somewhat as follows: "It is prima facie obligatory for society to cause pain or loss to every person who commits a morally objectionable act to an extent corresponding with the moral gravity of his offense." We can assume that other considerations, such as the obligation to avoid general insecurity, will require that punishment be imposed only for infractions of properly publicized laws, by specially authorized persons, and after a trial according to procedures selected in order to guarantee a fair application of the law.

Should we accept the retributive principle as a basic "axiom" about moral obligation (or else the assertion that it is intrinsically better for offenders to be punished than to go unpunished)? Various considerations suggest that we should answer this question *negatively*.

(1) Our ethical theory is *simpler* without this principle, and therefore it should be rejected unless it enables us to deduce, as theorems (when we combine it with true factual premises), ethical principles which are valid, and which cannot be deducted without it. But since our discussion of the rule-utilitarian theory of punishment has not disclosed any major objection to that theory, there is no reason to complicate our theory by adding a retributive principle.

(2) The retributive principle asserts in effect that a principal aim of the law is to punish moral guilt. But if so, then it ought to punish merely *attempted* crimes as severely as successful crimes, and since an attempt is a case of setting oneself to commit a crime, it is as much a deliberate deviation from subjective obligation as the successful commission of a crime. Assuming that this implication is incorrect, clearly the retributive principle alone will not do as a principle guiding legislative practice.

(3) According to retributivism, laws should be so framed that no one will be punished, no matter what he does, if he is morally blameless. This is objectionable. It is of great importance that the law be able to set up standards of conduct, and require all to conform, whether or not they are convinced of the desirability of the standards. The law must be in a position to demand certain conduct from individuals, say in the Defense Department, whose conscientious deliberations might lead them to betray secrets essential to the national defense. Again, the law must be in a position to ban some practice like polygamy, irrespective of the value judgments of any persons. Therefore we must again say that the retributive principle cannot be the only principle guiding the framing of law and judicial practice.

NOTES

1. In *Principles of Morals and Legislation*.

2. Act-utilitarians face some special problems. For instance, if I am an act-utilitarian and serve on a jury, I shall work to get a verdict that will do the most good, irrespective of the charges of the judge, and of any oath I may have taken to give a reasonable answer to certain questions on the basis of the evidence presented — unless I think my doing so will have indirect effects on the institution of the jury, public confidence in it, and so on. This is certainly not what we think a juror should do. Of course, neither a juror nor a judge can escape his prima facie obligation to do what good he can; this obligation is present in some form in every theory. The act-utilitarian, however, makes this the whole of one's responsibility.

3. See H. L. A. Hart, "Legal Responsibility and Excuses," in Sidney Hook (ed.), *Determinism and Freedom* (New York: New York University Press, 1958), pp. 81–104; and David Braybrooke, "Professor Stevenson, Voltaire, and the Case of Admiral Byng," *Journal of Philosophy,* LIII (1956), 787–96

4. The utilitarian must admit that the same thing is true for many deliberate murders and probably he should also admit that some people who commit a crime in the heat of anger would have found time to think had they known that a grave penalty awaited them.

5. In any case, a tenable theory of punishment must approve of punishing persons who are morally blameless. Suppose someone commits treason for moral reasons. We may have to say that his deed is not repre-

hensible at all, and might even (considering the risk he took for his principles) be morally admirable. Yet we think such persons must be punished no matter what their motives; people cannot be permitted to take the law into their own hands.

6. For some discussion of the grammar of "punish," see A. M. Quinton, "On Punishment," *Analysis,* XIV (1954), 133–42, and K. Baier, "Is Punishment Retributive?" *Analysis,* XVI (1955), 25–32.

Notes and Questions

EDMUND L. PINCOFFS, from *The Rationale of Legal Punishment*

1. Edmund L. Pincoffs sets out three fundamental tenets of classical retributivism. What are they? How do they compare to the fundamental elements of utilitarianism?

2. The retributive justification of punishment is based on the principle or value of justice. Pincoffs presents this foundation in a long quotation from Immanuel Kant. In this passage Kant represents justice as equality. What does it mean to view justice as equality in the context of punishment? How does this relate to the right of retaliation?

3. Notice that Pincoffs takes pains to limit the retributive theory to intentional acts. Why is this important? Could unintentional acts be accommodated as well? How would Kant handle the difference? What difference should it make? How would a utilitarian handle it?

4. Pincoffs points out that an important underlying assumption of retributivism is the direction of justification. To whom is justification directed, according to a retributivist? Why is that important?

5. What sort of justification must be offered if retributivism is based on justice? Can we justify incarcerating a criminal for his own good? Why or why not? Can we punish someone for the good of society? How about for the protection of society? If so, how so?

6. Pincoffs' discussion of Kant and Hegel illustrates that retributivists assume certain basic ideas about moral justification in general and about how any human being is entitled to be treated. What are Kant's and Hegel's views on universalizing the principle of one's action? Is this a mistaken view of moral justification? If not, does it lead to their view of punishment?

7. According to retributivists (including Kant and Hegel), any human being is entitled to be taken seriously as a competent adult who is responsible for his or her actions. No one is to be treated as a child who doesn't know any better, doesn't understand the implications of his or her actions, or as a harmful animal that can't be expected to control itself. This is what it means to be treated as a rational being and to be entitled to one's punishment (as strange as that may sound). It is not to be discounted or excused as defective. Should all sane adults be treated as rational, that is, as responsible human beings? If not, why not (for what reasons), and who should decide?

8. According to retributivists, the penalty you pay should be the penalty you owe. Your punishment should be exactly what you deserve, no more, no less. That is justice. How can we decide what someone deserves? Is the problem of measuring desert so severe as to undermine the whole theory of retributivism for all practical purposes?

[From] *The Rationale of Legal Punishment*

EDMUND L. PINCOFFS

Classical Retributivism

I

The classification of Kant as a retributivist[1] is usually accompanied by a reference to some part of the following passage from the *Rechtslehre*, which is worth quoting at length.

> Juridical punishment can never be administered merely as a means for promoting another good either with regard to the criminal himself or to civil society, but must in all cases be imposed only because the individual on whom it is inflicted *has committed a crime.* For one man ought never to be dealt with merely as a means subservient to the purpose of another, nor be mixed up with the subjects of real right. Against such treatment his inborn personality has a right to protect him, even though he may be condemned to lose his civil personality. He must first be found guilty and *punishable* before there can be any thought of drawing from his punishment any benefit for himself or his fellow-citizens. The penal law is a categorical imperative; and woe to him who creeps through the serpent-windings of utilitarianism to discover some advantage that may discharge him from the justice of punishment, or even from the due measure of it, according to the Pharisaic maxim: "It is better that *one* man should die than the whole people should perish." For if justice and righteousness perish, human life would no longer have any value in the world. . . .
>
> But what is the mode and measure of punishment which public justice takes as its principle and standard? It is just the principle of equality, by which the pointer of the scale of justice is made to incline no more to the one side than the other. It may be rendered by saying that the undeserved evil which any one commits on another, is to be regarded as perpetrated on himself. Hence it may be said: "If you slander another, you slander yourself; if you steal from another, you steal from yourself; if you strike another, you strike yourself; if you kill another, you kill yourself." This is the Right of RETALIATION (*jus talionis*); and properly understood,

it is the only principle which in regulating a public court, as distinguished from mere private judgement, can definitely assign both the quality and the quantity of a just penalty. All other standards are wavering and uncertain; and on account of other considerations involved in them, they contain no principle conformable to the sentence of pure and strict justice.[2]

Obviously we could mull over this passage for a long time. What, exactly, is the distinction between the Inborn and the Civil Personality? How is the Penal Law a Categorical Imperative: by derivation from one of the five formulations in the *Grundlegung*, or as a separate formulation? But we are on the trail of the traditional retributive theory of punishment and do not want to lose ourselves in niceties. There are two main points in this passage to which we should give particular attention:

   i. The only acceptable reason for punishing a man is that he has committed a crime.

   ii. The only acceptable reason for punishing a man in a given manner and degree is that the punishment is "equal" to the crime for which he is punished.

These propositions, I think it will be agreed, express the main points of the first and second paragraphs respectively. Before stopping over these points, let us go on to a third. It is brought out in the following passage from the *Rechtslehre*, which is also often referred to by writers on retributivism.

> Even if a civil society resolved to dissolve itself with the consent of all its members — as might be supposed in the case of a people inhabiting an island resolving to separate and scatter themselves throughout the whole world — the last murderer lying in prison ought to be executed before the resolution was carried out. This ought to be done in order that every one may realize the desert of his deeds, and that bloodguiltiness

may not remain upon the people; for otherwise they will all be regarded as participators in the murder as a public violation of justice.[3]

It is apparent from this passage that, so far anyway as the punishment of death for murder is concerned, the punishment awarded not only may but must be carried out. If it must be carried out "so that everyone may realize the desert of his deeds," then punishment for deeds other than murder must be carried out too. We will take it, then, that Kant holds that:

    iii. Whoever commits a crime must be punished in accordance with his desert.

Whereas (i) tells us what kind of reason we must have if we punish, (iii) now tells us that we must punish *whenever* there is desert of punishment. Punishment, Kant tells us elsewhere, is "The *juridical* effect or consequence of a culpable act of Demerit."[4] Any crime is a culpable act of demerit, in that it is an "*intentional* transgression — that is, an act accompanied with the consciousness that it is a transgression."[5] This is an unusually narrow definition of crime, since crime is not ordinarily limited to intentional acts of transgression, but may also include unintentional ones, such as acts done in ignorance of the law, and criminally negligent acts. However, Kant apparently leaves room for "culpable acts of demerit" outside of the category of crime. These he calls "faults," which are unintentional transgressions of duty, but "are nevertheless imputable to a person."[6] I can only suppose, though it is a difficulty in the interpretation of the *Rechtslehre*, that when Kant says that punishment must be inflicted "only because he has committed a crime" he is not including in "crime" what he would call a fault. Crime would, then, refer to any *intentional* imputable transgressions of duty; and these are what must be punished as involving ill desert. The difficulties involved in the definition of crime as the transgression of duty, as opposed to the mere violation of a legal prohibition, will be taken up later.

Taking the three propositions we have isolated as expressing the essence of the Kantian retributivistic position, we must now ask a direct and obvious question. What makes Kant hold this position? Why does he think it apparent that consequences should have *nothing to do* with the

decision whether, and how, and how much to punish? There are two directions an answer to this question might follow. One would lead us into an extensive excursus on the philosophical position of Kant, the relation of this to his ethical theory, and the relation of his general theory of ethics to his philosophy of law. It would, in short, take our question as one about the consistency of Kant's position concerning the justification of punishment with the whole of the Kantian philosophy. This would involve discussion of Kant's reasons for believing that moral laws must be universal and categorical in virtue of their form alone, and divorced from any empirical content; of his attempt to make out a moral decision-procedure based upon an "empty" categorical imperative; and, above all, of the concept of freedom as a postulate of practical reason, and as the central concept of the philosophy of law. This kind of answer, however, we must forgo here; for while it would have considerable interest in its own right, it would lead us astray from our purpose, which is to understand as well as we can the retributivist position, not as a part of this or that philosophical system but for its own sake. It is a position taken by philosophers with diverse philosophical systems; we want to take another direction, then, in our answer. Is there any *general* (nonspecial, nonsystematic) reason why Kant rejects consequences in the justification of punishment?

Kant believes that consequences have nothing to do with the justification of punishment partly because of his assumptions about the *direction* of justification; and these assumptions are, I believe, also to be found underlying the thought of Hegel and Bradley. Justification is not only *of* something, it is also *to someone*; it has an addressee. Now there are important confusions in Kant's and other traditional justifications of punishment turning on the question what the "punishment" *is* which is being justified. In Chapter IV, we will examine some of these. But if we are to feel the force of the retributivist position, we can no longer put off the question of the addressee of justification.

To whom is the Kantian justification of punishment directed? The question may seem a difficult one to answer, since Kant does not consider it himself as a separate issue. Indeed, it is not the kind of question likely to occur to a philosopher of Kant's formalistic leanings. A Kantian justification or rationale stands, so to speak, on its own. It is a structure which can be examined, tested, probed by any rational being. Even to speak of the addressee of justification has an uncomfortably relativistic sound, as if only persuasion of A or B or C is possible, and proof impossible. Yet, in practice, Kant does not address his proffered justification of punishment so much to any rational being (which, to put it otherwise, is to address it not at all), as to the being most affected: the criminal himself.

It is the criminal who is cautioned not to creep through the serpent-windings of utilitarianism. It is the criminal's rights which are in question in the debate with Beccaria over capital punishment. it is the criminal we are warned not to mix up with property or things: the "subjects of Real Right." In the *Kritik der Praktischen Vernunst*, the intended direction of justification becomes especially clear.

> Now the notion of punishment, as such, cannot be united with that of becoming a partaker of happiness; for although he who inflicts the punishment may at the same time have the benevolent purpose of directing this punishment to this end, yet it must be justified in itself as punishment, that is, as mere harm, so that if it stopped there, and the person punished could get no glimpse of kindness hidden behind this harshness, he must yet admit that justice was done him, and that his reward was perfectly suitable to his conduct. In every punishment, as such, there must first be justice, and this constitutes the essence of the notion. Benevolence may, indeed, be united with it, but the man who has deserved punishment has not the least reason to reckon upon this.[7]

Since this matter of the direction of justification is central in our understanding of traditional retributivism, and not generally appreciated, it will be worth our while to pause over this paragraph. Kant holds here, as he later holds in the *Rechtslehre*, that once it has been decided that a given "mode and measure" of punishment is justified, then "he who inflicts punishment" may do so in such a way as to increase the long-term happiness of the criminal. This could be accomplished, for example, by using a prison term as an opportunity for reforming the criminal. But Kant's point is that reforming the criminal has nothing to do with justifying the infliction of punishment. It is not inflicted because it will give an opportunity for reform, but because it is merited. The passage does not need my gloss; it is transparently clear. Kant wants the justification of punishment to be such that the criminal "who could get no glimpse of kindness behind this harshness" would have to admit that punishment is warranted.

Suppose we tell the criminal, "We are punishing you for your own good." This is wrong, because it is then open to him to raise the question whether he deserves punishment, and what you consider good to be. If he does not deserve punishment, we have no right to inflict it, especially in the name of some good of which the criminal may not approve. So long as we are to treat him as rational — a being with dignity — we cannot force our judgments of good upon him. This is what makes the appeal to supposedly good consequences "wavering and uncertain." They waver because the criminal has as much right as anyone to question them. They concern ends which he may reject, and means which he might rightly regard as unsuited to the ends.

In the "Supplementary Explanations of the Principles of Right" of the *Rechtslehre*, Kant distinguishes between "punitive justice (*justitia punitiva*), in which the ground of the penalty is moral (*quia peccatum est*)," and "punitive *expediency*, the foundation of which is merely pragmatic (*ne peccetur*) as being grounded upon the experience of what operates most effectively to prevent crime." Punitive justice, says Kant, has an "entirely distinct place (*locus justi*) in the topical arrangement of the juridical conceptions." It does not seem reasonable to suppose that Kant makes this distinction merely to discard punitive expediency entirely, that he has no concern at all for the *ne peccetur*. But he does hold that there is no place for it in the justification of punishment proper: for this can only be to show the criminal that the punishment is just.

How is this to be done? The difficulty is that on the one hand the criminal must be treated as a rational being, an end in himself; but on the other hand the justification we offer him cannot be allowed to appear as the opening move in a rational discussion. It cannot turn on the criminal's acceptance of some premise which, as rational being, he has a perfect right to question. If the end in question is the well-being of society, we are assuming that the criminal will not have a different view of what that well-being consists in, and we are telling him that he should sacrifice himself *to* that end. As a rational being, he can question whether any end we propose is a good end. And we have no right to demand that he sacrifice himself to the public well-being, even supposing he agrees with us on what that consists in. No man has a duty, on Kant's view, to be benevolent.[8]

The way out of the quandary is to show the criminal that we are not inflicting the punishment on him for some questionable purpose of our own choice, but that he, as a free agent, has exercised his choice in such a way as to make the punishment a necessary consequence. "His own evil deed draws the punishment upon himself."[9] "The undeserved evil which anyone commits on another, is to be regarded as perpetuated on himself."[10] But may not the criminal rationally question this asserted connection between crime and punishment? Suppose he wishes to regard the punishment *not* as "drawn upon himself" by his own "evil deed?" Suppose he argues that no good purpose will be served by punishing him? But this line of thought leads into the "serpent-windings of utilitarianism," for if it is good consequences that govern, then justice goes by the board. What may not be done to him in the name of good consequences? What proportion would remain between what he has done and what he suffers?[11]

But punishment is *inflicted*. To tell the criminal that he "draws it upon himself is all very well, only how do we justify *to ourselves* the infliction of it? Kant's answer is found early in the Rechtslehre.[12] There he relates punishment to crime via freedom. Crime consists in compulsion or constraint of some kind: a hindrance of freedom.[13] If it is wrong that freedom should be hindered, it is right to block this hindrance. But to block the constraint of freedom it is necessary to apply constraint. Punishment is a "hindering of a hindrance of freedom." Compulsion of the criminal is, then, justified only to the extent that it hinders his compulsion of another.

But how are we to understand Kant here? Punishment comes after the crime. How can it hinder the crime? The reference cannot be to the hindrance of future crime, or Kant's doctrine reduces to a variety of utilitarianism. The picture of compulsion *vs* compulsion is clear enough, but how are we to apply it? Our answer must be somewhat speculative, since there is no direct answer to be found in the *Rechtslehre*. The answer must begin from yet another extension of the concept of a crime. For the crime cannot consist merely in an act. What is criminal is acting in accordance with a wrong maxim: a maxim which would, if made universal, destroy freedom. The adoption of the maxim is criminal. Should we regard punishment, then, as the hindrance of a wrong maxim? But how do we hinder a maxim? We show, exhibit, its wrongness by taking it at face value. If the criminal has adopted it, he is claiming that it can be universalized. But if it is universalized it warrants the same treatment of the criminal as he has accorded to his victim. So if he murders he must be executed; if he steals we must "steal from" him.[14] What we do to him he willed, in willing to adopt his maxim as universalizable. To justify the punishment to the criminal is to show him that the compulsion we use on him proceeds according to the same rule by which he acts. This is how he "draws the punishment upon himself." In punishing, we are not adopting his maxim but demonstrating its logical consequences if universalized: We show the criminal *what* he has willed. This is the positive side of the Kantian rationale of punishment.

II

Hegel's version of this rationale has attracted more attention, and disagreement, in recent literature. It is the Hegelian metaphysical terminology which is in part responsible for the disagreement, and which has stood in the way of an understanding of the retributivist position. The difficulty turns around the notions of "annulment of crime," and of punishment as the "right" of the criminal. Let us consider "annulment" first.

In the *Philosophie des Rechts*[15] Hegel tells us that

> Abstract right is a right to coerce, because the wrong which transgresses it is an exercise of force against the existence of my freedom in an external thing. The maintenance of this existent against the exercise of force therefore itself takes the form of an external act and an exercise of force annulling the force originally brought against it.[16]

Holmes complains that by the use of his logical apparatus, involving the negation of negations (or annulment), Hegel professes to establish what is only a mystic (though generally felt) bond between wrong and punishment.[17] Hastings Rashdall asks how any rational connection can be shown between the evil of the pain of punishment, and the twin evils of the suffering of the victim and the moral evil which "pollutes the offender's soul," unless appeal is made to the probable good consequences of punishment. The notion that the "guilt" of the offense must be, in some mysterious way, wiped out by the suffering of the offender does not seem to provide it.[18] Crime, which is an evil, is apparently to be "annulled" by the addition to it of punishment, which is another evil. How can two evils yield a good?[19]

But in fact Hegel is following the *Rechtslehre* quite closely here, and his doctrine is very near to Kant's. In the notes taken at Hegel's lectures,[20] we find Hegel quoted as follows:

> If crime and its annulment . . . are treated as if they were unqualified evils, it must, of course, seem quite unreasonable to will an evil merely because "another evil is there already." . . . But it is not merely a question of an evil or of this, that, or the other good; the precise point at issue is wrong, and the righting of it. . . . The various considerations which are relevant to punishment as a phenomenon and to the bearing it has on the particular consciousness, and which concern its effects (deterrent, reformative, etcetera) on the imagination, are an essential topic for examination in their place, especially in connection with modes of punishment, but all these considerations presuppose as their foundation the fact that punishment is inherently and actually just. In discussing this matter the only important things are, first, that crime is to be annulled, not because it is the producing of an evil, but because it is the infringing of the right as right, and secondly, the question of what that positive existence is which crime possesses and which must be annulled; it is this existence which is the real evil to be removed, and the essential point is the question of where it lies. So long as the concepts here at issue are not clearly apprehended, confusion must continue to reign in the theory of punishment.[21]

While this passage is not likely to dethrone confusion, it does bring us closer to the basically Kantian heart of Hegel's theory. To "annul crime"

should be read "right wrong." Crime is a wrong which consists in an "infringement of the right as right."[22] It would be unjust, says Hegel, to allow crime, which is the invasion of a right, to go unrequited. For to allow this is to admit that the crime is "valid": that is, that it is not in conflict with justice. But this is what we do want to admit, and the only way of showing this is to pay back the deed to the agent: coerce the coercer. For by intentionally violating his victim's rights, the criminal in effect claims that the rights of others are not binding on him; and this is to attack *das Recht* itself: the system of justice in which there are rights which must be respected. Punishment not only keeps the system in balance, it vindicates the system itself.

Besides talking about punishment's "annulment" of crime, Hegel has argued that it is the "right of the criminal." The obvious reaction to this is that it is a strange justification of punishment which makes it someone's right, for it is at best a strange kind of right which no one would ever want to claim! McTaggart's explanation of this facet of Hegel's theory is epitomized in the following quotation:

> What, then, is Hegel's theory? It is, I think, briefly this: In sin, man rejects and defies the moral law. Punishment is pain inflicted on him because he has done this, and in order that he may, by the fact of his punishment, be forced into recognizing as valid the law which he rejected in sinning, and so repent of his sin — really repent, and not merely be frightened out of doing it again.[23]

If McTaggart is right, then we are obviously not going to find in Hegel anything relevant to the justification of legal punishment, where the notions of sin and repentance are out of place. And this is the conclusion McTaggart of course reaches. "Hegel's view of punishment," he insists, "cannot properly be applied in jurisprudence, and . . . his chief mistake regarding it lay in supposing that it could."[24]

But though McTaggart may be right in emphasizing the theological aspect of Hegel's doctrine of punishment, he is wrong in denying it a jurisprudential aspect. In fact, Hegel is only saying what Kant emphasized: that to justify punishment to the criminal is to show him that *he* has chosen to be treated as he is being treated.

The injury (the penalty) which falls on the criminal is not merely *implicitly* just—as just, it is *eo ipso* his implicit will, an embodiment of his freedom, his right; on the contrary, it is also a right *established* within the criminal himself, that is, in his objectively embodied will, in his action. The reason for this is that his action is the action of a rational being and this implies that it is something universal and that by doing it the criminal has laid down a law which he has explicitly recognized in his action and under which in consequence he should be brought as under his right.[25]

To accept the retributivist position, then, is to accept a thesis about the burden of proof in the justification of punishment. Provided we make the punishment "equal" to the crime it is not up to us to justify it to the criminal, beyond pointing out to him that it is what he willed. It is not that he initiated a chain of events likely to result in his punishment, but that in willing the crime he willed that he himself should suffer in the same degree as his victim. But what if the criminal simply wanted to commit his crime and get away with it (break the window and run, take the funds and retire to Brazil, kill but live?) Suppose we explain to the criminal that *really* in willing to kill he willed to lose his life; and, unimpressed, he replies that *really* he wished to kill and save his skin. The retributivist answer is that to the extent that the criminal understands freedom and justice he will understand that his punishment was made inevitable by his own choice. No moral theory can hope to provide a justification of punishment which will seem such to the criminal merely as a nexus of passions and desires. The retributivist addresses him as a rational being, aware of the significance of his action. The burden of proof, the retributivist would argue, is on the theorist who would not start from this assumption. For to assume from the beginning that the criminal is not rational is to treat him, from the beginning, as merely a "harmful animal."

What is involved in the action of the criminal is not only the concept of crime, the rational aspect present in crime as such whether the individual wills it or not, the aspect which the state has to vindicate, but also the abstract rationality of the individual's *volition* Since that is so, punishment is regarded as containing the criminal's right and

hence by being punished he is honored as a rational being. He does not receive this due of honor unless the concept and measure of his punishment are derived from his own act. Still less does he receive it if he is treated as a harmful animal who has to be made harmless, or with a view to deterring and reforming him.[26]

To address the criminal as a rational being aware of the significance of his action is to address him as a person who knows that he has not committed a "bare" act; to commit an act is to commit oneself to the universalization of the rule by which one acted. For a man to complain about the death sentence for murder is as absurd as for a man to complain that when he pushes down one tray of the scales, the other tray goes up; whereas the action, rightly considered, is of pushing down *and* up. "The criminal gives his consent already by his very act.[27] "The Eumenides sleep, but crime awakens them, and hence it is the very act of crime which vindicates itself."[28]

F. H. Bradley's contribution to the retributive theory of punishment adds heat but not much light. The central, and best-known, passage is the following:

If there is any opinion to which the man of uncultivated morals is attached, it is the belief in the necessary connection of Punishment and guilt. Punishment is punishment, only where it is deserved. We pay the penalty because we owe it, and for no other reason; and if punishment is inflicted for any other reason whatever than because it is merited by wrong, it is a gross immorality, a crying injustice, an abominable crime, and not what it pretends to be. We may have regard for whatever considerations we please—our own convenience, the good of society, the benefit of the offender; we are fools, and worse, if we fail to do so. Having once the right to punish, we may modify the punishment according to the useful and the pleasant; but these are external to the matter, they cannot give us a right to punish, and nothing can do that but criminal desert. This is not a subject to waste words over; if the fact of the vulgar view is not palpable to the reader, we have no hope, and no wish, to make it so.[29]

Bradley's sympathy with the "vulgar view" should be apparent.[30] And there is at least a seeming variation between the position he expresses here and that we have attributed to Kant and Hegel. For Bradley can be read here as leaving an open field for utilitarian reasoning, when the question is how and how much to punish. Ewing interprets Bradley this way, and argues at some length that Bradley is involved in an inconsistency.[31] However, it is quite possible that Bradley did not mean to allow kind and quantity of punishment to be determined by utilitarian considerations. He could mean, as Kant meant, that once punishment is awarded, then "it" (what the criminal must suffer: time in jail, for example) may be made use of for utilitarian purposes. But, it should by this time go without saying, the retributivist would then wish to insist that we not argue backward from the likelihood of attaining these good purposes to the rightness of inflicting the punishment.

Bradley's language is beyond question loose when he speaks, in the passage quoted, of our "modifying" the punishment, "having once the right to punish." But when he says that "we pay the penalty because we owe it, and for no other reason," Bradley must surely be credited with the insight that we may owe more or less according to the gravity of the crime. The popular view, he says, is "that punishment is justice; that justice implies the giving what is due."[32] And, "punishment is the complement of criminal desert; is justifiable only so far as deserved."[33] If Bradley accepts this popular view, then Ewing must be wrong in attributing to him the position that kind and degree of punishment may be determined by utilitarian considerations.[34]

III

Let us sum up traditional retributivism, as we have found it expressed in the paradigmatic passage we have examined. We have found no reason, in Hegel or Bradley, to take back or qualify importantly the *three propositions* we found central in Kant's retributivism:

i. The only acceptable reason for punishing a man is that he has committed a crime.
ii. The only acceptable reason for punishing a man in a given manner and degree is that the punishment is "equal" to the crime.
iii. Whoever commits a crime must be punished in accordance with his desert.

To these propositions should be added *two underlying assumptions*:

i. An assumption about the direction of justification: to the criminal.
ii. An assumption about the nature of justification: to show the criminal that it is he who has willed what he now suffers.

Though it may have been stated in forbidding metaphysical terms, traditional retributivism cannot be dismissed as unintelligible, or absurd, or implausible.[35] There is no obvious contradiction in it; and there are no important disagreements among the philosophers we have studied over what it contends. Yet in spite of the importance of the theory, no one has yet done much more than sketch it in broad strokes. If, as I have surmised, it turns mainly on an assumption concerning the direction of justification, then this assumption should be explained and defended.

And the key concept of "desert" is intolerably vague. What does it mean to say that punishment must be proportionate to what a man *deserves?* This seems to imply, in the theory of the traditional retributivists, that there is some way of measuring desert, or at least of balancing punishment against it. How this measuring or balancing is supposed to be done, we will discuss later. What we must recognize here is that there are alternative criteria of "desert," and that it is not always clear which of these the traditional retributivist means to imply.

When we say of a man that he "deserves severe punishment" how, if at all, may we support our position by arguments? What kinds of considerations tend to show what a man does or does not deserve? There are at least two general sorts: those which tend to show that what he has done is a member of a class of actions which is especially heinous; and those which tend to show that his doing of this action was, in (or because of) the circumstances, particularly wicked. The argument that a man deserves punishment may rest on the first kind of appeal alone, or on both kinds. Retributivists who rely on the first sort of consideration alone would say that anyone who would do a certain sort of thing, no matter what the circumstances may have been, deserves punishment. Whether there are any such retributivists I do not know. Kant, because of his insistence on *intention* as a necessary condition of committing a crime, clearly wishes to bring in considerations of the second sort as well. It is not, on his view, merely *what* was done, but the intention of the agent which must be taken into account. No matter what the intention, a man cannot commit a crime deserving punishment if his deed is not a transgression. But if he does commit a transgression, he must do so intentionally to commit a crime; and all crime is deserving of punishment. The desert of the crime is a factor both of the seriousness of the transgression, considered by itself, and the degree to which the intention to transgress was present. If, for Kant, the essence of morality consists in knowingly acting from duty, the essence of immorality consists in knowingly acting against duty.

The retributivist can perhaps avoid the question of how we decide that one crime is morally more heinous than another by hewing to his position that no such decision is necessary so long as we make the punishment "equal" to the crime. To accomplish this, he might argue, it is not necessary to argue to the *relative* wickedness of crimes. But at best this leaves us with the problem how we *do* make punishments equal to crimes, a problem which will not stop plaguing retributivists. And there is the problem *which* transgressions, intentionally committed, the retributivist is to regard as crimes. Surely not every morally wrong action![36]

And how is the retributivist to fit in appeals to punitive expediency? None of our authors denies that such appeals may be made, but where and how do they tie into punitive justice? It will not do simply to say that justifying punishment to the criminal is one thing, and justifying it to society is another. Suppose we must justify in both directions at once? And who are "we" anyway — the players of which roles, at what stage of the game? And has the retributivist cleared himself of the charge, sure to arise, that the theory is but a cover for a much less commendable motive than respect for justice: elegant draping for naked revenge?

NOTES

1. . . . since in our own time there are few defenders of retributivism, the position is most often referred to by writers who are opposed to it. This does not make for clarity. In the past few years, however, there has been an upsurge of interest, and some good articles have been written. Cf. esp. J. D. Mabbott, "Punishment," *Mind*, XLVIII (1939), pp. 152–67; C.S. Lewis, "The Humanitarian Theory of Punishment," *20th Century* (Australian), March, 1949; C. W. K. Mundle, "Punishment and Desert," *The Philosophical Quarterly*, IV (1954), pp. 216–228; A. S. Kaufman, "Anthony Quinton on Punishment," *Analysis*, October, 1959; and K. G. Armstrong, "The Retributivist Hits Back," LXX (1961), pp. 471–90.

2. *Rechtslehre*, Part Second, 49, E. Hastie translation, Edinburgh, 1887, pp. 195–7.

3. *Ibid.*, p. 198. Cf. also the passage on p. 196 beginning "What, then, is to be said of such a proposal as to keep a Criminal alive who has been condemned to death . . ."

4. *Ibid.*, Prolegomena, General Divisions of the Metaphysic of Morals, IV. (Hastie, p. 38).

5. *Ibid.*, p. 32.

6. *Ibid.*, p. 32.

7. Book I, Ch. I, Sect. VIII, Theorem IV, Remark II (T. K. Abbott translation, 5th ed., revised, London, 1898, p. 127).

8. *Rechtslehre*.

9. "Supplementary Explanation of The Principles of Right," V.

10. Cf. long quote from the *Rechtslehre*, above.

11. How can the retributivist allow utilitarian considerations even in the administration of the sentence? Are we not then opportunistically imposing our conception of good on the convicted man? How did we come by this right, which we did not have when he stood before the bar awaiting sentence? Kant would refer to the loss of his "Civil Personality;" but what rights remain with the "Inborn Personality," which is not lost? How is human dignity modified by conviction of crime?

12. Introduction to The Science of Right, General Definitions and Divisions, D. Right is Joined with the Title to Compel. (Hastie, p. 47).

13. This extends the definition of crime Kant has given earlier by specifying the nature of an imputable transgression of duty.

14. There are serious difficulties in the application of the "Principle of Equality" to the "mode and measure" of punishment. This will be considered . . .

15. I shall use this short title for the work with the formidable double title of *Naturrecht and Stattswissenchaft in Grundrisse; Grundlinien der Philosophie des Rechts (Natural Law and Political Science in Outline: Elements of The Philosophy of Right.)* References will be to the T. M. Knox translation (*Hegel's Philosophy of Right*, Oxford, 1942).

16. *Philosophie des Rechts*, Sect. 93 (Knox, p. 67).

17. O. W. Holmes, Jr., *The Common Law*, Boston, 1881, p. 42.

18. Hastings Rashdall, *The Theory of Good and Evil*, 2nd. Edn., Oxford, 1924, vol. 1, pp. 285–6.

19. G. E. Moore holds that, consistently with his doctrine of organic wholes, they might; or at least they might yield that which is less evil than the sum of the constituent evils. This indicates for him a possible vindication of the Retributive theory of punishment. (*Principia Ethica*, Cambridge, 1903, pp. 213–214).

20. Included in the Knox translation.

21. Knox translation, pp. 69–70.

22. There is an unfortunate ambiguity in the German word *Recht*, here translated as "right." The word can mean either that which is a right or that which is in accordance with the law. So when Hegel speaks of "infringing the right as right" it is not certain whether he means a right as such or the law as such, or whether, in fact, he is aware of the ambiguity. But to say that the crime infringes the law is analytic, so we will take it that Hegel uses *Recht* here to refer to that which is right. But what the criminal does is not merely to infringe a right, but "the right (*das recht*) as right," that is, to challenge by his action the whole system of rights. (On "*Recht*," Cf. J. Austin, *The Province of Jurisprudence Determined*, London, Library of Ideas edn., 1954), Note 26, pp. 285–288 esp. pp. 287–8).

23. J. M. E. McTaggart, *Studies in the Hegelian Cosmology*, Cambridge, 1901, Ch. V, p. 133.

24. *Ibid.*, p. 145.

25. *Op. Cit.*, Sect. 100 (Hastie, p. 70.)

26. *Ibid.*, Lecture-notes on Sect. 100, Hastie, p. 71.

27. *Ibid.*, Addition to Sect. 100, Hastie, p. 246.

28. *Ibid.*, Addition to Sect. 101, Hastie, p. 247. There is something ineradicably *curious* about retributivism. We keep coming back to the metaphor of the balance scale. Why is the metaphor powerful and the same time strange? Why do we agree so readily that "the assassination" cannot "trammel up the conse-

quence," that "even-handed justice comments th' ingredients of our poisoned chalice to our own lips?"

29. F. H. Bradley, *Ethical Studies*, Oxford, 1952, pp. 26–7.

30. Yet it may not be amiss to note the part played by the "vulgar view" in Bradley's essay. In "The Vulgar Notion of Responsibility in Connection with the Theories of Free Will and Necessity," from which this passage is quoted, Bradley is concerned to show that neither the "Libertarian" nor the "Necessitarian" position can be accepted. Both of these "two great schools" which "divide our philosophy" "stand out of relation to vulgar morality." Bradley suggests that perhaps the truth is to be found not in either of these "two undying and opposite one-sidednesses but in a philosophy which "thinks what the vulgar believe." Cf. also the contrasting of the "ordinary consciousness" with the "philosophical" or "debauched" morality (p. 4). On p. 3 he says that by going to "vulgar morality" we "gain in integrity" what we "lose in refinement." Nevertheless, he does say (p. 4) "seeing the vulgar are after all the vulgar, we should not be at pains to agree with their superstitions."

31. A. C. Ewing, *The Morality of Punishment*, London, 1929, pp. 41–42.

32. *Op. Cit.*, p. 29.

33. *Ibid.*, p. 30.

34. *Op. Cit.*, p. 41.

35. Or, more ingeniously, "merely logical," the "elucidation of the use of a word;" answering the question, "When (logically) *can* we punish?" as opposed to the question answered by the utilitarians, "When (morally) *may* or *ought* we to punish?" (Cf. A. M. Quinton, "On Punishment," *Analysis,* June, 1954, pp. 133–142)

36. Cf. Ch. V. [of *The Rationale of Legal Punishment*—eds.]

Notes and Questions

JEFFRIE G. MURPHY, "Marxism and Retribution"

1. According to Jeffrie G. Murphy, utilitarian theory cannot provide an acceptable justification for punishment. Interestingly, he argues that the utilitarian justification for punishment is as problematic applied to the guilty as to the innocent. Why?

2. In order to justify having a right to punish, respect for individual autonomy must be reconciled with state authority to punish. This issue, in general terms, has often been called the most fundamental problem of political philosophy. Robert Paul Wolff, for example, says precisely this in his article in Chapter One. Recall that it was this very concern which led Wolff to argue for direct democracy as the only possible justification for legitimate government authority in general. Murphy points out that social contract and general will theories try to provide this reconciliation

of individual autonomy with public authority and that Kant's theory uses elements of both. How exactly does Kant's theory offer justification for punishment, according to Murphy?

3. Murphy notes that we must be careful of the fascist tendencies of "rational will" theories. What does he mean? With this qualification noted, Murphy nevertheless concludes that retributive theory at least gives formal acknowledgment of the necessity for respecting individual autonomy and therefore respects individual rights. The reason he takes pains to make this position clear is so that his criticisms will not be mistaken for the usual utilitarian objections. Murphy's critique is based on a commitment to justice and freedom — the basis of retributive theory itself. Why is that important?

4. Following Marx on this point, Murphy argues that any theory of moral or political philosophy must take into account the nature of the real world to which it must apply. In what two ways do empirical facts impinge on retributive theory, according to Murphy?

5. To develop his thesis, Murphy uses William Bonger's analysis of the sources of crime. What are the two primary sources of crime, according to Bonger? What support is offered for this view?

6. If most crime is the result of economic class and social influence, how does that challenge the model of rational choice used by contractarian retributive theory?

7. Is it fair for society to punish people for acting on motives and mental attitudes inculcated and fostered by society itself? Why or why not?

8. Does it make sense to claim that a poverty-stricken and socially deprived criminal must repay his or her debt to society? What could that mean? How does Murphy characterize the model of community implied in retributive arguments? Are the poor part of this community? What does this suggest?

9. How does the notion of voluntary acceptance work in social contract theories? Can a social contract theory work without this device? Does it apply to the poor?

10. What is Murphy's radical conclusion? Why does he reject the alternative of therapy? Can you find any other alternative? In the next two selections alternatives are offered. See if any can meet Murphy's challenge.

Marxism and Retribution

JEFFRIE G. MURPHY

Punishment in general has been defended as a means either of ameliorating or of intimidating. Now what right have you to punish me for the amelioration or intimidation of others? And besides there is history — there is such a thing as statistics — which prove with the most complete evidence that since Cain the world has been neither intimidated nor ameliorated by punishment. Quite the contrary. From the point of view of abstract right, there is only one theory of punishment which recognizes human dignity in the abstract, and that is the theory of Kant, especially in the more rigid formula given to it by Hegel. Hegel says: "Punishment is the *right* of the crim-

inal. It is an act of his own will. The violation of right has been proclaimed by the criminal as his own right. His crime is the negation of right. Punishment is the negation of this negation, and consequently an affirmation of right, solicited and forced upon the criminal by himself."

There is no doubt something specious in this formula, inasmuch as Hegel, instead of looking upon the criminal as the mere object, the slave of justice, elevates him to the position of a free and self-determined being. Looking, however, more closely into the matter, we discover that German idealism here, as in most other instances, has but given a transcendental sanction to the rules of existing society. Is it not a delusion to substitute for the individual with his real motives, with multifarious social circumstances pressing upon him, the abstraction of "free will" — one among the many qualities of man for man himself? . . . Is there not a necessity for deeply reflecting upon an alteration of the system that breeds these crimes, instead of glorifying the hangman who executes a lot of criminals to make room only for the supply of new ones?

> — Karl Marx, "Capital Punishment"
> *New York Daily Tribune* (18 February 1853)[1]

Philosophers have written at great length about the moral problems involved in punishing the innocent — particularly as these problems raise obstacles to an acceptance of the moral theory of Utilitarianism. Punishment of an innocent man in order to bring about good social consequences is, at the very least, not always clearly wrong on utilitarian principles. This being so, utilitarian principles are then to be condemned by any morality that may be called Kantian in character. For punishing an innocent man, in Kantian language, involves using that man as a mere means or instrument to some social good and is thus not to treat him as an end in himself, in accord with his dignity or worth as a person.

The Kantian position on the issue of punishing the innocent, and the many ways in which the utilitarian might try to accommodate that position, constitute extremely well-worn ground in contemporary moral and legal philosophy.[2] I do not propose to wear the ground further by adding additional comments on the issue here. What I do want to point out, however, is something which seems to me quite obvious but which philosophical commentators on punishment have almost universally failed to see — namely, that problems of the very same kind and seriousness arise for the utilitarian theory with respect to the punishment of the *guilty*. For a utilitarian theory of punishment (Bentham's is a paradigm) must involve justifying punishment in terms of its social results — e.g., deterrence, incapacitation, and rehabilitation. And thus even a guilty man is, on this theory, being punished because of the instrumental value the action of punishment will have in the future. He is being used as a means to some future good — e.g., the deterrence of others. Thus those of a Kantian persuasion, who see the importance of worrying about the treatment of

persons as mere means, must, it would seem, object just as strenuously to the punishment of the guilty on utilitarian grounds as to the punishment of the innocent. Indeed the former worry, in some respects, seems more serious. For a utilitarian can perhaps refine his theory in such a way that it does not commit him to the punishment of the innocent. However, if he is to approve of punishment at all, he must approve of punishing the guilty in at least some cases. This makes the worry about punishing the guilty formidable indeed, and it is odd that this has gone generally unnoticed.[3] It has generally been assumed that if the utilitarian theory can just avoid entailing the permissibility of punishing the innocent, then all objections of a Kantian character to the theory will have been met. This seems to me simply not to be the case.

What the utilitarian theory really cannot capture, I would suggest, is the notion of persons having rights. And it is just this notion that is central to any Kantian outlook on morality. Any Kantian can certainly agree that punishing persons (guilty or innocent) may have either good or bad or indifferent consequences and that insofar as the consequences (whether in a particular case or for an institution) are good, this is something in favor of punishment. But the Kantian will maintain that this consequential outlook, important as it may be, leaves out of consideration entirely that which is most morally crucial — namely, the question of rights. Even if punishment of a person would have good consequences, what gives us (i.e., society) the moral right to inflict it? If we have such a right, what is its origin or derivation? What social circumstances must be present for it to be applicable? What does this right to punish tell us about the status of the person to be punished — e.g., how are we to analyze his rights, the sense in which he must deserve to be punished, his obligations in the matter? It is this family of questions which any Kantian must regard as morally central and which the utilitarian cannot easily accommodate into his theory. And it is surely this aspect of Kant's and Hegel's retributivism, this seeing of rights as basic, which appeals to Marx in the quoted passage. As Marx himself puts it: "What right have you to punish me for the amelioration or intimidation of others?" And he further praises Hegel for seeing that punishment if justified, must involve respecting the rights of the person to be punished.[4] Thus Marx, like Kant, seems prepared to draw the important distinction between (a) what it would be good to do on grounds of utility and (b) what we have a right to do. Since we do not always have the right to do what it would be good to do, this distinction is of the greatest moral importance; and missing the distinction is the Achilles heel of all forms of Utilitarianism. For consider the following example: A Jehovah's Witness needs a blood transfusion in order to live; but, because of his (we can agree absurd) religious belief that such transfusions are against God's commands, he instructs his doctor not to give him one. Here is a case where it would seem to be good or for the best to give the transfusion and yet, at the very least, it is highly doubtful that the doctor has a right to give it. This kind of distinction is elementary, and any theory which misses it is morally degenerate.[5]

To move specifically to the topic of punishment: How exactly does retributivism (of a Kantian or Hegelian variety) respect the rights of persons? Is Marx really correct on this? I believe that he is. I believe that retributivism can be formulated in such a way that it is the only morally defensible theory of punishment. I also believe that arguments, which may be regarded as Marxist at least in spirit, can be formulated which show that social conditions as they obtain in most societies make this form of retributivism largely inapplicable within those societies. As Marx says, in those societies retributivism functions merely to provide a "transcendental sanction" for the status quo. If this is so, then the only morally defensible theory of punishment is largely inapplicable in modern societies. The consequence: modern societies largely lack the moral right to punish.[6] The upshot is that a Kantian moral theory (which in general seems to me correct) and a Marxist analysis of crime (which, if properly qualified, also seems to me correct) produces a radical and not merely reformist attack not merely on the scope and manner of punishment in our society but on the institution of punishment itself. Institutions of punishment constitute what Bernard Harrison has called structural injustices[7] and are, in the absence of a major social change, to be resisted by all who take human rights to be morally serious — i.e., regard them as genuine action guides and not merely as rhetorical devices which allow people to morally sanctify institutions which in fact can only be defended on grounds of social expediency.

Stating all of this is one thing and proving it, of course, is another. Whether I can ever do this is doubtful. That I cannot do it in one brief article is certain. I cannot, for example, here defend in detail my belief that a generally Kantian outlook on moral matters is correct.[8] Thus I shall content myself for the present with attempting to render at least plausible two major claims involved in the view that I have outlined thus far: (1) that a retributive theory, in spite of the bad press that it has received, is a morally credible theory of punishment — that it can be, H. L. A. Hart to the contrary,[9] a reasonable general justifying aim of punishment; and (2) that a Marxist analysis of crime can undercut the practical applicability of that theory.

The Right of the State to Punish

It is strong evidence of the influence of a utilitarian outlook in moral and legal matters that discussions of punishment no longer involve a consideration of the right of anyone to inflict it. Yet in the eighteenth and nineteenth centuries, this tended to be regarded as the central aspect of the problem meriting philosophical consideration. Kant, Hegel, Bosanquet, Green — all tended to entitle their chapters on punishment along the lines explicitly used by Green: "The Right of the State to Punish."[10] This is not just a matter of terminology but reflects, I think, something of deeper philosophical substance. These theories, unlike the utilitarian, did not view man as primarily a maximizer of personal satisfactions — a maximizer of individual utilities. They were inclined, in various ways, to adopt a different model of man — man as a free or spontaneous creator, man as autonomous. (Marx, it may be noted, is much more in line with this tradition than with the utilitarian outlook.)[11] This being so, these theorists were inclined to view punishment (a certain kind of coercion by the state) as not merely a causal contributor to pain and suffering, but rather as presenting at least a *prima facie* challenge to the values of autonomy and personal dignity and self-realization — the very values which, in their view, the state existed to nurture. The problem as they saw it, therefore, was that of reconciling punishment as state coercion with the value of individual autonomy. (This is an instance of the more general problem which Robert Paul Wolff has called the central problem of political philosophy — namely, how is individual moral autonomy to be reconciled with legitimate political authority?)[12] This kind of problem, which I am inclined to agree is quite basic, cannot even be formulated intelligibly from a utilitarian perspective. Thus the utilitarian cannot even see the relevance of Marx's charge: Even if punishment has wonderful social consequences, what gives anyone the right to inflict it on me?

Now one fairly typical way in which others acquire rights over us is by our own consent. If a neighbor locks up my liquor cabinet to protect me against my tendencies to drink too heavily, I might well regard this as a presumptuous interference with my own freedom, no matter how good the result intended or accomplished. He had no right to do it and indeed violated my rights in doing it. If, on the other hand, I had asked him to do this or had given my free consent to his suggestion that he do it, the same sort of objection on my part would be quite out of order. I had given him the right to do it, and he had the right to do it. In doing it, he violated no rights of mine — even if, at the time of his doing it, I did not desire or want the action to be performed. Here then we seem to have a case where my autonomy may be regarded as intact even though a desire of mine is thwarted. For there is a sense in which the thwarting of the desire can be imputed to me (my choice or decision) and not to the arbitrary intervention of another.

How does this apply to our problem? The answer, I think, is obvious. What is needed, in order to reconcile my undesired suffering of punishment at the hands of the state with my autonomy (and thus with the state's right to punish me), is a political theory which makes the state's decision to punish me in some sense my own decision. If I have willed my own punishment (consented to it, agreed to it) then — even if at the time I happen not to desire it — it can be said that my autonomy and dignity remain intact. Theories of the General Will and Social Contract theories are two such theories which attempt this reconciliation of autonomy with legitimate state authority (including the right or authority of the state to punish). Since Kant's theory happens to

incorporate elements of both, it will be useful to take it for our sample.

Moral Rights and the Retributive Theory of Punishment

To justify government or the state is necessarily to justify at least some coercion.[13] This poses a problem for someone, like Kant, who maintains that human freedom is the ultimate or most sacred moral value. Kant's own attempt to justify the state, expressed in his doctrine of the *moral title* (*Befugnis*),[14] involves an argument that coercion is justified only in so far as it is used to prevent invasions against freedom. Freedom itself is the only value which can be used to limit freedom, for the appeal to any other value (e.g., utility) would undermine the ultimate status of the value of freedom. Thus Kant attempts to establish the claim that some forms of coercion (as opposed to violence) are morally permissible because, contrary to appearance, they are really consistent with rational freedom. The argument, in broad outline, goes in the following way. Coercion may keep people from doing what they desire or want to do on a particular occasion and is thus *prima facie* wrong. However, such coercion can be shown to be morally justified (and thus not absolutely wrong) if it can be established that the coercion is such that it could have been rationally willed even by the person whose desire is interfered with:

> Accordingly, when it is said that a creditor has a right to demand from his debtor the payment of a debt, this does not mean that he can *persuade* the debtor that his own reason itself obligates him to this performance; on the contrary, to say that he has such a right means only that the use of coercion to make anyone do this is entirely compatible with everyone's freedom, *including the freedom of the debtor*, in accordance with universal laws.[15]

Like Rousseau, Kant thinks that it is only in a context governed by social practice (particularly civil government and its Rule of Law) that this can make sense. Laws may require of a person some action that he does not desire to perform. This is not a violent invasion of his freedom, however, if it can be shown that in some antecedent position of choice (what John Rawls calls "the original position"),[16] he would have been rational to adopt a Rule of Law (and thus run the risk of having some of his desires thwarted) rather than some other alternative arrangement such as the classical State of Nature. This is, indeed, the only sense that Kant is able to make of classical Social Contract theories. Such theories are to be viewed, not as historical fantasies, but as ideal models of rational decision. For what these theories actually claim is that the only coercive institutions that are morally justified are those which a group of rational beings could agree to adopt in a position of having to pick social institutions to govern their relations:

> The contract, which is called *contractus originarius*, or *pactum sociale* . . . need not be assumed to be a fact, indeed it is not [even possible as such. To suppose that would be like insisting] that before anyone would be bound to respect such a civic constitution, it be proved first of all from history that a people, whose rights and obligations we have entered into as their descendants, had *once upon a time* executed such an act and had left a reliable document or instrument, either orally or in writing, concerning this contract. Instead, this contract is a *mere idea* of reason which has undoubted practical reality; namely, to oblige every legislator to give us laws in such a manner that the laws *could* have originated from the united will of the entire people and to regard every subject in so far as he is a citizen as though he had consented to such [an expression of the general] will. This is the testing stone of the rightness of every publicly-known law, for if a law were such that it was impossible for an entire people to give consent to it (as for example a law that a certain class of subjects, by inheritance, should have the privilege of the *status of lords*), then such a law is unjust. On the other hand, if there is a mere *possibility* that a people might consent to a (certain) law, then it is a duty to consider that the law is just even though at the moment the people might be in such a position or have a point of view that would result in their refusing to give their consent to it if asked.[17]

The problem of organizing a state, however hard it may seem, can be solved even for a race of devils, if only they are intelligent. The problem is: "Given a multiple of rational beings requiring universal laws for their preservation, but each of whom is secretly inclined to exempt himself from them, to establish a constitution in such a way that, although their private intentions conflict, they check each other, with the result that their public conduct is the same as if they had no such intentions."[18]

Though Kant's doctrine is superficially similar to Mill's later self-protection principle, the substance is really quite different. For though Kant in some general sense argues that coercion is justified only to prevent harm to others, he understands by "harm" only certain invasions of freedom and not simply disutility. Also, his defense of the principle is not grounded, as is Mill's, on its utility. Rather it is to be regarded as a principle of justice, by which Kant means a principle that rational beings could adopt in a situation of mutual choice:

> The concept [of justice] applies only to the relationship of a will to another person's will, not to his wishes or desires (or even just his needs) which are the concern of acts of benevolence and charity . . . In applying the concept of justice we take into consideration only the form of the relationship between the wills insofar as they are regarded as free, and whether the action of one of them can be conjoined with the freedom of the other in accordance with universal law. Justice is therefore the aggregate of those conditions under which the will of one person can be conjoined with the will of another in accordance with a universal law of freedom.[19]

How does this bear specifically on punishment? Kant, as everyone knows, defends a strong form of a retributive theory of punishment. He holds that guilt merits, and is a sufficient condition for, the infliction of punishment. And this claim has been universally condemned — particularly by utilitarians — as primitive, unenlightened and barbaric.

But why is it so condemned? Typically, the charge is that infliction of punishment on such grounds is nothing but pointless vengeance. But what is meant by the claim that the infliction is "pointless"? If "pointless" is tacitly being analyzed as "disutilitarian," then the whole question is simply being begged. You cannot refute a retributive theory merely by noting that it is a retributive theory and not a utilitarian theory. This is to confuse redescription with refutation and involves an argument whose circularity is not even complicated enough to be interesting.

Why, then, might someone claim that guilt merits punishment? Such a claim might be made for either of two very different reasons. (1) Someone (e.g., a Moral Sense theorist) might maintain that the claim is a primitive and unanalyzable proposition that is morally ultimate — that we can just intuit the "fittingness" of guilt and punishment. (2) It might be maintained that the retributivist claim is demanded by a general theory of political obligation which is more plausible than any alternative theory. Such a theory will typically provide a technical analysis of such concepts as crime and punishment and will thus not regard the retributivist claim as an indisputable primitive. It will be argued for as a kind of theorem within the system.

Kant's theory is of the second sort. He does not opt for retributivism as a bit of intuitive moral knowledge. Rather he offers a theory of punishment that is based on his general view that political obligation is to be analyzed, quasi-contractually, in terms of reciprocity. If the law is to remain just, it is important to guarantee that those who disobey it will not gain an unfair advantage over those who do obey voluntarily. It is important that no man profit from his own criminal wrongdoing, and a certain kind of "profit" (i.e., not bearing the burden of self-restraint) is intrinsic to criminal wrongdoing. Criminal punishment, then, has as its object the restoration of a proper balance between benefit and obedience. The criminal himself has no complaint, because he has rationally consented to or willed his own punishment. That is, those very rules which he has broken work, when they are obeyed by others, to his own advantage as a citizen. He would have chosen such rules for himself and others in the original position of choice. And, since he derives and voluntarily accepts benefits from their operation, he owes his own obedience as a debt to his fellow-citizens for their sacrifices in maintaining them. If he chooses not to sacrifice by exercising self-restraint and obedience, this is tantamount to his choosing to sacrifice in another way — namely, by paying the prescribed penalty:

> A transgression of the public law that makes him who commits it unfit to be a citizen is called ... a crime. ...
> What kind and what degree of punishment does public legal justice adopt as its principle and standard? None other than the principle of equality (illustrated by the pointer of the scales

of justice), that is, the principle of not treating one side more favorably than the other. Accordingly, any undeserved evil that you inflict on someone else among the people is one you do to yourself. If you vilify him, you vilify yourself; if you steal from him, you steal from yourself; if you kill him, you kill yourself ...
> To say, "I will to be punished if I murder someone" can mean nothing more than, "I submit myself along with everyone else to those laws which, if there are any criminals among the people, will naturally include penal laws."[20]

This analysis of punishment regards it as a debt owed to the law-abiding members of one's community; and, once paid, it allows re-entry into the community of good citizens on equal status.

Now some of the foregoing no doubt sounds implausible or even obscurantist. Since criminals typically desire not to be punished, what can it really mean to say that they have, as rational men, really willed their own punishment? Or that, as Hegel says, they have a right to it? Perhaps a comparison of the traditional retributivist views with those of a contemporary Kantian — John Rawls — will help to make the points clearer.[21] Rawls (like Kant) does not regard the idea of the social contract as an historical fact. It is rather a model of rational decision. Respecting a man's autonomy, at least on one view, is not respecting what he now happens, however uncritically, to desire; rather it is to respect what he desires (or would desire) as a rational man. (On Rawls' view, for example, rational men are said to be unmoved by feelings of envy; and thus it is not regarded as unjust to a person or a violation of his rights, if he is placed in a situation where he will envy another's advantage or position. A rational man would object, and thus would never consent to, a practice where another might derive a benefit from a position at his expense. He would not, however, envy the position *simpliciter*, would not regard the position as itself a benefit.) Now on Kant's (and also, I think, on Rawls') view, a man is genuinely free or autonomous only in so far as he is rational. Thus it is man's rational will that is to be respected.

Now this idea of treating people, not as they in fact say that they want to be treated, but rather in terms of how you think they would, if rational, will to be treated, has obviously dangerous (indeed Fascistic) implications. Surely we want to avoid cramming indignities down the throats of people with the offhand observation that, no matter how much they scream, they are really rationally willing every bit of it. It would be particularly ironic for such arbitrary repression to come under the mask of respecting autonomy. And yet, most of us would agree, the general principle (though subject to abuse) also has important applications — for example, preventing the suicide of a person who, in a state of psychotic depression, wants to kill himself. What we need, then, to make the general view work, is a check on its arbitrary application; and a start toward providing such a check would be in the formulation of a public, objective theory of rationality and rational willing. It is just this, according to both Kant and Rawls, which the social contract theory can provide. On this theory, a man may be said to rationally will X if, and only if, X is called for by a rule that the man would necessarily have adopted in the original position of choice — i.e., in a position of coming together with others to pick rules for the regulation of their mutual affairs. This avoids arbitrariness because, according to Kant and Rawls at any rate, the question of whether such a rule would be picked in such a position is objectively determinable given certain (in their view) noncontroversial assumptions about human nature and rational calculation. Thus I can be said to will my own punishment if, in an antecedent position of choice, I and my fellows would have chosen institutions of punishment as the most rational means of dealing with those who might break the other generally beneficial social rules that had been adopted.

Let us take an analogous example: I may not, in our actual society, desire to treat a certain person fairly — e.g., I may not desire to honor a contract I have made with him because so doing would adversely affect my own self-interest. However, if I am forced to honor the contract by the state, I cannot charge (1) that the state has no right to do this, or (2) that my rights or dignity are being violated by my being coerced into doing it. Indeed, it can be said that I rationally will it since, in the original position, I would have chosen rules of justice (rather than rules of utility) and the principle, "contracts are to be honored," follows from the rules of justice.

Coercion and autonomy are thus reconciled, at least apparently. To use Marx's language, we may say (as Marx did in the quoted passage) that one virtue of the retributive theory, at least as expounded by Kant and Hegel on lines of the General Will and Social Contract theory, is that it manifests at least a formal or abstract respect for rights, dignity, and autonomy. For it at least recognizes the importance of attempting to construe state coercion in such a way that it is a product of each man's rational will. Utilitarian deterrence theory does not even satisfy this formal demand.

The question of primary interest to Marx, of course, is whether this formal respect also involves a material respect; i.e., does the theory have application in concrete fact in the actual social world in which we live? Marx is confident that it does not, and it is to this sort of consideration that I shall now pass.

Alienation and Punishment

What can the philosopher learn from Marx? This question is a part of a more general question: What can philosophy learn from social science? Philosophers, it may be thought, are concerned to offer *a priori* theories, theories about how certain concepts are to be analyzed and their application justified. And what can the mundane facts that are the object of behavioral science have to do with exalted theories of this sort?

The answer, I think, is that philosophical theories, though not themselves empirical, often have such a character that their intelligibility depends upon certain empirical presuppositions. For example, our moral language presupposes, as Hart has argued,[22] that we are vulnerable creatures — creatures who can harm and be harmed by each other. Also, as I have argued elsewhere,[23] our moral language presupposes that we all share certain psychological characteristics — e.g., sympathy, a sense of justice, and the capacity to feel guilt, shame, regret, and remorse. If these facts were radically different (if, as Hart imagines for example, we all developed crustaceanlike exoskeletons and thus could not harm each other), the old moral language, and the moral theories which employ it, would lack application to the world in which we live. To use a crude example, moral prohibitions against killing presuppose that it is in fact possible for us to kill each other.

Now one of Marx's most important contributions to social philosophy, in my judgment, is simply his insight that philosophical theories are in peril if they are constructed in disregard of the nature of the empirical world to which they are supposed to apply.[24] A theory may be formally correct (i.e., coherent, or true for some possible world) but materially incorrect (i.e., inapplicable to the actual world in which we live). This insight, then, establishes the relevance of empirical research to philosophical theory and is a part, I think, of what Marx meant by "the union of theory and practice." Specifically relevant to the argument I want to develop are the following two related points:

(1) The theories of moral, social, political and legal philosophy presuppose certain empirical propositions about man and society. If these propositions are false, then the theory (even if coherent or formally correct) is materially defective and practically inapplicable. (For example, if persons tempted to engage in criminal conduct do not in fact tend to calculate carefully the consequences of their actions, this renders much of deterrence theory suspect.)

(2) Philosophical theories may put forth as a necessary truth that which is in fact merely an historically conditioned contingency. (For example, Hobbes argued that all men are necessarily selfish and competitive. It is possible, as many Marxists have argued, that Hobbes was really doing nothing more than elevating to the status of a necessary truth the contingent fact that the people around him in the capitalistic society in which he lived were in fact selfish and competitive.[25]

In outline, then, I want to argue the following: that when Marx challenges the material adequacy of the retributive theory of punishment, he is suggesting (a) that it presupposes a certain view of man and society that is false and (b) that key concepts involved in the support of the theory (e.g., the concept of "rationality" in Social Contract theory) are given analyses which, though they purport to be necessary truths, are in fact mere reflections of certain historical circumstances.

In trying to develop this case, I shall draw primarily upon Willem Bonger's *Criminality and Economic Conditions* (1916), one of the few sustained Marxist analyses of crime and punishment.[26] Though I shall not have time here to qualify my support of Bonger in certain necessary ways, let me make clear that I am perfectly aware that his analysis is not the whole story. (No monolithic theory of anything so diverse as criminal behavior could be the whole story.) However, I am convinced that he has discovered part of the story. And my point is simply that insofar as Bonger's Marxist analysis is correct, then to that same degree is the retributive theory of punishment inapplicable in modern societies. (Let me emphasize again exactly how this objection to retributivism differs from those traditionally offered. Traditionally, retributivism has been rejected because it conflicts with the moral theory of its opponent, usually a utilitarian. This is not the kind of objection I want to develop. Indeed, with Marx, I have argued that the retributive theory of punishment grows out of the moral theory — Kantianism — which seems to me generally correct. The objection I want to pursue concerns the empirical falsity of the factual presuppositions of the theory. If the empirical presuppositions of the theory are false, this does indeed render its application immoral. But the immorality consists, not in a conflict with some other moral theory, but immorality in terms of a moral theory that is at least close in spirit to the very moral theory which generates retributivism itself — i.e., a theory of justice.)[27]

To return to Bonger. Put bluntly, his theory is as follows. Criminality has two primary sources: (1) need and deprivation on the part of disadvantaged members of society, and (2) motives of greed and selfishness that are generated and reinforced in competitive capitalistic societies. Thus criminality is economically based — either directly in the case of crimes from need, or indirectly in the case of crimes growing out of motives or psychological states that are encouraged and developed in capitalistic society. In Marx's own language, such an economic system alienates men from themselves and from each other. It alienates men from themselves by creating motives and needs that are not "truly human." It alienates men from their fellows by encouraging a kind of competitiveness that forms an obstacle to the development of genuine communities to replace mere social aggregates.[28] And in Bonger's thought, the concept of community is central. He argues that moral relations and moral restraint are possible only in genuine communities characterized by bonds of sympathetic identification and mutual aid resting upon a perception of common humanity. All this he includes under the general rubric of reciprocity.[29] In the absence of reciprocity in this rich sense, moral relations among men will break down and criminality will increase.[30] Within bourgeois society, then, crimes are to be regarded as normal, and not psychopathological, acts. That is, they grow out of need, greed, indifference to others, and sometimes even a sense of indignation — all, alas, perfectly typical human motives.

To appreciate the force of Bonger's analysis, it is necessary to read his books and grasp the richness and detail of the evidence he provides for his claims. Here I can but quote a few passages at random to give the reader a tantalizing sample in the hope that he will be encouraged to read further into Bonger's own text:

> The abnormal element in crime is a social, not a biological, element. With the exception of a few special cases, crime lies within the boundaries of normal psychology and physiology . . .
>
> We clearly see that [the egoistic tendencies of the present economic system and of its consequences] are very strong. Because of these tendencies the social instinct of man is not greatly developed; they have weakened the moral force in man which combats the inclination towards egoistic acts, and hence toward the crimes which are one form of these acts — Compassion for the misfortunes of others inevitably becomes blunted, and a great part of morality consequently disappears . . .
>
> As a consequence of the present environment, man has become very egoistic and hence more *capable of crime*, than if the environment had developed the germs of altruism . . .
>
> There can be no doubt that one of the factors of criminality among the bourgeoisie is bad [moral] education . . . The children — speaking of course in a general way — are brought up with the idea that they must succeed, no matter how; the aim of life is presented to them as getting money and shining in the world . . .
>
> Poverty (taken in the sense of absolute want) kills the social sentiments in man, destroys in fact all relations between men. He who is abandoned by all can no longer have any feelings for those who have left him to his fate . . .
>
> [Upon perception that the system tends to

legalize the egoistic actions of the bourgeoisie and to penalize those of the proletariat], the oppressed resort to means which they would otherwise scorn. As we have seen above, the basis of the social feeling is reciprocity. As soon as this is trodden under foot by the ruling class the social sentiments of the oppressed become weak towards them . . .[31]

The essence of this theory has been summed up by Austin J. Turk. "Criminal behavior," he says, "is almost entirely attributable to the combination of egoism and an environment in which opportunities are not equitably distributed."[32]

No doubt this claim will strike many as extreme and intemperate — a sample of the old-fashioned Marxist rhetoric that sophisticated intellectuals have outgrown. Those who are inclined to react in this way might consider just one sobering fact: of the 1.3 million criminal offenders handled each day by some agency of the United States correctional system, the vast majority (80 percent on some estimates) are members of the lowest 15-percent income level — that percent which is below the "poverty level" as defined by the Social Security Administration.[33] Unless one wants to embrace the belief that all these people are poor because they are bad, it might be well to reconsider Bonger's suggestion that many of them are "bad" because they are poor.[34] At any rate, let us suppose for purposes of discussion that Bonger's picture of the relation between crime and economic conditions is generally accurate. At what points will this challenge the credentials of the contractarian retributive theory as outlined above? I should like to organize my answer to this question around three basic topics:

(1) *Rational Choice.* The model of rational choice found in Social Contract theory is egoistic — rational institutions are those that would be agreed to by calculating egoists ("devils" in Kant's more colorful terminology). The obvious question that would be raised by any Marxist is: Why give egoism this special status such that it is built, *a priori*, into the analysis of the concept of rationality? Is this not simply to regard as necessary that which may be only contingently found in the society around us? Starting from such an analysis, a certain result is inevitable — namely, a transcendental sanction for the status quo. Start with a bourgeois model of rationality

and you will, of course, wind up defending a bourgeois theory of consent, a bourgeois theory of justice, and a bourgeois theory of punishment.

Though I cannot explore the point in detail here, it seems to me that this Marxist claim may cause some serious problems for Rawls' well-known theory of justice, a theory which I have already used to unpack some of the evaluative support for the retributive theory of punishment. One cannot help suspecting that there is a certain sterility in Rawls' entire project of providing a rational proof for the preferability of a certain conception of justice over all possible alternative evaluative principles, for the description which he gives of the rational contractors in the original position is such as to guarantee that they will come up with his two principles. This would be acceptable if the analysis of rationality presupposed were intuitively obvious or argued for on independent grounds. But it is not. Why, to take just one example, is a desire for wealth a rational trait whereas envy is not? One cannot help feeling that the desired result dictates the premises.[35]

(2) *Justice, Benefits, and Community.* The retributive theory claims to be grounded on justice; but is it just to punish people who act out of those very motives that society encourages and reinforces? If Bonger is correct, much criminality is motivated by greed, selfishness, and indifference to one's fellows; but does not the whole society encourage motives of greed and selfishness ("making it," "getting ahead"), and does not the competitive nature of the society alienate men from each other and thereby encourage indifference — even, perhaps, what psychiatrists call psychopathy? The moral problem here is similar to one that arises with respect to some war crimes. When you have trained a man to believe that the enemy is not a genuine human person (but only a gook, or a chink), it does not seem quite fair to punish the man if, in a war situation, he kills indiscriminately. For the psychological trait you have conditioned him to have, like greed, is not one that invites fine moral and legal distinctions. There is something perverse in applying principles that presuppose a sense of community in a society which is structured to destroy genuine community.[36]

Related to this is the whole allocation of benefits in contemporary society. The retributive theory really presupposes what might be called a "gentlemen's club" picture of the relation between man and society — i.e., men are viewed as being part of a community of shared values and rules. The rules benefit all concerned and, as a kind of debt for the benefits derived, each man owes obedience to the rules. In the absence of such obedience, he deserves punishment in the sense that he owes payment for the benefits. For, as a rational man, he can see that the rules benefit everyone (himself included) and that he would have selected them in the original position of choice.

Now this may not be too far off for certain kinds of criminals — e.g., business executives guilty of tax fraud. (Though even here we might regard their motives of greed to be a function of societal reinforcement.) But to think that it applies to the typical criminal, from the poorer classes, is to live in a world of social and political fantasy. Criminals typically are not members of a shared community of values with their jailers; they suffer from what Marx calls alienation. And they certainly would be hard-pressed to name the benefits for which they are supposed to owe obedience. If justice, as both Kant and Rawls suggest, is based on reciprocity, it is hard to see what these persons are supposed to reciprocate for. Bonger addresses this point in a passage quoted earlier: "The oppressed resort to means which they would otherwise scorn . . . The basis of social feelings is reciprocity. As soon as this is trodden under foot by the ruling class, the social sentiments of the oppressed become weak towards them."

(3) *Voluntary Acceptance.* Central to the Social Contract idea is the claim that we owe allegiance to the law because the benefits we have derived have been voluntarily accepted. This is one place where our autonomy is supposed to come in. That is, having benefited from the Rule of Law when it was possible to leave. I have in a sense consented to it and to its consequences — even my own punishment if I violate the rules. To see how silly the factual presuppositions of this account are, we can do no better than quote a famous passage from David Hume's essay "Of the Original Contract":

> Can we seriously say that a poor peasant or artisan has a free choice to leave his country — when he knows no foreign language or manners, and lives from day to day by the small wages which he acquires? We may as well assert that a man,

by remaining in a vessel, freely consents to the dominion of the master, though he was carried on board while asleep, and must leap into the ocean and perish the moment he leaves her.

A banal empirical observation, one may say. But it is through ignoring such banalities that philosophers generate theories which allow them to spread iniquity in the ignorant belief that they are spreading righteousness.

It does, then, seem as if there may be some truth in Marx's claim that the retributive theory, though formally correct, is materially inadequate. At root, the retributive theory fails to acknowledge that criminality is, to a large extent, a phenomenon of economic class. To acknowledge this is to challenge the empirical presupposition of the retributive theory — the presupposition that all men, including criminals, are voluntary participants in a reciprocal system of benefits and that the justice of this arrangement can be derived from some eternal and ahistorical concept of rationality.

The upshot of all this seems rather upsetting, as indeed it is. How can it be the case that everything we are ordinarily inclined to say about punishment (in terms of utility and retribution) can be quite beside the point? To anyone with ordinary language sympathies (one who is inclined to maintain that what is correct to say is a function of what we do say), this will seem madness. Marx will agree that there is madness, all right, but in view the madness will lie in what we do say — what we say only because of our massive (and often self-deceiving and self-serving) factual ignorance or indifference to the circumstances of the social world in which we live. Just as our whole way of talking about mental phenomena hardened before we knew any neurophysiology — and this leads us astray, so Marx would argue that our whole way of talking about moral and political phenomena hardened before we knew any of the relevant empirical facts about man and society—and this, too, leads us astray. We all suffer from what might be called the *embourgeoisment* of language, and thus part of any revolution will be a linguistic or conceptual revolution. We have grown accustomed to modifying our language or conceptual structures under the impact of empirical discoveries in physics. There is no reason why discoveries in sociology, economics, or psychology could not and should not have the same effect on entrenched patterns of thought and speech. It is important to remember, as Russell remarked, that our language sometimes enshrines the metaphysics of the Stone Age.

Consider one example: a man has been convicted of armed robbery. On investigation, we learn that he is an impoverished black whose whole life has been one of frustrating alienation from the prevailing socio-economic structure — no job, no transportation if he could get a job, substandard education for his children, terrible housing and inadequate health care for his whole family, condescending-tardy-inadequate welfare payments, harassment by the police but no real protection by them against the dangers in his community, and near total exclusion from the political process. Learning all this, would we still want to talk — as many do — of his suffering punishment under the rubric of "paying a debt to society"? Surely not. Debt for what? I do not, of course, pretend that all criminals can be so described. But I do think that this is a closer picture of the typical criminal than the picture that is presupposed in the retributive theory — i.e., the picture of an evil person who, of his own free will, intentionally acts against those just rules of society which he knows, as a rational man, benefit everyone including himself.

But what practical help does all this offer, one may ask. How should we design our punitive practices in the society in which we now live? This is the question we want to ask, and it does not seem to help simply to say that our society is built on deception and inequity. How can Marx help us with our real practical problem? The answer, I think, is that he cannot and obviously does not desire to do so. For Marx would say that we have not focused (as all piecemeal reform fails to focus) on what is truly the real problem. And this is changing the basic social relations. Marx is the last person from whom we can expect advice on how to make our intellectual and moral peace with bourgeois society. And this is surely his attraction and his value.

What does Bonger offer? He suggests, near the end of his book, that in a properly designed society all criminality would be a problem "for the physician rather than the judge." But this surely will not do. The therapeutic state, where prisons are called hospitals and jailers are called psychiatrists, simply raises again all the old problems about the justification of coercion and its reconciliation with autonomy that we faced in worrying about punishment. The only difference is that our coercive practices are now surrounded with a benevolent rhetoric which makes it even harder to raise the important issues. Thus the move to therapy, in my judgment, is only an illusory solution — alienation remains and the problem of reconciling coercion with autonomy remains unsolved. Indeed, if the alternative is having our personalities involuntarily restructured by some state psychiatrist, we might well want to claim the "right to be punished" that Hegel spoke of.[37]

Perhaps, then, we may really be forced seriously to consider a radical proposal. If we think that institutions of punishment are necessary and desirable, and if we are morally sensitive enough to want to be sure that we have the moral right to punish before we inflict it, then we had better first make sure that we have restructured society in such a way that criminals genuinely do correspond to the only model that will render punishment permissible — i.e., make sure that they are autonomous and that they do benefit in the requisite sense. Of course, if we did this then — if Marx and Bonger are right — crime itself and the need to punish would radically decrease if not disappear entirely.

NOTES

1. In a sense, my paper may be viewed as an elaborate commentary on this one passage, excerpted from a discussion generally concerned with the efficacy of capital punishment in eliminating crime. For in this passage, Marx (to the surprise of many I should think) expresses a certain admiration for the classical retributive theory of punishment. Also (again surprisingly) he expresses this admiration in a kind of language he normally avoids — i.e., the moral language of rights and justice. He then, of course, goes on to reject the applicability of that theory. But the question that initially perplexed me is the following: what is the explanation of Marx's ambivalence concerning the retributive theory; why is he both attracted and repelled by it? (This ambivalence is not shared, for example, by utilitarians — who feel nothing but repulsion when the retributive theory is even mentioned.) Now except for some very brief passages in *The Holy Family*, Marx himself has nothing more to say on the topic of punishment beyond what is contained in this brief *Daily Tribune*

article. Thus my essay is in no sense an exercise in textual scholarship (there are not enough texts) but is rather an attempt to construct an assessment of punishment, Marxist at least in spirit, that might account for the ambivalence found in the quoted passage. My main outside help comes, not from Marx himself, but from the writings of the Marxist criminologist Willem Bonger.

2. Many of the leading articles on this topic have been reprinted in *The Philosophy of Punishment*, ed. H. B. Acton (London, 1969). Those papers not included are cited in Acton's excellent bibliography.

3. One writer who has noticed this is Richard Wasserstrom. See his "Why Punish the Guilty?" *Princeton University Magazine* 20 (1964), pp. 14–19.

4. Marx normally avoids the language of rights and justice because he regards such language to be corrupted by bourgeois ideology. However, if we think very broadly of what an appeal to rights involves — namely, a protest against unjustified coercion — there is no reason why Marx may not legitimately avail himself on occasion of this way of speaking. For there is surely at least some moral overlap between Marx's protests against exploitation and the evils of a division of labor, for example, and the claims that people have a right not be used solely for the benefit of others and a right to self-determination.

5. I do not mean to suggest that under no conceivable circumstances would the doctor be justified in giving the transfusion even though, in one clear sense, he had no right to do it. If, for example, the Jehovah's Witness was a key man whose survival was necessary to prevent the outbreak of a destructive war, we might well regard the transfusion as on the whole justified. However, even in such a case, a morally sensitive man would have to regretfully realize that he was sacrificing an important principle. Such a realization would be impossible (because inconsistent) for a utilitarian, for his theory admits only one principle — namely, do that which on the whole maximizes utility. An occupational disease of utilitarians is a blindness to the possibility of genuine moral dilemmas — i.e., a blindness to the possibility that important moral principles can conflict in ways that are not obviously resolvable by a rational decision procedure.

6. I qualify my thesis by the word "largely" to show at this point my realization, explored in more detail later, that no single theory can account for all criminal behavior.

7. Bernard Harrison, "Violence and the Rule of Law," in *Violence*, ed. Jerome A. Shaffer (New York, 1971), pp. 139–176.

8. I have made a start toward such a defense in my "The Killing of the Innocent," forthcoming in *The Monist* 57, no. 4 (October 1973).

9. H. L. A. Hart, "Prolegomenon to the Principles

of Punishment," from *Punishment and Responsibility* (Oxford, 1968), pp. 1–27.

10. Thomas Hill Green, *Lectures on the Principles of Political Obligation* (1885), (Ann Arbor, 1967), pp. 180–205.

11. For an elaboration of this point, see Steven Lukes, "Alienation and Anomie," in *Philosophy, Politics and Society* (Third Series), ed. Peter Laslett and W. G. Runciman (Oxford, 1967), pp. 134–156.

12. Robert Paul Wolff, *In Defense of Anarchism* (New York, 1970).

13. In this section, I have adapted some of my previously published material: *Kant: The Philosophy of Right* (London, 1970), pp. 109–112 and 140–144; "Three Mistakes About Retributivism," *Analysis* (April 1971): 166–169; and "Kant's Theory of Criminal Punishment," in *Proceedings of the Third International Kant Congress*, ed. Lewis White Beck (Dordrecht, 1972), pp. 434–441. I am perfectly aware that Kant's views on the issues to be considered here are often obscure and inconsistent — e.g., the analysis of "willing one's own punishment" which I shall later quote from Kant occurs in a passage the primary purpose of which is to argue that the idea of "willing one's own punishment" makes no sense! My present objective, however, is not to attempt accurate Kant scholarship. My goal is rather to build upon some remarks of Kant's which I find philosophically suggestive.

14. Immanuel Kant, *The Metaphysical Elements of Justice* (1797), trans. John Ladd (Indianapolis, 1965), pp. 35ff.

15. *Ibid.*, p. 37.

16. John Rawls, "Justice as Fairness," *The Philosophical Review* 67 (1958): 164–194; and *A Theory of Justice* (Cambridge, Mass., 1971), especially pp. 17–22.

17. Immanuel Kant, "Concerning the Common Saying: This May be True in Theory but Does Not Apply in Practice (1793)," in *The Philosophy of Kant*, ed. and trans. Carl J. Friedrich (New York, 1949), pp. 421–422.

18. Immanuel Kant, *Perpetual Peace* (1795), trans. Lewis White Beck in the Kant anthology *On History* (Indianapolis, 1963), p. 112.

19. Immanuel Kant, *The Metaphysical Elements of Justice*, p. 34.

20. *Ibid.*, pp. 99, 101, and 105, in the order quoted.

21. In addition to the works on justice by Rawls previously cited, the reader should consult the following for Rawls's application of his general theory to the problem of political obligation: John Rawls, "Legal Obligation and the Duty of Fair Play," in *Law and Philosophy*, ed. Sidney Hook (New York, 1964), pp. 3–18. This has been reprinted in my anthology *Civil Disobedience and Violence* (Belmont, Cal., 1971), pp. 39–52. For a direct application of a similar theory to the problem of punishment, see Herbert Morris, "Persons and Punishment," *The Monist* 52, no. 4 (October 1968): 475–501.

22. H. L. A. Hart, *The Concept of Law* (Oxford, 1961), pp. 189–195.

23. Jeffrie G. Murphy, "Moral Death: A Kantian Essay on Psychopathy," *Ethics* 82, no. 4 (July 1972): 284–298.

24. Banal as this point may seem, it could be persuasively argued that all Enlightenment political theory (e.g., that of Hobbes, Locke and Kant) is built upon ignoring it. For example, once we have substantial empirical evidence concerning how democracies really work in fact, how sympathetic can we really be to classical theories for the justification of democracy? For more on this, see C. B. Macpherson, "The Maximization of Democracy," in *Philosophy, Politics and Society* (Third Series), ed. Peter Laslett and W. G. Runciman (Oxford, 1967), pp. 83–103. This article is also relevant to the point raised in note 11 above.

25. This point is well developed in C. B. Macpherson, *The Political Theory of Possessive Individualism* (Oxford, 1962). In a sense, this point affects even the formal correctness of a theory, for it demonstrates an empirical source of corruption in the analyses of the very concepts in the theory.

26. The writings of Willem Adriaan Bonger (1876–1940), a Dutch criminologist, have fallen into totally unjustified neglect in recent years. Anticipating contemporary sociological theories of crime, he was insisting that criminal behavior is in the province of normal psychology (though abnormal society) at a time when most other writers were viewing criminality as a symptom of psychopathology. His major works are: *Criminality and Economic Conditions* (Boston, 1916); *An Introduction to Criminology* (London, 1936); and *Race and Crime* (New York, 1943).

27. I say, "at least in spirit" to avoid begging the controversial question of whether Marx can be said to embrace a theory of justice. Though (as I suggested in note 4) much of Marx's own evaluative rhetoric seems to overlap more traditional appeals to rights and justice (and a total lack of sympathy with anything like Utilitarianism), it must be admitted that he also frequently ridicules at least the terms "rights" and "justice" because of their apparent entrenchment in bourgeois ethics. For an interesting discussion of this issue, see Allen W. Wood, "The Marxian Critique of Justice," *Philosophy & Public Affairs* 1, no. 3 (Spring 1972): 244–282.

28. The importance of community is also, I think, recognized in Gabriel de Tarde's notion of "social similarity" as a condition of criminal responsibility. See his *Penal Philosophy* (Boston, 1912). I have drawn on de Tarde's general account in my "Moral Death: A Kantian Essay on Psychopathy."

29. By "reciprocity" Bonger intends something which includes, but is much richer than, a notion of "fair trading or bargaining" that might initially be read into the term. He also has in mind such things as sympathetic identification with others and tendencies to provide mutual aid. Thus, for Bonger, reciprocity and egoism have a strong tendency to conflict. I mention this lest Bonger's notion of reciprocity be too quickly identified with the more restricted notion found in, for example, Kant and Rawls.

30. It is interesting how greatly Bonger's analysis differs from classical deterrence theory—e.g., that of Bentham. Bentham, who views men as machines driven by desires to attain pleasure and avoid pain, tends to regard terror as the primary restraint against crime. Bonger believes that, at least in a healthy society, moral motives would function as a major restraint against crime. When an environment that destroys moral motivation is created. Even terror (as statistics tend to confirm) will not eradicate crime.

31. *Introduction to Criminology*, pp. 75–76, and *Criminality and Economic Conditions*, pp. 532, 402, 483–484, 436, and 407, in the order quoted. Bonger explicitly attacks Hobbes: "The adherents of [Hobbes's theory] have studied principally men who live under capitalism, or under civilization; their correct conclusion has been that egoism is the predominant characteristic of these men, and they have adopted the simplest explanation of the phenomenon and say that this trait is inborn." If Hobbists can cite Freud for modern support, Bonger can cite Darwin. For, as Darwin had argued in the *Descent of Man*, men would not have survived as a species if they had not initially had considerably greater social sentiments than Hobbes allows them.

32. Austin J. Turk, in the Introduction to his abridged edition of Bonger's *Criminality and Economic Conditions* (Bloomington, 1969), p. 14.

33. Statistical data on characteristics of offenders in America are drawn primarily from surveys by the Bureau of Census and the National Council on Crime and Delinquency. While there is of course wide disagreement on how such data are to be interpreted, there is no serious disagreement concerning at least the general accuracy of statistics like the one I have cited. Even government publications openly acknowledge a high correlation between crime and socio-economic disadvantages: "From arrest records, probation reports, and prison statistics a 'portrait' of the offender emerges that progressively highlights the disadvantaged character of his life. The offender at the end of the road in prison is likely to be a member of the lowest social and economic groups in the country, poorly educated and perhaps unemployed. . . . Material failure, then, in a culture firmly oriented toward material success, is the most common denominator of offenders" (*The Chal-*

lenge of Crime in a Free Society, A Report by the President's Commission on Law Enforcement and Administration of Justice, U.S. Government Printing Office, Washington, D. C., 1967, pp. 44 and 160). The Marxist implications of this admission have not gone unnoticed by prisoners. See Samuel Jorden, "Prison Reform: In Whose Interest?" *Criminal Law Bulletin* 7, no. 9 (November 1971): 779–787.

34. There are, of course, other factors which enter into an explanation of this statistic. One of them is the fact that economically disadvantaged guilty persons are more likely to wind up arrested or in prison (and thus be reflected in this statistic) than are economically advantaged guilty persons. Thus economic conditions enter into the explanation, not just of criminal behavior, but of society's response to criminal behavior. For a general discussion on the many ways in which crime and poverty are related, see Patricia M. Wald, "Poverty and Criminal Justice," *Task Force Report: The Courts*, U.S. Government Printing Office, Washington, D.C., 1967, pp. 139–151.

35. The idea that the principles of justice could be proved as a kind of theorem (Rawls's claim in "Justice as Fairness") seems to be absent, if I understand the work correctly, in Rawls's recent *A Theory of Justice*. In this book Rawls seems to be content with something less than a decision procedure. He is no longer trying to pull his theory of justice up by its own bootstraps, but now seems concerned simply to *exhibit* a certain elaborate conception of justice in the belief that it will do a good job of systematizing and ordering most of our considered and reflective intuitions about moral matters. To this, of course, the Marxist will want to say something like the following: "The considered and reflective intuitions current in our society are a product of bourgeois culture, and thus any theory based upon them begs the question against us and in favor of the status quo." I am not sure that this charge cannot be answered, but I am sure that it deserves an answer. Someday Rawls may be remembered, to paraphrase Georg Lukács's description of Thomas Mann, as the last and greatest philosopher of bourgeois liberalism. The virtue of this description is that it perceives the limitations of his outlook in a way consistent with acknowledging his indisputable genius. (None of my remarks here, I should point out, are to be interpreted as denying that our civilization derived major moral benefits from the tradition of bourgeois liberalism. Just because the freedoms and procedures we associate with bourgeois liberalism—speech, press, assembly, due process of law, etc.—are not the only important freedoms and procedures, we are not to conclude with some witless radicals that these freedoms are not terribly important and that the victories of bourgeois revolutions are not worth preserving. My point is much

more modest and noncontroversial—namely, that even bourgeois liberalism requires a critique. It is not self-justifying and, in certain very important respects, is not justified at all.)

36. Kant has some doubts about punishing bastard infanticide and dueling on similar grounds. Given the stigma that Kant's society attached to illegitimacy and the halo that the same society placed around military honor, it did not seem totally fair to punish those whose criminality in part grew out of such approved motives. See *Metaphysical Elements of Justice*, pp. 106–107.

37. This point is pursued in Herbert Morris, "Persons and Punishment." Bonger did not appreciate that "mental illness," like criminality, may also be a phenomenon of social class. On this, see August B. Hollingshead and Frederick C. Redlich, *Social Class and Mental Illness* (New York, 1958). On the general issue of punishment versus therapy, see my *Punishment and Rehabilitation* (Belmont, Cal., 1973).

Notes and Questions

KARL MENNINGER, from *The Crime of Punishment*

1. Karl Menninger argues that we should change our attitude about crime and criminals. We need to replace our punitive perspective, our inclination to retaliation and revenge, with a therapeutic attitude. What, according to Menninger, is the therapeutic attitude? What values are basic to it?

2. The obvious question is one Menninger anticipates. Why should we think there can be any effective treatment for criminal offenders? Why should we think offenders can be changed? What does Menninger think?

3. Of course, not all criminals are alike, just as not all mental patients are alike. Menninger reports a set of rough categories of criminal offenders set out by Howard Gill. What are these categories? How do these categories affect treatment?

4. How does Menninger suggest approaching the practical problems of providing rehabilitation services for the vast numbers of criminal offenders who need treatment? Are his suggestions realistic?

5. Menninger points out that community action groups appear to be the greatest deterrent to crime. He calls for more citizen involvement in this areas. What are some of his specific suggestions? What examples does he give? Do you see any deficiencies in his view?

6. Menninger claims that the present system is both unjust and inefficient. Is he right? How does he support his claim? If he is right, does the failure of the present system act as an argument for replacing it with another system, such as the one Menninger suggests? Can you think of any arguments against a therapeutic system? Would it violate justice or utility? If so, why? What does Murphy suggest?

7. Is Menninger viewing criminals as children or as harmful animals not responsible for their actions? If so, is he wrong to do so? Remember that there are two ways he could be wrong. He could be mistaken, or he could be immoral. Are these two ways separate, or do they depend on one another? What would a retributivist say? What do you think?

8. From a utilitarian point of view, does it make sense to rehabilitate offenders and then send them back to the environment that demoralized them, according to Menninger, in the first place? Can rehabilitation fulfill the utilitarian goals of reducing crime and increasing the general welfare? Is there any reason to think it would inhibit the general welfare?

[From] *The Crime of Punishment*

KARL MENNINGER

Doctors charge fees; they impose certain "penalties" or prices, but they have long since put aside primitive attitudes of retaliation toward offensive patients. A patient may cough in the doctor's face or may vomit on the office rug; a patient may curse or scream or even struggle in the extremity of his pain. But these acts are not "punished." Doctors and nurses have no time or thought for inflicting unnecessary pain even upon patients who may be difficult, disagreeable, provocative, and even dangerous. It is their duty to care for them, to try to make them well, and to prevent them from doing themselves or others harm. This requires love, not hate.

This is the deepest meaning of the therapeutic attitude. Every doctor knows this; every worker in a hospital or clinic knows it (or should). I once put this principle in a paragraph of directions for the workers in our psychiatric hospital:

> If we can love: this is the touchstone. This is the key to all the therapeutic programs of the modern psychiatric hospital; it dominates the behavior of its staff from director down to gardener. To our patient who cannot love, we must say by our actions that we do love him. "You can be angry here if you must be; we know you have had cause. We know you have been wronged. We know you are afraid of your own anger, your own self-punishment—afraid, too, that your anger will arouse our anger and that you will be wronged again and disappointed again and rejected again and driven mad once more. But we are not angry—and you won't be either, after a while. We are your friends; those about you are all friends; you can relax your defenses and your tensions. As you—and we—come to understand your life better, the warmth of love will begin to replace your present anguish—and you will find yourself getting well."

Right You Are If You Think You Are

There is another element in the therapeutic attitude not explicitly mentioned by me in that paragraph. It is the quality of hopefulness. If no one believes that the patient can get well, if no one—not even the doctor—has any hope, there probably won't be any recovery. Hope is just as important as love in the therapeutic attitude.

"But you were talking about the mentally ill," readers may interject, "those poor, confused, bereft, frightened individuals who yearn for help from you doctors and nurses. Do you mean to imply that willfully perverse individuals, our criminals, can be similarly reached and rehabilitated? Do you really believe that effective treatment of the sort you visualize can be applied to people *who do not want any help*, who are so willfully vicious, so well aware of the wrongs they are doing, so lacking in penitence or even common decency that punishment seems to be the only thing left?"

Do I believe there is effective treatment for offenders, and that they *can* be changed? Most *certainly and definitely I do*. Not all cases, to be sure; there are also some physical afflictions which we cannot cure at the moment. Some provision has to be made for incurables—pending new knowledge—and these will include some offenders. But I believe the majority of them would prove to be curable. The willfulness and the viciousness of offenders are part of the thing for which they have to be treated. These must not thwart the therapeutic attitude.

It is simply not true that most of them are "fully aware" of what they are doing, nor is it true that they want no help from anyone, although some of them say so. Prisoners are individuals: some want treatment, some do not. Some don't know what treatment is. Many are utterly despairing and hopeless. Where treatment is made available in institutions, many prisoners seek it even with the full knowledge that doing so will not lessen their sentences. In some prisons, seeking treatment by prisoners is frowned upon by the officials.

Various forms of treatment are even now being tried in some progressive courts and prisons over the country—educational, social, industrial, religious, recreational, and psychological treatments. Socially acceptable behavior, new work-play opportunities, new identity and companion patterns all help toward community reacceptance. Some parole officers and some wardens have been extremely ingenious in developing these modalities of rehabilitation and reconstruction — more than I could list here even if I knew them all. But some are trying. The secret of success in all programs, however, is the replacement of the punitive attitude with a therapeutic attitude.

A therapeutic attitude is essential regardless of the particular form of treatment or help. Howard Gill of the American University's Institute of Correctional Administration believes that thirty per cent of offenders are overwhelmed with situational difficulties, and for such individuals crisis intervention often works wonders. Case work, economic relief, or other social assistance often will induce a favorable behavior pattern change in these offenders. In another thirty per cent, he estimates, personal psychological problems exist in the offender which require technical treatment efforts. For these the help of psychiatrists, physicians, and psychologists are needed. Still another thirty per cent of prisoners are essentially immature individuals whose antisocial tendencies have never found the proper paths of distribution and transformation in socially acceptable ways. These men are usually amenable to redirection, education, and guidance. They can achieve development of self-control and social conformity by the various programs which we call milieu treatment. In other words, one can think of the categories of treatment as falling largely into the three modalities of sociological, psychological (medical), and educational.

The reflective reader, recalling the history of our mental hospital reformation, may now feel prompted to ask, "Could not sufficient diagnosis and treatment be provided for offenders who need it in our presently existing psychiatric hospitals? We read that the population in these hospitals is diminishing rapidly; could not this empty space be used to treat offenders who might be transferred there?"

Unfortunately, the answer is not clearly in the affirmative at present. In the first place, the victims of our penal system are usually so embittered and, indeed, so outright aggressive that a degree of security is necessary for them, especially in the beginning, which the average psychiatric hospital is not physically prepared to insure. Even more significantly, our psychiatric hospitals are not psychologically prepared at the present time to be assigned the task of detaining and treating patients who have been labeled prisoners. We have had a long, painful experience with this in my own State of Kansas.

Please remember that psychiatric hospitals have themselves only recently emerged from a state of public obloquy which was nearly as bad as that now affecting prisons. Those hospitals which have raised their standards are proud of their achievement, proud of their respectability and good name, proud of being known as places where people come to be made well by the best of scientific medical effort. Ailing, faltering, erring, or even dimly conscious patients brought to them are soon surrounded by new-found friends who take in the newcomer and minister to him as companions, aides, fellow sufferers, amateur repairmen.

But if, into such an environment, there is introduced an individual who is not only angry and unsocial and generally hostile but who has a public record of having been caught and convicted for something heinous, the atmosphere immediately changes. No matter how obvious his suffering, sympathy and therapeutic idealism will not always be sufficient to neutralize the suspicion and negative feelings aroused in patients and staff members alike.

Treatment for the Many

In thinking of ways to provide truly corrective therapy for large numbers of offenders at minimal expense, penologists might take a leaf from the book of modern psychiatry. It was long assumed that only under detention, i.e., *in the hospital*, was it possible to effectively control and treat and change severely disturbed individuals. Early in the twentieth century an experiment of "out patient" psychiatric treatment was made in Boston by Ernest Southard of Harvard. Today, half a century later, the *majority* of all psychiatric patients are in outpatient status! Furthermore, there is a steadily rising preponderance of outpatients over inpatients. "Day hospitals," where patients spend some daylight hours in scheduled activities with other patients but go home in the evening for sleep, privacy, and family adaptation, have also proved useful. Similarly, "night hospitals" came into use for patients who could adapt themselves well enough to a work situation or a school setting but who did better by spending their nights under the protective care of the friendly hospital.

Thus there has developed the outpatient principle, which holds that it is optimal for the patient to continue living and working in his ordinary, everyday-life ways as much as possible, seeing his psychiatrist, psychologist, social worker, therapist, teacher, or clergyman in successive sessions at intervals *in their offices*. Obviously this is a great saving of time and money for everyone. And, curiously, it has proved to be just as effective, statistically measured, in nurturing favorable change in patients as were our carefully planned and elaborated inpatient hospital programs. Not the least advantage was the diminished stigmatization of the non-confined patient.

All this the correctional system might emulate — and in some progressive jurisdictions it does. Some individuals have to be protected against themselves, some have to be protected from other prisoners, some even from the community. Some mental patients must be detained for a time even against their wishes, and the same is true of offenders. Offenders with propensities for impulsive and predatory aggression should not be permitted to live among us unrestrained by some kind of social control. *But the great majority of offenders, even "criminals," should never become prisoners if we want to "cure" them.*

What we want to accomplish is the reintegration of the temporarily suspended individual back into the main stream of social life, preferably a life at a higher level than before, just as soon as possible. Many, many precariously constituted individuals are trying to make it on the outside right now, with little help from us. We all have to keep reminding ourselves that *most offenders are never even apprehended*. Most of those who are caught and convicted, we must remember, are released either free or on probation. But they rarely have the benefit of treatment.

Parole and probation officers are thus indispensable, and the profession should be vastly elevated in numbers, in prestige, and in salary. Its responsibility is great and should be greater. By their counsel, encouragement, warning, and befriending, many one-time offenders, with whom they keep in touch, are supported in new life efforts by these skilled and experienced guides and friends.

It is a curious thing that, important as we all recognize probation and parole to be, they rarely get very much discussion. The President's Commission on Law Enforcement and Administration of Justice has many Task Force Reports, but not one on probation or parole, which are discussed in two chapters of the small volume on Corrections. There are numerous books on the subject, however, but not enough.

A New Trend

A recent development in psychiatry is referred to by some as our "Third Revolution." After the cruelties of witchcraft trials, even the dreariness of custodial asylums in remote places reflected a revolutionary progress. Then came the modern concept of psychiatric hospitals, described earlier, which latterly included the day hospital, the night hospital, the half-way house, supervised foster home placement, and affiliated outpatient diagnostic and treatment departments. All this was the "Second Revolution."

The "Third Revolution" occurred when the therapeutic success and the economic advantages of outpatient treatment led to a general and widespread demand for more of it, more easily accessible. Psychiatric hospitals had nearly always been located in widely separated and far removed places, often difficult of access for the majority of people. Psychiatrists in private practice were few, and located only in the larger cities. Consequently, psychiatric outpatient clinics began to develop in association with general hospitals and medical clinics.

These clinics often lacked provision for emergency care, temporary hospitalization for critically severe cases, and the special requirements for the treatment of children and young adults with psychiatric problems. They generally lacked, also, facilities for supervised work and recreation programs.

Thus, there arose the idea of *comprehensive mental-health centers* in various parts of every state (and in various locations within the big cities), heavily subsidized by the federal government, to make certain that no citizen would be more than a few hours from such a refuge, and could go there for any kind of psychiatric emergency at any time, and at a cost he could meet. The ideal staffing is a team of one or more psychiatrists, plus psychologists, social workers, therapists, secretaries, and others trained in the programs of scientific therapy described in earlier pages. To these clinics may come anyone in trouble or crisis: the depressed woman, the alcoholic man, the excited youth, the delinquent boy, the school failure, the discordant couple, the bewildered parent.

This description omits one essential feature. The mental-health center seeks to be in direct communication and in a working relationship with all the people of the area—not just the sick ones. Hence it will be in touch with all the institutions of the community which it serves—the schools, the hospitals, the police court, the prison, the industries, the churches—indeed with *every* form of organized human activity. The counsel of the clinic staff is available to the management of all these sister institutions.

It is the hope that a continuing improvement in the public attitude toward mental illness will follow and that instead of a dreaded affliction which strikes down some poor victims who must then be isolated in a state asylum somewhere, mental ill health will be seen as something which, in varying degrees, affects all citizens and which, in most instances, can be helped before reaching such extremities of manifestation or treatment requirement. Only the most severely disabled persons will have to be removed from the community for treatment, and they will be returned as swiftly as possible, not as tabooed objects, but as objects of the concern of local citizens.

* * *

Citizen Responsibility

There are throughout the country many citizen action groups and programs for the prevention and control of crime and delinquency. The National Council on Crime and Delinquency, founded in 1907 as the National Probation Association, since 1955 has established state citizen action councils in nineteen states and the District of Columbia, and over one hundred and fifty local citizen action committees. Its aim is eventually to establish state and local councils in all states.

In the state of Washington a strong public information and citizen involvement program was brought into being in about a five-year period. One newspaper wrote an editorial to the effect that "more had been accomplished during the past five years than the previous ninety-five from the standpoint of prison and correctional reform." A great many major reform pieces of legislation were passed. When the program was started, over half of the daily newspapers in the state wrote extremely negative news stories and editorials. However, after the involvement of several news-media people on the Washington Citizen's Council and the release of many reports to the public on problems and needs in the correctional field, every one of the daily newspapers in the state began to write approvingly of the program.

A significant change in public thinking was brought about. The state, which in 1955 was cited by United Press International as having the "worst prison system in the country," was, five years later, considered to have one of the nation's better correctional systems. Correction has been completely removed from partisan politics, and a merit system effected. Labor, for the first time in history, supported the first state prison industries program. The office of sheriff was removed from politics. A twenty-five-million-dollar bond issue, including several million dollars for correctional facilities, was voted by the people.

A group of concerned women formed an anti-crime crusade in Indianapolis in 1962, demanding of city officials safe streets for themselves and their children. Tired of the "We're doing our best" clichés, they acted on their own! They exerted their energies and efforts in many ways, including evaluation of the law enforcement agencies and their needs, and analyzing the operation of the courts. In 1965, the crime rate in Indianapolis dropped for the first time since 1959, while the national rate rose six per cent.

With such attitudes of inquiry and concern, the public could acquire information (and incentive) leading to a change of feeling about crime and criminals. It will discover how unjust is much so-called "justice," how baffled and frustrated many judges are by the ossified rigidity of old-fashioned, obsolete laws and state constitutions which effectively prevent the introduction of sensible procedures to replace useless, harmful ones. It will learn of the sentencing schools which some judges attend to try to make the best of a bad situation, and of the Model Penal Code evolved by so much painstaking effort by representatives of the American Bar Association and Bar Institute.

Will the public listen?

If the public does become interested, it will realize that we must have more facts, more trial projects, more checked results. It will share the dismay of the President's Commission in finding that no one knows much about even the incidence of crime with any definiteness or statistical accuracy. We are told that of two thousand *known* crimes the police are only notified in about fifty per cent of the cases; when notified they come about three-fourths of the time; and in four out of five times no arrest is made. Of the twenty per cent of offenders who are arrested, more than one-half are dismissed without a trial; of the forty per cent who are tried, about one-half are convicted, and *some* of these serve some kind of a sentence. Usually it is for the second or third or tenth time.

About all this, we need more information, more research, more experimental data. That research is the basis for scientific progress, no one any more disputes. Industry knows it; the military establishment knows it; all scientists know it. The public gives tacit approval to it, and in many instances pays the bills generously without being sure what the research is, where it is needed, or what is or should be done.

The average citizen finds it difficult to see how any research would in any way change his mind about a man who brutally murders his children. But just such inconceivably awful acts most dramatically point up the need for research. Why should — how can — a man become so dreadful as that in our culture? How is such a man made? Is it comprehensible that he can be born to become so depraved?

With so many different proposals of new programs and experiments in rehabilitation, there should be a way to check on how successful each of these actually is. Almost any program will get *some* results and is apt to be praised indiscriminately. But it is not so easy as it might appear to check accurately on the effectiveness of a rehabilitative program. Social research is a particularly

difficult field and requires careful planning and control. Even our present prisons, bad as many of them are, could be extensively used as laboratories for the study of many of the unsolved problems.

There are thousands of questions regarding crime and public protection which deserve scientific study. What makes some individuals maintain their interior equilibrium by one kind of disturbance of the social structure rather than by another kind, one that would have landed him in a hospital? Why do some individuals specialize in certain types of crime? Why do so many young people reared in areas of delinquency and poverty and bad example never become habitual delinquents? (Perhaps this is a more important question than why some of them do.) Why is there so little delinquency and crime in Greece and in China?

These and a great many other questions remain to be solved by the patient methods of scientific investigation. But, in the meantime, we need not wait for results of the new research findings. *For we have at hand great quantities of research findings which clearly indicate what we should be doing. Much indeed we don't know, but we are not doing one-tenth of what we should about what we already do know.*

Consuming Justice

What I am proposing here is simply that the public take seriously the difficulties and complexities of insuring the peace, and take a hand in the matter rather than dumping all the responsibility onto the police. They must help the police. They must help the judges. They must help the parole and probation officers. It is *our* safety and welfare which is involved.

The public, in short, could be and should be what Edmond Cahn called *consumers of justice*, instead of merely providers of it, supplying it, endorsing it, paying for it, and deploring its poor distribution. How does one become a consumer of justice? In these ways, answers Professor Cahn:

> He consumes justice by being safeguarded and regulated from day to day as one fills his place in society . . . [one consumes] public justice whenever one talks or writes, works or sleeps, buys or sells. One may also consume it in a more dramatic way, as by engaging in a lawsuit or being charged with a crime.

In a democracy, a citizen consumes justice still more extensively when he influences the shape of policy and legislation, casts his vote, and asserts the interests of a special group or of the whole community.

Finally, there is a third way to consume justice. It consists of the people's examining and assuming responsibility for what officials do in their name and by their authority—the unjust and evil acts as well as the beneficent and good.

Charles D. McAtee, director of Penal Institutions for the State of Kansas, recently declared:

If we really intend to combat the problem, let's start at the grassroots level with community action committees who can best pool and coordinate the local resources available to combat crime. I believe that an informed, concerned, and aroused citizenry can have a tremendous impact on the causative factors of crime and delinquency, and that local community committees, dedicated to this effort and utilizing local community resources, can not only prevent crime, but can more adequately provide reasonable alternatives to imprisonment, for some of those who are involved in criminal offenses.

I agree completely. Public education and involvement are the first steps in any permanent, constructive change in our wretchedly inadequate, self-destroying, self-injuring, crime-encouraging system. Not that the public will straightaway rise up and ask for the radical changes that ought to be made. But once it knows, once it really perceives that the present pretentious procedure is falling on its face and endangering us all, once it discovers that better methods are well known and available but ignored and unused by those in authority—once the public becomes informed, it will become correspondingly aroused. It will let its demands be known to legislatures and officials, and the situation will change.

I have seen it happen. I saw the reaction of the people of Kansas to the discovery of the facts about their wretched state hospitals as exposed by the newspapers in 1948, and I saw the legislators' reactions to the people's reaction. They promptly hired a director of state institutions at twice the Governor's salary and told him to do what was necessary to modernize Kansas mental hospitals. Furthermore, they voted him the money to do it, and he did it. And I saw the people of Kansas confound the legislature and the political leaders two years later by voting two to one in favor of a constitutional amendment for a permanent mill tax for hospital construction, an amendment which was "sure to be defeated."

What had happened? Simply a change of attitude based on adequate information. The public learned that their relatives were not getting effective treatment and that with such treatment these patients could return (or could have returned) home. True, effective treatment would cost some money, far more per day than the state had been spending, but since the number of days would be reduced from thousands to scores, the people would save money and the patients would be saved suffering.

The people believed what we said, and their legislators voted the additional money. The cost *per day* went up five times. But the cost *for each discharged patient* went down *more* than five times. The state mental hospital budget has never since then been an item of political controversy, and not once in nineteen years has it been seriously curtailed.

Today there are forty times as many psychiatrists and graduate nurses in the Kansas state hospitals as in 1948. More than forty times as much therapy is given—and there are forty times as many recoveries. And there are forty times forty more private citizens helping with the state mental-health programs as volunteers, companions, foster parents, or staff employees.

Some day, somewhere, the same thing will happen with respect to transgressors and offenders. It will be harder to bring about, for reasons we have given: the public has a fascination for violence, and clings tenaciously to its yen for vengeance, blind and deaf to the expense, futility, and dangerousness of the resulting penal system. But we are bound to hope that this will yield in time to the persistent, penetrating light of intelligence and accumulating scientific knowledge. The public will grow increasingly ashamed of its cry for retaliation, its persistent demand to punish. This is its crime, *our* crime against criminals—and incidentally our crime against ourselves. For before we can diminish our sufferings from the ill-controlled aggressive assaults of fellow citizens, we must renounce the philosophy of punishment, the obsolete, vengeful penal attitude. In its place we would seek a comprehensive, constructive social attitude — therapeutic in some instances, restraining in some instances, but preventive in its total social impact.

In the last analysis this becomes a question of personal morals and value. No matter how glorified or how piously disguised, vengeance as a human motive must be personally repudiated by each and every one of us. This is the message of old religions and new psychiatries. Unless this message is heard, unless we, the people — the man on the street, the housewife in the home — can give up our delicious satisfactions in opportunities for vengeful retaliation on scapegoats, we cannot expect to preserve our peace, our public safety, or our mental health....

* * *

Notes and Questions

RANDY E. BARNETT, from "Restitution: A New Paradigm of Criminal Justice"

1. What is the basic idea of a restitution response to crime? How does it differ from the traditional or current view of crime?

2. What is the difference between punitive restitution and pure restitution, according to Barnett? Which does he support? Which is the more radical departure from our current institution of punishment?

3. Barnett points out that a restitution system would be particularly flexible, in fact, inherently so. Why? What are some possible refinements of a basic restitution system that Barnett suggests?

4. Barnett recognizes that an important problem for any advocate of a restitution system is the problem of determining the standard of compensation for victims. To ask for the standard of compensation is to ask what restitution is. Thus, the problem is central. Furthermore, it is difficult. Why is it difficult? Is it unique to a restitution system, or do other systems face the same problem? Do you see analogous problems for a retributive or utilitarian system of punishment? Is the problem more fatal for a restitution system? If so, why?

5. Barnett lists several advantages to a restitution approach to punishment. What are they? Do you agree that they are indeed advantages? Are they realistic?

6. Barnett recognizes two different sorts of objections to restitution. The first sort of objections are practical. What are they, and how does Barnett attempt to meet them? Do you find his answers satisfactory?

7. The second sort of objections Barnett calls distributionary criticisms, but we might also call them moral criticisms. What is the potential moral objection, and how does Barnett respond to it?

8. Barnett sets out briefly some collateral considerations that serve to illustrate how great the change to a restitution system of criminal justice would be. As he points out, justice would focus on the rights and equal treatment of victims, not on the suffering or punishment of criminals as such. Would that be a better focus for justice? Would it be better or worse for other reasons, such as utility? One result would be that "victimless crimes" by definition could not be crimes. Why not? Barnett thinks that is a good thing. Do you? Is there any good reason we could not have a mixed system that would recognize crimes against society? Such crimes would have to be handled differently, of course.

9. Like Menninger, Barnett is suggesting that we abandon the punitive frame of mind with regard to crime and criminals. Beyond that, however, his view is quite different from the therapeutic model, is it not? What are the important differences? Are the two views flatly contradictory, or could they be compatible? If so, how? Does Barnett offer an answer to the challenge posed by Murphy? If so, in what way or with what limits?

[From] "Restitution: A New Paradigm of Criminal Justice"

RANDY E. BARNETT

* * *

Outline of a New Paradigm

The idea of restitution is actually quite simple. It views crime as an offense by one individual against the rights of another. The victim has suffered a loss. Justice consists of the culpable offender making good the loss he has caused. It calls for a complete refocusing of our image of crime. Kuhn would call it a "shift of world-view." Where we once saw an offense against society, we now see an offense against an individual victim. In a way, it is a common sense view of crime. *The armed robber did not rob society, he robbed the victim.* His debt, therefore, is not to society; it is to the victim. There are really two types of restitution proposals: a system of "punitive" restitution and a "pure" restitutional system.

1. Punitive Restitution. "Since rehabilitation was admitted to the aims of penal law two centuries ago, the number of penological aims has remained virtually constant. Restitution is waiting to come in."[1] Given this view, restitution should merely be added to the paradigm of punishment. Stephen Schafer outlines the proposal: "[Punitive] restitution, like punishment, must always be the subject of judicial consideration. Without exception it must be carried out by personal performance by the wrong-doer, and should even then be equally burdensome and just for all criminals, irrespective of their means, whether they be millionaires or labourers."[2]

There are many ways by which such a goal might be reached. The offender might be forced to compensate the victim by his own work, either in prison or out. If it came out of his pocket or from the sale of his property this would compensate the victim, but it would not be sufficiently unpleasant for the offender. Another proposal would be that the fines be proportionate to the earning power of the criminal. Thus, "A poor man would pay in days of work, a rich man by an equal number of days' income or salary."[3] Her-

bert Spencer made a proposal along similar lines in his excellent "Prison-Ethics," which is well worth examining.[4] Murray N. Rothbard and others have proposed a system of "double payments" in cases of criminal behavior.[5] While closer to pure restitution than other proposals, the "double damages" concept preserves a punitive aspect.

Punitive restitution is an attempt to gain the benefits of pure restitution, which will be considered shortly, while retaining the perceived advantages of the paradigm of punishment. Thus, the prisoner is still "sentenced" to some unpleasantness — prison labor or loss of X number of days' income. That the intention is to preserve the "hurt" is indicated by the hesitation to accept an out-of-pocket payment or sale of assets. This is considered too "easy" for the criminal and takes none of his time. The amount of payment is determined not by the *actual harm* but by the *ability of the offender to pay*. Of course, by retaining the paradigm of punishment this proposal involves many of the problems we raised earlier. In this sense it can be considered another attempt to salvage the old paradigm.

2. Pure Restitution. "Recompense or restitution is scarcely a punishment as long as it is merely a matter of returning stolen goods or money. . . . The point is not that the offender deserves to suffer; it is rather that the offended party desires compensation."[6] This represents the complete overthrow of the paradigm of punishment. No longer would the deterrence, reformation, disablement, or rehabilitation of the criminal be the guiding principle of the judicial system. The attainment of these goals would be incidental to, and as a result of, reparations paid to the victim. No longer would the criminal deliberately be made to suffer for his mistake. Making good that mistake is all that would be required. What follows is a possible scenario of such a system.

When a crime occurred and a suspect was apprehended, a trial court would attempt to determine his guilt or innocence. If found guilty, the criminal would be sentenced to make restitution to the victim.[7] If a criminal is able to make restitution immediately, he may do so. This would discharge his liability. If he were unable to make restitution, but were found by the court to be trustworthy, he would be permitted to remain at his job (or find a new one) while paying restitution out of his future wages. This would entail a legal claim against future wages. Failure to pay could result in garnishment or a new type of confinement.

If it is found that the criminal is not trustworthy, or that he is unable to gain employment, he would be confined to an employment project.[8] This would be an industrial enterprise, preferably run by a private concern, which would produce actual goods or services. The level of security at each employment project would vary according to the behavior of the offenders. Since the costs would be lower, inmates at a lower-security project would receive higher wages. There is no reason why many workers could not be permitted to live with their families inside or outside the facility, depending, again, on the trustworthiness of the offender. Room and board would be deducted from the wages first, then a certain amount for restitution. Anything over that amount the worker could keep or apply toward further restitution, thus hastening his release. If a worker refused to work, he would be unable to pay for his maintenance, and therefore would not in principle be entitled to it. If he did not make restitution he could not be released. The exact arrangement which would best provide for high productivity, minimal security, and maximum incentive to work and repay the victim cannot be determined in advance. Experience is bound to yield some plans superior to others. In fact, the experimentation has already begun.[9]

While this might be the basic system, all sorts of refinements are conceivable, and certainly many more will be invented as needs arise. A few examples might be illuminating. With such a system of repayment, victim *crime insurance* would be more economically feasible than at present and highly desirable. The cost of awards would be offset by the insurance company's right to restitution in place of the victim (right of subrogation). The insurance company would be better suited to supervise the offender and mark his progress than would the victim. To obtain an ear-

lier recovery, it could be expected to innovate so as to enable the worker to repay more quickly (and, as a result, be released that much sooner). The insurance companies might even underwrite the employment projects themselves as well as related industries which would employ the skilled worker after his release. Any successful effort on their part to reduce crime and recidivism would result in fewer claims and lower premiums. The benefit of this insurance scheme for the victim is immediate compensation, conditional on the victim's continued cooperation with the authorities for the arrest and conviction of the suspect. In addition, the centralization of victim claims would, arguably, lead to efficiencies which would permit the pooling of small claims against a common offender.

Another highly useful refinement would be *direct arbitration* between victim and criminal. This would serve as a sort of healthy substitute for plea bargaining. By allowing the guilty criminal to negotiate a reduced payment in return for a guilty plea, the victim (or his insurance company) would be saved the risk of an adverse finding at trial and any possible additional expense that might result. This would also allow an indigent criminal to substitute personal services for monetary payments if all parties agreed.

Arbitration is argued for by John M. Greacen, deputy director of the National Institute for Law Enforcement and Criminal Justice. He sees the possible advantages of such reform as the ". . . development of more creative dispositions for most criminal cases; for criminal victims the increased use of restitution, the knowledge that their interests were considered in the criminal process; and an increased satisfaction with the outcome; increased awareness on the part of the offender that his crime was committed against another human being, and not against society in general; increased possibility that the criminal process will cause the offender to acknowledge responsibility for his acts."[10] Greacen notes several places where such a system has been tried with great success, most notably Tucson, Arizona, and Columbus, Ohio.[11]

Something analogous to the medieval Irish system of *sureties* might be employed as well.[12] Such a system would allow a concerned person, group, or company to make restitution (provided the offender agrees to this). The worker might then be released in the custody of the surety. If the surety had made restitution, the offender would owe restitution to the surety who might enforce the whole claim or show mercy. Of course, the more violent and unreliable the offender, the more serious and costly the offense, the less likely it would be that anyone would take the risk. But for first offenders, good workers, or others that charitable interests found deserving (or perhaps unjustly convicted) this would provide an avenue of respite.

Restitution and Rights

These three possible refinements clearly illustrate the flexibility of a restitutional system. It may be less apparent that this flexibility is *inherent* to the restitutional paradigm. Restitution recognizes rights in the victim, and this is a principal source of its strength. The nature and limit of the victim's right to restitution at the same time defines the nature and limit of the criminal liability. In this way, the aggressive action of the criminal creates a *debt* to the victim. The recognition of rights and obligations make possible many innovative arrangements. Subrogation, arbitration, and suretyship are three examples mentioned above. They are possible because this right to compensation[13] is considered the property of the victim and can therefore be delegated, assigned, inherited, or bestowed. One could determine in advance who would acquire the right to any restitution which he himself might be unable to collect.

The natural owner of an unenforced death claim would be an insurance company that had insured the deceased. The suggestion has been made that a person might thus increase his personal safety by insuring with a company well known for tracking down those who injure its policy holders. In fact, the partial purpose of some insurance schemes might be to provide the funds with which to track down the malefactor. The insurance company, having paid the beneficiaries would "stand in their shoes." It would remain possible, of course, to simply assign or devise the right directly to the beneficiaries, but this would put the burden of enforcement on persons likely to be unsuited to the task.

If one accepts the Lockean trichotomy of property ownership,[14] that is, acquiring property via exchange, gifts, and *homesteading* (mixing one's labor with previously unowned land or objects), the possibility arises that upon a person's wrongful death, in the absence of any heirs or assignees, his right to compensation becomes unowned property. The right could then be claimed (homesteaded) by anyone willing to go to the trouble of catching and prosecuting the criminal. Firms might specialize in this sort of activity, or large insurance companies might make the effort as a kind of "loss leader" for public relations purposes.

This does, however, lead to a potentially serious problem with the restitutional paradigm: what exactly constitutes "restitution"? What is the *standard* by which compensation is to be made? Earlier we asserted that any such problem facing the restitutional paradigm faces civil damage suits as well. The method by which this problem is dealt with in civil cases could be applied to restitution cases. But while this is certainly true, it may be that this problem has not been adequately handled in civil damage suits either.

Restitution in cases of crimes against property is a manageable problem. Modern contract and tort doctrines of restitution are adequate. The difficulty lies in cases of personal injury or death. How can you put a price on life or limb, pain or suffering? Is not any attempt to do so of necessity arbitrary? It must be admitted that a fully satisfactory solution to this problem is lacking, but it should also be stressed that this dilemma, though serious, has little impact on the bulk of our case in favor of a restitutional paradigm. It is possible that no paradigm of criminal justice can solve every problem, yet the restitutional approach remains far superior to the paradigm of punishment or any other conceivable rival.

This difficulty arises because certain property is unique and irreplaceable. As a result, it is impossible to approximate a "market" or "exchange" value expressed in monetary terms. Just as there is no rational relationship between a wrongfully taken life and ten years in prison, there is little relationship between that same life and $20,000. Still, the nature of this possibly insoluble puzzle reveals a restitutional approach theoretically superior to punishment. For it must be acknowledged that a real, tangible loss *has* occurred. The problem is only one of incommensurability. Restitution provides *some* tangible, albeit inadequate, compensation for personal injury. Punishment provides none at all.[15]

It might be objected that to establish some "pay scale" for personal injury is not only somewhat arbitrary but also a disguised reimplementation of punishment. Unable to accept the inevitable consequences of restitutional punishment, the argument continues, I have retreated to a pseudorestitutional award. Such a criticism is unfair. The true test in this instance is one of primacy of intentions. Is the purpose of a system to compensate victims for their losses (and perhaps, as a consequence, punish the criminals), or is its purpose to punish the criminals (and perhaps, as a consequence, compensate the victims for their losses)? The true ends of a criminal justice system will determine its nature. In short, arbitrariness *alone* does not imply a retributive motive. And while arbitrariness remains to some extent a problem for the restitutional paradigm, it is less of a problem for restitution than for punishment, since compensation has *some* rational relationship to damages and costs.

Advantages of a Restitutional System

1. The first and most obvious advantage is the assistance provided to victims of crime. They may have suffered an emotional, physical, or financial loss. Restitution would not change the fact that a possibly traumatic crime has occurred (just as the award of damages does not undo tortious conduct). Restitution, however, would make the resulting loss easier to bear for both victims and their families. At the same time, restitution would avoid a major pitfall of victim compensation/welfare plans: Since it is the criminal who must pay, the possibility of collusion between victim and criminal to collect "damages" from the state would be all but eliminated.

2. The possibility of receiving compensation would encourage victims to report crimes and to appear at trial. This is particularly true if there were a crime insurance scheme which contractually committed the policyholder to testify as a condition for payment, thus rendering unnecessary oppressive and potentially tyrannical subpoenas and contempt citations. Even the actual reporting of the crime to police is likely to be a prerequisite for compensation. Such a require-

ment in auto theft insurance policies has made car thefts the most fully reported crime in the United States. Furthermore, insurance companies which paid the claim would have a strong incentive to see that the criminal was apprehended and convicted. Their pressure and assistance would make the proper functioning of law enforcement officials all the more likely.

3. Psychologist Albert Eglash has long argued that restitution would aid in the rehabilitation of criminals. "Restitution is something an inmate does, not something done for or to him. . . . Being reparative, restitution can alleviate guilt and anxiety, which can otherwise precipitate further offenses."[16] Restitution, says Eglash, is an active effortful role on the part of the offender. It is socially constructive, thereby contributing to the offender's self-esteem. It is related to the offense and may thereby redirect the thoughts which motivated the offense. It is reparative, restorative, and may actually leave the situation better than it was before the crime, both for the criminal and victim.[17]

4. This is a genuinely "self-determinative" sentence.[18] The worker would know that the length of his confinement was in his own hands. The harder he worked, the faster he would make restitution. He would be the master of his fate and would have to face that responsibility. This would encourage useful, productive activity and instill a conception of reward for good behavior and hard work. Compare this with the current probationary system and "indeterminate sentencing" where the decision for release is made by the prison bureaucracy, based only (if fairly administered) on "good behavior"; that is, passive acquiescence to prison discipline. Also, the fact that the worker would be acquiring *marketable* skills rather than more skillful methods of crime should help to reduce the shocking rate of recidivism.

5. The savings to taxpayers would be enormous. No longer would the innocent taxpayer pay for the apprehension and internment of the guilty. The cost of arrest, trial, and internment would be borne by the criminal himself. In addition, since now-idle inmates would become productive workers (able, perhaps, to support their families), the entire economy would benefit from the increase in overall production.[19]

6. Crime would no longer pay. Criminals, par-

ticularly shrewd white-collar criminals, would know that they could not dispose of the proceeds of their crime and, if caught, simply serve time. They would have to make full restitution plus enforcement and legal costs, thereby greatly increasing the incentive to prosecute. While this would not eliminate such crime it would make it rougher on certain types of criminals, like bank and corporation officials, who harm many by their acts with a virtual assurance of lenient legal sanctions.[20] It might also encourage such criminals to keep the money around for a while so that, if caught, they could repay more easily. This would make a full recovery more likely.

A restitutional system of justice would benefit the victim, the criminal, and the taxpayer. The humanitarian goals of proportionate punishment, rehabilitation, and victim compensation are dealt with on a *fundamental* level making their achievement more likely. In short, the paradigm of restitution would benefit all but the entrenched penal bureaucracy and enhance justice at the same time. What then is there to stop us from overthrowing the paradigm of punishment and its penal system and putting in its place this more efficient, more humane, and more just system? The proponents of punishment and others have a few powerful counterarguments. It is to these we now turn.

Objections to Restitution

1. Practical criticisms of restitution. It might be objected that "crimes disturb and offend not only those who are directly their victim, but also the whole social order."[21] Because of this, society, that is, individuals other than the victim, deserves some satisfaction from the offender. Restitution, it is argued, will not satisfy the lust for revenge felt by the victim or the "community's sense of justice." This criticism appears to be overdrawn. Today most members of the community are mere spectators of the criminal justice system, and this is largely true even of the victim.[22] One major reform being urged presently is more victim involvement in the criminal justice process.[23] The restitution proposal would necessitate this involvement. And while the public generally takes the view that officials should be tougher on criminals, with "tougher" taken by nearly everyone to mean more severe in punishing, one must view this "social fact" in light of

the lack of a known alternative. The real test of public sympathies would be to see which sanction people would choose: incarceration of the criminal for a given number of years or the criminal's being compelled to make restitution to the victim: While the public's choice is not clearly predictable, neither can it be assumed that it would reject restitution. There is some evidence to the contrary.

This brings us to a second practical objection: that monetary sanctions are insufficient deterrents to crime. Again, this is something to be discovered, not something to be assumed. There are a number of reasons to believe that our *current* system of punishment does not adequately deter, and for the reasons discussed earlier an increase in the level of punishment is unlikely. In fact, many have argued that the deterrent value of sanctions has less to do with *severity* than with *certainty*, and the preceding considerations indicate that law enforcement would be more certain under a restitutional system. In the final analysis, however, it is irrelevant to argue that more crimes may be committed if our proposal leaves the victim better off. It must be remembered: *Our goal is not the suppression of crime; it is doing justice to victims.*

A practical consideration which merits considerable future attention is the feasibility of the employment project proposal. A number of questions can be raised. At first blush, it seems naively optimistic to suppose that offenders will be able or willing to work at all, much less earn their keep and pay reparations as well. On the contrary, this argument continues, individuals turn to crime precisely because they lack the skills which the restitutional plan assumes they have. Even if these workers have the skills, but refuse to work, what could be done? Would not the use of force to compel compliance be tantamount to slavery? This criticism results in part from my attempt to sketch an "ideal" restitution system; that is, I have attempted to outline the type toward which every criminal justice system governed by the restitution paradigm should strive. This is not to say that every aspect of the hypothetical system would, upon implementation, function smoothly. Rather, such a system could only operate ideally once the paradigm had been fully accepted and substantially articulated.

With this in mind, one can advance several

responses. First, the problem as usually posed assumes the offender to be highly irrational and possibly mentally unbalanced. There is no denying that some segment of the criminal population fits the former description. What this approach neglects, however, is the possibility that many criminals are making rational choices within an irrational and unjust political system. Specifically I refer to the myriad laws and regulations which make it difficult for the unskilled or persons of transitory outlook to find legal employment. I refer also to the laws which deny legality to the types of services which are in particular demand in economically impoverished communities. Is it "irrational" to choose to steal or rob when one is virtually foreclosed from the legal opportunity to do otherwise? Another possibility is that the criminal chooses crime not because of foreclosure, but because he enjoys and obtains satisfaction from a criminal way of life. Though morally repugnant, this is hardly irrational.

Furthermore, it no longer can be denied that contact with the current criminal justice system is itself especially damaging among juveniles. The offenders who are hopelessly committed to criminal behavior are not usually the newcomers to crime but those who have had repeated exposure to the penal system. In Kuhn's words, "Existing institutions have ceased to meet the problems posed by an environment *they have in part created*." While a restitutionary system might not change these hard-core offenders, it could, by the early implementation of sanctions perceived by the criminal to be just, break the vicious circle which in large part accounts for their existence.

Finally, if offenders could not or would not make restitution, then the logical and just result of their refusal would be confinement until they could or would. Such an outcome would be entirely in their hands. While this "solution" does not suggest who should justly pay for this confinement, the problem is not unique to a restitutionary system. In this and other areas of possible difficulty we must seek guidance from existing pilot programs as well as from the burgeoning research in this area and in victimology in general.

2. Distributionary criticisms of restitution. There remains one criticism of restitution which is the most obvious and the most difficult with which to deal. Simply stated, it takes the following form: "Doesn't this mean that rich people will be able to commit crimes with impunity if they can afford it? Isn't this unfair?" The *practical* aspect of this objection is that whatever deterrent effect restitution payments may have, they will be less for those most able to pay. The *moral* aspect is that whatever retributive or penal effect restitution payments may have they will be less for those who are well off. Some concept of equality of justice underlies both considerations.

Critics of restitution fail to realize that the "cost" of crime will be quite high. In addition to compensation for pain and suffering, the criminal must pay for the cost of his apprehension, the cost of the trial, and the legal expenditures of *both* sides. This should make even an unscrupulous wealthy person think twice about committing a crime. The response to this is that we cannot have it both ways. If the fines would be high enough to bother the rich, then they would be so high that a project worker would have no chance of earning that much and would, therefore, have no incentive to work at all. If, on the other hand, you lower the price of crime by ignoring all its costs, you fail to deter the rich or fully compensate the victim.

This is where the option of arbitration and victim crime insurance becomes of practical importance. If the victim is uninsured, he is unlikely to recover for all costs of a very severe crime from a poor, unskilled criminal, since even in an employment project the criminal might be unable to earn enough. If he had no hope of earning his release, he would have little incentive to work very hard beyond paying for his own maintenance. The victim would end up with less than if he had "settled" the case for the lesser amount which a project worker could reasonably be expected to earn. If, however, the victim had full-coverage criminal insurance, he would recover his damages in full, and the insurance company would absorb any disparity between full compensation and maximal employment project worker's output. This cost would be reflected in premium prices, enabling the insurance company which settled cases at an amount which increased the recovery from the criminal to offer the lowest rates. Eventually a "maximum" feasible fine for project workers would be

Punishment: Justification and Alternatives 635

determined based on these considerations. The "rich," on the other hand, would naturally have to pay in full. This arrangement would solve the practical problem, but it should not be thought of as an imperative of the restitutional paradigm.

The same procedure of varying the payments according to ability to pay would answer the moral considerations as well (that the rich are not hurt enough) and this is the prime motive behind *punitive* restitution proposals. However, we reject the moral consideration outright. The paradigm of restitution calls not for the (equal) hurting of criminals, but for restitution to victims. Any appeal to "inadequate suffering" is a reversion to the paradigm of punishment, and by varying the sanction for crimes of the same magnitude according to the economic status of the offender it reveals its own inequity. *Equality of justice means equal treatment of victims.* It should not matter to the victim if his attacker was rich or poor. His plight is the same regardless. Any reduction of criminal liability because of reduced earning power would be for practical, not moral, reasons.

Equality of justice derives from the fact that the rights of men should be equally enforced and respected. Restitution recognizes a victim's right to compensation for damages from the party responsible. Equality of justice, therefore, calls for equal enforcement of each victim's right to restitution. *Even if necessary or expedient, any lessening of payment to the victim because of the qualities of the criminal is a violation of that victim's rights and an inequality of justice.* Any such expedient settlement is only a recognition that an imperfect world may make possible only imperfect justice. As a practical matter, a restitutional standard gives victims an enormous incentive to pursue wealthy criminals since they can afford quick, full compensation. Contrast this with the present system where the preference given the wealthy is so prevalent that most victims simply assume that nothing will be done.

The paradigm of restitution, to reiterate, is neither a panacea for crime nor a blueprint for utopia. Panaceas and utopias are not for humankind. We must live in a less than perfect world with less than perfect people. Restitution opens the possibility of an improved and more just society. The old paradigm of punishment, even reformed, simply cannot offer this promise.

Other Considerations

Space does not permit a full examination of other less fundamental implications of such a system. I shall briefly consider five.

1. Civil versus criminal liability. If one accepts a restitutionary standard of justice, what sense does it make to distinguish between crime and tort, since both call for payment of damages? For most purposes I think the distinction collapses. Richard Epstein, in a series of brilliant articles, has articulated a theory of strict liability in tort.[24] His view is that since one party has caused another some harm and one of the parties must bear the loss, justice demands that it falls on the party who caused the harm. He argues that intention is only relevant as a "third-stage" argument; that notwithstanding some fault on the part of the plaintiff (a second-stage argument), the defendant intended the harm and is therefore liable.[25] With a restitutional system I see no reason why Epstein's theory of tort liability could not incorporate criminal liability into a single "system of corrective justice that looks to the conduct, broadly defined, of the parties to the case with a view toward the protection of individual liberty and private property."

There would, at least initially, be some differences, however. The calculation of damages under the restitutionary paradigm which includes cost of apprehension, cost of trial, and legal costs of both parties would be higher than tort law allows. A further distinction would be the power of enforcers to confine unreliable offenders to employment projects.[26]

2. Criminal responsibility and competency. Once a criminal sanction is based not on the offender's badness but on the nature and consequences of his acts, Thomas Szasz's proposal that the insanity plea be abolished makes a great deal of sense,[27] as does his argument that "all persons charged with offenses—except those grossly disabled—[are fit to stand trial and] should be tried."[28] On this view, Epstein's concept of fairness as *between the parties* is relevant. A restitution proceeding like a "lawsuit is always a comparative affair. The defendant's victory ensures the plaintiff's [or victim's] defeat. . . . Why should we prefer the injurer to his victim in a case where one may win and the other lose? . . . As a matter of fairness between the parties, the defendant

should be required to treat the harms which he has inflicted upon another as though they were inflicted upon himself."[29]

3. Victimless crimes. The effect of restitutional standards on the legality of such crimes as prostitution, gambling, high interest loans, pornography, and drug use is intriguing. There has been no violation of individual rights, and consequently no damages and, therefore, no liability. While some may see this as a drawback, I believe it is a striking advantage of the restitutional standard of justice. So-called victimless crimes would in principle cease to be crimes. As a consequence, criminal elements would be denied a lucrative monopoly, and the price of these services would be drastically reduced. Without this enormous income, organized crime would be far less able to afford the "cost" of its nefarious activities than it is today.

4. Legal positivism. What is true for victimless crimes is true for the philosophy of legal positivism. On the positivist view, whatever the state (following all the correct political procedures) says is law, is law; hence, whatever the state makes a crime is a crime. A restitutional standard would hold the state to enforcing individual rights through the recovery of individual damages.

5. Legal process. Because the sanction for crime would no longer be punitive, the criminal process could explore less formal procedures for dispute settlement. Also, the voice of the victim would be added to the deliberations. One possible reform might be a three-tiered verdict: guilty, not proven, and not guilty. If found "guilty," the offender would pay all the costs mentioned above. If the charges are "not proven," then neither party would pay the other. If found "not guilty," the defendant would be reimbursed by the enforcement agency for his costs and inconvenience. This new interpretation of "not guilty" would reward those defendants who, after putting on a defense, convinced the trier that they were innocent.

These and many other fascinating implications of restitution deserve a more thorough examination. As any new paradigm becomes accepted, it experiences what Kuhn calls a period of "normal research," a period characterized by continuous expansion and perfection of the new paradigm as well as a testing of its limits. The experimentation with restitutionary justice will, however, differ from the trial and error of the recent past

since we will be guided by the principle that the purpose of our legal system is not to harm the guilty but to help the innocent — a principle which will above all restore our belief that our overriding commitment is to do justice.*

NOTES

1. Gerhard O. W. Mueller, "Compensation for Victims of Crime: Thought before Action," *Minnesota Law Review* 50 (1965): 221.

2. Schafer, p. 127.

3. Ibid.

4. Herbert Spencer, "Prison-Ethics," in *Essays: Scientific, Political and Speculative* (New York: D. Appleton & Co., 1907), 3:152–91.

5. Murray N. Rothbard, *Libertarian Forum* 14, no. 1 (January 1972): 7–8.

6. Kaufmann, p. 55.

7. The nature of judicial procedure best designed to carry out this task must be determined. For a brief discussion of some relevant considerations, see Laster, pp. 80–98; Burt Galaway and Joe Hudson, "Issues in the Correctional Implementation of Restitution to Victims of Crime," in *Considering the Victim*, pp. 351–60. Also to be dealt with is the proper standard of compensation. At least initially, the problem of how much payment constitutes restitution would be no different than similar considerations in tort law. This will be considered at greater length below.

8. Such a plan (with some significant differences) has been suggested by Kathleen J. Smith in *A Cure for Crime: The Case for the Self-determinate Prison Sentence* (London: Gerald, Duckworth & Co., 1965), pp. 13–29; see also Morris and Linda Tannehill, *The Market for Liberty* (Lansing, Mich.: Privately printed, 1970), pp. 44–108.

9. For a recent summary report, see Burt Galaway, "Restitution as an Integrative Punishment," in Barnett and Hagel, *Assessing the Criminal*, pp. 331–347.

10. John M. Greacen, "Arbitration: A Tool for Criminal Cases?" *Barrister* (Winter 1975), p. 53; see also Galaway and Hudson, pp. 352–55; "Conclusions and Recommendations, International Study Institute on Vic-

---

*The ideas presented in this selection are developed further in Randy E. Barnett, "Pursuing Justice in a Free Society: Part One — Power vs. Liberty," *Criminal Justice Ethics,* Summer/Fall 1985, at 50; Randy E. Barnett, "Pursuing Justice in a Free Society: Part Two — Crime Prevention and the Legal Order," *Criminal Justice Ethics,* Winter/Spring 1986, at 30; and Randy E. Barnett, "The Justice of Restitution," *American Journal of Jurisprudence* 25 (1980), at 117.

timology, Bellagio, Italy, July 1–12, 1975," *Victimology* 1 (1976): 150–51; Ronald Goldfarb, *Jails: The Ultimate Ghetto* (Garden City, N.Y.: Anchor Press/Doubleday, 1976), p. 480.

11. Greacen, p. 53.

12. For a description of the Irish system, see Joseph R. Peden, "Property Rights in Medieval Ireland: Celtic Law versus Church and State," *Journal of Libertarian Studies* 1 (1976):86.

13. Or, perhaps more accurately, the compensation itself.

14. For a brief explanation of this concept and several of its possible applications, see Murray N. Rothbard, "Justice and Property Rights," in *Property in a Humane Economy*, ed. Samuel L. Blumenfeld (La Salle, Ill.: Open Court Publishing Co., 1974), pp. 101–22.

15. That the "spiritual" satisfaction which punishment may or may not provide is to be recognized as a legitimate form of "compensation" is a claim retributionists must defend.

16. Albert Eglash, "Creative Restitution: Some Suggestions for Prison Rehabilitation Programs," *American Journal of Correction* 40 (November–December 1958): 20.

17. Ibid.; see also Eglash's "Creative Restitution: A Broader Meaning for an Old Term," *Journal of Criminal Law and Criminology* 48 (1958): 619–22; Burt Galaway and Joe Hudson, "Restitution and Rehabilitation—Some Central Issues," *Crime and Delinquency* 18 (1972): 403–10.

18. Smith, pp. 13–29.

19. An economist who favors restitution on efficiency grounds is Gary S. Becker, although he does not break with the paradigm of punishment. Those interested in a mathematical "cost-benefit" analysis should see his "Crime and Punishment," *Journal of Political Economy* 76 (1968): 169–217.

20. This point is also made by Minocher Jehangirji Sethna in his paper, "Treatment and Atonement for Crime," in *Victims and Society*, p. 538.

21. Del Vecchio, p. 198.

22. William F. McDonald, "Towards a Bicentennial Revolution in Criminal Justice: The Return of the Vic-

tim," *American Criminal Law Review* 13 (1976): 659; see also his paper "Notes on the Victim's Role in the Prosecutional and Dispositional Stages of the Criminal Justice Process" (paper presented at the Second International Symposium on Victimology, Boston, September 1976); Jack M. Kress, "The Role of the Victim at Sentencing" (paper presented at the Second International Symposium on Victimology, Boston, September 1976).

23. McDonald, pp. 669–73; Kress, pp. 11–15. Kress specifically analyzes restitution as a means for achieving victim involvement.

24. Richard A. Epstein, "A Theory of Strict Liability in Tort," *Journal of Legal Studies* 2 (1973): 151–204.

25. Richard A. Epstein, "Intentional Harms," *Journal of Legal Studies* 3 (1975): 402–8; see also his article "Defenses and Subsequent Pleas in a System of Strict Liability," ibid., 3 (1974): 174–85.

26. It would seem that the only way to account for these differences would be an appeal to the *mens rea* or badness of the criminal as opposed to the unintentional tortfeasor. Yet such an approach, it might be argued, is not available to a restitutionary system which considers the moral outlook of an offender to be irrelevant to the determination of the proper criminal sanction. A possible response is that this overstates the restitutionist claim. That a criminal's mental state does not justify punishment does not imply that it is not relevant to *any* aspect of the criminal justice process. It may well be that it is relevant to the consideration of methods by which one is justified in extracting what, on other grounds, is shown to be a proper sanction, that is, restitution.

27. Szasz, pp. 228–30.

28. Ibid., pp. 228–29. "The emphasis here is on gross disability: it should be readily apparent or easily explicable to a group of lay persons, like a jury" (p. 229). But even the qualification of gross disablement might be unjustified (see Yochelson and Samenow, pp. 227–35).

29. Epstein, p. 398. In his article "Crime and Tort: Old Wine in Old Bottles," he takes exactly this approach with the insanity defense in tort law.

Ideas for Class Projects, Papers, or Debates

1. Evaluate and attack or defend the Model Penal Code position on (a) prostitution or (b) pornography. (See the selection by Louis B. Schwartz in Section 1.)

2. In 1989 the U.S. Supreme Court in a 5 to 4 ruling struck down a Texas law prohibiting the desecration of the flag. This ruling triggered both a rash of flag burnings and a storm of protest. Many states introduced laws outlawing flag desecration. The Kentucky legislature, for example, recently proposed a bill that would make flag desecration a Class D felony, punishable by up to five years in prison and a fine of up to $10,000. One would expect that such laws would be

declared unconstitutional if they are ever used and challenged. Thus, resolutions have also been advanced in the U.S. Congress to institute a constitutional amendment allowing such laws to stand. Suppose such an amendment were passed. Defend or oppose the Kentucky bill against flag desecration, explaining the principles that justify your position.

3. In recent years the criminal use of automatic assault weapons has caused great concern for police and citizens alike. Many people have called for a ban on the possession and/or sale of such weapons, but opponents argue that such restrictions erode the constitutional right to bear arms. Argue for or against a law banning the sale or possession of automatic assault weapons.

4. Alternatively, consider the regulation of firearms in terms of the following proposal by former Chief Justice Warren Burger: (a) To acquire a firearm, application must be made reciting age, residence, employment, and prior criminal convictions. (b) There will be a ten-day waiting period between application and licensure. (c) Transfer of firearms will be made in the same way as transfer of automobiles. (d) Every firearm will have a "ballistic fingerprint" filed with the license so that bullets can be traced.

5. You are a legislator. Making sure to anticipate and respond to objections of opponents, prepare a statement for or against the following proposal. (You may wish to qualify or refine the proposal.) The criminal code of the state of X shall be amended to eliminate the criminal offense of (a) sodomy, (b) polygamy, (c) prostitution, or (d) drug possession.

6. Argue for or against the recognition of the insanity defense in the criminal law. (Refer to the articles by Brandt, Hall, and Friedman in Section 2.)

7. In terms of the categories set out by Packer in Section 2, argue for or against the recognition of strict liability in the criminal law.

Cases on Capital Punishment

Furman v. *Georgia*
408 U.S. 238 (1972)*

Per Curiam

. . . Certiorari was granted limited to the following question: "Does the imposition and carrying out of the death penalty in [these cases] constitute cruel and unusual punishment in violation of the Eight and Fourteenth Amendments?" 403 U.S. 952 (1971). The Court holds that the imposition and carrying out of the death penalty in these cases constitute cruel and unusual punishment in violation of the Eighth and Fourteenth Amendments. The judgment in each case is therefore reversed insofar as it leaves undisturbed the death sentence imposed, and the cases are remanded for further proceedings.

So ordered.

Mr. Justice Douglas, Mr. Justice Brennan, Mr. Justice Stewart, Mr. Justice White, and Mr. Justice Marshall have filed separate opinions in support of the judgments. The Chief Justice, Mr. Justice Blackmun, Mr. Justice Powell, and Mr. Justice Rehnquist have filed separate dissenting opinions.

Mr. Justice Douglas, concurring.

In these three cases the death penalty was imposed, one of them for murder, and two for

---

*Excerpts only. Footnote numbered as in the original. Two cases from Georgia and one from Texas were considered and decided together by the Supreme Court.

rape. In each the determination of whether the penalty should be death or a lighter punishment was left by the State to the discretion of the judge or of the jury. In each of the three cases the trial was to a jury. They are here on petitions for certiorari which we granted limited to the question whether the imposition and execution of the death penalty constitutes "cruel and unusual punishment" within the meaning of the Eighth Amendment as applied to the States by the Fourteenth. I vote to vacate each judgment, believing that the exaction of the death penalty does violate the Eighth and Fourteenth Amendments.

. . . We cannot say from facts disclosed in these records that these defendants were sentenced to death because they were black. Yet our task is not restricted to an effort to divine what motives impelled these death penalties. Rather, we deal with a system of law and of justice that leaves to the uncontrolled discretion of judges or juries the determination whether defendants committing these crimes should die or be imprisoned. Under these laws no standards govern the selection of the penalty. People live or die, dependent on the whim of one man or of 12.

. . . In a Nation committed to equal protection of the laws there is no permissible "caste" aspect of law enforcement. Yet we know that the discretion of judges and juries in imposing the death penalty enables the penalty to be selectively applied, feeding prejudices against the accused if he is poor and despised, and lacking political clout, or if he is a member of a suspect or unpopular minority, and saving those who by social position may be in a more protected position. In ancient Hindu law a Brahman was exempt from capital punishment, and in those days, "[g]enerally, in the law books, punishment increased in severity as social status diminished." We have, I fear, taken in practice the same position, partially as a result of making the death penalty discretionary and partially as a result of the ability of the rich to purchase the services of the most respected and most resourceful legal talent in the Nation.

The high service rendered by the "cruel and unusual" punishment clause of the Eighth Amendment is to require legislatures to write penal laws that are evenhanded, nonselective, and nonarbitrary, and to require judges to see to it that general laws are not applied sparsely, selectively, and spottily to unpopular groups.

A law that stated that anyone making more than $50,000 would be exempt from the death penalty would plainly fall, as would a law that in terms said that blacks, those who never went beyond the fifth grade in school, those who made less than $3,000 a year, or those who were unpopular or unstable should be the only people executed. A law which in the overall view reaches that result in practice has no more sanctity than a law which in terms provides the same.

Thus, these discretionary statutes are unconstitutional in their operation. They are pregnant with discrimination and discrimination is an ingredient not compatible with the idea of equal protection of the laws that is implicit in the ban on "cruel and unusual" punishment.

Any law which is nondiscriminatory on its face may be applied in such a way as to violate the Equal Protection Clause of the Fourteenth Amendment. *Yick Wo* v. *Hopkins*, 118 U.S. 356. Such conceivably might be the fate of a mandatory death penalty, where equal or lesser sentences were imposed on the elite, a harsher one on the minorities or members of the lower castes. Whether a mandatory death penalty would otherwise be constitutional is a question I do not reach.

I concur in the judgments of the Court.

Mr. Justice Brennan, concurring.

. . . There are, then, four principles by which we may determine whether a particular punishment is "cruel and unusual." The primary principle, which I believe supplies the essential predicate for the application of the others, is that a punishment must not by its severity be degrading to human dignity. The paradigm violation of this principle would be the infliction of a torturous punishment of the type that the Clause has always prohibited. Yet "[i]t is unlikely that any State at this moment in history," *Robinson* v. *California*, 370 U.S., at 666, would pass a law providing for the infliction of such a punishment. Indeed, no such punishment has ever been before this Court. The same may be said of the other principles. It is unlikely that this Court will confront a severe punishment that is obviously inflicted in wholly arbitrary fashion; no State would engage in a reign of blind terror. Nor is it likely that this Court will be called upon to review a severe punishment that is clearly and totally rejected throughout society; no legislature would be able even to authorize the infliction of such a punishment. Nor, finally, is it likely that this Court will have to consider a severe punishment that is patently unnecessary; no State today would inflict a severe punishment knowing that there was no reason whatever for doing so. In short, we are unlikely to have occasion to determine that a punishment is fatally offensive under any one principle.

Since the Bill of Rights was adopted, this Court has adjudged only three punishments to be within the prohibition of the Clause. See *Weems* v. *United States*, 217 U.S. 349 (1910) (12 years in chains at hard and painful labor); *Trop* v. *Dulles*, 356 U.S. 86 (1958) (expatriation); *Robinson* v. *California*, 370 U.S. 660 (1962) (imprisonment for narcotics addiction). Each punishment, of course, was degrading to human dignity, but of none could it be said conclusively that it was fatally offensive under one or the other of the principles. Rather, these "cruel and unusual punishments" seriously implicated several of the principles, and it was the application of the principles in combination that supported the judgment. That, indeed, is not surprising. The function of these principles, after all, is simply to provide means by which a court can determine whether a challenged punishment comports with human dignity. They are, therefore, interrelated, and in most cases it will be their convergence that will justify the conclusion that a punishment is "cruel and unusual." The test, then, will ordinarily be a cumulative one: If a punishment is unusually severe, if there is a strong probability that it is inflicted arbitrarily, if it is substantially rejected by contemporary society, and if there is no reason to believe that it serves any penal purpose more effectively than some less severe punishment, then the continued infliction of that punishment violates the command of the Clause that the State may not inflict inhuman and uncivilized punishments upon those convicted of crimes.

. . . The question, then, is whether the deliberate infliction of death is today consistent with the command of the Clause that the State may not inflict punishments that do not comport with human dignity. I will analyze the punishment of death in terms of the principles set out above and the cumulative test to which they lead: It is a denial of human dignity for the State arbitrarily to subject a person to an unusually severe punishment that society has indicated it does not

regard as acceptable, and that cannot be shown to serve any penal purpose more effectively than a significantly less drastic punishment. Under these principles and this test, death is today a "cruel and unusual" punishment.

Death is a unique punishment in the United States. In a society that so strongly affirms the sanctity of life, not surprisingly the common view is that death is the ultimate sanction. This natural human feeling appears all about us. There has been no national debate about punishment, in general or by imprisonment, comparable to the debate about the punishment of death. No other punishment has been so continuously restricted, nor has any State yet abolished prisons, as some have abolished this punishment. And those States that still inflict death reserve it for the most heinous crimes. Juries, of course, have always treated death cases differently, as have governors exercising their communication powers. Criminal defendants are of the same view. "As all practicing lawyers know, who have defended persons charged with capital offenses, often the only goal possible is to avoid the death penalty." *Griffin* v. *Illinois*, 351 U.S. 12, 28 (1956) (Burton and Minton, JJ., dissenting). Some legislatures have required particular procedures, such as two-stage trials and automatic appeals, applicable only in death cases. "It is the universal experience in the administration of criminal justice that those charged with capital offenses are granted special considerations." *Ibid.* See *Williams* v. *Florida*, 399 U.S. 78, 103 (1970) (all States require juries of 12 in death cases). This Court, too, almost always treats death cases as a class apart. And the unfortunate effect of this punishment upon the functioning of the judicial process is well known; no other punishment has a similar effect.

The only explanation for the uniqueness of death is its extreme severity. Death is today an unusually severe punishment, unusual in its pain, in its finality, and in its enormity. No other existing punishment is comparable to death in terms of physical and mental suffering. Although our information is not conclusive, it appears that there is no method available that guarantees an immediate and painless death. Since the discontinuance of flogging as a constitutionally permissible punishment, *Jackson* v. *Bishop*, 404 F. 2d 571 (CA8 1968), death remains as the only punishment that may involve the conscious infliction of physical pain. In addition, we know that mental pain is an inseparable part of our practice of punishing criminals by death for the prospect of pending execution exacts a frightful toll during the inevitable long wait between the imposition of sentence and the actual infliction of death. Cf *Ex parte Medley*, 134 U.S. 160, 172 (1890). As the California Supreme Court pointed out, "the process of carrying out a verdict of death is often so degrading and brutalizing to the human spirit as to constitute psychological torture." *People* v. *Anderson*, 6 Cal. 3d 628, 649, 493 P. 2d 880, 894 (1972). Indeed, as Mr. Justice Frankfurter noted, "the onset of insanity while awaiting execution of a death sentence is not a rare phenomenon." *Solesbee* v. *Balkcom*, 339 U.S. 9, 14 (1950) (dissenting opinion). The "fate of ever-increasing fear and distress" to which the expatriate is subjected, *Trop* v. *Dulles*, 356 U.S., at 102, can only exist to a greater degree for a person confined in prison awaiting death.

The unusual severity of death is manifested most clearly in its finality and enormity. Death, in these respects, is in a class by itself. Expatriation, for example, is a punishment that "destroys for the individual the political existence that was centuries in the development," that "strips the citizen of his status in the national and international political community," and that puts "[h]is very existence" in jeopardy. Expatriation thus inherently entails "the total destruction of the individual's status in organized society." *Id.*, at 101. "In short, the expatriate has lost the right to have rights." *Id.*, at 102. Yet, demonstrably, expatriation is not "a fate worse than death." *Id.*, at 125 (Frankfurter, J., dissenting). Although death, like expatriation, destroys the individual's "political existence" and his "status in organized society," it does more, for, unlike expatriation, death also destroys "[h]is very existence." There is, too at least the possibility that the expatriate will in the future regain "the right to have rights." Death forecloses even that possibility.

Death is truly an awesome punishment. The calculated killing of a human being by the State involves, by its very nature, a denial of the executed person's humanity. The contrast with the plight of a person punished by imprisonment is evident. An individual in prison does not lose "the right to have rights." A prisoner retains, for example, the constitutional rights to the free exercise of religion, to be free of cruel and unusual punishments, and to treatment as a "person" for purposes of due process of law and the equal protection of the laws. A prisoner remains a member of the human family. Moreover, he retains the right of access to the courts. His punishment is not irrevocable. Apart from the common charge, grounded upon the recognition of human fallibility, that the punishment of death must inevitably be inflicted upon innocent men, we know that death has been the lot of men whose convictions were unconstitutionally secured in view of later, retroactively applied, holdings of this Court. The punishment itself may have been unconstitutionally inflicted, see *Witherspoon* v. *Illinois*, 391 U.S. 510 (1968), yet the finality of death precludes relief. An executed person has indeed "lost the right to have rights." As one 19th century proponent of punishing criminals by death declared, "When a man is hung, there is an end of our relations with him. His execution is a way of saying, 'You are not fit for this world, take your chance elsewhere.'"

In comparison to all other punishments today, then, the deliberate extinguishment of human life by the State is uniquely degrading to human dignity. I would not hesitate to hold, on that ground alone, that death is today a "cruel and unusual" punishment, were it not that death is a punishment of longstanding usage and acceptance in this country. I therefore turn to the second principle—that the State may not arbitrarily inflict an unusually severe punishment.

. . . When the punishment of death is inflicted in a trivial number of the cases in which it is legally available, the conclusion is virtually inescapable that it is being inflicted arbitrarily. Indeed, it smacks of little more than a lottery system. The States claim, however, that this rarity is evidence not of arbitrariness, but of informed selectivity: Death is inflicted, they say, only in "extreme" cases.

Informed selectivity, of course, is a value not to be denigrated. Yet presumably the States could make precisely the same claim if there were 10 executions per year, or five, or even if there were but one. That there may be as many as 50 per year does not strengthen the claim. When the rate of infliction is at this low level, it is highly implausible that only the worst criminals or the criminals who commit the worst crimes are selected for this punishment. No one has yet suggested a rational basis that could differentiate in those terms the few who die from the many who go to prison. Crimes and criminals simply do not admit of a distinction that can be drawn so finely as to explain, on that ground, the execution of such a tiny sample of those eligible. Certainly the laws that provide for this punishment do not attempt to draw that distinction; all cases to which the laws apply are necessarily "extreme." Nor is the distinction credible in fact. If, for example, petitioner Furman or his crime illustrates the "extreme," then nearly all murderers and their murders are also "extreme."[48] Furthermore, our procedures in death cases, rather than resulting in the selection of "extreme" cases for this punishment, actually sanction an arbitrary selection. For this Court has held that juries may, as they do, make the decision whether to impose a death sentence wholly unguided by standards governing that decision. *McGautha* v. *California*, 402 U.S. 183, 196–208 (1971). In other words, our procedures are not constructed to guard against the totally capricious selection of criminals for the punishment of death.

Although it is difficult to imagine what further facts would be necessary in order to prove that death is, as my Brother Stewart puts it, "wantonly and . . . freakishly" inflicted, I need not conclude that arbitrary infliction is patently obvious. I am not considering this punishment by the isolated light of one principle. The probability of arbitrariness is sufficiently substantial that it can be relied upon, in combination with the other principles, in reaching a judgment on the constitutionality of this punishment.

When there is a strong probability that an unusually severe and degrading punishment is being inflicted arbitrarily, we may well expect that society will disapprove of its infliction. I turn, therefore, to the third principle. An examination of the history and present operation of the American practice of punishing criminals by death reveals that this punishment has been almost totally rejected by contemporary society. . . . The progressive decline in, and the current rarity of, the infliction of death demonstrate that our society seriously questions the appropriateness of this punishment today. The States point out that many legislatures authorize death as the punishment for certain crimes and that substantial segments of the public, as reflected in opinion polls and referendum votes, continue to support it. Yet the availability of this punishment through statutory authorization, as well as the polls and referenda, which amount simply to approval of that authorization, simply underscores the extent to which our society has in fact rejected this punishment. When an unusually severe punishment is authorized for wide-scale application but not, because of society's refusal, inflicted save in a few instances, the inference is compelling that there is a deep-seated reluctance to inflict it. Indeed, the likelihood is great that the punishment is tolerated only because of its disuse. The objective indicator of society's view of an unusually severe punishment is what society does with it, and today society will inflict death upon only a small sample of the eligible criminals. Rejection could hardly be more complete without becoming absolute. At the very least, I must conclude that contemporary society views this punishment with substantial doubt.

The final principle to be considered is that an unusually severe and degrading punishment may not be excessive in view of the purposes for which it is inflicted. This principle, too, is related to the others. When there is a strong probability that the State is arbitrarily inflicting an unusually severe punishment that is subject to grave societal doubts, it is likely also that the punishment cannot be shown to be serving any penal purpose that could not be served equally well by some less severe punishment.

The States' primary claim is that death is a necessary punishment because it prevents the commission of capital crimes more effectively than any less severe punishment. The first part of this claim is that the infliction of death is necessary to stop the individuals executed from committing further crimes. The sufficient answer to this is that if a criminal convicted of a capital crime poses a danger to society, effective administration of the State's pardon and parole laws can delay or deny his release from prison, and techniques of isolation can eliminate or minimize the danger while he remains confined.

The more significant argument is that the threat of death prevents the commission of capital crimes because it deters potential criminals who would not be deterred by the threat of imprisonment. The argument is not based upon evidence that the threat of death is a superior deterrent. Indeed, as my Brother Marshall establishes, the available evidence uniformly indicates, although it does not conclusively prove, that the threat of death has no greater deterrent effect than the threat of imprisonment. The States argue, however, that they are entitled to rely upon common human experience, and that experience, they say, supports the conclusion that death must be a more effective deterrent than any less severe punishment. Because people fear death the most, the argument runs, the threat of death must be the greatest deterrent.

It is important to focus upon the precise import of this argument. It is not denied that many, and probably most, capital crimes cannot be deterred by the threat of punishment. Thus the argument can apply only to those who think rationally about the commission of capital crimes. Particularly is that true when the potential criminal, under this argument, must not only consider the risk of punishment, but also distinguish between two possible punishments. The concern, then, is with a particular type of potential criminal, the rational person who will commit a capital crime knowing that the punishment is long-term imprisonment, which may well be for the rest of his life, but will not commit the crime knowing that the punishment is death. On the face of it, the assumption that such persons exist is implausible.

In any event, this argument cannot be appraised in the abstract. We are not presented with the theoretical question whether under any imaginable circumstances the threat of death might be a greater deterrent to the commission of capital crimes than the threat of imprisonment. We are concerned with the practice of punishing criminals by death as it exists in the United States today. Proponents of this argument necessarily admit that its validity depends upon the existence of a system in which the punishment of death is invariably and swiftly imposed. Our system, of course, satisfies neither condition. A rational person contemplating a murder or rape is confronted, not with the certainty of a speedy death, but with the slightest possibility that he will be executed in the distant future. The risk of death is remote and improbable; in contrast, the risk of long-term imprisonment is near and great. In short, whatever the

speculative validity of the assumption that the threat of death is a superior deterrent, there is no reason to believe that as currently administered the punishment of death is necessary to deter the commission of capital crimes. Whatever might be the case were all or substantially all eligible criminals quickly put to death, unverifiable possibilities are an insufficient basis upon which to conclude that the threat of death today has any greater deterrent efficacy than the threat of imprisonment.

There is, however, another aspect to the argument that the punishment of death is necessary for the protection of society. The infliction of death, the States urge, serves to manifest the community's outrage at the commission of the crime. It is, they say, a concrete public expression of moral indignation that inculcates respect for the law and helps assure a more peaceful community. Moreover, we are told, not only does the punishment of death exert this widespread moralizing influence upon community values, it also satisfies the popular demand for grievous condemnation of abhorrent crimes and thus prevents disorder, lynching, and attempts by private citizens to take the law into their own hands.

The question, however, is not whether death serves these supposed purposes of punishment, but whether death serves them more effectively than imprisonment. There is no evidence whatever that utilization of imprisonment rather than death encourages private blood feuds and other disorders. Surely if there were such a danger, the execution of a handful of criminals each year would not prevent it. The assertion that death alone is a sufficiently emphatic denunciation for capital crimes suffers from the same defect. If capital crimes require the punishment of death in order to provide moral reinforcement for the basic values of the community, those values can only be undermined when death is so rarely inflicted upon the criminals who commit the crimes. Furthermore, it is certainly doubtful that the infliction of death by the State does in fact strengthen the community's moral code; if the deliberate extinguishment of human life has any effect at all, it more likely tends to lower our respect for life and brutalize our values. That, after all, is why we no longer carry out public executions. In any event, this claim simply means that one purpose of punishment is to indicate social disapproval of crime. To serve that purpose our laws distribute punishments according to the gravity of crimes and punish more severely the crimes society regards as more serious. That purpose cannot justify any particular punishment as the upper limit of severity.

Mr. Justice White, concurring.

. . . Most important, a major goal of the criminal law — to deter others by punishing the convicted criminal — would not be substantially served where the penalty is so seldom invoked that it ceases to be the credible threat essential to influence the conduct of others. For present purposes I accept the morality and utility of punishing one person to influence another. I accept also the effectiveness of punishment generally and need not reject the death penalty as a more effective deterrent than a lesser punishment. But common sense and experience tell us that seldom-enforced laws become ineffective measures for controlling human conduct and that the death penalty, unless imposed with sufficient frequency, will make little contribution to deterring those crimes for which it may be exacted.

The imposition and execution of the death penalty are obviously cruel in the dictionary sense. But the penalty has not been considered cruel and unusual punishment in the constitutional sense because it was thought justified by the social ends it was deemed to serve. At the moment that it ceases realistically to further these purposes, however, the emerging question is whether its imposition in such circumstances would violate the Eighth Amendment. It is my view that it would, for its imposition would then be the pointless and needless extinction of life with only marginal contributions to any discernible social or public purposes. A penalty with such negligible returns to the State would be patently excessive and cruel and unusual punishment violative of the Eighth Amendment.

It is also my judgment that this point has been reached with respect to capital punishment as it is presently administered under the statutes involved in these cases. Concededly, it is difficult to prove as a general proposition that capital punishment, however administered, more effectively serves the ends of the criminal law than does imprisonment. But however that may be, I cannot avoid the conclusion that as the statutes before us are now administered, the penalty is so infrequently imposed that the threat of execution is too attenuated to be of substantial service to criminal justice.

I need not restate the facts and figures that appear in the opinions of my Brethren. Nor can I "prove" my conclusion from these data. But, like my Brethren, I must arrive at judgment; and I can do no more than state a conclusion based on 10 years of almost daily exposure to the facts and circumstances of hundreds and hundreds of federal and state criminal cases involving crimes for which death is the authorized penalty. That conclusion, as I have said, is that the death penalty is exacted with great infrequency even for the most atrocious crimes and that there is no meaningful basis for distinguishing the few cases in which it is imposed from the many cases in which it is not. The short of it is that the policy of vesting sentencing authority primarily in juries — a decision largely motivated by the desire to mitigate the harshness of the law and to bring community judgment to bear on the sentence as well as guilt or innocence — has so effectively achieved its aims that capital punishment within the confines of the statutes now before us has for all practical purposes run its course.

Mr. Chief Justice Burger, with whom Mr. Justice Blackmun, Mr. Justice Powell, and Mr. Justice Rehnquist join, dissenting.

. . . There are no obvious indications that capital punishment offends the conscience of society to such a degree that our traditional deference to the legislative judgment must be abandoned. It is not a punishment such as burning at the stake that everyone would ineffably find to be repugnant to all civilized standards. Nor is it a punishment so roundly condemned that only a few aberrant legislatures have retained it on the statute books. Capital punishment is authorized by statute in 40 States, the District of Columbia, and in the federal courts for the commission of certain crimes. On four occasions in the last 11 years Congress has added to the list of federal crimes punishable by death. In looking for reliable indicia of contemporary attitude, none more trustworthy has been advanced.

One conceivable source of evidence that legislatures have abdicated their essentially barometric role with respect to community values would be public opinion polls, of which there have been many in the past decade addressed to the question of capital punishment. Without assessing the reliability of such polls, or intimating that any judicial reliance could ever be placed on them, it need only be noted that the reported results have shown nothing approximating the universal condemnation of capital punishment that might lead us to suspect that the legislatures in general have lost touch with current social values.

Counsel for petitioners rely on a different body of empirical evidence. They argue, in effect, that the number of cases in which the death penalty is imposed, as compared with the number of cases in which it is statutorily available, reflects a general revulsion toward the penalty that would lead to its repeal if only it were more generally and widely enforced. It cannot be gainsaid that by the choice of juries — and sometimes judges — the death penalty is imposed in far fewer than half the cases in which it is available. To go further and characterize the rate of imposition as "freakishly rare," as petitioners insist, is unwarranted hyperbole. And regardless of its characterization, the rate of imposition does not impel the conclusion that capital punishment is now regarded as intolerably cruel or uncivilized.

It is argued that in those capital cases where juries have recommended mercy, they have given expression to civilized values and effectively renounced the legislative authorization for capital punishment. At the same time it is argued that where juries have made the awesome decision to send men to their deaths, they have acted arbitrarily and without sensitivity to prevailing standards of decency. This explanation for the infrequency of imposition of capital punishment is unsupported by known facts, and is inconsistent in principle with everything this Court has ever said about the functioning of juries in capital cases.

In *McGautha* v. *California*, decided only one year ago, the Court held that there was no mandate in the Due Process Clause of the Fourteenth Amendment that juries be given instructions as to when the death penalty should be imposed. After reviewing the autonomy that juries have traditionally exercised in capital cases and noting the practical difficulties of framing manageable instructions, this Court concluded that judicially articulated standards were not needed to insure a responsible decision as to penalty. Nothing in *McGautha* licenses capital juries to act arbitrarily or assumes that they have so acted in the past.

On the contrary, the assumption underlying the *McGautha* ruling is that juries "will act with due regard for the consequences of their decision." 402 U.S., at 208.

The responsibility of juries deciding capital cases in our system of justice was nowhere better described than in *Witherspoon* v. *Illinois, supra*:

"[A] jury that must choose between life imprisonment and capital punishment can do little more — and must do nothing less — than express *the conscience of the community* on the ultimate question of life or death."

"And one of the most important functions any jury can perform in making such a selection is to maintain a link between contemporary community values and the penal system — a link without which the determination of punishment could hardly reflect 'the evolving standards of decency that mark the progress of a maturing society'" 391 U.S., at 519 and n. 15 (emphasis added).

The selectivity of juries in imposing the punishment of death is properly viewed as a refinement on rather than a repudiation of, the statutory authorization for that penalty. Legislatures prescribe the categories of crimes for which the death penalty should be available, and, acting as "the conscience of the community," juries are entrusted to determine in individual cases that the ultimate punishment is warranted. Juries are undoubtedly influenced in this judgment by myriad factors. The motive or lack of motive of the perpetrator, the degree of injury or suffering of the victim or victims, and the degree of brutality in the commission of the crime would seem to be prominent among these factors. Given the general awareness that death is no longer a routine punishment for the crimes for which it is made available, it is hardly surprising that juries have been increasingly meticulous in their imposition of the penalty. But to assume from the mere fact of relative infrequency that only a random assortment of pariahs are sentenced to death, is to cast grave doubt on the basic integrity of our jury system.

It would, of course, be unrealistic to assume that juries have been perfectly consistent in choosing the cases where the death penalty is to be imposed, for no human institution performs with perfect consistency. There are doubtless prisoners on death row who would not be there had they been tried before a different jury or in a different State. In this sense their fate has been controlled by a fortuitous circumstance. However, this element of fortuity does not stand as an indictment either of the general functioning of juries in capital cases or of the integrity of jury decisions in individual cases. There is no empirical basis for concluding that juries have generally failed to discharge in good faith the responsibility described in *Witherspoon* — that of choosing between life and death in individual cases according to the dictates of community values.

. . . It seems remarkable to me that with our basic trust in lay jurors as the keystone in our system of criminal justice, it should now be suggested that we take the most sensitive and important of all decisions away from them. I could more easily be persuaded that mandatory sentences of death, without the intervening and ameliorating impact of lay jurors, are so arbitrary and doctrinaire that they violate the Constitution. The very infrequency of death penalties imposed by jurors attests their cautious and discriminating reservation of that penalty for the most extreme cases. I had thought that nothing was clearer in history, as we noted in *McGautha* one year ago, than the American abhorrence of "the common-law rule imposing a mandatory death sentence on all convicted murderers." 402 U.S., at 198. As the concurring opinion of Mr. Justice Marshall shows, *ante*, at 339, the 19th century movement away from mandatory death sentences marked an enlightened introduction of flexibility into the sentencing process. It recognized that individual culpability is not always measured by the category of the crime committed. This change in sentencing practice was greeted by the Court as a humanizing development. See *Winston* v. *United States*, 172 U.S. 303 (1899); cf. *Calton* v. *Utah*, 130 U.S. 83 (1889). See also *Andres* v. *United States*, 333 U.S. 740, 753 (1948) (Frankfurter, J., concurring). I do not see how this history can be ignored and how it can be suggested that the Eighth Amendment demands the elimination of the most sensitive feature of the sentencing system.

As a general matter, the evolution of penal concepts in this country has not been marked by great progress, nor have the results up to now been crowned with significant success. If anywhere in the whole spectrum of criminal justice fresh ideas deserve sober analysis, the sentencing and correctional area ranks high on the list. But it has been widely accepted that mandatory sentences for crimes do not best serve the ends of the criminal justice system. Now, after the long process of drawing away from the blind imposition of uniform sentences for every person convicted of a particular offense, we are confronted with an argument perhaps implying that only the legislatures may determine that a sentence of death is appropriate, without the intervening evaluation of jurors or judges. This approach threatens to turn back the progress of penal reform, which has moved until recently at too slow a rate to absorb significant setbacks.

NOTES

48. The victim surprised Furman in the act of burglarizing the victim's home in the middle of the night. While escaping, Furman killed the victim with one pistol shot fired through the closed kitchen door from the outside. At the trial, Furman gave his version of the killing:

> "They got me charged with murder and I admit, I admit going to these folks' home and they did caught me in there and I was coming back out, backing up and there was a wire down there on the floor. I was coming out backwards and fell back and I didn't intend to kill nobody. I didn't know they was behind the door. The gun went off and I didn't know nothing about no murder until they arrested me, and when the gun went off I was down on the floor and I got up and ran. That's all to it." App. 54–55.

The Georgia Supreme Court accepted that version:

> "The admission in open court by the accused . . . that during the period in which he was involved in the commission of a criminal act at the home of the deceased, he accidentally tripped over a wire in leaving the premises causing the gun to go off, together with other facts and circumstances surrounding the death of the deceased by violent means, was sufficient to support the verdict of guilty of murder. . . ." *Furman* v. *State*, 225 Ga. 253, 254, 167 S. E. 2d 628, 629 (1969).

About Furman himself, the jury knew only that he was black and that, according to his statement at trial, he was 26 years old and worked at "Superior Upholstery." App. 54. It took the jury one hour and 35 minutes to return a verdict of guilt and a sentence of death. *Id.*, at 64–65.

Gregg v. *Georgia*
428 U.S. 153 (1976)

Mr. Justice Stewart, Mr. Justice Powell, *and* Mr. Justice Stevens *announced the judgment of the Court and filed an opinion delivered by* Mr. Justice Stewart.

The issue in this case is whether the imposition of the sentence of death for the crime of murder under the law of Georgia violates the Eighth and Fourteenth Amendments.

I

The petitioner, Troy Gregg, was charged with committing armed robbery and murder. In accordance with Georgia procedure in capital cases, the trial was in two stages, a guilt stage and a sentencing stage. The evidence at the guilt trial established that on November 21, 1973, the petitioner and a traveling companion, Floyd Allen, while hitchhiking north in Florida, were picked up by Fred Simmons and Bob Moore. Their car broke down, but they continued north after Simmons purchased another vehicle with some of the cash he was carrying. While still in Florida, they picked up another hitchhiker, Dennis Weaver, who rode with them to Atlanta, where he was let out about 11 P.M. A short time later the four men interrupted their journey for a rest stop along the highway. The next morning the bodies of Simmons and Moore were discovered in a ditch nearby.

On November 23, after reading about the shootings in an Atlanta newspaper, Weaver communicated with the Gwinnett County police and related information concerning the journey with the victims, including a description of the car. The next afternoon, the petitioner and Allen, while in Simmons' car, were arrested in Asheville, N.C. . . . After receiving the warnings required by *Miranda*, and signing a written waiver of his rights, the petitioner signed a statement in which he admitted shooting, then robbing, Simmons and Moore. He justified the slayings on grounds of self-defense. . . . [The next day Allen gave police his version of the events at the scene of the slayings.] At the subsequent trial, the jury found the petitioner guilty of two counts of armed robbery and two counts of murder.

At the penalty stage, which took place before the same jury, . . . the judge instructed the jury that it "would not be authorized to consider [imposing] the sentence of death" unless it first found beyond a reasonable doubt one of these aggravating circumstances:

> One — That the offense of murder was committed while the offender was engaged in the commission o[f] two other capit[a]l felonies, to-wit the armed ro[b]bery of [Simmons and Moore].
>
> Two — That the offender committed the offense of murder for the purpose of receiving money and the automobile described in the indictment.
>
> Three — The offense of murder was outrageously and wantonly vile, horrible and inhuman, in that they [sic] involved the depravity of the mind of the defendant.

Finding the first and second of these circumstances, the jury returned verdicts of death on each count.

The Supreme Court of Georgia affirmed the convictions and the imposition of the death sentences for murder. . . . The death sentences imposed for armed robbery, however, were vacated on the grounds that the death penalty had rarely been imposed in Georgia for that offense. . . .

We granted the petitioner's application for a writ of certiorari challenging the imposition of the death sentences in this case as "cruel and unusual" punishment in violation of the Eighth and the Fourteenth Amendments. . . .

II

Before considering the issues presented it is necessary to understand the Georgia statutory scheme for the imposition of the death penalty. The Georgia statute, as amended after our decision in *Furman* . . . retains the death penalty for six categories of crime: murder, kidnapping for ransom or where the victim is harmed, armed robbery, rape, treason, and aircraft hijacking. . . . The capital defendant's guilt or innocence is determined in the traditional manner, either by a trial judge or a jury, in the first stage of a bifurcated trial.

If trial is by jury, the trial judge is required to charge lesser included offenses when they are supported by any view of the evidence. . . . After a verdict, finding, or plea of guilty to a capital crime, a presentence hearing is conducted before whomever made the determination of guilt. The sentencing procedures are essentially the same in both bench and jury trials. At the hearing,

> . . . the judge (or jury) shall hear additional evidence in extenuation, mitigation, and aggravation of punishment, including the record of any prior criminal convictions and pleas of guilty or pleas of nolo contendere of the defendant, or the absence of any prior conviction and pleas: Provided however, that only such evidence in aggravation as the State has made known to the defendant prior to his trial shall be admissible. . . .

In the assessment of the appropriate sentence to be imposed the judge is also required to consider or to include in his instructions to the jury "any mitigating circumstances or aggravating circumstances otherwise authorized by law and any of (10) statutory aggravating circumstances which may be supported by the evidence. . . ." The scope of the nonstatutory aggravating or mitigating circumstances is not delineated in the statute. Before a convicted defendant may be sentenced to death, however, except in cases of treason or aircraft hijacking, the jury, or the trial judge in cases tried without a jury, must find beyond a reasonable doubt one of the 10 aggravating circumstances specified in the statute. . . . If the verdict is death the jury or judge must specify the aggravating circumstance(s) found. . . . In jury cases, the trial judge is bound by the jury's recommended sentence. . . .

In addition to the conventional appellate process available in all criminal cases, provision is made for special expedited direct review by the Supreme Court of Georgia of the appropriateness of imposing the sentence of death in the particular case. The court is directed to consider "the punishment as well as any errors enumerated by way of appeal," and to determine:

(1) Whether the sentence of death was imposed under the influence of passion, prejudice, or any other arbitrary factor, and

(2) Whether, in cases other than treason or aircraft hijacking, the evidence supports the jury's or judge's finding of a statutory aggravating circumstance as enumerated in section 27.2534.1 (b), and

(3) Whether the sentence of death is excessive or disproportionate to the penalty imposed in similar cases considering both the crime and the defendant.

If the court affirms a death sentence, it is required to include in its decision reference to similar cases that it has taken into consideration. . . .

III

We address initially the basic contention that the punishment of death for the crime of murder is, under all circumstances, "cruel and unusual" in violation of the Eighth and Fourteenth Amendments of the Constitution. In Part IV of this opinion, we will consider the sentence of death imposed under the Georgia statutes at issue in this case.

The Court on a number of occasions has both assumed and asserted the constitutionality of capital punishment. In several cases that assumption provided a necessary foundation for the decision, as the Court was asked to decide whether a particular method of carrying out a capital sentence would be allowed to stand under the Eighth Amendment. But until *Furman* v. *Georgia*, the Court never confronted squarely the fundamental claim that the punishment of death always, regardless of the enormity of the offense or the procedure followed in imposing the sentence, is cruel and unusual punishment in violation of the Constitution. Although this issue was presented and addressed in *Furman*, it was not resolved by the Court. Four Justices would have reached the opposite conclusion; and three Justices, while agreeing that the statutes then before the Court were invalid as applied, left open the question whether such punishment may ever be imposed. We now hold that the punishment of death does not invariably violate the Constitution.

The history of the prohibition of "cruel and unusual" punishment already has been reviewed by this Court at length. . . .

In the earliest cases raising Eighth Amendment claims, the Court focused on particular methods of execution to determine whether they were too cruel to pass constitutional muster. The constitutionality of the sentence of death itself was not at issue, and the criterion used to evaluate the mode of execution was its similarity to "torture" and other "barbarous" methods. . . .

But the Court has not confined the prohibition embodied in the Eighth Amendment to "barbarous" methods that were generally outlawed in the 18th century. Instead, the Amendment has been interpreted in a flexible and dynamic manner. The Court early recognized that "a principle to be vital must be capable of wider application than the mischief which gave it birth." *Weems* v. *United States*, 217 U.S. 349, 373 (1910). Thus the clause forbidding "cruel and unusual" punishments "is not fastened to the obsolete but may acquire meaning as public opinion becomes enlightened by a humane justice." *Id.*, at 378. . . .

It is clear that the Eighth Amendment has not been regarded as a static concept. As Chief Justice Warren said, in an oft-quoted phrase, "[t]he Amendment must draw its meaning from the evolving standards of decency that mark the progress of a maturing society." *Trop* v. *Dulles*, 356 U.S. at 101. . . . Thus, an assessment of contemporary values concerning the infliction of a challenged sanction is relevant to the application of the Eighth Amendment. . . . It requires, rather, that we look to objective indicia that reflect the public attitude toward a given sanction.

But our cases also make clear that public perceptions of standards of decency with respect to criminal sanctions are not conclusive. A penalty also must accord with "the dignity of man," which is the "basic concept underlying the Eighth Amendment." . . . This means, at least, that the punishment not be "excessive." When a form of punishment in the abstract . . . is under consideration, the inquiry into "excessiveness" has two aspects. First, the punishment must not involve the unnecessary and wanton infliction of pain. . . . Second, the punishment must not be grossly out of proportion to the severity of the crime. . . .

* * *

We now consider specifically whether the sentence of death for the crime of murder is a *per se* violation of the Eighth and Fourteenth Amendments to the Constitution. We note first that history and precedent strongly support a negative answer to this question.

1

The imposition of the death penalty for the crime of murder has a long history of acceptance both in the United States and in England. The common-law rule imposed a mandatory death sentence on all convicted murderers. . . . And the penalty continued to be used into the 20th century by most American States, although the breadth of the common-law rule was diminished, initially by narrowing the class of murders to be punished by death and subsequently by widespread adoption of laws expressly granting juries the discretion to recommend mercy. . . .

It is apparent from the text of the Constitution itself that the existence of capital punishment was accepted by the Framers. At the time the Eighth Amendment was ratified, capital punishment was a common sanction in every State. Indeed, the First Congress of the United States enacted legislation providing death as the penalty for specified crimes. . . . The Fifth Amendment, adopted at the same time as the Eighth, contemplated the continued existence of the capital sanction by imposing certain limits on the prosecution of capital cases. . . . And the Fourteenth Amendment, adopted over three-quarters of a century later, similarly contemplates the existence of the capital sanction in providing that no State shall deprive any person of "life, liberty, or property" without due process of law.

For nearly two centuries, this Court, repeatedly and often expressly, has recognized that capital punishment is not invalid per se. . . .

Four years ago, the petitioners in *Furman* and its companion cases predicated their argument primarily upon the asserted proposition that standards of decency had evolved to the point where capital punishment no longer could be tolerated. . . . This view was accepted by two Justices. Three other Justices were unwilling to go so far. . . .

The petitioners . . . before the Court today renew the "standards of decency" argument, but developments during the four years since *Furman* have undercut substantially the assumptions upon which their argument rested. Despite the continuing debate, dating back to the 19th century, over the morality and utility of capital punishment, it is now evident that a large proportion of American society continues to regard it as an appropriate and necessary criminal sanction.

The most marked indication of society's endorsement of the death penalty for murder is the legislative response to *Furman*. The legislatures of at least 35 States have enacted new statutes that provide for the death penalty for at least some crimes that result in the death of another person. And the Congress of the United States, in 1974, enacted a statute providing the death penalty for aircraft piracy that results in death. These recently adopted statutes have attempted to address the concerns expressed by the Court in *Furman*. . . . But all of the post-*Furman* statutes make clear that capital punishment itself has not been rejected by the elected representatives of the people. In the only statewide referendum occurring since *Furman* and brought to our attention, the people of California adopted a constitutional amendment that authorized capital punishment. . . .

The jury also is a significant and reliable objective index of contemporary values because it is so directly involved. . . . Indeed, the actions of juries in many States since *Furman* is fully compatible with the legislative judgments, reflected in the new statutes, as to the continued utility and necessity of capital punishment in appropriate cases. At the close of 1974 at least 254 persons had been sentenced to death since *Furman*, and by the end of March 1976, more than 460 persons were subject to death sentences. . . .

The death penalty is said to serve two principal social purposes: retribution and deterrence of capital crimes by prospective offenders.

In part, capital punishment is an expression of society's moral outrage at particularly offensive conduct. This function may be unappealing to many, but it is essential in an ordered society that asks its citizens to rely on legal processes rather than self-help to vindicate their wrongs. . . . "Retribution is no longer the dominant objective of the criminal law," *Williams* v. *New York*, 337 U.S. 241, 248 (1949), but neither is it a forbidden objective nor one inconsistent with our respect for the dignity of men. . . . Indeed, the decision that capital punishment may be the appropriate sanction in extreme cases is an expression of the community's belief that certain crimes are themselves so grievous an affront to humanity that the only adequate response may be the penalty of death.

Statistical attempts to evaluate the worth of the death penalty as a deterrent to crimes by potential offenders have occasioned a great deal of debate. The results simply have been inconclusive. . . .

Although some of the studies suggest that the death penalty may not function as a significantly greater deterrent than lesser penalties, there is no convincing empirical evidence either supporting or refuting this view. We may nevertheless assume safely that there are murderers, such as those who act in passion, for whom the threat of death has little or no deterrent effect. But for many others, the death penalty undoubtedly is a significant deterrent. . . .

The value of capital punishment as a deterrent of crime is a complex factual issue the resolution of which properly rests with the legislatures, which can evaluate the results of statistical studies in terms of their own local conditions and with a flexibility of approach that is not available to the court. . . .

In sum, we cannot say that the judgment of the Georgia legislature that capital punishment may be necessary in some cases is clearly wrong. Considerations of federalism, as well as respect for the ability of a legislature to evaluate, in terms of its particular state the moral consensus concerning the death penalty and its social utility as a sanction, require us to conclude, in the absence of more convincing evidence, that the infliction of death as a punishment for murder is not without justification and thus is not unconstitutionally severe.

Finally, we must consider whether the punishment of death is disproportionate in relation to the crime for which it is imposed. There is no question that death as a punishment is unique in its severity and irrevocability. . . . When a defendant's life is at stake, the Court has been particularly sensitive to insure that every safeguard is observed. . . . But we are concerned here only with the imposition of capital punishment for the crime of murder, and when a life has been taken deliberately by the offender, we cannot say that the punishment is invariably disproportionate to the crimes. . . .

IV

[Here the Court reviews the mandate of *Furman* on sentencing discretion.]

B

We now turn to consideration of the constitutionality of Georgia's capital-sentencing procedures. In the wake of *Furman*, Georgia amended its capital punishment statute, but chose not to narrow the scope of its murder provisions. . . .

These procedures require the jury to consider the circumstances of the crime and the criminal before it recommends sentence. No longer can a Georgia jury do as *Furman's* jury did: reach a finding of the defendant's guilt and then, without guidance or direction, decide whether he should live or die. . . .

. . . Georgia's new sentencing procedures require as a prerequisite to the imposition of the death penalty, specific jury findings as to the circumstances of the crime or the character of the defendant. Moreover to guard further against a situation comparable to that presented in *Furman*, the Supreme Court of Georgia compares each death sentence with the sentences imposed on similarly situated defendants to ensure that the sentence of death in a particular case is not disproportionate. On their face these procedures seem to satisfy the concerns of *Furman*. . . .

[The concurring opinion of Mr. Justice White with whom the Chief Justice and Mr. Justice Rehnquist joined is not reprinted here.]

Mr. Justice Brennan, *dissenting.*

In *Furman* v. *Georgia*, . . . I read "evolving standards of decency" as requiring focus upon the essence of the death penalty itself and not primarily or solely upon the procedures under which the determination to inflict the penalty upon a particular person was made. I there said:

> . . . At bottom, the battle has been waged on moral grounds. The country has debated whether a society for which the dignity of the individual is the supreme value can, without a fundamental inconsistency, follow the practice of deliberately putting some of its members to death. In the United States, as in other nations of the western world, the struggle about this punishment has been one between ancient and deeply rooted beliefs in retribution, atonement or vengeance on the one hand, and, on the other, beliefs in the personal value and dignity of the common man that were born of the democratic movement of the eighteenth century, as well as beliefs in the scientific approach to an understanding of the motive

> forces of human conduct, which are the result of the growth of the sciences of behavior during the nineteenth and twentieth centuries. It is this essentially moral conflict that forms the backdrop for the past changes in and the present operation of our system of imposing death as a punishment for crime.

That continues to be my view. For the Clause forbidding cruel and unusual punishments under our constitutional system of government embodies in unique degree moral principles restraining the punishments that our civilized society may impose on those persons who transgress its laws. . . .

This Court inescapably has the duty, as the ultimate arbiter of the meaning of our Constitution, to say whether, when individuals condemned to death stand before our Bar, "moral concepts" require us to hold that the law has progressed to the point where we should declare that the punishment of death, like punishments on the rack, the screw and the wheel, is no longer morally tolerable in our civilized society. . . . I emphasize only that foremost among the "moral concepts" recognized in our cases and inherent in the Clause is the primary moral principle that the State, even as it punishes, must treat its citizens in a manner consistent with their intrinsic worth as human beings—a punishment must not be so severe as to be degrading to human dignity. A judicial determination whether the punishment of death comports with human dignity is therefore not only permitted but compelled by the Clause. . . .

I do not understand that the Court disagrees that "[i]n comparison to all other punishments today . . . the deliberate extinguishment of human life by the State is uniquely degrading to human dignity." . . . For three of my Brethren hold today that mandatory infliction of the death penalty constitutes the penalty cruel and unusual punishment. I perceive no principled basis for this limitation. Death for whatever crime and under all circumstances "is truly an awesome punishment. The calculated killing of a human being by the State involves, by its very nature, a denial of the executed person's humanity. . . ."

* * *

The fatal constitutional infirmity in the punishment of death is that it treats "members of the human race as nonhumans, as objects to be toyed with and discarded. [It] is thus inconsistent with the fundamental premise of the Clause that even the vilest criminal remains a human being possessed of common human dignity." . . . As such

it is a penalty that "subjects the individual to a fate forbidden by the principle of civilized treatment guaranteed by the [Clause]." . . .

Penry v. *Lynaugh*
847 U.S. 1233 (1988)

Justice O'Connor announced the judgment of the Court.

* * *

I

On the morning of October 25, 1979, Pamela Carpenter was brutally raped, beaten, and stabbed with a pair of scissors in her home in Livingston, Texas. She died a few hours later in the course of emergency treatment. Before she died, she described her assailant. Her description led two local sheriff's deputies to suspect Penry, who had recently been released on parole after conviction on another rape charge. Penry subsequently gave two statements confessing to the crime and was charged with capital murder.

At a competency hearing held before trial, a clinical psychologist, Dr. Jerome Brown, testified that Penry was mentally retarded. As a child, Penry was diagnosed as having organic brain damage, which was probably caused by trauma to the brain at birth. . . . Penry was tested over the years as having an IQ between 50 and 63, which indicates mild to moderate retardation. . . . Dr. Brown's own testing before the trial indicated that Penry had an IQ of 54. Dr. Brown's evaluation also revealed that Penry, who was 22 years old at the time of the crime, had the mental age of a 6½ year old, which means that "he has the ability to learn and the learning or the knowledge of the average 6½ year old kid." . . . Penry's social maturity, or ability to function in the world, was that of a 9 or 10 year old. Dr. Brown testified that "there's a point at which anyone with [Penry's] IQ is always incompetent, but, you know, this man is more in the borderline range."

* * *

We granted certiorari to resolve two questions. First, was Penry sentenced to death in violation of the Eighth Amendment because the jury was not adequately instructed to take into consideration all of his mitigating evidence and because the terms in the Texas special issues were not defined in such a way that the jury could consider and give effect to his mitigating evidence in answering them? Second, is it cruel and unusual punishment under the Eight Amendment to execute a mentally retarded person with Penry's reasoning ability?

* * *

IV

Penry's second claim is that it would be cruel and unusual punishment, prohibited by the Eighth Amendment, to execute a mentally retarded person like himself with the reasoning capacity of a 7 year old. He argues that because of their mental disabilities, mentally retarded people do not possess the level of moral culpability to justify imposing the death sentence. He also argues that there is an emerging national consensus against executing the mentally retarded. The State responds that there is insufficient evidence of a national consensus against executing the retarded, and that existing procedural safeguards adequately protect the interests of mentally retarded persons such as Penry.

* * *

B

The Eighth Amendment categorically prohibits the infliction of cruel and unusual punishments. At a minimum, the Eighth Amendment prohibits punishment considered cruel and unusual at the time the Bill of Rights was adopted. The prohibitions of the Eighth Amendment are not limited, however, to those practices condemned by the common law in 1789. The prohibition against cruel and unusual punishments also recognizes the "evolving standards of decency that mark the progress of a maturing society." . . . In discerning those "evolving standards," we have looked to objective evidence of how our society views a particular punishment today. The clearest and most reliable objective evidence of contemporary values is the legislation enacted by the country's legislatures. We have also looked to data concerning the actions of sentencing juries.

It was well settled at common law that "idiots," together with "lunatics," were not subject to punishment for criminal acts committed under those incapacities. As Blackstone wrote:

> "The second case of a deficiency in will, which excuses from the guilt of crimes, arises also from a defective or vitiated understanding, viz. in an *idiot* or a *lunatic*. . . . [I]diots and lunatics are not chargeable for their own acts, if committed when under these incapacities: no, not even for treason itself. . . . [A] total idiocy, or absolute insanity, excuses from the guilt, and of course from the punishment, of any criminal action committed under such deprivation of the senses. . . ." 4 W. Blackstone, Commentaries 24–25 (emphasis in original).

("[T]hose who are under a natural disability of distinguishing between good and evil, as . . . ideots, and lunaticks are not punishable by any criminal prosecution whatsoever"). Idiocy was understood as "a defect of understanding from the moment of birth," in contrast to lunacy, which was "a partial derangement of the intellectual faculties, the senses returning at uncertain intervals."

There was no one definition of idiocy at common law, but the term "idiot" was generally used to describe persons who had a total lack of reason or understanding, or an inability to distinguish between good and evil. Hale wrote that a person that is deaf and mute from birth "is in presumption of law an ideot . . . because he hath no possibility to understand what is forbidden by law to be done, or under what penalties: but if it can appear, that he hath the use of understanding, . . . then he may be tried, and suffer judgment and execution." ("[A] man that is totally deprived of his understanding and memory, and doth not know what he is doing, no more than an infant, than a brute, or a wild beast, such a one is never the object of punishment.")

The common law prohibition against punishing "idiots" and "lunatics" for criminal acts was the precursor of the insanity defense, which today generally includes "mental defect" as well as "mental disease" as part of the legal definition of insanity. ("A person is not responsible for criminal conduct if at the time of such conduct as a result of mental disease or defect he lacks substantial capacity either to appreciate the criminality [wrongfulness] of his conduct or to conform his conduct to the requirements of law") (it is an affirmative defense to federal prosecution if "the defendant, as a result of a severe mental disease or defect, was unable to appreciate the nature and quality or the wrongfulness of his acts" at the time the offense was committed).

In its emphasis on a permanent, congenital mental deficiency, the old common law notion of "idiocy" bears some similarity to the modern definition of mental retardation. The common law prohibition against punishing "idiots" generally applied, however, to persons of such severe disability that they lacked the reasoning capacity to form criminal intent or to understand the difference between good and evil. In the 19th and early 20th centuries, the term "idiot" was used to describe the most retarded of persons, corresponding to what is called "profound" and "severe" retardation today.

The common law prohibition against punishing "idiots" for their crimes suggests that it may indeed be "cruel and unusual" punishment to execute persons who are profoundly or severely retarded and wholly lacking the capacity to appreciate the wrongfulness of their actions. Because of the protections afforded by the insanity defense today, such a person is not likely to be convicted or face the prospect of punishment. Moreover, under *Ford* v. *Wainwright*, someone who is "unaware of the punishment they are about to suffer and why they are to suffer it" cannot be executed.

Such a case is not before us today. Penry was found competent to stand trial. In other words, he was found to have the ability to consult with his lawyer with a reasonable degree of rational understanding, and was found to have a rational as well as factual understanding of the proceedings against him. In addition, the jury rejected his insanity defense, which reflected their conclusion that Penry knew that his conduct was wrong and was capable of conforming his conduct to the requirements of the law.

Penry argues, however, that there is objective evidence today of an emerging national consensus against execution of the mentally retarded, reflecting the "evolving standards of decency that mark the progress of a maturing society." The federal Anti-Drug Abuse Act of 1988 prohibits execution of a person who is mentally retarded. Only one State, however, explicitly bans execution of retarded persons who have been found guilty of a capital offense.

In contrast, in *Ford* v. *Wainwright*, which held that the Eighth Amendment prohibits execution of the insane, considerably more evidence of a national consensus was available. No State permitted the execution of the insane, and 26 States had statutes explicitly requiring suspension of the execution of a capital defendant who became insane. Other States had adopted the common law prohibition against executing the insane. Moreover, in examining the objective evidence of contemporary standards of decency in *Thompson* v. *Oklahoma*, the plurality noted that 18 States expressly established a minimum age in their death penalty statutes, and all of them required that the defendant have attained at least the age of 16 at the time of the offense. In our view, the single state statute prohibiting execution of the mentally retarded, even when added to the 14 States that have rejected capital punishment completely, does not provide sufficient evidence at present of a national consensus.

Penry does not offer any evidence of the general behavior of juries with respect to sentencing mentally retarded defendants, nor of decisions of prosecutors. He points instead to several public opinion surveys that indicate strong public opposition to execution of the retarded. For example, a poll taken in Texas found that 86% of those polled supported the death penalty, but 73% opposed its application to the mentally retarded. A Florida poll found 71% of those surveyed were opposed to the execution of mentally retarded capital defendants, while only 12% were in favor. A Georgia poll found 66% of those polled opposed to the death penalty for the retarded, 17% in favor, with 16% responding that it depends how retarded the person is. In addition, the American Association on Mental Retardation (AAMP), the country's oldest and largest organization of professionals working with the mentally retarded, opposes the execution of persons who are men-

tally retarded. The public sentiment expressed in these and other polls and resolutions may ultimately find expression in legislation, which is an objective indicator of contemporary values upon which we can rely. But at present, there is insufficient evidence of a national consensus against executing mentally retarded people convicted of capital offenses for us to conclude that it is categorically prohibited by the Eighth Amendment.

C

Relying largely on objective evidence such as the judgments of legislatures and juries, we have also considered whether application of the death penalty to particular categories of crimes or classes of offenders violates the Eighth Amendment because it "makes no measurable contribution to acceptable goals of punishment and hence is nothing more than the purposeless and needless imposition of pain and suffering" or because it is "grossly out of proportion to the severity of the crime." *Gregg* noted that "[t]he death penalty is said to serve two principal social purposes: retribution and deterrence of capital crimes by prospective offenders." "The heart of the retribution rationale is that a criminal sentence must be directly related to the personal culpability of the criminal offender."

Penry argues that execution of a mentally retarded person like himself with a reasoning capacity of approximately a 7 year old would be cruel and unusual because it is disproportionate to his degree of personal culpability. Just as the plurality in *Thompson* reasoned that a juvenile is less culpable than an adult for the same crime, Penry argues that mentally retarded people do not have the judgment, perspective, and self-control of a person of normal intelligence. In essence, Penry argues that because of his diminished ability to control his impulses, to think in long-range terms, and to learn from his mistakes, he "is not capable of acting with the degree of culpability that can justify the ultimate penalty."

The American Association on Mental Retardation and other groups working with the mentally retarded agree with Penry. They argue as *amici* that all mentally retarded people, regardless of their degree of retardation, have substantial cognitive and behavioral disabilities that reduce their level of blameworthiness for a capital offense.

Amici do not argue that people with mental retardation cannot be held responsible or punished for criminal acts they commit. Rather, they contend that because of "disability in the areas of cognitive impairment, moral reasoning, control of impulsivity, and the ability to understand basic relationships between cause and effect," mentally retarded people cannot act with the level of moral culpability that would justify imposition of the death sentence. Thus, in their view, execution of mentally retarded people convicted of capital offenses serves no valid retributive purpose.

It is clear that mental retardation has long been regarded as a factor that may diminish an individual's culpability for a criminal act. In its most severe forms, mental retardation may result in complete exculpation from criminal responsibility. Moreover, virtually all of the States with death penalty statutes that list statutory mitigating factors include as a mitigating circumstance evidence that "[t]he capacity of the defendant to appreciate the criminality of his conduct or to conform his conduct to the requirements of law was substantially impaired." A number of States explicitly mention "mental defect" in connection with such a mitigating circumstance. Indeed, as the Court holds in Part III of this opinion, the sentencing body must be allowed to consider mental retardation as a mitigating circumstance in making the individualized determination whether death is the appropriate punishment in a particular case.

On the record before the Court today, however, I cannot conclude that all mentally retarded people of Penry's ability — by virtue of their mental retardation alone, and apart from any individualized consideration of their personal responsibility — inevitably lack the cognitive, volitional, and moral capacity to act with the degree of culpability associated with the death penalty. Mentally retarded persons are individuals whose abilities and experiences can vary greatly. As the AAMR's standard work, Classification in Mental Retardation, points out:

"The term *mental retardation*, as commonly used today, embraces a heterogeneous population, ranging from totally dependent to nearly independent people. Although all individuals so designated share the common attributes of low intelligence and inadequacies in adaptive behavior, there are marked variations in the degree of deficit manifested and the presence or absence of associated physical handicaps, stigmata, and psychologically disordered states." Classification in Mental Retardation, at 12.

In addition to the varying degrees of mental retardation, the consequences of a retarded person's mental impairment, including the deficits in their adaptive behavior, "may be ameliorated through education and habilitation." Although retarded persons generally have difficulty learning from experience, some are fully "capable of learning, working, and living in their communities." In light of the diverse capacities and life experiences of mentally retarded persons, it cannot be said on the record before us today that all mentally retarded people, by definition, can never act with the level of culpability associated with the death penalty.

Penry urges us to rely on the concept of "mental age," and to hold that execution of any person with a mental age of 7 or below would constitute cruel and unusual punishment. Mental age is "calculated as the chronological age of nonretarded children whose average IQ test performance is equivalent to that of the individual with mental retardation." Such a rule should not be adopted today. First, there was no finding below by the judge or jury concerning Penry's "mental age." One of Penry's expert witnesses, Dr. Brown, testified that he estimated Penry's "mental age" to be 6½. That same expert estimated that Penry's "social maturity" was that of a 9 or 10 year old. As a more general matter, the "mental age" concept, irrespective of its intuitive appeal, is problematic in several respects. As the AAMR acknowledges, "[t]he equivalence between nonretarded children and retarded adults is, of course, imprecise." The "mental age" concept may underestimate the life experiences of retarded adults, while it may overestimate the ability of retarded adults to use logic and foresight to solve problems. The mental age concept has other limitations as well. Beyond the chronological age of 15 or 16, the mean scores on most intelligence tests cease to increase significantly with age. As a result, "[t]he average mental age of the average 20 year old is not 20 but 15 years."

Not surprisingly, courts have long been reluctant to rely on the concept of mental age as a basis for exculpating a defendant from criminal responsibility. Moreover, reliance on mental age to measure the capabilities of a retarded person for purposes of the Eighth Amendment could have a disempowering effect if applied in other areas of the law. Thus, on that premise, a mildly mentally retarded person could be denied the opportunity to enter into contracts or to marry by virtue of the fact that he had a "mental age" of a young child. In light of the inherent problems with the mental age concept, and in the absence of better evidence of a national consensus against execution of the retarded, mental age should not be adopted as a line-drawing principle in our Eighth Amendment jurisprudence.

In sum, mental retardation is a factor that may well lessen a defendant's culpability for a capital offense. But we cannot conclude today that the Eighth Amendment precludes the execution of any mentally retarded person of Penry's ability convicted of a capital offense simply by virtue of their mental retardation alone. So long as sentencers can consider and give effect to mitigating evidence of mental retardation in imposing sentence, an individualized determination of whether "death is the appropriate punishment" can be made in each particular case. While a national consensus against execution of the mentally retarded may someday emerge reflecting the "evolving standards of decency that mark the progress of a maturing society," there is insufficient evidence of such a consensus today.

Accordingly, the judgment below is affirmed in part and reversed in part, and the case is remanded for further proceedings consistent with this opinion.

It is so ordered.

Justice Brennan, with whom Justice Marshall joins, concurring in part and dissenting in part.

* * *

A

I agree with Justice O'Connor that one question to be asked in determining whether the execution of mentally retarded offenders is always unconstitutional because disproportionate is whether the mentally retarded as a class "by virtue of their mental retardation alone, . . . inevitably lack the cognitive, volitional, and moral capacity to act with the degree of culpability associated with the death penalty." Justice O'Connor answers

that question in the negative, "[i]n light of the diverse capacities and life experiences of mentally retarded persons." It seems to me that the evidence compels a different conclusion.

For many purposes, legal and otherwise, to treat the mentally retarded as a homogeneous group is inappropriate, bringing the risk of false stereotyping and unwarranted discrimination. Nevertheless, there are characteristics as to which there is no danger of spurious generalization because they are a part of the clinical definition of mental retardation. "Mental retardation" is defined by the American Association on Mental Retardation (AAMR) as "significantly subaverage general intellectual functioning existing concurrently with deficits in adaptive behavior and manifested during the developmental period." To fall within this definition, an individual must be among the approximately two percent of the population with an IQ below 70 on standardized measures of intelligence, see *id.*, at 31, and *in addition* must be subject to "significant limitations in [his or her] effectiveness in meeting the standards of maturation, learning, personal independence, and/or social responsibility that are expected for his or her age level and cultural group." Thus, while as between the mildly, moderately, severely, and profoundly mentally retarded, with IQs ranging from 70 to below 20, there are indeed "marked variations in the degree of deficit manifested," it is also true that "*all* individuals [designated as mentally retarded] share the common attributes of low intelligence and inadequacies in adaptive behavior."

In light of this clinical definition of mental retardation, I cannot agree that the undeniable fact that mentally retarded persons have "diverse capacities and life experiences," is of significance to the Eighth Amendment proportionality analysis we must conduct in this case. "Every individual who has mental retardation" — irrespective of her precise capacities or experiences — has "a substantial disability in cognitive ability and adaptive behavior." This is true even of the "highest functioning individuals in the 'mild' retardation category," and of course of those like Penry whose cognitive and behavioral disabilities place them on the borderline between mild and moderate retardation. Among the mentally retarded, "reduced ability is found in every dimension of the individual's functioning, including his language, communication, memory, attention, ability to control impulsivity, moral development, self-concept, self-perception, suggestibility, knowledge of basic information, and general motivation." Though individuals, particularly those who are mildly retarded, may be quite capable of overcoming these limitations to the extent of being able to "maintain themselves independently or semi-independently in the community," nevertheless, the mentally retarded by definition "have a reduced ability to cope with and function in the everyday world." The impairment of a mentally retarded offender's reasoning abilities, control over impulsive behavior, and moral development in my view limits her culpability so that, whatever other punishment might be appropriate, the ultimate penalty of death is always and necessarily disproportionate to her blameworthiness and hence is unconstitutional.

Even if mental retardation alone were not invariably associated with a lack of the degree of culpability upon which death as a proportionate punishment is predicated, I would still hold the execution of the mentally retarded to be unconstitutional. If there are among the mentally retarded exceptional individuals as responsible for their actions as persons who suffer no such disability, the individualized consideration afforded at sentencing fails to ensure that they are the only mentally retarded offenders who will be picked out to receive a death sentence. The consideration of mental retardation as a mitigating factor is inadequate to guarantee, as the Constitution requires, that an individual who is not fully blameworthy for her crime because of a mental disability does not receive the death penalty.

That "sentencers can consider and give effect to mitigating evidence of mental retardation in imposing sentence" provides no assurance that an adequate individualized determination of whether the death penalty is a proportionate punishment will be made at the conclusion of each capital trial. At sentencing, the judge or jury considers an offender's level of blameworthiness only along with a host of other factors that the sentencer may decide outweigh any want of responsibility. The sentencer is free to weigh a mentally retarded offender's relative lack of culpability against the heinousness of the crime and other aggravating factors and to decide that even the most retarded and irresponsible of offenders should die. Indeed, a sentencer will entirely discount an offender's retardation as a factor mitigating against imposition of a death sentence if it adopts this line of reasoning:

> "It appears to us that there is all the more reason to execute a killer if he is also . . . retarded. Killers often kill again; [a] retarded killer is more to be feared than a . . . normal killer. There is also far less possibility of his ever becoming a useful citizen." Upholding Law and Order, Hartsville Messenger, June 24, 1987, p. 5B, col. 1.

Lack of culpability as a result of mental retardation is simply not isolated at the sentencing stage as a factor that determinatively bars a death sentence; for individualized consideration at sentencing is not designed to ensure that mentally retarded offenders are not sentenced to death if they are not culpable to the degree necessary to render execution a proportionate response to their crimes. When Johnny Penry is resentenced, absent a change in Texas law there will be nothing to prevent the jury, acting lawfully, from sentencing him to death once again—even though it finds his culpability significantly reduced by reason of mental retardation. I fail to see how that result is constitutional, in the face of the acknowledged Eighth Amendment requirement of proportionality.

* * *

CHAPTER SEVEN

The Nature of Civil Rights

What is a civil right? The most general definition is that civil rights are rights that are held (or ought to be held) by virtue of one's membership in a civil society. Civil rights are what your country owes you; they are what you are entitled to as a citizen. They may be distinguished from human rights, which are what you are entitled to as a human being. Civil rights include human rights, but extend beyond the latter to rights entailed by the form of government.

In many cases civil rights claims are straightforward legal disputes about the proper interpretation or application of statutory or constitutional provisions. For example: What is required by due process? What is the meaning of equal protection of the laws in terms of constitutional interpretation? What is covered by Title VII of the Civil Rights Act of 1964? Such dispute about interpretation is certainly what has been going on in the free speech and association cases in the U.S. Supreme Court since the 1920s. There is no question that the U.S. Constitution explicitly recognizes a right of free speech. But it is not absolute, so what is the scope of the right? What does it amount to in particular cases? Do I have a right to speak out against the government? A right to conspire to overthrow it? A right to cause unrest? To cause a riot? What does my right cover? That's the question—not whether I have a right of free speech, for I certainly do.

Some of the prominent civil rights cases of the 1960s can be construed the same way. I have a right to equal protection of the laws, explicit in the Constitution and Civil Rights Acts. But what does it mean? If it means anything at all, it must mean that the government cannot discriminate against me on irrelevant grounds. But what does that amount to in specific cases? Does it mean that public schools cannot be segregated on the basis of race? How about sex? How about wealth? Does it mean that the government must take affirmative action to correct segregation that results coincidentally from divided neighborhoods? Affirmative action to correct the injurious effects of a history of segregation? What is the scope of the right? That is the question. There is no question that I have the right. In such cases disputes over civil rights are disputes over the proper interpretation of the positive law.

Some civil rights claims, however, are not disputes about the interpretation of law but rather are protests that the law is wrong or inadequate. In such cases the civil right appealed to is a moral right. The claim is a claim that certain moral rights ought to be recognized as legal rights. Thus, civil rights are ambiguous in this respect. Some are disputes over the scope or application of generally recognized legal rights, whereas others are appeals to moral rights that are not legally recognized in general.

Moral claims of civil rights are always protests against the legal status quo. They are demands for legal change on the basis of immorality or injustice. This basis can be contrasted with other grounds that might be used to demand legal change, such as a change in public need, assertions of special interests, or a change in majority will. Times change and public demands change with it, but these are ordinary political claims, not concerned with the violation of rights. The claim of civil rights violation—even if it is a moral claim—is the assertion that government has exceeded its rightful jurisdiction or is not meeting its obligations to its citizens and is thereby unjust. Protestors against the Alien and Sedition Act, for example, did not just say that times have changed; they said that the act violated their right to free speech. Similarly, abolitionists claimed that slaves had a right to be free, no matter what the law said. Sit-ins at lunch counters and demonstrations at bus stops during the 1960s were protests against injustice — that is, rights violations — and not just the lobbying of a special interest group. Objections to apartheid have been based on the claim that every member of any society has a right to vote, whether the law recognizes it or not. Thus, some civil rights claims are moral claims, but they are always claims about what ought to be recognized by law in a just society.

Whether we are talking about moral rights or legal rights, certain important civil rights are directly connected with the value of freedom. These are often called civil liberties, but they are not mere liberties in Hohfeld's sense. Remember that a mere liberty is simply the absence of a duty. If you are at liberty to do something, that just means that you have no duty not to do that something. But civil liberties are much stronger. Most are, in fact, immunities against government interference or restriction, which, indeed, specifies their relation to freedom.

And what is freedom? It is often said freedom is the absence of restraints. Bentham and Mill define it as the absence of impediments to attaining one's desires. A more Kantian perspective construes political freedom as the noninterference due individuals out of respect for human autonomy. Positions like these form the basis of the classical liberal tradition, which takes individual freedom as its centerpiece. This concept of freedom is often called *negative freedom* and the rights associated with it *negative rights*. The emphasis is on what government or individuals may *not* (within the bounds of justice) do to one another.

In the classical liberal tradition, civil liberties act as presumptions against government in favor of individual freedom. The presumption of restricted government is inherent in the idea of a rule of law, but it is also embodied in the explicit civil rights catalogues of most modern constitutions — for example, the U.S. Bill of Rights. The result is that although the state may restrict individual liberty, it must first justify doing so. In some areas this justification must be very strong. In the United States, the First Amendment protections of thought and expression are considered stringent.

This chapter considers as a clear case of civil rights to freedom some of the liberties protected by the First Amendment, with the focus on the right to free speech. We will next look at a less clear case — the civil right to privacy. Both are examples of the liberal notion of civil rights as rights against interference.

The civil right to free speech is a clear case because of the focus of political history in Western civilization at least since the seventeenth century, and also because it is expressly declared in the U.S. Constitution. There can be no question that it is both a political and legal right of the first order of importance and certainty.

The right to privacy is unclear because of the absence of both of these factors. First, its emphasis in political discourse and advocacy is recent. Not only has this right not been fought for during the past three centuries (as has the right to free speech), it has not been discussed as such for more than fifty years. Concern about the right to privacy is recent. Second, there is no explicit reference to a right to privacy in the Constitution; nor is it laid out clearly in legislative enactment. Thus, both the political and legal grounding is unclear. Recognizing these differences between free speech and privacy, however, you should keep in mind that both are concerned with negative rights: Both involve claims against interference that are central to if not explicit in the classical liberal or individualist tradition. In this respect — that is, in their focus on freedom — they are alike.

Freedom is not the only value protected by civil rights. Section 2 of this chapter examines the civil right to justice. Like freedom, justice is a fundamental value that plays a prominent — indeed, indispensable — role in evaluating political (or legal) legitimacy. Since a legitimate state cannot be unjust, any government must answer claims of unjust treatment.

The history and development of such claims as well as their recognition is much like claims to freedom. Both are stories of gradually expanding ranges of application. Over time more and more objectives are taken to be appropriate for evaluation in terms of freedom and justice. And over time more and more groups of people are included in the scope of application. That is, over time the value of freedom is seen to apply to groups of people who were not included in it before. And over time the same standard of justice has come to be applied to groups who were previously considered essentially different.

Also like claims to freedom, claims to civil rights to just treatment have clear and unclear cases. We will consider as a clear case of the civil right to justice the right against discrimination. The formulation of what is entailed by a right against discriminatory treatment is much more recent than evaluations of what is required by a civil right to freedom, but it is nevertheless a clear case in two respects. First, like freedom, the claim to justice is one of the oldest political claims ever made against governments. What is required by justice is controversial. That we are all entitled to just treatment is clear. Second, legally in the United States the equal protection of the laws is explicitly guaranteed by the Constitution. Thus, the political and legal grounding for the civil right to justice is clear even if the content of the right is not.

As an unclear case of a civil right to justice we will look at claims for positive benefits such as medical care, education, housing, and minimum income. Although in some countries such benefits have been recognized as civil rights, in the United States no such general recognition has been forthcoming. These claims are doubly controversial in that they are claims to positive rights rather than to negative rights. They do not fit naturally or follow from the foundation laid by the liberal individualist tradition. Nevertheless, all these benefits have been provided by government to a certain extent in various forms. And claims to such civil rights have been raised in the courts. A consideration of these issues will provide us with the opportunity to examine the requirements of justice in law.

SECTION 1

Civil Rights and the Value of Freedom

In the United States certain basic rights and freedoms were considered so valuable that they were explicitly as well as implicitly built into the Constitution itself. Their inclusion made a strong commitment to freedom part of the basic structure of government, insulating the value of liberty from the vicissitudes of majority opinion. Freedom is the abiding value that permeates the Constitution, providing a clear legal foundation for some important civil liberties. The commitment to freedom is reflected in the rationale of the First Amendment, which states:

> Congress shall make no law respecting the establishment of religion, or the free exercise thereof; or abridging the freedom of speech, or of the press; or the right of the people peaceably to assemble, and to petition the Government for a redress of grievances.

The obvious purpose of this provision is to protect the freedom of individual thought, expression, and communication. Why is that so important and how far should it extend? In *On Liberty* John Stuart Mill offers some of the reasons for defending individual freedom in general and the freedom of thought and expression in particular. What was unusual about Mill's approach to the subject of freedom at the time was that he did not rely on any claim of natural right. Instead, as staunch utilitarian, he argues that the general welfare requires a strong protection of individual freedom. In fact, Mill argues that the only justification of state interference with individual freedom is self-protection. That is, society may restrict the freedom of an individual only to keep that individual from harming others. The state cannot justifiably restrict a competent adult in order to protect her from herself or to promote her own physical or moral well-being.

In regard to freedom of thought and expression, Mill argues for almost absolute protection. His thesis is that if we restrict the free expression of an idea, for all we know the idea that gets censored could be the truth or part of the truth. So long as we allow all ideas to be heard, each individual can evaluate the comparative worth of the various arguments. And if an idea is not true, the evaluation and defense against it enhances both our understanding of what is true and our conviction in maintaining it. Thus, the protection of freedom, especially the freedom of thought and expression, is required by a commitment to the general welfare or public good itself. This argument has a good and bad side. It makes no controversial metaphysical assumptions about natural rights, but it makes the protection of rights rely on the public interest.

Other philosophers, such as Tocqueville and Wolff (Chapter One, Section 3), have argued for the protection of free speech on other grounds, for example, democracy or autonomy. These grounds differ sharply from an appeal to the common good and can support free speech whether or not it is in the public interest. Respect for persons as autonomous individuals requires the recognition of free speech as well as other rights. The argument from democracy is an interesting approach for our purposes because it utilizes the same basis as that on which we founded civil rights. Free speech is implicit in the notion of democratic government. A commitment to democratic government carries with it a presumption of freedom to discuss, criticize, and change the government itself, since the legitimacy of democratic government is derived from the consent of the governed. Yet this right extends only within the legitimate processes of democratic government and not outside the law. Although very strong, the right to free speech is far from absolute. Thus, a major problem is how to determine the scope of the right. The Supreme Court approaches the problem by balancing individual interests against state interests (such as protection against breach of peace, breach of national security, or incitement to illegal acts), but recognizes that speech is entitled to greater protection than conduct that is not speech.

Determining the scope of the civil right to free expression becomes even more difficult when we move from verbal communication to symbolic speech. Focusing specifically on symbolic conduct as protected expression, Fred R. Berger argues for an even broader range of protection than that currently protected by the Supreme Court. Berger argues that some illegal acts should be protected as symbolic expression. What is needed, he thinks, is a jurisprudence of civil disobedience, which recognizes that within certain limits violating certain statutes or ordinances may be the most—or perhaps the only—effective means of conveying a particular message. For example, blacks in the 1960s frequented segregated establishments in violation of the law for the express purpose of objecting to the practice of segregation. In certain circumstances violating the law can be the most effective expression of protest, especially for minorities or others without access to mainstream channels of communication. But this practice raises a difficult problem for determining the scope of the right. Which illegal acts should be protected and which should not? Berger suggests that this problem is not insurmountable. Categories are already available (for example, in the form of libel or privacy law) for the purpose of regulating the content of expression, and analogous categories can be used for expressive conduct. As to protecting against the breach of peace or the violation of the rights of others, Berger suggests that we can balance these conflicting interests.

Berger's is an interesting and controversial position, which we may be more inclined to agree with when we agree with the cause or message being advanced. We may sympathize with depressed minorities violating immoral laws to fight for equal treatment, but nuisance and trespass may not be so agreeable when used for the benefit of the American Nazi Party or the Ku Klux

Klan. At the end of this section you will find a short article by Nat Hentoff discussing the importance of protecting unpopular speech, along with a series of cases intended to provide certain insights into this issue. First, the cases represent the development of the protection of free speech through the interpretation of the U.S. Constitution by the Supreme Court during the past seventy years or so. Clearly, these are difficult interpretations that are susceptible to the attitudes and pressures of the time in which they are written and the individuals who occupy the bench. Second, they illustrate that whether or not Mill is right that free speech is required for the common good in the long run, in the short run free speech can cause great harm to the country and to individuals and groups within it. Consider what the costs are, what interests are at issue, and how these should be balanced. Finally, note that although the scope and meaning of the right to free speech has always been subject to debate, the existence of the right has never been questioned. This tradition provides a sharp contrast with our next consideration, which is the right to privacy.

Privacy is a notoriously slippery concept, so the first objective to confront is the nature of privacy itself. There is no consensus on a proper definition or description, although quite a few proposals have been offered. The problem in coordinating these proposals is that the invasion of privacy covers a multitude of sins that are not related in any obvious way. Proposals tend to emphasize one aspect of privacy or another without covering all facets. Any definition broad enough to cover all aspects of privacy also includes things that are not privacy. (This is like the problem of defining personhood.) A few brief examples follow as a representative sample.

Privacy is often construed as the state of being let alone. The right to privacy has sometimes been called the right to be let alone. This makes it a right against intrusion in a very broad sense, which seems to cover all facets of privacy. But as a definition being let alone is much too broad, since it cannot distinguish privacy from liberty. Privacy and liberty are obviously distinct, and significantly so. Privacy can conflict with liberty. But more important, I can invade your privacy without invading your liberty — as long as you do not know it. That is the whole point of spying. Being let alone, therefore, cannot explain enough if it cannot explain what distinguishes privacy from liberty.

Another natural description of privacy is the absence of publicity, since publicity contrasts with privacy. This definition covers many aspects of privacy, and it is important. For example, three of the four torts recognizing the invasion of privacy center on the prevention of publicity. But the absence of publicity is too narrow a description, since a peeping tom or a private investigator for a private party can invade your privacy without ever making anything public.

Selective disclosure is another view of privacy. This view links privacy with power or control — most often control over the disclosure of information about ourselves, but also control over acquaintance with one's personal affairs or even control over when one is sensed by others. Again, this definition seems to offer some important insights into privacy, but it has problems. The most serious is that if privacy is construed in terms of control, then consent cancels privacy, thus implying that self-disclosure is not compatible with the loss of privacy. But that does not seem to be true: I may sell my memoirs and thereby lose my privacy. I may even regret this action or be embarrassed about it later.

Some theories, in fact, have defined privacy in terms of feelings or psychological states. Some have focused on feelings of embarrassment, shame, or humiliation. Others have emphasized the sense of separateness or the condition of "being apart from others," which is related to alienation. This approach has several advantages. It explains the apparent social relativity of what is considered a private matter. It also relates offenses against privacy with offenses against decency, which provides some helpful insights.

But the approach also contains problems, the worst of them having to do with the social relativity that otherwise seems so helpful. In situations offering little privacy — hospitals, prisons, concentration camps, even the armed forces — the sense of individuality and dignity, as well as feelings of embarrassment and shame, associated with feelings of privacy may be lost. But this theory seems to imply that there is no loss of privacy in the absence of the proper feelings. Thus, the very worst breaches of privacy, the annihilation of privacy, is unaccounted for. Another problem is that this view of privacy is hard to translate into the language of rights. If privacy is a feeling, just what is it that a right to privacy is supposed to protect?

Some attempts have been made to explain privacy as analogous to property. Privacy is exclusive access. It relates to a private domain or realm of one's own. A right to privacy thus entitles one to exclude others from intruding upon (watching, utilizing, or invading) this realm. From this point of view, lost privacy can be construed as wrongful appropriation or exploitation of one's personality or private affairs. This view has great intuitive appeal, but it also has at least three problems. First, some people object to human qualities being construed as property in any form. Second, property can be sold, so the analogy breaks down. Third (and worst), the theory relies on a private domain that is not itself defined, although it is precisely that domain which we need to understand. That is what is private. Therefore, we still do not know what it is that intruders can be excluded from.

Obviously there are many differing accounts of the nature and value of privacy. None is clearly superior and all have problems or deficiencies. For this reason some philosophers and legal theorists have characterized privacy as a derivative concept, a cluster concept, or a collection of interests irreducible to one another. This is the approach taken in tort law. The invasion of privacy can be claimed on any of four grounds in tort law (although conceptually these four grounds can easily be reduced to two: intrusion and publicity). In tort law the grounds for invasion of privacy are (1) intrusion upon the solitude or seclusion of private affairs; (2) commercial appropriation of one's name or likeness; (3) publicity placing one in a false light; and (4) public disclosure of embarrassing private facts.

Invasion of privacy is a dignitary tort, and it is often said that the interest protected is the dignity of the individual. In fact, most of the accounts of privacy we reviewed earlier also refer to the protection of what is personal: to the unique self, to the inviolate personality, to individual dignity. Although these ideas are not helpful as a definition since they cannot, for example, distinguish the invasion of privacy from all the other dignitary torts (libel, slander, and so on), they nevertheless are central to understanding the nature and value of privacy.

It is beyond question that privacy — whatever it is — is an important interest that people in fact want. But is it a right, and if it is, what justifies it? John Stuart Mill argues that the protection of individuality is justified by utility — the general welfare. Whether that makes privacy a moral or civil right is not clear, but utilitarians can consistently argue that it does. Some philosophers argue that a right to privacy is required by justice or respect for persons, and we can see from even our brief review of theories that this claim is not without support. Some people argue that privacy is a basic need (like food or shelter) or an intrinsic good (like freedom or security). There is support for these claims as well, but the right to privacy is not as well established as the traditional negative rights. It has not been fought over for centuries like freedom or property, although the demand for privacy has grown enormously as the population has exploded over the past century.

One important feature of the right of privacy, in terms of the need for justification, is its fundamental conflict with other rights, especially the rights to free speech and press. The rationale behind free speech and press is the promotion of unrestricted, public exchange of ideas. The rationale behind privacy is the exclusion of some areas of life from public access, discussion, acquisition, or knowledge. Privacy sets limits on other rights, especially First Amendment rights. What justifies this restriction on the exchange of ideas? No right is absolute. Speech and press are limited by libel, slander, defamation, and fraud. But all these limit the abuse of free speech for the promotion of falsehood or misinformation. Privacy is a prohibition of divulging, or even knowing, the truth. In this regard the right against the invasion of privacy is like the limits of treason or espionage, which also prohibit divulging the truth. The justification for these limits is national security. But the justification for the right to privacy is more complex than personal security.

Tort law has long recognized a legal right to privacy on behalf of individuals – private parties against other private parties. Constitutional protection against government intrusion is found in the Third and Fourth amendments prohibiting the quartering of soldiers and unwarranted searches and seizures on private property. These amendments have sometimes been interpreted as the protection of privacy, although privacy is not mentioned by name in the Constitution. In the early 1920s the Supreme Court interpreted the due process clause of the Fourteenth Amendment as a protection of certain private decisions from government interference. At that time the rationale was called *substantive due process,* and its major focus was labor law and contracts (as discussed in Chapter Three). Yet certain cases decided within this rubric provided the foundation of precedent for what would be called the *constitutional right to privacy* in the case of *Griswold* v. *Connecticut.* *Griswold* is one of the most controversial and important cases ever decided in American law. It is important because it provides the basis for restricting government regulation of individual private choices about personal and family life. It is controversial because it does not have a clear foundation in the Constitution. *Griswold* and the cases following it (especially *Roe* v. *Wade*) are activist decisions, accused of being judicial legislation, analogous to the now discredited doctrine of substantive due process. Selections from this line of cases are given at the end of this section.

The debate over *Griswold* and the constitutional right to privacy in general is represented by the selections by Hyman Gross and Judith Wagner DeCew. Gross argues that the so-called constitutional right to privacy muddles traditional legal analysis because it is not really about privacy at all. According to Gross (and other legal commentators), the right established in *Griswold* is really autonomy, or the right to make decisions without interference. Such an interpretation would make the right apparently indistinguishable from substantive due process. But in the next selection, DeCew argues that the connection with privacy is defensible. While liberty (or autonomy) determines the power of decision making, privacy determines its subject matter. Given that the Supreme Court does not protect all decisions, the rationale of privacy explains which ones will be protected. As you will see, the level of dispute goes much deeper over the right to privacy than over the right to free speech. Some people argue that no right to privacy exists at all, whereas others claim that privacy is the most important right a modern free society can guarantee its citizens.

Notes and Questions

JOHN STUART MILL, from *On Liberty*

1. According to John Stuart Mill, what is the only justification for state interference with individual freedom: Mill's "one very simple principle"? Notice that no society grants individuals so much freedom as Mill advocates. Is Mill's principle realistic? What other principles can you think of that could justify restricting individual freedom? (Consider Feinberg's "liberty limiting principles" cited in the introduction to Chapter Six.)

2. Mill argues that there is a particular sphere of human action, of great importance to individuals, in which society has only an indirect interest. What is it? Why does he think so? Is he right that society has only an indirect interest in this sphere? What would Mill's claim have to mean in order to be true?

3. What is Mill's ultimate justification for the (almost) absolute protection of individual freedom of thought and expression and of tastes and pursuits? Does he claim that such freedoms do not harm other individuals or society at large? In what respect? Do you agree with him? Many political writers and philosophers feel that society should mold the character of its citizens — in fact, that it must do so to survive. Is Mill's view compatible with such a claim? How might he respond to it?

4. It is often argued that society should "protect" (that is, regulate) the morals of its citizens. How would Mill respond? On Mill's account should prostitution be legal? How about bigamy? How about drug use or sale? Why or why not — that is, how should such questions be decided, according to Mill? Is Mill's defense of the freedom of thought and expression stronger than the same arguments applied to actions or lifestyles? Why does Mill think they should work the same way? Do you agree?

5. What four specific arguments does Mill give for the protection of free speech? This set of arguments supports a view often called *the marketplace of ideas*. What is presumed by a commitment to a marketplace of ideas? Is it a plausible view? What alternatives are there? Are the alternatives better?

6. Do you think that Mill is implicitly arguing that people have a right to the freedoms he argues for? (He is not doing so explicitly.) If so, what kind of a right would it be? If not, what kind of an argument is he making, and what would it add if you additionally claim that people have rights to the freedoms in question?

[From] *On Liberty*

JOHN STUART MILL

Liberty of Thought and Discussion

The object of this Essay is to assert one very simple principle, as entitled to govern absolutely the dealings of society with the individual in the way of compulsion and control, whether the means used be physical force in the form of legal penalties, or the moral coercion of public opinion. That principle is, that the sole end for which mankind are warranted, individually or collectively, in interfering with the liberty of action of any of their number is self-protection. That the only purpose for which power can be rightfully exercised over any member of a civilized community, against his will, is to prevent harm to others. His own good, either physical or moral, is not a sufficient warrant. He cannot rightfully be compelled to do or forbear because it will be better for him to do so, because it will make him happier, because, in the opinions of others, to do so would be wise, or even right. These are good reasons for remonstrating with him, or reasoning with him, or persuading him, or entreating him, but not for compelling him, or visiting him with any evil in case he do otherwise. To justify that, the conduct from which it is desired to deter him, must be calculated to produce evil to someone else. The only part of the conduct of anyone, for which he is amenable to society, is that which concerns others. In the part which merely concerns himself, his independence is, of right, absolute. Over himself, over his own body and mind, the individual is sovereign. . . .

It is proper to state that I forgo any advantage which could be derived to my argument from the idea of abstract right, as a thing independent of utility. I regard utility as the ultimate appeal on all ethical questions; but it must be utility in the largest sense, grounded on the permanent interests of man as a progressive being. Those interests, I contend, authorize the subjection of individual spontaneity to external control, only in respect to those actions of each, which concern the interest of other people. . . .

But there is a sphere of action in which society, as distinguished from the individual, has, if any, only an indirect interest; comprehending all that portion of a person's life and conduct which affects only himself, or if it also affects others, only with their free, voluntary, and undeceived consent and participation. When I say only himself, I mean directly, and in the first instance: for whatever affects himself, may affect others through himself; and the objection which may be grounded on this contingency will receive consideration in the sequel. This, then, is the appropriate region of human liberty. It comprises, first, the inward domain of consciousness; demanding liberty of conscience, in the most comprehensive sense; liberty of thought and feeling; absolute freedom of opinion and sentiment on all subjects, practical or speculative, scientific, moral, or theological. The liberty of expressing and publishing opinions may seem to fall under a different principle, since it belongs to that part of the conduct of an individual which concerns other people; but, being almost of as much importance as the liberty of thought itself, and resting in great part on the same reasons, is practically inseparable from it. Secondly, the principle requires liberty of tastes and pursuits; of framing the plan of our life to suit our own character; of doing as we like, subject to such consequences as may follow: without impediment from our fellow creatures, so long as what

we do does not harm them, even though they should think our conduct foolish, perverse, or wrong. Thirdly, from this liberty of each individual, follows the liberty, within the same limits, of combination among individuals; freedom to unite, for any purpose not involving harm to others: the persons combining being supposed to be of full age, and not forced or deceived.

No society in which these liberties are not, on the whole, respected, is free, whatever may be its form of government; and none is completely free in which they do not exist absolute and unqualified. The only freedom which deserves the name, is that of pursuing our own good in our own way, so long as we do not attempt to deprive others of theirs, or impede their efforts to obtain it. Each is the proper guardian of his own health, whether bodily, or mental and spiritual. Mankind are greater gainers by suffering each other to live as seems good to themselves, than by compelling each to live as seems good to the rest. . . .

Apart from the peculiar tenets of individual thinkers, there is also in the world at large an increasing inclination to stretch unduly the powers of society over the individual, both by the force of opinion and even by that of legislation: and as the tendency of all the changes taking place in the world is to strengthen society, and diminish the power of the individual, this encroachment is not one of the evils which tend spontaneously to disappear, but, on the contrary, to grow more and more formidable. The disposition of mankind, whether as rulers or as fellow citizens, to impose their own opinions and inclinations as a rule of conduct on others, is so energetically supported by some of the best and by some of the worst feelings incident to human nature, that it is hardly ever kept under restraint by anything but want of power; and as the power is not declining, but growing, unless a strong barrier of moral conviction can be raised against the mischief, we must expect, in the present circumstances of the world, to see it increase.

It will be convenient for the argument, if, instead of at once entering upon the general thesis, we confine ourselves in the first instance to a single branch of it, on which the principle here stated is, if not fully, yet to a certain point, recognized by the current opinions. This one branch is the Liberty of Thought: from which it is impossible to separate the cognate liberty of speaking and of writing. Although these liberties, to some considerable amount, form part of the political morality of all countries which profess religious toleration and free institutions, the grounds, both philosophical and practical, on which they rest, are perhaps not so familiar to the general mind, nor so thoroughly appreciated by many even of the leaders of opinion, as might have been expected. Those grounds, when rightly understood, are of much wider application than to only one division of the subject, and a thorough consideration of this part of the question will be found the best introduction to the remainder. . . .

The time, it is to be hoped, is gone by, when any defense would be necessary of the "liberty of the press" as one of the securities against corrupt or tyrannical government. No argument, we may suppose, can now be needed, against permitting a legislature or an executive, not identified in interest with the people, to prescribe opinions to them, and determine what doctrines or what arguments they shall be allowed to hear. This aspect of the question, besides, has been so often and so triumphantly enforced by preceding writers, that it needs not be specially insisted on in this place. . . . Let us suppose, therefore, that the government is entirely at one with the people, and never thinks of exerting any power of coercion unless in agreement with what it conceives to be their voice. But I deny the right of the people to exercise such coercion, either by themselves or by their government. The power itself is illegitimate. The best government has no more title to it than the worst. It is as noxious, or more noxious, when exerted in accordance with public opinion, than when in opposition to it. If all mankind minus one, were of one opinion, and only one person were of the contrary opinion, mankind would be no more justified in silencing that one person, than he, if he had the power, would be justified in silencing mankind. Were an opinion a personal possession of no value except to the owner; if to be obstructed in the enjoyment of it were simply a private injury, it would make some difference whether the injury was inflicted only on a few persons or on many. But the peculiar evil of silencing the expression of an opinion is, that it is robbing the human race; posterity as well as the existing generation; those who dissent

from the opinion, still more than those who hold it. If the opinion is right, they are deprived of the opportunity of exchanging error for truth: if wrong, they lose, what is almost as great a benefit, the clearer perception and livelier impression of truth, produced by its collision with error.

It is necessary to consider separately these two hypotheses, each of which has a distinct branch of the argument corresponding to it. We can never be sure that the opinion we are endeavoring to stifle is a false opinion; and if we were sure, stifling it would be an evil still.

First: the opinion which it is attempted to suppress by authority may possibly be true. Those who desire to suppress it, of course deny its truth; but they are not infallible. They have no authority to decide the question for all mankind, and exclude every other person from the means of judging. To refuse a hearing to an opinion, because they are sure that it is false, is to assume that *their* certainty is the same thing as *absolute* certainty. All silencing of discussion is an assumption of infallibility. Its condemnation may be allowed to rest on this common argument, not the worse for being common.

Unfortunately for the good sense of mankind, the fact of their fallibility is far from carrying the weight in their practical judgment, which is always allowed to it in theory; for while everyone well knows himself to be fallible, few think it necessary to take any precautions against their own fallibility, or admit the supposition that any opinion, of which they feel very certain, may be one of the examples of the error to which they acknowledge themselves to be liable. Absolute princes, or others who are accustomed to unlimited deference, usually feel this complete confidence in their own opinions on nearly all subjects. People more happily situated, who sometimes hear their opinions disputed, and are not wholly unused to be set right when they are wrong, place the same unbounded reliance only on such of their opinions as are shared by all who surround them, or to whom they habitually defer: for in proportion to a man's want of confidence in his own solitary judgment, does he usually repose, with implicit trust, on the infallibility of "the world" in general. And the world, to each individual, means the part of it with which he comes in contact; his party, his sect, his church, his class of society: the man may be called, by comparison, almost liberal and large-minded to whom it means anything so comprehensive as his own country or his own age. Nor is his faith in this collective authority at all shaken by his being aware that other ages, countries, sects, churches, classes, and parties have thought, and even now think, the exact reverse. He devolves upon his own world the responsibility of being in the right against the dissentient worlds of other people; and it never troubles him that mere accident has decided which of these numerous worlds is the object of his reliance, and that the same causes which make him a Churchman in London, would have made him a Buddhist or a Confucian in Peking. Yet it is as evident in itself, as any amount of argument can make it, that ages are no more infallible than individuals; every age having held many opinions which subsequent ages have deemed not only false but absurd; and it is as certain that many opinions, now general, will be rejected by future ages, as it is that many, once general, are rejected by the present.

The objection likely to be made to this argument would probably take some such form as the following. There is no greater assumption of infallibility in forbidding the propagation of error, than in any other thing which is done by public authority on its own judgment and responsibility. Judgment is given to men that they may use it. Because it may be used erroneously, are men to be told that they ought not to use it at all? To prohibit what they think pernicious, is not claiming exemption from error, but fulfilling the duty incumbent on them, although fallible, of acting on their conscientious conviction. If we were never to act on our opinions, because those opinions may be wrong, we should leave all our interests uncared for, and all our duties unperformed. An objection which applies to all conduct, can be no valid objection to any conduct, in particular. It is the duty of governments, and of individuals, to form the truest opinions they can; to form them carefully, and never impose them upon others unless they are quite sure of being right. But when they are sure (such reasoners may say), it is not conscientiousness but cowardice to shrink from acting on their opinions, and allow doctrines which they honestly think dangerous to the welfare of mankind, either in

this life or in another, to be scattered abroad without restraint, because other people, in less enlightened times, have persecuted opinions now believed to be true. Let us take care, it may be said, not to make the same mistake: but governments and nations have made mistakes in other things, which are not denied to be fit subjects for the exercise of authority: they have laid on bad taxes, made unjust wars. Ought we therefore to lay on no taxes, and, under whatever provocation, make no wars? Men, and governments, must act to the best of their ability. There is no such thing as absolute certainty, but there is assurance sufficient for the purposes of human life. We may, and must, assume our opinion to be true for the guidance of our own conduct: and it is assuming no more when we forbid bad men to pervert society by the propagation of opinions which we regard as false and pernicious.

I answer, that it is assuming very much more. There is the greatest difference between presuming an opinion to be true, because, with every opportunity for contesting it, it has not been refuted, and assuming its truth for the purpose of not permitting its refutation. Complete liberty of contradicting and disproving our opinion, is the very condition which justifies us in assuming its truth for purposes of action; and on no other terms can a being with human faculties have any rational assurance of being right.

When we consider either the history of opinion, or the ordinary conduct of human life, to what is it to be ascribed that the one and the other are no worse than they are? Not certainly to the inherent force of the human understanding; for, on any matter not self-evident, there are ninety-nine persons totally incapable of judging of it, for one who is capable; and the capacity of the hundredth person is only comparative; for the majority of the eminent men of every past generation held many opinions now known to be erroneous, and did or approved numerous things which no one will now justify. Why is it, then, that there is on the whole a preponderance among mankind of rational opinions and rational conduct? If there really is this preponderance — which there must be unless human affairs are, and have always been, in an almost desperate state — it is owing to a quality of the human mind, the source of everything respectable in man either as an intellectual or as a moral being, namely, that his errors are corrigible. He is capable of rectifying his mistakes, by discussion, and experience. Not by experience alone. There must be discussion, to show how experience is to be interpreted. Wrong opinions and practices gradually yield to fact and argument: but facts and arguments, to produce any effect on the mind, must be brought before it. Very few facts are able to tell their own story, without comments to bring out their meaning. The whole strength and value, then, of human judgment, depending on the one property, that it can be set right when it is wrong, reliance can be placed on it only when the means of setting it right are kept constantly at hand. In the case of any person whose judgment is really deserving of confidence, how has it become so? Because he has kept his mind open to criticism of his opinions and conduct. Because it has been his practice to listen to all that could be said against him; to profit by as much of it as was just, and expound to himself, and upon occasion to others, the fallacy of what was fallacious. Because he has felt, that the only way in which a human being can make some approach to knowing the whole of a subject, is by hearing what can be said about it by persons of every variety of opinion, and studying all modes in which it can be looked at by every character of mind. No wise man ever acquired his wisdom in any mode but this; nor is it in the nature of human intellect to become wise in any other manner. The steady habit of correcting and completing his own opinion by collating it with those of others, so far from causing doubt and hesitation in carrying it into practice, is the only stable foundation for a just reliance on it: for, being cognizant of all that can, at least obviously, be said against him, and having taken up his position against all gainsayers — knowing that he has sought for objections and difficulties, instead of avoiding them, and has shut out no light which can be thrown upon the subject from any quarter — he has a right to think his judgment better than that of any person, or any multitude, who have not gone through a similar process.

It is not too much to require that what the wisest of mankind, those who are best entitled to trust their own judgment, find necessary to warrant their relying on it, should be submitted to by that miscellaneous collection of a few wise and many foolish individuals, called the public. The most intolerant of churches, the Roman Catholic Church, even at the canonization of a saint, admits, and listens patiently to, a "devil's advocate." The holiest of men, it appears, cannot be admitted to posthumous honors, until all that the devil could say against him is known and weighed. If even the Newtonian philosophy were not permitted to be questioned, mankind could not feel as complete assurance of its truth as they now do. The beliefs which we have most warrant for, have no safeguard to rest on, but a standing invitation to the whole world to prove them unfounded. If the challenge is not accepted, or is accepted and the attempt fails, we are far enough from certainty still; but we have done the best that the existing state of human reason admits of; we have neglected nothing that could give the truth a chance of reaching us: if the lists are kept open, we may hope that if there be a better truth, it will be found when the human mind is capable of receiving it; and in the meantime we may rely on having attained such approach to truth, as is possible in our own day. This is the amount of certainty attainable by a fallible being, and this the sole way of attaining it.

Strange it is, that men should admit the validity of the arguments for free discussion, but object to their being "pushed to an extreme"; not seeing that unless the reasons are good for an extreme case, they are not good for any case. Strange that they should imagine that they are not assuming infallibility, when they acknowledge that there should be free discussion on all subjects which can possibly be *doubtful*, but think that some particular principle or doctrine should be forbidden to be questioned because it is so *certain*, that is, because *they are certain* that it is certain. To call any proposition certain, while there is any one who would deny its certainty if permitted, but who is not permitted, is to assume that we ourselves, and those who agree with us, are the judges of certainty, and judges without hearing the other side.

In the present age — which has been described as "destitute of faith, but terrified at scepticism" — in which people feel sure, not so much that their opinions are true, as that they should not know what to do without them — the claims of an opinion to be protected from public attack are rested not so much on its truth, as on its importance to society. There are, it is alleged, certain beliefs, so useful, not to say indispensable to well-being, that it is as much the duty of governments to uphold those beliefs, as to protect any other of the interests of society. In a case of such necessity, and so directly in the line of their duty, something less than infallibility may, it is maintained, warrant, and even bind, governments, to act on their own opinion, confirmed by the general opinion of mankind. It is also often argued, and still oftener thought, that none but bad men would desire to weaken these salutary beliefs; and there can be nothing wrong, it is thought, in restraining bad men, and prohibiting what only such men would wish to practice. This mode of thinking makes the justification of restraints on discussion not a question of the truth of doctrines, but of their usefulness; and flatters itself by that means to escape the responsibility of claiming to be an infallible judge of opinions. But those who thus satisfy themselves, do not perceive that the assumption of infallibility is merely shifted from one point to another. The usefulness of an opinion is itself a matter of opinion: as disputable, as open to discussion, and requiring discussion as much, as the opinion itself. There is the same need of an infallible judge of opinions to decide an opinion to be noxious, as to decide it to be false, unless the opinion condemned has full opportunity of defending itself. And it will not do to say that the heretic may be allowed to maintain the utility or harmlessness of his opinion, though forbidden to maintain its truth. The truth of an opinion is part of its utility. If we would know whether or not it is desirable that a proposition should be believed, is it possible to exclude the consideration of whether or not it is true? In the opinion, not of bad men, but of the best men, no belief which is contrary to truth can be really useful: and can you prevent such men from urging that plea, when they are charged with culpability for denying some doctrine which they are told is useful, but which they believe to be false? Those who are on the side of received opinions, never fail to take all possible advantage of this plea; you do not find *them* handling the question of utility as if it could be completely abstracted from that of truth: on the contrary, it is, above all, because

their doctrine is the "truth," that the knowledge or the belief of it is held to be so indispensable. There can be no fair discussion of the question of usefulness, when an argument so vital may be employed on one side, but not on the other. And in point of fact, when law or public feeling do not permit the truth of an opinion to be disputed, they are just as little tolerant of a denial of its usefulness. The utmost they allow is an extenuation of its absolute necessity, or of the positive guilt of rejecting it.

In order more fully to illustrate the mischief of denying a hearing to opinions because we, in our own judgment, have condemned them, it will be desirable to fix down the discussion to a concrete case; and I choose, by preference, the cases which are least favorable to me — in which the argument against freedom of opinion, both on the score of truth and on that of utility, is considered the strongest. Let the opinions impugned be the belief in a God and in a future state, or any of the commonly received doctrines of morality. To fight the battle on such ground, gives a great advantage to an unfair antagonist; since he will be sure to say (and many who have no desire to be unfair will say it internally), Are these the doctrines which you do not deem sufficiently certain to be taken under the protection of law? Is the belief in a God one of the opinions, to feel sure of which, you hold to be assuming infallibility? But I must be permitted to observe, that it is not the feeling sure of a doctrine (be it what it may) which I call an assumption of infallibility. It is the undertaking to decide that question *for others*, without allowing them to hear what can be said on the contrary side. And I denounce and reprobate this pretension not the less, if put forth on the side of my most solemn convictions. However positive anyone's persuasion may be, not only of the falsity but of the pernicious consequences — not only of the pernicious consequences, but (to adopt expressions which I altogether condemn) the immorality and impiety of an opinion; yet if, in pursuance of that private judgment, though backed by the public judgment of his country or his contemporaries, he prevents the opinion from being heard in its defense, he assumes infallibility. And so far from the assumption being less objectionable or less dangerous because the opinion is called immoral or impious, this is the case of all others in which it is most fatal. These are exactly the occasions on which the men of one generation commit those dreadful mistakes, which excite the astonishment and horror of posterity. It is among such that we find the instances memorable in history, when the arm of the law has been employed to root out the best men and the noblest doctrines; with deplorable success as to the men, though some of the doctrines have survived to be (as if in mockery) invoked, in defense of similar conduct towards those who dissent from *them*, or from their received interpretation.

Mankind can hardly be too often reminded, that there was once a man named Socrates, between whom and the legal authorities and public opinion of his time, there took place a memorable collision. Born in an age and country abounding in individual greatness, this man has been handed down to us by those who best knew both him and the age, as the most virtuous man in it; while we know him as the head and prototype of all subsequent teachers of virtue, the source equally of the lofty inspiration of Plato and the judicious utilitarianism of Aristotle, "*i maëstri di color che sanno*," the two headsprings of ethical as of all other philosophy. This acknowledged master of all the eminent thinkers who have since lived—whose fame, still growing after more than two thousand years, all but outweighs the whole remainder of the names which make his native city illustrious—was put to death by his countrymen, after a judicial conviction, for impiety and immorality. Impiety, in denying the gods recognized by the State; indeed his accuser asserted (see the *Apologia*) that he believed in no gods at all. Immorality, in being, by his doctrines and instructions, a "corruptor of youth." Of these charges the tribunal, there is every ground for believing, honestly found him guilty, and condemned the man who probably of all then born had deserved best of mankind, to be put to death as a criminal.

To pass from this to the only other instance of judicial iniquity, the mention of which, after the condemnation of Socrates, would not be an anticlimax: the event which took place on Calvary rather more than eighteen hundred years ago. The man who left on the memory of those who witnessed his life and conversation, such an impression of his moral grandeur, that eighteen subsequent centuries have done homage to him as the Almighty in person, was ignominiously put to death, as what? As a blasphemer. Men did not merely mistake their benefactor; they mistook him for the exact contrary of what he was, and treated him as that prodigy of impiety, which they themselves are now held to be, for their treatment of him. The feelings with which mankind now regard these lamentable transactions, especially the later of the two, render them extremely unjust in their judgment of the unhappy actors. These were, to all appearance, not bad men—not worse than men commonly are, but rather the contrary; men who possessed in a full, or somewhat more than a full measure, the religious, moral, and patriotic feelings of their time and people: the very kind of men who, in all times, our own included, have every chance of passing through life blameless and respected. The high-priest who rent his garments when the words were pronounced, which, according to all the ideas of his country, constituted the blackest guilt, was in all probability quite as sincere in his horror and indignation, as the generality of respectable and pious men now are in the religious and moral sentiments they profess; and most of those who now shudder at his conduct, if they had lived in his time, and been born Jews, would have acted precisely as he did. Orthodox Christians who are tempted to think that those who stoned to death the first martyrs must have been worse men than they themselves are, ought to remember that one of those persecutors was Saint Paul.

Let us add one more example, the most striking of all, if the impressiveness of an error is measured by the wisdom and virtue of him who falls into it. If ever anyone, possessed of power, had grounds for thinking himself the best and most enlightened among his contemporaries, it was the Emperor Marcus Aurelius. Absolute monarch of the whole civilized world, he preserved through life not only the most unblemished justice, but what was less to be expected from his Stoical breeding, the tenderest heart. The few failings which are attributed to him, were all on the side of indulgence: while his writings, the highest ethical product of the ancient mind, differ scarcely perceptibly, if they differ at all, from the most characteristic teachings of Christ. This man, a better Christian in all but the dogmatic sense of the word, than almost any of the ostensibly Christian sovereigns who have since reigned, persecuted Christianity. Placed at the summit of all the previous attainments of humanity, with an open, unfettered intellect, and a character which led him of himself to embody in his moral writings the Christian ideal, he yet failed to see that Christianity was to be a good and not an evil to the world, with his duties to which he was so deeply penetrated. Existing society he knew to be in a deplorable state. But such as it was, he saw, or thought he saw, that it was held together, and prevented from being worse, by belief and reverence of the received divinities. As a ruler of mankind, he deemed it his duty not to suffer society to fall in pieces; and saw not how, if its existing ties were removed, any others could be formed which could again knit it together. The new religion openly aimed at dissolving these ties: unless, therefore, it was his duty to adopt that religion, it seemed to be his duty to put it down. Inasmuch then as the theology of Christianity did not appear to him true or of divine origin; inasmuch as this strange history of a crucified God was not credible to him, and a system which purported to rest entirely upon a foundation to him so wholly unbelievable, could not be foreseen by him to be that renovating agency which, after all abatements, it has in fact proved to be; the gentlest and most amiable of philosophers and rulers, under a solemn sense of duty, authorized the persecution of Christianity. To my mind this is one of the most tragical facts in all history. It is a bitter thought, how different a thing the Christianity of the world might have been, if the Christian faith had been adopted as the religion of the empire under the auspices of Marcus Aurelius instead of those of Constantine. But it would be equally unjust to him and false to truth, to deny, that no one plea which can be urged for punishing anti-Christian teaching, was wanting to Marcus Aurelius for punishing, as he did, the propagation of Christianity. No Christian more firmly believes that Atheism is false, and tends to the dissolution of society, than Marcus Aurelius believed the same things of Christianity; he who, of all men then living, might have been thought the most capable of appreciating it. Unless anyone who approves of punishment for the promulgation of opinions, flatters himself that he is a wiser and better man than Marcus Aurelius — more deeply versed in the wisdom of his time, more elevated in his intellect above it — more earnest in his search for truth, or more singleminded in his devotion to it when found — let him abstain from that assumption of the joint infallibility of himself and the multitude, which the great Antoninus made with so unfortunate a result....

But, indeed, the dictum that truth always triumphs over persecution, is one of those pleasant falsehoods which men repeat after one another till they pass into commonplaces, but which all experience refutes. History teems with instances of truth put down by persecution. If not suppressed forever, it may be thrown back for centuries. To speak only of religious opinions: the Reformation broke out at least twenty times before Luther, and was put down. Arnold of Brescia was put down. Fra Dolcino was put down. Savonarola was put down. The Albigeois were put down. The Vaudois were put down. The Lollards were put down. The Hussites were put down. Even after the era of Luther, wherever persecution was persisted in, it was successful. In Spain, Italy, Flanders, the Austrian empire, Protestantism was rooted out; and, most likely, would have been so in England, had Queen Mary lived, or Queen Elizabeth died. Persecution has always succeeded, save where the heretics were too strong a party to be effectually persecuted. No reasonable person can doubt that Christianity might have been extirpated in the Roman Empire. It spread, and became predominant, because the persecutions were only occasional, lasting but a short time, and separated by long intervals of almost undisturbed propagandism. It is a piece of idle sentimentality that truth, merely truth, has any inherent power denied to error, of prevailing against the dungeon and the stake. Men are not more zealous for truth than they often are for error, and a sufficient application of legal or even of social penalties will generally succeed in stopping the propagation of either. The real advantage which truth has, consists in this, that when an opinion is true, it may be extinguished once, twice, or many times, but in the course of ages there will generally be found persons to rediscover it, until some one of its reappearances falls on a time when from favorable circumstances it escapes persecution until it has made such head as to withstand all subsequent attempts to suppress it.

It will be said, that we do not now put to death the introducers of new opinions: we are not like our fathers who slew the prophets, we even build sepulchers to them. It is true we no longer put heretics to death; and the amount of penal infliction which modern feeling would probably tolerate, even against the most obnoxious opinions, is not sufficient to extirpate them. But let us not flatter ourselves that we are yet free from the stain even of legal persecution. Penalties for opinion, or at least for its expression, still exist by law; and their enforcement is not, even in these times, so unexampled as to make it at all incredible that they may some day be revived in full force. In the year 1857, at the summer assizes of the county of Cornwall, an unfortunate man, said to be of unexceptionable conduct in all relations of life, was sentenced to twenty-one months' imprisonment, for uttering, and writing on a gate, some offensive words concerning Christianity. Within a month of the same time, at the Old Bailey, two persons, on two separate occasions, were rejected as jurymen, and one of them grossly insulted by the judge and by one of the counsel, because they honestly declared that they had no theological belief; and a third, a foreigner, for the same reason, was denied justice against a thief. This refusal of redress took place in virtue of the legal doctrine, that no person can be allowed to give evidence in a court of justice, who does not profess belief in a God (any god is sufficient) and in a future state; which is equivalent to declaring such persons to be outlaws, excluded from the protection of the tribunals; who may not only be robbed or assaulted with impunity, if no one but themselves, or persons of similar opinions, be present, but anyone else may be robbed or assaulted with impunity, if the proof of the fact depends on their evidence. The assumption on which this is grounded is that the oath is worthless, of a person who does not believe in a future state; a proposition which betokens much ignorance of history in those who assent to it (since it is historically true that a large proportion of infidels in all ages have been persons of distinguished integrity and honor); and would be maintained by no one who had the smallest conception how many of the persons in greatest repute with the world, both for virtues and for attainments, are well known, at least to their intimates, to be unbelievers. The rule, besides, is suicidal, and cuts away its own foundation. Under pretense that atheists must be liars, it admits the testimony of all atheists who are willing to lie, and rejects only those who brave the obloquy of publicly confessing a detested creed rather than affirm a falsehood. A rule thus self-convicted of absurdity so far as regards its professed purpose, can be kept in force only as a badge of hatred, a relic of persecution; a persecution, too, having the peculiarity, that the qualification for undergoing it, is the being clearly proved not to deserve it. The rule, and the theory it implies, are hardly less insulting to believers than to infidels. For if he who does not believe in a future state, necessarily lies, it follows that they who do believe are only prevented from lying, if prevented they are, by the fear of hell. We will not do the authors and abettors of the rule the injury of supposing, that the conception which they have formed of Christian virtue is drawn from their own consciousness.

These, indeed, are but rags and remnants of persecution, and may be thought to be not so much an indication of the wish to persecute, as an example of that very frequent infirmity of English minds, which makes them take a preposterous pleasure in the assertion of a bad principle, when they are no longer bad enough to desire to carry it really into practice. But unhappily there is no security in the state of the public mind, that the suspension of worse forms of legal persecution, which has lasted for about the space of a generation, will continue. In this age the quiet surface of routine is as often ruffled by attempts to resuscitate past evils, as to introduce new benefits. What is boasted of at the present time as the revival of religion, is always, in narrow and uncultivated minds, at least as much the revival of bigotry; and where there is the strong permanent leaven of intolerance in the feelings of a people, which at all times abides in the middle classes of this country, it needs but little to provoke them into actively persecuting those whom they have never ceased to think proper objects of persecution. For it is this — it is the opinions men entertain, and the feelings they cherish, respecting those who disown the beliefs they deem important, which makes this country not a place of mental freedom. For a long time past, the chief mischief of the legal penalties is that they strengthen the social stigma. It is that stigma which is really effective, and so effective is it, that the profession of opinions which are under the ban of society is much less common in

England, than is, in many other countries, the avowal of those which incur risk of judicial punishment. . . . Our merely social intolerance kills no one, roots out no opinions, but induces men to disguise them, or to abstain from any active effort for their diffusion. With us, heretical opinions do not perceptibly gain, or even lose, ground in each decade or generation; they never blaze out far and wide, but continue to smolder in the narrow circles of thinking and studious persons among whom they originate, without ever lighting up the general affairs of mankind with either a true or a deceptive light. And thus is kept up a state of things very satisfactory to some minds, because, without the unpleasant process of fining or imprisoning anybody, it maintains all prevailing opinions outwardly undisturbed, while it does not absolutely interdict the exercise of reason by dissentients afflicted with the malady of thought. A convenient plan for having peace in the intellectual world, and keeping all things going on therein very much as they do already. But the price paid for this sort of intellectual pacification, is the sacrifice of the entire moral courage of the human mind. A state of things in which a large portion of the most active and inquiring intellects find it advisable to keep the general principles and grounds of their convictions within their own breasts, and attempt, in what they address to the public, to fit as much as they can of their own conclusions to premises which they have internally renounced, cannot send forth the open, fearless characters, and logical, consistent intellects who once adorned the thinking world. The sort of men who can be looked for under it, are either mere conformers to commonplace, or time-servers for truth, whose arguments on all great subjects are meant for their hearers, and are not those which have convinced themselves. Those who avoid this alternative, do so by narrowing their thoughts and interest to things which can be spoken of without venturing within the region of principles, that is, to small practical matters, which would come right of themselves, if but the minds of mankind were strengthened and enlarged, and which will never be made effectually right until then: while that which would strengthen and enlarge men's minds, free and daring speculation on the highest subjects, is abandoned.

Those in whose eyes this reticence on the part of heretics is no evil, should consider in the first place, that in consequence of it there is never any fair and thorough discussion of heretical opinions; and that such of them as could not stand such a discussion, though they may be prevented from spreading, do not disappear. But it is not the minds of heretics that are deteriorated most, by the ban placed on all inquiry which does not end in the orthodox conclusions. The greatest harm done is to those who are not heretics, and whose whole mental development is cramped, and their reason cowed, by the fear of heresy. Who can compute what the world loses in the multitude of promising intellects combined with timid characters, who dare not follow out any bold, vigorous, independent train of thought, lest it should land them in something which would admit of being considered irreligious or immoral? Among them we may occasionally see some man of deep conscientiousness, and subtle and refined understanding, who spends a life in sophisticating with an intellect which he cannot silence, and exhausts the resources of ingenuity in attempting to reconcile the promptings of his conscience and reason with orthodoxy, which yet he does not, perhaps, to the end succeed in doing. No one can be a great thinker who does not recognize, that as a thinker it is his first duty to follow his intellect to whatever conclusions it may lead. Truth gains more even by the errors of one who, with due study and preparation, thinks for himself, than by the true opinions of those who only hold them because they do not suffer themselves to think. Not that it is solely, or chiefly, to form great thinkers, that freedom of thinking is required. On the contrary, it is as much and even more indispensable, to enable average human beings to attain the mental stature which they are capable of. There have been, and may again be, great individual thinkers, in a general atmosphere of mental slavery. But there never has been, nor even will be, in that atmosphere, an intellectually active people. When any people has made a temporary approach to such a character, it has been because the dread of heterodox speculation was for a time suspended. Where there is a tacit convention that principles are not to be disputed; where the discussion of the greatest questions which can occupy humanity is considered to be closed, we cannot hope to find that generally high scale of mental activity which has made some periods of history so remarkable. . . .

Let us now pass to the second division of the argument, and dismissing the supposition that any of the received opinions may be false, let us assume them to be true, and examine into the worth of the manner in which they are likely to be held, when their truth is not freely and openly canvassed. However unwillingly a person who has a strong opinion may admit the possibility that his opinion may be false, he ought to be moved by the consideration that however true it may be, if it is not fully, frequently, and fearlessly discussed, it will be held as a dead dogma, not a living truth.

There is a class of persons (happily not quite so numerous as formerly) who think it enough if a person assents undoubtingly to what they think true, though he has no knowledge whatever of the grounds of the opinion, and could not make a tenable defense of it against the most superficial objections. Such persons, if they can once get their creed taught from authority, naturally think that no good, and some harm, comes of its being allowed to be questioned. Where their influence prevails, they make it nearly impossible for the received opinion to be rejected wisely and considerately, though it may still be rejected rashly and ignorantly; for to shut out discussion entirely is seldom possible, and when it once gets in, beliefs not grounded on conviction are apt to give way before the slightest semblance of an argument. Waiving, however, this possibility — assuming that the true opinion abides in the mind, but abides as a prejudice, a belief independent of, and proof against, argument — this is not the way in which truth ought to be held by a rational being. This is not knowing the truth. Truth, thus held, is but one superstition the more accidentally clinging to the words which enunciate a truth.

If the intellect and judgment of mankind ought to be cultivated, a thing which Protestants at least do not deny, on what can these faculties be more appropriately exercised by anyone, than on the things which concern him so much that it is considered necessary for him to hold opinions on them? If the cultivation of the understanding consists in one thing more than in another, it is surely in learning the grounds of one's own opin-

ions. Whatever people believe, on subjects on which it is of the first importance to believe rightly, they ought to be able to defend against at least the common objections. But, some one may say, "Let them be *taught* the grounds of their opinions. It does not follow that opinions must be merely parroted because they are never heard controverted. Persons who learn geometry do not simply commit the theorems to memory, but understand and learn likewise the demonstrations; and it would be absurd to say that they remain ignorant of the grounds of geometrical truths, because they never hear anyone deny, and attempt to disprove them." Undoubtedly: and such teaching suffices on a subject like mathematics, where there is nothing at all to be said on the wrong side of the question. The peculiarity of the evidence of mathematical truths is, that all the argument is on one side. There are no objections, and no answers to objections. But on every subject on which difference of opinion is possible, the truth depends on a balance to be struck between two sets of conflicting reasons. Even in natural philosophy, there is always some other explanation possible of the same facts; some geocentric theory instead of heliocentric, some phlogiston instead of oxygen; and it has to be shown why that other theory cannot be the true one: and until this is shown, and until we know how it is shown, we do not understand the grounds of our opinion. But when we turn to subjects infinitely more complicated, to morals, religion, politics, social relations, and the business of life, three-fourths of the arguments for every disputed opinion consist in dispelling the appearances which favor some opinion different from it. The greatest orator, save one, of antiquity, has left it on record that he always studied his adversary's case with as great, if not with still greater, intensity than even his own. What Cicero practiced as the means of forensic success, requires to be imitated by all who study any subject in order to arrive at the truth. He who knows only his own side of the case, knows little of that. His reasons may be good, and no one may have been able to refute them. But if he is equally unable to refute the reasons on the opposite side; if he does not so much as know what they are, he has no ground for preferring either opinion. The rational position for him would be suspension of judgment, and unless he contents himself with that, he is either led by authority, or adopts, like the generality of the world, the side to which he feels most inclination. Nor is it enough that he should hear the arguments of adversaries from his own teachers, presented as they state them, and accompanied by what they offer as refutations. That is not the way to do justice to the arguments, or bring them into real contact with his own mind. He must be able to hear them from persons who actually believe them; who defend them in earnest, and do their very utmost for them. He must know them in their most plausible and persuasive form; he must feel the whole force of the difficulty which the true view of the subject has to encounter and dispose of; else he will never really possess himself of the portion of truth which meets and removes that difficulty. Ninety-nine in a hundred of what are called educated men are in this condition; even of those who can argue fluently for their opinions. Their conclusion may be true, but it might be false for anything they know: they have never thrown themselves into the mental position of those who think differently from them, and considered what such persons may have to say; and consequently they do not, in any proper sense of the word, know the doctrine which they themselves profess. They do not know those parts of it which explain and justify the remainder; the considerations which show that a fact which seemingly conflicts with another is reconcilable with it, or that, of two apparently strong reasons, one and not the other ought to be preferred. All that part of the truth which turns the scale, and decides the judgment of a completely informed mind, they are strangers to; nor is it ever really known, but to those who have attended equally and impartially to both sides, and endeavored to see the reasons of both in the strongest light. So essential is this discipline to a real understanding of moral and human subjects, that if opponents of all important truths do not exist, it is indispensable to imagine them, and supply them with the strongest arguments which the most skillful devil's advocate can conjure up.

To abate the force of these considerations, an enemy of free discussion may be supposed to say, that there is no necessity for mankind in general to know and understand all that can be said against or for their opinions by philosophers and theologians. That it is not needful for common men to be able to expose all the misstatements or fallacies of an ingenious opponent. That it is enough if there is always somebody capable of answering them, so that nothing likely to mislead uninstructed persons remains unrefuted. That simple minds, having been taught the obvious grounds of the truths inculcated in them, may trust to authority for the rest, and being aware that they have neither knowledge nor talent to resolve every difficulty which can be raised, may repose in the assurance that all those which have been raised have been or can be answered, by those who are specially trained to the task.

Conceding to this view of the subject the utmost that can be claimed for it by those most easily satisfied with the amount of understanding of truth which ought to accompany the belief of it; even so, the argument for free discussion is in no way weakened. For even this doctrine acknowledges that mankind ought to have a rational assurance that all objections have been satisfactorily answered; and how are they to be answered if that which requires to be answered is not spoken? or how can the answer be known to be satisfactory, if the objectors have no opportunity of showing that it is unsatisfactory? If not the public, at least the philosophers and theologians who are to resolve the difficulties, must make themselves familiar with those difficulties in their most puzzling form; and this cannot be accomplished unless they are freely stated, and placed in the most advantageous light which they admit of. The Catholic Church has its own way of dealing with this embarrassing problem. It makes a broad separation between those who can be permitted to receive its doctrines on conviction, and those who must accept them on trust. Neither, indeed, are allowed any choice as to what they will accept; but the clergy, such at least as can be fully confided in, may admissibly and meritoriously make themselves acquainted with the arguments of opponents, in order to answer them, and may, therefore, read heretical books; the laity, not unless by special permission, hard to be obtained. This discipline recognizes a knowledge of the enemy's case as beneficial to the teachers, but finds means, consistent with this, of denying it to the rest of the world: thus giving to the *élite* more mental culture, though not more mental freedom, than it allows to the mass. By this device it succeeds in obtaining the kind of mental superiority which its purposes require; for though culture without freedom never made a large and liberal mind, it can make a clever *nisi prius* advocate of a cause. But in countries professing Protestantism, this resource is denied; since Protestants hold, at least in theory, that the responsibility for the choice of a religion must be borne by each for himself, and cannot be thrown off upon teachers. Besides, in the present state of the world, it is practically impossible that writings which are read by the instructed can be kept from the uninstructed. If the teachers of mankind are to be cognizant of all that they ought to know, everything must be free to be written and published without restraint.

If, however, the mischievous operation of the absence of free discussion, when the received opinions are true, were confined to leaving men ignorant of the grounds of those opinions, it might be thought that this, if an intellectual, is no moral evil, and does not affect the worth of the opinions, regarded in their influence on the character. The fact, however, is, that not only the grounds of the opinion are forgotten in the absence of discussion, but too often the meaning of the opinion itself. The words which convey it, cease to suggest ideas, or suggest only a small portion of those they were originally employed to communicate. Instead of a vivid conception and a living belief, there remain only a few phrases retained by rote; or, if any part, the shell and husk only of the meaning is retained, the finer essence being lost. The great chapter in human history which this fact occupies and fills, cannot be too earnestly studied and meditated on.

It is illustrated in the experience of almost all ethical doctrines and religious creeds. They are all full of meaning and vitality to those who originate them, and to the direct disciples of the originators. Their meaning continues to be felt in undiminished strength, and is perhaps brought out into even fuller consciousness, so long as the struggle lasts to give the doctrine or creed an ascendancy over other creeds. At last it either prevails, and becomes the general opinion, or its progress stops; it keeps possession of the ground it has gained, but ceases to spread further. When either of these results has become apparent, controversy on the subject flags, and gradually dies away. The doctrine has taken its place, if not as a received opinion, as one of the admitted sects or divisions of opinion: those who hold it have generally inherited, not adopted it; and conversion from one of these doctrines to another, being now an exceptional fact, occupies little place in the thoughts of their professors. Instead of being, as at first, constantly on the alert either to defend themselves against the world, or to bring the world over to them, they have subsided into acquiescence, and neither listen, when they can help it, to arguments against their creed, nor trouble dissentients (if there be such) with arguments in its favor. From this time may usually be dated the decline in the living power of the doctrine. We often hear the teachers of all creeds lamenting the difficulty of keeping up in the minds of believers a lively apprehension of the truth which they nominally recognize, so that it may penetrate the feelings, and acquire a real mastery over the conduct. No such difficulty is complained of while the creed is still fighting for its existence: even the weaker combatants then know and feel what they are fighting for, and the difference between it and other doctrines; and in that period of every creed's existence, not a few persons may be found, who have realized its fundamental principles in all the forms of thought, have weighed and considered them in all their important bearings, and have experienced the full effect on the character, which belief in that creed ought to produce in a mind thoroughly imbued with it. But when it has come to be an hereditary creed, and to be received passively, not actively — when the mind is no longer compelled, in the same degree as at first, to exercise its vital powers on the questions which its belief presents to it, there is a progressive tendency to forget all of the belief except the formularies, or to give it a dull and torpid assent, as if accepting it on trust dispensed with the necessity of realizing it in consciousness, or testing it by personal experience; until it almost ceases to connect itself at all with the inner life of the human being. Then are seen the cases, so frequent in this age of the world as almost to form the majority, in which the creed remains as it were outside the mind, encrusting and petrifying it against all other influences addressed to the higher parts of our nature; manifesting its power by not suffering any fresh and living conviction to get in, but itself doing nothing for the mind or heart, except standing sentinel over them to keep them vacant.

To what an extent doctrines intrinsically fitted to make the deepest impression upon the mind may remain in it as dead beliefs, without being ever realized in the imagination, the feelings, or the understanding, is exemplified by the manner in which the majority of believers hold the doctrines of Christianity. By Christianity I here mean what is accounted such by all churches and sects—the maxims and precepts contained in the New Testament. These are considered sacred, and accepted as laws, by all professing Christians. Yet it is scarcely too much to say that not one Christian in a thousand guides or tests his individual conduct by reference to those laws. The standard to which he does refer it, is the custom of his nation, his class, or his religious profession. He has thus, on the one hand, a collection of ethical maxims, which he believes to have been vouchsafed to him by infallible wisdom as rules for his government; and on the other, a set of everyday judgments and practices, which go a certain length with some of those maxims, not so great a length with others, stand in direct opposition to some, and are, on the whole, a compromise between the Christian creed and the interests and suggestions of worldly life. To the first of these standards he gives his homage; to the other his real allegiance. All Christians believe that the blessed are the poor and humble, and those who are ill-used by the world; that it is easier for a camel to pass through the eye of a needle than for a rich man to enter the kingdom of heaven; that they should judge not, lest they be judged; that they should swear not at all; that they should love their neighbor as themselves; that if one take their cloak, they should give him their coat also; that they should take no thought for the morrow; that if they would be perfect, they should sell all that they have and give it to the poor. They are not insincere when they say that they believe these things. They do believe them, as people believe what they have always heard lauded and never discussed. But in the sense of that living belief which regulates conduct, they believe these doctrines just up to the point to which it is usual to act upon them. The doctrines in their integrity are serviceable to pelt adversaries with; and it is understood that they

are to put forward (when possible) as the reasons for whatever people do that they think laudable. But anyone who reminded them that the maxims require an infinity of things which they never even think of doing, would gain nothing but to be classed among those very unpopular characters who affect to be better than other people. The doctrines have no hold on ordinary believers—are not a power in their minds. They have an habitual respect for the sound of them, but no feeling which spreads from the words to the things signified, and forces the mind to take *them* in, and make them conform to the formula. Whenever conduct is concerned, they look round for Mr. *A* and *B* to direct them how far to go in obeying Christ.

Now we may be well assured that the case was not thus, but far otherwise, with the early Christians. Had it been thus, Christianity never would have expanded from an obscure sect of the despised Hebrews into the religion of the Roman empire. When their enemies said, "See how these Christians love one another" (a remark not likely to be made by anybody now), they assuredly had a much livelier feeling of the meaning of their creed than they have ever had since. And to this cause, probably, it is chiefly owing that Christianity now makes so little progress in extending its domain, and after eighteen centuries, is still nearly confined to Europeans and the descendants of Europeans. Even with the strictly religious, who are much in earnest about their doctrines, and attach a greater amount of meaning to many of them than people in general, it commonly happens that the part which is thus comparatively active in their minds is that which was made by Calvin, or Knox, or some such person much nearer in character to themselves. The sayings of Christ co-exist passively in their minds, producing hardly any effect beyond what is caused by mere listening to words so amiable and bland. There are many reasons, doubtless, why doctrines which are the badge of a sect retain more of their vitality than those common to all recognized sects, and why more pains are taken by teachers to keep their meaning alive; but one reason certainly is, that the peculiar doctrines are more questioned, and have to be oftener defended against open gainsayers. Both teachers and learners go to sleep at their post, as soon as there is no enemy in the field.

The same thing holds true, generally speaking, of all traditional doctrines — those of prudence and knowledge of life, as well as morals or religion. All languages and literatures are full of general observations on life, both as to what it is, and how to conduct oneself in it; observations which everybody knows, which everybody repeats, or hears with acquiescence, which are received as truisms, yet of which most people first truly learn the meaning, when experience, generally of a painful kind, has made it a reality to them. How often, when smarting under some unforeseen misfortune or disappointment, does a person call to mind some proverb or common saying, familiar to him all his life, the meaning of which, if he had ever before felt it as he does now, would have saved him from the calamity. There are indeed reasons for this, other than the absence of discussion: there are many truths of which the full meaning *cannot* be realized, until personal experience has brought it home. But much more of the meaning even of these would have been understood, and what was understood would have been far more deeply impressed on the mind, if the man had been accustomed to hear it argued *pro* and *con* by people who did understand it. The fatal tendency of mankind to leave off thinking about a thing when it is no longer doubtful, is the cause of half their errors. A contemporary author has well spoken of "the deep slumber of a decided opinion."

But what! (it may be asked) Is the absence of unanimity an indispensable condition of true knowledge? Is it necessary that some part of mankind should persist in error, to enable any to realize the truth? Does a belief cease to be real and vital as soon as it is generally received — and is a proposition never thoroughly understood and felt unless some doubt of it remains? As soon as mankind have unanimously accepted a truth, does the truth perish within them? The highest aim and best result of improved intelligence, it has hitherto been thought, is to unite mankind more and more in the acknowledgment of all important truths: and does the intelligence only last as long as it has not achieved its object? Do the fruits of conquest perish by the very completeness of the victory?

I affirm no such thing. As mankind improve, the number of doctrines which are no longer disputed or doubted will be constantly on the increase: and the well-being of mankind may almost be measured by the number and gravity of the truths which have reached the point of being uncontested. The cessation, on one question after another, of serious controversy, is one of the necessary incidents of the consolidation of opinion; a consolidation as salutary in the case of true opinions, as it is dangerous and noxious when the opinions are erroneous. But though this gradual narrowing of the bounds of diversity of opinion is necessary in both senses of the term, being at once inevitable and indispensable, we are not therefore obliged to conclude that all its consequences must be beneficial. The loss of so important an aid to the intelligent and living apprehension of a truth, as is afforded by the necessity of explaining it to, or defending it against, opponents, though not sufficient to outweigh, is no trifling drawback from, the benefit of its universal recognition. Where this advantage can no longer be had, I confess I should like to see the teachers of mankind endeavoring to provide a substitute for it; some contrivance for making the difficulties of the question as present to the learner's consciousness, as if they were pressed upon him by a dissentient champion, eager for his conversion.

But instead of seeking contrivances for this purpose, they have lost those they formerly had. The Socratic dialectics, so magnificently exemplified in the dialogues of Plato, were a contrivance of this description. They were essentially a negative discussion of the great questions of philosophy and life, directed with consummate skill to the purpose of convincing anyone who had merely adopted the commonplaces of received opinion, that he did not understand the subject — that he as yet attached no definite meaning to the doctrines he professed; in order that, becoming aware of his ignorance, he might be put in the way to attain a stable belief, resting on a clear apprehension both of the meaning of doctrines and of their evidence. The school disputations of the middle ages had a somewhat similar object. They were intended to make sure that the pupil understood his own opinion, and (by necessary correlation) the opinion opposed to it, and could enforce the grounds of the one and confute those of the other. These last-mentioned contests had indeed the incurable defect, that the premises appealed to were taken from authority, not from reason; and, as a discipline to the mind, they were in every respect inferior to the powerful dialectics which formed the intellects of the *"Socratici viri"*: but the modern mind owes far more to both than it is generally willing to admit, and the present modes of education contain nothing which in the smallest degree supplies the place either of the one or of the other. A person who derives all his instruction from teachers or books, even if he escape the besetting temptation of contenting himself with cram, is under no compulsion to hear both sides; accordingly it is far from a frequent accomplishment, even among thinkers, to know both sides; and the weakest part of what everybody says in defense of his opinion, is what he intends as a reply to antagonists. It is the fashion of the present time to disparage negative logic — that which points out weaknesses in theory or errors in practice, without establishing positive truths. Such negative criticism would indeed be poor enough as an ultimate result; but as a means to attaining any positive knowledge or conviction worthy the name, it cannot be valued too highly; and until people are again systematically trained to it, there will be few great thinkers, and a low general average of intellect, in any but the mathematical and physical departments of speculation. On any other subject no one's opinions deserve the name of knowledge, except so far as he has either had forced upon him by others, or gone through of himself, the same mental process which would have been required of him in carrying on an active controversy with opponents. That, therefore, which when absent, it is so indispensable, but so difficult, to create, how worse than absurd it is to forgo, when spontaneously offering itself! If there are any persons who contest a received opinion, or who will do so if law or opinion will let them, let us thank them for it, open our minds to listen to them, and rejoice that there is someone to do for us what we otherwise ought, if we have any regard for either the certainty or the vitality of our convictions, to do with much greater labor for ourselves.

It still remains to speak of one of the principal causes which make diversity of opinion advantageous, and will continue to do so until mankind shall have entered a stage of intellectual advancement which at present seems at an incalculable distance. We have hitherto considered only two possibilities: that the received opinion may be false, and some other opinion, consequently, true; or that, the received opinion being true, a conflict with the opposite error is essential to a clear apprehension and deep feeling of its truth. But there is a commoner case than either of these; when the conflicting doctrines, instead of being one true and the other false, share the truth between them; and the nonconforming opinion is needed to supply the remainder of the truth, of which the received doctrine embodies only a part. Popular opinions, on subjects not palpable to sense, are often true, but seldom or never the whole truth. They are a part of the truth; sometimes a greater, sometimes a smaller part, but exaggerated, distorted, and disjoined from the truths by which they ought to be accompanied and limited. Heretical opinions, on the other hand, are generally some of these suppressed and neglected truths, bursting the bonds which kept them down, and either seeking reconciliation with the truth contained in the common opinion, or fronting it as enemies, and setting themselves up, with similar exclusiveness, as the whole truth. The latter case is hitherto the most frequent, as, in the human mind, one-sidedness has always been the rule and many-sidedness the exception. Hence, even in revolutions of opinion, one part of the truth usually sets while another rises. Even progress, which ought to superadd, for the most part only substitutes, one partial and incomplete truth for another; improvement consisting chiefly in this, that the new fragment of truth is more wanted, more adapted to the needs of the time, than that which it displaces. Such being the partial character of prevailing opinions, even when resting on a true foundation, every opinion which embodies somewhat of the portion of truth which the common opinion omits, ought to be considered precious, with whatever amount of error and confusion that truth may be blended. No sober judge of human affairs will feel bound to be indignant because those who force on our notice truths which we should otherwise have overlooked, overlook some of those which we see. Rather, he will think that so long as popular truth is one-sided, it is more desirable than otherwise that unpopular truth should have one-sided asserters too; such being usually the most energetic, and the most likely to compel reluctant attention to the fragment of wisdom which they proclaim as if it were the whole. . . .

In politics, again, it is almost a commonplace, that a party of order or stability, and a party of progress or reform, are both necessary elements of a healthy state of political life; until the one or the other shall have so enlarged its mental grasp as to be a party equally of order and of progress, knowing and distinguishing what is fit to be preserved from what ought to be swept away. Each of these modes of thinking derives its utility from the deficiencies of the other; but it is in a great measure the opposition of the other that keeps each within the limits of reason and sanity. Unless opinions favorable to democracy and to aristocracy, to property and to equality, to cooperation and to competition, to luxury and to abstinence, to sociality and individuality, to liberty and discipline, and all the other standing antagonisms of practical life, are expressed with equal freedom, and enforced and defended with equal talent and energy, there is no chance of both elements obtaining their due; one scale is sure to go up, and the other down. Truth, in the great practical concerns of life, is so much a question of the reconciling and combining of opposites, that very few have minds sufficiently capacious and impartial to make the adjustment with an approach to correctness, and it has to be made by the rough process of a struggle between combatants fighting under hostile banners. On any of the great open questions just enumerated, if either of the two opinions has a better claim than the other, not merely to be tolerated, but to be encouraged and countenanced, it is the one which happens at the particular time and place to be in a minority. That is the opinion which, for the time being, represents the neglected interests, the side of human well-being which is in danger of obtaining less than its share. I am aware that there is not, in this country, any intolerance of differences of opinion on most of these topics. They are adduced to show, by admitted and multiplied examples, the universality of the fact, that only through diversity of opinion is there, in the existing state of human intellect, a chance of fair play to all sides of the truth. When there are persons to be found, who form an exception to the apparent unanimity of the world on any subject, even if the world is in the right, it is always prob-

able that dissentients have something worth hearing to say for themselves, and that truth would lose something by their silence. . . .

I do not pretend that the most unlimited use of the freedom of enunciating all possible opinions would put an end to the evils of religious or philosophical sectarianism. Every truth which men of narrow capacity are in earnest about, is sure to be asserted, inculcated, and in many ways even acted on, as if no other truth existed in the world, or at all events none that could limit or qualify the first. I acknowledge that the tendency of all opinions to become sectarian is not cured by the freest discussion, but is often heightened and exacerbated thereby; the truth which ought to have been, but was not, seen, being rejected all the more violently because proclaimed by persons regarded as opponents. But it is not on the impassioned partisan, it is on the calmer and more disinterested bystander, that this collision of opinions works its salutary effect. Not the violent conflict between parts of the truth, but the quiet suppression of half of it, is the formidable evil; there is always hope when people are forced to listen to both sides; it is when they attend only to one that errors harden into prejudices, and truth itself ceases to have the effect of truth, by being exaggerated into falsehood. And since there are few mental attributes more rare than that judicial faculty which can sit in intelligent judgment between two sides of a question, of which only one is represented by an advocate before it, truth has no chance but in proportion as every side of it, every opinion which embodies any fraction of the truth, not only finds advocates, but is so advocated as to be listened to.

We have now recognized the necessity to the mental well-being of mankind (on which all their other well-being depends) of freedom of opinion, and freedom of the expression of opinion, on four distinct grounds; which we will now briefly recapitulate.

First, if any opinion is compelled to silence, that opinion may, for aught we can certainly know, be true. To deny this is to assume our own infallibility.

Secondly, though the silenced opinion be an error it may, and very commonly does, contain a portion of truth, and since the general or prevailing opinion of any subject is rarely or never the whole truth, it is only by the collision of adverse opinions that the remainder of the truth has any chance of being supplied.

Thirdly, even if the received opinion be not only true, but the whole truth; unless it is suffered to be, and actually is, vigorously and earnestly contested it will, by most of those who receive it, be held in the manner of a prejudice with little comprehension or feeling of its rational grounds.

And not only this, but Fourthly, the meaning of the doctrine itself will be in danger of being lost, or enfeebled and deprived of its vital effect on the character and conducts the dogma becoming a mere formal profession, inefficacious for good, but cumbering the ground, and preventing the growth of any real and heartfelt conviction, from reason or personal experience.

* * *

Notes and Questions

FRED R. BERGER, "Symbolic Conduct and Freedom of Speech"

1. The First Amendment to the Constitution specifically guarantees freedom from government interference with speech. There is no question that a civil right to free speech is recognized and respected in this country, but it is far from clear what this right covers. Some limits are discussed in the cases following the article by Nat Hentoff, namely, the limits imposed by the need to protect state interests. To recognize these limits is to recognize that even important First Amendment rights are not absolute. They must be coordinated with other rights and with the general welfare. Fred R. Berger discusses a different kind of limit: the limit of meaning. The question is, What is to be included in the notion of speech? Is a parade speech? How about carrying a sign or wearing an armband, a political button, or a T-shirt with a message on it? Such conduct is often considered symbolic speech. How does Berger defend this position? What two features must a symbolic act have, according to Berger? Would these features enable you, or a court, to distinguish clearly symbolic acts from other acts? If the act has these two features, is it appropriate to call it speech? Why or why not?

2. Suppose we recognize symbolic conduct within Berger's limits as speech. How far should the protection go? What is Berger's position? Do you agree that violating a protested statute is a special kind of symbolic conduct? Should it be accorded special protection? Does it cause special problems for First Amendment protection?

3. What grounds for special protection of symbolic conduct are provided by the democratic idea of freedom of expression, according to Berger? Is there greater need for this protection now than in an earlier time? Why?

4. Does Berger successfully answer objections to his position? What major objections does he enumerate? Can you think of others? Even if the First Amendment protects speech, is it reasonable to think that it protects the expression or communication of ideas in any manner? What reasons are there to think so?

5. Berger argues that the legal doctrines needed to adjudicate the protection and restriction of symbolic conduct should be part of a unified theory of free expression that makes no distinction between conventional speech and symbolic conduct as such. He notes that conventional speech is restricted to protect conflicting individual rights and government interests in certain cases and that analogous criteria may be used to regulate all expression. What are these criteria? Would using them handle the objections Berger confronted earlier? Would they workably apply to all speech? Would you add or subtract from them? Why or why not?

6. Following the Berger essay is a brief comment by Nat Hentoff about an event that occurred in 1977.

Symbolic Conduct and Freedom of Speech

FRED R. BERGER

Civil disobedience is no longer the live topic it was in the United States during the 1960s. As the Vietnam war ended, and the civil rights struggle gave way to more intractable racial difficulties, public discussion of civil disobedience virtually died out. Civil disobedience long predated the sixties, however, and it will continue to be a mode of protest, resistance, or political change as long as governments exist. Moreover, there is much unfinished business in the area of the political and legal philosophy of American institutions which bears on civil disobedience. Despite years of litigation involving conscience-motivated disobedience, there still is no clearcut jurisprudence of civil disobedience to which the American legal system is committed. This is especially true of protest that involves symbolic conduct. The courts have been faced with claims to First Amendment protection of such conduct as distributing literature,[1] soliciting donations for a religious group,[2] parading,[3] picketing,[4] burning a flag,[5] wearing black armbands to school,[6] burning a draft card,[7] sitting-in at a segregated lunch counter,[8] and so on. Although the Supreme Court has at times shown admirable sensitivity to the claims of the protestors, it has also shown a remarkable flexibility in the decisions it has taken. The results have appeared to some observers quite anomalous or even bordering on the contradictory.

Part of the difficulty with the Court's position arises from an inadequate theoretical position. It has sometimes employed a distinction between "pure speech" and "speech plus" as a tool for deciding cases involving symbolic conduct. "Speech plus," presumably, cannot have the same protections afforded speech proper. We shall explore some difficulties with this treatment.

In this essay I shall seek: (1) to show up the inadequacy of the speech-conduct distinction; (2) to illuminate the nature of symbolic conduct; (3) to provide a philosophical justification for bringing symbolic conduct under First Amendment purview; (4) to answer some of the chief objections to doing so; and (5) to indicate the sorts of legal doctrines needed to intelligently deal with symbolic conduct. Some of this work has been done by others.[9] My intention is to present the issues in outline or capsule form, and to stress points that others have missed or have not dealt with. I maintain that the same criteria should apply to symbolic conduct and so-called pure speech. Just as one cannot be free to say anything one wants, wherever and whenever one wants, so too one cannot engage in symbolic conduct in any form, whenever and wherever one wants. However, the grounds for distinguishing the acceptable from the unacceptable cases should be the same for both conventional and symbolic communication.

I. The Nature of Symbolic Conduct

Symbolic conduct is a subject to which surprisingly little attention has been given. Moreover, there is one special form of symbolic conduct which, in my opinion, has very great importance in the contemporary world and which has not been adequately discussed in the literature.

In contemporary philosophical circles theories of "speech acts" are very popular. Such theories emphasize how, in engaging in *speech*, we perform certain acts, e.g., promising, insulting, contracting, etc. What is wanted is a theory that explains how, in engaging in *other* acts, e.g., burning a draft card, we accomplish what is done by speech acts, and why, sometimes, we do it *better* that way. Although I cannot provide such a theory, I shall indicate some ways in which actions may be symbolic and thus communicate ideas. One kind of symbolic action—a "demonstration" of an evil—I think is particularly important.

The simplest form of symbolic action takes place when what are normally noncommunicative acts are mingled with conventional speech or with conventional nonverbal symbols, e.g., banners, placards, flags, etc. Here, the nonverbal devices convey at least part of the message and give added meaning to the behavior. A group might, for example, wear black armbands in a sit-in at a police station to protest the shooting of a member of the group.

Special problems are raised if there is a temporal gap in the behavior and the appearance of the conventional symbols or speech. For example, one might have burned one's draft card during the Vietnam War and later marched to the draft board with the ashes to confront the state with the deed. At first glance, it appears there are two acts committed — the burning of the draft card, which is not communicative (it may have been done in secret), and the later announcement of the deed. Only the latter, some persons would say, counts as speech.

Such an approach seems overly hasty, for there are at least two important reasons for regarding the series of actions as aspects of one complex act, which, as a whole, carries the communicative force of the protest. First, the full impact of the conventional speech is tied in essential ways to the defiance of statute embodied in the earlier aspect of the complex. Second, the act was done (I am supposing), in part as an aspect of the attempt to confront the state in a dramatic way with its alleged iniquity. In other words, the force, effectiveness, and importance attached to the communication are altered and enhanced through the commission of the nonverbal act, and this was part of the actor's intention. By virtue of its properties, the nonverbal act influences the character of the communication and thus acquires communicative force. It does not have this force performed alone, but then the conventional speech does not fully convey its message when performed alone, either. So, though one can distinguish the nonverbal activities, from another perspective they are part of a chain of activities that together constitute the full communicative act.

If this reasoning seems implausible, consider that we would not find it acceptable as a defense in a murder case for the defendant to claim that all he did was to set an alarm clock, if we knew that the clock was connected to a bomb and that the defendant knew this and set the alarm with the intention of exploding the bomb and killing someone. It is the intended connections between what (from another point of view) appear as discrete events that justify us in part in identifying a single act of murder. Perhaps more a propos, we can note that the movements of our vocal chords, lips, and tongues are different from one another and from the sounds we make. We do not, however, separate any of these from the protected act of speaking, simply because if they occurred alone they would not convey any message. The sorts of acts we are talking of may be seen as a necessary means of conveying a message with full force, clarity, and urgency.

Alternatively, these cases, and a spectrum of others, could be characterized as ones in which objects or actions normally not symbolic are *given* a symbolic function. Presumably, any thing, action, or event can be arbitrarily assigned a meaning, but it is clear that the symbolic function usually requires that the "symbol" bear some relation to the object of the protest. For example, a draft card had a clear, obvious connection to the conduct of a war that protestors opposed. On the other hand, political assassination, though sometimes done with communicative purpose or effect, is not well suited for that purpose because the audience cannot readily identify the policies or programs being protested and is drawn away from the "message" by the nature of the deed.

There is one special kind of symbolic conduct that relies heavily on its connection with the protested injustice. This is an extremely important form of civil disobedience in contemporary society, and it has not been sufficiently recognized. These are statute-violating acts that *demonstrate*, in their commission, the protested injustice or policy. Such acts have sometimes been of great historical importance. When Gandhi marched to the sea and extracted a bit of salt from it — a violation of British colonial law — he was *demonstrating* the nature, extent, and burden of English colonial oppression and of the laws buttressing it. He showed that even so simple and harmless an act as making salt from sea water was made a crime in order to guarantee an open market for English salt manufacturers. Moreover, the Salt Acts were not the most oppressive laws Gandhi was protesting; his civil disobedience was doubly symbolic in that it pointed to the many ways in which colonial rule stifled native initiative and industry to turn British profits.

Similarly, when black students in the United

States refused to leave segregated lunch counters, they were demonstrating that, even in such matters as getting a cup of coffee in a department store, they were discriminated against. And, of course, the lunch counter sit-ins were symbolic of the various affronts to human dignity supported by racist local governments. A demonstration of this kind may be a more meaningful appeal to the electorate than conventional speech, and, indeed, these and other demonstrations helped pave the way for legislation and changed attitudes that decades of speeches, petitions, legal marches, etc., had been unable to accomplish.[10]

The impact of a demonstration, and thus its importance, is very much a function of the manner in which it serves to communicate ideas. A demonstration is very like what Charles Peirce called an *icon* or *iconic sign*: "a sign that represents its Object in resembling it."[11] The kinds of civil disobedience I am discussing create, through the violation of statute or orders of public officials, situations that have features in common with the protested wrong by virtue of being an instance of it. A demonstration *shows* people the injustice and signifies patterns of which it is an instance. With today's potential for media coverage, this can be a significant means of enlightening a complacent public — through either apprising it of facts or getting it to better appreciate facts of which it is already aware. The general public could readily identify with the situation of young blacks at the lunch counters and was literally confronted with injustices of which it previously had only an intellectual grasp.

In summary, there appear to be two general conditions for an act to be communicative or symbolic: (1) It has features (of the kinds indicated) that suit it for conveying ideas, and (2) the actor intends (perhaps among other things) to communicate ideas in that way.

II. The Argument for Protection

Does the democratic idea of freedom of expression give grounds for according special protection to symbolic conduct — e.g., under the umbrella of the First Amendment of the Constitution of the United States? I shall argue that it does.

First, let us concentrate on the point, purpose, and values that provide the rationale for the First Amendment. Freedom of speech, press, and assembly reflect the democratic principles that all citizens are sources of ideas and political influence, that all citizens have a right to participate in their governance, that freedom of expression is essential to the preservation and furtherance of other freedoms, and that certain kinds of liberties are crucial to a sense of dignity and self-determination. Moreover, the First Amendment is clearly intended to foster open, unfettered, informed debate — an obvious prerequisite for the determination of public policy and the election of public officials.[12]

Furthermore, to the extent that being oneself openly and honestly involves expressing oneself in one's own way, mutual respect for one another as persons dictates freedom of expression as something deserving of protection, in as many ways as is consistent with civic life. Democracy correctly professes to incorporate respect for persons as a value, and the protection of the right of free speech is one important way in which this is done.

If we take seriously the values underlying freedom of speech, there is no reason to limit its ambit to conventional modes of communication. And, indeed, the Supreme Court has not always insisted on a narrow interpretation of the legal term *speech*, certifying the free speech rights of persons wearing armbands; displaying banners, flags, or placards; holding parades; picketing; etc.

Moreover, there are reasons why, in the contemporary world, unconventional communications have increasing importance. With contemporary media technology, we are literally bombarded with communications of conventional kinds — a situation that has a numbing effect. Also, the "normal" techniques are too often controlled or monopolized by special groups. During the Vietnam War, the successive presidential administrations had continual access to sizable audiences, whereas critics were fortunate to be able to *buy* extremely expensive media time. When one bears in mind that administration platforms dealing with that issue were too often employed for implanting misleading or false beliefs, and for impugning the patriotism and honesty of the opposition, it is apparent that any countercommunication had an uphill battle to fight.[13] In such circumstances, shock tactics may be required.

We should add that many who have cause to protest in our society are unconventional persons who require unconventional modes to feel they are freely and fully expressing their views effectively. To the extent that freedom of speech is a form of respect for autonomous individuals, we should allow maximum tolerance to the need of individuals to express themselves in the manner *they* feel best suits their message. And, to the extent we are willing to take this stance, we will regard restrictions as to time, place, and manner as possible interferences with speech.

Finally, we must note that the conventional, or "normal" channels for mass communication can prove extremely costly and require considerable sophistication and knowledge for effective utilization. This is true of the process by which redress is to be had for legal as well as for social wrongs.

III. Objections and Replies

Though most persons with an interest in freedom of speech acknowledge some force to these arguments, many are unwilling to accept the general proposition that symbolic conduct is entitled to First Amendment protection. The chief objection is that recognition of such a principle would expand too broadly the range of activity that would be protected. "We cannot accept the view," Chief Justice Warren wrote in one of the draft-card burning cases, "that an apparently limitless variety of conduct can be labelled *speech* whenever the person engaging in the conduct intends thereby to express an idea."[14] The perceived defects of this expansion vary.

Professor Carl Cohen has argued that, in such cases as sitting-in, blocking traffic, etc., the "specific act . . . is not the sort of thing that requires constitutional protection." To insist that such an act is speech because the actor intends it to be, and "in spite of its specific nature, which is obvious and undeniable," is to bring any sort of action under the First Amendment, which was not its original or "proper present" intention.[15]

Such an argument is beside the point. It is not claimed that trespasses, burning cards or flags,

interferences with traffic, and so on, are per se the sorts of things that require constitutional protection. It is *communication* that must be protected. Moreover, it is not claimed that such acts become communicative simply because the actor intends them to be. Rather, they become communicative acts for that reason *and* the fact that they have features that suit them for the conveying of ideas. I have tried to indicate some of these, and Professor Cohen has listed several such features in another place in his book.[16] There is no good reason the courts cannot, at least under certain circumstances, investigate and take note of acts of such kinds and recognize the important communicative role they sometimes play in our social and political life. Finally, we should note that Cohen's point that these acts, in their "specific" descriptions, are not intended to be protected would destroy protection for all speech. Lip movements and the making of sounds are not specifically encompassed within the First Amendment. It is the functional connection of these with the production of communicative speech and the dissemination of ideas that is crucial. Where such a functional connection can be strongly made for acts with other specific descriptions, fidelity to the values for which protection is required makes it incumbent to extend protection to such acts.

A second variation on the theme was expressed by former Justice Fortas:

> The Supreme Court of the United States has said, over and over, that the words of the First Amendment mean what they say. But they mean what they say and not something else. They guarantee freedom to speak and freedom of the press — not freedom to club people or to destroy property. The First Amendment protects the right to assemble and to petition, but it requires — in plain words — that the right be peaceably exercised.[17]

A related, and perhaps more appealing, objection would stress the dangers to civil rights of *impartially* protecting symbolic conduct without regard to the protestor's political views. Impartial administration of the First Amendment requires protecting the expression of views of those with whom we disagree. If we protect as First Amendment activity a sit-in that protests racial discrimination, then, it may be argued, impartiality requires that we also protect those who seek to block attempts at racial equality.[18]

Such views will seem plausible only if one insists on ignoring important differences between such acts as clubbing people and destroying property, and (for example) making a spoonful of salt or remaining at a lunch counter when asked to leave. The second version will appeal only if we fail to distinguish acts that infringe no basic political and moral rights from those that do. Not all cases of statute-violating acts threaten the lives, property, or basic rights of others. There is simply no reason why the courts cannot recognize this fact; they could consistently protect symbolic conduct that poses no serious dangers while permitting punishment of conduct that does.

This point also bears on my final objection, raised also by Professor Cohen, which holds that an expansive view on symbolic conduct and the First Amendment would grant excessive autonomy to individuals, permitting anyone to ignore the law whenever the person claims his or her violation of law is a protest. This, Cohen thinks, is an absurd result and not in keeping with First Amendment principles. Cohen's objection is that the courts will balance interests *only* when there is a "natural" and "unavoidable" conflict between the two. Thus, there is a natural and unavoidable conflict between an individual's interest in being protected from injurious, libelous speech, and freedom of speech. Generally speaking, there is no such natural and unavoidable conflict between, say, prohibitions on trespass and freedom of speech. If, however, symbolic conduct is given First Amendment protection, the "natural and unavoidable conflict" requirement would fall away, protestors would be able to force on the courts *their* choice of which interests must be balanced against freedom of speech:

> But if any deliberate violation of a trespass statute chosen by the protestor to be a political act must be balanced against the larger need to protect free speech, then the deliberate violation of any statute, major or minor, if intended as a protest, will have also to be so balanced and may claim the same protection. To accept [the] argument, in short, is to allow a First Amendment defense for any statute violation whatever, if it could reasonably be argued that the violation was intended as

some form of protest. This would carry the extension of First Amendment guarantees to the point of absurdity, giving that Amendment as a protective weapon to whomever might wish to stage an illegal protest, whatever its form. . . .

This is not to say that where the interests of free speech conflict with property or other interests of lesser importance the latter should prevail, but only that unless there is a natural or normal conflict of community interests, such a balancing need not be undertaken.[19]

It is important to note that Cohen's argument, if it is to have prima facie plausibility, is directed against an extreme view not taken in this paper, namely, that First Amendment rights are absolute against all other interests. Indeed, all his mention of balancing interests is a smokescreen, for the position he is attacking in fact rejects balancing. If it asserts that all protest activity is speech *and* that the free speech guarantee *always* overrides contrary statutes "major or minor," then any further "balancing" is otiose. The account for which I have been arguing rejects so simplistic a view. It recognizes the fact that symbolic conduct can pose immediate dangers to important interests that citizens have, and that sometimes those dangers can be very great. Accepting symbolic conduct as protected speech need not commit one to asserting such a right holds even when according it protection in the circumstances of its occurrence would invade important rights of others.

Moreover, granting a certain amount of legal autonomy to citizens, conditioned on the circumstances and the dangers its exercise poses, would not have the absurd result Cohen claims. Once the disobedient can show that the action is a significant communicational act, he or she can then argue that it is the kind of thing the Constitution is meant to protect,[20] and the fact that it is unusual, or not normal, cannot by itself defeat the claim. The free speech guarantee is considerably weakened if excluded from its ambit are the remarkable, the unusual, and the unconventional. The choice exercised by the protestor should be put in proper perspective. That choice is of the *manner* of the exercise of the right. And, surely, freedom of speech is compromised if a fair measure of choice as to manner is not protected. There must be some limits, but they are not marked by what is a "normal" manner of expression.

At this stage, it is important to note that all the objections considered above have a feature in common. They all assume some fundamental difference between symbolic conduct and conventional speech hinging on the fact that physical activity is involved in the former but not in the latter — thus, the Supreme Court's distinction between "pure speech" and "speech plus." Not only is this view mistaken, but rigid adherence to it will make inexplicable First Amendment doctrine dealing with uncontested aspects of "pure speech."

As we have seen earlier, even conventional speech involves physical activity — the movement of one's vocal chords and mouth, the movements of one's hands, writing on paper, etc. As is the case with symbolic conduct, what gives these movements communicative force are the intended connections among them, the signs used, and the conveyance of ideas. Moreover, the deliverance of speech and writing involves a physical context. Speech always occurs in a given place, at a given *time*. Written or printed material consists of physical objects that must be distributed in a place, at a time, etc. All communication arises in, or as a result of, physical activity. What makes "pure speech" seem different from symbolic speech (when it is not merely the nature of the symbols employed that is the basis of the distinction) is that the sorts of physical activity involved — moving one's lips, etc. — do not normally impinge on others' rights or pose dangers to others. But — and this is of central importance — when the physical aspects of conventional speech *do* affect the interests and rights of others, regulation is in order. Even a defender of an "absolute" right of free speech agrees that one has no First Amendment right to give political speeches in a hospital operating room.[21] This is "pure speech," but properly proscribed because it poses a real and immediate danger to important interests of others.

I am urging, then, that a solution to the question of the legal doctrines needed to deal with symbolic conduct must be part of a unified theory of freedom of expression that makes no essential distinction between symbolic and conventional speech.[22] Though I cannot present and argue for the doctrines needed, I do want to make some points that bear on the selection of such doctrines.

IV. Legal Doctrines Needed

The choice of principles to govern First Amendment regulation must recognize an important, if imprecise, distinction between regulation of speech because of its *content*, and regulation of the *activity* of engaging in speech. Prosecutions based on such concepts as defamation, libel, invasion of privacy, and incitement to crime are all based in part on the nature of the speech involved. Although we like to think freedom of speech is perfectly neutral as to content, in fact, each such prosecution necessarily inquiries into what was said, and, in some cases, even into whether what was said was true or false. Such exemptions from First Amendment protection constitute specifiable classes of cases in which certain interests of persons are endangered by what is said and in which the values underlying free speech are not significantly furthered. Principles are needed for picking out such classes, but once identified, the principles for regulating protected speech will not necessarily apply to these cases.[23]

In cases where the *activity* is to be regulated, the interests of others may be endangered directly or through danger to the institutions in which persons have an interest. The conflict will normally be posed by a person engaging in speech in a context which, prima facie, constitutes a violation of an official statute, directive, or order that is directed at protecting or furthering interests other than interests in engaging in speech.[24] What is needed are guidelines for adjudicating these conflicts. The clear and present danger rule was one attempt to come up with such guidelines, the balancing of interests test another.

The Supreme Court in the *O'Brien* draft-card burning case set out the following criteria:

> a government regulation is sufficiently justified if it is within the constitutional power of the Government; if it furthers an important or substantial governmental interest; if the governmental interest is unrelated to the suppression of free expression; and if the incidental restriction on alleged First Amendment freedoms is no greater than is essential to the furtherance of that interest.[25]

At least one commentator has pointed out that an additional and important criterion was used in the case of *Tinker*, involving students wearing black armbands to school. The Court held that "where there is no finding and no showing that engaging in any of the forbidden conduct would 'materially and substantially interfere with the requirements of appropriate discipline in the operation of the school,' the prohibition cannot be sustained."[26] If one combines these points with the thrust of the clear and present danger rule that proscribed speech activity must pose a likely and imminent danger to interests it is appropriate for government to protect, criteria emerge that can form the basis of the legal doctrines needed to regulate speech—conventional *and* symbolic: (1) The speech activity must endanger interests the government may properly protect. (2) The interest protected must be important or substantial. (3) The government interest must be unrelated to the suppression of free speech. (4) The government regulation employed to further that interest must in fact do so, and not unnecessarily infringe speech. (5) The speech activity must present a likely danger of a material and substantial degree to the interests that government seeks to protect.

Much needs to be said concerning the interpretation of these points, and additional criteria may be needed. Moreover, ultimate clarification could only come from applying the principles to actual cases. These points do, however, provide a basis for the development of the needed legal doctrines. They are drawn from existing legal adjudication, and they can be applied to both conventional and symbolic speech.

NOTES

1. Lovell v. City of Griffin, 303 U.S. 444 (1938).

2. Cantwell v. Connecticut, 310 U.S. 296 (1940).

3. There are a great many cases bearing on this issue. See, e.g., Shuttlesworth v. City of Birmingham, 382 U.S. 87 (1965).

4. The classic case is Thornhill v. Alabama, 310 U.S. 88 (1940). The development and recent history of picketing doctrine is outlined in Thomas I. Emerson, *The System of Freedom of Expression* (New York: Random House, 1970), pp. 435–49.

5. Street v. New York, 394 U.S. 576 (1969).

6. Tinker v. Des Moines Independent Community School District, 393 U.S. 503 (1969).

7. United States v. O'Brien, 391 U.S. 367 (1968).

8. See Garner v. Louisiana, 368 U.S. 157, 201–202 (1961), where the issue was posed clearly by Justice Harlan. The relevant passage is quoted below, in note 11.

9. Some of the works I have found especially helpful are: Harry Kalven, Jr., "The Concept of the Public Forum: Cox v. Louisiana," *The Supreme Court Review, 1965,* ed. P. Kurland (Chicago: University of Chicago Press, 1966), pp. 1–32; Dean Alfange, Jr., "Free Speech and Symbolic Conduct: The Draft-Card Burning Case," *The Supreme Court Review, 1968.* ed. P. Kurland (Chicago University of Chicago Press, 1969), pp. 1–52; Lawrence R. Velvel, "Freedom of Speech and the Draft-Card Burning Cases," *Kansas Law Review XVI* (1968), pp. 149–79; James E. Leahy, "'Flamboyant Protest,' the First Amendment and the Boston Tea Party," *Brooklyn Law Review XXXVI* (Winter 1970), pp. 185–211; and Melville B. Nimmer, "The Meaning of Symbolic Speech Under the First Amendment," *UCLA Law Review XXI* (October 1973), pp. 29–62. Nimmer's article has the most extensive treatment of the nature of symbolic conduct.

10. In the case of Garner v. Louisiana, 368 U.S. 157, 201–202, Justice Harlan remarked:

"We would surely have to be blind not to recognize that petitioners were sitting at these counters, where they knew they would not be served, in order to demonstrate that their race was being segregated in dining facilities in this part of the country.

"Such a demonstration, in the circumstances of these two cases, is as much a part of the "free trade in ideas" as is verbal expression, more commonly thought of as "speech." It, like speech, appeals to good sense and to "the power of reason as applied through public discussion" just as much as, if not more than, a public oration delivered from a soapbox at a street corner."

11. Charles S. Peirce, *Values in a Universe of Chance,* ed. Philip P. Wiener (Garden City, N.Y.: Doubleday, 1958), p. 368. Cf. also, Charles W. Morris: "A sign is iconic to the extent to which it itself has the properties of its denotata." (*Signs, Language, and Behavior* [New York: George Braziller, 1946], p. 349.) Morris' work is an attempt to develop a general theory of signs that would have application to, among other things, the issues raised here. Even if one is unwilling to accept his behavioral approach, or his specific kind of behaviorism, there is a great deal in the book that is useful to problems of this kind.

12. All of the underlying values I have mentioned have been cited by the courts at some time or other in connection with the First Amendment. A helpful discussion of these is in Thomas I. Emerson, *Toward a*

General Theory of the First Amendment (New York: Random House, 1967), ch. I. Emerson has useful discussions of the sorts of First Amendment cases I have in mind in his monumental study, *The System of Freedom of Expression.*

13. To cite just one example, President Nixon asserted in a news conference on June 29, 1972, that, at the end of the French-Indochinese conflict, "15,000 French were never accounted for," indicating that the Vietnamese Communists had not released prisoners and that he would not remove American troops from Vietnam and let that happen to American POWs. Within days, the French government disputed the President's claim, stating that "we are certain that the North Vietnamese gave us back all the prisoners they had." It was further pointed out that, though there were approximately 6,200 troops unaccounted for, they were, for the most part, "Nazi SS officers who fled to Indochina to join the French Foreign Legion," and on whom no records had been kept. (San Francisco *Sunday Examiner and Chronicle*, July 2, 1972, Sec. A, p. 4.) It is a further irony that, very close to the time of the President's statement, a couple of cases were being decided in the Supreme Court concerning groups who, two years before, had tried to buy time on television to criticize presidential policies on Vietnam, and had been denied. Cf. Business Executives Move for Vietnam Peace v. FCC, and Democratic National Committee v. FCC, 450 F. 2d 642 (1971), for an appellate ruling on the case. Though the Court of Appeals held that these groups did have a right to be heard, the Supreme Court reversed the ruling, thus leaving dissenting groups at the mercy of the media even if they were able to raise the money for a presentation of their views. Cf. Columbia Broadcasting System, Inc. v. Democratic National Committee, 412 U.S. 94 (1972).

14. United States v. O'Brien, 391 U.S. 367, 376 (1968).

15. Carl Cohen, *Civil Disobedience, Conscience, Tactics, and the Law* (New York: Columbia University Press, 1971), pp. 188–89.

16. *Ibid.*, p. 53. Cohen correctly points out that symbolic force may be conveyed by the location or time of the act as well as by "the *nature* of the disobedient act."

17. Abe Fortas, *Concerning Dissent and Civil Disobedience* (New York: Signet, 1968), p. 34.

18. For a rather extreme statement of such a view, which seems to imply that the law cannot make *any* such distinctions, see the statement by former Solicitor General Irwin Griswold in "Dissent — 1968," *Tulane Law Review* XLII (1968), pp. 733–34. Griswold could see no legal difference between stopping a troop train and firing shots into a civil rights leader's home.

19. Cohen, *Civil Disobedience, Conscience, Tactics, and the Law*, pp. 190–92.

20. Note that the relevant notion of intention is that of "oblique intention." For example, the Framers could not have known of the coming of radio and television; yet it is clear the First Amendment is "meant" to have some applications to the media — the Founders did mean to protect the communication of ideas.

21. Alexander Meiklejohn, *Political Freedom: The Constitutional Powers of the People* (New York: Oxford University Press, 1965), p. 25. Somewhat paradoxically, Meiklejohn's "absolutist" position is consonant with the arguments I am making, as he makes an important (if arguable) distinction between the *regulation* of speech and the abridgment of speech. See also his essay "The First Amendment Is an Absolute, *The Supreme Court Review 1961,* ed. Philip B. Kurland (Chicago: University of Chicago Press, 1962), pp. 245–66.

22. I am not holding that no distinctions can be made, only that, *from the point of view of the objectives of the First Amendment*, there is no important distinction between the two.

23. In effect, the Supreme Court has classed pornography and obscenity with the "exemption" cases. (See, e.g., Paris Adult Theatre I v. Slaton, 413 U.S. 49.) This is an extremely questionable move. It is unclear that there are significant, real "harms" involved, and there are serious problems with identifying material as falling into the categories of pornography and obscenity without endangering First Amendment values. See David A. J. Richards, *The Moral Criticism of Law* (Encino and Belmont, Calif.: Dickenson Publishing Company, 1977), pp. 56–77; and my own essay "Pornography, Sex and Censorship," *Social Theory and Practice* IV (Spring 1977), pp. 183–209.

24. As Nimmer points out, the legislation may be directed at protecting "anti-speech" interests. See "The Meaning of Symbolic Speech Under the First Amendment," especially pp. 44–46. My own treatment of the legal doctrines is very much influenced by Nimmer's.

25. United States v. O'Brien, 391 U.S. 367, 377 (1968).

26. Tinker v. Des Moines Independent Community School District, 393 U.S. 503, 509 (1969).

The Enemy Within: The American Nazis and Symbolic Conduct
NAT HENTOFF

One night in the late 1960s, South Vietnam's ambassador to the United States, having been invited to speak at New York University, tried to do so but was received in the manner accorded dissidents in Saigon. Shouting and stamping made the words of Thieu's emissary inaudible; water laced with imprecations was poured over him; and the ambassador was otherwise manhandled while learning how a free society functions.

Some of his suppressors were authoritarian "revolutionaries," and that was no surprise. As has been shown in other contexts — Stalinists and storm troopers, Mark Rudd and Tom Charles Huston — all yearning totalitarians are fundamentally the same. However, among others who roaringly silenced the Vietnamese ambassador that night were unaffiliated anti-war activists characterizing themselves as true egalitarians. And it was with them in mind that I wrote here of how the assault on Thieu's vassal had revealed the attackers were beginning to resemble those they took so much price in calling their enemies. . . .

Now, in 1977, in a domestic war, or rather skirmish, the phenomenon recurs of decent people so intent on crushing a foul enemy that they are coming, in small but distinct ways, to resemble that enemy.

As detailed last week, the village of Skokie, just north of Chicago, has gone to court, many courts, to prevent the National Socialist Party of America from demonstrating anywhere in the village where some 40,000 of the 70,000 residents are Jews. (And 7,000 of those Jews are survivors of Hitler). At the moment, the homegrown Nazis have been banned by the Illinois Appellate Court from assembling and speaking in Skokie as long as they insist on wearing or displaying swastikas. The Nazis and their counsel, the American Civil Liberties Union, keep maintaining that the swastika is symbolic speech and so must be fully protected by the First Amendment.

* * *

Meanwhile, in Skokie, consider what these good folk have done to themselves in their zeal to entirely shut the village off from Nazi free expression. On May 3, Skokie passed a set of ordinances imposing criminal penalties on certain forms of speech and assembly. Without mentioning the Nazis by name, the ordinances first require that no parade or assembly involving more than 50 persons can be held unless there is at least 30 days' notice for a demonstration permit — and unless a $350,000 insurance policy is obtained by the demonstrators. The latter, covering public liability and property damage, costs anywhere from $100 to $900, depending on the risk. You also have to find an underwriter willing to insure you, and that is not always possible.

Also prohibited, under any circumstances, is any demonstration that will "incite violence, hatred, abuse, or hostility toward a person or group of persons by reason or reference to racial, ethnic, national, or religious affiliation." There's more in the ordinances, and it all transmogrifies Skokie into a village so sterilized to avoid controversy that it could almost be in Czechoslovakia.

The lengthy notice for a permit prevents ad hoc demonstrations, yet free speech often must be timely to be effective. The blanket definition of the kinds of "incitement" now banished from Skokie suffocates the First Amendment. And the insurance provision turns the Bill of Rights into a document disfavoring the lower economic classes. Suppose you don't have $100 or $900?

There is an escape clause. Skokie's governing body can waive any or all of these ordinances, if they so choose, for a particular demonstration. Terrific. As far as free speech is concerned, Skokie has become a tiny fascist state. Henceforth, a few people will decide what all the people in the village can safely hear. Given a town of their own, the National Socialist Party would do the same thing.

These ordinances will be challenged in court by the ACLU and will probably be struck down. Though you never know. But will Skokie itself ever fully recover its sense of liberty? How deep was that sense to begin with?

Before the courts' injunctions against the Nazis, some 18 Jewish organizations met in Skokie and planned a counterdemonstration in which 12,000 to 15,000 people were expected to participate on the same day some 30 to 50 Nazis were to appear for half an hour in front of the Village Hall. At the meeting of the Jewish organizations, also attended by village officials, it was made clear that the counterdemonstration would be peaceful so long as the Nazis did *not* appear. Otherwise, it was stated, there could well be bloodshed.

See, said the village officials, we won't be able to control the incited crowds so we must get an injunction against the Nazis. However, as the ACLU pointed out, "If the village was so sure that certain hostile groups would be hard to control, it is difficult to understand why the village did not seek an injunction against *those* persons to prohibit *their* unlawful activities." (Emphasis added.) Unless, of course, Skokie, through fear of free speech, is now under mob rule where vio-

lence and the threat of violence prevail over individual liberties.

In sour fact, this is indeed what Skokie has become.

To the once free, now fear-shackled people of that village, I commend an opinion in a 1961 case concerning George Lincoln Rockwell's right to speak in a New York City park. Said Judge Charles Breitel: "The unpopularity of views, their shocking quality, their obnoxiousness, and even their alarming impact is not enough [to prohibit speech]. Otherwise, the preacher of any strange doctrine could be stopped: the anti-racist himself could be suppressed if he undertakes to speak in 'restricted' areas; and one who asks the public schools be open indiscriminately to all ethnic groups could be lawfully suppressed, if only he chose to speak where persuasion is most needed."

It is from this indivisibility of liberty that Skokie, having become its own enemy, has chosen to secede.

Notes and Questions

Cases on Civil Liberties and the First Amendment

1. These cases are concerned with the grounds for limiting speech — especially political protest. A central function of the First Amendment is to protect political thought and expression, but political dissent can be disturbing, offensive, and even dangerous. Inciting violent acts is beyond constitutional protection, but what counts as incitement is not easily determined. The cases of *Schenck, Abrams, Dennis*, and *Brandenburg* show the development of judicial doctrine with regard to advocating the violent overthrow of government, or at least advocating violence to effect political or industrial change. The question here is, Where does abstract discussion or advocacy become incitement to criminal action? Much of the judicial treatment of this issue is tied in with the permutations of the "clear and present danger" test formulated by Justice Oliver Wendell Holmes, Jr., in *Schenck*. See if you can account for the various interpretations of this test.

The cases of *Feiner, Edwards*, and *Cox* are concerned with another form of incitement to violence: the direct confrontation of provocative protestors with a hostile audience. Can protestors be arrested for their own protection? Well, not exactly, but they can be arrested to prevent breach of the peace. The final case, *Skokie* v. *National Socialist Party* considers both grounds (inciting violence and breaching the peace) to decide whether the village of Skokie can enjoin the Neo-Nazi party from holding demonstrations in a community of holocaust survivors. See if you can find principled grounds for protecting or restricting speech in these cases.

2. Of what was Schenck charged and convicted? What exactly did he do? What law did he violate? What constitutional question did it raise?

3. What test does Justice Holmes formulate to determine whether sections 3 and 4 of the Espionage Act were constitutional as applied in the *Schenck* case? Is this a reasonable test for such cases? What sorts of situations might it apply to? Are there other factors that should be included?

4. Is it important that Schenck is attempting to persuade draftees to resist the authority of government and especially the military establishment *during a war*? How do his actions compare to the resistance movement during the Vietnam War? Was resistance to the draft more justified during the Vietnam War? Was there a less "clear and present danger" of draft evasion that might damage the war effort? Are laws such as the Espionage Act enforceable when dissent is widespread? If not, does it follow that the application of the clear and present danger test is effectively enforceable only when there is not really a clear and present danger? Why or why not?

5. Notice in the next case that Abrams and his associates were convicted of violating *amendments* to the Espionage Act that extended its coverage to "uttering, printing, writing, or publishing any disloyal, profane, scurrilous or abusive language or language intended to cause contempt, scorn, contumely or disrepute as regards the form of government of the United States. . . ." These amendments were repealed in 1921. Is there any criticism of government that they would not cover? Yet the majority of the Court assumed the constitutionality of the Espionage Act was settled by *Schenck*. Was that reasonable? Can such amendments be constitutionally justified?

6. What exactly did Abrams advocate, and how did he do so? How does this case compare with Schenck's actions and speech? Is the intent similar or not? How about the focus of the advocacy? How about the audience? Do these differences matter? Obviously Holmes thought the two cases should be decided differently. Why? Is his dissent persuasive? Notice that he is objecting to the use of the "clear and present danger" test that he himself formulated that same year in *Schenck*. Is the test too hard to apply, or is the Court clearly wrong to apply it in both cases? How can you decide? Do you agree with the Court's application of the Espionage Act in *Abrams*? Why or why not? Does the Constitution protect capitalism? If so, where is the language that provides this protection? If not, is it reasonable to view calling for the overthrow of capitalism as calling for the overthrow of government? Why or why not? Can economic issues be separated from political ones? In what way, if at all, is economic espionage different from political espionage?

7. Of what was Dennis convicted? What did he do? What law did this violate? Notice that this is no longer a wartime case but a "cold war" time case. Does that matter? Should the clear and present danger test (or something like it) apply here? Why or why not? How would you assess the relative immediacy and probability of danger to legitimate government interests in these three cases? Was the clear and present danger test applied as Holmes would have applied it? How should it have been applied? Is there any test that can avoid the pressure of popular sentiment?

8. Should a country or a government have the right of self protection from speech such as that presented in these cases? Should it matter whether it takes place during war or peace? Does it matter according to the Smith Act? Compare the Smith Act with the Espionage Act of 1917. Is one more defensible than the other? Would Mill's "harm principle" apply to either? Would Burger's view help?

9. A basic purpose of law is to preserve order. But the expression of unpopular views often tends to disrupt order. How are these two values to be balanced? In the case of *Feiner* v. *New York*, Mr. Feiner was arrested and convicted of "ignoring reasonable police orders given to control the crowd and to prevent a breach of the peace" (that is, disorderly conduct). Here is what happened. Feiner was standing on a box on a sidewalk addressing seventy-five or eighty people through an amplifier. His purpose was to urge the crowd to attend a meeting later that night, but

while doing so he made disparaging remarks about President Harry Truman, the mayor of Syracuse, and the American Legion. He also said that Negroes should fight for their rights. According to two police officers who had arrived to investigate the crowd, there was some pushing and unrest but no general disorder. After about twenty minutes one man threatened to remove Feiner if the police did not do so. At that point the police requested Feiner to stop talking. When he repeatedly refused, they arrested him. Feiner appealed his conviction for disorderly conduct. Should his right to speak have been better protected? The people could have walked away if they didn't like what they heard. But they were not walking away. When does a speech become inciting a riot?

10. In 1963 the assertion of black civil rights was exceedingly unpopular in segregated southern states. The demonstrators in *Edwards* v. *South Carolina* were peaceful, but there can be no doubt that the protest aroused strong and hostile feelings among the crowd of white onlookers. Suppose the crowd had not been peaceful? Would that be a good reason to arrest the protestors rather than violent members of the crowd? Can you distinguish this case from *Feiner*?

11. *Cox* v. *Louisiana* is much like *Edwards*, except for one factor. Cox urged his protestors to go sit at segregated lunch counters. Was that inflammatory speech, as the prosecution urged? It could hardly be more confrontive. It impeded business on private property. Should it be protected? When? Should blocking the entrance to abortion clinics be protected? Can you explain the difference between peaceful, unpopular protest and breach of the peace? The Court in both *Cox* and *Edwards* says that these situations are clearly and easily distinguishable from that in *Feiner*. What's the big difference? Were any of them advocating violence?

12. *Brandenburg* v. *Ohio* is about a gathering of the Ku Klux Klan that clearly posed no immediate danger, since it took place on a private farm with no outsiders present except media representatives who were invited. Brandenburg was initially convicted of "advocating the duty, necessity or propriety of crime, sabotage, violence, or unlawful methods of terrorism as a means of accomplishing industrial or political reform." The Supreme Court reversed his conviction and invalidated the Ohio statute on which it was based. Why? What is wrong with making such advocacy illegal? How is it different from conspiring to commit a crime? How is it different from the civil rights organizations in *Cox* or *Edwards*?

13. In the case of *Skokie* v. *National Socialist Party of America* the village of Skokie is asking for an injunction to prevent the Neo-Nazi NSPA from holding a demonstration in the predominantly Jewish town. The Court reviews both grounds that we have so far considered for restricting speech. What does the Court say about incitement to commit mass murder in this case? Is this like the approach in *Brandenburg*? There has been a great deal of discussion about the issue of "hate speech" — the advocacy of prejudice and hatred. Is it constitutionally protected? Should it be? If not, could it be adequately distinguished from other forms of unpopular speech to keep restriction from spreading?

14. The ground on which the Court restricts the wearing of the swastika as a symbol of genocide has been called the doctrine of "fighting words." What is the doctrine of "fighting words?" It applies potentially to any unpopular speech. What does it do? Could it have applied in *Edwards* or *Cox*? Is the *Skokie* case like the case of *Feiner*? What are the similarities and differences? What is the difference if any between fighting words and disorderly conduct (or breach of the peace)?

Cases on Civil Liberties and the First Amendment

Schenck v. United States
249 U.S. 47 (1919)

MR. JUSTICE HOLMES delivered the opinion of the court.

This is an indictment in three counts. The first charges a conspiracy to violate the Espionage Act of June 15, 1917, c. 30, §3, 40 Stat. 217, 219, by causing and attempting to cause insubordination, &c., in the military and naval forces of the United States, and to obstruct the recruiting and enlistment service of the United States, when the United States was at war with the German Empire, to-wit, that the defendants wilfully conspired to have printed and circulated to men who had been called and accepted for military service under the Act of May 18, 1917, a document set forth and alleged to be calculated to cause such insubordination and obstruction. The count alleges overt acts in pursuance of the conspiracy, ending in the distribution of the document set forth. The second count alleges a conspiracy to commit an offence against the United States, to-wit, to use the mails for the transmission of matter declared to be non-mailable by Title XII, §2 of the Act of June 15, 1917, to-wit, the above mentioned document, with an averment of the same overt acts. The third count charges an unlawful use of the mails for the transmission of the same matter and otherwise as above. The defendants were found guilty, on all the counts. They set up the First Amendment to the Constitution forbidding Congress to make any law abridging the freedom of speech, or of the press, and bringing the case here on that ground have argued some other points also of which we must dispose.

* * *

We admit that in many places and in ordinary times the defendants in saying all that was said in the circular would have been within their constitutional rights. But the character of every act depends upon the circumstances in which it is done. . . . The most stringent protection of free speech would not protect a man in falsely shouting fire in a theatre and causing a panic. It does not even protect a man from an injunction against uttering words that may have all the effect of force. . . . The question in every case is whether the words used are used in such circumstances and are of such a nature as to create a clear and present danger that they will bring about the substantive evils that Congress has a right to prevent. It is a question of proximity and degree. When a nation is at war many things that might be said in time of peace are such a hindrance to its effort that their utterance will not be endured so long as men fight and that no Court could regard them as protected by any constitutional right. it seems to be admitted that if an actual obstruction of the recruiting service were proved, liability for words that produced that effect might be enforced. The statute of 1917 in §4 punishes conspiracies to obstruct as well as actual obstruction. If the act, (speaking, or circulating a paper,) its tendency and the intent with which it is done are the same, we perceive no ground for saying that success alone warrants making the act a crime. . . .

The convictions were affirmed.

Abrams et al. v. United States
250 U.S. 616 (1919)

MR. JUSTICE CLARKE delivered the opinion of the court.

On a single indictment, containing four counts, the five plaintiffs in error, hereinafter designated the defendants, were convicted of conspiring to violate provisions of the Espionage Act of Congress §3, Title I, of Act approved June 15, 1917, as amended May 16, 1918, 40 Stat. 553).

* * *

It was admitted on the trial that the defendants had united to print and distribute the described circulars and that five thousand of them had been printed and distributed about the 22d day of August, 1918.

* * *

Thus the conspiracy and the doing of the overt acts charged were largely admitted and were fully established.

On the record thus described it is argued, somewhat faintly, that the acts charged against the defendants were not unlawful because within the protection of that freedom of speech and of the press which is guaranteed by the First Amendment to the Constitution of the United States, and that the entire Espionage Act is unconstitutional because in conflict with that Amendment.

This contention is sufficiently discussed and is definitely negatived in *Schenck* v. *United States* and *Baer* v. *United States*, 249 U.S. 47; and in *Frohwerk* v. *United States*, 249 U.S. 204.

The claim chiefly elaborated upon by the defendants . . . is that there is no substantial evidence in the record to support the judgment upon the verdict of guilty. . . . A question of law is thus presented, which calls for an examination of the record, not for the purpose of weighing conflicting testimony, but only to determine whether there was some evidence, competent and substantial, before the jury, fairly tending to sustain the verdict.

* * *

The first of the two articles attached to the indictment is conspicuously headed, "The Hypocrisy of the United States and her Allies." After denouncing President Wilson as a hypocrite and a coward because troops were sent into Russia, it proceeds to assail our Government in general, . . .

* * *

The second of the articles was printed in the Yiddish language and in the translation is headed, "Workers — Wake up." After referring to "his Majesty, Mr. Wilson, and the rest of the gang; dogs of all colors!", it continues:

"Workers, Russian emigrants, you who had the least belief in the honesty of *our* Government," which defendants admitted referred to the United States Government, "must now throw away all confidence, must spit in the face the false, hypocritic, military propaganda which has fooled you so relentlessly, calling forth your sympathy, your help, to the prosecution of the war."

The purpose of this obviously was to persuade the persons to whom it was addressed to turn a deaf ear to patriotic appeals in behalf of the Government of the United States, and to cease to render it assistance in the prosecution of the war.

* * *

These excerpts sufficiently show, that while the immediate occasion for this particular outbreak of lawlessness, on the part of the defendant alien anarchists, may have been resentment caused by our Government sending troops into Russia as a strategic operation against the Germans on the eastern battle front, yet the plain purpose of their propaganda was to excite, at the supreme crisis of the war, disaffection, sedition, riots, and, as they hoped, revolution, in this country for the purpose of embarrassing and if possible defeating the military plans of the Government in Europe. . . .

* * *

Thus it is clear not only that some evidence but that much persuasive evidence was before the jury tending to prove that the defendants were guilty as charged in both the third and fourth counts of the indictment and under the long established rule of law hereinbefore stated the judgment of the District Court must be *affirmed*.

MR. JUSTICE HOLMES dissented, saying:

* * *

"In this case sentences of twenty years imprisonment have been imposed for the publishing of two leaflets that I believe the defendants had as much right to publish as the Government has to publish the Constitution of the United States now vainly invoked by them. Even if I am technically wrong and enough can be squeezed from these poor and puny anonymities to turn the color of legal litmus paper; I will add, even if what I think the necessary intent were shown; the most nominal punishment seems to me all that possibly could be inflicted, unless the defendants are to be made to suffer not for what the indictment alleges but for the creed that they avow — a creed that I believe to be the creed of ignorance and immaturity when honestly held, as I see no reason to doubt that it was held here, but which, although made the subject of examination at the trial, no one has a right even to consider in dealing with the charges before the Court.

"Persecution for the expression of opinions seems to me perfectly logical. If you have no doubt of your premises or your power and want a certain result with all your heart you naturally express your wishes in law and sweep away all opposition. To allow opposition by speech seems to indicate that you think the speech impotent, as when a man says that he has squared the circle, or that you do not care whole-heartedly for the result, or that you doubt either your power or your premises. But when men have realized that time has upset many fighting faiths, they may come to believe even more than they believe the very foundations of their own conduct that the ultimate good desired is better reached by free trade in ideas—that the best test of truth is the power of the thought to get itself accepted in the competition of the market, and that truth is the only ground upon which their wishes safely can be carried out. That at any rate is the theory of our Constitution. It is an experiment, as all life is an experiment. Every year if not every day we have to wager our salvation upon some prophecy based upon imperfect knowledge. While that experiment is part of our system I think that we should be eternally vigilant against attempts to check the expression of opinions that we loathe and believe to be fraught with death, unless they so imminently threaten immediate interference with the lawful and pressing purposes of the law that an immediate check is required to save the country. I wholly disagree with the argument of the Government that the First Amendment left the common law as to seditious libel in force. History seems to me against the notion. I had conceived that the United States through many years had shown its repentance for the Sedition Act of 1978, by repaying fines that it imposed. Only the emergency that makes it immediately dangerous to leave the correction of evil counsels to time warrants making any exception to the sweeping command, 'Congress shall make no law . . . abridging the freedom of speech.' Of course I am speaking only of expressions of opinion and exhortations, which were all that were uttered here, but I regret that I cannot put into more impressive words my belief that in their conviction upon this indictment the defendants were deprived of their rights under the Constitution of the United States."

Dennis v. United States
341 U.S. 494 (1951)

[Dennis et al., leaders of the Communist Party, were convicted in a federal district court in New York of violating the *Smith Act* which provided:

"Sec. 2(a) It shall be unlawful for any person—

"(1) to knowingly or willfully advocate, abet, advise, or teach the duty, necessity, desirability, or propriety of overthrowing or destroying any government in the United States by force or violence, or by the assassination of any officer of any such government; . . .

"(3) to organize or help to organize any society, group, or assembly of persons who teach, advocate, or encourage the overthrow or destruction of any government in the United States by force or violence; or to be or become a member of, or affiliate with, any such society, group, or assembly of persons, knowing the purposes thereof. . . .

"Sec. 3. It shall be unlawful for any person to attempt to commit, or to conspire to commit, any of the acts prohibited by the provisions of this title."]

* * *

The plurality opinion was delivered by Chief Justice Vinson: The obvious purpose of the statute is to protect existing Government, not from change by peaceable, lawful and constitutional means, but from change by violence, revolution and terrorism. That it is within the *power* of the Congress to protect the Government of the United States from armed rebellion is a proposition which requires little discussion. . . .

* * *

"Obviously, the words cannot mean that before the Government may act, it must wait until the *putsch* is about to be executed, the plans have been laid and the signal is awaited. If Government is aware that a group aiming at its overthrow is attempting to indoctrinate its members and to commit them to a course whereby they will strike when the leaders feel the circumstances permit, action by the Government is required. The argument that there is no need for Government to concern itself, for Government is strong, it possesses ample power to put down a rebellion, it may defeat the revolution with ease needs no answer. For that is not the question. Certainly an attempt to overthrow the Government by force, even though doomed from the outset because of inadequate numbers of power of the revolutionists, is a sufficient evil for Congress to prevent. . . .

* * *

"CHIEF JUDGE LEARNED HAND, writing for the majority below, interpreted the phrase as follows: 'In each case [courts] must ask whether the gravity of the "evil," discounted by its improbability, justifies such invasion of free speech as is necessary to avoid the danger.' We adopt this statement of the rule. As articulated by CHIEF JUDGE HAND, it is as succinct and inclusive as any other we might devise at this time. It takes into consideration those factors which we deem relevant, and relates their significances. More we cannot expect from words.

"Likewise, we are in accord with the court below, which affirmed the trial court's finding that the requisite danger existed. The mere fact that from the period 1945 to 1948 petitioners' activities did not result in an attempt to overthrow the Government by force and violence is of course no answer to the fact that there was a group that was ready to make the attempt. The formation by petitioners of such a highly organized conspiracy, with rigidly disciplined members subject to call when the leaders, these petitioners, felt that the time had come for action, coupled with the inflammable nature of world conditions, similar uprisings in other countries, and the touch-and-go nature of our relations with countries with whom petitioners were in the very least ideologically attuned, convince us that their convictions were justified on this score. And this analysis disposes of the contention that a conspiracy to advocate, as distinguished from the advocacy itself, cannot be constitutionally restrained, because it comprises only the preparation. It is the existence of the conspiracy which creates the danger. . . . If the ingredients of the reaction are present, we cannot bind the Government to wait until the catalyst is added."

* * *

JUSTICE FRANKFURTER wrote an extensive concurring opinion:

* * *

"*First.* — Free speech cases are not an exception of the principle that we are not legislators, that direct policymaking is not our province. How best to reconcile competing interests is the business of legislatures, and the balance they strike is a judgment not to be displaced by ours, but to be respected unless outside the pale of fair judgment." . . . *Second.* — A survey of the relevant decisions indicates that the results which we have reached are on the whole those that would ensue from careful weighing of conflicting interests." . . . "It were far better that the [clear and present danger test] be abandoned than that it be sounded once more to hide from the believers in an absolute right of free speech the plain fact that the interest in speech, profoundly important as it is, is no more conclusive in judicial review than other attributes of democracy or than a determination of the peoples' representatives that a measure is necessary to assure the safety of government itself. *Third.* — Not every type of speech occupies the same position on the scale of values. . . . The defendants have been convicted of conspiring to organize a party of persons who advocate the overthrow of the Government by force and violence. The jury has found that the object of the conspiracy is advocacy as 'a rule or principle of action,' 'by language reasonably and ordinarily calculated to incite persons to such action,' and with the intent to cause the overthrow 'as speedily as circumstances would permit.' On any scale of values which we have hitherto recognized speech of this sort ranks low."

* * *

MR. JUSTICE DOUGLAS dissented, saying:

* * *

"There comes a time when even speech loses its constitutional immunity. Speech innocuous one year may at another time fan such destructive flames that it must be halted in the interests of the safety of the Republic. That is the meaning of the clear and present danger test. When conditions are so critical that there will be no time to avoid the evil that the speech threatens, it is time to call a halt. Otherwise, free speech which is the strength of the Nation will be the cause of its destruction. Yet free speech is the rule, not the exception. The restraint to be constitutional must be based on more than fear, on more than passionate opposition against the speech, on more than a revolted dislike for its contents. There must be some immediate injury to society that is likely if speech is allowed."

* * *

The convictions were affirmed by a vote of six to two.

Feiner v. New York
340 U.S. 315 (1951)

Mr. Chief Justice Vinson delivered the opinion of the Court. . . . We are not faced here with blind condonation by a state court of arbitrary police action. Petitioner was accorded a full, fair trial. The trial judge heard testimony supporting and contradicting the judgment of the police officers that a clear danger of disorder was threatened. After weighing this contradictory evidence, the trial judge reached the conclusion that the police officers were justified in taking action to prevent a breach of the peace. The exercise of the police officers' proper discretionary power to prevent a breach of the peace was thus approved by the trial court and later by two courts on review. The courts below recognized petitioner's right to hold a street meeting at this locality, to make use of loud-speaking equipment in giving his speech, and to make derogatory remarks concerning public officials and the American Legion. They found that the officers in making the arrest were motivated solely by a proper concern for the preservation of order and protection of the general welfare, and that there was no evidence which could lend color to a claim that the acts of the police were a cover for suppression of petitioner's views and opinions. Petitioner was thus neither arrested nor convicted for the making or the content of his speech. Rather, it was the reaction which it actually engendered. . . .

. . . It is one thing to say that the police cannot be used as an instrument for the suppression of unpopular views, and another to say that, when as here the speaker passes the bounds of argument or persuasion and undertakes incitement to riot, they are powerless to prevent a breach of the peace. Nor in this case can we condemn the considered judgment of three New York courts approving the means which the police, faced with a crisis, used in the exercise of their power and duty to preserve peace and order. The findings of the state courts as to the existing situa-

tion and the imminence of greater disorder coupled with petitioner's deliberate defiance of the police officers convince us that we should not reverse this conviction in the name of free speech.

Affirmed.

Mr. Justice Black, dissenting.

The record before us convinces me that petitioner, a young college student, has been sentenced to the penitentiary for the unpopular views he expressed. . . . The police of course have power to prevent breaches of the peace. But if, in the name of preserving order, they ever can interfere with a lawful public speaker, they first must make all reasonable efforts to protect him. Here the policemen did not even pretend to try to protect petitioner. According to the officers' testimony, the crowd was restless but there is no showing of any attempt to quiet it; pedestrians were forced to walk into the street, but there was no effort to clear a path on the sidewalk; one person threatened to assault petitioner but the officers did nothing to discourage this when even a word might have sufficed. Their duty was to protect petitioner's right to talk, even to the extent of arresting the man who threatened to interfere. Instead, they shirked that duty and acted only to suppress the right to speak. . . .

Mr. Justice Douglas, with whom Mr. Justice Minton concurs, dissenting. . . .

A speaker may not, of course, incite a riot any more than he may incite a breach of the peace by the use of "fighting words." See Chaplinsky v. New Hampshire, 315 U.S. 568. But this record shows no such extremes. It shows an unsympathetic audience and the threat of one man to haul the speaker from the stage. It is against that kind of threat that speakers need police protection. If they do not receive it and instead the police throw their weight on the side of those who would break up the meetings, the police become the new censors of speech. . . .

Edwards v. South Carolina
372 U.S. 229 (1963)

A group of black students marched to the State House to protest discrimination against the black population by white citizens and the legislature. They were arrested and convicted of breach of the peace. The Supreme Court reversed its conviction, saying in part:

"It has long been established that these First Amendment freedoms are protected by the Fourteenth Amendment from invasion by the States. . . . The circumstances in this case reflect an exercise of these basic constitutional rights in their most pristine and classic form. The petitioners felt aggrieved by laws of South Carolina which allegedly 'prohibited Negro privileges in this State.' They peaceably assembled at the site of the State Government and there peaceably expressed their grievances 'to the citizens of South Carolina, along with the Legislative Bodies of South Carolina.' Not until they were told by police officials that they must disperse on pain of arrest did they do more. Even then, they but sang patriotic and religious songs after one of their leaders had delivered a 'religious harangue.' There was no violence or threat of violence on their part, or on the part of any member of the crowd watching them. Police protection was 'ample.'

"This, therefore, was a far cry from the situation in Feiner v. New York, . . . where two policemen were faced with a crowd which was 'pushing, shoving, and milling around,' . . . where at least one member of the crowd 'threatened violence if the police did not act,' . . . where 'the crowd was pressing closer around petitioner and the officer,' . . . and where 'the speaker passes the bounds of argument or persuasion and undertakes incitement to riot.' . . . And the record is barren of any evidence of 'fighting words.' See Chaplinsky v. New Hampshire, 315 U.S. 568.

* * *

"The Fourteenth Amendment does not permit a State to make criminal the peaceful expression of unpopular views. [A] function of free speech under our system of government is to invite dispute. It may indeed best serve its high purpose when it induces a condition of unrest, creates dissatisfaction with conditions as they are, or even stirs people to anger. Speech is often provocative and challenging. It may strike at prejudices and preconceptions and have profound unsettling effects as it presses for acceptance of an idea. That is why freedom of speech, . . . is . . . protected against censorship or punishment, unless shown likely to produce a clear and present danger of a serious substantive evil that rises far above public inconvenience, annoyance, or unrest. . . . There is no room under our Constitution for a more restrictive view. For the alternative would lead to standardization of ideas either by legislatures, courts, or dominant political or community groups.' Terminiello v. Chicago, 337 U.S. 1, 4–5. As in the *Terminiello* case, the courts of South Carolina have defined a criminal offense so as to permit conviction of the petitioners if their speech 'stirred people to anger, invited public dispute, or brought about a condition of unrest. A conviction resting on any of those grounds may not stand.'" . . .

* * *

Cox v. Louisiana
379 U.S. 536 (1965)

* * *

Mr. Justice Goldberg delivered the opinion of the Court. . . .

II. The Breach of the Peace Conviction

Appellant was convicted of violating a Louisiana "disturbing the peace" statute. . . .

. . . We hold that Louisiana may not constitutionally punish appellant under this statute for engaging in the type of conduct which this record reveals, and also that the statute as authoritatively interpreted by the Louisiana Supreme Court is unconstitutionally broad in scope.

The Louisiana courts have held that appellant's conduct constituted a breach of the peace under state law and, as in Edwards, "we may accept their decision as binding upon us to that extent," Edwards v. South Carolina, supra, 372 U.S., at 235; but our independent examination of the record, which we are required to make, shows no conduct which the State had a right to prohibit as a breach of the peace.

Appellant led a group of young college students who wished "to protest segregation" and discrimination against Negroes and the arrest of 23 fellow students. They assembled peaceably at the State Capitol building and marched to the courthouse where they sang, prayed and listened to a speech. A reading of the record reveals agreement on the part of the State's witnesses that Cox had the demonstration "very well controlled," and until the end of Cox's speech, the group was perfectly "orderly." Sheriff Clemmons testified that the crowd's activities were not "objectionable" before that time. They became objectionable, according to the Sheriff himself, when Cox, concluding his speech, urged the students to go uptown and sit in at lunch counters. The Sheriff testified that the sole aspect of the program to which he objected was "[t]he inflammatory manner in which he [Cox] addressed that crowd and told them to go on up town, go to four places on the protest list, sit down and if they don't feed you, sit there for one hour." Yet this part of Cox's speech obviously did not deprive the demonstration of its protected character under the Constitution as free speech and assembly....

The State argues, however, that while the demonstrators started out to be orderly, the loud cheering and clapping by the students in response to the singing from the jail converted the peaceful assembly into a riotous one. The record, however, does not support this assertion. It is true that the students, in response to the singing of their fellows who were in custody, cheered and applauded. However, the meeting was an outdoor meeting and a key state witness testified that while the singing was loud, it was not disorderly. There is, moreover, no indication that the mood of the students was ever hostile, aggressive, or unfriendly. Our conclusion that the entire meeting from the beginning until its dispersal by tear gas was orderly and not riotous is confirmed by a film of the events taken by a television news photographer, which was offered in evidence as a state exhibit. We have viewed the film, and it reveals that the students, though they undoubtedly cheered and clapped, were well-behaved throughout. My Brother BLACK, concurring in this opinion . . . agrees "that the record does not show boisterous or violent conduct or indecent language on the part of the . . ." students. The singing and cheering do not seem to us to differ significantly from the constitutionally protected activity of the demonstrators in Edwards, who loudly sang "while stamping their feet and clapping their hands"

Finally, the State contends that the conviction should be sustained because of fear expressed by some of the state witnesses that "violence was about to erupt" because of the demonstration. It is virtually undisputed, however, that the students themselves were not violent and threatened no violence. The fear of violence seems to have been based upon the reaction of the group of white citizens looking on from across the street. . . . There is no indication, however, that any member of the white group threatened violence. And this small crowd estimated at between 100 and 300 was separated from the students by "seventy-five to eighty" armed policemen, including "every available shift of the City Police," the "Sheriff's Office in full complement," and "additional help from the State Police," along with a "fire truck and the Fire Department." As Inspector Trigg testified, they could have handled the crowd.

This situation, like that in Edwards, is "a far cry from the situation in Feiner v. [People of State of] New York."

There is an additional reason why this conviction cannot be sustained. The statute at issue in this case, as authoritatively interpreted by the Louisiana Supreme Court, is unconstitutionally vague in its overly broad scope.

* * *

For all these reasons we hold that appellant's freedoms of speech and assembly, secured to him by the First Amendment, as applied to the States by the Fourteenth Amendment, were denied by his conviction for disturbing the peace. The conviction on this charge cannot stand....

* * *

Brandenburg v. Ohio
395 U.S. 444 (1969)

Per Curiam

The appellant, a leader of a Ku Klux Klan group, was convicted under the Ohio Criminal Syndicalism statute for "advocat[ing] . . . the duty, necessity, or propriety of crime, sabotage, violence, or unlawful methods of terrorism as a means of accomplishing industrial or political reform" and for "voluntarily assembl[ing] with any society, group, or assemblage of persons formed to teach or advocate the doctrines of criminal syndicalism." Ohio Rev.Code Ann. §2923.13. He was fined $1,000 and sentenced to one to 10 years' imprisonment. The appellant challenged the constitutionality of the criminal syndicalism statute under the First and Fourteenth Amendments to the United States Constitution, but the intermediate appellate court of Ohio affirmed his conviction without opinion. The Supreme Court of Ohio dismissed his appeal, *sua sponte*, "for the reason that no substantial constitutional question exists herein." . . . Appeal was taken to this Court, . . . We reverse.

The record shows that a man, identified at trial as the appellant, telephoned an announcer-reporter on the staff of a Cincinnati television station and invited him to come to a Ku Klux Klan "rally" to be held at a farm in Hamilton County. With the cooperation of the organizers, the reporter and a cameraman attended the meeting and filmed the events. Portions of the films were later broadcast on the local station and on a national network.

The prosecution's case rested on the films and on testimony identifying the appellant as the person who communicated with the reporter and who spoke at the rally. The State also introduced into evidence several articles appearing in the film, including a pistol, a rifle, a shotgun, ammunition, a Bible, and a red hood worn by the speaker in the films.

One film showed 12 hooded figures, some of whom carried firearms. They were gathered around a large wooden cross, which they burned. No one was present other than the participants and the newsmen who made the film. Most of the words uttered during the scene were incomprehensible when the film was projected, but scattered phrases could be understood that were derogatory of Negroes and, in one instance, of Jews. Another scene on the same film showed the appellant, in Klan regalia, making a speech. The speech, in full, was as follows:

"This is an organizers' meeting. We have had quite a few members here today which are — we have hundreds, hundreds of members throughout the State of Ohio. I can quote from a newspaper clipping from the Columbus, Ohio Dispatch, five weeks ago Sunday morning. The Klan has more members in the State of Ohio than does any other organization. We're not a revengent organization, but if our President, our Congress, our Supreme Court, continues to suppress the white, Caucasian race, it's possible that there might have to be some revengeance taken.

"We are marching on Congress July the Fourth, four hundred thousand strong. From there we are dividing into two groups, one group to march on St. Augustine, Florida, the other group to march into Mississippi. Thank you."

The second film showed six hooded figures one of whom, later identified as the appellant, repeated a speech very similar to that recorded on the first film. The reference to the possibility of "revengeance" was omitted, and one sentence was added: "Personally, I believe the nigger should be returned to Africa, the Jew returned to Israel." Though some of the figures in the films carried weapons, the speaker did not.

The Ohio Criminal Syndicalism Statute was enacted in 1919. From 1917 to 1920, identical or quite similar laws were adopted by 20 States and two territories. In 1927, this Court sustained the constitutionality of California's Criminal Syndicalism Act, the text of which is quite similar to that of the laws of Ohio. Whitney v. California, 274 U.S. 357 (1927). The Court upheld the statute on the ground that, without more, "advocating" violent means to effect political and economic change involves such danger to the security of the State that the State may outlaw it. Cf. Fiske v. Kansas, 274 U.S. 380 (1927). But *Whitney* has been thoroughly discredited by later decisions. See Dennis v. United States, 341 U.S. 494, at 507 (1951). These later decisions have fashioned the principle that the constitutional guarantees of free speech and free press do not permit a State to forbid or proscribe advocacy of the use of force or of law violation except where such advocacy is directed to inciting or producing imminent lawless action and is likely to incite or produce such action. As we said in Noto v. . . . United States, "the mere abstract teaching . . . of the moral propriety or even moral necessity for a resort to force and violence, is not the same as preparing a group for violent action and steeling it to such action." A statute which fails to draw this distinction impermissibly intrudes upon the freedoms guaranteed by the First and Fourteenth Amendments. It sweeps within its condemnation speech which our Constitution has immunized from governmental control.

Measured by this test, Ohio's Criminal Syndicalism Act cannot be sustained. The Act punishes persons who "advocate or teach the duty, necessity, or propriety" of violence "as a means of accomplishing industrial or political reform"; or who publish or circulate or display any book or paper containing such advocacy; or who "justify" the commission of violent acts "with intent to exemplify, spread or advocate the propriety of the doctrines of criminal syndicalism"; or who "voluntarily assemble" with a group formed "to teach or advocate the doctrines of criminal syndicalism." Neither the indictment nor the trial judge's instructions to the jury in any way refined the statute's bald definition of the crime in terms of mere advocacy not distinguished from incitement to imminent lawless action.

Accordingly, we are here confronted with a statute which, by its own words and as applied, purports to punish mere advocacy and to forbid, on pain of criminal punishment, assembly with others merely to advocate the described type of action. Such a statute falls within the condemnation of the First and Fourteenth Amendments. The contrary teaching of Whitney v. California, *supra*, cannot be supported, and that decision is therefore overruled.

Reversed.

Mr. Justice Douglas, concurring.

While I join the opinion of the Court, I desire to enter a *caveat*.

* * *

. . . I see no place in the regime of the First Amendment for any "clear and present danger" test, whether strict and tight as some would make it, or free-wheeling as the Court in *Dennis* rephrased it.

When one reads the opinions closely and sees when and how the "clear and present danger" test has been applied, great misgiving are aroused. First, the threats were often loud but always puny and made serious only by judges so wedded to the *status quo* that critical analysis made them nervous. Second, the test was so twisted and perverted in *Dennis* as to make the trial of those teachers of Marxism an all-out political trial which was part and parcel of the cold war that has eroded substantial parts of the First Amendment. . . .

The line between what is permissible and not subject to control and what may be made impermissible and subject to regulation is the line between ideas and overt acts.

The example usually given by those who would punish speech is the case of one who falsely shouts fire in a crowded theatre.

This is, however, a classic case where speech is brigaded with action. They are indeed inseparable and a prosecution can be launched for the overt acts actually caused. Apart from rare instances of that kind, speech is, I think, immune from prosecution. Certainly there is no constitutional line between advocacy of abstract ideas as in *Yates* and advocacy of political action as in *Scales*. The quality of advocacy turns on the depth of the conviction; and government has no power to invade that sanctuary of belief and conscience.

Village of Skokie
v. *National Socialist Party of America*
366 NE 2nd 347 (1977)

The complaint alleged the following pertinent facts. The village of Skokie contains a population of approximately 70,000 persons, of whom approximately 40,500 are of the Jewish religion, Jewish ancestry, or both. Included within the Jewish population are hundreds of persons who are survivors of Nazi concentration camps and many thousands whose families and close relatives were murdered by the Nazis. A large percentage of the Jewish population of Skokie is organized into groups and organizations. At the hearing, the above allegations were stipulated to by both parties. The complaint further alleged the nature of defendant Party's purpose, and stated that the "uniform of the National Socialist Party of America consists of the storm trooper uniform of the German Nazi Party embellished with the Nazi swastika." It is alleged that on March 20, the village police chief was informed by defendant Collin of defendants' intention to march on the village's sidewalks on May 1. As a result of publicity from the news media and early morning phone calls purportedly made by members of the defendant Party to Skokie residents whose names indicated the probability of their Jewish faith or ancestry, it was common knowledge in the village, particularly among the Jewish population, that the defendant Party intended to march in Skokie on May Day.

* * *

The complaint prayed for the issuance of an injunction enjoining defendants from various activities in the village of Skokie on May 1.

Defendants filed a motion to dismiss stating that the complaint fails to state a cause of action upon which relief can be granted; seeks relief barred by the first and fourteenth amendments to the United States Constitution and alleges facts which are untrue. The motion to dismiss referred to an affidavit of one of the individual defendants appended thereto.

* * *

The circuit court of Cook County conducted a hearing on a motion by plaintiff for a preliminary injunction. The court considered the abovementioned affidavit and the testimony of a number of witnesses. A resident of Skokie, an officer in several Jewish organizations, testified that he learned about the planned demonstration from the newspapers. As a result, meetings of some 15 to 18 Jewish organizations, within Skokie and surrounding areas, were called, and a counter-demonstration was scheduled for the same day as the demonstration planned by defendants. The witness estimated that some 12,000 to 15,000 people were expected to participate. In the opinion of the witness, this counterdemonstration would be peaceful if defendants did not appear. However, if they did appear, the outrage of the participants might not be controllable.

* * *

Defendants' case consisted of the testimony of defendant Frank Collin, the leader of the defendant Party, and his affidavit previously described

as having been admitted into evidence. He testified, *inter alia*, that the purpose of the demonstration was to peacefully protest the Skokie Park District's ordinance which required a bond of $350,000 to be posted prior to the issuance of a park permit. If enjoined from marching on May 1, he planned a demonstration on May 22, three weeks hence, or on a future date yet undecided. After hearing arguments of counsel, the trial court entered an order enjoining defendants

> "from engaging in any of the following acts on May 1, 1977, within the Village of Skokie: Marching, walking or parading in the uniform of the National Socialist Party of America; Marching, walking or parading or otherwise displaying" the swastika on or off their person; Distributing pamphlets or displaying any materials which incite or promote hatred against persons of Jewish faith or ancestry or hatred against persons of any faith or ancestry, race or religion."

* * *

The question before the court is whether plaintiff, village of Skokie, has met its heavy burden of showing justification for the imposition of the circuit court's prior restraint upon defendants' rights to freedom of speech and public assembly.

* * *

As thusly framed, the first issue is whether plaintiff has overcome the presumptive invalidity of the prior restraint on defendants' planned demonstration to be held in front of the Skokie Village Hall if defendants would not wear their uniforms.

* * *

The law of our nation is clear as to the question of whether the presence of hostile spectators or bystanders may justify the restraint of otherwise legal first amendment activities. "As to the possibility of there being hostile audience members causing violence, the law is quite clear that such considerations are impermissible. . . . Starting with *Terminiello v. City of Chicago* (1949), and continuing through *Gregory v. City of Chicago* (1969), the rule has been that if the communications expressed do not fit into an exception stripping them of first amendment protections, then under our Constitution, the public expression of ideas may not be prohibited merely because the ideas themselves are offensive to the hearers. Since the plaintiff has failed to meet its burden of proof, in so far as the injunction order purports to enjoin defendants from marching, walking or parading in the village of Skokie without reference to the uniform of the National Socialist Party of America, it is reversed.

The second issue, therefore, is whether plaintiff has overcome the presumptive invalidity of the prior restraint on defendants' demonstrating while wearing the uniform of the National Socialist Party of America in the village of Skokie.

*   *   *

The wearing of distinctive clothing to express a thought or idea is generally the type of a symbolic act which is considered protected speech within the first amendment. For example, a black armband worn by schoolchildren to protest the Vietnam War was held protected speech in *Tinker v. Des Moines Independent Community School District* (1969). Similarly, a jacket bearing the words "Fuck the Draft" was held protected speech in *Cohen v. California* (1971). In both cases, as in *Schacht v. United States* (1970), and other cases, in the absence of other circumstances the wearing of distinctive clothing was considered only the communication of ideas and therefore protected speech. There are, of course, circumstances which could remove speech from the sphere of protection. The advocacy of abstract force or violence is generally protected speech "except where such advocacy is directed to inciting or producing imminent lawless action and is likely to incite or produce such action." . . .

In *Brandenburg*, a Ku Klux Klan meeting of individuals wearing the distinctive hood and uttering statements quite derogatory of Blacks and Jews was held protected speech. In the instant case, plaintiff argues that the Nazi uniform is the symbolic equivalent of a public call to kill all Jews and is a direct incitation to immediate mass murder, which is not entitled to first amendment protection. The record does not support this conclusion. There is not one bit of evidence in the record that the uniform without the swastika would have such an effect. There has been no showing that there are persons who would be directly and immediately incited to commit mass murder as a result of seeing defendants' storm trooper uniforms.

Other exceptions we need not concern ourselves with are the obscenity and libel exceptions. We do, however, need carefully consider the exception of fighting words. According to the rule in *Chaplinsky v. New Hampshire* (1942),

". . . it is well understood that the right of free speech is not absolute at all times and under all circumstances. There are certain well-defined and narrowly limited classes of speech, the prevention and punishment of which have never been thought to raise any Constitutional problem. These include the lewd and obscene, the profane, the libelous and the insulting or 'fighting' words — those which by their very utterance inflict injury or tend to incite an immediate breach of the peace. It has been well observed that such utterances are no essential part of any exposition of ideas, and are of such slight social value as a step to truth that any benefit that may be derived from them is clearly outweighed by the social interest in order and morality."

Such "fighting" words are those personally abusive epithets which, when addressed to an ordinary citizen, as a matter of common knowledge, are inherently likely to provoke violent reaction (*Cohen v. California* (1971). The evidence of record does not support a conclusion that the uniform *sans* swastika constitutes fighting words. There is no testimony that anyone in the village of Skokie would consider the uniform itself as an abusive epithet which would provoke him to violent reaction. Nor can this court say as a matter of law and common knowledge that the brown-shirt uniform stripped of all other symbols is inherently likely to provoke violent reaction.

*   *   *

The third issue on appeal is whether the plaintiff has overcome the presumptive invalidity of the prior restraint on defendants' "marching, walking or parading or otherwise displaying the swastika on or off their person," which is Part B of the injunction order. Since the display of the swastika is an expression of defendants' ideas, however odious and repulsive to most members of our society, it will generally be considered protected speech unless it falls within the exceptions discussed in connection with the wearing of the uniform. There is no showing that the display or wearing of the swastika will incite anyone to immediately commit mass murder in furtherance of the aims of the German Nazi Party, or to commit any unlawful act in furtherance of the goals of the defendant Party. *Brandenburg v. Ohio* (1969).

The original complaint filed in this cause

alleges that by reason of the ethnic and religious composition of the village and the particular circumstances of this case, the public display of the swastika by defendants will incite large numbers of Skokie residents to violence and retaliation. We understand this portion of the complaint, although inartfully drafted in haste, to allege under the circumstances of this case that the display of the swastika constitutes fighting words and is therefore not protected by the first amendment. The evidence taken at the hearing which relates to this allegation is illuminating.

One Skokie resident who was a survivor of German concentration camps testified that to him, the swastika is a symbol that his closest family was killed by the Nazis and that he presently fears his death and the death of his children at the hands of those displaying the swastika. He feels strongly about the defendants and their swastika and does not know if he can control himself should he see a swastika in the village where he lives. By implication, a great many of the other 5000 to 7000 survivors of the holocaust who reside in Skokie may not be able to control themselves under similar circumstances. The mayor of the plaintiff village (who testified that he is a Roman Catholic) stated at the hearing that there was a "terrible feeling of unrest regarding the parading of the swastika in the Village of Skokie, a terrible feeling expressed by people in words that they should not have to tolerate this type of demonstration, in view of their history as a people." The legal question, therefore, is whether the display of the swastika in the village of Skokie, under the circumstances of this case, would constitute "fighting words."

Since *Chaplinsky v. New Hampshire* (1942), the fighting words exception has been well established in our law and is a viable rule, but it has been noted that *Chaplinsky*

"has been significantly limited by cases which hold protected the peaceful expression of views which stirs people to anger because of the content of the expression, or perhaps of the manner in which it is conveyed, and that breach of the peace and disorderly conduct statutes may not be used to curb such expression."

* * *

It has been somewhat unclear . . . whether anti-Semitic or other similar derogatory statements may be considered as fighting words when intentionally delivered to and heard by the reviled party. There is a recent clue, however, in the opinion of the Court in *Cohen v. California* (1971)

"No individual actually or likely to be present could reasonably have regarded the words on appellant's jacket as a direct personal insult. Nor do we have here an instance of the exercise of the State's police power to prevent a speaker from intentionally provoking a given group to hostile reaction. There is, as noted above, no showing that anyone who saw Cohen was in fact violently aroused or that appellant intended such a result."

As stated earlier, *Cohen v. California* concisely stated the *Chaplinsky* fighting words test as follows:

"[T]hose personally abusive epithets which, when addressed to the ordinary citizen, are, as a matter of common knowledge, inherently likely to provoke violent reaction." 403 U.S. at 20, 91 S.Ct. at 1785.

As in *Cohen*, we shall determine whether the test has been subjectively and objectively satisfied.

The evidence conclusively shows that at least one resident of Skokie considered the swastika to be a personally abusive epithet which was, in light of his personal history, inherently likely to provoke a violent reaction in him if the swastika were intentionally displayed by defendants in the village of Skokie. Other evidence shows by implication that similar or identical feelings were shared by thousands of other residents of the village of Skokie. In *Cohen v. California*, it is stated: "We have been shown no evidence that substantial numbers of citizens are standing ready to strike out physically at whoever may assault their sensibilities with execrations like that uttered by Cohen." In the instant case, the evidence shows precisely that substantial numbers of citizens are standing ready to strike out physically at whoever may assault their sensibilities with the display of the swastika. We feel that the subjective portion of the fighting words test has been satisfied.

The objective portion of the fighting words test follows. Would the ordinary citizen be provoked to violent reaction? We cannot say more than the evidence shows that the average Jewish resident of the village of Skokie would be provoked. Yet, in *Cantwell v. Connecticut* (1940), Cantwell played a phonograph record for two Roman Catholic men in a Roman Catholic neighborhood, and the record singled out "the Roman Catholic Church for strictures couched in terms which naturally would offend not only persons of that persuasion, but all others who respect the honestly held religious faith of their fellows." The hearers were offended, but they had already consented to listen to the record. If the swastika would naturally offend thousands of Jewish persons in Skokie, then it must be said that it would offend all those who respect the honestly held faith of their fellows, including the ordinary citizen.

The remaining portion of the objective test is whether the swastika, as a matter of common knowledge, is inherently likely to provoke violent reactions among those of the Jewish persuasion or ancestry if brought in close proximity to their homes or places of worship. As stated in dissent to an unrelated issue in *Anderson v. Vaughn* (D.Conn. 1971).

> "By way of illustration, if one were to parade a Ku Klux Klan flag or other such emblem into an NAACP meeting it would quite likely provoke a riotous reaction; or to publicly carry a Nazi flag into a synagogue would certainly be calculated to incite disorder; or to display a Viet Cong flag at a political gathering of loyal Americans might well be calculated to provoke an incitement to violence. Contrary conclusions would be both unreal and naive."

*   *   *

The swastika is a symbol which, as demonstrated by the record in this case and as a matter of common knowledge, is inherently likely to provoke violent reaction among those of the Jewish persuasion or ancestry when intentionally brought in close proximity to their homes and places of worship. The swastika is a personal affront to every member of the Jewish faith, in remembering the nearly consummated genocide of their people committed within memory by those who used the swastika as their symbol. This is especially true for the thousands of Skokie residents who personally survived the holocaust of the Third Reich. They remember all too well the brutal destruction of their families and communities by those then wearing the swastika. So too, the tens of thousands of Skokie's Jewish residents must feel gross revulsion for the swastika and would immediately respond to the personally abusive epithets slung their way in the form of the defendants' chosen symbol, the swastika. The epithets of racial and religious hatred are not protected speech (*Beauharnais v. Illinois* (1952), and we find that the village of Skokie has met its heavy burden of justifying the prior restraint imposed upon the defendants' planned wearing and display of the swastika. So that there should be no confusion, Part B of the injunction order, dealing with the swastika, is modified to read: "Intentionally displaying the swastika on or off their persons, in the course of a demonstration, march, or parade within the Village of Skokie." As thus modified, the order is affirmed.

Notes and Questions

HYMAN GROSS, "Privacy and Autonomy"

1. With this article we move from the protection of speech to the protection of behavior from the interference of government in terms of the right to privacy. Rather than attempting a formal definition of privacy, Hyman Gross focuses on important questions about privacy to determine what legal treatment is appropriate. His first question is, When does the loss of privacy occur? What is his answer? Where does his answer place him in the catalogue of positions on privacy listed in the introduction to this section? Notice that privacy is not lost, according to Gross, until control over what is known is lost, no matter how much information is disclosed. Do you see any problems with this position?

2. Privacy can be lost in two ways, Gross suggests. It can be given up or taken away, but only the latter is an offensive loss of privacy. This seems like a sensible view, but it requires a clear

notion of what counts as abandonment or giving up privacy. How does Gross define abandonment of privacy? What is the significance of expectability in his account?

3. There are two sorts of things that we keep private: facts or impressions about ourselves as persons—our identity, personality, and so on—and facts about our lives—what we have done, what we are doing, what we plan to do, and so on. Each is important for different reasons, according to Gross. Why is privacy of the person important? Gross's reasons for the importance of privacy are reminiscent of Mill's plea in *On Liberty* for the significance of individuality. What other reasons does Gross offer for the value of privacy of person?

4. Why is privacy of personal life important, according to Gross? What is wrong, for example, with a data bank?

5. Gross thinks that both the privacy of personality and of personal affairs merit protection. What arguments does he offer for this protection? Do you agree that a society that is allowed no privacy at all would resemble George Orwell's in the novel *1984*?

6. Gross recognizes, of course, that privacy conflicts with other important interests, so some compromises must be made. One of the biggest problems is how to resolve the conflict between privacy and freedom of speech or freedom of the press. How has this compromise been handled in law so far? How does Gross defend the legal treatment? Are there problems with the distinction between use and mere exposure?

7. How does Gross suggest handling the conflict between privacy and security?

8. Gross argues that a distinction between privacy and autonomy should be maintained. He believes these are separate interests that were conflated in the case of *Griswold* v. *Connecticut*. What are his criticisms of *Griswold*? Keep these criticisms in mind when you read the cases at the end of this section.

Privacy and Autonomy

HYMAN GROSS

Why is privacy desirable? When is its loss objectionable and when is it not? How much privacy is a person entitled to? These questions challenge at the threshold our concern about protection of privacy. Usually they are pursued by seeking agreement on the boundary between morbid and healthy reticence, and by attempting to determine when unwanted intrusion or notoriety is justified by something more important than privacy. Seldom is privacy considered as the condition under which there is *control* over acquaintance with one's personal affairs by the one enjoying it, and I wish here to show how consideration of privacy in this neglected aspect is helpful in answering the basic questions. First I shall attempt to make clear this part of the idea of privacy, next suggest

why privacy in this aspect merits protection, then argue that some important dilemmas are less vexing when we do get clear about these things, and finally offer a cautionary remark regarding the relation of privacy and autonomy.

I

What in general is it that makes certain conduct offensive to privacy? To distinguish obnoxious from innocent interference with privacy we must first see clearly what constitutes loss of privacy at all, and then determine why loss of privacy when it does occur is sometimes objectionable and sometimes not.

Loss of privacy occurs when the limits one has

set on acquaintance with his personal affairs are not respected. Almost always we mean not respected by *others*, though in unusual cases we might speak of a person not respecting his own privacy — he is such a passionate gossip, say, that he gossips even about himself and later regrets it. Limits on acquaintance may be maintained by the physical insulation of a home, office, or other private place within which things that are to be private may be confined. Or such bounds may exist by virtue of exclusionary social conventions, for example those governing a private conversation in a public place; or through restricting conventions which impose an obligation to observe such limits, as when disclosure is made in confidence. Limits operate in two ways. There are restrictions on what is known, and restrictions on who may know it. Thus, a curriculum vitae furnished to or for a prospective employer is not normally an invitation to undertake a detective investigation using the items provided as clues. Nor is there normally license to communicate to others the information submitted. In both instances there would be disregard of limitations implied by considerations of privacy, unless the existence of such limitations is unreasonable under the circumstances (the prospective employer is the CIA, or the information is furnished to an employment agency). But there is no loss of privacy when such limits as do exist are respected, no matter how ample the disclosure or how extensive its circulation. If I submit a detailed account of my life while my friend presents only the barest résumé of his, I am not giving up more of privacy than he. And if I give the information to a hundred employers, I lose no more in privacy than my friend who confides to only ten, provided those informed by each of us are equally restricted. More people know more about me, so my *risk* of losing privacy is greater and the threatened loss more serious. Because I am a less private person than my friend, I am more willing to run that risk. But until there is loss of control over what is known, and by whom, my privacy is uncompromised — though much indeed may be lost in secrecy, mystery, obscurity, and anonymity.

Privacy is lost in either of two ways. It may be given up, or it may be taken away. Abandonment of privacy (though sometimes undesired) is an inoffensive loss, while deprivation by others is an offensive loss.

If one makes a public disclosure of personal matters or exposes himself under circumstances that do not contain elements of restriction on further communication, there is loss of control for which the person whose privacy is lost is himself responsible. Such abandonment may result from indifference, carelessness, or a positive desire to have others become acquainted. There are, however, instances in which privacy is abandoned though this was not intended. Consider indiscreet disclosures while drunk which are rued when sober. If the audience is not under some obligation (perhaps the duty of a confidant) to keep dark what was revealed, there has been a loss of privacy for which the one who suffers it is responsible. But to constitute an abandonment, the loss of privacy must result from voluntary conduct by the one losing it, and the loss must be an expectable result of such conduct. If these two conditions are not met, the person who suffers the loss cannot be said to be responsible for it. Accordingly, a forced revelation, such as an involuntary confession, is not an abandonment of privacy, because the person making it has not given up control but has had it taken from him.

Regarding the requirement of expectability, we may see its significance by contrasting the case of a person whose conversation is overheard in Grand Central Station with the plight of someone made the victim of eavesdropping in his living room. In a public place loss of control is expectable by virtue of the circumstances of communication: part of what we mean when we say a place is public is that there is not present the physical limitation upon which such control depends. But a place may be called private only when there is such limitation, so communication in it is expectably limited and the eavesdropping an offensive violation for which the victim is not himself responsible. And consider the intermediate case of eavesdropping on a conversation in a public place — a distant parabolic microphone focused on a street-corner conversation, or a bugging device planted in an airplane seat. The offensive character of such practices derives again from their disregard of expectable limitations, in this instance the force of an exclusionary social convention which applies to all except those whose immediate presence enables them to overhear.

So far there has been consideration of what constitutes loss of privacy, and when it is objectionable. But to assess claims for protection of privacy we must be clear also about *why* in general loss of privacy is objectionable. This becomes especially important when privacy and other things we value are in competition, one needing to be sacrificed to promote the other. It becomes important then to understand what good reasons there are for valuing privacy, and this is our next item of business.

II

There are two sorts of things we keep private, and with respect to each, privacy is desirable for somewhat different reasons. Concern for privacy is sometimes concern about which facts about us can become known, and to whom. This includes acquaintance with all those things which make up the person as he may become known — identity, appearance, traits of personality and character, talents, weaknesses, tastes, desires, habits, interests — in short, things which tell us who a person is and what he's like. The other kind of private matter is about our lives — what we've done, intend to do, are doing now, how we feel, what we have, what we need — and concern about privacy here is to restrict acquaintance with these matters. Together these two classes of personal matters comprise all those things which can be private. Certain items of information do indeed have aspects which fit them for either category. For example, a person's belief is something which pertains to him when viewed as characteristic of him, but pertains to the events of his life when viewed as something he has acquired, acts on, and endeavors to have others adopt.

Why is privacy of the person important? This calls mainly for consideration of what is necessary to maintain an integrated personality in a social setting. Although we are largely unaware of what influences us at the time, we are constantly concerned to control how we appear to others, and act to implement this concern in ways extremely subtle and multifarious. Models of image and behavior are noticed, imitated, adopted so that nuances in speech, gesture, facial expression, *politesse*, and much more become a person as known on an occasion. The deep motive is to influence the reactions of others, and this is at the heart of human social accommodation. Constraints to imitation and disguise can

become a pathological problem of serious proportions when concern with appearances interferes with normal functioning, but normal behavior allows, indeed requires, that we perform critically in presenting and withholding in order to effect certain appearances. If these editorial efforts are not to be wasted, we must have a large measure of control over what of us is seen and heard, when, where, and by whom. For this reason we see as offensive the candid camera which records casual behavior with the intention of later showing it as entertainment to a general audience. The victim is not at the time aware of who will see him and so does not have the opportunity to exercise appropriate critical restraint in what he says and does. Although subsequent approval for the showing eliminates grounds for objection to the publication as an offense to privacy, there remains the lingering objection to the prior disregard of limits of acquaintance which are normal to the situation and so presumably relied on by the victim at the time. The nature of the offense is further illuminated by considering its aggravation when the victim has been deliberately introduced unawares into the situation for the purpose of filming his behavior, or its still greater offensiveness if the setting is a place normally providing privacy and assumed to be private by the victim. What we have here are increasingly serious usurpations of a person's prerogative to determine how he shall appear, to whom, and on what occasion.

The same general objection applies regarding loss of privacy where there is information about our personal affairs which is obtained, accumulated, and transmitted by means beyond our control. It is, however, unlike privacy of personality in its untoward consequences. A data bank of personal information is considered objectionable, but not because it creates appearances over which we have no control. We are willing to concede that acquaintance with our reputation is in general not something we are privileged to control, and that we are not privileged to decide just what our reputation shall be. If the reputation is correct we cannot object because we do not appear as we would wish. What then are the grounds of objection to a data bank, an objection which indeed persists even if its information is correct and the inferences based on the information are sound? A good reason for objecting is that a data bank is an offense to self-determination. We are subject to being acted on by others because of conclusions about us which we do not know and whose effect we have no opportunity to counteract. There is a loss of control over reputation which is unacceptable because we no longer have the ability to try to change what is believed about us. We feel entitled to know what others believe, and why, so that we may try to change misleading impressions and on occasion show why a decision about us ought not to be based on reputation even if the reputation is justified. If our account in the data bank were made known to us and opportunity given to change its effect, we should drop most (though not all) of our objection to it. We might still fear the danger of abuse by public forces concerned more with the demands of administrative convenience than justice, but because we could make deposits and demand a statement reflecting them, we would at least no longer be in the position of having what is known and surmised about us lie beyond our control.

Two aspects of privacy have been considered separately, though situations in which privacy is violated sometimes involve both. Ordinary surveillance by shadowing, peeping, and bugging commonly consists of observation of personal behavior as well as accumulation of information. Each is objectionable for its own reasons, though in acting against the offensive practice we protect privacy in both aspects. Furthermore, privacy of personality and of personal affairs have some common ground in meriting protection, and this has to do with a person's role as a responsible moral agent.

In general we do not criticize a person for untoward occurrences which are a result of his conduct if (through no fault of his own) he lacked the ability to do otherwise. Such a person is similarly ineligible for applause for admirable things which would not have taken place but for his conduct. In both instances we claim that he is not responsible for what happened, and so should not be blamed or praised. The principle holds true regarding loss of privacy. If a person cannot control how he is made to appear (nor could he have prevented his loss of control), he is not responsible for how he appears or is thought of, and therefore cannot be criticized as displeasing or disreputable (nor extolled as the opposite). He

can, or course, be condemned for conduct which is the basis of the belief about him, but that is a different matter from criticism directed solely to the fact that such a belief exists. Personal gossip (even when believed) is not treated by others as something for which the subject need answer, because its existence defies his control. Responsible appraisal of anyone whose image or reputation is a matter of concern requires that certain private items illicitly in the public domain be ignored in the assessment. A political figure may, with impunity, be known as someone who smokes, drinks, flirts, and tells dirty jokes, so long (but only so long) as this is not the public image *he* presents. The contrasting fortunes of recent political leaders remind us that not being responsible for what is believed by others can be most important. If such a man is thought in his private life to engage in discreet though illicit liaisons he is not held accountable for rumors without more. However, once he has allowed himself to be publicly exposed in a situation which is in the slightest compromising, he must answer for mere appearances. And on this same point, we might consider why a woman is never held responsible for the way she appears in the privacy of her toilette.

To appreciate the importance of this sort of disclaimer of responsibility we need only imagine a community in which it is not recognized. Each person would be accountable for himself however he might be known, and regardless of any precautionary seclusion which was undertaken in the interest of shame, good taste, or from other motives of self-regard. In such a world modesty is sacrificed to the embarrassment of unwanted acclaim, and self-criticism is replaced by the condemnation of others. It is part of the vision of Orwell's *1984*, in which observation is so thorough that it forecloses the possibility of a private sector of life under a person's exclusionary control, and so makes him answerable for everything observed without limits of time or place. Because of this we feel such a condition of life far more objectionable than a community which makes the same oppressive social demands of loyalty and conformity but with the opportunity to be free of concern about appearances in private. In a community without privacy, furthermore, there can be no editorial privilege exercised in making oneself known to others. Consider, for example, the plight in which Montaigne would find himself. He observed that "No quality embraces us purely and universally. If it did not seem crazy to talk to oneself, there is not a day when I would not be heard growling at myself: 'Confounded fool!' And yet I do not intend that to be my definition." Respect for privacy is required to safeguard our changes of mood and mind, and to promote growth of the person through self-discovery and criticism. We want to run the risk of making fools of ourselves and be free to call ourselves fools, yet not be fools in the settled opinion of the world, convicted out of our own mouths.

III

Privacy is desirable, but rights to enjoy it are not absolute. In deciding what compromises must be made some deep quandaries recur, and three of them at least seem more manageable in light of what has been said so far.

In the first place, insistence on privacy is often taken as implied admission that there is cause for shame. The assumption is that the only reason for keeping something from others is that one is ashamed of it (although it is conceded that sometimes there is in fact no cause for shame even though the person seeking privacy thinks there is). Those who seek information and wish to disregard interests in privacy often play on this notion by claiming that the decent and the innocent have no cause for shame and so no need for privacy: "Only those who have done or wish to do something shameful demand privacy." But it is unsound to assume that demands for privacy imply such an admission. Pride, or at least wholesome self-regard, is the motive in many situations. The famous Warren and Brandeis article on privacy which appeared in the *Harvard Law Review* in 1890 was impelled in some measure, we are told, by Samuel Warren's chagrin. His daughter's wedding, a very social Boston affair, had been made available to the curious at every newsstand by the local press. Surely he was not ashamed of the wedding even though outraged by the publicity. Or consider Miss Roberson, the lovely lady whose picture was placed on a poster advertising the product of Franklin Mills with the eulogistic slogan "Flour of the family," thereby precipitating a lawsuit whose consequences included the first statutory

protection of privacy in the United States. What was exploited was the lady's face, undoubtedly a source of pride.

Both these encroachments on privacy illustrate the same point. Things which people like about themselves are taken by them to belong to them in a particularly exclusive way, and so control over disclosure or publication is especially important to them. The things about himself which a person is most proud of he values most, and thus are things over which he is most interested to exercise exclusive control. It is true that shame is not infrequently the motive for privacy, for often we do seek to maintain conditions necessary to avoid criticism and punishment. But since it is not the only motive, the quest for privacy does not entail tacit confessions. Confusion arises here in part because an assault on privacy always does involve humiliation of the victim. But this is because he has been deprived of control over something personal which is given over to the control of others. In short, unwilling loss of privacy always results in the victim being shamed, not because of what others learn, but because they and not he may then determine who else shall know it and what use shall be made of it.

Defining the privilege to make public what is otherwise private is another source of persistent difficulty. There is a basic social interest in making available information about people, in exploring the personal aspects of human affairs, in stimulating and satisfying curiosity about others. The countervailing interest is in allowing people who have not offered themselves for public scrutiny to remain out of sight and out of mind. In much of the United States the law has strained with the problem of drawing a line of protection which accords respect to both interests. The result, broadly stated, has been recognition of a privilege to compromise privacy for news and other material whose primary purpose is to impart information, but to deny such privileged status to literary and other art, to entertainment, and generally to any appropriation for commercial purposes. Development of the law in New York after Miss Roberson's unsuccessful attempt to restrain public display of her picture serves as a good example. A statute was enacted prohibiting unauthorized use of the name, portrait, or picture of any living person for purposes of trade or advertising, and the legislation has been interpreted by the courts along the general lines indicated. But it is still open to speculation why a writer's portrayal of a real person as a character in a novel could qualify as violative, while the same account in biographical or historical work would not. It has not been held that history represents a more important social interest than art and so is more deserving of a privileged position in making known personal matters, or, more generally, that edification is more important than entertainment. Nor is the question ever raised, as one might expect, whether an item of news is sufficiently newsworthy to enjoy a privilege in derogation of privacy. Further, it was not held that the implied statutory criterion of intended economic benefit from the use of a personality would warrant the fundamental distinctions. Indeed, the test of economic benefit would qualify both television's public affairs programs and its dramatic shows as within the statute, and the reportage of *Life* Magazine would be as restricted as the films of De Mille or Fellini. But in each instance the former is in general free of the legal prohibition while the latter is not. What, then, is the basis of distinction? Though not articulated, a sound criterion does exist.

Unauthorized *use* of another person — whether for entertainment, artistic creation, or economic gain — is offensive. So long as we remain in charge of how we are used, we have no cause for complaint. In those cases in which a legal wrong is recognized, there has been use by others in disregard of this authority, but in those cases in which a privilege is found, there is not *use* of personality or personal affairs at all, at least not use in the sense of one person assuming control over another, which is the gist of the offense to autonomy. We do indeed suffer a loss of autonomy whenever the power to place us in free circulation is exercised by others, but we consider such loss offensive only when another person assumes the control of which we are deprived, when we are used and not merely exposed. Failure to make clear this criterion of offensiveness has misled those who wish to define the protectable area, and they conceive the problem as one of striking an optimal balance between two valuable interests, when in fact it is a matter of deciding whether the acts complained of are offensive under a quite definite standard of offensiveness. The difficult cases here have not presented a dilemma of selecting the happy medium, but rather the slippery job of determining whether the defendant had used the plaintiff or whether he had merely caused things about him to become known, albeit to the defendant's profit. The difference is between managing another person as a means to one's own ends, which is offensive, and acting merely as a vehicle of presentation (though not gratuitously) to satisfy established social needs, which is not offensive. Cases dealing with an unauthorized biography that was heavily anecdotal and of questionable accuracy, or with an entertaining article that told the true story of a former child prodigy who became an obscure eccentric, are perplexing ones because they present elements of both offensive and inoffensive publication, and a decision turns on which is predominant.

There remains another balance-striking quandary to be dismantled. It is often said that privacy as an interest must be balanced against security. Each, we think, must sacrifice something of privacy to promote the security of all, though we are willing to risk some insecurity to preserve a measure of privacy. Pressure to reduce restrictions on wiretapping and searches by police seeks to push the balance toward greater security. But the picture we are given is seriously misleading. In the first place we must notice the doubtful assumption on which the argument rests. It may be stated this way: the greater the ability to watch what is going on, or obtain evidence of what has gone on, the greater the ability to prevent crime. It is a notion congenial to those who believe that more efficient law enforcement contributes significantly to a reduction in crime. We must, however, determine if such a proposition is in fact sound, and we must see what crimes are suppressible, even in principle, before any sacrifice of privacy can be justified. There is, at least *in limine*, much to be said for the conflicting proposition that, once a generally efficient system of law enforcement exists, an increase in its efficiency does not result in a corresponding reduction in crime, but only in an increase in punishments. Apart from that point, there is an objection relating more directly to what has been said here about privacy. Security and privacy are both desirable, but measures to promote each are on different moral footing. Men ought to be secure, we say, because only in that condition can they live a good life. Privacy, however, like peace and prosperity, is itself part of what we mean by a good life, a part having to do with self-respect and self-determination. Therefore, the appropriate attitudes when we are asked to sacrifice privacy for security are first a critical one which urges alternatives that minimize or do not at all require the sacrifice, and ultimately regret for loss of a cherished resource if the sacrifice proves necessary.

IV

In speaking of privacy and autonomy, there is some danger that privacy may be conceived as autonomy. Such confusion has been signaled in legal literature by early and repeated use of the phrase "right to be let alone" as a synonym for "right of privacy." The United States Supreme Court succumbed completely in 1965 in its opinion in *Griswold v. Connecticut*, and the ensuing intellectual disorder warrants comment.

In that case legislative prohibition of the use of contraceptives was said to be a violation of a constitutional right of privacy, at least when it affected married people. The court's opinion relied heavily on an elaborate *jeu de mots*, in which different senses of the word "privacy" were

punned upon, and the legal concept generally mismanaged in ways too various to recount here. In the *Griswold* situation there had been an attempt by government to regulate personal affairs, not get acquainted with them, and so there was an issue regarding autonomy and not privacy. The opinion was not illuminating on the question of what are proper bounds for the exercise of legislative power, which was the crucial matter before the court. It is precisely the issue of what rights to autonomous determination of his affairs are enjoyed by a citizen. The *Griswold* opinion not only failed to take up that question in a forthright manner, but promoted confusion about privacy in the law by unsettling the intellectual focus on it which had been developed in torts and constitutional law. If the confusion in the court's argument was inadvertent, one may sympathize with the deep conceptual difficulties which produced it, and if it was deliberately contrived, admire its ingenuity. Whatever its origin, its effect is to muddle the separate issues, which must be analyzed and argued along radically different lines when protection is sought either for privacy or for autonomy. Hopefully, further developments will make clear that while an offense to privacy is an offense to autonomy, not every curtailment of autonomy is a compromise of privacy.

Notes and Questions

JUDITH WAGNER DECEW, "The Scope of Privacy in Law and Ethics"

1. Judith Wagner DeCew's primary objective is to dispute the claim that the constitutional right of privacy developed through the *Griswold* line of cases is spurious for the reason that it does not really involve a claim for privacy but a claim for liberty (or autonomy). This was the position taken by Gross. Answering this charge compels DeCew to examine the scope of the concept of privacy.

2. To pursue her examination DeCew analyzes a position formulated by William Parent. Notice that Parent's definition differs from that offered by Gross. DeCew finds both strengths and weaknesses in Parent's definition. What are they? Would her critique work as well against Gross?

3. Ultimately the question comes down to the relation between privacy and liberty. How does DeCew explain that relation? How does she support her claim that the constitutional cases following *Griswold* do not conflate privacy with liberty but instead require the violation of both?

4. If DeCew's argument is convincing, then a broader account of privacy is needed to accommodate the full range of cases falling under the heading of privacy. DeCew suggests that there are two options for accomplishing this task. What are they? Which does she choose to pursue?

5. In attempting to find the common meaning among the diverse legal uses of privacy, DeCew

considers several candidates, such as control of information, exclusive access, and protection against intrusion into personal zones close to oneself. What are the virtues and deficiencies of these views?

6. Focusing finally on the intuition that what is private is what is not the legitimate concern of others, DeCew notes that this intuition allows a broad range of privacy interests — and provides a number of other benefits as well. What are they? Yet there is one major problem with this view. What is it?

7. To determine the subclass of areas beyond the legitimate concern of others that are privacy interests, DeCew suggests that we look to the reasons for wanting privacy. If the reasons given for wanting protection are the same as those given for wanting privacy, then privacy is the ground of the claim. What are the reasons she gives for wanting privacy? Are they the same as the reasons Gross offers? There is an interesting alignment between these reasons given for the value of privacy and the reasons some philosophers give for personhood or personality. For example, Mill gives such reasons in *On Liberty* for the value of individuality.

8. DeCew does not claim to have defined privacy, but she does claim to have provided criteria of identification that can accommodate the broad range of privacy interests in both tort and constitutional cases. Does she succeed?

The Scope of Privacy in Law and Ethics

JUDITH WAGNER DECEW

---

1. Introduction

In both laws and ethics, "privacy" is an umbrella term for a wide variety of interests. Due to the growth of computer technology and capacities for electronic surveillance, data collection and storage, concern has increased over protection from unwarranted observations and exploitation of personal communications and information including academic, medical, and employment records. In these areas privacy is most obviously at stake, and has traditionally been protected in tort law as an interest in "having control over information about oneself." In addition, privacy has been associated in recent constitutional law with such issues as possession of obscene matter in one's home, interracial marriage, attendance at public schools, sterilization, contraception, abortion, and other medical treatment.

We might agree that information such as the content of one's fantasies is private. There is also consensus that action such as wife-battering, even if done in the confines of one's home, is not wholly private. Nevertheless, there are troubling borderline cases. For example, should threats on another's life, made in confidence to a lawyer or psychiatrist, be protected in the name of privacy? Complexities concerning the relationship between privacy and harm or the risk of harm, and the conflict between privacy and social good, have yet to be sorted out to determine the scope of privacy in law and ethics.

Much of the discussion of privacy has evolved from a constellation of legal judgments. Philosophers then entered the debate, attempting to illuminate just what a right to privacy can and should mean. In two recent articles William Parent has attempted to clarify confusion surrounding the concept of privacy. He defends a definition of privacy focusing on personal knowledge not part of any public record. Subsequently he discredits alternate accounts of privacy, explains the importance of privacy as a moral value, and assesses recent privacy decisions in the law. Parent also claims that the constitutional cases since *Griswold v. Connecticut* (banning disbursement of contraceptive information, instruction, and medical advice to married persons) invoking a right to privacy are "spurious" privacy cases because attempts to explain them in terms of privacy conflate privacy and liberty. My central goal is to show that we may dispute this claim about the constitutional privacy cases. I begin by presenting Parent's definition of privacy and highlighting strengths as well as serious difficulties of his approach. I then show why we must reject Parent's as well as other narrow definitions, thus leaving it open to us to adopt a broader concept of privacy. After arguing that a notion of privacy relevant to the constitutional privacy cases need not merely confuse privacy and liberty, I discuss alternative conceptual bases for an account of privacy relevant to both tort and constitutional privacy claims.

Let me make two preliminary points. First, in this paper I shall not place special weight on privacy as a right, as opposed to a claim or interest. A claim is often described as an argument that someone deserves something. A right is then a justified claim; justified by laws or judicial decisions if it is a legal right, by moral principles if it is a moral right. However I am making moral and legal points which are significant independently of whether we can ultimately make sense of rights, explain when they are binding, or show they are reducible to utilitarian claims. Since the literature on privacy uses rights terminology I must accommodate that. But because I am making no claim about a theory of rights, whenever possible I shall refer to privacy as an interest (which can be invaded), by which I mean something it would be a good thing to have, leaving open how extensively it ought to be protected.

Second, nothing in my discussion requires assuming that one endorse all the decisions in cases I cite. One need not accept the actual rulings to inquire whether there is a common notion of privacy at stake. Indeed, disagreement over some decisions is likely for at least two reasons. (i) The notion of privacy has been so poorly articulated that it is not clear what is protected and what is not. (ii) Even if we develop a clearer concept of privacy, that will not dictate how it

should be balanced against other individual rights or public concerns. One may have an important interest in privacy that for legal or social reasons cannot be protected.

2. Privacy and the Public Record

Understanding Parent's reasonable but inadequate position on privacy will provide a helpful way of addressing more general issues about the scope and meaning of "privacy." Motivated by a concern to provide a definition of privacy that a) "is by and large consistent with ordinary language" and b) does "not usurp or encroach upon the basic meanings and functions" of other related concepts (PPA 269), Parent defines privacy as

> (P) the condition of not having undocumented personal information [knowledge] about oneself known [possessed] by others (LP 306, PPA 269)

He stresses that he is defining the "condition" of privacy as opposed to the right to privacy. The difference, he explains, is that the condition of privacy is a moral value for persons who also prize freedom and individuality which should be protected against unwarranted invasion in part by advocating a moral right to privacy. This moral right is in turn protected by law, and on Parent's view should be guaranteed more fully than it is at present. The distinction is important because it allows us to acknowledge that diminishing privacy need not violate a moral or legal right to privacy, and vice versa.

Let us get clearer on the significance of (P). "Personal" knowledge is, according to Parent, knowledge of personal information. Such information must be factual, he believes, because publicity of falsehoods or subjective opinions does not constitute an invasion of privacy; it is appropriately characterized as slander, libel, or defamation. Furthermore, information which is personal consists either a) of facts which most persons in a given society choose not to reveal about themselves (except to close friends, family . . .) or b) of facts about which a particular individual is acutely sensitive and which he therefore does not choose to reveal about himself, even though most people do not care if similar facts are widely known about themselves (LP 307, PPA 270). Thus in our culture facts about sexual preferences, salaries, physical or mental health, etc. are examples of personal information. While most of us do not consider our height or marital status to be instances of personal information, they will be for those sensitive about it.

Finally, personal information is "documented" just in case it belongs to the public record, that is, just in case it can be found in newspapers, court proceedings, and other official documents available to the public (LP 307, PPA 270). This characterization is meant to exclude information about individuals kept on file for a particular purpose, such as medical or employment records, which are not available for public perusal.

A valuable feature of Parent's account is that he not only sees privacy as a coherent concept but also takes the view that there is something unique, fundamental, and of special value in privacy. In contrast, "reductionists" such as Judith Thomson have argued that the right to privacy is not an independent right but is "derivative" from other rights, most notably property rights and rights to bodily security. According to this hypothesis there is no such thing as *the* right to privacy, for any violation of a right to privacy violates some right not identical with or included in the right to privacy. Privacy is "derivative" in the sense that it is possible to explain each right in the cluster of privacy rights without ever mentioning the right to privacy. Hence there is no need to find whatever might be in common in the rights in the privacy cluster. Commentators taking this approach differ of course, yet all agree that talk of privacy as an independent notion will not be illuminating. By considering Thomson's examples in detail Parent shows that it is surely *as* plausible that the reverse of reductionism is true, that other rights such as those of ownership or rights over one's person, are "derivative" from privacy rights. Indeed this is likely if there is a distinctive and important value designated by the term "privacy."

A second strength of Parent's approach is the extent to which he recognizes and accommodates the fact that privacy is a conventional or relative notion. Because what counts as personal information may vary from group to group or individual to individual, and may change over time, there is no fixed realm of the private. This relative feature of privacy is well known but not often emphasized. Nevertheless, it must be allowed for by an adequate account of privacy.

3. Beyond Information

In attempting to isolate the conceptual core of privacy, Parent is surely correct to abandon Judge Cooley's famous, but overbroad, characterization of privacy as a right "to be let alone." Yet he overreacts in the opposite direction and defends a definition of privacy that is much too narrow. To see this, consider first Parent's emphasis on *undocumented* personal knowledge. Imagine a case in which personal information about some individual has become part of the public record through a violation of privacy. A news agency, for example, surreptitiously taps an entertainer's telephone and subsequently publishes revealing information about that person's sex life or drug use habits. Given Parent's definition of privacy, once that information becomes part of the public record there is no violation of privacy in repeated publication of the information. The entertainer has no recourse for future protection; the information is no longer private even if the original disclosure was an error or a moral wrong.

In defense of his view, Parent says "[w]hat belongs to the public domain cannot without glaring paradox be called private and consequently should not be incorporated within a viable conception of privacy" (LP 308). If the original publication surfaced in a nationally syndicated daily, subsequent publication might seem only mildly invasive. But if the first disclosure occurred in publicly accessible but obscure documents, it is difficult to deny that a widely distributed reprint would be a further intrusion on the individual's privacy. The general point is that we are not likely to view perpetrating a violation as any less of a violation just because the agent is not the first one to invade the other's privacy. Thus, for example, during Margaret Heckler's divorce proceedings her husband claimed they had not had sexual relations in 20 years. Although this information was publicly available to reporters in the courtroom, it seems clear that the subsequent media coverage not only diminished Heckler's privacy but also violated her right to privacy.

Parent replies that similar publicity about a rape victim, for example, cannot be condemned on privacy grounds but should be criticized because it abridges her anonymity. It is far from clear that his account reflects our ordinary linguistic usage or is even applicable to Heckler's case. And even if we did talk of a "right to anonymity" in certain instances, surely it would be accorded to the victim so that her privacy would not be invaded. Indeed, there are legal counterexamples to Parent's position. Yet on Parent's account, once information becomes part of the public record, whether legitimately or not, further release of it is never a privacy invasion.

Moreover, if any personal information is part of the public record, then even the most insidious snooping to attain the information, by someone unaware that it is already documented, for example, does not constitute a privacy intrusion on Parent's account. There is no invasion of privacy as long as "the information revealed was publicly available and could have been found out by anyone, without resort to snooping or prying" (PPA 271). Parent's test depends on whether or not the personal information is part of the public domain. Yet most of us would find the snooping diminishes our privacy, even if it were based on error and unnecessary to learn the facts. Snooping, spying, and other methods of acquisition are not always determinative of a privacy invasion. For example, I may intrude on another's privacy by overhearing a quiet conversation on a subway. Nevertheless, the mode of acquisition cannot be said to be irrelevant, as it apparently may be given Parent's account of privacy.

These considerations introduce a more general concern. Because Parent has identified privacy invasions with possession of undocumented personal information, there is no way on his account to judge what should or should not be a part of the public record. His descriptive emphasis on what is *as a matter of fact* part of the public record leaves no room for a normative sense of privacy encompassing interests *worthy* of protection.

Thus, for example, Blue Cross/Blue Shield guidelines have recently been revised so that for psychological/psychiatric as well as physical treatment, specific descriptions of the ailment being treated are required in order for patients to receive reimbursement. While the Privacy Act of 1974 protects the content of medical and other records, if the detailed descriptions required by Blue Cross/Blue Shield should be deemed necessary as public verification of the legitimacy of any payments, they will not be private given Parent's definition. The point is that even very personal information can, through legislative action or decisions by agencies requiring its release, become nonprivate according to his definition, by virtue of its becoming documented. That account gives no normative standard for what it is legitimate for the public to know.

A second question we can ask is why Parent characterizes privacy as the condition of not having undocumented personal *knowledge* about one possessed by others. One problem is that it may be difficult to determine the truth of some statements. Setting aside such cases, however, we may still ask why knowledge must be disseminated for there to be a loss of privacy. Parent says, "[i]nvasion of privacy must consist of truthful disclosures about a person . . . privacy is invaded by certain kinds of intrusions, namely those of a cognitive nature that *result in the acquisition* of undocumented personal facts" (PPA 285, emphasis mine). It is never clear whether it is the acquisition or the disclosure of information that troubles Parent most deeply. But what if there is neither? If one secretly trains a telescope on another but discovers nothing that is not already public information, has there been no privacy invasion? Consider Parent's discussion of an example of Thomson's: a great opera singer, who no longer wants to be listened to, only sings quietly behind soundproof walls. If she is nonetheless heard through an ingenious and strategically placed amplifier, what knowledge about her is gained? Even if none, most of us would agree there has been a privacy invasion. Parent himself seems confused on such cases. In assessing this example he writes, "[i]f B's snooping is without justification it should be condemned as a violation of A's right to privacy" (PPA 280), indicating the unjustified spying itself, independently of any knowledge acquired, is determinative of a privacy violation. The problem then reduces to when such snooping is justified and when it is not. Yet according to Parent's definition we must agree that there have been no privacy invasions in cases where no undocumented personal facts become known.

We might make sense of his remarks by requiring information acquisition only for a loss of privacy, not for a violation of a right. Yet Parent does not give this reply, and he invites us to use his definition concerning when privacy is diminished as a legal standard presumably relevant for determining rights violations as well. He does suggest an alternative response, however, namely that knowledge *is* gained in many such cases. The snooper learns the person's posture and attire, for example, and learns of the opera singer what she sings, how often, etc. Nevertheless, with repeated observations it is less clear that *new* knowledge is gained. And when the information is trivial we have good reason to doubt that the knowledge gained helps explain *why* we consider privacy the issue. Parent concedes, moreover, that if one snoops and fails to gather information, then there is no privacy invasion although the action is condemnable as unwarranted trespass. But then the most he can say if the singer is practicing in a building owned by a third party is that the snooper committed a wrong against the owner, not the singer! If he tries to say there is a sense in which the listener does trespass against the singer, then "trespass" is merely standing in for a certain kind of privacy invasion, whether he admits it or not.

Third, even if we weaken Parent's definition so that we do not always require that knowledge be gained for privacy to be invaded, we may wonder why it is reasonable to focus on possession of *information* as central to privacy. If privacy is merely the condition of not having others possess certain information, it appears that privacy is tantamount to *secrecy*, though Parent hopes to deny such an identification. Nearly every dictionary includes a definition of privacy as secrecy or concealment. According to the *Oxford English Dictionary*, that which is private is "removed from public view or knowledge; not within the cognizance of people generally." Private information is often that which conceals, and interests in not being seen or overheard seem central to many privacy cases. However, this merely shows that the concepts overlap. Privacy and secrecy are not coextensional. First, whatever is secret is concealed or withheld from others, and it may not always be private. Thus a secret treaty or military plans kept from the public are not private transactions or information. Second, privacy does not always imply secrecy. For private information about one's debts or odd behavior may be publicized. Although it is no longer concealed, it is no less private. Characterizing privacy as what is *intended* to be concealed is no help. Similar counterexamples follow. Mili-

tary secrets are intended to be concealed; it does not follow that they are private. Information or intimate caresses may be private even if there is no intention to conceal them.

Historically, protection of information has been prominent but not exhaustive in the development of privacy law. Warren and Brandeis first sought protection from publication, without consent or adequate justification, not only of personal information, but also of one's name or likeness. The Fourth and Fifth Amendment protection against unreasonable search and seizures and self-incrimination protect potentially oppressive governmental surveillance as well as information gathering. They now limit wiretapping and other forms of electronic eavesdropping in addition to the physical intrusions on privacy that were once their primary target.

Moreover, it is widely recognized that others' physical access to one can limit one's privacy in other ways as well. Ruth Gavison has argued that one can lose privacy merely by becoming the object of attention, even if no new information becomes known and whether the attention is conscious and purposeful, or inadvertent. More obviously, one's privacy is diminished when others gain physical proximity to them, as Peeping Toms for example, through observation of their bodies, behavior, or interactions, through entry into a home under false pretenses, or even by a move from a single-person office to a shared one. In none of these cases is it necessary for new information to be acquired for there to be a privacy intrusion. Scanlon makes the point graphically.

> If you press personal questions on me in a situation in which this is conventionally forbidden, I can always refuse to answer. But the *fact that no information is revealed* does not remove the violation, which remains just as does the analogous violation when you peek through my bathroom window but fail to see me because I have taken some mildly inconvenient evasive action.

Parent responds that privacy is irrelevant here. At best there is harassment (and possibly trespass). Parent's general strategy, then, in cases where no new information is acquired, is to urge that while there is a violation, it is unrelated to privacy — either anonymity (rape victim), trespass (insidious snooping, opera singer), or harassment (Scanlon's case). But as an argument for a conclusion about privacy, this hardly suffices. That an act involves harassment, trespass, or infringes one's anonymity implies nothing about whether it also diminishes or violates one's privacy.

It might seem that the above cases compel characterization of privacy as *seclusion* or the state or condition of being withdrawn from others, the observations of others, or the public interest. This definition may come closest to Judge Cooley's characterization of the right as "the right to be let alone." But even if a conversation or activity is private, it will fail to be secluded if it is in public view or if it is overheard, seen or otherwise observed by others. Discussion or activity intended to be private, such as child abuse or consenting sadomasochism, may be observed or may be of public concern. Analogously, even if a conversation or action is not in view of others, it may not be a private one in any sense except that it happens not to be observed or known about even if it is of great public interest.

Some aspect of seclusion is clearly protected by privacy law. The American Law Institute's *Restatement of the Law of Torts*, Second (1976) includes a section titled "Intrusion on Seclusion" (§ 652B), which reads:

> One who intentionally intrudes, physically or otherwise, upon the solitude or seclusion of another, or his private affairs or concerns, is subject to liability to the other for invasion of his privacy, if the invasion would be highly offensive to a reasonable person.

But this legal protection can be limited. What would ordinarily be considered privacy interests are not always protected if the individual involved is a public figure or if the information is not confidential. A clandestine search (without a warrant) through office files was not considered an invasion of privacy, despite a loss of privacy, since the information gathered and publicized was needed to judge the individual as a candidate for the U.S. Senate. And when Ralph Nader complained that prior to his publication of *Unsafe at Any Speed*, General Motors agents interviewed acquaintances about his political, racial and sexual views, kept him under surveillance in public places, attempted to entrap him with women, made threatening, harassing, and obnoxious telephone calls to him, tapped his telephone, and eavesdropped on private conversations by means

of mechanical and electronic equipment, the court asserted that

> . . . mere gathering of information about a particular individual does not give rise to a cause of action under this theory. Privacy is invaded only if the information sought is of a confidential nature and the defendant's conduct was unreasonably intrusive.

According to the opinion in Nader's case, *confidential content* is crucial to privacy. Yet other tort privacy claims are upheld because of the intrusiveness of the behavior, even if the information or photographs obtained are not at all confidential. For example, in *Dïetemann v. Time Inc.*, two *Life* magazine reporters entered a disabled veteran's home under false pretenses and took clandestine photographs and recordings to learn about and publicize the quackery being practiced. It was held and affirmed on appeal that this was an invasion of privacy even though the content was not confidential and whether or not the material was published.

The courts are clearly puzzled over the relationship between privacy and confidential content, publicity, and intrusiveness. Secrecy, seclusion, and confidential content alone cannot give an adequate picture of the realm of the private, although each may be a crucial aspect of some subset of privacy invasions. Unfortunately, Parent has neither acknowledged nor addressed this confusion. I wish to suggest that most of us find the *Nader* decision outrageous, the *Dïetemann* result reasonable, and believe the opera singer's privacy has been invaded. If so, then we can agree that acquisition of undocumented personal knowledge is not always relevant to a privacy intrusion. Our privacy interests are both more extensive and deeper than Parent's definition allows. He can at best capture much of the legal extension of the concept of privacy, not the nature of our moral notion of privacy.

4. Privacy and Liberty

I have argued that we must reject information acquisition and publication as solely determinative of privacy invasions. If we do so, and acknowledge that privacy concerns encompass not only information but activity and physical access as well, then we have good reason to consider whether the realm of the private can properly be taken to include the sort of privacy interests protected in constitutional law as well as those associated with tort law. Tort privacy, developed over the past 90 years, covers interests individuals have in protection not only from publication of information but also from unwarranted observations of themselves, their activities, materials, and conversations, whether those observations occur in person or through electronic surveillance. There has also been increased protection from having one's communications reproduced or misused without authorization and from having information about oneself appropriated or exploited.

The constitutional right to privacy, first announced by the Supreme Court twenty years ago in the *Griswold* case, has continued to be elusive. It has been used not only to guard rights to use and distribute contraceptives, but also to protect abortion rights and to defend subsequent decisions concerning funding, father's rights, third party consent for minors, and protection of the fetus. Furthermore, the right to privacy was cited as one major reason for allowing "possession of obscene matter" in one's home and it has been associated with cases on sterilization laws, interracial marriage, and attendance at public schools.

Paradigmatically, tort privacy cases involve concerns with information, either conveyed by or about an individual. The more diverse constitutional privacy cases involve issues related to one's body, family relations, life style, or child rearing. In 1977, in *Whalen v. Roe*, the Court made its most comprehensive effort thus far to define the right to privacy, embracing both (i) an "individual interest in avoiding disclosure of personal matters" and (ii) an "interest in independence in making certain kinds of important decisions." (The case was deemed to involve both aspects of privacy, yet the Court upheld New York statutes for maintaining computerized records of prescriptions for certain dangerous but lawful drugs, even though the records included the patients' names.)

Since its inception the constitutional right to privacy has been severely criticized. It has been called "pernicious," "a malformation of constitutional law which thrives because of the conceptual vacuum surrounding the legal notions of privacy," and "a composite term whose sense is illusory." There is general worry that the right

flagrantly expresses subjective judicial ideology and is a form of legislative policy-making not properly a function of the courts, because there is no explicit passage in the Constitution or Bill of Rights justifying the right as described by the Court. Worse still, while other legal rights (such as the right to travel from state to state) are not mentioned in the Constitution, they are plausibly inferable in some way. But the constitutional right to privacy, it is claimed, cannot be inferred from the intent of the framers or from the governmental system depicted by the Constitution.

There is also a philosophically more important concern which I wish to address, namely that the line of constitutional cases since *Griswold* involve rights which have "no basis in any meaningful conception of privacy." Parent objects specifically to an account of privacy relevant to the constitutional cases which he describes as "control over significant personal matters" on the grounds that it is based on a conceptual error: confusing privacy and liberty. He argues,

> The defining idea of liberty is the absence of external restraints or coercion. A person who is behind bars or locked in a room or physically pinned to the ground is unfree to do many things. Similarly, a person who is prohibited by law from making certain choices should be described as having been denied the liberty or freedom to make them. The loss of liberty in these cases takes the form of a deprivation of autonomy. Hence we can meaningfully say that the right to liberty embraces in part the right of persons to make fundamentally important choices about their lives and therewith to exercise significant control over different aspects of their behavior. It is clearly distinguishable from the right to privacy, which condemns the unwarranted acquisition of undocumented personal knowledge (PPA 274–5). . . . All of these [constitutional privacy] cases conflate the right to privacy with the right to liberty. (PPA 284, LP 316).

We can readily concur with Parent that an adequate account of privacy should not confuse it with other related concepts such as liberty or autonomy. And of course his concept of liberty is distinguishable from privacy as he has described it. But it is not at all that Parent has shown that the constitutional privacy cases involve no "genuine" privacy interests. His argument is not new, yet it has often been accepted with little comment.

There is a practical reason why the Court avoided using liberty as the defense of the *Griswold* line of cases, although it does not provide a rationale for why privacy was used. According to the Fourteenth Amendment no state shall deprive any person of life, liberty or property, without due process of law. It was the "liberty" of this due process clause that was most commonly cited in a sequence of cases in the early 1900's striking down nearly 200 economic regulations, such as those fixing minimum wages for women. But the Court was not in those cases merely addressing fair procedures, and critics (led by Justice Oliver Wendell Holmes) felt that the due process clause was there being used in a substantive way to scrutinize economic regulation carefully and to hold laws unconstitutional if the Court believed they were unwise. This substantive due process doctrine, allowing courts to intrude on legislative value judgments, was widely discredited and discarded by the late 1930's.

Given early association of a legal right to privacy as a right to be let alone and the well-known explanation of a concept of negative liberty in terms of freedom from interference, it is hardly surprising that privacy and liberty should often be equated. But our intuitive notion of privacy can be shown to be distinct from liberty. For example, one's privacy may constantly be invaded by surreptitious surveillance without affecting one's liberty, and one's liberty may be invaded by assault, by conferring undesired benefits, or by limiting one's choices (such as to burn one's draft card) without violating privacy interests. There are all sorts of liberties we do not have. I cannot leave the country without a passport nor is George Carlin free to parody dirty words on the airwaves during daytime hours. In neither case are we inclined to believe a privacy interest is at stake. While the word "privacy" could be used to mean freedom to live one's life without governmental interference, the Supreme Court cannot so use it since such a right is at stake in *every* case. Our lives are continuously limited, often seriously, by governmental regulation. Privacy may not always be well-protected either, but it is not understood by the Court or in our ordinary language to be as comprehensive an interest as freedom from governmental regulation.

Perhaps concern about the relation between privacy and liberty in the *Griswold* line of cases can be understood as the view that the constitutional right of privacy protects certain liberties, namely freedom to perform acts that do not affect the interests of others, what J. S. Mill in *On Liberty* called "self-regarding" actions. With his juxtaposition of terms, Mill himself gave the impression that both "liberty" and "privacy" characterize the realm of action he was most concerned to protect. He first described

> . . . a sphere of action in which society, as distinguished from the individual, has, if any, only an indirect interest: comprehending all that portion of a person's life and conduct which affects only himself, or, if it also affects others, only with their free, voluntary, and undeceived consent and participation. When I say only himself, I mean directly and in the first instance; for whatever affects himself may affect others through himself; . . . This, then, is the appropriate region of human *liberty*. (my emphasis)

Yet only two paragraphs later, while defending the necessity of maintaining such liberty, he cautioned that while modern states have prevented great "interference by law in the details of *private* life," traditional tendencies have been just the opposite. "The ancient Commonwealths thought themselves entitled to practise, and the ancient philosophers countenanced, the regulation of every part of *private* conduct by public authority." (my emphasis)

However, in *Paris Adult Theatre* the Court clearly and effectively rejects the idea that constitutional privacy is just freedom with respect to self-regarding acts. It says, first, that the Constitution does not incorporate the proposition that conduct involving consenting adults is always beyond regulation, whereas the Constitution does provide a right of privacy. Hence the latter is not just a Mill-like right to freedom from legislative or other governmental interference in behavior that does not harm nonconsenting others. Second, the Court lays out the sort of things it takes the constitutional privacy right to protect. Some of the activities protected such as child-rearing, are not protected by a Mill-like right. It also appears from the Court's reasoning that some things protected by the Mill-like right, eating what one pleases, for example, or watching obscene movies in a public cinema in *Paris*, are not protected by the privacy right. Thus the constitutional right to privacy as it has developed is not even coextensional with a Mill-type right to freedom from governmental interference with behavior that does not prejudicially affect the welfare of others.

The constitutional privacy cases generally involve an interest in independence in making certain fundamental or personal decisions, and in virtue of that they do concern, as Parent recognizes, autonomy to determine for oneself what to do. But because privacy does *not* just consist in possession of undocumented personal knowledge, and because an intuitive notion of privacy invoked in the constitutional privacy cases does *not* conflate privacy and liberty, we need not deny that there is a sense of privacy relevant to those cases. To the contrary, I wish to show that it is more intuitive to agree that privacy is related to liberty in the following way. Many privacy issues, such as protection from electronic surveillance, have no connection with autonomous decision-making. Also, many self-determined choices, to drive a loudspeaker through a quiet neighborhood, for example, can be made by an individual but are not in any further sense private decisions. A subset of autonomy cases, however, certain personal decisions regarding one's basic lifestyle, can plausibly be said to involve privacy interests as well. They should be viewed as liberty cases in virtue of their concern over decision-making *power*, whereas privacy is at stake because of the *nature* of the decision. More needs to be said about which decisions and activities are private ones, but it is no criticism or conflation of concepts to say that an act can be both a theft and a trespass. Similarly, acknowledging that in some cases there is both an invasion of privacy and a violation of liberty need not confuse those concepts.

Parent has not shown that a notion of privacy encompassing the constitutional cases must conflate privacy and liberty. If one already accepts his definition of privacy, the conclusion that privacy is irrelevant to the constitutional cases follows trivially. That conclusion, though, is unhelpful at best and question-begging at worst. It would be more productive to determine whether there is a broader sense of privacy which is relevant to the full range of cases where privacy is claimed to be at stake.

5. Toward a Broad Conception of Privacy

If we agree to reject the claim that the constitutional privacy cases cannot be said to be "genuine" privacy cases without conflating privacy and liberty, we have (at least) these two options: (i) We might draw on similarities between tort and constitutional privacy claims in order to develop a notion of privacy fundamental to informational and Fourth Amendment privacy concerns as well as the constitutional cases. Certain examples indicate this will be promising. Consider consenting homosexuality in one's home, for instance. We view it as a private matter whether the state is seeking to regulate the behavior, or if others are attempting to gain or exploit information about it. (ii) We could concede that whatever "privacy" means in the tort and Fourth Amendment cases, it means something different in the constitutional cases. Nevertheless, we might take that "something else" seriously as a distinct but legitimate use of the term which is not "spurious" but is reflected in our ordinary language.

Alternative (ii) may seem more fruitful since the wide diversity of privacy claims enumerated, as well as the use of the term in such varied aspects of social life including information, property, parts, decisions, activity, and enterprise, indicate why it is so difficult to isolate common elements in the full range of cases where privacy is central. Note, however, that even in tort law there is no fixed way of using "privacy" which we then proceed to analyze; yet the term has not in those cases been taken to be meaningless or empty. Hence I shall conclude this paper by exploring (i).

In an effort to distinguish privacy as a descriptive term from a normative use of the word encompassing interests *worthy* of protection (some subset of which, depending on the circumstances, actually are protected), it has sometimes been suggested that privacy concerns not merely the absence of others having information, but individual *control* over knowledge others have about one. While the interest was first discussed as control over *information* others have about oneself, it has been extended to include control over *actions* as well. On this view, privacy is a power to deny or grant access. But surely not every loss or gain of control over information about us, or what we do or have done to us, is a loss or gain of privacy. Consider a writer whose research unexpectedly reveals his shabby or inaccurate scholarship. Information about him has become known to others without his consent. He loses control of it, yet we would not say he has suffered a loss of privacy. Similarly, if a policeman pushes me out of the way of an ambulance, I have lost control of what has been done to me, but we would not say that my privacy has been invaded. Not just any touching is a privacy intrusion. Characterization of a privacy interest as an ability to control is thus much too broad.

Nevertheless, it may be that control of some aspect of ourselves is a necessary condition for a loss of privacy. Perhaps for every privacy invasion the individual loses control over what is seen, heard, or read about him, over what is done with information, recordings, or photographs of her, over what is done to him (e.g., he is wired, or operated on without consent), or over what she does (e.g., uses contraceptives, reads pornography).

If this is so, then we might extend a traditional notion of property to include whatever one has control over. On this account every privacy invasion would also be a property invasion, but not the reverse, so that privacy interests would form a subset of property interests. We would be claiming not only that our bodies and minds and written work, but our reputations, information about us, and so on, are our property, stretching considerably our common notion of property. This is apparently Van den Haag's view. "Privacy is best treated as a property right," he says, and he focuses on exclusivity as the core of privacy when he defines privacy as exclusive access of a person to a realm of his own.

I am concerned, however, that our intuitive sense of property rights breaks down in privacy contexts. Do we own behavior we do not want observed, or all information we want or have a right to suppress? Do we own our bodies in as straightforward and uncomplicated a sense as we own letters or land, or as the wealthy once owned slaves? It is more worrisome that even if this thesis could be defended adequately, focus on control or property ownership may not offer a *full explanation* of privacy issues. It may fail to capture what is distinctive and most fundamental in the diverse privacy cases.

Noting that mention of "personal" rights is prominent in the Court's explanation of constitutional privacy, one might think that whether a privacy invasion involves information about oneself, bodily security, or choices about one's lifestyle, it always intrudes on a special zone close to oneself, something very personal. According to the *Oxford English Dictionary*, what is private affects "a person, or a small intimate body or group of persons apart from the general community; [it is] individual, personal." One feature of Parent's definition which we have not yet rejected is his focus on "personal" information. While information is personal in this sense, we might attempt to extend his characterization of what is personal to cover activities as well as information, in order to generate a broader notion of privacy. Recall, however, that for Parent what is personal is relativized to individuals, and includes not only what most would choose to share, but also what that individual is "acutely sensitive" about. There are of course well-known difficulties with legal protection of peculiar sensitivities, and we might do better to adopt a "reasonable person" standard of what is personal.

There are still problems with this latter suggestion. If you tap my phone, but merely hear me placing an order for pizza, it seems reasonable to agree you violated my privacy although you heard no personal information and had no physical access to me. A decision to merge one's business with another may be a private but not a personal one. Such cases indicate that focus on what is personal to an individual will either be vacuous or will not adequately circumscribe what we understand as the scope of privacy.

We do, however, have a crude intuition that what is private is that which is nobody else's business. In view of this, we might take the realm of the private to be whatever is not the legitimate concern of others, where those others may be private individuals in tort cases, the government for constitutional claims. Despite the vagueness of this characterization, we can agree that information as well as activities and decisions can be private in this sense, allowing a basic conceptual relationship between tort and constitutional privacy interests. On this account privacy claims can be made by individuals, couples or small groups. Because some trivial claims can on this interpretation be private, there will be a broad spectrum of more and less important privacy interests. Moreover, what is legitimately the concern of others can vary according to circumstances and culture. Thus we might agree that in this country a couple's decision about whether or not to use contraceptives is beyond the legitimate concern of others. Whereas it is at least arguable that governmental intrusion in such a decision could be legitimate in overpopulated countries such as China or India.

The obvious worry is that this account is overbroad. Consider, for example, Locke's principle that religious ends are not a legitimate state concern. If we wish to differentiate privacy and religious claims, among others, we must seek an explanation of which subclass of issues beyond the legitimate concern of others comprise the private ones. This is a very difficult task and not one that can be completed in this article. Yet I believe we can make progress if we attend to the various reasons people have for wanting privacy. Moreover, the similarity of reasons for protecting tort and constitutional privacy claims gives further evidence that those claims are related in an important way, and strengthens my position that an important interest in privacy is at stake in the constitutional privacy cases.

People have many different reasons for wanting to control information about themselves, ranging from freedom from defamation to commercial gain. When freedom from scrutiny, embarrassment, judgment, even ridicule, are at stake, as well as protection from pressure to conform, prejudice, emotional distress, and loss in self-esteem, opportunities, or finances arising from them, we are more inclined to view the claim to control information as a privacy claim. A tort privacy action is one mechanism society has created to accomplish such protection. By itself it is not wholly adequate, however, because the interests that provide the reasons for the screen on information include the interest in being free to decide free of the threat of the same problems which accompany an information leak. In other words, it is plausible to maintain that worries about what information others have are often *due* to worries about social control. What

you can do to me or what I can do free of the threat of scrutiny, judgment, etc. may often depend on what information, personal or not, you, the state, or others have about me. Since my behavior is also affected by the extent to which I can make my own choices, both the threat of an information leak and the threat of decreased control over decision-making can have a chilling effect on my behavior. Thus protecting a sanctuary for ourselves, a refuge within which we can shape and carry on our lives and relationships with others — intimacies as well as other activities — without the threat of scrutiny, embarrassment, judgment, and the deleterious consequences they might bring, is a major underlying reason for protecting *both* information control and control over decision-making. Furthermore, since people want control over many things, and freedom is far broader than privacy, this similarity of reasons for protecting tort and constitutional privacy is more fundamental than the idea that both involve freedom or control.

While this examination of reasons for protecting privacy does not give a unified definition of privacy, it does indicate that privacy claims can be identified by looking at the justifications for such claims. An interest in privacy is at stake when intrusion by others is not legitimate *because* it jeopardizes or prohibits protection of a realm free from scrutiny, judgment, and the pressure, distress, or losses they can cause. While I have not given an exhaustive list of reasons for protecting privacy, I believe I have said enough to show there is a certain range of similar reasons for guarding tort and constitutional privacy claims which can be used to demarcate which intrusions are privacy invasions.

Of course if this characterization of the private is to be useful we need further explanation of the notion of legitimacy. Many cases will be clear. Thus, for example, neither my bathroom behavior nor information about it can be justified as the legitimate concern of others, given that I have no communicable disease or dangerous tendencies. In contrast, there is wide disagreement over whether a decision to have an abortion is a proper concern of anyone except the mother. Even if we believe details about one's sex life do not comprise the kind of information that is the legitimate concern of the state, we might have great difficulty determining whether or not, for an individual with AIDS, the danger of the disease and our lack of knowledge about its transmission justify viewing detailed information about that individual's sex life as legitimately of public concern.

Unfortunately there is a more serious difficulty with this proposal. As presented, it does not allow us to account for the existence of *justifiable* invasions of privacy. If, for example, we determine that when an individual has AIDS, details about his sex life are legitimately the concern of state health officials, then according to the explanation given we must agree that there is no privacy invasion when they inquire about those intimacies. But this seems incorrect. What we want to say in such a case is that seeking such information is an invasion of the Aids victim's privacy, but that the intrusion is justified because of the seriousness of the health threat.

Perhaps the best way to handle this difficulty is to characterize the realm of the private as whatever is not generally, that is, according to a reasonable person under normal circumstances, or according to certain social conventions, a legitimate concern of others because of the threat of scrutiny or judgment and the potential problems following from them. Privacy would thus be a property of *types* of information and activities, and we could say that any interference with them would be a privacy invasion, although particular interferences could be justified. Much more needs to be said, however, about determining relevant circumstances, conventions, and descriptions of types of acts, to fill out this more general description.

This sort of account does have the advantage of allowing us to clarify an important relationship between privacy and liberty. As we have seen, loss of privacy can diminish freedom. Nevertheless, defending privacy cannot always protect liberty. It cannot guard against public assault, for example. If however, privacy protects against intrusions of others for a certain set of reasons, and if one has liberty when one is free of external restraints and interferences, then pro-

tection of privacy can preserve some liberty. We can in this way make sense of Parent's claim "that privacy is a moral value for persons who also prize freedom and individuality" (PPA 278).

An additional consequence is worth noting. Parent objects that currently informational privacy is less well protected than the constitutional right to privacy. If a reasonable person would not be troubled by publicity about a family wedding of the sort Warren and Brandeis sought to protect, then in such cases privacy may well be a petty tort. And if in the balance it is more important to exclude the state from decisions about whether or not to have a vasectomy, or to acquire contraceptive information and devices, than to have security against embarrassment arising from the use of one's name, correspondence, or photograph, then we may be able to support this recent trend over complaints against it.

6. Conclusion

I have not provided a constitutional defense for citing privacy as one right at stake in the *Griswold* line of cases. Nor have I attempted to enter the debate about how strictly to interpret the Constitution. Yet I have urged that it is reasonable for us to agree that there is an interest in privacy at issue in the constitutional cases because (1) privacy does *not* just consist in possession and acquisition of undocumented personal knowledge, (2) taking privacy to be relevant in the constitutional cases need *not* conflate the concepts privacy and liberty, and (3) similar interests provide reasons for protecting *both* tort privacy over information and constitutional privacy over decision-making. The implications of this view are significant. Current constitutional standards, controversial though they may be, require "strict scrutiny" for cases concerning "fundamental values," and privacy has been judged one such value. Thus these privacy claims have *a greater* chance of being protected when they conflict with other rights or general interests than they would have if only liberty, or freedom from governmental interference, were involved.

Notes and Questions

Cases on the Constitutional Right of Privacy

1. A number of interesting questions may be asked about these cases as a group. What are the object and scope of the subject matter? That is, what are these cases about, what thread connects them, and how far can they legitimately extend? Second, what kinds of rights are being discussed? Natural rights? Civil rights? Constitutional rights? The Court uses flamboyant language about certain basic or fundamental rights. What is its referent? What is the constitutional justification for any or all of these cases? Can it be distinguished from substantive due process as rejected in *West Coast Hotel* v. *Parrish*? If it cannot be conceptually distinguished, is there nevertheless reason to support it for privacy cases but not for economic cases?

2. The line of cases begins with *Meyer* v. *Nebraska* in 1923. Upholding the right to teach or study German (or other foreign languages), the Court sets out a list of protected liberties. What are they? What, if anything, do they have in common?

3. Two years later, in *Pierce*, the Court relies on *Meyer* and its general doctrine of substantive due process to strike down a statute allowing only public school education for children up to the age of eighteen. What argument does the Court offer to support its opinion? What assumptions or claims does it make?

4. Almost twenty years later, in *Skinner* v. *Oklahoma*, the Court discusses procreation as one of the basic civil rights of man. Notice that the *ratio decidendi* is different from that used in *Meyer* and *Pierce*, which is hardly surprising since substantive due process was discredited in 1937. The ground for this case is equal protection, so the discussion you read here is dicta except insofar as it applies to the equal protection clause. Nevertheless, the language is powerful. What rationale is advanced, and what follows from it? Suppose that Oklahoma revised its penal statute, making it perfectly consistent, so as to undermine any equal protection objection. Would it then be constitutional? That is, is it constitutional to sterilize robbers as long as embezzlers are sterilized as well?

5. The pivotal case in establishing the right to privacy is *Griswold* v. *Connecticut*. Delivering the opinion for a sharply divided Court (with two concurring opinions and two dissents), Justice William O. Douglas argues that the right of privacy is implicit in the protections of the Bill of Rights. Consider his support for his position and explain what, if anything, is wrong with his analysis. How can he answer the objections in Justice Hugo Black's dissent? Is Justice Arthur Goldberg's concurring opinion any stronger than Douglas's opinion?

6. The argument, of course, is not over whether Connecticut's prohibition of contraceptive use was a good law (apparently no one on the Court thought that it was) but over whether the Court had the authority to strike the law down. Is the Court acting as a superlegislature in limiting the power of states to regulate the private behavior of individuals? If not, what is the difference between the privacy cases and the economic due process cases following *Lochner*? Is there a better constitutional ground for one than the other?

7. There are two basic questions to ask about the constitutional right to privacy. First, how — if at all — is it justified? The answer involves assessing *Griswold* and the cases before it. Second, assuming that there is such a right (since *Griswold* has not been reversed), what does it cover? What is the scope of this right? The answer involves examining the cases following *Griswold*. Douglas discusses this problem in terms of "zones of privacy" created by the penumbras of the First, Third, Fourth, and Fifth amendments. Consider what these zones of privacy are and how they specify the right to privacy. Is the right subject to unlimited expansion? Could the right be

expanded in a way that would be worse than not having the right protected at all? In this respect is it the same or different than economic due process?

8. Notice that some cases use the language of *Griswold* but actually rely on other grounds. *Loving* v. *Virginia*, for example, speaks of marriage as a vital personal right and as one of the basic civil rights of man, but in fact relies on the equal protection clause as interpreted in *Skinner*. *Stanley* v. *Georgia* is another example when it speaks of the fundamental right to be free of government intrusion into the privacy of one's home, but relies on the Fourth Amendment. These cases are also about privacy, are they not? Are the interests in these cases more alike or different?

9. Many of the cases following *Griswold* are even more controversial than the original decision. *Eisenstadt* v. *Baird* extends the right against government intrusion into personal decisions such as procreation to unmarried persons. And *Roe* v. *Wade* extends this right to cover decisions to terminate pregnancies within certain limits. But in *Bowers* v. *Hardwick* the Court refuses to extend the right to cover private consensual sex by refusing to declare sodomy statutes unconstitutional. Are all of these cases natural extensions of the rationale set out in *Griswold*? See if you can find any principled rationale that can make these cases consistent. Notice (as illustrated in *Bowers*) that the disposition (or result) of the case depends crucially on how the issue is framed.

Cases on the Constitutional Right of Privacy

Meyer v. Nebraska
262 U.S. 390 (1923)

Meyer was convicted of violating a Nebraska law which prohibited teaching any language other than English in the first eight grades of school. Meyer taught German. The Court reversed his conviction, saying (in part):

"While this court has not attempted to define with exactness the liberty thus guaranteed, the term has received much consideration, and some of the included things have been definitely stated. Without doubt, it denotes not merely freedom from bodily restraint, but also the right of the individual to contract to engage in any of the common occupations of life to acquire useful knowledge to marry, establish a home and bring up children, to worship God according to the dictates of his own conscience, and, generally, to enjoy those privileges long recognized at common law as essential to the orderly pursuit of happiness by free men. . . . The established doctrine is that this liberty may not be interfered with under the guise of protecting the public interest, by legislative action which is arbitrary or without reasonable relation to some purpose within the competency of the state to effect. Determination by the legislature of what constitutes proper exercise of police power is not final or conclusive, but is subject to supervision by the courts. . . ."

Pierce v. Society of Sisters
268 U.S. 510 (1925)

An Oregon statute requiring parents to send children between 8 and 16 to public school was enjoined in a suit brought by a parochial school and a private military academy. The Supreme Court affirmed the lower court injunction, saying:

"Under the doctrine of Meyer v. Nebraska, 262 U.S. 390 (1923), we think it entirely plain that the Act of 1922 unreasonably interferes with the liberty of parents and guardians to direct the upbringing and education of children under their control. As often heretofore pointed out, rights guaranteed by the Constitution may not be abridged by legislation which has no reasonable relation to some purpose within the competency of the state. The fundamental theory of liberty upon which all governments in this Union repose excludes any general power of the state to standardize its children by forcing them to accept instruction from public teachers only. The child is not the mere creature of the state; those who nurture him and direct his destiny have the right, coupled with the high duty, to recognize and prepare him for additional obligations."

Skinner v. *Oklahoma*
316 U.S. 535 (1942)

Sterilization of habitual criminals who had been convicted two or more times of crimes of moral turpitude was required by an Oklahoma law, which also held that grand larceny was a crime of moral turpitude, but embezzlement was not. The Court reversed an order to sterilize a man convicted of grand larceny and robbery on the ground that it violated the equal protection of the law by treating those convicted of grand larceny as significantly different from those convicted of embezzlement. The Court remarked:

"But the instant legislation runs afoul of the equal protection clause, though we give Oklahoma that large deference which the rule of the foregoing cases requires. We are dealing here with legislation which involves one of the basic civil rights of man. Marriage and procreation are fundamental to the very existence and survival of the race. The power to sterilize, if exercised, may have subtle, far-reaching and devastating effects. In evil or reckless hands it can cause races or types which are inimical to the dominant group to wither and disappear. There is no redemption for the individual whom the law touches. Any experiment which the State conducts is to his irreparable injury. He is forever deprived of a basic liberty. We mention these matters not to reexamine the scope of the police power of the States. We advert to them merely in emphasis of our view that strict scrutiny of the classification which a State makes in a sterilization law is essential, lest unwittingly or otherwise invidious discriminations are made against groups or types of individuals in violation of the constitutional guaranty of just and equal laws. . . ."

Griswold v. *Connecticut*
381 U.S. 479 (1965)

Mr. Justice Douglas delivered the opinion of the Court.

Appellant Griswold is Executive Director of the Planned Parenthood League of Connecticut. Appellant Buxton is a licensed physician and a professor at the Yale Medical School who served as Medical Director for the League at its Center in New Haven—a center open and operating from November 1 to November 10, 1961, when appellants were arrested.

They gave information, instruction, and medical advice to *married persons* as to the means of preventing conception. They examined the wife and prescribed the best contraceptive device or material for her use. Fees were usually charged, although some couples were serviced free.

The statutes whose constitutionality is involved in this appeal are §§ 53–32 and 54–196 of the General Statutes of Connecticut (1938). The former provides:

"Any person who uses any drug, medicinal article or instrument for the purpose of preventing conception shall be fined not less than fifty dollars or imprisoned not less than sixty days nor more than one year or be both fined and imprisoned."

Section 54–196 provides:

"Any person who assists, abets, counsels, causes, hires or commands another to commit any offense may be prosecuted and punished as if he were the principal offender."

The appellants were found guilty as accessories and fined $100 each, against the claim that the accessory statute as so applied violated the Fourteenth Amendment. The Appellate Division of the Circuit Court affirmed. The Court of Errors affirmed that judgment. 151 Conn. 544, 200 A.2d 479. We noted probable jurisdiction. 379 U.S. 926.

* * *

Coming to the merits, we are met with a wide range of questions that implicate the Due Process Clause of the Fourteenth Amendment. Overtones of some arguments suggest that Lochner v. State of New York, 198 U.S. 45, should be our guide. But we decline that invitation as we did in West Coast Hotel Co. v. Parrish, 300 U.S. 379; Olsen v. State of Nebraska, 313 U.S. 236; Lincoln Federal Labor Union v. Northwestern Co., 335 U.S.

525; Williamson v. Lee Optical Co., 348 U.S. 483; Giboney v. Empire Storage Co., 336 U.S. 490. We do not sit as a super-legislature to determine the wisdom, need, and propriety of laws that touch economic problems, business affairs, or social conditions. This law, however, operates directly on an intimate relation of husband and wife and their physician's role in one aspect of that relation.

The association of people is not mentioned in the Constitution nor in the Bill of Rights. The right to educate a child in a school of the parents' choice — whether public or private or parochial — is also not mentioned. Nor is the right to study any particular subject or any foreign language. Yet the First Amendment has been construed to include certain of those rights.

By Pierce v. Society of Sisters, *supra*, the right to educate one's children as one chooses is made applicable to the States by the force of the First and Fourteenth Amendments. By Meyer v. State of Nebraska, *supra*, the same dignity is given the right to study the German language in a private school. In other words, the State may not, consistently with the spirit of the First Amendment, contract the spectrum of available knowledge. The right of freedom of speech and press includes not only the right to utter or to print, but the right to distribute, the right to receive, the right to read (Martin v. City of Struthers, 319 U.S. 141, 143) and freedom of inquiry, freedom of thought, and freedom to teach (see Wieman v. Updegraff, 344 U.S. 183, 195) — indeed the freedom of the entire university community. Sweezy v. State of New Hampshire, 354 U.S. 234, 249–250, 261–263; Barenblatt v. United States, 360 U.S. 109, 112; Baggett v. Bullitt, 377 U.S. 360, 369. Without those peripheral rights the specific rights would be less secure. And so we reaffirm the principle of the Pierce and the Meyer cases.

* * *

The foregoing cases suggest that specific guarantees in the Bill of Rights have penumbras, formed by emanations from those guarantees that help give them life and substance. See Poe v. Ullman, 367 U.S. 497, 516–522 (dissenting opinion). Various guarantees create zones of privacy. The right of association contained in the penumbra of the First Amendment is one, as we have seen. The Third Amendment in its prohibition against the quartering of soldiers "in any house" in time of peace without the consent of the owner is another facet of that privacy. The Fourth Amendment explicitly affirms the "right of the people to be secure in their persons, houses, papers, and effects, against unreasonable searches and seizures." The Fifth Amendment in its Self-Incrimination Clause enables the citizen to create a zone of privacy which government may not force him to surrender to his detriment. The Ninth Amendment provides: "The enumeration in the Constitution, of certain rights, shall not be construed to deny or disparage others retained by the people."

The Fourth and Fifth Amendments were described in Boyd v. United States, 116 U.S. 616, 630, as protection against all governmental invasions "of the sanctity of a man's home and the privacies of life." We recently referred in Mapp v. Ohio, 367 U.S. 643, 656, to the Fourth Amendment as creating a "right to privacy, no less important than any other right carefully and particularly reserved to the people." See Beaney, The Constitutional Right to Privacy, 1962 Sup.Ct.Rev. 212; Griswold, The Right to be Let Alone, 55 N.W.U.L.Rev. 216 (1960).

We have had many controversies over these penumbral rights of "privacy and repose." . . . These cases bear witness that the right of privacy which presses for recognition here is a legitimate one.

The present case, then, concerns a relationship lying within the zone of privacy created by several fundamental constitutional guarantees. And it concerns a law which, in forbidding the *use* of contraceptives rather than regulating their manufacture or sale, seeks to achieve its goals by means having a maximum destructive impact upon that relationship. Such a law cannot stand in light of the familiar principle, so often applied by this Court, that a "governmental purpose to control or prevent activities constitutionally subject to state regulation may not be achieved by means which sweep unnecessarily broadly and thereby invade the area of protected freedoms." NAACP v. Alabama, 377 U.S. 288, 307. Would we allow the police to search the sacred precincts of marital bedrooms for telltale signs of the use of contraceptives? The very idea is repulsive to the notions of privacy surrounding the marriage relationship.

We deal with a right of privacy older than the Bill of Rights — older than our political parties, older than our school system. Marriage is a coming together for better or for worse, hopefully enduring, and intimate to the degree of being sacred. It is an association that promotes a way of life, not causes; a harmony in living, not political faiths; a bilateral loyalty, not commercial or social projects. Yet it is an association for as noble a purpose as any involved in our prior decisions.

Reversed.

Mr. Justice Goldberg, whom The Chief Justice and Mr. Justice Brennan join, concurring.

I agree with the Court that Connecticut's birth control law unconstitutionally intrudes upon the right of marital privacy, and I join in its opinion and judgment. Although I have not accepted the view that "'due process' as used in the Fourteenth Amendment includes all of the first eight Amendments," *id.*, 367 U.S. at 516 (see my concurring opinion in Pointer v. Texas, 380 U.S. 400, 410, and the dissenting opinion of Mr. Justice Brennan in Cohen v. Hurley, 366 U.S. 117), I do agree that the concept of liberty protects those personal rights that are fundamental, and is not confined to the specific terms of the Bill of Rights. My conclusion that the concept of liberty is not so restricted and that it embraces the right of marital privacy though that right is not mentioned explicitly in the Constitution is supported both by numerous decisions of this Court, referred to in the Court's opinion, and by the language and history of the Ninth Amendment. In reaching the conclusion that the right of marital privacy is protected, as being within the protected penumbra of specific guarantees of the Bill of Rights, the Court refers to the Ninth Amendment, ante, at 1681. I add these words to emphasize the relevance of that Amendment to the Court's holding.

* * *

The Ninth Amendment reads, "The enumeration in the Constitution, of certain rights, shall not be construed to deny or disparage others retained by the people." . . .

While this Court has had little occasion to interpret the Ninth Amendment, "[i]t cannot be presumed that any clause in the constitution is intended to be without effect." Marbury v. Madison, 1 Cranch 137, 174. In interpreting the Constitution, "real effect should be given to all the words

it uses." Myers v. United States, 272 U.S. 52, 151. The Ninth Amendment to the Constitution may be regarded by some as a recent discovery but since 1791 it has been a basic part of the Constitution which we are sworn to uphold. To hold that a right so basic and fundamental and so deep-rooted in our society as the right of privacy in marriage may be infringed because that right is not guaranteed in so many words by the first eight amendments to the Constitution is to ignore the Ninth Amendment and to give it no effect whatsoever. Moreover, a judicial construction that this fundamental right is not protected by the Constitution because it is not mentioned in explicit terms by one of the first eight amendments or elsewhere in the Constitution would violate the Ninth Amendment, which specifically states that "[t]he enumeration in the Constitution, of certain rights shall not be *construed* to deny or disparage others retained by the people." (Emphasis added.)

* * *

The entire fabric of the Constitution and the purposes that clearly underlie its specific guarantees demonstrate that the rights to marital privacy and to marry and raise a family are of similar order and magnitude as the fundamental rights specifically protected.

Although the Constitution does not speak in so many words of the right of privacy in marriage, I cannot believe that it offers these fundamental rights no protection. The fact that no particular provision of the Constitution explicitly forbids the State from disrupting the traditional relation of the family — a relation as old and as fundamental as our entire civilization — surely does not show that the Government was meant to have the power to do so. Rather, as the Ninth Amendment expressly recognizes, there are fundamental personal rights such as this one, which are protected from abridgment by the Government though not specifically mentioned in the Constitution.

* * *

The logic of the dissents would sanction federal or state legislation that seems to me even more plainly unconstitutional than the statute before us. . . . [I]f upon a showing of a slender basis of rationality, a law outlawing voluntary birth control by married persons is valid, then, by the same reasoning, a law requiring compulsory birth control also would seem to be valid. In my view, however, both types of law would unjustifiably intrude upon rights of marital privacy which are constitutionally protected.

* * *

In sum, I believe that the right of privacy in the marital relation is fundamental and basic—a personal right "retained by the people" within the meaning of the Ninth Amendment. Connecticut cannot constitutionally abridge this fundamental right, which is protected by the Fourteenth Amendment from infringement by the States. I agree with the Court that petitioners' convictions must therefore be reversed.

* * *

Mr. Justice Black, with whom Mr. Justice Steward joins, dissenting.

I agree with my Brother STEWART's dissenting opinion. And like him I do not to any extent whatever base my view that this Connecticut law is constitutional on a belief that the law is wise or that its policy is a good one. In order that there may be no room at all to doubt why I vote as I do, I feel constrained to add that the law is every bit as offensive to me as it is to my Brethren of the majority and my Brothers HARLAN, WHITE and GOLDBERG who, reciting reasons why it is offensive to them, hold it unconstitutional. There is no single one of the graphic and eloquent strictures and criticisms fired at the policy of this Connecticut law either by the Court's opinion or by those of my concurring Brethren to which I cannot subscribe—except their conclusion that the evil qualities they see in the law make it unconstitutional.

* * *

The Court talks about a constitutional "right of privacy" as though there is some constitutional provision or provisions forbidding any law ever to be passed which might abridge the "privacy" of individuals. But there is not. . . .

* * *

I realize that many good and able men have eloquently spoken and written, sometimes in rhapsodical strains, about the duty of this Court to keep the Constitution in tune with the times. The idea is that the Constitution must be changed from time to time and that this Court is charged with a duty to make those changes. For myself, I must with all deference reject that philosophy. The Constitution makers knew the need for change and provided for it. Amendments suggested by the people's elected representatives can be submitted to the people or their selected agents for ratification. That method of change was good for our Fathers, and being somewhat old-fashioned I must add it is good enough for me. And so, I cannot rely on the Due Process Clause or the Ninth Amendment or any mysterious and uncertain natural law concept as a reason for striking down this state law. The Due Process Clause with an "arbitrary and capricious" or "shocking to the conscience" formula was liberally used by this Court to strike down economic legislation in the early decades of this century, threatening, many people thought, the tranquility and stability of the Nation. See, e. g., Lochner v. State of New York, 198 U.S. 45. That formula, based on subjective considerations of "natural justice," is no less dangerous when used to enforce this Court's views about personal rights than those about economic rights. I had thought that we had laid that formula, as a means for striking down state legislation, to rest once and for all in cases like West Coast Hotel Co. v. Parrish, 300 U.S. 379; Olsen v. State of Nebraska ex rel. Western Reference & Bond Assn., 313 U.S. 236, and many other opinions. . . .

* * *

The late Judge Learned Hand, after emphasizing his view that judges should not use the due process formula suggested in the concurring opinions today or any other formula like it to invalidate legislation offensive to their "personal preferences," made the statements, with which I fully agree, that:

"For myself it would be most irksome to be ruled by a bevy of Platonic Guardians, even if I knew how to choose them, which I assuredly do not." So far as I am concerned, Connecticut's law as applied here is not forbidden by any provision of the Federal Constitution as that Constitution was written, and I would therefore affirm.

Loving v. Virginia
388 U.S. 1 (1967)

A black woman and a white man were convicted of violating a Virginia law against interracial marriage. The Court reversed the conviction. Although the primary foundation of the opinion was the equal protection clause, the Court also found the statute in violation of the due process clause, as follows:

"Marriage is one of the 'basic civil rights of

man' fundamental to our very existence and survival. Skinner v. State of Oklahoma, 316 U.S. 535, 541 (1942). See also Maynard v. Hill, 125 U.S. 190, (1882). To deny this fundamental freedom on so unsupportable a basis as the racial classifications embodied in these statutes, classifications so directly subversive of the principle of equality at the heart of the Fourteenth Amendment, is surely to deprive all the State's citizens of liberty without due process of law. The Fourteenth Amendment requires that the freedom of choice to marry not be restricted by invidious racial discriminations. Under our Constitution, the freedom to marry or not marry, a person of another race resides with the individual and cannot be infringed by the State."

Stanley v. Georgia
394 U.S. 557 (1969)

Stanley was convicted of knowing possession of obscene material on the basis of film taken from his bedroom in the course of a search warranted for bookmaking activity. The Court reversed the conviction as a violation of the First Amendment, remarking that the First Amendment takes on an added dimension in the context of printed or filmed materials viewed in the privacy of one's home, because ". . . the right to be free, except in very limited circumstances, from unwanted governmental intrusions into one's privacy" is fundamental. The Court also added:

". . . we think that mere categorization of these films as 'obscene' is insufficient justification for such a drastic invasion of personal liberties guaranteed by the First and Fourteenth Amendments. Whatever may be the justifications for other statutes regulating obscenity we do not think they reach into the privacy of one's home. If the First Amendment means anything, it means that a State has no business telling a man, sitting alone in his own house, what books he may read or what films he may watch."

Eisenstadt v. Baird
405 U.S. 438 (1972)

The Court in *Eisenstadt* established the right to give contraceptives to unmarried persons. Although the case was decided on the basis of equal protection, the Court also observed:

"If the right of privacy means anything, it is the right of the *individual,* married or single, to be free from unwarranted governmental intrusion into matters so fundamentally affecting a person as the decision whether to bear or beget a child."

Roe v. Wade
410 U.S. 113 (1973)

Mr. Justice Blackmun delivered the opinion of the Court.

This Texas federal appeal and its Georgia companion, Doe v. Bolton, *post,* 410 U.S. 179, present constitutional challenges to state criminal abortion legislation. The Texas statutes under attack here are typical of those that have been in effect in many States for approximately a century. The Georgia statutes, in contrast, have a modern cast and are a legislative product that, to an extent at least, obviously reflects the influences of recent attitudinal change, of advancing medical knowledge and techniques, and of new thinking about an old issue. . . .

VII

Three reasons have been advanced to explain historically the enactment of criminal abortion laws in the 19th century and to justify their continued existence.

It has been argued occasionally that these laws were the product of a Victorian social concern to discourage illicit sexual conduct. Texas, however, does not advance this justification in the present case, and it appears that no court or commentator has taken the argument seriously. . . .

A second reason is concerned with abortion as a medical procedure. When most criminal abortion laws were first enacted, the procedure was a hazardous one for the woman. . . .

Modern medical techniques have altered this situation. Appellants and various *amici* refer to medical data indicating that abortion in early pregnancy, that is, prior to the end of first trimester, although not without its risk, is now relatively safe. Mortality rates for women undergoing early abortions, where the procedure is legal, appear to be as low as or lower than the rates for normal childbirth. . . .

The third reason is the State's interest — some phrase it in terms of duty — in protecting prenatal life. Some of the argument for this justification rests on the theory that a new human life is present from the moment of conception. The State's interest and general obligation to protect life then extends, it is argued, to prenatal life. Only when the life of the pregnant mother herself is at stake, balanced against the life she carries within her, should the interest of the embryo or fetus not prevail. Logically, of course, a legitimate state interest in this area need not stand or fall on acceptance of the belief that life begins at conception or at some other point prior to live birth. In assessing the State's interest, recognition may be given to the less rigid claim that as long as at least *potential* life is involved, the State may assert interests beyond the protection of the pregnant woman alone. . . .

VIII

The Constitution does not explicitly mention any right of privacy. In a line of decisions, however, going back perhaps as far as Union Pacific R. Co. v. Botsford, 141 U.S. 250, 251 (1891), the Court has recognized that a right of personal privacy, or a guarantee of certain areas or zones of privacy, does exist under the Constitution. In varying contexts the Court or individual Justices have indeed found at least the roots of that right in the First Amendment; in the Fourth and Fifth Amendments; in the penumbras of the Bill of Rights; in the Ninth Amendment; or in the concept of liberty guaranteed by the first section of the Fourteenth Amendment. These decisions make it clear that only personal rights that can be deemed "fundamental" or "implicit in the concept of ordered liberty" are included in this guarantee of personal privacy. They also make it clear that the right has some extension to activities relating to marriage, procreation, contraception, family relationships, and child rearing and education.

* * *

A. The appellee and certain *amici* argue that the fetus is a "person" within the language and meaning of the Fourteenth Amendment. In support of this they outline at length and in detail the well-known facts of fetal development. If this suggestion of personhood is established, the appellant's case, of course, collapses, for the fetus' right to life is then guaranteed specifically by the Amend-ment. The appellant conceded as much on reargument. On the other hand, the appellee conceded on reargument that no case could be cited that holds that a fetus is a person within the meaning of the Fourteenth Amendment.

The Constitution does not define "person" in so many words. Section 1 of the Fourteenth Amendment contains three references to "person." The first, in defining "citizens," speaks of "persons born or naturalized in the United States." The word also appears both in the Due Process Clause and in the Equal Protection Clause. "Person" is used in other places in the Constitution: in the listing of qualifications for representatives and senators, Art. I, § 2, cl. 2, and § 3, cl. 3; in the Apportionment Clause, Art. I, § 2, cl. 3; in the Migration and Importation provision, Art. I, § 9, cl. 1; in the Emolument Clause, Art. I, § 9, cl. 8; in the Electors provisions, Art. II, § 1, cl. 2, and the superseded cl. 3; in the provision outlining qualifications for the office of President, Art. II, § 1, cl. 5; in the Extradition provisions, Art. IV, § 2, cl. 2, and the superseded Fugitive Slave cl. 3; and in the Fifth, Twelfth, and Twenty-second Amendments as well as in §§ 2 and 3 of the Fourteenth Amendment. But in nearly all these instances, the use of the word is such that it has application only postnatally. None indicates, with any assurance, that it has any possible prenatal application.[1]

All this, together with our observation, *supra,* that throughout the major portion of the 19th century prevailing legal abortion practices were far freer than they are today, persuades us that the word "person," as used in the Fourteenth Amendment, does not include the unborn. . . .

This conclusion, however, does not of itself fully answer the contentions raised by Texas, and we pass on to other considerations.

B. The pregnant woman cannot be isolated in her privacy. She carries an embryo and, later, a fetus, if one accepts the medical definitions of the developing young in the human uterus. The situation therefore is inherently different from marital intimacy, or bedroom possession of obscene material, or marriage, or procreation, or education, with which *Eisenstadt, Griswold, Stanley, Loving, Skinner, Pierce,* and *Meyer* were respectively concerned. As we have intimated above, it is reasonable and appropriate for a State to decide that at some point in time another interest, that of health of the mother or that of potential human life, becomes significantly involved. The woman's privacy is no longer sole and any right of privacy she possesses must be measured accordingly.

Texas urges that, apart from the Fourteenth Amendment, life begins at conception and is present throughout pregnancy, and that, therefore, the State has a compelling interest in protecting that life from and after conception. We need not resolve the difficult question of when life begins. When those trained in the respective disciplines of medicine, philosophy, and theology are unable to arrive at any consensus, the judiciary, at this point in the development of man's knowledge, is not in a position to speculate as to the answer.

It should be sufficient to note briefly the wide divergence of thinking on this most sensitive and difficult question. There has always been strong support for the view that life does not begin until live birth. This was the belief of the Stoics. It appears to be the predominant, though not the unanimous, attitude of the Jewish faith. It may be taken to represent also the position of a large segment of the Protestant community, insofar as that can be ascertained; organized groups that have taken a formal position on the abortion issue have generally regarded abortion as a matter for the conscience of the individual and her family. As we have noted, the common law found greater significance in quickening. Physicians and their scientific colleagues have regarded that event with less interest and have tended to focus either upon conception or upon live birth or upon the interim point at which the fetus becomes "viable," that is, potentially able to live outside the mother's womb, albeit with artificial aid. Viability is usually placed at about seven months (28 weeks) but may occur earlier, even at 24 weeks. The Aristotelian theory of "mediate animation," that held sway throughout the Middle Ages and the Renaissance in Europe, continued to be official Roman Catholic dogma until the 19th century, despite opposition to this "ensoulment" theory from those in the Church who would recognize the existence of life from the moment of conception. The latter is now, of course, the official belief of the Catholic Church. As one of the briefs *amicus* discloses, this is a view strongly held by many non-Catholics as well, and by many physicians. Substantial problems for precise definition of this

view are posed, however, by new embryological data that purport to indicate that conception is a "process" over time, rather than an event, and by new medical techniques such as menstrual extraction, the "morning-after" pill, implantation of embryos, artificial insemination, and even artificial wombs.

In areas other than criminal abortion the law has been reluctant to endorse any theory that life, as we recognize it, begins before live birth or to accord legal rights to the unborn except in narrowly defined situations and except when the rights are contingent upon live birth.

*   *   *

X

In view of all this, we do not agree that, by adopting one theory of life, Texas may override the rights of the pregnant woman that are at stake. We repeat, however, that the State does have an important and legitimate interest in preserving and protecting the health of the pregnant woman, whether she be a resident of the State or a non-resident who seeks medical consultation and treatment there, and that it has still *another* important and legitimate interest in protecting the potentiality of human life. These interests are separate and distinct. Each grows in substantiality as the woman approaches term and, at a point during pregnancy, each becomes "compelling."

With respect to the State's important and legitimate interest in the health of the mother, the "compelling" point, in the light of present medical knowledge, is at approximately the end of the first trimester. This is so because of the now established medical fact, referred to above . . . that until the end of the first trimester mortality in abortion is less than mortality in normal childbirth. It follows that, from and after this point, a State may regulate the abortion procedure to the extent that the regulation reasonably relates to the preservation and protection of maternal health.

*   *   *

This means, on the other hand, that, for the period of pregnancy prior to this "compelling" point, the attending physician, in consultation with his patient, is free to determine, without regulation by the State, that in his medical judgment the patient's pregnancy should be terminated. If that decision is reached, the judgment may be effectuated by an abortion free of interference by the State.

With respect to the State's important and legitimate interest in potential life, the "compelling" point is at viability. This is so because the fetus then presumably has the capability of meaningful life outside the mother's womb. State regulation protective of fetal life after viability thus has both logical and biological justifications. If the State is interested in protecting fetal life after viability, it may go so far as to proscribe abortion during that period except when it is necessary to preserve the life or health of the mother.

*   *   *

XI

To summarize and to repeat:

1. A state criminal abortion statute of the current Texas type, that excepts from criminality only a *life saving* procedure on behalf of the mother, without regard to pregnancy stage and without recognition of the other interests involved, is violative of the Due Process Clause of the Fourteenth Amendment.

(a) For the stage prior to approximately the end of the first trimester, the abortion decision and its effectuation must be left to the medical judgment of the pregnant woman's attending physician.

(b) For the stage subsequent to approximately the end of the first trimester, the State, in promoting its interest in the health of the mother, may, if it chooses, regulate the abortion procedure in ways that are reasonably related to maternal health.

(c) For the stage subsequent to viability the State, in promoting its interest in the potentiality of human life, may, if it chooses, regulate, and even proscribe, abortion except where it is necessary, in appropriate medical judgment, for the preservation of the life or health of the mother.

2. The State may define the term "physician," as it has been employed in the preceding numbered paragraphs of this Part XI of this opinion, to mean only a physician currently licensed by the State, and may proscribe any abortion by a person who is not a physician as so defined.

*   *   *

Mr. Justice Rehnquist, dissenting.

I have difficulty in concluding, as the Court does, that the right of "privacy" is involved in this case. Texas by the statute here challenged bars the performance of a medical abortion by a licensed physician on a plaintiff such as Roe. A transaction resulting in an operation such as this is not "private" in the ordinary usage of that word. Nor is the "privacy" which the Court finds here even a distant relative of the freedom from searches and seizures protected by the Fourth Amendment to the Constitution which the Court has referred to as embodying a right to privacy. Katz v. United States, 389 U.S. 347 (1967).

If the Court means by the term "privacy" no more than that the claim of a person to be free from unwanted state regulation of consensual transactions may be a form of "liberty" protected by the Fourteenth Amendment, there is no doubt that similar claims have been upheld in our earlier decisions on the basis of that liberty. I agree with the statement of MR. JUSTICE STEWART in his concurring opinion that the "liberty," against deprivation of which without due process the Fourteenth Amendment protects, embraces more than the rights found in the Bill of Rights. But that liberty is not guaranteed absolutely against deprivation, but only against deprivation without due process of law. The test traditionally applied in the area of social and economic legislation is whether or not a law such as that challenged has a rational relation to a valid state objective. Williamson v. Lee Optical Co., 348 U.S. 483, 491 (1955). The Due Process Clause of the Fourteenth Amendment undoubtedly does place a limit on legislative power to enact laws such as this, albeit a broad one. If the Texas statute were to prohibit an abortion even where the mother's life is in jeopardy, I have little doubt that such a statute would lack a rational relation to a valid state objective under the test stated in *Williamson, supra.* But the Court's sweeping invalidation of any restrictions on abortion during the first trimester is impossible to justify under that standard, and the conscious weighing of competing factors which the Court's opinion apparently substitutes for the established test is far more appropriate to a legislative judgment than to a judicial one.

*   *   *

NOTE

1. When Texas urges that a fetus is entitled to Fourteenth Amendment protection as a person, it faces a dilemma. Neither in Texas nor in any other State are all abortions prohibited. Despite broad proscription, an exception always exists. The exception contained in Art. 1196, for an abortion procured or attempted by medical advice for the purpose of saving the life of the mother, is typical. But if the fetus is a person who is not to be deprived of life without due process of law, and if the mother's condition is the sole determinant, does not the Texas exception appear to be out of line with the Amendment's command?

There are other inconsistencies between Fourteenth Amendment status and the typical abortion statute. It has already been pointed out, n. 49, *supra*, that in Texas the woman is not a principal or an accomplice with respect to an abortion upon her. If the fetus is a person, why is the woman not a principal or an accomplice? Further, the penalty for criminal abortion specified by Art. 1195 is significantly less than the maximum penalty for murder prescribed by Art. 1257 of the Texas Penal Code. If the fetus is a person, may the penalties be different?

Bowers v. *Hardwick*
478 U.S. 186 (1986)

Michael Hardwick, a practicing homosexual, brought action challenging the constitutionality of Georgia's sodomy statute.

Justice White delivered the opinion of the Court.

*   *   *

This case does not require a judgment on whether laws against sodomy between consenting adults in general, or between homosexuals in particular, are wise or desirable. It raises no question about the right or propriety of state legislative decisions to repeal their laws that criminalize homosexual sodomy, or of state-court decisions invalidating those laws on state constitutional grounds. The issue presented is whether the Federal Constitution confers a fundamental right upon homosexuals to engage in sodomy and hence invalidates the laws of the many States that still make such conduct illegal and have done so for a very long time. The case also calls for some judgment about the limits of the Court's role in carrying out its constitutional mandate.

We first register our disagreement with the Court of Appeals and with respondent that the Court's prior cases have construed the Constitution to confer a right of privacy that extends to homosexual sodomy and for all intents and purposes have decided this case. The reach of this line of cases was sketched in *Carey v. Population Services International. Pierce v. Society of Sisters* and *Meyer v. Nebraska* were described as dealing with child rearing and education; *Prince v. Massachusetts*, with family relationships; *Skinner v. Oklahoma ex rel. Williamson*, with procreation; *Loving v. Virginia*, with marriage; *Griswold v. Connecticut* and *Eisenstadt v. Baird*, with contraception; and *Roe v. Wade*, with abortion. The latter three cases were interpreted as construing the Due Process Clause of the Fourteenth Amendment to confer a fundamental individual right to decide whether or not to beget or bear a child.

Accepting the decisions in these cases and the above description of them, we think it evident that none of the rights announced in those cases bears any resemblance to the claimed constitutional right of homosexuals to engage in acts of sodomy that is asserted in this case. No connection between family, marriage, or procreation on the one hand and homosexual activity on the other has been demonstrated, either by the Court of Appeals or by respondent. Moreover, any claim that these cases nevertheless stand for the proposition that any kind of private sexual conduct between consenting adults is constitutionally insulated from state proscription is unsupportable. Indeed, the Court's opinion in *Carey* twice asserted that the privacy right, which the *Griswold* line of cases found to be one of the protections provided by the Due Process Clause, did not reach so far.

Precedent aside, however, respondent would have us announce, as the Court of Appeals did, a fundamental right to engage in homosexual sodomy. This we are quite unwilling to do. It is true that despite the language of the Due Process Clauses of the Fifth and Fourteenth Amendments, which appears to focus only on the processes by which life, liberty, or property is taken, the cases are legion in which those Clauses have been interpreted to have substantive content, subsuming rights that to a great extent are immune from federal or state regulation or proscription. Among such cases are those recognizing rights that have little or no textual support in the constitutional language. *Meyer, Prince*, and *Pierce* fall in this category, as do the privacy cases from *Griswold* to *Carey.*

Striving to assure itself and the public that announcing rights not readily identifiable in the Constitution's text involves much more than the imposition of the Justices' own choice of values on the States and the Federal Government, the Court has sought to identify the nature of the rights qualifying for heightened judicial protection. In *Palko v. Connecticut*, it was said that this category includes those fundamental liberties that are "implicit in the concept of ordered liberty," such that "neither liberty nor justice would exist if [they] were sacrificed." A different description of fundamental liberties appeared in *Moore v. East Cleveland*, where they are characterized as those liberties that are "deeply rooted in this Nation's history and tradition."

It is obvious to us that neither of these formulations would extend a fundamental right to homosexuals to engage in acts of consensual sodomy. Proscriptions against that conduct have ancient roots. . . .

. . . In fact, until 1961, all 50 States outlawed sodomy, and today, 24 States and the District of Columbia continue to provide criminal penalties for sodomy performed in private and between consenting adults. Against this background, to claim that a right to engage in such conduct is "deeply rooted in this Nation's history and tradition" or "implicit in the concept of ordered liberty" is, at best, facetious.

Nor are we inclined to take a more expansive view of our authority to discover new fundamental rights imbedded in the Due Process Clause. The Court is most vulnerable and comes nearest to illegitimacy when it deals with judge-made constitutional law having little or no cognizable roots in the language or design of the Constitution. . . .

* * *

Even if the conduct at issue here is not a fundamental right, respondent asserts that there must be a rational basis for the law and that there is none in this case other than the presumed belief of a majority of the electorate in Georgia that homosexual sodomy is immoral and unacceptable. This is said to be an inadequate rationale to support the law. The law, however, is constantly based on notions of morality, and if all laws representing essentially moral choices are to be invalidated under the Due Process Clause, the courts will be very busy indeed. Even respondent makes no such claim, but insists that majority sentiments about the morality of homosexuality should be declared inadequate. We do not agree, and are unpersuaded that the sodomy laws of some 25 States should be invalidated on this basis.

Accordingly, the judgment of the Court of Appeals is

Reversed.

Justice Blackmun, with whom Justice Brennan, Justice Marshall, and Justice Stevens join, dissenting.

This case is no more about "a fundamental right to engage in homosexual sodomy," as the Court purports to declare, than *Stanley v. Georgia* was about a fundamental right to watch obscene movies, or *Katz v. United States* was about a fundamental right to place interstate bets from a telephone booth. Rather, this case is about "the most comprehensive of rights and the right most valued by civilized men," namely, "the right to be let alone."

* * *

Justice Stevens, with whom Justice Brennan and Justice Marshall join, dissenting.

Because the Georgia statute expresses the traditional view that sodomy is an immoral kind of conduct regardless of the identity of the persons who engage in it, I believe that a proper analysis of its constitutionality requires consideration of two questions: First, may a State totally prohibit the described conduct by means of a neutral law applying without exception to all persons subject to its jurisdiction? If not, may the State save the statute by announcing that it will only enforce the law against homosexuals? The two questions merit separate discussion.

I

Our prior cases make two propositions abundantly clear. First, the fact that the governing majority in a State has traditionally viewed a particular practice as immoral is not a sufficient reason for upholding a law prohibiting the practice; neither history nor tradition could save a law prohibiting miscegenation from constitutional attack. Second, individual decisions by married persons, concerning the intimacies of their physical relationship, even when not intended to produce offspring, are a form of "liberty" protected by the Due Process Clause of the Fourteenth Amendment. Moreover, this protection extends to intimate choices by unmarried as well as married persons.

In consideration of claims of this kind, the Court has emphasized the individual interest in privacy, but its decisions have actually been animated by an even more fundamental concern. As I wrote some years ago:

> "These cases do not deal with the individual's interest in protection from unwarranted public attention, comment, or exploitation. They deal, rather, with the individual's right to make certain unusually important decisions that will affect his own, or his family's, destiny. The Court has referred to such decisions as implicating 'basic values,' as being 'fundamental,' and as being dignified by history and tradition. The character of the Court's language in these cases brings to mind the origins of the American heritage of freedom — the abiding interest in individual liberty that makes certain state intrusions on the citizen's right to decide how he will live his own life intolerable. Guided by history, our tradition of respect for the dignity of individual choice in matters of conscience and the restraints implicit in the federal system, federal judges have accepted the responsibility for recognition and protection of these rights in appropriate cases."

*   *   *

Paradoxical as it may seem, our prior cases thus establish that a State may not prohibit sodomy within "the sacred precincts of marital bedrooms," *Griswold*, 381 U.S., at 485, 85 S.Ct., at 1682, or, indeed, between unmarried heterosexual adults. *Eisenstadt*, 405 U.S., at 453, 92 S.Ct., at 1038. In all events, it is perfectly clear that the State of Georgia may not totally prohibit the conduct proscribed by § 16–6–2 of the Georgia Criminal Code.

II

If the Georgia statute cannot be enforced as it is written — if the conduct it seeks to prohibit is a protected form of liberty for the vast majority of Georgia's citizens — the State must assume the burden of justifying a selective application of its law. Either the persons to whom Georgia seeks to apply its statute do not have the same interest in "liberty" that others have, or there must be a reason why the State may be permitted to apply a generally applicable law to certain persons that it does not apply to others.

The first possibility is plainly unacceptable. Although the meaning of the principle that "all men are created equal" is not always clear, it surely must mean that every free citizen has the same interest in "liberty" that the members of the majority share. . . .

The second possibility is similarly unacceptable. A policy of selective application must be supported by a neutral and legitimate interest — something more substantial than a habitual dislike for, or ignorance about, the disfavored group. Neither the State nor the Court has identified any such interest in this case.

*   *   *

III

The Court orders the dismissal of respondent's complaint even though the State's statute prohibits all sodomy; even though that prohibition is concededly unconstitutional with respect to heterosexuals; and even though the State's *post hoc* explanations for selective application are belied by the State's own actions. At the very least, I think it clear at this early stage of the litigation that respondent has alleged a constitutional claim sufficient to withstand a motion to dismiss.

I respectfully dissent.

Planned Parenthood of S.E. Pennsylvania v. Casey
112 S.Ct. 2791 (1992)

Justice O'Connor, Justice Kennedy, and Justice Souter announced the judgment of the Court:

*   *   *

At issue in these cases are five provisions of the Pennsylvania Abortion Control Act of 1982 as amended in 1988 and 1989. The Act requires that a woman seeking an abortion give her informed consent prior to the abortion procedure, and specifies that she be provided with certain information at least 24 hours before the abortion is performed. For a minor to obtain an abortion, the Act requires the informed consent of one of her parents, but provides for a judicial bypass option if the minor does not wish to or cannot obtain a parent's consent. Another provision of the Act requires that, unless certain exceptions apply, a married woman seeking an abortion must sign a statement indicating that she has notified her husband of her intended abortion. The Act exempts compliance with these three requirements in the event of a "medical emergency," which is defined in s 3203 of the Act. In addition to the above provisions regulating the performance of abortions, the Act imposes certain reporting requirements on facilities that provide abortion services.

* * *

After considering the fundamental constitutional questions resolved by Roe, principles of institutional integrity, and the rule of stare decisis, we are led to conclude this: the essential holding of Roe v. Wade should be retained and once again reaffirmed.

It must be stated at the outset and with clarity that Roe's essential holding, the holding we reaffirm, has three parts. First is a recognition of the right of the woman to choose to have an abortion before viability and to obtain it without undue interference from the State. Before viability, the State's interests are not strong enough to support a prohibition of abortion or the imposition of a substantial obstacle to the woman's effective right to elect the procedure. Second is a confirmation of the State's power to restrict abortions after fetal viability, if the law contains exceptions for pregnancies which endanger a woman's life or health. And third is the principle that the State has legitimate interests from the outset of the pregnancy in protecting the health of the woman and the life of the fetus that may become a child. These principles do not contradict one another; and we adhere to each.

* * *

The Court's duty in the present case is clear. In 1973, it confronted the already divisive issue of governmental power to limit personal choice to undergo abortion, for which it provided a new resolution based on the due process guaranteed by the Fourteenth Amendment. Whether or not a new social consensus is developing on that issue, its divisiveness is no less today than in 1973, and pressure to overrule the decision, like pressure to retain it, has grown only more intense. A decision to overrule Roe's essential holding under the existing circumstances would address error, if error there was, at the cost of both profound and unnecessary damage to the Court's legitimacy, and to the Nation's commitment to the rule of law. It is therefore imperative to adhere to the essence of Roe's original decision, and we do so today. . . .

From what we have said so far it follows that it is a constitutional liberty of the woman to have some freedom to terminate her pregnancy. We conclude that the basic decision in Roe was based on a constitutional analysis which we cannot now repudiate. The woman's liberty is not so unlimited, however, that from the outset the State cannot show its concern for the life of the unborn, and at a later point in fetal development the State's interest in life has sufficient force so that the right of the woman to terminate the pregnancy can be restricted.

That brings us, of course, to the point where much criticism has been directed at Roe, a criticism that always inheres when the Court draws a specific rule from what in the Constitution is but a general standard. We conclude, however, that the urgent claims of the woman to retain the ultimate control over her destiny and her body, claims implicit in the meaning of liberty, require us to perform that function. Liberty must not be extinguished for want of a line that is clear. And it falls to us to give some real substance to the woman's liberty to determine whether to carry her pregnancy to full term.

We conclude the line should be drawn at viability, so that before that time the woman has a right to choose to terminate her pregnancy. We adhere to this principle for two reasons. First, as we have said, is the doctrine of stare decisis. Any judicial act of line-drawing may seem somewhat arbitrary, but Roe was a reasoned statement, elaborated with great care. We have twice reaffirmed it in the face of great opposition. Although we must overrule those parts of Thornburgh and Akron I which, in our view, are inconsistent with Roe's statement that the State has a legitimate interest in promoting the life or potential life of the unborn, the central premise of those cases represents an unbroken commitment by this Court to the essential holding of Roe. It is that premise which we reaffirm today.

The second reason is that the concept of viability, as we noted in Roe, is the time at which there is a realistic possibility of maintaining and nourishing a life outside the womb, so that the independent existence of the second life can in reason and all fairness be the object of state protection that now overrides the rights of the woman. Consistent with other constitutional norms, legislatures may draw lines which appear arbitrary without the necessity of offering a justification. But courts may not. We must justify the lines we draw. And there is no line other than viability which is more workable. To be sure, as we have said, there may be some medical developments that affect the precise point of viability, but this is an imprecision within tolerable limits given that the medical community and all those who must apply its discoveries will continue to explore the matter. The viability line also has, as a practical matter, an element of fairness. In some broad sense it might be said that a woman who fails to act before viability has consented to the State's intervention on behalf of the developing child.

The woman's right to terminate her pregnancy before viability is the most central principle of Roe v. Wade. It is a rule of law and a component of liberty we cannot renounce.

* * *

Yet it must be remembered that Roe v. Wade speaks with clarity in establishing not only the woman's liberty but also the State's "important and legitimate interest in potential life." That portion of the decision in Roe has been given too little acknowledgement and implementation by the Court in its subsequent cases. Those cases decided that any regulation touching upon the abortion decision must survive strict scrutiny, to be sustained only if drawn in narrow terms to further a compelling state interest. Not all of the cases decided under that formulation can be reconciled with the holding in Roe itself that the State has legitimate interests in the health of the woman and in protecting the potential life within her. In resolving this tension, we choose to rely upon Roe, as against the later cases.

Roe established a trimester framework to govern abortion regulations. Under this elaborate but rigid construct, almost no regulation at all is permitted during the first trimester of pregnancy; regulations designed to protect the woman's health, but not to further the State's interest in potential life, are permitted during the second trimester; and during the third trimester, when the fetus is viable, prohibitions are permitted provided the life or health of the mother is not at stake. Most of our cases since Roe have involved the application of rules derived from the trimester framework.

The trimester framework no doubt was erected to ensure that the woman's right to choose not become so subordinate to the State's interest in promoting fetal life that her choice exists in theory but not in fact. We do not agree, however, that the trimester approach is necessary to accomplish this objective. A framework of this rigidity was unnecessary and in its later interpretation sometimes contradicted the State's permissible exercise of its powers.

Though the woman has a right to choose to terminate or continue her pregnancy before viability, it does not at all follow that the State is prohibited from taking steps to ensure that this choice is thoughtful and informed. Even in the earliest stages of pregnancy, the State may enact rules and regulations designed to encourage her to know that there are philosophic and social arguments of great weight that can be brought to bear in favor of continuing the pregnancy to full term and that there are procedures and institutions to allow adoption of unwanted children as well as a certain degree of state assistance if the mother chooses to raise the child herself. "'[T]he Constitution does not forbid a State or city, pursuant to democratic processes, from expressing a preference for normal childbirth.'" Webster v. Reproductive Health Services.

* * *

We reject the trimester framework, which we do not consider to be part of the essential holding of Roe. Measures aimed at ensuring that a woman's choice contemplates the consequences for the fetus do not necessarily interfere with the right recognized in Roe, although those measures have been found to be inconsistent with the rigid trimester framework announced in that case. A logical reading of the central holding in Roe itself, and a necessary reconciliation of the liberty of the woman and the interest of the State in promoting prenatal life, require, in our view, that we abandon the trimester framework as a rigid prohibition on all previability regulation aimed at the protection of fetal life. The trimester framework suffers from these basic flaws: in its formulation it misconceives the nature of the pregnant woman's interest; and in practice it undervalues the State's interest in potential life, as recognized in Roe.

As our jurisprudence relating to all liberties save perhaps abortion has recognized, not every law which makes a right more difficult to exercise is, ipso facto, an infringement of that right. An example clarifies the point. We have held that not every ballot access limitation amounts to an infringement of the right to vote. Rather, the States are granted substantial flexibility in establishing the framework within which voters choose the candidates for whom they wish to vote.

The abortion right is similar. Numerous forms of state regulation might have the incidental effect of increasing the cost or decreasing the availability of medical care, whether for abortion or any other medical procedure. The fact that a law which serves a valid purpose, one not designed to strike at the right itself, has the incidental effect of making it more difficult or more expensive to procure an abortion cannot be enough to invalidate it. Only where state regulation imposes an undue burden on a woman's ability to make this decision does the power of the State reach into the heart of the liberty protected by the Due Process Clause.

* * *

For the most part, the Court's early abortion cases adhered to this view. In Maher v. Roe, the Court explained: "Roe did not declare an unqualified 'constitutional right to an abortion,' as the District Court seemed to think. Rather, the right protects the woman from unduly burdensome interference with her freedom to decide whether to terminate her pregnancy."

* * *

These considerations of the nature of the abortion right illustrate that it is an overstatement to describe it as a right to decide whether to have an abortion "without interference from the State,"

Planned Parenthood of Central Mo. v. Danforth. All abortion regulations interfere to some degree with a woman's ability to decide whether to terminate her pregnancy. It is, as a consequence, not surprising that despite the protestations contained in the original Roe opinion to the effect that the Court was not recognizing an absolute right, the Court's experience applying the trimester framework has led to the striking down of some abortion regulations which in no real sense deprived women of the ultimate decision. Those decisions went too far because the right recognized by Roe is a right "to be free from unwarranted governmental intrusion into matters so fundamentally affecting a person as the decision whether to bear or beget a child." Eisenstadt v. Baird. Not all governmental intrusion is of necessity unwarranted; and that brings us to the other basic flaw in the trimester framework: even in Roe's terms, in practice it undervalues the State's interest in the potential life within the woman. Roe v. Wade was express in its recognition of the State's "important and legitimate interest[s] in preserving and protecting the health of the pregnant woman [and] in protecting the potentiality of human life." The trimester framework, however, does not fulfill Roe's own promise that the State has an interest in protecting fetal life or potential life. Roe began the contradiction by using the trimester framework to forbid any regulation of abortion designed to advance that interest before viability. Before viability, Roe and subsequent cases treat all governmental attempts to influence a woman's decision on behalf of the potential life within her as unwarranted. This treatment is, in our judgment, incompatible with the recognition that there is a substantial state interest in potential life throughout pregnancy.

The very notion that the State has a substantial interest in potential life leads to the conclusion that not all regulations must be deemed unwarranted. Not all burdens on the right to decide whether to terminate a pregnancy will be undue. In our view, the undue burden standard is the appropriate means of reconciling the State's interest with the woman's constitutionally protected liberty.

* * *

A finding of an undue burden is a shorthand for the conclusion that a state regulation has the purpose or effect of placing a substantial obstacle in the path of a woman seeking an abortion of a nonviable fetus. A statute with this purpose is invalid because the means chosen by the State to further the interest in potential life must be calculated to inform the woman's free choice, not hinder it. And a statute which, while furthering the interest in potential life or some other valid state interest, has the effect of placing a substantial obstacle in the path of a woman's choice cannot be considered a permissible means of serving its legitimate ends. To the extent that the opinions of the Court or of individual Justices use the undue burden standard in a manner that is inconsistent with this analysis, we set out what in our view should be the controlling standard. In our considered judgment, an undue burden is an unconstitutional burden. . . .

Some guiding principles should emerge. What is at stake is the woman's right to make the ultimate decision, not a right to be insulated from all others in doing so. Regulations which do no more than create a structural mechanism by which the State, or the parent or guardian of a minor, may express profound respect for the life of the unborn are permitted, if they are not a substantial obstacle to the woman's exercise of the right to choose. Unless it has that effect on her right of choice, a state measure designed to persuade her to choose childbirth over abortion will be upheld if reasonably related to that goal. Regulations designed to foster the health of a woman seeking an abortion are valid if they do not constitute an undue burden.

Even when jurists reason from shared premises, some disagreement is inevitable. That is to be expected in the application of any legal standard which must accommodate life's complexity. We do not expect it to be otherwise with respect to the undue burden standard. We give this summary:

(a) To protect the central right recognized by Roe v. Wade while at the same time accommodating the State's profound interest in potential life, we will employ the undue burden analysis as explained in this opinion. An undue burden exists, and therefore a provision of law is invalid, if its purpose or effect is to place a substantial obstacle in the path of a woman seeking an abortion before the fetus attains viability.

(b) We reject the rigid trimester framework of Roe v. Wade. To promote the State's profound interest in potential life, throughout pregnancy the State may take measures to ensure that the woman's choice is informed, and measures designed to advance this interest will not be invalidated as long as their purpose is to persuade the woman to choose childbirth over abortion. These measures must not be an undue burden on the right.

(c) As with any medical procedure, the State may enact regulations to further the health or safety of a woman seeking an abortion. Unnecessary health regulations that have the purpose or effect of presenting a substantial obstacle to a woman seeking an abortion impose an undue burden on the right.

(d) Our adoption of the undue burden analysis does not disturb the central holding of Roe v. Wade, and we reaffirm that holding. Regardless of whether exceptions are made for particular circumstances, a State may not prohibit any woman from making the ultimate decision to terminate her pregnancy before viability.

(e) We also reaffirm Roe's holding that "subsequent to viability, the State in promoting its interest in the potentiality of human life may, if it chooses, regulate, and even proscribe, abortion except where it is necessary, in appropriate medical judgment, for the preservation of the life or health of the mother." Roe v. Wade, 410 U.S., at 164–165, 93 S.Ct., at 732.

These principles control our assessment of the Pennsylvania statute. . . .

* * *

The Court of Appeals applied what it believed to be the undue burden standard and upheld each of the provisions except for the husband notification requirement. We agree generally with this conclusion. . . .

* * *

SECTION 2

Civil Rights and the Value of Justice

Justice is the most fundamental virtue of government. A government that genuinely disregards the requirements of justice — an unjust government — cannot be legitimate. In this regard, political justice simply is what government owes its citizens, and civil rights are what justice guarantees, although the matter has not always been put in these terms. Recall from Chapter One that the notion of a right is an individualistic concept that was not introduced into political theory until the Middle Ages and was not part of the broader political discourse until the time of John Locke. At least since that time, however, justice and rights have been recognized as essentially linked. Those who view duty as the foundation of political theory say that rights are what follow from the requirements of justice. On the other hand, those who take rights as fundamental say that justice is the enforcement of rights. Either way, rights and duties of justice are two sides of the same coin. But what is justice? What must a government do to be just?

Since the time of the ancient Greeks there has been a close and uneasy relation between justice and equality. Just treatment is in some sense equal treatment. But no one is quite sure exactly what that means. Sometimes just treatment means identical treatment. When cases or individuals or classes are judged to be relevantly similar, then justice requires that they be treated the same. But some circumstances or characteristics deserve different treatment. The important questions are, When should people be treated the same or differently and why? What circumstances or characteristics are relevant to issues of justice?

Aristotle grapples with these questions in his seminal work on the nature of justice, *The Nicomachean Ethics*. In this work he sets out the classical formulation of formal justice: Justice requires that equal, or like, cases be treated equally, or alike, and that unequal cases be treated differently in proportion to their differences. This formal definition is not disputed. It is agreed that this is the form of justice; this is what justice means. But we still don't know what justice requires until we fill in the content of the formula, and the content has been a source of continuous and unending dispute for centuries. Which cases are alike? What is a relevant difference? How are the proportions of differences determined?

Aristotle does not deal with these substantive questions, but he makes some important distinctions that clarify the meaning of justice. First, he distinguishes universal justice from particular justice. Universal justice he describes as comprehending all other virtues as applied to one's neighbor. In this regard it is the greatest of all virtues. Aristotle calls this form of justice lawfulness because the law, rightly formed, is intended to accomplish this end. His primary interest, however, is particular justice, which he further divides into distributive justice and rectificatory justice. Distributive justice is concerned with the just distribution of social benefits and burdens, such as wealth, office, military service, and taxation. Aristotle says that distributive justice involves an "equality of proportions" by which, in terms of the way we use the terms today, he means something more like fairness than equality. Rectificatory justice (also called corrective or compensatory justice) is concerned with correcting unjust gains and losses that occur when one party receives an unfair gain at the expense of another. Rectificatory justice, Aristotle says, requires that such cases be equalized, and he suggests a formula for doing so. The formula is abstract, and determining compensation in actual cases may not be as simple as Aristotle suggests. Nevertheless, it provides a starting point for further developments in the analysis of compensation.

Throughout the selection Aristotle struggles with the relation among justice, equality, and merit — a struggle that continues to this day.

Contemporary philosopher John Rawls characterizes justice in terms of two principles: (1) Each person participating in a practice, or affected by it, has an equal right to the most extensive liberty compatible with a like liberty for all; and (2) inequalities are arbitrary unless it is reasonable to expect that they will work out for everyone's advantage, and provided the positions and offices to which they attach are open to all. These principles, Rawls says, represent justice as a complex of three ideas: liberty, equality, and reward for service contributing to the common good. Compare Rawls's views to Aristotle's analysis of justice. Like Aristotle, Rawls is concerned with distributive justice, and, like Aristotle, he argues that the fundamental idea in distributive justice is fairness, or equal treatment. By fair principles Rawls means those basic principles of judgment that would be mutually acknowledged by free persons who have no authority over one another but are engaged in a common practice. Rawls contends that it is this idea of fairness that utilitarian theory cannot accommodate, thus making it unable to account for the requirements of justice. He believes, however, that a social contract model, properly formulated, could explain the idea of fairness, and he proposes a social contract model designed to do just that. His social contract model has two important features. The first is the character and situation of the parties, which are intended to represent the conditions under which questions of justice arise. The second is the decision procedure, which represents the constraints morality would place on their decisions. As with any social contract theory, Rawls's model is a thought experiment. He asks us to imagine certain people (rational, nonenvious heads of families) coming together from time to time to discuss their practices and institutions and to agree on the principles by which their judgments will be made. Rawls's idea is that if we imagine these people in a situation that requires them to agree permanently in advance on the principles that will be used to settle all claims or complaints before any claims or complaints can be made, we will arrive at the two principles he suggests. The reason is that no one will be able to tailor the principles to his or her own advantage and so will choose principles that are fair to all. Rawls's theory has been both influential and controversial.

Robert Nozick, for example (see Chapter Four on property), specifically argues against what Rawls calls a duty of fair play and further denies that the idea of distributive justice is a defensible idea at all. According to Nozick, corrective justice is all there is. Distributive justice is a legislative matter, and Nozick denies, while Rawls and Aristotle affirm, that states should legislate the distribution of certain benefits and burdens.

All, nevertheless, accept Aristotle's formal definition of justice. That definition has judicial as well as legislative application and returns us to the questions raised earlier. Which cases are relevantly alike? Which are relevantly different, and how are the proportions of differences determined? Everyone agrees that equals should be treated equally and unequals unequally. The question is, Who is equal, and who is unequal, and for what purposes? Since 1868 when the Fourteenth Amendment was passed the U.S. Constitution has explicitly guaranteed equal protection of the law. Presumably, the idea that the protection of the law extends equally to all citizens has in some sense always been embraced in this country as an abstract ideal. In fact, however, several groups have been excluded from the rights of full citizenship — or from any rights of citizenship, for that matter. Indeed, the black race was held in slavery, the Native Americans were annihilated, the Chinese were oppressed or deported, and women were denied basic rights of citizenship on the ground that they were different. Were these people treated unjustly? We would certainly think so today, but at the time their treatment was thought to be justified because they were thought by those in power to be different in ways relevant to treating them differently.

In considering questions of equality, the first question, then, is what characteristics make someone different? Who is entitled to equal treatment? It took a civil war and a constitutional amendment to remove race (even formally) as a ground for different treatment. Even after the Civil War amendments were passed — abolishing slavery, granting equal protection of the law to all races, and specifically providing the right of black men to vote — Chinese, Native Americans, and blacks were systematically segregated, oppressed, and terrorized. Courts originally upheld segregation of blacks on the ground that "separate but equal" facilities were not discriminatory.

This raises the second question. Suppose you are entitled to equal treatment (you are an equal); what does equal treatment require? Is "separate but equal" good enough, or must facilities be the same? The Court determined eventually that exclusion or segregation is inherently discriminatory to oppressed races and that all races must be treated the same, thus determining that equal means the same. Therefore, races are equal because they are the same. Since there is no relevant difference between them, they are entitled to equal treatment, which means identical treatment. This analysis seems basically right as applied to race so long as our standards and institutions that comprise the status quo are neutral as they stand. But, of course, there is no reason to think that they are neutral. Instead, there is every reason to think that they represent the standards and judgments of the white, the male, and the privileged. The basic question therefore remains: What constitutes equal treatment or equal protection of the law in the first place?

Kimberlé Crenshaw discusses this issue in the specific context of American equal protection law. She notes that the idea of equal protection is ambiguous, an ambiguity that runs through the law in the form of two standards or visions of equal treatment. Crenshaw calls these the expansive view and the restrictive view. The expansive view is concerned with both formal inequality and the substantive conditions of material inequality that have resulted from discrimination in the past and continued racial prejudice and stereotyping in the present. The expansive view argues that equal protection of the law requires compensation for these disadvantages, that the goal of racial equality is far from being met, and that therefore affirmative measures are needed.

The conservative or restrictive view focuses on the notion of equal protection as equal process — the removal of formal barriers, such as prohibitions against voting and educational segregation — and argues that this goal has already been accomplished and therefore affirmative action measures are unjust. In fact, conservatives regularly charge that the expansive view is a perversion of "true law," which deviates from the original understanding of equal protection and equal opportunity. Crenshaw points out, however, that both the expansive and the restrictive visions have been part of equal protection law from the beginning and that choosing between them is entirely a function of interpretations, which depend upon one's vision of the just society and the meaning of equality. Crenshaw's worry is that reforms for oppressed people can be promoted only in the discourse of dominant institutions that entrench inequality in the long run. Formal reforms make present circumstances appear fair and open, but mask continuing racial prejudice and fragment the black community, dissipating its strength to press further claims and leaving it without clear arguments on behalf of those who are still most disadvantaged.

Thus, we are confronted today with the ambiguity of justice and equality, as we have been since the time of Aristotle. Racial discrimination was once considered clearly justified on the ground that races differ and therefore should be treated differently. We have slowly concluded that this idea is wrong. But what must be done to correct it when racial prejudice systematically permeates our history and institutions? Is changing the formalities of law — the words and the symbolic barriers — enough? Or must we address the material inequality that has resulted from our unjust history?

The cases that follow the Crenshaw article present some major Supreme Court decisions dealing with the issue of racial injustice. Like free speech and religion, equal protection of the law is a clear mandate of the Constitution in the sense that it is explicitly stated in the text of the document. But what this phrase means or requires is far from clear, as you will see from the Court opinions. That is, whereas the right to equal protection is stated in the Constitution, the scope of the right is an unresolved question.

Although it still has far to go, the fight against racial discrimination has met with some success so long as it has remained in the area of negative rights: rights against harassment, interference, or discriminatory limitations. Claims to positive benefits, however, have been much less successful. This problem is particularly illustrated by the plight of a large percentage of blacks, where a history of discrimination and deprivation has made a disproportionate number of that race into a disadvantaged class, with only a few hard-won exceptions. Given this disadvantaged status, a large percentage of blacks do not compete well, even when formal barriers are removed. Thus, they become exactly like disadvantaged classes of every race. Whether we are discussing disadvantaged whites in Appalachia, migrant workers across the country, Chicanos in southwestern cities, or poor women in the sweatshops of New York, the poor and disadvantaged do not compete well.

The question is not one of race but of class, and it raises again the issue of equal treatment. What does equal treatment in law amount to when gross inequalities of social and economic means have always divided society into classes, even when such social stratification is not legally recognized? Should law do anything about this situation or leave everyone equally alone? Is there a civil right to material equality or material well-being in a society that can afford it? Is everyone entitled — or should everyone be entitled — to a minimal share of the national wealth or a minimum standard of living as a right of membership in that society?

Frank Michelman asks this question in addressing the possibility of using the Fourteenth Amendment to protect the poor. He points out that although the equal protection clause is a natural ground for claims to satisfy certain basic needs of disadvantaged persons, the approach has some clear drawbacks. First, such protection suggests the possibility of extensive interference toward a goal of income or wealth equalization, which would be a radical idea even for a legislature, let alone a court. Second, it seems to justify no assistance to anyone — no matter how great the need or substantial the interest — since that, after all, would be equal treatment.

Michelman suggests instead what he calls a "minimum protection" approach, which would protect all citizens against the deprivation of certain vital needs or fundamental interests. This approach, he argues, better accounts for past decisions of the Court that deal with guaranteeing certain rights (especially voting and criminal defense) to the indigent. Michelman also sees it as more promising for dealing with the devastating effects of poverty in a manner that could still be limited in a more manageable way by the Supreme Court.

Since Michelman wrote his article in 1968, there have been great changes in the composition of the Supreme Court and what might be considered a reversal — although not an explicit one — of judicial policy in the area of equal protection. (This shift in direction is a primary concern of Crenshaw.) The fundamental rights analysis has not been expanded as Michelman suggested. Instead, as he feared the Court has suggested that the Constitution guarantees nothing but equal process. If that is true, is the Constitution consistent with the requirements of justice? Does it allow injustice? Can a society tolerate gross inequality of wealth and opportunity without guaranteeing, as Michelman suggested, even minimum protections of vital interests and still be a just society?

And historically has the legal treatment of disadvantaged classes had nothing to do with their present status? Lawrence Friedman outlines the legal treatment of the poor and of minority races in this country until the turn of the century, illustrating the disadvantages to which these groups have been legally subjected. The summary by L. J. Barker and T. W. Barker, Jr., updates the legal treatment of the poor in the areas of housing, schools, and access to courts, showing clearly that disadvantage is not addressed by the Constitution as currently interpreted.

Finally, the cases that conclude this section pick up where the racial discrimination cases leave off and together trace the history of the equal protection clause of the Constitution from 1896 when the Court supported the segregation of blacks through the doctrine of separate but equal facilities to 1980 when the Court supported the denial of funds for abortions for poor women. Equal protection, as presently interpreted, clearly does not mean equal opportunity, especially for the poor. These cases may leave you wondering exactly what, as a requirement of justice, equal treatment means.

Notes and Questions

ARISTOTLE, from *The Nicomachean Ethics*

1. Pointing out that the term *justice* (or *injustice*) is ambiguous, Aristotle divides the term into universal justice and particular justice and discusses the two separately. Universal justice he describes as lawfulness. What makes the lawful the just, according to Aristotle? What is the "rightly framed law" supposed to do? Why does Aristotle claim that this form of justice is complete virtue?

2. Aristotle's main interest is what he calls particular justice, which he views as the sense of justice concerned with fairness and equality. (In Aristotle's time the Greek word for *fair* also meant *equal*.) Particular justice he further divides into distributive justice and rectificatory justice. Distributive justice is justice in accord with geometrical proportion, according to Aristotle. By this he means that a just distribution of burdens or benefits is not absolutely equal but instead is an equality of ratios between two pairs. Every distribution, he explains, involves at least four terms: two people and two things (or shares of things). If the two people are equal, then their shares should be equal. If they are not equal (say, one member of a pair works more hours or produces more goods or invests more capital), then their shares should reflect their inequality. Thus, justice, according to Aristotle, requires equal cases to be treated equally and unequal cases to be treated unequally in proportion to their differences. Does this sound like what we mean by distributive justice today? Does it sound like what we mean by equality?

3. Aristotle points out that distributive justice as proportional equality, or distribution according to merit, is the source of quarrels because people cannot agree on what counts as merit. What proposals does he list for what might count as merit? What other proposals can you think of? Is there any way to resolve a dispute over the nature of merit?

4. The second sense of particular justice is rectificatory, or compensatory, justice. This kind of justice is also concerned with a certain sort of equality — namely, with equalizing or restoring balance between two parties where one has gained unfairly from the other's loss. When this happens in voluntary transactions it corresponds to damages in contract cases. Where involuntary transactions are concerned it corresponds to tort actions. According to Aristotle, it is up to the judge in such cases to restore equality. But what does he mean by equality here? How, if at all, does equality relate to equality of distribution?

5. Aristotle divides political justice into natural justice and legal justice. What does he mean by this distinction? How does the distinction fit into his overall discussion of justice? Note that the distinction is the classical basis for the natural law theory discussed in Chapters One and Two.

6. According to Aristotle, just and unjust acts are always voluntary. Why does he think so? Is he right? What does he mean by *voluntary*? Can a person voluntarily be treated unjustly?

7. Equity is the correction of legal justice necessary when the generality of law produces injustice in particular cases. What is the relation between equity and justice, according to Aristotle?

[From] *The Nicomachean Ethics*

ARISTOTLE

Justice: Its Sphere and Outer Nature: In What Sense It Is a Mean

The Just as the Lawful (Universal Justice) and the Just as the Fair and Equal (Particular Justice): The Former Considered

1. With regard to justice and injustice we must consider (1) what kind of actions they are concerned with, (2) what sort of mean justice is, and (3) between what extremes the just act is intermediate. Our investigation shall follow the same course as the preceding discussions.

We see that all men mean by justice that kind of state of character which makes people disposed to do what is just and makes them act justly and wish for what is just; and similarly by injustice that state which makes them act unjustly and wish for what is unjust. Let us too, then, lay this down as a general basis. For the same is not true of the sciences and the faculties as of states of character. A faculty or a science which is one and the same is held to relate to contrary objects, but a state of character which is one of two contraries does *not* produce the contrary results; for example, as a result of health we do not do what is the opposite of healthy, but only what is healthy; for we say a man walks healthily, when he walks as a healthy man would.

Now often one contrary state is recognized from its contrary, and often states are recognized from the subjects that exhibit them; for (A) if good condition is known, bad condition also becomes known, and (B) good condition is known from the things that are in good condition, and they from it. If good condition is firm-ness of flesh, it is necessary both that bad condition should be flabbiness of flesh and that the wholesome should be that which causes firmness in flesh. And it follows for the most part that if one contrary is ambiguous the other also will be ambiguous; for example, that if "just" is so, "unjust" will be so too.

Now "justice" and "injustice" seem to be ambiguous, but because their different meanings approach near to one another the ambiguity escapes notice and is not obvious as it is, comparatively, when the meanings are far apart, for example, (for here the difference in outward form is great) as the ambiguity in the use of κλείζ for the collarbone of an animal and for that with which we lock a door. Let us take as a starting-point, then, the various meanings of "an unjust man." Both the lawless man and the grasping and unfair man are thought to be unjust, so that evidently both the law-abiding and the fair man will be just. The just, then, is the lawful and the fair, the unjust the unlawful and the unfair.

Since the unjust man is grasping, he must be concerned with goods—not all goods, but those with which prosperity and adversity have to do, which taken absolutely are always good, but for a particular person are not always good. Now men pray for and pursue these things; but they should not, but should pray that the things that are good absolutely may also be good for them, and should choose the things that *are* good for them. The unjust man does not always choose the greater, but also the less—in the case of things bad absolutely; but because the lesser evil is itself thought to be in a sense good, and graspingness is directed at the good, therefore he is thought to be grasping. And he is unfair; for this contains and is common to both.

Since the lawless man was seen to be unjust and the law-abiding man just, evidently all lawful acts are in a sense just acts; for the acts laid down by the legislative art are lawful, and each of these, we say, is just. Now the laws in their enactments on all subjects aim at the common advantage either of all or of the best or of those who hold power, or something of the sort; so that in one sense we call those acts just that tend to produce and preserve happiness and its components for the political society. And the law bids us do both the acts of a brave man (for example, not to desert our post nor take a flight nor throw away our arms), and those of a temperate man (for example, not to commit adultery nor to gratify one's lust), and those of a good-tempered man (for example, not to strike another nor to speak evil), and similarly with regard to the other virtues and forms of wickedness, commanding some acts and forbidding others; and the rightly-framed law does this rightly, and the hastily conceived one less well.

This form of justice, then, is complete virtue, but not absolutely, but in relation to our neighbour. And therefore justice is often thought to be the greatest of virtues, and "neither evening nor morning star" is so wonderful; and proverbially "in justice is every virtue comprehended." And it is complete virtue in its fullest sense because it is the actual exercise of complete virtue. It is complete because he who possesses it can exercise his virtue not only in himself but towards his neighbour also; for many men can exercise virtue in their own affairs, but not in their relations to their neighbour. This is why the saying of Bias is thought to be true, that "rule will show the man"; for a ruler is necessarily in relation to other men, and a member of a society. For this same reason justice, alone of the virtues, is thought to be "another's good," because it is related to our neighbour; for it does what is advantageous to another, either a ruler or a co-partner. Now the worst man is he who exercises his wickedness both towards himself and towards his friends, and the best man is not he who exercises his virtue towards himself but he who exercises it towards another; for this is a difficult task. Justice in this sense, then, is not part of virtue but

virtue entire, nor is the contrary injustice a part of vice but vice entire. What the difference is between virtue and justice in this sense is plain from what we have said; they are the same but their essence is not the same; what, as a relation to one's neighbour, is justice is, as a certain kind of state without qualification, virtue.

The Just as the Fair and Equal: Divided into Distributive and Rectificatory Justice

2. But at all events what we are investigating is the justice which is a *part* of virtue; for there is a justice of this kind, as we maintain. Similarly it is with injustice in the particular sense that we are concerned.

That there is such a thing is indicated by the fact that while the man who exhibits in action the other forms of wickedness acts wrongly indeed, but not graspingly (for example, the man who throws away his shield through cowardice or speaks harshly through bad temper or fails to help a friend with money through meanness), when a man acts graspingly he often exhibits none of these vices—no, nor all together, but certainly wickedness of some kind (for we blame him) and injustice. There is, then, another kind of injustice which is a part of injustice in the wide sense, and a use of the word "unjust" which answers to a part of what is unjust in the wide sense of "contrary to the law." Again, if one man commits adultery for the sake of gain and makes money by it, while another does so at the bidding of appetite though he loses money and is penalized for it, the latter would be held to be self-indulgent rather than grasping, but the former is unjust, but not self-indulgent; evidently, therefore, he is unjust by reason of his making gain by his act. Again, all other unjust acts are ascribed invariably to some particular kind of wickedness, for example, adultery to self-indulgence, the desertion of a comrade in battle to cowardice, physical violence to anger; but if a man makes gain, his action is ascribed to no form of wickedness but injustice. Evidently, therefore, there is apart from injustice in the wide sense another, "particular," injustice which shares the name and nature of the first, because its definition falls within the same genus; for the significance of both consists in a relation to one's neighbour, but the one is concerned with honour or money or safety — or that which includes all these, if we had a single name for it — and its motive is the pleasure that arises from gain; while the other is concerned with all the objects with which the good man is concerned.

It is clear, then, that there is more than one kind of justice, and that there is one which is distinct from virtue entire; we must try to grasp its genus and differentia.

The unjust has been divided into the unlawful and the unfair, and the just into the lawful and the fair. To the unlawful answers the aforementioned sense of injustice. But since the unfair and the unlawful are not the same, but are different as a part is from its whole (for all that is unfair is unlawful, but not all that is unlawful is unfair), the unjust and injustice in the sense of the unfair are not the same as but different from the former kind, as part from whole; for injustice in this sense is a part of injustice in the wide sense, and similarly justice in the one sense of justice in the other. Therefore we must speak also about particular justice and particular injustice, and similarly about the just and the unjust. The justice, then, which answers to the whole of virtue, and the corresponding injustice, one being the exercise of virtue as a whole, and the other that of vice as a whole, towards one's neighbour, we may leave on one side. And how the meanings of "just" and "unjust" which answer to these are to be distinguished is evident; for practically the majority of the acts commanded by the law are those which are prescribed from the point of view of virtue taken as a whole; for the law bids us practise every virtue and forbids us to practise any vice. And the things that tend to produce virtue taken as a whole are those of the acts prescribed by the law which have been prescribed with a view to education for the common good. But with regard to the education of the individual as such, which makes him without qualification a good *man*, we must determine later whether this is the function of the political art or of another; for perhaps it is not the same to be a good man and a good citizen of any state taken at random.

Of particular justice and that which is just in the corresponding sense, (A) one kind is that which is manifested in distributions of honour or money or the other things that fall to be divided among those who have a share in the constitution (for in these it is possible for one man to have a share either unequal or equal to that of another), and (B) one is that which plays a rectifying part in transactions between man and man. Of this there are two divisions; of transactions (1) some are voluntary and (2) others involuntary — voluntary such transactions as sale, purchase, loan for consumption, pledging, loan for use, depositing, letting (they are called voluntary because the *origin* of these transactions is voluntary), while of the involuntary *(a)* some are clandestine, such as theft, adultery, poisoning, procuring, enticement of slaves, assassination, false witness, and *(b)* others are violent, such as assault, imprisonment, murder, robbery with violence, mutilation, abuse, insult.

Distributive Justice, in Accordance with Geometrical Proportion

3. (A) We have shown that both the unjust man and the unjust act are unfair or unequal; now it is clear that there is also an intermediate between the two unequals involved in either case. And this is the equal; for in any kind of action in which there is a more and a less there is also what is equal. If, then, the unjust is unequal, the just is equal, as all men suppose it to be, even apart from argument. And since the equal is intermediate, the just will be an intermediate. Now equality implies at least two things. The just, then, must be both intermediate and equal and relative (for example, for certain persons). And *qua* intermediate it must be between certain things (which are respectively greater and less); *qua* equal, it involves *two* things; *qua* just, it is for certain people. The just, therefore, involves at least four terms; for the persons for whom it is in fact just are two, and the things in which it is manifested, the objects distributed, are two. And the same equality will exist between the persons and between the things concerned; for as the latter — the things concerned — are related, so are the former; if they are not equal, they will not have what is equal, but this is the origin of quarrels and complaints — when either equals have and are awarded unequal shares, or unequals equal shares. Further, this is plain from the fact that awards should be "according to merit"; for all men agree that what is just in distribution must be according to merit in some sense, though they do not all specify the same sort of merit, but

democrats identify it with the status of freemen, supporters of oligarchy with wealth (or with noble birth), and supporters of aristocracy with excellence.

The just, then, is a species of the proportionate (proportion being not a property only of the kind of number which consists of abstract units, but of number in general). For proportion is equality of ratios, and involves four terms at least (that discrete proportion involves four terms is plain, but so does continuous proportion, for it uses one term as two and mentions it twice; for example, "as the line A is to the line B, so is the line B to the line C"; the line B, then, has been mentioned twice, so that if the line B be assumed twice, the proportional terms will be four); and the just, too, involves at least four terms, and the ratio between one pair is the same as that between the other pair; for there is a similar distinction between the persons and between the things. As the term A, then, is to B, so will C be to D, and therefore, *alternando*, as A is to C, B will be to D. Therefore also the whole is in the same ratio to the whole;[1] and this coupling the distribution effects, and, if the terms are so combined, effects justly. The conjunction, then, of the term A with C and of B with D is what is just in distribution,[2] and this species of the just is intermediate, and the unjust is what violates the proportion; for the proportional is intermediate, and the just is proportional. (Mathematicians call this kind of proportion geometrical; for it is in geometrical proportion that it follows that the whole is to the whole as either part is to the corresponding part.) This proportion is not continuous; for we cannot get a single term standing for a person and a thing.

This, then, is what the just is—the proportional; the unjust is what violates the proportion. Hence one term becomes too great, the other too small, as indeed happens in practice; for the man who acts unjustly has too much, and the man who is unjustly treated too little, of what is good. In the case of evil the reverse is true; for the lesser evil is reckoned a good in comparison with the greater evil, since the lesser evil is rather to be chosen than the greater, and what is worthy of choice is good, and what is worthier of choice a greater good.

This, then, is one species of the just.

Rectificatory Justice in Accordance with Arithmetical Progression

4. (B) The remaining one is the rectificatory, which arises in connexion with transactions both voluntary and involuntary. This form of the just has a different specific character from the former. For the justice which distributes common possessions is always in accordance with the kind of proportion mentioned above (for in the case also in which the distribution is made from the common funds of a partnership it will be according to the same ratio which the funds put into the business by the partners bear to one another); and the injustice opposed to this kind of justice is that which violates the proportion. But the justice in transactions between man and man is a sort of equality indeed, and the injustice a sort of inequality; not according to that kind of proportion, however, but according to arithmetical proportion. For it makes no difference whether a good man has defrauded a bad man or a bad man a good one, nor whether it is a good or a bad man that has committed adultery; the law looks only to the distinctive character of the injury, and treats the parties as equal, if one is in the wrong and the other is being wronged, and if one inflicted injury and the other has received it. Therefore, this kind of injustice being an inequality, the judge tries to equalize it; for in the case also in which one has received and the other has inflicted a wound, or one has slain and the other been slain, the suffering and the action have been unequally distributed; but the judge tries to equalize things by means of the penalty, taking away from the gain of the assailant. For the term "gain" is applied generally to such cases—even if it be not a term appropriate to certain cases, for example, to the person who inflicts a wound—and "loss" to the sufferer; at all events when the suffering has been estimated, the one is called loss and the other gain. Therefore the equal is intermediate between the greater and the less, but the gain and the loss are respectively greater and less in contrary ways; more of the good and less of the evil are gain, and the contrary is loss; intermediate between them is, as we saw, the equal, which we say is just; therefore corrective justice will be the intermediate between loss and gain. This is why, when people dispute, they take refuge in the judge; and to go to

the judge is to go to justice; for the nature of the judge is to be a sort of animate justice; and they seek the judge as an intermediate, and in some states they call judges mediators, on the assumption that if they get what is intermediate they will get what is just. The just, then, is an intermediate, since the judge is so. Now the judge restores equality; it is as though there were a line divided into unequal parts, and he took away that by which the greater segment exceeds the half, and added it to the smaller segment. And when the whole has been equally divided, then they say they have "their own"—that is, when they have got what is equal. The equal is intermediate between the greater and the lesser line according to arithmetical proportion. It is for this reason also that it is called just δίκαιον, because it is a division into two equal parts δίχα, just as if one were to call it διχαιον; and the judge δικαστής is one who bisects διχαστής. For when something is subtracted from one of two equals and added to the other, the other is in excess by these two; since if what was taken from the one had not been added to the other, the latter would have been in excess by one only. It therefore exceeds the intermediate by one, and the intermediate exceeds by one that from which something was taken. By this, then, we shall recognize both what we must subtract from that which has more, and what we must add to that which has less; we must add to the latter that by which the intermediate exceeds it, and subtract from the greatest that by which it exceeds the intermediate. Let the lines AA', BB', CC' be equal to one another; from the line AA' let the segment AE have been subtracted, and to the line CC' let the segment CD' have been added, so that the whole line DCC' exceeds the line EA' by the segment CD and the segment CF; therefore it exceeds the line BB' by the segment CD.

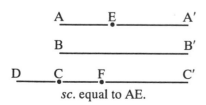

sc. equal to AE.

These names, both loss and gain, have come from voluntary exchange; for to have more than

one's own is called gaining, and to have less than one's original share is called losing, for example, in buying and selling and in all other matters in which the law has left people free to make their own terms; but when they get neither more nor less but just what belongs to themselves, they say that they have their own and that they neither lose nor gain.

Therefore the just is intermediate between a sort of gain and a sort of loss, to wit, those which are involuntary;[3] it consists in having an equal amount before and after the transaction.

Justice in Exchange, Reciprocity in Accordance with Proportion

5. Some think that *reciprocity* is without qualification just, as the Pythagoreans said; for they defined justice without qualification as reciprocity. Now "reciprocity" fits neither distributive nor rectificatory justice—yet people *want* even the justice of Rhadamanthus to mean this:

> Should a man suffer what he did, right justice would be done.

—for in many cases reciprocity and rectificatory justice are not in accord; for example, (1) if an official has inflicted a wound, he should not be wounded in return, and if someone has wounded an official, he ought not to be wounded only but punished in addition. Further (2) there is a great difference between a voluntary and an involuntary act. But in associations for exchange this sort of justice does hold men together—reciprocity in accordance with a proportion and not on the basis of precisely equal return. For it is by proportionate requital that the city holds together. Men seek to return either evil for evil—and if they cannot do so, think their position mere slavery—or good for good—and if they cannot do so there is no exchange, but it is by exchange that they hold together. This is why they give a prominent place to the temple of the Graces—to promote the requital of services; for this is characteristic of grace—we should serve in return one who has shown grace to us, and should another time take the initiative in showing it.

Now proportionate return is secured by cross-conjunction.[4] Let A be a builder, B a shoemaker, C a house, D a shoe. The builder, then, must get from the shoemaker the latter's work, and must himself give him in return his own. If, then, first there is proportionate equality of goods, and then reciprocal action takes place, the result we mention will be effected. If not, the bargain is not equal, and does not hold; for there is nothing to prevent the work of the one being better than that of the other; they must therefore be equated. (And this is true of the other arts also; for they would have been destroyed if what the patient suffered had not been just what the agent did, and of the same amount and kind.) For it is not two doctors that associate for exchange, but a doctor and a farmer, or in general people who are different and unequal; but these must be equated. This is why all things that are exchanged must be somehow comparable. It is for this end that money has been introduced, and it becomes in a sense an intermediate; for it measures all things, and therefore the excess and the defect — how many shoes are equal to a house or to a given amount of food. The number of shoes exchanged for a house [or for a given amount of food] must therefore correspond to the ratio of builder to shoemaker. For if this be not so, there will be no exchange and no intercourse. And this proportion will not be effected unless the goods are somehow equal. All goods must therefore be measured by some one thing, as we said before. Now this unit is in truth demand, which holds all things together (for if men did not need one another's goods at all, or did not need them equally, there would be either no exchange or not the same exchange); but money has become by convention a sort of representative of demand; and this is why it has the name "money" (νόμισμα) — because it exists not by nature but by law (νόμος) and it is in our power to change it and make it useless. There will, then, be reciprocity when the terms have been equated so that as farmer is to shoemaker, the amount of the shoemaker's work is to that of the farmer's work for which it exchanges. But we must not bring them into a figure of proportion when they have already exchanged (otherwise one extreme will have both excesses), but when they still have their own goods. Thus they are equals and associates just because this equality can be effected in their case. Let A be a farmer, C food, B a shoemaker, D his product equated to C. If it had not been possible for reciprocity to be thus effected, there would have been no association of the parties.

That demand holds things together as a single unit is shown by the fact that when men do not need one another, that is, when neither needs the other or one does not need the other, they do not exchange, as we do when someone wants what one has oneself, for example, when people permit the exportation of corn in exchange for wine. This equation therefore must be established. And for the future exchange — that if we do not need a thing now we shall have it if ever we do need it — money is as it were our surety; for it must be possible for us to get what we want by bringing the money. Now the same thing happens to money itself as to goods — it is not always worth the same; yet it tends to be steadier. This is why all goods must have a price set on them for then there will always be exchange, and if so, association of man with man. Money, then, acting as a measure, makes goods commensurate and equates them; for neither would there have been association if there were not exchange, nor exchange if there were not equality, nor equality if there were not commensurability. Now in truth it is impossible that things differing so much should become commensurate, but with reference to demand they may become so sufficiently. There must, then, be a unit, and that fixed by agreement (for which reason it is called money); for it is this that makes all things commensurate, since all things are measured by money. Let A be a house, B ten minae, C a bed. A is half of B, if the house is worth five minae or equal to them; the bed, C, is a tenth of B; it is plain, then, how many beds are equal to a house, to wit, five. That exchange took place thus before there was money is plain; for it makes no difference whether it is five beds that exchange for a house, or the money value of five beds.

We have now defined the unjust and the just. These having been marked off from each other, it is plain that just action is intermediate between acting unjustly and being unjustly treated; for the one is to have too much and the other to have too little. Justice is a kind of mean, but not in the same way as the other virtues, but because it relates to an intermediate amount, while injustice relates to the extremes. And justice is that in virtue of which the just man is said to be a doer, by choice, of that which is just, and one who will distribute either between himself and another or between two others not so as to give more of what is desirable to himself and less to his neighbour (and conversely with what is harmful), but so as to give what is equal in accordance with proportion; and similarly in distributing between two other persons. Injustice on the other hand is similarly related to the unjust, which is excess and defect, contrary to proportion, of the useful or hurtful. For which reason injustice is excess and defect, to wit, because it is productive of excess and defect — in one's own case excess of what is in its own nature useful and defect of what is hurtful, while in the case of others it is a whole like what it is in one's own case, but proportion may be violated in either direction. In the unjust act to have too little is to be unjustly treated; to have too much is to act unjustly.

Let this be taken as our account of the nature of justice and injustice, and similarly of the just and the unjust in general.

Political Justice and Analogous Kinds of Justice

6. Since acting unjustly does not necessarily imply being unjust, we must ask what sort of unjust acts imply that the doer is unjust with respect to each type of injustice, for example, a thief, an adulterer, or a brigand. Surely the answer does not turn on the difference between these types. For a man might even lie with a woman knowing who she was, but the origin of his act might be not deliberate choice but passion. He acts unjustly, then, but is not unjust; for example, a man is not a thief, yet he stole, nor an adulterer, yet he committed adultery; and similarly in all other cases.

Now we have previously stated how the reciprocal is related to the just, but we must not forget that what we are looking for is not only what is just without qualification but also political justice. This is found among men who share their life with a view to self-sufficiency, men who are free and either proportionately or arithmetically equal, so that between those who do not fulfil this condition there is no political justice but justice in a special sense and by analogy. For justice exists only between men whose mutual relations are governed by law; and law exists for men between whom there is injustice; for legal justice is the discrimination of the just and the unjust. And between men between whom injustice is done there is also unjust action (though there is not injustice

between all between whom there is unjust action), and this is assigning too much to oneself of things good in themselves and too little of things evil in themselves. This is why we do not allow a *man* to rule, but *rational principle*, because a man behaves thus in his own interests and becomes a tyrant. The magistrate on the other hand is the guardian of justice, and, if of justice, then of equality also. And since he is assumed to have no more than his share, if he is just (for he does not assign to himself more of what is good in itself, unless such a share is proportional to his merits — so that it is for others that he labours, and it is for this reason that men, as we stated previously, say that justice is "another's good"), therefore a reward must be given him, and this is honour and privilege; but those for whom such things are not enough become tyrants.

The justice of a master and that of a father are not the same as the justice of citizens, though they are like it; for there can be no injustice in the unqualified sense towards things that are one's own, but a man's chattel,[5] and his child until it reaches a certain age and sets up for itself, are as it were part of himself, and no one chooses to hurt himself (for which reason there can be no injustice towards oneself). Therefore the justice or injustice of citizens is not manifested in these relations; for it was as we saw according to law, and between people naturally subject to law, and these as we saw are people who have an equal share in ruling and being ruled. Hence justice can more truly be manifested towards a wife than towards children and chattels, for the former is household justice; but even this is different from political justice.

Natural and Legal Justice

7. Of political justice part is natural, part legal, — natural, that which everywhere has the same force and does not exist by people's thinking this or that; legal, that which is originally indifferent, but when it has been laid down is not indifferent, for example, that a prisoner's ransom shall be a mina, or that a goat and not two sheep shall be sacrificed, and again all the laws that are passed for particular cases, for example, that sacrifice shall be made in honour of Brasidas, and the provisions of decrees. Now some think that all justice is of this sort, because that which is by nature is

unchangeable and has everywhere the same force (as fire burns both here and in Persia), while they see change in the things recognized as just. This, however, is not true in this unqualified way, but is true in a sense; or rather, with the gods it is perhaps not true at all, while with us there is something that is just even by nature, yet all of it is changeable; but still some is by nature, some not by nature. It is evident which sort of thing, among things capable of being otherwise, is by nature; and which is not but is legal and conventional, assuming that both are equally changeable. And in all other things the same distinction will apply; by nature the right hand is stronger, yet it is possible that all men should come to be ambidextrous. The things which are just by virtue of convention and expediency are like measures; for wine and corn measures are not everywhere equal, but larger in wholesale and smaller in retail markets. Similarly, the things which are just not by nature but by human enactment are not everywhere the same, since constitutions also are not the same, though there is but one which is everywhere by nature the best.

Of things just and lawful each is related as the universal to its particulars; for the things that are done are many, but of *them* each is one, since it is universal.

There is a difference between the act of injustice and what is unjust, and between the act of justice and what is just; for a thing is unjust by nature or by enactment; and this very thing, when it has been done, is an act of injustice, but before it is done is not yet that but is unjust. So, too, with an act of justice (though the general term is rather "just action," and "act of justice" is applied to the correction of the act of injustice).

Each of these must later be examined separately with regard to the nature and number of its species and the nature of the things with which it is concerned.

Justice: Its Inner Nature as Involving Choice

The Scale of Degrees of Wrongdoing

8. Acts just and unjust being as we have described them, a man acts unjustly or justly whenever he does such acts voluntarily; when involuntarily, he acts neither unjustly nor justly except in an incidental way; for he does things which happen to be just or unjust. Whether an act is or is not one of injustice (or of justice) is determined by its voluntariness or involuntariness; for when it is voluntary it is blamed, and at the same time is then an act of injustice; so that there will be things that are unjust but not yet acts of injustice, if voluntariness be not present as well. By the voluntary I mean, as has been said before, any of the things in a man's own power which he does with knowledge, that is, not in ignorance either of the person acted on or of the instrument used or of the end that will be attained (for example, whom he is striking, with what, and to what end), each such act being done not incidentally nor under compulsion (for example, if A takes B's hand and therewith strikes C, B does not act voluntarily; for the act was not in his own power). The person struck may be the striker's father, and the striker may know that it is a man or one of the persons present, but not know that it is his father; a similar distinction may be made in the case of the end, and with regard to the whole action. Therefore that which is done in ignorance, or though not done in ignorance is not in the agent's power, or is done under compulsion, is involuntary (for many natural processes, even, we knowingly both perform and experience, none of which is either voluntary or involuntary; for example, growing old or dying). But in the case of unjust and just acts alike the injustice or justice may be only incidental; for a man might return a deposit unwillingly and from fear, and then he must not be said either to do what is just or to act justly, except in an incidental way. Similarly the man who under compulsion and unwillingly fails to return the deposit must be said to act unjustly, and to do what is unjust, only incidentally. Of voluntary acts we do some by choice, others not by choice; by choice those which we do after deliberation, not by choice those which we do without previous deliberation. Thus there are three kinds of injury in transactions between man and man; those done in ignorance are mistakes when the person acted on, the act, the instrument, or the end that will be attained is other than the agent supposed; the agent thought either that he was not hitting any one or that he was not hitting with this missile or not hitting this person or to this end, but a result followed other than that which he though likely (for example, he threw

not with intent to wound but only to prick), or the person hit or the missile was other than he supposed. Now when (1) the injury takes place contrary to reasonable expectation, it is *misadventure*. When (2) it is not contrary to reasonable expectation, but does not imply vice, it is a *mistake* (for a man makes a mistake when the fault originates in him, but is the victim of accident when the origin lies outside him). When (3) he acts with knowledge but not after deliberation, it is an *act of injustice*—for example, the acts due to anger or to other passions necessary or natural to man; for when men do such harmful and mistaken acts they act unjustly, and the acts are acts of injustice, but this does not imply that the doers are unjust or wicked; for the injury is not due to vice. But when (4) a man acts from choice, he is an *unjust man* and a vicious man.

Hence acts proceeding from anger are rightly judged not to be done of malice aforethought; for it is not the man who acts in anger but he who enraged him that starts the mischief. Again, the matter in dispute is not whether the thing happened or not, but its justice; for it is apparent injustice that occasions rage. For they do not dispute about the occurrence of the act—as in commercial transactions where one of the two parties *must* be vicious[6]—unless they do so owing to forgetfulness; but, agreeing about the fact, they dispute on which side justice lies (whereas a man who has deliberately injured another cannot help knowing that he has done so), so that one thinks he is being treated unjustly and the other disagrees.

But if a man harms another by choice, he acts unjustly; and *these* are the acts of injustice which imply that the doer is an unjust man, provided that the act violates proportion or equality. Similarly, a man *is just* when he acts justly by choice; but he *acts justly* if he merely acts voluntarily.

Of involuntary acts some are excusable, others not. For the mistakes which men make not only in ignorance but also from ignorance are excusable, while those which men do not from ignorance but (though they do them *in* ignorance) owing to a passion which is neither natural nor such as man is liable to, are not excusable.

Can a man be voluntarily treated unjustly? Is it the distributor or the recipient that is guilty of injustice in distribution? Justice is not so easy as it might seem, because it is not a way of acting but an inner disposition.

9. Assuming that we have sufficiently defined the suffering and doing of injustice, it may be asked (1) whether the truth is expressed in Euripides' paradoxical words:

"I slew my mother, that's my tale in brief."
"Were you both willing, or unwilling both?"

Is it truly possible to be willingly treated unjustly, or is all suffering of injustice on the contrary involuntary, as all unjust action is voluntary? And is all suffering of injustice of the latter kind or else all of the former, or is it sometimes voluntary, sometimes involuntary? So, too, with the case of being justly treated; all just action is voluntary, so that it is reasonable that there should be a similar opposition in either case—that both being unjustly and being justly treated should be either alike voluntary or alike involuntary. But it would be thought paradoxical even in the case of being justly treated, if it were always voluntary; for some are unwillingly treated justly. (2) One might raise this question also, whether everyone who has suffered what is unjust is being unjustly treated, or on the other hand it is with suffering as with acting. In action and in passivity alike it is possible for justice to be done incidentally, and similarly (it is plain) injustice; for to do what is unjust is not the same as to act unjustly, nor to suffer what is unjust as to be treated unjustly, and similarly in the case of acting justly and being justly treated; for it is impossible to be unjustly treated if the other does not act unjustly, or justly treated unless he acts justly. Now if to act unjustly is simply to harm someone voluntarily, and "voluntarily" means "knowing the person acted on, the instrument, and the manner of one's acting," and the incontinent man voluntarily harms himself, not only will he voluntarily be unjustly treated but it will be possible to treat oneself unjustly. (This also is one of the questions in doubt, whether a man can treat himself unjustly.) Again, a man may voluntarily, owing to incontinence, be harmed by another who acts voluntarily, so that it would be possible to be voluntarily treated unjustly. Or is our definition incorrect; must we to "harming another, with knowledge both of the person acted on, of the instrument, and of the manner" add "contrary to the wish of the person acted on?" Then a man may be voluntarily harmed and voluntarily suffer what is unjust, but no one is voluntarily treated unjustly; for no one wishes to be unjustly treated, not even the incontinent man. He acts contrary to his wish; for no one *wishes* for what he does not think to be good, but the incontinent man does *do* things that he does not think he ought to do. Again, one who gives what is his own, as Homer says Glaucus gave Diomede

> Armour of gold for brazen, the price of a hundred beeves for nine,

is not unjustly treated; for though to give is in his power, to be unjustly treated is not, but there must be someone to treat him unjustly. It is plain, then, that being unjustly treated is not voluntary.

Of the questions we intended to discuss two still remain for discussion; (3) whether it is the man who has assigned to another more than his share that acts unjustly, or he who has the excessive share, and (4) whether it is possible to treat oneself unjustly. The questions are connected; for if the former alternative is possible and the distributor acts unjustly and not the man who has the excessive share, then if a man assigns more to another than to himself, knowingly and voluntarily, he treats himself unjustly; which is what modest people seem to do, since the virtuous man tends to take less than his share. Or does this statement too need qualification? For (*a*) he perhaps gets more than his share of some other good, for example, of honour or of intrinsic nobility. (*b*) The question is solved by applying the distinction we applied to unjust action, for he suffers nothing contrary to his own wish, so that he is not unjustly treated so far as this goes, but at most only suffers harm.

It is plain too that the distributor acts unjustly, but not always the man who has the excessive share; for it is not he to whom injustice is done that acts unjustly, but he to whom it appertains to do the unjust act voluntarily, that is, the person in whom lies the origin of the action, and this lies in the distributor, not in the receiver. Again, since the word "do" is ambiguous, and there is a sense in which lifeless things, or a hand, or a servant who obeys an order, may be said to slay, he who gets an excessive share does not act unjustly, though he "does" what is unjust.

Again, if the distributor gave his judgement in ignorance, he does not act unjustly in respect of legal justice, and his judgement is not unjust in this sense, but in a sense it *is* unjust (for legal justice and primordial justice are different); but if with the knowledge he judged unjustly, he is himself aiming at an excessive share either of gratitude or of revenge. As much, then, as if he were to share in the plunder, the man who has judged unjustly for these reasons has got too much; the fact that what he gets is different from what he distributes makes no difference, for even if he awards land with a view to sharing in the plunder he gets not land but money.

Men think that acting unjustly is in their power, and therefore that being just is easy. But it is not; to lie with one's neighbour's wife, to wound another, to deliver a bribe, is easy and in our power, but to do these things as a result of a certain state of character is neither easy nor in our power. Similarly to know what is just and what is unjust requires, men think, no great wisdom, because it is not hard to understand the matters dealt with by the laws (though these are not the things that are just, except incidentally); but how actions must be done and distributions effected in order to be just, to know *this* is a greater achievement than knowing what is good for the health; though even there, while it is easy to know that honey, wine, hellebore, cautery, and the use of the knife are so, to know how, to whom, and when these should be applied with a view to producing health, is no less an achievement than that of being a physician. Again, for this very reason[7] men think that acting unjustly is characteristic of the just man no less than of the unjust, because he would be not less but even more capable of doing each of these unjust acts, for he could lie with a woman or wound a neighbour; and the brave man could throw away his shield and turn to flight in this direction or in that. But to play the coward or to act unjustly consists not in doing these things, except incidentally, but in doing them as the result of a certain state of character, just as to practice medicine and healing consists not in applying or not applying the knife, in using or not using medicines, but in doing so in a certain way.

Just acts occur between people who participate in things good in themselves and can have too much or too little of them; for some beings (for example, presumably the gods) cannot have too much of them, and to others, those who are incurably bad, not even the smallest share in them is beneficial but all such goods are harmful, while to others they are beneficial up to a point; therefore justice is essentially something human.

Equity, A Corrective of Legal Justice

10. Our next subject is equity and the equitable and their respective relations to justice and the just. For on examination they appear to be neither absolutely the same nor generically different; and while we sometimes praise what is equitable and the equitable man, at other times, when we reason it out, it seems strange if the equitable, being something different from the just, is yet praiseworthy; for either the just or the equitable is not good, if they are different; or, if both are good, they are the same.

These, then, are pretty much the considerations that give rise to the problem about the equitable; they are all in a sense correct and not opposed to one another; for the equitable, though it is better than one kind of justice, yet is just, and it is not as being a different class of thing that it is better than the just. The same thing, then, is just and equitable, and while both are good the equitable is superior. What creates the problem is that the equitable is just, but not the legally just but a correction of legal justice. The reason is that all law is universal but about some things It is not possible to make a universal statement which shall be correct. In those cases, then, in which it is necessary to speak universally, but not possible to do so correctly, the law takes the usual case, though it is not ignorant of the possibility of error. And it is none the less correct; for the error is not in the law nor in the legislator but in the nature of the thing, since the matter of practical affairs is of this kind from the start. When the law speaks universally, then, and a case arises on it which is not covered by the universal statement, then it is right, where the legislator fails us and has erred by over-simplicity, to correct the omission—to say what the legislator himself would have said had he been present, and would have put into his law if he had known. Hence the equitable is just, and better than one kind of justice—not better than absolute justice, but better than the error that arises from the absoluteness of the statement. And this is the

nature of the equitable, a correction of law where it is defective owing to its universality. In fact this is the reason why all things are not determined by law, to wit, that about some things it is impossible to lay down a law, so that a decree is needed. For when the thing is indefinite the rule also is indefinite, like the leaden rule used in making the Lesbian moulding; the rule adapts itself to the shape of the stone and is not rigid, and so too the decree is adapted to the facts.

It is plain, then, what the equitable is, and that it is just and is better than one kind of justice. It is evident also from this who the equitable man is; the man who chooses and does such acts, and is no stickler for his rights in a bad sense but tends to take less than his share though he has the law on his side, is equitable, and this state of character is equity, which is a sort of justice and not a different state of character.

Can a Man Treat Himself Unjustly?

11. Whether a man can treat himself unjustly or not, is evident from what has been said. For *(a)* one class of just acts are those acts in accordance with any virtue which are prescribed by the law, for example, the law does not expressly permit suicide, and what it does not expressly permit it forbids. Again, when a man in violation of the law harms another (otherwise than in retaliation) voluntarily, he acts unjustly, and a voluntary agent is one who knows both the person he is affecting by his action and the instrument he is using; and he who through anger voluntarily stabs himself does this contrary to the right rule of life, and this the law does not allow; therefore he is acting unjustly. But towards whom? Surely towards the state, not towards himself. For he suffers voluntarily, but no one is voluntarily treated unjustly. This is also the reason why the state punishes; a certain loss of civil rights attaches to the man who destroys himself, on the ground that he is treating the state unjustly.

Further, *(b)* in that sense of "acting unjustly" in which the man who "acts unjustly" is unjust only and not bad all round, it is not possible to treat oneself unjustly (this is different from the former sense; the unjust man in one sense of the term is wicked in a particularized way just as the coward is, not in the sense of being wicked all round, so that his "unjust act" does not manifest wickedness in general). For (i) that would imply the possibility of the same thing's having been subtracted from and added to the same thing at the same time; but this is impossible — the just and the unjust always involve more than one person. Further; (ii) unjust action is voluntary and done by choice, and *takes the initiative* (for the man who because he has suffered does the same in return is not thought to act unjustly); but if a man harms himself he suffers and does the same things *at the same time.* Further, (iii) if a man could treat himself unjustly, he could be voluntarily treated unjustly. Besides, (iv) no one acts unjustly without committing particular acts of injustice; but no one can commit adultery with his own wife or housebreaking on his own house or theft on his own property.

In general, the question "Can a man treat himself unjustly?" is solved also by the distinction we applied to the question "Can a man be voluntarily treated unjustly?"

(It is evident too that both are bad, being unjustly treated and acting unjustly; for the one means having less and the other having more than the intermediate amount, which plays the part here that the healthy does in the medical art, and the good condition does in the art of bodily training. But still acting unjustly is the worse, for it involves vice and is blameworthy — involves vice which is either of the complete and unqualified kind or almost so (we must admit the latter alternative, because not all voluntary unjust action implies injustice as a state of character), while being unjustly treated does not involve vice and injustice in oneself. In itself, then, being unjustly treated is less bad, but there is nothing to prevent its being incidentally a greater evil. But theory cares nothing for this; it calls pleurisy a more serious mischief than a stumble; yet the latter may become incidentally the more serious, if the fall due to it leads to your being taken prisoner or put to death by the enemy.)

Metaphorically and in virtue of a certain resemblance there is a justice, not indeed between a man and himself, but between certain parts of him; yet not every kind of justice but that of master and servant or that of husband and wife. For these are the ratios in which the part of the soul that has a rational principle stands to the irrational part; and it is with a view to these parts that people also think a man can be unjust to himself, to wit, because these parts are liable to suffer something contrary to their respective desires; there is therefore thought to be a mutual justice between them as between ruler and ruled.

Let this be taken as our account of justice and the other, that is, the other moral, virtues.

NOTES

1. Person A + thing C to person B + thing D.
2. The problem of distributive justice is to divide the distributable honour or reward into parts which are to one another as are the merits of the persons who are to participate. If

> A (first person) : B (second person) :: C (first portion) : D (second portion),
> then (*alternando*) A : C :: B : D,
> and therefore (*componendo*) A + C : B + D :: A : B.

In other words the position established answers to the relative merits of the parties.
3. that is, for the loser.
4. The working of "proportionate reciprocity" is not very clearly described by Aristotle, but seems to be as follows. A and B are workers in different trades, and will normally be of different degrees of "worth." Their products, therefore, will also have unequal worth, that is (though Aristotle does not expressly reduce the question to one of time) if A = nB, C (what A makes, say, in an hour) will be worth n times as much as D (what B makes in an hour). A fair exchange will then take place if A gets nD and B gets 1 C; that is, if A gives what it takes him an hour to make, in exchange for what it takes B n hours to make.
5. that is, his slave.
6. The plaintiff, if he brings a false accusation; the defendant, if he denies a true one.
7. that is, that stated in 11.4 f., that acting unjustly is in our own power.

Notes and Questions

JOHN RAWLS, "Justice as Fairness"

1. John Rawls claims that the fundamental idea of justice is fairness. He also proposes that utilitarian theory cannot handle this idea but that a version of the social contract theory, properly formulated, can do so. After giving some preliminary qualifications, he defends his theory of justice by discussing the two principles that specify it. What are these principles?

2. The first principle requires justification for any departure from equal liberty, but it also guarantees the most extensive liberty compatible with like liberty for all. How extensive would such protection be? Would it be like Mill's position? Do you think justice requires maximum freedom?

3. The second principle tells how to rebut the presumption of equal liberty established by the first principle: It tells when inequality is allowed. What two requirements must be met to justify inequality? Why are they important? Would you agree to an unequal practice if it met these two requirements? Would you require something more or something different? If so, what?

4. Rawls suggests that these principles might be derived from reason or intuition, but since this source would not be helpful in understanding the basis of the concept of justice, he formulates a version of the social contract as a foundation for the two principles of justice. There are two important features of this social contract. The first is the character and situation of the parties, which Rawls intends to reflect the conditions under which questions of justice arise. Describe the character and situation of the parties. Do they reflect the conditions relevant to questions of justice? The second significant feature of Rawls's social contract is the procedure for arriving at agreement, which is intended to represent the constraints of morality. What is this procedure? How does it function, and in what way does it represent the constraints of morality?

5. Rawls believes that by showing that his two principles are derived from his formulation of the social contract, he has demonstrated that the concept of fairness is fundamental to justice. What does he mean by fairness? What is the connection between fairness and freedom? Why does a *prima facie* duty of fair play (that is, an obligation to follow the rules) arise in practices that are fair? Does this duty require actual consent, according to Rawls? How does the duty of fair play apply to just practices?

6. What is the difference between the principles of justice and the principle of utility (that is, act so as to maximize the greatest happiness for the greatest number of people)? Why can't the principle of utility accommodate the notion of fairness, according to Rawls? Why is that a significant failure?

Justice as Fairness

JOHN RAWLS

I

It might seem at first sight that the concepts of justice and fairness are the same, and that there is no reason to distinguish them, or to say that one is more fundamental than the other. I think that this impression is mistaken. In this paper I wish to show that the fundamental idea in the concept of justice is fairness; and I wish to offer an analysis of the concept of justice from this point of view. To bring out the force of this claim, and the analysis based upon it, I shall then argue that it is this aspect of justice for which utilitarianism, in its classical form, is unable to account, but which is expressed, even if misleadingly, by the idea of the social contract.

To start with I shall develop a particular conception of justice by stating and commenting upon two principles which specify it, and by considering the circumstances and conditions under which they may be thought to arise. The principles defining this conception, and the conception itself, are, of course, familiar. It may be possible, however, by using the notion of fairness as a framework, to assemble and to look at them in a new way. Before stating this conception, however, the following preliminary matters should be kept in mind.

Throughout I consider justice only as a virtue of social institutions, or what I shall call practices.[1] The principles of justice are regarded as formulating restrictions as to how practices may define positions and offices, and assign thereto powers and liabilities, rights, and duties. Justice as a virtue of particular actions or of persons I do not take up at all. It is important to distinguish these various subjects of justice, since the meaning of the concept varies according to whether it is applied to practices, particular actions, or persons. These meanings are, indeed, connected, but they are not identical. I shall confine my discussion to the sense of justice as applied to practices, since this sense is the basic one. Once it is understood, the other senses should go quite easily.

Justice is to be understood in its customary sense as representing but *one* of the many virtues of social institutions, for these may be antiquated, inefficient, degrading, or any number of other things, without being unjust. Justice is not to be confused with an all-inclusive vision of a good society; it is only one part of any such conception. It is important, for example, to distinguish that sense of equality which is an aspect of the concept of justice from that sense of equality which belongs to a more comprehensive social ideal. There may well be inequalities which one concedes are just, or at least not unjust, but which, nevertheless, one wishes, on other grounds, to do away with. I shall focus attention, then, on the usual sense of justice in which it is essentially the elimination of arbitrary distinctions and the establishment, within the structure of a practice, of a proper balance between competing claims.

Finally, there is no need to consider the principles discussed below as *the* principles of justice. For the moment it is sufficient that they are typical of a family of principles normally associated with the concept of justice. The way in which the principles of this family resemble one another, as shown by the background against which they may be thought to arise, will be made clear by the whole of the subsequent argument.

II

The conception of justice which I want to develop may be stated in the form of two principles as follows: First, each person participating in a practice, or affected by it, has an equal right to the most extensive liberty compatible with a like liberty for all; and second, inequalities are arbitrary unless it is reasonable to expect that they will work out for everyone's advantage, and provided the positions and offices to which they attach, or from which they may be gained, are open to all. These principles express justice as a complex of three ideas: liberty, equality, and reward for services contributing to the common good.[2]

The term "person" is to be construed variously depending on the circumstances. On some occasions it will mean human individuals, but in others it may refer to nations, provinces, business firms, churches, teams, and so on. The principles of justice apply in all these instances, although there is a certain logical priority to the case of human individuals. As I shall use the term "person," it will be ambiguous in the manner indicated.

The first principle holds, of course, only if other things are equal: That is, while there must always be a justification for departing from the initial position of equal liberty (which is defined by the pattern of rights and duties, powers and liabilities, established by a practice), and the burden of proof is placed on him who would depart from it, nevertheless, there can be, and often there is, a justification for doing so. Now, that similar particular cases, as defined by a practice, should be treated similarly as they arise, is part of the very concept of a practice; it is involved in the notion of an activity in accordance with rules.[3] The first principle expresses an analogous conception, but as applied to the structure of practices themselves. It holds, for example, that there is a presumption against the distinctions and classifications made by legal systems and other practices to the extent that they infringe on the original and equal liberty of the persons participating them. The second principle defines how this presumption may be rebutted.

It might be argued at this point that justice requires only an equal liberty. If, however, a greater liberty were possible for all without loss or conflict, then it would be irrational to settle on a lesser liberty. There is no reason for circumscribing rights unless their exercise would be incompatible, or would render the practice defining them less effective. Therefore no serious distortion of the concept of justice is likely to follow from including within it the concept of the greatest equal liberty.

The second principle defines what sorts of inequalities are permissible; it specifies how the presumption laid down by the first principle may be put aside. Now by inequalities it is best to understand not *any* differences between offices and positions, but differences in the benefits and burdens attached to them either directly or indirectly, such as prestige and wealth, or liability to taxation and compulsory services. Players in a game do not protest against there being different positions, such as batter, pitcher, catcher, and the like, nor to there being various privileges and powers as specified by the rules; nor do the citizens of a country object to there being the different offices of government such as president, senator, governor, judge, and so on, each with its special rights and duties. It is not differences of this kind that are normally thought of as inequalities, but differences in the resulting distribution established by a practice, or made possible by it, of the things men strive to attain or avoid. Thus they may complain about the pattern of honors and rewards set up by a practice (for example, the privileges and salaries of government officials) or they may object to the distribution of power and wealth which results from the various ways in which men avail themselves of the opportunities allowed by it (for example, the concentration of wealth which may develop in a free price system allowing large entrepreneurial or speculative gains).

It should be noted that the second principle holds that an inequality is allowed only if there is

reason to believe that the practice with the inequality, or resulting in it, will work for the advantage of *every* party engaging in it. Here it is important to stress that *every* party must gain from the inequality. Since the principle applies to practices, it implies that the representative man in every office or position defined by a practice, when he views it as a going concern, must find it reasonable to prefer his condition and prospects with the inequality to what they would be under the practice without it. The principle excludes, therefore, the justification of inequalities on the grounds that the disadvantages of those in one position are outweighed by the greater advantages of those in another position. This rather simple restriction is the main modification I wish to make in the utilitarian principle as usually understood. When coupled with the notion of a practice, it is a restriction of consequence,[4] and one which some utilitarians, for example, Hume and Mill, have used in their discussions of justice without realizing apparently its significance, or at least without calling attention to it.[5] Why it is a significant modification of principle, changing one's conception of justice entirely, the whole of my argument will show.

Further, it is also necessary that the various offices to which special benefits or burdens attach are open to all. It may be, for example, to the common advantage, as just defined, to attach special benefits to certain offices. Perhaps by doing so the requisite talent can be attracted to them and encouraged to give its best efforts. But any offices having special benefits must be won in a fair competition in which contestants are judged on their merits. If some offices were not open, those excluded would normally be justified in feeling unjustly treated, even if they benefited from the greater efforts of those who were allowed to compete for them. Now if one can assume that offices are open, it is necessary only to consider the design of practices themselves and how they jointly, as a system, work together. It will be a mistake to focus attention on the varying relative positions of particular persons, who may be known to us by their proper names, and to require that each such change, as a once for all transaction viewed in isolation, must be in itself just. It is the system of practices which is to be judged, and judged from a general point of view: Unless one is prepared to criticize it from the standpoint of a representative man holding some particular office, one has no complaint against it.

III

Given these principles one might try to derive them from a priori principles of reason, or claim that they were known by intuition. These are familiar enough steps and, at least in the case of the first principle, might be made with some success. Usually, however, such arguments, made at this point, are unconvincing. They are not likely to lead to an understanding of the basis of the principles of justice, not at least as principles of justice. I wish, therefore, to look at the principles in a different way.

Imagine a society of persons amongst whom a certain system of practices is *already* well established. Now suppose that by and large they are mutually self-interested; their allegiance to their established practices is normally founded on the prospect of self-advantage. One need not assume that, in all senses of the term "person," the persons in this society are mutually self-interested. If the characterization as mutually self-interested applies when the line of division is the family, it may still be true that members of families are bound by ties of sentiment and affection and willingly acknowledge duties in contradiction to self-interest. Mutual self-interestedness in the relations between families, nations, churches, and the like, is commonly associated with intense loyalty and devotion on the part of individual members. Therefore, one can form a more realistic conception of this society if one thinks of it as consisting of mutually self-interested families, or some other association. Further, it is not necessary to suppose that these persons are mutually self-interested under all circumstances, but only in the usual situations in which they participate in their common practices.

Now suppose also that these persons are rational: they know their own interests more or less accurately; they are capable to tracing out the likely consequences of adopting one practice rather than another; they are capable of adhering to a course of action once they have decided upon it; they can resist present temptations and the enticements of immediate gain; and the bare knowledge or perception of the difference between their condition and that of others is not, within certain limits and in itself, a source of great dissatisfaction. Only the last point adds anything to the usual definition of rationality. This definition should allow, I think, for the idea that a rational man would not be greatly downcast from knowing, or seeing, that others are in a better position than himself, unless he thought their being so was the result of injustice, or the consequence of letting chance work itself out for no useful common purpose, and so on. So if these persons strike us as unpleasantly egoistic, they are at least free in some degree from the fault of envy.[6]

Finally, assume that these persons have roughly similar needs and interests, or needs and interests in various ways complementary, so that fruitful cooperation amongst them is possible; and suppose that they are sufficiently equal in power and ability to guarantee that in normal circumstances none is able to dominate the others. This condition (as well as the others) may seem excessively vague; but in view of the conception of justice to which the argument leads, there seems no reason for making it more exact here.

Since these persons are conceived as engaging in their common practices, which are already established, there is no question of our supposing them to come together to deliberate as to how they will set these practices up for the first time. Yet we can imagine that from time to time they discuss with one another whether any of them has a legitimate complaint against their established institutions. Such discussions are perfectly natural in any normal society. Now suppose that they have settled on doing this in the following way. They first try to arrive at the principles by which complaints, and so practices themselves, are to be judged. Their procedure for this is to let each person propose the principles upon which he wishes his complaints to be tried with the understanding that, if acknowledged, the complaints of others will be similarly tried, and that no complaints will be heard at all until everyone is roughly to one mind as to how complaints are to be judged. They each understand further that the principles proposed and acknowledged on this occasion are binding on future occasions. Thus each will be wary of proposing a principle which would give him a peculiar advantage, in his present circumstances, supposing it to be accepted. Each person knows that he will be bound by it in future circumstances the peculiarities of which cannot be known, and which might well be such that the principle is then to his disadvantage. The idea is that everyone should be required to make *in advance* a firm commitment, which others also may reasonably be expected to make, and that no one be given the opportunity to tailor the canons of a legitimate complaint to fit his own special condition, and then to discard them when they no longer suit his purpose. Hence each person will propose principles of a general kind which will, to a large degree, gain their sense from the various applications to be made of them, the particular circumstances of which being as yet unknown. These principles will express the conditions in accordance with which each is the least unwilling to have his interests limited in the design of practices, given the competing interests of the others, on the supposition that the interests of others will be limited likewise. The restrictions which would so arise might be thought of as those a person would keep in mind if he were designing a practice in which his enemy were to assign him his place.

The two main parts of his conjectural account have a definite significance. The character and respective situations of the parties reflect the typical circumstances in which questions of justice arise. The procedure whereby principles are proposed and acknowledged represents constraints, analogous to those of having a morality, whereby rational and mutually self-interested persons are brought to act reasonably. Thus the first part reflects the fact that questions of justice arise when conflicting claims are made upon the design of a practice and where it is taken for granted that each person will insist, as far as possible, on what he considers his rights. It is typical of cases of justice to involve persons who are pressing on one another their claims, between which a fair balance or equilibrium must be found. On the other hand, as expressed by the second part, having a morality must at least imply the acknowledgment of principles as impartially applying to one's own conduct as well as to another's, and moreover principles which may constitute a constraint, or limitation, upon the pursuit of one's own interests. There are, of course, other aspects of having a morality:

The acknowledgment of moral principles must show itself in accepting a reference to them as reasons for limiting one's claims, in acknowledging the burden of providing a special explanation, or excuse, when one acts contrary to them, or else in showing shame and remorse and a desire to make amends, and so on. It is sufficient to remark here that having a morality is analogous to having made a firm commitment in advance; for one must acknowledge the principles of morality even when to one's disadvantage.[7] A man whose moral judgments always coincided with his interests could be suspected of having no morality at all.

Thus the two parts of the foregoing account are intended to mirror the kinds of circumstances in which questions of justice arise and the constraints which having a morality would impose upon persons so situated. In this way one can see how the acceptance of the principles of justice might come about, for given all these conditions as described, it would be natural if the two principles of justice were to be acknowledged. Since there is no way of anyone to win special advantages for himself, each might consider it reasonable to acknowledge equality as an initial principle. There is, however, no reason why they should regard this position as final; for if there are inequalities which satisfy the second principle, the immediate gain which equality would allow can be considered as intelligently invested in view of its future return. If, as is quite likely, these inequalities work as incentives to draw out better efforts, the members of this society may look upon them as concessions to human nature: they, like us, may think that people ideally should want to serve one another. But as they are mutually self-interested, their acceptance of these inequalities is merely the acceptance of the relations in which they actually stand, and a recognition of the motives which lead them to engage in their common practices. *They* have no title to complain of one another. And so provided that the conditions of the principle are met, there is no reason why they should not allow such inequalities. Indeed, it would be short-sighted of them to do so, and could result, in most cases, only from their being dejected by the bare knowledge, or perception, that others are better situated. Each person will, however, insist on an advantage to himself, and so on a common advantage, for none is willing to sacrifice anything for the others.

These remarks are not offered as a proof that persons so conceived and circumstanced would settle on the two principles, but only to show that these principles could have such a background, and so can be viewed as those principles which mutually self-interested and rational persons, when similarly situated and required to make in advance a firm commitment, could acknowledge as restrictions governing the assignment of rights and duties in their common practices, and thereby accept as limiting their rights against one another. The principles of justice may, then, be regarded as those principles which arise when the constraints of having a morality are imposed upon parties in the typical circumstances of justice.

IV

These ideas are, of course, connected with a familiar way of thinking about justice which goes back at least to the Greek Sophists, and which regards the acceptance of the principles of justice as a compromise between persons of roughly equal power who would enforce their will on each other if they could, but who, in view of the equality of forces amongst them and for the sake of their own peace and security, acknowledge certain forms of conduct insofar as prudence seems to require. Justice is thought of as a pact between rational egoists the stability of which is dependent on a balance of power and a similarity of circumstances.[8] While the previous account is connected with this tradition, and with its most recent variant, the theory of games,[9] it differs from it in several important respects which, to forestall misinterpretations, I will set out here.

First, I wish to use the previous conjectural account of the background of justice as a way of analyzing the concept. I do not want, therefore, to be interpreted as assuming a general theory of human motivation: When I suppose that the parties are mutually self-interested, and are not willing to have their (substantial) interests sacrificed to others, I am referring to their conduct and motives as they are taken for granted in cases where questions of justice ordinarily arise. Justice is the virtue of practices where there are assumed to be competing interests and conflicting claims, and where it is supposed that persons

will press their rights on each other. That persons are mutually self-interested in certain situations and for certain purposes is what gives rise to the question of justice in practices covering those circumstances. Amongst an association of saints, if such a community could really exist, the disputes about justice could hardly occur; for they would all work selflessly together for one end, the glory of God as defined by their common religion, and reference to this end would settle every question of right. The justice of practices does not come up until there are several different parties (whether we think of these as individuals, associations, or nations and so on, is irrelevant) who do press their claims on one another, and who do regard themselves as representatives of interests which deserve to be considered. Thus the previous account involves no general theory of human motivation. Its intent is simply to incorporate into the conception of justice the relations of men to one another which set the stage for questions of justice. It makes no difference how wide or general these relations are, as this matter does not bear on the analysis of the concept.

Again, in contrast to the various conceptions of the social contract, the several parties do not establish any particular society or practice; they do not covenant to obey a particular sovereign body or to accept a given constitution.[10] Nor do they, as in the theory of games (in certain respects a marvelously sophisticated development of this tradition), decide on individual strategies adjusted to their respective circumstances in the game. What the parties do is to *jointly* acknowledge certain *principles* of appraisal relating to their common *practices* either as already established or merely proposed. They accede to standards of judgment, not to a given practice; they do not make any specific agreement, or bargain, or adopt a particular strategy. The subject of their acknowledgment is, therefore, very general indeed; it is simply the acknowledgment of certain principles of judgment, fulfilling certain general conditions, to be used in criticizing the arrangement of their common affairs. The relations of mutual self-interest [among] the parties who are similarly circumstanced mirror the conditions under which questions of justice arise, and the procedure by which the principles of judgment are proposed and acknowledged reflects the constraints of having a morality. Each aspect, then, of preceding hypothetical account serves the purpose of bringing out a feature of the notion of justice. One could, if one liked, view the principles of justice as the "solution" of this highest order "game" of adopting, subject to the procedure described, principles of argument for all coming particular "games" whose peculiarities one can in no way foresee. But this comparison, while no doubt helpful, must not obscure the fact that this highest order "game" is of a special sort.[11] Its significance is that its various pieces represent aspects of the concept of justice.

Finally, I do not, of course, conceive the several parties as necessarily coming together to establish their common practices for the first time. Some institutions may, indeed, be set up *de novo;* but I have framed the preceding account so that it will apply when the full complement of social institutions already exists and represents the result of a long period of development. Nor is the account in any way fictitious. In any society where people reflect on their institutions they will have an idea of what principles of justice would be acknowledged under the conditions described, and there will be occasions when the questions of justice are actually discussed in this way. Therefore if their practices do not accord with these principles, this will affect the quality of their social relations. For in this case there will be some recognized situations wherein the parties are mutually aware that one of them is being forced to accept what the other would concede is unjust. The foregoing analysis may then be thought of as representing the actual quality of relations [among] persons as defined by practices accepted as just. In such practices the parties will acknowledge the principles on which it is constructed, and the general recognition of this fact shows itself in the absence of resentment and in the sense of being justly treated. Thus one common objection to the theory of the social contract, its apparently historical and fictitious character, is avoided.

V

That the principles of justice may be regarded as arising in the manner described illustrates an important fact about them. Not only does it bring out the idea that justice is a primitive moral notion in that it arises once the concept of morality is imposed on mutually self-interested agents similarly circumstanced, but it emphasizes that, fundamental to justice, is the concept of fairness which relates to right dealing between persons who are cooperating with or competing against one another, as when one speaks of fair games, fair competition, and fair bargains. The question of fairness arises when free persons, who have no authority over one another, are engaging in a joint activity and amongst themselves settling or acknowledging the rules which define it and which determine the respective shares in its benefits and burdens. A practice will strike the parties as fair if none feels that, by participating in it, they or any of the others are taken advantage of, or forced to give in to claims, which they do not regard as legitimate. This implies that each has a conception of legitimate claims which he thinks it reasonable for others as well as himself to acknowledge. If one thinks of the principles of justice as arising in the manner described, then they do define this sort of conception. A practice is just or fair, then, when it satisfies the principles which those who participate in it could propose to one another for mutual acceptance under the aforementioned circumstances. Persons engaged in a just, or fair, practice can face one another openly and support their respective positions, should they appear questionable, by reference to principles which it is reasonable to expect each to accept.

It is this notion of the possibility of mutual acknowledgment of principles by free persons who have no authority over one another which makes the concept of fairness fundamental to justice. Only if such acknowledgment is possible can there be true community between persons in their common practices; otherwise their relations will appear to them as founded to some extent on force. If, in ordinary speech, fairness applies more particularly to practices in which there is a choice whether to engage or not (for example, in games, business competition), and justice to practices in which there is no choice (for example, in slavery), the element of necessity does not render the conception of mutual acknowledgment inapplicable, although it may make it much more urgent to change unjust than unfair institutions. For one activity in which one can always engage is that of proposing and acknowledging principles to one another supposing each to be similarly circumstanced; and to judge practices by the principles so arrived at is to apply the standard of fairness to them.

Now if the participants in a practice accept its rules as fair, and so have no complaint to lodge against it, there arises a prima facie duty (and a corresponding prima facie right) of the parties to each other to act in accordance with the practice when it falls upon them to comply. When any number of persons engage in a practice, or conduct a joint undertaking according to rules, and thus restrict their liberty, those who have submitted to these restrictions when required have the right to a similar acquiescence on the part of those who have benefited by their submission. These conditions will obtain if a practice is correctly acknowledged to be fair, for in this case all who participate in it will benefit from it. The rights and duties so arising are special rights and duties in that they depend on previous actions voluntarily undertaken, in this case on the parties having engaged in a common practice and knowingly accepted its benefits.[12] It is not, however, an obligation which presupposes a deliberate performative act in the sense of a promise, or contract, and the like.[13] An unfortunate mistake of proponents of the idea of the social contract was to suppose that political obligation does require some such act, or at least to use language which suggests it. It is sufficient that one has knowingly participated in and accepted the benefits of a practice acknowledged to be fair. This prima facie obligation may, of course, be overridden: It may happen, when it comes one's turn to follow a rule, that other considerations will justify not doing so. But one cannot, in general, be released from this obligation by denying the justice of the practice only when it falls on one to obey. If a person rejects a practice, he should, so far as possible, declare his intention in advance, and avoid participating in it or enjoying its benefits.

This duty I have called that of fair play, but it should be admitted that to refer to it in this way is, perhaps, to extend the ordinary notion of fairness. Usually acting unfairly is not so much the breaking of any particular rule, even if the infraction is difficult to detect (cheating), but taking advantage of loopholes or ambiguities in rules, availing oneself of unexpected or special circumstances which make it impossible to enforce them, insisting that rules be enforced to one's advantage when they should be suspended, and more generally, acting contrary to the intention of a practice. It is for this reason that one speaks of the sense of fair play: Acting fairly requires more than simply being able to follow rules; what is fair must often be felt, or perceived, one wants to say. It is not, however, an unnatural extension of the duty of fair play to have it include the obligation which participants who have knowingly accepted the benefits of their common practice owe to each other to act in accordance with it when their performance falls due; for it is usually considered unfair if someone accepts the benefits of a practice but refuses to do his part in maintaining it. Thus one might say of the tax-dodger that he violates the duty of fair play: He accepts the benefits of government but will not do his part in releasing resources to it; and members of labor unions often say that fellow workers who refuse to join are being unfair: They refer to them as "free riders," as persons who enjoy what are the supposed benefits of unionism, higher wages, shorter hours, job security, and the like, but who refuse to share in its burdens in the form of paying dues, and so on.

The duty of fair play stands beside other prima facie duties such as fidelity and gratitude as a basic moral notion; yet it is not to be confused with them.[14] These duties are all clearly distinct, as would be obvious from their definitions. As with any moral duty, that of fair play implies a constraint on self-interest in particular cases; on occasion it enjoins conduct which a rational egoist strictly defined would not decide upon. So while justice does not require of anyone that he sacrifice his interests in that *general position* and procedure whereby the principles of justice are proposed and acknowledged, it may happen that in particular situations, arising in the context of engaging in a practice, the duty of fair play will often cross his interests in the sense that he will be required to forgo particular advantages which the peculiarities of his circumstances might permit him to take. There is, of course, nothing surprising in this. It is simply the consequence of the firm commitment which the parties may be supposed to have made, or which they would make, in the general position, together with the fact that they have participated in and accepted the benefits of a practice which they regard as fair.

Now the acknowledgment of this constraint in particular cases, which is manifested in acting fairly or wishing to make amends, feeling ashamed, and the like, when one has evaded it, is one of the forms of conduct by which participants in a common practice exhibit their recognition of each other as persons with similar interests and capacities. In the same way that, failing a special explanation, the criterion for the recognition of suffering is helping one who suffers, acknowledging the duty of fair play is a necessary part of the criterion of recognizing another as a person with similar interests and feelings as oneself.[15] A person who never under any circumstances showed a wish to help others in pain would show, at the same time, that he did not recognize that they were in pain; nor could he have any feelings of affection or friendship for anyone; for having these feelings implies, failing special circumstances, that he comes to their aid when they are suffering. Recognition that another is a person in pain shows itself in sympathetic action; this primitive natural response of compassion is one of those responses upon which the various forms of moral conduct are built.

Similarly, the acceptance of the duty of fair play by participants in a common practice is a reflection in each person of the recognition of the aspirations and interests of the others to be realized by their joint activity. Failing a special explanation, their acceptance of it is a necessary part of the criterion for their recognizing one another as persons with similar interests and capacities, as the conception of their relations in the general position supposes them to be. Otherwise they would show no recognition of one another as persons with similar capacities and interests, and indeed, in some cases perhaps hypothetical, they would not recognize one another as persons at all, but as complicated objects involved in a complicated activity. To recognize another as a person one must respond to him and act towards him in certain ways; and these ways are intimately connected with the various prima facie duties. Acknowledging these duties in *some* degree, and so having the ele-

ments of morality, is not a matter of choice, or of intuiting moral qualities, or a matter of the expression of feelings or attitudes (the three interpretations between which philosophical opinion frequently oscillates); it is simply the possession of one of the forms of conduct in which the recognition of others as persons is manifested.

These remarks are unhappily obscure. Their main purpose here, however, is to forestall, together with the remarks in section IV, the misinterpretation that, on the view presented, the acceptance of justice and the acknowledgment of the duty of fair play depends in every day life solely on their being a *de facto* balance of forces between the parties. It would indeed be foolish to underestimate the importance of such a balance in securing justice; but it is not the only basis thereof. The recognition of one another as persons with similar interests and capacities engaged in a common practice must, failing a special explanation, show itself in the acceptance of the principles of justice and the acknowledgment of the duty of fair play.

The conception at which we have arrived, then, is that the principles of justice may be thought of as arising once the constraints of having a morality are imposed upon rational and mutually self-interested parties who are related and situated in a special way. A practice is just if it is in accordance with the principles which all who participate in it might reasonably be expected to propose or to acknowledge before one another when they are similarly circumstanced and required to make a firm commitment in advance without knowledge of what will be their peculiar condition, and thus when it meets standards which the parties could accept as fair should occasion arise for them to debate its merits. Regarding the participants themselves, once persons knowingly engage in a practice which they acknowledge to be fair and accept the benefits of doing so, they are bound by the duty of fair play to follow the rules when it comes their turn to do so, and this implies a limitation on their pursuit of self-interest in particular cases.

Now one consequence of this conception is that, where it applies, there is no moral value in the satisfaction of a claim incompatible with it. Such a claim violates the conditions of reciprocity and community amongst persons, and he who presses it, not being willing to acknowledge it when pressed by another, has no grounds for complaint when it is denied; whereas he against whom it is pressed can complain. As it cannot be mutually acknowledged it is a resort to coercion; granting the claim is possible only if one party can compel acceptance of what the other will not admit. But it makes no sense to concede claims the denial of which cannot be complained of in preference to claims the denial of which can be objected to. Thus in deciding on the justice of a practice it is not enough to ascertain that it answers to wants and interests in the fullest and most effective manner. For if any of these conflict with justice, they should not be counted, as their satisfaction is no reason at all for having a practice. It would be irrelevant to say, even if true, that it resulted in the greatest satisfaction of desire. In tallying up the merits of a practice one must toss out the satisfaction of interests the claims of which are incompatible with the principles of justice.

VI

The discussion so far has been excessively abstract. While this is perhaps unavoidable, I should now like to bring out some of the features of the conception of justice as fairness by comparing it with the conception of justice in classical utilitarianism as represented by Bentham and Sidgwick, and its counterpart in welfare economics. This conception assimilates justice to benevolence and the latter in turn to the most efficient design of institutions to promote the general welfare. Justice is a kind of efficiency.[16]

Now it is said occasionally that this form of utilitarianism puts no restrictions on what might be a just assignment of rights and duties in that there might be circumstances which, on utilitarian grounds, would justify institutions highly offensive to our ordinary sense of justice. But the classical utilitarian conception is not totally unprepared for this objection. Beginning with the notion that the general happiness can be represented by a social utility function consisting of a sum of individual utility functions with identical weights (this being the meaning of the maxim that each counts for one and no more than one),[17] it is commonly assumed that the utility functions of individuals are similar in all essential respects.

Differences [among] individuals are ascribed to accidents of education and upbringing, and they should not be taken into account. This assumption, coupled with that of diminishing marginal utility, results in a prima facie case for equality, for example, of equality in the distribution of income during any given period of time, laying aside indirect effects on the future. But even if utilitarianism is interpreted as having such restrictions built into the utility function, and even if it is supposed that these restrictions have in practice much the same result as the application of the principles of justice (and appear, perhaps, to be ways of expressing these principles in the language of mathematics and psychology), the fundamental idea is very different from the conception of justice as fairness. For one thing, that the principles of justice should be accepted is interpreted as the contingent result of a higher order administrative decision. The form of this decision is regarded as being similar to that of an entrepreneur deciding how much to produce of this or that commodity in view of its marginal revenue, or to that of someone distributing goods to needy persons according to the relative urgency of their wants. The choice between practices is thought of as being made on the basis of the allocation of benefits and burdens to individuals (these being measured by the present capitalized value of their utility over the full period of the practice's existence), which results from the distribution of rights and duties established by a practice.

Moreover, the individuals receiving these benefits are not conceived as being related in any way: They represent so many different directions in which limited resources may be allocated. The value of assigning resources to one direction rather than another depends solely on the preferences and interests of individuals as individuals. The satisfaction of desire has its value irrespective of the moral relations between persons, say as members of a joint undertaking, of the claims which, in the name of these interests, they are prepared to make on one another;[18] and it is this value which is to be taken into account by the (ideal) legislator who is conceived as adjusting the rules of the system from the center so as to maximize the value of the social utility function.

It is thought that the principles of justice will not be violated by a legal system so conceived provided these executive decisions are correctly made. In this fact the principles of justice are said to have their derivation and explanation; they simply express the most important general features of social institutions in which the administrative problem is solved in the best way. These principles have, indeed, a special urgency because, given the facts of human nature, so much depends on them; and this explains the peculiar quality of the moral feelings associated with justice.[19] This assimilation of justice to a higher order executive decision, certainly a striking conception, is central to classical utilitarianism; and it also brings out its profound individualism, in one sense of this ambiguous word. It regards persons as so many *separate* directions in which benefits and burdens may be assigned; and the value of the satisfaction or dissatisfaction of desire is not thought to depend in any way on the moral relations in which individuals stand, or on the kinds of claims which they are willing, in the pursuit of their interests, to press on each other.

VII

Many social decisions are, of course, of an administrative nature. Certainly this is so when it is a matter of social utility in what one may call its ordinary sense: that is, when it is a question of the efficient design of social institutions for the use of common means to achieve common ends. In this case either the benefits and burdens may be assumed to be impartially distributed, or the question of distribution is misplaced, as in the instance of maintaining public order and security or national defense. But as an interpretation of the basis of the principles of justice, classical utilitarianism is mistaken. It *permits* one to argue, for example, that slavery is unjust on the grounds that the advantages to the slaveholder as slaveholder do not counterbalance the disadvantages to the slave and to society at large burdened by a comparatively inefficient system of labor. Now the conception of justice as fairness, when applied to the practice of slavery with its offices of slaveholder and slave, would not allow one to consider the advantages of the slaveholder in the first place. As that office is not in accordance with principles which could be mutually acknowledged, the gains accruing to the slave-

holder, assuming them to exist, cannot be counted as in *any* way mitigating the injustice of the practice. The question whether these gains outweigh the disadvantages to the slave and to society cannot arise, since in considering the justice of slavery these gains have no weight at all which requires that they be overridden. Where the conception of justice as fairness applies, slavery is *always* unjust.

I am not, of course, suggesting the absurdity that the classical utilitarians approved of slavery. I am only rejecting a type of argument which their view allows them to use in support of their disapproval of it. The conception of justice as derivative from efficiency implies that judging the justice of a practice is always, in principle at least, a matter of weighing up advantages and disadvantages, each having an intrinsic value or disvalue as the satisfaction of interests, irrespective of whether or not these interests necessarily involve acquiescence in principles which could not be mutually acknowledged. Utilitarianism cannot account for the fact that slavery is always unjust, nor for the fact that it would be recognized as relevant in defeating the accusation of injustice for one person to say to another, engaged with him in a common practice and debating its merits, that nevertheless it allowed of the greatest satisfaction of desire. The charge of injustice cannot be rebutted in this way. If justice were derivative from a higher order executive efficiency, this would not be so.

But now, even if it is taken as established that, so far as the ordinary conception of justice goes, slavery is always unjust (that is, slavery by definition violates commonly recognized principles of justice), the classical utilitarian would surely reply that these principles, as other moral principles subordinate to that of utility, are only generally correct. It is simply for the most part true that slavery is less efficient than other institutions; and while common sense may define the concept of justice so that slavery is unjust, nevertheless, where slavery would lead to the greatest satisfaction of desire, it is not wrong. Indeed, it is then right, and for the very same reason that justice, as ordinarily understood, is usually right. If, as ordinarily understood, slavery is always unjust, to this extent the utilitarian conception of justice might be admitted to differ from that of common moral opinion. Still the utilitarian would want to hold that, as a matter of moral principle, his view is correct in giving no special weight to considerations of justice beyond that allowed for by the general presumption of effectiveness. And this, he claims, is as it should be. The everyday opinion is morally in error, although, indeed, it is a useful error, since it protects rules of generally high utility.

The question, then relates not simply to the analysis of the concept of justice as common sense defines it, but the analysis of it in the wider sense as to how much weight considerations of justice, as defined, are to have when laid against other kinds of moral considerations. Here again I wish to argue that reasons of justice have a *special* weight for which only the conception of justice as fairness can account. Moreover, it belongs to the concept of justice that they do have this special weight. While Mill recognized that this was so, he thought that it could be accounted for by the special urgency of the moral feelings which naturally support principles of such high utility. But it is a mistake to resort to the urgency of feeling; as with the appeal to intuition, it manifests a failure to pursue the question far enough. The special weight of considerations of justice can be explained from the conception of justice as fairness. It is only necessary to elaborate a bit what has already been said as follows.

If one examines the circumstances in which a certain tolerance of slavery is justified, or perhaps better, excused, it turns out that these are of a rather special sort. Perhaps slavery exists as an inheritance from the past and it proves necessary to dismantle it piece by piece; at times slavery may conceivably be an advance on previous institutions. Now while there may be some excuse for slavery in special conditions, it is never an excuse for it that it is sufficiently advantageous to the slaveholder to outweigh the disadvantages to the slave and to society. A person who argues in this way is not perhaps making a wildly irrelevant remark; but he is guilty of a moral fallacy. There is disorder in his conception of the ranking of moral principles. For the slaveholder, by his own admission, has no moral title to the advantages which he receives as a slaveholder. He is no more prepared than the slave to acknowledge the principle upon which is founded the respective positions in which they both stand. Since slavery does not accord with

principles which they could mutually acknowledge, they each may be supposed to agree that it is unjust: it grants claims which it ought not to grant and in doing so denies claims which it ought not to deny. Amongst persons in a general position who are debating the form of their common practices, it cannot, therefore, be offered as a reason for a practice that, in conceding these very claims that ought to be denied, it nevertheless meets existing interests more effectively. By their very nature the satisfaction of these claims is without weight and cannot enter into any tabulation of advantages and disadvantages.

Furthermore, it follows from the concept of morality that, to the extent that the slaveholder recognizes his position vis-à-vis the slave to be unjust, he would not choose to press his claims. His not wanting to receive his special advantages is one of the ways in which he shows that he thinks slavery is unjust. It would be fallacious for the legislator to suppose, then, that it is a ground for having a practice that it brings advantages greater than disadvantages, if those for whom the practice is designed, and to whom the advantages flow, acknowledge that they have no moral title to them and do not wish to receive them.

For these reasons the principles of justice have a special weight; and with respect to the principle of the greatest satisfaction of desire, as cited in the general position amongst those discussing the merits of their common practices, the principles of justice have an absolute weight. In this sense they are not contingent; and this is why their force is greater than can be accounted for by the general presumption (assuming that there is one) of the effectiveness, in the utilitarian sense, of practices which in fact satisfy them.

If one wants to continue using the concepts of classical utilitarianism, one will have to say, to meet this criticism, that at least the individual or social utility functions must be so defined that no value is given to the satisfaction of interests the representative claims of which violate the principles of justice. In this way it is no doubt possible to include these principles within the form of the utilitarian conception; but to do so is, of course, to change its inspiration altogether as a moral conception. For it is to incorporate within it principles which cannot be understood on the basis of a higher order executive decision aiming at the greatest satisfaction of desire.

It is worth remarking, perhaps, that this criticism of utilitarianism does not depend on whether or not the two assumptions, that of individuals having similar utility functions and that of diminishing marginal utility, are interpreted as psychological propositions to be supported or refuted by experience, or as moral and political principles expressed in a somewhat technical language. There are, certainly, several advantages in taking them in the latter fashion.[20] For one thing, one might say that this is what Bentham and others really meant by them, as least as shown by how they were used in arguments for social reform. More importantly, one could hold that the best way to defend the classical utilitarian view is to interpret these assumptions as moral and political principles. It is doubtful whether, taken as psychological propositions, they are true of men in general as we know them under normal conditions. On the other hand, utilitarians would not have wanted to propose them merely as practical working principles of legislation, or as expedient maxims to guide reform, given the egalitarian sentiments of modern society.[21] When pressed they might well have invoked the idea of a more or less equal capacity of men in relevant respects if given an equal chance in a just society. But if the argument above regarding slavery is correct, then granting these assumptions as moral and political principles makes no difference. To view individuals as equally fruitful lines for the allocation of benefits, even as a matter of moral principle, still leaves the mistaken notion that the satisfaction of desire has value in itself irrespective of the relations between persons as members of a common practice, and irrespective of the claims upon one another which the satisfaction of interests represents. To see the error of this idea one must give up the conception of justice as an executive decision altogether and refer to the notion of justice as fairness: that participants in a common practice be regarded as having an original and equal liberty and that their common practices be considered unjust unless they accord with principles which persons so circumstanced and related could freely acknowledge before one another, and so could accept as fair. Once the emphasis is put upon the concept of the mutual recognition of principles by participants in common practice the rules of which are to define their several rela-

tions and give form to their claims on one another, then it is clear that the granting of a claim the principle of which could not be acknowledged by each in the general position (that is, in the position in which the parties propose and acknowledge principles before one another) is not a reason for adopting a practice. Viewed in this way, the background of the claim is seen to exclude it from consideration; that it can represent a value in itself arises from the conception of individuals as separate lines for the assignment of benefits, as isolated persons who stand as claimants on an administrative or benevolent largesse. Occasionally persons do so stand to one another; but this is not the general case, nor, more importantly, is it the case when it is a matter of the justice of practices themselves in which participants stand in various relations to be appraised in accordance with standards which they may be expected to acknowledge before one another. Thus however mistaken the notion of the social contract may be as history, and however far it may overreach itself as a general theory of social and political obligation, it does express, suitably interpreted, an essential part of the concept of justice.[22]

VIII

By way of conclusion I should like to make two remarks: first, the original modification of the utilitarian principle (that it require of practices that the offices and positions defined by them be equal unless it is reasonable to suppose that the representative man in *every* office would find the inequality to his advantage), slight as it may appear at first sight, actually has a different conception of justice standing behind it. I have tried to show how this is so by developing the concept of justice as fairness and by indicating how this notion involves the mutual acceptance, from a general position, of the principles on which a practice is founded, and how this in turn requires the exclusion from consideration of claims violating the principles of justice. Thus the slight alteration of principle reveals another family of notions, another way of looking at the concept of justice.

Second, I should like to remark also that I have been dealing with the *concept* of justice. I have tried to set out the kinds of principles upon which judgments concerning the justice of practices may be said to stand. The analysis will be successful to the degree that it expresses the principles involved in these judgments when made by competent persons upon deliberation and reflection.[23] Now every people may be supposed to have the concept of justice, since in the life of every society there must be at least some relations in which the parties consider themselves to be circumstanced and related as the concept of justice as fairness requires. Societies will differ from one another not in having or in failing to have this notion but in the range of cases to which they apply it and in the emphasis which they give to it as compared with other moral concepts.

A firm grasp of the concept of justice itself is necessary if these variations, and the reasons for them, are to be understood. No study of the development of moral ideas and of the differences between them is more sound than the analysis of the fundamental moral concepts upon which it must depend. I have tried, therefore, to give an analysis of the concept of justice which should apply generally, however large a part the concept may have in a given morality, and which can be used in explaining the course of men's thoughts about justice and its relations to other moral concepts. How it is to be used for this purpose is a large topic which I cannot, of course, take up here. I mention it only to emphasize that I have been dealing with the concept of justice itself and to indicate what use I consider such an analysis to have.

NOTES

1. I use the word "practice" throughout as a sort of technical term meaning any form of activity specified by a system of rules which defines offices, roles, moves, penalties, defenses, and so on, and which gives the activity its structure. As examples one may think of games and rituals, trials and parliaments, markets and systems of property. I have attempted a partial analysis of the notion of a practice in a paper "Two Concepts of Rules," *Philosophical Review*, LXIV (1955), 3–32.

2. These principles are, of course, well known in one form or another and appear in many analyses of justice even where the writers differ widely on other matters. Thus if the principle of equal liberty is commonly associated with Kant (see *The Philosophy of Law*, tr. by W. Hastie, Edinburgh, 1887, pp. 56 f.), it may be claimed that it can also be found in J. S. Mill's *On Liberty* and

elsewhere, and in many other liberal writers. Recently H. L. A. Hart has argued for something like it in his paper "Are There Any Natural Rights?" *Philosophical Review*, LXIV (1955), 175–191. The injustice of inequalities which are not won in return for a contribution to the common advantage is, of course, widespread in political writings of all sorts. The conception of justice here discussed is distinctive, if at all, only in selecting these two principles in this form; but for another similar analysis, see the discussion by W. D. Lamont, *The Principles of Moral Judgment* (Oxford, 1946), ch. v.

3. This point was made by Sidgwick, *Methods of Ethics*, 6th ed. (London, 1901), Bk. III, ch. v, sec. 1. It has recently been emphasized by Sir Isaiah Berlin in a symposium, "Equality," *Proceedings of the Aristotelian Society*, n.s. LVI (1955–56), 305 f.

4. In the paper referred to above, footnote 1, I have tried to show the importance of taking practices as the proper subject of the utilitarian principle. The criticisms of so-called "restricted utilitarianism" by J. J. C. Smart, "Extreme and Restricted Utilitarianism," *Philosophical Quarterly*, VI (1956), 344–354, and by H. J. McCloskey, "An Examination of Restricted Utilitarianism," *Philosophical Review*, LXVI (1957), 466–485, do not affect my argument. These papers are concerned with the very general proposition, which is attributed (with what justice I shall not consider) to S. E. Toulmin and P. H. Nowell-Smith (and in the case of the latter paper, also, apparently, to me); namely, the proposition that particular moral actions are justified by appealing to moral rules, and moral rules in turn by reference to utility. But clearly I meant to defend no such view. My discussion of the concept of rules as maxims is an explicit rejection of it. What I did argue was that, in the *logically special* case of practices (although actually quite a common case) where the rules have special features and are not moral rules at all but legal rules or rules of games and the like (except, perhaps, in the case of promises), there is a peculiar force to the distinction between justifying particular actions and justifying the system of rules themselves. Even then I claimed only that restricting the utilitarian principle to practices as defined strengthened it. I did not argue for the position that this amendment alone is sufficient for a complete defense of utilitarianism as a general theory of morals. In this paper I take up the question as to how the utilitarian principle itself must be modified, but here, too, the subject of inquiry is not all of morality at once, but a limited topic, the concept of justice.

5. It might seem as if J. S. Mill, in paragraph 36 of Chapter v of *Utilitarianism*, expressed the utilitarian principle in this modified form, but in the remaining two paragraphs of the chapter, and elsewhere, he would appear not to grasp the significance of the change. Hume often emphasizes that *every* man must

benefit. For example, in discussing the utility of general rules, he holds that they are requisite to the "well-being of every individual"; from a stable system of property "every individual person must find himself a gainer in balancing the account. . . ." "Every member of society is sensible of this interest; everyone expresses this sense to his fellows along with the resolution he has taken of squaring his actions by it, on the conditions that others will do the same." *A Treatise of Human Nature*, Bk. III, Pt. II, Section II, paragraph 22.

6. It is not possible to discuss here this addition to the usual conception of rationality. If it seems peculiar, it may be worth remarking that it is analogous to the modification of the utilitarian principle which the argument as a whole is designed to explain and justify. In the same way that the satisfaction of interests, the representative claims of which violate the principles of justice, is not a reason for having a practice (see sec. VII), unfounded envy, within limits, need not to be taken into account.

7. The idea that accepting a principle as a moral principle implies that one generally acts on it, failing a special explanation, has been stressed by R. M. Hare, *The Language of Morals* (Oxford, 1952). His formulation of it needs to be modified, however, along the lines suggested by P. L. Gardiner, "On Assenting to a Moral Principle," *Proceedings of the Aristotelian Society*, n.s. LV (1955), 23–44. See also C. K. Grant, "Akrasia and the Criteria of Assent to Practical Principles," *Mind*, LXV (1956), 400–407, where the complexity of the criteria for assent is discussed.

8. Perhaps the best known statement of this conception is that given by Glaucon at the beginning of Book II of Plato's *Republic*. Presumably it was, in various forms, a common view among the Sophists; but that Plato gives a fair representation of it is doubtful. See K. R. Popper, *The Open Society and Its Enemies*, rev. ed. (Princeton, 1950), pp. 112–118. Certainly Plato usually attributes to it a quality of manic egoism which one feels must be an exaggeration; on the other hand, see the Melian Debate in Thucydides, *The Peloponnesian War*, Book V, ch. vii, although it is impossible to say to what extent the views expressed there reveal any current philosophical opinion. Also in this tradition are the remarks of Epicurus on justice in *Principal Doctrines*, XXXI–XXXVIII. In modern times elements of the conception appear in a more sophisticated form in Hobbes's *The Leviathan* and in Hume's *A Treatise of Human Nature*, Book III, Pt. II, as well as in the writings of the school of natural law such as Pufendorf's *De jure naturae et gentium*. Hobbes and Hume are especially instructive. For Hobbes's argument see Howard Warrender's *The Political Philosophy of Hobbes* (Oxford, 1957). W. J. Baumol's *Welfare Economics and the Theory of the State* (London, 1952) is valuable in showing the wide

applicability of Hobbes's fundamental idea (interpreting his natural law as principles of prudence), although in this book it is traced back only to Hume's *Treatise*.

9. See J. von Neumann and O. Morgenstern, *The Theory of Games and Economic Behavior*, 2nd ed. (Princeton, 1947). For a comprehensive and not too technical discussion of the developments since, see R. Duncan Luce and Howard Raiffa, *Games and Decisions: Introduction and Critical Survey* (New York, 1957). Chs. vi and xiv discuss the developments most obviously related to the analysis of justice.

10. For a general survey see J. W. Gough, *The Social Contract*, 2nd ed. (Oxford, 1957), and Otto von Gierke, *The Development of Political Theory*, tr. by B. Freyd (London, 1939), Pt. II, ch. II.

11. The difficulty one gets into by a mechanical application of the theory of games to moral philosophy can be brought out by considering among several possible examples, R. B. Braithwaite's study, *Theory of Games as a Tool for the Moral Philosopher* (Cambridge, 1955). On the analysis there given, it turns out that the fair division of playing time between Matthew and Luke depends on their preferences, and these in turn are connected with the instruments they wish to play. Since Matthew has a threat advantage over Luke, arising purely from the fact that Matthew, the trumpeter, prefers both of them playing at once to neither of them playing, whereas Luke, the pianist, prefers silence to cacophony, Matthew is allotted 26 evenings of play to Luke's 17. If the situation were reversed, the threat advantage would be with Luke. See pp. 36 f. But now we have only to suppose that Matthew is a jazz enthusiast who plays the drums, and Luke a violinist who plays sonatas, in which case it will be fair, on this analysis, for Matthew to play whenever and as often as he likes, assuming, of course, as it is plausible to assume, that he does not care whether Luke plays or not. Certainly something has gone wrong. To each according to his threat advantage is hardly the principle of fairness. What is lacking is the concept of morality, and it must be brought into the conjectural account in some way or other. In the text this is done by the form of the procedure whereby principles are proposed and acknowledged (section III). If one starts directly with the particular case as known, and if one accepts as given and definitive the preferences and relative positions of the parties, whatever they are, it is impossible to give an analysis of the moral concept of fairness. Braithwaite's use of the theory of games, insofar as it is intended to analyze the concept of fairness, is, I think, mistaken. This is not, of course, to criticize in any way the theory of games as a mathematical theory, to which Braithwaite's book certainly contributes, nor as an analysis of how rational (and amoral) egoists might behave (and so as an analysis of how people sometimes actually do behave). But it is to say that if the theory of games is to

be used to analyze moral concepts, its formal structure must be interpreted in a special and general manner as indicated in the text. Once we do this, though, we are in touch again with a much older tradition.

12. For the definition of this prima facie duty, and the idea that it is a special duty, I am indebted to H. L. A. Hart. See his paper "Are There Any Natural Rights?" *Philosophical Review*, LXIV (1955), 185 f.

13. The sense of "performative" here is to be derived from J. L. Austin's paper in the symposium, "Other Minds," *Proceedings of the Aristotelian Society*, Supplementary Volume (1946), pp. 170–174.

14. This, however, commonly happens. Hobbes, for example, when invoking the notion of a "tacit covenant," appeals not to the natural law that promises should be kept but to his fourth law of nature, that of gratitude. On Hobbes's shift from fidelity to gratitude, see Warrender, *Political Philosophy of Hobbes* (footnote 8), pp. 51–52, 233–237. While it is not a serious criticism of Hobbes, it would have improved his argument had he appealed to the duty of fair play. On his premises he is perfectly entitled to do so. Similarly Sidgwick thought that a principle of justice, such as every man ought to receive adequate requital for his labor, is like gratitude universalized. See *Methods of Ethics*, Bk. III, ch. v, Sec. 5. There is a gap in the stock of moral concepts used by philosophers into which the concept of the duty of fair play fits quite naturally.

15. I am using the concept of criterion here in what I take to be Wittgenstein's sense. See *Philosophical Investigations* (Oxford, 1953); and Norman Malcolm's review, "Wittgenstein's *Philosophical Investigations,*" *Philosophical Review*, LXIII (1954), 543–547. That the response of compassion, under appropriate circumstances, is part of the criterion for whether or not a person understands what "pain" means, is, I think, in the *Philosophical Investigations*. The view in the text is simply an extension of this idea. I cannot, however, attempt to justify it here. Similar thoughts are to be found, I think, in Max Scheler, *The Nature of Sympathy*, tr. by Peter Heath (New Haven, 1954). His way of writing is often so obscure that I cannot be certain.

16. While this assimilation is implicit in Bentham's and Sidgwick's moral theory, explicit statements of it as applied to justice are relatively rare. One clear instance in *The Principles of Morals and Legislation* occurs in ch. x, footnote 2 to section XL: ". . . justice, in the only sense in which it has a meaning, is an imaginary personage, feigned for the convenience of discourse, whose dictates are the dictates of utility, applied to certain particular cases. Justice, then, is nothing more than an imaginary instrument, employed to forward on certain occasions, and by certain means, the purposes of benevolence. The dictates of justice are nothing more than a part of the dictates of benevolence, which, on certain occasions, are applied to cer-

tain subjects. . . ." Likewise in *The Limits of Jurisprudence Defined*, ed. by C. W. Everett (New York, 1945), pp. 117 f., Bentham criticizes Grotius for denying that justice derives from utility; and in *The Theory of Legislation*, ed. by C. K. Ogden (London, 1931), p. 3, he says that he uses the words "just" and "unjust" along with other words "simply as collective terms including the ideas of certain pains or pleasures." That Sidgwick's conception of justice is similar to Bentham's is admittedly not evident from his discussion of justice in Book III, ch. v of *Methods of Ethics*. But it follows, I think, from the moral theory he accepts. Hence C. D. Broad's criticism of Sidgwick in the matter of distributive justice in *Five Types of Ethical Theory* (London, 1930), pp. 249–253, do not rest on a misinterpretation.

17. This maxim is attributed to Bentham by J. S. Mill in *Utilitarianism*, ch. v, paragraph 36. I have not found it in Bentham's writings, nor seen such a reference. Similarly James Bonar, *Philosophy and Political Economy* (London, 1893), p. 234 n. But it accords perfectly with Bentham's ideas. See the hitherto unpublished manuscript in David Baumgardt, *Bentham and the Ethics of Today* (Princeton, 1952), Appendix IV. For example, "the total value of the stock of pleasure belonging to the whole community is to be obtained by multiplying the number expressing the value of it as respecting any one person, by the number expressing the multitude of such individuals" (p. 556).

18. An idea essential to the classical utilitarian conception of justice. Bentham is firm in his statement of it: "It is only upon that principle [the principle of asceticism], and not from the principle of utility, that the most abominable pleasure which the vilest of malefactors ever reaped from his crime would be reprobated, if it stood alone. The case is, that it never does stand alone; but is necessarily followed by such a quantity of pain (or, what comes to the same thing, such a chance for a certain quantity of pain) that the pleasure in comparison of it, is as nothing: and this is the true and sole, but perfectly sufficient, reason for making it a ground for punishment" (*The Principles of Morals and Legislation*, ch. II, sec. iv. See also ch. x, sec. x, footnote I). The same point is made in *The Limits of Jurisprudence Defined*, pp. 115 f. Although much recent welfare economics, as found in such important works as I. M. D. Little, *A Critique of Welfare Economics*, 2nd ed. (Oxford, 1957) and K. J. Arrow, *Social Choice and Individual Values* (New York, 1951), dispenses with the idea of cardinal utility, and uses instead the theory of ordinal utility as stated by J. R. Hicks, *Value and Capital*, 2nd ed. (Oxford, 1946), Pt. I, it assumes with utilitarianism that individual preferences have value as such, and so accepts the idea being criticized here. I hasten to add, however, that this is no objection to it as a means of analyzing

economic policy, and for that purpose it may, indeed, be a necessary simplifying assumption. Nevertheless it is an assumption which cannot be made insofar as one is trying to analyze moral concepts, especially the concept of justice, as economists would, I think, agree. Justice is usually regarded as a separate and distinct part of any comprehensive criterion of economic policy. See, for example, Tibor Scitovsky, *Welfare and Competition* (London, 1952), pp. 59–69, and Little, *Critique of Welfare Economics* (this footnote), ch. VII.

19. See J. S. Mill's argument in *Utilitarianism,* ch. v, pars. 16–25.

20. See D. G. Ritchie, *Natural Rights* (London, 1894), pp. 95 ff., 249 ff. Lionel Robbins has insisted on this point on several occasions. See *An Essay on the Nature and Significance of Economic Science,* 2nd ed. (London, 1935), pp. 134–43, "Interpersonal Comparisons of Utility: A Comment," *Economic Journal,* XLVIII (1938), 635–41, and more recently, "Robertson on Utility and Scope," *Economica,* n.s. XX (1953), 108 f.

21. As Sir Henry Maine suggested Bentham may have regarded them. See *The Early History of Institutions* (London, 1875), pp. 398 ff.

22. Thus Kant was not far wrong when he interpreted the original contract merely as an "Idea of Reason"; yet he still thought of it as a *general* criterion of right and as providing a general theory of political obligation. See the second part of the essay, "On the Saying 'That may be right in theory but has no value in practice'" (1793), in *Kant's Principles of Politics,* tr. by W. Hastie (Edinburgh, 1891). I have drawn on the contractarian tradition not for a general theory of political obligation but to clarify the concept of justice.

23. For a further discussion of the idea expressed here, see my paper, "Outline of a Decision Procedure for Ethics," in the *Philosophical Review,* LX (1951), 177–197. For an analysis, similar in many respects but using the notion of the ideal observer instead of that of the considered judgment of a competent person, see Roderick Firth, "Ethical Absolutism and the Ideal Observer," *Philosophy and Phenomenological Research,* XII (1952), 317–345. While the similarities between these two discussions are more important than the differences, an analysis based on the notion of a considered judgment of a competent person, as it is based on a kind of judgment, may prove more helpful in understanding the features of moral judgment than an analysis based on the notion of an ideal observer, although this remains to be shown. A man who rejects the conditions imposed on a considered judgment of a competent person could no longer profess to *judge* at all. This seems more fundamental than his rejecting the conditions of observation, for these do not seem to apply, in an ordinary sense, to making a moral judgment.

Notes and Questions

KIMBERLÉ WILLIAMS CRENSHAW, from "Race, Reform, and Retrenchment"

1. Kimberlé Williams Crenshaw pursues a middle path between commentators on the left and those on the right on the issue of civil rights for blacks in the United States today. What three considerations does she stress throughout the article?

2. The New Right, she points out, is hostile to prior civil rights policies, but claims not to be antiblack or anticivil rights. In fact, the New Right claims to be re-establishing civil rights and equal protection law, not dismantling them. How do the neoconservatives, such as Thomas Sowell, support this claim? What is the distinction between equal process and equal results, according to Sowell, and how does it relate to the politics of law?

3. How does Crenshaw attack Sowell and the conservative view in general? Can Sowell explain what is the "true law" or the "correct" interpretation that he claims to be defending? Why or why not? How does one choose between a restrictive view and an expansive view of equal protection and civil rights law, according to Crenshaw? What is the significance of this distinction? Could Sowell recognize it and defend his "true law" position?

4. Since both the restrictive and the expansive views are contained in the history of equal protection law, what dilemma is created for civil rights visionaries? What does "equal opportunity" mean, given these two possible interpretations? What is Crenshaw's suggestion for reformulating the conflict between the restrictive, or equal process, view and the expansive, or equal result, view? Does her suggestion help to clarify the debate?

5. What, according to Crenshaw, is the position of the left, or the Critical Legal Scholars, regarding legal reform as a means of ending domination? Why don't they think legal rights discourse will help dominated people in the long run? How does Crenshaw respond?

6. What are the function and significance of race consciousness, according to Crenshaw? What does it mean to say that blacks function as the "other" to whites? How does racism create an illusion of unity among whites?

7. What is the distinction between symbolic and material oppression, and how does it interact with the doctrine of formal equality to make the situation of the poor blacks more difficult to articulate and correct? Can formal equality correct material inequality, according to Crenshaw? Should a just society be concerned with material inequality in Crenshaw's view? In Sowell's? In yours?

8. Crenshaw is worried about losing black unity. How have formal reforms worsened this problem? If the goal of oppressed people is inclusion and those who succeed first join the dominant class and forget their former common interests with those who are still oppressed, why is it even harder for those who have not succeeded? Why does Crenshaw think that it is important for the black community to create and maintain a distinct consciousness or identity?

9. For Crenshaw, the crucial question is how to use rights discourse as necessary to fight discrimination against blacks without legitimating the very institutions that preserve racial inequality. Another version of this question is, If our institutions are systematically racist, how can we use racist institutions (when it is the only way to fight for improvements for oppressed people — the only game in town, so to speak) without reaffirming those racist institutions? How can you use the system to correct the system if the problem is systemic? What does Crenshaw suggest?

[From] "Race, Reform, and Retrenchment: Transformation and Legitimation in Antidiscrimination Law"

KIMBERLÉ WILLIAMS CRENSHAW

I. Introduction

In 1984, President Reagan signed a bill that created the Martin Luther King, Jr. Federal Holiday Commission. The Commission was charged with the responsibility of issuing guidelines for states and localities to follow in preparing their observances of Martin Luther King's birthday. The Commission's task would not be easy. Although King's birthday had come to symbolize the massive social movement that grew out of efforts of African-Americans to end the long history of racial oppression in America, the first official observance of the holiday would take place in the face of at least two disturbing obstacles: first, a constant, if not increasing, socioeconomic disparity between the races, and second, a hostile administration devoted to changing the path of civil rights reforms that some believe responsible for most of the movement's progress.[1] A focus on the continuing disparities between Blacks and whites might call, not for celebration, but for strident criticism of America's failure to make good on its promise of racial equality. Yet such criticism would overlook the progress that has been made, progress which the holiday itself represents. The Commission apparently resolved this dilemma by calling for a celebration of progress toward racial equality while urging continued commitment to this ideal. This effort to reconcile the celebration of an ideal with conditions that bespeak its continuing denial was given the ironic, but altogether appropriate title "Living the Dream." The "Living the Dream" directive aptly illustrates Professor Derrick Bell's observation that "[m]ost Americans, black and white, view the civil rights crusade as a long, slow, but always upward pull that must, given the basic precepts of the country and the commitment of its people to equality and liberty, eventually end in the full enjoyment by blacks of all rights and privileges of citizenship enjoyed by whites."[2]

Commentators on both the Right and the Left, however, have begun to cast doubt upon the continuing vitality of this shopworn theme. The position of the New Right, articulated by members of the Reagan Administration and by neoconservative scholars such as Thomas Sowell, is that the goal of the civil rights movement — the extension of formal equality to all Americans regardless of color — has already been achieved. Therefore, the vision of a continuing struggle under the banner of civil rights is inappropriate.[3] The position of the New Left, presented in the work of scholars associated with the Conference on Critical Legal Studies ("CLS"), also challenges the perception that the civil rights struggle represents a long, steady march toward social transformation. CLS scholars do not significantly disagree with the goal of racial equality, but assert only the basic counterproductivity of seeking that objective through the use of legal rights. Indeed, CLS scholars claim that even engaging in rights discourse is incompatible with a broader strategy of social change. They view the extension of rights, although perhaps energizing political struggle or producing apparent victories in the short run, as ultimately legitimating the very racial inequality and oppression that such extension purports to remedy.[4]

This Article challenges both the New Left and New Right critiques of the civil rights movement.

* * *

In the course of my analysis, I wish to stress three crucial aspects of the consideration of race in the American legal context. First, racism is a central ideological underpinning of American society. Critical scholars who focus on legal consciousness alone thus fail to address one of the most crucial ideological components of the dominant order. The CLS practice of delegitimating false and constraining ideas[5] must include race consciousness if the accepted objective is to transcend oppressive belief systems. Second, the definitional tension in antidiscrimination law, which

attempts to distinguish equality as process from equality as result,[6] is more productively characterized as a conflict between the stated *goals* of antidiscrimination law. Is the goal limited to the mere rejection of white supremacy as a normative vision, or may the goal be expanded to include a societal commitment to the eradication of the substantive conditions of Black subordination? Finally, the Black community must develop and maintain a distinct political consciousness in order to prevail against the co-opting force of legal reform. History has shown that the most valuable political asset of the Black community has been its ability to assert a collective identity and to name its collective political reality. Liberal reform discourse must not be allowed to undermine the Black collective identity.

II. The New Right Attack: Civil Rights as "Politics"

A. The Neoconservative Offensive

The Reagan Administration arrived in Washington in 1981 with an agenda that was profoundly hostile to the civil rights policies of the previous two decades. The principal basis of its hostility was a formalistic, color-blind view of civil rights that had developed in the neoconservative "think tanks" during the 1970's.[7] Neoconservative doctrine singles out race-specific civil rights policies as one of the most significant threats to the democratic political system. Emphasizing the need for strictly color-blind policies, this view calls for the repeal of affirmative action and other race-specific remedial policies, urges an end to class-based remedies, and calls for the Administration to limit remedies to what it calls "actual victims" of discrimination.[8]

A number of early episodes sent a clear message that the Reagan Administration would be inhospitable to the civil rights policies adopted by earlier administrations. For example, the Civil Rights Division of the Justice Department, under Deputy Attorney General William Bradford Reynolds, abruptly changed sides in several cases. Other serious attacks on the civil rights constituency included Reagan's attempt to fire members of the United States Commission on Civil Rights, the Administration's opposition to the 1982 amendment of the Voting Rights Act, and Reagan's veto of the Civil Rights Restoration Act.

These fervent attempts to change the direction of civil rights law generated speculation that the Reagan Administration was anti-Black and ideologically opposed to civil rights. Yet the Administration denied that any racial animus motivated its campaign. Far from viewing themselves as opponents of civil rights, Reagan, Reynolds, and others in the Administration apparently saw themselves as "true" civil rights advocates seeking to restore the original meaning of civil rights.

Neoconservative scholar Thomas Sowell[9] perhaps best articulates the philosophy underlying the New Right policies on race and law. Sowell presents the neoconservative struggle against prevailing civil rights policies as nothing less than an attempt to restore law to its rightful place and to prevent the descent of American society into fascism. Sowell suggests that the growing popularity of white hate groups is evidence of the instability wrought by improvident civil rights policies. To Sowell, the growth of anti-Black sentiment is an understandable reaction to a vision that has threatened to undermine democratic institutions, delegitimize the court system, and demoralize the American people.

The culprit in this epic struggle is a political view which Sowell has dubbed "the civil rights vision." According to Sowell, this view developed as the leaders of the civil rights movement shifted the movement's original focus on equal treatment under the law to a demand for equal results notwithstanding genuine differences in ability, delegitimizing the movement's claim in a democratic society. The civil rights vision has nothing to do with the achievement of civil rights today, according to Sowell, because in reality "the battle for civil rights was fought and won — at great cost — many years ago."[10] Sowell's central criticism is that the visionaries have attempted to infuse the law with their own political interpretation, which Sowell characterizes as separate from and alien to the true meaning of civil rights. He argues that, although these visionaries have struggled and sacrificed in the name of civil rights, they nonetheless merit censure for undermining the stability of American society through their politicization of the law.[11]

Sowell singles out the judiciary for especially harsh criticism. Judges, according to Sowell, have ignored the original understanding of title VII and imposed their own political views instead. "The perversions of the law by federal judges . . . have been especially brazen," Sowell charges. According to Sowell, judges have participated in a process by which "law, plain honesty and democracy itself [have been] sacrificed on the altar of missionary self-righteousness."[12] Sowell cautions that when judges allow law to be overriden by politics, the threat of fascism looms ever large:

> When judges reduce the law to a question of who has the power and whose ox is gored, they can hardly disclaim responsibility, or be morally superior, when others respond in kind. We can only hope that the response will not someday undermine our whole concept of law and freedom. Fascism has historically arisen from the utter disillusionment of the people with democratic institutions.[13]

B. A Critique of the Critique: The Indeterminacy of Civil Rights Discourse

Given the seriousness of his accusations, particularly those against the judiciary, one would expect Sowell's proof of subversion to be substantial. His repeated accusations that the true law has been subverted raise expectations that he will eventually identify some determinate, clearly discernible version of that law. Sowell's true law would presumably stand apart from the politics of race, yet control it, without being influenced by inappropriate political factors. Sowell's only "proof" that the law has been subverted, however, rests on his assumption that such subversion is self-evident. In the context of voting, for example, Sowell declares simply: "The right to vote is a civil right. The right to win is not. Equal treatment does not mean equal results."[14]

Sowell fails to substantiate his accusations because he cannot tell us *what* the real law is, or whether it ever existed as he claims. He simply embraces language from antidiscrimination texts, imports his own meaning of its purpose, and ignores contradictory purposes and interpretations. Here Sowell, apparently without realizing it, merely embraces one aspect of a tension that runs throughout antidiscrimination law — the tension between equality as a process and equality as a result.

This basic conflict has given rise to two distinct rhetorical visions in the body of antidiscrimination law — one of which I have termed the expansive view, the other the restrictive view. The expansive view stresses equality as a result, and looks to real consequences for African-Americans. It interprets the objective of antidiscrimination law as the eradication of the substantive conditions of Black subordination and attempts to enlist the institutional power of the courts to further the national goal of eradicating the effects of racial oppression.[15]

The restrictive vision, which exists side by side with this expansive view, treats equality as a process, downplaying the significance of actual outcomes. The primary objective of antidiscrimination law, according to this vision, is to prevent future wrongdoing rather than to redress present manifestations of past injustice. "Wrongdoing," moreover, is seen primarily as isolated actions against individuals rather than as a societal policy against an entire group. Nor does the restrictive view contemplate the courts playing a role in redressing harms from America's racist past, as opposed to merely policing society to eliminate a narrow set of proscribed discriminatory practices. Moreover, even when injustice is found, efforts to redress it must be balanced against, and limited by, competing interests of white workers — even when those interests were actually created by the subordination of Blacks. The innocence of whites weighs more heavily than do the past wrongs committed upon Blacks and the benefits that whites derived from those wrongs.[16] In sum, the restrictive view seeks to proscribe only certain kinds of subordinating acts, and then only when other interests are not overly burdened.

Although the tension between the expansive and restrictive vision is present throughout antidiscrimination law, Sowell dismisses the full complexity of the problem by simply declaring that equal process is completely unrelated to equal results. Yet it is not nearly as clear as Sowell suggests that the right to vote, for instance, has nothing to do with winning; no measure of a process' effectiveness can be wholly separated from the purpose for which it was initiated. Sowell implicitly acknowledges that voting is related to some notion of actual representation. Having done so, he cannot completely sever that process from its admitted purpose. Depending on how one views society, democracy, and the historic significance of racial disenfranchisement, the "appropriate" relationship between voting and representation can be defined to require anything from at-large representation to full proportional representation. Sowell's attempt to sever voting from winning merely *raises* the question of process and results; it does not answer it.

As the expansive and restrictive views of antidiscrimination law reveal, there simply is no self-evident interpretation of civil rights inherent in the terms themselves. Instead, specific interpretations proceed largely from the world view of the interpreter. For example, to believe, as Sowell does, that color-blind policies represent the only legitimate and effective means of ensuring a racially equitable society, one would have to assume not only that there is only one "proper role" for law, but also that such a racially equitable society already exists. In this world, once law had performed its "proper" function of assuring equality of process, differences in outcomes between groups would not reflect past discrimination but rather real differences between groups competing for societal rewards. Unimpeded by irrational prejudices against identifiable groups and unfettered by government-imposed preferences, competition would ensure that any group stratification would reflect only the cumulative effects of employers' rational decisions to hire the best workers for the least cost. The deprivations and oppression of the past would somehow be expunged from the present. Only in such a society, where all other societal functions operate in a nondiscriminatory way, would equality of process constitute equality of opportunity.

This belief in color-blindness and equal process, however, would make no sense at all in a society in which identifiable groups had actually been treated differently historically and in which the effects of this difference in treatment continued into the present. If employers were thought to have been influenced by factors other than the actual performance of each job applicant, it would be absurd to rely on their decisions as evidence of true market valuations. Arguments that differences in economic status cannot be redressed, or are legitimate because they reflect cultural rather than racial inferiority, would have to be rejected; cultural disadvantages themselves would be seen as the consequence of historical discrimination. One could not look at outcomes as a fair measure of merit since one would recognize that everyone had not been given an equal start. Because it would be apparent that institutions had embraced discriminatory policies in order to produce disparate results, it would be necessary to rely on results to indicate whether these discriminatory policies have been successfully dismantled.

These two visions of society correspond closely to those held by Sowell and the civil rights visionaries. In each vision, all arguments about what the law *is* are premised upon what the law *should be*, given a particular world view. The conflict is not, as Sowell has suggested, between the true meaning of the law and a bastardized version, but between two different interpretations of society. Thus, though they attempt to lay claim to an apolitical perch from which to accuse civil rights visionaries of subverting the law to politics, the neoconservatives as well rely on their own political interpretations to give meaning to their respective concepts of rights and oppression. The crucial point that Sowell overlooks is that law itself does not dictate which of various visions will be adopted as an interpretive base. The choice between various visions and the values that lie within them is not guided by any determinate organizing principle. Consequently, Sowell has no basis from which to argue that color-conscious, result-oriented remedies are political perversions of the law, but that his preference, color-blind, process-oriented remedies are not.

C. The Constituency's Dilemma

The passage of civil rights legislation nurtured the impression that the United States had moved decisively to end the oppression of Blacks. The fanfare surrounding the passage of these Acts, however, created an expectation that the legislation would not and could not fulfill. The law accommodated and obscured contradictions that led to conflict, countervision, and the current vacuousness of antidiscrimination law.

Because antidiscrimination law contains both the expansive and the restrictive view, equality of opportunity can refer to either. This uncertainty means that the societal adoption of racial equality

rhetoric does not itself entail a commitment to end racial inequality. Indeed, to the extent that antidiscrimination law is believed to embrace color-blindness, equal opportunity rhetoric constitutes a formidable obstacle to efforts to alleviate conditions of white supremacy. As Alfred Blumrosen observes, "it [is] clear that a 'color-blind' society built upon the subordination of persons of one color [is] a society which [cannot] correct that subordination because it [can] never recognize it."[17] In sum, the very terms used to proclaim victory contain within them the seeds of defeat. To demand "equality of opportunity" is to demand nothing specific because "equality of opportunity" has assimilated both the demand and the object against which the demand is made; it is to participate in an abstracted discourse which carries the moral force of the movement as well as the stability of the institutions and interests which the movement opposed.

Society's adoption of the ambivalent rhetoric of equal opportunity law has made it that much more difficult for Black people to name their reality. There is no longer a perpetrator, a clearly identifiable discriminator. Company X can be an equal opportunity employer even though Company X has no Blacks or any other minorities in its employ. Practically speaking, all companies can now be equal opportunity employers by proclamation alone. Society has embraced the rhetoric of equal opportunity without fulfilling its promise; creating a break with the past has formed the basis for the neoconservative claim that present inequities cannot be the result of discriminatory practices because this society no longer discriminates against Blacks.

Equal opportunity law may have also undermined the fragile consensus against white supremacy. To the extent that the objective of racial equality was seen as lifting formal barriers imposed against participation by Blacks, the reforms appear to have succeeded. Today, the claim that equal opportunity does not yet exist for Black America may fall upon deaf ears — ears deafened by repeated declarations that equal opportunity exists. Even Alfred Blumrosen — himself a civil rights visionary — demonstrates how the rhetoric of formal racial equality, by bringing about the collapse of overt obstacles, convinced people that things have changed significantly:

The public sympathy for the plight of black Americans circa 1965 cannot be recreated, because the condition of black American[s] in 1985 is so much improved, as a result of the 1964 legislation. The success of the Civil Rights Act contained the seeds of its loss of public support. *Racism alone simply will no longer do as an explanation for the current condition of depressed minorities.* The rhetoric of the sixties sounds hollow to Americans of the eighties because it is hollow.[18]

Blumrosen and others may be correct in pointing out that many things have changed under the political, legal, and moral force of the civil rights movement. Formal barriers have constituted a major aspect of the historic subordination of African-Americans and, as I discuss below, the elimination of those barriers was meaningful. Indeed, equal opportunity rhetoric gains its power from the fact that people can point to real changes that accompanied its advent. As the indeterminacy of doctrine reveals, however, what at first appears an unambiguous commitment to antidiscrimination conceals within it many conflicting and contradictory interests. In antidiscrimination law, the conflicting interests actually reinforce existing social arrangements, moderated to the extent necessary to balance the civil rights challenge with the many interests still privileged over it.

The recognition on the part of civil rights advocates that deeper institutional changes are required has come just as the formal changes have begun to convince people that enough has been done. Indeed, recent cases illustrate that the judiciary's commitment to racial equality has waned considerably.[19] These doctrinal and procedural developments, taken along with the overall political climate, indicate that the policy of redressing discrimination no longer has the high priority it once had. As Derrick Bell argues, "At heart, many of the cases seem to reflect an unwillingness that has been evident since *Washington v. Davis* to further expand remedies for discrimination." In discussing what he views as the waning of the commitment to achieve a non-racist society, Bell observes, "Discrimination claims, when they are dramatic enough, and do not greatly threaten majority concerns, are given a sympathetic hearing, but there is a pervasive

sense that definite limits have been set on the weight that minority claims receive when balanced against majority interests."[20]

The flagging commitment of the courts and of many whites to fighting discrimination may not be the only deleterious effect of the civil rights reforms. The lasting harm must be measured by the extent to which limited gains hamper efforts of African-Americans to name their reality and to remain capable of engaging in collective action in the future. The danger of adopting equal opportunity rhetoric on its face is that the constituency incorporates legal and philosophical concepts that have an uneven history and an unpredictable trajectory. If the civil rights constituency allows its own political consciousness to be completely replaced by the ambiguous discourse of antidiscrimination law, it will be difficult for it to defend its genuine interests against those whose interests are supported by opposing visions that also lie within the same discourse. The struggle, it seems, is to maintain a contextualized, specified world view that reflects the experience of Blacks. The question remains whether engaging in legal reform precludes this possibility.

III. The New Left Attack: The Hegemonic Function of Legal Rights Discourse

Various scholars connected with the Critical Legal Studies movement[21] have offered critical analyses of law and legal reform which provide a broad framework for explaining how legal reforms help mask and legitimate continuing racial inequality. The Critics present law as a series of ideological constructs that operate to support existing social arrangements by convincing people that things are both inevitable and basically fair. Legal reform, therefore, cannot serve as a means for fundamentally restructuring society. This theory, however, is a general one, the utility of which is limited in the context of civil rights by its insufficient attention to racial domination. Removed from the reality of oppression and its overwhelming constraints, the Critics cannot fairly understand the choices the civil rights movement confronted or, still less, recommend solutions to its current problems. . . .

In broadest terms, Critical scholars have

attempted to analyze legal ideology and discourse as a social artifact which operates to recreate and legitimate American society. In order to discover the contingent character of the law, CLS scholars unpack legal doctrine to reveal both its internal inconsistencies (generally by exposing the incoherence of legal arguments) and its external inconsistencies (often by laying bare the inherently paradoxical and political world views imbedded within legal doctrine). Having thus exposed the inadequacies of legal doctrine, CLS scholars go on to examine the political character of the choices that were made in the doctrine's name. This inquiry exposes the ways in which legal ideology has helped create, support, and legitimate America's present class structure

* * *

The Critical emphasis on deconstruction as *the* vehicle for liberation leads to the conclusion that engaging in legal discourse should be avoided because it reinforces not only the discourse itself but also the society and the world that it embodies. Yet Critics offer little beyond this observation. Their focus on delegitimating rights rhetoric seems to suggest that, once rights rhetoric has been discarded, there exists a more productive strategy for change, one which does not reinforce existing patterns of domination.

Unfortunately, no such strategy has yet been articulated, and it is difficult to imagine that racial minorities will ever be able to discover one. As Frances Fox Piven and Richard Cloward point out in their excellent account of the civil rights movement, popular struggles are a reflection of institutionally determined logic and a challenge to that logic. People can only demand change in ways that reflect the logic of the institutions that they are challenging. Demands for change that do not reflect the institutional logic — that is, demands that do not engage and subsequently reinforce the dominant ideology — will probably be ineffective.[22]

The possibility for ideological change is created through the very process of legitimation, which is triggered by crisis. Powerless people can sometimes trigger such a crisis by challenging an institution internally, that is, by using its own logic against it.[23] Such crisis occurs when powerless people force open and politicize a contradiction between the dominant ideology and

their reality. The political consequences of maintaining the contradictions may sometimes force an adjustment — an attempt to close the gap or to make things appear fair. Yet, because the adjustment is triggered by the political consequences of the contradiction, circumstances will be adjusted only to the extent necessary to close the apparent contradiction.

This approach to understanding legitimation and change is applicable to the civil rights movement. Because Blacks were challenging their exclusion from political society, the only claims that were likely to achieve recognition were those that reflected American society's institutional logic: legal rights ideology. Articulating their formal demands through legal rights ideology, civil rights protestors exposed a series of contradictions — the most important being the promised privileges of American citizenship and the practice of absolute racial subordination. Rather than using the contradictions to suggest that American citizenship was itself illegitimate or false, civil rights protestors proceeded as if American citizenship were real, and demanded to exercise the "rights" that citizenship entailed. By seeking to restructure reality to reflect American mythology, Blacks relied upon and ultimately benefited from politically inspired efforts to resolve the contradictions by granting formal rights. Although it is the need to maintain legitimacy that presents powerless groups with the opportunity to wrest concessions from the dominant order, it is the very accomplishment of legitimacy that forecloses greater possibilities. In sum, the potential for change is both created and limited by legitimation.

The central issue that the Critics fail to address, then, is how to avoid the "legitimating" effects of reform if engaging in reformist discourse is the only effective way to challenge the legitimacy of the social order. Perhaps the only situation in which powerless people may receive any favorable response is where there is a political or ideological need to restore an image of fairness that has somehow been tarnished. Most efforts to change an oppressive situation are bound to adopt the dominant discourse to some degree. On the other hand, Peter Gabel may well be right in observing that the reforms which come from such demands are likely to transform a given situation only to the extent necessary to legitimate those elements of the situation that "must" remain unchanged.[24] Thus, it might just be the case that oppression means "being between a rock and a hard place" — that there are risks and dangers involved both in engaging in the dominant discourse *and* in failing to do so. What subordinated people need is an analysis which can inform them how the risks can be minimized, and how the rocks and the very hard places can be negotiated.

IV. The Context Defined: Racist Ideology and Hegemony

The failure of the Critics to consider race in their account of law and legitimacy is not a minor oversight: race consciousness is central not only to the domination of Blacks, but also to whites' acceptance of the legitimacy of hierarchy and to their identity with elite interest. Exposing the centrality of race consciousness is crucial to identifying and delegitimating beliefs that present hierarchy as inevitable and fair. Moreover, exposing the centrality of race consciousness shows how the options of Blacks in American society have been limited, and how the use of rights rhetoric has emancipated Blacks from some manifestations of racial domination.

* * *

Blacks are ultimately presented with a dilemma: liberal reform both transforms and legitimates. Even though legal ideology absorbs, redefines, and limits the language of protest, African-Americans cannot ignore the power of legal ideology to counter some of the most repressive aspects of racial domination.

A. The Hegemonic Role of Racism: Establishing the "Other" in American Ideology

Throughout American history, the subordination of Blacks was rationalized by a series of stereotypes and beliefs that made their conditions appear logical and natural. Historically, white supremacy has been premised upon various political, scientific, and religious theories, each of which relies on racial characterizations and stereotypes about Blacks that have coalesced into an extensive legitimating ideology.[25] Today, it is probably not controversial to say that these stereotypes were developed primarily to rationalize the oppression of Blacks. What *is* overlooked, however, is the extent to which these stereotypes serve a hegemonic function by perpetuating a mythology about both Blacks *and* whites even today, reinforcing an illusion of a white community that cuts across ethnic, gender, and class lines.

As presented by Critical scholars, hegemonic rule succeeds to the extent that the ruling class world view establishes the appearance of a unity of interests between the dominant class and the dominated. Throughout American history, racism has identified the interests of subordinated whites with those of society's white elite. Racism does not support the dominant order simply because all whites want to maintain their privilege at the expense of Blacks, or because Blacks sometimes serve as convenient political scapegoats. Instead, the very existence of a clearly subordinated "other" group is contrasted with the norm in a way that reinforces identification with the dominant group. Racism helps create an illusion of unity through the oppositional force of a symbolic "other."[26] The establishment of an "other" creates a bond, a burgeoning common identity of all non-stigmatized parties — whose identity and interests are defined in opposition to the other.

According to the philosophy of Jacques Derrida, a structure of polarized categories is characteristic of Western thought:

> Western thought . . . has always been structured in terms of dichotomies or polarities: good vs. evil, being vs. nothingness, presence vs. absence, truth vs. error, identity vs. difference, mind vs. matter, man vs., woman, soul vs. body, life vs. death, nature vs. culture, speech vs. writing. These polar opposites do not, however, stand as independent and equal entities. The second term in each pair is considered the negative, corrupt, undesirable version of the first, a fall away from it. . . . In other words, the two terms are not simply opposed in their meanings, but are arranged in a hierarchical order which gives the first term *priority.* . . .[27]

Racist ideology replicates this pattern of arranging oppositional categories in a hierarchical order; historically, whites represented the dominant antinomy while Blacks came to be seen as separate and subordinate. This hierarchy is reflected in the chart below. Note how each traditional negative image of Blacks correlates with a counter-image of whites:

Historical Oppositional Dualities

White Images	Black Images
Industrious	Lazy
Intelligent	Unintelligent
Moral	Immoral
Knowledgeable	Ignorant
Enabling Culture	Disabling Culture
Law-Abiding	Criminal
Responsible	Shiftless
Virtuous/Pious	Lascivious

The oppositional dynamic symbolized by this chart was created and maintained through an elaborate and systematic process. Laws and customs helped create "races" out of a broad range of human traits. In the process of creating races, the categories came to be filled with meaning — Blacks were characterized one way, whites another. Whites became associated with normatively positive characteristics; Blacks became associated with the subordinate, even aberrational characteristics. The operation of this dynamic, along with the important political role of racial oppositionalism, can be illustrated through a few brief historical references.

Edmund Morgan provides vivid illustration of how slaveholders from the seventeenth century onward created and politicized racial categories to maintain the support of non-slaveholding whites. Morgan recounts how the planters "lump[ed] Indians, mulattoes, and Negroes in a single slave class," and how these categories became "an essential, if unacknowledged, ingredient of the republican ideology that enabled Virginians to lead the nation."[28] Having accepted a common interest with slaveholders in keeping Blacks subordinated, even whites who had material reasons to object to the dominance over the slaveholding class could challenge the regime only so far. The power of race consciousness convinced whites to support a system that was opposed to their own economic interests. As George Fredrickson put it, "racial privilege could and did serve as a compensation for class disadvantage."[29]

* * *

The political and ideological role that race consciousness continues to play is suggested by racial polarization in contemporary presidential politics. Several political commentators have suggested that many whites supported Ronald Reagan in the belief that he would correct a perceived policy imbalance that unjustly benefited Blacks, and some argue further that Reagan made a direct racist appeal to white voters. Manning Marable notes, for example, that "[a]ppeals to the 'race consciousness' of white workers were the decisive factor in Reagan's 1984 victory, especially in the South."[30] Reagan received nearly 70% of the white vote whereas 90% of Black voters cast their ballots for Mondale. Similarly, the vast majority of Blacks — 82% — disapproved of Reagan's performance, whereas only 32% of whites did.

Even the Democratic Party, which has traditionally relied on Blacks as its most loyal constituency, has responded to this apparent racial polarization by seeking to distance itself from Black interests. Although it has been argued that the racial polarization demonstrated in the 1984 election does not represent a trend of white defections from the Democratic Party, it is significant that, whatever the cause of the Party's inability to attract white votes, Democratic leaders have expressed a willingness to moderate the Party's stand on key racial issues in attempts to recapture the white vote.[31]

B. The Role of Race Consciousness in a System of Formal Equality

The previous section emphasizes the continuity of white race consciousness over the course of American history. This section, by contrast, focuses on the partial transformation of the functioning of race consciousness that occurred with the transition from Jim Crow to formal equality in race law.

Prior to the civil rights reforms, Blacks were formally subordinated by the state. Blacks experienced being the "other" in two aspects of oppression, which I shall designate as symbolic and material. Symbolic subordination refers to the formal denial of social and political equality to all Blacks, regardless of their accomplishments. Segregation and other forms of social exclusion — separate restrooms, drinking fountains, entrances, parks, cemeteries, and dining facilities — reinforced a racist ideology that Blacks were simply inferior to whites and were therefore not included in the vision of America as a community of equals.

Material subordination, on the other hand, refers to the ways that discrimination and exclusion economically subordinated Blacks to whites and subordinated the life chances of Blacks to those of whites on almost every level. This subordination occurs when Blacks are paid less for the same work, when segregation limits access to decent housing, and where poverty, anxiety, poor health care, and crime create a life expectancy for Blacks that is five to six years shorter than for whites.

Symbolic subordination often created material disadvantage by reinforcing race consciousness in everything from employment to education. In fact, the two are generally not thought of separately: separate facilities were usually inferior facilities, and limited job categorization virtually always brought lower pay and harder work. Despite the pervasiveness of racism, however, there existed even before the civil rights movement a class of Blacks who were educationally, economically, and professionally equal — if not superior — to many whites, and yet these Blacks suffered social and political exclusion as well.

It is also significant that not all separation resulted in inferior institutions. School segregation — although often presented as the epitome of symbolic and material subordination — did not always result in inferior education. It is not separation *per se* that made segregation subordinating, but the fact that it was enforced and supported by state power, and accompanied by the explicit belief in African-American inferiority.

The response to the civil rights movement was the removal of most formal barriers and symbolic manifestations of subordination. Thus, "White Only" notices and other obvious indicators of the societal policy of racial subordination disappeared — at least in the public sphere. The disappearance of these symbols of subordination reflected the acceptance of the rhetoric of formal equality and signaled the demise of the rhetoric of white supremacy as expressing America's normative vision. In other words, it could no

longer be said that Blacks were not included as equals in the American political vision.

Removal of these public manifestations of subordination was a significant gain for all Blacks, although some benefited more than others. The eradication of formal barriers meant more to those whose oppression was primarily symbolic than to those who suffered lasting material disadvantage. Yet despite these disparate results, it would be absurd to suggest that no benefits came from these formal reforms, especially in regard to racial policies, such as segregation, that were partly material but largely symbolic. Thus, to say that the reforms were "merely symbolic" is to say a great deal. These legal reforms and the formal extension of "citizenship" were large achievements precisely because much of what characterized Black oppression was symbolic and formal.

Yet the attainment of formal equality is not the end of the story. Racial hierarchy cannot be cured by the move to facial race-neutrality in the laws that structure the economic, political, and social lives of Black people. White race consciousness, in a new form but still virulent, plays an important, perhaps crucial, role in the new regime that has legitimated the deteriorating day-to-day material conditions of the majority of Blacks.

The end of Jim Crow has been accompanied by the demise of an explicit ideology of white supremacy. The white norm, however, has not disappeared; it has only been submerged in popular consciousness. It continues in an unspoken form as a statement of the positive social norm, legitimating the continuing domination of those who do not meet it. Nor have the negative stereotypes associated with Blacks been eradicated. The rationalizations once used to legitimate Black subordination based on a belief in racial inferiority have now been reemployed to legitimate the domination of Blacks through reference to an assumed cultural inferiority.

* * *

White race consciousness, which includes the modern belief in cultural inferiority, acts to further Black subordination by justifying all the forms of unofficial racial discrimination, injury, and neglect that flourish in a society that is only formally dedicated to equality. In more subtle ways, moreover, white race consciousness reinforces and is reinforced by the myth of equal opportunity that explains and justifies broader class hierarchies.

Race consciousness also reinforces whites' sense that American society is really meritocratic and thus helps prevent them from questioning the basic legitimacy of the free market. Believing both that Blacks are inferior and that the economy impartially rewards the superior over the inferior, whites see that most Blacks are indeed worse off than whites are, which reinforces their sense that the market is operating "fairly and impartially"; those who should logically be on the bottom are on the bottom. This strengthening of whites' belief in the system in turn reinforces their beliefs that Blacks are *indeed* inferior. After all, equal opportunity *is* the rule, and the market *is* an impartial judge; if Blacks are on the bottom, it must reflect their relative inferiority. Racist ideology thus operates in conjunction with the class components of legal ideology to reinforce the status quo, both in terms of class and race.

To bring a fundamental challenge to the way things are, whites would have to question not just their own subordinate status, but also both the economic and the racial myths that justify the status quo. Racism, combined with equal opportunity mythology, provides a rationalization for racial oppression, making it difficult for whites to see the Black situation as illegitimate or unnecessary. If whites believe that Blacks, because they are unambitious or inferior, get what they deserve, it becomes that much harder to convince whites that something is wrong with the entire system. Similarly, a challenge to the legitimacy of continued racial inequality would force whites to confront myths about equality of opportunity that justify for them whatever measure of economic success they may have attained.

Thus, although Critics have suggested that legal consciousness plays a central role in legitimating hierarchy in America, the otherness dynamic enthroned within the maintenance and perpetuation of white race consciousness seems to be at least as important as legal consciousness in supporting the dominant order. Like legal consciousness, race consciousness makes it difficult—at least for whites—to imagine the world differently. It also creates the desire for identification with privileged elites. By focusing on a distinct, subordinate "other," whites include themselves in the dominant circle—an arena in which most hold no real power, but only their privileged racial identity. Consider the case of a dirt-poor, southern white, shown participating in a Ku Klux Klan rally in the movie *Resurgence*, who declared: "Every morning, I wake up and thank God I'm white." For this person, and for others like him, race consciousness—manifested by his refusal even to associate with Blacks—provides a powerful explanation of why he fails to challenge the current social order.

C. Rights Discourse as a Challenge to the Oppositional Dynamic

The oppositional dynamic, premised upon maintaining Blacks as an excluded and subordinated "other," initially created an ideological and political structure of formal inequality against which rights rhetoric proved to be the most effective weapon. Although rights rhetoric may ultimately have absorbed the civil rights challenge and legitimated continued subordination, the otherness dynamic provides a fuller understanding of how the very transformation afforded by legal reform itself has contributed to the ideological and political legitimation of continuing Black subordination.

Rights discourse provided the ideological mechanisms through which the conflicts of federalism, the power of the Presidency, and the legitimacy of the courts could be orchestrated against Jim Crow. Movement leaders used these tactics to force open a conflict between whites that eventually benefited Black people. Casting racial issues in the moral and legal rights rhetoric of the prevailing ideology helped create the political controversy without which the state's coercive function would not have been enlisted to aid Blacks.

Simply critiquing the ideology from without or making demands in language outside the rights discourse would have accomplished little. Rather, Blacks gained by using a powerful combination of direct action, mass protest, and individual acts of resistance, along with appeals to public opinion and the courts couched in the language of the prevailing legal consciousness. The result was a series of ideological and political crises. In these crises, civil rights activists and lawyers induced the federal government to aid Blacks and triggered efforts to legitimate and reinforce the authority of the law in ways that benefited Blacks. Simply insisting that Blacks be integrated or speaking in the language of "needs" would have endangered the lives of those who were already taking risks — and with no reasonable chance of success. President Eisenhower, for example, would not have sent federal troops to Little Rock simply at the behest of protesters demanding that Black schoolchildren receive an equal education. Instead, the successful manipulation of legal rhetoric led to a crisis of federal power that ultimately benefited Blacks.

Some critics of legal reform movements seem to overlook the fact that state power has made a significant difference — sometimes between life and death — in the efforts of Black people to transform their world. Attempts to harness the power of the state through the appropriate rhetorical/legal incantations should be appreciated as intensely powerful and calculated political acts. In the context of white supremacy, engaging in rights discourse should be seen as an act of self-defense. This was particularly true because the state could not assume a position of neutrality regarding Black people once the movement had mobilized people to challenge the system of oppression: either the coercive mechanism of the state had to be used to support white supremacy, or it had to be used to dismantle it. We know now, with hindsight, that it did both.

Blacks did use rights rhetoric to mobilize state power to their benefit against symbolic oppression through formal inequality and, to some extent, against material deprivation in the form of private, informal exclusion of the middle class from jobs and housing. Yet today the same legal reforms play a role in providing an ideological framework that makes the present conditions facing underclass Blacks appear fair and reasonable. The eradication of barriers has created a new dilemma for those victims of racial oppression who are not in a position to benefit from the move to formal equality. The race neutrality of the legal system creates the illusion that racism is no longer the primary factor responsible for the condition of the Black underclass; instead, as we have seen, class disparities appear to be the consequence of individual and group merit within a supposed system of equal opportunity. Moreover, the fact that there are Blacks who are economically successful gives credence both to the assertion that opportunities exist, and to the backlash attitude that Blacks have "gotten too far."[32] Psychologically, for Blacks who have not made it, the lack of an explanation for their underclass status may result in self-blame and other self-destructive attitudes.

Another consequence of the formal reforms may be the loss of collectivity among Blacks. The removal of formal barriers created new opportunities for some Blacks that were not shared by various other classes of African-Americans. As Blacks moved into different spheres, the experience of being Black in America became fragmented and multifaceted, and the different contexts presented opportunities to experience racism in different ways. The social, economic, and even residential distance between the various classes may complicate efforts to unite behind issues as a racial group. Although "White Only" signs may have been crude and debilitating, they at least presented a readily discernible target around which to organize. Now, the targets are obscure and diffuse, and this difference may create doubt among some Blacks whether there is enough similarity between their life experiences and those of other Blacks to warrant collective political action.

Formal equality significantly transformed the Black experience in America. With society's embrace of formal equality came the eradication of symbolic domination and the suppression of white supremacy as the norm of society. Future generations of Black Americans would no longer be explicitly regarded as America's second-class citizens. Yet the transformation of the oppositional dynamic — achieved through the suppression of racial norms and stereotypes, and the recasting of racial inferiority into assumptions of cultural inferiority — creates several difficulties for the civil rights constituency. The removal of formal barriers, although symbolically significant to all and materially significant to some, will do little to alter the hierarchical relationship between Blacks and whites until the way in which white race consciousness perpetuates norms that legitimate Black subordination is revealed. This is not to say that white norms alone account for the conditions of the Black underclass. It is instead an acknowledgment that, until the distinct racial nature of class ideology is itself revealed and debunked, nothing can be done about the underlying structural problems that account for the disparities. The narrow focus of racial exclusion— that is, the belief that racial exclusion is illegitimate only where the "White Only" signs are explicit—coupled with strong assumptions about equal opportunity, makes it difficult to move the discussion of racism beyond the societal self-satisfaction engendered by the appearance of neutral norms and formal inclusion.

D. Self-Conscious Ideological Struggle

Rights have been important. They may have legitimated racial inequality, but they have also been the means by which oppressed groups have secured both entry as formal equals into the dominant order and the survival of their movement in the face of private and state repression. The dual role of legal change creates a dilemma for Black reformers. As long as race consciousness thrives, Blacks will often have to rely on rights rhetoric when it is necessary to protect Black interests. The very reforms brought about by appeals to legal ideology, however, seem to undermine the ability to move forward toward a broader vision of racial equality. In the quest for racial justice, winning and losing have been part of the same experience.

The Critics are correct in observing that engaging in rights discourse has helped to deradicalize and co-opt the challenge. Yet they fail to acknowledge the limited range of options presented to Blacks in a context where they were deemed "other," and the unlikelihood that specific demands for inclusion and equality would be heard if articulated in other terms. This abbreviated list of options is itself contingent upon the ideological power of white race consciousness and the continuing role of Black Americans as "other." Future efforts to address racial domination, as well as class hierarchy, must consider the continuing ideology of white race consciousness by uncovering the oppositional dynamic and by chipping away at its premises. Central to this task is revealing the contingency of race and exploring the connection between white race consciousness and the other myths that legitimate both class and race hierarchies. Critics and others whose agendas include challenging hierarchy and legitimation must not overlook the importance of revealing the contingency of race.

Optimally, the deconstruction of white race consciousness might lead to a liberated future for both Blacks and whites. Yet, until whites recognize the hegemonic function of racism and turn their efforts toward neutralizing it, African-American people must develop pragmatic political strategies—self-conscious ideological struggle—to minimize the costs of liberal reform while maximizing its utility. A primary step in engaging in self-conscious ideological struggle must be to transcend the oppositional dynamic in which Blacks are cast simply and solely as white's subordinate "other."

The dual role that rights have played makes strategizing a difficult task. Black people can afford neither to resign themselves to, nor to attack frontally, the legitimacy and incoherence of the dominant ideology. The subordinate position of Blacks in this society makes it unlikely that African-Americans will realize gains through the kind of direct challenge to the legitimacy of American liberal ideology that is now being waged by Critical scholars. On the other hand, delegitimating race consciousness would be directly relevant to Black needs, and this strategy will sometimes require the pragmatic use of liberal ideology.

This vision is consistent with the views forwarded by theoreticians such as Frances Fox Piven and Richard Cloward, Antonio Gramsci, and Roberto Unger. Piven and Cloward observe that oppressed people sometimes advance by creating ideological and political crisis, but that the form of the crisis-producing challenge must reflect the institutional logic of the system. The use of rights rhetoric during the civil rights movement created such a crisis by presenting and manipulating the dominant ideology in a new and transformative way. Challenges and demands made from outside the institutional logic would have accomplished little because Blacks, as the subordinate "other," were already perceived as being outside the mainstream. The struggle of Blacks, like that of all subordinated groups, is a struggle for inclusion, an attempt to manipulate elements of the dominant ideology to transform the experience of domination. It is a struggle to create a new status quo through the ideological and political tools that are available.

Gramsci called this struggle a "War of Position" and he regarded it as the most appropriate strategy for change in Western societies. According to Gramsci, direct challenges to the dominant class accomplish little if ideology plays such a central role in establishing authority that the legitimacy of the dominant regime is not challenged. Joseph Femia, interpreting Gramsci, states that "the dominant ideology in modern capitalist societies is highly institutionalized and widely internalized. It follows that a concentration on frontal attack, on direct assault against the bourgeois state ('war of movement' or 'war of manoeuvre') can result only in disappointment and defeat."[33] Consequently, the challenge in such societies is to create a counter-hegemony by maneuvering within and expanding the dominant ideology to embrace the potential for change.

Gramsci's vision of ideological struggle is echoed in part by Roberto Unger in his vision of deviationist doctrine. Unger, who represents another strand of the Critical approach, argues that, rather than discarding liberal legal ideology, we should focus and develop its visionary undercurrents:

> [T]he struggle over the form of social life, through deviationist doctrine, creates opportunities for experimental revisions of social life in the direction of the ideals we defend. An implication of our ideas is that the elements of a formative institutional or imaginative structure may be replaced piecemeal rather than only all at once.[34]

Liberal ideology embraces communal and liberating visions along with the legitimating hegemonic visions. Unger, like Gramsci and Piven and Cloward, seems to suggest that the strategy toward meaningful change depends on skillful use of the liberating potential of dominant ideology.

V. Conclusion

For Blacks, the task at hand is to devise ways to wage ideological and political struggle while minimizing the costs of engaging in an inherently legitimating discourse. A clearer understanding of the space we occupy in the American political consciousness is a necessary prerequisite to the development of pragmatic strategies for political and economic survival. In this regard, the most serious challenge for Blacks is to minimize the political and cultural cost of engaging in an inevitably co-optive process in order to secure material benefits. Because our present predicament gives us few options, we must create conditions for the maintenance of a distinct political thought that is informed by the actual conditions of Black people. Unlike the civil rights vision, this new approach should not be defined and thereby limited by the possibilities of dominant political discourse, but should maintain a distinctly progressive outlook that focuses on the needs of the African-American community.

NOTES

1. The principal civil rights reforms are the Civil Rights Act of 1964, Pub. L. No. 88–352, 18 Stat. 243 (codified as amended at 42 U.S.C. §§ 2000(e)–2000(h)(6) (1982)); the Voting Rights Act of 1965, Pub. L. No. 89–110, 79 Stat. 437 (codified as amended at 42 U.S.C. §§ 1971–1974 (1982)); U.S. CONST. amends. XIII–XV; 42 U.S.C. §§ 1981, 1983, 1985 (1982); Exec. Order No. 11,246, 3 C.F.R. 339 (1964–1965 comp.); and the Equal Employment Opportunity Commission regulations, 29 C.F.R. §§ 1600–1691 (1987).

2. D. BELL, RACE, RACISM, AND AMERICAN LAW, § 1.2, at 7 (2d ed. 1981).

3. *See, e.g.*, Abram, *Affirmative Action: Fair Shakers and Social Engineers*, 99 HARV. L. REV. 1312 (1986); *infra* note 23.

4. *See* Freeman, *Legitimizing Racial Discrimination Through Antidiscrimination Law: A Critical Review of Supreme Court Doctrine*, 62 MINN. L. REV. 1049 (1978); *infra* pp. 1349–69.

5. This practice of deconstruction, or, more irreverently, "trashing," is a principal tactic of Critical scholars. *See, e.g.*, Kelman, *Trashing*, 36 STAN. L. REV. 293 (1984); *infra* pp. 1354–56.

6. *See, e.g.*, Belton, *Discrimination and Affirmative Action: An Analysis of Competing Theories of Equality* and Weber, 59 N.C.L. REV. 531, 539–41 (1981); Freeman, *supra* note 4 at 1052–53; Fallon & Weiler, Firefighters v. Stotts: *Conflicting Models of Racial Justice*, 1984 SUP. CT. REV. i.

7. Prominent among these was the Heritage Foundation. *See, e.g.*, S. BUTLER, M. SANERA & W. WEINROD, MANDATE FOR LEADERSHIP II: CONTINUING THE CONSERVATIVE REVOLUTION (Heritage Foundation) (1984); HERITAGE FOUNDATION, MANDATE FOR LEAD-

ERSHIP: POLICY MANAGEMENT IN A CONSERVATIVE ADMINISTRATION (C. Heatherly ed. 1981) (hereinafter HERITAGE FOUNDATION REPORT).

8. For scholarship generally supportive of this restrictive view, see generally Abram, cited in note 3 above; Cooper, *The Coercive Remedies Paradox*, 9 HARV. J.L. & PUB. POL'Y 77 (1986).

9. *See* T. SOWELL, CIVIL RIGHTS: RHETORIC OR REALITY? 116 (1984).

10. *Id.* at 13–35, 37–48, 109.

11. *Id.* at 120. Although Sowell is apparently convinced that law is fundamentally separate from politics, he believes that it can be captured by politics. Sowell's position appears to ignore both the critique of law as politics and ethics developed by the Legal Realists; *see, e.g.*, Cohen, *Transcendental Nonsense and the Functional Approach*, 35 COLUM. L. REV. 809 (1935); Cook, *The Logic and Bases of the Conflict of Laws*, 33 YALE L.J. 457 (1924), and the work of European structuralist and post-structuralist philosophical schools showing the general indeterminate "meaning" of texts, *see, e.g.*, J. DERRIDA, OF GRAMMATOLOGY (G. Spivak trans. 1976); V. LEITCH, DECONSTRUCTIVE CRITICISM: AN ADVANCED INTRODUCTION (1983). Both of these approaches have been extended as specific critiques of American legal ideology by Critical legal scholars.

12. *Id.* at 119, 120.

13. *Id.*

14. *Id.* at 109.

15. Accordingly, the Supreme Court declared that district courts hold "not merely the power but the duty to render a decree which will so far as possible eliminate the discriminatory effects of the past as well as bar like discrimination in the future." Louisiana v. United States, 380 U.S. 145, 154 (1965).

16. This concern has gained special solicitude from the Supreme Court in the context of layoffs. *See* Wygant v. Jackson Bd. of Educ., 476 U.S. 267, 280–84 (1986) (plurality opinion).

Derrick Bell describes this tendency through the following equation: "White Racism v. Justice = White Racism; White Racism v. White Self-Interest = Justice." *See* D. BELL, *supra* note 2, § 1.12, at 41.

17. A. Blumrosen, Twenty Years of Title VII Law: An Overview 26 (April 18, 1985) (unpublished manuscript on file in the Harvard Law Library).

18. *Id.* at 13 (emphasis added).

19. Recent Supreme Court decisions have placed severe limitations on civil rights suits. *See, e.g.*, Firefighters Local Union No. 1784 v. Stotts, 467 U.S. 561 (1984); Ford Motor Co. v. EEOC, 458 U.S. 219 (1982); General Tel. Co. v. Falcon, 457 U.S. 147 (1982).

20. D. BELL, *supra* note 2, § 9.11.3, at 117 (2d ed. Supp. 1984) (citing Washington v. Davis, 426 U.S. 229 (1976)).

21. This brief summary does not begin to represent a full description of Critical literature. For an introduction to Critical Legal Studies, see, for example, M. KELMAN, A GUIDE TO CRITICAL LEGAL STUDIES (1987).

22. Reforms necessarily come from an existing repertoire of options. As Piven and Cloward note, "if impoverished southern blacks had demanded land reform, they would probably have still gotten the vote." F. Piven and R. Cloward, *Poor People's Movements*, 22–25 (1977).

23. Conversely, groups that do not engage the institutional logic are unlikely to create such a crisis; indeed, they are routinely infiltrated, isolated, and destroyed. Compare, for example, the history of the NAACP with that of the Black Panthers.

24. *See* Gabel, "The Phenomenology of Rights—Consciousness and the Pact of the Withdrawn Selves," 62 TEX. L. REV. 1563 (1984).

25. *See, e.g.*, S. DRAKE, i, BLACK FOLK: HERE AND THERE 28–30 (1987).

26. The notion of Blacks as a subordinated "other" in Western culture has been a major theme in scholarship exploring the cultural and sociological structure of racism. *See* Trost, *Western Metaphysical Dualism as an Element in Racism*, in CULTURAL BASES OF RACISM AND GROUP OPPRESSION 49 (J. Hodge, D. Struckmann & L. Trost eds. 1975).

27. J. DERRIDA, DISSEMINATION viii (B. Johnson trans. 1981) (emphasis in original). Otherness is a corollary to the bipolar conceptualizations that characterize structuralist analysis of Western thought. Some Critical legal scholars have seized these bipolar conceptualizations and used them to explain how doctrine attempts to mediate opposing tendencies in the law. *See, e.g.*, Kennedy, *Form and Substance in Private Law Adjudication*, 89 HARV. L. REV. 1685 (1976).

28. *See* E. MORGAN, AMERICAN SLAVERY—AMERICAN FREEDOM (1975) at 386.

29. G. FREDRICKSON, WHITE SUPREMACY (1981), at 87.

30. *See, e.g.*, M. Marable, Race and Realignment in American Politics (1985) (unpublished manuscript available in Harvard Law School library).

31. This effort to minimize Black influence reflects what Derrick Bell has called the principle of "involuntary sacrifice." *See* D. BELL, *supra* note 2, § 1.9, at 29–30. Bell asserts that throughout American history, Black interests have been sacrificed when necessary to reestablish the bonds of the white community, "so that identifiably different groups of whites may settle a dispute and establish or reestablish their relationship." *Id.* at 30.

32. This phenomenon is undoubtedly exacerbated by periods of economic hardship. It was in this context that the U.S. Commission on Civil Rights commented that some whites "believe that their hard times result

from 'reverse discrimination' in employment and a tax burden imposed upon them to support government programs that in their view provide undeserved advantages to minorities." U.S. COMM'N ON CIVIL RIGHTS, *supra note 3, at ii.*

33. J. FEMIA, GRAMSCI'S POLITICAL THOUGHT: HEGEMONY, CONSCIOUSNESS, AND THE REVOLUTIONARY PROCESS 51 (1981).

34. Unger, The Critical Legal Studies Movement, 96 HARVARD LAW REV. 561 (1983), at 666.

Notes and Questions

Cases on Discrimination and Equal Protection of the Law

1. In *Plessy* v. *Ferguson* the Supreme Court upheld a Louisiana statute requiring the separation of races on public transportation. Recognizing that the object of the Fourteenth Amendment is "to enforce the absolute equality of the two races before the law," the Court argued that laws requiring segregation of the races do not necessarily imply inequality or inferiority of one race to another. Isn't that true? If so, what is wrong with the argument? What does Justice John Harlan say is wrong with it?

2. Given Justice Harlan's dissent in *Plessy* how can we account for the Court's hands-off policy toward enforcing the Fourteenth Amendment in this case? In the civil rights cases thirteen years earlier the Court struck down as an unconstitutional restriction on interstate commerce a public accommodations law that would have prohibited racial discrimination. You may also recall from Chapter Three that at this time the Court was beginning a strong protection of private enterprise through the freedom of contract doctrine. Therefore, keep in mind that many factors are interacting in the courts at any given time. Sympathy for blacks quickly dissipated after the Civil War, and concern for private enterprise and economic development loomed large in the courts by the turn of the century. The short commentary by Lawrence Friedman outlines the legal treatment of minority races around the time of *Plessy*. Does the case simply represent institutionalized racism?

3. By 1948 the Court began to turn around its policy on civil rights, addressing the issue of private agreements restricting the sale of property to the white race. Recognizing that the decision in the civil rights cases of 1883 clearly restricts application of the Fourteenth Amendment to state action, the Court in *Shelley* v. *Kraemer* was faced with the question whether private contracts are ever affected. To what extent and on what grounds does the Court say they are? Keep in mind here the distinction between an illegal contract and an invalid one. Does the Court prohibit restrictive covenants? Will it enforce them? How useful is an unenforceable contract?

4. Six years after *Shelley*, in the landmark case of *Brown* v. *Board of Education*, the Supreme Court explicitly reverses itself on the "separate but equal" doctrine and establishes a requirement of racial integration in the public schools. What argument does the Court advance to support its conclusion that segregation in the schools deprives minority children of an equal opportunity to receive an education, and thus of equal protection of the law?

5. Implementing the goal of equal treatment in general and equal educational opportunity in particular has proved to be a difficult and complex task. Corrective measures were unevenly and begrudgingly adopted while social prejudice remained strong. Integrated schools were largely ineffective in supplying equal education to disadvantaged children, whether black or white. Socially and economically disadvantaged children did not compete well for jobs or higher education. In response, some universities and businesses adopted affirmative action policies that sometimes included quotas, or slots set aside for minority applicants. Many individuals objected to such policies as themselves discriminatory. In the *Bakke* case, the Court considered one such challenge to the quota system adopted by the University of California medical school. What limits does the

Court place on affirmative action programs in general and racial quotas in particular? What arguments support its holding? What objections can be raised to it?

Cases on Discrimination and Equal Protection of the Law

Plessy v. Ferguson
163 U.S. 537 (1896)

Mr. Justice Brown delivered the opinion of the court.   This case turns upon the constitutionality of an act of the general assembly of the state of Louisiana, passed in 1890, providing for separate railway carriages for the white and colored races. Acts 1890, No. 111, p. 152. . . .

* * *

The petition for the writ of prohibition averred that petitioner was seven-eighths Caucasian and one-eighth African blood; that the mixture of colored blood was not discernible in him; and that he was entitled to every right, privilege, and immunity secured to citizens of the United States of the white race; and that, upon such theory, he took possession of a vacant seat in a coach where passengers of the white race were accommodated, and was ordered by the conductor to vacate said coach, and take a seat in another, assigned to persons of the colored race, and, having refused to comply with such demand, he was forcibly ejected, with the aid of a police officer, and imprisoned in the parish jail to answer a charge of having violated the above act.

The constitutionality of this act is attacked upon the ground that it conflicts . . . with . . . the fourteenth amendment. . . .

* * *

The object of the amendment was undoubtedly to enforce the absolute equality of the two races before the law, but, in the nature of things, it could not have been intended to abolish distinctions based upon color, or to enforce social, as distinguished from political, equality, or a commingling of the two races upon terms unsatisfactory to either. Laws permitting, and even requiring, their separation, in places where they are liable to be brought into contact, do not necessarily imply the inferiority of either race to the other, and have been generally, if not universally, recognized as within the competency of the state legislatures in the exercise of their police power. The most common instance of this is connected with the establishment of separate schools for white and colored children, which have been held to be a valid exercise of the legislative power even by courts of states where the political rights of the colored race have been longest and most earnestly enforced.

* * *

Laws forbidding the intermarriage of the two races may be said in technical sense to interfere with the freedom of contract, and yet have been universally recognized as within the police power of the state. State v. Gibson, 36 Ind. 389. . . .

* * *

In this connection, it is also suggested by the learned counsel for the plaintiff in error that the same argument that will justify the state legislature in requiring railways to provide separate accommodations for the two races will also authorize them to require separate cars to be provided for people whose hair is of a certain color, or who are aliens, or who belong to certain nationalities, or to enact laws requiring colored people to walk upon one side of the street, and white people upon the other, or requiring white men's houses to be painted white, and colored men's black, or their vehicles or business signs to be of different colors, upon the theory that one side of the street is as good as the other, or that a house or vehicle of one color is as good as one of another color. The reply to all this is that every exercise of the police power must be reasonable, and extend only to such laws as are enacted in good faith for the promotion of the public good, and not for the annoyance or oppression of a particular class. . . .

So far, then, as a conflict with the fourteenth amendment is concerned, the case reduces itself to the question whether the statute of Louisiana is a reasonable regulation, and with respect to this there must necessarily be a large discretion on the part of the legislature. In determining the question of reasonableness, it is at liberty to act with reference to the established usages, customs, and traditions of the people, and with a view to the promotion of their comfort, and the preservation of the public peace and good order. Gauged by this standard, we cannot say that a law which authorizes or even requires the separation of the two races in public conveyances is unreasonable, or more obnoxious to the fourteenth amendment than the acts of congress requiring separate schools for colored children in the District of Columbia, the constitutionality of which does not seem to have been questioned or the corresponding acts of state legislatures.

We consider the underlying fallacy of the plaintiff's argument to consist in the assumption that the enforced separation of the two races stamps the colored race with a badge of inferiority. If this be so, it is not by reason of anything found in the act, but solely because the colored race chooses to put that construction upon it. The argument necessarily assumes that if, as has been more than once the case, and is not unlikely to be so again, the colored race should become the dominant power in the state legislature, and should enact a law in precisely similar terms, it would thereby relegate the white race to an inferior position. We imagine that the white race, at least, would not acquiesce in this assumption. The argument also assumes that social prejudices may be overcome by legislation, and that equal rights cannot be secured to the negro except by an enforced commingling of the two races. We cannot accept this proposition. If the two races are to meet upon terms of social equality, it must be the result of natural affinities, a mutual appreciation of each other's merits, and a voluntary consent of individuals. . . . Legislation is powerless to eradicate racial instincts, or to abolish distinctions based upon physical differences, and the attempt to do so can only result in accentuating the difficulties of the present situation. If the civil and political rights of both races be equal, one cannot be inferior to the other civilly or politically. If one race be inferior to the other socially, the constitution of the United States cannot put them upon the same plane.

* * *

The judgment of the court below is therefore affirmed.

Mr. Justice Harlan dissenting. . . .

In respect of civil rights, common to all citizens, the constitution of the United States does not, I think, permit any public authority to know the race of those entitled to be protected in the enjoyment of such rights. Every true man has pride of race, and under appropriate circumstances, when the rights of others, his equals before the law, are not to be affected, it is his privilege to express such pride and to take such action based upon it as to him seems proper. But I deny that any legislative body or judicial tribunal may have regard to the race of citizens when the civil rights of those citizens are involved. Indeed, such legislation as that here in question is inconsistent not only with that equality of rights which pertains to citizenship, national and state, but with the personal liberty enjoyed by every one within the United States. . . .

[The thirteenth, fourteenth, and fifteenth amendments] were welcomed by the friends of liberty throughout the world. They removed the race line from our governmental systems. . . .

It was said in argument that the statute of Louisiana does not discriminate against either race, but prescribes a rule applicable alike to white and colored citizens. But this argument does not meet the difficulty. Everyone knows that the statute in question had its origin in the purpose, not so much to exclude white persons from railroad cars occupied by blacks, as to exclude colored people from coaches occupied by or assigned to white persons. Railroad corporations of Louisiana did not make discrimination among whites in the matter of accomodation for travelers. The thing to accomplish was, under the guise of giving equal accommodation for whites and blacks, to compel the latter to keep to themselves while traveling in railroad passenger coaches. No one would be so wanting in candor as to assert the contrary. The fundamental objection, therefore, to the statute, is that it interferes with the personal freedom of citizens. . . . If a white man and a black man choose to occupy the same public conveyance on a public highway, it is their right to do so; and no government, proceeding alone on grounds of race, can prevent it without infringing the personal liberty of each. . . .

The white race deems itself to be the dominant race in this country. And so it is, in prestige, in achievements, in education, in wealth, and in power. So, I doubt not, it will continue to be for all time, if it remains true to its great heritage, and holds fast to the principles of constitutional liberty. But in view of the constitution, in the eye of the law, there is in this country no superior, dominant, ruling class of citizens. There is no caste here. Our constitution is color-blind, and neither knows nor tolerates classes among citizens. In respect of civil rights, all citizens are equal before the law. The humblest is the peer of the most powerful. The law regards man as man, and takes no account of his surroundings or of his color when his civil rights as guaranteed by the supreme law of the land are involved. It is therefore to be regretted that this high tribunal, the final expositor of the fundamental law of the land, has reached the conclusion that it is competent for a state to regulate the enjoyment by citizens of their civil rights solely upon the basis of race.

* * *

If evils will result from the commingling of the two races upon public highways established for the benefit of all, they will be infinitely less than those that will surely come from state legislation regulating the enjoyment of civil rights upon the basis of race. We boast of the freedom enjoyed by our people above all other peoples. But it is difficult to reconcile that boast with a state of the law which, practically, puts the brand of servitude and degradation upon a large class of our fellow citizens, — our equals before the law. The thin disguise of "equal" accommodations for passengers in railroad coaches will not mislead any one, nor atone for the wrong this day done. . . .

Shelley v. Kraemer
334 U.S. 1 (1948)

Mr. Chief Justice Vinson delivered the opinion of the Court.

These cases present for our consideration questions relating to the validity of court enforcement of private agreements, generally described as restrictive covenants, which have as their purpose the exclusion of persons of designated race or color from the ownership or occupancy of real property. Basic constitutional issues of obvious importance have been raised.

The first of these cases comes to this Court on certiorari to the Supreme Court of Missouri. On February 16, 1911, thirty out of a total of thirty-nine owners of property fronting both sides of Labadie Avenue between Taylor Avenue and Cora Avenue in the city of St. Louis, signed an agreement, which was subsequently recorded providing in part:

". . . the said property is hereby restricted to the use and occupancy for the term of Fifty (50) years from this date, so that it shall be a condition all the time and whether recited and referred to as [sic] not in subsequent conveyances and shall attach to the land, as a condition precedent to the sale of the same, that hereafter no part of said property or any portion thereof shall be, for said term of Fifty-years, occupied by any person not of the Caucasian race, it being intended hereby to restrict the use of said property for said period of time against the occupancy as owners or tenants of any portion of said property for resident or other purpose by people of the Negro or Mongolian Race."

* * *

On August 11, 1945, pursuant to a contract of sale, petitioners Shelley, who are Negroes, for valuable consideration received from one Fitzgerald a warranty deed to the parcel in question. The trial court found that petitioners had no actual knowledge of the restrictive agreement at the time of the purchase.

On October 9, 1945, respondents, as owners of other property subject to the terms of the restrictive covenant, brought suit in the Circuit Court of the city of St. Louis praying that petitioners Shelley be restrained from taking possession of the property and that judgment be entered divesting title out of petitioners Shelley and revesting title in the immediate grantor or in such other person as the court should direct. The trial court denied the requested relief on the ground that the restrictive agreement, upon which respondents based their action, had never become final and complete. . . .

The Supreme Court of Missouri sitting *en banc* reversed and directed the trial court to grant the relief for which respondents had prayed. That court held the agreement effective and concluded that enforcement of its provisions violated no rights guaranteed to petitioners by the Federal Constitution. At the time the court rendered its decision, petitioners were occupying the property in question.

* * *

Petitioners have placed primary reliance on their contentions, first raised in the state courts, that judicial enforcement of the restrictive agreements in these cases has violated rights guaranteed to petitioners by the Fourteenth Amendment of the Federal Constitution and Acts of Congress passed pursuant to that Amendment. Specifically, petitioners urge that they have been denied the equal protection of the laws, deprived of property without due process of law, and have been denied privileges and immunities of citizens of the United States. We pass to a consideration of those issues.

I

Whether the equal protection clause of the Fourteenth Amendment inhibits judicial enforcement by state courts of restrictive covenants based on race or color is a question which this Court has not heretofore been called upon to consider. . . .

* * *

It should be observed that these covenants do not seek to proscribe any particular use of the affected properties. Use of the properties for residential occupancy, as such, is not forbidden. The restrictions of these agreements, rather are directed toward a designated class of persons and seek to determine who may and who may now own or make use of the properties for residential purposes. The excluded class is defined wholly in terms of race or color; "simply that and nothing more."

It cannot be doubted that among the civil rights intended to be protected from discriminatory state action by the Fourteenth Amendment are the rights to acquire, enjoy, own and dispose of property. . . .

It is likewise clear that restrictions on the right of occupancy of the sort sought to be created by the private agreements in these cases could not be squared with the requirements of the Fourteenth

Amendment if imposed by state statute or local ordinance. We do not understand respondents to urge the contrary. In the case of Buchanan v. Warley [245 U.S. 60] a unanimous Court declared unconstitutional the provisions of a city ordinance which denied to colored persons the right to occupy houses in blocks in which the greater number of houses were occupied by white persons, and imposed similar restrictions on white persons with respect to blocks in which the greater number of houses were occupied by colored persons. During the course of the opinion in that case, this Court stated: "The Fourteenth Amendment and these statutes enacted in furtherance of its purpose operate to qualify and entitle a colored man to acquire property without state legislation discriminating against him solely because of color."

* * *

But the present cases, unlike those just discussed, do not involve action by state legislatures or city councils. Here the particular patterns of discrimination and the areas in which the restrictions are to operate, are determined, in the first instance, by the terms of agreements among private individuals. Participation of the State consists in the enforcement of the restrictions so defined. The crucial issue with which we are here confronted is whether this distinction removes these cases from the operation of the prohibitory provisions of the Fourteenth Amendment.

Since the decision of this Court in the Civil Rights Cases, 1883, 109 U.S. 3, the principle has become firmly embedded in our constitutional law that the action inhibited by the first section of the Fourteenth Amendment is only such action as may fairly be said to be that of the States. That Amendment erects no shield against merely private conduct, however discriminatory or wrongful.

We conclude, therefore, that the restrictive agreements standing alone cannot be regarded as a violation of any rights guaranteed to petitioners by the Fourteenth Amendment. So long as the purposes of those agreements are effectuated by voluntary adherence to their terms, it would appear clear that there has been no action by the State and the provisions of the Amendment have not been violated. Cf. Corrigan v. Buckley, *supra*.

But here there was more. These are cases in which the purposes of the agreements were secured only by judicial enforcement by state courts of the restrictive terms of the agreements. The respondents urge that judicial enforcement of private agreements does not amount to state action; or, in any event, the participation of the State is so attenuated in character as not to amount to state action within the meaning of the Fourteenth Amendment. Finally, it is suggested, even if the States in these cases may be deemed to have acted in the constitutional sense, their action did not deprive petitioners of rights guaranteed by the Fourteenth Amendment. We move to a consideration of these matters.

II

That the action of state courts and of judicial officers in their official capacities is to be regarded as action of the State within the meaning of the Fourteenth Amendment, is a proposition which has long been established by decisions of this Court. That principle was given expression in the earliest cases involving the construction of the terms of the Fourteenth Amendment. . . .

* * *

The short of the matter is that from the time of the adoption of the Fourteenth Amendment until the present, it has been the consistent ruling of this Court that the action of the States to which the Amendment has reference, includes action of state courts and state judicial officials. Although, in construing the terms of the Fourteenth Amendment, differences have from time to time been expressed as to whether particular types of state action may be said to offend the Amendment's prohibitory provisions, it has never been suggested that state court action is immunized from the operation of those provisions simply because the act is that of the judicial branch of the state government.

III

Against this background of judicial construction, extending over a period of some three-quarters of a century, we are called upon to consider whether enforcement by state courts of the restrictive agreements in these cases may be deemed to be the acts of those States; and, if so, whether that action has denied these petitioners the equal protection of the laws which the Amendment was intended to insure.

We have no doubt that there has been state action in these cases in the full and complete sense of the phrase. The undisputed facts disclose that petitioners were willing purchasers of properties upon which they desired to establish homes. The owners of the properties were willing sellers; and contracts of sale were accordingly consummated. It is clear that but for the active intervention of the state courts, supported by the full panoply of state power, petitioners would have been free to occupy the properties in question without restraint.

These are not cases, as has been suggested, in which the States have merely abstained from action, leaving private individuals free to impose such discriminations as they see fit. Rather, these are cases in which the States have made available to such individuals the full coercive power of government to deny to petitioners, on the grounds of race or color, the enjoyment of property rights in premises which petitioners are willing and financially able to acquire and which the grantors are willing to sell. The difference between judicial enforcement and nonenforcement of the restrictive covenants is the difference to petitioners between being denied rights of property available to other members of the community and being accorded full enjoyment of those rights on an equal footing.

* * *

We hold that in granting judicial enforcement of the restrictive agreements in these cases, the States have denied petitioners the equal protection of the laws and that, therefore, the action of the state courts cannot stand. We have noted that freedom from discrimination by the States in the enjoyment of property rights was among the basic objectives sought to be effectuated by the framers of the Fourteenth Amendment. That such discrimination has occurred in these cases is clear. Because of the race or color of these petitioners they have been denied rights of ownership or occupancy enjoyed as a matter of course by other citizens of different race or color. . . .

Respondents urge, however, that since the state courts stand ready to enforce restrictive covenants excluding white persons from the ownership or occupancy of property covered by such agreements, enforcement of covenants excluding colored persons may not be deemed a denial of equal protection of the laws to the colored persons who are thereby affected. This contention does not bear scrutiny. The parties have directed our attention to no case in which a court, state or federal, has been called upon to enforce a covenant excluding members of the white majority from ownership or occupancy of real property on grounds of race or color. But there are more fundamental considerations. The rights created by the first section of the Fourteenth Amendment are, by its terms, guaranteed to the individual. The rights established are personal rights. It is, therefore, no answer to these petitioners to say that the courts may also be induced to deny white persons rights of ownership and occupancy on grounds of race or color. Equal protection of the laws is not achieved through indiscriminate imposition of inequalities. . . .

* * *

For the reasons stated, the judgment of the Supreme Court of Missouri and the judgment of the Supreme Court of Michigan must be reversed.

Brown v. Board of Education of Topeka, Kansas I
347 U.S. 483 (1954)

Chief Justice Warren delivered the opinion of the Court.

These cases came to us from the States of Kansas, South Carolina, Virginia, and Delaware. They are premised on different facts and different local conditions, but a common legal question justifies their consideration together in this consolidated opinion.

In each of the cases, minors of the Negro race, through their legal representatives, seek aid of the courts in obtaining admission to the public schools of their community on a non-segregated basis. . . . In each of the cases other than the Delaware case, a three-judge federal district court denied relief to the plaintiffs on the so-called "separate but equal" doctrine announced by the Court in *Plessy* v. *Ferguson*. . . . In the Delaware case, the Supreme Court of Delaware adhered to that doctrine, but ordered that the plaintiffs be admitted to the white schools because of their superiority to the Negro schools.

The plaintiffs contend that segregated public schools are not "equal" and cannot be made "equal," and that hence they are deprived of the equal protection of the laws. Because of the obvious importance of the question presented, the Court took jurisdiction. Argument was heard in the 1952 Term, and re-argument was heard this Term on certain questions propounded by the Court.

Reargument was largely devoted to the circumstances surrounding the adoption of the Fourteenth Amendment in 1868. It covered exhaustively consideration of the Amendment in Congress, ratification by the states, then existing practices in racial segregation, and the views of proponents and opponents of the Amendment. This discussion and our own investigation convince us that, although these sources cast some light, it is not enough to resolve the problem with which we are faced. At best, they are inconclusive. The most avid proponents of the post-War Amendments undoubtedly intended them to remove all legal distinctions among "all persons born or naturalized in the United States." Their opponents just as certainly were antagonistic to both the letter and spirit of the Amendments and wished them to have the most limited effect. What others in Congress and the state legislatures had in mind cannot be determined with any degree of certainty.

An additional reason for the inconclusive nature of the Amendment's history, with respect to segregated schools, is the status of public education at that time. In the South, the movement toward free common schools, supported by general taxation, had not yet taken hold. Education for white children was largely in the hands of private groups. Education for Negroes was almost nonexistent, and practically all of the race was illiterate. In fact, any education of Negroes was forbidden by law in some states. Today, in contrast, many Negroes have achieved outstanding success in the arts and sciences as well as in the business and professional world. It is true that public education had already advanced further in the North, but the effect of the Amendment on Northern States was generally ignored in the Congressional debates. Even in the North, the conditions of public education did not approximate those existing today. The curriculum was usually rudimentary; ungraded schools were common in rural areas; the school term was but three months a year in many states; and compulsory school attendance was virtually unknown. As a consequence, it is not surprising that there should be so little in the history of the Fourteenth Amendment relating to its intended effect on public education.

In the first cases in this Court construing the Fourteenth Amendment, decided shortly after its adoption, the Court interpreted it as proscribing all state-imposed discriminations against the Negro race. The doctrine of "separate but equal" did not make its appearance in the Court until 1896 in the case of *Plessy* v. *Ferguson*, . . . involving not education but transportation. American courts have since labored with the doctrine for over half a century. In this Court, there have been six cases involving the "separate but equal" doctrine in the field of public education. In *Cumming* v. *Board of Education of Richmond County* and *Gong Lum* v. *Rice*, the validity of the doctrine itself was not challenged. In more recent cases, all on the graduate school level, inequality was found in that specific benefits enjoyed by white students were denied to Negro students of the same educational qualifications (*State of Missouri ex. rel. Gaines* v. *Canada, Sipuel* v. *Board of Regents of University of Oklahoma, Sweatt* v. *Painter,* and *McLaurin* v. *Oklahoma State Regents*). In none of these cases was it necessary to re-examine the doctrine to grant relief to the Negro plaintiff. And in *Sweatt* v. *Painter*, . . . the Court expressly reserved decision on the question whether *Plessy* v. *Ferguson* should be held inapplicable to public education.

In approaching this problem, we cannot turn the clock back to 1868 when the Amendment was adopted, or even to 1896 when *Plessy* v. *Ferguson* was written. We must consider public education in the light of its full development and its present place in American life throughout the Nation. Only in this way can it be determined if segregation in public schools deprives these plaintiffs of the equal protection of the laws.

Today, education is perhaps the most important function of state and local governments. Compulsory school attendance laws and the great expenditures for education both demonstrate our recognition of the importance of education to our democratic society. It is required in the performance of our most basic public responsibilities, even service in the armed forces. It is the very foundation of good citizenship. Today it is a principal instrument in awakening the child to cultural values, in preparing him for later pro-

fessional training, and in helping him to adjust normally to his environment. In these days, it is doubtful that any child may reasonably be expected to succeed in life if he is denied the opportunity of an education. Such an opportunity, where the state has undertaken to provide it, is a right which must be made available to all on equal terms.

We come then to the question presented: Does segregation of children in public schools solely on the basis of race, even though the physical facilities and other "tangible" factors may be equal, deprive the children of the minority group of equal educational opportunities? We believe that it does.

In *Sweatt* v. *Painter* . . . in finding that a segregated law school for Negroes could not provide them equal educational opportunities, this Court relied in large part on "those qualities which are incapable of objective measurement but which make for greatness in a law school." In *McLaurin* v. *Oklahoma State Regents* . . . the Court, in requiring that a Negro admitted to a white graduate school be treated like all other students, again resorted to intangible considerations: " . . . his ability to study, to engage in discussion and exchange views with other students, and, in general, to learn his profession." Such considerations apply with added force to children in grade and high schools. To separate them from others of similar age and qualifications solely because of their race generates a feeling of inferiority as to their status in the community that may affect their hearts and minds in a way unlikely ever to be undone. The effect of this separation on their educational opportunities was well stated by a finding in the Kansas case by a court which nevertheless felt compelled to rule against the Negro plaintiffs:

> Segregation of white and colored children in public schools has a detrimental effect upon the colored children. The impact is greater when it has the sanction of the law; for the policy of separating the races is usually interpreted as denoting the inferiority of the negro group. A sense of inferiority affects the motivation of a child to learn. Segregation with the sanction of law, therefore, has a tendency to retard the educational and mental development of negro children and to deprive them of the benefits they would receive in a racial[ly] integrated school system.

Whatever may have been the extent of psychological knowledge at the time of *Plessy* v. *Ferguson*, this finding is amply supported by modern authority. Any language in *Plessy* v. *Ferguson* contrary to this finding is rejected.

We conclude that in the field of public education the doctrine of "separate but equal" has no place. Separate educational facilities are inherently unequal. Therefore, we hold that the plaintiffs and others similarly situated for whom the actions have been brought are, by the reason of the segregation complained of, deprived of the equal protection of the laws guaranteed by the Fourteenth Amendment. This disposition makes unnecessary any discussion whether such segregation also violates the Due Process Clause of the Fourteenth Amendment.

* * *

Regents of The University of California v. Bakke
98 S. Ct. 2733 (1978)

Mr. Justice POWELL announced the judgment of the Court.

This case presents a challenge to the special admissions program of the petitioner, the Medical School of the University of California at Davis, which is designed to assure the admission of a specified number of students from certain minority groups.

* * *

For the reasons stated in the following opinion, I believe that so much of the judgment of the California court as holds petitioner's special admissions program unlawful and directs that respondent be admitted to the Medical School must be affirmed. For the reasons expressed in a separate opinion, my Brothers THE CHIEF JUSTICE, Mr. Justice STEWART, Mr. Justice REHNQUIST, and Mr. Justice STEVENS concur in this judgment.

I also conclude for the reasons stated in the following opinion that the portion of the court's judgment enjoining petitioner from according any consideration to race in its admissions process must be reversed. For reasons expressed in separate opinions, my Brothers Mr. Justice BRENNAN, Mr. Justice WHITE, Mr. Justice MARSHALL, and Mr. Justice BLACKMUN concur in this judgment.

Affirmed in part and reversed in part.

* * *

Allan Bakke is a white male who applied to the Davis Medical School in both 1973 and 1974. In both years Bakke's application was considered by the general admissions program, and he received an interview. His 1973 interview was with Dr. Theodore H. West, who considered Bakke "a very desirable applicant to [the] medical school." Despite a strong benchmark score of 468 out of 500, Bakke was rejected. His application had come late in the year, and no applicants in the general admissions process with scores below 470 were accepted after Bakke's application was completed. There were four special admissions slots unfilled at that time, however, for which Bakke was not considered. . . .

Bakke's 1974 application was completed early in the year. . . . Again, Bakke's application was rejected. . . . In both years, applicants were admitted under the special program with grade point averages, MCAT scores, and benchmark scores significantly lower than Bakke's.

After the second rejection, Bakke filed the instant suit in the Superior Court of California.

* * *

Turning to Bakke's appeal, the court ruled that since Bakke had established that the University had discriminated against him on the basis of his race, the burden of proof shifted to the University to demonstrate that he would not have been admitted even in the absence of the special admissions program. . . . [T]he University conceded its inability to carry that burden. The California court [directed] that the trial court enter judgment ordering Bakke's admission to the medical school. . . .

* * *

This semantic distinction is beside the point: the special admissions program is undeniably a classification based on race and ethnic background. To the extent that there existed a pool of at least minimally qualified minority applicants to fill the 16 special admissions seats, white applicants could compete only for 84 seats in the entering class, rather than the 100 open to minority applicants. Whether this limitation is described as a quota or a goal, it is a line drawn on the basis of race and ethnic status.

. . . The guarantee of equal protection cannot mean one thing when applied to one individual and something else when applied to a person of another color. If both are not accorded the same protection, then it is not equal.

Nevertheless, petitioner argues that the court below erred in applying strict scrutiny to the special admissions programs because white males, such as respondent, are not a "discrete and insular minority" requiring extraordinary protection from the majoritarian political process. *Carolene Products Co.*, at 152–153, n. 4. This rationale, however, has never been invoked in our decisions as a prerequisite to subjecting racial or ethnic distinctions to strict scrutiny. Nor has this Court held that discreteness and insularity constitute necessary preconditions to a holding that a particular classification is invidious. These characteristics may be relevant in deciding whether or not to add new types of classifications to the list of "suspect" categories or whether a particular classification survives close examination. Racial and ethnic classifications, however, are subject to stringent examination without regard to these additional characteristics. . . . Racial and ethnic distinctions of any sort are inherently suspect and thus call for the most exacting judicial examination.

* * *

Petitioner urges us to adopt for the first time a more restrictive view of the Equal Protection Clause and hold that discrimination against members of the white "majority" cannot be suspect if its purpose can be characterized as "benign." The clock of our liberties, however, cannot be turned back to 1868. It is far too late to argue that the guarantee of equal protection to *all* persons permits the recognition of special wards entitled to a degree of protection greater than that accorded others. . . .

Once the artificial line of a "two-class theory" of the Fourteenth Amendment is put aside, the difficulties entailed in varying the level of judicial review according to a perceived "preferred" status of a particular racial or ethnic minority are intractable. The concepts of "majority" and "minority" necessarily reflect temporary arrangements and political judgments. . . . There is no principled basis for deciding which groups would merit "heightened judicial solicitude" and which would not. Courts would be asked to evaluate the extent of the prejudice and consequent harm suffered by various minority groups. . . .

The kind of variable sociological and political analysis necessary to produce such rankings simply does not lie within the judicial competence — even if they otherwise were politically feasible and socially desirable.

Moreover, there are serious problems of justice connected with the idea of preference itself. First, it may not always be clear that a so-called preference is in fact benign. Courts may be asked to validate burdens imposed upon individual members of particular groups in order to advance the group's general interest. Nothing in the Constitution supports the notion that individuals may be asked to suffer otherwise impermissible burdens in order to enhance the societal standing of their ethnic groups. Second, preferential programs may only reinforce common stereotypes holding that certain groups are unable to achieve success without special protection based on a factor having no relationship to individual worth. Third, there is a measure of inequity in forcing innocent persons in respondent's position to bear the burdens of redressing grievances not of their making.

By hitching the meaning of the Equal Protection Clause to these transitory considerations, we would be holding, as a constitutional principle, that judicial scrutiny of classifications touching on racial and ethnic background may vary with the ebb and flow of political forces. Disparate constitutional tolerance of such classifications well may serve to exacerbate racial and ethnic antagonisms rather than alleviate them. . . .

If it is the individual who is entitled to judicial protection against classifications based upon his racial or ethnic background because such distinctions impinge upon personal rights, rather than the individual only because of his membership in a particular group, then constitutional standards may be applied consistently. . . . When [political judgments] touch upon an individual's race or ethnic background, he is entitled to a judicial determination that the burden he is asked to bear on that basis is precisely tailored to serve a compelling governmental interest. The Constitution guarantees that right to every person regardless of his background. . . .

Petitioner contends that on several occasions this Court has approved preferential classifications without applying the most exacting scrutiny. Most of the cases upon which petitioner relies are drawn from three areas: school desegregation, employment discrimination, and sex discrimination. Each of the cases cited presented a situation materially different from the facts of this case.

The school desegregation cases are inapposite. Each involved remedies for clearly determined constitutional violations. . . . Here, there was no judicial determination of constitutional violation as a predicate for the formulation of a remedial classification.

The employment discrimination cases also do not advance petitioner's cause. For example, in *Franks v. Bowman Transportation Co.*, 425 U. S. 747 (1975), we approved a retroactive award of seniority to a class of Negro truck drivers who had been the victims of discrimination — not just by society at large, but by the respondent in that case. While this relief imposed some burdens on other employees, it was held necessary "'to make [the victims] whole for injuries suffered on account of unlawful employment discrimination.'" The courts of appeals have fashioned various types of racial preferences as remedies for constitutional or statutory violations resulting in identified, race-based injuries to individuals held entitled to the preference. Such preferences also have been upheld where a legislative or administrative body charged with the responsibility made determinations of past discrimination by the industries affected, and fashioned remedies deemed appropriate to rectify the discrimination. *E. g., Contractors Association of Eastern Pennsylvania v. Secretary of Labor*, 442 F.2d 159 (CA3), cert. denied, 404 U. S. 954 (1971). But we have never approved preferential classifications in the absence of proven constitutional or statutory violations.

Nor is petitioner's view as to the applicable standard supported by the fact that gender-based classifications are not subjected to this level of scrutiny. Gender-based distinctions are less likely to create the analytical and practical problems present in preferential programs premised on racial or ethnic criteria. . . . More importantly, the perception of racial classifications as inherently odious stems from a lengthy and tragic history that gender-based classifications do not share. In sum, the Court has never viewed such classification as inherently suspect or as comparable to racial or ethnic classifications for the purpose of equal-protection analysis.

Petitioner also cites *Lau v. Nichols*, 414 U. S. 563 (1974), in support of the proposition that discrimination favoring racial or ethnic minorities has received judicial approval without the exacting inquiry ordinarily accorded "suspect" classifications.

* * *

Lau provides little support for petitioner's argument. The decision rested solely on the statute, which had been construed by the responsible administrative agency to reach educational practices "which have the effect of subjecting individuals to discrimination." . . . Moreover, the "preference" approved did not result in the denial of the relevant benefit — "meaningful participation in the educational program" — to anyone else. No other student was deprived by that preference of the ability to participate in San Francisco's school system, and the applicable regulations required similar assistance for all students who suffered similar linguistic deficiencies.

* * *

In this case, unlike *Lau*, . . . there has been no determination by the legislature or a responsible administrative agency that the University engaged in a discriminatory practice requiring remedial efforts. Moreover, the operation of petitioner's special admissions program is quite different from the remedial measures approved in those cases. It prefers the designated minority groups at the expense of other individuals who are totally foreclosed from competition for the 16 special admissions seats in every medical school class. Because of that foreclosure, some individuals are excluded from enjoyment of a state-provided benefit — admission to the medical school — they otherwise would receive. When a classification denies an individual opportunities or benefits enjoyed by others solely because of his race or ethnic background, it must be regarded as suspect. . . .

We have held that in "order to justify the use of a suspect classification, a State must show that its purpose or interest is both constitutionally permissible and substantial, and that its use of the classification is 'necessary . . . to the accomplishment' of its purpose or the safeguarding of its interest." The special admissions program purports to serve the purposes of: (i) "reducing the historic deficit of traditionally disfavored minorities in medical schools and the medical profession"; (ii) countering the effects of societal discrimination; (iii) increasing the number of physicians who will practice in communities currently underserved; and (iv) obtaining the educational benefits that flow from an ethnically diverse student body. It is necessary to decide which, if any, of these purposes is substantial enough to support the use of a suspect classification. . . .

. . . If petitioner's purpose is to assure within its student body some specified percentage of a particular group merely because of its race or ethnic origin, such a preferential purpose must be rejected not as insubstantial but as facially invalid. Preferring members of any one group for no reason other than race or ethnic origin is discrimination for its own sake. This the Constitution forbids. . . .

The State certainly has a legitimate and substantial interest in ameliorating, or eliminating where feasible, the disabling effects of identified discrimination. . . .

We have never approved a classification that aids persons perceived as members of relatively victimized groups at the expense of other innocent individuals in the absence of judicial, legislative, or administrative findings of constitutional or statutory violations. . . . Without such findings of constitutional or statutory violations, it cannot be said that the government has any greater interest in helping one individual than in refraining from harming another. Thus, the government has no compelling justification for inflicting such harm.

* * *

Petitioner simply has not carried its burden of demonstrating that it must prefer members of particular ethnic groups over all other individuals in order to promote better health care delivery to deprived citizens. Indeed, petitioner has not shown that its preferential classification is likely to have any significant effect on the problem. . . .

The fourth goal asserted by petitioner is the attainment of a diverse student body. . . . An otherwise qualified medical student with a particular background — whether it be ethnic, geographic, culturally advantaged or disadvantaged — may bring to a professional school of medicine experiences, outlooks and ideas that enrich the training of its student body and better equip its gradu-

ates to render with understanding their vital service to humanity.

Ethnic diversity, however, is only one element in a range of factors a university properly may consider in attaining the goal of a heterogeneous student body. Although a university must have wide discretion in making the sensitive judgments as to who should be admitted, constitutional limitations protecting individual rights may not be disregarded. Respondent urges — and the courts below have held — that petitioner's dual admissions program is a racial classification that impermissibly infringes his rights under the Fourteenth Amendment. As the interest of diversity is compelling in the context of a university's admissions program, the question remains whether the program's racial classification is necessary to promote this interest. . . .

It may be assumed that the reservation of a specified number of seats in each class for individuals from the preferred ethnic groups would contribute to the attainment of considerable ethnic diversity in the student body. But petitioner's argument that this is the only effective means of serving the interest of diversity is seriously flawed. In a most fundamental sense the argument misconceives the nature of the state interest that would justify consideration of race or ethnic background. It is not an interest in simple ethnic diversity, in which a specified percentage of the student body is in effect guaranteed to be members of selected ethnic groups, with the remaining percentage an undifferentiated aggregation of students. The diversity that furthers a compelling state interest encompasses a far broader array of qualifications and characteristics of which racial or ethnic origin is but a single though important element. Petitioner's special admissions program, focused *solely* on ethnic diversity, would hinder rather than further attainment of genuine diversity.

Nor would the state interest in genuine diversity be served by expanding petitioner's two-track system into a multitrack program with a prescribed number of seats set aside for each identifiable category of applicants. Indeed, it is inconceivable that a university would thus pursue the logic of petitioner's two-track program to the illogical end of insulating each category of applicants with certain desired qualifications from competition with all other applicants.

The experience of other university admissions programs, which take race into account in achieving the educational diversity valued by the First Amendment, demonstrates that the assignment of a fixed number of places to a minority group is not a necessary means toward that end. An illuminating example is found in the Harvard College program. . . .

In such an admissions program, race or ethnic background may be deemed a "plus" in a particular applicant's file, yet it does not insulate the individual from comparison with all other candidates for the available seats. The file of a particular black applicant may be examined for his potential contribution to diversity without the factor of race being decisive when compared, for example, with that of an applicant identified as an Italian-American if the latter is thought to exhibit qualities more likely to promote beneficial educational pluralism. Such qualities could include exceptional personal talents, unique work or service experience, leadership potential, maturity, demonstrated compassion, a history of overcoming disadvantage, ability to communicate with the poor, or other qualifications deemed important. In short, an admissions program operated in this way is flexible enough to consider all pertinent elements of diversity in light of the particular qualifications of each applicant, and to place them on the same footing for consideration, although not necessarily according them the same weight. Indeed, the weight attributed to a particular quality may vary from year to year depending upon the "mix" both of the student body and the applicants for the incoming class.

This kind of program treats each applicant as an individual in the admissions process. The applicant who loses out on the last available seat to another candidate receiving a "plus" on the basis of ethnic background will not have been foreclosed from all consideration for that seat simply because he was not the right color or had the wrong surname. It would mean only that his combined qualifications, which may have included similar nonobjective factors, did not outweigh those of the other applicant. His qualifications would have been weighed fairly

and competitively, and he would have no basis to complain of unequal treatment under the Fourteenth Amendment.

It has been suggested that an admissions program which considers race only as one factor is simply a subtle and more sophisticated—but no less effective—means of according racial preference than the Davis program. A facial intent to discriminate, however, is evident in petitioner's preference program and not denied in this case. No such facial infirmity exists in an admissions program where race or ethnic background is simply one element—to be weighed fairly against other elements—in the selection process. . . . In short, good faith would be presumed in the absence of a showing to the contrary in the manner permitted by our cases. . . .

In summary, it is evident that the Davis special admission program involves the use of an explicit racial classification never before countenanced by this Court. It tells applicants who are not Negro, Asian, or "Chicano" that they are totally excluded from a specific percentage of the seats in an entering class. No matter how strong their qualifications, quantitative and extracurricular, including their own potential for contribution to educational diversity, they are never afforded the chance to compete with applicants from the preferred groups for the special admission seats. At the same time, the preferred applicants have the opportunity to compete for every seat in the class.

The fatal flaw in petitioner's preferential program is its disregard of individual rights as guaranteed by the Fourteenth Amendment. Such rights are not absolute. But when a State's distribution of benefits or imposition of burdens hinges on the color of a person's skin or ancestry, that individual is entitled to a demonstration that the challenged classification is necessary to promote a substantial state interest. Petitioner has failed to carry this burden. For this reason, that portion of the California court's judgment holding petitioner's special admissions program invalid under the Fourteenth Amendment must be affirmed.

In enjoining petitioner from ever considering the race of any applicant, however, the courts below failed to recognize that the State has a substantial interest that legitimately may be served by a properly devised admissions program involving the competitive consideration of race and ethnic origin. For this reason, so much of the California court's judgment as enjoins petitioner from any consideration of the race of any applicant must be reversed.

With respect to respondent's entitlement to an injunction directing his admission to the Medical School, petitioner has conceded that it could not carry its burden of proving that, but for the existence of its unlawful special admissions program, respondent still would not have been admitted. Hence, respondent is entitled to the injunction, and that portion of the judgment must be affirmed.

* * *

Notes and Questions

FRANK I. MICHELMAN, from "On Protecting the Poor through the Fourteenth Amendment"

1. Writing in 1968, when the Supreme Court was much more open to addressing claims of inequality than it is now, Frank I. Michelman asks what a just society should aim to guarantee: equality or minimum welfare? With regard to differences in wealth or income, he suggests that justice does not necessarily require equality. He further argues that the Court's equal protection approach to issues of poverty or unequal wealth has serious potential problems, as the Court itself soon concluded. Why does Michelman claim that it may be paradoxical to base a claim for relief from deprivation due to poverty on the equal protection clause, given a commitment to a free market economy?

2. Unlike the Court, which simply backed away from the poverty problem, Michelman argues that certain basic goods should be considered fundamental rights that must be allocated by need and not by the market. Why does he think that this is not an equal protection issue?

3. Proposing a minimum protection theory rather than an equal protection theory for approaching the poverty problem, Michelman draws on Rawls's theory of justice as fairness. How does Michelman apply this general theory to the poverty problem? What are "just wants," according to Michelman, and how would a decision-making body, such as a court or a legislature go about determining what they are? Is this a plausible way of deciding the requirements of justice? If not, why not? If so, what sorts of requirements — that is, "just wants," might such a method indicate?

4. Michelman argues that there are good reasons to consider *de jure* wealth classifications to be like *de jure* race classifications, but not to consider *de facto* wealth classifications to be like *de facto* race classifications. Why? Note that *de jure* means "by law," whereas *de facto* means basically "in fact"; that is, the term *de facto* applies to circumstances that pertain in fact but that are not enforced by law. What are the similarities in the two *de jure* classifications? The Court does not recognize any wealth classifications as suspect today, not even *de jure* ones. Should it? If so, under what circumstances? Consider the discussion of the *James* v. *Valtierra* case in the article by L.J. Barker and T.W. Barker, Jr. at the end of this section. Would such a classification have made a difference in that case?

5. What are the important differences between *de facto* race classifications and *de facto* wealth classifications, according to Michelman? What does a *de facto* wealth classification amount to in practice? Why does Michelman think that the exceptions prove his point rather than undermine it?

6. Explain Michelman's comparison of equal protection with minimum protection analysis. What are the areas of overlap? More to the point, what areas of equal protection are not covered by minimum protection, and vice versa? Think about what that would amount to in cases of deprivation due to poverty. How does it apply to Michelman's "golf and opera" case? How would it be different in the "school allocation" case? What conclusion does Michelman draw? Do you agree?

7. As Michelman notes in passing, equal protection is consistent with the government doing nothing for anyone. Michelman concludes that this makes equal protection analysis an unacceptable tool for meeting the requirements of justice in regard to deprivation of fundamental interests, or "just wants." The current members of the Supreme Court apparently believe that it is not their business either to define fundamental interests or to protect them. If equal protection is the standard, then the government may do nothing at all about the deprivation of basic needs as long as it is done equally. On this model state governments could close the schools and privatize fire and police services. Congress could end social services, food stamps, housing assistance, and medical programs. Is there anything wrong with that?

8. In fact, elected legislators are unlikely to do what they think will be unpopular with the majority. Poor people, however, are rarely well organized or powerful constituencies. Should any branch of government protect their interests? If not, why not? Isn't everyone supposed to count? If so, which branch of government should protect them?

[From] "On Protecting the Poor through the Fourteenth Amendment"

FRANK I. MICHELMAN

The equal protection clause is the constitutional text which most naturally suggests itself to one who would claim a legal right to have certain wants satisfied out of the public treasury, insofar as he means to found his argument upon a comparison of burdens and opportunities which must otherwise accrue to the relatively rich and the relatively poor. And equal protection is, of course, the text which the Supreme Court has preferred in upholding such claims with respect to criminal defense needs and voting rights. Yet it could well be thought paradoxical to infer from a general statement of duty on the government's part to treat all persons "equally" a more particular duty to satisfy certain wants irrespective of the recipient's readiness to pay the associated costs.

The paradox and its resolution are most clearly seen by noting first that when a government's practice of, say, charging tuition fees or otherwise requiring persons to pay for their (or their dependents') education out of their own means is challenged, there may be ambiguity about the intended scope and focus of the attack. The target might consist of the government's assertedly "discriminatory" actions in setting conditions of access to that education which it is visibly engaged in providing. Alternatively, the attack might concentrate on the poor person's predicament of being unable to afford a certain amount of education. Now, given a prevalent assumption that the "proper" allocation of resources results when consumers of goods are required to pay a "market" price for goods consumed — one which fairly reflects and reconciles the cost of providing those goods and the felt benefits of consuming them — it would seem that *if the "treatment" immediately at issue is the setting of conditions under which a person will be granted access to a good*, "equality" would normally reside in access to goods at the same market price which everyone else must pay, while "discrimination" would consist of price discrimination. Bringing the claim within the locutions of the equal protection clause thus involves obvious strains on usage, *as long as the focus of attack is the official act of setting conditions of access.*

Of course, we remain free to say that there is a list of select goods which are "properly" rationed according to need rather than according to a consumer's readiness to purchase at market prices, and that for *these* goods "equality" (the norm) consists of a compensatory assurance of access to universally "needed" amounts, while "discrimination" (departure from the norm) exists wherever access to the universally needed portion is so straitened, by a uniform price or other impediment, that some persons are effectively deprived of it. But our undoubted freedom to state the matter in this fashion does not lead to any Lewis Carroll punch line, because that linguistic freedom is significantly burdened: *in shaping the statement of our claim so as to fit it to the locutions of the equal protection clause, we must find an "inequality" to complain about; and the only inequality turns out to be that some persons, less than all, are suffering from inability to satisfy certain "basic" wants which presumably are felt by all alike.* But if we define the inequality that way, we can hardly avoid admitting that the injury consists more essentially of deprivation than of discrimination, that the cure accordingly lies more in provision than in equalization, and that the reality of injury and need for cure are to be determined largely without reference to whether the complainant's predicament is somehow visibly related to past or current governmental activity. A focus on a government's access-determining practices implies, or at least is consistent with, an overriding concern with the moral and psychological harms uniquely associated with official nonevenhandedness. But a focus on the predicament of nonaccess is consistent only with an overriding concern for the impairments of welfare or effectiveness flowing from the exclusion — which seem the same no matter whether the government is or is not actively engaged in satisfying the want in question. And that, Dear Reader (plus a suggestion that the Court has not been as clear on the point as seems desirable), is in essence my story. All that follows is a scramble of restatement, development, and recapitulation.

An Imperfect Theory of Social Justice

Before proceeding to an examination of the Court's work, and that of some of its scholarly kibitzers, it will be helpful to dwell briefly on a proposition about social justice which I shall call "minimum protection against economic hazard."

As applied to economic hazards, a claim to "minimum protection" would mean that persons are entitled to have certain wants satisfied — certain existing needs filled — by government, free of any direct charge over and above the obligation to pay general taxes (and perhaps free of conditions referring to past idleness, prodigality, or other economic "misconduct"). Wants to which this claim applies we shall call "just wants." The claimant does not, except in a quite limited sense, try to show that an overall distributional configuration is improper. He claims a right to have *a specific, existing want* provided for,

* * *

We might take our cue from Professor Rawls' idea of "justice as fairness."[1] Rawls grants that social institutions and practices may be just, even though they produce unequal incomes and accumulations. Yet for an unequal system to be just, it must be the case that a rational person, hypothetically ignorant of what particular place in society awaits him, would find the inequalities acceptable. To Rawls this means that inequalities of wealth and income are unjust unless they are necessary to a system which assures to those who turn out to occupy society's least advantageous positions a better situation than they could reasonably expect under a system which distributed the net social product in equal shares. In particular, such inequalities might be just insofar as they were necessary to incentives and market allocations thought to make the economy more efficient and productive than it could otherwise be. But a just arrangement would be grudging in its allowance of such inequalities and would go as far as possible in the direction of channeling the additional outputs generated by an incentive system into a generous guarantee of a minimum welfare for all (entailing, very likely, redistributions which to some extent limit incentive effects). Accordingly, an arrangement would not be just insofar as it overlooked means whereby persons could be insured against the risk of relatively grave need with relatively little damage to efficiency and incentives.

The identity of "just wants" would then be determined according to a judgment arrived at through the following process of reasoning. Assume that a man has no idea what his social and economic station in a predominantly competitive society is to be and that he fully recognizes the role of income incentives and free markets in maximizing social productivity. Will he nevertheless wish to have each person insured against the risk that certain needs will remain unfulfilled as and when they accrue — and what specific risks of that sort, if any, will he say should be insured against? Might he, for example, say that insofar as the society provides for "democratic" political participation through such means as voting and standing for office, access to these activities should never be blocked by economic vicissitude? Or that persons must at all times be assured of effective access to some impartial and remedially competent forum for the peaceful settlement of bona fide legal disputes? Or that everyone at all times must be assured of facilities for a modicum of privacy, intimacy, confidentiality, self-expression? Or that each child must be guaranteed the means of developing his competence, self-knowledge, and tastes for living?

Our immediate purpose is not to try to answer these or any cognate questions. It is, rather, a much more limited one: . . .

* * *

. . . our purpose is to show how the possibility of propounding such questions might affect the elaboration of constitutional rights pertaining to the status of being poor.

* * *

II. Discrimination against the Poor — Pecuniary Circumstance as an "Invidious" or "Suspect" Classifying Trait

* * *

. . . I shall use the words "invidious" and "suspect" in the following somewhat specialized fashion: "Invidious," a term of opprobrium, refers generally to legislative or administrative behavior as reflected in an act of classifying, and specifically to certain obnoxious tendencies or implications which the classification is thought to harbor. "Suspect," a neutral term, refers to judicial behavior, and specifically to certain variations in that behavior which are supposed to result from a classification's invidiousness. An "invidious" classification or trait is one which combines, in greater or lesser degree and in varying proportions, three qualities: (1) a general illsuitedness to the advancement of any proper governmental objective; (2) a high degree of adaptation to uses which are oppressive in the sense of systematic and unfair devaluation, through majority rule, of the claims of certain persons to nondiscriminatory sharing in the benefits and burdens of social existence; (3) a potency to injure through an effect of stigmatizing certain persons by implying popular or official belief in their inherent inferiority or undeservingness. A law requiring racial segregation epitomizes the idea of "invidiousness." The operational meaning of "suspect" is, roughly, that a court will invalidate the classification unless it is shown to be "necessary" in the service of some "compelling" state interest (rather than merely "rationally related" to some "permissible" governmental objective). This form of "special judicial scrutiny" is said to be due when invidious classifications are employed, particularly if certain "fundamental" interests are also at stake. Since there are, obviously, degrees of invidiousness, it would seem to follow that there are also degrees of suspectness — that is, of judicial stringency in the evaluation of the "compellingness" of state interests and the "necessity" in their pursuit of certain classifications. Of these related continuums, more anon.

A limited assimilation of impecuniousness to membership in a racial, ethnic, or national minority is not lacking in plausibility. The convincing reasons which can be offered for extremely skeptical judicial inspection of official acts which explicitly classify by race (or have the obvious purpose of doing so, although not explicitly) seem applicable to statutes which explicitly or designedly classify by wealth or income, *in the sense of deliberately subdividing the population according to a wealth or income criterion for the purpose of extending different treatment to the groups so distinguished.* For if money is power, then a class deliberately defined so as to include everyone who has less wealth or income than any person outside it may certainly be deemed, as racial minorities are by many observers deemed, to be especially susceptible to abuse by majoritarian process; and classification of "the poor" as such may, like classification of racial minorities as such, be popularly understood as a badge of inferiority. Especially is this so in light of the extreme difficulty of imagining proper governmental objectives which require for their achievement the explicit carving out, for relatively disadvantageous treatment, of a class defined by relative paucity of wealth or income.

But if there are good reasons for treating de jure wealth classifications as specially suspect irrespective of the interests particularly involved, there are also good reasons (to which we shall presently turn) for doubting whether a doctrine has yet emerged or ought to be encouraged which would draw pecuniary circumstance into an "inner circle" of invidious and therefore suspect classifying traits insofar as de facto classifications are concerned.

* * *

Such a doctrine is not only gratuitous insofar as an ordering of the data is concerned. It is also endemically troublesome as a matter of principle. The trouble is that, unlike a de facto racial classification which usually must seek its justifications in purposes completely distinct from its race-related impacts, a de facto pecuniary classification typically carries a highly persuasive justification inseparable from the very effect which excites antipathy — *i.e.*, the hard choices it forces upon the financially straitened. For the typical form assumed by such a classification is simply the charging of a price, reasonably approximating cost, for some good or service which the complaining person may freely choose to purchase or not to purchase. A de facto pecuniary classification, that is, is usually nothing more or less than the making of a market (*e.g.*, in trial transcripts) or the failure to relieve someone of the vicissitudes of market pricing (*e.g.*, for appellate legal services). But the risk of exposure to markets and their "decisions" is not normally deemed objectionable, to say the least, in our society. Not only do we not inveigh generally against unequal distribution of income or full-cost pricing for most goods. We usually regard it as both the fairest and most efficient arrangement to require each consumer to pay the full market price of what he consumes, limiting his consumption to what his income permits. Exceptions, of course, exist. The point is precisely that such "commodities" as a vote, an effective defense to criminal prosecution, perhaps education, conceivably some others, *are* exceptional,

and that the exceptions depend on the special qualities of the excepted commodities. It is uninformative at best, and very likely misleading as well, to defend such exceptional holdings through formulas of disparagement ("invidious" or "suspect classification"; "lines . . . drawn on the basis of wealth"; "discrimination against the indigent") which apply non-selectively to the pricing practice and refer not at all to any exceptional attributes in the excepted commodities.

The disparaging phraseology seems aptly designed for instances of de jure wealth discrimination, and also, perhaps, for instances of de facto wealth discrimination (should the Court ever meet up with one) other than those implicit in payment requirements. Most typically, these latter might be cases of unequal provision of municipal services to neighborhoods significantly segregated (though without official complicity) by wealth or income. If a resident of the north side of town complains that police, sanitation, or recreational services are inferior to those provided on the south side, no doubt his complaint is significantly strengthened by an allegation that the relatively poor are disproportionately concentrated on the north side, while the richer citizens congregate on the south side. The situation is visibly suggestive of oppression and stigma, and may have a high invidiousness quotient, to the point where convincing justifications ought to be required to dispel one's irrepressible suspicions. In fact, it seems to me questionable whether these cases should be classed together with those of payment requirements, in a collection labeled "de facto," rather than along with cases of explicit discrimination against the poor under the "de jure" label. Although the official lines (if any) were supposedly drawn with reference to geography rather than income, the geographical distinctions in themselves seem prima facie random and purposeless. It is precisely the *wealth* distinctions which strike an observer as probably nonrandom and purposeful. Thus we should perhaps call this an instance of quasi de jure wealth discrimination, subject to possible dissolution of the de jure inference by adequate justification.

But this treatment seems wholly inappropriate for cases involving payment requirements. No doubt we could conceive of such cases as having historically presented state officials with a choice between requiring and not requiring payment. Then, noting that decisions to require payment are always specially burdensome to the poor, we could say that such decisions always come freighted with intimations of oppression and stigma which demand special justification. But this line of thought seems unhelpful, since in every such case *except for those involving just wants (or "fundamental interests") or nonscarce values*, a convincing justification is present. The proper conclusion, then, seems to be not that it is helpful to emphasize and weigh invidiousness factors in disposing of payment-requirements cases, but that one ought to be appropriately cautious about equating the set of such cases with the set of cases involving de facto wealth discriminations.

* * *

III. Classification and "Discrimination" in the New Equal Protection

We have been considering a legal problem — a set of circumstances giving rise to legal claims — which can be stated in the following general form: a person is denied access to certain goods or activities because of some trait or situation which he is powerless to change currently and which is not the result of any decision freely made by him in the proximate past. A special case of the general problem, in which we have a particular interest, is that of the impecunious person denied access because of inability to pay a price. Two different strategies for thought about the problem, and the legal claim against the state which arises from it, may be sketched and compared. The first somewhat resembles that which has become associated with litigation under the equal protection clause, and I shall label it "equal protection." The second is the one which I have styled "minimum protection."

"Equal protection" radar is sensitized to governmental implication in systematic inequality. It blips whenever a government seems (a) to be "classifying" persons so as to extend to them unequal treatments, or (b) otherwise to be acting in a way which results in systematic inequality in treatments received by definable groups of persons. Here we are primarily concerned with cases in category (b). When a blip — a warning signal —

occurs, the ensuing inspection focuses first upon the criteria which, explicitly or implicitly, are used to classify the affected population. If those criteria are free of invidiousness, the case is to be treated, in effect, as one of "substantive due process."[2] If, however, they are in noticeable degree suggestive of oppression or stigmatization, that fact is to be borne in mind as attention shifts to the actual clash of interests involved in the case: the personal interests which are adversely affected by unequal treatment and the interest of the government in continuing the "unequal" practice. We are concerned about the degree of special importance (in some sense) which attaches to the unequally served personal interest; we factor this with the degree of invidiousness of the classifying trait. The resultant is a kind of "prejudice" variable which, if it exceeds a certain critical magnitude, we are to balance against the governmental interest — a procedure crudely described by the statement that in such cases the governmental interest can prevail only if it is "compelling."

* * *

"Minimum protection" radar scans, not for inequalities, but for instances in which persons have important needs or interests which they are prevented from satisfying because of traits or predicaments not adopted by free and proximate choice. Such instances, when located, are subject to inspection to see whether, in a just society, the hazard is tolerable that the trait or predicament in question will be burdened by nonsatisfaction of the want in question. If the Rawlsian conception of justice is accepted, the question will be whether a person would insist on the relevant assurances assuming that he was (a) deprived of knowledge about whether he personally will find himself in the relevant predicament, but (b) sufficiently informed about the organizing principles of the society to be able to appraise (i) the frequency of the predicament and (ii) the gravity, in such a society, of the particular unfulfilled want. On the answer to this question, the existence and content of governmental duties will depend.

In comparing the two conceptual strategies, it is well to begin by noting relationships of overlap and correspondence. The area of overlap, of common scanning and simultaneous blipping, may be described as that covered by equal protection except for (a) the area occupied by cases of "irrationally" imposed disadvantage not affecting specially important interests, and (b) the area occupied by cases of de jure classification so invidious as to require invalidation irrespective of the importance of the affected interest. The overlapped area may also be described, from an equal protection viewpoint, as that covered by the "new equal protection" method of cross-hatching the "invidiousness" of classifying traits with the "importance" of the affected interests to derive composite prejudice variables. Alternatively, the overlapped area may be described from a minimum-protection standpoint as including all cases which tentatively excite minimum-protection concern, except for those in which a clear absence of "state action" would turn off equal protection.

Within the overlapped area, the two strategies have some tendency to arrive, ultimately, at closely similar interest balancings to determine validity. An example may make this clear. Suppose that a government is charging admission fees as a condition of access to the golf course it operates in a public park or the grand opera being staged in a civic auditorium, thus making it difficult or impossible for poor persons to enjoy the facility. Equal protection might detect a degree of invidiousness in the implicit wealth classification, which it would factor together with the degree of importance (probably not exceeding "1") of the interest in golf playing or opera going. The resultant prejudice variable would probably be found less weighty than the governmental interest in optimizing the allocation of resources to the golf course or opera stage (for maintenance, improvement, expansion of facilities, etc.). Minimum protection would proceed directly to the question whether assurance would be consensually demanded against the risk that preclusion from golf or opera may be an accompaniment of a low income — taking into account the general social advantages of allocating resources in accordance with dollar-expressed demand, but also bearing in mind the possibilities of systematic oppression of the poor in the guise of admission fees and of harmful stigmatization by exclusion of the poor from public facilities. The determinative mental calculus (or should we say chemistry) seems hard to distinguish from that employed under equal protection.

But the two approaches do not always tend toward identical outcomes. Consider the following case. The average annual per-pupil expenditure in all of a state's public schools is $800. Two juvenile institutions, one of the protective and one of the corrective variety, are situated in a county which annually spends $1100 per child in attendance at its public schools. The institutions are state-operated and state-financed, but each serves a "constituency" defined by county boundaries. Each of the "homes" operates its own school program. The orphanage spends $900 per child per year, while the reform school spends $500. Suits are brought on behalf of children confined in each institution, complaining of unequal protection. The orphan plaintiff points to the $1100 standard established by "his" county. The delinquent points to that and also to the $800 state average and the $900 orphanage expenditures.

We have, I think, good reason to fear that the "new equal protection" will make a mess of these cases — especially if we imagine that the orphan's case is decided first with full appellate opinions. The orphan will argue, with great plausibility, that the effect of the combined state and county practices is to "classify" school-age children resident in the county into those who are and those who are not orphans. Indeed, the classification is de jure. He will then claim, quite convincingly, that orphanage is a distinctly invidious classifying trait. Since educational resource seems to be a "fundamental" good, the cross-hatching of suspect classification with damage to a favored interest is likely to yield a decision in favor of the orphan plaintiff. The opinion, naturally, will lay great stress on the presence in the case of the invidious classification. The delinquent, when his turn comes, of course can argue to similar effect that he has been disadvantageously classified; but the argument that delinquency is an invidious classifying trait will be much harder to sustain, and he therefore may well find that his case will be distinguished.

Two elements in this fantasy are noteworthy. First, equal protection seems somewhat undiscriminatingly sensitized to any and all inequalities affecting "favored" interests. The quality of an inequality — in this case, the fact that orphans already receive an educational expenditure which is average for the state — does not seem to concern it. We might say that equal protection responds to relative deprivation, even though the presence of a quasi-symptomatic and severe absolute deprivation is doubtful. Second, once doctrinal reliance has been reposed in the "invidiousness" of some classification, issues are likely to be confused in subsequent cases which are somewhat analogous but which involve different, and noninvidious, classifications. A severe and quasi-symptomatic absolute deprivation may beget no response unless a "discrimination" suggestive of prevalent, institutionalized, relative deprivation is also present.

Minimum protection avoids both these effects. For each of the two cases it poses a custom-built question, eschewing equality as an end but focusing instead upon just what it is that institutionalized children seek but do not get. In a supposedly just society, it would ask, which risk is the more likely to be consensually deemed unacceptable: the risk that orphanage will entail deprivation of stratospheric educational expenditure (assuming a guaranty of at least that expenditure which is normal for the state), or the risk that conviction of delinquency will entail an educational expenditure as low as 63% of the state average?

In sum, it can be said that in the area of overlapping concern, where governmental action is somehow associated with a person's exclusion from an important good, minimum protection leads to inquiry at least as refined and sensitive to relevant factors as does equal protection, and that equal protection, conversely, cannot ultimately avoid reliance on judgments as complex, subjective, and ineffable as those arising under minimum protection. Yet there are, even in the overlapped area, differences between the two methods which seem to me quite significant. They are that minimum protection goes about its work without pretension to general pursuit of an "equality" goal, that minimum protection does not employ, as a separate and doctrinally packaged step in the reasoning, any attempt to rank classifying traits according to their "invidiousness," and most particularly, that minimum protection avoids general declarations to the effect that inequalities in treatment are "specially suspect" or "discriminatory" when born of inequalities in wealth.

Minimum protection, in short, imports no doctrine, worthy of separate statement, which inveighs generally against "de facto discriminations against the poor." It thus answers the argument made earlier that recognition of any such general doctrine ought to be given grudgingly, if at all.

We may now summarize the theoretical and practical consequences of approaching the denial-of-access problem by way of a "minimum protection" thought process — one not regimented, as equal protection thinking has come to be, by categories of *governmental involvement* and *invidious discriminations* (including in the latter category discriminations bearing adversely upon the fundamental interests of some "judicially favored" class). These consequences fall under two major heads: (1) *Minimum protection is likely to demand correction of certain practices or conditions which equal protection would tolerate.* This may come about, most notably, under either of two interesting sets of circumstances: (a) when, although there is governmental complicity in an inequality which affects important interests, the disadvantaged class is deemed to have no special claim to judicial favor; or (b) when, although the important interests of a class meriting special protection are comparatively ill-served, no governmental action has occurred which proximately caused (or crystallized) the troublesome disadvantage (?) *Minimum protection is likely to demand remedies which cannot be directly embodied in judicial decrees.* This may come about either because (a) justiciable standards are lacking whereby a court can say whether a government has done its duty, or (b) the remedy entails positive action, of a substantially discretionary or indeterminate character, by a legislative body.

* * *

An additional effect of minimum protection thinking may be to help the decisionmaker understand how to differentiate education from other goods, say opera and golf, which persons will have to continue to pay for out of their own means or do without. Evenhandedness tends to be an all-encompassing value, to become an end in itself, to be "not easily cabined" once loosed. Education, golf, and opera may tend to seem but fungible objects upon which evenhandedness can work, or vehicles through which evenhandedness can realize itself. The distinctive psychic and moral evils of relative deprivation may not seem significantly less present when golf or opera is made available through a governmental facility, but only to those who can and will pay, than when schooling is similarly offered. What we may call the "Harlan syndrome" is an indubitably real phenomenon. The notion of protection against severe deprivation may seem helpfully selective when laid beside that of evenhandedness. It is insistent upon getting what is basic, but is outspokenly explicit in claiming nothing more. It reacts more hospitably than evenhandedness to the question: why education and not golf?

NOTES

1. *See* Rawls, *Distributive Justice: Some Addenda,* 13 Nat. L. Forum 51 (1968); Rawls, *Constitutional Liberty and the Concept of Justice,* in Nomos VI: Justice 96 (C. Friedrich & J. Chapman eds. 1963); Rawls, *The Sense of Justice,* 72 Phil. Rev. 281 (1963); Rawls, *Justice as Fairness,* 67 Phil. Rev. 164 (1958).

2. That is, the challenged acts of government will be invalidated only if (i) not rationally related to any proper governmental purpose, or (ii) so damaging to some judicially favored interest as not (in the court's judgment) to be justified by whatever tendency they do have to advance a proper governmental end. Invalidation on either of these grounds is unconcerned with whether the governmental acts in question entail any "classification" or disparity of treatment.

Notes and Questions

LAWRENCE FRIEDMAN, from *A History of American Law*

1. It has been said that the morality of a society can be judged by how it treats its young, its old, and its weak. By this criterion a purely capitalistic society will not do well, since it responds to the desires of the strongest. How were the poor dealt with in this country initially? Is selling to the lowest bidder likely to produce sympathetic care? Is this approach substantively different from the way we treat institutionalized people who are on welfare today?

2. Lawrence M. Friedman observes that there was a gradual move from private care to institutional care in this country. Was this a good move for the poor? What are the benefits and drawbacks?

3. Friedman points out that general attitudes toward public relief have always been hostile in the United States. What does he say the attitudes have been? Have these attitudes changed in your judgment? Is charity incompatible with the work ethic?

4. Friedman explains that general progress has been made through singling out certain categories of poor, such as war veterans, the handicapped, the old, the insane, and children and designating them as worthy of help. He says that this is the only politically sound way to humanize welfare. Why is that true? Where does that leave the "unworthy poor"—those who are left? Is there sympathy today for the homeless in general? Or for welfare recipients? Should there be?

5. A disproportionate percentage of the poor today are members of minority groups. Friedman traces the repressive legal treatment of some minorities, particularly blacks, during the nineteenth century. It is worth noting that at least in the case of blacks, this repression continued legally until the mid-twentieth century, and in many forms until the civil rights movement of the 1960s. Informally, it is still widespread. You may want to consider the interaction of hostile attitudes toward blacks with disparaging attitudes toward the poor.

[From] *A History of American Law*

LAWRENCE FRIEDMAN

CHAPTER 7

The Underdogs: 1847–1900

The Dependent Poor

The American system provided a voice and a share in the economy to everyone; but for the unorganized and the powerless the share was niggardly indeed. The basis of politics, and law, was the pressure of interest groups; the loudest, most powerful voices won the most. Old people, transients, the feebleminded, dirt-poor and crippled families — all these stayed by and large at the bottom of the social pit. Tort law blossomed, corporation law swelled in pride; the poor laws were local, haphazard, backward, and cruel. There were, however, some gradual improvements.

In some counties of some states, the poor, in the age of the railroad and the telegraph, were still bound out "like cattle at so much per head, leaving the keeper to make his profit out of their petty needs." Sometimes this was a simple matter of necessity, in the absence of institutional alternatives. Trempealeau County, Wisconsin, in the 1870's, and 1880's, boarded out the handful of the "permanently demented" that the state's asylum could not or would not hold. The auction system, in its most blatant form, was dying. "Indoor" relief, that is, relief inside the walls of institutions, was clearly, by 1850, in the ascendancy; "outdoor" relief was on the wane. The trend meant poor farms and poorhouses, if not more specialized institutions. One reason for the change in policy was ideological: outdoor relief was not stigmatic enough. "Men who before had eaten the bread of industry saw their fellows receiving sustenance from the overseer of the poor. . . . The pauper came to look upon the aid given as his by right." Many no doubt through poorhouses would work an improvement in the quality of care; outdoor relief made moral training, medical treatment and rehabilitation more difficult.

These high hopes were frequently disappointed. In 1850, Rhode Island made a study of its poor-law system at work. The results were harrowing. There were fifteen almshouses which spent, on the average, $51.50 per inmate per year. Some of the poor were still "vendued" to keepers who made the lowest bid for their care. There was testimony about one keeper who beat and abused his charges: "He used to drag John Davis, an old man as much as sixty years old up stairs with a rope and kept him there in the cold for days and nights together until he died, having one of his legs frozen. . . . [H]e died before midnight, with no person watching with him and he lay until the sun was 2 or 3 hours high in the morning, on a very cold morning before they came to him." Public poor farms, in general, were not much better than the facilities provided by these private keepers. The public poor farms too were run cheaply, sometimes callously. In the words of one observer, they housed "the most sodden driftwood from the social wreckage of the time. . . . In some of the country almshouses, no clergyman comes the year round; and no friendly visitor appears to encourage the superintendent to be faithful, or to bring to light abuses that may exist." The Ulster County poorhouse (New York) was in 1868 an "old, dilapidated two-story wooden structure." The rooms were small, "ceilings low, ventilation imperfect"; there were no "suitable bathing conveniences." The little wooden house for the insane contained "twenty-five small unventilated cells." The inmates were all "noisy and filthy"; several were "nearly nude." The beds were disordered and torn, and the halls littered with straw and bits of clothing. The water closet, used by both sexes, was out of repair, and the air in the room was "foul and impure." In the Schoharie County poorhouse, "an insane woman was chained to the floor, and a man to a block of wood in the yard." Twenty years later, some of these hovels had been improved; some had not. The poor got almost no medical care in many counties. In Michigan, in 1894, a former county physician reported the auction system at work; many counties awarded contracts to supply medicine, give medical care, and perform surgery for the poor, to the local doctor who put in the lowest bid.

After the Civil War, some states began to reform their poor laws, by centralizing administration. Massachusetts created a State Board of Charities in 1863, Illinois in 1869. A Connecticut law of 1873 set up a five-member board of charities — "three gentlemen and two ladies" — appointed by the governor. The board was to visit and inspect "all institutions in the state, both public and private, in which persons are detained by compulsion for penal, reformatory, sanitary or humanitarian purposes." The board had to see whether inmates were "properly treated," and whether they were "unjustly placed" or "improperly held" in the institution. The board had some vague powers to "correct any abuses that shall be found to exist," but were told to work, "so far as practicable, through the persons in charge of such institutions. This was something less than iron discipline over charitable institutions. But the boards had the power of publicity. They could, if they wished, evoke scandal. In the late 19th century, for these areas of apathy and neglect, the enthusiasm of a small band of people, inside and outside of government — men and women like Florence Kelley, Lawrence Veiller, and many others — was one of the few real forces of reform. The reformers used words, charts, and pictures as their weapons. They aimed for the sympathy of a wider public, or, more tellingly, at a public sense of social cost. They tried to show that callousness, in the long run, did not pay. Welfare improvement came about mostly on this social-cost basis. In the 1890's, when some counties were still selling medical care of the poor to the lowest bidder, Amos G. Warner and associates noted that 10 American cities, with an aggregate population of 3,327,323, spent $1,034,576.50 in one year on medical relief. Warner thought there were "three strong motives" at work: "the desire to aid the destitute, the desire to educate students and build up medical reputations, and the desire to protect the public health. The latter has

often been the leading cause of public appropriations for medical charities." The reformers, then, were valuable not only because they touched the heart, but because they persuaded the selfish soul too. They played on fear of crime, plague, and social disorganization that poverty might breed. Still, reformers had to struggle against strongly held attitudes, unfriendly to public relief. These attitudes infected even public agencies. The Illinois board of charities, in 1886, voiced a common fear, that the "inevitable consequences of substituting the machinery of state for the spontaneous impulses of private benevolence," would be to "paralyze" the "charitable activity" of the private sector. Josephine Shaw Lowell, writing in 1890, thought that public relief was justified only when "starvation is imminent." How could one tell when this was the case? "Only by putting such conditions upon the giving of public relief that, presumably, persons not in danger of starvation will not consent to receive it. The less that is given, the better for everyone, the giver and the receiver."

The poor were thus impaled on the horns of a 19th-century dilemma: society refused to tolerate the idea of pay without work, but no one was supposed to starve. Relief was, in theory, available to everyone who really needed it. But this right was not to be too freely exercised. Consciously or not, relief was made so degrading and obnoxious that no one with an alternative, and some pride, would choose it voluntarily. Mostly, in fact, family and friends had to sustain the urban poor; private charity took care of some others; the public sector lagged behind. In times of depression, however, there were soup kitchens in the major cities. Some relief agencies protested that these kitchens were too indiscriminate; it was "impossible" to tell the "worthy" from the "unworthy poor." Soup presumably corrupted the one but not the other. The big city machines had no such qualms. Boss Tweed of New York City personally donated $50,000 to provide the poor with Christmas dinners, in the harsh winter of 1870. He used his position in the state legislature to squeeze appropriations for charities in his city; and city funds, too, were distributed to welfare institutions. Some of this money, of course, had been extorted from the public, rich and poor. Caustically, the *New York Times* compared Tweed to a medieval baron, "who swept a man's land of his crops, and then gave him a crust of dry bread." There were hard times in the 90's, which brought forth a few new ideas from reform governments, too. Mayor Hazen Pingree of Detroit had a garden plan; the poor grew vegetables on vacant lots. San Francisco spent $3,000 a month in 1893 to help the unemployed. Some of these jobless men were put to work cleaning streets and building roads.

There were some substantive improvements in the law of settlement and removal. The main trend, however, was to continue to redefine the worthy as opposed to the unworthy poor. Worthy meant, in essence, guiltless. These were the blind, children, veterans, the deaf and dumb, the epileptic. Temporary sufferers, fallen from the middle class, were likely to catch the fancy and sympathy of legislatures. Kansas, for example, was as stingy as any toward its destitute poor. But in 1869, it appropriated $15,000 to buy seed wheat for impoverished settlers on the western frontier; more was appropriated in 1874; in 1875, the state passed a "seed and feed" law. Townships could float bonds to provide "destitute citizens . . . with grain for seed and feed." Another law authorized counties to sell bonds for relief purposes. (The farmers were expected to pay the money back.) In the 1890's, the state gave away seed wheat, and sold grain and coal to farmers hurt by drought and crop failures.

War veterans were another meritorious class. There had been both state and federal pensions for veterans of every American war, including, of course, the Civil War. Wounded war veterans, and their families, were singled out for special benefits, in a federal pension law of 1862. The organized veterans continued to press for bonuses, pensions and bounties; after 1876, they won a number of signal victories. They were a potent lobby in the states, too. Connecticut, for example, granted some tax relief to former soldiers (1869); small pensions to orphans of soldiers, up to age twelve; and incorporated, in 1864, a soldiers' orphans' home. In 1889, Civil War veterans were given job preferences for state jobs. In 1895, veterans were exempted from peddlers' licenses.

Government participation in the care of special classes of the poor took more and more direct forms: first, granting charters to private charities, then donating money to these agencies, finally running state institutions. In Massachusetts, the state lunatic hospital at Worcester was founded in the 1830's. In the 1840's, Dorothea Dix bravely roamed the country, pleading that something be done for the mentally ill. In New Jersey, she talked the legislature into creating an insane asylum at Trenton; it opened its doors in 1848. After 1850, other states established institutions for these neglected people. Kansas set up a hospital for the insane at Osawatomie in 1863; later, four more such hospitals were created, and in 1881, a state home for the feebleminded. But even in states with statewide institutions, most of the insane who were not at home were at the tender mercies of county officials of the poor. The state institutions themselves were of varying quality. Government, reflecting its constituencies, was niggardly; and its span of attention was short. Neglected, some state institutions turned into snake pits. Their only advance on local institutions was that they centralized abuse.

Legislatures did, however, create or finance other kinds of "home." Particularly, there was a special effort to ease the lot of the children. Pennsylvania, in 1860, donated $5,000 to the "Northern Home for friendless children," a typical act of largess. Children were a natural object of sympathy and, in the city, were the stuff of which the "dangerous classes" were made, if they were not taken care of. The old apprenticeship system was not suitable in the factory age. In New York, the Children's Aid Society, founded by Charles Loring Brace in 1853, gathered up homeless children from the streets and sent them into the country — many to the Midwest — to work and build character on clean, honest, Protestant farms. Some foster parents were perhaps cruel and exploitive; other orphans found what were probably passable homes, and a decent way to earn their bread. Western farm life was in any event to be preferred to street life, hunger, and an early, violent death. Up to 1892, the Children's Aid Society had "emigrated" 84,318 children; most of these (51,427) were boys.

On the whole, the categorical approach was the only way to humanize welfare that was at all politically sound. This approach consisted of constantly pinching off a class of the more or less guiltless or worthy poor. It was therefore devastating to those left over, the unworthy or guilty poor. No programs dealt with their problems in any meaningful way. Special aids to others drained away whatever sympathy and political clout this residue could muster. It was a story to be endlessly repeated. The fate of families on relief was later matched by the fate of ADC and public housing in the 1950's, which became more and more controversial and degraded, the more they became last-stop programs for the lowest dependents of them all.

* * *

The Races

The war, the Emancipation Proclamation, and the 13th, 14th, and 15th amendments ended American slavery and gave the blacks the right to vote. The 14th amendment also gave them (ostensibly) the equal protection of the laws. The basic promises of Reconstruction, however, were not kept. Until well into the 20th century, much of the history of Reconstruction was written by white Southerners, in a style unfriendly to blacks and to the radical North. Historians have only recently begun to peel away misconceptions in earnest, and reconstruct Reconstruction in a more generous, balanced way.

Clearly, leaders of the old South who survived the war were in no mood for racial equality. It was a bitter enough pill that the slaves were legally free; there was no indication to go beyond the formal status. The Black Codes of 1865 and the following years meant to replace slavery with some kind of caste system, and to preserve as much as possible of the prewar way of life. Mississippi led the way. Its statutes in 1865 looked to a system in which the freedmen would enter into long-term written contracts of labor. Any black laborer who later quit "without good cause" could be arrested, and taken back to his employer. The Black Codes kept on some of the old legal disabilities of blacks. Negroes could not sit on juries, for example. The Southern states also passed stringent vagrancy laws to control the movement of the freedmen.

The North—at least the radicals—were not ready to concede this much to the South. The Black Codes were erased; Congress enacted a strong Civil Rights Act (1866), anticipating the 14th amendment (1868); the South was put under military government. The Freedmen's Bureaus, established by Congress, were an experiment in social planning, to help blacks adapt to the white man's society and economy. Blacks were elected to Congress and held state offices. But Recon-

struction did not last. The Freedmen's Bureaus practically ceased operation by 1869; they were at all times understaffed and underfinanced; and their boldest moves—for example, land redistribution on the sea islands of South Carolina—were frustrated by the Johnson administration's policies. By 1875, the North's passion for equality had unfortunately dribbled away. The North lost interest in the welfare of the black; Northern racism, briefly and thinly covered over, came to the surface once more. As for the white South, it eagerly embraced the new situation. The Klan terrorized the blacks. The South destroyed Negro suffrage, and enforced Negro poverty, with the help of lien laws for landlords and merchants, and the sharecropping system.

Reconstruction of legal apartheid proceeded slowly but inexorably in other areas of southern life. C. Vann Woodward has described the strange career of Jim Crow. Woodward argued that the end of Radical Reconstruction did not mean a complete, immediate Jim Crow system in the South. Many of the most blatant Jim Crow laws, on the contrary, belonged to the very end of the 19th century. Woodward did not claim that race relations were smooth before that, or that the Negro was ever welcomed into white society. He merely pointed out a period of trial and error, ambiguity, and complexity; the decisive instruments of segregation were nailed into law at a date rather later than some historians had assumed. But in South Carolina, according to Joel Williamson, though Negroes could, by the letter of the law, use all public facilities between 1868 and 1889, there is evidence that few actually dared to do so. Probably the South was not of one mind or one practice on segregation. In some parts of the South, it was when the black man dared to protest against his social position that Jim Crow's grip tended to tighten. Georgia required separate railroad cars for blacks and whites in 1891; white and black prisoners could not even be chained together in the chain gangs. Law and social custom defined a place—a subordinate place—for blacks; those who violated the code were severely punished. Major infractions could mean death. Four Negroes were lynched in South Carolina in 1876 for killing an old white couple. The Columbia *Daily Register* approved: "Civilization" was "in banishment . . . a thing apart, cowering in a corner"; there was a need for the "equity" of "Judge Lynch." Later the blood-letting increased. Between 1888 and 1903, 241 blacks died at the hands of lynch mobs.

The South proceeded, in fact, to ensure white supremacy on every front. Amendments to Southern constitutions took away, through one device or another, the black man's right to vote. The surviving black legislators, judges, members of Congress lost their offices. By 1900, not even many voters were left. In Louisiana, the number of blacks registered to vote fell from 127,000 in 1896 to 3,300 in 1900, after the imposition of the "grandfather clause." The North acquiesced. In the Senate, in 1900, Ben Tillman of South Carolina told the North, "You do not love them any better than we do. You used to pretend that you did, but you no longer pretend it." He defended the constitutional change: "We took the government away. We stuffed ballot boxes. We shot them. . . . With that system . . . we got tired ourselves. So we called a constitutional convention, and we eliminated . . . all of the colored people whom we could."

The federal courts probably could not have stood, for long, in the way of Jim Crow, or prevented murder and oppression of America's untouchables. But the Supreme Court hardly tried. In 1878, the Court faced a Louisiana statute (1869) which forbade "discrimination on account of race or color" in common carriers. The court felt this law was an unconstitutional "burden" on interstate commerce. The case arose when the owner of a steamboat, bound for Vicksburg from New Orleans, refused plaintiff, "a person of color," a place "in the cabin specially set apart for white persons." In 1883, the Court declared the Civil Rights Act of 1875 — a public accommodations law — unconstitutional. *Plessy* v. *Ferguson* (1896) was a dark decision. It put the Supreme Court's stamp of approval on apartheid. This was another case from Louisiana. But the underlying facts were different; it was no longer a civil-rights statute that the Court confronted, but a law which called for "equal but separate accommodation for the white, and colored races," in railway carriages. The Court upheld the statute.

The blacks were not the only race to feel the lash of white hatred. The shock-word genocide, so loosely and so often used, comes embarrassingly close to describing the white man's treatment of the Indian. The Indians were driven from their lands and frequently slaughtered. By 1880, they were no longer a military threat. They were herded onto reservations, usually land the white man did not want. Even so, treaties with the Indian tribes were constantly broken by the white man; and the allotment statutes, supposedly safeguarding the Indian's property rights, themselves spoke with forked tongue, and were frequently and adversely amended.

In California (and in the West generally), there was virulent hatred against Orientals, which manifested itself in countless ordinances and laws. A California statute of 1872 authorized school districts to establish separate schools for Orientals. A San Francisco ordinance of 1880, aimed at the Chinese, made it unlawful to carry on a laundry in the city, without the "consent of the board of supervisors," unless the laundry was "located in a building constructed either of brick and stone." Almost every San Francisco laundry was in fact in a wooden building. The Board turned down all applications of Chinese and granted all those of Caucasians. In the famous case of *Yick Wo* v. *Hopkins* (1886), the Supreme Court struck down the discrimination; it was "illegal," and the public administration which enforced it was "a denial of the equal protection of the laws and a violation of the Fourteenth Amendment."

But such victories were rare. Fear of the competition of Chinese labor was one root cause of anti-Chinese feeling; and it ran deep. The hostility, wrote John R. Commons, "is not primarily racial in character. It is the competitive struggle for standards of living." True enough, organized labor in the North was almost as anti-Chinese as Southern populists were anti-Negro. Labor, indeed, lent its support to federal restrictions on Chinese immigration. The "coming of Chinese laborers to this country," proclaimed a federal law of 1882, "endangers the good order of certain localities." Everyone knew what was meant. This law suspended the immigration of Chinese laborers. It also provided that no state or federal court "shall admit Chinese to citizenship." The Scott Act of 1888 prohibited some 20,000 Chinese (who had temporarily left the country) from coming back. An act of 1892, "to prohibit the coming of Chinese persons into the United States," suspended immigration for another ten years, and provided that Chinese laborers were to be deported unless they applied for and obtained a "certificate of residence." A statute of 1902 made the ban on Chinese entry and Chinese citizenship permanent. Whatever the original causes, race did become part of the story: xenophobia, fear of the strange, and the eugenic madness of the 1890's. In the 1880's, riots in Rock Springs, Wyoming, ended with twenty-eight dead Chinese; then the whites in Tacoma, Washington, put their Chinatown to the torch. The blacks and Chinese, voteless or powerless, were strangers at the pluralist table.

Notes and Questions

Cases on Poverty and Equal Protection of the Law

1. The thrust of *Shelley* v. *Kraemer* is that state power cannot be used to aid discrimination in housing, but in 1971, in *James* v. *Valtierra*, the Court upheld a California statute requiring majority approval by community referendum before any low-rent housing can be developed. Doesn't this ruling lend state power to a community desire to block low-income housing? Is that consistent with *Shelley*? The statute in *Valtierra* does not discriminate against minorities as such, only against the poor. The plaintiff argued that subjecting only low-income housing to popular vote puts an unconstitutional burden on only one class — the poor — thus denying equal protection of the law. Is there any constitutional protection against economic inequality? Or against discrimination against the poor? Does it matter if the impact of the California statute falls disproportionately on racial minorities? How does the Court support its position in *Valtierra*?

2. Two years after *Valtierra* limited equal protection in the area of housing, a challenge was raised to unequal funding of public schools. In *San Antonio Public School District* v. *Rodriguez* the plaintiffs argued that poor school districts do not receive equal educational opportunity because rich school districts receive far more funds. The Court decided not to interfere in the state educational system in this case, for at least three reasons. First, wealth is not a suspect class (that is, equal protection of the law does not require special judicial protection in cases of economic inequality), and furthermore, there is no absolute denial of education, only a difference in quality. Second, education is not a fundamental right protected by the Constitution. Third, the case does not involve any state obstacle to education, but merely the differential distribution of a benefit. Do these sound like good reasons to you? Why does the Court think that they are — that is, how does it support its position? Is this case compatible with *Brown*? Why or why not?

3. Notice that *United States* v. *Kras* and *Ortwein* v. *Schwab* make clear that there is no guarantee of general access to the civil court system for the poor, either to file bankruptcy or to protect themselves against errors in welfare or old-age assistance. *Harris* v. *McRae* shows that there is no constitutional protection of medical benefits to the poor. State or federal legislatures can structure benefits programs for the poor as they see fit. The Court will not interfere. These cases demonstrate that there is no constitutional right to affirmative benefits (except certain procedural ones, such as a criminal trial). Constitutionally speaking, there is no fundamental right to Social Security, disability pay, medical care, affordable housing, education, or free legal services. Equal protection of the law requires only that a person not be denied access to such benefits by a state agency, if and only if the individual can afford to pay for such benefits. If a person cannot afford the benefits, however, the state need not provide them. No matter how crucial these basic benefits are, there is no constitutional right to them. Does that mean that there is no civil right to them? Certainly not. In fact, all of these benefits are provided in one form or another by state or federal programs, funded by taxes, and all citizens who meet the eligibility requirements are entitled to them. But as far as the law is concerned, in the United States these entitlements are subject to

majority rule through legislative enactment (as constitutional rights are not). This means that legally an individual is not protected from majority will in the enjoyment of these rights. We hold them at the pleasure of the majority. Is this fair to the poor?

4. These cases begin with a brief note by L. J. Barker and T. W. Barker, Jr., that surveys the Court's consideration of constitutional rights or other legal protections for the poor during the 1970s. What are the major issues raised by the Court, and on what grounds does it make its dispositions? Are the poor a particularly vulnerable class? Is poverty a discernible class characteristic? How does it differ from race? Is the Court correct to treat race and class so differently?

Cases on Poverty and Equal Protection of the Law

[From] *Civil Liberties and the Constitution*
L. J. BARKER AND T. W. BARKER, JR.

Civil Rights and the Poor

Poor people in America experience deprivation and discrimination solely because of their low socio-economic status. In the most affluent nation on earth the poor barely subsist. Their everyday life is burdened by inadequate food and clothing, dilapidated housing, high unemployment, grossly inferior schools, and high crime rates. It is as if they lived in another country, another world — and most of them do! In actual numbers, whites form the majority of poor people in this country. Nonetheless, because blacks and other minority groups constitute a disproportionate number of those in poverty, the drive to eliminate poverty and live a decent life may be viewed as part of the overall civil rights struggle. Consequently, the nation's poor have also resorted to the judiciary (in addition to other political institutions) in attempting to achieve their objectives. This section reviews the stance of the Supreme Court with respect to certain problems affecting the rights of the poor.

Poverty, Public Schools, and Property Tax

In *San Antonio Independent School District* v. *Rodriguez*, a 1973 decision, the Supreme Court rejected challenges to the property tax that pro-

vides a significant part of public school finance in 49 of the 50 states. Here, Rodriguez contended that the Texas system of supplementing state aid to school districts by means of an *ad valorem* tax on property within the jurisdiction of the individual school district violated the equal protection clause. Rodriguez, whose children attended schools in a district with lower per pupil expenditures but higher property tax rates than in other area districts, argued that substantial differences in per pupil expenditures among the districts resulted from the differences in the value of the property taxed within each district. Justice Lewis Powell, speaking for a 5–4 majority of the Court, said that the financing system, although not perfect, "abundantly satisfies" the constitutional standard for equal protection since the system "rationally furthers a legitimate state purpose or interest." Powell said that the traditional equal protection standard applied, since "the Texas system does not operate to the peculiar disadvantage of any suspect class" and since education, although an important state service, is not a "fundamental" right because it is not "explicitly or implicitly guaranteed by the Constitution." Justices Brennan, White, Douglas, and Marshall dissented.

One real effect of *Rodriguez* is that relief from

such inequities would perhaps best be sought in state courts and legislatures. And some relief has come about. A number of states, through court rulings and legislative enactments, have made sweeping reforms in this regard. But the fact that other states have refused to overturn existing methods of financing public education must temper any notion of circumventing *Rodriguez* on a massive scale. (Cf. *Serrano* v. *Priest,* 487 P.2d 1241, 1977, cert. denied in *Clowes* v. *Serrano,* 97 S. Ct. 2951, 1977.)

The Poor and Housing

Several decisions of the Supreme Court held considerable importance for the poor with respect to housing. In *James* v. *Valtierra* (402 U.S. 137,) in 1971, for example, the Court upheld a California statute that "provided that no low-rent [federally-financed] housing project should be developed, constructed or acquired in any manner by a state public body until the project was approved by a majority of those voting at a community election." A federal district court agreed with plaintiffs who contended the statute denied them equal protection of the laws and enjoined its enforcement. But in appeal the Supreme Court reversed. In his opinion for the majority, Justice Black rejected the plaintiff's argument "that the mandatory nature of the . . . referendum constitutes unconstitutional discrimination because it hampers persons desiring public housing from achieving their objective when no such roadblock faces other groups seeking to influence other public decisions to their advantage." To him, it was clear that the referendum procedure "ensures that all the people of a community will have a voice in a decision which may lead to large expenditures of local governmental funds for increased public services and to lower tax revenues." The California referendum statute, he concluded, is a "procedure for democratic decision-making" that does not violate the equal protection clause.

Justice Marshall, joined by Justices Brennan and Blackmun, dissented. Marshall said that the California statute "on its face constitutes invidious discrimination which the Equal Protection Clause of the Fourteenth Amendment plainly prohibits." He contended further that "singling out the poor to bear a burden not placed on any other

class of citizens tramples the values that the Fourteenth Amendment was designed to protect."

At issue in *Warth* v. *Seldin* (422 U.S. 490, 1975) was the allegedly discriminatory zoning laws of Penfield, New York, a Rochester suburb, which effectively prevented low- and middle-income blacks and Puerto Ricans from moving in. The suit was brought by several groups. These included several area residents with low or middle incomes who were members of racial minorities; several Rochester taxpayers who claimed that the discriminatory practices of Penfield resulted in higher taxes; and a nonprofit organization whose purpose was to alleviate the housing shortage in the Rochester area for lower income persons. In a 5–4 decision the Court ruled that the above groups did not have the standing requisite to bring such action. Justice Powell, who wrote the majority opinion, held that none of the petitioners had met the "threshold requirement" of "clearly . . . demonstrating that he is a proper party to invoke judicial resolution of the dispute and the exercise of the court's remedial powers."

The decision in *Warth,* especially considered in light of *San Antonio,* illustrates the plight of the poor in trying to achieve parity with their wealthier "neighbors." On the one hand the poor are denied relief with respect to financial inequities which exist between different school districts or communities. On the other hand, it is possible for the wealthy to exclude the poor through certain zoning regulations. Thus, the options for poor people to achieve some sense of parity on the local level have been greatly narrowed by these Court actions. (But some hope might be found in the 1976 Court decision in *Hills* v. *Gauthreaux.* . . .

A long-standing concern of the poor came before the Supreme Court in the 1970s. That concern involves the rights of indigent renters. In *Lindsey* v. *Normet* (405 U.S. 56, 1972) Lindsey and other tenants refused to pay their monthly rent unless certain substandard conditions were remedied, and Normet threatened to evict them. The appellants filed a class action suit seeking a declaratory judgment that three provisions of the Oregon Forcible Entry and Wrongful Detainer statute (FED) were unconstitutional. The appellants attacked primarily (1) the requirement of a trial no later than six days after service of the complaint unless security for the accruing rent is provided, (2) the limitation of triable issues to the tenant's default (the landlord's breach of duty to maintain the premises was excluded), and (3) the requirement of posting bond on appeal which amounted to twice the rent expected to accrue pending the appellate decision. The entire bond was forfeited if the lower court decision was affirmed.

Justice White, delivering the opinion for the Court, ruled that the first two issues did not violate either the Due Process or the Equal Protection Clause. However, White argued that the double bond prerequisite for appealing an FED action violated the Equal Protection Clause because it arbitrarily discriminated against tenants wishing to appeal adverse FED decisions without effectuating the state's purpose of preserving the property issue.

Also at issue was the refusal of a judge to deny a jury trial to a renter who was being sued by his landlord for repossession of property [*Pernell* v. *Southhall Realty* (416 U.S. 363, 1974)]. The appellant refused payments to "set-off" costs he had incurred in performing certain repair work and for the landlord's failure to maintain the premises in compliance with District of Columbia housing regulations. In the majority opinion, Justice Marshall stated that either party has the right to a jury trial by the Seventh Amendment. In general, *Lindsey* and *Pernell* recognize that renters too have certain rights and are entitled to seek redress on constitutional grounds.

Access to the Courts

In *Boddie* v. *Connecticut* (401 U.S. 371, 1971) the Court held that states cannot deny access to their courts to persons seeking divorces solely because of inability to pay court costs. The case involved indigent welfare recipients who desired divorces but who were unable to pay the necessary filing and other court fees (about $60 in all) in order to obtain a hearing. They claimed that the due process and equal protection clauses required Connecticut to grant them access to courts. In accepting Boddie's due process contention, Justice John Harlan's opinion for the Court emphasized the state's authority over the marriage status. "Given the basic position of the marriage relationship in this society's hierarchy

of values and the concomitant state monopolization of the means for legally dissolving [it]," he asserted, "due process does prohibit the State from denying, solely because of inability to pay, access to its courts to individuals who seek judicial dissolution of their marriages." Harlan's opinion in *Boddie,* however, is self-limiting, since two important factors must be present in cases attempting to use the result as a binding precedent: (1) the presence of a fundamental or basic interest, and (2) "state monopolization" over resolution of the dispute.

Several of the other opinions in *Boddie,* however, were not so limited. Justice Douglas, for example, concurred, saying that the decision should have rested on the broader base of equal protection. "An invidious discrimination based on poverty," said Douglas, "is adequate for this case." Justice Brennan, in another concurring opinion, said that "[t]he right to be heard in some way at some time extends to all proceedings entertained by courts." "The possible distinctions suggested by the Court today," cautioned Brennan, "will not withstand analysis." Brennan was concerned over the "state monopolization" language used by Harlan in the majority opinion.

But the Burger Court moved away from this "access" trend in civil matters with two 5–4 decisions in 1973. In each instance, the four Nixon appointees were joined by Justice Byron White of the Warren Court. First, in *United States* v. *Kras* (409 U.S. 434, 1973), the inability of an unemployed indigent to pay the $50 filing fee in a bankruptcy petition was at issue. A federal district court had agreed with the petitioner's argument that denying him the opportunity to file for bankruptcy because of his inability to pay the filing fee violated the due process and equal protection guarantees of the Fifth Amendment. Relying on the *Boddie* decision, the district court concluded that "a discharge in bankruptcy was a 'fundamental interest' that could be denied only when a 'compelling government interest' was demonstrated." But a five-member majority of the Supreme Court rejected this reliance upon *Boddie* as misplaced. Speaking for them, Justice Harold Blackmun maintained that bankruptcy should not be regarded as a fundamental right that demands the showing of a "compelling governmental interest" to justify significant regulation. Furthermore, he contended, this subject does not touch upon "the suspect criteria of race, nationality or alienage." Hence, he argued, "rational justification" was the appropriate standard and Congress had met it. For example, while the court action sought in *Boddie* was the only way to dissolve the marriage, the statute involved in *Kras* permits "negotiated agreements" and very low installment payments. In short, the indigent bankrupt is offered effective alternatives. In the end, he held, any extension of the *Boddie* principle to bankruptcy proceedings should start with the Congress.

The dissenting justices (Douglas, Stewart, Brennan, and Marshall) were sharply critical of the majority for in effect holding, as Justice Stewart remarked, "that some of the poor are too poor even to go bankrupt." Because they believed that access to the courts to determine the claim of a legal right is fundamental, any denial of that access because of inability to pay filing fees, constituted for them the kind of invidious discrimination between rich and poor contrary to equal protection.

The second case, *Ortwein* v. *Schwab* (410 U.S. 656), involved an action by welfare recipients to have a court review of Oregon administrative action reducing their benefits without payment of the required $25 filing fee. The Supreme Court affirmed the Oregon courts' denial of relief. In its per curiam opinion, the Court cited *Kras* rather than *Boddie* as the governing precedent, noting that the interest alleged by the welfare recipients (to have administrative action reducing their benefits judicially reviewed), was far less significant than that asserted by the indigent divorce seekers in *Boddie*.

The same four dissenters restated their argument advanced in *Kras*. As Justice William O. Douglas noted, the majority's action simply "broadens and fortifies the 'private preserve' for the affluent . . . [by upholding] a scheme of judicial review whereby justice remains a luxury for the wealthy." Furthermore, Douglas noted, *Kras* should not be considered applicable to this case because relief through "nonjudicial accommodation" was not available. Even more crucial was the fact that the majority's ruling permits a state to deny "initial access to the courts for review of an adverse administrative determination."

The Supreme Court did not exhibit this kind of deference to state procedures permitting pre-judgment garnishment of wages (in Wisconsin and about 20 other states) and pre-judgment seizure of goods under writs of replevin (in Pennsylvania and Florida) without any prior hearing. In 1969, in *Sniadach* v. *Family Finance Corporation* (395 U.S. 337), the Court indicated that wages were "a specialized type of property" and that the consequences of wage garnishment (e.g., hardship on wage earners with families to support) were quite severe. Justice Douglas's brief majority opinion stated that "[w]here the taking of one's property is so obvious, it needs no extended argument to conclude that absent notice and a prior hearing this pre-judgment garnishment procedure violates the fundamental principles of due process."

Three years later, in *Fuentes* v. *Shevin* (407 U.S. 67, 1972), the Court in a 4–3 decision ruled that due process requires that an opportunity for a hearing be provided before the State can authorize its agents to seize property in the possession of a debtor upon the application of his creditor. Justice Stewart's majority opinion noted that "essential reason for the hearing requirement is to prevent unfair and mistaken deprivations of property." "Due process," said Stewart, "is afforded only by the kinds of 'notice' and 'hearing' that are aimed at establishing the validity, or at least the probable validity, of the underlying claim against the alleged debtor *before* he can be deprived of his property." Chief Justice Burger and Justices White and Blackmun did not believe that the Constitution guarantees such a right to a defaulting buyer-debtor. In Justice White's dissenting opinion, supported by Burger and Blackmun, the creditor's property interest is considered just "as deserving as that of the debtor." White argued that under the Court's historic view of what procedures due process requires "under any given set of circumstances," the creditors had the right under state laws to take possession of the property *pending final hearing*. White chided the majority that it should best leave such legislative matters to the experts employed by legislative bodies. Certainly, he did not think the procedures struck down were "some barbaric hangover from bygone days."

By 1974, Justice White's dissent in *Fuentes* was, in great measure, accepted by the Court majority in *Mitchell* v. *W. T. Grant Co.* (416 U.S.

600, 1974). Here the Court upheld a Louisiana sequestration statute permitting creditors to secure a court order for immediate repossession of goods without prior notice to the defaulting debtor. However, the statute gives the debtor the opportunity for full hearing subsequent to the repossession. Speaking for a 5–4 court majority, Justice White rejected the "petitioner's broad assertion that the Due Process Clause of the United States Constitution guaranteed to him the use and possession of the goods until all issues in the case were judicially resolved after full adversary proceedings had been completed." "The very nature of due process," said White, "negates any concept of inflexible procedures universally applicable to every imaginable situation." Applying this principle to the instant case, White observed:

> The question is not whether a debtor's property may be seized by his creditors, *pendente lite,* where they hold no present interest in the property sought to be seized. The reality is that both seller and buyer had rights as a matter of state law. Resolution of the due process question must take account not only of the interests of the buyer of the property but those of the seller as well.

Prior cases upon which the petitioner relied, reasoned White, "merely stand for the proposition that a hearing must be had before one is *finally* [emphasis added] deprived of his property." "Considering the Louisiana procedure as a whole," said White, "we are convinced that the State has reached a constitutional accommodation of the respective interests of buyer and seller."

Justice Stewart, in a dissent joined by Justices Douglas and Marshall, strongly attacked the majority for not following *Fuentes.* Said Stewart: "The only perceivable change that has occurred since *Fuentes* is in the makeup of this Court." Stewart pinpointed this membership change by indicating in a footnote (8) that although Justices Powell and Rehnquist were on the Court when *Fuentes* was announced, they were not on the Court when the case was argued and hence did not participate in its consideration or decision. "A basic change in the law upon a ground no firmer than a change in our membership," warned Stewart, "invites the popular misconception that this institution is little different from the two political branches of the Government." "No misconception," concluded Stewart, "could do

more lasting injury to this Court and to the system of law which it is our abiding mission to serve."

The cases that follow focus on some of the significant issues reviewed in this commentary.

Ortwein v. *Schwab*
410 U.S. 656 (1973)

Ortwein, a recipient of old-age assistance had his award reduced by the county welfare agency. As provided by state law he appealed to the state public welfare agency which held a hearing and upheld the county agency's decision. Judicial review of the state agency decision was provided by law in the state appellate court. Ortwein sought to appeal to that court without paying the $25 filing fee required in all civil cases filed in that court, alleging that he was indigent and unable to pay the fee. The state court denied this contention and refused to hear the appeal without the fee. The Supreme Court, in a *per curiam* opinion, affirmed, indicating that *Kras* rather than *Boddie* was the controlling precedent. The Court gave three principal reasons for its decision:

(1) The interest in increased welfare benefits "has far less constitutional significance" than the inability to dissolve one's marriage except through the courts.

(2) Ortwein did receive a pre-termination evidentiary hearing (the required due process minimum) not conditioned on the payment of a fee. "This Court has long recognized that, even in criminal cases, due process does not require a State to provide an appellate system."

(3) The filing fee does not violate the Equal Protection Clause by discriminating against the poor. The litigation, which deals with welfare payments, is in the area of economics and social welfare. "No suspect classification, such as race, nationality, or alienage, is present. . . . The applicable standard is that of rational justification." The filing fee makes a contribution toward the cost of operating the court system, hence the "requirement of rationality is met."

JUSTICES STEWART, DOUGLAS, BRENNAN and MARSHALL dissented.

United States v. Kras
409 U.S. 434 (1973)

An indigent petitioner seeking voluntary bankruptcy sought to proceed without paying the fees (not more than $50 in this case) which were a condition of discharge. The district court found for the petitioner, relying on *Boddie*. The Supreme Court reversed, JUSTICE BLACKMUN, speaking for the Court, said, in part:

"We agree with the Government that our decision in *Boddie* does not control the disposition of this case and that the District Court's reliance upon *Boddie* is misplaced.

"A. *Boddie* was based on the notion that a State cannot deny access, simply because of one's poverty, to a 'judicial proceeding [that is] the only effective means of resolving the dispute at hand.' Throughout the opinion there is constant and recurring reference to Connecticut's exclusive control over the establishment, enforcement, and dissolution of the marital relationship. The Court emphasized that 'marriage involves interests of basic importance in our society', and spoke of 'state monopolization of the means for legally dissolving this relationship.' '[R]esort to the state courts [was] the only avenue to dissolution of . . . marriages,' which was 'not only the paramount dispute-settlement technique, but, in fact the only available one.' . . . In the light of all this, we concluded that resort to the judicial process was 'no more voluntary in a realistic sense than that of the defendant called upon to defend his interests in court' and we resolved the case 'in light of the principles enunciated in our due process decisions that delimit rights of defendants compelled to litigate their differences in the judicial forum.'

"B. The appellants in *Boddie,* on the one hand, and Robert Kras, on the other, stand in materially different postures. The denial of access to the judicial forum in *Boddie* touched directly, as has been noted, on the marital relationship and on the associational interests that surround the establishment and dissolution of that relationship. On many occasions we have recognized the fundamental importance of these interests under our Constitution. See, for example, Loving v. Virginia, 388 U.S. 1 (1967). . . . The *Boddie* appellants' inability to dissolve their marriages seriously impaired their freedom to pursue other protected associational activities. Kras' alleged interest in the elimination of his debt burden, and in obtaining his desired new start in life, although important and so recognized by the enactment of the Bankruptcy Act, does not rise to the same constitutional level. See Dandridge v. Williams, 397 U.S. 471 (1970); Richardson v. Belcher, 404 U.S. 78 (1971). If Kras is not discharged in bankruptcy, his position will not be materially altered in any constitutional sense. Gaining or not gaining a discharge will effect no change with respect to basic necessities. We see no fundamental interest that is gained or lost depending on the availability of a discharge in bankruptcy.

"C. Nor is the government's control over the establishment, enforcement, or dissolution of debts nearly so exclusive as Connecticut's control over the marriage relationship in *Boddie*. In contrast with divorce, bankruptcy is not the only method available to a debtor for the adjustment of his legal relationship with his creditors. The utter exclusiveness of court access and court remedy, as has been noted, was a potent factor in *Boddie*. But '[w]ithout a prior judicial imprimatur, individuals may freely enter into and rescind commercial contracts. . . .'

"However unrealistic the remedy may be in a particular situation, a debtor, in theory, and often in actuality, may adjust his debts by negotiated agreement with his creditors. At times the happy passage of the applicable limitation period, or other acceptable creditor arrangement, will provide the answer. Government's role with respect to the private commercial relationship is qualitatively and quantitatively different than its role in the establishment, enforcement, and dissolution of marriage.

"Resort to the Court, therefore, is not Kras' sole path to relief. *Boddie's* emphasis on exclusivity finds no counterpart in the bankrupt's situation. . . .

"D. We are also of the opinion that the filing fee requirement does not deny Kras the equal protection of the laws. Bankruptcy is hardly akin to free speech or marriage or to those other rights, so many of which are imbedded in the First Amendment, that the Court has come to regard as fundamental and that demand the lofty requirement of a compelling governmental interest before they may be significantly regulated. See Shapiro v. Thompson, 394 U.S. 618, 638 (1969). Neither does it touch upon what has been said to be the suspect criteria of race, nationality or alienage. Graham v. Richardson, 403 U.S. 365, 375 (1971). Instead, bankruptcy legislation is in the area of economics and social welfare. This being so, the applicable standard, in measuring the propriety of Congress' classification, is that of rational justification."

JUSTICES STEWART, DOUGLAS, and MARSHALL, dissented.

San Antonio Independent School District
v. Rodriquez
411 U.S. 1 (1973)

Mr. Justice Powell delivered the opinion of the Court.

This suit attacking the Texas system of financing public education was initiated by Mexican-American parents whose children attend the elementary and secondary schools in the Edgewood Independent School District, an urban school district in San Antonio, Texas. They brought a class action on behalf of school children throughout the State who are members of minority groups or who are poor and reside in school districts having a low property tax base. Named as defendants were the State Board of Education, the Commissioner of Education, the State Attorney General, and the Bexar County (San Antonio) Board of Trustees. The complaint was filed in the summer of 1968 and a three-judge court was impaneled in January 1969. In December 1971 the panel rendered its judgment in a *per curiam* opinion holding the Texas school finance system unconstitutional under the Equal Protection Clause of the Fourteenth Amendment. . . . For the reasons stated in this opinion we reverse the decision of the District Court.

I

* * *

The case comes to us with no definitive description of the classifying facts or delineation of the disfavored class. Examination of the District Court's opinion and of appellees' complaint, briefs, and contentions at oral argument suggests, however, at least three ways in which the discrimination claimed here might be described. The Texas system of school finance might be regarded as discriminating (1) against "poor"

persons whose incomes fall below some identifiable level of poverty or who might be characterized as functionally "indigent," or (2) against those who are relatively poorer than others, or (3) against all those who, irrespective of their personal incomes, happen to reside in relatively poorer school districts. Our task must be to ascertain whether, in fact, the Texas system has been shown to discriminate on any of these possible bases and, if so, whether the resulting classification may be regarded as suspect.

The precedents of this Court provide the proper starting point. The individuals or groups of individuals who constituted the class discriminated against in our prior cases shared two distinguishing characteristics: because of their impecunity they were completely unable to pay for some desired benefit, and as a consequence, they sustained an absolute deprivation of a meaningful opportunity to enjoy that benefit. In Griffin v. Illinois, 351 U.S. 12 (1956), and its progeny, the Court invalidated state laws that prevented an indigent criminal defendant from acquiring a transcript, or an adequate substitute for a transcript, for use at several stages of the trial and appeal process. The payment requirements in each case were found to occasion *de facto* discrimination against those who, because of their indigency, were totally unable to pay for transcripts. And, the Court in each case emphasized that no constitutional violation would have been shown if the State had provided some "adequate substitute" for a full stenographic transcript. . . .

* * *

Only appellees' first possible basis for describing the class disadvantaged by the Texas school finance system—discrimination against a class of definably "poor" persons—might arguably meet the criteria established in these prior cases. Even a cursory examination, however, demonstrates that neither of the two distinguishing characteristics of wealth classifications can be found here. First, in support of their charge that the system discriminates against the "poor," appellees have made no effort to demonstrate that it operates to the peculiar disadvantage of any class fairly definable as indigent, or as composed of persons whose incomes are beneath any designated poverty level. Indeed, there is reason to believe that the poorest families are not necessarily clustered in the poorest property districts. A recent and exhaustive study of school districts in Connecticut concluded that "[i]t is clearly incorrect . . . to contend that the 'poor' live in 'poor' districts. . . . Thus, the major factual assumption of *Serrano*—that the educational finance system discriminates against the 'poor'—is simply false in Connecticut." Defining "poor" families as those below the Bureau of the Census "poverty level," the Connecticut study found, not surprisingly, that the poor were clustered around commercial and industrial areas—those same areas that provide the most attractive sources of property tax income for school districts. Whether a similar pattern would be discovered in Texas is not known, but there is no basis on the record in this case for assuming that the poorest people—defined by reference to any level of absolute impecunity—are concentrated in the poorest districts.

Second, neither appellees nor the District Court addressed the fact that, unlike each of the foregoing cases, lack of personal resources has not occasioned an absolute deprivation of the desired benefit. The argument here is not that the children in districts having relatively low assessable property values are receiving no public education; rather, it is that they are receiving a poorer quality education than that available to children in districts having more assessable wealth. . . .

For these two reasons—the absence of any evidence that the financing system discriminates against any definable category of "poor" people or that it results in the absolute deprivation of education—the disadvantaged class is not susceptible to identification in traditional terms.

As suggested above, appellees and the District Court may have embraced a second or third approach, the second of which might be characterized as a theory of relative or comparative discrimination based on family income. Appellees sought to prove that a direct correlation exists between the wealth of families within each district and the expenditures therein for education. That is, along a continuum, the poorer the family the lower the dollar amount of education received by the family's children.

* * *

If, in fact, these correlations could be sustained, then it might be argued that expenditures on education—equated by appellees to the quality of educa-

tion—are dependent on personal wealth. . . . These questions need not be addressed in this case, however, since appellees' proof fails to support their allegations or the District Court's conclusions.

Professor Berke's affidavit is based on a survey of approximately 10% of the school districts in Texas. His findings, set out in the margin,[1] show only that the wealthiest few districts in the sample have the highest median family incomes and spend the most on education, and that the several poorest districts have the lowest family incomes and devote the least amount of money to education. For the remainder of the districts—96 districts comprising almost 90% of the sample—the correlation is inverted, *i. e.*, the districts that spend next to the most money on education are populated by families having next to the lowest median family incomes while the districts spending the least have the highest median family incomes. It is evident that, even if the conceptual questions were answered favorably to appellees, no factual basis exists upon which to found a claim of comparative wealth discrimination.

This brings us, then, to the third way in which the classification scheme might be defined—*district* wealth discrimination. Since the only correlation indicated by the evidence is between district property wealth and expenditures, it may be argued that discrimination might be found without regard to the individual income characteristics of district residents. Assuming a perfect correlation between district property wealth and expenditures from top to bottom, the disadvantaged class might be viewed as encompassing every child in every district except the district that has the most assessable wealth and spends the most on education.[2] Alternatively, as suggested in MR. JUSTICE MARSHALL's dissenting opinion, *post*, . . . the class might be defined more restrictively to include children in districts with assessable property which falls below the statewide average, or median, or below some other artificially defined level.

However described, it is clear that appellees' suit asks this Court to extend its most exacting scrutiny to review a system that allegedly discriminates against a large, diverse, and amorphous class, unified only by the common factor of residence in districts that happen to have less taxable wealth than other districts. The system of alleged discrimination and the class it defines have none of the traditional indicia of suspect- ness: the class is not saddled with such disabili- ties, or subjected to such a history of purposeful unequal treatment, or relegated to such a position of political powerlessness as to command extra- ordinary protection from the majoritarian politi- cal process.

We thus conclude that the Texas system does not operate to the peculiar disadvantage of any suspect class. But in recognition of the fact that this Court has never heretofore held that wealth discrimination alone provides an adequate basis for invoking strict scrutiny, appellees have not relied solely on this contention. They also assert that the State's system impermissibly interferes with the exercise of a "fundamental" right and that accordingly the prior decisions of this Court require the application of the strict standard of judicial review. . . . It is this question — whether education is a fundamental right, in the sense that it is among the rights and liberties protected by the Constitution — which has so consumed the atten- tion of courts and commentators in recent years.

B

In Brown v. Board of Education, a unanimous Court recognized that "education is perhaps the most important function of state and local gov- ernments." What was said there in the context of racial discrimination has lost none of its vitality with the passage of time: . . .

Nothing this Court holds today in any way detracts from our historic dedication to public education. We are in complete agreement with the conclusion of the three-judge panel below that "the grave significance of education both to the individual and to our society" cannot be doubted. But the importance of a service per- formed by the State does not determine whether it must be regarded as fundamental for purposes of examination under the Equal Protection Clause. Mr. Justice Harlan, dissenting from the Court's application of strict scrutiny to a law impinging upon the right of interstate travel, admonished that "[v]irtually every state statute affects important rights." Shapiro v. Thompson. In his view, if the degree of judicial scrutiny of state legislation fluctuated depending on a major- ity's view of the importance of the interest affected, we would have gone "far toward mak-

ing this Court a 'super-legislature.'" *Ibid.* We would indeed then be assuming a legislative role and one for which the Court lacks both authority and competence. But MR. JUSTICE STEWART'S response in *Shapiro* to Mr. Justice Harlan's con- cern correctly articulates the limits of the funda- mental rights rationale employed in the Court's equal protection decisions:

"The Court today does *not* 'pick out particular human activities, characterize them as "funda- mental," and give them added protection. . . .' To the contrary, the Court simply recognizes, as it must, an established constitutional right, and gives to that right no less protection than the Constitution itself demands." (Emphasis from original.)

* * *

. . . The right to interstate travel had long been recognized as a right of constitutional signifi- cance, and the Court's decision therefore did not require an *ad hoc* determination as to the social or economic importance of that right.

* * *

The lesson of these cases in addressing the question now before the Court is plain. It is not the province of this Court to create substantive constitutional rights in the name of guaranteeing equal protection of the laws. Thus the key to dis- covering whether education is "fundamental" is not to be found in comparisons of the relative societal significance of education as opposed to subsistence or housing. Nor is it to be found by weighing whether education is as important as the right to travel. Rather, the answer lies in assessing whether there is a right to education explicitly or implicitly guaranteed by the Constitution.

Education, of course, is not among the rights afforded explicit protection under our Federal Constitution. Nor do we find any basis for saying it is implicitly so protected. . . .

* * *

We have carefully considered each of the arguments supportive of the District Court's finding that education is a fundamental right or liberty and have found those arguments unper- suasive. In one further respect we find this a par- ticularly inappropriate case in which to subject state action to strict judicial scrutiny. The present case, in another basic sense, is significantly dif- ferent from any of the cases in which the Court has applied strict scrutiny to state or federal leg-

islation touching upon constitutionally protected
rights. Each of our prior cases involved legislation which "deprived," "infringed," or "interfered" with the free exercise of some such fundamental personal right or liberty. See Skinner v.
Oklahoma, *supra*, at 536; Shapiro v. Thompson,
supra at 634; Dunn v. Blumstein, *supra*, at
338–343. A critical distinction between those
cases and the one now before us lies in what
Texas is endeavoring to do with respect to education. . . . The Texas system of school finance
. . . was implemented in an effort to *extend* public education and to improve its quality. Of
course, every reform that benefits some more
than others may be criticized for what it fails to
accomplish. But we think it plain that, in substance, the thrust of the Texas system is affirmative and reformatory and, therefore, should be
scrutinized under judicial principles sensitive to
the nature of the State's efforts and to the rights
reserved to the States under the Constitution.

C

It should be clear, for the reasons stated above
and in accord with the prior decisions of this
Court, that this is not a case in which the challenged state action must be subjected to the
searching judicial scrutiny reserved for laws that
create suspect classifications or impinge upon
constitutionally protected rights.

We need not rest our decision, however, solely
on the inappropriateness of the strict scrutiny test.
A century of Supreme Court adjudication under
the Equal Protection Clause affirmatively supports the application of the traditional standard of
review, which requires only that the State's system be shown to bear some rational relationship
to legitimate state purposes. This case represents
far more than a challenge to the manner in which
Texas provides for the education of its children.
We have here nothing less than a direct attack on
the way in which Texas has chosen to raise and
disburse state and local tax revenues. We are
asked to condemn the State's judgment in conferring on political subdivisions the power to tax
local property to supply revenues for local interests. In so doing, appellees would have the Court
intrude in an area in which it has traditionally
deferred to state legislatures. This Court has often
admonished against such interferences with the

State's fiscal policies under the Equal Protection
Clause. . . .

Thus we stand on familiar ground when we
continue to acknowledge that the Justices of this
Court lack both the expertise and the familiarity
with local problems so necessary to the making
of wise decisions with respect to the raising and
disposition of public revenues. . . .

In addition to matters of fiscal policy, this case
also involves the most persistent and difficult
questions of educational policy, another area in
which this Court's lack of specialized knowledge
and experience counsels against premature interference with the informed judgments made at the
state and local levels. . . .

* * *

The foregoing considerations buttress our conclusion that Texas' system of public school
finance is an inappropriate candidate for strict
judicial scrutiny. These same considerations are
relevant to the determination whether that system, with its conceded imperfections, nevertheless bears some rational relationship to a legitimate state purpose. It is to this question that we
next turn our attention.

III

* * *

In sum, to the extent that the Texas system of
school finance results in unequal expenditures
between children who happen to reside in different districts, we cannot say that such disparities
are the product of a system that is so irrational as
to be invidiously discriminatory. Texas has
acknowledged its shortcomings and has persis-
tently endeavored—not without some success—to
ameliorate the differences in levels of expenditures without sacrificing the benefits of local participation. The Texas plan is not the result of hur-
ried, ill-conceived legislation. It certainly is not
the product of purposeful discrimination against
any group or class. On the contrary, it is rooted in
decades of experience in Texas and elsewhere,
and in major part is the product of responsible
studies by qualified people. In giving substance to
the presumption of validity to which the Texas
system is entitled, it is important to remember that
at every stage of its development it has constituted
a "rough accommodation" of interests in an effort
to arrive at practical and workable solutions. One

also must remember that the system here challenged is not peculiar to Texas or to any other State. In its essential characteristics the Texas plan for financing public education reflects what many educators for a half century have thought was an enlightened approach to a problem for which there is no perfect solution. We are unwilling to assume for ourselves a level of wisdom superior to that of legislators, scholars, and educational authorities in 49 States, especially where the alternatives proposed are only recently conceived and nowhere yet tested. The constitutional standard under the Equal Protection Clause is whether the challenged state action rationally furthers a legitimate state purpose or interest. We hold that the Texas plan abundantly satisfies this standard.

* * *

Reversed.

Mr. Justice Stewart, concurring.

* * *

Unlike other provisions of the Constitution, the Equal Protection Clause confers no substantive rights and creates no substantive liberties.[3] The function of the Equal Protection Clause, rather, is simply to measure the validity of *classifications* created by state laws.

There is hardly a law on the books that does not affect some people differently from others. But the basic concern of the Equal Protection Clause is with state legislation whose purpose or effect is to create discrete and objectively identifiable classes. And with respect to such legislation, it has long been settled that the Equal Protection Clause is offended only by laws that are invidiously discriminatory — only by classifications that are wholly arbitrary or capricious.

* * *

Mr. Justice Brennan, dissenting.

Although I agree with my BROTHER WHITE that the Texas statutory scheme is devoid of any rational basis, and for that reason is violative of the Equal Protection Clause, I also record my disagreement with the Court's rather distressing assertion that a right may be deemed "fundamental" for the purposes of equal protection analysis only if it is "explicitly or implicitly guaranteed by the Constitution." . . . As my BROTHER MARSHALL convincingly demonstrates, our prior cases stand for the proposition that "fundamentality" is, in large measure, a function of the right's importance in terms of the effectuation of those

rights which are in fact constitutionally guaranteed. Thus, "[a]s the nexus between the specific constitutional guarantee and the nonconstitutional interest draws closer, the nonconstitutional interest becomes more fundamental and the degree of judicial scrutiny applied when the interest is infringed on a discriminatory basis must be adjusted accordingly." . . .

Here, there can be no doubt that education is inextricably linked to the right to participate in the electoral process and to the rights of free speech and association guaranteed by the First Amendment. . . . This being so, any classification affecting education must be subjected to strict judicial scrutiny, and since even the State concedes that the statutory scheme now before us cannot pass constitutional muster under this stricter standard of review, I can only conclude that the Texas school financing scheme is constitutionally invalid.

Mr. Justice White, with whom Mr. Justice Douglas and Mr. Justice Brennan join, dissenting.

* * *

The Equal Protection Clause permits discriminations between classes but requires that the classification bear some rational relationship to a permissible object sought to be attained by the statute. It is not enough that the Texas system before us seeks to achieve the valid, rational purpose of maximizing local initiative; the means chosen by the State must also be rationally related to the end sought to be achieved. . . .

Neither Texas nor the majority heeds this rule. If the State aims at maximizing local initiative and local choice, by permitting school districts to resort to the real property tax if they choose to do so, it utterly fails in achieving its purpose in districts with property tax bases so low that there is little if any opportunity for interested parents, rich or poor, to augment school district revenues. Requiring the State to establish only that unequal treatment is in furtherance of a permissible goal, without also requiring the State to show that the means chosen to effectuate that goal are rationally related to its achievement, makes equal protection analysis no more than an empty gesture. In my view, the parents and children in Edgewood, and in like districts, suffer from an invidious discrimination violative of the Equal Protection Clause.

* * *

Mr. Justice Marshall, with whom Mr. Justice Douglas concurs, dissenting.

NOTES

1.

Market Value of Taxable Property Per Pupil	Median Family Income in 1960	State and Local Expenditures Per Pupil
Above $100,000 (10 districts)	$5,900	$815
$100,000–$50,000 (26 districts)	$4,425	$544
$50,000–$30,000 (30 districts)	$4,900	$483
$30,000–$10,000 (40 districts)	$5,050	$462
Below $10,000 (4 districts)	$3,325	$305

2. Indeed, this is precisely how the plaintiffs in Serrano v. Priest defined the class they purported to represent: "Plaintiff children claim to represent a class consisting of all public school pupils in California, 'except children in that school district . . . which . . . affords the greatest educational opportunity of all school districts within California.'" 96 Cal.Rptr., at 604, 487 P.2d, at 1244, 5 Cal.3d, at 580. See also Van Dusartz v. Hatfield, 334 F.Supp., at 873.

3. There is one notable exception to the above statement: It has been established in recent years that the Equal Protection Clause confers the substantive right to participate on an equal basis with other qualified voters whenever the State has adopted an electoral process for determining who will represent any segment of the State's population. See, *e.g.*, Reynolds v. Sims, 377 U.S. 533; Kramer v. Union School District, 395 U.S. 621; Dunn v. Blumstein, 405 U.S. 330, 336. But there is no constitutional right to vote, as such. Minor v. Happersett, 88 U.S. 162. If there were such a right, both the Fifteenth Amendment and the Nineteenth Amendment would have been wholly unnecessary.

Harris v. Mc Rae
448 U.S. 297 (1980)

Mr. Justice Stewart delivered the opinion of the Court.

This case presents statutory and constitutional questions concerning the public funding of abortions under Title XIX of the Social Security Act, commonly known as the "Medicaid" Act, and recent annual Appropriations Acts containing the so-called "Hyde Amendment." The statutory question is whether Title XIX requires a State that participates in the Medicaid program to fund the cost of medically necessary abortions for which federal reimbursement is unavailable under the Hyde Amendment. The constitutional question, which arises only if Title XIX imposes no such requirement, is whether the Hyde Amendment, by denying public funding for certain medically necessary abortions, contravenes the liberty or equal protection guarantees of the Due Process Clause of the Fifth Amendment, or either of the Religion Clauses of the First Amendment.

* * *

C

It remains to be determined whether the Hyde Amendment violates the equal protection component of the Fifth Amendment. This challenge is premised on the fact that, although federal reimbursement is available under Medicaid for medically necessary services generally, the Hyde Amendment does not permit federal reimbursement of all medically necessary abortions. The District Court held, and the appellees argue here, that this selective subsidization violates the constitutional guarantee of equal protection.

The guarantee of equal protection under the Fifth Amendment is not a source of substantive rights or liberties,[1] but rather a right to be free from invidious discrimination in statutory classifications and other governmental activity. It is well settled that where a statutory classification does not itself impinge on a right or liberty protected by the Constitution, the validity of classification must be sustained unless "the classification rests on grounds wholly irrelevant to the achievement of [any legitimate governmental] objective." This presumption of constitutional validity, however, disappears if a statutory classification is predicated on criteria that are, in a constitutional sense, "suspect," the principal example of which is a classification based on race.

1

For the reasons stated above, we have already concluded that the Hyde Amendment violates no constitutionally protected substantive rights. We now conclude as well that it is not predicated on a constitutionally suspect classification. In reaching this conclusion, we again draw guidance from the Court's decision in Maher v Roe. As to whether the Connecticut welfare regulation providing funds for childbirth but not for nontherapeutic abortions discriminated against a suspect class, the Court in Maher observed:

> An indigent woman desiring an abortion does not come within the limited category of disadvantaged classes so recognized by our cases. Nor does the fact that the impact of the regulation falls upon those who cannot pay lead to a different conclusion. In a sense, every denial of welfare to an indigent creates a wealth classification as compared to nonindigents who are able to pay for the desired goods or services. But this Court has never held that financial need alone identifies a suspect class for purposes of equal protection analysis.

Thus, the Court in Maher found no basis for concluding that the Connecticut regulation was predicated on a suspect classification.

It is our view that the present case is indistinguishable from Maher in this respect. Here, as in Maher, the principal impact of the Hyde Amendment falls on the indigent. But that fact does not itself render the funding restriction constitutionally invalid, for this Court has held repeatedly that poverty, standing alone, is not a suspect classification. That Maher involved the refusal to fund nontherapeutic abortions, whereas the present case involved the refusal to fund medically necessary abortions, has no bearing on the factors that render a classification "suspect" within the meaning of the constitutional guarantee of equal protection.

* * *

IV

For the reasons stated in this opinion, we hold that a State that participates in the Medicaid program is not obligated under Title XIX to continue to fund those medically necessary abortions

for which federal reimbursement is unavailable under the Hyde Amendment. We further hold that the funding restrictions of the Hyde Amendment violate neither the Fifth Amendment nor the Establishment Clause of the First Amendment. It is also our view that the appellees lack standing to raise a challenge to the Hyde Amendment under the Free Exercise Clause of the First Amendment. Accordingly, the judgment of the District Court is reversed, and the case is remanded to that court for further proceedings consistent with this opinion.

It is so ordered.

* * *

Mr. Justice Marshall dissenting.

* * *

The Court resolves the equal protection issue in this case through a relentlessly formalistic catechism. Adhering to its "two-tiered" approach to equal protection, the Court first decides that so-called strict scrutiny is not required because the Hyde Amendment does not violate the Due Process Clause and is not predicated on a constitutionally suspect classification. Therefore "the validity of classification must be sustained unless 'the classification rests on grounds wholly irrelevant to the achievement of [any legitimate governmental] objective.'" Observing that previous cases have recognized "the legitimate governmental objective of protecting potential life," the Court concludes that the Hyde Amendment "establishe[s] incentives that make childbirth a more attractive alternative than abortion for persons eligible for Medicaid," ibid., and is therefore rationally related to that governmental interest.

I continue to believe that the rigid "two-tiered" approach is inappropriate and that the Constitution requires a more exacting standard of review than mere rationality in cases such as this one. Further, in my judgment the Hyde Amendment cannot pass constitutional muster even under the rational-basis standard of review.

A

This case is perhaps the most dramatic illustration to date of the deficiencies in the Court's obsolete "two-tiered" approach to the Equal Protection Clause.

With all deference, I am unable to understand

how the Court can afford the same level of scrutiny to the legislation involved here — whose cruel impact falls exclusively on indigent pregnant women — that it has given to legislation distinguishing opticians from opthalmologists, or to other legislation that makes distinctions between economic interests more than able to protect themselves in the political process. Heightened scrutiny of legislative classifications has always been designed to protect groups "saddled with such disabilities, or subjected to such a history of purposeful unequal treatment, or relegated to such a position of political powerlessness as to command extraordinary protection from the majoritarian political process." And while it is now clear that traditional "strict scrutiny" is unavailable to protect the poor against classifications that disfavor them, I do not believe that legislation that imposes a crushing burden on indigent women can be treated with the same deference given to legislation distinguishing among business interests.

* * *

B

The class burdened by the Hyde Amendment consists of indigent women, a substantial proportion of whom are members of minority races. As I observed in Maher non-white women obtain abortions at nearly double the rate of whites. Ibid. In my view, the fact that the burden of the Hyde Amendment falls exclusively on financially destitute women suggests "a special condition, which tends seriously to curtail the operation of those political processes ordinarily to be relied upon to protect minorities, and which may call for a correspondingly more searching judicial inquiry." For this reason, I continue to believe that "a showing that state action has a devastating impact on the lives of minority racial groups must be relevant" for purposes of equal protection analysis.

As I explained in Maher, the asserted state interest in protecting potential life is insufficient to "outweigh the deprivation or serious discouragement of a vital constitutional right of especial importance to poor and minority women." In Maher, the Court found a permissible state interest in encouraging normal childbirth. The governmental interest in the present case is substan-

tially weaker than in Maher, for under the Hyde Amendment funding is refused even in cases in which normal childbirth will not result: one can scarcely speak of "normal childbirth" in cases where the fetus will die shortly after birth, or in which the mother's life will be shortened or her health otherwise gravely impaired by the birth. Nevertheless, the Hyde Amendment denies funding even in such cases. In these circumstances, I am unable to see how even a minimally rational legislature could conclude that the interest in fetal life outweighs the brutal effect of the Hyde Amendment on indigent women. Moreover, both the legislation in Maher and the Hyde Amendment were designed to deprive poor and minority women of the constitutional right to choose abortion. That purpose is not constitutionally permitted under Roe v Wade.

C

Although I would abandon the strict-scrutiny/rational-basis dichotomy in equal protection analysis, it is by no means necessary to reject that traditional approach to conclude, as I do, that the Hyde Amendment is a denial of equal protection. My Brother Brennan has demonstrated that the Amendment is unconstitutional because it impermissibly infringes upon the individual's constitutional right to decide whether to terminate a pregnancy. (Dissenting opinion.) And as my Brother Stevens demonstrates (dissenting opinion), the Government's interest in protecting fetal life is not a legitimate one when it is in conflict with "the preservation of the life or health of the mother," Roe v Wade, 410 US, at 165, 35 L Ed 2d 147, 93 S Ct 705, and when the Government's effort to make serious health damage to the mother "a more attractive alternative than abortion," ante, at 325, 65 L Ed 2d, at 810, does not rationally promote the governmental interest in encouraging normal childbirth.

The Court treats this case as though it were controlled by Maher. To the contrary, this case is the mirror image of Maher. The result in Maher turned on the fact that the legislation there under consideration discouraged only nontherapeutic, or medically unnecessary, abortions. In the Court's view, denial of Medicaid funding for nontherapeutic abortions was not a denial of equal protection because Medicaid funds were available only for medically necessary procedures. Thus the plaintiffs were seeking benefits which were not available to others similarly situated. I continue to believe that Maher was wrongly decided. But it is apparent that while the plaintiffs in Maher were seeking a benefit not available to others similarly situated, appellees are protesting their exclusion from a benefit that is available to all others similarly situated. This, it need hardly be said, is a crucial difference for equal protection purposes.

Under Title XIX and the Hyde Amendment, funding is available for essentially all necessary medical treatment for the poor. Appellees have met the statutory requirements for eligibility, but they are excluded because the treatment that is medically necessary involves the exercise of a fundamental right, the right to choose an abortion. In short, these appellees have been deprived of a governmental benefit for which they are otherwise eligible, solely because they have attempted to exercise a constitutional right. The interest asserted by the Government, the protection of fetal life, has been declared constitutionally subordinate to appellees' interest in preserving their lives and health by obtaining medically necessary treatment. Roe v Wade, supra. And finally, the purpose of the legislation was to discourage the exercise of the fundamental right. In such circumstances the Hyde Amendment must be invalidated because it does not meet even the rational-basis standard of review.

III

The consequences of today's opinion — consequences to which the Court seems oblivious — are not difficult to predict. Pregnant women denied the funding necessary to procure abortions will be restricted to two alternatives. First, they can carry the fetus to term — even though that route may result in severe injury or death to the mother, the fetus, or both. If that course appears intolerable, they can resort to self-induced abortions or attempt to obtain illegal abortions — not because bearing a child would be inconvenient, but because it is necessary in order to protect their health. The result will not be to protect what the Court describes as "the legiti-

mate governmental objective of protecting potential life," ante, but to ensure the destruction of both fetal and maternal life. "There is another world 'out there,' the existence of which the Court . . . either chooses to ignore or fears to recognize." Beal v Doe, 432 US, at 463, 53 L Ed 2d 464, 97 S Ct 2366 (Blackmun, J., dissenting). In my view, it is only by blinding itself to that other world that the Court can reach the result it announces today.

Ultimately, the result reached today may be traced to the Court's unwillingness to apply the constraints of the Constitution to decisions involving the expenditure of governmental funds. In today's decision, as in Maher v Roe, the Court suggests that a withholding of funding imposes no real obstacle to a woman deciding whether to exercise her constitutionally protected procreative choice, even though the Government is prepared to fund all other medically necessary expenses, including the expenses of childbirth. The Court perceives this result as simply a distinction between a "limitation on governmental power" and "an affirmative funding obligation." For a poor person attempting to exercise her "right" to freedom of choice, the difference is imperceptible. As my Brother Brennan has shown (dissenting opinion), the differential distribution of incentives — which the Court concedes is present here — can have precisely the same effect as an outright prohibition. It is no more sufficient an answer here than it was in Roe v Wade to say that "'the appropriate forum'" for the resolution of sensitive policy choices is the legislature.

More than 35 years ago, Mr. Justice Jackson observed that the "task of translating the majestic generalities of the Bill of Rights . . . into concrete restraints on officials dealing with the problems of the twentieth century, is one to disturb self-confidence." These constitutional principles, he observed for the Court, "grew in soil which also produced a philosophy that the individual['s] . . . liberty was attainable through mere absence of governmental restraints." Ibid. Those principles must be "transplant[ed] . . . to a soil in which the laissez-faire concept or principle of non-interference has withered at least as to economic affairs, and social advancements are increasingly sought through closer integration of society and through expanded and strengthened governmental controls."

In this case, the Federal Government has taken upon itself the burden of financing practically all medically necessary expenditures. One category of medically necessary expenditure has been singled out for exclusion, and the sole basis for the exclusion is a premise repudiated for purposes of constitutional law in Roe v Wade. The consequence is a devastating impact on the lives and health of poor women. I do not believe that a Constitution committed to the equal protection of the laws can tolerate this result. I dissent.

NOTE

1. An exception to this statement is to be found in Reynolds v Sims, 377 US 533, 12 L Ed 2d 506, 84 S Ct 1362, and its progeny. Although the Constitution of the United States does not confer the right to vote in state elections, see Minor v Happersett, 21 Wall 162, 178, 22 L Ed 627, Reynolds held that if a State adopts an electoral system, the Equal Protection Clause of the Fourteenth Amendment confers upon a qualified voter a substantive right to participate in the electoral process equally with other qualified voters. See, e.g., Dunn v. Blumstein, 405 US 330, 336, 31 L Ed 2d 274, 92 S Ct 995.

Ideas for Class Projects, Papers, or Debates

1. Should speech advocating hatred, racism, and discrimination, but without any direct violence, be protected? Evaluate the *Skokie* case and defend or oppose the judicial decision on that question.

2. Is the government required to provide a public forum (specifically public access television) for groups dedicated to the discrimination and "defamation" of other groups of the public (recognizing that there is no legal category of group defamation)? Read the newspaper article following these questions and defend or oppose the action of the city council of Kansas City, which shut down its public access channel rather than broadcast "hate TV" for the Ku Klux Klan or the White American Political Association. Should other alternatives be available to cities or states that are trying to retard hatred?

3. In 1989 the Supreme Court's 5 to 4 ruling striking down a Texas law prohibiting the desecration of the flag triggered a rash of flag burnings and a storm of protest. Many states introduced laws outlawing flag desecration. Kentucky, for example, recently introduced a bill that would make flag desecration a Class D felony, punishable by up to five years in prison and a fine of up to $10,000. One would have to expect that such laws would also be declared unconstitutional if they are ever used and challenged. Thus, resolutions have also been advanced in Congress to institute a constitutional amendment making it illegal to desecrate the flag. Formulate and defend or oppose such an amendment.

4. In 1989 a planned showing, initially funded by a grant from the National Endowment for the Arts (NEA), of the art work of Robert Mapplethorpe at a Washington gallery was closed on the ground that it was homoerotic. This touched off a volatile controversy over whether the NEA should be restricted or regulated by Congress in evaluating or censoring the art that this government foundation will fund. Ultimately, some regulatory measures were passed under the guidance (helmsmanship?) of Jesse Helms, who was much offended at the thought of government funding for art of questionable moral character. Such restriction, or even outright censorship, is not a violation of any constitutional right because it simply regulates funding. Should the NEA be regulated by Congress to eliminate funding for morally offensive work?

5. Defend or oppose the *Griswold* case. Anticipate and respond to your opponents' arguments.

6. Assuming that the *Griswold* line is valid law, explain why the Court was justified in not extending it to cover private, consensual sex acts in *Bowers* v. *Hardwick*. Or explain why the Court was not justified.

7. Defend or oppose *Roe* v. *Wade*.

"Hate TV"

Supremacist Groups Use Cable to Spread Views

LOS ANGELES (AP) — Geraldo and Oprah might heat up their TV talk shows with controversial guests, but many cable channels are aflame these days as white supremacists use public-access channels for their own programs.

Dubbed "hate TV" by some, shows such as "Race and Reason" with host Tom Metzger, a former grand dragon of the Ku Klux Klan, are popping up on public-access cable channels nationwide.

The programs, usually featuring guests with the same views as their outspoken hosts, are triggering debates on free speech and race relations, according to a recent study by the Baltimore-based National Institute Against Prejudice and Violence.

"Race and Reason" is seen in 55 cities, said Metzger, a Southern California TV repairman and a leader of the White American Political Association.

Other groups, such as the KKK, also are trying to move from the soapbox to the tube, using cable access channels set aside to be open theoretically to anyone. It is causing chagrin among local cable operators and government officials.

In Kansas City, Mo., the city council shut down its public access channel rather than show "Kansas City," a local KKK program proposed after "Race and Reason" was rejected.

In response, the American Civil Liberties Union will represent the Klan in a lawsuit challenging termination of the channel, the ACLU's Dick Kurtenbach said.

In Florida, the Klan unsuccessfully sued a local cable system for $2,500 after company officials refused to show the KKK-produced "Florida Klan News," said Tony Pupo of Storer Cable Communications near Orlando.

The show opened with pictures of a burning cross.

"Derogatory terms like nigger, honky, spook and cracker may be used," Tony Bastanzio, grand wizard of the Knights of the Ku Klux Klan, said of the show. "But we won't allow any profanity."

J. Allen Moran, grand dragon of the Missouri White Knights of the Ku Klux Klan, who has seen 53 "Race and Reason" tapes, said: "It's not a debate. They are advocacy programs. There is no controversy at all."

Metzger, who began "Race and Reason" in 1984, calls it "a small island of free speech in a sea of controlled and managed news."

Moran said the Missouri KKK was turning to cable "because the day of the street walk is over. If we're on the street and are attacked, it seems that the news media like to take pictures of us defending ourselves under the headline 'Klan Violence.'

"With electronic media, those who oppose us cannot physically attack us. Cable allows us the unique opportunity to present our side of the story."

Lorraine Meyer of the American Jewish Committee in Cincinnati said such groups "don't need a lot of members to get their message across. The use and abuse of technology to spread extremist hate rhetoric has a disturbing potential."

Human rights and cable access groups united in Cincinnati after the White American Skin Heads cablecast a video "bulletin board" message, "Join the American Nazis and smash Red, Jew and Black power," the National Institute Against Prejudice and Violence reported.

Moran termed his views as "racialist," not racist.

"We chose the term 'racialist' because the word 'racist' in the dictionary is one who hates," Moran said. "A racialist loves. We love our race. We are proud of our heritage."

He advocates "a separate country" for whites, adding "the Pacific Northwest is what we have our eyes on."

The Northwest Knights of the Ku Klux Klan has a cable program in Spokane, Wash. "Race and Reason" and "Ernest Zundel on National

Socialism" are shown on the public-access channel.

In Pocatello, Idaho, counterprograms were used, said Randy Ammon, access coordinator for Pocatello Cablevision 12.

"The very first installment of 'Race and Reason' was followed by a film of Bill Cosby on stage in an anti-prejudice film that was followed by a live call-in discussion," said Ammon. "The community spoke out against the racism advocated in 'Race and Reason' and for the First Amendment."

APPENDIX

The Constitution of the United States of America

Article I

Section 1. All legislative Powers herein granted shall be vested in a Congress of the United States, which shall consist of a Senate and House of Representatives.

Section 2. [1] The House of Representatives shall be composed of Members chosen every second Year by the People of the several States, and the Electors in each State shall have the Qualifications requisite for Electors of the most numerous Branch of the State Legislature.

[2] No Person shall be a Representative who shall not have attained to the Age of twenty five Years, and been seven Years a Citizen of the United States, and who shall not, when elected, be an Inhabitant of that State in which he shall be chosen.

[3] Representatives and direct Taxes shall be apportioned among the several States which may be included within this Union, according to their respective Numbers, which shall be determined by adding to the whole Number of free Persons, including those bound to Service for a Term of Years, and excluding Indians not taxed, three fifths, of all other Persons. The actual Enumeration shall be made within three Years after the first Meeting of the Congress of the United States, and within every subsequent Term of ten Years, in such Manner as they shall by Law direct. The Number of Representatives shall not exceed one for every thirty Thousand, but each State shall have at Least one Representative; and until such enumeration shall be made, the State of New Hampshire shall be entitled to chuse three, Massachusetts eight, Rhode Island and Providence Plantations one, Connecticut five, New York six, New Jersey four, Pennsylvania eight, Delaware one, Maryland six, Virginia ten, North Carolina five, South Carolina five, and Georgia three.

[4] When vacancies happen in the Representation from any State, the Executive Authority thereof shall issue Writs of Election to fill such Vacancies.

[5] The House of Representation shall chuse their Speaker and other Officers; and shall have the sole Power of Impeachment.

Section 3. [1] The Senate of the United States shall be composed of two Senators from each State, chosen by the Legislature thereof, for six Years; and each Senator shall have one Vote.

[2] Immediately after they shall be assembled in Consequence of the first Election, they shall be divided as equally as may be into three Classes. The Seats of the Senators of the first Class shall be vacated at the Expiration of the Second Year, of the second Class at the Expiration of the fourth Year, and of the third Class at the Expiration of the sixth Year, so that one third may be chosen every second Year; and if Vacancies happen by Resignation, or otherwise, during the Recess of the Legislature of any State, the Executive thereof may make temporary Appointments until the next Meeting of the Legislature, which shall then fill such Vacancies.

[3] No Person shall be a Senator who shall not have attained to the Age of thirty Years, and been nine Years a Citizen of the United States, and who shall not, when elected, be an Inhabitant of that State for which he shall be chosen.

[4] The Vice President of the United States shall be President of the Senate, but shall have no Vote, unless they be equally divided.

[5] The Senate shall chuse their other Officers, and also a President pro tempore, in the Absence of the Vice President, or when he shall exercise the Office of President of the United States.

[6] The Senate shall have the sole Power to try all Impeachments. When sitting for that Purpose, they shall be on Oath or Affirmation. When the President of the United States is tried, the Chief Justice shall preside: And no Person shall be convicted without the Concurrence of two thirds of the Members present.

[7] Judgment in Cases of Impeachment shall not extend further than to removal from Office, and disqualification to hold and enjoy any Office of honor, Trust, or Profit under the United States: but the Party convicted shall nevertheless be liable and subject to Indictment, Trial, Judgment, and Punishment, according to Law.

Section 4. [1] The Times, Places and Manner of holding Elections for Senators and Representatives, shall be prescribed in each State by the Legislature thereof; but the Congress may at any time by Law make or alter such Regulations, except as to the Places of chusing Senators.

[2] The Congress shall assemble at least once in every Year, and such Meeting shall be on the first Monday in December, unless they shall by Law appoint a different Day.

Section 5. [1] Each House shall be the Judge of the Elections, Returns, and Qualifications of its own Members, and a Majority of each shall constitute a Quorum to do Business; but a smaller Number may adjourn from day to day, and may be authorized to compel the Attendance of absent Members, in such Manner, and under such Penalties as each House may provide.

[2] Each House may determine the Rules of its Proceedings, punish its Members for disorderly Behavior, and, with the Concurrence of two thirds, expel a Member.

[3] Each House shall keep a Journal of its Proceedings, and from time to time publish the same, excepting such Parts as may in their Judgment require Secrecy; and the Yeas and Nays of the Members of either House on any question shall, at the Desire of one fifth of those Present, be entered on the Journal.

[4] Neither House, during the Session of Congress, shall, without the Consent of the other, adjourn for more than three days, nor to any other Place than that in which the two Houses shall be sitting.

Section 6. [1] The Senators and Representatives shall receive a Compensation for their Services, to be ascertained by Law, and paid out of the Treasury of the United States. They shall in all Cases, except Treason, Felony and Breach of the Peace, by privileged from Arrest during their Attendance at the Session of their respective Houses, and in going to and returning from the same; and for any Speech or Debate in either House, they shall not be questioned in any other Place.

[2] No Senator or Representative shall, during the Time for which he was elected, be appointed to any civil Office under the Authority of the United States, which shall have been created, or the Emoluments whereof shall have been encreased during such time; and no Person holding any Office under the United States, shall be a Member of either House during his Continuance in Office.

Section 7. [1] All Bills for raising Revenue shall originate in the House of Representatives; but the Senate may propose or concur with Amendments as on other Bills.

[2] Every Bill which shall have passed the House of Representatives and the Senate, shall, before it become a Law, be presented to the President of the United States; If he approve he shall sign it, but if not he shall return it, with his Objections to the House in which it shall have originated, who shall enter the Objections at large on their Journal, and proceed to reconsider it. If after such Reconsideration two thirds of that House shall agree to pass the Bill, it shall be sent together with the Objections, to the other House, by which it shall likewise be reconsidered, and if

approved by two thirds of that House, it shall become a Law. But in all such Cases the Votes of both Houses shall be determined by yeas and Nays, and the Names of the Persons voting for and against the Bill shall be entered on the Journal of each House respectively. If any Bill shall not be returned by the President within ten Days (Sundays excepted) after it shall have been presented to him, the Same shall be a Law, in like Manner as if he had signed it, unless the Congress by their Adjournment prevent its Return in which Case it shall not be a Law.

[3] Every Order, Resolution, or Vote, to Which the Concurrence of the Senate and House of Representatives may be necessary (except on a question of Adjournment) shall be presented to the President of the United States; and before the Same shall take Effect, shall be approved by him, or being disapproved by him, shall be repassed by two thirds of the Senate and House of Representatives, according to the Rules and Limitations prescribed in the Case of a Bill.

Section 8. [1] The Congress shall have Power To lay and collect Taxes, Duties, Imports and Excises, to pay the Debts and provide for the common Defence and general Welfare of the United States; but all Duties, Imposts and Excises shall be uniform throughout the United States;

[2] To borrow money on the credit of the United States;

[3] To regulate Commerce with foreign Nations, and among the several States, and with the Indian Tribes;

[4] To establish an uniform Rule of Naturalization, and uniform Laws on the subject of Bankruptcies throughout the United States;

[5] To coin Money, regulate the Value thereof, and of foreign Coin, and fix the Standard of Weights and Measures;

[6] To provide for the Punishment of counterfeiting the Securities and current Coin of the United States;

[7] To Establish Post Offices and Post Roads;

[8] To promote the Progress of Science and useful Arts, by securing for limited Times to Authors and Inventors the exclusive Right to their respective Writings and Discoveries;

[9] To constitute Tribunals inferior to the supreme Court;

[10] To define and punish Piracies and Felonies committed on the high Seas, and Offenses against the Law of Nations:

[11] To declare War, grant Letters of Marque and Reprisal, and make Rules concerning Captures on Land and Water;

[12] To raise and support Armies, but no Appropriation of Money to that Use shall be for a longer Term than two Years;

[13] To provide and maintain a Navy;

[14] To make Rules for the Government and Regulation of the land and naval Forces;

[15] To provide for calling forth the Militia to execute the Laws of the Union, suppress Insurrections and repel Invasions;

[16] To provide for organizing, arming, and disciplining, the Militia, and for governing such Part of them as may be employed in the Service of the United States, reserving to the States respectively, the Appointment of the Officers, and the Authority of training the Militia according to the discipline prescribed by Congress;

[17] To exercise exclusive Legislation in all Cases whatsoever, over such District (not exceeding ten Miles square) as may, by Cession of particular States, and the Acceptance of Congress, become the Seat of the Government of the United States, and to exercise like Authority over all Places purchased by the Consent of the Legislature of the State in which the Same shall be, for the Erection of Forts, Magazines, Arsenals, dock-Yards, and other needful Buildings; — And

[18] To make all Laws which shall be necessary and proper for carrying into Execution the foregoing Powers, and all other Powers vested by this Constitution in the Government of the United States, or in any Department or Officer thereof.

Section 9. [1] The Migration or Importation of Such Persons as any of the States now existing shall think proper to admit, shall not be prohibited by the Congress prior to the Year one thousand eight hundred and eight, but a Tax or duty may be imposed on such Importation, not exceeding ten dollars for each Person.

[2] The privilege of the Writ of Habeas Corpus shall not be suspended, unless when in Cases of Rebellion or Invasion the public Safety may require it.

[3] No Bill of Attainder or ex post facto Law shall be passed.

[4] No Capitation, or other direct, Tax shall be laid, unless in Proportion to the Census or Enumeration herein before directed to be taken.

[5] No Tax or Duty shall be laid on Articles exported from any State.

[6] No Preference shall be given by any Regulation of Commerce or Revenue to the Ports of one State over those of another: nor shall Vessels bound to, or from, one State be obliged to enter, clear, or pay Duties in another.

[7] No money shall be drawn from the Treasury, but in Consequence of Appropriations made by Law; and a regular Statement and Account of the Receipts and Expenditures of all public Money shall be published from time to time.

[8] No Title of Nobility shall be granted by the United States: And no Person holding any Office of Profit or Trust under them, shall, without the Consent of the Congress, accept of any present, Emolument, Office, or Title, of any kind whatever, from any King, Prince, or foreign State.

Section 10. [1] No State shall enter into any Treaty, Alliance, or Confederation; grant Letters of Marque and Reprisal; coin Money; emit Bills of Credit; make any Thing but gold and silver Coin a Tender in Payment of Debts; pass any Bill of Attainder, ex post facto Law, or Law impairing the Obligation of Contracts, or grant any Title of Nobility.

[2] No State shall, without the Consent of the Congress, lay any Imposts or Duties on Imports or Exports, except what may be absolutely necessary for executing its inspection Laws: and the net Produce of all Duties and Imposts, laid by any State on Imports or Exports, shall be for the Use of the Treasury of the United States; and all such Laws shall be subject to the Revision and Controul of the Congress.

[3] No State shall, without the Consent of Congress, lay any Duty of Tonnage, keep Troops, or Ships of War in time of Peace, enter into any Agreement or Compact with another State, or with a foreign Power, or engage in War, unless actually invaded, or in such imminent Danger as will not admit of delay.

Article II

Section 1. [1] The executive Power shall be vested in a President of the United States of America. He shall hold his Office during the Term of four Years, and, together with the Vice President, chosen for the same Term, be elected, as follows:

[2] Each State shall appoint, in such Manner as the Legislature thereof may direct, a Number of Electors, equal to the whole Number of Senators and Representatives to which the State may be entitled in the Congress; but no Senator or Representative, or Person holding an Office of Trust or Profit under the United States, shall be appointed an Elector.

[3] The Electors shall meet in their respective States, and vote by Ballot for two Persons, of

whom one at least shall not be an Inhabitant of the same State with themselves. And they shall make a List of all the Persons voted for, and of the Number of Votes for each; which List they shall sign and certify, and transmit sealed to the Seat of the Government of the United States, directed to the President of the Senate. The President of the Senate shall, in the Presence of the Senate and House of Representatives, open all the Certificates, and the Votes shall then be counted. The Person having the greatest Number of Votes shall be the President, if such Number be a Majority of the whole Number of Electors appointed; and if there be more than one who have such Majority, and have an equal Number of Votes, then the House of Representatives shall immediately chuse by Ballot one of them for President; and if no Person have a Majority, then from the five highest on the List the said House shall in like Manner chuse the President. But in chusing the President, the Votes shall be taken by States, the Representation from each State having one Vote; A quorum for this Purpose shall consist of a Member or Members from two thirds of the States, and a Majority of all the States shall be necessary to a Choice. In every Case, after the Choice of the President, the Person having the greater Number of Votes of the Electors shall be the Vice President. But if there should remain two or more who have equal Votes, the Senate shall chuse from them by Ballot the Vice President.

[4] The Congress may determine the Time of chusing the Electors, and the Day on which they shall give their Votes; which Day shall be the same throughout the United States.

[5] No person except a natural born Citizen, or a Citizen of the United States, at the time of the Adoption of this Constitution, shall be eligible to the Office of President; neither shall any Person be eligible to that Office who shall not have attained to the Age of thirty five Years, and been fourteen Years a Resident within the United States.

[6] In case of the removal of the President from Office, or of his Death, Resignation or Inability to discharge the Powers and Duties of the said Office, the Same shall devolve on the Vice President, and the Congress may by Law provide for the Case of Removal, Death, Resignation or Inability, both of the President and Vice President, declaring what Officer shall then act as President, and such Officer shall act accordingly, until the Disability be removed, or a President shall be elected.

[7] The President shall, at stated Times, receive for his Services, a Compensation, which shall neither be encreased nor diminished during the Period for which he shall have been elected, and he shall not receive within that Period any other Emolument from the United States, or any of them.

[8] Before he enter on the Execution of his Office, he shall take the following Oath or Affirmation: "I do solemnly swear (or affirm) that I will faithfully execute the Office of President of the United States, and will to the best of my Ability, preserve, protect and defend the Constitution of the United States."

Section 2. [1] The President shall be Commander in Chief of the Army and Navy of the United States, and of the militia of the several States, when called into the actual Service of the United States; he may require the Opinion, in writing, of the principal Officer in each of the executive Departments, upon any Subject relating to the Duties of their respective Offices, and he shall have Power to grant Reprieves and Pardons for Offenses against the United States, except in Cases of Impeachment.

[2] He shall have Power, by and with the Advice and Consent of the Senate, to make Treaties, provided two thirds of the Senators present concur; and he shall nominate, and by and with the Advice and Consent of the Senate, shall appoint Ambassadors, other public Ministers and Consuls, Judges of the supreme Court, and all other Officers of the United States, whose Appoint-

ments are not herein otherwise provided for, and which shall be established by Law; but the Congress may by Law vest the Appointment of such inferior Officers, as they think proper, in the President alone, in the Courts of Law, or in the Heads of Departments.

[3] The President shall have Power to fill up all Vacancies that may happen during the Recess of the Senate, by granting Commissions which shall expire at the End of their next Session.

Section 3. He shall from time to time give to the Congress Information of the State of the Union, and recommend to their Consideration such Measures as he shall judge necessary and expedient; he may, on extraordinary Occasions, convene both Houses, or either of them, and in Case of Disagreement between them, with Respect to the Time of Adjournment, he may adjourn them to such Time as he shall think proper; he shall receive Ambassadors and other public Ministers; he shall take Care that the Laws be faithfully executed, and shall Commission all the Officers of the United States.

Section 4. The President, Vice President and all civil Officers of the United States, shall be removed from Office on Impeachment for, and Conviction of, Treason, Bribery, or other high Crimes and Misdemeanors.

Article III

Section 1. The judicial Power of the United States, shall be vested in one supreme Court, and in such inferior Courts as the Congress may from time to time ordain and establish. The Judges, both of the supreme and inferior Courts, shall hold their Offices during good Behaviour, and shall, at stated Times, receive for their Services a Compensation, which shall not be diminished during their Continuance in Office.

Section 2. [1] The judicial Power shall extend to all Cases, in Law and Equity, arising under this Constitution, the Laws of the United States, and Treaties made, or which shall be made, under their Authority; — to all Cases affecting Ambassadors, other public Ministers and Consuls; — to all Cases of admiralty and maritime Jurisdiction; — to Controversies to which the United States shall be a Party; — to Controversies between two or more States; — between a State and Citizens of another State; — between Citizens of different States; — between Citizens of the same State claiming Lands under the Grants of different States, and between a State, or the Citizens thereof, and foreign States, Citizens or Subjects.

[2] In all Cases affecting Ambassadors, other public Ministers and Consuls, and those in which a State shall be a Party, the supreme Court shall have original Jurisdiction. In all the other Cases before mentioned, the supreme Court shall have appellate Jurisdiction, both as to Law and Fact, with such Exceptions, and under such Regulations as the Congress shall make.

[3] The trial of all Crimes, except in Cases of Impeachment, shall be by Jury; and such Trial shall be held in the State where the said Crimes shall have been committed; but when not committed within any State, the Trial shall be at such Place or Places as the Congress may by Law have directed.

Section 3. [1] Treason against the United States, shall consist only in levying War against them, or, in adhering to their Enemies, giving them Aid and Comfort. No Person shall be convicted of Treason unless on the Testimony of two Witnesses to the same overt Act, or on Confession in open Court.

[2] The Congress shall have Power to declare the Punishment of Treason, but no Attainder of Treason shall work Corruption of Blood, or Forfeiture except during the Life of the Person attainted.

Article IV

Section 1. Full Faith and Credit shall be given in each State to the public Acts, Records, and judicial Proceedings of every other State. And the Congress may by general Laws prescribe the Manner in which such Acts, Records and Proceedings shall be proved, and the Effect thereof.

Section 2. [1] The Citizens of each State shall be entitled to all Privileges and Immunities of Citizens in the several States.

[2] A Person charged in any State with Treason, Felony, or other Crime, who shall flee from Justice, and be found in another State, shall on demand of the executive Authority of the State from which he fled, be delivered up, to be removed to the State having Jurisdiction of the Crime.

[3] No Person held to Service or Labour in one State, under the Laws thereof, escaping into another, shall, in Consequence of any Law or Regulation herein, be discharged from such Service or Labour, but shall be delivered up on Claim of the Party to whom such Service or Labour may be due.

Section 3. [1] New States may be admitted by the Congress into this Union; but no new State shall be formed or erected within the Jurisdiction of any other State; nor any State be formed by the Junction of two or more States, or Parts of States, without the Consent of the Legislatures of the States concerned as well as of the Congress.

[2] The Congress shall have Power to dispose of and make all needful Rules and Regulations respecting the Territory or other Property belonging to the United States; and nothing in this Constitution shall be so construed as to Prejudice any Claims of the United States, or of any particular State.

Section 4. The United States shall guarantee to every State in this Union a Republican Form of Government, and shall protect each of them against Invasion; and on Application of the Legislature, or of the Executive (when the Legislature cannot be convened) against domestic Violence.

Article V

The Congress, whenever two thirds of both Houses shall deem it necessary, shall propose Amendments to this Constitution, or, on the Application of the Legislatures of two thirds of the several States, shall call a Convention for proposing Amendments, which, in either Case, shall be valid to all Intents and Purposes, as part of this Constitution, when ratified by the Legislatures of three fourths of the several States, or by Conventions in three fourths thereof, as the one or the other Mode of Ratification may be proposed by the Congress; Provided that no Amendment which may be made prior to the Year One thousand eight hundred and eight shall in any Manner affect the first and fourth Clauses in the Ninth Section of the first Article; and that no State, without its Consent, shall be deprived of its equal Suffrage in the Senate.

Article VI

[1] All Debts contracted and Engagements entered into, before the Adoption of this Constitution shall be as valid against the United States under this Constitution, as under the Confederation.

[2] This Constitution, and the Laws of the United States which shall be made in Pursuance thereof; and all Treaties made, or which shall be made, under the Authority of the United States, shall be the supreme Law of the Land; and the Judges in every State shall be bound thereby, any Thing in the Constitution or Laws of any State to the Contrary notwithstanding.

[3] The Senators and Representatives before mentioned, and the Members of the several State Legislatures, and all executive and judicial Officers, both of the United States and of the several States, shall be bound by Oath or Affirmation, to support this Constitution; but no religious Test shall ever be required as a Qualification to any Office or public Trust under the United States.

Article VII

The Ratification of the Conventions of nine States shall be sufficient for the Establishment of this Constitution between the States so ratifying the Same.

Articles in Addition to, and Amendment of, the Constitution of the United States of America, Proposed by Congress, and Ratified by the Legislatures of the Several States Pursuant to the Fifth Article of the Original Constitution

Amendment I [1791]

Congress shall make no law respecting an establishment of religion, or prohibiting the free exercise thereof; or abridging the freedom of speech, or of the press; or the right of the people peaceably to assemble, and to petition the Government for a redress of grievances.

Amendment II [1791]

A well regulated Militia, being necessary to the security of a free State, the right of the people to keep and bear Arms, shall not be infringed.

Amendment III [1791]

No Soldier shall, in time of peace be quartered in any house, without the consent of the Owner, nor in time of war, but in a manner to be prescribed by law.

Amendment IV [1791]

The right of the people to be secure in their persons, houses, papers, and effects, against unreasonable searches and seizures, shall not be violated, and no Warrants shall issue, but upon probable cause, supported by Oath or affirmation, and particularly describing the place to be searched, and the persons or things to be seized.

Amendment V [1791]

No person shall be held to answer for a capital, or otherwise infamous crime, unless on a presentment or indictment of a Grand Jury, except in cases arising in the land or naval forces, or in the Militia, when in actual service in time of War or public danger; nor shall any person be subject for the same offense to be twice put in jeopardy of life or limb; nor shall be compelled in any criminal case to be a witness against himself, nor be deprived of life, liberty, or property, without due process of law; nor shall private property be taken for public use, without just compensation.

Amendment VI [1791]

In all criminal prosecutions, the accused shall enjoy the right to a speedy and public trial, by an impartial jury of the State and district wherein the crime shall have been committed, which district shall have been previously ascertained by law, and to be informed of the nature and cause of the accusation; to be confronted with the witnesses against him; to have compulsory process for obtaining witnesses in his favor, and to have the Assistance of Counsel for his defence.

Amendment VII [1791]

In Suits at common law, where the value in controversy shall exceed twenty dollars, the right of trial by jury shall be preserved, and no fact tried by jury, shall be otherwise re-examined in any Court of the United States, than according to the rules of the common law.

Amendment VIII [1791]

Excessive bail shall not be required, nor excessive fines imposed, nor cruel and unusual punishments inflicted.

Amendment IX [1791]

The enumeration in the Constitution, of certain rights, shall not be construed to deny or disparage others retained by the people.

Amendment X [1791]

The powers not delegated to the United States by the Constitution, nor prohibited by it to the States, are reserved to the States respectively, or to the people.

*   *   *

The Declaration of Independence
[July 4, 1776]

The Unanimous Declaration of the Thirteen United States of America

When in the course of human events, it becomes necessary for one people to dissolve the political bands which have connected them with another, and to assume among the Powers of the earth, the separate and equal station to which the Laws of Nature and of Nature's God entitle them, a decent respect to the opinions of mankind requires that they should declare the causes which impel them to the separation.

We hold these truths to be self-evident, that all men are created equal, that they are endowed by their Creator with certain unalienable Rights, that among these are Life, Liberty, and the pursuit of Happiness. That to secure these rights, Governments are instituted among Men, deriving their just powers from the consent of the governed; That whenever any Form of Government becomes destructive of these ends, it is the Right of the People to alter or to abolish it, and to institute new Government, laying its foundation on such principles and organizing its powers in such form, as to them shall seem most likely to effect their Safety and Happiness. Prudence, indeed, will dictate that Governments long established should not be changed for light and transient causes; and accordingly all experience hath shown, that mankind are more disposed to suffer, while evils are sufferable, than to right themselves by abolishing the forms to which they are accustomed. But when a long train of abuses and usurpations, pursuing invariably the same Object evinces a design to reduce them under absolute Despotism, it is their right, it is their duty, to throw off such Government, and to provide new Guards for their future security.—Such has been the patient sufferance of these Colonies; and such is now the necessity which constrains them to alter their former Systems of Government. The history of the present King of Great Britain is a history of repeated injuries and usurpations, all having in direct object the establishment of an absolute Tyranny over these States. To prove this, let Facts be submitted to a candid world.

He has refused his Assent to Laws, the most wholesome and necessary for the public good.

He has forbidden his Governors to pass Laws of immediate and pressing importance, unless suspended in their operation till his Assent should be obtained; and when so suspended, he has utterly neglected to attend to them.

He has refused to pass other Laws for the accommodation of large districts of people, unless those people would relinquish the right of Representation in the Legislature, a right inestimable to them and formidable to tyrants only.

He has called together legislative bodies at places unusual, uncomfortable, and distant from the depository of their Public Records, for the sole purpose of fatiguing them into compliance with his measures.

He has dissolved Representative Houses repeatedly, for opposing with manly firmness his invasions on the rights of the people.

He has refused for a long time, after such dissolutions, to cause others to be elected; whereby the Legislative Powers, incapable of Annihilation, have returned to the People at large for their exercise; the State remaining in the meantime exposed to all the dangers of invasion from without, and convulsions within.

He has endeavoured to prevent the population of these States; for that purpose obstructing the Laws of Naturalization of Foreigners; refusing to pass others to encourage their migration hither, and raising the conditions of new Appropriations of Lands.

He has obstructed the Administration of Justice, by refusing his Assent to Laws for establishing Judiciary Powers.

He has made Judges dependent on his Will alone, for the tenure of their offices, and the amount and payment of their salaries.

He has erected a multitude of New Offices, and sent hither swarms of Officers to harass our People, and eat out their substance.

He has kept among us, in times of peace, Standing Armies without the Consent of our legislature.

He has affected to render the Military independent of and superior to the Civil Power.

He has combined with others to subject us to a jurisdiction foreign to our constitution, and unacknowledged by our laws; giving his Assent to their acts of pretended legislation:

For quartering large bodies of armed troops among us:

For protecting them, by a mock Trial, from Punishment for any Murders which they should commit on the Inhabitants of these States:

For cutting off our Trade with all parts of the world:

For imposing taxes on us without our Consent:

For depriving us in many cases, of the benefits of Trial by Jury:

For transporting us beyond Seas to be tried for pretended offences:

For abolishing the free System of English Laws in a neighbouring Province, establishing therein an Arbitrary government, and enlarging its Boundaries so as to render it at once an example and fit instrument for introducing the same absolute rule into these Colonies:

For taking away our Charters, abolishing our most valuable Laws, and altering fundamentally the Forms of our Governments:

For suspending our own Legislature, and declaring themselves invested with Power to legislate for us in all cases whatsoever.

He has abdicated Government here, by declaring us out of his Protection and waging War against us.

He has plundered our seas, ravaged our Coasts, burnt our towns, and destroyed the lives of our people.

He is at this time transporting large armies of foreign mercenaries to compleat the works of death, desolation and tyranny, already begun with circumstances of Cruelty & perfidy scarcely paralleled in the most barbarous ages, and totally unworthy the Head of a civilized nation.

He has constrained our fellow Citizens taken Captive on the high Seas to bear Arms against their Country, to become the executioners of their friends and Brethren, or to fall themselves by their Hands.

He has excited domestic insurrections amongst us, and has endeavoured to bring on the inhabitants of our frontiers, the merciless Indian Savages, whose known rule of warfare, is an undistinguished destruction of all ages, sexes and conditions.

In every stage of these Oppressions We have Petitioned for Redress in the most humble terms: Our repeated Petitions have been answered only by repeated injury. A Prince, whose character is thus marked by every act which may define a Tyrant, is unfit to be the ruler of a free People.

Nor have We been wanting in attention to our British brethren. We have warned them from time to time of attempts by their legislature to extend an unwarrantable jurisdiction over us. We have reminded them of the circumstances of our emigration and settlement here. We have appealed to their native justice and magnanimity, and we have conjured them by the ties of our common kindred to disavow these usurpations, which would inevitably interrupt our connections and correspondence. They too have been deaf to the voice of justice and of consanguinity. We must, therefore, acquiesce in the necessity, which denounces our Separation, and hold them, as we hold the rest of mankind, Enemies in War, in Peace Friends.

We, therefore, the Representatives of the united States of America, in General Congress, Assembled, appealing to the Supreme Judge of the world for the rectitude of our intentions, do, in the Name, and by Authority of the good People of these Colonies, solemnly publish and declare, That these United Colonies are, and of Right ought to be Free and Independent States; that they are Absolved from all Allegiance to the British Crown, and that all political connection between them and the State of Great Britain, is and ought to be totally dissolved; and that as Free and Independent States, they have full Power to levy War, conclude Peace, contract Alliances, establish Commerce, and to do all other Acts and Things which Independent States may of right do. And for the support of this Declaration, with a firm reliance on the Protection of Divine Providence, we mutually pledge to each other our Lives, our Fortunes and our sacred Honor.

JOHN HANCOCK.

New Hampshire

JOSIAH BARTLETT
WM. WHIPPLE
MATTHEW THORNTON

Massachusetts Bay

SAML. ADAMS
JOHN ADAMS
ELBRIDGE GERRY
ROBT. TREAT PAINE

Rhode Island

STEP. HOPKINS
WILLIAM ELLERY

Connecticut

ROGER SHERMAN
SAM'EL HUNTINGTON
WM. WILLIAMS
OLIVER WOLCOTT

New York

WM. FLOYD
PHIL. LIVINGSTON
FRANS. LEWIS
LEWIS MORRIS

New Jersey

RICHD. STOCKTON
JNO. WITHERSPOON
FRAS. HOPKINSON
JOHN HART
ABRA. CLARK

Pennsylvania

ROBT. MORRIS
BENJAMIN RUSH
BENJA. FRANKLIN
JOHN MORTON
GEO. CLYMER
JAS. SMITH
GEO. TAYLOR
JAMES WILSON
GEO. ROSS

Delaware

CESAR RODNEY
GEO. READ
THO. M'KEAN

Maryland

SAMUEL CHASE

WM. PACA

THOS. STONE

CHARLES CARROLL of Carrollton

Virginia

GEORGE WYTHE

RICHARD HENRY LEE

TH. JEFFERSON

BENJA. HARRISON

THOS. NELSON, jr.

FRANCIS LIGHTFOOT LKE

CARTER BRAXTON

North Carolina

WM. HOOPER

JOSEPH HEWES

JOHN PENN

South Carolina

EDWARD RUTLEDGE

THOS. HEYWARD, JUNR.

ARTHUR MIDDLETON

THOMAS LYNCH, junr.

Georgia

BUTTON GWINNETT

LYMAN HALL

GEO. WALTON

Universal Declaration of Human Rights

Adopted on December 10th, 1948 by General Assembly of United Nations at the Palais de Chaillot, Paris

Whereas Member States have pledged themselves to achieve, in co-operation with the United Nations, the promotion of universal respect for and observance of human rights and fundamental freedoms,

Whereas a common understanding of these rights and freedoms is of the greatest importance for the full realisation of this pledge,

Now, therefore, the General Assembly, Proclaim this Universal Declaration of Human Rights as a common standard of achievement for all peoples and all nations, to the end that every individual and every organ of society, keeping this Declaration constantly in mind, shall strive by teaching and education to promote respect for these rights and freedoms and by progressive measures, national and international, to secure their universal and effective recognition and observance, both among the peoples of Member States themselves and among the peoples of territories under their jurisdiction.

Article 1

All human beings are born free and equal in dignity and rights. They are endowed with reason and conscience and should act towards one another in a spirit of brotherhood.

Article 2

1. Everyone is entitled to all the rights and freedoms set forth in this Declaration, without distinction of any kind, such as race, colour, sex, language, religion, political or other opinion, national or social origin, property, birth or other status.

2. Furthermore, no distinction shall be made on the basis of the political, jurisdictional or international status of the country or territory to which a person belongs, whether it be independent, trust, non-self-governing or under any other limitation of sovereignty.

Article 3

Everyone has the right to life, liberty and security of person.

Article 4

No one shall be held in slavery or servitude; slavery and the slave trade shall be prohibited in all their forms.

Article 5

No one shall be subjected to torture or to cruel, inhuman or degrading treatment or punishment.

Article 6

Everyone has the right to recognition everywhere as a person before the law.

Article 7

All are equal before the law and are entitled without any discrimination to equal protection of the law. All are entitled to equal protection against any discrimination in violation of this Declaration and against any incitement to such discrimination.

Article 8

Everyone has the right to an effective remedy by the competent national tribunals for acts violating the fundamental rights granted him by the constitution or by law.

Article 9

No one shall be subjected to arbitrary arrest, detention or exile.

Article 10

Everyone is entitled in full equality to a fair and public hearing by an independent and impartial tribunal, in the determination of his rights and obligations and of any criminal charge against him.

Article 11

1. Everyone charged with a penal offence has the right to be presumed innocent until proved guilty according to law in a public trial at which he has had all the guarantees necessary for his defence.
2. No one shall be held guilty of any penal offence on account of any act or omission which did not constitute a penal offence, under national or international law, at the time when it was committed. Nor shall a heavier penalty be imposed than the one that was applicable at the time the penal offence was committed.

Article 12

No one shall be subjected to arbitrary interference with his privacy, family, home or correspondence, nor to attacks upon his honour and reputation. Everyone has the right to the protection of the law against such interference or attacks.

Article 13

1. Everyone has the right to freedom of movement and residence within the borders of each State.
2. Everyone has the right to leave any country, including his own, and to return to his country.

Article 14

1. Everyone has the right to seek and to enjoy in other countries asylum from persecution.

2. This right may not be invoked in the case of prosecutions genuinely arising from non-political crimes or from acts contrary to the purposes and principles of the United Nations.

Article 15

1. Everyone has the right to a nationality.

2. No one shall be arbitrarily deprived of his nationality nor denied the right to change his nationality.

Article 16

1. Men and women of full age, without any limitation due to race, nationality or religion, have the right to marry and to found a family. They are entitled to equal rights as to marriage, during marriage and at its dissolution.

2. Marriage shall be entered into only with the free and full consent of the intending spouses.

3. The family is the natural and fundamental group unit of society and is entitled to protection by society and the State.

Article 17

1. Everyone has the right to own property alone as well as in association with others.

2. No one shall be arbitrarily deprived of his property.

Article 18

Everyone has the right to freedom of thought, conscience and religion; this right includes freedom to change his religion or belief, and freedom, either alone or in community with others and in public or private, to manifest his religion or belief in teaching, practice, worship and observance.

Article 19

Everyone has the right to freedom of opinion and expression; this right includes freedom to hold opinions without interference and to seek, receive and impart information and ideas through any media and regardless of frontiers.

Article 20

1. Everyone has the right to freedom of peaceful assembly and association.

2. No one may be compelled to belong to an association.

Article 21

1. Everyone has the right to take part in the government of his country, directly or through freely chosen representatives.

2. Everyone has the right of equal access to public service in his country.

3. The will of the people shall be the basis of the authority of government; this will shall be expressed in periodic and genuine elections which shall be by universal and equal suffrage and shall be held by secret vote or by equivalent free voting procedures.

Article 22

Everyone, as a member of society, has the right to social security and is entitled to realization, through national effort and international co-operation and in accordance with the organization and resources of each State, of the economic, social and cultural rights indispensable for his dignity and the free development of his personality.

Article 23

1. Everyone has the right to work, to free choice of employment, to just and favorable conditions of work and to protection against unemployment.

2. Everyone, without any discrimination, has the right to equal pay for equal work.

3. Everyone who works has the right to just and favorable remuneration ensuring for himself and his family an existence worthy of human dignity, and supplemented, if necessary, by other means of social protection.

4. Everyone has the right to form and to join trade unions for the protection of his interests.

Article 24

Everyone has the right to rest and leisure, including reasonable limitation of working hours and periodic holidays with pay.

Article 25

1. Everyone has the right to a standard of living adequate for the health and well-being of himself and of his family, including food, clothing, housing and medical care and necessary social services, and the right to security in the event of unemployment, sickness, disability, widowhood, old age or other lack of livelihood in circumstances beyond his control.

2. Motherhood and childhood are entitled to special care and assistance. All children, whether born in or out of wedlock, shall enjoy the same social protection.

Article 26

1. Everyone has the right to education. Education shall be free, at least in the elementary and fundamental stages. Elementary education shall be compulsory. Technical and professional education shall be made generally available and higher education shall be equally accessible to all on the basis of merit.

2. Education shall be directed to the full development of the human personality and to the strengthening of respect for human rights and fundamental freedoms. It shall promote understanding, tolerance and friendship among all nations, racial or religious groups, and shall further the activities of the United Nations for the maintenance of peace.

3. Parents have a prior right to choose the kind of education that shall be given to their children.

Article 27

1. Everyone has the right freely to participate in the cultural life of the community, to enjoy the arts and to share in scientific advancement and its benefits.

2. Everyone has the right to the protection of the moral and material interests resulting from any scientific, literary or artistic production of which he is the author.

Article 28

Everyone is entitled to a social and international order in which the rights and freedoms set forth in this Declaration can be fully realised.

Article 29

1. Everyone has duties to the community in which alone the free and full development of his personality is possible.

2. In the exercise of his rights and freedoms, everyone shall be subject only to such limitations as are determined by law solely for the purpose of securing due recognition and respect for the rights and freedoms of others and of meeting the just requirements of morality, public order and the general welfare in a democratic society.

3. These rights and freedoms may in no case be exercised contrary to the purposes and principles of the United Nations.

Article 30

Nothing in this Declaration may be interpreted as implying for any State, group or person any right to engage in any activity or to perform any act aimed at the destruction of any of the rights and freedoms set forth herein.